Italy

Helen Gillman & Stefano Cavedoni
Damien Simonis
Sally Webb

LONELY PLANET PUBLICATIONS
Melbourne • Oakland • London • Paris

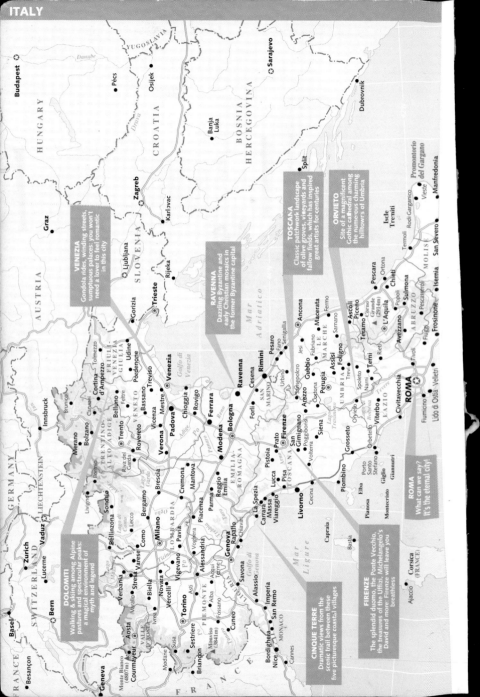

ITALY

DOLOMITI
Walking & skiing among Alpine pastures and spectacular peaks; a magical environment of myth and legend

VENEZIA
Gondola rides, winding streets, sumptuous palaces; you won't need a lover to feel romantic in this city

RAVENNA
Dazzling Byzantine and early Christian mosaics in the former Byzantine capital

TOSCANA
Classic patchwork landscape of olive groves, vineyards and fallow fields, which has inspired great artists for centuries

ORVIETO
Site of a magnificent Gothic cathedral among the numerous charming hilltowns of Umbria

ROMA
What can we say? It's the eternal city!

FIRENZE
The splendid duomo, the Ponte Vecchio, the treasures of the Uffizi, Michelangelo's David and more. Firenze will leave you breathless

CINQUE TERRE
Dramatic views from the scenic trail between these five picturesque coastal villages

MATERA
Fascinating sassi (stone houses), home to up to 20,000, half the town's population, until the 1950s

SICILIA
Greek temples at Agrigento, Selinunte and Segesta standing as testament to the glory of Magna Grecia

COSTIERA AMALFITANA
Striking cliffs and deep blue waters along a coastline of citrus and olive groves, vineyards and timeless Mediterranean villages

SARDEGNA
Sandy beaches, dramatic gorges and isolated coves compete with archaeological sites, rugged mountains and ancient village traditions

KEY

National Park

Elevation

3000m
2000m
1000m
500m
0

0   50   100 km

Mar Ionio

Mar Tirreno

MAR MEDITERRANEO

LAZIO
CAMPANIA
PUGLIA
BASILICATA
CALABRIA
SICILIA
SARDEGNA

ISOLE EOLIE
ISOLE EGADI
ISOLE PELAGIE

MALTA
TUNISIA
ALGERIA

Brindisi, Lecce, Otranto, Gallipoli, Taranto, Bari, Barletta, Andria, Cerignola, Foggia, Lucera, Benevento, Avellino, Salerno, Caserta, Napoli, Pompei, Sorrento, Amalfi, Capri, Ischia, Campobasso, Potenza, Matera, Altamura, Crotone, Cosenza, Catanzaro, Reggio di Calabria, Messina, Catania, Siracusa, Noto, Ragusa, Modica, Gela, Agrigento, Palermo, Trapani, Marsala, Mazara del Vallo, Sciacca, Licata, Enna, Caltanissetta, Caltagirone, Cefalù, Mt Etna (3350m), Taormina, Stromboli, Panarea, Lipari, Salina, Filicudi, Alicudi, Vulcano

Cagliari, Oristano, Nuoro, Sassari, Alghero, Olbia, Arbatax, Muravera, Villasimius, Iglesias, Carbonia, Sant'Antioco

Tunis, Bizerte, Sousse, Kelibia, Annaba, Valletta, Pantelleria, Lampedusa, Linosa

Italy
4th edition – April 2000
First published – September 1993

Published by
Lonely Planet Publications Pty Ltd ABN 36 005 607 983
90 Maribyrnong St, Footscray, Victoria 3011, Australia

Lonely Planet Offices
Australia Locked Bag 1, Footscray, Victoria 3011
USA 150 Linden St, Oakland, CA 94607
UK 10a Spring Place, London NW5 3BH
France 1 rue du Dahomey, 75011 Paris

Photographs
Many of the images in this guide are available for licensing from Lonely
Planet Images.
email: lpi@lonelyplanet.com.au

Front Cover Photograph
One of the unique images of Italy – the Torre Pendente (Leaning
Tower) in Pisa (Jon Davison)

ISBN 0 86442 692 5

text & maps © Lonely Planet 2000
photos © photographers as indicated 2000

Printed by Colorcraft Ltd, Hong Kong

Contents – Text

4 Contents – Text

SICILIA (SICILY) 741

SARDEGNA (SARDINIA) 803

LANGUAGE 834

GLOSSARY 840

ACKNOWLEDGMENTS 844

INDEX 856

MAP LEGEND back page

METRIC CONVERSION inside back cover

Contents – Maps

INTRODUCTION

GETTING AROUND

ROMA

LIGURIA, PIEMONTE & VALLE D'AOSTA

LOMBARDIA (LOMBARDY) & THE LAKES

TRENTINO-ALTO ADIGE

IL VENETO

FRIULI-VENEZIA GIULIA

EMILIA-ROMAGNA & SAN MARINO

TOSCANA (TUSCANY)

MAP LEGEND – SEE BACK PAGE

MAPS

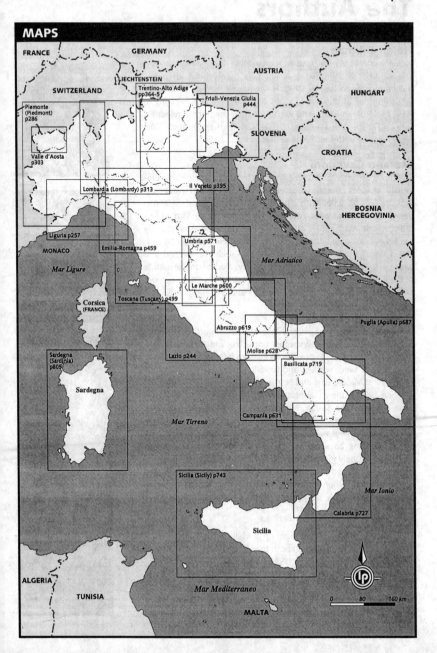

The Authors

Helen Gillman

Helen works as a writer and editor, based in Italy. For many years she worked as a journalist in Australia (her country of birth), before moving to Italy in 1990. Helen has worked on all the previous editions of this book as well as Lonely Planet's *Walking in Italy* and *Rome* guides, and wrote the Italy chapter for *Mediterranean Europe* and *Western Europe*. On all of these guides she works closely with her husband Stefano.

Stefano Cavedoni

Stefano is an actor and writer. In the late 1970s, while still a university student, Stefano's career in the Italian entertainment industry was launched with a bang when his rock band, *Skiantos*, became a major success. After this he wrote and performed humorous one-man shows. But while on stage he was secretly thinking about travel, forests and mountains. He has worked with Helen on all the previous editions of this guide, researched and wrote many of the walks in *Walking in Italy*, worked on the update of the Italy chapter for *Mediterranean Europe* and *Western Europe*, and wrote the Walks chapter in Lonely Planet's *Rome* guide.

Damien Simonis

With a degree in languages and several years' reporting and sub-editing on Australian newspapers (including the *Australian* and the *Age*) behind him, Sydney-born Damien left Australia in 1989. He has since lived, worked and travelled extensively throughout Europe, the Middle East and North Africa.

Since 1992, Lonely Planet has kept him busy writing *Jordan & Syria*, *Egypt & the Sudan*, *Morocco*, *North Africa*, *Italy*, *Spain*, *Canary Islands* and *Barcelona*. As well as this edition of *Italy*, he has written the *Venice*, *Florence* and *Tuscany* guides. At last report he was heading back to Spain, where among other things he is working on Lonely Planet's new guide to Madrid. Damien has also written and snapped for other publications in Australia, the UK and North America. When not on the road, Damien resides in splendid Stoke Newington, deep in the heart of north London.

Sally Webb

Sally Webb was born and brought up in Melbourne, Australia, but has spent many years living in both the UK and Italy and has travelled throughout Europe, the USA and Asia.

In a former life she was an art historian, having studied at Melbourne University and at the Courtauld Institute of Art in London, where she graduated in 1990 with an MA in Art History. She moved to Italy in 1994 and became a journalist, editor and travel writer.

Until recently Sally lived in Trastevere in the heart of Rome where she was working as a journalist and editor for *Wanted in Rome*, an English-language fortnightly magazine. She is a regular contributor to the *Australian Gourmet Traveller* and has written for several other Australian publications, including the *Qantas Club* magazine and Ansett Airline's *Vive*. She also contributes to publications in the USA and Italy.

Sally is co-author of Lonely Planet's guide to *Rome* and has also updated the Malta chapter of *Mediterranean Europe*. She is currently working on the first edition of *Corfu & the Ionian Islands*.

FROM THE AUTHORS

From Helen Gillman & Stefano Cavedoni We would like to thank the following friends for their valuable assistance. Special thanks from Stefano to Dott. Sandro Privitera for his expert guidance and advice on the Sicilia chapter and to Hans and Mariangela for their hospitality in Noto. Thanks to Massimo Tua and his family – their enthusiastic approach to life gave us a new perspective on Cortina. Thanks a lot to Laura Clark for her competent collaboration and great patience.

Thanks also to the following tourist offices and staff in Italy for their help: ENIT (Ente Nazionale Italiano per il Turismo); ESIT (Ente Sardo Industrie Turistiche), in particular Rag. Mario Pinna, Sig. Marco Grippo, Sig. Costantino Nardi; APT Palermo, in particular Arch. Sortino, Dott.ssa Salfi, Sig.a Verdina, Sig.a Visconti; AAPIT Catania, in particular Dott. Sciacca, Dott.ssa Francese, Sig.a Zappala'; Comando Ripartimentale Foreste di Catania, in particular Dott. Riggi; APT Messina, in particular Dott.ssa D'Amico; AAST Isole Eolie, in particular Sig. Ziino; APT Trapani, in particular Dott. Butera, Sig. Paolo Sciortino and Sig.a Geraci; APT Marsala, in particular Sig.a Parrinello; APT Marche, in particular Dott.ssa Dorigati; APT Alto Adige-Sud Tirolo, in particular Sig.a Boninsegna; APT Trentino, in particular Dott.ssa Maraschin, Sig.a Barozzi and Sig.a Gloria; APT Madonna di Campiglio, in particular Sig.a Fabrizia Caola; Pro Loco Lardaro, in particular Sig.a Rossella; APT Val di Fassa, in particular Dott. Weiss; APT San Martino di Castrozza, in particular Sig. Vinante; Alta Badia, in particular Dott. Da Punt; Alpe di Siusi – Sciliar, in particular Sig.a Mahlknecht; Azienda Promozione Turistica Dolomiti, in particular Sig. Ennio Soccal; Pro Loco Valzoldana, in particular Sig.Fabrizio Votta and Sig. Paolo Lazzarin.

From Damien Simonis Thanks go first and foremost to the lads and lasses in Milano: Anna and Guido Cerutti, Daniela Antongiovanni and Sergio Bosio, Caroline Heidler and Stefano Falletti (thanks for the boat ride!). Anna in particular gets a bucket of gold stars for rolling out the welcome lounge on occasions too numerous to count – there aren't enough cheeses in the world I could give you to express my gratitude. Daniela and Sergio also did their share, and housed various goods and chattels of mine while I dithered about my next lodgings. To all I am indebted for their suggestions and above all their friendship.

Alberto Stassi, one of the Milano gang, seems to have been fated to shadow my movements … or to have me shadow his. Having shifted to Torino to work he found himself putting up with yours truly on the lounge. He moved to Padova, only to find old trusty Iob in nearby Venezia seemingly with the express purpose of dogging him at every turn! In Torino also special thanks to Chiara Cerutti. The team at Turismo Torino, especially Gaia Enria, was terrific.

In Firenze I had the great fortune to stumble across Barbara, Ottobrina, Michela, Silvia and Ruggero. They all made me feel more than welcome – *grazie*.

Anthony Haywood was kind enough to provide some info from Germany. As usual, Paul Gowan from the RAC kindly provided information on motoring issues in Italy.

Finally, thanks to Katharine Leck and the crew at the Lonely Planet office in London for giving me free run of the office in times of (seemingly unending) computer crises! David Green happily assisted with my nagging little technological doubts.

From Sally Webb I am indebted to Fiorenza Lodi at ENIT (Ente Nazionale Italiano per il Turismo) in Roma for providing me with invaluable assistance and contacts which helped me enormously in my research.

In Salerno, special thanks to Vito Caponigro and Ciro Adinolfi from the EPT and to Pasquale Splendori and Carlo Sacchi. In Napoli, thanks to Assessore Giuliana Parente and Pino Imperatore from the Comune di Napoli, to Gianni Ciabatti from the Napoli EPT and to Catherine Horsby for an insider's view of the city. In Puglia, thanks to Michele Abbatescianni (Foggia APT) and to COTUP's Luigi Manzionna, Dr Pantano, Donato Esposito and Luciana Brescia. A big thank you to Gino Fusco (Vieste EPT), who went well beyond the call of duty, making my research on the Promontorio del Gargano peninsula comparable to a day on the film set with Roberto Benigni. In Basilicata I was assisted by numerous people from the APT including Romano Toppana, Ivo Persichella, Giovanni Gonnella, Matteo Visceglia, Rosanna Moliterni and Sig.a Iannini. Thanks also to Tina Festa and Marilena in Matera and to Mario Atzori in Melfi.

On a personal note, I would like to thank my colleagues at *Wanted in Rome*, all of whom shouldered a significant extra burden during my research. I am indebted to friends in Roma who put up with my absences and exhaustion, especially Sari and Alessandro Taddei, Adrian Arena and Orla Guerin. Last but not least, thanks to my family for their love and support, and especially to Kirsty Webb for her company on our Calabrian road trip and to Anna Webb for changing her plans to accommodate my deadline.

This Book

This is the fourth edition of Lonely Planet's *Italy* guide. The first edition was written by Helen Gillman and John Gillman. Helen Gillman and Damien Simonis updated the second edition. The third edition was revised and expanded by Helen Gillman, Damien Simonis and Stefano Cavedoni. For this edition Helen Gillman teamed up with Damien Simonis, Sally Webb and Stefano Cavedoni.

Helen coordinated the project once again and, along with Stefano, updated sections of the Facts about Italy, Facts for the Visitor and Emilia-Romagna & San Marino chapters as well as the Rome, Trentino-Alto Adige, Le Marche, Abruzzo & Molise, Sicilia and Sardegna chapters. Damien updated some of the Facts about Italy, Facts for the Visitor and Emilia-Romagna & San Marino chapters and also the Getting There & Away, Liguria, Piemonte & Valle d'Aosta, Lombardia & the Lakes, Il Veneto, Friuli-Venezia Giulia and Toscana chapters. Sally updated the History section of the Facts about Italy chapter along with the Getting Around, Umbria, Campania and Puglia, Basilicata & Calabria chapters. Sally also revised the colour Art & Architecture section based on Ann Moffat's work in the last edition.

From the Publisher

This edition of *Italy* was produced in the London office. David Rathborne, Katrina Browning and Wendy Bashford coordinated the editing and proofing with assistance from Arabella Bamber, Claire Hornshaw, Claudia Martin, Sally O'Brien, Wendy Owen and Christine Stroyan. David Wenk coordinated the mapping and design and was assisted by Paul Edmunds, Ed Pickard, Angie Watts and Sara Yorke. Tim Ryder compiled the index while Claudia, Sam Trafford and Adam McCrow helped out with last-minute layout corrections. David and Gadi Farfour designed the cover, David produced the climate charts and Jim Miller drew the back-cover map. Most of the photographs were supplied by Lonely Planet Images, with additional images for the Art & Architecture section from Scala Picture Library. Quentin Frayne cast his expert Italian eye over the Language chapter and Imogen Franks and Anna Sutton chipped in with some extra research. Thanks to Charles Page from Rail Europe. The Rome transport map is by kind permission of ATAC-Contral, Rome. A final thanks to Helen, Damien, Sally and Stefano for all their hard work to produce this edition – we think it's the best yet.

THANKS
Many thanks to the travellers who used the last edition and wrote to us with helpful hints, advice and interesting anecdotes. Your names appear in the back of this book.

Foreword

ABOUT LONELY PLANET GUIDEBOOKS

The story begins with a classic travel adventure: Tony and Maureen Wheeler's 1972 journey across Europe and Asia to Australia. Useful information about the overland trail did not exist at that time, so Tony and Maureen published the first Lonely Planet guidebook to meet a growing need.

From a kitchen table, then from a tiny office in Melbourne (Australia), Lonely Planet has become the largest independent travel publisher in the world, an international company with offices in Melbourne, Oakland (USA), London (UK) and Paris (France).

Today Lonely Planet guidebooks cover the globe. There is an ever-growing list of books and there's information in a variety of forms and media. Some things haven't changed. The main aim is still to help make it possible for adventurous travellers to get out there – to explore and better understand the world.

At Lonely Planet we believe travellers can make a positive contribution to the countries they visit – if they respect their host communities and spend their money wisely. Since 1986 a percentage of the income from each book has been donated to aid projects and human rights campaigns.

Updates Lonely Planet thoroughly updates each guidebook as often as possible. This usually means there are around two years between editions, although for more unusual or more stable destinations the gap can be longer. Check the imprint page (following the colour map at the beginning of the book) for publication dates.

Between editions up-to-date information is available in two free newsletters – the paper *Planet Talk* and email *Comet* (to subscribe, contact any Lonely Planet office) – and on our Web site at www.lonelyplanet.com. The *Upgrades* section of the Web site covers a number of important and volatile destinations and is regularly updated by Lonely Planet authors. *Scoop* covers news and current affairs relevant to travellers. And, lastly, the *Thorn Tree* bulletin board and *Postcards* section of the site carry unverified, but fascinating, reports from travellers.

Correspondence The process of creating new editions begins with the letters, postcards and emails received from travellers. This correspondence often includes suggestions, criticisms and comments about the current editions. Interesting excerpts are immediately passed on via newsletters and the Web site, and everything goes to our authors to be verified when they're researching on the road. We're keen to get more feedback from organisations or individuals who represent communities visited by travellers.

Lonely Planet gathers information for everyone who's curious about the planet – and especially for those who explore it first-hand. Through guidebooks, phrasebooks, activity guides, maps, literature, newsletters, image library, TV series and Web site we act as an information exchange for a worldwide community of travellers.

Research Authors aim to gather sufficient practical information to enable travellers to make informed choices and to make the mechanics of a journey run smoothly. They also research historical and cultural background to help enrich the travel experience and allow travellers to understand and respond appropriately to cultural and environmental issues.

Authors don't stay in every hotel because that would mean spending a couple of months in each medium-sized city and, no, they don't eat at every restaurant because that would mean stretching belts beyond capacity. They do visit hotels and restaurants to check standards and prices, but feedback based on readers' direct experiences can be very helpful.

Many of our authors work undercover, others aren't so secretive. None of them accept freebies in exchange for positive write-ups. And none of our guidebooks contain any advertising.

Production Authors submit their raw manuscripts and maps to offices in Australia, USA, UK or France. Editors and cartographers – all experienced travellers themselves – then begin the process of assembling the pieces. When the book finally hits the shops some things are already out of date, we start getting feedback from readers, and the process begins again ...

WARNING & REQUEST

Things change – prices go up, schedules change, good places go bad and bad places go bankrupt – nothing stays the same. So, if you find things better or worse, recently opened or long since closed, please tell us and help make the next edition even more accurate and useful. We genuinely value all the feedback we receive. Julie Young coordinates a well-travelled team that reads and acknowledges every letter, postcard and email and ensures that every morsel of information finds its way to the appropriate authors, editors and cartographers for verification.

Everyone who writes to us will find their name in the next edition of the appropriate guidebook. They will also receive the latest issue of *Planet Talk*, our quarterly printed newsletter, or *Comet*, our monthly email newsletter. Subscriptions to both newsletters are free. The very best contributions will be rewarded with a free guidebook.

Excerpts from your correspondence may appear in new editions of Lonely Planet guidebooks, the Lonely Planet Web site, *Planet Talk* or *Comet*, so please let us know if you *don't* want your letter published or your name acknowledged.

Send all correspondence to the Lonely Planet office closest to you:

Australia: Locked Bag 1, Footscray, Victoria 3011
USA: 150 Linden St, Oakland, CA 94607
UK: 10a Spring Place, London NW5 3BH
France: 1 rue du Dahomey, 75011 Paris

Or email us at: talk2us@lonelyplanet.com.au

For news, views and updates see our Web site: www.lonelyplanet.com

HOW TO USE A LONELY PLANET GUIDEBOOK

The best way to use a Lonely Planet guidebook is any way you choose. At Lonely Planet we believe the most memorable travel experiences are often those that are unexpected, and the finest discoveries are those you make yourself. Guidebooks are not intended to be used as if they provide a detailed set of infallible instructions!

Contents All Lonely Planet guidebooks follow roughly the same format. The Facts about the Destination chapter or section gives background information ranging from history to weather. Facts for the Visitor gives practical information on issues like visas and health. Getting There & Away gives a brief starting point for researching travel to and from the destination. Getting Around gives an overview of the transport options when you arrive.

The peculiar demands of each destination determine how subsequent chapters are broken up, but some things remain constant. We always start with background, then proceed to sights, places to stay, places to eat, entertainment, getting there and away, and getting around information – in that order.

Heading Hierarchy Lonely Planet headings are used in a strict hierarchical structure that can be visualised as a set of Russian dolls. Each heading (and its following text) is encompassed by any preceding heading that is higher on the hierarchical ladder.

Entry Points We do not assume guidebooks will be read from beginning to end, but that people will dip into them. The traditional entry points are the list of contents and the index. In addition, however, some books have a complete list of maps and an index map illustrating map coverage.

There may also be a colour map that shows highlights. These highlights are dealt with in greater detail in the Facts for the Visitor chapter, along with planning questions and suggested itineraries. Each chapter covering a geographical region usually begins with a locator map and another list of highlights. Once you find something of interest in a list of highlights, turn to the index.

Maps Maps play a crucial role in Lonely Planet guidebooks and include a huge amount of information. A legend is printed on the back page. We seek to have complete consistency between maps and text, and to have every important place in the text captured on a map. Map key numbers usually start in the top left corner.

Although inclusion in a guidebook usually implies a recommendation we cannot list every good place. Exclusion does not necessarily imply criticism. In fact there are a number of reasons why we might exclude a place – sometimes it is simply inappropriate to encourage an influx of travellers.

Introduction

A unified nation only for the past century, Italy is a highly complex, if unevenly woven, tapestry.

While Roma continued to exercise extraordinary power and attract enormous wealth as seat of the Catholic Church, its influence over the rest of the peninsula after the collapse of the empire in 476 AD was far from complete. City-states to the north and feudal kingdoms to the south shared control and left a legacy of unparalleled richness in diversity.

Centuries ago, well-to-do northern Europeans were drawn to the Mediterranean light and so the Grand Tour was born. What they found in Italy was an extraordinary cocktail: next to the artistic wealth of Roma, Venezia and Firenze, they often saw decadence, poverty and swindlers.

The economic miracles of recent decades have transformed the country, but beneath all the style, fine food and delicious wine, there remains, a certain chaotic air. Not everything is wonderful – expanding industry, poor urban planning, unchecked resort construction and an indifference to the nation's art treasures have too often blighted the cities and countryside.

You could not hope to experience all the wonders of the country in even a year's non-stop travel. From the majestic peaks of the Dolomiti to the rainbow-coloured sea of Sardegna, there is much more to Italy than San Pietro and the Uffizi.

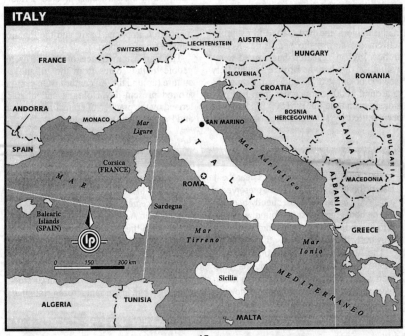

Facts about Italy

HISTORY

Italy's strategic position in the Mediterranean made it a target for colonisers and invaders, whose comings and goings over thousands of years created a people with a diverse ethnic background. But it also gave the Romans, and later the Christian Church, an excellent base from which to expand. Italy's history is therefore a story of powerful empires and foreign domination and, from the fall of the Roman Empire to the formation of the Kingdom of Italy in 1861, the country was never a unified entity.

Prehistoric Italy

The Italian peninsula has supported human life for thousands of years. Archaeological finds show that Palaeolithic Neanderthals lived in Italy about 70,000 years ago. By around 4000 BC, the Neolithic humans in the area were no longer exclusively nomadic hunters and had started to establish settlements across the peninsula. Recent archaeological research has forced a re-evaluation of when the Bronze Age hit Italy (see the boxed text 'The Iceman Cometh'), to around 1000 years earlier than had previously been thought. By 1800 BC Italy had been settled by several Italic tribes which had frequent contact with eastern and other Mediterranean cultures and were eventually absorbed into the Roman Empire. The major indigenous Italic tribes relevant to the later prehistorical period are: the Apulians, Umbrians and Latins (Lazio region); the Samnites (Calabria, Campania and Abruzzo); the Marsi, Aequi, Volsci, Sabines and Oscans (Central Italy); the Picenums (northern Abruzzo and Le Marche); and the Veneti and Ligurians.

The Etruscans

Historians differ on the origins of the Etruscan people and when they reached the Italian peninsula, although it is widely agreed that they migrated from the Aegeo-Asian area at the end of the 12th century BC. It is known that the Etruscans created a flourishing civilisation between the Arno and Tevere valleys, with other important settlements in Campania, Lazio and the Pianura Padana (the Po plain).

The earliest evidence of the Etruscan people in Italy dates from the Villanovan culture (around the 9th century BC), centred around present-day Bologna and characterised by the practice of cremating the dead and burying their ashes in urns.

The Iceman Cometh

In 1991 tourists in the mountains near the Italy-Austria border came across the body of a prehistoric hunter, remarkably well-preserved in ice, together with weapons, leather clothing and a basket. The hunter subsequently became known as the Iceman.

The body, the oldest yet found, was taken to Innsbruck, in Austria, where scientists dated it to around 3000 BC – thus forcing a re-evaluation of when the Bronze Age arrived in Italy. Previously this was generally thought to have been around 1800 BC.

The Austrians were intent on keeping the body until surveyors discovered that the site where it was found is 11m inside the Italian border. After a six year custody battle, the Iceman was transported to the northern Italian city of Bolzano in 1998, where museum curators have created a special refrigerated showcase that will keep him in the same frozen state that preserved his body for 5000 years.

From the 7th to the 6th century BC, Etruscan culture was at its height. Etruria was based on large city-states, among them Caere (Cerveteri), Tarquinii (Tarquinia), Veii (Veio), Volsinii (believed to be either Bolsena or Orvieto), Felsina (Bologna), Perusia (Perugia), Volaterrae (Volterra), Faesulae (Fiesole) and Arretium (Arezzo), which were collectively known as the Etruscan League. The Etruscans were predominantly navigators and traders, competing against the Phoenicians and Greeks for markets in the Mediterranean.

A good deal of what is known about Etruscan culture has been learned from the archaeological evidence unearthed at the sites of their tombs and religious sanctuaries, many of which can be visited today. Their belief in life after death necessitated the burial of the dead with everything they might need in the afterlife. This included such items as food and drink, clothing, ornaments and weapons. Painted tombs depicting scenes of everyday life, notably those discovered at Tarquinia, near Roma, provide important information about how the Etruscans lived.

The long period of Etruscan decline began in the 5th century BC, when they began to lose control of their trade routes to the more powerful Greeks. By the 4th century BC they had lost their northern territories to Gallic invaders and their settlements in Campania to the Samnites, confining Etruria to its original territories in central Italy. While Etruscan civilisation continued to flourish during this period, its development was by then greatly determined by its relationship with the ever growing Roman power.

The Romans had long been profoundly influenced by Etruscan culture and three of the seven Roman kings who ruled before the Republic (see The Roman Republic later in this section) were Etruscans, known as the Tarquins.

The Etruscan and Roman civilisations coexisted relatively peacefully until the defeat of Veii and its incorporation into Roman territory in 396 BC. During the ensuing century, Etruscan cities were either defeated or entered into peaceful alliances with the increasingly powerful Romans, although they maintained a fair degree of autonomy until 90 BC, when the Etruscans (along with all the Italic peoples of the peninsula) were granted Roman citizenship.

The separate Etruscan culture and language rapidly disappeared partly because scholars of the day attached little importance to the need to preserve the Etruscan language and few translations into Latin were made. No Etruscan literature survived and the only remaining samples of the written language are related to religious and funerary customs.

Etruscan warriors: by the 4th century BC Etruscan territories were being invaded by the Gauls.

Greek Colonisation

The first Greek settlements in Italy were established in the early 8th century BC; first on the island of Ischia in the Golfo di Napoli (Bay of Naples), followed by other settlements along the peninsula's southern coast and in Sicilia. What became known as Magna Graecia (Greater Greece) was, in fact, a group of independent city-states, established by colonists from the independent city-states of Greece itself. The founders of the colonies at Ischia and Cumae were from the island of Euboea, the great city of Siracusa was founded by the Corinthians and Spartan exiles founded the wealthy city of Taranto.

The civilisation of Magna Graecia, which flourished in territories that had previously been colonised by Pheonicians or occupied by local peoples, spanned about six centuries. The ruins of magnificent Doric temples in Italy's south (at Paestum) and in Sicilia (Agrigento, Selinunte and Segesta), and other monuments such as the Greek theatre at Siracusa, stand as testament to its splendour.

Siracusa became so powerful that Athens considered it enough of a threat to launch an attack on the city. In one of history's great maritime battles, Siracusa managed to destroy the Athenian fleet in 413 BC. By the end of the 3rd century BC, Magna Graecia had succumbed to the might of the advancing Roman Republic, though not before playing a major role in introducing Hellenic culture to the Romans in the form of philosophy, literature, art, architecture and coinage.

The Roman Republic

Aeneas, a refugee from Troy whose mother was the goddess Venus, is said to have landed in Italy in 1184 BC. Through alliances and warfare, the Trojans established a kingdom based at Alba Longa. The last of this line produced the twins Romulus and Remus, allegedly sired by Mars himself.

The traditional date of the foundation of Roma by Romulus is 753 BC. The next seven kings were elected from the ranks of the nobles. Most notably, Numa Pompilius is credited with the creation of the whole legal and religious civic structure. The Etruscan Servius Tullius built the first walls around the city-state and established the basic organisation of the political and military system.

Servius Tullius was assassinated by a rival, Tarquinius Superbus (Tarquin the Proud), whose delinquent son, in 509 BC, broke all rules of hospitality and good manners by raping his host's wife when her husband was out of the city. Lucretia was so mortified that she committed suicide after telling the story to her male relatives. One of them, Lucius Junius Brutus, decided that enough was enough and incited the overthrow and expulsion of the Etruscan royal house. The Roman Republic was born and the first temple was built on the Campidoglio (Capitoline Hill).

The mixed constitution of the Roman Republic was considered the best of all known political systems because it combined elements of all the others, with each element acting as a counterbalance to the others. Monarchy was represented by the two consuls, who were also the alternating commanders-in-chief; oligarchy came from the Senate, to which all the higher magistrates, including the consuls, belonged; and democracy came from direct election to almost all political offices.

To keep the magistrates in check, all offices were held for one year only and re-election was originally forbidden (it was later allowed only after a 10 year gap). No man was permitted to stand for high office until he had progressed through the sequence of junior posts and all magistracies were held jointly.

Unlike the US constitution, which was consciously modelled on it, the Roman original was never codified and recorded. This left many constitutional issues open to interpretation and led to interesting situations such as the creation of an imperial system of government within the legal framework of a republic.

A basic principle of political philosophy

introduced with the first Republic was that of the sovereign rights of the people. In modern Roma, the initials SPQR (*Senatus Populusque Romanus*; the Senate and People of Roma), visible on ancient Roman monuments and stamped on municipal property to this day, stand as testimony to an ideal of continuity with the first Senate.

The Romans also developed a unique system for dealing with the other peoples in the region (the Sabines and Etruscans to the north and the Oscans, Samnites and Greek colonies to the south). Defeated city-states were not taken over, but became allies, part of the Latin League. Allowed to retain their own government and lands, they were required to provide troops on demand to serve alongside Roman soldiers. This naturally increased the Republic's military strength, and the protection offered by Roman hegemony induced many cities to become allies voluntarily.

The civic structure also expanded. In 450 BC the existing laws were codified as the Law of the Twelve Tables. These covered public and private life and remained in force for the next 1000 years.

The Punic Wars

The other Mediterranean power during this period was Carthage, a kingdom of traders based in North Africa (modern Tunis). Although they were in close proximity, it was not inevitable that the Romans would come into conflict with Carthage. The problem was Sicilia, the western cities of which were allied with Carthage, while those on the east were linked to Roma.

The First Punic War (264-241 BC) was the result of the internal politics of Messina, a Greek colony on Sicilia. One faction was thrown out of the city and appealed to the Carthaginians for help. The city was besieged and the inhabitants turned to the Romans. During the resulting 23 year war the Romans realised the importance of naval power. Eventually victorious, they forced the Carthaginians to abandon their colonies in western Sicilia and also seized Sardegna.

One of the defeated and aggrieved Punic (Carthaginian) generals, Hamilcar Barca, was based in southern Spain. His son Hannibal inherited command of the army and initiated a violent campaign. This escalated into the Second Punic War (218-202 BC) when the Roman Senate once again declared war on Carthage.

With the Romans controlling the seas, Hannibal daringly crossed into Italy by leading his army over the Alpi (Alps). Despite losing up to half his troops and almost all of his war elephants in the crossing, the Punic general was able to inflict several crushing defeats on the Romans, notably at Lago di Trasimeno (in present-day Umbria) in 217 BC, and at Cannae (in Puglia) the following year, when the Romans lost 30,000 soldiers.

During the stalemate that followed, the Romans discovered a military genius of their own to match Hannibal – Publius Cornelius Scipio. Backed by a strong army, the 23-year-old general struck first at Hannibal's power base in Spain and then, in 204 BC, attacked Africa, forcing the Carthaginians to recall Hannibal to defend their own capital. In 202 BC Scipio won the decisive battle of Zama over Hannibal, who committed suicide in exile some 20 years later.

During the following years, the Roman Republic added Macedonian Greece to its provinces after a decisive defeat of Perseus, the son of Philip V of Macedon, in a three year war. The Third Punic War (149-146 BC) dealt the final blow to Carthage. Vengeful in victory, the Romans' destruction of Carthaginian civilisation was total and we know little about it today.

From Republic to Empire

With the Romans' eastward expansion came the rise of the generalissimo. In 107 BC Gaius Marius replaced the increasingly unpopular system of conscription by accepting volunteers from the ranks of the landless urban poor. Roman armies now looked to their individual generals for recompense after a campaign and the commanders realised the unlimited political potential of conquest.

Meanwhile, Roman politics was increasingly polarised into two factions, linked as much by marriage as by policies: the Optimates (conservatives), who upheld the primacy of the Senate, and the Populares (populists), who preferred to take their bills before the people's assemblies. This split in political allegiances was the cause of civil conflict between the supporters of Marius, a Populare, and his erstwhile lieutenant Cornelius Sulla, an Optimate. Sulla twice threatened to invade Roma and in 82 BC, after he committed a string of political murders, the Senate gave in to his demands, and he was voted dictator for the extraordinary period of 10 years.

One of Sulla's protégés, Gnaeus Pompeius Magnus (Pompey the Great) was allowed by Sulla to leapfrog his way up the political ladder. In 71 BC the fabulously wealthy Marcus Licinius Crassus finally mopped up the dramatic slave rebellion led by the gladiator Spartacus, which had been raging through Italy for two years. At its conclusion, 6000 slaves who did not die in battle were crucified along the Via Appia.

Julius Caesar, general, statesman, historian and dictator of the Roman Empire (49-44 BC)

Crassus and Pompey together then campaigned (and bribed) their way to the consulships of 70 BC. Pompey later took an army as far east as Syria.

In 59 BC Gaius Julius Caesar was running for the consulship and made a deal with Crassus and the newly returned Pompey. In return for their electoral and financial support, Caesar as consul would ensure that his allies' interests would be looked after despite Optimate opposition. The three men became known as the First Triumvirate and their pact was reinforced by Pompey's marriage to Caesar's daughter, Julia. After his consulship, Caesar left to win military glory in Gaul. The First Triumvirate was renewed in 56 BC and, with Caesar's electoral support, Crassus and Pompey shared another consulship in 55 BC. The alliance was shaken, however, when Julia died in 54 BC and Crassus was heavily defeated and killed in Parthia the following year.

Pompey came increasingly under the influence of Optimates, who wanted to impeach Caesar for irregularities in Gaul, and civil war began when Caesar crossed into Italy with his army of devoted veterans in 49 BC. Pompey and his supporters evacuated Italy for Spain, Africa and Greece, where their main force was defeated by Caesar at Pharsalus a year later. Pompey fled to Egypt, where he was assassinated.

In 47 BC Caesar returned to Roma, where he began to institute a series of reforms, overhauling the calendar and the Senate. Of his extensive building programme, the Curia (Senate House) and the Basilica Giulia remain. Initially declared dictator for one year, Caesar had this extended to 10 years and then, in 44 BC, was proclaimed dictator for life. This accumulation of power fatally alienated even those political allies who had initially supported him and Caesar was famously assassinated in the portico of the Teatro di Pompeo (Theatre of Pompey) on the Ides of March (15 March), 44 BC.

However, the Liberators, as Caesar's assassins called themselves, found that they had severely underestimated Caesar's popularity with the military and the general populace; the people regarded the dead dictator as a new god. Caesar's lieutenant, Marcus Antonius (Mark Antony), took command of the city, aided by troops under the command of Lepidus. Caesar's will had declared the adoption of his 18-year-old great-nephew, Octavian, as his son and heir. Octavian, then studying in Greece, returned to Roma to claim his inheritance. Now calling himself Gaius Julius Caesar Octavianus, the young man first sided with the Liberators against Antony, then switched sides and fought with Antony when Brutus and Cassius were defeated at Philippi. The orator Cicero, who had attacked Antony in a series of speeches and then underestimated Octavian, became a victim of the political murders which followed.

Lepidus was quickly frozen out of the Second Triumvirate and the Roman world was divided in two, with the new Caesar raising troops in the western half while Antony administered the wealthy provinces and client kingdoms of the east. Although Antony married Octavian's sister, the situation inevitably deteriorated into another civil war, with Octavian making brilliant propagandistic use of Antony's affair with Cleopatra VII, Queen of Egypt.

Octavian's general Marcus Agrippa defeated Antony and Cleopatra in a naval battle off the coast of Actium in 31 BC and they committed suicide in Alexandria the following year.

The Empire

Octavian was left as sole ruler of the Roman world but, remembering Caesar's fate, trod very carefully. In 27 BC he officially surrendered his extraordinary powers to the Senate, which promptly gave most of them back. Four years later his position was regularised again, with the Senate voting him the unique title Augustus (Your Eminence).

The new era of political stability which followed allowed the arts to flourish. Augustus was exceptionally lucky in having as his contemporaries the poets Virgil, Horace and Ovid, as well as the historian Livy. He also encouraged the visual arts, restoring existing buildings and constructing many new ones. Agrippa built the original Pantheon, while Augustus himself dedicated the Teatro di Marcello in honour of his nephew, Marcellus, and commissioned the Ara Pacis (Altar of Peace) explicitly to commemorate his achievement. He boasted in his memoirs that he 'found Roma in brick and left it in marble'.

Augustus succeeded because instead of trying to reinvent the political system, he simply made room for himself at the top. He never called himself a king or an emperor, but only *princeps* (the leading man). The Republic (as it was still known) continued as usual from the consuls down. He died aged 75 after a 40 year reign.

His successor Tiberius' reign (14-37 AD) was stable (he ruled from his villa in Capri for the last decade). Gaius Caligula (ruled 37-45 AD) had little time for the political niceties which the Senate expected; his increasingly extravagant and bizarre behaviour led to his assassination by an officer of the Praetorian Guard, the imperial bodyguard.

A return to a truly republican form of government was contemplated, but the Praetorians, with an eye on job security, declared Claudius, Gaius' uncle, emperor. Despite his unexpected elevation, Claudius proved to be a conscientious ruler. He extended the port facilities at Ostia and built a new aqueduct, the Acqua Claudia, to service the growing population of Roma. He also strengthened the Romans' hold on Britain, first invaded by Caesar.

Probably poisoned in 58 AD by his wife, Agrippina, Claudius was succeeded by Nero, her 17-year-old son by a previous marriage. Nero gradually showed his preference for Gaius Caligula's style of government. In the ultimate act of youthful rebellion he had his mother assassinated, then began to impose his passion for all things Greek on an increasingly resentful Roman aristocracy. With revolt spreading among the provincial governors, who commanded armies, the Senate declared Nero a public enemy in 68 AD and he committed suicide while on the run. In the Year of the Four Emperors which followed, Galba, Otho and Vitellius came and went in quick succession.

Stability was restored when Vespasian, sent to Judaea to crush the Great Rebellion of 66 AD, was proclaimed emperor by his troops and the exhausted Senate agreed. A practical man, Vespasian (ruled 69-79 AD) made a point of rebuilding the temple on the Campidoglio, which had been burned down during the civil wars, and constructing a huge amphitheatre in the grounds of Nero's Domus Aurea. He also re-dedicated the enormous statue in front of the Colosseo, originally of Nero and destined for his entrance hall, to Apollo, the sun god.

As a parallel to Augustus' Ara Pacis, Vespasian celebrated the return of normality by building the Foro di Pace (Forum of Peace). The brief reign of his successor, Titus (79-81 AD), is chiefly remembered for the catastrophic eruption of Vesuvio. He did find time to construct public baths, as well as the Arco di Tito, which commemorates him as the captor of Jerusalem.

Domitian, Titus' younger brother, built the Forum Transitorio (for which his successor, Nerva, took the credit and the name, calling it the Foro di Nerva) and greatly extended the palace complex on the Palatino; he had the corridors lined with highly polished stone to allow him to detect lurking assassins. This paranoia was justified in 96 AD when he was murdered in a palace plot.

After the brief reign of Nerva, the elderly stop-gap emperor (96-98 AD), came Trajan, an experienced general of Spanish birth. His victories over the Dacians are depicted on the column erected in the forecourt of his forum, which also contained separate Greek and Latin libraries. Other public works constructed during this time included his market, and the Via Traiana linking Benevento with Brindisi. Trajan was the first Roman general to conquer Parthia, the traditional eastern enemy. He died while on campaign in 117 and his ashes were buried in the base of his column.

Hadrian (117-138) is known as a prodigious traveller, but he was also a keen architect who remodelled the Pantheon in its current form and built an extensive and elaborate holiday villa at Tivoli, outside Roma. This era was the peak of the Roman Empire, when stability on the borders was matched in internal politics. By 100 AD, the city of Roma had more than 1.5 million inhabitants and all the trappings of the capital of an empire, its wealth and prosperity obvious in the rich mosaics, marble temples, public baths, theatres, circuses and libraries. An extensive network of aqueducts fed the baths and provided private houses with running water and flushing toilets.

The reigns of Antonius Pius (138-161) and the philosopher-emperor Marcus Aurelius (161-180) were stable, but the latter ominously spent 14 years fighting northern invaders. A slow decline began with the disturbed Commodus (180-192) and, with his assassination, the events of 68-69 repeated themselves. Pertinax, Didius Julianus and Pescennius Niger came and went before Septimius Severus (193-211), born in North Africa, defeated the other challengers to become emperor. Serious cracks were beginning to appear in the Empire.

Severus was jointly succeeded by the brothers Caracalla and Geta, with Caracalla predictably having his sibling assassinated. Despite financial problems, his building programme included refurbishing roads as well as building his monumental public baths. When he was throttled in 213, chaos ensued. Some 24 emperors and pretenders violently rose and fell until Diocletian (ruled 284-305) realised that increasing instability on the borders made central government impossible. He therefore split the administration of the Empire, looking after the east himself and allocating the west to Maximian, who based himself in Milano. This arrangement worked so well that in 293 Diocletian created two junior rulers, Caesars to the senior Augustuses.

In 305 Maximian and Diocletian abdicated simultaneously, leaving the Empire to Constantius in the west and Galerius in the east. A four-way tug-of-war ensued until, in 312, Constantine (Constantius' son) faced Maxentius, his last rival, just outside Roma at Saxa Rubra. After his celebrated vision of the Christian monogram and the message 'with this sign you will conquer', Constantine prevailed at the Battle of the Milvian Bridge. The new emperor converted to Christianity and in 313 granted the Edict of Milan, which enshrined religious freedom in law.

Constantine's highly ambitious building programme included churches such as San Pietro, San Lorenzo Fuori le Mura and Santa Croce, the Basilica di Costantino in the Foro Romano, and his own triumphal arch, the Arco di Costantino. However, he accepted Diocletian's view that Roma could no longer serve as the Empire's capital, being too far removed from the northern and eastern frontiers, and in 324 he founded the new Christian capital – Constantinople – in Byzantium.

Division of the Empire

The demise of the Roman Empire continued when the ruling brothers Valentian and Valens divided the Empire into western and eastern halves in 364, a division that was formalised after the death of Emperor Theodosius I in 395. One of his sons, Honorius, ruled the Western Roman Empire, while his other son, Arcadius, ruled the Eastern Roman Empire.

Separated from its Roman roots, the Eastern Roman Empire embraced Hellenistic culture and went on to develop into the mighty Byzantine Empire, the most powerful Mediterranean state throughout the Middle Ages. It existed until the capture of Constantinople by the Turks in 1453.

Early Middle Ages (400-600)

A population decline throughout the 2nd and 3rd centuries was exacerbated in the 4th century by plague, famine and war. The arrival of the Vandals in North Africa cut off the Romans' corn supplies, while a western Teutonic tribe, the Visigoths, consolidated control of much of the northern

Mediterranean coast and northern Italy. In 452 Attila the Hun, leader of a tribe from the Central Asian steppes, invaded and, it is said, caused the people of Aquileia and Grado to found a city of refuge called Venezia. This city was to become a great trading and seafaring centre and the birthplace, in 1254, of one of Italy's most well known adventurers, Marco Polo.

In 476, the year traditionally recognised as the end of the great period of the Roman Empire, the last Western Roman Emperor, Romulus Augustulus, was deposed by Odvacar, a mutinous Germanic captain of mercenaries.

Gothic rule in Italy reached its zenith with the Ostrogothic emperor Theodoric (493-526). The greatest of the Ostrogothic rulers, Theodoric had spent several years as a hostage in Constantinople, where he acquired great respect for Roman culture. When the Eastern Roman Emperor Zeno put him in charge of Italy, Theodoric, ruling from Ravenna, brought peace and prosperity to the area.

After Theodoric's death, the Eastern Roman Emperor Justinian (527-565) and his wife, Theodora, reconquered Italy and laid the groundwork for the Byzantine era. Among the early examples of Byzantine art in Italy are the mosaic portraits of Justinian and Theodora in the Basilica di San Vitale at Ravenna. Though the Justinian reconquest was soon rolled back by the Lombards, Byzantine emperors and empresses managed to hold on to parts of southern Italy until the 11th century.

During the middle years of the 5th century, Pope Leo I 'the Great' (440-461), known as the founder of Catholicism, had ensured the secular power of the papacy by persuading Attila not to attack Roma. Using a document known as the *Donation of Constantine*, Leo I secured the Western Roman Empire for the fledgling Catholic Church.

In 590 Pope Gregory I, son of a rich Roman family, returned from self-imposed exile in a monastery, having given all his wealth to the poor. He set the pattern of Church administration which was to guide

Goths (left) and Swabians were just two of the ethnic groups to invade the Italian peninsula.

Catholic services and rituals throughout history. Gregory oversaw the Christianisation of Britain, improved conditions for slaves, provided free bread in Roma and repaired Italy's extensive network of aqueducts, as well as leaving an enormous volume of writing on which much Catholic dogma was subsequently based.

Lombard Italy & the Papal States (600-800)

Even before Gregory became pope the Lombard invasion of Italy had begun. The Lombards were a Swabian people who appear to have originally inhabited the lower basin of the Elbe but, as so often happened with conquerors of the Italian peninsula, rather than imposing their culture on the locals, they adopted the local culture. Thus their language did not last long after their arrival and their culture too was almost completely integrated. Their more communal concept of land and property tenure was soon overthrown by the Romans' high regard for private property, either absolute or leased, and the Lombards, who mainly settled around Milano, Pavia and Brescia, soon became city dwellers, building many churches and public baths which still grace these cities. They eventually expanded their control further down the peninsula – taking over the important duchies of Spoleto and Benevento – although they were unable to take Roma.

In an effort to unseat the Lombards, the pope invited the Franks to invade Italy, which they did in 754 and 756 under the command of their king, Pepin, disenfranchising the Lombards and establishing the Papal States, which were to survive until 1870. Using the *Donation of Constantine* as his precedent, Pepin issued the *Donation of Pepin* in 756, which gave land that was still nominally under the Byzantine Empire to Pope Stephen II and proclaimed the pope heir of the Roman emperors.

When Pepin's son and successor, Charlemagne, visited Roma in 774 he confirmed the *Donation of Pepin*. Charlemagne was crowned emperor by Pope Leo III on Christmas Day 800 in the Basilica di San Pietro and the concept of the Holy Roman Empire came into being. The bond between the papacy and the Byzantine Empire was thus forever broken and political power in what had been the Western Roman Empire shifted north of the Alpi, where it would remain for more than 1000 years. However, on Charlemagne's death his successors were unable to hold together his vast Carolingian Empire. In 843 the Partition of Verdun divided the Empire between his three nephews and Italy became a battleground of rival powers and states. The imperial crown was ruthlessly fought over and Roma's aristocratic families also engaged in battle for the papacy.

An Oasis of Calm

Meanwhile, Muslim Arabs had invaded Sicilia and in 831 took Palermo as their capital, while Siracusa, an important city since the first Greek settlements, fell to them in 878. They established a splendid civilisation, restoring the fundamentals of Greek culture elaborated by Muslim scholars such as the physician and philosopher Avicenna, the astronomer and geographer Al-Battani and the mathematician Al-Kovarizmi. Cotton, sugar cane, oranges and lemons were introduced in the south, taxes there were lower and the Sicilians lived relatively peacefully under their Arab lords for more than two centuries. Hundreds of mosques were built and the elegant Arabian architecture survived even after Sicilia was returned to Christian powers.

Amalfi, which had secured independence from Napoli in the 840s, soon became a major trading republic in the western Mediterranean. It also became a centre of great cosmopolitan civilisation and learning, as did the republics of Gaeta and Napoli, and Salerno, which was still a Lombard principality. In the 11th century Salerno was famous for its medical school, where Greek and Hebrew, Arab and Christian teachers worked together.

While the south prospered under Arab rule, the rest of Italy was not so calm. Following the demise of the Carolingian Empire in 887, warfare broke out in earnest between local Italian rulers, who were divided in their support of Frankish and Germanic claimants – all of whom were absentee landlords – to the imperial title and throne. Italy became the battleground of Europe, the stage on which rival factions fought for ascendancy and refugees flooded into safe cities from the devastated countryside. Many of Italy's medieval hill towns developed in this period as easily defendable safe havens.

In 962 the Saxon Otto I was crowned emperor in Roma and formally founded the Holy Roman Empire. His son, Otto II, and later his grandson, Otto III, also took the title Holy Roman Emperor, cementing a tradition that was to remain the privilege of Germanic emperors until 1806.

In the early 11th century the fanatically Christian Normans began arriving. First, they served as mercenaries in southern Italy, where they fought against the Arabs, but they were willing to change their allegiance as profit dictated.

The Norman & Holy Roman Eras

The campaign of Hildebrand (who was to become Pope Gregory VII in 1073) to bring the world under the rule of Christianity was, in reality, a struggle for power between Church and State. In order to be legitimate, every new emperor had to be sworn in and 'crowned' by the pope. The papacy, based in Roma, and the Holy Roman Empire, with its power base north of the Alpi, were compelled to agree in order to reconstruct the political and cultural unity which had been lost with the fall of the Western Roman Empire. In reality, the two powers were in perennial conflict and the consequences of this dual leadership were to dominate the Middle Ages.

However, both the Frankish and Germanic claimants to the crown were temporarily distracted by the summons of Christendom to recapture the Holy Land from the Muslims. The First Crusade, a tragic disaster, emanated primarily from modern-day Germany and France.

Having already established themselves firmly in Puglia and Calabria, the Normans moved into Sicilia, which they progressively managed to wrest from the Arab Muslims. But, rather than banish the Arabs, the Normans tended to assimilate eastern traditions and systems and established what was to be a long period of religious tolerance in the south. When Roger II was crowned king of Sicilia in 1130, he established his court at Palermo, which had been the capital of the Arab emirate and, before long, church towers stood beside the domes of the mosques.

The Normans brought with them an appreciation of majestic structures, characterised by their Romanesque architecture, but they also liberally adapted many Arab and Byzantine architectural features. The Chiesa di San Giovanni degli Eremiti in Palermo might equally pass as a mosque or a Greek or Norman basilica. King Roger's magnificent Cappella Palatina and the cattedrale at Monreale (just outside Palermo) are excellent examples of how the Normans combined the vitality of eastern influences with the glory of Byzantine architecture and the simple beauty of Romanesque.

Norman rule in the south gave way to Germanic claims due to the foresight of Holy Roman Emperor Frederick I (known as Barbarossa), who married off his son Henry to Constance de Hauteville, heir to the Norman throne in Sicilia. Barbarossa's grandson, Frederick II, became Holy Roman Emperor in 1220. An enlightened ruler, Frederick, who became known as Stupor Mundi (Wonder of the World), was both a warrior and a scholar. A profound admirer of Arabic culture, he allowed freedom of worship to Muslims, as well as to Jews. He studied philosophy and magic, wrote laws and earned a place in Italian history as one of the country's earliest poets. In 1224 Frederick founded the University of Napoli, with the idea of educating administrators for his kingdom. As a half-Norman southerner, Frederick rejected the tradition that Holy Roman Emperors lived north of the Alpi. He moved his exotic, multicultural court (complete with Saracen guard) between Sicilia and southern Italy, where he built several castles, notably the superb octagonal Castel del Monte in Puglia.

City-States & Comuni

Between the 12th and 14th centuries, government in Italy evolved into a new kind of political institution – the city-states or city-republics, whose political organisation became known as the *comune*, or the town council.

The cities of northern Italy were highly favoured commercially by their position on the route into Europe from the Mar Mediterraneo. They were also a long way from both the pope and the emperor. With the resulting new wealth, some cities freed themselves from feudal control. Milano, Crema, Bologna, Firenze, Pavia, Modena, Parma, Lodi and many other cities set themselves up as autonomous powers, but with the protection of either the pope or the emperor. The middle class was born, composed of rich merchants and artisans who, very soon, passed from commercial rivalry to internal political struggles. These conflicts ended up favouring restricted oligarchies in which one family prevailed, charged by the city with exercising a form of government called the *Signoria*. This was the highest level of republican government of the city-states and was particularly prevalent in Firenze. The various Signorie were reinforced internally, persecuting rival families and opponents while simultaneously expanding their territories at the expense of weaker neighbours.

The five great Italian regional divisions began to take shape: Veneto, Lombardia, Toscana, the Papal States, and the Southern Kingdom.

In the south, Charles of Anjou, who had defeated and beheaded Conradin, Frederick II's 16-year-old grandson and heir, ousted Germanic rule. French dominion under Charles brought heavy taxes, particularly on rich landowners, who did not accept such measures graciously. Although always a hated foreigner, Charles supported much-needed road repairs, reformed the coinage, imposed standard weights and measures, improved the equipment of ports and opened silver mines.

Despite his grip on papal power and his subsequent conquests of Jerusalem and Constantinople, Charles of Anjou was to become infamous throughout Italy for a popular uprising, sparked off by the assault of a Sicilian woman by a French soldier in Palermo on 30 March 1282. A crowd gathered, killing the soldier, and a widespread massacre of the French ensued as communities throughout Sicilia rose against their warlords. Known as the Sicilian Vespers, the events of this time led to the citizens of Palermo breaking away from French domination and endorsing Peter of Aragon as king, effectively separating themselves from the Neapolitan mainland and bringing themselves under Spanish rule.

The latter decades of the 13th century were marked by decreasing economic vitality as Europeans battled an invasion far more deadly than that of a mere army. The effects of plague (later to be known as the

Black Death), along with famine and deprivation from years of war, wiped out over half the population of many major cities.

Meanwhile, in northern and central Italy, the city-states were growing in importance. The Republic of Venezia increased its possessions. Trading with its powerful fleet towards the Byzantine east, it securely managed its own independence in the ports of Dalmatia, Greece, Cyprus and the Aegean.

The legal debate of this time and the ensuing changes to Italian society, together with the dawning of a new era of powerful literary and artistic expression, were to form the basis of the humanist culture which ushered in the Renaissance.

Humanism

The artist whose works signify the breakthrough from the Byzantine or Gothic style to the Renaissance was Giotto. In literature, Averroës, a Muslim philosopher born in Córdoba in southern Spain in 1126, resurrected Aristotle's doctrine that immortality was gained through individual efforts towards universal reason. This emphasis on the autonomy of human reason, based on the theories of the classical philosophers instead of the increasingly self-serving dogmas of the Church hierarchy, was a revolutionary philosophical position that became known as humanism.

The Church had chosen to embrace only those classical philosophers whose thinking fitted its theological purposes. Instead humanist thinkers were discovering ancient Roman and Greek works, which had been transcribed by religious orders during the Middle Ages and remained hidden away, often thought lost, in monasteries throughout Europe. These classical works were not necessarily those which were accepted by the Church and they inspired great debate among intellectuals of the day.

Translated into Latin, Averroës' work strongly influenced another interpreter of Aristotelian thought, St Thomas Aquinas, who was educated at Monte Cassino by the Benedictines and at the University of Bologna, before joining the Dominicans

in 1243. Aquinas bridged the gap between the Christian belief in God and Aristotle's respect for the validity of reason with his *Summa Theologiae*. This resulted in Italian Christianity never losing either its grip on the real world or its respect for good works.

The new era saw independent artisans flourish and their guilds became influential in the power structure of the cities, particularly in Firenze, which retained the trappings of the new republicanism until 1434, when the Medici family brought back a comparatively mild despotism. The Florentine houses of Peruzzi and Bardi were the business powers of Europe, minting some 400,000 units of their currency, the *firenze* (florin) each year.

Florentine prosperity was based on the wool trade, finance and general commerce, allowing craft and trade guilds to become increasingly powerful in the affairs of the city. The Arte della Lana (wool guild) of Firenze employed a workforce of more than 5000, but these workers did not have the status of citizens and could not take part in elections in the republic. In 1378 the poorest workers, the wool-carters *(ciompi)*, revolted against their city fathers, taking power in the city-state for at least six weeks, during which time they created new guilds to represent them.

Meanwhile, a greater power struggle was taking place between the pope and the Holy Roman Emperor. This conflict formed the focal point of Italian politics in the late Middle Ages which saw two camps emerge: Guelfi (Guelph, in support of the pope) and Ghibellini (Ghibelline, in support of the emperor). Dante Alighieri, the great poet and writer, whom Italians see as the father of the Italian language, was one of the casualties of the Guelph-Ghibelline struggle. A dedicated Guelph supporter, Dante was exiled from his birthplace, Firenze, in 1301 because he belonged to the wrong faction.

While the first decades of the 14th century were years of economic and cultural growth, not all cities employed the relatively liberal style of the government of

Firenze. Like many of the Italian comuni, Milano was still strictly dominated by the Signorie. The Della Torre family, which represented the popular party of the city-state, came into fierce conflict with the Visconti family, representing the Ghibelline nobility. Ottone Visconti had been made Archbishop of Milano in 1262 and his nephew, Matteo, was made imperial vicar by Henry VII. He subsequently destroyed the power of the Della Torre, extending Milanese control over Pavia and Cremona, and later Genova and Bologna. Giangaleazzo Visconti (1351-1402) would turn Milano from a city-state into a strong European power and, although the Visconti were disliked as dictators, Milano managed to resist French attempts at invasion.

The policies of the Visconti (up to 1450), followed by those of the Sforza family, allowed Milano an economic and territorial development that extended the borders of the Signoria from Genova to Bologna and from Ticino in Switzerland to Lago di Garda. During those years of tireless labour, the entire area of the Pianura Padana (the Po plain) was transformed. Massive hydraulic and irrigation projects (involving Leonardo da Vinci) converted the plain from a swampy woodland into an extremely productive agricultural collective with some of the most fertile farmland in Italy. Among other things, the cultivation of rice and mulberries was introduced. In the 15th century parmesan cheese, a product of Parma, Reggio Emilia and Lodi, was among the most precious cheeses in Europe, and butter from the plains of Lombardia was exported as far as Roma.

The Babylonian Captivity

During this period, the Church was going through a profound crisis. The papacy's ongoing crusades against Muslims during the 13th century had turned into campaigns against European heretics in the 14th, campaigns which in Italy were thinly disguised grabs for wealth and prosperity by claimants from Italian ruling families and the related nobility of Europe.

Pope Boniface VIII (1294-1303) came from Italian nobility and his efforts were directed at ensuring his family's continuing wealth and power. His papal bull of 1302, *Unam Sanctum*, claimed papal supremacy in worldly and spiritual affairs – claims of secular power which achieved its ends by eliminating heretics.

In 1309 Pope Clement V chose to base the papacy in Avignon. When the French Pope John XXII (1316-34) established this on a permanent basis, the Roman Catholic Church, and indeed Roma in general, suddenly lost its *raison d'être*. Goats and cows grazed on the Campidoglio and in the Foro Romano, and public support for the city's many churches and cathedrals disappeared. The city became a battleground for the struggles between the powerful Orsini and Colonna families. The ruling families challenged the papacy's claim to be secular rulers of Roma and the Papal State began to fall apart.

There were seven popes in Avignon between 1309 and 1377. This period became known as the Babylonian Captivity, a phrase coined by the Roman poet laureate Petrarch to castigate the evils of the French papal court.

After the failed attempt of Cola di Rienzo, a popular leader, to wrest control of Roma from the nobility, Cardinal Egidio d'Albornoz managed to restore the Papal State with his *Egidian Constitutions*, thereby enabling Pope Gregory XI to return to Roma in 1377. Finding a ruined and almost deserted city, Gregory made Il Vaticano his base because it was fortified and had the formidable Castel Sant'Angelo nearby.

On Gregory's death, a year after he returned to Roma, Roman cardinals moved to retain their power. They elected Urban VI as pope, but he proved to be unpopular. This sparked off a renegade movement of cardinals, mainly French, who, a few months later, elected a second pope, Clement VII, who set up his claim in Avignon. So began the Great Schism, and the papacy was not to be reconciled with Roma until 1417.

The Borgia Family

It seems surprising, if not shocking, by today's standards, that the popes of 15th century Italy fought wars to maintain their territories, had their enemies killed, kept mistresses and even had children by them.

But if the Church was to survive the effects of the Great Schism (1378-1417), it was considered necessary for the pontiff to be noted more for his political and diplomatic skills than for his spiritual and moral qualities. Thus he was chosen for his leadership abilities and capacity to compete with the various ferocious rulers of the peninsula at that time. In other words, the popes of the period were no saints.

The Spaniard Rodrigo Borgia was elected Pope Alexander VI in 1492, in what is said to have been the most corrupt election in papal history. He went on to establish a notoriously corrupt and immoral court, and throughout his papacy he maintained a mistress, Vannozza Catanei, who bore him the infamous Borgia family. It all seemed to make little difference to the Christian pilgrims who flocked to Rome to honour Alexander in the jubilee year of 1500.

Alexander's son Cesare, who killed his own brother, terrorised Italy in a campaign to consolidate and expand the papal states. Ruthless and brilliant, he was at one point admired by Machiavelli. But his sister, Lucrezia, has gone down in history as the embodiment of Borgia cruelty, lust and avarice. It is said that Pope Alexander was obsessed with his daughter almost to the point of incest. He ensured that she lived in incredible luxury and considered no man worthy of her. Nevertheless, Lucrezia did marry several times, though one of her husbands was assassinated by Cesare and another was publicly declared impotent by Alexander.

The Renaissance

With the end of the Great Schism in the 15th century, the newly influential papacy initiated the transformation of Roma. Reduced during the Middle Ages to a conglomeration of majestic ruins and wretched dwellings, the city assumed a new elegance. In 1455 Bernardo Rossellino began construction of Palazzo Venezia, Sixtus IV initiated an urban plan which was to link the areas that had been cut off from one another during the Middle Ages and Donatello, Sandro Botticelli and Fra Angelico lived and worked in Roma at this time.

At the beginning of the 16th century, Pope Julius II opened Via del Corso and Via Giulia and gave Bramante the task of beginning work on the second Basilica di San Pietro, which was to take more than a century to finish. In 1508 Raphael started painting the rooms in Il Vaticano which are now known as Le Stanze di Raffaello, while between 1508 and 1512 Michelangelo worked on the vaults of the Cappella Sistina

(Sistine Chapel). All the great artists of the epoch were influenced by the increasingly frequent discoveries of marvellous pieces of classical art, such as the *Laocoön*, found in 1506 in the area of Nero's Domus Aurea (the sculpture is now in the Musei Vaticani).

Roma had 100,000 inhabitants at the height of the Renaissance and became the major centre for Italian political and cultural life. Pope Julius II was succeeded by Leo X, of the Medici family, and the Roman Curia (or Papal Court) became a meeting place for learned men such as Baldassar Castiglione and Ludovico Ariosto.

As the Renaissance dawned, Italians found they could no longer accept the papal domination of earlier times. A remarkable treatise by the humanist Lorenzo Valla revealed the *Donation of Constantine* to be a forgery. Serious study of the Greek classics and Hebrew and Arabic scholars influenced the literary works of the later 15th century and the idea of the place of the individual in the universe grew in importance.

The 15th and early 16th centuries showed unparalleled creativity and visionary accomplishments in all aspects of political, cultural and social life. In Firenze, Cosimo de' Medici, private citizen and wealthy merchant, took over the Signoria in 1434. His nephew, Lorenzo Il Magnifico (the Magnificent), is remembered as a great politician who laid importance on the economic and financial security of Firenze. In his refined diplomacy he focused on building the prestige of the city by enriching it with the presence, and the works, of the greatest artists of the time, thus becoming the greatest art patron of the Renaissance.

Feudal lords such as Federico da Montefeltro in Urbino, a merchant as rich as the Medicis, and Francesco Sforza, military commander of Milano, shifted their allegiance between the pope and the emperor as best suited them. They became wealthy bankers and, revitalised by the profits from increased commerce, they competed with each other for the services of artists, writers, poets and musicians.

This phenomenal creativity was disrupted in Firenze by Savonarola, a Dominican monk who preached fire and brimstone against humanist thinking and allied himself with the French King Charles VIII to overthrow the Medici family and declare a republic in Firenze in 1494. Although the monk eventually met a gruesome end, he wielded tremendous power in Florentine politics in the later 15th century.

The Medicis, briefly reinstated, could not reassert their positive influence over the Florentines, who eventually rejected them, setting up a second democratic republic in 1527. In 1530 this republic was in turn overthrown when Emperor Charles V, who had sacked Roma in 1527, brought back the Medicis, who ruled over Firenze for the next 210 years.

The first Florentine Republic produced Niccolò Machiavelli (1469-1527), a public official whose short handbook, *Il Principe* (The Prince), outlined somewhat cynically the prerequisite skills for securing and retaining power. Machiavelli advocated the end of all foreign rule in Italy and urged the people to employ their native wit and cunning to achieve this end. He also wrote a history of Firenze, in Italian rather than Latin, although his efforts in this field were less original than those of his contemporary and friend, Francesco Guicciardini (1483-1532).

Not all Italian states experienced the great social blossoming of the Renaissance. In the south, quarrels over power and land between the Visconti family (in league with Alfonso V of Aragon) and the house of Angevin ensured repression of the liberty and free thinking which had inspired the new sense of creativity and productivity in other parts of the country.

The Counter-Reformation

By the third decade of the 16th century, the broad-minded curiosity of the Renaissance had begun to give way to the intolerance of the Counter-Reformation. This was the response of the Church to the Reformation, a collective term for the movement led by Martin Luther that aimed to reform the Church and which led to the rise of Protestantism in its many forms. The transition was epitomised by the reign of Pope Paul III (1534-49), who promoted the building of the classically elegant Palazzo Farnese in Roma but who also, in 1540, allowed the establishment of Ignatius Loyola's order of the Jesuits and the organisation in 1542 of the Holy Office. This was the final (and ruthless) court of appeal in the trials of suspected heretics. These trials began to gather momentum with the increased activities of the Inquisition (1232-1820), the notorious judicial arm of the Church whose aim was to suppress heresy.

Pope Paul III's fanatical opposition to Protestantism and his purging of clerical abuse, as he saw it, resulted in a widespread campaign of torture and fear. In 1559 the Church published the *Index Librorum Prohibitorum* (Index of Prohibited Books) and the persecution of intellectuals and free thinkers intensified as part of the Roman Church's strategy to regain papal supremacy over the Protestant churches.

Two of the great Italian intellectuals to suffer during the Counter-Reformation were Giordano Bruno (1548-1600) and Galileo Galilei (1564-1642). Bruno, a Dominican monk, was forced to flee Italy for Calvinist Geneva, from where he travelled extensively throughout Europe before being arrested by the Inquisition in Venezia in 1592. In 1870 the Kingdom of Italy erected a statue of Bruno in Roma's Campo de' Fiori, where he had been burnt at the stake.

An advocate of Aristotelian science, Galileo was forced by the Church to renounce his approval of the Copernican astronomical system, which held that the earth moved round the sun rather than the reverse. But where Bruno had rejected the Catholic Church, Galileo never deviated from the faith which rejected him.

The latter years of the 16th century were not all counterproductive. Pope Gregory XIII (1572-85) replaced the Julian calendar with the Gregorian one in 1582, fixing the start of the year on 1 January and adjusting the system of leap years to align the 365 day year with the seasons. In addition, the city of Roma was greatly embellished by the architectural and sculptural achievements of Gian Lorenzo Bernini (1598-1680).

However, despite these exceptions, Italy no longer determined European cultural expression. Epidemics and wars, in particular the War of the Spanish Succession (1701-14), tossed the nation from Spanish domination in the 17th century to Austrian occupation in the 18th century, beginning with the conquest of Napoli in 1707.

The Enlightenment

The Italy of the 18th century, although mainly ruled from abroad, was set to play its part in an era which broke down many of the national barriers of Europe, a development which was as much due to the intermarriage of its monarchies as to new trading laws necessitated by bad harvests in many areas of the continent. The papacy became less influential, especially following the expulsion of the Jesuits from Portugal, France and Spain.

The Enlightenment swept away the dark days of the Counter-Reformation, producing great philosophers and writers such as Cesare Beccaria (1738-94), whose masterpiece *Of Crimes & Punishments* attacked torture and capital punishment as barbarism and advocated reform of the criminal code, a proposal taken up by Grand Duke Leopold of Toscana, who abolished the death sentence.

In the field of economics, ideas advocating the liberalisation of trade laws were put forward by the influential writer Pietro Verri (1728-97) who, with his brother Alessandro, introduced reforms in schools and universities as well as in the government of Lombardia. Alessandro Volta (1745-1827), after whom the unit of electric potential, the volt, is named, invented the battery while he was professor of natural philosophy at the University of Bologna.

Napoleon

Italy had been the source of many enlightened political ideas, but the concept of national sovereignty had not been one of them. However, when the 27-year-old, Corsican-born French general Napoleon Bonaparte invaded Italy in 1796 and unilaterally declared himself its dictator, a nationalist movement began in earnest. Inspired by the ideas of Jean-Jacques Rousseau, the French leftist Jacobin movement gained significant support in Italy when, in his first year of occupation, Napoleon used Italy as the base for his expedition into Egypt.

The Jacobin movement established a republic in Roma, renewing the debate about Italy as a nation and the sovereign rights of its people. This movement was dubbed the Risorgimento, or Revival, by Italian dramatist Vittorio Alfieri (1749-1803). However, the mainly middle-class movement found itself unable to bring about social reforms quickly enough for the peasants, particularly the very poor of Napoli. A peasant army sacked the city, littering its streets with dead Jacobins.

Although he had declared himself first consul of Italy in 1799, Napoleon acceded to the calls of Italian deputies in the north to proclaim a republic and, for the first time in history, the political entity known as Italy came into being, albeit with Napoleon as its first, self-elected president.

When, in 1804, Napoleon made himself emperor of France he established the Kingdom of Italy and made himself its first sovereign, inviting Pope Pius VII to crown him king in Paris. Pius delayed his visit, reluctant to give his endorsement to the power brokers of the French Revolution, which had greatly curtailed the power of the Catholic Church. He was also loath to endorse the marriage of Napoleon to the divorcée Josephine. When the pope finally arrived several days late, Napoleon was not amused. As the pope raised the emperor's crown to his head, Napoleon took it and crowned himself.

Unification

During the final years of Napoleon's domination of Italy, hopes grew that his regime would be replaced with independence and constitutional rule. It was not to be: following Napoleon's defeat at Waterloo in 1815, all of the peninsula's former rulers were reinstated by the Congress of Vienna. It was a backward step that had terrible consequences for the country, but it encouraged the rapid growth of secret societies which were, in the main, comprised of disaffected middle-class intellectuals. In the south, one of these societies, the republican Carbonari society, pushed hard and often ruthlessly for a valid constitution, leading a revolutionary uprising in Napoli in 1820.

One of the leading revolutionary figures of the secret societies of the time was Filippo Buonarroti, who strove for independence from Austria and the establishment of a communist society devoid of private-property interests.

A Genovese, Giuseppe Mazzini (1805-72), emerged as a key proponent of nationhood and political freedom. Having quit the Carbonari movement in 1830, Mazzini founded Young Italy, a society of young men whose aims were the liberation of Italy from foreign and domestic tyranny and its unification under a republican government. This was to be achieved through education and, where necessary, revolt by guerrilla bands. Exiled from his homeland for his former activities with the Carbonari, Mazzini was responsible for organising a number of abortive uprisings throughout Italy during the 1830s and 1840s. These left dead many of the young men who had flocked to join Young Italy. Twice sentenced to death, Mazzini was to live out his days in England, from where he wrote articles and solicited as much support as he could from influential allies to raise the consciousness of Europeans about the Italian question.

In 1848 there were revolutions in almost every major city and town of Europe. In their newspaper, *Il Risorgimento* – one of several publications to have sprung up as the Italian nationalist movement gained ground among citizens of all classes – nationalist writer Cesare Balbo and Count Camillo Benso di Cavour of Torino pressed for a constitution. In 1848 they published their *Statuto* (Statute) advocating a two chamber parliament, with the upper chamber to be appointed by the Crown and the lower chamber to be elected by educated

NICKY CAVEN

Mazzini formed his nationalist Young Italy movement while in exile in Marseilles.

taxpayers. In 1861 the *Statuto* was to become the constitutional basis of the Kingdom of Italy, but not before 13 more years of warring between the various European princes had resulted in the deaths of a great many more Italians.

Returning to Italy in 1848 from his famous exploits in South America, where he is still remembered as one of the founding fathers of Uruguay, Giuseppe Garibaldi (1807-82) was to become the hero Italians needed to lead them towards unification. Garibaldi's personal magnetism, the result of his respect for people, rich and poor, drew more Italians into the fight for nationhood than ever before.

Despite significant personal animosity, Garibaldi and Cavour fought side by side, each in their chosen arena, to break the stranglehold of foreign domination. The brilliant diplomacy of Cavour, coupled with the independent efforts of Garibaldi and his popular base, finally caught the attention of European communities, particularly the British, who became staunch supporters of a free and united Italy.

When King Carlo Alberto, the sympathetic Piemontese monarch, granted a constitution based on the *Statuto* in March 1848, Cavour stood for election. In 1850 he was given three ministries – navy, commerce and finance – in the government headed by Massimo d'Azeglio. When Cavour's centre-left faction joined forces with the centre-right, headed by Urbano Rattazzi, behind d'Azeglio's back, the prime minister resigned and Cavour was asked by the king to take the top government post. As prime minister, Cavour focused on forging an alliance with the French emperor Napoleon III, in a move destined to overthrow Austrian domination of Piemonte.

Meanwhile the unification movement was literally on the move, as Garibaldi led his Expedition of One Thousand, which took Sicilia and Napoli in 1860. The Kingdom of Italy was declared on 17 March 1861 and Vittorio Emanuele II, who had been king of Sardegna-Piemonte from 1849, was proclaimed king. But Italy was not completely united: Venezia remained in the hands of the Austrians and Roma was held by France.

Cavour died within six months of leading the first parliament of the Kingdom of Italy. He had been betrayed by his French allies when Napoleon III signed the armistice of Villafranca, ending the Franco-Austrian war (fought in Italy, largely by Italians) without consulting Cavour, who resigned his post. Venezia was wrested from the Austrians in 1866, but it wasn't until the Franco-Prussian War of 1870 that Napoleon III's hold over Italy was broken. Needing all available troops elsewhere, he withdrew from Roma, leaving the way clear for the Italian army to reclaim the capital.

The only resistance to the push on Roma came from the papal soldiers of Pope Pius IX, who refused to recognise the Kingdom of Italy. The pope was eventually stripped of his remaining secular powers as well as his palace, the Quirinale. The papacy regained some autonomy in the 1920s when the Fascist dictator, Benito Mussolini, restored the independent papal state, but in the interim, the papacy forbade Catholics to participate in governmental elections.

As the 20th century approached, the economic crisis of Europe was reflected in Italian politics by constant fluctuations as socialist democrats and right-wing imperialists in turn gained and lost the support of the populace. In the general elections of 1894, Pope Pius X formally gave Catholics the right to vote (although many had already been doing just that) and there was a widespread backlash against socialism. Giovanni Giolitti, one of Italy's longest-serving prime ministers (heading five governments between the years 1892 and 1921), managed to bridge the political extremes and was able to embark on parliamentary reforms which gave the vote to all literate men aged 21 or over and all illiterate men who had completed military service or were aged 30 or over. But although male suffrage had been achieved, Italian women were denied the right to vote until after WWII.

Fascism

When war broke out in Europe in July 1914, Italy chose to remain neutral rather than become caught between old enemies. But senior politicians soon allied themselves with the British, Russians and French, while the papacy spoke out against the 'atheist' French in favour of Catholic Austria.

In October 1914 the editor of the socialist newspaper *Avanti!* also declared himself strongly in favour of alignment with the Allied forces. For his views, young Benito Mussolini was forced to resign. He started his own newspaper in November, *Il Popolo d'Italia*, a propaganda publication financed by French, British and Russian interests.

In 1919 he founded the Fascist Party, with its hallmarks of the black shirt and Roman salute. These were to become symbols of violent oppression and aggressive nationalism for the next 23 years. In 1921 the party won 35 of the 135 seats in parliament. In October 1922 the king asked Mussolini to form a government, and thus began his domination of Italy. With an expedition of 40,000 Fascist militia, he began the famous march on Roma to 'free the nation from the socialists'.

In April 1924, following a campaign marked by violence and intimidation, the Fascist Party won the national elections and Mussolini created the world's first Fascist regime. By 1925 the term 'totalitarianism' had come into use. By the end of that year Mussolini had expelled opposition parties from parliament, gained control of the press and trade unions and had rescinded the right to vote from two-thirds of the electorate. In 1929 Mussolini and Pope Pius XI signed the Lateran Pact, whereby Catholicism was declared the sole religion of Italy and Il Vaticano was recognised as an independent state. In return, the papacy finally acknowledged the united Kingdom of Italy.

In the 1920s Mussolini embarked on an aggressive foreign policy, leading to skirmishes with Greece over the island of Corfu and to military expeditions against nationalist forces in the Italian colony of Libya. In 1935 Italy sought a new colonial conquest through the invasion of Abyssinia (present-day Ethiopia) from the Italian base in Eritrea, but took seven months to capture Addis Ababa. The act was condemned by the League of Nations, which imposed limited sanctions on Italy.

Fearful of international isolation, Mussolini formed the Axis with Hitler in 1936. They were soon joined by Japan and Italy entered WWII in June 1941 as an ally of Germany.

After a series of military disasters and the landing of the Allied armies on Sicilia on 10 July 1943, Mussolini was faced not only with increasing discontent among Italians and diminishing support for Fascism, but also with Hitler's refusal to assign more troops to defend southern Italy. Two weeks after the Allied landing, the King of Italy, Vittorio Emanuele III, led a coup against Mussolini and had him arrested.

In the confused period that followed, now known as the 45 Days, Italy erupted in a series of massive demonstrations demanding an end to the war. The king signed an armistice with the Allies that amounted to an unconditional surrender and declared war on Germany, but it was too late to prevent the takeover of northern Italy by Nazi troops. As the Allies moved up through the south of the Italian peninsula, the Germans began their campaign of brutal suppression in the north, prompting the formation of the Resistance.

The Germans rescued Mussolini from his prison on the Gran Sasso in what is now Abruzzo and installed him as head of the Republic of Salò in the north. By now completely demoralised, Mussolini was nothing more than a German puppet. He was eventually captured and shot by partisans, along with his mistress, Clara Petacci, in April 1945, and hung upside down from the roof of a petrol station in Milano's Piazzale Loreto.

The Resistance

Members of the Resistance, which numbered more than 100,000 by conservative estimates in early 1945, managed to gain control of small areas of the north and played a significant role in liberating Firenze from the Germans in August 1944. The Nazi response to partisan attacks was savage. Whole villages were exterminated: in one of the most notorious reprisals, 1830 men, women and children were murdered by an SS battalion at Marzabotto, south of Bologna, on 1 October 1944. In March of that year urban partisans had blown up 32 military police in Roma. In reprisal, the Germans shot 335 prisoners at the Fosse Ardeatine, just outside the city.

Northern Italy was finally liberated by the end of May 1945, after Allied troops broke through German lines. The Resistance had suffered huge losses and its contribution to the Allied victory did not go unacknowledged. These people had fought not only against German and Fascist oppression, but also for an ideal of social and political change, and after the war they wanted to put that ideal into action. The Allies, meanwhile, were wondering how to deal with what amounted to a massive, armed, left-wing movement whose leaders spoke often of insurrection.

The Republic

The Resistance was disarmed, either voluntarily or by force, as Italy's political forces scrambled to regroup and the USA, through the Marshall Plan, was exerting a profound effect on the country both economically and politically. Immediately after the war there was a series of three coalition governments. The third, which came to power in December 1945, was dominated by the newly formed Democrazia Cristiana (DC; Christian Democrats), led by Alcide de Gasperi, who remained prime minister until 1953.

In 1946, following a referendum, the constitutional monarchy was abolished and a republic established, with the DC winning the majority of votes at the first post-war elections. The Partito Comunista Italiano (PCI; Communist Party), led by Palmiro Togliatti, and the Partito Socialista Italiano (PSI; Socialist Party), led by Pietro Nenni, participated in coalition governments until

1947, when de Gasperi formed a government which excluded the left.

Economic Recovery

By the early 1950s the country's economy had begun to show strong signs of recovery, although the more impoverished and less industrialised south lagged behind. To counter this, the government formed the Cassa per il Mezzogiorno (State Fund for the South) in 1950, which would eventually pour trillions of lire into development projects in the southern regions. In 1958 Italy became a founding member of the European Economic Community (EEC) and this signalled the beginning of the Economic Miracle, a period of significant economic growth which saw unemployment drop as industry expanded. A major feature of this period was the development of Italy's automobile industry and, more particularly, of Fiat in Torino, which sparked a massive migration of peasants from the south to the north in search of work.

The early 1950s also saw the formation of a new extreme right-wing party called the Movimento Sociale Italiano (MSI), which was basically neo-Fascist.

Although it was the only major party not to participate in the government of the country, the PCI nevertheless played a crucial role in Italy's social and political development well into the 1980s. The party steadily increased its share of the poll at each election and always had more card-carrying members than the DC, but the spectre of European communism and the Cold War continued to undermine its chances of participating in government.

By the mid-1960s Italy's economic strength was waning and social unrest was becoming commonplace. Togliatti, the long-serving leader of the PCI, died in 1964. His policy of cooperation with the DC in the interests of national unity had played a significant role in avoiding serious social conflict. One year earlier, Aldo Moro had been appointed prime minister, a position he held until 1968. It was Moro who invited the PSI into government in 1963 and

NICKY CAVEN

Kidnap victim Aldo Moro was killed by the Brigate Rosse after the government refused to release 13 of their colleagues jailed in Torino.

more than a decade later he was moving towards a historic compromise which would have allowed the communists to enter government for the first time. This prompted his kidnapping and murder by the Brigate Rosse (BR; Red Brigades) terrorist group.

Protest & Terrorism

Influenced by similar events in France, in 1967 and 1968 Italian university students rose up in protest, ostensibly against poor conditions in the universities. However, the protests were really aimed at authority and the perceived impotence of the left. The movement resulted in the formation of many small revolutionary groups which attempted to fill what the students saw as an ideological gap in Italy's political left wing. The uprising was closely followed in 1969 by what has become known as the Autunno Caldo (Hot Autumn), when factory workers embarked on a series of strikes and protests which continued into 1971.

But as the new decade began, a new phenomenon, terrorism, began to overshadow this turbulent era of protest and change. By 1970, a group of young left-wing militants had formed the Brigate Rosse (a modern version of this terrorist group resurfaced in Italy towards the end of the 1990s – see later in this section).

Neo-Fascist terrorists had already struck. On 12 December 1969, a bomb was set off in a bank in Milano's Piazza Fontana, killing 16 people. Controversy and mystery shrouded this incident, but it is now certain that it was an act of right-wing extremists directed by forces within the country's secret services. The bombing formed part of what was known as the Strategy of Tension, which culminated in the 1980 bombing of the Bologna train station by right-wing terrorists, in which 84 people died.

The Brigate Rosse were by no means the only terrorists operating in the country during the Anni di Piombo (Years of Lead) from 1973 to 1980, but they were certainly the most prominent. While many of the BR's original members were dead or in prison by the mid-1970s, 1977 saw a major recruiting campaign give new life to the movement. That year was also marked by student protests, sparked largely by their opposition to education reforms proposed by the government. As opposed to Sessantotto (1968), this was more an anti-political than an ideological movement. Universities were occupied in Roma, Bologna and Milano and the *centro sociale* – a type of left-wing cultural centre established through the occupation of unused buildings – had its origin in this period.

In 1978 the Brigate Rosse claimed their most important victim – Aldo Moro. During the 54 days that Moro was held captive by the BR, his colleagues laboured over whether to bargain with the terrorists to save his life, or to adopt a position of no compromise. In the end, they took the latter path and the BR killed Moro on 9 May 1978, leaving his body in the boot of a car parked in a street in the centre of Roma which was equidistant from the headquarters of the DC and the PCI.

Finally, the *carabinieri* general Carlo Alberto dalla Chiesa was appointed to wipe out the terrorist groups. Using a new law which allowed *pentiti* (repentants) much-reduced prison sentences, he convinced key terrorists to aid his efforts. In 1980 dalla Chiesa was appointed by the government to fight the Mafia in Sicilia. He and his wife were assassinated in Palermo within a few months of his taking up the job.

The 1970s also produced much positive political and social change. In 1970 the country was divided into administrative regions and regional governments were elected. In the same year divorce became legal and efforts by conservative Catholics to have the law repealed were defeated in a referendum in 1974. In 1978 abortion was legalised, following anti-sexist legislation which allowed women to keep their own names after marriage.

The compromise with the communists was never to come about, but in 1983 the DC government was forced by its diminishing share of the electoral vote to hand over the prime ministership to a socialist. Bettino Craxi became the longest serving prime minister since de Gasperi, holding the post from 1983 to 1989. A skilled politician, Craxi continued to wield considerable power in government until he fled the country in 1993 after being implicated in the Tangentopoli national bribery scandal (see the following section). Convicted *in absentia* on corruption charges, he remains in self-imposed exile in Tunisia.

Italy benefitted from significant economic growth in the 1980s, during which it became one of the world's leading economic powers (see the Economy section later in this chapter). However, the 1990s heralded a new period of crisis for the country, both economically and politically. High unemployment and inflation rates, combined with a huge national debt and an extremely unstable lira, led the government to introduce draconian measures to revive the economy.

In this period the PCI reached a watershed. Internal ideological disagreements led

to a split in the party in the early 1990s. The old guard now goes by the title Partito Rifondazione Comunista (PRC; Refounded Communist Party), under the leadership of Fausto Bertinotti. The breakaway, more moderate wing of the party reformed itself under the title Partito Democratico della Sinistra (PDS; Democratic Party of the Left). Under the leadership of Massimo d'Alema, the party went on to become the largest in the centre-left Ulivo (Olive Tree) coalition, which came to power in 1996 (see later in this section).

Tangentopoli

The scandal of Tangentopoli (literally 'kickback cities') broke in Milano in early 1992 when a functionary of the PSI was arrested on charges of accepting bribes in exchange for public works contracts. Led by Milanese magistrate Antonio di Pietro, who was dubbed 'the reluctant hero', investigations known as Mani Pulite (Clean Hands) eventually implicated thousands of politicians, public officials and businesspeople.

Charges ranged from bribery, making illicit political payments and receiving kickbacks, to blatant theft. It is worth noting that few ordinary Italians were surprised that many politicians, at all levels of government, were entrenched in a system whereby they demanded secret payments as a matter of course. The corruption went to the very highest levels of government and few of the country's top politicians escaped the taint of scandal.

In elections just after the scandal broke in 1992, voters expressed their discontent and the DC's share of the vote dropped by 5%. In this election Umberto Bossi's Lega Nord (Northern League) made its first appearance as a force to be reckoned with at the national level, winning 7% of the vote on a federalist, anti-corruption platform.

As Tangentopoli continued to unfold, the main parties – the DC and the PSI – were in tatters and the centre of the Italian political spectrum was effectively demolished.

At the 1994 national elections, voters took the opportunity to express their disgust with the old order. The elections were won by a new right-wing coalition known as the Polo per le Libertà (Freedom Alliance), whose members included the newly formed Forza Italia (Go Italy) and the neo-Fascist Alleanza Nazionale (National Alliance, a repackaged and sanitised MSI), as well as the federalist Northern League. The leader of the alliance, billionaire media magnate Silvio Berlusconi, who had entered politics only three months before the elections, was appointed prime minister. After a turbulent nine months in power, Berlusconi's volatile coalition government disintegrated when Bossi, in what was a very controversial move, withdrew the support of his Northern League.

Berlusconi himself had been notified that he was under investigation by the Milano Mani Pulite judges and various court proceedings against him continued into 1999.

In the chaos following the fall of the Berlusconi government, President Oscar Luigi Scalfaro appointed an interim government of technocrats which set about confronting the country's economic problems: it introduced pension reforms as one measure aimed at reducing the public debt.

New Beginning

The technocrats ran the country until elections were held in April 1996. By that time, the electoral system had resulted in a fairly clear division of the parties into two main groups: *centro-destra* (centre-right) and *centro-sinistra* (centre-left). Berlusconi's party, Forza Italia, remained aligned with the Alleanza Nazionale in the Polo per le Libertà, which has gathered other small parties of the centre right under its umbrella.

However, it was the centre-left Ulivo coalition, led by Bolognese university professor Romano Prodi, which won the 1996 elections. Prodi immediately promised that Italy would join Europe's economic and monetary union (EMU) in the first intake. His government drastically reduced public spending and introduced new taxes, and Italy participated in the single currency from its inception in 1999.

Despite the minor economic miracle, the road was far from smooth for Prodi's government and saw a succession of trials of strength between the Ulivo and its coalition partner, the far-left PRC, which made its support conditional on increased spending on welfare and job creation. The impasse reached its height in September 1998. Faced with the prospect of bringing down the second longest-lasting government of the Republic, the PRC divided into those who supported the PRC leader, Fausto Bertinotti, and a new grouping, Comunisti Italiani, who wanted to maintain the Prodi government. At the same time, the Unione Democratica per la Repubblica (UDR), a centrist group seeking a share of political power, offered its (conditional) support. Prodi refused to compromise and opted to face parliament in a ballot, which he lost by one vote.

During the Prodi government the PDS, under party secretary Massimo D'Alema, had remodelled itself as the Democratici della Sinistra (DS; Democrats of the Left), moving yet further from its communist roots. D'Alema had been manoeuvring for months (if not years) into a position where he could take over from Prodi. Prepared to compromise where Prodi wouldn't, he put forward an agreement with the centrist UDR, and was asked by President Scalfaro to form a government. Thus Italy gained its first former communist prime minister (ironically leading a governing coalition closer to the centre than that of his predecessor), who clearly believes that it is better to be in power with an uncomfortable ally than not be in power at all.

The election in May 1999 of Carlo Azeglio Ciampi as 10th president of the republic marked a new age in Italian politics. The former Bank of Italy governor, highly respected both in Italy and abroad, was elected by a strong parliamentary consensus of both left and right. The NATO war with Yugoslavia threw Italy into the international spotlight and political squabbling was minimised in the country's attempts to cope with its frontline position.

However, a shadow of the past reared its ugly head only days after the new president was sworn in, with the assassination of a senior government advisor, Massimo D'Antona, who had been closely involved with the labour ministry, especially in the area of strike legislation. The Brigate Rosse, long thought to be extinct, claimed responsibility for this attack, and the country was left wondering whether political terrorism was set to return.

GEOGRAPHY

Italy's boot shape makes it one of the most recognisable countries in the world, with the island of Sicilia appearing somewhat like a football at the toe of the boot and Sardegna situated in the middle of the Mar Tirreno to the west of the mainland.

The country is bounded by four seas, all part of the Mediterranean. The Mar Adriatico separates Italy from Slovenia, Croatia and Montenegro, the Mar Ionio laps the southern coasts of Puglia, Basilicata and Calabria and the Mar Ligure and Mar Tirreno are to the west of the country. Coastal areas vary from the cliffs of Liguria and Calabria to the generally flat, low-lying Adriatic coast.

More than 75% of Italy is mountainous, with the Alpi stretching from the Golfo di Genova (Gulf of Genoa) to the Mar Adriatico north of Trieste and dividing the peninsula from France, Switzerland, Austria and Slovenia. The highest Alpine peak is Monte Bianco (Mont Blanc) on the border with France, standing at 4807m, while the highest mountain in the Italian Alpi is Monte Rosa (4634m), on the Swiss border.

The Alpi are divided into three main groups – western, central and eastern – and undoubtedly the most spectacular scenery is found in the Dolomiti (Dolomites) in the eastern Alpi in Trentino-Alto Adige and the Veneto. There are more than 1000 glaciers in the Alpi, remnants of the last ice age, but they are in a constant state of retreat. The best known in the Italian Alpi is the Marmolada glacier on the border of Trentino and the Veneto, popular for summer skiing.

The Appennini (Apennine range) form a backbone extending for 1220km from near Genova, in Liguria, to the tip of Calabria and into Sicilia. The highest peak is the Corno Grande (2914m) in the Gran Sasso d'Italia group in Abruzzo. Another interesting group of mountains, the Alpi Apuane (Apuan Alps), is in north-western Toscana and constitutes a part of the sub-Appennini. These mountains are composed almost entirely of marble and have been mined almost continuously since Roman times. Michelangelo selected his blocks of perfect white marble at Carrara in the Alpi Apuane.

Lowlands, or plains, make up less than a quarter of Italy's total land area. The largest is the Pianura Padana, bounded by the Alpi, the Appennini and the Mar Adriatico. The plain is heavily populated and industrialised and through it run Italy's largest river, the Po, and its tributaries, the Reno, Adige, Piave and Tagliamento rivers. Other plains include the Tavoliere di Puglia and the Pianura Campana around Vesuvio.

GEOLOGY

Italy has a complex geological history, characterised by marked environmental and climatic changes. Around 100 million years

Rock Varieties

Even though Italy is not a large country, it contains a great variety of rock types. The Alpi are largely formed of crystalline rocks, such as granite and porphyry, and there are also sedimentary rocks, such as limestone, dolomite and sandstone, in the eastern Alpi. Sedimentary rocks are also found throughout the Appennini and on Sicilia and Sardegna. Crystalline and volcanic rocks predominate in Sardegna. Volcanic rocks are also common on Sicilia and along the Tyrrhenian side of the country, consistent with the volcanic activity in these parts of Italy. The country's plains are mainly formed from mixed deposits of gravel, sand and clay.

ago the area now occupied by the peninsula was covered by a tropical sea, the Tethys, which separated the Euro-Asiatic and African continental plates. As the ocean began to recede, various types of materials were deposited, including limestones, dolomites and sandstones, as well as the extensive coral reefs to the north-east from which the Dolomite mountain range was later formed (see the boxed text 'Rock Varieties' on the previous page).

Although earlier volcanic activity had resulted in the formation of the original nucleus of the Alpine chain and other mountains further south, the crucial moment came around 40 million years ago when the African and European continental plates collided. The collision forced the respective borders of the plates and part of the bed of the Tethys to fold and rise up, beginning the formation of the Alpine and Appennine chains. The Alpi rose up relatively quickly, at first forming an archipelago of tropical islands in the Tethys Sea. The curvature of the Alpine and Appennine chains, as well as the transverse orientation of the peninsula itself in the Mediterranean basin, reflect the manner in which the continental plates collided.

Both mountain chains underwent significant erosion, resulting in huge deposits of sand, gravel and clay at their feet and in part preparing the way for the development of land areas including Toscana. It is interesting to note that around six million years ago, when both the Alpi and the Appennini were still largely submerged, the Straits of Gibraltar closed up completely. As a result, the Mar Mediterraneo, which was all that remained of the vast Tethys, began to dry up. The Straits of Gibraltar reopened some two million years ago, allowing the Atlantic Ocean to refill the Mediterraneo. Some scholars have suggested that this ancient geological event could have given rise much later to the Atlantis myth, as well as the biblical story of Noah and the great flood.

By around two million years ago, after

Earthquakes & Volcanoes

A fault line runs through the entire Italian peninsula, from eastern Sicilia, following the Appennini up into the Alpi of Friuli-Venezia Giulia in the north-east of the country. The fault line corresponds to the collision point of the European and African continental plates and subjects a good part of the country to seismic activity. Central and southern Italy, including Sicilia, are subject to sometimes devastating earthquakes. The worst this century was in 1908, when Messina and Reggio di Calabria were destroyed by a seaquake registering seven on the Richter scale. Almost 86,000 people were killed by the quake and subsequent tidal wave. In November 1980 an earthquake south-east of Naples destroyed several villages and killed 2570 people. A more recent earthquake in the Appennini in September 1997, which affected Umbria and Le Marche, killed 10 people and caused part of the vaulted ceiling of the Basilica di San Francesco d'Assisi, in Assisi, to collapse, destroying important frescoes.

Italy has six active volcanoes: Stromboli and Vulcano (on the Isole Eolie), Vesuvio, the Campi Flegrei and the island of Ischia (near Napoli), and Etna (on Sicilia). Stromboli and Etna are among the world's most active volcanoes, while Vesuvio has not erupted since 1944. However, this has become a source of concern for scientists, who estimate that it should erupt every 30 years. Etna's most recent major eruption occurred in 1992, when a trail of lava on its eastern flank threatened to engulf the town of Zafferana Etnea.

Related volcanic activity produces thermal and mud springs, notably at Viterbo in Lazio and in the Isole Eolie. The Campi Flegrei near Napoli are an area of intense volcanic activity, including hot springs, gas emissions and steam jets.

much modelling by the combined forces of continental plate movement and erosion, the Italian peninsula had almost arrived at its present-day form. The level of the sea continued to rise and fall with the alternation of ice ages and periods of warm climate, until the end of the last ice age around 10,000 to 12,000 years ago.

CLIMATE

Situated in the temperate zone and jutting deep into the Mediterranean, Italy is regarded by many tourists as a land of sunny, mild weather. The country's climate is, however, quite variable due to the north-south orientation of the peninsula and the fact that it is largely mountainous.

In the Alpi, temperatures are lower and winters are long and severe. Generally the weather is warm from July to September, although rainfall can be high in September. While the first snowfall is usually in November, light snow sometimes falls in mid-September and the first heavy falls can occur in early October.

The Alpi shield northern Lombardia and the Lakes area, including Milano, from the extremes of the northern European winter, and Liguria enjoys a mild, Mediterranean climate similar to southern Italy because it has protection from both the Alpi and the Appennini.

Winters are severe and summers very hot in the Pianura Padana. Venezia can be hot and humid in summer and, although not extremely cold in winter, it can be unpleasant as the sea level rises and *acqua alta* (literally 'high water') inundates the city.

Farther south, at Firenze, which is encircled by hills, the weather can be extreme, but as you travel towards the tip of the boot, temperatures and weather conditions become milder.

Roma, for instance, has an average July and August temperature in the mid-20s (Celsius), although the impact of the *scirocco*, a hot, humid wind blowing from Africa, can produce stiflingly hot weather in August, with temperatures in the high 30s for days on end. Winters are moderate

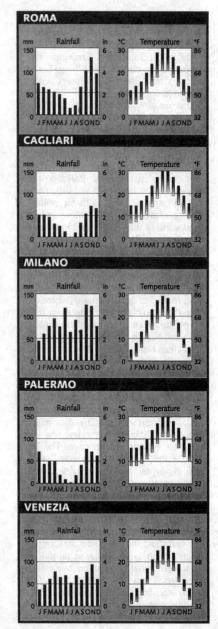

and snow is very rare in Roma, although winter clothing (or at least a heavy overcoat) is still a requirement.

The south, Sicilia and Sardegna have a Mediterranean climate, with long, hot, dry summers, and moderate winters with an average temperature of around 10°C. These regions are also affected by the scirocco in summer.

ECOLOGY & ENVIRONMENT

Italy is a dramatically beautiful country, but since Etruscan times humans have left their mark on the environment. Pollution problems caused by industrial and urban waste exist throughout Italy, with air pollution proving a problem in the more industrialised north of the country and in the major cities such as Roma, Milano and Napoli, where car emissions poison the atmosphere with carbon monoxide and lead. The seas, and therefore many beaches, are fouled to some extent, particularly on the Ligurian coast, in the northern Adriatic (where there is an algae problem resulting from industrial pollution) and near major cities such as Roma and Napoli. However, it is possible to find a clean beach, particularly on Sardegna and Sicilia. Litter-conscious visitors will be astounded by the extraordinary Italian habit of discarding and dumping rubbish when and where they like.

The Italian government's record on ecological and environmental issues has not been good, although in the last few years things have begun to improve. The Ministry for the Environment, created only in 1986, is now taking a tougher line concerning the environment, partly in response to European Union (EU) directives. However, environmental groups maintain that the increase in the number of devastating floods which have hit parts of northern Italy in recent years and the landslides in Campania are due not only to increased rainfall, but also to deforestation and excessive building near rivers. From 1984 to 1995, 20% of new houses were built without planning permits and environmental groups blamed this on the ministry's failure to regulate urban plan-

ning. Environmental organisations active in Italy include the Lega Ambiente (Environment League), the World Wide Fund for Nature (WWF) and the Lega Italiana Protezione Uccelli (LIPU; Italian Bird Protection League).

1998 saw an increase in the number of summer forest fires, especially in the south and on the islands. Due in part to the lack of rain and intense heat during the summer months, forest fires are no novelty in Italy. Not a few of the fires are started by arsonists – some of them wanting to clear forest land, others hoping to find work when it's time to replant the trees destroyed by the fire.

FLORA & FAUNA
Flora

The long presence of humans on the Italian peninsula has had a significant impact on the environment, resulting in widespread destruction of original forests and vegetation and their replacement with crops and orchards. Aesthetically the result is not displeasing – much of the beauty of Toscana, for instance, lies in the interaction of olive groves with vineyards, fallow fields and stands of cypress and pine.

Fauna

The Alpi are home to marmots and an increasing number of ibex (mountain goat), chamois and roe deer. In the Parco delle Foreste Casentinesi, in Emilia-Romagna, there are about 1000 deer. Among the native animals on Sardegna are wild boar, the mouflon sheep, deer and a variety of wild cat. You will find evidence of wild boar (and the people who hunt them) throughout the hills and countryside in Italy. Commonly available maps in national parks in the Alpi and Appennini detail the local wildlife and indicate areas where they might be found.

Hunters continue to plunder the countryside for birds. However, enough remain to make bird-watching an interesting pastime. A large variety of falcons and hawks are found throughout Italy, as are many varieties of small birds. The irony is that it is often easier to spot the colourful smaller birds in city parks – among the few refuges they have from the Italian hunter – than in their natural habitats in the countryside. Good spots to observe water birds include the Parco Nazionale del Circeo, just south of Roma, and huge flocks of flamingoes can be seen on Sardegna, just outside Cagliari and near Oristano.

Italy is home to remarkably little dangerous fauna. It has only one poisonous snake, the viper. While the great white shark is known to exist in the waters of the Mediterraneo, particularly in the southern waters, attacks are extremely rare. Italians will generally respond with a blank stare if you inquire about the presence of sharks. The seas around southern Italy and Sicilia have been used as breeding grounds since ancient times by blue-fin tuna and swordfish. The Isole Egadi (Egadi Islands), off the southern coast of Sicilia, are famous for the bloody netting and killing of tuna which occurs annually between May and June (see the boxed text 'La Mattanza' in the Isole Egadi section of the Sicilia chapter).

For information on animals and birds which have become extinct or are in danger of extinction in Italy see the boxed text 'Endangered Species' below.

National Parks

Italy has 17 national parks, with three more on the way, and 421 smaller nature reserves, natural parks and wetlands. Altogether, almost two million hectares of land is protected (6.63% of the country), of which about 1.2 million hectares, or just over 4% of the country, is national parks and nature reserves. Italy's environmentalists have been campaigning for years to bring the total protected area up to 10% of the land.

Endangered Species

Changes to the environment, combined with the Italians' passion for hunting *(la caccia)*, has led to many native animals and birds becoming extinct, rare or endangered. Hunters constitute a powerful lobby group in Italy and continue to win regular referendums on whether hunting should be banned.

In the 20th century, 13 species have become extinct in Italy, including the Alpine lynx, the *aquila di mare* (white-tailed eagle) and the crane. Under laws progressively introduced over the years, many animals and birds are now protected. The World Wild Fund for Nature (WWF) has released a *Lista Rossa* (Red List) of threatened vertebrates in Italy. The 120 page document claims that 60% of Italy's vertebrates are at risk.

Among those which are very slowly making a comeback after being reintroduced in the wild are the brown bear, which survives only in the Brenta area of Trentino, the Marsican bear, which has been reintroduced in Abruzzo, and the lynx, which is extremely rare and found mainly in the area around Tarvisio in Friuli-Venezia Giulia. Efforts are also under way to reintroduce the lynx in Abruzzo. Wolves are slightly more common, although you will still be very hard pressed to spot one in the wild. They can be seen in a large enclosure at Civitella Alfedena in the Parco Nazionale d'Abruzzo.

There are only about 100 otters left in Italy and most live protected in the Parco Nazionale del Cilento in Campania. Another extremely rare animal is the monk seal: only about 10 are thought to survive in sea caves on the eastern coast of Sardegna. The magnificent golden eagle was almost wiped out by hunters and now numbers about 300 pairs spread throughout the country. A colony of griffon vultures survives on the western coast of Sardegna, near Bosa. The bearded vulture, known in Italy as the *gipeto*, has been reintroduced in the Alpi in the past decade.

They have had some success. In the period from 1922 to 1991, only five national parks were created in Italy and their management left a lot to be desired. However, a law on protected areas passed in 1991 allowed for the creation of 14 new national parks. A few of these projects are shrouded in controversy and have yet to be realised; others have been created but management infrastructure is still to be established.

The five long-standing national parks are the Parco Nazionale del Gran Paradiso, the Parco Nazionale d'Abruzzo, the Parco Nazionale del Circeo, the Parco Nazionale dello Stelvio and the Parco Nazionale della Calabria. The new national parks include the Parco della Val Grande (Piemonte), the Parco delle Dolomiti Bellunesi (Veneto), the Parco delle Foreste Casentinesi (Emilia-Romagna), the Parco dei Monti Sibillini (Le Marche/Umbria), the Parco del Gran Sasso-Monti della Laga (Abruzzo), the Parco della Maiella (Abruzzo), the Parco del Vesuvio (Campania), the Parco del Cilento e Vallo di Diano (Campania), the Parco del Gargano (Puglia), the Parco dell'Aspromonte (Calabria) and the Parco del Pollino (Basilicata/Calabria). Numerous other parks on the peninsula and the islands are currently being planned.

GOVERNMENT & POLITICS

Italy is a parliamentary republic, headed by a president who appoints the prime minister. The parliament consists of two houses – a senate and a chamber of deputies – both with equal legislative power. Neither house has formal precedence over the other. The seat of national government is in Roma. The president resides in the Palazzo del Quirinale, the Chamber of Deputies sits in the Palazzo Montecitorio and the Senate in the Palazzo Madama, near Piazza Navona.

Political Scandals

The heritage of consistent one-party domination was a system which Italians called *partitocrazia* (partyocracy), which operated on the basis of *lottizzazione* (share-out), by which the major parties divided control of

the country's public bodies and utilities. The resulting patronage system meant that government jobs and other positions of power and influence were handed out virtually as political favours, and all government services were open to manipulation.

The *tangenti* (kickbacks or bribes to government officials and politicians) were another unfortunate offshoot of the system. These ranged from payments by companies wanting to secure government building contracts to payments by individuals wanting to speed up bureaucracy. The Tangentopoli scandal which erupted in 1992 dramatically changed the face of Italian politics (see History earlier in this chapter).

Political renewal has brought about greater efficiency in the running of institutions and it seems that the level of corruption in the public sector at least has decreased. However, June 1999 brought news of a new high-level corruption scandal. Moreover, bureaucracy and minor civil servants continue to bog down the system and minor corruption – ranging from the exchange of favours *(clientelismo)* to recommendations – still looks to be rife.

Reforms

Until reforms were introduced in 1994, members of parliament were elected by what was probably the purest system of proportional representation in the world – the aim of the country's intensely democratic constitution. The reforms mean that now 75% of both houses of parliament are elected on the basis of who receives the most votes in their district, basically the same system as the first-past-the-post system in the UK. The other 25% is elected by proportional representation. Italians are conscientious voters, with an average 88% turnout at the frequent elections.

The old system generally produced unstable coalition governments – Italy had 53 governments in the 48 years from the declaration of the republic to the introduction of the electoral reforms. But even under the new system there has been instability.

In 1997 Italian politicians passed up the

chance to significantly reform the country's system of government. A parliamentary commission, known as the *bicamerale*, spent six months considering reforms to Italy's 1947 constitution. But after a series of corruption scandals had brought down many from the country's ruling class, those who had been heralding a fresh start were badly disappointed. Instead of the expected sweeping changes to the system of government and major reforms to the judicial system, the bicamerale made a series of weak proposals which were seen by many as the result of political compromise. After months of consultations the bicamerale dissolved without having reached an agreement. In June 1999 D'Alema's government was planning a series of wholesale reforms to the government and the federal and judicial systems.

The Regions

For administrative purposes, Italy is divided into 20 regions *(regioni)* which roughly correspond to the historical regions of the country. The regions are divided into provinces *(province)*, which are further divided into town councils *(comuni)*.

Five regions (Sicilia, Sardegna, Trentino-Alto Adige, Friuli-Venezia Giulia and Valle d'Aosta) are semi-autonomous or autonomous, with special powers granted under the constitution. Their regional assemblies are similar to parliaments and they have a wider range of economic and administrative powers than those of the other 15 Italian regions.

Elections for all three tiers of local government are held simultaneously every five years.

ECONOMY

Italy's economy lay in ruins at the close of WWII, but the country wasted little time in setting about repairing the damage. By the early 1950s Italy had regained prewar levels of production. The boom of the 1950s and early 1960s, known as the Economic Miracle, relied to a great extent on the masses of workers who migrated from the poorer south of the country to the industrial north, providing an ample but low-paid workforce.

Today, services and public administration account for 63.7% of GDP, industry 33% and agriculture 3.3%. Most raw materials for industry and more than three-quarters of energy needs are imported. Tourism remains an important source of income. In 1996 estimated takings were about US$27.5 million and Italy ranked fourth in income from international tourism.

Following sustained growth of 3% through much of the 1980s, Italy became the fifth-largest economy in the world, made possible largely by a national tendency to produce entrepreneurs. As well as the household names, such as Agnelli (Fiat), De Benedetti (Olivetti) and Berlusconi (media), numerous ordinary Italians run their own businesses. Some 90% of Italian firms have fewer than 100 workers, and many of these firms are family businesses – officially in any case. There are those who suggest that many companies artificially divide themselves into smaller units to sidestep tax and labour laws which apply to larger firms.

Some would say that Italian business succeeds in spite of the national government. Massive public debt, widespread corruption and arcane legal and tax systems have always combined to restrain economic progress. As well as this, many of the country's top business people were implicated in the Tangentopoli corruption scandals in the early and mid-90s. Foreign firms have long found all this combined with the country's seemingly endless political wrangling a strong deterrent to investment in Italy.

The common European currency, the euro, came into being on 1 January 1999 (see the boxed text 'Introducing the Euro' in the Money section of the Facts for the Visitor chapter). After serious doubts about whether Italy would qualify under the strict terms of the Maastricht Treaty, it was one of 11 EU countries to commit to the currency. This was seen as a reward for years of government belt-tightening. However, reining in government debt financing (the external debt stands at US$4.5 billion) and waste remain among the most intractable problems facing the country. Finance has been raised through privatisations. Telecom left the state's protective grip in 1998, and the main electricity body, ENEL, was set to go the same way in 1999.

That the country is already firmly locked into Europe is also illustrated by the fact that more than half its exports go to EU partners. But not everyone is glowing with optimism. Industry was slowing in 1998 to 1999 and Italy was said to be dragging the overall EU economic stats downward – at 1.4%, the Italian economy's growth was the lowest in Euroland. Indeed, at the time of writing there were suggestions that Italy might have to withdraw from the euro project. Like farmers elsewhere in the EU, Italy's dairy farmers in particular were on the warpath, demanding an end to the milk quotas that they have for years ignored – running up hefty fines in the process.

In spite of all the postwar efforts to promote growth in the poor south, the gap between north and south remains as great as ever. Although the desperate poverty of the past is a memory and regions like Puglia and Abruzzo have seen real economic progress, the fact remains that Italy's richest regions (Piemonte, Emilia-Romagna and Lombardia) are all northern and its poorest (Calabria, Campania and Sicilia) are all southern. Unemployment in the south (which was on the rise again in 1999) is double the national average of 12.2% and three times the level in the north. Infrastructure remains poorer and several attempts to establish industry in the south have come to little, in spite of the trillions of lire poured into the *Mezzogiorno* (south) in the form of subsidies, tax breaks and loans.

POPULATION & PEOPLE

The population of Italy is 56.7 million, according to 1998 estimates. The birth rate was put at 9.13 per thousand the same year, one of the lowest in Europe and below the EU average of about 12 per thousand – surprising given the Italians' preoccupation with children and family. The figures show that the country's population is actually shrinking. More children are born in the south than in the north: the birth rate in Emilia-Romagna is half that of Campania, for instance.

Heavily populated areas include those around Roma, Milano and Napoli, Liguria, Piemonte and parts of Lombardia, the Veneto and Friuli-Venezia Giulia. The most densely populated spot in Italy – in fact the most populous in the world after Hong Kong – is Portici, a suburb of Napoli, directly under Vesuvio.

There is only a small minority of non-Italian speakers, including those who speak German in Alto Adige (in the province of Bolzano) and a tiny French-speaking minority in the Valle d'Aosta. Slovene is spoken by some around Trieste and along the border with Slovenia. The south has pockets of Greeks and Albanians whose ancestors arrived in the 14th and 15th centuries.

Italy has traditionally been a country of emigrants, with Italians leaving in search of work in the USA, Argentina, Brazil, Australia and Canada. Southern Italians have also traditionally moved to the north of the country to work in the factories of Piemonte and Lombardia. In recent years, however, Italy has become a country of immigration. Long coastlines and a fairly relaxed attitude to enforcement of immigration laws by the Italian authorities have made Italy an easy point of entry into Europe. It is estimated that more than 1.5 million immigrants (of whom at least 300,000 are clandestine) now live in Italy. Illegal immigrants are known in Italy as *extracomunitari*. This state of affairs has come to worry not only the Italians (65% demanded 'stern measures' in a 1999 poll) but the rest of the EU. In early 1997 parliament approved tougher immigration rules that envisage a more determined programme of expulsion for illegal immigrants. The numbers turfed out rose from 8394 in 1997 to 44,770 in 1998.

Italians, however, are still more concerned with the traditional hostility of northern Italians towards southerners. Many northerners feel the richer north subsidises the poorer south. A minority of northerners have expressed their resentment in terms of votes for secessionist parties over the past few years, notably Umberto Bossi's Lega Nord.

EDUCATION

The Italian state-school system is free of charge and consists of several levels. Attendance is compulsory from the ages of six to 14 years, although children can attend a *scuola materna* (nursery school) from the ages of three to five years before starting the *scuola elementare* (primary school) at six. After five years they move on to the *scuola media* (secondary school) until they reach the age of 14.

The next level, the *scuola secondaria superiore* (higher secondary school), is voluntary and lasts a further five years, until the student is 19 years old. It is, however, essential if young people want to study at university. At this higher school level there are several options: four types of *liceo* (humanities-based school), four types of technical school, and teacher-training school.

The government is in the process of reforming the education system. The standards of education in the state-run system compare well with those in other countries, although the system does have its problems, compounded by relatively low standards in teacher training and poor government management. Officially at least, 3% of Italians over the age of 15 cannot read or write.

Private schools in Italy are run mainly by religious institutions, notably the Jesuits.

Italy has a long tradition of university education and can claim to have the world's oldest university, established at Bologna in the 11th century. Courses usually last from four to six years, although students are under no obligation to complete them in that time. In fact, students often take many more years to fulfil their quota of exams and submit their final thesis. Attendance at inevitably overcrowded lectures is optional

and for scientific courses practical experimentation is rare. Students therefore tend to study at home from books. All state-school and university examinations are oral, rather than written.

Italy produces far fewer graduates per capita than most other countries in the west. Despite that, unemployment among graduates is estimated at higher than 40%.

ARTS
Literature

Roman The roots of ancient Latin literature lie in simple popular songs, religious rites and official documents. As Latin evolved and the Romans came into contact with the Greek world, the emerging empire's upper classes began to acquire more sophisticated tastes. Plautus (259-184 BC) adapted classic Greek themes to create his own plays – a step forward from the translations of Greek literature that had come before.

The classical period did not start until well into the 1st century BC. Cicero (106-43 BC) stands out during the early years of this period as the Roman Republic collapsed into civil war and gave way to dictatorial government. Cicero's writing, infused with political commitment, explored new terrain in Latin prose with works such as *Brutus*. More concerned with affairs of the heart, particularly his own, Catullus (c84-54 BC) devoted his creative power to passionate love poetry. Julius Caesar combined conquest with commentary in recording his campaigns in Gaul and the disintegration of the Republic.

The reign of Augustus (27 BC-14 AD) marked the emergence of a new wave of intellectuals. Among them was Virgil, whose epic poem, *The Aeneid*, links the founding of Roma with the fall of Troy. Some years later Ovid addressed love in his *Amores* poems, annoyed Emperor Augustus with descriptions of lewd lifestyles in *Ars Amatoria* after the emperor's daughter had been banished for vice, and wrote about transformation myths in *Metamorphoses*. Horace commented on military matters while

Livy chronicled the emergence of the new empire.

Seneca the Younger (4 BC-65 AD), a philosopher from Spain, introduced a more introspective, even existential, note into Latin writing in the early years of the Christian era. Petronius (died 66 AD) conveyed the decadence of the Nero era in his *Satyricon*, although only a fragment still exists, and it is to Pliny the Younger (62-113 AD) that we owe first-hand descriptions of the disaster of Pompei. The years following the downfall of Nero are detailed in the *Histories* of Tacitus (55-120 AD), while his *Annales* reveal the astounding court intrigues of the early emperors. Marcus Aurelius' *Meditations* were the musings of the last philosopher-king of the crumbling empire.

The Middle Ages From before the final collapse of the Roman Empire until well into the Middle Ages, creative literary production declined, kept barely alive in Western Europe by clerics and erudites who debated theology, wrote history, translated or interpreted classical literature and used Latin as their lingua franca. Above all, however, theology and philosophy were what preoccupied the great minds of medieval Italy and Europe.

The most outstanding Italian figure in this field was San Tommaso d'Aquino (St Thomas Aquinas, 1224-1274). He wrestled with Aristotelian thinking and in works like *De Aeternitate Mundi* (On the Eternity of the World) sought to expound his vision of our existence. He was also a gifted poet.

The Birth of Italian Literature By the time Aquinas was penning his theses, Latin had ceased to be a living language. The genius of Dante Alighieri (1265-1321), probably the greatest figure in Italian literature, confirmed the Italian vernacular (in its Florentine form) as a serious medium for poetic expression, particularly his *Divina Commedia* – an allegorical masterpiece that takes his protagonist on a search for God through hell, purgatory and paradise. His Latin work *De Monarchia* reflects his desire for a return of imperial power and his vision of a world where the roles of pope and emperor complement each other.

Another master writer of this time was Francesco Petrarca (Petrarch, 1304-74), son of a lawyer exiled from Firenze at the same time as Dante. Petrarch was crowned poet laureate in Roma in 1341 after earning a reputation throughout Europe as a classical scholar. His epic poem, *Africa*, and the sonnets of *Il Canzoniere* are typical of his formidable lyricism, which has permanently influenced Italian poetry.

Completing the triumvirate is Giovanni Boccaccio (1313-75). Author of *Il Decamerone*, 100 short stories ranging from the bawdy to the earnest that chronicle the exodus of 10 young Florentines from their plague-ridden city, Boccaccio is considered the first Italian novelist.

The Renaissance The 15th century produced several treatises on architecture and politics, but perhaps more important was the feverish study and translation of Greek classics along with the work of more recent Hebrew and Arabic scholars. The advent of the printing press accelerated the spread of knowledge. In Italy, the industry was most highly developed in Venezia, where Aldo Manuzio (c1450-1515) flooded the market with Greek classics from his Aldine Press and introduced italic type in 1501, along with the octavo, half the size of a standard quarto page and more suitable for printed books.

Machiavelli's *Il Principe* (The Prince), although purely political, has proved the most lasting of the Renaissance works. Surprisingly for many, Machiavelli (1469-1527) was also an accomplished playwright and his *Mandragola* is a masterpiece.

Machiavelli's contemporary Ludovico Ariosto (1474-1533) is arguably the star of the Italian Renaissance. His *Orlando Furioso* is a subtle tale of chivalry, told in exquisite verse and laced with subplots. Torquato Tasso (1544-95) continued a strong tradition of narrative poetry with his *Gerusalemme Liberata*, for which he drew inspiration from Italy's increasingly precarious political situation towards the end of the 16th century.

The 18th & 19th Centuries At a time when French playwrights ruled the stage, the Venetian Carlo Goldoni (1707-93) attempted to bring Italian theatre back into the limelight. He combined realism and a certain literary discipline with a popular feel rooted in the *commedia dell'arte*, the tradition of improvisational theatre based on a core of set characters.

The heady winds of Romanticism that prevailed in Europe in the first half of the 19th century did not leave Italy untouched. In the small town of Recanati in Le Marche, Giacomo Leopardi (1798-1837) penned verses heavy with longing and melancholy, but equally erudite (although he was largely self-taught). The best of them, the *Canti*, constitute a classic of Italian verse.

Poetry remained the main avenue of literary expression for much of the century, but Milano's Alessandro Manzoni (1785-1873) changed all that with his *I Promessi Sposi* (The Betrothed), a historical novel on a grand scale. Manzoni laboured hard to establish a narrative language accessible to all Italians, lending the manuscript a barely disguised nationalist flavour lost on no-one when it appeared in the 1840s. In 1881 Giovanni Verga (1840-1922) announced the arrival of the realist novel in Italy with *I Malavoglia*.

The 20th Century The turbulence of political and social life in Italy throughout most of the 20th century produced a wealth of literature, much of it available in translation for English speakers.

Theatre On Sicilia, Luigi Pirandello (1867-1936) began his career writing novels and short stories along realist lines, but soon moved to theatre. With such classics as *Sei Personaggi in Cerca d'Autore* (Six Characters in Search of an Author) he threw into question every preconception of what theatre should be. A Nobel-prize winner in

1934, Pirandello's influence continues to assert itself in the west; from Brecht to Beckett, few modern playwrights could claim to have escaped his influence.

Modern Italian theatre is very much the junior member of Italy's literary family. Its most enduring contemporary representative is Dario Fo (born 1926), who has been writing, directing and performing since the 1950s. Often in the form of a one-man show, but also in company (most often with Franca Rame), his work is laced with political and social critique. He has had a number of hits in London's West End, including *Morte Accidentale di un Anarchista* (Accidental Death of an Anarchist), *Non Si Paga, Non Si Paga* (Can't Pay, Won't Pay) and *Mistero Buffo*. Much to the consternation of the Italian literary establishment, Fo won the 1997 Nobel Prize for Literature.

Poetry Gabriele d'Annunzio (1863-1938) is in a class of his own. An ardent nationalist, his often virulent poetry was perhaps not of the highest quality, but his voice was a prestige tool for Mussolini's Fascists.

Giuseppe Ungaretti (1888-1970), whose creative and personal baptism of fire took place on the battlefields of WWI, produced a robust, spare poetry, far from the wordy complexity of his predecessors. The sum of his work is contained in *Vita d'un Uomo* (Life of a Man).

Two other 'hermetic' poets stand out, both Nobel-prize winners. Eugenio Montale (1896-1981) is less accessible than Ungaretti and devoted much of his time after WWII to journalism. Sicilian poet Salvatore Quasimodo (1901-68) reached a high point after WWII, when he believed poetry could and should empathise with human suffering. The myth exploded; his later work is heavy with melancholy and nostalgia.

Fiction Italy's richest contribution to modern literature has been in the novel and short story. Torino especially has produced a wealth of authors. Cesare Pavese, born in a Piemonte farmhouse in 1908, took Walt Whitman as his guiding light. Involved in the anti-Fascist circles of prewar Torino, his greatest novel, *La Luna e Il Falò* (The Moon and the Bonfire), was published in 1950, the year he took his life.

Like Pavese, the Torino doctor Carlo Levi (1902-75) experienced internal exile in southern Italy under the Fascists. The result was a moving account of a world oppressed and forgotten by Roma, *Cristo si è Fermato a Eboli* (Christ Stopped at Eboli).

Primo Levi, a Torino Jew, ended up in Auschwitz during the war. *Se Quest'è Un Uomo* (If This is a Man) is the dignified account of his survival, while *La Tregua* (The Truce) recounts his long road back home through Eastern Europe. Born in 1919, Levi committed suicide in 1987.

Palermo-born Natalia Ginzburg (1916-90) spent most of her life in Torino. Much of her writing is semi-autobiographical. *Tutti I Nostri Ieri* (All Our Yesterdays), *Valentino* and *Le Voci della Sera* (Voices in the Evening) are just three novels from her range of fiction, plays and essays. Her particular gift is in capturing the essence of gestures and moments in everyday life.

A writer of a different ilk is Italo Calvino (1923-85), who was born in Cuba. A Resistance fighter and then Communist Party member until 1957, Calvino's works border on the fantastical, thinly veiling his main preoccupations with human behaviour in society. *I Nostri Antenati* (Our Ancestors), a collection of three such tales, is perhaps his greatest success.

Alberto Moravia (1907-90) describes Roma and its people in his prolific writings. Such novels as *La Romana* (A Woman of Roma) convey the detail of place and the sharp sense of social decay that make his storytelling so compelling.

Il Gattopardo (The Leopard) is the only work of lasting importance by Sicilia's Giuseppe Tomasi di Lampedusa (1896-1957). Set at the time of Italian unification, it is a moving account of the decline of the virtually feudal order in Sicilia, embodied in the slow ruin of Prince Fabrizio Salina, later played by Burt Lancaster in Luchino Visconti's 1963 film of the same name.

Leonardo Sciascia (1921-89) has dedicated most of his career to his native Sicilia, attacking all facets of its past and present in novels and essays. His first great success was *Il Giorno della Civetta* (The Day of the Owl), a kind of whodunit illustrating the extent of the Mafia's power.

The novels of Roma's Elsa Morante (1912-85), characterised by a subtle psychological appraisal of her characters, can be seen too as a personal cry of pity for the sufferings of individuals and society. Her 1948 novel *Menzogna e Sortilegio* (Lies and Incantations) brought her to prominence. In it she recounts the slow decay of the southern Italian noble family.

Italian literature of the 1980s was briefly dominated by Bologna intellectual Umberto Eco (born 1932), who shot to popularity with his first and best known work, *Il Nome della Rosa* (The Name of the Rose). It was made into a successful film starring Sean Connery.

Pisa-born Antonio Tabucchi (born 1943) is emerging as a writer of some stature, with more than a dozen books to his credit. Possibly one of his most endearing works is *Sostiene Pereira* (Pereira Maintains), set in prewar Lisbon and made into a charming film starring Marcello Mastroianni.

The 1998 Strega Prize (the Italian equivalent of the Booker) went to Claudio Magris (born 1939) for his *Microcosmi*, a sometimes dizzying journey through time and place, visiting people past and present, places, animals and numerous other 'microcosms'. Rosetta Loy (born 1931) made a splash with her novel *La Parola Ebreo* (The Word Jew), a touching account of the fate of Jews in Mussolini's Italy. Another name to watch is Daniele Del Giudice (born 1949), whose most recent collection of short stories, *Mania*, revolves around the theme of death.

Music

Classical Music & Opera The Italians have played a pivotal role in the history of music: they invented the system of musical notation in use today, a 16th century Venetian printed the first musical scores, Stradivari (Stradivarius) and others produced violins in Cremona and Italy is the birthplace of the piano.

The 16th century brought a musical revolution in the development of opera, which began as an attempt to recreate the drama of ancient Greece. One of the earliest successful composers in this genre, Claudio Monteverdi (c1567-1643), drew from a variety of sources.

In the 17th and early 18th centuries, instrumental music became established, helped by the concertos of Arcangelo Corelli (1653-1713) and Antonio Vivaldi (1675-1741). Vivaldi, whose best known work is *Le Quattro Stagioni* (The Four Seasons), created the concerto in its present form while he was teaching in Venezia. Domenico Scarlatti (1685-1757) wrote more than 500 sonatas for harpsichord and Giovanni Battista Sammartini (1700-75) experimented with the symphony.

Verdi (1813-1901), Puccini (1858-1924), Bellini (1801-1835), Donizetti (1797-1848) and Rossini (1792-1868) are all stars of the modern operatic era. Giuseppe Verdi became an icon midway through his life; his achievements include *Aïda* and one of the most popular operas of all, *La Traviata*. Rossini's *Barber of Seville* is an enduring favourite, with a lively score, and *Madame Butterfly* ensures Puccini a firm place in musical history.

The composer Gian Carlo Menotti (born 1911) is famed for creating the Festival dei Due Mondi (Festival of Two Worlds; see the Special Events section in the Facts for the Visitor chapter), at Spoleto in Umbria. One of the greatest conductors of the past two centuries was, with little doubt, Italy's Arturo Toscanini (1867-1957). See Parma in the Emilia-Romagna chapter section for more about him.

Classical Music & Opera Today The main opera season in Italy runs from December to June. The country's premier opera theatres include La Scala in Milano, San Carlo in Napoli, the Teatro dell'Opera in Roma and La Fenice (closed at the time of writing) in Venezia. With restoration partially complete, Sicilia's prestigious Teatro Massimo in Palermo is now finally back in action. Tenor Luciano Pavarotti (born 1935) is today's luminary of Italian opera.

The remarkable blind tenor Andrea Bocelli (born 1958) has taken his fine voice to the pop charts. His *Con Te, Partirò* was a karaoke hit in 1998, but he is every bit as serious as Pavarotti and some critics see Bocelli as Pavarotti's natural successor. Cecilia Bartolli (born 1966) meanwhile, has been making great strides as Italy's latest mezzo-soprano sensation.

Among the country's leading conductors, Napoli-born Riccardo Muti (born 1941) has a distinguished career behind him both at home and abroad. Since 1986 he has been musical director at La Scala in Milano and continues to tour widely across Europe and the USA. He is equally at home conducting opera or symphonic music. Claudio Abbado (born 1933) comes from a long line of Milanese musicians. He has been the main conductor for some of the most prestigious orchestras in the world, including the Berlin Philharmonic and the London Symphony Orchestra, and has been musical director of the Vienna State Opera.

Canzone Napoletana If a great many rock and pop greats in the English-speaking world have their roots in the blues tradition, Italian popular music has much the same relation to the *canzone Napoletana* (Neapolitan song).

By the late 18th century, an annual pilgrimage in September to the Chiesa di Santa Maria di Piedigrotta, in Pozzuoli, had become an occasion for merriment and song. At a time when the Neapolitan dialect had the status of a language in its own right, bands played in impromptu competitions that soon began to produce what could be considered the year's top hits. In 1840 came the first real classic, *Te Voglio Bene Assaje*, a song that remains enshrined in the city's musical imagination. But surely the best known Neapolitan song is *O Sole Mio*.

Contemporary Music Few modern Italian singers or groups have made any impact outside Italy. The best vocalist to emerge since WWII is probably Mina. During the 1960s she cut dozens of records. Many of her songs were written by Giulio Rapetti, better known as Mogol, the undisputed king of Italian songwriters.

The 1960s and 1970s produced various *cantautori* (singer-songwriters) who were vaguely reminiscent of some of the greats of the UK and USA. Lucio Dalla, Vasco Rossi and Pino Daniele have been successfully hawking their versions of protest music since the early 1970s. While they are not of the stature of, say, Bob Dylan, the strength of their music lies in lyrics occasionally laced with venom portraying the shortcomings of modern Italian society. Daniele, whose Neapolitan roots are clearly on display, brings an unmistakably bluesy flavour to his music.

Lucio Battisti's material is much softer and less inclined towards social comment, but has been highly popular since the end of the 1960s. Some of the early stuff (the classics) may make your hair stand on end (*very* 1970s). His later material (he died in 1994), innovative and against the grain of the musical establishment, has been dismissed by some critics as simply crazy.

Ivano Fossati is another well-established *cantautore*, but some of his most agreeable material is purely instrumental.

Zucchero (Adelmo Fornaciari) is a phenomenon on the Italian music scene. Starting out as a session musician with the likes of Joe Cocker, he has aimed at both the Italian and international market as few other Italians have. He sings many of his songs in Italian *and* English.

Other names to look out for include Luca Carboni, Francesco de Gregori, Antonello Venditti and Franco Battiato. A much rockier sound comes from Vasco Rossi, a big concert draw.

The grand public face of Italian pop is the annual San Remo song fest (held in February), but most would agree that the veteran performers and new hopefuls who appear at this glitzy spectacle are not always of the best quality.

As well as these melody-makers, a whole jungle of new bands ranging from rock to punk to hip-hop has thrived in Italy over the past few years. Litfiba is a high-profile indie Florentine duo that has been around for most of the 90s. Ligabue is more of a straight rock band with a big following.

There are plenty of other rock 'n' roll bands doing the rounds. Among the better known ones are Prozac+ (whose songs have been described as hallucinogenic pop-rock), CSI and the somewhat surreal Afterhours, whose lyrics tend to concentrate on sex.

Jovanotti's thoughtful and entertaining lyrics make him the top exponent of rap in Italy. He recently declared that Italian music was largely uninspired because the younger generation was too rich and privileged to produce the necessary sentiment to make good music.

Cinema

Born in Torino in 1904, the Italian film industry initially made an impression with silent spectaculars. By 1930 it was virtually bankrupt and Mussolini began moves to nationalise the industry. These culminated in 1940, when Roma's version of Hollywood, Cinecittà, was ceded to the state. Set up in 1937, this huge complex was fitted out with the latest in film equipment. Half the nation's production took place here – 85 films in 1940 alone.

Abandoned later in the war, Cinecittà only went timidly back into action in 1948 – its absence had not bothered the first of Italy's neo-realist directors anyway (see the following section). In 1950 an American team arrived to make *Quo Vadis?*, and for the rest of the 1950s film-makers from Italy and abroad moved in to use the site's huge lots. By the early 1960s, however, this symbol of Italian cinema had again begun to wane as location shooting became more common.

Neo-Realism Even before the fall of Mussolini in 1943, those who were about to launch Italy's most glorious cinematic era were at work. Luchino Visconti (1906-76) came to cinema late, after meeting Jean Renoir, the French film-maker, in France in 1936. His first film, *Ossessione*, based on James M Cain's *The Postman Always Rings Twice*, was one of the earliest examples of the new wave in cinema.

In the three years following the close of hostilities in Europe, Roberto Rossellini (1906-77) produced a trio of neo-realist masterpieces. The first, in 1945, was *Roma Città Aperta* (Rome, Open City), which was set in German-occupied Roma and starred Anna Magnani. For many cinophiles this film marks the true beginning of neo-realism, uniting a simplicity and sincerity peculiar to Italian film-making; often heart-rending without ever descending into the bathos to which so many Hollywood products fall victim.

Paisà (1946) follows the course of war from Sicilia to the Po river in a series of powerful vignettes, while *Germania Anno Zero* (Germany Year Zero, 1947) pulls no punches in looking at a country left crushed by the war it had launched.

Vittorio de Sica (1901-74) kept the neo-realist ball rolling with another classic in 1948, *Ladri di Biciclette* (Bicycle Thieves), the story of a man's frustrated fight to earn enough to keep his family afloat. It is one of 10 films he made between 1939 and 1950.

The 1950s to the 1970s Federico Fellini (1920-94) took the creative baton from the masters of neo-realism and carried it into the following decades. His disquieting style is slightly more demanding of audiences, abandoning realistic shots for pointed images at once laden with humour, pathos and double-meaning – all cleverly capturing not only the Italy of the day, but the human foibles of his protagonists. Fellini's greatest international hit was *La Dolce Vita* (1968), with Anita Ekberg and Marcello Mastroianni. Others include *8½* (1963), *Satyricon* (1969), *Roma* (1972) and *Amarcord* (1973). Fellini's wife, Giulietta Masina, starred in many of his pictures.

Luchino Visconti made movies from 1942 until his death in 1976, including the memorable adaptation of Tomasi di Lampedusa's *Il Gattopardo* (The Leopard, 1963).

Michelangelo Antonioni (born 1912) began directing in 1950; his films explore existential themes and individual crises, reaching a climax with *Blow-Up* in 1967. Pier Paolo Pasolini (1922-75) had some altogether different themes: preoccupied at first with the condition of the subproletariat in films like *Accattone* (1961) and *Teorema* (1968), he later dealt with human decay and death in such films as *Il Decamerone*, *I Racconti di Canterbury* and *Il Fiore delle Mille e Una Notte*.

In 1974 Lina Wertmüller (born 1928) incurred the wrath of feminists with her work *Swept Away* (*Travolti da un Insolito Destino nell'Azzurro Mare di Agosto* in Italian!). Bernardo Bertolucci (born 1940) first made a splash on the international scene with *Last Tango in Paris* (1972).

On a different note, Sergio Leone (1929-89) ended up specialising in a particular brand of rough Western in the late 1960s. Critical approval for movies such as *The Good, the Bad and the Ugly* (1968) came late, but the films were highly successful at the box office.

1980 to the Present Bertolucci's foreign profile has continued to grow with English-language blockbusters such as *The Last Emperor* (1987), *Little Buddha* (1992) and *Stealing Beauty* (1996). Another Italian director who has worked extensively outside his home country is Franco Zeffirelli (born 1923), among whose better known films are *Othello* (1986), *Hamlet* (1990) and *Jane Eyre* (1995).

Paolo (born 1931) and Vittorio Taviani (born 1929) got started in the 1960s and in 1976 produced *Padre Padrone*, a heart-rending account of peasant life on Sardegna and one man's escape. Their biggest hits of the 1980s were *Good Morning Babilonia* (1986), an account of the creation of WD Griffiths' *Intolerance*, and *Kaos* (1984), inspired by stories by Luigi Pirandello.

Stars of the Screen

One of the earliest international Italian stars was Rudolph Valentino (actually Rodolfo Pietro Filiberto Guglielmi), whose brief career in Hollywood lasted from about 1920 until his death in 1926 and spanned 10 silent movies. A migrant from Puglia in southern Italy, where he was born in 1895, he was a true American success story, arriving at the age of 18 and working as a waiter and professional dance partner before being discovered.

Among Italy's greatest actors since WWII is Marcello Mastroianni (1924-1996), who starred in *La Dolce Vita* and countless other films, including Robert Altman's *Prêt-à-Porter*. Vittorio Gassman (born 1922) is of similar stature in Italy but less acclaimed outside his homeland. Now a grand old man of Italian cinema and comedy, he most recently appeared as a New York gangland boss in the American flick *Sleepers*. Other notable Italian thespians include Anna Magnani (1908-73), who won an Academy Award for *The Rose Tattoo*, Gina Lollobrigida (born 1927) best known for *Go Naked in the World* and *Come September* and, of course, Sophia Loren (born 1934), whose innumerable films include *It Started In Naples*, *Houseboat* and *Boy on a Dolphin*.

NICKY CAVEN

The Italian star of the Hollywood screen – Sophia Loren

For a long time Totò (1898-1967) was the undisputed king of film comedy. Until his death, Totò was for Italy what Chaplin became internationally. That he never achieved similar recog-

---

Nuovo Cinema Paradiso (1988), by Giuseppe Tornatore (born 1956) is a wonderful homage to film-making. He was back in 1998 with *La Leggenda del Pianista sull'Oceano* (The Legend of the Pianist Over the Ocean), a quirky tale of a genius piano player born and raised in the bowels of a huge ocean-going liner.

Nanni Moretti (born 1953), who first came to the silver screen in the late 1970s, has proven a highly individualistic actor-director. *Caro Diario* (Dear Diary), his whimsical, self-indulgent, autobiographical three-part film won the prize for best director at Cannes in 1994. He followed it up in 1999 with *Aprile*, an equally quirky exploration of his mental meanderings.

Il Postino (The Postman), which starred Massimo Troisi, released in 1995, was ac-

claimed as one of the most striking Italian films of the 1990s.

Internationally, the bright new star is Roberto Benigni (see the boxed text 'Stars of the Screen' above).

SOCIETY & CONDUCT

It is difficult to make blanket assertions about Italian culture, if only because Italians have only lived as one nation for little over 100 years. Prior to unification, the peninsula was long subject to a widely varied mix of masters and cultures. This lack of unity contributed to the maintenance of local dialects and customs. Only with the advent of national TV did the spread of a standard Italian begin. Previously it was not unusual to find farmers and villagers who spoke only their local dialect.

Stars of the Screen

nition can perhaps be attributed to the special appeal for Italian audiences of his quick Neapolitan wit, the kind of thing that does not translate well.

Who, however, has not seen at least one spaghetti western with 160kg Bud Spencer and his thin, blue-eyed counterpart, Terence Hill? The names are pseudonyms – these cowboys are actually all-Italian. From 1970, when *They Called Him Trinity* was released, until 1986, they kept Italy and much of the rest of the world in stitches with their version of how the West was won.

The contemporary scene has thrown up few actors of international stature, but there are some names to watch. Massimo Troisi (1953-1994) brought a striking human touch to his characters, who were nearly always Neapolitan.

One who has occasionally appeared out of the Italian context is Roberto Benigni (born 1952), a highly popular Tuscan comedian. Long established as one of Italy's favourite comedic actors, he must be the first director to try to get a laugh out of the Holocaust – and succeed. He picked up three Oscars in 1999, including that for best actor, an honour rarely bestowed by Hollywood upon anyone but its own, for his *La Vita è Bella* (Life is Beautiful, 1998). The film, which he directed and starred in, is the story of an Italian Jewish family that ends up in the camps, where the father tries to hide its horrors from his son by pretending it's all a game. Benigni was already known to cinema-goers outside Italy for his appearances in Jim Jarmusch's *Down By Law* and *Night On Earth*. Charlie Chaplin's daughter, Geraldine, declared months after the Oscars that Benigni had inherited her father's cinematic poetry. Quite an accolade.

Following in the steps of Loren, Isabella Rossellini (born 1952), film director Roberto Rossellini's daughter, has carved out a career for herself in Hollywood. She came to particular attention with her role in David Lynch's disturbing 1986 film, *Blue Velvet*, but has appeared in many other pictures.

Italians at a World Cup football match may present a patriotic picture, but most Italians identify more with their region or even home town – a phenomenon known as *campanilismo* (an attachment to one's local bell tower!). An Italian is first and foremost a Sicilian or Tuscan, or even a Roman, Milanese or Neapolitan, before being Italian.

Confronted with a foreigner, however, Italians will energetically reveal a national pride difficult to detect in the relationships they have with each other.

Stereotypes

Foreigners may think of Italians as passionate, animated people who gesticulate wildly when speaking, love to eat, and drive like maniacs. There's a lot more to it than that, however.

Journalist Luigi Barzini has defined his compatriots as a hard-working, resilient and resourceful people, optimistic and with a good sense of humour. If you really feel that you have to subscribe to a national stereotype, Barzini's description is probably closer to the truth.

Italians are also passionately loyal to their friends and families – all-important qualities, noted Barzini, since 'a happy private life helps people to tolerate an appalling public life'.

Italians have a strong distrust of authority and, when confronted with a silly rule, an unjust law or a stupid order (and they are regularly confronted with many of them), they do not complain or try to change rules, but rather try to find the quickest way around them.

Family

The family remains of central importance in the fabric of Italian society, particularly in the south. Most young Italians tend to stay at home until they marry, a situation admittedly partly exacerbated by the lack of affordable housing. Still, modern attitudes have begun to erode the traditions. Statistics show that one in three married couples have no children and one in nine children is born out of wedlock. In Milano, more than one-third of families are headed by a single parent, two-thirds of whom are women.

Dos & Don'ts

Italians tend to be tolerant but, despite an apparent obsession with (mostly female) nakedness, especially in advertising, they are not excessively free and easy.

In some parts of Italy, particularly in the south, women will be harassed if they wear skimpy or see-through clothing.

Topless sunbathing, while not uncommon on some Italian beaches, is not always acceptable. Take your cue from other sunbathers. Nude sunbathing is likely to be offensive anywhere but on appropriately designated beaches. Walking the streets near beaches in a bikini or skimpy costume is also not on, and on the Venezia Lido it'll get you a fine.

In churches you are expected to dress modestly. This means no shorts (for men or women) or short skirts, and shoulders should be covered. Those that are major tourist attractions, such as San Pietro in Roma and San Francesco in Assisi, enforce strict dress codes. Churches are places of worship, so if you visit one during a service (which you should refrain from doing), try to be as inconspicuous as possible.

The police and *carabinieri* (see Dangers & Annoyances in the Facts for the Visitor chapter) have the right to arrest you for insulting a state official if they believe you have been rude or offensive, so be diplomatic in your dealings with them!

THE MAFIA

A journalist once noted that 'the Mafia and the establishment are intertwined, and that this marriage is one of the pillars of politi-

Mummy's Boys

The rough charm of the unshaven Italian Lothario mounted jauntily on his Vespa is an inescapable image; one redolent of the Latin lover. The truth is perhaps a little less alluring.

According to figures published in 1997 by Istat (Istituto Centrale di Statistica), the country's main statistics body, Italian men actually constitute an *esercito di mammoni* (army of mummy's boys). Forget Oedipus, these boys know which side their bread is buttered. Perhaps they are not so different from men the world over, but the numbers are certainly telling.

If you can believe Istat, 66.5% of single Italian men remain at home with mum (and dad) up to the age of 34 at least. Granted, this is partly caused by problems of unemployment, the cost of housing and so on. Of the remainder who do move out of home, some 42% do not shift more than 1km away and only 20% dare to move more than 50km beyond the maternal home. Of all these 'independent' single men, 70% manage to stop by mum's place every day of the week. The unkind might be led to believe (as was the author of at least one newspaper story on the subject) that apart from filial devotion, the lads might well bring with them a bag of dirty washing and time the visit to coincide with lunch.

But even if the washing and lunch are taken care of by their wives (not an uncommon situation among Italian couples), those men who are married still find time to pop in to see mamma at least a few times a week. And when marriage fails, a quarter of ex-husbands go home to mother, as opposed to 17% of wives.

cal life in Italy. The Mafia is not only omnipotent, it is omnipresent'.

The multiple crises that have rocked Italy's political establishment, from the stream of revelations linking Mafia figures to politicians, through to Tangentopoli (see History earlier in this chapter), have only served to increase people's awareness of the problem.

The term Mafia can be used to describe five distinct groups of organised criminals: the original Sicilian Mafia, also known as the Cosa Nostra; the Calabrian 'ndrangheta; the Camorra of Napoli; and two relatively new organisations, the Sacra Corona Unita (United Holy Crown) and La Rosa (the Rose), in Puglia. These groups operate both separately and together.

Their activities range from contraband to protection rackets and monopolising lucrative contracts in just about every field. Narcotics is another big source of income. By the early 1990s, the estimated combined worth of the Italian Mafia groups was around L100,000 billion, or about 12% of GNP. It comes as little comfort to the EU to know that similar organisations which have recently emerged in Russia appear to match, or even outdo, their Italian counterparts in ruthlessness and the scope of their activities throughout Europe.

Cosa Nostra

The Sicilian Mafia has its roots in the oppression of the Sicilian people and has a history extending back as far as the 13th century. Its complex system of justice is based on the code of silence known as *omertà*.

In the early 1930s, Mussolini moved against the Mafia in a way no-one has attempted since, appointing a proconsul with dictatorial powers and a brief to destroy the Mafia and eliminate it from the Sicilian mentality. A tall order. Mussolini managed to drive the Mafia so far underground that its activities became negligible.

From the devastation of WWII, however, grew the modern version of the organisation, known as Cosa Nostra. This has spread its tentacles worldwide and is far more ruthless and powerful than its predecessor. It is involved in drug-trafficking and arms deals, as well as finance, construction and tourist development, not to forget public-sector projects and Italian politics. Few Italians doubt the claim that the Mafia's influence extends into almost every part of the country, and well beyond.

When, in the early 1990s, the Mafia assassinated two anti-Mafia judges in Palermo in separate bomb blasts, the central government was finally moved to act. The first big success of this operation was the arrest of Salvatore 'Toto' Riina, the Sicilian godfather. Riina, head of the powerful Corleonese clan, had been the world's most wanted man since 1969. More recently, the venerable ex-prime minister Giulio Andreotti, one of the longest serving and most dominant political figures in post-war Italy, was put on trial in Palermo in the mid-1990s for alleged links with the Mafia. In late 1999 he was cleared of all charges. In June 1997 Pietro Aglieri, who was widely regarded as Riina's number two, was also finally arrested.

The policy of clemency for *pentiti*, arrested Mafia members who grass, has raised uncomfortable questions. On more than one occasion the pentiti have been found to be lying. Spilling the beans (or pretending to) doesn't necessarily get them off scot-free: Mafia killer Giovanni Brusca was imprisoned for 30 years in 1999.

Still, however much the judiciary have clamped down, Cosa Nostra is alive and well, so much so that it is claimed that Riina is running it from inside his jail cell. One of their more original activities is trafficking in antiquities, of which Sicilia is full. Mafiosi steal mosaics, ceramics or anything else they can from such sites as Piazza Armerina. They then pass them on to experts who have been bought off (and at least one of whom is now in prison) to be exported and sold in foreign auction houses. On a more old-fashioned note, several top regional politicians in Catania were arrested in May 1999 for accepting kickbacks in return for channelling building contracts to the Mafia. One of them had been on an anti-Mafia commission.

'ndrangheta

Until the late 1980s, the 'ndrangheta was a disorganised group of bandits and kidnappers; today it controls an organised crime network specialising in arms, drug-dealing and construction. In the 1970s, 16-year-old oil heir J Paul Getty III was kidnapped and held by the 'ndrangheta, having his ear severed before his release. The organisation continues to kidnap for profit. Based in the villages of Calabria, the 'ndrangheta is notorious for its savage violence: in the early 1990s they carried out an average of one execution a day.

Camorra

This secret society grew to power in Napoli in the 19th century. It was all but completely suppressed around the turn of the century, but enjoyed a renaissance after WWII, dealing mainly in contraband cigarettes. After the earthquake of 1980, the Camorra diverted hundreds of millions of dollars of the aid money that poured in for reconstruction around Napoli and built a criminal empire that has since diversified into drugs, construction, finance and tourist developments. It has worked closely with the Sicilian Mafia.

As the Camorra clans began to fragment in the mid-90s, their internecine squabbles over territory left a trail of death across Napoli. To make matters somewhat worse, 20 policemen from the Napoli *questura* (police station) stood accused in early 1997 of collusion with the Camorra. The mayor of Napoli at that time, Antonio Bassolino, was not surprised that the Camorra's tentacles had reached into the ranks of the police. 'It would have been strange had that not been the case – there is not one sector of society that has been spared by the system of corruption in Campania,' he said. Nor was the mayor impressed when, in mid-1997, Roma decided to send 600 troops into Napoli to protect sensitive points of the city and free

up police to pursue the bandits. For Antonio Bassolino, it was too little, too late.

Sacra Corona Unita & La Rosa

Puglia had managed to escape the clutches of organised crime that had terrorised the rest of the south, but by the late 1980s the Mafia had arrived in the form of the Sacra Corona Unita in the south of the region and La Rosa in the north. As a gateway to Eastern Europe through its main ports of Bari and Brindisi, Puglia was a natural target following the collapse of communism. It quickly supplanted Napoli as a base for smuggling, chiefly of cigarettes, and an early consequence of large-scale organised drug-running activities has been a massive upsurge in the number of heroin addicts in Bari, Brindisi and Taranto.

RELIGION

Under the terms of the Lateran Treaty of 1929 between Mussolini and the Catholic Church, the city of Roma was recognised as the centre of the Catholic world. The treaty resolved the uncomfortable standoff that had resulted from Italian unification and the effective removal from the Church's hands of secular power. The pope recognised the Italian state with Roma as its capital, Il Vaticano was made an independent state and Catholicism the state religion of Italy.

Times change, and in 1985 Il Vaticano and the Socialist prime minister Bettino Craxi renegotiated the treaty. As a result, Catholicism is no longer the state religion and compulsory religious education was dropped.

In a sense, this only reflected reality. Church attendance had fallen from 70% after the war to 25%, and nowadays many children are not baptised. But the Church moves slowly. Since 1978 the Polish Pope John Paul II has been at the helm. An archconservative, he is seen as having played a major role in the collapse of the communist bloc in the 1980s and 1990s. On social policy issues he has not been afraid to confront critics and has remained steadfast in his opposition to contraception, abortion, the idea of women priests and a host of other novelties. In Italy especially, he has been quick to criticise hedonism and consumerism, fuelling the impression some have of him as overly puritanical. At the same time, however, he has won the hearts of Catholics around the world with his indefatigable papal tours, taking the faith to the faithful. He continues to undertake a punishing schedule, in spite of his advanced age and speculation over his health.

Religiosity among the Italians appears often to be more a matter of form. First communions, church weddings and religious feast days are an integral part of Italian ritual. In the same way, the royal family is part of the ritual scenery in the life of many Britons, so the papacy is a kind of royal family to Italians.

It is sometimes hard to draw the line between faith and superstition. Busloads of Italians still crisscross the country in pilgrimage to venerate one saint or another. The present pope is big on beatification: the latest to receive the honour is Padre Pio (see San Giovanni Rotondo in the Puglia, Calabria & Basilicata chapter), beatified in May 1999, and at the time of writing a tribunal was considering the beatification of Mother Teresa of Calcutta, who died in 1997. In general, it is hard to escape the conclusion that the majority of people who express their faith in this regard are hoping for a little intervention on earth rather than spiritual improvement.

Some 85% of Italians professed to be Catholic in a census taken in the early 1980s. Of the remaining 15%, there were about 500,000 evangelical Protestants, about 220,000 Jehovah's Witnesses, and other, smaller groups, including a Jewish community in Roma and the Valdesi (Waldenses) – Swiss-Protestant Baptists living in small communities in Piemonte. There are also communities of orange-clad followers of the

Stray Flock

Most Italians claim to be Catholic, but ask them about the *malocchio* (evil eye) and see what happens. Most will make a simple hand movement (index and little finger pointing down, with the middle and ring fingers folded under the thumb) which is designed to ward off evil spirits. Others, if pressed, might admit to wearing amulets. A pregnant woman might wear a chicken's neck hanging around her own neck to ensure that her child is not born with the umbilical cord around its neck. Insurance agents can have difficulty discussing life insurance policies with clients, as many of them don't want to discuss their eventual death, or the possibility of suffering serious accidents. This phenomenon is known to sociologists as Catholic paganism.

Bhagwan Rajneesh who are known in Italy as the *arancioni*.

The big surprise to emerge from the census is the growth of the Muslim population, estimated at 700,000 and thus the second largest religious community in Italy after the Catholics. A fitting symbol for this novelty in the heart of Christendom was the inauguration in 1995 of a big Saudi-financed mosque in Roma.

LANGUAGE

Many Italians speak some English because they study it in school, but it is more widely understood in the north, particularly in major centres such as Milano, Firenze and Venezia, than in the south. Staff at hotels and restaurants often speak a little English, but you will be better received if you at least attempt to communicate in Italian. See the Language chapter for an introduction to the Italian language and some vocabulary.

ART &
ARCHITECTURE

ARCHITECTURE
The Etruscans, the Latins & the Greeks

The earliest well-preserved Italian art and architecture dates from the 1st millennium BC. It is the product of three cultures: Latin and Roman culture in Lazio, Etruscan culture in what is now northern Lazio and southern Toscana, and the culture of Magna Graecia in southern Italy and Sicilia, where city-states were founded in the 8th and 7th centuries BC by Greek colonists.

Like the Greeks, the early Romans built temples of stone. However, whereas the Greek temples had steps and colonnades on all sides, the Roman variety had a high podium with steps and columns only at the front, forming a deep porch. The Romans also favoured fluted Ionic columns with volute capitals and Corinthian columns with acanthus leaf capitals (rather than the Doric columns with cushion-like capitals used by the Greeks).

Etruscan temples followed the Greek style but were more elaborately decorated. However, almost no Etruscan architectural remains are visible today except for fragments of temple friezes.

Title page: The world's most famous frescoes – Michelangelo's *Creation* on the barrel-vaulted ceiling of the Cappella Sistina in Il Vaticano.

Below: Construction of Roma's Colosseo was begun by Emperor Vespasian in 72 AD.

The Roman Empire

In terms of style, the Romans invented little; their great achievement was to perfect existing construction techniques to create aqueducts and arches on a grandiose scale, the likes of which had never been seen before.

From the 1st century BC they used a quick-curing, strong concrete for vaults, arches and domes to roof vast areas like the Pantheon. Dry stone masonry was used for some temples, aqueducts and for the supporting vaults of theatres and amphitheatres, such as the Colosseo in Roma and the amphitheatres in Verona, Lucca and Capua.

Marble was used from the 2nd century BC until the 2nd century AD. As Roma's power grew, new buildings were needed to reflect the city's status in the Mediterranean world and the Romans started building forums, public baths, colonnaded streets and theatres, and complexes for both commercial and political activities.

JON DAVISON

Early Christian & Byzantine

Middle: Venezia's Basilica di San Marco embodies a magnificent blend of architectural styles, dominated by the Byzantine.

Bottom: Pisa's baptistry, started in 1153, was finally completed in the 14th century – a mix of Pisan-Romanesque and Gothic styles.

The early Christians practised their religion in private houses (many of which later became churches) and catacombs. In the 4th century, under the Christian emperor Constantine, several places of worship were constructed, the architecture of which was based on the buildings of Imperial Roma, in particular the rectangular basilica or public hall. Over time, transepts were added to create the shape of a cross.

The domed baptistry of San Giovanni in Laterano (in Roma), built by Constantine between 315 and 324 and remodelled into its present octagonal shape in the 5th century, became the model for many baptistries throughout the Christian world. The starkly simple Basilica di Santa Sabina in Roma, built in the 5th century, is one of the best preserved churches of this period.

When Ravenna became the Imperial capital in 402, several churches were built there, some in the basilican style. The Byzantine dome was freely adopted, often supported on a square rather than a round base (which the Romans had used). The innovative plan for the Basilica di San Vitale used an octagon within an octagon.

The Byzantine architectural style reached its peak in Venezia, with the magnificent Basilica di San Marco (consecrated in 1094). In the 10th and 11th centuries, the Greeks in the south built several small, cross-shaped and domed churches in the Byzantine style.

JON DAVISON

Romanesque (c1050-1200)

The Romanesque period saw a revival of buildings whose size and structure resembled those of the Roman Empire. Large basilicas were built by the Norman rulers in Puglia at Bari, Molfetta, Trani, Barletta, Bitonto and Canosa, often with the outside walls decorated with typically Romanesque blind arcading and whimsical sculptural ornament.

Architecture on Sicilia was a unique combination of Byzantine and Romanesque, illustrated by the cathedral in Monreale, with its beautiful cloister, carved capitals and dazzling mosaics; the cathedrals in Cefalù and Palermo; and the Palazzo dei Normanni and Palazzo La Zisa in Palermo.

Among the most stunning buildings of the period are Pisa's magnificently carved marble cathedral (begun in 1064), baptistry and (leaning) bell tower.

DAMIEN SIMONIS

ART & ARCHITECTURE

Gothic

Because of the influence of classical antiquity, the pointed arches and vaults of Gothic architecture never flourished in Italy to the same extent as they did north of the Alpi.

The most outstanding early Gothic church in Italy is the Basilica di San Francesco in Assisi, begun in the mid-13th century, which combines a heavily vaulted, dark and mysterious lower church with a light-filled upper church.

The Dominican and Franciscan orders built vast Gothic churches on the outskirts of medieval cities, such as Santa Maria Novella and Santa Croce in Firenze and the Frari and San Zanipolo in Venezia. The best examples of late medieval Gothic architecture can be found in the cathedrals at Siena (1196-1215), arguably the most sumptuous Gothic cathedral ever built, Orvieto, Milano and Roma (Santa Maria sopra Minerva).

With the growth of trade and city government, town halls were built, such as the Palazzo Vecchio in Firenze (1298-1310) and the imposing Palazzo Pubblico in Siena (begun in 1298), and many patrician families built impressive Gothic mansions.

The Gothic style in Italy lingered longest in Venezia. A fine example is the Palazzo Ducale (Doges' Palace) built in the 14th and early 15th centuries, which combines Gothic and Islamic styles in its façade. The elegant Ca' d'Oro (1420-34) on the Canal Grande was freely based on the Palazzo Ducale.

JON DAVISON

Left: Milano's cathedral has some 135 spires and 3200 statues crammed onto the roof and into the façade, but interestingly no bell tower.

Early Renaissance (c1400-1500)

Domes, vaults and arches are typical of Renaissance architecture.

The first major architectural achievement of the early Renaissance was Filippo Brunelleschi's (1377-1446) bold experiment in 1436 to span the *duomo* (cathedral) of Firenze with a double-skinned, segmented dome. It was followed by other domes: the Tempietto of Donato Bramante (c1504-10) beside San Pietro in Montorio, on the

Gianicolo in Roma, and the large, centrally planned Santa Maria della Consolazione, near Todi. The latter was begun in 1508 when Bramante was designing the Basilica di San Pietro; originally conceived as centrally planned and domed, the basilica was finally built in the form of a long Latin cross, with a 42m-diameter dome designed by Michelangelo Buonarroti (1475-1564).

A *palazzo* (palace) in the city was a very visible sign of a family's success. In Firenze, Michelozzo di Bartolommeo (1396-1472) designed influential urban buildings, including the Palazzo Medici-Riccardi, which features severe façades and rusticated stonework. Leon Battista Alberti (1404-72) wrote treatises on architecture, the harmony of classical forms and the ratio of measurements. He employed his theories in church façades such as Santa Maria Novella in Firenze, Sant'Andrea and San Sebastiano in Mantova and the Tempio Malatestiano in Rimini, as well as in the Palazzo Rucellai in Firenze.

Above: Brunelleschi's vast dome of Firenze's magnificent duomo consists of an outer shell supported by a thicker inner shell.

Giuliano da Sangallo (1445-1516) was the first architect to use Renaissance principles in the planning of villas, including the Palazzo Strozzi in Firenze, the most ambitious palace of the century.

High Renaissance (c1500-1600)

With the revival of the papacy, Roma became the centre of the High Renaissance. The popes of the 15th century summoned the leading artistic and architectural masters to rebuild the city. The Venetian Pope Paul II (1464-71) commissioned many works, including Palazzo Venezia, Roma's first great Renaissance palazzo (1455-64). Other important buildings include the Palazzo della Cancelleria, Palazzo Farnese, Palazzo Spada and Villa (Palazzo) Farnesina.

The lengthy construction of the Basilica di San Pietro occupied most of the other notable architects of the High Renaissance, including Raphael (1483-1520), Giuliano da Sangallo, Baldassarre Peruzzi (1481-1537) and Antonio da Sangallo the Younger (1483-1546).

Jacopo Sansovino (1486-1570) introduced the High Renaissance to Venezia, leaving his mark in various public buildings around Piazza San Marco. In the mid-16th century, Andrea Palladio applied Ancient Roman temple design to the façades of his churches in Venezia and also to his villas in Vicenza and the Veneto. His La Rotonda, outside Vicenza, a cardinal's party-house, imitates the Pantheon in Roma.

BETHUNE CARMICHAEL

During the Counter-Reformation, both art and architecture were entirely at the service of the Church. In Roma, the Jesuits created massive and impressive places of worship to attract and overawe the faithful. Giacomo della Porta (1539-1602), the last architect of the Renaissance tradition, designed the Mannerist façade of the main Jesuit church in Roma, the Gesù (1568-75), with elements creating a play of light and shade. Both the exterior and the interior – a wide nave and side chapels instead of aisles – were widely copied throughout Italy.

Baroque

The baroque style is synonymous with Roma. The two great architects of this period were the Naples-born Gian Lorenzo Bernini (1598-1680) and Francesco Borromini (1599-1667), from Lombardia.

No other architect before or since has had such an impact on a city as Bernini did on Roma. He was patronised by the Barberini pope, Urban VIII, who in 1629 appointed him official architect of San Pietro, for which he designed the *baldacchino* (altar canopy) above San Pietro's grave. Bernini transformed the face of the city, and his churches, palaces, piazzas and fountains (such as the Fontana dei Quattro Fiumi in Piazza Navona) are Roman landmarks to this day.

Bernini's great rival was Borromini, who created buildings involving complex shapes and exotic geometry. His most memorable works are the Chiesa di San Carlo alle Quattro Fontane (1641), which has an oval

SALLY WEBB

interior, and the Chiesa di Sant'Ivo alla Sapienza, which combines a unique arrangement of convex and concave surfaces and is topped by an innovative spiral campanile.

On Sicilia, following the 1693 earthquake, new churches and public buildings were erected in a derivative late-baroque style.

Neoclassicism

The early 18th century saw a brief flurry of surprisingly creative architecture, such as the Scalinata di Spagna (Spanish Steps, 1726) and the exuberant Fontana di Trevi, which was designed in 1732 by Nicola Salvi (1697-1751) and completed three decades later.

The neoclassical style is generally considered to have begun in the mid-18th century. It returned to the fundamental principles of classicism and was a direct reaction against the frivolous excesses of baroque.

In Napoli, the ruling Spanish dynasty, the Bourbons, built the Palazzo Reale di Capodimonte and at Caserta, north of Napoli, Luigi Vanvitelli (1700-73) designed another vast royal palace and grounds, the Reggia di Caserta, combining an ornate baroque interior with a restrained neoclassical exterior. In Milano, Vanvitelli's pupil Giuseppe Piermarini (1734-1808) became the most popular architect, building, among other edifices, La Scala opera theatre (1778). La Fenice opera house, in Venezia, was completed in 1792, and Napoli's San Carlo had opened in 1738, but was rebuilt in 1816 after a fire.

Facing page, above: Bernini's Piazza San Pietro is bounded by two semicircular colonnades, each made up of four rows of Doric columns.

Facing page, below: It is reputed that the statues of Bernini's Fontana dei Quattro Fiumi in Roma are shielding their eyes in disgust from Borromini's Chiesa di Sant' Agnese in Agone, but Bernini finished the fountain before work on the church was even begun.

Right: Nicola Salvi's Fontana di Trevi, finished in 1762, is a fabulous fusion of architecture and sculpture.

BETHUNE CARMICHAEL

The 19th & 20th Centuries

Architecture in 19th century Italy was fairly unremarkable, although there were interesting developments in town planning in Torino, Trieste and Milano.

The beginning of modern architecture in Italy is epitomised by the late 19th century shopping galleries in Milano, Napoli, Genova and Torino, with their distinctive iron-and-glass roofs. This fashion never quite made it to Roma, which instead got the massive white marble monument to Vittorio Emanuele II – the so-called wedding cake – built between 1885 and 1911. As the new capital of Italy, Roma got its own dose of urban planning, including massive apartment blocks, monumental public buildings and the Tevere river embankment.

In the 20th century Art Nouveau, known in Italy as Lo Stilo Liberty, made a brief appearance before Mussolini and the Fascist era inaugurated grandiose building schemes such as EUR (Esposizione Universale di Roma), a complete district on the outskirts of Roma.

The internationally celebrated Pier Luigi Nervi (1891-1979) made reinforced concrete one of his chief materials in his designs for Roma's Stadio Olimpico (1960) and the papal audience chamber in Il Vaticano.

Italy's two leading contemporary architects are Renzo Piano (born 1937), whose new music auditorium in Roma is almost complete, and Paolo Portoghesi (born 1931), who designed Roma's mosque, but both seem to do more work abroad than in their native country.

Left: The late 19th century and early 20th century brought huge change to Milano with the introduction of colossal buildings such as the neobaroque Stazione Centrale building completed in 1931 and the glass-domed Galleria Vittorio Emanuele.

PAINTING & MOSAICS
The Etruscans & the Greeks

A surprising number of Etruscan wall paintings have survived in various tombs. Decorated in vibrant colours, the tombs were intended as a pleasing environment for the dead, who were buried with their favourite worldly goods around them. The earliest subject matter was of a religious nature; representations of the afterlife became more common in later centuries. The best tomb paintings, dating from the 6th to the 1st centuries BC, can be seen at Tarquinia (Lazio). There are others at Chiusi (Toscana).

Tomb decorations discovered at Paestum, in Campania, dating mainly from the 6th and 5th centuries BC, are extremely well-preserved but are almost the only examples of Greek painting in Italy to have survived. They represent mythological and narrative scenes, and include the famous Tomba del Tuffatore, now in the Museo di Paestum.

Below: The famous Tomba del Tuffatore (Tomb of the Diver), found at Paestum in Campania, is made up of four panels decorated with a banqueting scene and a fifth panel showing a youth diving into the sea.

Republican to Imperial Rome

The Romans used painting and mosaic work, both legacies from the Greeks, to decorate houses and palaces from at least the 1st century BC. Although very little decoration from this period survives, there are some magnificent examples in the Museo Nazionale Romano collection at Palazzo Massimo alle Terme in Roma (such as the Villa Livia frescoes of an imaginary garden) and in the Museo Nazionale Archeologico in Napoli. Traces of mosaics and frescoes *in situ* can be found at Roma's ancient port of Ostia, as well as at Pompei and Ercolano (in Campania).

SCALA

Christian Art

Roman painting went into decline from the 2nd century AD, when mosaics and coloured marble veneers became a popular decorative medium. At first, black and white mosaic cubes were used for floors in both public and private buildings. Later, coloured stones were employed, as in the villa at Piazza Armerina, south of Enna on Sicilia, and in the early churches of Aquileia and Grado, near Trieste.

By the 4th century, glass tesserae were used to splendid effect in the apses of the early Christian churches of Roma (including Santa Costanza, Santa Pudenziana, SS Cosma e Damiano and the Basilica di Santa Maria Maggiore) and in Ravenna (Mausoleo di Galla Placidia, the Basilica di San Vitale and the Basilica di Sant'Apollinare Nuovo).

During the 5th and 6th centuries, only Christian art was permitted. This changed little in style but broadened its subject matter, including scenes from the Old Testament and the Passion of Christ. At this time Ravenna was the centre of artistic innovation.

The Middle Ages

The tradition of decorating churches with mosaics continued from the 7th to the 9th centuries and is seen in Roma at Santa Maria in Cosmedin, Santa Prassede and the Basilica di Santa Cecilia, in Trastevere. The influence of imported Byzantine mosaic artists, who created images against a gold background, began to spread.

Interesting frescoes survive from the 10th and 11th centuries in the small domed churches built in the Byzantine style by Greeks in the south: the Cattolica (Stilo), San Marco (Rossano) and San Pietro (Otranto), all of which have frescoed decoration on a blue background. There are, of course, the stunning mosaics in Venezia's Basilica di San Marco, dating from the 11th to the 15th centuries.

From the mid-12th century, panel paintings became increasingly important, especially in Toscana, as frescoes were so expensive to produce.

In Roma in the 12th century, the Cosmati – originally a single family of artisans, but eventually a name for a whole school – used fragments of coloured glass and marble from ancient ruins to create intricately patterned pavements, altars, paschal candlesticks and pulpits. Their work is referred to as 'cosmatesque' and can be found in churches all over Roma, as well as in other regions.

Above: The 12th century frescoes in the Cripta degli Affreschi of Aquileia's basilica depict scenes of the life of Christ.

Below: The gleaming mosaics in the Basilica di San Marco in Venezia cover the walls, cupolas and even the floors.

Early Renaissance

The Firenze-born artist Cimabue (c1240-1302) blurred the distinction between Gothic and the Renaissance, using rounded, modelled forms in his frescoes in the Basilica di San Francesco in Assisi (1228-53). Other artists who worked on the upper and lower churches of San Francesco in the first part of the 14th century included Simone Martini (c1284-1344), Pietro Lorenzetti and Giotto di Bondone (1266-1337) and his pupils.

The innovative Giotto cast aside the two-dimensional restrictions of painting and created an illusion of depth. He represented gesture and emotion in a completely new way and was the first artist to come to terms fully with foreshortening, modelling and the effects of light and shade, evident also in his frescoes in the Cappella degli Scrovegni in Padova (1305). In Firenze, Giotto's followers included Taddeo and Agnolo Gaddi.

In Siena, artists were occupied with entirely different concerns. Their work was a direct continuation of the Byzantine tradition of icon paintings, traditionally painted on wooden panels with tempera (pigments with

an egg binder), often with gold-leaf backgrounds, such as the *Rucellai Madonna* by Duccio (c1285), now in the Galleria degli Uffizi in Firenze.

Altarpieces during the 14th century became less like Byzantine icons, incorporating larger individual panels. Simone Martini's refined, graceful style is evident in his *Annunciation* (1333), in the Uffizi, which depends on line, colour and decorative effects. Ambrogio Lorenzetti's *Presentation in the Temple* (1342), also in the Uffizi, shows a lively interest in

Above: The Cappella dei Principi (Princes' Chapel), sumptuously decorated with marble and semi-precious stones, was once the main burial place of Firenze's Medici rulers.

perspective, but there is no consistent vanishing point, a concept only mastered in the next century. His *Allegories of Good and Bad Government*, in the Palazzo Pubblico in Siena, was the first purely secular painting and it gave a new importance to landscape.

Experimentation with optics and perspective was a feature of the early Renaissance. This is evident in the work of Masaccio (1401-28), who achieved a perfect sense of depth and perspective in his *Trinity* fresco in Santa Maria Novella, in Firenze, and in his fresco cycle in Santa Maria del Carmine, which uses a single light source and realistic shadows. Also in Firenze, the Dominican friar Fra Angelico (c1400-55) created ethereal and beautifully coloured religious works, while his pupil, Benozzo Gozzoli (c1421-97), painted decorative frescoes in the Palazzo Medici-Riccardi.

Classical mythology was of great interest to the Florentine painters, none more so than Sandro Botticelli (1445-1510), whose *Allegria della Primavera* (Joy of Spring) and *Birth of Venus* in the Uffizi remain enigmatic to this day.

Artistic activity elsewhere in Italy came nowhere near the rich style of Firenze, although Piero della Francesca (c1410-92) did produce magnificent fresco cycles in Arezzo and Urbino, and Luca Signorelli (c1441-1523) drew on a deep understanding of anatomy for his frescoes in the Orvieto duomo.

In northern Italy, Andrea Mantegna (c1431-1506) was outstanding; his *Cristo Morto* (Dead Christ) in the Pinacoteca di Brera, Milano, took foreshortening and perspective to a new level. In Venezia, the various members of the Bellini family achieved lasting influence, especially Giovanni (c1430-1516), who employed a unique use of colour and an innovative use of picture planes, one behind the other, to create depth and recession.

Above: Sandro Botticelli's *Allegria della Primavera* (Joy of Spring, 1478) is painted on a panel of poplar, using both tempera and oil, and presents a mythological ode to spring.

High Renaissance

Leonardo da Vinci (1452-1519) painted his *Cenacolo* (Last Supper) in the refectory of Santa Maria delle Grazie in Milano at the end of the 15th century. The artist's ability to represent the psychological characteristics of his subjects and create illusions of space marked the beginning of the High Renaissance but, unfortunately, his unconventional fresco technique, the ravages of time and irresponsible restoration have left the work in a pitiful state.

Between 1481 and 1483 some of the country's greatest painters were employed by Pope Sixtus IV to decorate the walls in his newly rebuilt Cappella Sistina in Il Vaticano. The frescoes of the lives of Moses and Christ and portraits of popes, were done by Perugino (1446-1523), Sandro Botticelli (1444-1510), Domenico Ghirlandaio (1449-94), Cosimo Rosselli (1439-1507) and Luca Signorelli.

The decoration of the official apartments of Pope Julius II (the Stanze di Raffaello) marked the beginning of the brilliant Roman career of Urbino-born Raphael (Raffaello Sanzio, 1483-1520), who arrived from Firenze in 1508. In the true spirit of the Renaissance, he absorbed the grand manner of classical Roma and became the most influential painter of his time.

Raphael was also adept at portraiture and mythological paintings, and there are wonderful frescoes in this vein from 1508 to 1511 in the

Villa Farnesina in Roma. Other leading artists who worked on the villa designed by Baldassarre Peruzzi were Sebastiano del Piombo (c1485-1547), Sodoma (1477-1549) and Giulio Romano (c1492-1546), one of the few native Roman artists of the Renaissance.

The greatest artistic achievement of the period (and arguably of all time) was by Raphael's contemporary, Michelangelo Buonarotti (1475-1564), on the Cappella Sistina ceiling (1508-12), which is crammed with dramatically foreshortened statuesque figures. Three decades later Michelangelo returned to adorn the altar wall of the Cappella Sistina with the *Giudizio Universale* (Last Judgment) between 1535 and 1541.

A distinct artistic school emerged in mid-16th century Venezia which placed emphasis on colour rather than drawing and line. Tiziano Vecelli (Titian, 1493-1576) painted the huge panel of the *Assumption of the Virgin* (1516-18) in the Frari, Venice, in which the composition is built up with colours as much as by form. The artist was sought after as a portraitist and produced sensuous paintings such as the *Venere d'Urbino* (Venus of Urbino,1538), in the Uffizi.

Below: In Titian's *Venere d'Urbino* (Venus of Urbino) the softness and light hues of the reclining nude contrast with the deep plum-coloured fabrics, typical of certain Venetian artists.

The Scuola Grande di San Rocco houses an overwhelming cycle of biblical scenes by Tintoretto (Jacopo Robusti, 1518-94), including the 12m-wide *Crucifixion*, in which a pool of light in the centre is ringed by a crowd of figures.

Another striking canvas of the period is Veronese's (c1528-88) *Feast in the House of Levi* (1573), in the Gallerie dell'Accademia, Venezia, which depicts the Last Supper, with Christ seated at a banquet in a lavish palazzo with a crowd in contemporary Venetian dress.

SCALA

Baroque

The late 16th century saw few highlights in painting, although Annibale Carracci (1560-1609) created magnificent frescoes of mythological subjects in the Palazzo Farnese, Roma, between 1597 and 1603.

Michelangelo Merisi da Caravaggio (1573-1610) heralded a move away from the confines of the High Renaissance towards a new naturalism. His paintings, using street urchins and prostitutes as models for biblical subjects, were often rejected for being too real. However, his innovative sense of light and shade and supreme drawing ability meant that he was courted by contemporary collectors and was influential for centuries.

More successful in their day, although less highly revered since, were the drily academic painters Guido Reni (1575-1642) and Domenichino (1581-1641), who were considered by their contemporaries and immediate successors to be on level par with Raphael and Michelangelo. Domenichino, a native of Bologna and a pupil of Annibale Carracci, received innumerable commissions from the aristocratic clergy and his best works adorn nine churches in Roma.

Michelangelo had started a fashion for ceiling frescoes which continued for some time into the 17th century. Pietro da Cortona (1596-1669) was one of the most sought-after decorators of baroque Roma, completing the ceiling frescoes in the Salone Grande of Palazzo Barberini as well as in the Chiesa Nuova and many private palaces.

The Jesuit artist Andrea dal Pozzo (1642-1709) made a name for himself by creating trompe l'oeil perspectives on ceilings and walls in the many Jesuit churches being erected in Roma, while serene landscapes were produced by Salvator Rosa (1615-73) and the Italianised French painters Nicolas Poussin (1594-1665) and Claude Lorrain (1600-82).

Below: Caravaggio's *Madonna dei Palafrenieri* (Madonna of the Grooms), painted in 1605 and showing the Virgin Mary stamping on a serpent's head, was criticised in Roma's ecclesiastical circles due to its subject matter.

SCALA

The 18th to 20th Centuries

In the 18th century the attention of the many foreign artists who settled in Italy turned to the antique. The widely disseminated etchings of Roma and its ancient ruins by Giovanni Battista Piranesi (1720-78) attracted Grand Tourists and artists alike. The only notable artistic endeavours of the early 19th century were produced by academic history painters such as Francesco Hayez (1791-1882).

The years from 1855 to 1865 saw the heyday of the *Macchiaioli* (from the Italian for 'stain' or 'blot'), who produced a version of pointillism using thousands of dots of pure colour to build up the picture, and the end of the century saw the rise of the Italian Symbolists. Painting since Italian unification in 1870 is most readily found in Roma's Galleria Nazionale d'Arte Moderna.

The Italian Futurists were inspired by urbanism, industry and the idea of progress. Umberto Boccioni (1882-1916) and Giacomo Balla (1871-1958) aligned themselves with the *Futurist Manifesto* (1909) of the writer Emilio Marinetti, while Carlo Carrà (1881-1996) had much in common with Cubists such as Pablo Picasso. Giorgio Morandi (1890-1964) consistently depicted tangible objects, such as bottles and jars, and made them appear as abstract forms, while the Surrealist Giorgio De Chirico (1888-1978) painted visionary empty streetscapes with elements disconcertingly juxtaposed, often incorporating allusions to classical Antiquity.

Amedeo Modigliani (1884-1920) spent most of his adult life in Paris. However, his art – mainly arresting portraits and sensuous reclining female nudes – was firmly rooted in the tradition of the Italian Renaissance and Mannerist masters.

Important post-WWII artists include Burri, Colla, Manzoni and Pascali, as well as the *Transavanguardia*, whose exponents include Enzo Cucchi, Francesco Clemente, Mimmo Paladino and Sandro Chia, many of whom have worked and gained success both in Italy and abroad.

Right: Giorgio De Chirico's *Piazza d'Italia* epitomises the usual style of his work – views of seemingly uninhabited cities, painted in dark, earthy tones.

SCALA

SCULPTURE
The Etruscans & the Greeks

JOHN HAY

Most evidence of Etruscan art has come from their tombs, richly furnished with carved stone sarcophagi, fabulous gold jewellery, ceramics and bronzes. The Etruscan artists took Greek artistic techniques and used them to create a unique style of their own.

The 7th century BC saw ceramics decorated with geometric and oriental motifs with lions and sphinxes, but by the end of the century there was a growing interest in the human figure. Terracotta and stone sculpture and bronze figurines often followed Greek styles, from the rather stiff figures of the archaic period (6th century BC) to the almost idealised naturalism of the classical (5th and 4th centuries). Finally a more naturalistic and even expressive realism surfaced in the Hellenistic period (from 323 BC to 31 BC).

The Etruscans were famous for metalwork, such as the bronze *Lupa Capitolina* (She-Wolf) in the Musei Capitolini in Roma, although such large sculptures are rare. Most of the surviving pieces are smaller figurines or jewellery with intricate filigree work. The Museo Nazionale Etrusco di Villa Giulia in Roma, the Museo Gregoriano Etrusco (part of the Musei Vaticani) in Roma and the Museo Archeologico in Firenze have the richest collections of Etruscan art. The height of creativity and skill that the Etruscan artists could reach is demonstrated at Villa Giulia by the beautifully sculpted *Sarcofago degli Sposi* (Sarcophagus of the Married Couple), presumably made for a husband and wife, from a tomb at Cerveteri.

SCALA

Above left: According to legend, Siena (Toscana) was founded by the son of Remus. The symbol of the wolf feeding the twins Romulus and Remus is found throughout the city.

Left: The composition of the *Sarcofago degli Sposi* (Sarcophagus of the Married Couple) highlights the exceptional skill of the Etruscan artists.

Republican to Imperial Roma

In both the Republican and Imperial eras, sculpture was very much at the service of Roma and, more than any other art form, provides a compelling historical record.

The first Roman sculptures were actually made by Greek artists brought to Roma or were copies of imported classical Greek works. An exception was portrait sculpture, which was derived from the Etruscans, who aimed for naturalism. The Romans often had statues made of themselves in the guise of Greek gods or heroes. However, the most interesting Roman sculpture was that of the 1st and 2nd centuries AD which commemorated the history of the city and its citizens or which was made for specific architectural settings such as the Villa Adriana at Tivoli.

Emperor Augustus was the first to exploit the possibilities of sculpture as a propaganda tool. One of the most important works of Roman sculpture is the Ara Pacis (13 BC) in Roma, made to celebrate Augustus' victories in Spain and Gaul and the peace that he had established in the Empire. The carved reliefs of scenes from Augustus' reign, exemplified by clarity and classical restraint, mark the point at which Roman sculpture gained its own identity.

Later commemorative works include the Colonna di Traiana (early 2nd century AD), erected to celebrate Emperor Trajan's military achievements in the Dacian campaigns, and the Colonna Antonina (180-196) built to commemorate Marcus Aurelius' victories over the Germans and Sarmations between 169 and 176 AD.

In the 3rd and 4th centuries there was little public sculpture, although a notable exception was the 4th century statue of Emperor Constantine, a 10m-high colossus which stood at his basilica in the Foro Romano. Pieces of it (namely the head, a hand and a foot) are in Roma's Musei Capitolini.

Above right: The Museo Pio-Clementino in the Musei Vaticano holds one of the largest collections of classical statues.

Right: The marble Ara Pacis (Altar of Peace) is decorated with reliefs showing historical scenes on the sides and mythological scenes on the ends.

Christian Art to the Middle Ages

The early Christian period saw an almost total rejection of sculpture, except for carved decoration on Christian sarcophagi. The carved wooden panels depicting scenes of the Passion of Christ on the doors of the Basilica di Santa Sabina in Roma and dating from the 5th century are a significant but rare exception.

Sculpture took centuries to recover, and did so first in Lombardia and Emilia, with church portals decorated with intricate bas-reliefs by Wiligelmo (at Modena) and his pupil Nicolò, who carved, among others, the portals of cathedrals in Verona, Ferrara, Piacenza and Cremona.

Nicola Pisano (c1220-84) created an illusion of space by using different levels of relief, and also created voluminous figures. His pulpits in the baptistry in Pisa and in Siena's cathedral have a creative expression not seen in sculpture since Roman times.

Giovanni Pisano (1250-1314), Nicola's son, was also an innovative sculptor. His statues for the façade of the cathedral in Siena broke away from the static figures used for similar purpose elsewhere. Posed in dramatic ways, they were placed high up on the façade and were designed to be viewed from a distance.

SCALA

Left: This early 14th century pulpit in the Pisa's duomo highlights Giovanni Pisano's synthesis of Gothic and classical elements.

The Renaissance

Firenze was the heart of sculptural activity during the early Renaissance, with the limelight falling on sculptors such as Lorenzo Ghiberti (1398-1455), responsible for the magnificent cast bronze baptistry doors of the duomo, and the prolific Donatello (Donato Bardi, 1386-1466), many of whose works are now in the Museo del Bargello in Firenze. Donatello's large equestrian statue, the *Gattamelata* (1453), in front of the Basilica del Santo in Padova is considered the first great bronze of the Italian Renaissance.

Three generations of the Della Robbia family produced distinctive terracotta sculpture (from the 15th to the mid-16th centuries) using blue and white enamel glazes, sometimes with the addition of yellow and green.

Michelangelo already had an established reputation as a sculptor when he arrived in Roma from Firenze at the end of the 15th century. His staggeringly beautiful *Pietà*, now in the Basilica di San Pietro, was sculpted when he was only 25 years old. He was put to work immediately by Julius II on the massive project of creating a tomb for the pope, involving 40 sculptures. The tomb occupied the artist for his entire career but was never completed.

JOHN HAY

Baroque

In terms of sculpture, the baroque meant one person – Gian Lorenzo Bernini. Baroque sensibilities gave a new importance to exaggerated poses, cascading drapery and primacy of emotions, and Bernini was an unequalled master. His were not sculptures but rather theatrical and emotional spectacles set in stone which unfold before the viewer's eyes. His *Davide*, *Il Ratto di Proserpina* and *Apollo e Dafne*, all in Roma's Museo Borghese, and the *Santa Teresa trafitta dall'amor di Dio* (The Ecstasy of St Teresa) in Santa Maria della Vittoria (also in Roma) are cases in point.

Right: The doors of Firenze's duomo and battistero are richly decorated with sculptures and reliefs.

Bologna-born Alessandro Algardi (1595-1654) was one of the few sculptors not totally overshadowed by Bernini, a great rival. His bronzes and marbles grace several Roman churches and palazzi. His white marble monument to Pope Leo XI (1650) is in the Basilica di San Pietro.

Neoclassicism

The neoclassicism of the late 18th and early 19th centuries was a reaction to the excesses of the baroque and a response to the renewed interest in the classical world which had been sparked by the excavations of Pompei and Ercolano.

The neoclassical sculptural style was adopted by many foreign artists who had come to Roma, but among the Italians it was best represented by Antonio Canova (1757-1822). He was an accomplished modeller, but his work is sometimes devoid of obvious emotion. His most famous work is a daring sculpture of Pauline Bonaparte Borghese as a reclining *Venere Vincitrice*, in the Museo e Galleria Borghese, which is typical of the slightly erotic sculptures for which the sculptor became known.

The 20th Century

Giacomo Manzù (1908-91) revived the Italian religious tradition. His best known work is a bronze door (to the left of the central Holy Door) in the Basilica di San Pietro.

Many of Italy's important post-WWII artists incorporate sculpture into their oeuvre. The best panorama can be found at Roma's Galleria Nazionale d'Arte Moderna, which includes works by Alberto Giacometti, Lucio Fontana and Mimmo Paladino.

Sally Webb & Ann Moffatt

Below: Canova's famous statue of Pauline Bonaparte Borghese is one of several statues of members of Napoleon's family, which were based on classical figures.

SCALA

Facts for the Visitor

SUGGESTED ITINERARIES

However you decide to approach the country, and whatever itinerary you map out, remember that the determined monument zealot could spend days and in some cases weeks in any one Italian city. No human being can 'do' all of Italy, probably not even in a lifetime dedicated to the project! So do some research before you go and assemble a package of cities, monuments and countryside you particularly wish to see – and build in time for detours, long lunches and the unexpected!

One week

A week is not a long time in Italy, but speedy travellers have been known to arrive in Roma and undertake a whistle-stop tour of the tried and true. After a couple of days in Roma you could make for Firenze by train, spend two nights there (allowing time for a quick excursion to Siena or Pisa) and then push on to Venezia, where another two days would allow you to sample the place. The ultra-keen might stop en route for a day in Bologna. Such a trip could be a one-way journey or end with a return trip by rail to the point of departure.

Two weeks

With two weeks the options widen a little. The same route could be used as a basis, with further side trips thrown in to suit. Between Roma and Firenze, Perugia suggests itself as a stop, while Firenze itself can be used as a base for a whole range of exploratory touring – why not try the medieval village of San Gimignano? It is one among many in the Tuscan and Umbrian countryside worth poking about in.

Digging deeper

Those who know Italy or simply want to 'specialise' a little could devote three to four weeks to one or two regions. Sicilia, for example, offers plenty. After arriving by charter flight in Palermo, you could undertake a circuit taking in (heading east) Cefalù, the Isole Eolie (where

Highlights

The Best

Coming up with a Top 10 hit list for Italy is a little like trying to find the 10 shiniest gold ingots in Fort Knox. Bearing that in mind, these are some of the places, sights and experiences that make Italy so special:

1. Firenze (Toscana)
2. Isole Eolie (Sicilia)
3. Costiera Amalfitana (Campania)
4. Siena (Toscana)
5. Italian food
6. The Cinque Terre (Liguria)
7. The ancient ruins of Roma (Lazio), Pompei and Paestum (Campania)
8. Venezia (Il Veneto)
9. Parco Naturale Fanes-Sennes-Braies (Trentino-Alto Adige)
10. Carnevale in Ivrea (Piemonte)

The Worst

Obviously you should make of the following what you will. It is just possible that the thought of driving headlong down a Pianura Padana (Po plain) autostrada in dense fog will turn some people on:

1. Potenza (Basilicata)
2. Reggio di Calabria (Calabria)
3. Italian bureaucracy
4. Italian drivers
5. Autostrada tolls
6. Roman men
7. Driving through fog in the Pianura Padana (Emilia-Romagna)
8. Tourist crowds in the Cappella Sistina (hard to avoid!)
9. Italian beaches in August (so packed you can't breathe!)
10. Italian queues

you could easily chew up a week alone), Taormina, Etna, Siracusa, Ragusa, Agrigento, Trapani (for the Isole Egadi), Erice and the Riserva Naturale dello Zingaro. Speedy travellers can accomplish this in less time and add in the villages and hill country of the interior – a world little observed by foreigners. Another area to consider for a concentrated visit is Campania. Basing yourself in Italy's fascinating southern metropolis, Napoli (itself worthy of several days' investigation), you could easily spend a week or two taking in the wonders of: Vesuvio; the ancient cities of Pompei, Ercolano and, farther south, Paestum; the captivating islands of Capri, Ischia and Procida; the seaside resort of Sorrento and the dazzling Costiera Amalfitana; and the regal town of Caserta.

A 'Grand Tour'
Those with a month or more have unlimited options. Backpackers often wander into the north of Italy from France and make their way south to Brindisi to catch a boat on to the next obvious destination – the Greek isles. You might begin with some exploration of the Ligurian coast, including chic Portofino and the charming Cinque Terre, then head eastward for Bologna and on to Venezia. Or you could simply maintain a straightforward south-easterly course. This would allow you to take in Pisa, Firenze, Siena, Perugia, perhaps some excursions in the Tuscan and Umbrian countryside, Roma and Napoli, before cutting east across to Brindisi and the ferries for Greece.

PLANNING
When to Go
The best time to visit Italy is from April to June, when prices are lower and competition from other tourists is not as great. Late July and August is the time to avoid Italy, when the weather boils, prices are inflated and the whole country swarms with holidaymakers. Most Italians go on holiday in the month of August, abandoning the cities (and leaving many shops, hotels and restaurants closed) and packing out the coastal and mountain resorts.

July and September are the best months for walking in the Alpi and Appennini – like everywhere else, walking trails and *rifugi* (mountain accommodation) are crowded in August. During these months the weather is generally good, although you should always

allow for cold snaps. Rifugi are usually open from late June to the end of September for walkers, and at Easter (March/April) for skiers.

Italy's southern regions can be mild in winter, but you shouldn't bank on it. Inland especially, freezing conditions, heavy rain and snow can prevail. Your best chance of mild weather in winter is on Sicilia or Sardegna, although even on these islands cast-iron guarantees are impossible.

You may prefer to organise your trip or itinerary to coincide with one or more of the many festivals that litter the Italian calendar (see the Special Events section later in this chapter).

When we refer to winter and summer opening hours throughout this book, by summer we mean Easter to late September/early October.

What Kind of Trip
Virtually any kind of trip is possible in Italy and what you decide on will depend on your budget, time, how well you know the country and whether or not you have specific interests. The top tourist cities (such as Roma, Venezia and Firenze) are popular destinations for short excursions from Europe – many travel agencies and companies offer travel-and-accommodation packages for this kind of weekend break. In winter, you can get some great deals.

The budget traveller could spend months slowly touring around the whole country using local transport and sticking to *ostelli per la gioventù* (youth hostels) and basic *pensioni* (small hotels). Those with less time might prefer instead to concentrate on a single region (Toscana or the island of Sicilia, for instance) or make up an itinerary taking in some of the great cities. Having your own vehicle is a great advantage, allowing you to explore off-the-beaten-track places – and Italy is great motorcycling country.

Skiers often spend a week or two in the mountains of northern Italy and pretty much ignore the rest of the country.

There is no shortage of organised-tour

possibilities. They reduce hassle but can be restricting and pricey (see Organised Tours in the Getting There & Away chapter). Some tours are theme-based, such as art tours or cookery courses in rural Italy. Another approach is to undertake language and culture courses in cities like Perugia and Firenze and fit in travel around study (for some ideas see the Courses section later in this chapter).

Maps

Small-Scale Maps Michelin has a series of good fold-out country maps. Map No 988 covers the whole country on a scale of 1:1,000,000. You could also consider the series of area maps at 1:400,000 – Nos 428 to 431 cover the mainland, 432 covers Sicilia and 433 Sardegna. The Touring Club Italiano (TCI) publishes a decent map covering Italy, Switzerland and Slovenia at 1:800,000.

Road Atlases If you are driving around Italy, the AA's *Big Road Atlas – Italy*, available in the UK for UK£9.99, is scaled at 1:250,000 and includes 39 town maps. Pretty much as good is Michelin's *Tourist and Motoring Atlas Italy*, which is scaled at 1:300,000, has 78 town maps and retails for UK£9.95 (L30,000). In Italy, the Istituto Geografico de Agostini's *Atlante Stradale d'Italia* (1:600,000) contains city plans and sells for L24,500. For L43,000 the same publisher offers the much more comprehensive *Atlante Turistico Stradale d'Italia* (1:250,000). TCI publishes an *Atlante Stradale d'Italia* (1:200,000) divided into three parts – Nord, Centro and Sud. Each costs L34,000.

City Maps City maps in this book, combined with tourist office maps, are generally adequate. More detailed maps are available in Italy at good bookshops (like Feltrinelli, which has branches throughout the country) or newspaper stands. Excellent city plans and maps are published by de Agostini, TCI and Michelin. Other decent city-map publishers include FMB (with the yellow cov-

ers) and Milano's Vincitorio Editore. TCI publishes *200 Piante di Città* (L20,000), a handy book of street plans covering pretty much any city that might otherwise be a source of confusion.

Walking Maps Maps of walking trails in the Alpi and Appennini are available in major Italian bookshops, but the best by far are the TCI bookshops (especially the head office in Milano). Otherwise, you can usually locate maps of specific zones once you are in the area.

The best walking maps are the 1:25,000 scale series published by Tabacco; they mainly cover the north. Kompass publishes 1:25,000 scale maps of various parts of Italy, as well as a 1:50,000 series and several in other scales (including one at 1:7500 of Capri!). Edizioni Multigraphic Firenze produces a series of walking maps concentrating mainly on the Appennini. All cost from around L10,000 to L12,000 each. The series of *Guide dei Monti d'Italia*, grey hardbacks published by the TCI and Club Alpino Italiano, are exhaustive walking guides with maps.

What to Bring

Pack as little as possible. A backpack is an advantage since petty thieves prey on the luggage-laden tourists with no free hands. Backpacks whose straps and openings can be zipped inside a flap are less awkward and more secure than the standard ones.

Suitcases with wheels or trolleys may be fine in airports but otherwise you won't get far on foot with them. If you must carry a suitcase/bag, make sure it's lightweight and not too big. Remember that most everyday necessities can be found easily in Italy.

A small pack (with a lock) for day trips and sightseeing is preferable to a handbag or shoulder bag, especially in the southern cities, where motorcycle bandits are particularly active.

Clothes Except in the mountains, Italy is uniformly hot in summer but variable in winter. In most areas, during the months ⌐

July and August a light jacket will do for cool evenings. In winter you will need a heavy coat, hat, gloves and scarf for the north, while a lined raincoat will do on Sicilia. Roma has a mild climate, so you will need heavy woollens in January/February only.

Italians dress up just to do the daily food shopping, so if you plan to hang around in cafés and bars or enjoy some of the nightlife you'll feel more comfortable with a set of casually dressy clobber.

You'll need a pair of hardy, comfortable walking shoes with rubber soles – trainers are fine except for going out, so something a little more presentable, though practical, might cover all bases.

People planning to walk in the Alpi should bring the necessary clothing and equipment, in particular a pair of walking boots (lightweight and waterproof). Even in mid-summer you will need warm clothing on long walks or if you plan to go to high altitudes on cable cars – even if it's sweltering in the valley, the temperature can drop to below 0°C at 3000m. Inexperienced walkers should check with a local mountaineering group for a list of essentials before leaving home. Otherwise, the list provided in the Walking in the Dolomiti section of the Trentino-Alto Adige chapter should be adequate.

Unless you plan to spend large sums in dry-cleaners and laundrettes, it's wise to pack a portable clothesline. Many pensioni and hotels ask guests not to wash clothes in the room, but such rules are rarely enforced. Consider packing a light travel iron or crease-proof clothes.

Useful Items As well as any special personal needs, consider the following:

- an under-the-clothes money belt or shoulder wallet, useful for protecting your money and documents in cities
- a towel and soap, which are sometimes lacking in cheap accommodation
- ¬mall Italian dictionary and/or phrasebook
- ¬s army knife
- ¬ical kit (see Health later in this chapter)
- ¬apter plug for electrical appliances

- a padlock or two to secure your luggage to racks and to close hostel lockers
- a sleeping sheet to save on sheet rental costs if you're using youth hostels (a sleeping bag is unnecessary unless you're camping)
- a torch (flashlight)
- an alarm clock
- sunglasses and a hat
- a universal sink plug

RESPONSIBLE TOURISM

It would be nice to see more travellers wandering around with an awareness of local sensibilities. Visitors all too often seem to leave manners and common sense at home. In the main tourist centres, locals are by now used to the sight of men wandering around in little more than a pair of shorts and (maybe) sandals. But you have to ask yourself, if you wouldn't walk around like that in your town, why do so in someone else's? Sun-scorched bellies do not a pretty sight make, and less still to a people known for their preoccupation with dressing well.

When visiting ancient sites such as Pompei, every care should be taken to minimise your impact on these precious reminders of the world's ancient heritage. Clambering all over walls and handling objects all helps speed decay. The sheer volume of people visiting these places is already problematic – in Venezia it has been suggested some sort of restriction should be placed on the number of visitors entering the city on any one day. The moral of the story is, simply, respect the monuments and works of art you see as you would your own most prized possessions. Tread softly.

TOURIST OFFICES
Local Tourist Offices

The quality of tourist offices in Italy varies dramatically. One office might have enthusiastic staff but no useful printed information, while indifferent and even hostile staff in another might keep a gold mine of brochures hidden under the counter.

Three tiers of office exist: regional, provincial and local. The names of tourist boards are different throughout the country, but they all offer roughly the same services.

Regional offices are generally concerned with promotion, planning, budgeting and other projects far removed from the daily concerns of the humble tourist. Provincial offices are known either as the Ente Provinciale per il Turismo (EPT) or, more commonly, as the Azienda di Promozione Turistica (APT) and usually have information on both the province and the town. Local offices generally have information only about the town you're in and go by various names. Increasingly common is Informazioni e Assistenza ai Turisti (IAT), but you may also come across Azienda Autonoma di Soggiorno e Turismo (AAST) offices. These are the places to go if you want specific information about bus routes, museum opening times and so on.

In many small towns and villages, the local tourist office is called a Pro Loco; these are often similar to the IAT or AAST offices, but on occasion are little more than a meeting place for the local elderly men.

Most EPT, APT and AAST offices will respond to written and telephone requests for information about hotels, apartments for rent and so on.

Tourist offices are generally open from 8.30 am to 12.30 or 1 pm and from 3 to around 7 pm Monday to Friday. Hours are usually extended in summer, when some offices also open on Saturday or Sunday.

Information booths at most major train stations and some smaller stations tend to keep similar hours, but in some cases operate only in summer. Staff can usually provide a *pianta della città* (map), *elenco degli alberghi* (list of hotels) and *informazioni sulle attrazioni turistiche* (information on the major sights). Many will help you find a hotel.

English, and sometimes French or German, is spoken at offices in larger towns and major tourist areas. German is, of course, spoken in Alto Adige. Printed information is generally provided in a variety of languages.

If you are arriving in Roma, you can obtain limited information about the major destinations throughout the country from the EPT office (☎ 06 488 99 253, fax 06 488 99 228), Via Parigi 11, 00185 Roma, and at the headquarters of Italy's national tourist office, Ente Nazionale Italiano per il Turismo (ENIT; ☎ 06 4 97 11, fax 06 446 33 79), Via Marghera 2, 00185 Roma. ENIT has Web sites at www.enit.it and www.piu italia2000.it. Both offices are near Roma's central train station, Stazione Termini.

The addresses and telephone numbers of local, provincial and some useful regional tourist offices are listed under towns and cities throughout this book.

Tourist Offices Abroad

Information on Italy is available from the Italian State Tourist Office in the following countries:

Austria
(☎ 01-505 16 39)
Kaerntnerring 4, 1010 Vienna
Canada
(☎ 514-866 7669, email initaly@ican.net)
Suite 1914, 1 Place Ville Marie,
Montreal, Quebec H3B 2C3
France
(☎ 01 42 66 66 68, email 106616.131@
compuserve.com)
23 rue de la Paix, 75002 Paris
Germany
(☎ 030-247 83 97, email enit-berlin@
t-online.de)
Karl Liebknecht Strasse 34, 10178 Berlin
(☎ 069-25 93 32, email enit.ffm@t-online.de)
Kaisertstrasse 65, 60329 Frankfurt am Main
(☎ 089-53 13 17)
Goethe Strasse 20, 80336 Munich
Netherlands
(☎ 020-616 8244)
Stadhouderskade 2, 1054 ES Amsterdam
Spain
(☎ 91 559 9750)
Gran Via 84, 28013 Madrid
Switzerland
(☎ 01-211 7917, email enit@bluewin.ch)
Uraniastrasse 32, 8001 Zurich
UK
(☎ 020-7408 1254, 0891 600 280, email
enitlond@globalnet.co.uk)
1 Princes St, London W1R 8AY
USA
(☎ 312-644 0996, email enitch@
italiantourism.com)
500 North Michigan Ave, Chicago, IL 60611

(☎ 310-820 2977)
Suite 550, 12400 Wilshire Blvd,
Los Angeles, CA 90025
(☎ 212-245 4822, email enitny@bway.net)
Suite 1565, 630 Fifth Ave,
New York, NY 10111

Sestante CIT (Compagnia Italiana di Turismo), Italy's national travel agency, also has offices throughout the world (known as CIT or Citalia outside Italy). Staff can provide extensive information on travelling in Italy and will organise tours, as well as book individual hotels. CIT staff can also make train bookings and sell Eurail passes and discount passes for train travel in Italy. Offices include:

Australia
    (☎ 03-9650 5510)
    Level 4, 227 Collins St, Melbourne 3000
    (☎ 02-9267 1255)
    263 Clarence St, Sydney 2000
Canada
    (☎ 514-845 4310, 800 361 7799)
    Suite 750, 1450 City Councillors St,
    Montreal, Quebec H3A 2E6
    (☎ 905-415 1060, 800 387 0711)
    Suite 401, 80 Tiverton Court, Markham,
    Toronto, Ontario L3R 0G4
France
    (☎ 01 44 51 39 00)
    5 blvd des Capucines, Paris 75002
Germany
    (☎ 0211-690030)
    Geibelstrasse 39, 40235 Düsseldorf
UK
    (☎ 020-8686 0677, 8686 5533)
    Marco Polo House, 3-5 Lansdowne Rd,
    Croydon, Surrey CR9 1LL
USA
    (☎ 310-338 8615)
    Suite 980, 6033 West Century Blvd,
    Los Angeles, CA 90045
    (☎ 212-730 2121)
    10th Floor, 15 West 44th St,
    New York, NY 10036

Italian cultural institutes in major cities throughout the world have extensive information on study opportunities in Italy. See the Courses section later in this chapter for more details.

VISAS & DOCUMENTS

For information on driving licences and permits see under Paperwork & Preparations in the Car & Motorcycle section of the Getting There & Away chapter.

Passport

Citizens of the 15 European Union (EU) member states can travel to Italy with their national identity cards alone. People from countries that do not issue ID cards, such as the UK, must be in possession of a valid passport. All non-EU nationals must have a full valid passport.

If you've had your passport for a while, check that the expiry date is at least some months off, otherwise you may not be granted a visa (if you need one). If you travel a lot, keep an eye on the number of pages you have left in the passport. US consulates will generally insert extra pages into your passport if you need them, but other consulates require you to apply for a new passport.

If your passport is stolen or lost while in Italy, notify the police and obtain a statement, and then contact your embassy or consulate as soon as possible.

Visas

Italy is one of 15 countries that have signed the Schengen Convention, an agreement whereby all EU member countries (except the UK and Ireland) plus Iceland and Norway have agreed to abolish checks at common borders by the end of 2000. The other EU countries are Austria, Belgium, Denmark, Finland, France, Germany, Greece, Luxembourg, the Netherlands, Portugal, Spain and Sweden. Legal residents of one Schengen country do not require a visa for another Schengen country. Citizens of the UK and Ireland are also exempt from visa requirements for Schengen countries. In addition, nationals of a number of other countries, including Canada, Japan, New Zealand and Switzerland, do not require visas for tourist visits of up to 90 days to any Schengen country.

Various other nationals not covered by

the Schengen exemption can also spend up to 90 days in Italy without a visa. These include Australian, Israeli and US citizens. However, all non-EU nationals entering Italy for any reason other than tourism (such as study or work) should contact an Italian consulate, as they may need a specific visa. They should also insist on having their passport stamped on entry as, without a stamp, they could encounter problems when trying to obtain a *permesso di soggiorno* (see Permits). If you are a citizen of a country not mentioned in this section, you should check with an Italian consulate whether you need a visa.

The standard tourist visa issued by Italian consulates is the Schengen visa, valid for up to 90 days. A Schengen visa issued by one Schengen country is generally valid for travel in all other Schengen countries. However, individual Schengen countries may impose additional restrictions on certain nationalities. It is, therefore, worth checking visa regulations with the consulate of each Schengen country you plan to visit.

Rules for obtaining Schengen visas have been tightened and it's now mandatory that you apply in your country of residence. You can apply for no more than two Schengen visas in any 12 month period and they are not renewable inside Italy. If you are going to visit more than one Schengen country, you are supposed to apply for the visa at a consulate of your main destination country or, if you have no main destination, the first country you intend to visit. It's worth applying early for your visa, especially in the busy summer months.

Study Visas Non-EU citizens who want to study at a university or language school in Italy must have a study visa. These visas can be obtained from your nearest Italian embassy or consulate. You will normally require confirmation of your enrolment and proof of payment of fees and adequate funds to support yourself before a visa is issued. The visa will then cover only the period of the enrolment. This type of visa is renewable within Italy but, again, only with

confirmation of ongoing enrolment and proof that you are able to support yourself – bank statements are preferred.

Permits

EU citizens do not require any permits to live, work or start a business in Italy. They are, however, advised to register with a *questura* (police station) if they take up residence, in accordance with an anti-Mafia law that aims at keeping a watch on everyone's whereabouts in the country. Failure to do so carries no consequences, although some landlords may be unwilling to rent out a flat to you if you cannot produce proof of registration.

Those considering long-term residence will eventually want to consider getting a permesso di soggiorno (see the next page), a necessary first step to acquiring a *carta d'identità* (ID card). While you're at it, you'll need a *codice fiscale* (tax-file number) if you wish to be paid for most work in Italy.

Work Permits Non-EU citizens wishing to work in Italy will need to obtain a *permesso di lavoro* (work permit). If you intend to work for an Italian company and will be paid in lire, the company must organise the permesso and forward it to the Italian embassy or consulate in your country – only then will you be issued with an appropriate visa.

If non-EU citizens intend to work for a non-Italian company, will be paid in foreign currency or wish to go freelance, they must organise the visa and permesso in their country of residence through an Italian embassy or consulate. This process can take many months, so look into it early.

It is in any case advisable to seek detailed information from an Italian embassy or consulate on the exact requirements before attempting to organise a legitimate job in Italy. Many foreigners, however, don't bother with such formalities, preferring to work illegally in areas such as teaching English, bar work and seasonal jobs. See the Work section later in this chapter.

Permesso di Soggiorno If you intend to stay at the same address for more than one week, you are technically obliged to report to a questura and obtain a permesso di soggiorno. Tourists who are staying in hotels do not need to do this, because hotel owners are required to register all guests with the police.

A permesso di soggiorno only becomes a necessity if you plan to study, work (legally) or live in Italy. Obtaining one is never a pleasant experience, although for EU citizens it is fairly straightforward and success is guaranteed. Other nationals may find it involves enduring long queues, rude police officers and the frustration of arriving at the counter (after a two hour wait) to find that you don't have all the necessary documents.

The exact requirements, such as which documents and *marche da bollo* (official stamps), vary from city to city. In general, you will need a valid passport containing a visa stamp indicating your date of entry into Italy, a special visa issued in your own country if you are planning to study, four passport-style photographs and proof of your ability to support yourself financially.

It is best to go to the questura to obtain precise information on what is required. Sometimes a list is posted; otherwise you will need to queue at the information counter.

The main Roma questura, in Via Genova, is notorious for delays and is best avoided if possible. In Roma, try instead the questura closest to where you are staying.

Travel Insurance
Don't, as they say, leave home without it. It will cover you for medical expenses, theft or loss of luggage, and for cancellation of and delays in your travel arrangements. Cover depends on your insurance and type of ticket, so ask both your insurer and ticket-issuing agency to explain where you stand. Ticket loss is also covered by travel insurance, but keep a separate record of your ticket details (see also Photocopies on the next page). Buy travel insurance as early

as possible. If you buy it the week before you fly or hop on the bus, you may find, for example, that you are not covered for delays to your trip caused by strikes or other industrial action.

Travel insurance papers, and the international medical aid numbers that generally accompany them, are valuable documents, so treat them like your passport.

Paying for your ticket with a credit card often provides limited travel insurance and you may be able to reclaim the payment if the operator doesn't deliver. Ask your credit card company what it will cover. See also Medical Cover under Health later in this chapter.

Hostel Card
A valid Hostelling International (HI) card is required if you want to stay in any of the ostelli per la gioventù run by the Associazione Italiana Alberghi per la Gioventù (AIG) in Italy. You can get this in your home country by becoming a member of your national Youth Hostel Association (YHA) or at youth hostels in Italy. In the latter case, you must collect six stamps in the card at L5000 each. You pay for a stamp on each of the first six nights you spend in a hostel, on top of the hostel fee. With six stamps you are considered a full international member. Membership also entitles the holder to various discounts and benefits in Italy, including train travel, car hire with Hertz and reduced entry prices to various attractions around the country. HI is on the Web at www.iyhf.org.

Student, Teacher & Youth Cards
The International Student Identity Card (ISIC), for full-time students, and the International Teacher Identity Card (ITIC), for full-time teachers and professors, are issued by more than 5000 organisations around the world. The cards entitle you to a range of discounts, from reduced museum entry charges to cheap air fares.

Student travel organisations such as STA Travel (Australia, the UK and the USA), Council Travel (the UK and USA) and

Travel CUTS/Voyages Campus (Canada) can issue these cards. See Air in the Getting There & Away chapter for more details.

Anyone aged under 26 can get a Euro<26 card. This gives similar discounts to the ISIC card and is issued by most of the same organisations. The Euro<26 has a variety of names, such as the Under 26 Card (England and Wales) and the CartaGiovani (Italy).

Centro Turistico Studentesco e Giovanile (CTS) youth and student travel organisation branches in Italy can issue ISIC, ITIC and Euro<26 cards (see Information under major cities for addresses). You have to join CTS first, however, which costs L45,000.

Seniors' Cards

If you are aged over 60 or 65 (depending on what you are seeking a discount for) you can get many discounts simply by presenting your passport or ID card as proof of age. For discounted international train travel in Europe, you could apply for a Rail Europe Senior card (see the boxed text 'Rail Passes & Discounted Tickets' in the Land section of the Getting There & Away chapter).

Photocopies

All important documents (passport, credit cards, travel insurance policy, driving licence etc) should be photocopied before you leave home. Leave one copy at home and keep another with you, separate from the originals.

Another way of storing your travel documents details is with Lonely Planet's free on-line Travel Vault. Storing details of your important documents in the vault is the best option if you travel in a country with easy Internet access. Your password-protected vault is accessible on line at anytime. Create your own vault at www.ekno.lonely planet.com.

EMBASSIES & CONSULATES
Italian Embassies & Consulates

The following is a selection of Italian diplomatic missions abroad. Bear in mind that Italy maintains consulates in additional cities in many of the countries listed here:

Australia
  Embassy:
  (☎ 02-6273 3333, fax 6273 4223,
  email ambital2@dynamite.com.au)
  12 Grey St, Deakin, Canberra 2600
  Consulates:
  (☎ 03-9867 5744, fax 9866 3932,
  email itconmel@netlink.com.au)
  509 St Kilda Rd, Melbourne 3004
  (☎ 02-9392 7900, fax 9252 4830,
  email itconsyd@armadillo.com.au)
  Level 45, The Gateway, 1 Macquarie Place,
  Sydney 2000
Austria
  Embassy:
  (☎ 01-712 51 21, fax 713 97 19,
  email ambitalviepress@via.at)
  Metternichgasse 13, Vienna 1030
Canada
  Embassy:
  (☎ 613-232 2401, fax 233 1484,
  email ambital@trytel.com)
  21st Floor, 275 Slater St,
  Ottawa, Ontario KIP 5H9
  Consulates:
  (☎ 514-849 8351, fax 499 9471,
  email consitmtl@cyberglobe.net)
  3489 Drummond St,
  Montreal, Quebec H3G 1X6
  (☎ 416-977 2569, fax 977 1119,
  email consolato.it@toronto.italconsulate.org)
  136 Beverley St, Toronto, Ontario M5T 1Y5
France
  Embassy:
  (☎ 01 49 54 03 00, fax 01 45 49 35 81,
  email stampa@dial.oleane.com)
  47-51 rue de Varenne, Paris 75007
Germany
  Embassy:
  (☎ 0228-82 20, fax 82 22 10,
  email italia.ambasciata.bonn@t-online.de)
  Karl Finkelnburgstrasse 49-51, Bonn 53173
  Consulate:
  (☎ 030-25 44 00, fax 25 44 01 00,
  email italcons.berlino@t-online.de)
  Hiroshimastrasse 1-7, Berlin 10785
Ireland
  Embassy:
  (☎ 01-660 1744, fax 668 2759,
  email italianembassy@tinet.ie)
  63/65 Northumberland Rd, Dublin 4
Netherlands
  Embassy:
  (☎ 070-302 1030, fax 361 4932,
  email italemb@worldonline.nl)
  Alexanderstraat 12, The Hague 2514 JL

New Zealand
  Embassy:
    (☎ 04-473 5339, fax 472 7255,
    email ambwell@xtra.co.nz)
    34 Grant Rd, Thorndon, Wellington
Slovenia
  Embassy:
    (☎ 061-126 21 94, fax 125 33 02)
    Snezniska Ulica 8, Ljubljana 61000
Spain
  Embassy:
    (☎ 91 577 6529, fax 91 575 7776,
    email ambital.sp@nauta.es)
    Calle Lagasca 98, Madrid 28006
Switzerland
  Embassy:
    (☎ 031-352 4151, fax 351 1026,
    email ambital.berna@spectraweb.ch)
    Elfenstrasse 14, Bern 3006
UK
  Embassy:
    (☎ 020-7312 2209, fax 7312 2230,
    email emblondon@embitaly.org.uk)
    14 Three Kings Yard, London W1Y 2EH
  Consulate:
    (☎ 020-7235 9371, fax 7823 1609)
    38 Eaton Place, London SW1X 8AN
USA
  Embassy:
    (☎ 202-328 5500, fax 328 5593,
    email itapress@ix.netcom.com)
    1601 Fuller St, NW,
    Washington, DC 20009
  Consulates:
    (☎ 213-820 0622, fax 820 0727,
    email cglos@aol.com)
    Suite 300, 12400 Wilshire Blvd,
    Los Angeles, CA 90025
    (☎ 212-737 9100, fax 249 4945,
    email italconsny@aol.com)
    690 Park Ave, New York, NY 10021/5044
    (☎ 415-931 4924, fax 931 7205)
    2590 Webster St, San Francisco, CA 94115

Embassies & Consulates in Italy

It's important to realise what your embassy
– the embassy of the country of which you
are a citizen – can and can't do to help you.

Generally speaking, it won't be much
help in emergencies if the trouble you're in
is even remotely your own fault. Remember
that you are bound by the laws of the country you are in. Your embassy will not be
sympathetic if you end up in jail after committing a crime locally.

In genuine emergencies you might get
some assistance, but only if other channels
have been exhausted. For example, if you
need to get home urgently, a free ticket
home is exceedingly unlikely – the embassy
would expect you to have insurance. If you
have all your money and documents stolen,
it might assist with getting a new passport,
but not with a loan for onward travel.

The following is a list of embassies and
consulates in major Italian cities:

Albania
  Embassy:
    (☎ 06 862 14 475)
    Via Asmara 9, 00199 Roma
Australia
  Embassy:
    (☎ 06 85 27 21, fax 06 852 72 300)
    Via Alessandria 215, 00198 Roma
  Consulate:
    (☎ 02 77 70 41, fax 02 777 04 242)
    3rd Floor, Via Borgogna 2, 20122 Milano
Austria
  Embassy:
    (☎ 06 844 01 41)
    Via Pergolesi 3, 00189 Roma
  Consulate:
    (☎ 02 481 20 66)
    Via Tranquillo Cremona 27, 20145 Milano
Canada
  Embassy:
    (☎ 06 44 59 81, fax 06 445 98 750)
    Via GB de Rossi 27, 00198 Roma
  Consulate:
    (☎ 02 6 75 81, fax 02 675 83 900)
    Via Vittorio Pisani 19, 20124 Milano
Croatia
  Embassy:
    (☎ 06 363 07 300)
    Via Luigi Bodio 74-76, 00189 Roma
France
  Embassy:
    (☎ 06 68 60 11, fax 06 686 01 360)
    Piazza Farnese 67, 00186 Roma
  Consulates:
    (☎ 02 655 91 41, fax 02 655 61 344)
    Via Mangili 1, 20121 Milano
    (☎ 081 761 22 75, fax 081 761 48 83)
    Piazza della Repubblica 2, 80122 Napoli
    (☎ 041 522 43 19, fax 041 522 17 98)
    Ramo del Pestrin, Castello 6140, Venezia
Germany
  Embassy:
    (☎ 06 49 21 31, fax 06 884 74 320)

Via San Martino della Battaglia 4, Roma
Consulates:
(☎ 055 29 47 22, fax 055 28 17 89)
Lungarno Vespucci 30, 50123 Firenze
(☎ 02 623 11 01, fax 02 655 42 13)
Via Solferino 40, 20121 Milano
(☎ 081 61 33 93, fax 081 761 46 87)
Via Francesco Crispi 69, 80121 Napoli
(☎ 091 625 46 60)
Viale Scaduto 2d, 90144 Palermo
(☎ 041 523 76 75, fax 041 522 76 55)
Campo S Solia, Cannaregio 4201,
30131 Venezia

Greece
Embassy:
(☎ 06 855 85 89, fax 06 841 59 27)
Via S Mercadante 36, 00198 Roma
Consulates:
(☎ 02 659 86 24, fax 02 290 00 833)
Via Turati 6, 20121 Milano
(☎ 081 761 10 75, fax 081 66 68 35)
Viale G Gramsci 5, 80122 Napoli
(☎ 041 523 72 60, fax 041 523 88 37)
San Polo 720, 30125 Venezia

Ireland
Embassy:
(☎ 06 697 91 21)
Piazza Campitelli 3, 00186 Roma
Consulate:
(☎ 02 551 87 569)
Piazza F Pietro in Gessate 2, 20122 Milano

Malta
Embassy:
(☎ 06 687 99 90)
Lungotevere Marzio 12, 00186 Roma
Consulates:
(☎ 055 21 78 75, fax 055 24 41 87)
Via dei Servi 13, 50122 Firenze
(☎ 02 78 24 01)
Via Bianca Maria 35, 20100 Milano
(☎ 081 552 15 73, fax 081 552 11 83)
Via Nuova Ponte di Tappia 82, 80133 Napoli
(☎ 091 58 48 30, fax 091 45 49 57)
Via Principe Belmonte 55, 90139 Palermo
(☎ 041 522 26 44)
Piazzale Roma, S Croce 515, 30100 Venezia

Netherlands
Embassy:
(☎ 06 322 11 41, fax 06 321 91 43)
Via Michele Mercati 8, 00197 Roma
Consulates:
(☎ 081 551 30 03, fax 081 551 07 76)
Via Agostino Depretis 114, 80133 Napoli
(☎ 091 58 15 21, fax 091 58 12 30)
Via Roma 489, 90139 Palermo

New Zealand
Embassy:
(☎ 06 441 71 71, fax 06 440 29 84)

Via Zara 28, 00198 Roma
Consulate:
(☎ 02 480 12 544, fax 02 480 12 577)
Via Guido d'Arezzo 6, 20145 Milano

Slovenia
Embassy:
(☎ 06 808 12 75)
Via Leonardo Pisano 10, 00197 Roma
Consulate:
(☎ 040 30 78 55)
Via S Georgio 1, 34123 Trieste

Spain
Embassy:
(☎ 06 683 21 68)
Largo Fontanella di Borghese 19,
00186 Roma
Consulates:
(☎ 02 632 88 31)
Via Fatebenefratelli 26-1, 20121 Milano
(☎ 081 41 11 57)
Via dei Mille 40, 80121 Napoli

Switzerland
Embassy:
(☎ 06 80 95 71)
Via Barnarba Oriani 61, 00197 Roma
Consulates:
(☎ 055 22 24 34)
Piazzale Galileo 5, 50125 Firenze
(☎ 02 777 91 61)
Via Palestro 2, 20121 Milano
(☎ 081 761 45 33)
Via Pergolesi 1, 80122 Napoli

Tunisia
Embassy:
(06 860 30 60)
Via Asmara 7, 00199 Roma

UK
Embassy:
(☎ 06 482 54 41, fax 06 487 33 24)
Via XX Settembre 80a, 00187 Roma
Consulates:
(☎ 055 28 41 33, fax 055 21 91 12)
Lungarno Corsini 2, 50123 Firenze
(☎ 02 72 30 01, fax 02 720 20 153)
Via San Paolo 7, 20121 Milano
(☎ 081 66 35 11, fax 081 761 37 20)
Via Francesco Crispi 122, 80122 Napoli
(☎ 091 32 64 12)
S Tagiavia & Co, Via Cavour 117,
90133 Palermo
(☎ 041 522 72 07, fax 041 522 26 17)
Palazzo Querini, Dorsoduro 1051,
30123 Venezia

USA
Embassy:
(☎ 06 4 67 41)
Via Vittorio Veneto 119a, 00187 Roma

Consulates:
(☎ 055 239 82 76)
Lungarno Amerigo Vespucci 38,
50123 Firenze
(☎ 02 29 03 51)
Largo Donegani 1, Milano
(☎ 081 583 81 11)
Piazza della Repubblica, 80122 Napoli
(☎ 091 611 00 20)
Via Re Federico 18b, 90141 Palermo

For other foreign embassies in Roma and consulates in other cities, look under 'Ambasciate' or 'Consolati' in the telephone directory or, in Roma, Milano, Genova, Napoli, Bologna or Firenze, check the *English Yellow Pages*. Tourist offices will generally also have a list.

CUSTOMS

As of 1 July 1999, duty-free sales within the EU were abolished. Under the rules of the single market, goods bought in and exported within the EU incur no additional taxes, provided duty has been paid somewhere within the EU and the goods are for personal consumption.

Travellers coming into Italy from outside the EU, on the other hand, can import, duty free, 200 cigarettes, 1L of spirits, 2L of wine, 60mL of perfume, 250mL of toilet water, and other goods up to a total value of L340,000 (€175); anything over this limit must be declared on arrival and the appropriate duty paid (it is advisable to carry all receipts).

MONEY
Currency

Italy is one of 11 EU countries in the first intake for Economic and Monetary Union (EMU), which includes the introduction of a single currency, the euro (see the boxed text 'Introducing the Euro'). The present unit of currency in Italy is the *lira* (plural *lire*). The smallest note is L1000. Other denominations in notes are L2000, L5000, L10,000, L20,000, L50,000, L100,000 and L500,000. Coin denominations are L50, L100, L200, L500 and L1000.

Like other Continental Europeans, the

Introducing the Euro

Since 1 January 1999, the lira and the euro – the new currency in 11 European Union (EU) countries – have both been legal tender in Italy. Euro coins and banknotes have not been issued yet, but you can already get billed in euros and opt to pay in euros by credit card. Essentially, if there's no hard cash involved, you can deal in euros. Travellers should check bills carefully to make sure that any conversion has been calculated correctly.

The whole idea behind the current paperless currency is to give euro-fearing punters a chance to limber up arithmetically before euro coins and banknotes are issued on 1 January 2002. The same euro coins (one to 50 cents, €1 and €2) and banknotes (€5 to €500) will then be used in Euroland's 11 countries: Austria, Belgium, Finland, France, Germany, Ireland, Italy, Luxembourg, the Netherlands, Portugal and Spain. The lira will remain legal currency alongside the euro until 1 July 2002, when it will be hurled on the scrapheap of history.

Until then, the 11 currencies have been fixed to the euro at the following rates: Austria AS13.76, Belgium BF40.34, Finland 5.95 mk, France 6.56FF, Germany DM1.96, Ireland IR£0.79, Italy L1936, Luxembourg flux40.34, Netherlands f2.2, Portugal 200$48 and Spain 166.39 ptas.

The Lonely Planet Web site at www .lonelyplanet.com has a link to a currency converter and up-to-date news on the integration process. Alternatively, you can check out the official Web site of the European Union at europa.eu.int/euro/html/entry.html.

Euro exchange rates include:

Australia	A$1	=	€0.62
Canada	C$1	=	€0.64
Japan	¥100	=	€0.83
New Zealand	NZ$1	=	€0.50
UK	UK£1	=	€1.52
USA	US$1	=	€0.95

Italians indicate decimals with commas and thousands with points.

Exchange Rates

country	unit		lira
Australia	A$1	=	L1183
Canada	C$1	=	L1221
euro	€1	=	L1936
France	1FF	=	L295
Germany	DM1	=	L989
Ireland	IR£1	=	L2458
Japan	¥100	=	L1608
New Zealand	NZ$1	=	L835
UK	UK£1	=	L2904
USA	US$1	=	L1824

Exchanging Money

The best thing to do is to take a combination of travellers cheques and credit cards. It is also worth bringing some lire with you (especially if you're arriving by air) to avoid the hassles of having to change money immediately on arrival.

You can change money in banks, at post offices or in bureaux de change. Banks are generally the most reliable and tend to offer the best rates. However, you should look around and ask about commissions. These can fluctuate considerably and a lot depends on whether you are changing cash or cheques. The charge for a cash transaction starts at about L2500, and travellers cheques attract even higher fees. Some banks charge L1000 per cheque with a L3000 minimum, others have a flat rate of L7500. In all cases you should compare the exchange rates too. The post office charges a flat rate of L5000 for all transactions, cash and cheque. Currency exchange booths often advertise 'no commission', but the rate of exchange can often be inferior to that of banks.

Balanced against the desire to save on such fees by making occasional large transactions should be a healthy fear of pickpockets – you don't want to be robbed the very day you have exchanged a huge amount of money which was intended to last you for weeks!

Cash There is little advantage in bringing foreign cash into Italy. True, exchange commissions are often lower than for travellers cheques, but the danger of losing the lot far outweighs such petty gains.

Travellers Cheques These are a safe way to carry money and are easily cashed at banks and bureaux de change throughout Italy. Always keep the bank receipt listing the cheque numbers separate from the cheques and keep a list of the numbers of those you have already cashed – this will reduce problems in the event of loss or theft. Check the conditions applying to such circumstances before buying the cheques. Take along your passport when you go to cash travellers cheques.

If you buy your travellers cheques in lire (which you could do if your trip is to be restricted to Italy), there should be no commission charge when cashing them. Buying cheques in a third currency (such as US dollars if you are not coming from the USA), means you pay commission when you buy the cheques and again when cashing them in Italy.

Travellers who use the better-known cheques, such as Visa, American Express (Amex) and Thomas Cook, will have little trouble in Italy. Amex, in particular, has offices in all the major Italian cities and agents in many smaller cities. If you lose your Amex cheques, you can call a 24 hour toll-free number (☎ 800 87 20 00) anywhere in Italy.

Credit/Debit Cards & ATMs Carrying plastic (whether a credit or ATM card) is the simplest way to organise your holiday funds. You don't have large amounts of cash or travellers cheques to lose, you can get money after hours and at weekends and the exchange rate is better than that offered for travellers cheques or cash exchanges. By arranging for payments to be made into your card account while you are travelling, you can avoid paying interest.

Major credit cards, such as Visa, MasterCard, Eurocard, Cirrus and Eurocheque cards, are accepted throughout Italy. They can be used for many purchases in shops and supermarkets, and in hotels and restaurants (although pensioni and smaller restaurants and pizza places tend to accept cash only). Credit cards can also be used in ATMs (automated teller machines, or *bancomat*) displaying the appropriate sign, or (if you have no PIN) to obtain cash advances over the counter in many banks – Visa and MasterCard are among the most widely recognised for such transactions. Check charges with your bank but, as a rule, there is no charge for purchases on major cards and a 1.5% charge on cash advances and ATM transactions in foreign currencies.

It is not uncommon for ATMs in Italy to reject foreign cards. Don't despair or start wasting money on international calls to your bank. Try a few more ATMs (at major banks) displaying your credit card's logo before assuming the problem lies with your card rather than with the local system.

If your credit card is lost, stolen or swallowed by an ATM, you can telephone toll-free to have an immediate stop put on its use. For MasterCard the number in Italy is ☎ 800 870 866, or make a reverse-charge call to St Louis in the USA on ☎ 314-542 7111; for Visa, phone ☎ 800 87 72 32 in Italy. Credit cards issued in Italy by an Italian bank can be blocked by calling ☎ 800 82 20 56.

Amex cards are also widely accepted (although they are not as common as Visa or MasterCard). Amex's full-service offices (such as in Roma and Milano) will issue new cards, usually within 24 hours and sometimes immediately, if yours has been lost or stolen.

Some Amex offices have ATMs that you can use to obtain cash advances if you have made the necessary arrangements in your own country. The toll-free emergency number to report a lost or stolen Amex card varies according to where the card was issued. Check with Amex in your home country or contact the office in Roma on ☎ 06 7 22 82, which itself has a 24 hour cardholders' service.

International Transfers It is inadvisable to send cheques by mail to Italy, because of the unreliability of the country's postal service. One reliable method is to send money by 'urgent telex' through the foreign office of a large Italian bank, or through major banks in your own country, to a nominated bank in Italy. It is important to have an exact record of all details associated with the money transfer, particularly the exact address of the Italian bank to which the money has been sent. The money will always be held at the head office of the bank in the town to which it has been sent. Urgent-telex transfers should take only a few days, while other means, such as telegraphic transfer, or draft, can take weeks.

It is also possible to transfer money through Amex and Thomas Cook. You will be required to produce identification, usually a passport, in order to collect the money. It is also a good idea to take along the details of the transaction.

A speedy option is to send money through Western Union. This service functions in Italy through the Mail Boxes Etc chain of stores and other outlets, although the list of affiliates is constantly changing. Call ☎ 800 46 44 64 toll-free to get the address of the nearest outlet; the operators are helpful and some of them speak English. The sender and receiver have to turn up at their respective Western Union outlets with passport or other form of ID. The fees charged for the virtually immediate transfer depend on the amount sent.

Security

Petty theft is a problem throughout Italy and tends to get worse the farther south you travel. Keep only a limited amount of your money as cash and the bulk in more easily replaceable forms, such as credit cards or travellers cheques. If your accommodation has a safe, use it. If you must leave money and documents in your room, divide the former into several stashes and hide them in different places. Lockable luggage is a good deterrent.

On the streets, keep as little on you as

possible. The safest thing is a shoulder wallet or under-the-clothes money belt or pouch. External money belts tend to attract attention to your belongings rather than deflect it. If you eschew the use of any such device, keep money in your front pockets and watch out for people who seem to brush close to you. Teams of delinquents employ an infinite number of tricks whereby one distracts you and the other deftly empties your pockets. See Theft under Dangers & Annoyances later in this chapter for more advice.

Costs

Italy isn't cheap. Accommodation charges and high entrance fees for many museums and monuments keep daily expenditure high. Prices also vary significantly between north and south (in the north they are generally higher), and between cities and provincial or rural areas. A *very* prudent backpacker might scrape by on around L70,000 a day, but only by staying in youth hostels, eating one simple meal a day (at the youth hostel), buying a sandwich or pizza slice for lunch, travelling slowly to keep transport costs down and minimising visits to museums and galleries.

One rung up, you can get by on L100,000 per day if you stay in the cheaper pensioni or small hotels and keep sit-down meals and museum visits to one a day. Lone travellers may find even this budget hard to maintain, since single rooms tend to be pricey.

If money is no object, you'll find your niche in Italy. There's no shortage of luxury hotels, expensive restaurants and pricey shops. Realistically, a traveller wanting to stay in comfortable mid-range hotels, eat two square meals a day, not feel restricted to one museum visit a day and be able to enjoy the odd drink and other minor indulgences should reckon on a minimum daily average of between L200,000 and L250,000 a day – possibly more if you are driving.

A basic breakdown of costs per person during an average day for the budget to mid-range traveller could be: accommodation L25,000 (youth hostel) to L60,000 (single in pensione or per person in comfortable double), breakfast L3000 (coffee and croissant), lunch (sandwich and mineral water) L6000, bottle of mineral water L1500, public transport (bus or underground railway in a major town) up to L6000, entrance fee for one museum up to L12,000, cost of long-distance train or bus travel (spread over three days) L15,000 to L20,000, sit-down dinner L14,000 to L30,000.

Accommodation Budget travellers can save by staying in youth hostels (open to people of all ages) or camp sites. If you are travelling in a group and staying in pensioni or hotels, always ask for triples or quads. The cost per person drops the more people you have in a room. Avoid, where possible, pensioni and hotels that charge for a compulsory breakfast. A *cappuccino* and *cornetto* (croissant) at a bar cost less and are undoubtedly better.

If you plan to ski, it may be cheaper to organise accommodation as part of a Settimana Bianca (White Week) skiing package. These deals offer accommodation, meals and a ski pass.

Food In Italian bars, prices can double (sometimes even triple) if you sit down and are served at the table. Stand at the bar to drink your coffee or eat a sandwich, or buy a sandwich or slice of pizza and head for the nearest piazza.

Read the fine print on menus (usually posted outside eating establishments) to check if there's a *coperto* (cover charge) and *servizio* (service fee). These can make a big difference to the bill and it is best to avoid restaurants that charge both. Shop in markets and *alimentari* (grocery shops) for picnic lunches and the odd meal in your room. Steer clear of the 'touristy' food-and-drink kiosks in major cities: the 'fresh' food is rarely fresh and the mark-up is extortionate.

Travel If you're travelling by train and have time to spare, take a *regionale* or *diretto*: they are slower but cheaper than the Intercity trains, for which you have to pay a *supplemento* (supplement). It's best to travel overnight if possible to save on a night's accommodation. See the Getting Around chapter for information about the different types of trains and various discounts on train travel within Italy. See the boxed text 'Rail Passes & Discounted Tickets' in the Getting There & Away chapter for information about discounts on European train travel.

When catching ferries (say to Sardegna, Corsica or Greece) in summer, travelling *passaggio ponte* (deck class) is cheapest.

In cities, where you need to use a lot of public transport, buy a daily tourist ticket (up to L6000).

Other Cost-Savers Aerograms (on sale only at post offices for L900) are the cheapest way to send international mail.

At museums, never hesitate to ask if there are discounts for students (you will be asked to produce an ISIC card to prove your student status), young people, children, families or the elderly. When sightseeing, where possible buy a *biglietto cumulativo*, a ticket that allows entrance to a number of associated sights for less than the combined cost of separate admission fees. Details of such tickets are listed throughout the book; otherwise ask at the local tourist office.

Avoid buying food and drinks at service stations on the *autostrade* (motorways), where they can cost up to 30% more. Petrol also tends to be slightly more expensive on the autostrade.

Tipping & Bargaining

You are not expected to tip on top of restaurant service charges, but it is common to leave a small amount, perhaps L2000 per person. If there is no service charge, the customer might consider leaving a 10% tip, but this is by no means obligatory. In bars, Italians often leave any small change as a tip, maybe only L100 or L200. Tipping taxi drivers is not common practice, but you should tip the porter at top-end hotels.

Bargaining is common throughout Italy in flea markets, but not in shops. At the Porta Portese market in Roma, for instance, don't hesitate to offer half the asking price for any given item. Don't be deterred by stallholders who dismiss you with a wave of the arm: the person at the next stall may well accept your offer after a brief (and obligatory) haggle. While bargaining in shops is not acceptable, you might find that the proprietor is disposed to give a discount if you are spending a reasonable amount of money.

It is quite acceptable (and advisable) to ask if there is a special price for a room in a pensione if you plan to stay for more than a few days.

Taxes & Refunds

A value-added tax of around 19%, known as Imposta di Valore Aggiunto (IVA), is slapped onto just about everything in Italy. If you are resident outside the EU and you spend in the same shop on the same day more than a certain amount (L300,000 in 1999), you may claim a refund on this tax when you leave the EU. The refund applies only to items purchased at retail outlets affiliated to the system – these shops display a 'Tax-free for tourists' sign. If you don't see a sign, ask the shopkeeper. You must fill out a form at the point of purchase and have it stamped and checked by Italian customs when you leave the country (you will need to show the receipt and your purchases). At major airports and some border crossings you can then get an immediate cash refund at specially marked booths; alternatively, return the form by mail to the vendor, who will make the refund, either by cheque or to your credit card.

For information call ☎ 0332 87 07 70 or consult the rules brochure available in affiliated stores.

Receipts

Laws aimed at tightening controls on the payment of taxes in Italy mean that the onus is on the buyer to ask for and retain receipts for all goods and services. This applies to everything from a litre of milk to a haircut. Although it rarely happens, you could be

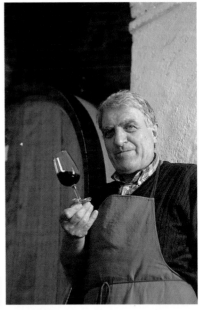

From vegetable farmers to Tuscan viticulturists, snake charmers to villagers going about their daily chores, the people of Italy are passionate about life.

Scenes of Italian life: frothy cappuccini, outdoor cafés on piazze, gelato in the summer, mopeds on the go and a night's entertainment at the theatre

asked by an officer of the Guardia di Finanza (Fiscal Police) to produce the receipt immediately after you leave a shop. If you don't have it, you may be obliged to pay a fine of up to L300,000.

POST & COMMUNICATIONS
Post

Italy's postal service is notoriously slow, unreliable and expensive. Don't expect to receive every letter sent to you, or that every letter you send will reach its destination. Information (in Italian) about postal services can be obtained by calling ☎ 160.

Francobolli (stamps) are available at post offices and authorised tobacconists (look for the official *tabacchi* sign: a big 'T', often white on black). For letters that need to be weighed, what you get at the tobacconist's for international air mail will often be an approximation of the proper rate.

Postal Rates The cost of sending a letter *via aerea* (air mail) depends on its weight and where it is being sent. Letters up to 20g cost L800 to EU countries (L900 to the rest of Europe), L1300 to the USA and L1400 to Australia and New Zealand. Postcards cost the same. Aerograms cost L900 to send anywhere and can be purchased at post offices.

Sending letters *espresso* (express) costs a standard extra L3600 and may help speed a letter on its way, but only within Italy, after which it will go by normal airmail. See Express Mail later in this section for more on sending urgent items.

If you want to post more important items by *raccomandato* (registered mail) or by *assicurato* (insured mail), remember that they will take as long as normal mail. Raccomandato costs L4000 on top of the normal cost of the letter. The cost of assicurato depends on the weight of the object being sent (L6400 for letters up to 20g) and is not available to the USA.

Sending Mail An air-mail letter can take up to two weeks to reach the UK or the USA, while a letter to Australia will take between two and three weeks. Postcards take even longer because they are classed as low-priority mail. One of the authors of this book sent a postcard from Australia to Italy for Christmas – it did not arrive until September of the following year.

The service within Italy is no better: local letters take at least three days and up to a week to get to another city. Past surveys on postal efficiency in Europe found that next-day delivery did not exist in Italy. Sending a letter espresso (see Postal Rates) can help.

In Roma you can avoid this frustration by using the Poste Vaticane (Vatican Post). There are offices on Piazza San Pietro and in the Musei Vaticani. The Poste Vaticane has a good record for prompt delivery but doesn't accept poste restante mail. Rates are similar to those of the Italian postal system.

Express Mail Urgent mail (maximum 20kg for international destinations) can be sent by an express mail service known as CAI Post, or *posta celere*, available at most main post offices. Letters up to 500g cost L30,000 to the UK, L46,000 to the USA and Canada, and L68,000 to Australia and New Zealand. A parcel weighing 1kg will cost L34,000 to the UK, L54,000 to the USA and Canada, and L80,000 to Australia and New Zealand. CAI Post is not necessarily as fast as private services. It will take two to three days for a parcel to reach European destinations, two to five days to the USA and four to eight days to Australia. You can follow your parcel on its journey overseas on-line at www.postacelere.com or by calling ☎ 800 00 99 66 toll-free.

Couriers Several international couriers operate in Italy: DHL is on the 24 hour toll-free number ☎ 800 34 53 45 and Federal Express is on toll-free ☎ 800 83 30 40; for UPS call toll-free ☎ 800 82 20 54. Look in the telephone book for addresses. Note that if you are having articles sent to you by courier in Italy, you might be obliged to pay IVA of up to 20% to retrieve the goods.

Receiving Mail Poste restante is known as *fermo posta* in Italy. Letters marked thus will be held at the counter of the same name in the main post office in the relevant town. Poste restante mail to Verona, for example, should be addressed as follows:

John SMITH,
Fermo Posta,
37100 Verona
Italy

Postcodes are provided throughout this guide. You will need to pick up your letters in person and you must present your passport as ID.

Amex card or travellers cheque holders can use the free client mail-holding service at Amex offices throughout Italy. You can obtain a list of these from Amex offices inside or outside Italy. Take your passport when you go to pick up mail.

Telephone

The state-run Telecom Italia is the largest telecommunications organisation in Italy and its orange public payphones are liberally scattered about the country. The most common accept only *carte/schede telefoniche* (telephone cards), although you will still find some that accept both cards and coins (L100, L200 and L500). Some card phones now also accept special Telecom credit cards and even commercial credit cards. Among the latest generation of payphones are those that also send faxes. If you call from a bar or shop, you may still encounter old-style metered phones, which

count *scatti*, the units used to measure the length of a call.

Telecom payphones can be found in the streets, train stations and some big stores, as well as in Telecom offices. Where these offices are staffed, it is possible to make international calls and pay for them at the desk afterwards. A few have telephone directories for other parts of the country. Addresses of telephone offices are listed throughout the book.

You can buy phonecards at post offices, tobacconists, newspaper stands and from vending machines in Telecom offices. To avoid the frustration of trying to find fast-disappearing coin telephones, always keep a phonecard on hand. They come with a value of L5000, L10,000 or L15,000. You must break the top left-hand corner of the card before you can use it.

Public telephones operated by a new telecommunications company, Infostrada, can be found in airports and train stations. These phones accept Infostrada phonecards (available from post offices, tobacconists and newspaper stands), which come with a value of L3000, L5000 or L10,000. Infostrada's rates are slightly cheaper than Telecom's for long-distance and international calls, but you cannot make local calls from these phones.

Costs Rates, particularly for long-distance calls, are among the highest in Europe. Peak time for domestic calls is from 8 am to 6.30 pm Monday to Friday and from 8 am to 1 pm Saturday. Cheap rates apply from 6.30 pm to 8 am Monday to Friday, on Saturday afternoon and on Sunday and public holidays. For international calls, different times apply. Cheap rates to the UK apply from 10 pm to 8 am Monday to Saturday and all day Sunday, to the US and Canada from 7 pm to 2 pm Monday to Friday and all day Saturday and Sunday, and to Australia from 11 pm to 8 am Monday to Saturday and all day Sunday.

A *comunicazione urbana* (local call) from a public phone will cost L200 for three minutes 40 seconds during peak hours and

Emergency Numbers

Wherever you are in Italy, these are the numbers to ring in an emergency:

Ambulance (Ambulanza)	☎ 118
Carabinieri	☎ 112
Fire Brigade (Vigili del Fuoco)	☎ 115
Highway Rescue (Soccorso Stradale)	☎ 116
Police (Polizia)	☎ 113

six minutes 40 seconds off-peak. The same call made from a private phone will cost you L152.

Rates for *comunicazione interurbana* (long-distance calls within Italy) depend on the time of day and the distance involved. At the most, one minute will cost about L340 in the peak period.

If you need to call overseas, beware of the cost – a five minute call to Australia at 11 pm will cost around L10,000 from a private phone (more from a public phone). Calls to most of the rest of Europe cost around L1250 for the first minute and L762 thereafter (more from a public phone).

Domestic Calls At the moment telephone area codes all begin with 0 and consist of up to four digits. Area codes are now an integral part of all telephone numbers in Italy (see the boxed text 'Telephone Shake-Up' on this page for more information).

Mobile-telephone numbers in Italy begin with a four digit prefix, such as 0330, 0335 or 0347. *Numeri verdi* (freephone or toll-free numbers) begin with 800. The prefix 147 indicates a national number that is charged at a local rate. To reach directory inquiries dial ☎ 12.

International Calls Direct international calls can easily be made from public telephones by using a phonecard. Dial 00 to get out of Italy, then the relevant country and city codes, followed by the telephone number. Useful country codes are: Australia 61, Canada and the USA 1, and New Zealand 64. Codes for countries in Europe include: France 33, Germany 49, Greece 30, Ireland 353, Spain 34 and the UK 44. Other codes are listed in Italian telephone books.

To make a reverse-charge (collect) international call from a public telephone, dial ☎ 15 for European countries and ☎ 170 for elsewhere. All operators speak English.

It can be easier to use the Country Direct service. You dial the number and request a reverse-charge call through the operator in your home country. Numbers for this service include:

Telephone Shake-Up

A new dialling procedure has been introduced. Area codes are now an integral part of the phone number, even if you are making a local call. So, for instance, if you dial a number in Rome, you must first dial 06, even if you are dialling from within the city.

Changes to telephone codes have been planned, with a 4 due to replace the initial 0. At the time of writing, these changes are expected to be implemented on 29 December 2000, but this date may change.

Australia	– Telstra	☎ 172 10 61
	– Optus	☎ 172 11 61
Canada		☎ 172 10 01
France		☎ 172 00 33
New Zealand		☎ 172 10 64
UK	– BT	☎ 172 00 44
	– BT Chargecard Operator	☎ 172 01 44
USA	– AT&T	☎ 172 10 11
	– IDB	☎ 172 17 77
	– MCI	☎ 172 10 22
	– Sprint	☎ 172 18 77

For international directory inquiries call ☎ 176.

Call Centres There are cut-price call centres all over Italy, especially in the major cities. These are run by various companies and rates are significantly lower than Telecom payphones for international calls. Other advantages are that it's usually a little less noisy than making a call from a payphone in a busy street and you don't need a phonecard. You simply place your call from a private booth inside the centre and pay for it when you've finished.

International Phonecards The Lonely Planet eKno Communication Card (visit its Web site at www.ekno.lonelyplanet.com for details) is aimed specifically at travellers and provides cheap international calls, a range of messaging services and free email (though for local calls, you're usually better off with a local card). You can join on line at www.ekno.lonelyplanet.com, or by phone from Italy by dialling ☎ 800 87 56 91. Once you have joined, to use eKno from Italy dial ☎ 800 87 56 83.

Several other private companies now distribute international phonecards, which are mostly linked to US phone companies such as Sprint and MCI. The cards come in a variety of unit sizes and are sold in some bars and tobacconists in the bigger cities.

Calling Italy from Abroad The country code for Italy is 39 and you must always include the initial 0 in area codes. For mobile phones, however, drop the initial 0.

Telegram

These dinosaurs can be sent from post offices or dictated by phone (☎ 186) and are an expensive, but sure, way of having important messages delivered by the same or next day.

Fax

There is no shortage of fax offices in Italy, but the country's high telephone rates make faxes an expensive mode of communication. Some offices charge per page while others charge per minute, and still others charge for both! In all cases, prices vary considerably from one office to another. However, in general, to send a fax within Italy you can expect to pay L4000 for the first page and L1500 for each page thereafter, or L3000 for the first minute and L1500 for the subsequent minutes. International faxes can cost from L8000 for the first page and L5000 per page thereafter, depending on the destination. Per minute, a fax to an EU country can cost L7000 for the first minute and L3500 thereafter; to the US it can cost L9000 for the first minute and L4500 thereafter. Faxes can also be sent from some Telecom public phones.

It usually costs about L1000 per page to receive a fax.

Email & Internet Access

Italy has been a little slower than some parts of Western Europe to march down the Infobahn. Nevertheless, email has definitely arrived. If you plan to carry your notebook or palmtop computer with you, remember that the power-supply voltage in your hotel may vary from that at home, risking damage to your equipment. The best investment is a universal AC adapter for your appliance, which will enable you to plug it in anywhere without frying the innards. You'll also need a plug adapter – often it's easiest to buy these before you leave home.

Also, your PC-card modem may or may not work once you leave your home country – and you won't know for sure until you try. The safest option is to buy a reputable 'global' modem before you leave home, or buy a local PC-card modem if you're spending an extended time in Italy. Bear in mind that the telephone socket will probably be different from that at home, so ensure that you have at least a US RJ-11 telephone adapter that works with your modem. You can almost always find an adapter that will convert from RJ-11 to the local variety. For more information on travelling with a portable computer, see www.teleadapt.com or www.warrior.com.

Major Internet service providers (ISPs), such as CompuServe, at www.compuserve.com, and IBM Net, at www.ibm.net, have dial-in nodes throughout Italy; it's best to download a list of the dial-in numbers before you leave home. Some Italian servers can provide short-term accounts for Internet access. Flashnet (☎ 06 66 05 41) offers 20-hour renewable subscriptions for L30,000 (valid for one year); their Web site at www.flashnet.it has a list of authorised sales points in Italy. Agora (☎ 06 699 17 42) has two-month subscriptions for L84,000. Both of these providers have English-speaking staff.

If you intend to rely on cybercafés, you'll need to carry three pieces of information with you to enable you to access your Internet mail account: your incoming (POP or IMAP) mail server name, your account name and your password. Your ISP or network supervisor will be able to give you these. Armed with this information, you should be able to access your Internet mail account from any Net-connected machine in the world, provided it runs some kind of email software (remember that Netscape and Internet Explorer both have mail modules). It pays to become familiar with the process for doing this before you leave home. A better option for collecting mail through cybercafés is to open a free eKno Web-based email account on line at www .ekno.lonelyplanet.com. You can then access your mail from anywhere in the world from any Net-connected machine running a standard Web browser.

There are cybercafés throughout Italy: check out Web site www.netcafeguide.com for an up-to-date list. You may find public Internet access in post offices, libraries, hostels, hotels, universities and so on.

INTERNET RESOURCES

The World Wide Web is a rich resource for travellers. You can research your trip, hunt down bargain air fares, book hotels, check on weather conditions or chat with locals and other travellers about the best places to visit (or avoid!).

One of the best places to start your Web explorations is the Lonely Planet Web site (www.lonelyplanet.com). Here you'll find succinct summaries on travelling to most places on earth, postcards from other travellers and the Thorn Tree bulletin board, where you can ask questions before you go or dispense advice when you get back. You can also find travel news and updates to many of our most popular guidebooks, and the subWWWay section links you to the most useful travel resources elsewhere on the Web. Lonely Planet's Italy page is at www.lonelyplanet.com/dest/eur/ita.htm.

The following are a few of the huge number of useful Web sites for visitors to Italy:

Alfanet
  www.alfanet.it
  (has a Welcome Italy page, with a link to information about a number of cities)

CTS
  www.cts.it
  (useful information from Italy's leading student travel organisation)
English Yellow Pages
  www.mondoweb.it/eyp
  (directory of English-speaking professionals, commercial activities, organisations and services in Roma, Milano, Firenze, Napoli, Genova and Bologna, plus lots of links)
Excite Reviews
  www.excite.com
  (key in Italy for a selection of useful sites, as well as brief reviews and ratings)
Roma
  www.informaroma.it
  (information on the city's monuments and museums, virtual tours and links to other pertinent sites)
Travel Italy
  www.travel.it
  (useful tourist information)
Il Vaticano
  www.christusrex.org
  (information about the Jubilee 2000 and virtual tours of the main monuments in the Città del Vaticano and the Musei Vaticani)
Wanted in Rome Magazine
  www.wantedinrome.com
  (includes listings and reviews of current exhibitions and cultural events, and a classified section, which is helpful if you want to find a room in a shared apartment)

BOOKS

Most books are published in different editions by different publishers in different countries. Your local bookshop or library is best placed to advise you on the availability of the following recommendations.

For information on Italian literature from the Roman epic poem to the modern novel, see Literature in the Arts section of the Facts about Italy chapter.

Lonely Planet

Europe on a shoestring, *Mediterranean Europe* and *Western Europe* include chapters on Italy and are recommended for those planning further travel in Europe. The *Italian phrasebook* lists all the words and phrases you're likely to need in Italy. *Walking in Italy* is a useful guide for experienced and not-so-experienced walkers who want to explore Italy's great outdoors. If you're intending to limit your travelling to one city or region, look out for *Rome, Florence, Venice* and *Tuscany*, which provide in-depth, detailed coverage.

Lonely Planet's *World Food Italy* is a full-colour book with information on the whole range of Italian food and drink. It includes a useful language section, with the definitive culinary dictionary and a handy quick-reference glossary.

Guidebooks

The paperback Companion Guides are excellent and include *Rome* by Georgina Masson and *Venice* by Hugh Honour. The Blue Guide series gives very good detailed information about the art and monuments of Italy. If you can read Italian you can't get better than the excellent red guides published by the Touring Club Italiano.

Rome: An Oxford Archaeological Guide is an extremely detailed guide to the ruins of Roma, with descriptions, maps, plans and photos of more than 150 archaeological sites.

Travel

Three 'Grand Tour' classics are Johann Wolfgang von Goethe's *Italian Journey*, Charles Dickens' *Pictures from Italy* and Henry James' *Italian Hours*. DH Lawrence wrote three short travel books while living in Italy, now combined in one volume entitled *DH Lawrence and Italy*.

Other interesting travel books include: *Venice* by James Morris, *The Stones of Florence and Venice Observed* by Mary McCarthy, *On Persephone's Island* by Mary Taylor Simeti, *Old Calabria* by Norman Douglas, *North of Naples, South of Rome* by Paolo Tullio and *A Traveller in Southern Italy* by HV Morton. Although written in the 1960s, the latter remains a valuable guide to the south and its people. See also *A Traveller in Italy* by the same author.

A Small Place in Italy and *Love and War in the Apennines* by Eric Newby make good introductory reading, as do Lisa St Aubin de Terán's *A Valley in Italy*, Frances Maye's

chart-topping *Under the Tuscan Sun*, and *Night Letters*, Robert Dessaix's 1990s counterpart to Thomas Mann's *Death in Venice*.

History & Politics

For a simple introduction to the ancient history of the country try *The Oxford History of the Roman World*, edited by John Boardman, Jasper Griffin & Oswyn Murray, or *A History of Rome*, compiled by M Carey and HH Scullard. *Daily Life in Ancient Rome* by Jerome Carcopino and Robert Graves' classics *I, Claudius* and *Claudius the God* are on the same subject. Other interesting titles include *Italy: A Short History* by Harry Hearder; *The Horizon Concise History of Italy* by Vincent Cronin; *History of the Italian People* by Giuliano Procacci; *The Oxford Dictionary of Popes*, compiled by JND Kelly; and *Rome: Biography of a City*, *Venice: Biography of a City* and *The House of Medici*, all by Christopher Hibbert. *A History of Contemporary Italy: Society and Politics 1943-1988* by Paul Ginsborg is an absorbing and very well-written book that will help Italophiles place the country's modern society in perspective.

The Mafia is the subject of a number of titles, including *The Honoured Society* by Norman Lewis. *Excellent Cadavers: The Mafia and the Death of the First Italian Republic* by Alexander Stille is a shocking and absorbing account of the Mafia in Sicilia, focusing on the years leading up to the assassinations of anti-Mafia judges Giovanni Falcone and Paolo Borsellino in 1992 and the subsequent fall of Italy's First Republic. *Midnight in Sicily* by Peter Robb is also recommended.

Art & Architecture

The Penguin Book of the Renaissance by JH Plumb, *The Italian Painters of the Renaissance* by Bernard Berenson and Giorgio Vasari's *Lives of the Artists* should be more than enough for people interested in the Renaissance. Other useful books include *A Handbook of Roman Art* edited by Martin Henig, *Roman Architecture* by Frank Sear and *Art and Architecture in Italy 1600-1750* by Rudolf Wittkower.

There is also a series of guides to Italian art and architecture published under the general title World of Art. These include: *Palladio and Palladianism* by Robert Tavernor, *Michelangelo* by Linda Murray, *Italian Renaissance Sculpture* by Roberta JM Olson and *Roman Art and Architecture* by Mortimer Wheeler.

General

People For background on Italian people and their culture there is the classic by Luigi Barzini, *Italians*. *Italian Labyrinth* by John Haycraft looks at Italy in the 1980s. *Getting it Right in Italy: Manual for the 1990s* by William Ward aims, with considerable success, to provide accessible, useful information about Italy, while also providing a reasonable social profile of the people. *An Italian Education* by Tim Parks is an often hilarious account of the life of an expatriate in Verona.

Food & Drink *The Food of Italy* by Waverly Root is an acknowledged classic. Mitchell Beazley does a very good guide to Italian wines called *Wines of Italy* and has also recently published a guide called *The New Italy: A Complete Guide to Contemporary Italian Wines*.

See Lonely Planet earlier in this section for information on *World Food Italy*.

FILMS

If you want to get in the mood before heading off to Italy, here are a few suggestions: *Roman Holiday* (Gregory Peck and Audrey Hepburn scootering around Roma), *Three Coins in the Fountain* (three American women get their men at the Fontana di Trevi), *It Started in Naples* (Sophia Loren), *La Dolce Vita* (Fellini's study of Roman society), *Come September* (Rock, Gina, Sandra and Bobby romp around the Costiera Amalfitana), *The Pink Panther* (set in Cortina and Roma), *The Agony and the Ecstasy* (Charlton Heston as Michelango) and *Death in Venice* (Dirk Bogarde). More re-

cently there's been *A Room with a View* (not a view in the world can beat the one from Fiesole over Firenze), *Cinema Paradiso* (the story of a young boy in a small Italian town soon after WWII), *Enchanted April* (two women escape from London to a Tuscan villa), *Stealing Beauty* (a pretty dumb film, but a great Tuscan travelogue) and *The Wings of the Dove* (Henry James' story of love and betrayal in Venice).

If you want to see what Sicilia and Sardegna are like before you go, watch the Lonely Planet video *Corsica, Sicily and Sardinia*.

NEWSPAPERS & MAGAZINES

Italian newspapers can be frustratingly impenetrable, even for proficient Italian readers. Milano-based *Corriere della Sera* (L1500, or L2200 if a supplement is included) is the country's leading daily and has the best foreign-news pages and the most comprehensive and comprehensible political coverage.

Il Messaggero (L1500/2200) is the most popular broadsheet in Roma. The tabloid-format *La Repubblica* (L1500/2200), also a Roma-based paper, usually has great photos but also has a reputation for sloppy reporting. Its *Trovaroma* supplement on Thursday provides entertainment listings.

L'Unità (L1700), once the voice of the political left, now wobbles somewhere in the centre of the spectrum. Its cultural pages are always a good read.

The conservative *L'Osservatore Romano* (L1500) is published daily in Italian (with weekly editions in English and other foreign languages) and is Il Vaticano's official voice.

The English-language *International Herald Tribune* (L3000) is available from Monday to Saturday and has a daily four page supplement on Italian news. The *European* (L5000) is available on Friday.

British daily papers such as the *Guardian* (L3500), the *Times* (L5000) and the *Daily Telegraph* (L5500), and the various British tabloids, are sent from London, usually arriving in Italy's major cities on the day of publication. Elsewhere, they are generally a few days old.

The US press is represented by *USA Today* (L2800), the *Wall Street Journal* (European edition, L3700) and the weekly *New York Times* (L19,500). The major German, French and Spanish dailies are also available. News magazines such as *Time* (L6200), *Newsweek* (L6500) and the *Economist* (L8000) are available weekly.

RADIO & TV

There are three state-owned radio stations: RAI-1 (1332 AM or 89.7 FM), RAI-2 (846 AM or 91.7 FM) and RAI-3 (93.7 AM). They offer a combination of classical and light music, news broadcasts and discussion programmes. RAI-2 broadcasts news in English at three minutes past the hour from 1 to 5 am.

You can pick up the BBC World Service on medium wave at 648kHz, on short wave at 6.195MHz, 9.410MHz, 12.095MHz or 15.575MHz, and on long wave at 198kHz, depending on where you are and the time of day. Voice of America (VOA) can usually be found on short wave at 15.205MHz. Radio Vaticano (1530 AM, 93.3 FM and 105 FM) broadcasts the news in English at 7 am, 8.30 am, 6.15 pm and 9.50 pm. Pick up a pamphlet at the Vaticano information office for details.

The state-run television channels are Rai 1, Rai 2 and Rai 3. The main commercial stations are Canale 5, Italia 1, Rete 4 and Telemontecarlo (TMC). The choice and quality of the broadcasts on Italian television are painfully inadequate, but it is ideal if you want to unwind after a hard day's sightseeing.

CNN is broadcast nightly on TMC from around 3 am. On Channel 41, known as Autovox, the American PBS McNeill Lehrer News Hour is broadcast nightly at around 8 pm. BBC World, Sky Channel, CNN and NBC Superchannel are also available by satellite in many better hotels.

The French-language TV channel Antenne 2 can sometimes be received on Channel 10.

VIDEO SYSTEMS

Italy uses the PAL video system (the same as Australia and the rest of Europe, except France). This system is not compatible with NTSC (used in the USA, Japan and Latin America) or Secam (used in France and other French-speaking countries). Modern video players are often multi-system and can read all three.

PHOTOGRAPHY & VIDEO
Film & Equipment

There are numerous outlets that sell and process films, but beware of poor-quality processing. Many places claim to process films in one hour but you will rarely get your photos back that quickly – count on late the next day if the outlet has its own processing equipment, or three to four days if it hasn't.

A roll of film is called a *pellicola*, but you will be understood if you ask for 'film'. A 100 ASA Kodak film will cost around L7000/8000 for 24/36 exposures. Developing costs around L11,000/14,000 for 24/36 exposures in standard format. A roll of 36 slides costs L10,000 to buy and L8000 to develop.

Tapes for video cameras, including V8, are often available at the same outlets or can be found at stores selling cameras, videos and electrical goods.

Restrictions

Photography is not allowed in many churches, museums and galleries. Look out for signs as you go in. These restrictions do not normally apply to archaeological sites.

In military zones you will encounter signs in Italian warning you not to trespass and not to take photographs. Realistically, photography in these areas carries little risk in peace time – although the enforcement of restrictions is left to the discretion of the soldiers.

Photographing People

The standard rules about photographing people apply in Italy. In the south, you need to be particularly sensitive to the fact that people – especially women and the elderly – are traditionally more reserved. Children, on the other hand, will often come running to have their photo taken (and probably ask to try out your camera themselves).

Airport Security

The major Italian airports are all fully equipped with modern inspection systems that do not damage film or other photographic material carried in hand luggage.

TIME

Italy operates on a 24 hour clock, which will take travellers used to a 12 hour clock some getting used to.

Italy is one hour ahead of GMT/UTC. France, Germany, Austria and Spain are on the same time as Italy. Greece, Egypt and Israel are one hour ahead. When it's noon in Roma, it's 3 am in San Francisco, 6 am in New York and Toronto, 11 am in London, 7 pm in Perth, 9 pm in Sydney and 11 pm in Auckland.

Daylight-saving time starts on the last Sunday in March, when clocks are moved forward one hour. Clocks are put back an hour on the last Sunday in October. When telephoning home, remember to make allowances for daylight-saving in your own country.

ELECTRICITY
Voltages & Cycles

The electric current in Italy is 220V, 50Hz, but make a point of checking with your hotel management because in some areas – for instance, in some older hotels in Roma – they may still use 125V. Travellers from the USA need a voltage converter (although many of the more expensive hotels have provision for 110V appliances such as shavers).

Plugs & Sockets

Power sockets have two or three holes and do not have their own switches, while plugs have two or three round pins. Some sockets have larger holes than others. If you find that the plug and socket are incompatible,

do not despair: electrical and hardware stores sell special adapter plugs that cater for every conceivable combination.

Make sure you bring plug adapters for appliances that you bring with you into the country. It is a good idea to buy these *before* leaving home as they are virtually impossible to get in Italy. If you do forget, there is always the option of taking your appliance to an electrical store and having them replace the foreign plug with an Italian one.

WEIGHTS & MEASURES

Italy uses the metric system. Basic terms for weight include *un etto* (100g) and *un chilo* (1kg). Travellers from the USA (and often the UK) will have to cope with the change from pounds to kilograms, miles to kilometres and gallons to litres. A standard conversion table can be found on the inside back cover of this book.

Note that for numbers, Italians indicate decimals with commas and thousands with points.

LAUNDRY

Coin-operated laundrettes, where you can do your own washing, are catching on in Italy and you'll find them in most of the main cities. A load will cost around L8000.

Lavasecco (dry-cleaning) charges range from around L6000 for a shirt to L15,000 for a jacket. Be careful, though: the quality can be unreliable.

TOILETS

Public toilets are not exactly widespread in Italy, although coin-operated toilets are becoming increasingly common in major tourist areas. Most people use the toilets in bars and cafés, although you might need to buy a coffee first.

HEALTH
Medical Services

If you need an ambulance anywhere in Italy call ☎ 118.

The quality of medical treatment in public hospitals varies in Italy. Simply put, the farther north, the better the care.

Private hospitals and clinics throughout the country generally provide excellent services but are expensive for those without medical insurance. That said, certain treatments in public hospitals may also have to be paid for, and in such cases can be equally costly.

Your embassy or consulate in Italy can provide a list of recommended doctors in major cities; however, if you have a specific health complaint, it would be wise to obtain the necessary information and referrals for treatment before leaving home.

The public health system is administered along provincial lines by centres generally known as Unità Sanitarie Locali (USL) or Unità Soci Sanitarie Locali (USSL). Increasingly they are being reorganised as Aziende Sanitarie Locali (ASL). Through them you find out where your nearest hospital, medical clinics and other services are. Look under 'U' or 'A' in the telephone book (sometimes the USL and USSL are under 'A' too, as Azienda USL).

Under these headings you'll find long lists of offices – look for Poliambulatorio (Polyclinic) and the telephone number for Accetazione Sanitaria. You need to call this number to make an appointment: there is no point in just rolling up. Clinic opening hours vary widely, with the minimum generally being about 8 am to 12.30 pm Monday to Friday. Some open for a couple of hours in the afternoon and on Saturday mornings too.

Each ASL/USL area has its own Consultorio Familiare (Family Planning Centre) where you can go for contraceptives, pregnancy tests and information about abortion (legal up to the 12th week of pregnancy).

For emergency treatment, go straight to the *pronto soccorso* (casualty) section of a public hospital, where you can also get emergency dental treatment. Sometimes hospitals are listed in the phone book under Aziende Ospedaliere. In major cities you are likely to find doctors who speak English, or a volunteer translator service. Often, first aid is also available at train stations, airports and ports.

Medical Cover

Citizens of EU countries are covered for emergency medical treatment in Italy on presentation of an E111 form. Treatment in private hospitals is not covered and charges are also likely for medication, dental work and secondary examinations, including X-rays and laboratory tests. Ask about the E111 at your local health services department a few weeks before you travel (in the UK, the form is available at post offices).

Australia also has a reciprocal arrangement with Italy so that emergency treatment is covered – Medicare in Australia publishes a brochure with the details. The USA, Canada and New Zealand do not have reciprocal arrangements, and citizens of these countries will be required to pay for any treatment in Italy themselves. Advise medical staff of any reciprocal arrangements *before* they begin treating you. Most travel insurance policies include medical cover. See Travel Insurance under Visas & Documents earlier in this chapter.

General Preparations

Make sure you are healthy before you leave home. If you are embarking on a long trip, make sure your teeth are OK, because dental treatment is particularly expensive in Italy.

If you wear glasses, take a spare pair and your prescription. If you lose your glasses, you will be able to have them replaced within a few days by an *ottico* (optician).

Travellers who require a particular medication should take an adequate supply as well as the prescription, with the generic rather than the brand name, as this will make getting replacements easier. Basic drugs are widely available and indeed many items requiring prescriptions in countries such as the USA can be obtained over the counter in Italy. Tampons and condoms are freely available in pharmacies and supermarkets.

No vaccinations are required for entry into Italy unless you have been travelling through a part of the world where yellow fever or cholera is prevalent.

Basic Rules

Stomach upsets are the most likely travel health problem, but in Italy the majority of these will be relatively minor and probably due to overindulgence in the local food. Some people take a while to adjust to the regular use of olive oil in the food.

Water Tap water is drinkable throughout Italy, although Italians themselves have taken to drinking the bottled stuff. The sign *acqua non potabile* tells you that water is not drinkable (you may see the sign in trains and at some camp sites). Water from drinking fountains is safe unless there is a sign telling you otherwise.

Everyday Health Normal body temperature is 37°C or 98.6°F; more than 2°C (4°F) higher indicates a 'high' fever. Normal adult pulse rate is 60 to 100 beats per minute (children 80 to 100; babies 100 to 140). As a general rule, the pulse increases by about 20 beats per minute for each °C (2°F) rise in fever.

Environmental Hazards

Heatstroke This serious and sometimes fatal condition can occur if the body's heat-regulating mechanism breaks down and the body temperature rises to dangerous levels. Long, continuous periods of exposure to high temperatures can leave you vulnerable to heatstroke. Avoid excessive alcohol or strenuous activity when you first arrive in Italy during mid-summer.

The symptoms of heatstroke are feeling unwell, not sweating much or at all and a high body temperature (39 to 41°C or 102 to 106°F). Where sweating has ceased, the skin becomes flushed. Severe, throbbing headaches and lack of coordination will also occur. The sufferer may become confused or aggressive. Eventually the victim will become delirious or convulse. Hospitalisation is essential and, meanwhile, patients should be kept out of the sun, have their clothing removed, and be covered with a wet sheet or towel and fanned continuously to lower their temperature.

Medical Kit Check List

The following is a list of items you should consider including in your medical kit – consult your pharmacist for brands available in your country.

☐ **Aspirin** or **paracetamol** (acetaminophen in the USA) – for pain or fever

☐ **Antihistamine** – for allergies; to ease the itch from insect bites or stings; and to prevent motion sickness

☐ **Antibiotics** – consider these if you're travelling off the beaten track; see your doctor, as they must be prescribed, and carry the prescription

☐ **Loperamide** or **diphenoxylate** –'blockers' for diarrhoea

☐ **Prochlorperazine** or **metaclopramide** – for nausea and vomiting

☐ **Rehydration mixture** – to prevent dehydration, eg due to severe diarrhoea; particularly important when travelling with children

☐ **Insect repellent, sunscreen, lip balm** and **eye drops**

☐ **Calamine lotion, sting-relief spray** or **aloe vera** – to ease irritation from sunburn and insect bites or stings

☐ **Antifungal cream** or **powder** – for fungal skin infections and thrush

☐ **Antiseptic** (such as povidone-iodine) – for cuts and grazes

☐ **Bandages, Band-Aids (plasters)** and other wound dressings

☐ **Water-purification tablets** or **iodine**

☐ **Scissors, tweezers** and a **thermometer** (note that mercury thermometers are prohibited by airlines)

☐ **Cold** and **flu tablets, throat lozenges** and **nasal decongestant**

☐ **Multivitamins** – consider for long trips, when dietary vitamin intake may be inadequate

Hypothermia Too much cold can be just as dangerous as too much heat. If you are walking at high altitudes, particularly at night, be prepared.

Hypothermia occurs when the body loses

heat faster than it can produce it and the core temperature of the body falls. It is surprisingly easy to progress from very cold to dangerously cold due to a combination of wind, wet clothing, fatigue and hunger, even if the air temperature is above freezing. It is best to dress in layers: silk, wool and some of the new artificial fibres are all good insulating materials. A hat is important, as a lot of heat is lost through the head. A strong, waterproof outer layer (and a 'space' blanket for emergencies) is essential. Carry basic supplies, including food containing simple sugars to generate heat quickly and fluid to drink.

Symptoms of hypothermia are exhaustion, numb skin (particularly toes and fingers), shivering, slurred speech, irrational or violent behaviour, lethargy, stumbling, dizzy spells, muscle cramps and violent bursts of energy. Irrationality may take the form of sufferers claiming they are warm and trying to take off their clothes.

To treat mild hypothermia, first get the person out of the wind and/or rain, remove their clothing if it's wet and replace it with dry, warm clothing. Give them hot liquids – not alcohol – and some high-kilojoule, easily digestible food. Do not rub victims; instead, allow them to slowly warm themselves. This should be enough to treat the early stages of hypothermia. The early recognition and treatment of mild hypothermia is the only way to prevent severe hypothermia, which is a critical condition.

Motion Sickness Eating lightly before and during a trip will reduce the chances of motion sickness. If you are prone to motion sickness, try to find a place that minimises disturbance – near the wing on aircraft, close to midships on boats, near the centre on buses. Fresh air usually helps; reading and cigarette smoke definitely don't. Commercial antimotion-sickness preparations, which can cause drowsiness, have to be taken before the trip commences. Ginger (available in capsule form) and peppermint (including mint-flavoured sweets) are natural preventatives.

Prickly Heat Prickly heat is an itchy rash caused by excessive perspiration trapped under the skin. It usually strikes people who have just arrived in a hot climate. Keeping cool by bathing often, using a mild talcum powder or even resorting to spending time in air-conditioning may help.

Sunburn In the south of Italy during summer or at high altitude in the Alpi you can get sunburnt surprisingly quickly, even through cloud. Use a sunscreen, a hat and some barrier cream for your nose and lips. Calamine lotion is good for soothing mild sunburn. Don't forget to protect your eyes with good-quality sunglasses.

Infectious Diseases

Diarrhoea Despite all your precautions, you may still have a bout of mild travellers' diarrhoea. Dehydration is the main danger with any diarrhoea, particularly for children and the elderly, so fluid replenishment is the number-one treatment. Weak black tea with a little sugar, soda water or soft drinks allowed to go flat and diluted 50% with water are all good. With severe diarrhoea, a rehydrating solution is necessary to replace minerals and salts and you should see a doctor. Stick to a bland diet as you recover.

Hepatitis Hepatitis is a general term for inflammation of the liver. The symptoms are fever, chills, headache, fatigue, feelings of weakness and aches and pains, followed by loss of appetite, nausea, vomiting, abdominal pain, dark urine, light-coloured faeces, jaundiced (yellow) skin and the whites of the eyes may turn yellow. Hepatitis A is transmitted by contaminated food and drinking water. You should seek medical advice but there is not much you can do apart from resting, drinking lots of fluids, eating lightly and avoiding fatty foods. Those who have had hepatitis should avoid alcohol for some time after the illness as the liver needs time to recover.

Hepatitis B is spread through contact with infected blood, blood products or body fluids – for example, through sexual contact, unsterilised needles, blood transfusions or contact with blood via small breaks in the skin. Other risk situations include getting a tattoo and body piercing. Hepatitis B may lead to long-term problems.

There is no treatment for hepatitis, but vaccination against the disease is readily available in most countries. The problem has been complicated in recent years by the discovery of a plethora of new strains of the disease: C, D, E and a rumoured G. Recent reports have shown a sharp rise in Italy in the incidence of hepatitis C through sexual contact.

Rabies Rabies is still found in Italy, but only in isolated areas of the Alpi. It is transmitted through a bite or scratch by an infected animal. Dogs are noted carriers. Any bite, scratch or even lick from a mammal in an area where rabies does exist should be cleaned immediately and thoroughly. Scrub with soap and running water and then clean with an alcohol solution. Medical help should be sought immediately.

Sexually Transmitted Diseases If you require treatment or tests for a suspected STD or for HIV/AIDS, contact the provincial ASL. The Human Immunodeficiency Virus (HIV) may develop into Acquired Immune Deficiency Syndrome (AIDS). Exposure to infected blood, blood products or bodily fluids may put the individual at risk. In Italy, transmission is most likely through sexual contact with homosexual or bisexual males, or via contaminated needles shared by IV drug users. Apart from abstinence, the most effective preventative is always to practise safe sex using condoms. It's impossible to detect the HIV-positive status of an otherwise healthy-looking person without a blood test.

HIV/AIDS can be spread through infected blood transfusions, but in Italy blood is screened and they are safe. It can also be spread by dirty needles – acupuncture, tattooing and ear and nose piercing can potentially be as dangerous as intravenous drug use if the equipment isn't clean. The needles used in Italian hospitals are reliable. Fear of HIV infection should never preclude treatment for serious medical conditions.

Insect-Borne Diseases

Leishmaniasis This is a group of parasitic diseases transmitted by sandflies and found in coastal parts of Italy. Cutaneous leishmaniasis affects the skin tissue, and causes ulceration and disfigurement; visceral leishmaniasis affects the internal organs. Avoiding sandfly bites by covering up and using repellent is the best precaution against this disease.

Lyme Disease Lyme disease is an infection transmitted by ticks that can be acquired throughout Europe, including in forested areas of Italy. The illness usually begins with a spreading rash at the site of the tick bite and is accompanied by fever, headache, extreme fatigue, aching joints and muscles and mild neck stiffness. If untreated, these symptoms usually resolve over several weeks but, over subsequent weeks or months, disorders of the nervous system, heart and joints may develop. Treatment works best early in the illness. Medical help should be sought.

Bites & Stings

Jellyfish Italian beaches are occasionally inundated with jellyfish. Their stings are painful but not dangerous. Dousing in vinegar will de-activate any stingers that have not fired. Calamine lotion, antihistamines and analgesics may reduce the reaction and relieve pain. If in doubt about swimming, ask locals if any jellyfish are in the water.

Snakes Italy's only dangerous snake, the viper, is found throughout the country (except on Sardegna). To minimise the possibilities of being bitten, always wear boots, socks and long trousers when walking through undergrowth where snakes may be present. Don't put your hands into holes and crevices and do be careful when collecting firewood.

Viper bites do not cause instantaneous death and an antivenene is widely available in pharmacies. Keep the victim calm and still, wrap the bitten limb tightly, as you would for a sprained ankle, and attach a splint to immobilise it. Seek medical help, if possible with the dead snake for identification. Don't attempt to catch the snake if there is a possibility of being bitten again. Tourniquets and sucking out the poison are now comprehensively discredited.

Ticks Always check your body if you have been walking through a tick-infested area. In recent years there have been several reported deaths on Sardegna related to tick bites. Health authorities have yet to pinpoint the cause.

Women's Health

Women travellers often find that their menstrual periods become irregular or even cease while they're on the road. Remember that a missed period in these circumstances doesn't necessarily indicate pregnancy.

If you use contraceptive pills, don't forget to take time zones into account and do be aware that the pills may not be absorbed if you suffer intestinal problems. Ask your physician about these matters. If you think you've run into problems in Italy, contact the nearest Consultorio Familiare, attached to each USL or ASL (see Medical Services earlier in this section for details).

Most miscarriages occur during the first three months of pregnancy, so this is the most risky time to travel as far as your own health is concerned. Miscarriage is not uncommon and can occasionally lead to severe bleeding. The last three months of pregnancy should also be spent within reasonable distance of good medical care. A baby born as early as 24 weeks into the pregnancy stands a chance of survival, but only in a good, modern hospital. Pregnant women should avoid all unnecessary medication. Additional care should be taken to prevent illness and particular attention should be paid to diet and nutrition. Alcohol and nicotine should be avoided.

WOMEN TRAVELLERS

Italy is not a dangerous country for women, but women travelling alone will often find themselves plagued by unwanted attention from men. This attention usually involves catcalls, hisses and whistles and, as such, is more annoying than anything else. Lone women will also find it difficult to remain alone: you will have Italian men harassing you as you walk along the street, drink a coffee in a bar or try to read a book in a park. Usually the best response is to ignore them, but if that doesn't work, politely tell them that you are waiting for your *marito* (husband) or *fidanzato* (boyfriend) and, if necessary, walk away.

Avoid becoming aggressive as this almost always results in an unpleasant confrontation. If all else fails, approach the nearest member of the police or *carabinieri*. Watch out for men with wandering hands on crowded buses. Either keep your back to the wall or make a loud fuss if someone starts fondling your backside.

Basically, most of the attention falls into the nuisance/harassment category. However, women on their own should use their common sense. Avoid walking alone in deserted and dark streets and look for hotels that are central and within easy walking distance of places where you can eat at night (unsafe areas for women are noted throughout this book). Women should also avoid hitchhiking alone.

Women will find that the farther south they travel, the more likely they are to be harassed. It is advisable to dress more conservatively in the south, particularly if you are travelling to small towns and villages. Skimpy clothing is a sure attention-earner – you should take your cue from the Italian women on this one.

In cities where there is a high petty-crime rate, such as Roma, Napoli, Palermo, Siracusa and Bari, women on their own are regarded as prime targets for bag-snatchers (on foot or on *motorino*). Use a backpack if you can (it's harder to pull off) or keep one hand on your bag (preferably carried diagonally across the body with the bag on the side away from the road), and be very careful about walking in deserted streets.

Recommended reading is the *Handbook for Women Travellers* by M & G Moss.

GAY & LESBIAN TRAVELLERS

Homosexuality is legal in Italy and well tolerated in major cities, particularly in the north. Friendships between Italian men tend to involve physical contact, so the sight of two men (or two women) walking down a street arm in arm is not unusual. However, overt displays of affection by homosexual couples could attract a negative response in smaller towns.

Cities such as Roma, Firenze and Milano have several gay clubs, which may be listed in newspapers but can be more reliably tracked down through local gay organisations (see below) or the national monthly gay magazine *Babilonia*. This, along with the annual *Guida Gay Italia*, is available at most newsstands. *Babilonia* also has a Web site at www.babilonia.net.

International gay and lesbian guides worth checking out are the *Spartacus International Gay Guide* (the Spartacus list also includes the comprehensive *Spartacus National Edition Italia*, in English and German), published by Bruno Gmünder Verlag, Mail Order, PO Box 61 01 04, D-10921 Berlin, Germany, and *Places for Women*, published by Ferrari Publications, Phoenix, Arizona, USA.

More information about gay and lesbian venues can be found in the Entertainment sections of individual cities in this book.

Organisations

The national organisations for gay men and lesbians are ArciGay and ArciLesbica (☎ 051 644 70 54, fax 051 644 67 22), Piazza di Porta Saragozza 2, 40123 Bologna.

You'll find any number of Italian gay sites on the Internet, but some are all but useless. However, ArciGay's Web site, at www.gay.it/arcigay, has general information on the gay and lesbian scene in Italy and plenty of useful links. ArciLesbica's Web site can be found at www.women.it/

~arciles. Another interesting site with plenty of links is that of La Comunità Gay/Lesbica/Trans Italiana. Go to www.webring.org and search on 'itgay'.

DISABLED TRAVELLERS

The Italian State Tourist Office in your country may be able to provide advice on Italian associations for the disabled and information on what help is available in the country. It may also carry a small brochure, *Services for Disabled People*, published by the Italian railways company, Ferrovie dello Stato, which details facilities at stations and on trains. Some of the better trains, such as the ETR460 and ETR500 trains, have a carriage for passengers in wheelchairs and their companions.

The Italian travel agency CIT can advise on hotels with special facilities, such as ramps. It can also request that wheelchair ramps be provided on arrival of your train if you book travel through CIT.

Organisations

The UK-based Royal Association for Disability & Rehabilitation (RADAR) publishes a useful guide called *Holidays & Travel Abroad: A Guide for Disabled People*, which provides a good overview of facilities available to disabled travellers in Europe. Contact RADAR (☎ 020-7250 3222), Unit 12, City Forum, 250 City Rd, London EC1V 8AS.

Another UK organisation worth calling is Holiday Care Service (☎ 01293-774535). It produces an information pack on Italy for disabled people and other travellers with special needs.

Mobility International (☎ 02-201 5608, fax 201 5763), 18 blvd Baudouin, Brussels, Belgium, organises all sorts of activities and events throughout Europe for the disabled.

In Italy itself, you may be able to get help from Co.In. (Cooperative Integrate), a national voluntary group with links to the government and branches all over the country. It publishes a quarterly magazine for disabled tourists, *Turismo per Tutti* (Tourism for All), in Italian and English. It has details of accessible accommodation, transport and attractions. Co.In. (☎ 06 232 67 505) is at Via Enrico Giglioli 54a, Roma. Its Web site is at andi.casaccia.enea.it/andi/COIN/TUR/hometur.htm.

The Associazione Italiana Assistenza Spastici (☎ 02 550 17 564), Via S Barnaba 29, Milano, operates an information service for disabled travellers called the Sportello Vacanze Disabili. They have information for disabled travellers in Milano and around the country.

Promotur – Accessible Italy (☎ 011 309 63 63, fax 011 309 12 01), Piazza Pitagora 9, 10137 Torino, is a private company which specialises in holiday services for the disabled, ranging from tours to hiring of adapted-transport rental. Check out their Web site at www.tour-web.com/accitaly.

SENIOR TRAVELLERS

Senior citizens are entitled to discounts on public transport and on admission fees at some museums in Italy. It is always important to ask. The minimum qualifying age is generally 60 years. You should also seek information in your own country on travel packages and discounts for senior travellers through senior citizens' organisations and travel agencies.

TRAVEL WITH CHILDREN

Successful travel with children can require a special effort. Don't try to overdo things by packing too much into the time available, and make sure activities include the kids as well. Remember that visits to museums and galleries can be tiring, even for adults. Children might be more interested in some of the major archaeological sites, such as Pompei, the Colosseo and the Foro in Roma, and Greek temples in the south and Sicilia. If you're travelling in northern Italy, you might want to make a stopover at Gardaland, the amusement park near Lago di Garda in Lombardia, or at Italia in Miniatura at Viserba near Rimini in Emilia-Romagna.

Allow time for the kids to play, either in a park or in the hotel room; taking a toddler to a playground for an hour or so in the morning can make an amazing difference to their tolerance for sightseeing in the afternoon. When travelling long distances by car or public transport, take plenty of books and other activities, such as colouring pencils and paper. Include older children in the planning of the trip – if they have helped to work out where they will be going, they are likely to be much more interested when they get there.

Discounts are available for children (usually aged under 12) on public transport and for admission to museums, galleries and other sites.

There are special sections on activities for families in the Roma, Firenze and Venezia sections, as well as in several other cities and towns. These include activities that might interest the kids and usually point out where you can find a playground for young children. Always make a point of asking staff at tourist offices if they know of any special family or children's activities and for suggestions on hotels that cater for kids. Families should book accommodation in advance, where possible, to avoid unnecessary inconvenience.

You can buy baby formula in powder or liquid form, as well as sterilising solutions such as Milton, at *farmacie* (chemists). Disposable nappies (diapers) are widely available at supermarkets, *farmacie* (where they are more expensive) and sometimes in larger *cartolerie* (stores selling paper goods). A pack of around 30 disposable nappies costs about L18,000. Fresh cow's milk is sold in cartons in bars (which have a '*Latteria*' sign) and in supermarkets. If it is essential that you have milk, you should carry an emergency carton of UHT milk, since bars usually close at 8 pm. In many out-of-the-way areas in southern Italy, the locals use only UHT milk.

You can hire children's safety seats from many car-rental firms. It is strongly advised that you book them in advance.

For more information, see Lonely Planet's *Travel with Children* by Maureen Wheeler.

DANGERS & ANNOYANCES
Theft

This is the main problem for travellers in Italy. Pickpockets and bag-snatchers operate in most major cities and are particularly active in Napoli and Roma. The best way to avoid being robbed is to wear a money belt under your clothing. You should keep all important items, such as money, passport, other papers and tickets, in your money belt at all times. If you are carrying a bag or camera, ensure that you wear the strap across your body and have the bag on the side away from the road to deter snatchers, who often operate from motorcycles and scooters. Since the aim of young motorcycle bandits is often fun rather than gain, you are just as likely to find yourself relieved of your sunglasses – or worse, of an earring – as something more valuable. Motorcycle bandits are very active in Napoli, Roma, Siracusa and Palermo.

You should also watch out for groups of dishevelled-looking women and children. They generally work in groups of four or five and carry paper or cardboard which they use to distract your attention while they swarm around and rifle through your pockets and bag. Never underestimate their skill – they are lightning fast and very adept. Their favourite haunts are in and near major train stations, at tourist sights (such as the Colosseo) and in shopping areas. If you notice that you have been targeted by a group, either take evasive action, such as crossing the street, or shout 'Va via!' (Go away!) in a loud, angry voice.

Pickpockets often hang out on busy buses (the No 64 in Roma, which runs from Stazione Termini to Il Vaticano, is notorious) and in crowded areas such as markets. There is only one way to deter pickpockets: simply *do not* carry any money or valuables in your pockets, and be very careful with your bags.

Horror tales abound about women being dragged to the ground by thieves trying to snatch their bags and of people losing wallets, watches and cameras on crowded buses or in a flurry of newspaper-waving children. These things really do happen! Certainly, even the most cautious travellers are still prey to expert thieves, but there is no need to be paranoid. By taking a few basic precautions, you can greatly lessen the risk of being robbed.

Be careful even in hotels and don't leave valuables lying around your room. You should also be cautious of sudden friendships, particularly if it turns out that your new-found *amico* or *amica* wants to sell you something.

Parked cars are also prime targets for thieves, particularly those with foreign number plates or rental-company stickers. Try removing the stickers, or cover them and leave a local newspaper on the seat to make it look like a local car. *Never* leave valuables in your car – in fact, try not to leave anything in the car if you can help it and certainly not overnight. It is a good idea to pay extra to leave your car in supervised car parks, although there is no guarantee it will be completely safe. Throughout Italy, particularly in the south, service stations along the autostrade are favourite haunts of thieves who can clean out your car in the time it takes to have a cup of coffee. If possible, park your car where you can keep an eye on it.

In recent years there have been isolated incidences of armed robberies on the autostrade south of Napoli, when travellers have been forced off the road or tricked into pulling over, and have then been robbed at gunpoint.

When driving in cities you also need to beware of thieves when you pull up at traffic lights. Keep the doors locked and, if you have the windows open, ensure that there is nothing valuable on the dashboard. Car theft is a major problem in the regions of Campania and Puglia, particularly in the cities of Napoli, Bari, Foggia and Brindisi. Beware also of unofficial parking attendants who say you can leave your car double-parked as long as you leave them your keys: you will return to find that both the attendant and your car have disappeared.

Some Italians practise a more insidious

form of theft: short-changing. Numerous travellers have reported losing money in this way. If you are new to the Italian currency, take the time to acquaint yourself with the denominations. When paying for goods, tickets, a meal or whatever, keep an eye on the bills you hand over and then count your change carefully. One popular means of short-changing goes something like this: you hand over L50,000 for a newspaper that costs L2800; you are handed change for L10,000 and, while the person who sold you the paper hesitates, you hurry off without counting it. If you'd stayed for another five seconds, the rest of the change probably would have been handed over without you needing to say anything.

In case of theft or loss, always report the incident at the questura (police station) within 24 hours and ask for a statement, otherwise your travel insurance company won't pay out.

Traffic

Italian traffic can at best be described as chaotic, at worst downright dangerous, for the unprepared tourist. Drivers are not keen to stop for pedestrians, even at pedestrian crossings, and are more likely to swerve. Italians simply step off the footpath and walk through the (swerving) traffic with determination. It is a practice that seems to work, so if you feel uncertain about crossing a busy road, wait for the next Italian. In many cities, roads that appear to be for one-way traffic have lanes for buses travelling in the opposite direction – always look both ways before stepping onto the road.

Pollution

Tourists will be affected in a variety of ways by the surprising disregard Italians have for their country (see Ecology & Environment in the Facts about Italy chapter). Noise and air pollution are problems in the major cities, caused mainly by heavy traffic. A headache after a day of sightseeing in Roma is likely to be caused by breathing carbon monoxide and lead, rather than simple tiredness. While cities such as Roma,

Firenze and Milano have banned normal traffic from their historic centres, there are still more than enough cars, buses and motorcycles in and around the inner city areas to pollute the air.

Particularly in summer, there are periodic pollution alerts. The elderly, children and people who have respiratory problems are warned to stay indoors. If you fit into one of these categories, keep yourself informed through the tourist office or your hotel.

When booking a hotel room it is a good idea to ask if it is quiet, although this might mean you will have to decide between a view and sleep.

One of the most annoying things about Roma is that the pavements are littered with dog pooh – so be careful where you plant your feet.

Italy's beaches are generally heavily polluted by industrial waste, sewage and oil spills from the Mediterraneo's considerable sea traffic. There are clean beaches on Sardegna, Sicilia, and in the less populated areas of the south and around Elba.

Italian-Style Service

It requires a lot of patience to deal with the Italian concept of service. What for Italians is simply a way of life can be horrifying for the foreigner. For example, the bank clerk who wanders off to have a cigarette just as it is your turn (after a one hour wait) to be served, or the postal worker who has too much important work to do at a desk to sell stamps to customers. Anyone in a uniform or behind a counter (including police officers, waiters and shop assistants) is likely to regard you with imperious contempt. Long queues are the norm in banks, post offices and any government offices.

It pays to remain calm and patient. Aggressive, demanding and angry customers stand virtually no chance of getting what they want.

LEGAL MATTERS

For many Italians, finding ways to get around the law (any law) is a way of life. They are likely to react with surprise, if not annoyance, if you point out that they might be breaking a law. Few people pay attention to speed limits; most motorcyclists and many drivers don't stop at red lights – and certainly not at pedestrian crossings. No-one bats an eyelid about littering or dogs pooping in the middle of the pavement, even though many municipal governments have introduced laws against these things. But these are minor transgressions when measured up against the country's organised crime, the extraordinary levels of tax evasion and the corruption in government and business.

The average tourist will probably have a brush with the law only if they are robbed by a bag-snatcher or pickpocket.

Drugs

Italy has introduced new drug laws which are lenient on drug users and heavy on pushers. If you're caught with drugs which the police determine are for your personal use, you'll be let off with a warning – and, of course, the drugs will be confiscated. If, instead, it is determined that you intend to sell the drugs in your possession, you could find yourself in prison. It's up to the discretion of the police to determine whether or not you're a pusher, since the law is not specific about quantities. It's best to avoid illicit drugs altogether.

Drink Driving

The legal limit for blood alcohol level is 0.08% and random breath tests do occur. See Road Rules in the Getting Around chapter for more information.

Police

To call the *polizia* (police) dial the toll-free emergency number ☎ 113. To report a non-violent theft or incident that doesn't endanger life, call the carabinieri on ☎ 112. Addresses and local telephone numbers of police stations are given in the Emergency sections throughout this book.

If you run into trouble in Italy, you're likely to end up dealing with either the polizia or the carabinieri. The polizia are a

civil force and take their orders from the Ministry of the Interior, while the carabinieri fall under the Ministry of Defence. There is a considerable duplication of their roles, despite a 1981 reform of the police forces which intended to merge the two. Both forces are responsible for public order and security, which means that you can visit either in the event of a robbery or attack.

The carabinieri wear a dark-blue uniform (changing to black) with a red stripe and drive dark-blue cars with a red stripe. They are well trained and tend to be helpful. You are more likely to be pulled over by the carabinieri than the polizia if you are speeding. Their police station is called a *caserma* (barracks), a reflection of their military status.

The polizia wear powder-blue trousers with a fuchsia stripe and a navy-blue jacket, and drive light-blue cars with a white stripe, with 'polizia' written on the side. People wanting to get a residence permit will have to deal with them. Their headquarters is called the questura.

Other varieties of police in Italy include the *vigili urbani*, who are basically traffic police. You will have to deal with them if you get a parking ticket or your car is towed away. The *guardia di finanza* are responsible for fighting tax evasion and drug smuggling. It's a long shot, but you could be stopped by one of them if you leave a shop without a receipt for your purchase.

The *guardia forestale* are responsible for enforcing laws concerning forests and their fauna and flora and the environment in general. Like the carabinieri, their headquarters is called a caserma. They are often found in isolated townships bordering on areas of environmental interest. They are armed and can fine law-breakers.

Your Rights

Italy still has some anti-terrorism laws on its books which could make life very difficult if you happen to be detained by the police. You can be held for 48 hours without a magistrate being informed and you can be interrogated without the presence of a lawyer. It is difficult to obtain bail and you

euro currency converter L10,000 = €5.16

can be held legally for up to three years without being brought to trial.

BUSINESS HOURS

Business hours vary from city to city, but generally shops are open from around 9 am to 1 pm and 3.30 to 7.30 pm (or 4 to 8 pm) Monday to Saturday. In some cities, grocery shops might not reopen until 5 pm and, during the warmer months, they could stay open until 9 pm. They may close on Saturday afternoon and on Thursday or Monday afternoon (depending on the town). Other shops, department stores and supermarkets also close for a half-day during the week – it varies from city to city, but is usually either Monday morning or Thursday afternoon. Some department stores, such as Coin and Rinascente, and most supermarkets now have continuous opening from 9 am to 7.30 pm Monday to Saturday. Some even open from 9 am to 1 pm on Sunday.

Banks tend to open from 8.30 am to 1.30 pm and 3.30 to 4.30 pm (although hours can vary) Monday to Friday. They are closed at weekends, but it is always possible to find a bureau de change open in the larger cities and in major tourist areas.

Major post offices open from 8.30 am to 5 or 6 pm Monday to Friday, and also from 8.30 am to 1 or 2 pm on Saturday. Smaller post offices generally open from 8.30 am to 1.50 pm Monday to Friday, and also from 8.30 to 11.50 am on Saturday. All post offices close two hours earlier than normal on the last business day of each month (not including Saturday).

Pharmacies are usually open from 9 am to 12.30 pm and 3.30 to 7.30 pm. They are always closed on Sunday and usually on Saturday afternoon. When closed, pharmacies are required to display a list of pharmacies in the area that are open.

Bars (in the Italian sense, coffee and sandwich places) and cafés generally open from 7.30 am to 8 pm, although some stay open after 8 pm and turn into pub-style drinking-and-meeting places. Clubs and discos might open around 10 pm, but often there'll be no-one there until around mid-

night. Restaurants open from noon to 3 pm and 7.30 to 11 pm (later in summer and in the south). Restaurants and bars are required to close for one day each week, which varies between establishments.

The opening hours of museums, galleries and archaeological sites vary, although there is a trend towards continuous opening from 9.30 am to 7 pm. Many close on Monday. Increasingly, during summer the major national museums and galleries remain open until 10 pm.

PUBLIC HOLIDAYS

Most Italians take their annual holiday in August, deserting the cities for the cooler coastal or mountain resorts. This means that many businesses and shops close for at least a part of the month, particularly during the week around Ferragosto (Feast of the Assumption) on 15 August. Larger cities, notably Milano and Roma, are left to the tourists, who may be frustrated that many restaurants and shops are closed until early September. The Settimana Santa (Easter Week) is another busy holiday period for Italians. To give you an idea of when this period will fall in the next few years, Good Friday is April 21 in 2000, April 13 in 2001 and March 29 in 2002.

National public holidays include the following:

New Year's Day	1 January
Epiphany	6 January
Easter Monday	March/April
Liberation Day	25 April
Labour Day	1 May
Feast of the Assumption	15 August
All Saints' Day	1 November
Feast of the Immaculate Conception	8 December
Christmas Day	25 December
Feast of Santo Stefano	26 December

Individual towns also have public holidays to celebrate the feasts of their patron saints. See the following Special Events section for details.

SPECIAL EVENTS

Italy's calendar bursts with cultural events ranging from colourful traditional celebrations, with a religious and/or historical flavour, through to festivals of the performing arts, including opera, music and theatre.

Many towns celebrate the feasts of their patron saints in eye-catching fashion. These include: the Feast of St Mark on 25 April in Venezia; the Feast of St John the Baptist on 24 June in Firenze, Genova and Torino; the Feast of Saints Peter and Paul on 29 June in Roma; the Feast of St Gennaro (Janarius) on 19 September in Napoli; and the Feast of St Ambrose on 7 December in Milano. Religious festivals are particularly numerous on Sicilia and Sardegna, notably Le Feste di Pasqua (Holy Week) in Sicilia.

Among the important opera seasons are those at Verona's Arena and at La Scala in Milano. Major music festivals include Umbria Jazz in Perugia and Maggio Musicale Fiorentino in Firenze, while the Festival dei Due Mondi (Festival of Two Worlds) in Spoleto is worth visiting. Venezia plays host to an international film festival and the Biennale visual arts festival, the latter held every odd year.

If you wish to time your visit with a particular festival, contact the Italian State Tourist Office in your country or write to ENIT in Roma (see Tourist Offices earlier in this chapter) for dates. ENIT publishes an annual booklet, *An Italian Year*, which lists most festivals and music, opera and ballet seasons, as well as art and film festivals.

The Millennium

Amid all the hype about the biggest party in 1000 years, the religious significance to Christians of the year 2000 lies in the commemoration of the birth of Christ. It is not surprising, then, that Roma (or, more precisely, Il Vaticano), as home to the Catholic Church, has geared up for the millennium in a big way. A seemingly endless array of events, exhibitions and celebrations has been planned for this Anno Santo (Holy Year) or Giubileo (Jubilee), as it is variously known in Italy. Italian tourist offices in and outside Italy should have information on the programming, or check the Web site at www.enit.it/giubileo.htm.

Festivals

The following is a selection of Italy's main festivals:

February/March/April

Carnevale
During the period before Ash Wednesday, many towns stage carnivals and enjoy their last opportunity to indulge before Lent. The carnival held in Venezia during the 10 days before Ash Wednesday is the most famous, but more traditional and popular carnival celebrations are held at Viareggio, on the northern coast of Toscana, and at Ivrea, near Torino. The Venezia Carnevale will take place from 29 February to 7 March in 2000, 20 to 27 February in 2001 and 5 to 12 February in 2002. In a couple of towns (such as Milano), the celebrations take place a week later.

Sartiglia
This is the highlight of carnival celebrations at Oristano on Sardegna, held on the Sunday and Tuesday before Lent. It involves a medieval tournament of horsemen in masquerade.

Sagra del Mandorlo in Fiore
(Festival of the Almond Blossoms)
This traditional festival features a historical pageant and fireworks. It is held at Agrigento, Sicily, in early/mid-February.

Le Feste di Pasqua (Holy Week)
Holy Week in Italy is marked by solemn processions and Passion plays. On Holy Thursday at Taranto in Puglia there is the Procession of the Addolorata, and on Good Friday the Procession of the Mysteries, when statues representing the Passion of Christ are carried around the town. One of Italy's oldest and most evocative Good Friday processions is held at Chieti in Abruzzo. On Sicilia, the week is marked by numerous events, including a Procession of the Mysteries at Trapani and the celebration of Easter according to Byzantine rites at Piana degli Albanesi, near Palermo. Women in colourful 15th century costume give out Easter eggs to the public.

Scoppio del Carro (Explosion of the Cart)
Held in Firenzece on the Piazza del Duomo at noon on Easter Sunday, this event features the explosion of a cart full of fireworks, which is a tradition dating back to the crusades. It is seen as a good omen for the city if it works.

May

Festa di San Nicola

On 2 and 3 May, the people of Bari in Puglia process in traditional costume to re-enact the delivery of the bones of their patron saint to Dominican friars. The next day a statue of the saint is taken to sea.

Processione dei Serpari
(Snake-Charmers' Procession)

Held at Cocullo in Abruzzo on the first Thursday of May, this famous and traditional festival honours the village's patron saint, San Domenico. His statue is draped with live snakes and carried in procession.

Festa di San Gennaro

Three times a year (the first Sunday in May, 19 September and 16 December), the faithful gather in Napoli's Duomo to wait for the blood of San Gennaro to liquefy. If the miracle occurs, it is considered a good omen for the city.

Corsa dei Ceri

This exciting, traditional race is held at Gubbio in Umbria on 15 May. Groups of men carrying huge wooden shrines race uphill to the town's basilica, which is dedicated to the patron saint, Ubaldo.

Cavalcata Sarda (Sardinian Procession)

Hundreds of Sardi wearing colourful traditional costume gather at Sassari on Sardegna on the second-last Sunday in May to mark a victory over the Saracens in the year 1000.

Palio della Balestra (Crossbow Contest)

Held in Gubbio on the last Sunday in May, this contest is between the men of Gubbio and Sansepolcro, who dress in medieval costume and use antique weapons. There is a rematch at Sansepolcro in September.

Maggio Musicale Fiorentino (Musical May)

Held in Firenze in May and June.

June

Palio delle Quattro Antiche Repubbliche Marinare (Regatta of the Four Ancient Maritime Republics)

This event sees a procession of boats and a race between the four historical maritime rivals – Pisa, Venezia, Amalfi and Genova. The event rotates between the four towns: Genova in 2000, Amalfi in 2001, Pisa in 2002 and Venezia in 2003. Although usually held in June, it has been known to be delayed as late as September.

Festa di Sant'Antonio

Fans of Sant'Antonio, patron saint of Padova and of lost things, might want to attend the procession of the saint's relics, held annually on 13 June.

Infiorata (Flower Festival)

To celebrate Corpus Domini on 21 June, some towns decorate a street with colourful designs made with flower petals. Towns include Genzano, near Roma, and Spello in Umbria.

Gioco del Ponte (Game of the Bridge)

Two groups in medieval costume contend for the Ponte di Mezzo, a bridge over the Arno river in Pisa.

Festival dei Due Mondi
(Festival of Two Worlds)

This is an international arts event held in June and July at Spoleto, a beautiful hill town in Umbria. It was created by Gian Carlo Menotti and features music, theatre, dance and art.

July

Il Palio (The Banner)

The pride and joy of Siena, this famous traditional event is held twice a year – on 2 July and 16 August – in the town's beautiful Piazza del Campo. It involves a dangerous bareback horse race around the piazza, preceded by a parade of supporters in traditional costume.

Ardia

More dangerous than Il Palio, this impressive and chaotic horse race at Sedilo on Sardegna on 6 and 7 July celebrates the victory of the Roman Emperor Constantine over Maxentius in 312 AD (the battle was actually at the Ponte Milvio in Roma). A large number of horsemen race around town while onlookers shoot guns into the ground or air.

Festa del Redentore (Feast of the Redeemer)

Fireworks and a procession over the bridge to the Chiesa del Redentore on Isola della Giudecca in Venezia take place on the third weekend in July.

Umbria Jazz

Held at Perugia in Umbria in July, this week-long festival features performers from around the world.

International Ballet Festival

This festival held at Nervi, near Genova, features international performers.

August

Quintana (Medieval Joust)

This historical pageant features a parade of hundreds of people in 15th century costume, followed by a spectacular jousting tournament. It is held at Ascoli Piceno in Le Marche on the first Sunday in August.

I Candelieri (The Candlesticks)

Held on 14 August at Sassari on Sardegna, I Candelieri features town representatives in medieval costume carrying huge wooden columns through the town. The celebrations are held to honour a vow made in 1652 for deliverance from a plague.

Il Palio

This repeat of Siena's famous horse race is held on 16 August.

Festa del Redentore

Held at Nuoro on Sardegna, this folk festival and parade is attended by thousands of people from all over the island, who dress in traditional regional costume.

Mostra del Cinema di Venezia (International Film Festival)

Held at the Lido, Venezia, the festival attracts the international film scene.

September

Partita a Scacchi (Living Chess Game)

The townspeople of Marostica in the Veneto dress as chess figures and participate in a match on a chessboard marked out in the town square. Games are held in even years on the first weekend in September.

Palio della Balestra

A rematch of the crossbow competition between Gubbio and Sansepolcro is held at Sansepolcro on the first Sunday in September.

Regata Storica (Historic Regatta)

This gondola race along Venezia's Canal Grande is preceded by a parade of boats decorated in 15th century style. It is held on the first Sunday in September.

Giostra della Quintana (Medieval Joust)

This medieval pageant held in Foligno, near Perugia, involves a parade and jousting event with horsemen in traditional costume. It is held on the second Sunday in September.

Festa di San Gennaro

On 19 September the faithful of Napoli gather for the second time to await the miraculous liquefaction of San Gennaro's blood.

October

Festa di San Francesco d'Assisi

Special religious ceremonies are held in the churches of San Francesco and Santa Maria degli Angeli in Assisi on 3 and 4 October.

November

Festa della Madonna della Salute

Held in Venezia on 21 November, this procession over a bridge of boats across the Canal Grande to the Basilica di Santa Maria della Salute is to give thanks for the city's deliverance from plague in 1630.

Festa di Santa Cecilia

A series of concerts and exhibitions takes place

in Siena in Toscana to honour the patron saint of musicians.

December

Festa di San Nicola

Various religious ceremonies as well as traditional folk celebrations take place at Bari on 6 December.

Festa di San Gennaro

On 16 December the faithful of Napoli gather for a third and final time to await the liquefaction of the blood of San Gennaro.

Natale (Christmas)

During the weeks preceding Christmas there are numerous processions and religious events. Many churches set up elaborate cribs or nativity scenes known as *presepi*.

ACTIVITIES

If the museums, galleries and sights are not enough for you, there are numerous options for getting off the beaten tourist track. From mountaineering to water sports, Italy offers a wide range of outdoor pursuits.

Walking

The Alpi, in particular the spectacular Dolomiti, offer well-marked walking routes and strategically placed *rifugi* (mountain

NICKY CAVEN

Italy's rich history lives on in the annual Giostra della Quintana at Foligno.

accommodation) for long-distance walkers. With careful planning, it is possible to walk for as many days as you want, without carrying large quantities of supplies, by staying in and buying your food at the rifugi. However, walkers still need to be well prepared in the Alpi: even at the height of summer the weather can change suddenly. Walkers planning to tackle longer and more difficult trails, particularly at high altitudes, should ensure that they leave basic details of their route with someone. They should also be well informed on weather predictions and prepared for cold weather, rain and snow (the first snow can fall in September). See Walking in the Dolomiti in the Trentino-Alto Adige chapter for more information.

The Appennini also have good walking trails. Interesting areas include the Parco Nazionale d'Abruzzo and La Sila (Sila massif) in Calabria. Toscana's Alpi Apuane also have well-marked and challenging trails. On Sardegna, the rugged landscape offers some spectacular walks in the eastern ranges, such as Gennargentu, and the gorges near Dorgali. See the relevant sections for further information. If you plan to do a lot of walking, have a look at Lonely Planet's *Walking in Italy* – it has in-depth information and advice on walking trails throughout the country.

Guided walks are a good idea for inexperienced walkers. See the Alpine sections of the northern Italy chapters for details.

Check with tourist offices in each city for information about local groups that organise walking tours. Numerous mountainguide groups throughout the Alpi offer guided walks, ranging from nature walks to demanding week-long walks which may or may not require some mountaineering skills. Information about mountain guides can always be obtained from tourist offices throughout the Alpi. Many guides are also listed in the Alpine sections of the northern Italy chapters.

Skiing

There are numerous excellent ski resorts in the Italian Alpi and, again, the Dolomiti provide the most dramatic scenery. Options include *lo sci* (downhill skiing) and *sci di fondo* (cross-country skiing), as well as *sci alpinismo* (ski mountaineering). Sci alpinismo is only for the adventurous and advanced: skiers head well away from the organised runs and combine their mountaineering and skiing skills.

Skiing is quite expensive because of the costs of ski lifts and accommodation, but a Settimana Bianca (White Week) package can reduce the expense. It is not expensive, on the other hand, to hire ski equipment – and this factor should be weighed up against the inconvenience of bringing your own gear. Sci di fondo costs less because you don't pay for the lifts.

The season in Italy generally runs from December to late March, although at higher altitudes and in particularly good years it can be longer. There is year-round skiing in areas such as the Marmolada glacier in Trentino-Alto Adige and on Monte Bianco (Mont Blanc) and Monte Cervino (the Matterhorn) in the Valle d'Aosta.

The five major (read most fashionable and expensive) ski resorts in Italy are Cortina d'Ampezzo in the Veneto; Madonna di Campiglio, San Martino di Castrozza and Canazei in Trentino; and Courmayeur in the Valle d'Aosta. There are many other, less expensive resorts that also offer excellent facilities (see the Alpine sections of the northern Italy chapters for details).

Water Sports

Windsurfing and sailing are extremely popular in Italy and at most beach resorts it is possible to hire boats and equipment. There are also various diving schools, but the scenery above water is much more interesting. See the Things to See & Do and Activities sections throughout this book for information on boat and windsurfing-equipment hire at water resorts.

Cycling

The only problem with cycling in Italy is that more than 75% of the country is mountainous or hilly, so you will need plenty of stamina and a good bike. A mountain bike is a good idea, as it would enable you to tackle some of the Alpine trails as well. Cycling and mountain biking are becoming increasingly popular in Italy and you'll find that most tourist offices will be able to offer information on mountain-bike trails and guided mountain-bike rides. For information on hiring or buying a bike and on travelling around Italy with one, see the Bicycle section of the Getting Around chapter.

The hills of Toscana are very popular for cycling, particularly around Firenze and Siena, from where you could explore the countryside around Fiesole, San Gimignano and Chianti, just to name a few possibilities. A bike would be particularly useful for getting around Sardegna. In Umbria, areas such as the Valnerina and the Piano Grande at Monte Vettore have beautiful trails and quiet country roads to explore. Serious cyclists will know where to go for the most challenging routes – the tortuous, winding road up to the Passo Stelvio is one of the most famous.

COURSES

Many people come to Italy to study the language. Courses are run by private schools and universities throughout the country and are a great way to learn Italian while enjoying the opportunity to live in an Italian city or town.

Among the cheapest options is the Università per Stranieri in Perugia (☎ 075 5 74 61), where the cost per month is L350,000 (at a private school in Roma you can expect to pay a minimum of L800,000). Individual schools and universities are listed under the relevant towns throughout this book. The schools can usually also arrange accommodation in a student residence or with an Italian family. Inquire about extracurricular or full-time courses in painting, art history, sculpture and architecture; however, all these courses can be expensive.

The Istituto Italiano di Cultura (IIC), which has branches all over the world, is a government-sponsored organisation aimed at promoting Italian culture and language.

They put on classes in Italian and provide a library and information service. This is a good place to start your search for places to study in Italy. Try the IIC's Web sites at www.iicmelau.org (Australia), www.iictoca.org/istituto.htm (Canada), www.italynet.com/cultura/istcult (France) and www.italcultny.org (USA). IIC branches include:

Australia
(☎ 03-9866 5931) 233 Domain Rd, South Yarra, Melbourne, Victoria 3141
(☎ 02-9392 7939) Level 45, The Gateway, 1 Macquarie Place, Sydney, NSW 2000
Belgium
(☎ 02-538 7704) rue de Livourne 38, 1000 Brussels
Canada
(☎ 514-849 3473) 1200 Penfield Drive, Montreal, Quebec H3A 1A9
(☎ 416-921 3802) 496 Huron St, Toronto, Ontario M5R 2R3
France
(☎ 01 44 39 49 39) Hôtel Galliffet, 50 rue de Varenne, Paris 75007
Germany
(☎ 030-261 78 75) Hildebrandstrasse 1, 10785 Berlin
(☎ 089-76 45 63) Hermann Schmid Strasse 8, 80336 Munich
Ireland
(☎ 01-676 6662) 11 Fitzwilliam Square, Dublin 2
Japan
(☎ 03-3264 6011) 2-1-30 Kudan Minami, Chiyoda-ku, Tokyo 102
Switzerland
(☎ 01-202 4846) Gotthardstrasse 27, 8002 Zurich
USA
(☎ 310-443 3250) 1023 Hildegard Ave, Los Angeles, CA 90024
(☎ 212-879 4242) 686 Park Ave, New York, NY 10021-5009
(☎ 202-387 5261) 1717 Massachussets Ave NW, S104, Washington, DC 20036

Another option is to check with travel agencies in your country for organised study tours to Italy. In England, Italian Study Tours (☎ 020-7916 7323, fax 7916 7327, email bonallack@compuserve.com), 35 Murray Mews, London NW1 9RH, runs courses in art and architecture, painting and cooking in

euro currency converter L10,000 = €5.16

a farmhouse near Lucca, in Toscana. Courses run in spring and autumn and cost around L835,000 for seven days, including food and accommodation. For full course details check out the Italian Study Tours Web site at www.vallicorte.demon.co.uk.

Cookery courses are becoming increasingly popular and can be an excellent, if expensive, introduction to the local cuisine. In Roma, published cookery writer Diane Seed (☎ 06 679 71 03, fax 06 679 71 09) runs seven-day nonresidential courses for L1,400,000, including lessons in shopping and olive oil tasting.

For the hefty sum of L5,900,000 you can learn the art of Tuscan cuisine in a 9th century former monastery in the Chianti area with Lorenza de Medici (☎ 0577 74 94 98, fax 0577 74 92 35, email cuisineint@aol .com) – and you get to sleep in a monk's cell to boot.

The more adventurous traveller might want to take a course in rock climbing, ski mountaineering or hang-gliding, just to name a few of the possibilities. Mountainguide groups offering courses are listed in the Alpine sections of the northern Italy chapters, or you can always get information from local tourist offices in the relevant areas.

WORK
It is illegal for non-EU citizens to work in Italy without a permesso di lavoro (work permit), but trying to obtain one can be time-consuming. EU citizens are allowed to work in Italy, but they still need to obtain a permesso di soggiorno (residence permit) from the main questura in the town, ideally before they look for employment. See Work Permits and Permesso di Soggiorno in the Visas & Documents section earlier in this chapter for more information. New immigration laws require foreign workers to be 'legalised' through their employers, which can apply even to cleaners and babysitters. The employers then pay pension and health-insurance contributions. This doesn't mean, however, that there aren't employers willing to take people without the right papers.

Work options depend on a number of factors – location, length of stay, nationality and qualifications, for example – but, in the major cities at least, job possibilities for English speakers can be surprisingly plentiful. Go armed with a CV (if possible in Italian) and be persistent. Research potential employers before going to Italy; however, expect to have to follow up any speculative written applications with a visit once you have arrived.

Jobs are advertised in local newspapers and magazines, such as *Porta Portese* (published on Tuesday and Friday) or *Wanted in Rome* (fortnightly) in Roma, or *Secondamano* in Milano, and you can also place an ad yourself.

A very useful guide is *Living, Studying and Working in Italy* by Travis Neighbour & Monica Larner. You could also have a look at *Work Your Way Around the World* by Susan Griffith.

Nannying & Au Pair Work
Babysitting is a good possibility, and in the major cities you can try to pick up a summer job accompanying a family on their annual beach holiday. Look in magazines such as *Wanted in Rome*, or even place an advertisement. Another option is au pair work, organised before you come to Italy. A useful guide is *The Au Pair and Nanny's Guide to Working Abroad* by S Griffith & S Legg.

English Tutoring
The most obvious source of work for foreigners is teaching English, but even with full qualifications an American, Australian, Canadian or New Zealander might find it difficult to secure a permanent position. Most of the larger, more reputable language schools will hire only people with a permesso di lavoro, but their attitude can become more flexible if the demand for teachers is high and they come across someone with good qualifications. The more professional schools will require a TEFL (Teaching English as a Foreign Language) certificate. It is advisable to apply for work early in the year, in order to be considered for positions

available in October (language-school years correspond roughly to the Italian school year: late September to the end of June).

There are numerous schools throughout the country that hire people without a valid permesso or qualifications, but the pay is usually low (around L15,000 an hour). It is more lucrative to teach private students. Rates, however, can vary hugely: in a large city like Roma, the average rate is around L30,000, while in smaller provincial towns, where the market is more limited, even qualified private teachers will have to charge as low as L15,000 to L20,000 in order to attract students. Although you can get away with absolutely no qualifications or experience, it might be a good idea to bring along a few English grammar books (including exercises) to help you at least appear professional.

Most people get started by placing advertisements in English-language bookshops and churches, on university notice boards or in the local press.

Bar Work

A good option is to look for employment in a bar, nightclub or restaurant during the tourist season. The plethora of Irish pubs that have sprung up in Italy recently is a good starting point.

Street Performing

Busking is common in Italy, although theoretically buskers require a municipal permit. Italians tend not to stop and gather around street performers, but they are usually quite generous.

Other Work

Freelance translation work is a possibility if you have good Italian and access to a word processor. Advertise in a local paper or contact the local agencies (listed in the phone directory). People with secretarial skills and a good knowledge of Italian sometimes manage to pick up part or full-time secretarial work with international companies in the major cities. Look in the local papers for advertisements.

There are plenty of markets around the country where you can set up a stall and sell your wares, although you may need to pay a fee. Selling goods on the street is illegal unless you have a municipal permit, and it is quite common to see municipal police moving people along. Another option is to head for beach resorts in summer, particularly if you have handicrafts or jewellery you want to sell.

ACCOMMODATION

Prices for accommodation quoted in this book are intended as a guide only. There is generally a fair degree of fluctuation in hotel prices throughout Italy, depending on the season and whether establishments raise prices when they have the opportunity. It is not unusual for prices to remain fixed for years on end, (and in some cases they even go down), but it is more common that they rise by around 5 or 10% annually.

In budget hotels it can sometimes be worth bargaining. Try mentioning the names of a few close competitors and see how the owner miraculously finds an identical room at half the original price.

Reservations

It is a good idea to book a room if you're planning to travel during peak tourist times such as summer, Easter or Christmas. Hotels usually require confirmation by fax or letter, as well as a deposit. Fax numbers for larger hotels in major cities are listed in this book. Staff at tourist offices will generally send out information about hotels, camping, apartments and so on, if you need more choice than we provide. Another option is to use one of the local hotel-booking services – you'll find some listed under Places to Stay in Roma and Firenze.

Camping

Most camping facilities in Italy are major complexes with swimming pools, tennis courts, restaurants and supermarkets. Like hotels, they are graded according to a star system. Prices at even the most basic camp sites can be surprisingly expensive during the peak periods, once you add up the various charges for each person and for a site for your tent or caravan and a car, but they can generally still work out cheaper than a double room in a one star hotel. Charges range from L8000 to L18,000 per adult, L6000 to L15,000 for children aged under 12, and L10,000 to L20,000 for a site. You'll also often have to pay to park your car and there is sometimes a charge for use of the showers (usually around L2000).

Locations are usually good, ranging from beach or lakeside to valleys in the Alpi. In major cities, camp sites are often a long way from the historic centres, and the inconvenience, plus the additional cost of using public transport, should be weighed up against the price of a hotel room.

Independent camping is generally not permitted in protected areas and you might find yourself disturbed during the night by the carabinieri if you attempt it. But, out of the main tourist season, independent campers who choose spots not visible from the road, who don't light fires and do try to be inconspicuous shouldn't have too much trouble. Always get permission from the landowner if you want to camp on private property. Camper vans are very popular in Italy (see Car & Motorcycle in the Getting Around chapter for details on hiring them).

Full lists of camp sites in and near cities and towns are usually available from local tourist offices. The tourist boards of Sicilia and Sardegna publish annual booklets listing all facilities on the islands. TCI publishes an annual book listing all camp sites in Italy, *Campeggi in Italia* (L32,000), and the Istituto Geografico de Agostini publishes the annual *Guida ai Campeggi in Europa*, sold together with *Guida ai Campeggi in Italia* (L29,900). These books are available in major bookshops in Italy.

Hostels

Ostelli per la gioventù (youth hostels) are run by the Associazione Italiana Alberghi per la Gioventù (AIG), which is affiliated to Hostelling International (HI). An HI card is not always required, but it is recommended that you have one. For details on how to get a card see Hostel Card in the Visas & Documents section earlier in this chapter. Pick up a booklet on Italian hostels, with details of prices, locations and so on, from the AIG national head office (☎ 06 487 11 52, email aig@uni.net), Via Cavour 44, Roma. Their Web sites at www.travel.it/hostels and www.hostels-aig.org explain all the facilities on offer.

Many Italian hostels are beautifully located, some in castles and villas. Many have bars and with few exceptions they have restaurants or kitchens (for self-catering) or both. Nightly rates vary from L13,000 to L24,000, which often includes breakfast. If not, breakfast will cost around L2000. In some hostels there is an extra charge for use of heating and hot water, usually around L1000. A meal will cost from L14,000.

Accommodation is in segregated dormitories, although some hostels offer family rooms (at a higher price per person).

Hostels are usually closed between 9 am and 3.30 pm, although there are many exceptions. Check-in is from 6 to 10.30 pm, although some hostels will allow you a morning check-in before they close for the day (it is best to find out beforehand). Curfew is usually 10.30 or 11 pm in winter and 11.30 pm or midnight in summer. It is usually necessary to pay before 9 am on the day of your departure, otherwise you could be charged for another night.

Pensioni & Alberghi

It is very important to remember that prices quoted in this book are intended as a guide only. *Alberghi* (hotels) and pensioni are allowed to increase their prices twice a year, although many don't. Travellers should always check on prices before deciding to stay. Make a complaint to the local tourist office if you believe you're being overcharged. Remember that many proprietors employ various methods of bill-padding, such as charging for showers or making breakfast compulsory.

There is often no difference between a pensione and an albergo; in fact, some hotels use both titles. However, a pensione will generally be of one to three star quality, while an albergo can be awarded up to five stars. *Locande* (inns) and *affittacamere* (rooms for rent), also known as *alloggi*, are generally cheaper, but not always. Locande and affittacamere are not included in the star classification system, although in some areas (such as the Isole Eolie and the Alpi) the standard of affittacamere is very high.

While the quality of accommodation can vary a great deal, one-star alberghi/pensioni tend to be very basic and usually do not have a private bathroom attached to rooms. Standards at two-star places are often only slightly better, but rooms will generally have a private bathroom. Once you arrive at three stars you can assume that standards will be reasonable, although quality still varies dramatically. Four and five-star hotels are usually part of a chain and offer facilities such as room service, laundry and dry-cleaning.

Overall, prices are highest in Roma, Firenze, Milano and Venezia, and at other major tourist destinations. They also tend to be higher in northern Italy. Prices can soar in the high season at beach resorts and during the ski season in the Alpi.

A *camera singola* (single room) is uniformly expensive in Italy, costing from around L40,000. A *camera doppia* (double room with twin beds) and a *camera matrimoniale* (double room with a double bed) cost from around L65,000. It is much cheaper to share with two or more people. In most parts of Italy, proprietors will charge no more than 15% of the cost of a double room for each additional person.

Tourist offices have booklets listing all local pensioni and 'alberghi, including prices (although they might not always be up-to-date). Ask for lists of the locande and affittacamere.

Agriturismo

This is a holiday on a working farm and is becoming increasingly popular in Italy. Traditionally, the idea was that families rented out rooms in their farmhouses, and it is still possible to find this type of accommodation. However, more commonly now the term refers to a restaurant in a restored farm complex with rooms available for rent. All agriturismo establishments are operating farms and you will usually be able to sample the local produce.

Agriturismo is quite well organised in Trentino-Alto Adige, Toscana and Umbria, and increasingly so in parts of Sicilia and Sardegna. Local tourist offices will usually have information. For detailed information on all agriturismo facilities in Italy contact Agriturist (☎ 06 68 52 33 37), Corso Vittorio Emanuele 89, 00186 Roma. It publishes a book with agriturismo listings for the whole country (L40,000), available at the office and in selected bookshops.

Rifugi

If you are planning to walk in the Alpi, Appennini or other mountains in Italy, obtain information on the network of rifugi. The various kinds of rifugi are detailed in the relevant Alpine sections of the northern Italy chapters. It should be noted that most are only open from July to September.

Accommodation is generally in dormitories, but some of the larger rifugi have double rooms. The price per person for an overnight stay plus breakfast varies from around L18,000 to around L40,000 (more if you are staying in a double room). Meals are always available, but a hearty post-walking dinner will set you back about L40,000. Note that the average price of a bottle of mineral water is around L4000 and the beer will be the highest in price that you have ever come across.

The locations of rifugi are marked on good walking maps. Some are close to chair lifts and cable-car stations, which means they are usually expensive and crowded with tourists. Others are at high altitude, involving hours of hard walking or climbing from the nearest village or another rifugio. These tend to be a little bit cheaper and, in general, are used by serious walkers and mountaineers. It is important to book a bed in advance, otherwise you could end up walking for an unplanned extra few hours to the next one. Additional information, including telephone numbers, can be obtained from local tourist offices.

Religious Institutions

Known as *casa religiosa per l'ospitalità*, these institutions offer accommodation in major cities and in many monasteries in the country. The standard is usually good, but prices are no longer low. You can expect to pay about the same as for a one star hotel, if not more. Information can be obtained through local tourist offices or through the archdiocese of the relevant city. The Associazione Cattolica al Servizio della Giovane (or Protezione della Giovane) can organise accommodation for women in hostels. The organisation has offices in most major towns and often at major train stations, although these can be open at irregular hours.

Student Accommodation

People planning to study in Italy can usually organise accommodation through the school or university they will be attending. Options include a room with an Italian family or a share arrangement with other students in an independent apartment. Some Italian universities operate a *casa dello studente*, which houses Italian students throughout the school year and lets out rooms during the summer break (July to the end of September). It can be very difficult to organise a room in one of these institutions. The best way is to attempt to book through your own university or to contact the relevant Italian university directly.

Landmark Trust

If you fancy staying in the building where the poet Keats died, one of Palladio's villas or the poet Browning's house, contact the Landmark Trust in the UK. Established as a charity in 1965, the trust restores and conserves a host of architectural marvels in the UK, as well as three in Italy: the 3rd floor apartment where Keats died in Piazza di Spagna, Roma; the Casa Guidi in Firenze, where Browning lived; and the Villa Sara-

ceno near Vicenza, an early Palladio commission. For any further information contact the Landmark Trust (☎ 01628-825925), Shottesbrooke, Maidenhead, Berkshire SL6 3SW, UK.

Rental Accommodation

Finding rental accommodation in the major cities can be difficult and time-consuming, but not impossible. There are rental agencies that will assist, for a fee (some agencies are listed under major cities). Rental rates are higher for short-term leases. A small apartment anywhere near the centre of Roma will cost around L1,800,000 a month and it is usually necessary to pay a deposit (generally at least one month in advance). Apartments and villas for rent are listed in local publications such as the weekly *Porta Portese* and fortnightly *Wanted in Rome* in Roma. You will find that many owners want to rent to foreigners because the let is short term or because they intend to charge a high rent. Another option is to answer an advertisement in any of the local publications to share an apartment.

In major resort areas, such as the Isole Eolie and other parts of Sicilia, the coastal areas of Sardegna and in the Alpi, the tourist offices have lists of local apartments and villas for rent. Most offices will be more than cooperative if you telephone beforehand for information on how to book an apartment.

People wanting to rent a villa in the countryside can seek information from specialist travel agencies in their own country or contact an organisation in Italy directly. One of the major companies in Italy is Cuendet, which has villas in Toscana, Umbria, the Veneto, Roma, Le Marche, the Costiera Amalfitana, Puglia, Sicilia and Sardegna. This reliable company publishes a booklet listing all the villas in its files, with photos of most of them. Prices for a villa for four to six people range from around US$400 a week in winter up to US$1200 a week in August. For details, write to Cuendet & Cie spa (☎ 0577 57 63 30, fax 0577 30 11 93, email cuede@tin.it),

Strada di Strove 17, 53035 Monteriggioni, Siena. They also have a Web site at www.cuendet.com. In the UK, you can order Cuendet's catalogues and make reservations by calling ☎ 0800 891573 toll free. In the USA, Cuendet bookings are handled by Rentals in Italy (☎ 805 987 5278, fax 482 7976), 1742 Calle Corva, Camarillo, CA 93010.

CIT offices throughout the world have lists of villas and apartments available for rent in Italy. Alternatively, in Australia, try an organisation called Cottages & Castles (☎ 03-9853 1142, fax 9853 0509, email cottages@vicnet.net.au), 11 Laver St, Kew 3101, Victoria.

Don't expect to land in Italy and find an apartment or villa immediately: unless you are staying for an indefinite period, you might find that your holiday is taken up with flat-hunting.

FOOD

Eating is one of life's great pleasures for Italians. Be adventurous and don't ever be intimidated by eccentric waiters or indecipherable menus and you will find yourself agreeing with the locals that nowhere in the world is the food as good as in Italy – and, more specifically, as in their own town. See the Regional Cuisines special section for information on how Italian food varies from region to region. For an extensive glossary of food and culinary terms, see the Language chapter at the end of this book.

Restaurants

These fall into several categories. A *tavola calda* (literally 'hot table') usually offers cheap, pre-prepared meat, pasta and vegetable dishes in a self-service style. A *pizzeria* will of course serve pizza, but usually also has a full menu. An *osteria* is likely to be either a wine bar offering a small selection of dishes, or a small *trattoria*. A trattoria is basically a cheaper version of a *ristorante* (restaurant), which in turn generally has a wider selection of dishes and a higher standard of service. The problem is that many of the establishments that are in

fact restaurants call themselves trattorie and vice versa for reasons best known to themselves. It is best to check the menu, usually posted by the door, for prices.

Don't judge the quality of a ristorante or trattoria by its appearance. You are likely to eat your most memorable meal at a place with plastic tablecloths in a tiny backstreet, a dingy piazza or on a back road in the country. And don't panic if you find yourself in a trattoria that has no printed menu: they are often the ones that offer the best and most authentic food and have menus which change daily to accommodate the availability of fresh produce. Just hope that the waiter will patiently explain the dishes and cost.

Most eating establishments have a cover charge (usually from around L2000 to L3000) and a service charge of 10 to 15%. Restaurants usually open for lunch from 12.30 to 3 pm, but many are not keen to take orders after 2 pm. In the evening, opening hours vary from north to south. In the north, dinner starts at around 7.30 pm, but on Sicilia you will be hard-pressed to find a restaurant open before 8.30 pm.

Many restaurants offer tourist menus, with an average price of between L20,000 and L30,000 (usually not including drinks). Generally the food is of a reasonable standard, but choices will be limited and you can usually get away with paying less if you want only pasta, salad and wine.

Bars & Ice-Cream Parlours

Round off the meal with a *gelato* (ice cream) from a *gelateria* – a crowd outside is always a good sign – followed by a *digestivo* (digestive liqueur) or *caffè* at a bar. Most bars also serve *cornetti* (croissants), *panini* (rolls) and sweets and chocolate.

Fast Food & Takeaways

There are numerous outlets where you can buy pizza *al taglio* (by the slice). You could also try one of the *alimentari* (grocery stores) and ask them to make a panino with the filling of your choice.

[continued on page 132]

REGIONAL CUISINES

What the world regards as Italian cooking is really a collection of regional *cucine* (cuisines). Cooking styles continue to vary notably from region to region and significantly between the north and south. In the north the food is rich and often creamy, while in the south it becomes hotter and spicier and the *dolci* (cakes and pastries) are sweeter and more substantial. Here is a brief look at the specialities of the regions covered in this guide.

Emilia-Romagna The regional specialities of Emilia-Romagna, including *tagliatelle al ragù* (and its adaptation, *spaghetti bolognese*), *lasagne* and *tortellini*, are among the best-known Italian dishes abroad. Parma is the home of the best *prosciutto* (cured ham) and also of *parmigiano reggiano* (parmesan cheese).

Liguria The cuisine of this coastal region makes good use of the products of the Mediterraneo: fresh herbs, olive oil and seafood. Culinary specialities include *pesto*, a delicious uncooked pasta sauce of fresh basil, garlic, oil, pine nuts and cheese, ground together with a mortar and pestle. Also try the *farinata*, a tart made with chickpea flour, and the *focaccia*, a flat bread.

Piemonte In Piemonte the cuisine is influenced to some extent by nearby France. It is often delicate and always flavoursome. *Tartufo bianco* (white truffle) is used in a wide variety of dishes. Traditional specialities make good use of game birds and animals, including chamois, pheasant and quail, as well as more unusual meats, such as horse, donkey and frog (there is even such a dish as frog *risotto*).

Trentino-Alto Adige The cuisine in this region has quite a heavy Austrian influence, and alongside *minestrone* and *spaghetti* you will find *canerdeli* (a soup with noodles in it), *goulash* soup and *Wiener schnitzel*. Local specialities include smoked meats, which are eaten with heavy, black-rye bread.

Il Veneto This region is renowned for its boiled meats and the *radicchio trevisano* (bitter red lettuce), eaten baked, in *risotto* or with pasta. *Risotto* comes in many varieties in Il Veneto: with mushrooms, zucchini (courgettes), sausage, quail, trout and other seafood, chicken and spring vegetables. Not to be missed is *risotto nero*, coloured and flavoured with the ink of squid. The popular dolce *tiramisù* comes from this region.

Toscana Here, as in neighbouring Umbria, the locals use a lot of olive oil and herbs, and regional specialities are noted for their simplicity, fine flavour and the use of fresh produce. Try *bistecca fiorentina*, a huge T-bone steak usually 3 to 4cm thick. It is quite acceptable, and in fact advisable, to order one steak for two people. Among the staples of

JOHN HAY

JOHN HAY

JON DAVISON

BETHUNE CARMICHAEL

JON DAVISON

From fresh cheese direct from the shepherd and lamb alfresco to Sicilian gelato and the ubiquitous pizza and all that falls in-between, Italian food is regarded as one of the finest cuisines in the world.

One of the best ways to savour the Italian way of life is to head to the local market, pick up some fresh produce, find a park, relax under a tree and enjoy.

Nonna Rosa's Lasagne

Ingredients (for four people):
For the pasta:
  3 eggs
  plain flour
For the filling:
  200g minced meat
  1 400g tin chopped tomatoes
  1 small onion, chopped
  1 clove garlic, chopped
  125g mozzarella, sliced
  100g parmesan, grated
  2 tablespoons olive oil
For the béchamel sauce:
  25g plain flour
  40g butter
  425ml milk
  salt and pepper to taste

Method:
To make the pasta, beat the eggs in a basin and add the flour, stirring and then kneading the mixture to form a dough. Roll out the dough into thin sheets and cut into wide strips. Boil the strips three or four at a time in salted water for approximately 1½ minutes (or until the pasta rises to the surface). Remove the pasta and spread on a cloth to dry.

Next, fry the minced meat with the onion and garlic, then add the tomato, salt to taste and allow to cook for about 45 minutes. To make the béchamel, place the butter, flour, milk and seasoning together in a separate pan over a medium heat and stir until the sauce begins to thicken. Continue to stir vigorously for a couple of minutes, then turn the heat down low and allow to cook for six minutes.

In a baking dish layer the ingredients as follows: tomato sauce, pasta, mozzarella, béchamel, parmesan, pasta, tomato sauce, béchamel, pasta, tomato sauce, béchamel, parmesan. Cook for 20 minutes at 180°C/350°F and serve immediately.

Tuscan cuisine are small white *cannellini* beans, although all types of beans are widely used. There is also a wide range of soups, from the simple *acquacotta*, which translates as 'cooked water', to the rich *minestrone alla fiorentina*, flavoured with pork and chicken giblets. Don't miss the incredibly rich *panforte*, Siena's famous Christmas fruitcake.

Umbria In Umbria both the *tartufo* and *porcini* mushrooms (like the French *cèpes*) are abundant: both turn up in pasta, rice and a large number of other dishes. While many Umbrian dishes are based upon vegetables, the locals eat more meat than other Italians. A local speciality is *porchetta*, a whole roast piglet stuffed with rosemary. Umbrian cakes and pastries are worth a try, as are the chocolates produced by the Perugina factory at Perugia, notably the famous *baci* (chocolate-coated hazelnuts).

Lazio The cuisine in this region sits heavily on the stomach but is no less mouthwatering for all that. Traditional pasta dishes include *spaghetti carbonara* (with egg yolk, cheese and bacon) and *alla matriciana* (with a sauce of tomato, bacon and a touch of chilli). Offal is popular in Roma – if you can stomach it, try the pasta *pajata*, made with the entrails of very young veal, which are considered a delicacy since they contain the mother's congealed milk.

Campania Napoli is home to that most famous of Italian dishes, the pizza. Though the Romans hotly contest the supremacy of their own version (thin and crispy), the general consensus is that Neapolitan pizza *is* the best. Don't miss the *melanzane parmigiana* (eggplant layered with a tomato sauce and mozzarella and baked), another classic Neapolitan dish. A favourite *dolce* (dessert) in Napoli is *sfogliatelle*, layers of fine pastry with a ricotta filling.

Puglia The cuisine here is simple and hearty, featuring a lot of vegetables. Try the *orecchiette* (pasta in the shape of 'little ears') with a sauce of sautéed green vegetables. Another popular local dish is made from puréed broad beans topped with chicory. The Pugliesi also eat a lot of seafood.

Sicilia The focus on Sicilia is on seafood and fresh produce. Try the *pesce spada* (swordfish), which is usually sliced into thick steaks and cooked on an open grill. Pasta *con le sarde* (with sardines) is a speciality in Palermo. Eggplant is popular on Sicilia, turning up in pasta or as *melanzane alla siciliana*, filled with olives, anchovies, capers and tomato.

The Sicilians are masters when it comes to their dolci. Don't leave the island without trying *cassata*, a rich sponge cake filled with a cream of ricotta cheese, liqueur and candied fruits. Another speciality is *cannoli*, tubes of sweet pastry filled with a rich cream, often made from a mixture of cream cheese, honey and almond paste with pieces of candied fruit. Also try the assortment of *paste di mandorle* (almond pastries) and the *zabaione*, native to Marsala. Another speciality is

---

Tiramisù

This simple *dolce* (dessert) translates as 'pick me up' – and it really does!

Ingredients (for four people):
  400g savoyard biscuits (ladies' fingers)
  2 egg yolks
  60g caster sugar
  200g mascarpone
  6 small cups of espresso coffee,
    sweetened
  cocoa powder

Method:
Beat the yolks with the sugar, add the mascarpone and stir to obtain a creamy mixture. Layer the bottom of a dish with savoyard biscuits dipped in the sweetened coffee and cover with a layer of the creamy mixture, followed by a sprinkling of cocoa. Repeat the procedure, finishing with the layer of creamy mixture and cocoa. Place in the refrigerator and leave to sit for at least two hours before serving.

Pasta

Pasta is the mainstay of the Italian diet and the common element in a land of culinary diversity. Italian pasta is infinitely varied. It is divided into two types, *lunga* (long), such as *spaghetti* and *linguine*, and *corta* (short), including *penne* and *rigatoni* (tube shaped), *conchiglie* (shell shaped), *farfalle* (literally 'butterflies'), *fusilli* (corkscrew shaped) and

Farfalle

many others. The correct match of pasta type and sauce is as important as the quality of the sauce itself.

Ravioli

Packet, or dried pasta, is made with high-quality durum wheat and water. Pasta *all'uovo* or *fatto a mano* (fresh egg pasta), on the other hand, is made with eggs and flour and is used to make stuffed pasta such as *tortellini* and *ravioli*, or is cut into strips and called *tagliatelle* (thinner strips are also called *taglionini* or *tagliarini*). Egg pasta is usually served with richer, creamier sauces than those that usually accompany dried pasta, which are most likely to be tomato based.

Pasta-sauce ingredients traditionally vary quite dramatically between the north and south of the country. In the north, sauces are richer, often creamy and frequently use red meat (such as in the delicious *ragù* of Bologna, known outside Italy as *bolognese*), while, as you head farther

Gnocchetti

south, they tend to contain more vegetables and, on the coast, lots of seafood.

Conchiglie

Freshly grated cheese is the magic ingredient for most pasta. *Parmigiano* is the most widely used cheese, particularly in the north. Look for the words '*parmigiano reggiano*' on the rind, because there is also the similar, but lower-quality, *grana padano*. On Sardegna and around Roma there is a tendency to use the sharp *pecorino*, an aged sheep's cheese, while *ricotta salata* (salted ricotta) is widely used in the south and on Sicilia.

Cooking good pasta is no mean feat. First, the pasta has to be of the highest quality, and second, it has to be cooked for precisely the correct length of time, so that it is *al dente* (literally 'to the teeth', or with a bite to it). Italians almost always add salt to the boiling water before adding the pasta and they never throw in the pasta until everyone is present. Don't complain if your pasta takes a while to arrive when you are in a restaurant – you'll need to wait the 10 to 12 minutes it takes to cook.

Fusilli

ILLUSTRATIONS BY TRUDI CANAVAN

marzapane (marzipan), which Sicilian pastry chefs whip into every imaginable shape. Sicilian *gelato* (ice cream) is absolutely heavenly.

Sardegna One of the island's best-known dishes is *porcheddu*, baby pig roasted on a spit. Try the *carte musica*, a thin, crisp bread eaten warm and sprinkled with salt and oil. *Pecorino sardo* is a sharp, aged sheep's cheese which the Sardi sprinkle on pasta instead of *parmigiano*.

Stand or Sit?

Remember that as soon as you sit down in Italy prices go up considerably, since you have to pay for the service. A *cappuccino* at the bar will cost from around L1200 to L1500, but if you sit down you will pay anything from L2500 to L8000, and more than L12,000 on Piazza San Marco in Venezia. Italians rarely sit down in bars and, consequently, many bars do not even have seating. In some bars where it is obvious that no-one is serving the tables, you can sometimes sit down without paying extra.

[continued from page 127]

Fast food is becoming increasingly popular in Italy. There are McDonald's outlets throughout the country, along with other chain restaurants and hamburger joints.

Vegetarian

Vegetarians will have no problems eating in Italy. While there are very few restaurants devoted to them, vegetables are a staple of the Italian diet. Most eating establishments serve a good selection of *antipasti* (starters) and *contorni* (vegetables prepared in a variety of ways) and the farther south you go, the more excellent vegetable dishes you will find. Vegetarian restaurants and alimentari are listed throughout this book.

Self-Catering

If you have access to cooking facilities, it is best to buy fruit and vegetables at markets (usually open in the mornings only), and salami, cheese and wine at alimentari or *salumerie*, which are a cross between a grocery store and a delicatessen. Fresh bread is available at a *forno* or *panetteria* (bakeries that sell bread, pastries and sometimes groceries) and usually at alimentari. At a *pasticceria* you can buy pastries, cakes and biscuits. A *rosticceria* sells cooked meats. There are also supermarkets in most towns

and these are listed in the relevant sections throughout this book. Remember that most food shops close for lunch.

Eating Habits

Breakfast Italians rarely eat a sit-down *colazione* (breakfast). They tend to drink a cappuccino, usually *tiepido* (warm), and eat a cornetto or other type of pastry while standing at a bar.

Lunch *Pranzo* (lunch) is traditionally the main meal of the day and many shops and businesses close for three to four hours every afternoon to accommodate the meal and the siesta which is traditionally supposed to follow. A full meal will consist of an *antipasto* (starter), which can vary from *bruschetta*, a type of garlic bread with various toppings, to fried vegetables or *prosciutto e melone* (cured ham wrapped around melon). Next comes the *primo piatto*, a pasta or *risotto*, followed by the *secondo piatto* of meat or fish. Italians often then eat an *insalata* (salad) or *contorno* (vegetable side dish), and round off the meal with fruit, or occasionally with a *dolce* (dessert), and caffè, often at a bar on the way back to work.

Dinner *Cena* (the evening meal) was traditionally a simpler affair, but in recent years habits have been changing because of the inconvenience of travelling home for lunch every day.

In-Between Times In general, Italians are not big snackers, although it is not uncommon for them to have a quick bite – usually a *tramezzino* (sandwich), slice of pizza or *merendina* (cake or biscuit) – halfway through the morning or afternoon.

DRINKS
Nonalcoholic Drinks

Tea Italians don't drink a lot of *tè* (tea) and generally do so only in the late afternoon, when they might take a cup with a few *pasticcini* (small cakes). You can order tea in bars, although it will usually arrive in the form of a cup of warm water with an accompanying tea bag. If this doesn't suit your taste, ask for the water *molto caldo* (very hot) or *bollente* (boiling). The good-quality packaged teas, such as Twinings tea bags and leaves, as well as packaged herbal teas, such as camomile, are often sold in alimentari and sometimes in bars. You can find a wide range of herbal teas in an *erboristeria* (herbalist's shop); these sometimes also stock health foods.

Granita *Granita* is a drink made of crushed ice with fresh lemon or other fruit juices, or with coffee topped with whipped cream.

Water Despite the fact that tap water is reliable throughout the country, most Italians prefer to drink bottled *acqua minerale* (mineral water). This is available either *frizzante* (sparkling) or *naturale* (still) and you will be asked in restaurants and bars which you prefer. If you just want a glass of tap water, you should ask for *acqua dal rubinetto*, although simply asking for *acqua naturale* will also suffice.

Alcoholic Drinks

Wine & Spirits *Vino* (wine) is an essential accompaniment to any meal, and *digestivi* (liqueurs) are a popular way to end one. Italians are very proud of their wines and find it hard to believe that anyone else in the world could produce wines as good as theirs. Many Italians drink only alcohol with meals and the foreign custom of going out for a drink is still considered unusual, although in some parts of Italy it is common to see men starting their day with a *grappa* for breakfast and continuing to consume strong drinks throughout the day.

Wine is reasonably priced and you will rarely pay more than L15,000 for a good bottle of wine, although prices go up to more than L30,000 for really good quality. There are three main classifications of wine – DOCG (*denominazione d'origine controllata e garantita*), DOC (*denominazione di origine controllata*) and *vino da tavola* (table wine) – which will be marked on the label. A DOC wine is produced subject to certain specifications, although the label

Caffè Society

The first-time visitor to Italy is likely to be confused by the many ways in which the locals consume their caffeine.

An *espresso* is a small amount of very strong black coffee. If you want more to drink, you can ask for a *doppio espresso*, which will be 'double' the amount, or a *caffè lungo* (literally 'long coffee', although this can sometimes mean a slightly diluted espresso). If you want a long black coffee (as in a weaker, watered-down version), ask for a *caffè Americano*. If you are in an isolated village on Sardegna where they have no name for diluted coffee, try asking for an *espresso con molta acqua calda* (coffee with a lot of hot water). A *corretto* is an espresso with a dash of *grappa* or some other spirit, and a *macchiato* is espresso with a small amount of milk – on the other hand, *latte macchiato* is milk with a spot of coffee. *Caffè freddo* is a long glass of cold black coffee.

Then, of course, there is *cappuccino* – coffee with hot, frothy milk. If you want it without the froth, ask for a *caffè latte* or a *cappuccino senza schiuma* (without froth). Italians tend to drink cappuccino only with breakfast and during the morning. They never drink it after meals or in the evening, so if you order one after dinner, don't be surprised if the waiter asks you two or three times, just to make sure that he or she heard correctly. You will also find it difficult to convince bartenders to make your cappuccino hot rather than lukewarm. Ask for it *molto caldo* and wait for the same 'tut-tut' response that you attracted when you ordered a cappuccino after dinner.

does not certify quality. DOCG is subject to the same requirements as normal DOC but it is also tested by government inspectors. While there are table wines better left alone, there are also many that are of excellent quality, notably the Sicilian Corvo red and white.

Although some excellent wines are produced in Italy, most trattorie stock only a limited selection of bottled wines and generally only cheaper varieties. Most people tend to order the *vino della casa* (house wine) or the *vino locale* (local wine) when they go out to dinner.

The style of wine varies throughout the country, so make a point of sampling the local produce in your travels. Try the many varieties of the famous Chianti wines produced in Toscana, the white Vernaccia of San Gimignano, the excellent Brunello of Montalcino, the Vino Nobile of Montepulciano, the Soave in Verona and Valpolicella around Venezia. Piemonte and Trentino-Alto Adige both produce excellent wines, notably the Barolo in Piemonte. The wines of Orvieto in Umbria are good. In Roma try the local Frascati and other wines of the Castelli Romani. Sicilia is the home of Marsala.

Before dinner, Italians might drink a Campari and soda or a fruit cocktail, usually pre-prepared and often without alcohol. After dinner, try a shot of grappa, a very strong, clear brew made from grapes, or an *amaro*, a dark liqueur prepared from herbs. If you prefer a sweeter liqueur, try the almond-flavoured *amaretto* or the sweet aniseed *sambuca*. On the Costiera Amalfitana and the islands of the Golfo di Napoli, the fragrant local lemons are used to produce *limoncello*.

Beer The main local labels are Peroni, Dreher and Moretti, all very drinkable and cheaper than the imported varieties. If you want a local beer, ask for a *birra nazionale*, which will be either in a bottle or *alla spina* (on tap). Italy also imports beers from throughout Europe and the rest of the world. For example, all the main German beers are available in bottles or cans, English beers and Guinness are often found on tap in *birrerie* (bars specialising in beer), and Australians might be pleased to know that you can even find Foster's and Castlemaine XXXX. There has lately been a proliferation of pubs that specialise in beers from all around the world.

ENTERTAINMENT
Bars & Pubs
Italians cannot be said to have a 'drinking culture' but, in the bigger cities especially, you'll find plenty of bars all over. You can get a beer, wine or anything else at practically any bar, where you might just as likely have a cup of coffee. They range from workaday grungy through to chic places to be seen in. Those places operating first and foremost as nocturnal drinking establishments can be expected to stay open until about 1 am in most cases, sometimes later.

The Italian version of an Irish pub has taken off in a big way. Basically places where you can get Guinness on tap or select from a wide range of international beers, they are becoming more numerous by the month in major cities such as Roma, Firenze and Milano. Some pubs, in particular those where you are likely to meet up with other young foreigners, are listed under the major cities in this book.

Perhaps one reason why Italians don't tend to wander out of bars legless is the price of a drink. A tiny glass of beer can start at around L4000! For a pint you are looking at an average of L8000.

Discos & Clubs
Discos (what Brits think of as clubs, not necessarily some awful retro 80s scene) are expensive: entrance charges range from around L30,000 up to L100,000 for hotspots in places such as Rimini during the summer. This usually covers the cost of the first drink; after that you will pay up to L6000 just for a glass of wine. Venues are usually enormous, with big dance floors, and the music ranges from mainstream Top 40 fare to hip-hop, trip-hop and so on.

You'll find a wide assortment of smaller clubs and bars too, some of which have live music. Entrance fees vary from free to around L20,000.

Be aware that the Italians mean something far seedier by the word 'nightclub'.

Rock

The world's major performers are constantly passing through Italy on tour. Keep an eye on local newspapers. Information on the important venues and how to book tickets is listed under the major cities throughout the book.

Jazz

Italians love jazz and some of the numerous jazz venues are listed in the course of this book. The country's premier jazz festival is Umbria Jazz, held in Perugia in July and Orvieto in December/January.

Classical Music

The main concert seasons are usually during the winter months, although there are always plenty of classical music concerts included in major summer entertainment festivals, such as Roma's Estate Romana (see Special Events in the Roma chapter).

Cinemas

There is no shortage of cinemas in Italy, but quite a dearth of original-language ones. Even in a large city like Milano, only three or four cinemas show subtitled original-language movies, and then only once a week. The dubbing industry is justifiably proud in Italy, but that doesn't help foreigners who don't want to hear John Cleese spout Italian! The only other option in larger cities is the foreign cultural centres, which often put on film seasons. A cinema ticket costs up to L13,000 in a normal cinema, although this can come down to L6000 on the cheap day, which is often Wednesday.

Theatre

If you understand Italian, you'll have plenty of options in all the major cities. Performances in languages other than Italian are hard to come by, although in Roma the Agora has an international season. Tourist offices should be able to help out with information. In summer, there are performances of Greek theatre on Sicilia at Siracusa (biannually), Taormina, Segesta and Palazzolo Acreide. A ticket costs from L30,000 upwards. The future of the Siracusa event is under threat now, so check.

Opera

There are opera seasons in the major cities, including Roma, Milano, Palermo, Bologna and Venezia. In summer, there are special seasons at the Arena in Verona and in Piazza Siena in Roma. An opera is also usually performed as part of the Festival dei Due Monde at Spoleto in June and July. A ticket to the opera costs from L50,000 to more than L100,000 for better seats. At La Scala, in Milano, the top seats on opening night can go for L1,500,000!

SPECTATOR SPORTS
Motor Racing

Italy is one of the homes of prestige motor racing. The Italian Formula One Grand Prix races are held at the Monza race track, just north of Milano, each September. The San Marino Grand Prix (to all intents and purposes, if not technically, an Italian race) is held at the 5km Imola circuit in May.

Italy has provided some of the world's greatest driving machines. Ferrari, more than any other manufacturer, continues to dominate the Grand Prix in the popular imagination, even if it has not been in the winner's circle so often in recent years. Alfa Romeo has also been up there. For a while back in the 1950s, Maserati was on top, until the company ran into difficulties in 1958. Maserati has continued to contribute motors, as have Lamborghini and Lancia. Bugatti surfaced briefly in the 1950s, but never took line honours.

Monza has been a venue since 1922. Every few years the administrators of the circuit have to do battle with the Monza town authorities to renew the rent agreement. They did so in 1997, guaranteeing the

Goooooooooooaaaaaaaaaalllllll!

Il calcio excites Italian souls more than politics, religion, good food and dressing up all put together. Football (soccer) is one of the great forces in Italian life, so if you can get to one of the big games you'll be in for a treat. Tempers run high and at times overflow, and not just on the pitch either. Accusations that referees had favoured the 1998 championship winners, Torino-based Juventus, led to parliamentary punch-ups!

Italy's national team, the Azzuri (Blues) have long been one of the front-running teams (ranked 13th in the world), although ultimate success has been elusive in the past few World Cup contests. In 1998 they failed to make the finals and in the 1994 tussle in the USA they lost 3-2 on penalties to Brazil after an agonising 0-0 draw. Almost as frustrating for them in 1990, they managed to come in third by defeating England 2-1. However, Italy has picked up the World Cup three times, in 1934, 1938 and 1982.

On the home front, 18 teams tough out the Italian football honours in Serie A (the top division). Serie B consists of a further 20 teams, while another 90 teams dispute the medals at Serie C level, itself split up into several more manageable sub-competitions.

Predictably enough, Serie A is dominated by an elite group of *squadre* (teams) that generally take most of the silverware. To provide some idea of how a few teams monopolise the top honours, AC Milan has been champion in five of the last 11 seasons, and runner-up twice. Juventus took the laurels three times and came in second three times. Their closest rivals are Inter, with one *scudetto* (shield) and two second-places. After running neck and neck with Lazio in the final rounds of competition, AC Milan took the scudetto in 1999.

Of course, not everyone can be top all the time. At the close of the 1998-99 season, Inter had so disappointed its fans that at one stage they were howling for Brazilian captain Ronaldo's blood. Genova's Sampdoria did even worse. After 17 years as one of the top league's better teams, it was relegated to Serie B in 1999.

In between the World Cup and the local league there is a bewildering array of competitions and cups at both national and European level. The Coppa Italia (Italy Cup) is one of the most prestigious of these, and in 1999 five-times cup-winner Fiorentina was pipped at the post by Parma.

Whatever the form or place on the ladder of the various teams, some local derbies make for particularly hot clashes – for instance, when AC Milan and rivals Inter come face to face, or when Roma takes on Lazio. Both are traditionally excuses for a little sporting lunacy – with *tifosi* (fans) even more vociferous than usual.

Tickets for games start at around L20,000 for the lousiest positions and rise to well over L100,000. They are best purchased through specific ticketing agencies, some of which are listed in this guide; if not, staff at the local tourist office can tell you where to find them.

NICKY CAVEN

Modern-day gladiators: the stadium atmosphere at Serie A games is second to none.

Goooooooooooaaaaaaaaaalllllll!

The 18 teams in Serie A in 1999-2000 are as follows (with stadium details):

AC Milan
  Stadio Giuseppe Meazza/San Siro
  (☎ 02 487 07 123) Via Piccolomini 5,
  Milano
Bari
  Stadio San Nicola
  (☎ 080 505 51 44) Strada Torrebella, Bari
Bologna
  Stadio Renato dall'Ara
  (☎ 051 43 08 36) Via Andrea Costa 174,
  Bologna
Cagliari
  Stadio Sant'Elia
  (☎ 070 37 44 39) Via Vespucci,
  Borgo Sant'Elia, Cagliari
Fiorentina (Firenze)
  Stadio Artemio Franchi
  (☎ 055 58 78 58) Viale Manfredo Fanti 4/6,
  Firenze
Inter (FC Internazionale Milano)
  Stadio Giuseppe Meazza/San Siro
  (☎ 02 487 07 123) Via Piccolomini 5,
  Milano
Juventus (Torino)
  Stadio delle Alpi
  (☎ 011 739 57 59) Viale Grande Torino,
  Torino
Lazio
  Stadio Olimpico
  (☎ 06 3 68 51) Viale del Foro Italico, Roma
Lecce
  Stadio Via del Mare
  (☎ 0832 39 61 40) Via per San Cataldo,
  Lecce

Parma
  Stadio Ennio Tardini
  (☎ 0521 23 38 49) Viale Partigiani d'Italia 1,
  Parma
Perugia
  Stadio Renato Curi
  (☎ 075 500 66 42) Località Pian di
  Massiano, Perugia
Piacenza
  Stadio Galleana
  (☎ 0523 75 70 10) Via Gorra 25, Piacenza
Reggina (Reggio di Calabria)
  Stadio Oreste Granillo
  (☎ 0965 59 44 39) Via Galileo Galilei,
  Reggio di Calabria
Roma
  Stadio Olimpico
  (☎ 06 3 68 51) Viale del Foro Italico, Roma
Torino
  Stadio delle Alpi
  (☎ 011 738 00 81) Strada Altessano 131,
  10151 Torino
Udinese
  Stadio Friuli
  (☎ 0432 40 12 41) Piazzale Repubblica
  Argentina, Udine
Venezia
  Stadio Pierluigi Penzo
  (☎ 041 523 90 104) Isola Sant'Elena,
  Venezia
Verona
  Stadio Marc'Antonio Bentegodi
  (☎ 045 56 77 22) Piazzale Olimpia,
  Verona

Monza track as the exclusive site for Formula One racing into the new millennium.

Next to the present track is the crumbling reminder of more dangerous days: a circuit with slopes at such a steep gradient that it was the scene of enough accidents to convince all concerned it should be closed – it was last used in 1969. This dinosaur has long been destined for demolition, but as yet remains an intact, if overgrown, curio for bicycle riders doing more relaxed circuits of the adjacent Parco di Monza.

Tickets for the Monza Grand Prix go on

sale months in advance and cost up to L550,000 for a good seat in the grandstand; a spot on the grass costs L80,000. For ticket details, call the Monza track direct on ☎ 039 2 48 21, or a FIA Formula One Grand Prix organisation in your country.

The classic Italian motor race was the long-distance Mille Miglia, which took place annually (interrupted by WWII) from 1927 to 1957. Nowadays it's held as a nostalgic competition in which vintage racing cars career 1000 miles around Italy from Brescia to Roma and back again.

euro currency converter L10,000 = €5.16

Cycling

Second only to the Tour de France, the Giro d'Italia is *the* event on the summer cycling calendar. Little wonder, since Italy has a long record of producing world-class riders.

The race was first held in 1909 and has been staged every year since, interrupted predictably enough by WWI and WWII. It was initially a mostly Italian affair and the 1909 winner, Luigi Ganna, was followed by a long succession of local victors. Only in 1950 did a non-Italian finally break the home side's long winning streak, when the Swiss Hugo Koblet took the finishing-line honours. In total, the Giro has been won by non-Italians 24 times and by Italian riders 57 times. The latest Italian winner was Ivan Gotti in 1999.

This event is one of the few things in life that are free: if you want to watch, find out when the race is passing a location convenient to you and wait for the cyclists – it's as simple as that.

Skiing

Most people would probably rather do it than watch it, but skiing is something of a prestige spectator sport in Italy. Maybe that has something to do with the fact that Italy has had some stars who are particularly good at it.

For a decade, the brash Alberto Tomba (*'Tomba la bomba!'*, literally 'The bomb is falling!') dominated the world ski scene, despite (or because of) his off-piste antics. Before retiring in 1997, he won Olympic gold as well as the World Cup, but his performance was visibly sliding towards the end. Since his exit, Italian skiing has gone, if you'll pardon the expression, down hill.

Deborah Compagnoni and Isolde Kostner were world champions in 1997. Compagnoni had won five gold medals in her career, but both skiers were comprehensively outclassed in the 1999 World Cup. There was widespread speculation that Compagnoni was about ready to bow out of competition. Only Stefania Belmondo managed gold in the cross-country in an otherwise sad year for Italian skiing.

Several Italian ski fields host annual World Cup competitions. It doesn't cost anything to watch – just a fortune to find accommodation! Torino will witness world-class skiing in 2006 when it hosts the Winter Olympics.

SHOPPING

Shopping in Italy is probably not what you are used to back home. The vast majority of shops are small businesses: large department stores and supermarkets tend to be very thin on the ground. If you need necessities such as underwear, pantyhose, pyjamas, T-shirts and toiletries, head for one of the large retail stores, such as Standa, Upim, Oviesse or Rinascente. Otherwise, you can pick up underwear, pantyhose and pyjamas in a *merceria* (haberdashery), toiletries and condoms in a farmacia, a supermarket or sometimes in an alimentari, and items such as T-shirts in a normal clothing store. Hardware items can be purchased at a *ferramenta* (ironmonger's), and air-mail paper, notepads, pens and greeting cards at a *cartoleria* (paper-goods shop).

Clothing & Accessories

Italy is synonymous with elegant, fashionable and high-quality clothing. However, fashions tend to be conservative and middle of the range, and cheaper clothing can be downright boring for English, US and Australian travellers accustomed to a wide variety of styles and tastes. You will find that most of the better-quality clothes are very expensive. However, if you can manage to be in the country during the summer sales in July and August and the winter sales in December and January, you can pick up incredible bargains. By mid-sale, prices are often slashed by up to 60 or 70%. Roma, Firenze and Milano have the greatest variety of clothing, shoes and accessories. Main shopping areas are detailed under the relevant cities throughout this book.

The same applies to shoes. Expect to pay dearly (although still considerably less than at home) for the best quality at shops such as Beltrami and Pollini. Again, prices drop dramatically during the sales, but expect to have some difficulty finding shoes to fit if you take a larger size.

Italy is particularly noted for the quality of its leather goods, so plan to stock up on bags, wallets, purses, belts and gloves. At markets such as Porta Portese in Roma, you can find some incredible second-hand bargains. The San Lorenzo leather market in Firenze has a vast array of goods, including jackets, bags, wallets and belts, although the variety can be limited and you should check carefully for quality before buying.

Glassware & Ceramics
Some might call the famous and expensive Venetian glass grotesque – and it is certainly an acquired taste. Shops all over Venezia are full of it but, if you listen to the claims of the shop assistants, most of it (except for the glass in *their* shop) is not the real thing. If you want to buy Venetian glass, shop around and compare prices and quality. The merchandise at the larger factories is generally not cheaper, but you can be sure it is authentic. And remember you will probably have to pay customs duty on your purchase when you arrive home. For more information see Shopping in the Venezia section of the Il Veneto chapter.

Ceramics and pottery are less costly and more rustic. There is a great diversity of traditional styles associated with villages or areas, where designs have been handed down through many centuries. Some of the major centres are: Deruta, near Perugia in

Umbria; Faenza, in Emilia-Romagna; Vietri sul Mare, near Salerno at the start of the Costiera Amalfitana; and Grottaglie, near Taranto in Puglia. Sicilian pottery is particularly interesting; Caltagirone and Santo Stefano di Camastra are two of the important ceramic-producing towns.

Jewellery
Popular jewellery tends to be chunky and cheap looking, but more expensive, gold jewellery can be beautiful. The best-known haunt for tourists wanting to buy gold in Italy is the Ponte Vecchio in Firenze, which is lined with tiny shops full of both modern and antique jewellery. Jewellery and ornaments carved from coral can be found at Torre del Greco, just out of Napoli, and on the western coast of Sardegna, although overharvesting and pollution threaten this once thriving industry.

Souvenirs & Handicrafts
The beautiful Florentine paper goods, with their delicate flower design, and the Venetian, with a marbled design, are reasonably priced and make wonderful gifts. Specialist shops are dotted around both Firenze and Venezia, although it is possible to buy these paper goods in cartolerie throughout the country.

Local handicrafts include lace and embroidery, notably found on the Isola Maggiore in Lago di Trasimeno, Umbria, and the woodcarvings of the Val Gardena in Trentino-Alto Adige.

Getting There & Away

Competition between airlines on intercontinental routes means you should be able to pick up a reasonably priced fare, even if you are coming from as far away as Australia. If you live in Europe, you can easily enough go overland to Italy, but don't ignore the flight option, as you can often find enticing deals.

AIR
Airports & Airlines
Italy's main intercontinental gateway is Leonardo da Vinci (Fiumicino) airport in Roma, but regular intercontinental flights also serve Milano's airports. Plenty of flights (scheduled and charter) from other European cities also go direct to regional capitals.

Many European and international airlines compete with the country's national carrier, Alitalia.

Buying Tickets
World aviation has never been so competitive, making air travel better value than ever, but you have to research the options carefully to make sure you get the best deal.

The Internet is a useful source for checking air fares: many travel agencies and airlines have a Web site.

Some airlines now sell discounted tickets direct to the customer, and it's worth contacting airlines anyway for information on routes and timetables. However, sometimes there is nothing to be gained by going direct to the airline – specialist discount agencies often offer fares that are lower and/or carry fewer conditions than the airline's published prices. You can expect to be offered a wider range of options than a single airline would provide and, at worst, you will just end up paying the official airline fare.

The exception to this rule is the new breed of 'no-frills' carriers, which mostly sell direct. Unlike the 'full-service' airlines, the no-frills carriers often make one-way

tickets available at around half the return fare, meaning that it is easy to stitch together an open-jaw itinerary. Regular airlines may also offer open jaws, particularly if you are flying in from outside Europe.

If you're booking a charter flight, remember to check what time of day or night you'll be flying: many charter flights arrive late at night. If you're flying into Roma by charter, you will probably land at Ciampino airport, from where there is no public transport into the city centre after about 11 pm. Remember, if you miss your charter flight, you've lost your money.

Round-the-World (RTW) tickets are another possibility and are comparable in price to an ordinary return long-haul ticket. RTW tickets start at about UK£800, A$1800 or US$1300 and can be valid for up to a year. They can be economical if you're flying from Australia or New Zealand. Special conditions might be attached to such tickets (such as not being able to backtrack on a route). Also, beware of cancellation penalties for these and other tickets.

You may find that the cheapest flights are being advertised by obscure agencies. Most such firms are honest and solvent, but there are some rogue fly-by-night outfits around. Paying by credit card generally offers protection, since most card issuers will provide refunds if you don't get what you've paid for. Similar protection can be obtained by buying a ticket from a bonded agent, such as one covered by the Air Transport Operators Licence (ATOL) scheme in the UK. If you feel suspicious about a firm, it's best to steer clear or only pay a deposit before you get your ticket, then ring the airline to confirm that you are actually booked on the flight before you pay the balance. Established outfits, such as those mentioned in this book, offer more security and are about as competitive as you can get.

The cheapest deals are available at certain times of the year only or on weekdays.

Always ask about the route: the cheapest tickets may sometimes involve an inconvenient stopover. Don't take schedules for granted, either: airlines usually change their schedules twice a year, at the end of March and the end of October.

Ticketless travel, whereby your reservation details are contained within an airline computer, is becoming more common. On simple return trips the absence of a ticket can be a benefit – it's one less thing to worry about; however, if you are planning a complicated itinerary which you may wish to amend en route, there is no substitute for the good old paper version.

Student & Youth Fares

Full-time students and people aged under 26 have access to better deals than other travellers. The better deals may not always be cheaper fares, but can include more flexibility to change flights and/or routes. You have to show a document proving your date of birth or a valid International Student Identity Card (ISIC) when buying your ticket and boarding the plane.

Frequent Fliers

Most airlines offer frequent-flier deals that can earn you a free air ticket or other goodies. To qualify, you have to accumulate sufficient mileage with the same airline or airline alliance. Many airlines have blackout periods or times when you cannot fly for free on your frequent-flier points (Christmas and Chinese New Year, for example). The worst thing about frequent-flier programmes is that they tend to lock you into one airline, and that airline may not always have the cheapest fares or most convenient flight schedule.

Courier Flights

Courier flights are a great bargain if you're lucky enough to find one; see the boxed text 'Air Travel Glossary' on the next page. There are restrictions and you should check before you fly which apply to your ticket.

Booking a courier ticket takes some effort. They are not always readily available

and arrangements have to be made a month or more in advance. Courier flights are occasionally advertised in newspapers, or you could contact air freight companies listed in the phone book, although they aren't always interested in giving out information over the phone.

Travel Unlimited (PO Box 1058, Allston, MA 02134, USA) is a monthly travel newsletter that publishes quite a few courier flight deals from destinations worldwide. A 12 month subscription to *Travel Unlimited* costs US$25, or US$35 for those resident outside the US.

Travellers with Special Needs

If you have a broken leg, are a vegetarian or require a special diet (such as kosher food), are travelling in a wheelchair or have some other special need, let the airline know so that they can make arrangements. You should call to remind them of your requirements at least 72 hours before departure and again when you check in at the airport. It may also be worth ringing round the airlines before you make your booking to find out how they can handle your particular needs. Some airlines publish brochures on the subject. Ask your travel agency for details.

Guide dogs for the blind will often have to travel in a specially pressurised baggage compartment and are subject to quarantine laws (six months in isolation and so on) when entering, or returning to, countries currently free of rabies, such as Britain or Australia.

Deaf travellers can ask for airport and in-flight announcements to be written down for them.

Children aged under two travel for 10% of the standard fare (or free on some airlines), as long as they don't occupy a seat. They don't get a baggage allowance. Skycots, baby food and nappies (diapers) should be provided by the airline if requested in advance. Children aged between two and 12 can usually occupy a seat for half to two-thirds of the full fare and do get a baggage allowance. Pushchairs (strollers) can often be carried as hand luggage.

Air Travel Glossary

Baggage Allowance This will be written on your ticket and usually includes one 20kg item to go in the hold, plus one item of hand luggage, also generally of a specified size or weight.

Bucket Shops These are unbonded travel agencies specialising in discounted airline tickets.

Bumped Just because you have a confirmed seat doesn't mean you're going to get on the plane (see Overbooking).

Cancellation Penalties If you have to cancel or change a discounted ticket, there are often heavy penalties involved; insurance can sometimes be taken out against these penalties. Some airlines impose penalties on regular tickets as well, particularly against no-show passengers.

Check-In Airlines ask you to check in a certain time ahead of the flight departure (usually one to two hours on intercontinental flights). If you fail to check in on time and the flight is overbooked, the airline can cancel your booking and give your seat to somebody else.

Confirmation Having a ticket written out with the flight and date you want doesn't mean you have a seat until the agency has checked with the airline that your status is OK or confirmed. Meanwhile you could just be on request.

Courier Fares Businesses often need to send urgent documents or freight securely and quickly. Courier companies hire people to accompany the package through customs and, in return, offer a discount ticket which is sometimes a phenomenal bargain. In effect, what the companies do is ship their freight as your luggage on regular commercial flights. This is a legitimate operation, but there are two shortcomings – the short turnaround time of the ticket (usually not longer than a month) and the limitation on your luggage allowance. You may have to surrender all your allowance and take only carry-on luggage.

Full Fares Airlines traditionally offer 1st class (coded F), business class (coded J) and economy class (coded Y) tickets. These days there are so many promotional and discounted fares available that few passengers pay full economy fare.

ITX An ITX, or independent inclusive tour excursion, is often available on tickets to popular holiday destinations. Officially it's a package deal combined with hotel accommodation, but many agencies will sell you one of these for the flight only and give you phoney hotel vouchers in the unlikely event that you're challenged at the airport.

Lost Tickets If you lose your ticket an airline will usually treat it like a travellers cheque and, after inquiries, issue you with another one. Legally, however, an airline is entitled to treat it like cash and if you lose it then it's gone for ever. Take good care of your tickets.

MCO An MCO, or miscellaneous charge order, is a voucher that looks like an airline ticket but carries no destination or date. It can be exchanged through any International Association of Travel Agents (IATA) airline for a ticket on a specific flight. It's a useful alternative to an onward ticket in those countries that demand one and is more flexible than an ordinary ticket if you're unsure of your route.

No-Shows No-shows are passengers who fail to show up for their flight. Full-fare passengers who fail to turn up are sometimes entitled to travel on a later flight. The rest are penalised (see Cancellation Penalties).

On Request This is an unconfirmed booking for a flight.

Air Travel Glossary

Onward Tickets An entry requirement for many countries is that you have a ticket out of the country. If you're unsure of your next move, the easiest solution is to buy the cheapest onward ticket to a neighbouring country or a ticket from a reliable airline that can later be refunded if you do not use it.

Open-Jaw Tickets These are return tickets where you fly out to one place but return from another. If available, this can save you backtracking to your arrival point.

Overbooking Airlines hate to fly with empty seats and, since every flight has some passengers who fail to show up, airlines often book more passengers than they have seats. Usually excess passengers make up for the no-shows, but occasionally somebody gets 'bumped' onto the next available flight. Guess who it is most likely to be? The passengers who didn't check in early enough.

Point-to-Point Tickets These are discount tickets that can be bought on some routes in return for passengers waiving their rights to a stopover.

Promotional Fares These are officially discounted fares, available from travel agencies or direct from the airline.

Reconfirmation If you don't reconfirm your flight at least 72 hours prior to departure, the airline may delete your name from the passenger list. Ring to find out if your airline requires reconfirmation. Most flights within Europe no longer need to be reconfirmed.

Restrictions Discounted tickets often have various restrictions on them, such as needing to be paid for in advance and incurring a penalty for alteration. Others have restrictions on the minimum and maximum period you must be away, such as a minimum of 14 days or a maximum of one year.

Round-the-World Tickets RTW tickets give you a limited period (usually a year) in which to circumnavigate the globe. You can go anywhere the carrying airlines go, as long as you don't backtrack. They usually cost a bit more than a basic return flight and the number of stopovers or total number of separate flights is decided before you set off.

Stand-by This is a discounted ticket where you fly only if there is a seat free at the last moment. Stand-by fares are usually available only on domestic routes.

Transferred Tickets Airline tickets cannot be transferred from one person to another. Travellers sometimes try to sell the return half of their ticket, but officials can ask you to prove that you are the person named on the ticket. This is less likely to happen on domestic flights, but on an international flight tickets are compared with passports.

Travel Agencies Travel agencies vary widely and you should choose one that suits your needs. Some simply handle tours, while full-service agencies handle everything from tours and tickets to car rental and hotel bookings. If all you want is a ticket at the lowest possible price, then go to an agency specialising in discounted fares.

Travel Periods Ticket prices vary with the time of year. There is a low (off-peak) season and a high (peak) season, and often a low-shoulder season and a high-shoulder season as well. Usually the fare depends on your outward flight – if you depart in the high season and return in the low season, you pay the high-season fare.

Departure Tax

The departure tax payable when you leave Italy by air is factored into your airline ticket.

The UK & Ireland

Discount ticket agencies are known as bucket shops in the UK. Despite the name, there is nothing under-the-counter about them. Discount air travel is big business in London. Advertisements for many travel agencies appear in the travel pages of the weekend broadsheet newspapers, such as the *Independent* on Saturday and the *Sunday Times*, as well as in publications such as *Time Out* and *Exchange & Mart*. Look out for the free magazines, such as *TNT*, which are widely available in London – start by looking outside the main train and underground stations. Those with access to Teletext on television will find a host of travel agencies advertising.

For students or for travellers aged under 26, popular travel agencies in the UK include STA Travel (☎ 020-7361 6161), 86 Old Brompton Rd, London SW7 3LQ, which has offices throughout the UK. Visit its Web site at www.statravel.co.uk. Usit CAMPUS (☎ 020-7730 3402), 52 Grosvenor Gardens, London SW1W 0AG, also has branches throughout the UK. The Web address is www.usitcampus.com. Both of these agencies sell tickets to all travellers, but cater especially to young people and students.

Other recommended travel agencies include: Trailfinders (☎ 020-7937 5400), 215 Kensington High St, London W8 6BD; Flightbookers (☎ 020-7757 2000), 177-178 Tottenham Court Rd, London W1P 0LX; and Bridge the World (☎ 020-7734 7447), 4 Regent Place, London W1R 5F.

As fare competition in Europe grows, a gaggle of small airlines jostles for custom. In 1998 British Airways set up a 'no-frills', low-budget airline, Go (☎ 0845 6054321 in the UK, ☎ 147 88 77 66 in Italy), which flies to Roma, Milano, Venezia and Bologna from London Stansted. Standard returns (no changes, no refunds) start at UK£100, including taxes. You can book on line at www.go-fly.com or by phone.

The Irish airline Ryanair (☎ 0870 3331250, UK, ☎ 050 50 37 70, Italy) flies to Genova, Pisa, Rimini, Torino and Venezia from Stansted, with flights to each destination at least once daily. At the time of writing, a one-way mid-week fare to Venezia cost around UK£30, including taxes. Visit its Web site at www.ryanair.ie.

KLM uk's new no-frills airline buzz (☎ 0870 240 7070, UK, ☎ 02 696 82 222, Italy) flies to Milano from Stansted. At the time of writing, a return cost around UK£60 although several special deals were available. Buzz's Web site is at www.buzzaway.com.

Virgin Express (☎ 020-7744 0004, UK, ☎ 800 097097, Italy) flies to Milano and Roma from London's Gatwick, Heathrow and Stansted airports. At the time of writing, one-way fares started at UK£90. You can also book on line at www.virgin-express.com.

The two national airlines linking the UK and Italy are British Airways (BA; ☎ 020-7434 4700, ☎ 0845 222111 for 24 hour local-rate line), 156 Regent St, London W1R, and Alitalia (☎ 020-7602 7111), 4 Portman Square, London W1H 9PS. They operate regular flights (usually several a day) to Roma, Milano, Venezia, Firenze, Torino, Napoli and Pisa, as well as other cities, including Palermo, during the summer. Returns with either airline cost from UK£200. However, both airlines generally have special deals and you shouldn't need to resort to standard fares. For example, at the time of writing, BA was offering a return to Roma for as little as UK£120, with certain conditions.

Italy Sky Shuttle (☎ 020-8748 1333), 227 Shepherd's Bush Rd, London W6 7AS, specialises in charter flights to 22 destinations in Italy. The best return flight in the high season from London to Milano costs around UK£190, while a similar ticket to Roma costs from UK£170.

The Charter Flight Centre (☎ 020-7565 6755), 15 Gillingham St, London SW1V 1HN, has return flights for around UK£130 to main Italian destinations, valid for up to four weeks in the low season.

Another specialist in flights and holidays to Italy is Skybus Italia (☎ 020-7631 3444), 37 Harley St, London W1 1DB.

If you're coming from Ireland, it might be worth comparing the cost of flying direct with the cost of travelling to London first and then flying to Italy.

Youth Passes Alitalia offers people aged under 26 (and students aged under 31 with a valid ISIC) a Europa Pass from London and Dublin. The pass is valid for up to six months and allows unlimited one-way flights to all the airline's European and Mediterranean destinations for UK£62 per flight, with a minimum of four flights. The first flight has to be to Italy and the last flight back to the UK or Ireland from Italy. Internal flights in Italy on this pass cost UK£45 a pop. Lufthansa Airlines, British Midland and Scandinavian Airlines (SAS) have a similar pass called Young Europe Special (YES). There are eight Italian destinations included in the programme. The Alitalia deal is more cost-efficient if you plan to do most of your flying and travelling in Italy.

Continental Europe

Air travel between Italy and other places in Continental Europe is worth considering if you are pushed for time. Short hops can be expensive, but good deals are available from some major hubs.

Several airlines, including Alitalia, Qantas Airways and Air France, offer cut-rate fares between cities on the European legs of long-haul flights. These are usually cheap, but often involve flying at night or early in the morning.

France The student travel agency OTU Voyages (☎ 01 44 41 38 50) has a central Paris office at 39 ave Georges Bernanos and another 42 offices around the country. Its Web address is www.otu.fr. USIT (☎ 01 42 44 14 00) is a safe bet for reasonable student and cut-price travel. They have four addresses in Paris, including 85 blvd St Michel, and other offices around the country. STA Travel's Paris agent is Voyages Wasteels (☎ 01 43 25 58 35).

There are regular flights between Paris and Roma or Milano. The train is generally an easier bet for Milano, but to Roma you can occasionally find good air deals. A low-season return flight with Alitalia costs around 1300FF. Air Littoral (☎ 0803 83 48 34) operates flights from Bologna, Firenze, Milano, Napoli, Roma and Venezia to Nice, with onward connections all over France and to Spain.

Germany Munich is a haven of bucket shops and more mainstream budget travel outlets. Council Travel (☎ 089-39 50 22), Adalbertstrasse 32, near the university, is one of the best. STA Travel (☎ 089-39 90 96), Königstrasse 49, is also good.

In Berlin, Kilroy Travel-ARTU Reisen (☎ 030-310 00 40), Hardenbergstrasse 9, near Berlin Zoo (with three more branches around the city), is good. There is also a branch of STA Travel (☎ 030-311 09 50, fax 313 09 48) at Goethestrasse 73.

In Frankfurt am Main, you could try STA Travel (☎ 069-70 30 35), Bockenheimer Landstrasse 133.

KLM-Royal Dutch Airlines flies from Munich to Roma via Amsterdam from around DM400 (no changes, no refunds). Lufthansa flies direct for around DM450.

Greece Try ISYTS (☎ 01-322 12 67, fax 323 37 67), Upper Floor, 11 Nikis St, Syntagma Square, Athens. Alternatively, shop around the travel agencies in the backstreets of Athens between Syntagma and Omonia squares. At the time of writing, Alitalia was offering a return to Roma for around 125,000 dr for those aged under 26.

The Netherlands The student travel agency NBBS Reiswinkels (☎ 020-620 5071), Rokin 38, Amsterdam, offers reasonably low fares. Compare with the bucket shops along Rokin before making your decision. Another recommended travel agency in Amsterdam is

Malibu Travel (☎ 020-626 3230), Prinsengracht 230. At the time of writing, Air France was offering a return to Roma via Paris for f440.

Spain In Madrid, one of the most reliable budget travel agencies is Viajes Zeppelin (☎ 91 547 7903), Plaza de Santo Domingo 2. Return flights to Roma in the low season start at about 30,000 ptas. Flights to Milano tend to be pricier.

The USA

The North Atlantic is the world's busiest long-haul air corridor and the flight options are bewildering. Several airlines fly direct to Italy, landing at either Roma or Milano. These include Alitalia, Lufthansa, Air France, TWA and Delta Air Lines. If your trip will not be confined to Italy, check for cheaper flights to other European cities.

Discount travel agencies in the USA are known as consolidators (although you won't see a sign on the door saying 'Consolidator'). San Francisco is the ticket consolidator capital of America, although some good deals can be found in Los Angeles, New York and other big cities. Consolidators can be found through the phone book or the major daily newspapers. The *New York Times*, the *Los Angeles Times,* the *Chicago Tribune* and the *San Francisco Examiner* all produce weekly travel sections in which you will find a number of travel agency ads. Look out for an SOT number: if they have one of these they are probably legitimate.

Council Travel (☎ 800 2268624), 205 E 42 St, New York, NY 10017, America's largest student travel organisation, has around 60 offices in the USA. Call for the office nearest you or visit the Web site at www.counciltravel.com. STA Travel (☎ 800 7770112) has offices in Boston, Chicago, Miami, New York, Philadelphia, San Francisco and other major cities. Call the toll-free 800 number for office locations or visit the Web site at www.statravel.com.

At the time of writing, you could get return fares from Los Angeles to Roma, Firenze or Milano for around US$530 with Lufthansa via Frankfurt in the low season (roughly January to March). With a little luck you can do better still from the east coast. KLM, for instance, was offering return fares of around US$300 from New York to Milano in the low season. After March, prices begin to rise rapidly and availability declines.

Discount and rock-bottom options from the USA include charter, stand-by and courier flights. Stand-by fares are often sold at 60% of the normal price for one-way tickets. Airhitch (☎ 212-864 2000, ☎ 1 800 3262009 toll-free), 3rd Floor, 2641 Broadway, New York, NY 10025, specialises in this. Have a look at the Web site at www.airhitch.org. You will need to give a general idea of where and when you need to go, and a few days before your departure you will be presented with a choice of two or three flights.

A New York to Roma return on a courier flight can cost about US$300 (more from the west coast). Now Voyager (☎ 212-431 1616), Suite 307, 74 Varrick St, New York, NY 10013, specialises in courier flights, but you must pay an annual membership fee (around US$50) that entitles you to take as many courier flights as you like.

The Colorado-based Air Courier Association (☎ 303-215 9000) offers similar deals.

Also worth considering are Europe by Air coupons (☎ 1 888 3872479). Their Web site can be found at www.eurair.com. You purchase a minimum of three US$90 coupons before leaving North America. Each coupon is valid for a one-way flight within the combined system of 10 participating regional airlines in Europe (exclusive of local taxes, which you will be charged when you make the flight). The coupons are valid for 120 days from the day you make your first flight. A few words of caution – using one of these coupons for a one-way flight won't always be better value than local alternatives, so check them out before committing yourself to any given flight.

If you can't find a particularly cheap flight, it is always worth considering a cheap transatlantic hop to London to prowl around the bucket shops there. See The UK & Ireland section earlier in this chapter.

Canada

Both Alitalia and Air Canada have direct flights to Roma and Milano from Toronto and Montreal. Scan the budget travel agencies' ads in the *Toronto Globe & Mail*, the *Toronto Star* and the *Vancouver Province*.

Canada's main student travel organisation is Travel CUTS (☎ 800 6672887), which has offices in all major cities. It is known as Voyages Campus in Quebec. The Travel CUTS Web address is www.travel cuts.com.

For courier flights which originate in Canada, contact FB on Board Courier Services (☎ 514-631 2077).

Low-season return fares from Toronto to Roma or Milano start from around C$630 for students and other young people. From Montreal, KLM had a student deal for C$540 at the time of writing.

Australia

Cheap flights from Australia to Europe generally go via South-East Asian capitals, involving a stopover at Kuala Lumpur, Bangkok or Singapore. If a long stopover between connections is necessary, transit accommodation is sometimes included in the price of the ticket. If it's at your own expense, it may be worth considering a more expensive but direct ticket.

Many European airlines throw in a return flight to another European city, so, for instance, BA may fly you return to London with a London-Roma-London flight included in the price.

Quite a few travel offices specialise in discount air tickets. Some travel agencies, particularly smaller ones, advertise cheap air fares in the travel sections of weekend newspapers, such as the *Age* in Melbourne and the *Sydney Morning Herald*.

STA Travel and Flight Centre are well known for cheap fares. STA Travel (☎ 03-9349 2411), 224 Faraday St, Carlton, Melbourne, has offices in all major cities and on

many university campuses. Call ☎ 131 776 Australia-wide for the location of your nearest branch or visit its Web site at www.statravel.com.au. Flight Centre (☎ 131 600 Australia-wide), 82 Elizabeth St, Sydney, has dozens of offices throughout Australia. Its Web address is www.flightcentre .com.au. Compagnia Italiana di Turismo (CIT) can also help out with cheap fares (see Tourist Offices Abroad in the Facts for the Visitor chapter for details of its offices in Australia).

Discounted return fares on mainstream airlines through reputable agencies can be surprisingly cheap. A low-season return fare can be as low as A$1300 with an airline like Garuda Indonesia. In the high season you could be looking at around A$2500.

Qantas and Alitalia fly from Melbourne and Sydney to Roma three times a week. Flights from Perth are generally a few hundred dollars cheaper.

For courier flights try Jupiter (☎ 02-9317 2230), Unit 3, 55 Kent Rd, Sydney 2020.

New Zealand

RTW and Circle Pacific fares for travel to or from New Zealand are usually the best value. Depending on which airline you choose, you may fly across Asia, with possible stopovers in India, Thailand, Singapore or Australia, or across the USA, with possible stopovers in Honolulu or one of the Pacific Islands.

The *New Zealand Herald* has a travel section in which travel agencies advertise fares. Flight Centre (☎ 09-309 6171) has a large central office in Auckland at National Bank Towers (corner of Queen and Darby Sts) and many branches throughout the country. STA Travel (☎ 09-309 0458), 10 High St, Auckland, has other offices in Auckland, as well as in Hamilton, Palmerston North, Wellington, Christchurch and Dunedin. Its Web address is www.statravel .com.au.

Asia

Although you can find some fairly competitive air-fare deals in most Asian countries,

Bangkok, Singapore and Hong Kong are still the best places to shop around for discount tickets.

In Bangkok, try STA Travel (☎ 02-236 0262), 33 Surawong Rd. In Hong Kong many travellers use the Hong Kong Student Travel Bureau (☎ 2730 3269), 8th Floor, Star House, Tsimshatsui. You could also try Phoenix Services (☎ 2722 7378), 7th Floor, Milton Mansion, 96 Nathan Rd, Tsimshatsui. In Singapore a safe bet is STA Travel (☎ 737 7188), Orchard Parade Hotel, 1 Tanglin Rd.

Africa

Nairobi and Johannesburg are probably the best places in East and South Africa to buy tickets. Flight Centres (☎ 02-21 00 24), Lakhamshi House, Biashara St, Nairobi, has been in business for many years. In Johannesburg, the South African Students' Travel Services (☎ 011-716 30 45) has an office at the University of Witwatersrand. STA Travel (☎ 011-447 55 51) has an office on Tyrwhitt Ave in Rosebank.

Italy is no great source of budget air tickets to Africa. Tunisia is the most popular North African destination for Italians, so you might dig up something for Tunis; typically, return tickets from Roma to Tunis cost around L350,000 with Alitalia.

LAND

Not quite all roads lead to Roma, but there are plenty of options for entering Italy by train, bus or private vehicle. Bus is generally the cheapest, but services are less frequent and considerably less comfortable than the train.

If you are travelling by bus, train or car to Italy it will be necessary to check whether you require visas to the countries you intend to pass through.

Bus

Eurolines Eurolines, in conjunction with local bus companies across Europe, is the main international carrier. See its Web site at www.eurolines.com. You can contact them in your own country (see under The UK or Continental Europe later in this section) or in Italy. Eurolines' Italian headquarters (☎ 055 35 71 10, fax 055 35 05 65) is at Via Mercadante 2B, 50144 Firenze. Ticket offices around Italy include:

Firenze
  (☎ 055 21 51 55) Autostazione, Piazza
  Stazione 1, on the corner of Piazza Adua
Milano
  (☎ 02 720 01 304) Autostradale Viaggi,
  Piazza Castello 1
Roma
  (☎ 06 884 08 40) Lazzi Express,
  Via Tagliamento 27/r
  (☎ 06 440 40 09) Agenzia Elios,
  Circonvallazione Nomentana 574,
  Lato Stazione Tiburtina
Torino
  (☎ 011 433 25 25) Autostazione Comunale,
  Corso Inghilterra
Venezia
  (☎ 041 522 97 73) Agenzia Brusutti,
  Piazzale Roma 497/e

Eurolines Pass Eurolines offers the Eurolines Pass, a useful option for travellers planning to pack in a lot of kilometres touring Europe. A pass valid for 30/60 days costs UK£199/249 (UK£159/199 for those aged under 26 and senior citizens). It allows unlimited travel between up to 30 European cities, including Roma, Milano, Venezia and Firenze. Prices for all these passes cost from between UK£30 and UK£50 more from June to September.

Busabout This company offers passes of varying duration allowing you to use their bus network within designated zones of Western Europe. The make-up of the zones changes from summer to winter. The passes are of interest only to those who intend to travel a lot beyond Italy as well.

In summer (April to October) you have the choice of four colour-coded zones, or loops, and a circular route from Paris that takes in German, and some northern Italian, destinations. The idea of the zones is to make seat reservations and planning easier – your pass actually entitles you to use buses on any of the loops.

The Green Loop is the main one covering Italy, with buses arriving/departing Brindisi, Firenze, Milano, Pisa, Roma, Sorrento and Venezia every few days. It also includes Nice (France), Munich (Germany) and various stops in Switzerland. You also have the choice of add-ons (including buses into Greece, and beyond to Istanbul) for an extra one-off fee.

Busabout's summer passes cost UK£249 (15 days), UK£345 (21 days), UK£425 (one month), UK£595 (two months), UK£755 (three months) and UK£895 (over three months). Students and young people with appropriate ID (such as ISIC, GO25 and Euro<26) pay UK£199/275/325/485/595/720 respectively.

For information contact Busabout (☎ 020-7950 1661, fax 7950 1662, email info@busabout.co.uk), 258 Vauxhall Bridge Rd, London SW1V 1BS. Its Web site is at www .busabout.com.

The UK Eurolines (☎ 0870 514 3219), 52 Grosvenor Gardens, London SW1W 0AU, runs buses twice a week (Wednesday and Saturday) at 9 am to Milano (22 hours), Roma (33 hours) and other destinations. Up to five services run in summer. Other destinations include Torino, Firenze, Siena, Bologna and Venezia and may involve a change at Milano. The lowest youth/under-26 fares from London to Roma cost around UK£80 one way and UK£110 return. The full adult fares cost around UK£90/130. To Milano, the youth fare costs around UK£70/100 and the adult fare UK£80/110.

Prices rise in the peak summer season (July and August) and in the week before Christmas.

Continental Europe You will find Eurolines' main European offices at:

Austria
(☎ 01-712 04 53) Schalter 2 (Window 2), Autobusbahnhof Wien-Mitte, Hauptstrasse 1b, Vienna
France
(☎ 0836 69 52 52) 28 ave du Général de Gaulle, Paris

Germany
(☎ 089-545 87 00) Deutsche Touring GmbH, Arnulfstrasse 3 (Stamberger Bahnhof), Munich
Netherlands
(☎ 020-627 5151) Rokin 10, Amsterdam
Spain
(☎ 91 528 1105) Estación Sur de Autobuses, Calle de Méndez Alvaro 83, Madrid
Switzerland
(☎ 01 431 57 24) Carplatz am Sihlquai, 8005 Zurich

In Austria, you could also try contacting the Italian company SITA (☎ 01-533 13 60), Fangokur Reisen, Wipplingerstrasse 12, Vienna. It has a weekly service from Vienna to Padova (9 hours), with connections to Venezia. An adult one-way/return fare to Padova costs around AS800/1200.

From France, the Eurolines adult low-season one-way/return fare from Paris to Milano (16 hours, four times a week) costs around 550/900FF.

In Germany, you can contact SITA (☎ 069-790 32 40), Am Römerhof 17, Frankfurt. It has buses between Frankfurt am Main and Padova, with connections possible for destinations further into Italy. The adult one-way/return fare costs around DM200/350.

From the Netherlands, the Eurolines adult one-way/return fare from Amsterdam to Milano (19 hours, twice a week) costs around f200/300.

For buses from Slovenia contact the Ljubljana bus station (☎ 061-134 3838). From Slovenia the only destination in Italy is Trieste, for which the adult one-way/return fare costs 1600/2400 SIT. Buses from Koper (near the border) leave for Trieste 17 times a day, Monday to Friday, and once on Saturday.

Eurolines services connect Roma and Barcelona once a day except Sunday, with stops en route and onward connections to Madrid and Alicante. An adult one-way/return fare from Barcelona to Roma costs around 20,000/30,000 ptas.

There's not a great deal of bus traffic between Switzerland and Italy. In general, train is the way to go.

Rail Passes & Discount Tickets

If you're planning a wider European trip, it makes financial sense to get a rail pass. Remember that, even with a pass, you must still pay for seat and couchette reservations, full fare on the Eurostar and supplements on express trains such as Italy's Eurostar Italia and France's TGV. Treat your pass like gold, as it is virtually impossible to obtain replacements or refunds in the event of loss or theft. If you intend to travel mainly or only within Italy, consider a discount ticket or an Italian domestic rail pass (see Train in the Getting Around chapter).

Rail Passes

The InterRail Pass and Rail Europe Senior Card are available to people who have lived in Europe for six months or more. They can be bought at most major stations and student travel outlets or, within the UK, from the Rail Europe Travel Centre (☎ 0870 584 8848), 179 Piccadilly, London W1V 0BA.

Eurail Passes and Europasses are for those who have lived in Europe for less than six months. These passes are supposed to be bought outside Europe, and are cheaper if you do so. They are available from Sestante CIT offices (see Tourist Offices Abroad in the Facts for the Visitor chapter) and other leading travel agencies. You can review passes and special deals for Eurail passes on line at www.eurail.on.ca. In the USA and Canada you can purchase passes over the phone on ☎ 1 888 6679734 and have them sent to your home by courier.

InterRail Pass The InterRail map of Europe is divided into zones, one of which comprises Italy, Greece, Slovenia and Turkey.

The pass is designed for people aged under 26, but there is a more expensive version for older folk, the InterRail 26+. Twenty-two days of unlimited 2nd class travel in one zone costs UK£159/229 respectively. Better value is the one month ticket for two zones for UK£209/279 (which from the UK would get you across France too). A three zone pass for one month costs UK£229/309. If you think you can stand careering around virtually all of Europe, you could go for the one month all-in UK£259/349 ticket.

Cardholders get discounts on travel in the country where they purchase the ticket, as well as on a variety of other services, such as ferry travel.

Rail Europe Senior Card Seniors can get a Rail Europe Senior Card, which is valid for a year for trips that cross at least one border. In the UK the card costs UK£5; you must already have a Senior Citizens Rail Card (UK£18), which is available to anyone who can prove they are aged over 60. The pass entitles you to roughly 30% off standard fares. The card is known in Italy as Carta Rail Europ Senior and it costs L33,000.

Eurail Passes Eurail passes are expensive, so look at the options before committing yourself. The cards are good for travel in 17 European countries (not including the UK), but forget it

Train

If you plan to travel extensively by train in Europe it might be worth getting hold of the *Thomas Cook European Timetable*, which has a complete listing of train schedules. It is updated monthly and available from Thomas Cook offices worldwide. On overnight hauls you can book a couchette for around UK£10 to UK£15 on most international trains. In 1st class there are four bunks per cabin and in

Rail Passes & Discount Tickets

if you intend to travel mainly in Italy. People aged over 26 pay for a 1st class pass (Eurailpass) and those aged under 26 for a 2nd class pass (Eurail Youthpass). Passes are valid for 15 or 21 days or for one, two or three months. These cost US$538/698/864/1224/1512 respectively for the Eurailpass. Children aged between four and 11 pay half-price for 1st class passes. The Eurail Youthpass comes in at US$376/489/605/857/1059. You'll need to cover more than 2400km within two weeks to get value for money.

Eurail also offers Flexipasses, with which the traveller is entitled to 10 or 15 days of train travel over a two month period. These cost US$444/585 for those under 26 in 2nd class and US£634/836 for those aged over 26 in 1st class.

Eurail Saverpass is for two to five people travelling together and is available for 15 or 21 days, or one, two or three months. The price per person is US$458/594/734/1040/1286 respectively.

The Eurail Saver Flexipass entitles the travellers (up to five on one pass) using the pass to 10 or 15 days of train travel over a two month period. The pass costs US$540/710 (children half-price) per person.

The EurailDrive Pass gives the bearer four days of unlimited 1st class train travel combined with three days of car rental. There are various permutations on this and prices start at US$350 per person (if two are travelling together).

Europass This provides between five and 15 days of unlimited travel within a two month period in five 'core' countries (France, Spain, Germany, Switzerland and Italy).

As with Eurail passes, adults pay for a 1st class pass, while those aged under 26 can get a cheaper Europass Youth for travel in 2nd class. In the UK, the basic five country pass costs UK£229/152 for the adult/youth version.

Discount Tickets

Those aged under 26 can get Billets Internationaux de Jeunesse (BIJ), which cut fares by up to 30%. Wasteels (☎ 020-7834 7066) in London's Victoria station sells them. In Italy, BIJ tickets can be purchased from Transalpino offices at most major train stations and from travel agencies. Always check them out, because in Continental Europe they can be a good deal.

Wasteels also offers a series of set-route passes valid for unlimited stops over two months. One of these Mini-Tour tickets includes Italy. Leaving from London, for instance, the ticket would take you through Belgium, Switzerland, Italy and back to London through France. It costs UK£129/228 for those aged under/over 26.

Rail Inclusive Tours, available from Citalia (see Tourist Offices Abroad in the Facts for the Visitor chapter), offer up to 30% discounts on train tickets, but only as part of an accommodation package.

Always ask about discounts for children. As a rule, toddlers aged under four go for free. Kids aged four to 11 travel for half the adult fare.

2nd class there are six bunks. It is always advisable, and sometimes compulsory, to book seats on international trains to and from Italy. Some of the main international services include transport for private cars – an option

worth examining to save wear and tear on your vehicle before it arrives in Italy.

The UK The Channel Tunnel allows for land transport links between Britain and

Continental Europe. The Eurostar passenger train service (☎ 0870 518 6186) travels between London and Paris and London and Brussels. Visit its Web site at www.euro star.com. The Eurotunnel vehicle service (☎ 0870 535 3535) travels between terminals in Folkestone and Calais. Its Web address is www.eurotunnel.com.

Alternatively, you can get a train ticket that includes the Channel crossing by ferry, SeaCat or hovercraft. After that, you can travel via Paris and southern France or by swinging from Belgium down through Germany and Switzerland.

The cheapest standard fares to Roma at the time of writing were around UK£80/160 one-way/return for those aged under 26, while the full adult fares were UK£100/170. You need to add the price of a couchette onto this fare. To Milano, the respective fares were around UK£70/130 and UK£85/140.

For the latest fare information on journeys including the Eurostar, call the Rail Europe Travel Centre (☎ 0870 584 8848). For information on trips using normal trains and ferries only, call Wasteels (☎ 020-7834 7066). The Wasteels office is opposite platform 2 at Victoria station in London.

Continental Europe Regular trains on two lines connect Italy with main cities in Austria and on into Germany, France or Eastern Europe. Those crossing the frontier at the Brenner pass go to Innsbruck, Stuttgart, Munich and on. Those crossing at Tarvisio in the east proceed to Vienna, Salzburg and Prague. Trains from Milano head for Switzerland and on into France and the Netherlands. The main international train line to Slovenia crosses near Trieste. You can get trains to Ljubljana and onwards to Zagreb (Croatia), Budapest (Hungary) and as far as Moscow.

From Austria, the adult one-way 2nd class fare from Vienna to Roma (14 hours) costs around AS1200.

From France, adult one-way, 2nd class fares from Paris to Roma range from around 650FF (in the overnight sleeper train with couchette) to 900FF (TGV to Milano and a

Eurostar Italia connection from there to Roma; the journey takes 12 hours). The one-way 2nd class fare on the TGV to Milano (six hours 40 minutes) costs around 500FF.

From the Netherlands, an adult one-way 2nd class ticket from Amsterdam to Roma costs around f500.

From Slovenia, the adult one-way 2nd class fare from Ljubljana to Roma (nine hours) costs around 2500 SIT.

From Spain, an adult one-way, 2nd class ticket from Barcelona to Roma (20 hours) costs 18,000 ptas.

Cisalpino trains run at speeds of up to 200km/h from Milano to major Swiss destinations. The hub is Milano, but one Cisalpino train a day starts in Firenze and another in Venezia. The lines are: Firenze-Milano-Zurich, Venezia-Milano-Geneva, Milano-Bern-Basle and Milano-Zurich-Stuttgart (Germany). The one-way adult 2nd class fares from Zurich to Roma is around Sfr150.

Car & Motorcycle

Coming from the UK, you can take your car across to France by ferry or the Channel Tunnel car train, Eurotunnel (☎ 0870 535 3535). The latter runs around the clock, with up to four crossings (35 minutes) an hour between Folkestone and Calais in the high season. You pay for the vehicle only and fares vary according to time of day and season. The cheapest economy fare (January to May) is around UK£170 return (valid for a year) and the most expensive (May to late September) around UK£220, if you depart during the day Friday to Sunday.

The main points of entry to Italy are: the Mont Blanc tunnel from France at Chamonix (closed at the time of writing following a fire in March 1999 and not due to reopen until autumn 2000 at the earliest), which connects with the A5 for Torino and Milano; the Grand St Bernard tunnel from Switzerland (Sfr27), which also connects with the A5; and the Brenner pass from Austria (AS130), which connects with the A22 to Bologna. Mountain passes in the Alpi are often closed in winter and sometimes in autumn and spring, making the tunnels a less scenic but more reliable way to arrive in Italy. Make sure you have snow chains in winter.

Europe is made for motorcycle touring and Italy is no exception. Motorcyclists literally swarm into the country in summer to tour the scenic roads. Motorcyclists rarely have to book ahead for ferries. You will be able to enter restricted traffic areas in Italian cities without any problems and Italian traffic police generally turn a blind eye to motorcycles parked on footpaths. Crash helmets are compulsory in Italy.

An interesting Web site loaded with advice for people planning to drive in Europe is www.ideamerge.com/motoeuropa. If you want help with route planning, check out www.euroshell.com.

Paperwork & Preparations When driving in Europe you should always carry proof of ownership of a private vehicle (a Vehicle Registration Document for UK registered cars). All EU member states' driving licences (not the old-style UK green licence) are fully recognised throughout Europe, regardless of your length of stay. Those with a non-EU licence are supposed to obtain an International Driving Permit (IDP) to accompany their national licence. In practice, you will probably be OK with national licences from countries such as Australia, Canada and the USA. If you decide to get an IDP, your national automobile association can issue them. It is valid for 12 months and must be kept with your proper licence.

Third-party motor insurance is a minimum requirement in Italy and throughout Europe. The Green Card, an internationally recognised proof of insurance obtainable from your insurer, is mandatory. Also ask your insurer for a European Accident Statement form, which can simplify matters in the event of an accident. Never sign statements you can't read or understand – insist on a translation and sign that only if it's acceptable.

A European breakdown assistance policy is a good investment, such as the AA Five Star Service (☎ 0870 550 0600) or the RAC's Eurocover Motoring Assistance (☎ 0870 572 2722) in the UK. In Italy, assistance can be obtained through the Automobile Club Italiano. See Organisations under Car & Motorcycle in the Getting Around chapter for details.

Every vehicle travelling across an international border should display a nationality plate of its country of registration (GB for Great Britain, F for France etc). A warning triangle (to be used in the event of a breakdown) is compulsory throughout Europe. Recommended accessories are a first-aid kit, a spare-bulb kit and a fire extinguisher.

Rental There is a mind-boggling variety of special deals and terms and conditions attached to car rental. Here are a few pointers to help you through.

Multinational agencies – Hertz, Avis, Budget and Europe's largest rental agency, Europcar – will provide a reliable service and good standard of vehicle. However, if you walk into an office and ask for a car on the spot, you will always pay high rates, even allowing for special weekend deals. National and local firms can sometimes undercut the multinationals, but make sure you examine the rental agreement carefully (although this might be difficult if it is in Italian).

Planning ahead and pre-booking a rental car through a multinational agency before leaving home will enable you to find the best deals. Pre-booked and prepaid rates are always cheaper. Fly/drive combinations and other packages are worth looking into. You will simply pick up the vehicle on your arrival in Italy and return it to a nominated point at the end of the rental period. Ask your travel agency for information or contact one of the major rental agencies.

Holiday Autos sometimes has good rates for Europe, for which you need to pre-book; its main office is in the UK (☎ 0870 530 0400). At the time of writing, they were charging UK£332 (all-inclusive) for a small car (such as a Renault Twingo) for two weeks, with the option of one-way rental.

Car Rental Direct (☎ 020-7625 7166) is another possibility. Have a look at its Web site at www.car-rental-direct.com.

If you don't know exactly when you will want to rent, you could call back home from Italy (more or less affordable to the UK and the US) and reserve through an agency there. This way you get the benefits of booking from home.

If you do wait until you are travelling before deciding on car hire, you could add Switzerland in your driving itinerary. Car-hire costs can be much lower than in Italy, and generally there is no problem with cross-border travel in rental cars (confirm this before signing on the dotted line).

No matter where you hire your car, make sure you understand what is included in the price (unlimited kilometres, tax, insurance, collision damage waiver and so on) and what your liabilities are. Insurance can be a vexed issue. Are you covered for theft, vandalism and fire damage? Since the most common and convenient way to pay for rental is by credit card, check whether or not you have car insurance with the credit card provider and what the conditions are. The extra cover provided may pick up the slack in any local cover.

The minimum rental age in Italy is 21 years. A credit card is usually required.

Motorcycle and moped rental is common in Italy and there are specialist rental agencies in most cities (see Rental under Car & Motorcycle in the Getting Around chapter).

Purchase It is illegal for nonresidents to purchase vehicles in Italy. The UK is probably the best place to buy second-hand cars (prices are not so competitive for new cars). Bear in mind that you will be getting a left-hand-drive car (with the steering wheel on the right).

If you want a right-hand-drive car and can afford to buy new, prices are relatively low in Belgium, the Netherlands and Luxembourg. Paperwork can be tricky wherever you buy.

Camper Van Travelling in a camper van can kill several birds with one stone, taking care of eating, sleeping and travelling in one package. Among Europeans it is quite a popular way to get around.

London is a good place to buy. Look in *TNT* magazine or the ads paper *Loot*, or go to the daily van market on Market Rd, London N7 (near Caledonian Rd tube station). Expect to spend at least UK£2000. The most common camper van is the VW based on the 1600cc/2000cc Transporter, for which spare parts are widely available in Europe.

There are drawbacks. Camper vans can be expensive to buy in spring and hard to get rid of in autumn. They are difficult to manoeuvre around towns. A car and tent may do just as well for some people.

If you want to rent, organise it before reaching Italy, as it is next to impossible to hire vans there.

SEA

Ferries connect Italy to Albania, Croatia, France, Greece, Malta, Spain, Tunisia and Turkey. Tickets are most expensive in summer. Prices for cars, camper vans and motorcycles vary according to the size of the vehicle. Bicycles can sometimes be taken free of charge. Eurail and InterRail pass holders pay only a supplement on the Italy-Greece routes, but must travel with approved companies. Ticket prices are competitive on the heavily serviced Brindisi-Greece route.

For detailed information, see the Getting There & Away sections for: Brindisi, Bari and Ancona (ferries to/from Greece, Albania, Croatia and Turkey); Otranto (to/from Albania); Napoli (to/from Tunisia and Corsica); Trapani (to/from Tunisia via Pantelleria); Siracusa (to/from Malta); Porto Torres (to/from Marseille and Toulon); Livorno, La Spezia and Santa Teresa di Gallura (to/from Corsica); Genova (to/from Corsica, Spain and Tunisia); and Trieste (to/from Albania, Croatia and Greece).

ORGANISED TOURS

Options for organised travel to Italy abound. The Italian State Tourist Office (see Tourist Offices Abroad in the Facts for the Visitor chapter) can provide a list of tour operators, noting what each specialises in. Tours can save you hassles, but they rob you of independence and generally do not come cheap.

General

A couple of big specialists in the UK are Magic of Italy (☎ 020-8748 7575), 227 Shepherd's Bush Rd, London W6 7AS, and Alitalia's subsidiary, Italiatour (☎ 01883-621900). Between them they offer a wide range of tours, city breaks and resort-based holidays covering most of the country.

Sestante CIT (known as CIT or Citalia outside Italy), with offices worldwide (see Tourist Offices Abroad in the Facts for the Visitor chapter), organises a variety of tours.

Tours for Under-35s

Top Deck Travel (☎ 020-7370 4555), 131-135 Earls Court Rd, London SW5 9RH, and Contiki Travel Ltd (☎ 020-7637 0802), c/o Royal National Hotel, Bedford Way, London WC1H 0DG, do a range of coach tours across Europe for young people – they are generally aimed at the high-speed, party-minded crowd. Both companies have offices in North America, Australia, New Zealand and South Africa.

An outfit called Tracks offers budget coach/camping tours for under US$40 per day, plus food fund. It has a London office (☎ 020-7937 3028) and is represented in Australia and New Zealand by Adventure World. In North America call ☎ 800 2336046.

In the USA, New Frontiers (☎ 1 800 3666387), 12 East 33rd St, New York, offers train-travel packages and other tours in Italy.

Tours for Seniors

For people aged over 60, Saga Holidays offers holidays ranging from cheap coach tours to luxury cruises. Saga has offices in the UK (☎ 0800 300456), Saga Building, Middelburg Square, Folkestone, Kent CT20 1AZ; the USA (☎ 1 800 3430273), 222 Berkeley St, Boston, MA 02116; and Australia (☎ 02-9957 4266), Level 1, Suite 2, 110 Pacific Highway, North Sydney, Sydney 2061.

Warning

The information in this chapter is particularly vulnerable to change: prices for international travel are volatile, special deals come and go, and routes, schedules and visa requirements change. Airlines and governments seem to take a perverse pleasure in making price structures and regulations as complicated as possible. You should check with the airline or a travel agency to make sure you understand how a fare (and ticket you may buy) works. The travel industry is highly competitive and there are many lurks and perks.

Get quotes and advice from as many airlines and travel agencies as possible before you part with your hard-earned cash. The pointers in this chapter are no substitute for your own careful research.

Walking Tours

Several companies offer organised walking tours in selected areas. Explore Worldwide (☎ 01252-319448), 1 Frederick St, Aldershot, Hants GU11 1LQ, is one.

Also in the UK, Alternative Travel Group (☎ 01865-315678) offers a series of escorted and unescorted walking and cycling tours in many parts of Italy. With the unescorted version, accommodation is pre-booked and luggage is forwarded while you walk or cycle. Prices for the unescorted tours start at around UK£300 for eight days (excluding flights). Another UK company organising guided walking holidays is Ramblers Holidays (☎ 01707-331133).

Short Breaks

Kirker Travel Ltd (☎ 020-7231 3333), at 3 New Concordia Wharf, Mill St, London SE1 2BB, offers pricey short breaks from London in exclusive hotels in the main cities of Italy. Such a trip starts at about UK£400 per person for three nights in twin accommodation with air fare, transfers and breakfast included. Depending on the hotel you choose, the price can rise considerably.

Prices also rise in summer. CIT can also organise city breaks to 21 cities in Italy.

Other Tours

There are many tours for those people with specific interests. Tasting Places (☎ 020-7460 0077), Unit 40, Buspace Studios, Conlan St, London W10 5AP, offers one-week trips led by cooking instructors. You cook and eat your way to a better understanding of a chosen region. You won't get much change from UK£1000.

Voyages Jules Verne (☎ 020-7616 1000), 1 Dorset Square, London NW1 6QG, organises a tour taking in Venezia, Firenze and Roma for seven days, including three nights spent cruising the Venetian lagoon. At the time of writing, the price was UK£595 per person, including travel and accommodation.

The European Bike Express is a coach service for cyclists and their bikes. It runs in summer from north-eastern England to Italy or Spain, with pick-up/drop-off points en route. The return fare is UK£164 (UK£154 for Cyclists' Touring Club members); contact ☎ 01642-251440 in the UK or bolero@bolero.demon.co.uk for details.

Getting Around

Domestic air travel is expensive and probably worth it only if you are trying to cover long distances or are really short of time. You can reach almost any destination in Italy by train or bus and services are efficient and relatively cheap (though not always quick). Trains are the most straightforward method of travel and stations are usually in or near the historic centre of towns. Bus travel can be a little more complicated to work out because there are so many different companies, but it is a cheap method of transport. Your own wheels give you the most freedom and flexibility, and you can stray off the main routes to discover out-of-the-way hill towns or deserted beaches. However, be aware that both petrol and *autostrada* (motorway) tolls are expensive and that the stress of driving and parking your car in a big Italian city could easily ruin your trip.

AIR

The domestic lines are Alitalia and Meridiana. The main airports are in Roma, Pisa, Milano, Napoli, Catania and Cagliari, and there are other, smaller airports throughout the country. Domestic flights can be booked through any travel agency, including Sestante CIT (☎ 06 47 86 41, fax 06 478 64 200), Via Barberini 86, Roma, and Centro Turistico Studentesco e Giovanile (CTS; ☎ 06 687 26 72), Corso Vittorio Emanuele II 297, Roma. For further addresses see Information in individual cities.

There are no domestic air passes in Italy. Alitalia offers a range of discounts for young people, families, seniors and weekend travellers, as well as occasional promotional fares. It should be noted that airline fares fluctuate and that special deals sometimes apply only when tickets are bought in Italy, or for return fares only. The Domestic Airfares map on this page will give you an idea of return fares at the time of writing. Barring special deals, a one-way fare is generally half the cost of the return fare.

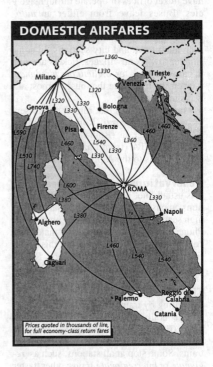

DOMESTIC AIRFARES

Prices quoted in thousands of lire, for full economy-class return fares

Departure (or airport) taxes are factored into the price of your ticket.

BUS

Bus services within Italy are provided by numerous companies and vary from local routes linking small villages to fast and reliable intercity connections. By utilising the local services, it is possible to get to just about any location throughout the country. Buses can be a cheaper and faster way to get around if your destination is not on a main train line (on major routes, trains tend to be cheaper).

It is usually possible to get bus timetables for the provincial and intercity services from local tourist offices. In larger cities, most of the main intercity bus companies have ticket offices or operate through agencies. Buses leave from either an *auto-stazione* (bus station) or from a particular piazza or street. Details are provided in the individual town and city sections. In some smaller towns and villages, tickets are sold in bars – just ask for *biglietti per il pullman* – or on the bus. Note that buses almost always leave on time.

Major companies that run long-haul services include Marozzi (Roma to Brindisi), SAIS and Segesta (Roma to Sicilia), and Lazzi and SITA (from Lazio, Toscana and other regions to the Alpi).

Reservations & Costs

It is usually not necessary to make reservations on buses, although it is advisable in the high season for overnight or long-haul trips. Phone numbers and addresses of major bus companies are listed throughout this book. Examples of bus ticket prices are: Roma-Palermo L65,000 and Roma-Siena L25,000.

TRAIN

Travelling by train in Italy is simple, cheap and generally efficient. The Ferrovie dello Stato (FS) is the partially privatised state train system. There are several types of trains. Some stop at all stations, such as *regionale* or *interregionale* trains; other, faster trains, such as the Intercity (IC) or very fast Eurostar Italia (ES), Italy's answer to the TGV in France, stop only at major cities. There are also several private train lines in Italy; these are noted throughout this book.

Travellers should note that all tickets must be validated *before* you board your train. You simply punch them in the yellow machines installed at the entrance to all train platforms. If you don't validate them, you risk a large fine. The rule does not apply to tickets purchased outside Italy.

There are left-luggage facilities at all train stations. They are often open 24 hours but, if not, they usually close only for a few hours after midnight. They are open seven days and charge from L5000 per day for each piece of luggage.

Rail Passes

It is not worth buying a Eurail or InterRail pass (see the boxed text Rail Passes & Discount Tickets in the Getting There & Away chapter) if you are going to travel only in Italy, since train fares are reasonably cheap. The FS offers its own discount passes for travel within the country. CIT offices around the world (see under Tourist Offices Abroad in the Facts for the Visitor chapter) also sell them.

FS passes include the Carta Verde, for people aged between 12 and 26. It costs L40,000, is valid for one year and entitles you to a 20% discount on all train travel, but you'll need to do a fair bit of travelling to get your money's worth. Children aged between four and 12 are automatically entitled to a 50% discount on rail fares, and those under four years can travel for free.

The Carta d'Argento entitles people aged 60 and over to a 20% discount on 1st and 2nd class travel for one year. It also costs L40,000.

A *biglietto chilometrico* (kilometric card) is valid for two months and allows you to cover 3000km, with a maximum of 20 trips. It costs L206,000 (2nd class) and you must pay a supplement if you catch an Intercity or Eurostar train. Its main attraction is that it can be used by up to five people, either singly or together.

Two other useful passes are the Italy Railcard and Italy Flexi Rail (both of which can be purchased in Italy and the UK). With both passes, prices include supplements for travel on Intercity trains but not for Eurostar trains. You should have your passport for identification when purchasing either pass. Italy Railcard is valid for eight, 15, 21 or 30 days and is available in 1st or 2nd class. An eight day pass costs L438,000/292,000 in 1st/2nd class, a 15 day pass costs L717,000/477,000, a 21 day pass L635,000/423,000 and a 30 day pass L1,500,000/L657,000. Italy Flexi Rail is valid for four, eight or 12 days of travel within one month. A four day pass costs L356,000/237,000 in 1st/2nd class, an eight day pass costs L627,000/387,000 and a 12 day pass costs L641,000/427,000.

TRAIN ROUTES

— Principal Train Lines
— Local Train Lines

The Euro-Domino pass, known as a Freedom pass in the UK, is available for any one of 28 European countries and is valid for three, five or 10 days of travel over a month. For Italy, a 1st class, 10 day pass costs UK£265. Second class is UK£182 and for those aged under 26 it's UK£140.

Classes

There are 1st and 2nd classes on all Italian trains, with a 1st class ticket costing a bit less than double the price of 2nd class. On Eurostar trains, 2nd class is much like 1st class on other trains.

Reservations

It is recommended that you book train tickets for long trips, particularly if you're travelling at the weekend or during holiday periods, otherwise you could find yourself standing in the corridor for the entire journey. Reservations are obligatory for many Eurostar trains. You can get timetable information and make train bookings at most travel agencies, including CTS and Sestante CIT, or you can simply buy your ticket on arrival at the station. There are special booking offices for Eurostar trains at the relevant train stations. If you are doing a reasonable amount of travelling, it is worth buying a train timetable. There are several available, including the official FS timetables, which can be bought at newspaper stands in or near train stations for around L5000.

Costs

To travel on Intercity and Eurostar trains you are required to pay a *supplemento*, an additional charge determined by the distance you are travelling. For instance, on the Roma-Firenze Intercity train you will pay an extra L15,000. On the Eurostar, the cost of the ticket includes the supplement and booking fee. The one-way fare from Roma to Firenze on the Eurostar is L78,500/51,000 in 1st/2nd class. The difference in price between the Eurostar (1½ hours) and the Intercity (around two hours) is only L12,500. For the extra money you get a faster, much more comfortable service. The Eurostar always takes priority over other trains, so there's less risk of long delays in the middle of nowhere.

Always check whether the train you are about to catch is an Intercity and pay the supplement before you get on, otherwise you will pay extra on the train. On overnight trips within Italy, it can be worth paying extra for a *cuccetta* (sleeping berth, commonly known as a couchette), which costs L30,500 for a bed in a four berth compartment and L21,500 in a six berth compartment, on top of your ticket. It is possible to take your bicycle in the baggage compartment on some trains for L10,000.

Some prices for one-way train fares are as follows (return fares are double the one-way fare):

from	to	fare (lire)
Milano	Firenze	38,500
	Venezia	34,000
Roma	Firenze	38,500
	Milano	68,000
	Napoli	28,500
	Venezia	68,000

The FS services and fare structures are about to be revised at the time of writing. This will probably result in more expensive fares and the introduction of peak and off-peak travel, bringing train travel in Italy in line with other EU countries. Changes could be introduced from early 2000. Check at the information office at any train station.

CAR & MOTORCYCLE
Documents

If you want to hire a car or motorcycle, you will generally need to produce your driving licence. Certainly you will need to produce it if you are pulled over by the police or *carabinieri*, who, if it's a non-EU licence, may well want to see an International Driving Permit (IDP).

To drive your own vehicle in Italy you need an International Insurance Certificate, also known as a Carta Verde (Green Card).

Your car insurance company will issue this. For further details see Paperwork & Preparations under Car & Motorcycle in the Getting There & Away chapter.

Roads

Roads are generally good throughout the country and there is an excellent network of autostrade (motorways). The main north-south link is the Autostrada del Sole, which extends from Milano to Reggio di Calabria (called the A1 from Milano to Napoli and the A3 from Napoli to Reggio di Calabria). Drivers usually travel at very high speeds in the fast (left-hand) lane on autostrade, so use that lane only to pass other cars.

There's a toll to use Italy's network of autostrade. For example, depending on the size of your car, it will cost approximately L30,000 from Roma to Bologna, L50,000 from Roma to Milano, L18,000 from Roma to Napoli, L23,000 from Milano to Venezia, L18,000 from Milano to Bologna and L14,000 from Genova to La Spezia. For more information call the Società Autostrade (☎ 06 436 32 121).

Travellers with time to spare could consider using the system of *strade statali* (state roads), which are often multilane dual carriageways and are toll free. They are represented on maps as 'S' or 'SS'. The *strade provinciali* (provincial roads) are sometimes little more than country lanes, but provide access to some of the more beautiful scenery and the many small towns and villages. They are represented as 'P' or 'SP' on maps.

Road Rules

Motoring in Europe (UK£4.99), published in the UK by the RAC, gives an excellent summary of road regulations in each European

Road Distances (km)

	Bari	Bologna	Brindisi	Firenze	Genova	Livorno	Milano	Napoli	Palermo	Perugia	Reggio di Calabria	Roma	Siena	Torino	Trento	Trieste	Venezia	Verona
Bari	---																	
Bologna	670	---																
Brindisi	114	785	---															
Firenze	662	101	776	---														
Genova	889	291	1004	227	---													
Livorno	742	176	857	84	179	---												
Milano	877	207	992	296	146	296	---											
Napoli	253	568	368	466	694	547	762	---										
Palermo	665	1234	669	1132	1360	1213	1429	683	---									
Perugia	565	235	679	150	378	231	447	369	1036	---								
Reggio di Calabria	445	1014	449	912	1140	993	1209	463	220	816	---							
Roma	413	369	527	267	495	305	563	217	884	170	664	---						
Siena	616	168	731	70	275	118	362	420	1087	103	867	221	---					
Torino	995	325	1109	394	168	345	139	860	1527	545	1307	661	460	---				
Trento	890	220	1005	309	354	384	223	775	1442	459	1222	576	375	355	---			
Trieste	891	290	1006	390	536	465	405	857	1523	465	1303	658	457	536	284	---		
Venezia	754	154	868	255	400	329	269	721	1388	327	1168	522	321	401	159	153	---	
Verona	808	137	922	226	289	301	158	693	1359	377	1139	494	293	290	97	250	114	---

Note
Distances between Palermo and mainland towns do not take into account the ferry from Reggio di Calabria to Messina. Add an extra hour to your journey time to allow for this crossing.

country, including parking rules. The motoring organisations in other countries have similar publications.

In Italy, as in the rest of Continental Europe, drive on the right side of the road and overtake on the left. Unless otherwise indicated, you must always give way to cars coming from the right. It is compulsory to wear seat belts if fitted to the car (front seat belts on all cars, rear seat belts on cars built after 26 April 1990). If you are caught not wearing a seat belt, you will be required to pay an on-the-spot L58,000 fine, although this doesn't seem to deter Italians, many of whom use them only on the autostrade.

Random breath tests now take place in Italy. If you're involved in an accident while under the influence of alcohol, the penalties can be severe. The blood-alcohol limit is 0.08%.

Speed limits, unless otherwise indicated by local signs, are as follows: on autostrade 130km/h for cars of 1100cc or more, 110km/h for smaller cars and for motorcycles under 350cc; on all main, non-urban highways 110km/h; on secondary, non-urban highways 90km/h; and in built-up areas 50km/h. Speeding fines follow EU standards and are L59,000 for up to 10km/h over the limit, L235,000 for up to 40km/h, and L587,000 for more than 40km/h. Driving through a red light will set you back L117,000.

You don't need a licence to ride a moped under 50cc, but you should be aged 14 or over; a helmet is compulsory for those aged under 18. You can't carry passengers or ride on autostrade. The speed limit for a moped is 40km/h. To ride a motorcycle or scooter up to 125cc, you must be aged 16 or over and have a licence (a car licence will do). Helmets are compulsory for everyone riding a motorcycle bigger than 50cc, although this is a rule that Italians choose to ignore. For motorcycles over 125cc you will need a motorcycle licence.

On a motorcycle, you will be able to enter restricted traffic areas in Italian cities without any problems, and traffic police generally turn a blind eye to motorcycles parked on footpaths. There is no lights-on requirement for motorcycles during the day.

City Driving

Driving in Italian towns and cities is quite an experience and may well present the unprepared with headaches. The Italian attitude to driving bears little similarity to the English concept of traffic in ordered lanes (a normal two-lane road in Italy is likely to carry three or four lanes of traffic), and the farther south you travel, the less drivers seem to pay attention to road rules. Instead, the main factor in determining right of way is whichever driver is more *prepotente* (forceful). If you must drive in an Italian city, particularly in Roma or Napoli, remain calm and keep your eyes on the car in front and you should be OK. Once you arrive in a city, follow the *centro* (city centre) signs. Most roads are well signposted.

Parking

Be extremely careful where you park your car, especially in major cities. If you leave it in an area marked with a sign reading *Zona Rimozione* (Removal Zone) and featuring a tow truck, it will almost certainly be towed away and you will pay a heavy fine. A stopover in a medieval hill town will generally mean leaving the car in a car park some distance from the town centre. It is a good idea to leave your car in a supervised car park if you have luggage, but even then it is a risk to leave your belongings in an unattended car.

Car parks in the major cities are indicated in this book. They are denoted on signs throughout Italy by a white 'P' on a blue background. There are parking meters in most cities and even in the historic centres of small towns. You are likely to have to pay in advance for the number of hours you think you will stay. Per hour, they can cost anything from L500 to L2000 (all over Roma, for example).

Petrol

The cost of petrol in Italy is very high. You'll pay around L2000 per litre for leaded

Free Wheelers

There was something magical about driving into Italy from France for the first time and something rather disturbing about the simultaneous red and green traffic lights at a choked intersection just beyond Ventimiglia. Judging by the irritated honking behind me, red and green meant green for go and red for watch out for what everyone else is doing.

Driving in Italy, especially in the cities, is special. It's a little like a combination of Formula One and bumper cars. Out on the autostrade it's pretty straightforward: when your rear-view mirror suddenly fills with the flashing headlights of an angry Audi doing 180km/h right up your caboose while you are overtaking a truck at 130km/h, just smile and complete your manoeuvre. Resist the temptation to lightly touch the brakes and have the Audi crumple itself into your rear end. Tailgating is *de rigueur* and speeding a matter of honour (in spite of the occasional fine), so things get a little hairy in dense fog with zero visibility. On the subject of honour, many locals look upon the seat belt with considerable disdain. This, as even most Italians will admit, is foolish in the extreme.

Most other aspects of Italian driving are infectious. You soon realise that what at first seems like clueless indiscipline is, in fact, the height of driving skill. When you begin to see how traffic flows, how drivers seem to have a sixth sense for what is happening around them and so generally proceed without having accidents, you begin to understand that, actually, these guys are good … and masters of entering the impossible parking spot.

The rules of the road are certainly subject to interpretation. For instance, stopping at pedestrian crossings is for pedestrians, not cars. In cities such as Napoli, stopping only occurs during gridlock – you can be sure everyone is running red lights. In most other cities red lights are respected, but scooters tend to slow rather than stop on a red. Nippy lane crossing, and even lane-creation on wide boulevards (and some narrow ones) and roundabouts, is the norm. Decisiveness is the key. Even when you have no clue where you are going, go there with brio – otherwise the guy going with brio behind you may wind up in your behind.

Perhaps the spirit of Italian driving is best illustrated by a late-night habit in cities such as Milano and Roma. All traffic lights flash orange in the wee hours, no matter how complex the intersection. Keep your eyes peeled, feet poised over accelerator and brake (you never know which will come in most handy) and go. Get enough of this and you'll never be able to drive in that staid Anglo-Saxon fashion again.

Damien Simonis

petrol, L2000 for unleaded and L1600 for diesel.

Petrol is called *benzina*, unleaded petrol is *benzina senza piombo* and diesel is *gasolio*. If you are driving a car that uses LPG (liquid petroleum gas), you will need to buy a special guide to service stations that have *gasauto* or GPL. By law these must be in nonresidential areas and are usually in the country or on city outskirts, although you'll find plenty on the autostrade. GPL costs around L1000 per litre.

Rental

Rental agencies are listed under the major cities in this book. Most tourist offices can provide information about car or motorcycle rental; otherwise, look in the local *Pagine Gialle* (*Yellow Pages*).

Car It is cheaper to arrange car rental before leaving your own country, for instance through some sort of fly/drive deal. Most of the major car-hire firms, including Hertz, Avis and Budget, can arrange this for you.

All you have to do is pick up the vehicle at a nominated point when you arrive in Italy. Foreign offices of Sestante CIT can also help to organise car or camper van rental before you leave home (see Tourist Offices Abroad in the Facts for the Visitor chapter for contact details).

You have to be aged 21 or over (23 or over for some companies) to hire a car in Italy and you will find the deal far easier to organise if you have a credit card. Most firms will accept your standard licence, sometimes with an Italian translation (which can usually be provided by the agencies themselves), or IDP.

At the time of writing, Avis offered a special weekend rate for unlimited kilometres which compared well with rates offered by other firms: L285,000 for a Fiat Uno or Renault Clio, or L320,500 for a Fiat Brava, from 9 am Friday to 9 am Monday. Maggiore Budget offered a weekend deal of L147,000 for a Renault Clio, with a limit of 300km. The same car for five to seven days, with a limit of 1400km, costs L497,000. If you pick up or drop off the car at an airport there is a 12% surcharge.

Motorcycle You'll have no trouble hiring a small motorcycle such as a scooter (Vespa) or moped. There are numerous rental agencies in cities, where you'll also usually be able to hire larger motorcycles for touring, and at tourist destinations such as seaside resorts. The average cost for a 50cc scooter (for one person) is around L60,000/300,000 per day/week. For a 125cc (for two people) you will pay from around L80,000/400,000 per day/week. For a moped (virtually a motorised bicycle) you'll pay around L45,000/220,000 per day/week.

Most agencies will not rent motorcycles to people aged under 18. Note that many places require a sizeable deposit and that you could be responsible for reimbursing part of the cost of the bike if it is stolen. Always check the fine print in the contract. See Road Rules earlier in this section for more details about age, licence and helmet requirements.

Purchase
Car It's very difficult for foreigners to buy a car in Italy, as the law requires that you be a resident to own and register one. You can get round this by having a friend who is resident in Italy buy one for you.

It is possible to buy a cheap, small 10-year-old car for as little as L1,500,000, though you'll pay up to around L7,000,000 for a reasonable five-year-old Fiat Uno and up to L10,000,000 for a two-year-old Fiat Uno. Look in the classified section of local newspapers to find cars for sale.

Motorcycle The same laws apply to owning and registering a motorcycle as apply to purchasing a car. The cost of a second-hand Vespa ranges from L500,000 to L1,500,000, and a moped will cost from L300,000 to L1,000,000. Prices for more powerful bikes start at L1,500,000.

Organisations
The Automobile Club Italiano (ACI) no longer offers free roadside assistance to tourists. Residents of the UK and Germany should organise assistance through their own national organisations, which entitles them to use ACI's emergency assistance number ☎ 116 for a small fee. Without this entitlement, you'll pay a minimum fee of L150,000 if you call ☎ 116. ACI has offices at Via Marsala 8, Roma (☎ 06 4 99 81) and Corso Venezia 43, Milano (☎ 02 7 74 51).

BICYCLE
Cycling is a national pastime in Italy and can be a great way to see the countryside as well as get around busy town centres. See the Activities section in the Facts for the Visitor chapter for suggestions on places to cycle. There are no special road rules for cyclists. Helmets and lights are not obligatory, but you would be wise to equip yourself with both. You cannot take bikes onto the autostrade. If you plan to bring your own bike, check with your airline for any additional costs. The bike will need to be disassembled and packed for the journey.

Bikes can be taken very cheaply on trains (L10,000), although only certain trains will actually carry them. Fast trains (IC, EC and Eurostar etc) will generally not accommodate bikes and they must be sent as registered luggage, which can take a few days. Check with the FS for more information. Bikes can be transported for free on ferries to Sicilia and Sardegna.

A primary consideration on a cycling tour is to travel light, but you will still need to take a few tools and spare parts, including a puncture-repair kit and a spare inner tube. Panniers are essential to balance your possessions on either side of the bike frame.

A bike helmet is a very good idea, as is a very solid bike lock and chain, although even that might not prevent your bike from being stolen if you leave it unattended. Theft of mountain bikes is a major problem in the big cities.

Rental

Bikes are available for hire in most Italian towns and many places have both city and mountain bikes. Rental costs for a city bike start at L15,000/100,000 per day/week. A good mountain bike will cost more. See Getting Around in individual cities for more information.

Purchase

If you shop around, bargain prices range from L190,000 for a ladies' bike without gears to L400,000 for a mountain bike with 16 gears, but you will pay a lot more for a very good bike. A good place to shop for bike bargains is Tacconi Sport, which buys in bulk. It has large outlets near Perugia, Arezzo, Trento and in the Republic of San Marino.

Organisations

There are organisations that can help you plan your bike tour or through which you can organise guided tours. In England, you should contact the Cyclists' Touring Club (☎ 01483-417217), Cotterell House, 69 Meadrow, Godalming, Surrey GU7 3HS. Its Web site is at www.ctc.org.uk. The club can

supply members with information on cycling conditions, itineraries and cheap insurance. Membership costs UK£25 per year or UK£15 for students and those aged under 18.

HITCHING

Hitching is never safe in any country and we don't recommend it. Travellers who decide to hitchhike should understand they are taking a small, but potentially serious, risk. People who do choose to hitchhike will be safer if they travel in pairs and let someone know where they are planning to go. A man and a woman travelling together is probably the best combination. Women travelling alone should be extremely cautious about hitching anywhere. Hitchhiking is not a major pastime in Italy, but Italians are friendly people and you will generally find a lift.

It is illegal to hitchhike on Italy's autostrade, but quite acceptable to stand near the entrance to the toll booths. Never hitchhike where drivers can't stop in good time or without causing an obstruction. You could also approach drivers at petrol stations and truck stops. Look presentable, carry as little luggage as possible and hold a sign in Italian indicating your destination.

It is sometimes possible to arrange lifts in advance – ask around at youth hostels. The International Lift Centre in Firenze (☎ 055 28 06 26) and Enjoy Rome (see the Tourist Offices section under Information in the Roma chapter) may be able to help. Dedicated hitchhikers might also like to get hold of Simon Calder's *Europe – A Manual for Hitchhikers*.

BOAT

Navi (large ferries) service the islands of Sicilia and Sardegna, and *traghetti* (smaller ferries) and *aliscafi* (hydrofoils) service areas such as the Isole Eolie, Isola d'Elba, the Isole Tremiti, Isola de Capri and Isola d'Ischia. The main embarkation points for Sardegna are Genova, Livorno, Civitavecchia and Napoli; for Sicilia the main points are Napoli and Villa San Giovanni in Calabria. The main points of arrival in Sardegna are Cagliari,

Arbatax, Olbia and Porto Torres; in Sicilia they are Palermo and Messina.

Tirrenia Navigazione is the major company servicing the Mediterranean and it has offices throughout Italy. The FS operates ferries to Sicilia and Sardegna. Detailed information on ferry companies, prices and times is provided in the Getting There & Away sections of the Sicilia and Sardegna chapters and other relevant destinations.

Many ferry services are overnight and travellers can choose between cabin accommodation (men and women are usually segregated in 2nd class, although families will be kept together) or a *poltrona*, an airline-type armchair. Deck class is available only in summer and only on some ferries, so ask when making your booking. Restaurant, bar and recreation facilities, including cinemas, are available on the larger, long-haul ferries. All ferries carry vehicles.

LOCAL TRANSPORT

All major cities have good transport systems, with bus and underground-train networks usually integrated. However, in Venezia your only options are by boat or on foot.

Bus & Underground

City bus services are usually frequent and reliable. You must always buy bus tickets before you board the bus and validate them once aboard. It is common practice among Italians and many tourists to ride buses for free by not validating their tickets – just watch how many people rush to punch their tickets when an inspector boards the bus. However, if you get caught with an unvalidated ticket, you will be fined on the spot (up to L50,000 in most cities, but between L100,000 and L500,000 in Roma). Efficient provincial and regional bus services also operate between towns and villages. Tourist offices will provide information on bus routes.

There are underground systems in Roma, Milano (MM) and Napoli (Metropolitana). You must buy tickets and validate them before getting on the train. You can get a map of the network from tourist offices in the relevant city.

Tickets Tickets can be bought at most *tabaccheria* (tobacconists), at many newspaper stands and at ticket booths or dispensing machines at bus stations (for instance, outside Stazione Termini in Roma, where many of the city buses stop) and in underground stations. They are valid both for buses and for the underground systems in Roma, Milano and Napoli. Tickets generally cost from L1500 to L2000 for one hour to 90 minutes (it varies from city to city). Most cities offer 24-hour tourist tickets which can mean big savings.

Taxi

Taxis in Italy are expensive and it is usually possible to catch a bus instead. You can usually find a taxi in taxi ranks at train and bus stations or you can telephone (radio-taxi phone numbers are listed in the Getting Around sections of the major cities). However, if you book a taxi by phone, you will be charged for the trip the driver makes to reach you. Taxis will rarely stop when hailed on the street and generally will not respond to telephone bookings if you are calling from a public phone.

Rates vary from city to city. A good indication of the average is Roma, where the minimum charge is L4500 for the first 3km, then L1200 per kilometre. There are supplements of L5000 from 10 pm to 7 am, and L2000 from 7 am to 10 pm on Sunday and public holidays. No more than four or five people will be allowed in one taxi, depending on the size of the car.

There is a Roma airports supplement: L15,000 on travel to and from the airports, because they are outside the city limits.

Watch out also for taxi drivers who take advantage of new arrivals and stretch out the length of the trip, and consequently the size of the fare.

ORGANISED TOURS

People wanting to travel around Italy on a fully organised package tour have a wide range of options and it is best to discuss these with your travel agent. A selection of companies that offer tours of Italy can be found in the Organised Tours section of the Getting There & Away chapter.

Once in Italy, it is often less expensive and usually more enjoyable to see the sights independently, but if you are in a hurry or prefer guided tours, go to the Sestante CIT office (in all major cities). They organise city tours for an average price of L40,000. They also offer an eight day Sicilia tour for L1,230,000, and a three day tour taking in Roma, Assisi, Firenze, Pisa, Padova and Venezia for L670,000. The prices include twin-share accommodation, transport and some meals.

CTS, which has offices in all major cities, offers six or seven-day tours of various destinations, including northern Italy (Roma, Venezia, Firenze, Siena and much more), southern Italy (Capri, Napoli and Pompei) or Sicilia, for around L1,500,000. The price includes twin-share accommodation, half-board, transport by bus, and admission to museums and sites.

Tourist offices can generally assist with information on local agencies that offer tours. There are also organisations in Italy that can offer guided bike tours, including I Bike Italy, which organises rides in the countryside around Firenze (see Cycling in the Firenze section of the Toscana chapter).

Roma

'I now realise all the dreams of my youth,' wrote Goethe on his arrival in Roma (Rome) in the winter of 1786. Perhaps Roma today is more chaotic, but it's certainly no less romantic or fascinating. In this city, a phenomenal concentration of history, legend and monuments coexists with an equally phenomenal concentration of people busily going about everyday life.

Modern-day Roma is a city of about four million residents and, as the capital of Italy, it is the centre of national government. Tourists usually spend their time in the historic centre, thereby avoiding the sprawling and architecturally anonymous suburbs.

While the look of central Roma is most obviously defined by the baroque style of the many fountains, churches and palaces, there are also ancient monuments, and beautiful churches and buildings of the medieval, Gothic and Renaissance periods, along with the architectural embellishments of the post-Risorgimento and Fascist eras.

Realistically, a week is probably a reasonable amount of time to explore the city. Whatever time you devote to Roma, put on your walking shoes, buy a good map and plan your time carefully and the city will seem less overwhelming than it first appears. If you are planning to visit Roma in July or August, remember that the suffocatingly hot and humid weather can make sightseeing an unpleasant pastime. The upside is that most Romans head for the beaches or mountains at this time, leaving the city quieter and more tolerable.

HISTORY

In Roma, there is visible evidence of the two great empires of the western world: the Roman Empire and the Christian Church. From the Foro Romano and the Colosseo to the Basilica di San Pietro and Il Vaticano, and in almost every piazza, lies history on so many levels that the saying 'Rome, a lifetime is not enough' must certainly be true.

Highlights

- Marvel at the scene from the dome of San Pietro, from where the view of Roma is unrivalled, before descending to the splendours of the Musei Vaticani

- Wander through the ruins of the Foro Romano, the Palatino and the Colosseo and imagine the glory of ancient Roma

- Take a seat at an outdoor café in Piazza Navona and enjoy a wine, cappuccino or gelato while you admire the fabulous fountains and watch Romans and tourists going about their business: you'll pay through the nose, but it's worth it!

- Stand with your back to the Fontana di Trevi and throw in a coin

- Stroll along Via Appia Antica on Sunday, when it is closed to traffic

- Explore the fascinating ruins of the port city of Ostia Antica, just outside Roma

Roma (Rome)	
Map 1	p193
Map 2	pp194-5
Map 3	pp198-9
Map 4	pp203-3
Map 5	pp204-5
Map 6	p206
Roma Transport Map	p208
Foro Romano (Roman Forum) & Palatino	p183
Roma Walking Tour	p175
Lazio	p244

LE MARCHE

TOSCANA   UMBRIA

Viterbo
p251

ABRUZZO

Greater Roma
p240

MOLISE

Mar
Tirreno

CAMPANIA

It is generally agreed that Roma had its origins in a group of Etruscan, Latin and Sabine settlements on the Palatino, Esquilino and Quirinale hills. These and surrounding hills constitute the now-famous seven hills of the city. Ancient Romans put the date of their city's foundation as 21 April 753 BC and, indeed, archaeological discoveries have confirmed the existence of a settlement on the Palatino in that period.

However, it is the legend of Romulus and Remus which prevails. According to this legend, the twin sons of Rhea Silvia and the war god Mars were raised by a she-wolf after being abandoned on the banks of the Tevere (Tiber) river. The myth says Romulus killed his brother during a battle over who should govern and then established the city of Roma on the Palatino, with himself as the first king. Later, he disappeared one day, enveloped in a cloud that was believed to have carried him back to the domain of the gods.

Out of the legend grew an empire which eventually controlled almost the entire world known to Europeans at the time, an achievement described by a historian of the day as 'without parallel in human history'.

Roma has always inspired wonder and awe in its visitors. Its ruined, but still quite imposing, monuments represent a point of reference for a city which, through the imperial, medieval, Renaissance and baroque periods and beyond, has undergone many transformations. The cultured and wealthy Europeans who, from the mid-17th century onwards, rediscovered Roma, found in the Eternal City a continuity from the pagan to the Christian worlds. In fact, from the time of the Roman Empire, through the development of Christianity to the present day – a period of more than 2500 years – Roma has built up an archaeological archive of Western culture.

The historical sites of Roma are merely the tip of the iceberg. Tourists wandering around the city with their eyes raised to admire its monuments should know that about 4m under their feet exists another city, with traces of other settlements deeper still. The

NICKY CAVEN

Capitoline Wolf – Romulus and his brother Remus with their adoptive mother

Basilica di San Pietro stands on the site of an earlier basilica built by Emperor Constantine in the 4th century over the necropolis where San Pietro was buried. Castel Sant'Angelo was the tomb of Emperor Hadrian before it was converted into a fortress. The form of Piazza Navona is suggestive of a hippodrome and, in fact, it was built on the ruins of Emperor Domitian's stadium. To know all this can help you interpret and understand this chaotic and often frustrating city.

ORIENTATION

Roma is a vast city, but the historic centre is relatively small, defined by the twisting Tevere (Tiber) river to the west, the sprawling Villa Borghese park to the north, the Foro Romano (Roman Forum) and Palatino (Palatine Hill) to the south and the central train station, Stazione Termini, to the east. Most of the major sights are within a reasonable distance of the station. It is, for instance, possible to walk from the Colosseo, through the Foro Romano and the Palatino, up to Piazza di Spagna and across to Il Vaticano in one day, although such a full itinerary is hardly recommended, even for the most dedicated tourist. One of the great pleasures of being in Roma is wandering through the many beautiful *piazze*, stopping now and again for a *caffè* or a *gelato*.

Most new arrivals in Roma will end up at Stazione Termini, which is the terminal for

ROMA

all international and national trains. The station is commonly referred to as Termini. The main city bus station is on Piazza dei Cinquecento, directly in front of the station. Many intercity buses depart from and arrive at the front of Stazione Tiburtina, accessible from Termini on the Metropolitana Linea B. This should not be confused with Piazzale Tiburtino, at the top of Via Tiburtina near Stazione Termini. Buses serving towns in the region of Lazio depart from various points throughout the city, usually corresponding to stops on Metro lines. See the Getting There & Away section later in this chapter for details.

The main airport is Leonardo da Vinci (also known as Fiumicino airport) at Fiumicino. From the city centre, it's about half an hour by the special airport-Termini train or 45 minutes to one hour by car. A second airport, Ciampino, south of the city on the Via Appia Nuova, handles most charter flights to Roma. It is not as easily accessible as Fiumicino (see the Getting Around section later in this chapter).

If you plan to arrive in Roma by car, invest in a good road map of the city beforehand, so as to have an idea of the various routes into the city centre. Roma is encircled by a ring road, called the Grande Raccordo Anulare (GRA), which is connected to the A1 autostrada, the main north-south route in Italy. The main access routes from the GRA into the city centre include Via Salaria from the north, Via Aurelia from the northwest and Via Cristoforo Colombo from the south.

Local traffic is not permitted into the city centre, but tourists are allowed to drive to their hotels (see under Car & Motorcycle in the Getting Around section later in this chapter for more details).

The majority of cheap hotels and *pensioni* are concentrated around Stazione Termini. The area is seedy, particularly to the west, but the number of hotels makes it the most popular area for budget travellers and tour groups. However, it is not much more expensive, and definitely more enjoyable, to stay closer to the city centre.

Maps

Invest L6000 in the street map and bus guide entitled *Roma*, which is published by Editrice Lozzi in Roma; it is available at any newspaper stand in Termini. It lists all streets, with map references, as well as all bus routes. There is also an excellent free map called *Roma Centro*, which details the city's public transport routes. This can be picked up at the APT office or at one of the many information booths in the centre.

INFORMATION
Tourist Offices

There is an APT office (Map 3; ☎ 06 487 12 70), in the central hall at Stazione Termini, which is open from 8.15 am to 7.15 pm daily. The main APT office (Map 3; ☎ 06 488 99 253, 06 488 99 255) is at Via Parigi 5 and is open from 8.15 am to 7 pm Monday to Friday and from 8.15 am to 1.45 pm on Saturday. It has information on accommodation, museums, festivals and concert seasons, as well as details on local and intercity transport. Brochures, maps and hotel lists for other Italian cities are sometimes available at this office. There's also an APT branch office (☎ 06 659 54 471) in the arrivals hall at Fiumicino airport.

A good alternative is Enjoy Rome (Map 3; ☎ 06 445 18 43, fax 06 445 07 34, email info@enjoyrome.com), Via Varese 39 (a few minutes walk north-east of Stazione Termini), a privately run tourist office brimming with information about the city and its environs. It offers a free hotel reservation service and can also organise alternative accommodation, such as rental apartments. There's always someone who speaks English and staff are helpful. The office is open from 8.30 am to 2 pm and 3.30 to 6.30 pm Monday to Friday and from 8.30 am to 2 pm on Saturday. Enjoy Rome also publishes a very useful *Enjoy Rome* city guide and has a Web site at www.enjoyrome.com, with lots of practical information.

Tourist information booths can also be found at Largo Corrado Ricci (opposite the entrance to the Foro Romano), Largo Goldoni (on Via del Corso at the end of Via

Condotti) and next to the Palazzo del Esposizione on Via Nazionale.

Foreign Embassies

For addresses and telephone numbers, see Embassies & Consulates in Italy in the Facts for the Visitor chapter. All embassies and consulates are listed in the Roma telephone book under Ambasciate and Consolati. The Australian, Canadian and New Zealand embassies can be reached from Stazione Termini on bus No 36, which travels along Via Nomentana. This bus also passes the British embassy. The US, British and German embassies are easily accessible on foot from the station. The French embassy and consulate are in Roma's historic centre.

Money

Banks are open from 8.30 am to 1.30 pm and usually from 2.45 to 3.45 pm Monday to Friday. You will find a bank and several currency exchange booths at Stazione Termini. There is also a Banca di Roma exchange booth at Fiumicino airport, to the right as you exit from the customs area. Numerous other exchange booths are scattered throughout the city, including American Express on Piazza di Spagna (Map 3) and Thomas Cook on Piazza Barberini and Piazza della Repubblica (both Map 3).

Most people use *bancomats* (ATMs) to get cash advances on their credit cards and you should have no problems in Roma. It is straightforward and most ATMs give you the option of conducting the transaction in English, French or German. MasterCard and Visa card holders should also be able to get cash advances at most banks.

It is also possible to transfer money through Western Union (☎ 800 46 44 64). This service functions in Roma through a number of different outlets. See International Transfers under Money in the Facts for the Visitor chapter for details.

Post

See Post & Communications in the Facts for the Visitor chapter for more detailed information about postal services in Italy.

The main post office (Map 3) is at Piazza San Silvestro 20, just off Via del Tritone, and is open from 9 am to 6 pm Monday to Friday and to 2 pm on Saturday. *Fermo posta* (the Italian version of poste restante) is available here. Address letters to Fermo Posta – Roma Centrale, 00186, Roma. Telegrams can be sent from the office next door at No 18 (open from 8 am to midnight) or dictated by phone 24 hours a day on ☎ 186. Il Vaticano post office on Piazza San Pietro (Map 2) is open from 8.30 am to 7 pm Monday to Friday and to 6 pm on Saturday. The service from here is faster and more reliable than anywhere else, but there's no poste restante.

The postcode for central Roma is 00100.

Telephone

There are Telecom offices at Stazione Termini, from where you can make international calls either direct or through an operator, and near the train station on Via San Martino della Battaglia. International calls are also easily made (with a phonecard) from any public telephone. Phonecards can be purchased at tobacconists and newspaper stands or from dispensing machines at Telecom offices.

Fax

There are public fax services at major post offices. Otherwise, there are numerous private services, which usually also offer photocopying and film processing.

Email & Internet Access

Roma has several Internet cafés. These allow you to surf the Net and in most cases permit you to send email. Some places also provide email accounts. If they don't, receiving email can be difficult, unless you have your own email account to log on to.

Hackers (Map 2; ☎ 06 397 39 268) is a huge Internet café/restaurant near the Musei Vaticani at Via San Veniero 10-16. Internet access costs L8000 an hour or L50,000 for 10 hours. You can get snacks or a full meal by placing your order on the computer. It is open every day from 7.30 am until 1 am (with later closing on Friday and Saturday nights).

euro currency converter L10,000 = €5.16

Bibli bookshop (Map 4; ☎ 06 588 40 97), Via dei Fienaroli 28, Trastevere, offers 10 hours of Internet access (over a period of three months) for L60,000. For that you get your own email address and access to the Web, plus 10 MB of personal disk space. It's open from 11 am to midnight Tuesday to Sunday and from 5.30 pm to midnight on Monday.

Itaca Multimedia (☎ 06 686 14 64, fax 06 689 60 96) is at Via della Fosse di Castello 8, next to the Castel Sant'Angelo. It allows access to the Web and email and costs L15,000 per hour or L100,000 for a 10 hour subscription, which includes a personal mail box for email. Internet phone and video phone services are also available.

The Netgate (Map 6; ☎ 06 689 34 45), Piazza Firenze 25, in the heart of the historic centre, offers Internet access at L10,000 per hour, including an email account. If you pay for 10 hours you get another six hours free and there are discounts for students. In summer, it's open from 10.30 am to 10.30 pm Monday to Saturday. In winter, it's open from 10.40 am to 9 pm Monday to Saturday and from 3 to 9 pm Sunday.

Internet Café (Map 3; ☎ 06 445 49 53), Via dei Marrucini 12, in the San Lorenzo area, is another option. For L8000 (L10,000 after 9 pm) you can use a computer for one hour, as well as order one sandwich and one drink. It's open from 9 am to 2 am Monday to Friday and from 5 pm to 2 am on Saturday and Sunday.

Internet Resources

There is a page dedicated to Roma on Lonely Planet's Web site at www.lonely planet.com. Another good place to look is *Excite Reviews* at www.excite.com. Call this up and key in 'Rome, Italy' and it will give you a long selection of sites. The Web site www.vatican.va is the official home page of the Holy See. (See also Internet Resources in the Facts for the Visitor chapter.)

Travel Agencies

There is a CIT office (Map 3; ☎ 06 474 65 55) at Piazza della Repubblica 64, where you can make bookings for trains, ferries and planes. The staff speak English and can provide information on fares and discounts for students and young people. The office also handles tours of Roma and surrounding areas.

CTS (Map 3; ☎ 06 462 04 31), Via Genova 16, off Via Nazionale, offers much the same services and will also make hotel reservations, but focuses on discount and student travel. Good deals on air fares are available, but you will need to pay a membership fee to take advantage of them. It's a good idea to check if other agencies are offering similar discounts. There are CTS branch offices at the Stazione Ostiense air terminal and at Corso Vittorio Emanuele 297. The staff at both offices speak English.

American Express (Map 3; ☎ 06 6 76 41 for travel information, ☎ 06 7 22 82 for 24 hour line for reporting lost or stolen cards, ☎ 800 87 20 00 for lost or stolen travellers cheques), Piazza di Spagna 38, has a travel service similar to CIT and CTS, as well as a hotel reservation service, and can arrange tours of the city and surrounding areas.

Bookshops

The Corner Bookshop (Map 6; ☎ 06 583 69 42), Via del Moro 48, Trastevere, has an excellent range of English-language books and travel guides. The Anglo-American Bookshop (Map 3; ☎ 06 678 96 57), Via della Vite 27, off Piazza di Spagna, also has an excellent range of literature, travel guides and reference books, and is also the Thomas Cook agent for Italy.

The Lion Bookshop (Map 2; ☎ 06 326 54 007) is at Via dei Greci 33-36 and stocks a good range of books and magazines.

Feltrinelli International (Map 3; ☎ 06 487 01 71), Via VE Orlando 84, just off Piazza della Repubblica, has an extensive range of books for adults and children in English, Spanish, French, German and Portuguese, plus lots of guidebooks to Roma, Italy and the rest of the world. There's another Feltrinelli in Largo Argentina (Map 6).

The Economy Book & Video Center (Map 3), Via Torino 136, also has a good selection of books, including some second-hand paperbacks.

For travellers, Libreria del Viaggiatore (Map 6; ☎ 06 688 01 048), Via del Pellegrino 78, is a real find. This intimate bookshop is devoted to travelling and is crammed with travel guides and travel literature. It carries a huge range of maps for countries, regions and towns around the world, as well as walking maps. Some books are available in English and French.

Libraries

The British Council (☎ 06 47 81 41), Via delle Quattro Fontane 20, allows free public use of its large reference library. At the time of writing it had closed down its lending service and was in the process of setting up a multimedia information service. This will offer such services as use of CD ROMs, Internet access and, perhaps, email facilities.

Universities

There are a number of international universities in Roma. Tuition fees and course requirements vary from one institution to another. The American University of Rome (Map 4; ☎ 06 583 30 919, fax 06 583 30 992), Via Pietro Roselli 4, offers degree programmes in international business, international relations and liberal arts.

John Cabot University (Map 2; ☎ 06 681 91 221, email jcu@johncabot.edu) is in Trastevere at Via della Lungara 233, and has courses in business administration, international affairs, political science and art history. It has a Web site at www.johncabot .edu.

St John's University (Map 2; ☎ 06 63 69 37, email info@st johns.edu), Via Santa Maria Mediatrice 24 (near Il Vaticano) has MBA degrees and MA programmes in government and politics.

Cultural Centres

There are a large number of foreign cultural academies and institutes in Roma, where artists, writers, performers and academics come from their home countries to spend time in the city, creating, researching and absorbing Italian history and culture. The academies organise exhibitions, poetry readings, drama and dance performances, lectures and conferences. Both *Time Out Roma* and *Wanted in Rome* carry regular listings of the events and they are sometimes listed in *Roma C'è* (see the Entertainment section later in this chapter).

Laundry

There is an Onda Blu coin laundrette at Via Lamarmora 10, between Stazione Termini and Piazza Vittorio Emanuele II, open from 8 am to 10 pm. Bolle Blu has two outlets, at Via Palestro 59-61 and Via Malazzo 20b, also open from 8 am to 10 pm.

Toilets

Public toilets are not exactly widespread in Roma. A recent report estimated that there were less than 40 of them in the whole of the city. Most people use the toilets in bars and cafés, although you might need to buy a coffee first!

Left Luggage

There are left luggage services at Stazione Termini. The daily rate is L1500 per item.

Fiumicino airport has a 24 hour left luggage facility in the international arrivals area on the ground floor. It costs L4100 per item per day. For luggage over 160cm long, you pay an extra L4100 per day. Make sure you have your passport handy, as a photocopy will be made when you leave your luggage.

Medical Services

Emergency medical treatment is available in the casualty sections of public hospitals, including Policlinico Umberto I (Map 3; ☎ 06 4 99 71), Viale del Policlinico 155, near Stazione Termini, and Policlinico A Gemelli (☎ 06 3 01 51), Largo A Gemelli 8 (some distance from the centre). For skin problems go to Ospedale San Gallicano (Map 4; ☎ 06 588 23 90), Via di San Gallicano 25/A, in Trastevere. The hospital also has a venereal diseases clinic.

For HIV/AIDS treatment, contact Ospedale Spallanzani (Map 1; ☎ 06 582 37 639), Via Portuense 292. For information about abortion, go to the free clinic at Ospedale San Camillo (Map 1; ☎ 06 5 87 01), Circonvallazione Gianicolense 87. There are gynaecological clinics, known by the acronym AIED, at Via Toscana 30 (☎ 06 428 25 314) and at Viale Gorizia 14 (☎ 06 855 77 31), where foreign women can seek medical assistance. English-speaking doctors work there twice a week, but you need to phone to make an appointment.

The American Hospital (☎ 06 2 25 51), Via E Longoni 69, is a long way east of the city centre, off Via Collatina. It's private and you should use its services only if you have health insurance and have consulted your insurance company. Roma's paediatric hospital is Ospedale Bambino Gesù (Map 2; ☎ 06 6 85 91), on the Gianicolo (Janiculum Hill) at Piazza Sant'Onofrio 4.

In general, the casualty sections of Roma's hospitals give free treatment to emergency patients. However, if you are admitted, or are referred to a specialist, you may be charged a fee. See Health in the Facts for the Visitor chapter for further details.

Your embassy will be able to recommend where to go for medical treatment and should be able to refer you to doctors who speak your language.

There is a 24 hour pharmacy (☎ 06 488 00 19) just outside Stazione Termini at Piazza dei Cinquecento 51, on the corner with Via Cavour. Inside the station, a pharmacy opens from 7.30 am to 10 pm daily (closed in August). Otherwise, *farmacie* (pharmacies or chemists) are usually open from 9 am to 1 pm and 4 to 7.30 pm Monday to Saturday. They open on Sunday and at night on a rotation basis. Night pharmacies are listed in the daily newspapers. When pharmacies are shut, they are required by law to post a list of others open nearby.

Emergency

The questura (police station; Map 3; ☎ 06 4 68 61) is at Via San Vitale 11. The Ufficio Stranieri (Foreigners' Bureau; Map 3; ☎ 06 468 63 216) is around the corner at Via Genova 2. It is open 24 hours and thefts can be reported here. This office can issue you with a *permesso di soggiorno* (see Visas & Documents in the Facts for the Visitor chapter).

Dangers & Annoyances

Thieves are very active around Stazione Termini, at major sights such as the Colosseo and Foro Romano, and in the city's more expensive shopping streets, such as those around Piazza di Spagna. Be careful in crowded shops and watch out for motorcycle-riding bag and camera snatchers. Pickpockets like to work on crowded buses (the No 64 from Stazione Termini to San Pietro is notorious). For more comprehensive information on how to avoid being robbed see Dangers & Annoyances in the Facts for the Visitor chapter.

Although Roma's traffic is nowhere near as chaotic as that in Napoli, some drivers, particularly motorcyclists, do not stop at red lights. Don't expect them to stop at pedestrian crossings either. The accepted mode of crossing a road is to step into the traffic and walk at a steady pace. If in doubt, follow a Roman.

The heavy traffic also means heavy pollution which, in summer, can rise to such high levels that elderly people, children and people with respiratory complaints are warned to stay indoors. Check with your hotel for daily information.

Oh Poo!

Just a short note on another pollution problem which tourists will doubtless encounter in Roma – dog poo! No footpath is clear of it, so watch your step. A brief effort by the city council at raising public awareness of this issue came and went with little effect and, although fines of L200,000 can be imposed on the owners of offending pooches, no-one seems to worry much, not least the *vigili urbani* (urban police), who do little to enforce the law.

WALKING TOUR

The following is a short walking tour through the heart of Roma, an area dense with important monuments. It explores the courtyards of patrician palaces and the narrow streets of one of the city's more characteristic areas. The walk starts at the Largo di Torre Argentina and ends with Michelangelo's beautiful Piazza del Campidoglio and a breathtaking view over the Foro Romano.

It is easy to get to Largo di Torre Argentina, since it is well-served by public transport, including buses from Piazza Venezia and Stazione Termini (Nos H, 64 and 640), from Il Vaticano (Nos 64 and 62), from San Giovanni in Laterano and the Colosseo (No 87) and from Via del Corso and Via Veneto (No 56). The No 8 tram from Trastevere-Casaletto terminates in Largo di Torre Argentina.

Start on the southern side of the square and walk down past the junction of Via delle Botteghe Oscure and Via Florida. Cross Piazza della Enciclopedia Italiana, skirting the elegant **Palazzo Mattei di Paganica** (1 on Walking Tour map), built in 1541 and now housing the Istituto per l'Enciclopedia Italiana. This is one of five palaces built by the patrician Mattei family in the area, causing it to be renamed L'Isola dei Mattei (Mattei Island) in the mid-16th century.

Continue south to the charming **Piazza Mattei**, with its elegant **Fontana delle Tartarughe** (4), designed by Giacomo della Porta. The bronzes, by Taddeo Landini, were added between 1581 and 1584. Legend has it that the fountain was built in a single night for the Duke of Mattei, who owned the surrounding palaces. The duke had, apparently, just lost all his money and consequently his fiancée, and wanted to prove to her father that he was still capable of great things. In

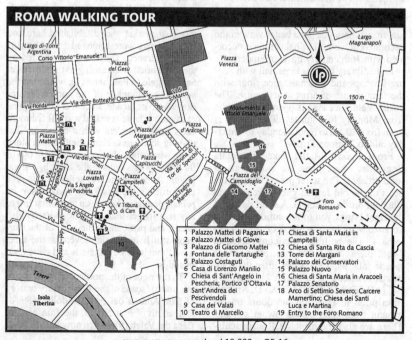

ROMA WALKING TOUR

1 Palazzo Mattei di Paganica
2 Palazzo Mattei di Giove
3 Palazzo di Giacomo Mattei
4 Fontana delle Tartarughe
5 Palazzo Costaguti
6 Casa di Lorenzo Manilio
7 Chiesa di Sant'Angelo in Pescheria; Portico d'Ottavia
8 Sant'Andrea dei Pescivendoli
9 Casa dei Valati
10 Teatro di Marcello
11 Chiesa di Santa Maria in Campitelli
12 Chiesa di Santa Rita da Cascia
13 Torre dei Margani
14 Palazzo dei Conservatori
15 Palazzo Nuovo
16 Chiesa di Santa Maria in Aracoeli
17 Palazzo Senatorio
18 Arco di Settimio Severo; Carcere Mamertino; Chiesa dei Santi Luca e Martina
19 Entry to the Foro Romano

the piazza at No 10 is the 16th century **Palazzo Costaguti** (5) and, at Nos 17-19, **Palazzo di Giacomo Mattei** (3). Through the entrance on the right of this palace is a beautiful 15th century courtyard with a staircase and an open gallery.

Go east along Via dei Funari and enter the **Palazzo Mattei di Giove** (2) at No 3. Built by Carlo Maderno in 1598, it now houses the Centro Italiano di Studi Americani (the Italian Centre for American Studies) and parts of it are open to the public. The palazzo, which is adorned with numerous pieces of ancient Roman sculpture, bas-relief and stucco, is a good example of the taste of the noble classes for all things classical, which flowered along with humanism during the Renaissance. The courtyards contain ancient Roman bas-reliefs set into the walls, and busts and statues from what remains of the Mattei collection, once one of the most valuable collections of Roman antiquities. The monumental staircase, decorated with classical stucco and ancient sculptures, leads to a library. There is a loggia, from where you get a better view of the decorative scheme. The balustrade is decorated with 16th century busts of emperors.

In the library there is large hall with ceiling frescoes and a Renaissance floor with the family coat of arms at its centre. The palace's entrance area is open to the public from Monday to Saturday. The library is open from 10 am to 6 pm Monday to Thursday and to 2 pm on Friday.

From Piazza Mattei take Via della Reginella, where there are workshops of local artisans. The street passes through the heart of the old Jewish ghetto area around Via del Portico d'Ottavia. A short detour to the right brings you to the curious **Casa di Lorenzo Manilio** (6) at Via del Portico d'Ottavia 1. The building was constructed in 1468, or, as the Latin inscription on its façade tells us, 2221 years after the traditional founding of Roma on 21 April 753 BC (AB URB CON MMCCXXI). Another inscription in Latin on the doors on the ground floor tells us the owner's name. There are also fragments of Roman sculpture, an inscription in Greek set into the wall, a relief depicting a lion killing a fallowdeer, a Greek stele with two dogs and a funereal relief with four busts.

Return to the junction with Via della Reginella and follow Via del Portico d'Ottavia. Go past the **Case dei Fabi** with their beautiful 16th century windows and the 13th century **Torre dei Grassi**, until you reach the remains of an entrance to the **Portico d'Ottavia** (7), built by Quintus Cecilius Metellus in 146 BC and rebuilt in 27-23 BC by Augustus, the first emperor of Roma, who dedicated it to his sister Octavia. It was rebuilt for the third and final time by Settimus Severus and Caracalla in 203 AD. Once a vast rectangular portico measuring 132m by 119m, it enclosed temples dedicated to Juno and Jupiter, the latter being the first temple in Roma to be built entirely of marble. It also contained a Latin and a Greek library and numerous magnificent statues and works of art.

By the Middle Ages the portico had already been sacked and pulled down. The city fish market was established here and two columns were removed from the surviving entrance. They were substituted by the large brick arch leading to the **Chiesa di Sant'Angelo in Pescheria** (7), which has the surviving colonnade of the portico incorporated into its façade. Recent archaeological excavations have revealed a small fishmonger's stand complete with a bench for displaying the wares, clam shells and a stone basin where the fish were washed. On one of the brick pillars outside the church, a stone plaque states that the fish-sellers had to give city officials the head and body *usque ad primas pinnas inclusive* (up to the first fin) of any fish longer than the plaque itself. Fish heads, and particularly the head of the sturgeon still living in the Tevere at the time, were thought to be delicious and were used in soups.

To the right of the portico you will notice the stucco façade of the 17th century oratory of **Sant'Andrea dei Pescivendoli** (1689; 8) and, south of it at No 29, the 14th century **Casa dei Valati** (9), which now houses the X

Circoscrizione of the Comune di Roma, which oversees the city's cultural patrimony. The building stands in isolation, since the surrounding buildings were demolished in 1927 during the restoration of the Teatro di Marcello at the rear. Wander along the narrow street by the portico to get a feeling for the traditional atmosphere of the ghetto.

The narrow passage opens onto the deserted Via Sant'Angelo in Pescheria. From here head along Via Tribuna di Campitelli, go around the back of the church and then bear right until you come to a dead end. From this isolated spot you get a view of the arches of the **Teatro di Marcello** (10). Only twelve of the original 41 arches, which are made of large travertine blocks, remain. You can also see the three marble columns with Corinthian capitals and beams of the Tempio di Apollo Sosiano, dedicated in 431 BC and rebuilt in 34 BC.

Retrace your steps out of the dead end street and take Via Tribuna di Campitelli to the right. At No 23 is a house incorporating a medieval portico with granite columns and Ionian capitals. After a short walk you come to **Piazza Campitelli**. On the western and north-eastern sides of the piazza stand a row of fine palaces belonging to five noble families: the Gaetani-Lovatelli family at Via Tribuna di Campitelli 16 (16th century), the Patrizi-Clementi family at Via Cavaletti 2 (16th century), the Cavaletti family at Piazza Campitelli 1 (16th century), the Albertoni family (early 17th century) and the Capizucchi famil y (late 16th century).

The **Chiesa di Santa Maria in Campitelli** (11), on the other side of the piazza, was built by Carlo Rainaldi and is a masterpiece of late baroque style. The church was built in 1662 in honour of the Virgin Mary, who was believed to have halted the plague of 1656. On the main altar there is an image of the miraculous Madonna in silver leaf and enamel. To the left of the church there is a pretty fountain designed in 1589 by Giacomo della Porta.

The 17th century façade of the building at No 6 was designed by the architect Flaminio Ponzio and once adorned his house in what

is now the Via dei Fori Imperiali. It was rebuilt here after the house was demolished in 1933. From the internal courtyard of the building next door (open to the public) there is a view of the archaeological area around the Teatro di Marcello against the backdrop of a medieval house.

Slightly further on, 0n Via Montanara, is the **Chiesa di Santa Rita da Cascia** (12), now deconsecrated. Built by Carlo Fontana in 1665, it was originally situated at the foot of the nearby Scalinata dell'Aracoeli and rebuilt on this spot in 1940 to allow for an urban revamp. Via Montanara brings you out onto Via del Teatro di Marcello, from where you have another good view of the Teatro di Marcello, crowned by Palazzo Orsini. Turn back and take Via Capizucchi to the right. This takes you through narrow streets into Piazza Capizucchi. Head diagonally across the piazza into Piazza Margana, where you'll see the **Torre dei Margani** (13). Together with the surrounding buildings, the tower looks like a fortified medieval residence. In the wall you will notice an ancient column with an Ionian capital. In the next door along are large pieces of Roman cornice from buildings of the late Empire.

Turn right into Via di Tor Margana and then right again into the darkness of Vicolo Margana. Go under an arch and you emerge into Via Tribuna di Tor de' Specchi. Here at No 3 is another medieval tower. Turn left to reach the chaotic Piazza d'Aracoeli, from where you have a splendid 180 degree view extending from the Palazzo Venezia to the Campidoglio. Turn right and go past the 16th century façade of Palazzo Pecci-Blunt at No 3 and the 17th century Palazzo Massimo di Rignano. This brings you to the monumental flight of steps designed by Michelangelo and leading up to the Campidoglio. If you are making this tour by bicycle, a road to the right of the stairway leads up to the square (closed to ordinary traffic).

The flight of steps is guarded at the bottom by two Egyptian basalt lions (turned into fountains in 1588), and almost touches the older staircase on the left, which leads up to the **Chiesa di Santa Maria in Aracoeli**

Hidden Treasures

Few tourists know that tucked away in Roma's medieval churches are some of the most beautiful Byzantine-style mosaics in Italy. Most of these mosaics decorate the apses of the city's important churches, such as Santa Maria Maggiore, Santa Maria in Trastevere and San Clemente. The oldest mosaics date from the 4th century (Mausoleo di Santa Costanza and Chiesa di Santa Pudenziana), the period in which the Roman art of mosaic-making was evolving into the early Christian and Byzantine styles. Those depicting Santa Costanza retain some characteristics of Roman mosaics: a white background, geometric composition and ornamental motifs.

During the reign of Constantine (306-37), when the Christian religion was decriminalised, many churches were built and ornamental mosaic became the main form of decoration. Often used to cover vast areas of wall inside the new churches, they were a form of architectural tapestry which, with their uneven tesserae of coloured glass and gold, brilliantly reflected light to create strong effects and sharp contrasts of colour.

Roma's early Christian mosaics also illustrate the progression from the naturalism of Roman art to the symbolism of Christian art, reflected, for example, in the various ways in which Jesus Christ was represented. A very early Christian mosaic in a mausoleum under the Basilica di San Pietro shows Christ in the form of Apollo. In Chiesa di Santa Pudenziana (390), he is represented enthroned between the apostles, but his magisterial air is reminiscent of Jupiter and the apostles are dressed as Roman senators. By the 9th century, as in Chiesa di Santa Prassede, he has become the Lamb and the faithful his flock.

The mosaics of Roma's medieval churches are a fascinating and often overlooked treasure for the tourist who might not have time to visit Ravenna or Monreale. The following is a suggested itinerary of some of the lesser-known churches. The mosaics in major churches are described in the relevant sections of this chapter.

The **Mausoleo di Santa Costanza** was built in the mid-4th century by Costantia, daughter of Constantine, as a mausoleum for herself and her sister Helen. This round church is in the same grounds as Basilica di Sant'Agnese Fuori le Mura, on Via Nomentana, a few kilometres north of the centre (catch bus No 60 from Piazza Venezia). As well as the fascinating palaeo-Christian mosaics on the barrel-vaulting of the ambulatory, the 7th century mosaics of St

(16), also accessible from the Campidoglio. Climb the **Cordonata di Michelangelo**, noticing the shift in perspective on the colossal Dioscuri, Castor and Pollux, and their horses that await your arrival at the top. They are Roman statues, dating from the late Empire, and were found in a temple complex dedicated to them near Monte dei Cenci. In a symmetrical arrangement on the same balustrade are the **Trofei di Mario**, representing Saracen weapons, that date back to the reign of Domitian, and statues of the Emperor Constantine and his son Constans II, found at the Terme di Costantino. There are also two milestones taken from the

Via Appia Antica, which bear inscriptions of the emperors Nerva and Vespasian. Once you reach the top of the stairs, the piazza, also designed by Michelangelo, will take your breath away. It is bordered by the **Palazzo Nuovo** (15), also known as Palazzo del Museo Capitolino, on the northern side, the **Palazzo Senatorio** (17) at the rear and the **Palazzo dei Conservatori** (14) on the southern side. In its centre stands a very good copy of an original bronze equestrian statue of the Roman Emperor Marcus Aurelius.

Walk towards the Palazzo Senatorio which is at the far end of the piazza, the official seat of Roma's mayor. In front of the

Hidden Treasures

Agnes and Popes Symmachus and Honorius I in the apse of the basilica are also worth taking a look at.

Tradition says that **Chiesa di Santa Pudenziana**, one of the oldest churches in Roma, was founded on the site of a house where San Pietro was given hospitality. The structure actually incorporated the internal thermal hall of the house. The mosaic in the apse dates from 390 and is the earliest of its kind in Roma but, unfortunately, was partially destroyed by a 16th century restoration. The church is on Via Urbana.

Basilica di SS Cosma e Damiano, on Via dei Fori Imperiali, harbours magnificent 6th century mosaics on the triumphal arch (Christ as the Lamb enthroned, surrounded by candlesticks and angels, as well as the symbols of the evangelists). In the apse you can see Cosma and Damian being presented to Christ and, underneath, Christ as the Lamb, with the 12 apostles also represented as lambs. Bethlehem and Jerusalem are represented on either side.

The 9th century **Chiesa di Santa Prassede**, on Via Santa Prassede, was founded by Pope Paschal I, who transferred the bones of 2000 martyrs there from the catacombs. The rich mosaics of the apse feature Christ in the centre of the semi-dome, surrounded by SS Pietro, Pudentiana and Zenone (to the right) and SS Paolo, Prassede and Pasquale (to the left). Underneath is Christ the Lamb and his flock. The **Cappella di San Zenone**, inside the church, is the most important Byzantine monument in Roma, built by Paschal I as a mausoleum for his mother. Known as the Garden of Paradise, the chapel has a vaulted interior completely covered in mosaics, including the *Madonna with Saints*, *Christ with Saints* and, in the vault, *Christ with Angels*. The pavement of the chapel is one of the earliest examples of opus sectile, and, in a small niche on the right, there are fragments of a column brought from Jerusalem in 1223, said to be the column at which Christ was scourged.

Across the Tevere, on Piazza dei Mercanti, is the **Basilica di Santa Cecilia in Trastevere**, built in the 9th century by Paschal I over the house of Santa Cecilia, where she was martyred in 230. The impressive mosaic in the apse was executed in 870 and features Christ giving a blessing. To his right are SS Pietro, Valerio (husband of Santa Cecilia) and Cecilia herself. To his left are SS Paolo, Agata and Pasquale. The holy cities are depicted underneath.

---

palace's double staircase is a fountain displaying a marble and porphyry statue of a sitting Minerva which dates from the time of Domitian. There is a colossal statue of the Tevere on the right and one of the Nile on the left. Martino Longhi il Vecchio's bell tower replaced an old medieval tower in 1578. This had been part of the fortress built by the Corsi family on top of the remains of the Tabularium, the ancient Roman state archive, built in 78 BC and turned into a salt deposit and prison in the early Middle Ages. Incorporated into the rear of the building, the monumental façade of the Tabularium, with 11 large supports in tufa blocks, formed

an imposing architectural backdrop to the Foro Romano.

Take the road downhill to the right of the Palazzo Senatorio. This takes you past the impressive entrance of the Tabularium and brings you to a crowded terrace overlooking the ancient Foro Romano and the Colosseo against the backdrop of the city and the Colli Albani (Alban Hills) – definitely one of the best views in Roma.

The route ends here. However, if you want to visit the Foro Romano (admission is free), go back to the Piazza del Campidoglio and descend to the left of Palazzo Senatorio. Via di San Pietro in Carcere begins here. Note

ROMA

the column bearing a reproduction of the famous *Capitoline Wolf* suckling Romulus and Remus. In front of you is a view of the Foro and **Arco di Settimio Severo** (18). Steps lead down into the area of the **Carcere Mamertino**, where San Pietro was held captive. You pass the baroque **Chiesa dei Santi Luca e Martina** before reaching the Via dei Fori Imperiali. Head right for the entrance to the **Foro Romano** (19).

PIAZZA DEL CAMPIDOGLIO (Map 3)

Designed by Michelangelo in 1538 and located on the Campidoglio (Capitoline Hill), this piazza is bordered by three palaces, also designed by Michelangelo: the Palazzo dei Conservatori on the southern side, the Palazzo Senatorio to the south-east and the Palazzo Nuovo (Palazzo del Museo Capitolino) to the north. It was on this hill, which was the seat of the ancient Roman government and is now the seat of the city's municipal government, that Brutus spoke of the death of Julius Caesar and Nelson hoisted the British flag in 1799 before he prevented Napoleon from entering the city. For the greatest visual impact, approach the piazza from Piazza d'Aracoeli and ascend the *cordonata*, a stepped ramp also designed by Michelangelo.

The bronze equestrian statue of Emperor Marcus Aurelius in the centre of the piazza is a copy of the original, which has been restored and is now on display inside the Palazzo Nuovo.

Musei Capitolini (Capitoline Museums) is the collective name for the two museums on the Campidoglio: **Palazzo del Museo Capitolino** and **Palazzo dei Conservatori** (☎ 06 671 02 071) opposite. The museums are made up of the Sale dei Conservatori, the Museo Nuovo, the Braccio Nuovo and the Pinacoteca. They hold one of the most impressive collections of ancient sculpture in the world, founded in 1471 when Pope Sixtus IV donated the first group of bronze sculptures to the city. The most famous piece in the Palazzo dei Conservatori is the *Capitoline Wolf*, an Etruscan bronze statue from

the 6th century BC. Romulus and Remus were added in 1509. Also of interest in this wing are the *Spinario*, a statue of a boy taking a thorn from his foot, dating from the 1st century BC, and a bronze bust of Julius Caesar's assassin, Brutus. The inner court of the ground floor contains the remains of a colossal statue of Emperor Constantine – the head, a hand and a foot – which were removed from the Basilica di Costantino in the Foro Romano.

Major works in the **Museo Nuovo** in the Palazzo del Museo Capitolino, include the impressive *Dying Gaul* and the *Capitoline Venus*, a Roman copy of a 3rd century BC Greek original. The collection of busts of Roman emperors and other famous people of the day is well worth a look.

If you walk to the right of Palazzo Senatorio on Via del Campidoglio, you'll see one of the best views in Roma – a panorama of the Foro Romano. To the left of the palace is Via di San Pietro in Carcere and the ancient Roman **Carcere Mamertino** (Mammertine Prison), where prisoners were put through a hole in the floor to starve to death. San Pietro was believed to have been imprisoned here and to have created a miraculous stream of water to baptise his jailers. It is now the site of Chiesa di San Pietro in Carcere.

The **Chiesa di Santa Maria in Aracoeli** is between the Piazza del Campidoglio and the Monumento a Vittorio Emanuele II, at the highest point of the hill. It is accessible either by a long flight of steps from the Piazza d'Aracoeli or from behind the Palazzo del Museo Capitolino. Built on the site where legend says the Tiburtine Sybil told Augustus of the coming birth of Christ, it features frescoes by Pinturicchio in the first chapel of the south aisle. The church is noted for a statue of the baby Jesus, said to have been carved from the wood of an olive tree from the garden of Gethsemane. The statue was stolen in 1994 and a replica is on display.

PIAZZA VENEZIA (Map 3)

Piazza Venezia is overshadowed by the unusual **Monumento a Vittorio Emanuele II**.

Often referred to by Italians as the *macchina da scrivere* – because of its resemblance to a typewriter – the monument was built to commemorate Italian unification. It incorporates the Altare della Patria (Altar of the Fatherland) and the tomb of the unknown soldier.

On the western side of the piazza is the Renaissance-era **Palazzo Venezia**, which was partially built with materials quarried from the Colosseo. Mussolini used it as his official residence and made some of his famous speeches from the balcony. Major exhibitions are held here. **Museo di Palazzo Venezia** (☎ 06 679 88 65), entrance at Via del Plebiscito 118, has an interesting collection of works of art. The museum is open from 9 am to 2 pm Monday to Saturday. Tickets cost L8000.

The **Basilica di San Marco** was founded in the 4th century in honour of San Marco l'Evangelista. After undergoing several major transformations over the centuries, the church has a Renaissance façade, a Romanesque bell tower and a largely baroque interior. The main attraction is the 9th century mosaic in the apse, which depicts Christ with saints and Pope Gregory IV.

The **Palazzo Doria Pamphili** is just north of Piazza Venezia on the corner of Via del Corso and Via del Plebiscito. Inside is the **Galleria Doria Pamphili** (☎ 06 679 73 23), which contains the private collections of the Doria and Pamphili families, including paintings by Titian, Tintoretto and Caravaggio, as well as a collection of sculptures. The gallery is open from 10 am to 5 pm daily except Thursday. The entrance is at Piazza del Collegio Romano 2 and admission costs L13,000. Guided tours of the private apartments take place between 10.30 am and 12.30 pm and cost L5000.

Linking Piazza Venezia with the Colosseo is the Via dei Fori Imperiali. This was one of Mussolini's projects and involved the destruction of many 16th century buildings and the levelling of part of the Velia hill. It has been proposed that the ill-considered road should be closed between Via Cavour and Piazza Venezia. At present, traffic is limited and the entire stretch from the Colosseo to

Piazza Venezia becomes a pedestrian zone on most Sundays and public holidays.

FORO DI TRAIANO (Map 3)

Designed by Apollodorus of Damascus for Emperor Trajan and constructed at the beginning of the 2nd century AD, the Foro di Traiano (Trajan's Forum) was a vast complex measuring 300m by 185m that extended from what is now Piazza Venezia. It comprised a basilica for the judiciary, two libraries – one Greek and one Latin – a temple, a triumphal arch in honour of the emperor, and the **Colonna di Traiano** (Trajan's Column). Restored in the late 1980s, the column was erected to mark Trajan's victories over the Dacians. It was used to house the ashes of the emperor, which were contained in a golden urn placed on a marble slab at the base of the column. The urn and ashes disappeared during one of the Saracen sacks of Roma.

The column is decorated with a series of reliefs depicting the battles between the Roman and Dacian armies, which are regarded as among the finest examples of ancient Roman sculpture. A golden statue of Trajan once topped the column but was lost during the Middle Ages and replaced with a statue of San Pietro. Apart from the column, all that remains of the grand imperial forum are some of the pillars which once formed part of the Basilica Ulpia, the largest basilica built in the ancient city.

The **Mercati di Traiano** (Trajan's Markets) were also designed by Apollodorus and constructed on three levels, comprising six floors of shops and offices in a semicircle. You can get an idea of their grandeur from the high vaulted roofs. It's worth paying the admission fee, if only to get to the upper levels, which afford spectacular views of the Foro Romano. The tall red brick tower above the market buildings, the **Torre delle Milizie**, was built in the 13th century for defensive purposes. The markets and forum are open from 9 am to 6 pm Tuesday to Sunday from April to October, and to one hour before sunset the rest of the year. Admission costs L3750. The entrance to the markets is at Via IV Novembre 94.

Just to the south-east of Trajan's forum and markets are the **Foro d'Augusto** and the **Foro di Nerva**, although very little remains of either complex. The 30m-high wall behind the Foro d'Augusto was built to protect the area from the fires which frequently swept through the area.

There is a delightful **walkway** beneath the loggia of the 12th century Casa dei Cavalieri di Rodi (ancient seat of the Knights of St John of Jerusalem), which is between the forums of Trajan and Augustus and accessible from either Via dei Fori Imperiali or Piazza del Grillo. In summer the three forums are illuminated at night.

FORO ROMANO & PALATINO
Foro Romano

The ancient Roman commercial, political and religious centre, the Foro Romano (Roman Forum), stands in a valley between the Capitoline and Palatine hills (see the Foro Romano & Palatino map). The forum was constructed over 900 years, with later emperors erecting buildings next to those from the Republican era. Its importance declined along with the Roman Empire after the 4th century AD, and the temples, monuments and buildings constructed by successive emperors, consuls and senators fell into ruin, eventually leading to the site being used as pasture land. In the Middle Ages the area was known as the Campo Vaccino (literally 'cow field') – ironic, since the valley in which the forum stood had been used as pasture land in the earliest days of the city's development.

During medieval times the area was extensively plundered for its stone and precious marbles. Many temples and buildings were converted to other uses, while other monuments lay half revealed. The physical destruction of Roma's ancient city can be blamed not on invaders or natural disasters, but on the Romans themselves. Over the centuries, in the name of what they called progress, the Romans dismantled the city brick by brick and marble block by marble block in order to build their new palaces, churches and monuments.

During the Renaissance, with the renewed appreciation of all things classical, the Foro Romano provided inspiration for artists and architects. The area was systematically excavated in the 18th and 19th centuries, and excavations continue.

Access to the Foro Romano is from Via dei Fori Imperiali or from Piazza di Santa Maria Nova, near the Arco di Tito. The forum is open from 9 am to 7 pm Monday to Saturday (closing earlier in winter) and from 9 am to 2 pm on Sunday and holidays. From 1 June to 30 September it also opens from 9 pm to midnight on Saturday. Admission is free. Guided tours in all major languages are available for L6000 per person. Phone the Centro Servizi per l'Archeologia (☎ 06 481 55 76) for information in English and to book tickets and guided tours in English.

As you enter the Foro Romano from Via dei Fori Imperiali, to your left is **Tempio di Antonino e Faustina**, erected by the Senate in 141 AD and dedicated to the Empress Faustina and later, after his death, to the Emperor Antoninus Pius. It was transformed into the Chiesa di San Lorenzo in Miranda in the 8th century. To your right is **Basilica Aemilia**, built in 179 BC. The building was 100m long and its façade was a two storey portico lined with shops. Destroyed and rebuilt several times, the basilica was almost completely demolished during the Renaissance, when it was plundered for its precious marbles.

The **Via Sacra**, which traverses the Foro Romano from north-west to south-east, runs in front of the basilica. Continuing along Via Sacra in the direction of the Campidoglio, you will reach the **Curia**, on the right just after the Basilica Aemilia. Once the meeting place of the Roman Senate, it was rebuilt successively by Julius Caesar, Augustus and Domitian and converted into a Christian church in the Middle Ages. The church was dismantled and the Curia restored in the 1930s. The bronze doors are copies – the Roman originals were moved by Borromini to the Basilica di San Giovanni in Laterano.

In front of the Curia is the famous **Lapis Niger**, a large piece of black marble that

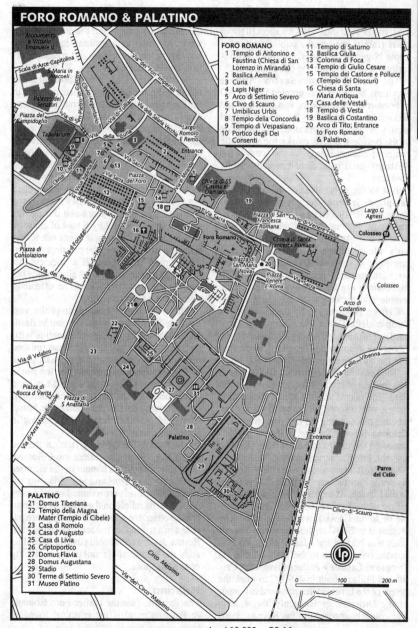

FORO ROMANO & PALATINO

FORO ROMANO
1 Tempio di Antonino e Faustina (Chiesa di San Lorenzo in Miranda)
2 Basilica Aemilia
3 Curia
4 Lapis Niger
5 Arco di Settimio Severo
6 Clivo di Scauro
7 Umbilicus Urbis
8 Tempio della Concordia
9 Tempio di Vespasiano
10 Portico degli Dei Consenti
11 Tempio di Saturno
12 Basilica Giulia
13 Colonna di Foca
14 Tempio di Giulio Cesare
15 Tempio dei Castore e Polluce (Tempio dei Dioscuri)
16 Chiesa di Santa Maria Antiqua
17 Casa delle Vestali
18 Tempio di Vesta
19 Basilica di Costantino
20 Arco di Tito; Entrance to Foro Romano & Palatino

PALATINO
21 Domus Tiberiana
22 Tempio della Magna Mater (Tempio di Cibele)
23 Casa di Romolo
24 Casa d'Augusto
25 Casa di Livia
26 Criptoportico
27 Domus Flavia
28 Domus Augustana
29 Stadio
30 Terme di Settimio Severo
31 Museo Platino

0   100   200 m

euro currency converter L10,000 = €5.16

covered a sacred area which legend says was the tomb of Romulus. Down a short flight of stairs (rarely open to the public) under the Lapis Niger is the oldest known Latin inscription, dating from the 6th century BC.

The **Arco di Settimio Severo** (Arch of Septimus Severus) was erected in 203 AD in honour of the emperor and his sons and is considered one of Italy's major triumphal arches. A circular base stone, the **umbilicus urbis**, beside the arch marks the symbolic centre of ancient Roma. To the south is the **Rostrum**, used in ancient times by public speakers.

Just to the north-west of the arch is the **Tempio di Saturno** (Temple of Saturn), inaugurated in 497 BC and one of the most important ancient Roman temples. It was used as the city's treasury and during Caesar's rule contained 13 tonnes of gold, 114 tonnes of silver and 30 million silver *sesterzi* (an ancient Roman coin). Eight granite columns are all that remain. Behind the temple and backing onto the Campidoglio are (from north to south) the ruins of the **Tempio della Concordia** (Temple of Concord), the three remaining columns of the **Tempio di Vespasiano** (Temple of Vespasian) and the **Portico degli Dei Consenti**.

The remains of the **Basilica Giulia**, which was the seat of civil justice, are on **Piazza del Foro**. The piazza was the site of the original forum, which served as the main market and meeting place during the Republican era. The **Colonna di Foca** (Column of Phocus), which stands on the piazza and dates from 608 AD, was the last monument erected in the Foro Romano. It honoured the Eastern Roman Emperor Phocus, who donated the Pantheon to the Church. At the south-eastern end of the piazza is the **Tempio di Giulio Cesare** (Temple of Julius Caesar), which was erected by Augustus in 29 BC on the site where Caesar's body was burned and Mark Antony read his famous speech. Just to the south-west is the **Tempio di Castore e Polluce** (Temple of Castor and Pollux), built in 489 BC to mark the defeat of the Etruscan Tarquins and in honour of the Dioscuri, or Heavenly Twins, who miraculously appeared to the Roman troops

during an important battle. Three elegant Corinthian columns from the temple, which served at times as a banking hall and also housed the city's weights and measures office, survive today.

South of the temple is the **Chiesa di Santa Maria Antiqua**, the oldest Christian church in the Foro Romano. Inside the church are some early Christian frescoes. This area has been closed to the public since 1992. Back towards the Via Sacra is the **Casa delle Vestali** (House of the Vestal Virgins), home of the virgins who tended the sacred flame in the adjoining **Tempio di Vesta**. The six priestesses were selected from patrician families when aged between six and 10 years. They had to serve in the temple for 30 years and during this time they were bound by a vow of chastity. If the flame in the temple went out it was seen as a bad omen and the priestess responsible would be flogged. If a priestess lost her virginity she was buried alive, since her blood could not be spilled. The offending man was flogged to death.

The next major monument is the vast **Basilica di Costantino**, also known as Basilica di Massenzio. Emperor Maxentius initiated work on the basilica and it was finished in 315 AD by Constantine. A colossal statue of Constantine was unearthed at the site in 1487. Pieces of this statue – a head, a hand and a foot – are on display in the courtyard of the Palazzo dei Conservatori in the Musei Capitolini (see the Piazza del Campidoglio section earlier in this chapter).

The **Arco di Tito** (Arch of Titus), at the end of the Foro Romano nearest the Colosseo, was built in 81 AD in honour of the victories of the emperors Titus and Vespasian against Jerusalem. Titus is represented with Victory on one of the reliefs on the inside of the arch. On the other, the spoils of Jerusalem are paraded in a triumphal procession. In the past, Roman Jews would avoid passing under this arch, the historical symbol of the beginning of the Diaspora.

Palatino

The Palatino (see the earlier Foro Romano & Palatino map) is the mythical founding place of Roma. You can reach the Palatino from the Foro Romano by following Clivio Palatino to the right from the Arco di Tito, or from another entrance on Via di San Gregorio VII. Wealthy Romans built their homes here during the era of the Republic and it later became the realm of the emperors. Like those of the Foro Romano, the temples and palaces of the Palatino fell into ruin and in the Middle Ages a few churches and castles were built over the remains.

During the Renaissance, members of the wealthy families established gardens on the hill, notably Cardinal Alessandro Farnese, who had his **Orti Farnesiani**, Europe's first botanical gardens, laid out over the ruins of the Domus Tiberiana. South-west of the gardens is **Tempio della Magna Mater**, also known as the Tempio di Cibele, built in 204 BC to house a black stone connected with the Asiatic goddess of fertility, Cybele. Nearby are some holes, reputedly left by the supporting posts of **Casa di Romolo** (Huts of Romulus), from the 9th century BC. To the east of here is **Casa di Livia**, thought to have been the house of the wife of Emperor Augustus. In front of the Casa di Livia is **Casa d'Augusto**, the actual residence of Augustus. Casa d'Augusto and Casa di Livia can sometimes be visited by appointment; ask at the entrance to the Palatino. Several rooms have frescoes which are very well preserved and of significant interest.

North of Casa di Livia is the **Criptoportico**, or cryptoporticus, a 128m-long tunnel built by Nero to connect his Domus Aurea (see the Esquilino section later in this chapter) with the imperial palaces on the Palatino. Farther east are the remains of the **Domus Flavia**, the residence of Domitian, and the vast **Domus Augustana**, which was the private residence of the emperors. Continuing south-east, you will find the **Stadio**, probably used by the emperors for private games and events, and next to it the ruins of the **Terme di Settimio Severo** bath complex.

The **Museo Palatino** houses works of art and artefacts found on the Palatino. Between the Domus Flavia and the Domus Augustana, this former convent was established as

a museum in the 1860s. The museum closes 80 minutes earlier than the Palatino site.

The Palatino has the same opening hours as the Foro Romano. Admission costs L12,000 and includes entry to the Museo Palatino.

CHIESA DI SS COSMA E DAMIANO & CHIESA DI SANTA FRANCESCA ROMANA

Near the Colosseo, along Via dei Fori Imperiali, is the 6th century Basilica di SS Cosma e Damiano (see the Foro Romano & Palatino map). The church once incorporated a large hall which formed part of Vespasian's Foro della Pace (Forum of Peace). In the apse are 6th century mosaics which are among the most beautiful in Roma. In a room off the 17th century cloisters is a vast Neapolitan *presepio* (nativity scene), dating from the 18th century.

Past the Basilica di Costantino there is a small stairway leading to Chiesa di Santa Francesca Romana. Built in the 9th century over an earlier oratory, the church incorporates part of the Tempio di Venere e Roma (Temple of Venus and Roma). It has a lovely Romanesque bell tower. In the apse is a 12th century mosaic of the Madonna and child and saints, and there's a 7th century painting of the Madonna and child above the high altar. During restoration work in 1949, another painting of the Madonna and child was discovered beneath the 7th century work. Dating from the early 5th century and probably taken from the Chiesa di Santa Maria Antiqua in the Foro Romano, this precious painting is now in the sacristy, which you can enter if the sacristan is around.

COLOSSEO

Construction of the Colosseo (Colosseum; see the Foro Romano & Palatino map) was started by Emperor Vespasian in 72 AD in the grounds of Nero's private Domus Aurea. Originally known as the Anfiteatro Flavio (Flavian Amphitheatre), after the family name of Vespasian, it was inaugurated by his son Titus in 80 AD. The massive structure could seat more than 80,000, and the bloody

Gladiators

Gladiatorial combat originated as part of Etruscan funerary rites as a form of human sacrifice. By the 1st century BC, gladiatorial games had far outstripped this ritual context: Caesar exhibited 320 pairs of gladiators in 65 BC, while Augustus and Trajan each showed 5000 pairs of gladiators on different occasions.

Gladiators were prisoners of war, slaves sold to gladiatorial schools or volunteers. They were differently equipped, some with heavy swords and shields and others almost naked, armed with a net and a trident. Pairings were made to match a heavily armed gladiator against a lightly armed one.

Bouts were not necessarily to the death. A defeated gladiator could appeal to the crowd and the presiding magistrate, who could signal that he had fought well and deserved to be spared. Thumbs down, however, meant death, which the defeated man was expected to face quietly and bravely.

Although gambling was technically illegal in Rome, vast sums were wagered on gladiatorial combats. Successful gladiators were popular heroes and lived to enjoy a comfortable retirement, with some running their own training schools.

As with the other blood sports held in Rome, gladiatorial games were more than just particularly gruesome entertainment. This state-run public spectacle was a demonstration of empire through the display of exotic beasts and prisoners of war and allowed the people, through their judgment of the defeated, to share in the Roman state's authority over life and death.

TAMSIN WILSON

The Colosseo, home to Roma's gladiator fights

gladiator combat and wild beast shows held there give some insight into the attitudes of the day. The games held to mark the inauguration of the Colosseo lasted for 100 days and nights, during which some 5000 animals were slaughtered. The Emperor Trajan once held games which lasted for 117 days, during which some 9000 gladiators fought to the death. However, with the fall of the Roman Empire, the Colosseo was abandoned and gradually became overgrown.

In the Middle Ages the Colosseo became a fortress, occupied by two of the city's warrior families, the Frangipani and the Annibaldi. Its reputation as a symbol of Roma, the Eternal City, also dates from the Middle Ages, when Christian pilgrims are said to

have predicted that when the Colosseo fell, Roma would also fall. Damaged several times by earthquake, it was later used as a quarry for travertine and marble to be used in the Palazzo Venezia and other buildings. Pollution and the vibrations caused by traffic and the Metro have also taken their toll. The Colosseo is currently undergoing restoration, expected to be finished in 2004.

Opening hours in summer are 9 am to 7 pm daily (to 4 pm in winter). Admission costs L10,000 and guided tours, in English, cost L6000 per person.

ARCO DI COSTANTINO

On the western side of the Colosseo is the triumphal arch built to honour Constantine following his victory over Maxentius at the battle of the Milvian Bridge (near the Zona Olimpica, north-west of the Villa Borghese) in 312 AD.

ESQUILINO (Map 3)

The Esquilino (Esquiline Hill) covers the area stretching from the Colosseo across Via Cavour, which links Via dei Fori Imperiali with Stazione Termini. Not the best known of Roma's seven hills, it incorporates the Parco del Colle Oppio, now a haunt of homeless people and drug users, but once the site of part of Nero's fabled **Domus Aurea** (Golden House), which the emperor had built after the fire of 64 AD. This was a vast complex of buildings covering an area of some 50 hectares which stretched from the Colle Oppio to the Celio (Celian Hill) and the Palatino (Map 5). The gardens, which contained a lake and game animals, occupied the valley where the Colosseo now stands.

After Nero's death in 68 AD, his successors were quick to destroy the complex, which had occupied a major part of the ancient city's centre. Vespasian drained the lake to build the Colosseo, Domitian demolished the buildings on the Palatino and Trajan built his baths over the buildings on the Colle Oppio. During the Renaissance, artists descended into the ruins of the wing of the Domus Aurea on the Colle Oppio to study its architectural features and the rich paintings which adorned its walls.

The Domus Aurea can be visited only by appointment – call ☎ 06 397 49 907 for reservations. Guided groups leave approximately every 15 minutes and the entire visit takes about one hour. Tickets cost L12,000.

From the Colle Oppio, follow Via Terme di Tito and turn left into Via del Monte Oppio to reach the **Basilica di San Pietro in Vincoli**, built in the 5th century by the Empress Eudoxia, wife of Valentinian III, to house the chains of San Pietro. Legend has it that when a second part of the chains was returned to Roma from Constantinople, the two pieces miraculously joined together. The church also offers another great treasure

– Michelangelo's unfinished tomb of Pope Julius II, with his powerful *Moses* and unfinished statues of *Leah* and *Rachel* on either side. Michelangelo was frustrated for many years by his inability to find time to complete work on the tomb. In the end, Pope Julius was buried in the Basilica di San Pietro without the great tomb he had envisioned. A flight of steps through a low arch leads down from the church to Via Cavour.

BASILICA DI SANTA MARIA MAGGIORE (Map 3)

One of Roma's four patriarchal basilicas, Santa Maria Maggiore was built on the Esquilino in the 5th century, during the time of Pope Sixtus III. Its main façade was added in the 18th century, although the mosaics of an earlier, 13th century, façade were preserved. The interior is baroque and the bell tower Romanesque. The basilican form of the vast interior, a nave and two aisles, remains intact and the most notable feature is the cycle of mosaics dating from the 5th century which decorate the triumphal arch and nave. They depict biblical scenes; in particular, events in the lives of Abraham, Jacob and Isaac (to the left), and Moses and Joshua (to the right). Note also the Cosmatesque pavement, dating from the 12th century. The sumptuously decorated Cappella Sistina, last on the right, was built in the 16th century and contains the tombs of popes Sixtus V and Pius V. Opposite is the Cappella Borghese (or Cappella Paolina), also full of elaborate decoration, erected in the 17th century by Pope Paul V. The *Madonna and Child* above the altar is believed to date from the 12th to the 13th century.

BASILICA DI SAN GIOVANNI IN LATERANO (Map 5)

Founded by Constantine in the 4th century, this was the first Christian basilica constructed in Roma and, as the city's cathedral, it remains one of the most important in the Christian world. It has been destroyed by fire twice and rebuilt several times. Borromini was commissioned to transform its interior into the baroque style in the mid-17th century. The eastern façade, which contains the basilica's main entrance, faces onto Piazza di Porta San Giovanni. The bronze main doors were moved here by Borromini from the Curia in the Foro Romano. The heads of SS Pietro and Paolo are contained in a tabernacle over the papal altar.

The beautiful 13th century **cloister** was decorated by the Cosma family. The cloister is usually open from 9 am to 5 pm (6 pm in summer) and admission costs L4000. At the time of writing it was under restoration.

There's a second entrance into the basilica in the northern façade, which faces onto Piazza San Giovanni in Laterano. Leaving the church by this door you come to the domed **baptistry**, which was also built by Constantine. Sixtus III gave it its present octagonal shape, which became the model for many baptistries throughout the Christian world. **Cappella di Santa Rufina** is decorated with a stunning 5th century mosaic of vines and foliage against a deep blue background, while the vault of **Cappella di San Giovanni Evangelista** has a mosaic of the Lamb of God surrounded by birds and flowers. **Cappella di San Venanzio** was added by Pope John IV in the 7th century. It has extremely well-preserved mosaics; in the apse are Christ with angels and the Madonna and saints, and on the triumphal arch are Christian martyrs. Right at the top are views of Jerusalem and Bethlehem. The baptistry is open from 9 am to 1 pm and 4 to 6 pm Monday to Thursday and from 9 am to 1 pm on Friday and Saturday.

The **Palazzo Laterano**, which adjoins the basilica, was the papal residence until the pope moved to Avignon early in the 14th century. It was largely destroyed by fire in 1308 and most of what remained was demolished in the 16th century.

The building on the eastern side of Piazza San Giovanni in Laterano contains the **Scala Santa** and the **Sancta Sanctorum**. The Scala Santa (Holy Staircase) is said to come from Pontius Pilate's palace in Jerusalem and people are allowed to climb it only on their knees. The Sancta Sanctorum was the popes'

private chapel and contains 13th century frescoes and mosaics. The Sancta Sanctorum is open from 10.30 to 11.30 am and 3 to 4 pm on Tuesday, Thursday and Saturday. Admission costs L5000.

CELIO (Map 3)

The Celio (Celian Hill) is accessible either from Via di San Gregorio VII to the west or from Via della Navicella on the east. The **Villa Celimontana** is a large public park on top of the hill, perfect for a quiet picnic. There is also a children's playground. The 4th century **Chiesa di SS Giovanni e Paolo**, on the piazza of the same name on Via di San Paolo della Croce, is dedicated to two Romans who had served in the court of Emperor Constantine II and were beheaded by his anti-Christian successor, Emperor Julian, for refusing to serve as officers in his court. The church was built over their houses. The 8th century **Chiesa di San Gregorio Magno** was built in honour of Pope Gregory the Great on the site where he dispatched St Augustine to convert the people of Britain to Christianity. The church was remodelled in the baroque style in the 17th century.

The fascinating circular **Chiesa di Santo Stefano Rotondo** is on Via di S Stefano Rotondo. Inside are two rings of antique granite and marble columns. The wall is lined with frescoes depicting the various ways in which saints were martyred. The vivid scenes are quite grotesque and you might not make it through all 34 of them.

At the base of the Celio, near the Colosseo, is the **Basilica di San Clemente**, on Via San Giovanni in Laterano. Dedicated to one of the earliest popes, the church exemplifies how history in Roma exists on many levels. The 12th century church at street level was built over a 4th century church which was, in turn, built over a 1st century Roman house, to which was added a late 2nd century temple to the pagan god Mithras (imported to Roma by soldiers returning from the east). Furthermore, it is believed that foundations from the era of the Roman Republic lie beneath the house.

It is possible to visit the first three levels.

In the medieval church, note the marble choir screen, originally in the older church below, and the early Renaissance frescoes by Masolino in the Cappella di Santa Caterina, which depict the life of Santa Caterina of Alexandria. The stunning mosaics in the apse date from the 12th century. On the triumphal arch are Christ and the symbols of the four Evangelists. There is also a depiction of the Triumph of the Cross, with 12 doves symbolising the apostles. Figures around the cross include the Madonna and San Giovanni, as well as San Giovanni Battista (St John the Baptist) and other saints, encircled by a vine growing from the foot of the cross.

The church below was mostly destroyed by Norman invaders in the 11th century, but some Romanesque frescoes remain. Descend farther and you reach the Roman house and temple of Mithras. You need a ticket to descend to the lower levels (L4000).

TERME DI CARACALLA (Map 5)
These baths are on Via delle Terme di Caracalla, south of the Celio, accessible by bus Nos 160 and 628 from Piazza Venezia. Covering 10 hectares, Caracalla's Baths could hold 1600 people and had shops, gardens, libraries and entertainment. Begun by Antonius Caracalla and inaugurated in 217 AD, the baths were used until the 6th century AD. From the 1930s until 1993 they were an atmospheric venue for opera performances in summer. These have now been banned to prevent further damage to the ruins. The baths are open from 9 am to 6 pm (to 3 pm in winter) Tuesday to Saturday and to 1 pm on Sunday and Monday. Admission costs L8000.

AVENTINO (Maps 4 & 5)
South of the Circo Massimo is the Aventino (Aventine Hill), best reached from Via del Circo Massimo by either Via di Valle Murcia or Clivo de Publici to Via di Santa Sabina. It is also easily accessible by bus No 27 from Stazione Termini and the Colosseo, or on the Metro Linea B, disembarking at Circo Massimo. Along the way, you will pass the **Roseto Comunale**, a beautiful public rose garden, best seen in spring and summer, and the pretty, walled **Parco Savello** (Map 4), planted with orange trees. There is a stunning view of Roma from the park. Next to the park is the 5th century **Basilica di Santa Sabina** (Map 4). Of particular note is the carved wooden door to the far left as you stand under the 15th century portico facing the church. Dating from the 5th century, the door features panels depicting biblical scenes; the crucifixion scene is one of the oldest in existence.

TOWARDS THE JEWISH GHETTO
The recently refurbished **Chiesa di Santa Maria in Cosmedin** (Map 5), on Piazza Bocca della Verità, is regarded as one of the finest medieval churches in Roma. It has a 12th century, seven storey bell tower and its interior, including the beautiful floor, was heavily decorated with inlaid marble. There are 12th century frescoes in the aisles. Under the portico is the famous **Bocca della Verità** (Mouth of Truth), a large, round, marble mask which probably served as the cover of an ancient drain. Legend says that if you put your right hand into the mouth while telling a lie, it will snap shut. Opposite the church are two tiny Roman temples: the round Tempio di Ercole Vincitore and the Tempio di Portunus.

Just off the piazza are the **Arco di Giano** (Arch of Janus; Map 5), a four sided Roman arch which once covered a crossroads, and the medieval **Chiesa di San Giorgio in Velabro**.

From Piazza Bocca della Verità, follow Via Petroselli to reach the **Teatro di Marcello** (Map 6; see also the Walking Tour earlier in this chapter), built in around 13 BC to plans by Julius Caesar and dedicated by Emperor Augustus. It was converted into a fortress and residence during the Middle Ages, and a palace built on the site in the 16th century preserved the original form of the theatre. In recent years open-air concerts have been held here nightly in summer.

From the theatre, head north along Via Montanara to Piazza Campitelli and then take Via dei Funari to Piazza Mattei. In the piazza is the **Fontana delle Tartarughe** (Fountain of the Tortoises; Map 6), a fountain designed by Giacomo della Porta and sculpted in bronze by Taddeo Landini in the 16th century (see the Walking Tour earlier in this chapter). The tortoises were added in the 17th century and are thought to be by Gian Lorenzo Bernini.

The area just south of here, around Via del Portico d'Ottavia, is known as the Jewish Ghetto. In the 16th century Pope Paul IV ordered the confinement of Jewish people to this area, marking the beginning of a time of intolerance which continued well into the 19th century. Follow Via del Portico d'Ottavia to the river and the 19th century **synagogue** (Map 6). Along the way, note the medieval houses. There is a 15th century house at No 1 which incorporates pieces of ancient Roman sculpture in its façade. See the Walking Tour earlier in this chapter if you are interested in exploring the ghetto area more thoroughly.

From here, you can reach the **Isola Tiberina** across the **Ponte Fabricio**, which was built in 62 BC and is Roma's oldest standing bridge. The island has been associated with healing since the 3rd century BC, when the Romans adopted Aesculapius, the Greek god of healing, as their own and erected a temple to him on the island. Today it is the site of the Ospedale Fatebenefratelli (hospital). The **Chiesa di San Bartolomeo** (Map 4) was built on the island in the 10th century on the ruins of the Roman temple. It has a Romanesque bell tower and a marble

Recognising the Evangelists

The four evangelists, Matthew, Mark, Luke and John, who wrote the gospels which record events in the life of Christ, are very often represented in early Christian art with symbols. Matthew is depicted as an eagle, Mark as a lion, Luke as a bull and John as a man. Look for the symbols of the evangelists in mosaics and bas-relief decorations and on capitals in Romanesque churches.

wellhead, believed to have been built over the same spring which provided healing waters for the temple. The **Ponte Cestio**, built in 46 BC, connects the island to Trastevere, to the south. It was rebuilt in the late 19th century. Also to the south of the island are the remains of part of the **Ponte Rotto** (Broken Bridge), ancient Roma's first stone bridge.

TRASTEVERE (Maps 4 & 6)

The settlement at Trastevere (on the other side of the river) was, in early times, separate from Roma. Although it was soon swallowed by the growing city, this sense of separation continued during medieval times, when the area developed its own identity.

The **Basilica di Santa Maria in Trastevere** (Map 4), in the lovely piazza of the same name, is believed to be the oldest place of worship dedicated to the Virgin in Roma. Although the first basilica was built on this site in the 4th century AD, the present structure was built in the 12th century and contains a Romanesque bell tower and façade, with a mosaic of the Virgin from the 12th century. The impressive interior features 21 ancient Roman columns. Of particular interest are the 17th century wooden ceiling and the vibrant 12th century mosaics in the apse and on the triumphal arch. Note the richly patterned dress of the Madonna in the apse. A badly deteriorated painting of the Madonna and angels, dating from the Byzantine era, is displayed in a room to the left of the altar.

Also well worth visiting is the **Basilica di Santa Cecilia in Trastevere** (Map 4; see also the boxed text 'Hidden Treasures' earlier in this chapter). There's a magnificent 13th century fresco of the Last Supper by Pietro Cavallini in the nuns' choir, entered through the convent. The fresco can be seen from 10 to 11.30 am on Tuesday and Thursday and from around 11.15 (after Mass) to 11.45 am on Sunday. Admission costs L2000. The church itself is open from 10 to 11.45 am and 4 to 5.30 pm daily.

PALAZZO SPADA (Map 6)

South of the Campo de' Fiori on Piazza Capodiferro, this 16th century palace has an elaborately decorated façade. It was restored by Francesco Borromini after Cardinal Bernardino Spada had acquired the palace. Note the optical illusion created by Borromini's colonnade, which he built to give an impression of greater space by linking two courtyards within the palace. The **Galleria Spada** contains the private collection of the Spada family, which was acquired by the state in 1926 and features works by Titian, Andrea del Sarto, Guido Reni and Caravaggio. It is open from 9 am to 7 pm Tuesday to Saturday and to 1 pm on Sunday. Admission costs L10,000.

CAMPO DE' FIORI (Map 6)

This is a lively piazza with a flower and vegetable market every morning except Sunday. The piazza was a place of execution during the Inquisition. In 1600 the monk Giordano Bruno was burned at the stake here for heresy and his statue now stands at the piazza's centre.

Nearby is the **Palazzo Farnese**, in the piazza of the same name. A magnificent Renaissance building, it was started in 1514 by Antonio da Sangallo and work was continued by Michelangelo and completed by Giacomo della Porta. Built for Cardinal Alessandro Farnese (later Pope Paul III), the palace is now the French embassy. The façade features elegant geometrical decorations, the meaning of which remains a mystery. The piazza contains two fountains, which were enormous granite baths taken from the Terme di Caracalla.

CHIESA DEL GESÙ (Map 6)

The Chiesa del Gesù on the piazza of the same name was the first Jesuit church in Roma. The Jesuits were founded in 1540 by the Spanish soldier Ignatius Loyola, who had joined the Church after being wounded in battle. He came to Roma in 1537 and three years later founded the Society of Jesus (the Jesuits).

Construction of the church began in 1568 and it was consecrated in 1584. The interior was designed by Vignola and the façade by Giacomo della Porta. The high point of Counter-Reformation baroque architecture, the Gesù was extremely important to the subsequent design of churches in Roma and throughout the Catholic world. The church's interior is elaborate, following the Jesuits' intention to attract worshippers with splendour and spectacle. The church is open from 6 am to 12.30 pm and 4 to 7.15 pm daily. At the time of writing much of the interior was under restoration.

PIAZZA NAVONA (Map 6)

Lined with baroque palaces, this vast and beautiful piazza was laid out on the ruins of Domitian's stadium and contains three fountains, including Bernini's masterpiece, the **Fontana dei Quattro Fiumi** (Fountain of the Four Rivers), in the centre, depicting the Nile, Ganges, Danube and the Rio Plata. Facing the piazza is the **Chiesa di Sant'Agnese in Agone**, its façade designed by Bernini's bitter rival, Borromini. It's traditionally held that the statues of Bernini's Fontana dei Quattro Fiumi are shielding their eyes in disgust from Borromini's church, but actually Bernini completed the fountain two years before his contemporary started work on the façade.

PALAZZO ALTEMPS (Map 6)

Palazzo Altemps, on Piazza Sant'Apollinare, at the northern end of Piazza Navona, was begun around 1477 for Girolamo Riario. Antonio da Sangallo the Elder, Baldassarre Peruzzi and Martino Longhi all had a hand in its design. For centuries the palace housed the notable Altemps family collection of antiquities as well as an extensive library. It was acquired by the Italian state in 1982 and underwent a careful and lengthy restoration, before opening in 1997 as the new home of part of the **Museo Nazionale Romano** collection (the rest of the collection is in Palazzo Massimo alle Terme). The sculptures are displayed in a way that is very similar to common 16th century exhibition criteria, so you get a good idea of how a Renaissance palazzo and collection would have looked. The entrance to Palazzo Altemps (☎ 06 689 70 91) is at Piazza Sant'Apollinare 44. It opens from 9 am to 7 pm Tuesday to Sunday (opening hours are usually extended in summer). Admission costs L10,000.

THE PANTHEON (Map 6)

This is the best-preserved building of ancient Roma. The original temple was built by Marcus Agrippa, son-in-law of Augustus, in 27 BC and dedicated to the planetary gods. Although the temple was rebuilt by Emperor Hadrian around 120 AD, Agrippa's name remained inscribed over the entrance, leading historians to believe it was the original building until excavations in the early 19th century revealed traces of the earlier temple.

After being abandoned under the first Christian emperors, the temple was given to the Church by the Eastern emperor, Phocus, in 608 AD and dedicated to the Madonna and all martyrs. Over the centuries the temple was consistently plundered and damaged. The gilded bronze roof tiles were removed by an emperor of the Eastern empire and, in the 17th century, the Barberini pope, Urban VIII, had the bronze ceiling of the portico melted down to make the *baldacchino* (canopy) over the main altar in San Pietro and 80 cannons for Castel Sant'Angelo. The height and diameter of the building's interior both measure 43.3m and the extraordinary dome is considered the most important achievement of ancient Roman architecture. The Italian kings Vittorio Emanuele II and Umberto I and the artist Raphael are buried here.

The Pantheon is on the Piazza della Rotonda and is open from 9 am to 6.30 pm Monday to Saturday and to 1 pm on Sunday and holidays. Admission is free.

CHIESA DI SANTA MARIA SOPRA MINERVA (Map 6)

On Piazza della Minerva, just east of the Pantheon, this 13th century Dominican church was built on the site of an ancient temple of Minerva. It was heavily restored in the Gothic style in the 19th century and contains a number of important art treasures. The body of Santa Caterina di Siena, minus her head (which is in the Chiesa di San Domenico in Siena) lies under the high altar. In the piazza in front of the church is a de-

lightful Bernini statue of an elephant supporting an Egyptian obelisk. The church is open from 7 am to 7 pm daily.

FONTANA DI TREVI (Map 3)

This high-baroque fountain is one of Roma's most famous monuments. Completely dominating a tiny piazza, it was designed by Nicola Salvi in 1732. Its water is supplied by one of the city's earliest aqueducts. Work to clean the fountain and its water supply was completed in 1991, but the effects of pollution have already dulled the brilliant white of the clean marble. The famous custom is to throw a coin into the fountain (over your shoulder while facing away) to ensure you return to Roma. If you throw a second coin you can make a wish.

PIAZZA DI SPAGNA & SCALINATA DELLA TRINITÀ DEI MONTI (Map 3)

The piazza, church and famous Spanish Steps have long provided a gathering place for foreigners. The piazza was named after the Spanish Embassy to the Holy See, although the staircase, built with a legacy from the French in 1725, lead to the French church, Trinità dei Monti.

To the right as you face the steps is the house where Keats died in 1821, now the **Keats-Shelley Memorial House**. It is open from 9 am to 1 pm and 2.30 to 5.30 pm Monday to Friday. Admission costs L5000. In the piazza is the boat-shaped fountain called the **Barcaccia**, believed to be by Pietro Bernini, father of the famous Gian Lorenzo.

PIAZZA DEL POPOLO (Map 2)

This vast piazza was laid out in the early 16th century at the point of convergence of the three roads – Via di Ripetta, Via del Corso and Via del Babuino – which form a trident at what was the main entrance to the city from the north. The two baroque churches between the three roads are Santa Maria dei Miracoli and Santa Maria in Montesanto. The piazza was redesigned in the neoclassical

[continued on page 209]

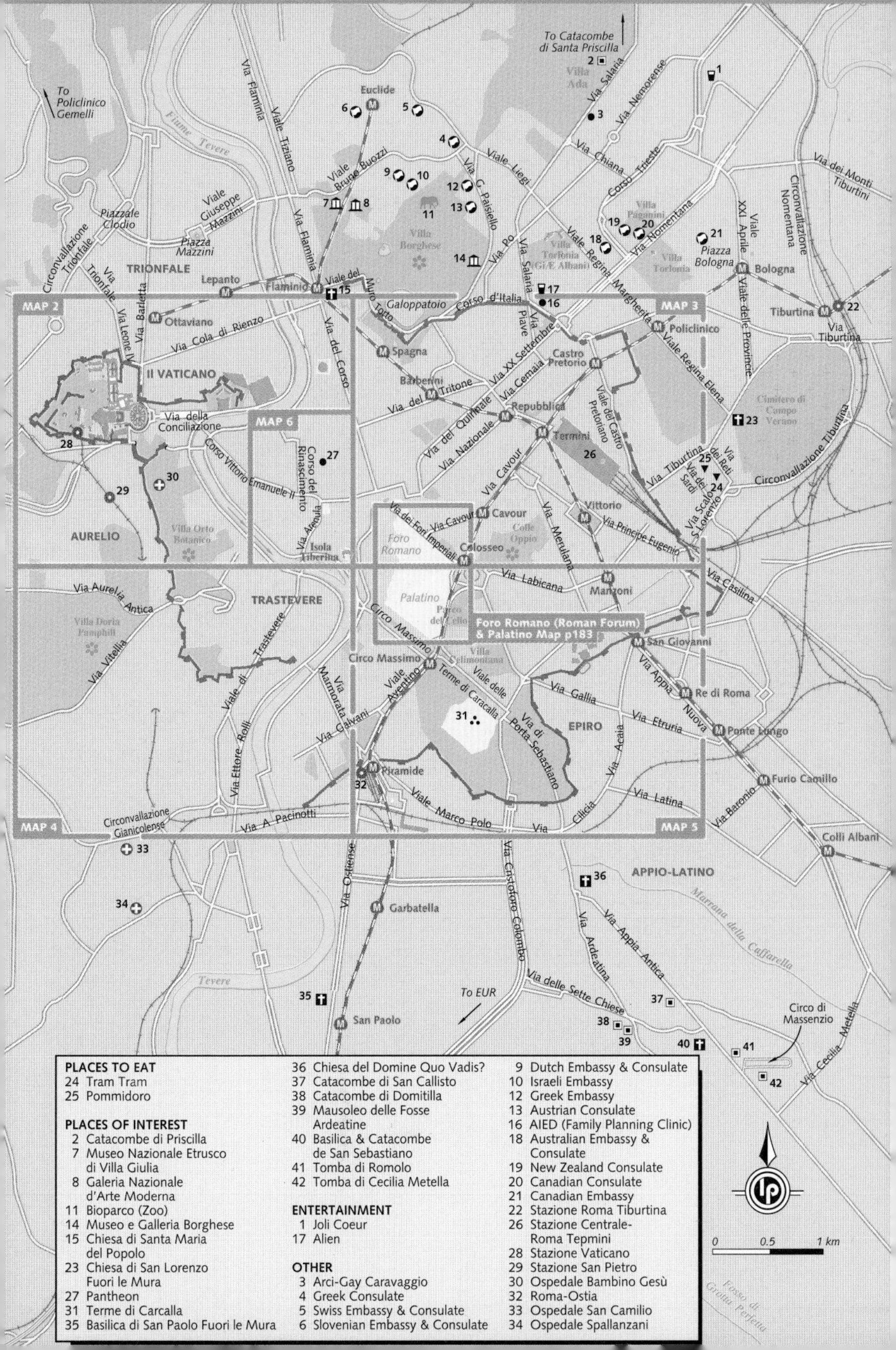

MAP 1

To Catacombe
di Santa Priscilla

To
Policlinico
Gemelli

Euclide

TRIONFALE

Piazzale
Clodio

Piazza
Mazzini

Lepanto

Flaminio

MAP 2

Ottaviano

Via Cola di Rienzo

IL VATICANO

Via della Conciliazione

MAP 6

AURELIO

TRASTEVERE

MAP 4

To Catacombe
di Santa Priscilla

Villa
Ada

Piazza
Bologna

Bologna

Tiburtina

MAP 3

Policlinico

Castro
Pretorio

Republica

Termini

Vittorio

Cavour

Colosseo

Colle
Oppio

Manzoni

San Giovanni

Re di Roma

EPIRO

Ponte Longo

Furio Camillo

Colli Albani

Piramide

Garbatella

APPIO-LATINO

MAP 5

San Paolo

To EUR

Circo di
Massenzio

Foro Romano (Roman Forum)
& Palatino Map p183

PLACES TO EAT
24 Tram Tram
25 Pommidoro

PLACES OF INTEREST
2 Catacombe di Priscilla
7 Museo Nazionale Etrusco
  di Villa Giulia
8 Galeria Nazionale
  d'Arte Moderna
11 Bioparco (Zoo)
14 Museo e Galleria Borghese
15 Chiesa di Santa Maria
  del Popolo
23 Chiesa di San Lorenzo
  Fuori le Mura
27 Pantheon
31 Terme di Carcalla
35 Basilica di San Paolo Fuori le Mura

36 Chiesa del Domine Quo Vadis?
37 Catacombe di San Callisto
38 Catacombe di Domitilla
39 Mausoleo delle Fosse
  Ardeatine
40 Basilica & Catacombe
  de San Sebastiano
41 Tomba di Romolo
42 Tomba di Cecilia Metella

ENTERTAINMENT
1 Joli Coeur
17 Alien

OTHER
3 Arci-Gay Caravaggio
4 Greek Consulate
5 Swiss Embassy & Consulate
6 Slovenian Embassy & Consulate

9 Dutch Embassy & Consulate
10 Israeli Embassy
12 Greek Embassy
13 Austrian Consulate
16 AIED (Family Planning Clinic)
18 Australian Embassy &
  Consulate
19 New Zealand Consulate
20 Canadian Consulate
21 Canadian Embassy
22 Stazione Roma Tiburtina
25 Stazione Centrale-
  Roma Tepmini
28 Stazione Vaticano
29 Stazione San Pietro
30 Ospedale Bambino Gesù
32 Roma-Ostia
33 Ospedale San Camillo
34 Ospedale Spallanzani

0   0.5   1 km

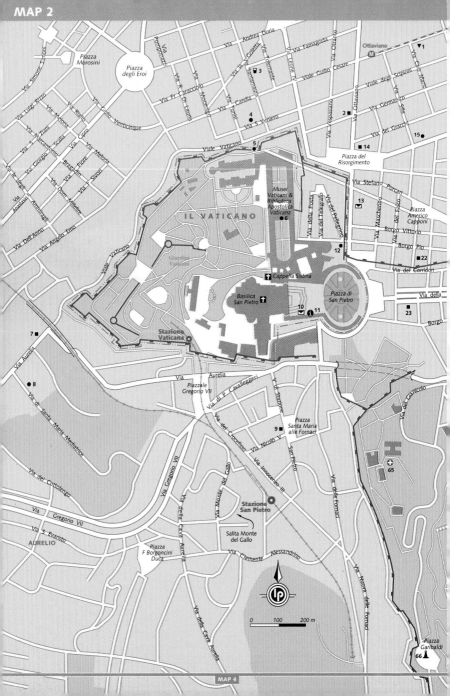

MAP 2

MAP 4

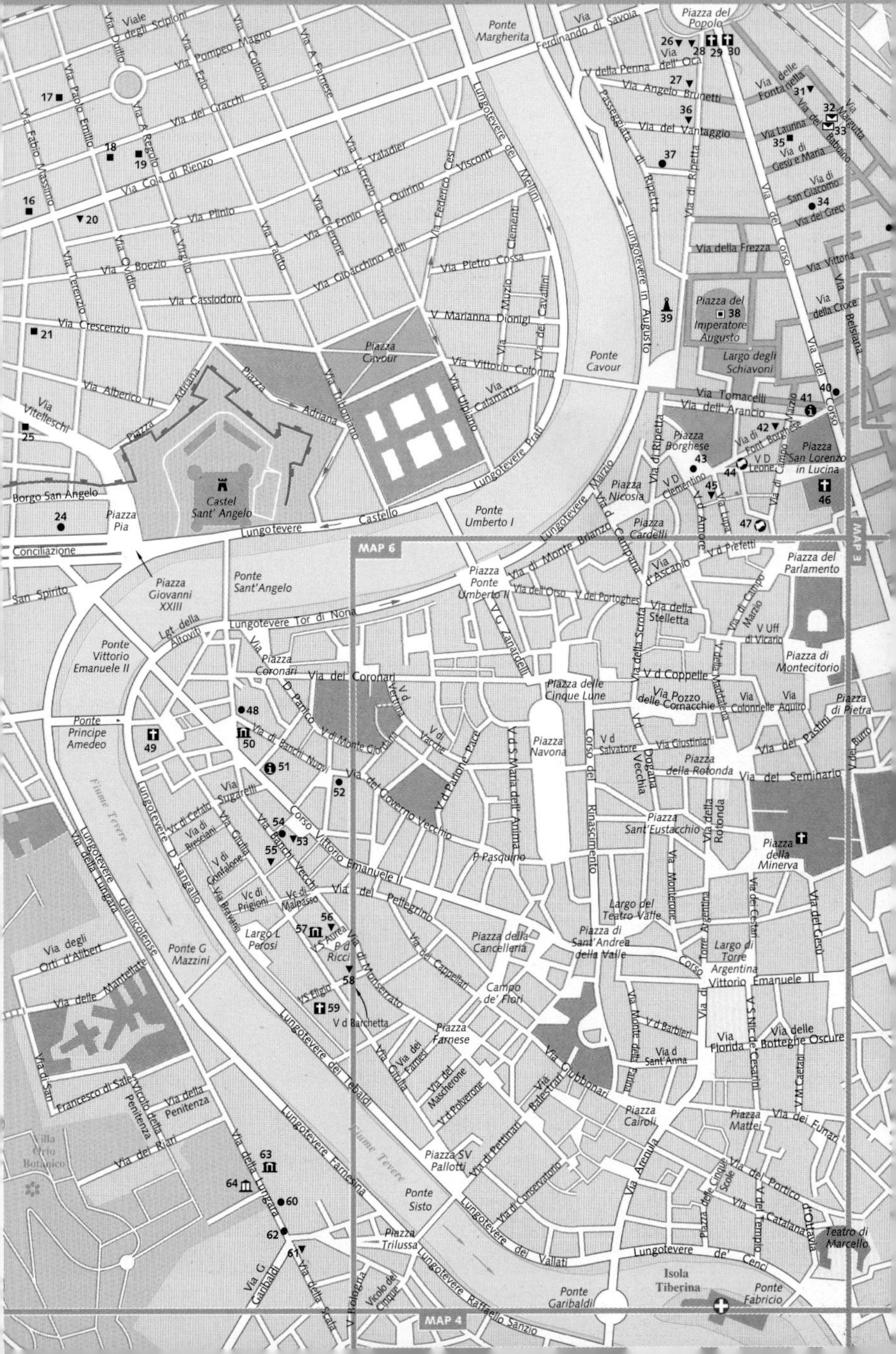
Viale degli Scipioni
Via Duilio
Via Pompeo Magno
Via Colonna
Via A Farnese
Ponte Margherita
Via Ferdinando di Savoia
Piazza del Popolo
Via della Penna
Via dell' Oca
Via Angelo Brunetti
Via delle Fontanella
Via Margutta
Via del Babuino
Via Laurina
Via di Gesù e Maria
Via di San Giacomo
Via dei Greci
Via del Vantaggio
Passeggiata di Ripetta
Via di Ripetta
Via del Corso
Via Paolo Emilio
Via Fabio Massimo
Via Ezio
Via A Regolo
Via dei Gracchi
Via Cola di Rienzo
Via Valadier
Via Lucrezio Caro
Via Visconti
Via Federico Cesi
Lungotevere dei Mellini
Via Quirino
Via Ennio
Via Cicerone
Via Plinio
Via Tacito
Via Virgilio
Via Ovidio
Via Boezio
Via Terenzio
Via Gioacchino Belli
Via Pietro Cossa
Via Muzio Clementi
Via dei Cavallini
Via Cassiodoro
V Marianna Dionigi
Lungotevere in Augusto
Via della Frezza
Via Vittoria
Via della Croce
Via Belsiana
Piazza del Imperatore Augusto
Via Crescenzio
Piazza Cavour
Via Vittorio Colonna
Ponte Cavour
Largo degli Schiavoni
Via Alberico II
Piazza Adriana
Via Tiboniano
Via Ulpiano
Via Calamatta
Via Tomacelli
Via dell' Arancio
Via Vitelleschi
Piazza Borghese
Via di Font Borghese
Via di Campo Marzio
Piazza San Lorenzo in Lucina
V D Leone
Lungotevere Prati
Lungotevere Marzio
Piazza Nicosia
V D Clementino
Castel Sant' Angelo
Borgo San Angelo
Piazza Pia
Lungotevere Castello
Ponte Umberto I
Via d Campana
V d Amore
Via Lupa
Piazza Cardelli
V d Prefetti
Conciliazione
Via di Monte Brianzo
Via d'Ascanio
Piazza del Parlamento
Piazza Ponte Umberto II
Via dell'Orso
V dei Portoghesi
San Spirito
Piazza Giovanni XXIII
Ponte Sant'Angelo
Lungotevere Tor di Nona
Via della Stelletta
Via della Scrofa
V Uff di Vicario
Lgt della Altoviti
V G Zanardelli
Piazza di Montecitorio
Ponte Vittorio Emanuele II
Piazza Coronari
Via dei Coronari
Via D Panico
V d Vecchia
V d Coppelle
V d Maddalena
Piazza delle Cinque Lune
Via Pozzo delle Cornacchie
Via Colonnelle
Via Aquiro
Piazza di Pietra
Ponte Principe Amedeo
Via di Banchi Nuovi
V di Monte Giordano
V di Vacche
Piazza Navona
V d S Maria dell' Anima
Corso del Rinascimento
V d Salvatore
V d Dogana Vecchia
Via Giustiniani
Piazza della Rotonda
Via del Seminario
Via dei Pastini
V dei Burro
Fiume Tevere
Via Sugarelli
V d Parione Pace
Via del Governo Vecchio
Lungotevere D Sangallo
Vc di Cefalo
Vc di Bresciani
Via Giulia
Via Banchi Vecchi
Corso Vittorio Emanuele II
P Pasquino
Piazza Sant'Eustacchio
Via della Rotonda
Piazza della Minerva
Lungotevere
Via della Lungara
V di Gonfalone
Vc di Prigioni
Vc di Malpasso
Via Bravaria
Via del Pellegrino
Via Monterone
Largo del Teatro Valle
Via dei Cestari
Via del Gesù
Lungotevere Gianicolense
Largo L Perosi
V S Aurea
P d Ricci
Via di Monserrato
Piazza della Cancelleria
Piazza di Sant'Andrea della Valle
Via di Torre Argentina
Largo di Torre Argentina
Via degli Orti d'Alibert
Ponte G Mazzini
Via dei Cappellari
Corso Vittorio Emanuele II
Via delle Mantellate
V S Eligio
V d Barchetta
Campo de' Fiori
Via Monte della Farina
V d Barbieri
Via Florida
V S Nic de Cesarini
Via delle Botteghe Oscure
Piazza Farnese
Via dei Farnesi
Via d Sant'Anna
V M Caetani
Via di San Francesco di Sales
Vicolo della Penitenza
Via della Penitenza
Via del Mascherone
V d Polverone
Via Balestrari
Via Giubbonari
Piazza Cairoli
Piazza Mattei
Via dei Funari
Lungotevere dei Tebaldi
Villa Orto Botanico
Via dei Riari
Via della Lungara
Piazza SV Pallotti
Via di Pettinari
Via Arenula
Via di Conservatorio
Piazza delle Cinque Scole
Via del Portico d'Ottavia
Via Catalana
V d Tempio
Lungotevere Farnesina
Ponte Sisto
Fiume Tevere
Piazza Trilussa
Lungotevere dei Vallati
Lungotevere de' Cenci
Teatro di Marcello
Via G Garibaldi
Via della Scala
V Bologna
Vicolo del Cinque
Lungotevere Raffaello Sanzio
Ponte Garibaldi
Isola Tiberina
Ponte Fabricio
MAP 3
MAP 4
MAP 6
16
17
18
19
20
21
24
25
26
27
28
29
30
31
32
33
34
35
36
37
38
39
40
41
42
43
44
45
46
47
48
49
50
51
52
53
54
55
56
57
58
59
60
61
62
63
64

MAP 2

Marcus Aurelius statue, Piazza del Campidoglio

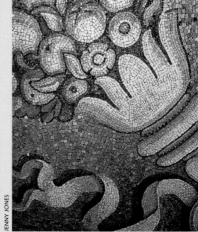

Intricate mosaic inside the Basilica di San Pietro

The peace of Roma's backstreets

Ancient Roma's well-preserved Pantheon

Lose yourself in Villa Lante's garden, Lazio.

Pick up an Italian masterpiece, Piazza Navona.

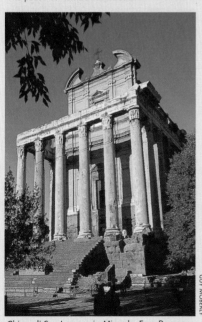

Chiesa di San Lorenzo in Miranda, Foro Romano

Virgins on guard, Casa delle Vestali

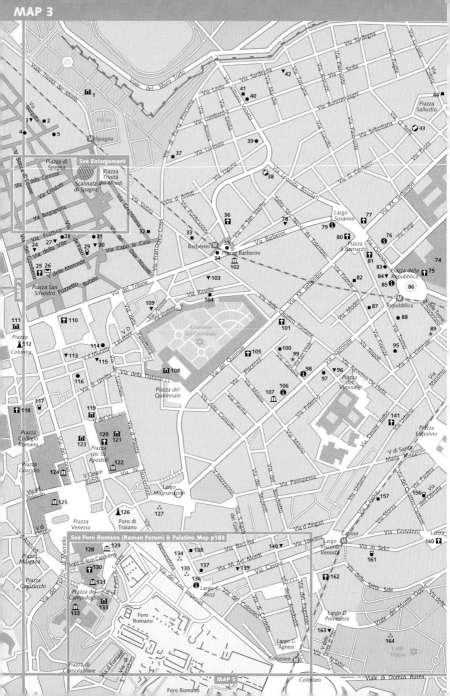

MAP 3

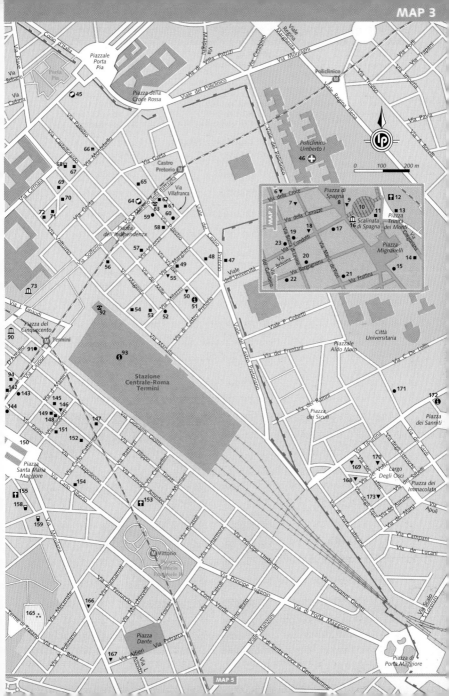

MAP 3

Piazzale
Porta Pia

Porta
Pia

Corso d'Italia

Via Pave

Via Belsiana

Via Cadorna

■ 45

Piazza della
Croce Rossa

Via Patrizi

Via di Villa Patrizi

Viale Regina Margherita

Via Morgagni

Viale Regina Elena

Policlinico

Via Treviso

Via Pavia

Via Imperia

Via A. Borelli

Viale del Policlinico

Policlinico
Umberto I
46 ✚

0   100   200 m

■ 66

■ 68   ■ 67

■ 69

■ 70

■ 72   ■ 71

Via Castelfidardo

Via Palestro

Via Cernaia

Via Montebello

Via Gaeta

Via Curtatone

Via Volturno

Castro
Pretorio

Via Villafranca

■ 65

■ 64

■ 62
■ 63   ■ 61

59 ■   ■ 60

■ 58

Via S. Martino della Battaglia

Via Marghera

Via Magenta

Via dei Mille

Via Vicenza

Piazza
dell'Indipendenza

57 ■

■ 56

Via dei Mille

Via Solferino

Via Magenta

Viale Castro Pretorio

Via del Castro

Viale dell'Università

■ 48

■ 47

▼ 49

▼ 55

50 ⓘ

51 ⓘ

🏛 73

Via L. Einaudi

Piazza del
Cinquecento

🏛 90

91 ●

Via Marsala

Via di Castro Pretorio

54 ■   ■ 53   52 ●

🛉 92

Termini

ⓘ 93

Stazione
Centrale-Roma
Termini

Viale P. Gioberti

Città
Universitaria

Piazzale
Aldo Moro

Via dei Frentani

Via C. De Lollis

171 ●

172
ⓘ

Piazza
dei Sanniti

94 ●

■ 142

● 143

● 91

Via D'Azeglio

Via Cavour

Via Gaeta

● 144

145 ■
146 ■
149 ▼
148 ■
● 151

● 147

150 ●

● 152

154 ●

🛉 155

158 🛉

● 159

🛉 153

Via Giovanni Giolitti

Via Filippo Turati

Via Principe Amedeo

Via Gioberti

Via Cattaneo

Via Napoleone III

Via Carlo Alberto

Via Manin

Via Ricasoli

Piazza
Santa Maria
Maggiore

Viale del Castro Pretorio

Via del Viminale

Via dei Ramni

Piazza
dei Siculi

Via Tiburtina

Via dei Volsci

170
169 ▼   ▼

168 ▼

173 ▼

Largo
Degli Osci

Via degli Equi

Piazza dei
Immacolata

Via dei Marsi

Via Apuli

Via Campani

Via de Lucani

Ⓜ Vittorio

Via Mamiani

Via Rattazzi

Via Ferruccio

166 ▼

165 ∴

Terme di Traiano

Via Machiavelli

167 ●

Via Buonarroti

Via Alfieri

Via L. Alberti

Piazza
Dante

Via Petrarca

Via Emanuele Filiberto

Via Principe Umberto

Via Conte Verde

Via Principe Eugenio

Via Carlo

Via Statilia

Via di Porta Labicana

Via Giovanni Giolitti

Via di Porta Maggiore

Via Campani

Via di Santa Croce in Gerusalemme

Piazza di
Porta Maggiore

Via Scalo
Tiburtino

MAP 2

6 ▼   Via della Croce

7 ▼

8 ▼

Piazza di
Spagna

10 ●

9 ▼

11 ■

🛉 12

■ 13

Via del Babuino

Via della Carrozze

Via della Croce

Via Condotti

18 ●

23 ▼   19 ▼

16 Ⓜ

Scalinata
di Spagna

● 17

Piazza
Trinità
dei Monti

Via Gregoriana

Piazza
Mignanelli

■ 14

20 ●

Via Belsiana

Via Mario de' Fiori

Via Borgognona

21 ●

● 15

▼ 22

Via Frattina

MAP 5

MAP 3

PLACES TO STAY
- 2 Hotel Forte
- 11 Hotel Scalinata di Spagna
- 13 Hassler Villa Medici
- 14 Gregoriana
- 32 Hotel Pensione Suisse
- 33 Hotel Sistina
- 37 Hotel Eden
- 41 Hotel Pensione Merano
- 44 Pensione Tizi; Hotel Ercoli
- 47 Pensione Ester
- 48 Hotel Ventura
- 49 Hotel Venezia
- 53 Fawlty Towers
- 54 Hotel Rimini
- 56 Pensione Giamaica; Hotel New York
- 57 Hotel Piemonte
- 58 Pensione Restivo; Hotel Cervia
- 61 Albergo Sandra
- 62 Hotel Positano; Hotel Continentale; Hotel Romae; Pensione Lachea; Hotel Dolomiti; Tre Stelle
- 65 Hotel Oceania
- 66 Hotel Montecarlo
- 67 Hotel Castelfidardo
- 69 Hotel Floridia
- 70 Albergo Mari 2
- 71 Papa Germano
- 72 Hotel Ascot
- 82 Hotel Seiler
- 87 Hotel Elide
- 94 Hotel Giada

- 104 Hotel Julia
- 137 Hotel Forum
- 138 Hotel Nerva
- 142 Pensione Everest
- 145 Hotel Dina
- 147 Hotel Kennedy
- 148 Hotel Acropoli
- 149 Hotel Sweet Home; Albergo Onella
- 151 Hotel Palladium Palace
- 152 Hotel Igea
- 154 Hotel d'Este
- 157 Hotel Sandy

PLACES TO EAT
- 3 Osteria Margutta
- 6 Otello alla Concordia
- 7 Al 34
- 9 Babington's Tea Rooms
- 18 Caffè Greco
- 24 Centro Macrobiotico Italiano
- 27 Mario
- 30 Sogo Asahi
- 42 Andrea
- 50 Trattoria da Bruno
- 55 Da Gemma alla Lupa
- 78 Tullio
- 84 Dagnino
- 96 Il Golosone
- 103 Colline Emiliane
- 109 Golden Crown
- 113 Al Moro
- 115 Pizza a Taglio
- 139 Alle Carrette

- 140 Osteria Gli Angeletti
- 146 Hostaria Angelo
- 163 Hostaria di Nerone
- 166 Panella L'Arte del Pane
- 167 La Tana del Grillo
- 168 Formula 1
- 169 Pizzeria L'Economica
- 170 Le Maschere
- 173 Il Dito e la Luna

OTHER
- 1 Villa Medici
- 4 Emporio Armani
- 5 Alinari
- 8 American Express
- 10 Scalinata della Trinità dei Monti
- 12 Chiesa della Trinità dei Monti
- 15 Mandarina Duck
- 16 Keats Shelley Memorial House
- 17 Gucci
- 19 Ferragamo (Women)
- 20 Fratelli Rossetti
- 21 La Cicogna
- 22 Fendi
- 23 Ferragamo (Men)
- 25 Chiesa di San Silvestro in Capite
- 26 Post Office
- 28 MaxMara
- 29 Gilda
- 31 Anglo-American Bookshop
- 34 Fontana del Tritone
- 35 Fontana delle Api

DAMIEN SIMONIS

Named after an angelic vision, Castel Sant'Angelo

GEOFF STRINGER

Wander through the Villa d'Este gardens, Tivoli.

MAP 3

The magnificent Piazza Navona, the social centre of Roma

GUY MOBERLY

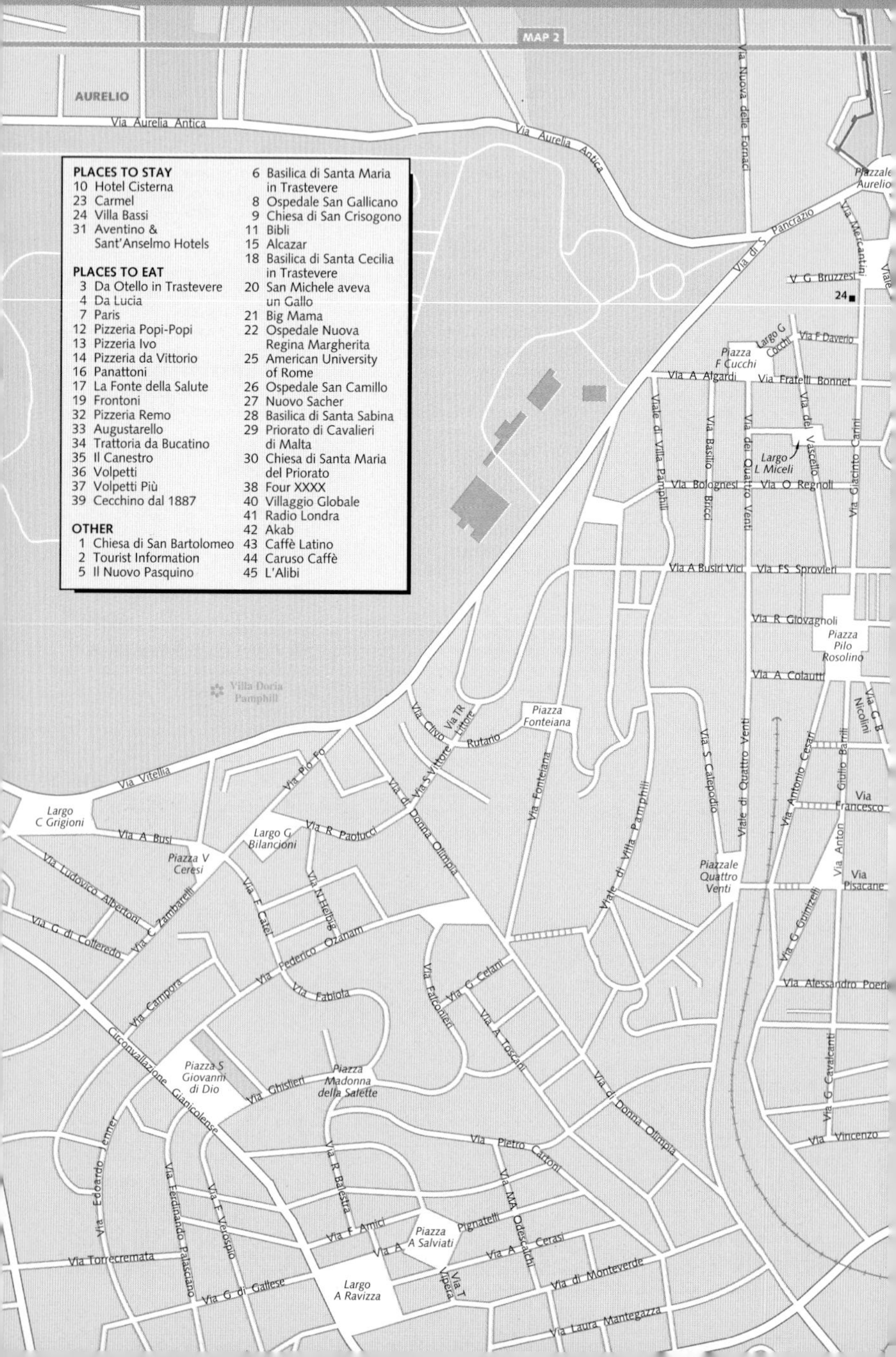

MAP 4

MAP 2

AURELIO

Via Aurelia Antica

Via Aurelia Antica

PLACES TO STAY
10 Hotel Cisterna
23 Carmel
24 Villa Bassi
31 Aventino &
    Sant'Anselmo Hotels

PLACES TO EAT
3   Da Otello in Trastevere
4   Da Lucia
7   Paris
12 Pizzeria Popi-Popi
13 Pizzeria Ivo
14 Pizzeria da Vittorio
16 Panattoni
17 La Fonte della Salute
19 Frontoni
32 Pizzeria Remo
33 Augustarello
34 Trattoria da Bucatino
35 Il Canestro
36 Volpetti
37 Volpetti Più
39 Cecchino dal 1887

OTHER
1   Chiesa di San Bartolomeo
2   Tourist Information
5   Il Nuovo Pasquino

6   Basilica di Santa Maria
    in Trastevere
8   Ospedale San Gallicano
9   Chiesa di San Crisogono
11 Bibli
15 Alcazar
18 Basilica di Santa Cecilia
    in Trastevere
20 San Michele aveva
    un Gallo
21 Big Mama
22 Ospedale Nuova
    Regina Margherita
25 American University
    of Rome
26 Ospedale San Camillo
27 Nuovo Sacher
28 Basilica di Santa Sabina
29 Priorato di Cavalieri
    di Malta
30 Chiesa di Santa Maria
    del Priorato
38 Four XXXX
40 Villaggio Globale
41 Radio Londra
42 Akab
43 Caffè Latino
44 Caruso Caffè
45 L'Alibi

Piazzale
Aurelio

Via di S. Pancrazio

V G Bruzzesi

24

Largo G
Cucchi   Via F Daverio
Piazza
F Cucchi   Via Fratelli Bonnet
Via A Algardi

Largo
L Vascello
Via O Regnoli

Via Basilio Bricci
Viale dei Quattro Venti
Via Bolognesi

Villa Doria
Pamphilj

Via A Busiri Vici   Via FS Sprovieri

Piazza
Pilo
Rosolino

Via R Giovagnoli

Via A Colautti

Piazza
Fonteiana

Via Clivia   Via TR
di Villa   Latina
Via Pio Fo   Rutano
Via Vitellia

Largo
C Grigioni
Via A Busi
Piazza V
Ceresi
Largo G
Bilancioni

Via di Villa Pamphilj

Piazzale
Quattro
Venti

Via
Francesco

Via
Pisacane

Via G Gioberti

Via Alessandro Poerio

Via G Castelvi

Via G di Colloredo
Via Ludovico Albertoni
Via C Zambarelli

Via Federico Ozanam

Via Fabiola

Via A Toscani

Via di Donna Olimpia

Circonvallazione Gianicolense

Piazza S
Giovanni
di Dio
Via Ghisleri
Piazza
Madonna
della Salette

Via Pietro Cartoni

Via di Donna Olimpia

Via Vincenzo

Via Torrecremata
Via G di Gaffese
Via R Balestra
Via F Amici
Piazza
A Salviati
Largo
A Ravizza
Piazza Pignatelli
Via A Cerasi
Via di Monteverde

Via Laura Mantegazza

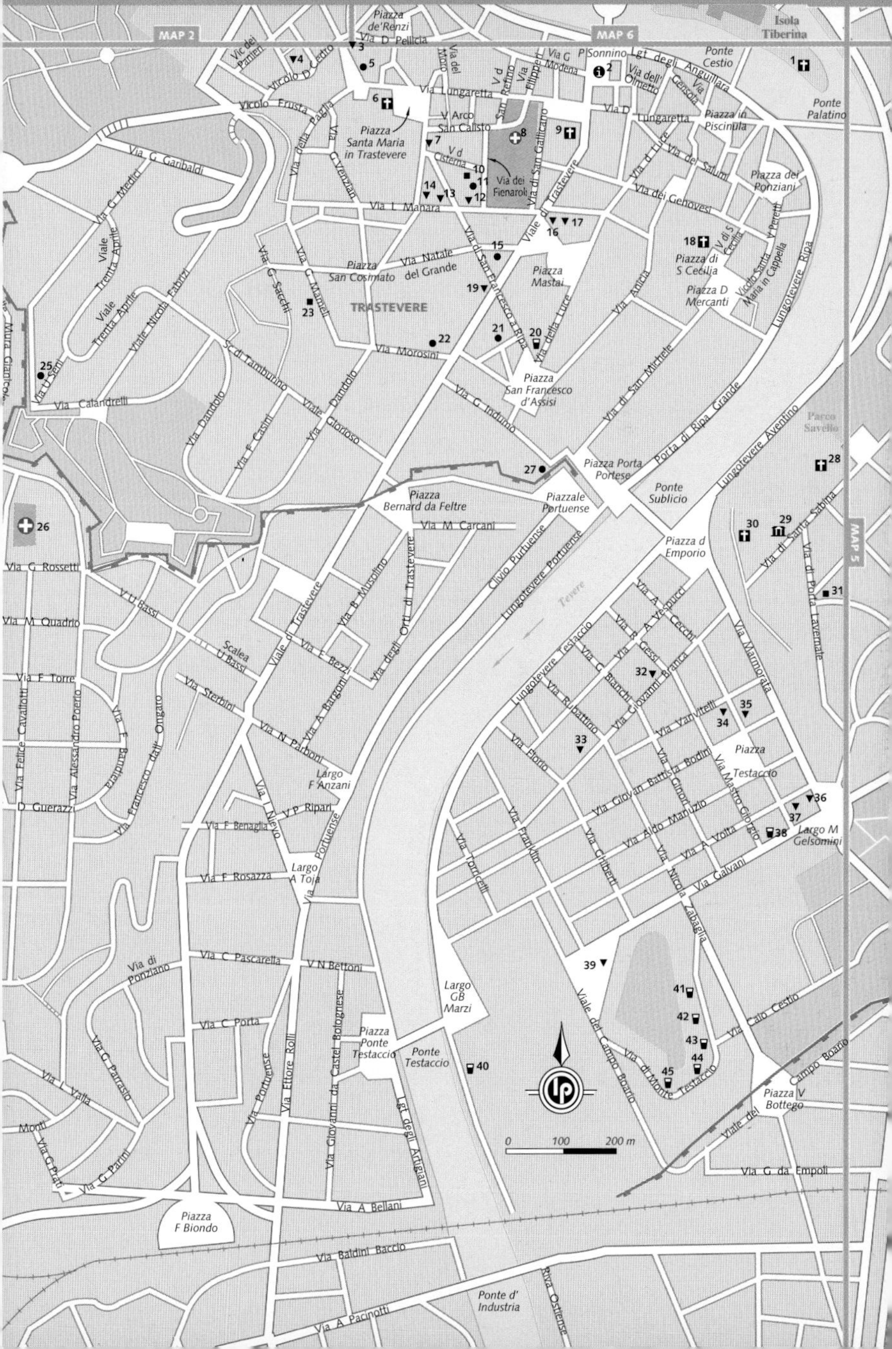

MAP 4

Isola
Tiberina

MAP 2

Piazza
de' Renzi
Via D. Pellicia

MAP 6

Ponte
Cestio

1

Ponte
Palatino

Vic dei
Panieri

Via del
Moro

Vicolo D. Cedro

Vicolo Frusta

Via della Paglia

Via G. Medici

Via G. Garibaldi

4

5

Via Lungaretta

6

V Arco
San Calisto

Piazza
Santa Maria
in Trastevere

7

V d
Cisterna

8

Via d Politeama

9

Piazza in
Piscinula

Ponte
Cestio

Via D. Tungaretta

Via dei Salumi

Piazza dei
Ponziani

10

14   13

11
12

Via I. Manara

16

17

Via dei Genovesi

18

Piazza di
S Cecilia

Piazza D
Mercanti

Viale Trenta Aprile

Viale Trenta Aprile

Viale Nicola Fabrizi

Via G. Stecchi

Piazza
San Cosimato

Via Natale del Grande

15

Piazza
Mastai

Via Anicia

Via di S
Maria in Cappella

Lungotevere Ripa

23

TRASTEVERE

19

Sc di Tambulino

Viale Dandolo

Vs di Porta S Pancrazio

Via Dandolo

Via G. Casini

Via Morosini

Via G. Induno

22

21   20

Piazza
San Francesco
d'Assisi

Via di San Michele

Porta di Ripa Grande

Parco
Savello

25

Via Calandrelli

27

Piazza Porta
Portese

Piazzale
Portuense

Ponte
Sublicio

Lungotevere Aventino

28

MAP 5

26

Via G. Rossetti

Piazza
Bernard da Feltre

Via M Carcani

Piazza d
Emporio

30

29

Via di Santa Sabina

Via G. Quadri

Lt Bassi

Lt Bassi

Scalea
V Bassi

Viale Trastevere

Via di Mastorino

Via degli Orti di Trastevere

Via G. B. Bodoni

31

Via Marmorata

Via F Torre

Via F Cavallotti

Via Felice

Via Alessandro Poerio

Via Francesco Orsini in Orsaro

Via Sterbini

Via N Parboni

Via F Benaglia

Largo
F Anzani

Via P. Ripari

Largo
A Toja

Clivio Portuense

Lungotevere Testaccio

Via A Volta

Via A. Y Cecchi

Via G Gesù

Via Rubattino

Via V Vitelli

Via G. Branca

Via Giovanni Battista Bodoni

Via Aldo Manuzio

Via Galvani

Via Beniamino Franklin

32

33

34

35

Piazza
Testaccio

36

37   38

Largo M
Gelsomini

D. Guerazzi

Via G. Rosazza

Via F Rosazza

Via di
Ponziano

Via C. Pascarella

V N Bettoni

Via C. Porta

Via Ettore Rolli

Via Giacinto Carini

Via Pordenone

Piazza
Ponte
Testaccio

Ponte
Testaccio

Largo
GB
Marzi

Viale del Campo Boario

Via Nicola Zabaglia

39

40

41

42

43   44

45

Piazza V
Bottego

Via di Valla

Via C C A

Monti

Via G. Parini

Via di Monte Testaccio

Via Caio Cestio

Via di Campo Boario

Via Galeno Becchino

Piazza
F Biondo

Via A Bellani

Viale di Campo Boario

Via G da Empoli

Ponte d'
Industria

Via Baldini Baccio

Via A Pacinotti

0   100   200 m

MAP 5

Via dei Fienili

Foro Romano **MAP 3**

Colosseo

Piazza del Colosseo

🏛 6

Via di Velabro

🏛 7

Piazza Bocca di Verità

Via L Petroselli

Via di Arco di Giano

Piazza di S Anastasia

Palatino

🏛 9

Via del Foro Ercole

Via di Santa Sabina

Clivo di Rocca Savella

Via del Cerchi

Circo Massimo

Via del Circo Massimo

▲ 5

Via Celio Vibenna

Piazza del Colosseo

▼ 4

Via In Giovanni

🏛 3

Via M Aurelio

Via Annia

Via Celimontana

Via Claudia

🏛 11

Parco del Celio

Clivo di Scauro

10 🏛

Piazza di SS Giovanni e Paolo

Via della Croce

🏛 18

Via di Valle delle Camene

19 🏛

See Foro Romano (Roman Forum) & Palatino Map p183

Via San Domenica

Largo Arrigo VII

Via di Publio

🄼 Circo Massimo

Via di Valle delle Camene

Villa Celimontana

Piazza Porta Metronia

Via Druso

20 🏛

Via Thiene

Viale Aventino

Via Aventino

Via di San Anselmo

Via M Celsomini

Piazza Albania

Via P Peruzzi

Via di Licinia

Via S Saba

Via Flaminio Ponzio

Via A Pollaio

21 🏛

Parco di Porta Capena

Via della Terme di Caracalla

Via Antonina

Via Guido

Piazzale Numa Pompilio

Terme di Caracalla

Piazzale Numa Pompilio

Via di Piramide Cestia

Via di Faustina

Via Armia

Via A Pollaio

Via P Branmante

Via Bramante

Piazza GL Bernini

Via G Mariotta

Pomelli Baccio

Via E Rosa

Via di Villa Pepoli

Via delle Terme di Caracalla

Piazza Porta San Paolo

Viale Giotto

Via Tata Giovanni

Viale Guido Baccelli

Piazzale Ostiense

Viale di Porta Ardeatina

🄼 Piramide

Via G Milani

Via di Porta Ardeatina

Viale Fabio L Clone

Stazione Roma-Ostia

Via Girolamo Dandini

Viale Marco Polo

Viale di Olberto Beccari

Piazzale dei Partigiani

Largo Terme di Caracalla

Via Cristoforo Colombo

Viale

Viale Marco Polo

MAP 5

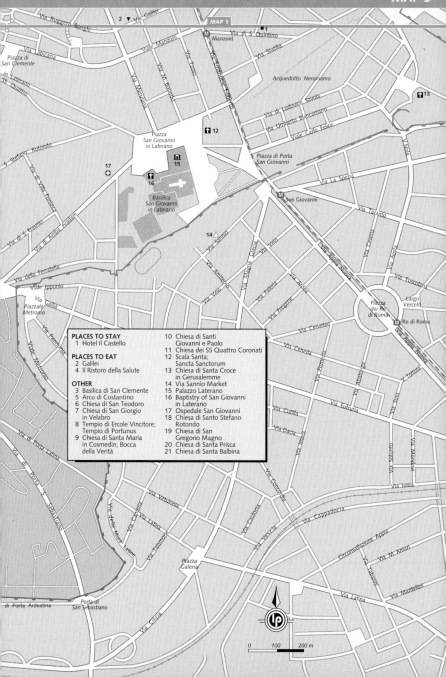

MAP 3

PLACES TO STAY
1 Hotel Il Castello

PLACES TO EAT
2 Galilei
4 Il Ristoro della Salute

OTHER
3 Basilica di San Clemente
5 Arco di Costantino
6 Chiesa di San Teodoro
7 Chiesa di San Giorgio
   in Velabro
8 Tempio di Ercole Vincitore;
   Tempio di Portunus
9 Chiesa di Santa Maria
   in Cosmedin; Bocca
   della Verità
10 Chiesa di Santi
   Giovanni e Paolo
11 Chiesa dei SS Quattro Coronati
12 Scala Santa;
   Sancta Sanctorum
13 Chiesa di Santa Croce
   in Gerusalemme
14 Via Sannio Market
15 Palazzo Laterano
16 Baptistry of San Giovanni
   in Laterano
17 Ospedale San Giovanni
18 Chiesa di Santo Stefano
   Rotondo
19 Chiesa di San
   Gregorio Magno
20 Chiesa di Santa Prisca
21 Chiesa di Santa Balbina

0   100   200 m

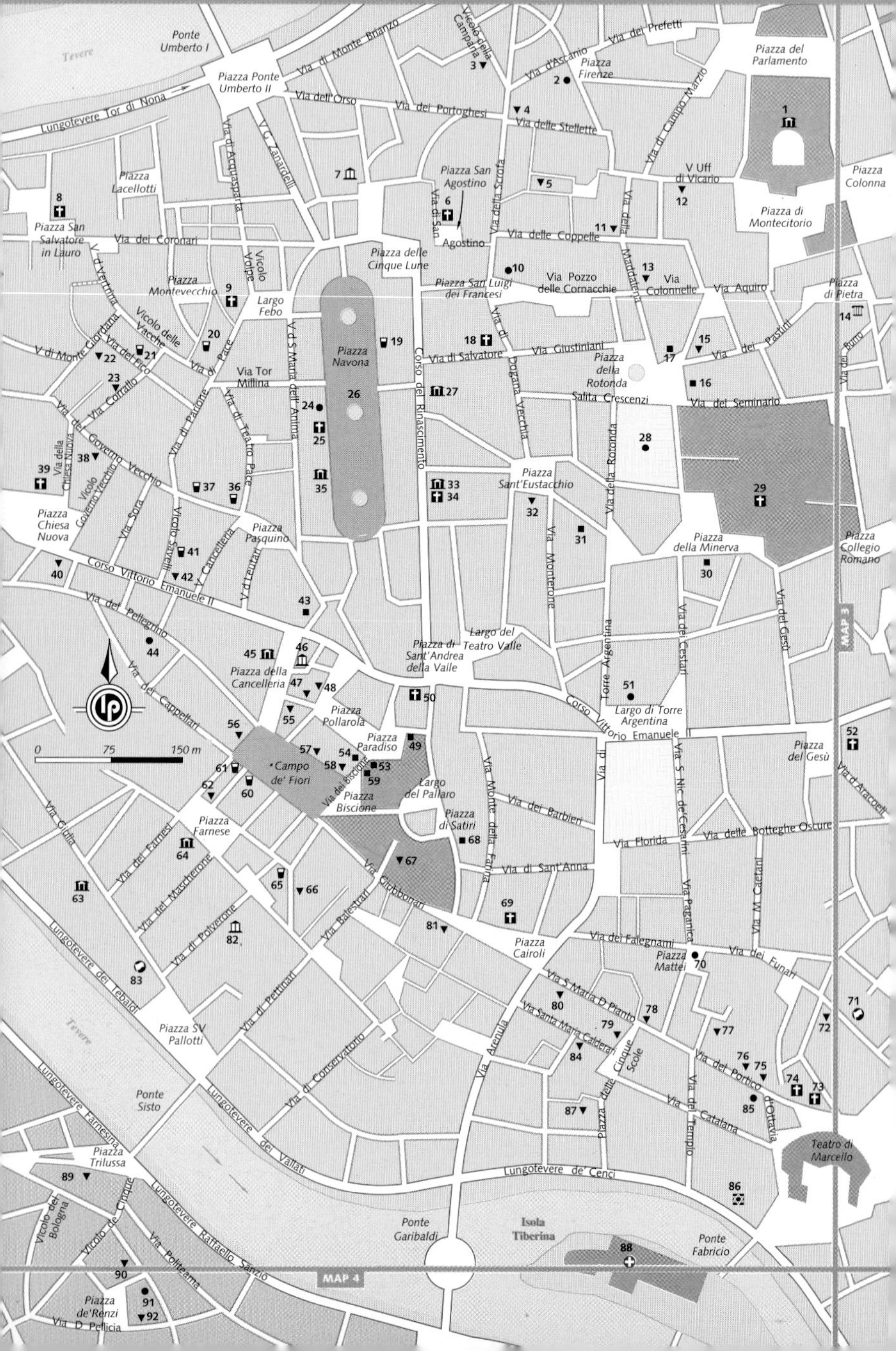

MAP 6

Tevere

Ponte Umberto I

Piazza Ponte Umberto II

Lungotevere Tor di Nona

Via di Monte Branzo

Vicolo della Campana

Via dei Prefetti

Via d'Ascanio

Piazza Firenze

Piazza del Parlamento

Via dell'Orso

Via dei Portoghesi

Via delle Stellette

Via di Campo Marzio

1

V Uff di Vicario

Piazza di Montecitorio

Piazza Colonna

Piazza Lacellotti

8

Piazza San Salvatore in Lauro

Via dei Coronari

Piazza San Agostino

6

Agostino

5

12

Via delle Coppelle

11

Piazza delle Cinque Lune

Piazza San Luigi dei Francesi

10

Via Pozzo delle Cornacchie

13

Via Colonnelle

Via Aquiro

Piazza di Pietra

Piazza Montevecchio

9

Largo Febo

14

Vicolo delle Vacche

20

21

22

23

Via Tor Millina

Piazza Navona

19

18

Via di Salvatori

Via Giustiniani

Piazza della Rotonda

15

17

16

Via del Seminario

26

27

24

25

28

29

35

33

34

32

Piazza Sant'Eustachio

31

Piazza della Minerva

30

Piazza Collegio Romano

39

38

37

36

Piazza Chiesa Nuova

Piazza Pasquino

41

42

40

Corso Vittorio Emanuele II

Via del Pellegrino

43

44

45

Piazza della Cancelleria

46

47

48

Largo del Teatro Valle

Piazza di Sant'Andrea della Valle

51

Largo di Torre Argentina

52

Piazza del Gesù

55

57

54

53

56

61

62

60

58

59

50

49

Piazza Pollarola

Piazza Paradiso

Campo de' Fiori

Largo del Pallaro

Piazza Biscione

Piazza di Satiri

68

67

Piazza Farnese

64

63

65

66

Piazza della Botteghe Oscure

82

83

Piazza SV Pallotti

Ponte Sisto

69

81

Piazza Cairoli

Piazza Mattei

70

71

72

80

78

79

77

76

75

74

73

84

85

87

86

Piazza Trilussa

89

Ponte Garibaldi

Isola Tiberina

88

Ponte Fabricio

Teatro di Marcello

90

91

92

Piazza de' Renzi

Via D. Pellicia

0   75   150 m

Tevere

Lungotevere de' Tebaldi

Lungotevere dei Vallati

Lungotevere de' Cenci

MAP 4

MAP 3

MAP 6

The top of the Basilica di San Pietro provides the perfect vantage point to see all of Roma.

JON DAVISON

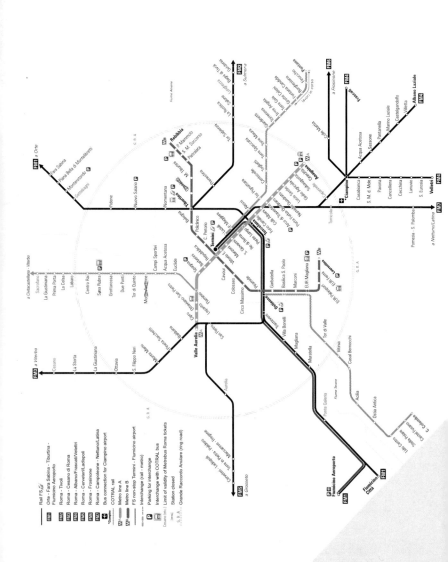

[continued from page 192]

style by Giuseppe Valadier in the early 19th century. In its centre is an obelisk brought by Augustus from Heliopolis, in ancient Greece, and moved here from the Circo Massimo in the mid-16th century. To the east is a ramp leading up to the **Pincio Hill**, which affords a stunning view of the city.

The **Chiesa di Santa Maria del Popolo** (Map 1), next to the Porta del Popolo at the northern side of the piazza, was originally a chapel built in 1099 on the site where Nero was buried. It was enlarged in the 13th century and rebuilt during the early Renaissance. In the 17th century the interior was renovated by Bernini. The Cappella Chigi (the second chapel in the north aisle after you enter the church) was designed by Raphael for the famous banker Agostino Chigi, but the artist died leaving the chapel unfinished. It was completed more than 100 years later by Bernini. The apse was designed by Donato Bramante and contains the tombs of Cardinal Ascanio Sforza and Cardinal Girolamo Basso della Rovere, both signed by the Florentine sculptor Andrea Sansovino. The frescoes in the vault are by Bernardino Pinturicchio. In the first chapel to the left of the high altar are paintings by Caravaggio.

VILLA BORGHESE (Map 1)

This beautiful park, just north-east of the Piazza del Popolo, was once the estate of Cardinal Scipione Borghese. The main entrance is from Piazzale Flaminio, but it is also accessible through the park at the top of the Pincio hill. It's a good place to have a picnic or to take children for a break from sightseeing.

The cardinal's 17th century villa houses the **Museo e Galleria Borghese**. A sculpture section on the ground floor features numerous important classical works and several sculptures by Bernini and Canova. In Room One is Canova's famous statue of Pauline Borghese (wife of Camillo Borghese and sister of Napoleon Bonaparte) depicted as Venus Victrix.

The museum is on Piazzale Museo Borghese in the Villa Borghese park. Opening hours vary by season (always call to check) and booking is compulsory (☎ 06 3 28 10, fax 06 326 51 329 for groups). If you book by telephone, you have to pay at the ticket office at least one hour before the starting time of your visit. Don't just turn up as you won't get in. Admission costs L12,000. The museum is equipped for disabled visitors and there's a bar/café which serves snacks and light meals.

Also in the park is the **Bioparco** (☎ 06 321 65 64), the former Zoological Gardens, at the northern end of the park in Viale del Giardino Zoologico. There are better ways to spend L10,000 (L7000 for children aged five to 12, free for children under five) but kids might enjoy it. It's open from 9.30 am to 5 pm daily.

Just outside the park, on Viale delle Belle Arti, is the **Galleria Nazionale d'Arte Moderna**, which houses an impressive collection of Italian art from the 19th century to the present day. It is open from 9 am to 8 pm Tuesday to Sunday. Admission costs L8000.

MUSEO NAZIONALE ETRUSCO DI VILLA GIULIA (Map 1)

Situated in the 16th century villa of Pope Julius III at the top end of the Villa Borghese at Piazzale di Villa Giulia 9, this museum houses the national collection of Etruscan treasures, many found in tombs at sites throughout Lazio. If you plan to visit Etruscan sites near Roma, a visit to the museum before setting out will give you a good understanding of Etruscan culture. The museum (☎ 06 320 19 51) is open from 9 am to 7 pm Tuesday to Saturday and to 2 pm on Sunday. Admission costs L8000.

AROUND VIA VITTORIO VENETO (Map 3)

This is still Roma's most fashionable street, although the atmosphere of the 1960s is long dead.

The **Chiesa di Santa Maria della Concezione** is an austere 17th century church, but the Capuchin cemetery beneath (access is on the right of the church steps) features a bizarre display of the bones of some 4000 monks, used to decorate the walls of a series of chapels between 1528 and 1870.

euro currency converter L10,000 = €5.16

In the centre of **Piazza Barberini**, at the southern end of Via Veneto, is the spectacular **Fontana del Tritone** (Fountain of the Triton), created by Bernini in 1643 for Pope Urban VIII, patriarch of the Barberini family. It features a Triton blowing a stream of water from a conch shell. In the north-eastern corner of the piazza is another fountain, the **Fontana delle Api** (Fountain of the Bees), created by the same artist for the Barberini family, whose crest, which features three bees, can be seen on many buildings throughout Roma.

The 17th century **Palazzo Barberini**, on Via delle Quattro Fontane, is well worth a visit. Carlo Maderno was commissioned by Urban VIII to build the palace and both Bernini and Borromini worked on its construction for the Barberini family. The building houses part of the **Galleria Nazionale d'Arte Antica**. The collection includes paintings by Raphael, Caravaggio, Guido Reni, Guercino, Bronzino, Bernini, Filippo Lippi and Holbein. A highlight is the ceiling of the main salon of the palace (part of the gallery), entitled the *Triumph of Divine Providence*, painted by Pietro da Cortona. A recent addition to the collection is Jacopo Zucchi's *Il Bagno di Betsabea*, dating from the late 1580s, which was lost after WWII, found in Paris, bought by an American museum and returned to Italy in 1998. The palace and gallery are open from 9 am to 7 pm Tuesday to Saturday and to 1 pm on Sunday. Admission is from Via Barberini 18 and costs L8000.

PALAZZO DEL QUIRINALE (Map 3)

The Palazzo del Quirinale, on the piazza of the same name, is the official residence of the president of the Republic. Built and added to from 1574 to the early 18th century, the palace was the summer residence of the popes until 1870, when it became the royal palace of the kings of Italy. It is open to the public from 8.30 am to 12.30 pm on the second and fourth Sunday of the month. Arrive early, as it is usually not possible to join the queue after about 11 am. Admission costs L10,000.

The obelisk in the centre of the piazza was moved here from the Mausoleo di Augusto in 1786. It is flanked by the large statues of the Dioscuri, Castor and Pollux, which are Imperial-era copies of 5th century BC Greek originals.

Along the Via del Quirinale are two excellent examples of baroque architecture: the churches of **Sant'Andrea al Quirinale**, designed by Bernini, and **San Carlo alle Quattro Fontane**, designed by Borromini. The Chiesa di Sant'Andrea is considered one of Bernini's masterpieces. He designed it with an elliptical floor plan and with a series of chapels opening onto the central area. The interior is decorated with polychrome marble, stucco and gilding. Note the cherubs which adorn the lantern of the dome.

The Chiesa di San Carlo was the first church designed by Borromini in Roma and was completed in 1641. The small cloister was also designed by Borromini. The church stands at the intersection known as Quattro Fontane, after the late 16th century fountains at its four corners.

TERME DI DIOCLEZIANO (Map 3)

Started by Emperor Diocletian, these baths were completed in the early 4th century. The complex of baths, libraries, concert halls and gardens was the largest in ancient Roma, covering about 13 hectares and with a capacity of 3000 people. After the aqueduct that fed the baths was destroyed by invaders in about 536 AD, the complex fell into disrepair. However, large sections of the baths were incorporated into the Basilica di Santa Maria degli Angeli, which faces Piazza della Repubblica. At the time of writing most of the baths complex was closed for restoration.

The **Museo Nazionale Romano**, which opened in 1889 and incorporated several halls of the ancient baths, houses a valuable collection of ancient art, including Greek and Roman sculpture (see also the following Palazzo Massimo alle Terme section).

The **Basilica di Santa Maria degli Angeli** was designed by Michelangelo and incorporates what was the great central hall and *tepidarium* (lukewarm room) of the original baths. During the following centuries his work was drastically changed and little evidence of his design, apart from the great vaulted ceiling, remains. An interesting feature of the church is a double meridian in the transept, one tracing the polar star and the other telling the precise time of the sun's zenith, visible at noon (solar time). The church is open from 7.30 am to 12.30 pm and 4 to 6.30 pm. A plaque near the stairway records the traditional belief that the baths were built by thousands of Christian slaves.

PALAZZO MASSIMO ALLE TERME (Map 3)

Palazzo Massimo, the new home of part of the Museo Nazionale Romano collection, boasts some of the best examples of Roman art in the city. It took 16 years and L68 billion for the 19th century building, a former Jesuit college, to be transformed into a museum. It is one of Roma's best: light-filled, spacious and blissfully air-conditioned in summer. The highlight is the collection of Roman paintings and mosaics, displayed on the 2nd floor. Palazzo Massimo is open from 9 am to 7 pm Tuesday to Sunday. Opening hours are usually extended (to 10 pm) in the summer. Admission costs L12,000.

IL VATICANO (Map 2)

After unification, the Papal States of central Italy became part of the new Kingdom of Italy, causing a considerable rift between Church and State. In 1929 Mussolini, under the Lateran Treaty, gave the pope full sovereignty over what is now the Città del Vaticano (Vatican City).

The city has its own postal service, currency, newspaper, radio station, train station and army of Swiss Guards, responsible for security.

Information & Services

The tourist office (☎ 06 698 84 466), on Piazza San Pietro to the left of the basilica, is open from 8.30 am to 7 pm daily and has general information about the Basilica di San Pietro and Il Vaticano. Guided tours of Il Vaticano can be organised here.

Il Vaticano post office, said to provide a much faster and more reliable service than the normal Italian postal system, is a few doors from the tourist office (there is another office on the other side of the piazza). Letters will be carried by this service only if they carry Vaticano stamps.

Papal Audiences

The pope usually gives a public audience at 11 am every Wednesday in the Aula delle Udienze Pontificie (Papal Audience Hall). For permission to attend, go to the Prefettura della Casa Pontifica (☎ 06 698 83 017), through the bronze doors under the colonnade to the right of the basilica as you face it. The office is open from 9 am to 1 pm and you can apply on the Tuesday before the audience (or, at a push, on the morning of the audience). You can also apply in writing to the Prefettura della Casa Pontifica, 00120 Città del Vaticano. You should specify the date you'd like to attend and the number of tickets required. If you have a hotel in Roma, the office will forward the tickets there. Individuals shouldn't have too much trouble obtaining a ticket at short notice. The pope also occasionally says Mass in the basilica and information can be obtained from the same office. You will be required to leave your passport with the Swiss Guards at the bronze doors.

People wanting to attend a normal Mass at San Pietro can ask for the times of daily Masses at the tourist office on the piazza.

Piazza San Pietro

Bernini's piazza is considered a masterpiece. Laid out in the 17th century as a place for the Christians of the world to gather, the immense square is bounded by two semicircular colonnades, each of which is made up of four rows of Doric columns. In the centre of the piazza is an obelisk brought to Roma by Caligula from Heliopolis in ancient Egypt.

Basilica di San Pietro

Nero's Circo Vaticano once stood in the area now occupied by the Basilica di San Pietro (St Peter's Basilica). The body of the saint was buried in an anonymous grave next to the wall of the circus and his fellow Christians built a humble red wall to mark the site. In 160 AD the stadium was abandoned and a small monument erected on the grave. In 315 Emperor Constantine ordered the construction of a basilica on the site of the apostle's tomb. This first Basilica di San Pietro was consecrated in 326.

After more than 1000 years, the church was in a poor state of repair and, in the mid-15th century, Pope Nicholas V put architects, including Alberti, to work on its reconstruction. But it was not until 1506, when Pope Julius II employed Donato Bramante, that serious work began. Bramante designed a new basilica on a Greek cross plan, with a central dome and four smaller domes. He oversaw the demolition of much of the old basilica and attracted great criticism for the unnecessary destruction of many of its precious works of art.

It took more than 150 years to complete the new basilica, with contributions from Bramante, Raphael, Antonio da Sangallo, Michelangelo, Giacomo della Porta and Carlo Maderno. It is generally held that San Pietro owes most to Michelangelo, who took over the project in 1547 at the age of 72 and was responsible for the design of the dome. He died before the church was completed.

The façade and portico were designed by Carlo Maderno, who took over the project after Michelangelo's death. He was also instructed to lengthen the nave towards the piazza, effectively altering Bramante's original Greek cross plan to a Latin cross. Restoration work on the façade was carried out between 1997 and 1999. This mainly consisted of cleaning the travertine marble and repairing damage caused by age and pollution.

The cavernous interior, decorated by Bernini and Giacomo della Porta, can hold up to 60,000 people. It contains art treasures including Michelangelo's superb *Pietà*, at the beginning of the right aisle, sculpted when he was only 25 years old and the only work to carry his signature (on the sash across the breast of the Madonna). It is now protected by bulletproof glass after a hammer-wielding

vandal attacked it in 1972. The red porphyry disk just inside the main door marks the spot where Charlemagne and later Holy Roman Emperors were crowned by the pope.

Bernini's baroque *baldacchino* (canopy) stands 29m high in the centre of the church and is an extraordinary work of art. The bronze used to make it was taken from the Pantheon. The high altar, which only the pope can use, stands over the site of San Pietro's grave.

To the right as you face the high altar is a famous bronze statue of San Pietro, believed to be a 13th century work by Arnolfo di Cambio. The statue's right foot has been worn down by the kisses and touch of many pilgrims.

Michelangelo's dome, a majestic architectural masterpiece, soars 119m above the high altar. Its balconies are decorated with reliefs depicting the Reliquie Maggiori (major relics) – the lance of San Longino, which he used to pierce Christ's side; the cloth of Santa Veronica, which bears a miraculous image of Christ; and a piece of the True Cross, collected by Sant'Elena, the mother of Emperor Constantine. Entry to the dome is to the right as you climb the stairs to the atrium of the basilica. Access to the roof of the church is by elevator (admission L6000) or stairs (admission L5000). From there, you ascend the stairs to the base of the dome for a view down into the basilica. A narrow staircase leads eventually to the top of the dome and San Pietro's lantern, from where you have an unequalled view of Roma. It is well worth the effort, but bear in mind that it's a long and tiring climb. You can climb the dome from 8 am to one hour before the basilica closes.

The entrance to the **Sacre Grotte Vaticane** (Sacred Grottoes), the resting place of numerous popes, is next to the pier of San Longino (one of four piers supporting the arches at the base of Michelangelo's cupola), to the right as you approach the papal altar. The tombs of many early popes were moved here from the old Basilica di San Pietro, and later popes, including John XXIII, Paul VI and John Paul I, are also buried here. The grottoes are open daily from 8 am to 6 pm (April to September) and 8 am to 5 pm (September to March).

The excavations beneath San Pietro, which began in 1940, have uncovered part of the original church, an early Christian cemetery and pagan tombs. Archaeologists believe they have also found the tomb of San Pietro; the site of the empty tomb is marked by a shrine and a wall plastered with red. Nearby is another wall, scrawled with the graffiti of pilgrims, under which were found the bones of an elderly, strongly built man. Pope Paul VI declared these to be the bones of the saint.

The excavations can be visited only by appointment, which can be made either in writing or in person at the Ufficio Scavi (☎ 06 698 85 318, fax 06 698 85 518), in Piazza Braschi. Address your letter to Ufficio Scavi, 00120 Città del Vaticano, Roma, and stipulate the date you'd like to visit. The office will then get back in contact with you to confirm the time and date. You need to book at least one week ahead. The office is open from 8 am to 5 pm Monday to Saturday. Small groups are taken most days between 9 am and noon and 2 and 5 pm. It costs L10,000 to visit the excavations with a guide.

Dress regulations are stringently enforced in San Pietro. It is forbidden to enter the church in shorts, wearing a short skirt or with bare shoulders.

Musei Vaticani

From San Pietro, follow the wall of Il Vaticano north to the entrance to the Vatican Museums. From mid-March to the end of October, they are open from 8.45 am to 4.45 pm Monday to Friday (last admission 3.45 pm) and to 1.45 pm on Saturday (last admission 12.45 pm). The rest of the year they are open from 8.45 am to 1.45 pm Monday to Saturday (last admission at 12.45 pm). Admission costs L15,000. The museums are closed on Sunday and holidays, but open from 9 am to 1.45 pm on the last Sunday of every month (admission is free, but queues are always very long).

A regular bus service runs from outside the Arco delle Campane (to the left of the basilica, just near the tourist office) to the museum about every half-hour from 8.45 am to 12.45 pm. Tickets cost L2000 and it is certainly the easiest way to make the journey. The bus passes through an area of Il Vaticano and its gardens.

One visit is probably not enough to appreciate the full value of the collections; it's worth trying to make at least two visits if you have the time. There are four itineraries which Il Vaticano has mapped out with the aim of simplifying visits and containing the huge number of visitors. Basically, it is compulsory that you follow the itineraries, but you may be able to make some deviations.

Another point to note is that the Cappella Sistina comes towards the end of a full visit. If you want to spend most of your time in the chapel, or you want to get there early to avoid the crowds, it is possible to walk straight there and then walk back to the Quattro Cancelli to pick up one of the itineraries. Most tour groups (and there are many!) head straight for the chapel and it is almost always very crowded. It is also important to note that the guards at the Cappella Sistina often refuse to let people in well before closing time. Of great assistance and well worth the L16,000 investment is the *Guide to the Vatican Museums and City*, on sale at the Musei.

The **Museo Gregoriano Egizio** (Egyptian Museum) contains many pieces taken from Egypt in Roman times. The collection is small, but there are interesting pieces.

Il Vaticano's enormous collection of ancient sculpture is contained in a series of galleries. The long corridor which forms the **Museo Chiaramonti** contains hundreds of marble busts, while the **Braccio Nuovo** (New Wing) contains important works, including a famous statue of Augustus and a statue depicting the Nile as a reclining god with 16 babies playing on him, which are supposed to represent the number of cubits the Nile rose when in flood.

The **Museo Pio-Clementino** is in the Belvedere Pavilion and accessible through the Egyptian Museum. In the Cortile Otta-gono (Octagonal Courtyard) is part of the Vaticano sculpture collection: the *Apollo Belvedere*, a 2nd century Roman copy in marble of a 4th century BC Greek bronze, considered one of the great masterpieces of classical sculpture, and, notably, the *Lao-coön*, depicting a Trojan priest of Apollo and his two sons in mortal struggle with two sea serpents.

In the Sala delle Muse (Room of the Muses) is the *Belvedere Torso*, a Greek sculpture of the 1st century BC, which was found in the Campo de' Fiori during the time of Pope Julius II and was much admired by Michelangelo and other Renaissance artists. In the Sala a Croce Greca (Greek Cross Room) are the porphyry sarcophagi of Con-stantine's daughter, Constantia, and his mother, Sant'Elena.

Up one flight of the Simonetti staircase is the **Museo Gregoriano Etrusco** (Etruscan Museum), which contains artefacts from Etruscan tombs in southern Etruria. Of par-ticular interest are those from the Regolini-Galassi tomb, discovered in 1836 south of

Michelangelo in Roma

Michelangelo Buonarotti was born in Caprese, near Arrezzo in Toscana, in 1475, the son of a Tuscan magistrate. He was a moody and solitary figure, easily offended and irritated. The true Renaissance man, he was a supremely talented architect and painter, but he regarded himself as a sculptor above all else.

It was as a sculptor that Michelangelo achieved his early recognition. One of his greatest early carvings is the *Pietà* in the Basilica di San Pietro, which he completed when he was 25 years old.

Michelangelo went to work in Roma for Pope Julius II, who wanted a grand marble tomb for himself which would surpass any funerary monument that had ever been built. Michelan-gelo was dispatched to the marble quarries of Carrara, in northern Toscana (which still pro-vide stone for sculptors today), and spent eight months selecting and excavating suitable marble blocks which, when taken to Roma, filled half of Piazza San Pietro.

Although the tomb preoccupied Michelangelo throughout his working life, it was never completed and Julius II lies in an unadorned grave in San Pietro. The original design included 40 statues. The famous figure of Moses, as well as statues of Leah and Rachel, are in the Chiesa di San Pietro in Vincoli. Two of the slaves are now in the Louvre and several famous unfinished slaves are in the Accademia in Firenze.

Despite claiming to be a reluctant painter, Michelangelo's single greatest artistic achieve-ment, one of the most awe-inspiring acts of individual creativity in the history of the visual arts, is the ceiling of the Cappella Sistina, painted between 1508 and 1512. Michelangelo never wanted the commission (also from Julius II) and the project was problematic from the outset. First the artist rejected the scaffolding that Bramante had built for him, then he con-sidered his assistants so incompetent that he dismissed them all, scraped off their work and ended up painting the entire ceiling single-handedly. The artist was pushed to his physical and emotional limits, and was continually harassed by the pope and his court, who wanted the job finished.

Michelangelo returned to Roma aged 59 at the request of Pope Clement VII to paint the *Giudizio Universale* (Last Judgment) on the altar wall of the Cappella Sistina. Once again he accepted the commission against his will, preferring to continue sculpting figures for Julius II's tomb, which he did secretly while he prepared the Last Judgment sketches.

Cerveteri. Those buried in the tomb included a princess and among the finds on display are gold jewellery and a funeral carriage with a bronze bed and funeral couch. A collection of Greek vases and Roman antiquities is also displayed in the museum.

Through the **Galleria degli Arazzi** (Tapestry Gallery) and the **Galleria delle Carte Geografiche** (Map Gallery) are the magnificent **Stanze di Raffaello**, the private apartments of Pope Julius II. Raphael painted the Stanza della Segnatura and the Stanza d'Eliodoro, while the Stanza dell'Incendio was painted

by his students to his designs and the ceiling was painted by his master, Perugino. In the Stanza della Segnatura is one of Raphael's masterpieces, *The School of Athens*, featuring philosophers and scholars gathered around Plato and Aristotle. Opposite is *Disputation on the Sacrament*, also by Raphael. In the Stanza d'Eliodoro is another Raphael masterpiece, *Expulsion of Heliodorus from the Temple*, on the main wall (to the right as you enter from the Sala dei Chiaroscuri), which depicts Julius' military victory over foreign powers. To the left is *Mass of Bolsena*,

Michelangelo in Roma

TRUDI CANAVAN

Now behind protective glass – Michelangelo's beautiful *Pietà*

On Clement VII's death, his successor, Paul III, was determined to have Michelangelo working exclusively for him and have the Cappella Sistina completed. In 1535 he appointed Michelangelo as chief architect, sculptor and painter to Il Vaticano and the artist started working on the Last Judgment, which was unveiled in 1541 and claimed by some as surpassing not only the other masters who had decorated the chapel walls but also Michelangelo's own ceiling frescoes.

Paul III then commissioned Michelangelo to create a new central square for the city on the Campidoglio and to design a suitably grand approach to it. The work was not finished until the middle of the 17th century, but successive architects closely followed the original plans.

Michelangelo's design for the upper storey of the Palazzo Farnese was also realised posthumously when Giacomo della Porta completed the building, and his design for the city gateway at Porta Pia was finished a year after his death.

The artist spent his last years working – unhappily – on the Basilica di San Pietro; he felt that it was penance from God. He disapproved of the plans that had been drawn up by Antonio da Sangallo the Younger before his death, claiming that they deprived the basilica of light, and argued with Sangallo's assistants, who wanted to retain their master's designs. Instead, Michelangelo created the magnificent light-filled dome, based on Brunelleschi's design for the cupola of Firenze's duomo.

In old age he was said to work with the same strength and concentration that he had as a young man. He continued to direct the work until his death on 18 February 1564. He was buried in the Chiesa dei Santi Apostoli, although his remains were later moved to Firenze. The dome of San Pietro was completed to his designs by Vignola, Giacomo della Porta and Carlo Fontana.

showing Julius II paying homage to a relic from a 13th century miracle in that town. Next is *Leo X Repulsing Attila*, by Raphael and his school, and on the fourth wall is *Liberation of San Pietro*, which depicts the saint being freed from prison, but is actually an allusion to Pope Leo's imprisonment after the battle of Ravenna (also the real subject of the Attila fresco).

Cappella Sistina

The private papal chapel, the Cappella Sistina (Sistine Chapel), was completed in 1484 for Pope Sixtus IV and is now used for some papal functions and for the conclave which elects the popes. However, it is best known for two of the most famous works of art in the world: Michelangelo's wonderful frescoes of the *Creation* on the barrel-vaulted ceiling, and the *Last Judgment* on the end wall. Both were restored during the 1980s and 90s and the rich, vibrant colours used by Michelangelo have been brought back to the surface.

Michelangelo was commissioned by the Pope Julius II to paint the ceiling and, although very reluctant to take on the job as he never considered himself a painter, he started work on it in 1508. The complex and grand composition that Michelangelo devised to cover the 800 sq metres of ceiling took him four years to complete. He worked on scaffolding which the restorers believe was inserted into holes under the windows. The restorers also learned much about the way in which the artist worked and how his painting skill developed as he progressed through the great project.

Twenty-four years later, Michelangelo was commissioned by Pope Clement VII to paint the *Last Judgment* (the pope died shortly afterwards and the work was executed under Pope Paul III). Two frescoes by Perugino were destroyed to make way for the new painting, which caused great controversy in its day. Criticism of its dramatic, swirling mass of predominantly naked bodies was summarily dismissed by Michelangelo, who depicted one of his greatest critics, Paul III's master of ceremonies, as

Minos with the ears of an ass. As with the *Creation*, the *Last Judgment* was blackened by candle smoke and incense, but it was also damaged by poor restorations and by the addition of clothes to cover some of the nude figures.

The walls of the chapel were painted by famous Renaissance artists, including Botticelli, Domenico Ghirlandaio, Pinturicchio and Luca Signorelli. These paintings, which were executed in the late 15th century, depict events in the life of Moses (to the right with your back to the *Last Judgment)* and Christ (to the left). Note particularly Botticelli's *Burning Bush* on the right wall, as well as his *Cleansing of the Leper*, Domenico Ghirlandaio's *Calling of Peter and Andrew* and Perugino's *Christ Giving the Keys to St Peter*.

CASTEL SANT'ANGELO (Map 2)

Originally the mausoleum of Emperor Hadrian, this building was converted into a fortress for the popes in the 6th century AD. It was named Castel Sant'Angelo by Pope Gregory the Great in 590 AD, after he saw a vision of an angel above the structure heralding the end of a plague in Roma. The fortress was linked to the Vatican palaces in 1277 by a wall and passageway, often used by the popes to escape to the fortress in times of threat. During the 16th century sacking of Roma by Emperor Charles V, hundreds of people lived in the fortress for months.

Castel Sant'Angelo is open from 9 am to 8 pm Tuesday to Sunday (last admission 7 pm). Admission costs L8000.

Hadrian built the **Ponte Sant'Angelo** across the Tevere river in 136 AD to provide an approach to his mausoleum. It collapsed in 1450 and was subsequently rebuilt, incorporating parts of the ancient bridge. In the 17th century Bernini and his pupils sculpted the figures of angels which now line the pedestrian-only bridge.

ARA PACIS (Map 2)

The Ara Pacis (Altar of Peace) was sculpted and erected during the four years after Augustus' victories in Spain and Gaul and dedicated in 9 BC. The marble altar is enclosed by a marble screen decorated with reliefs showing historical scenes on the sides and mythological scenes on the ends, all protected in a glass building. Of particular interest are the stories related to the discovery and eventual reconstruction of the Ara Pacis.

Sculpted marble panels were first unearthed in the 16th century and more panels were unearthed in the early 19th century during excavations under a palace at the corner of Via del Corso and Via di Lucina. The Italian government continued excavations until the surrounding palaces were in danger of collapse. It was not until Mussolini ordered the excavation to be resumed that the remainder of the monument was unearthed and the Ara Pacis reconstructed at its present site.

The monument is open from 9 am to 5 pm Tuesday to Saturday and from 9 am to 1 pm on Sunday. Admission costs L4000.

Just east of the monument is the **Mausoleo d'Augusto** (Mausoleum of Augustus), built by the emperor for himself and his family. It was originally faced with marble and was converted into a fortress during the Middle Ages. It then served various purposes until restored to its original state in 1936.

OTHER BASILICAS & CHURCHES

Chiesa di San Paolo Fuori le Mura (Map 1) is on Via Ostiense, some distance from the city centre (take Metro Linea B to San Paolo). The original church was built in the 4th century AD by Emperor Constantine over the burial place of San Paolo and, until the construction of the present-day Basilica di San Pietro, was the largest church in the world. The church was destroyed by fire in 1823 and the present structure was erected in its place. The beautiful cloisters of the adjacent Benedictine abbey, decorated with 13th century mosaics, survived the fire.

The **Chiesa di Santa Croce in Gerusalemme** (Map 5), on the piazza of the same name (take Metro Linea A to San Giovanni), dates from the 4th century but was completely remodelled in baroque style in the 18th century. A modern chapel inside the church contains what are said to be fragments of the cross on which Christ was crucified. The fragments were found in the Holy Land by Sant'Elena .

The **Chiesa di San Lorenzo Fuori le Mura** (Map 1) is dedicated to the martyred San Lorenzo. The original structure was built by Constantine, but the church was rebuilt on many occasions. Of note are the 13th century pulpits and bishop's throne. The remains of SS Lorenzo and Stefano are in the church crypt.

The opening hours of Roma's churches vary, but they are generally open daily from 7 or 8 am to noon and 4 to 7 pm.

GIANICOLO & VILLA DORIA PAMPHILI (Map 2)

For a panoramic view of Roma, go to the top of the Gianicolo hill, between the Basilica di San Pietro and Trastevere. At the top of the hill, just off Piazza Garibaldi, there are pony rides and a permanent merry-go-round. Puppet shows are often held here on Sunday. There is a small bar on the piazza. To reach Piazza Garibaldi, catch bus No 41 from Via della Conciliazione in front of San Pietro or walk up the steps from Via Mameli in Trastevere. The bus will also take you within easy walking distance of the nearby Villa Doria Pamphili (Map 4), the largest park in Roma and a lovely quiet spot for a walk and a picnic. Built in the 17th century for the Pamphili family, the villa is now used for official government functions.

VIA APPIA ANTICA (Map 1)

Known to ancient Romans as the *regina viarum* (queen of roads), the Via Appia Antica (Appian Way) runs from the Porta di San Sebastiano, near the Terme di Caracalla, to Brindisi, on the coast of Puglia. It was started around 312 BC by the censor Appius Claudius Caecus, but did not connect with Brindisi until around 190 BC. The first section of the road, which extended 90km to Terracina, was considered revolutionary in its day because it was almost perfectly straight.

Every Sunday a long section of the Via Appia Antica becomes a car-free zone. You can walk or ride a bike for the several kilometres from the Porta di San Sebastiano.

Monuments along the road near Roma include catacombs and Roman tombs. The **Chiesa del Domine Quo Vadis?** is built at the point where San Pietro is said to have met Gesù (Jesus) as he was leaving Roma. The saint consequently returned to Roma, where he was martyred.

Circo di Massenzio

This arena was built around 309 AD by Emperor Maxentius. In front of the it is the **Tomba di Romolo** (Tomb of Romulus), built by the same emperor for his son, and next to both are the ruins of the imperial residence. The circus is open from 9 am to 1.30 pm Tuesday to Saturday and to 12.30 pm on Sunday. Admission costs L3750.

Tombe di Cecilia Metella

Farther along Via Appia is this famous tomb of a Roman noblewoman. The tomb was incorporated into the castle of the Caetani family in the early 14th century. It is open from 9 am to 6 pm (to 4 pm in winter) Tuesday to Saturday and to 1 pm on Sunday and Monday. Admission is free.

Not far past the tomb is a section of the actual ancient road, excavated in the mid-19th century. It is very picturesque, lined with fragments of ancient tombs. Once littered with rubbish and vandalised ruins, this section of the Via Appia has recently been restored. It is advisable not to wander there alone after dark.

To get to Via Appia Antica, catch bus No 218 from Piazza San Giovanni in Laterano.

CATACOMBE

There are several *catacombe* (catacombs) along and near Via Appia – kilometres of tunnels carved out of the soft tufa rock, which acted as meeting and burial places of early Christians in Roma from the 1st century to the early 5th century. Corpses were wrapped in simple white sheets and usually placed in rectangular niches carved into the tunnel walls, which were then closed with marble or terracotta slabs.

To get to the area of the catacombs, catch bus No 218 from Piazza San Giovanni in Laterano (at the Basilica di San Giovanni in Laterano) or Metro Linea A from Stazione Termini to the Colli Albani Metro station and then bus No 660 to the Via Appia Antica.

Catacombe di San Callisto

These catacombs at Via Appia Antica 110 are the largest and most famous, and contain the tomb of the martyred Santa Cecilia (although her body was moved to the Basilica di Santa Cecilia in Trastevere). There is also a crypt containing the tombs of seven popes martyred in the 3rd century. In the 20km of tunnels explored to date, archaeologists have found the sepulchres of some 500,000 people.

The catacombs (☎ 06 513 01 580) are open from 8.30 am to noon and 2.30 to 5.30 pm daily except Wednesday. Admission is with a guide only and costs L8000. The catacombs are closed in February.

Basilica & Catacombe di San Sebastiano

The basilica was built in the 4th century over the catacombs, which were used as a safe haven for the remains of SS Pietro and Paolo during the reign of the Emperor Vespasian, who repressed and persecuted the Christians. San Sebastiano was buried here in the late 3rd century. The church and catacombs (☎ 06 788 70 35), at Via Appia Antica 136, just past the main entrance to the Catacombe di San Callisto, are open from 8.30 am to noon and 2.30 to 5.30 pm (to 5 pm in winter) daily except Sunday. Admission to the catacombs is with a guide only and costs L8000. The catacombs are closed from mid-November to mid-December.

Catacombe di San Domitilla

Among the largest and oldest in Roma, these catacombs were established on the private burial ground of Flavia Domitilla, niece of the Emperor Domitian and a member of the wealthy Flavian family. They contain Christian wall paintings and the underground Chiesa di SS Nereus e Achilleus. The cata-

The Catacombs

Scholars today claim that the theory that the catacombs were used by the early Christians to hide from persecution by the Roman emperors is totally unfounded.

It is possible that the early Christians felt the need to distinguish themselves from pagans by being buried in a communal *coemeterium* (cemetery, from the Greek *koimao*, meaning to sleep), in anticipation of their resurrection to eternal life. The choice of underground graves was probably influenced by the practices of the time – think of the Etruscans and the Roman columbaria – but also by practical and economic concerns. Catacombs were often established in areas where there were existing quarries or underground passages: the soft volcanic earth of the Roman countryside enabled the Christians to dig to a depth of 20m. They maximised the land made available by rich Christians by digging on numerous levels, while retaining only a few easily controllable entrances.

During the periods of persecution, martyrs were often buried beside the fathers of the Church and the first popes. Many Christians wanted to be buried in the same place as these martyrs and consequently a trade in tombs developed, becoming increasingly unethical until Pope Gregory the Great issued a decree in 597 to abolish the sale of graves. However, Christians had already started to abandon the catacombs as early as 313, when Emperor Constantine issued the decree legalising the Christian religion. Increasingly, Christians opted to bury their dead near the churches and basilicas that were being built, often above pagan temples. This became common practice under Theodosius, who made Christianity the state religion in 394.

In about 800 the increasingly frequent incursions by invaders necessitated the removal of the saintly bodies of the martyrs and the first popes to the basilicas inside the city walls. The catacombs were thus left abandoned and eventually many were forgotten and filled up with earth. In the Middle Ages only three catacombs were known; those of San Sebastiano were the most frequented as a place of pilgrimage, since they had earlier been the burial place of SS Pietro and Paolo.

The Catacombe di Santa Priscilla on Via Salaria were discovered by chance at the end of the 16th century, following the collapse of a tufa quarry. Groups of curious aristocrats began to lower themselves into the dark underground passages on a regular basis, often risking losing themselves permanently in the underground labyrinths. From the mid-19th century onwards, passionate scholars of Christian archaeology began a programme of scientific research and more than 30 catacombs in the Roma area have been uncovered.

combs (☎ 06 511 03 42) are at Via delle Sette Chiese 283 (take bus No 218) and are open from 8.30 am to noon and from 2.30 to 5.30 pm daily except Tuesday (closed from late December to January). Admission costs L8000.

MAUSOLEO DELLE FOSSE ARDEATINE (Map 1)

Near the catacombs, on Via Ardeatine, is the site of one of the worst Nazi atrocities in Italy during WWII. After a brigade of

Roman urban partisans blew up 32 German military police in Via Rasella, the Germans took 335 prisoners, who had no connection with the incident, to the Ardeatine Caves and shot them. The Germans then used mines to explode sections of the caves and thus bury the bodies. After the war, the bodies were exhumed, identified and reburied in a mass grave at the site, now marked by a huge concrete slab and sculptures. The Mausoleo delle Fosse Ardeatine (☎ 06 513 67 42) is open from 8.15 am to 5.45 pm

Monday to Saturday and from 8.45 am to 5.15 pm on Sunday and public holidays. Admission is free.

EUR

This acronym, which stands for Esposizione Universale di Roma, has become the name of a peripheral suburb south of Roma, interesting for its many examples of Fascist architecture. These include the **Palazzo della Civiltà del Lavoro** (Palace of the Workers), a square building with arched windows known as the Square Colosseum.

Mussolini ordered the construction of the satellite city for an international exhibition, which was to have been held in 1942. Work was suspended with the outbreak of war and the exhibition never took place; however, many buildings were completed during the 1950s.

The **Museo della Civiltà Romana** (☎ 06 592 61 35), Piazza G Agnelli, reconstructs the development of Roma with the use of models. It's open from 9 am to 7 pm Tuesday to Saturday and to 1.30 pm on Sunday. Admission costs L5000. Also of interest is the **Museo Nazionale Preistorico Etnografico Luigi Pigorini** (☎ 06 54 95 21), Piazza Marconi 14. Its Museo Preistorico covers the development of civilisation in the region, while its ethnographical collection includes exhibits from around the world. The museum is open from 9 am to 2 pm Tuesday to Saturday and to 1 pm on Sunday. Admission costs L8000.

EUR is accessible on Metro Linea B.

ROMA FOR CHILDREN

Sightseeing in Roma will wear out adults, so imagine how the kids feel! If the weather isn't too hot, children of all ages should appreciate a wander through the Foro Romano and up to the Palatino. Also take them to visit the port city of Ostia Antica (see the Lazio section later in this chapter). Another interesting, if somewhat tiring, experience is the climb to the top of the dome of Basilica di San Pietro for a spectacular view of the city. There is a Luna Park at EUR, as well as a couple of museums which older children might find interesting.

During the Christmas period Piazza Navona is transformed into a festive market place, with stalls selling puppets, figures for nativity scenes and Christmas stockings. Most churches set up nativity scenes, many of them elaborate arrangements which will fascinate kids and adults alike. The most elaborate of these is an 18th century Neapolitan presepio at the Basilica di SS Cosma e Damiano.

If you can spare the money, take the family on a tour of Roma by horse and cart. You'll pay through the nose at around L180,000 for what the driver determines is the full tour of the city. Make sure you agree on a price and itinerary before you get in the cart – even though prices are supposedly regulated, horror stories abound about trusting tourists who forgot to ask the price!

Fortunately the city has plenty of parks. Take a break for a picnic lunch and an afternoon in the Villa Borghese. Near the Porta Pinciana there are bicycles for hire, as well as pony rides, train rides and a merry-go-round. In the Villa Celimontana, on the western slopes of the Celio (entrance from Piazza della Navicella), is a lovely public park and a children's playground. See also the Gianicolo & Villa Doria Pamphili section earlier in this chapter.

LANGUAGE COURSES

The Dante Alighieri school (☎ 06 687 37 22), Piazza Firenze 27, 00186, is Roma's best known Italian language school. It has intensive one-month courses (eight hours a week) for L270,000, or two-month courses (four hours a week) for the same price. Write or phone for a programme and enrolment forms.

The Centro Linguistico Dante Alighieri (☎ 06 442 31 400, fax 06 442 31 007, email clidar@tin.it), Piazza Bologna 1, offers courses in Italian language and culture. One-month intensive courses cost L1,050,000 (80 hours) or L700,000 (60 hours). A one month course of 20 hours costs L270,000. The school sends out brochures and enrolment forms on request and can find accommodation for students.

ORGANISED TOURS

Bus

ATAC operates a special air-conditioned tourist bus, No 110, which leaves from the bus terminus in front of Stazione Termini daily at 2, 3, 5 and 6 pm. Commentary is provided on board in English, Italian and several other languages. The tour takes three hours and the bus stops at Piazza del Popolo, Piazza San Pietro, Piazza del Campidoglio, Circo Massimo and the Colosseo. Tickets cost L15,000 and are available from the ATAC information booth on stand C at the terminus. For information call ☎ 06 469 52 252 or ☎ 06 469 52 256.

Stop'n'Go City Tours, run by CSR Consorzio Sightseeing Roma (☎ 06 321 70 54), Piazza del Cinquecento 60, has nine city tours daily (hourly from 9.30 am to 5.30 pm) with 14 stops en route. Tours depart from Stazione Termini and cost L20,000.

CIT Green Line Tours (☎ 06 482 74 80), Via Farini 5a, near Piazza Esquilino, operates two city tours – a religious tour and a scenic tour – with recorded commentary in 10 languages. Each tour costs L30,000 (the ticket is valid for 24 hours) and you can hop on and off, when and where you want.

Ciao Roma (☎ 06 474 37 95), Via Cavour 113, organises classical and religious tours with recorded commentary in 10 languages. Each tour costs L30,000. Ciao Roma also has a short river cruise which can be taken together with the classical bus tour.

Walking & Cycling

Enjoy Rome organises walking tours of the major sights for groups of 15 to 20 people most days of the week. The tour lasts three hours and tickets cost L30,000/25,000 for those aged over/under 26. Enjoy Rome also organises bicycle tours, which last 3½ hours. Tickets (L30,000) include bike and helmet rental. See Tourist Offices earlier in this chapter for contact details.

Scala Reale (☎ 06 447 00 898), Via Varese 52, organises archaeological walks in small groups with knowledgeable guides. Walks on other themes and bicycle and scooter tours can also be arranged.

SPECIAL EVENTS

Although Romans desert their city in summer, particularly in August when the weather is relentlessly hot and humid, cultural and musical events liven up the place and many performances and festivals are held in the open. The Comune di Roma coordinates a diverse series of concerts, performances and events throughout summer under the general title of Estate Romana (Roman Summer). Information is published in Roma's daily newspapers and tourist offices have details.

One of the more interesting and pleasant summer events is the jazz festival in the Villa Celimontana, a lovely park on top of the Celio (enter from Piazza della Navicella).

The Festa de Noantri, in honour of Our Lady of Mt Carmel, is held in Trastevere in the last two weeks of July. If you stick to Viale di Trastevere it is not much more than a line of street stalls. Head for the back streets, however, and you will find street theatre, live music and locals enjoying their food alfresco.

The Festa di San Giovanni is held on 23 and 24 June in the San Giovanni area and features much dancing and eating in the streets. Part of the ritual is to eat stewed snails and suckling pig.

Holy Week events include the famous procession of the cross between the Colosseo and the Palatino on Good Friday, and the pope's blessing of the city and the world in Piazza San Pietro on Easter Sunday.

The area around the Spanish Steps becomes a sea of flowers during the Spring Festival in May.

Keep an eye out for Italian Cultural Heritage Week, which in recent years has been held in mid-April. The museums, galleries, archaeological zones and monuments overseen by the Ministero dei Beni Culturali can be visited free of charge throughout the week and numerous monuments normally closed to the public open their doors.

PLACES TO STAY

Roma has a vast number of *pensioni* and hotels, but it is always best to book. If you haven't already booked, you can do so at the tourist offices at Stazione Termini or Fiumicino airport, the main APT office or Enjoy Rome (see Tourist Offices earlier in this chapter). A hotel booking service is available free of charge for new arrivals in Roma. Called HR Hotel Reservations, the service is offered by a consortium of Roma hotel owners and has booths in the international arrivals hall at Fiumicino airport, in Stazione Termini opposite platform 10 and on the Autostrada del Sole (A1) at the Tevere Ovest service station. The service (☎ 06 699 10 00) operates from 7.30 am to 9.30 pm daily. It will also make bookings at hotels in other major Italian cities.

Avoid the people at the train station who claim to be tourism officials and offer to find you a room.

The Associazione Cattolica Internazionale al Servizio della Giovane (also known as Protezione della Giovane), downstairs at Stazione Termini, offers young women accommodation and is usually open from 9 am to 1 pm and 2 to 8 pm. If the office is closed, try contacting the head office (☎ 06 488 00 56) at Via Urbana 158, which runs parallel to Via Cavour, off Piazza Esquilino.

Most of the budget pensioni and larger hotels which cater for tour groups are near Stazione Termini. The area south-west of the station (to the left as you leave) can be noisy and unpleasant. It teems with pickpockets and snatch thieves and women may find it unsafe at night. To the north-east you can find accommodation in quieter and somewhat safer streets in a more pleasant residential area. However, the historic centre of Roma is far more appealing and the area around Il Vaticano is much less chaotic; both of these areas are only a short bus or Metro ride away from Stazione Termini.

You will often find three or four budget pensioni in the same building, although many are small establishments of 12 rooms or less which fill up quickly in summer. The number of budget hotels in the area should, however, ensure that you find a room.

Most hotels accept bookings in advance, although some demand a deposit for the first night. Many Roman pensioni proprietors are willing to bargain over the price of a room. Generally, prices go down if you stay for more than three days. Prices quoted here are for the high season (June to September).

The year 2000 is a Holy Year (Jubilee) and about 20 million Catholic pilgrims are expected to travel to Roma and surrounds throughout the year. It is, therefore, strongly recommended that you book accommodation well in advance.

PLACES TO STAY – BUDGET

Unless otherwise stated, the prices quoted for hotels in this section are for rooms without a shower or bath. Many pensioni charge an extra L1000 to L2000 for use of the communal bathroom.

Camping

All of Roma's camp sites are a fair distance from the centre. *Seven Hills (☎ 06 303 10 826, Via Cassia 1216)* charges L10,000/8000/5000 per person/tent/car and is open from 15 March to 30 October. It's a bit of a hike from Termini: catch the Metro Linea A to Ottaviano, walk to Piazza del Risorgimento and take bus No 907 (ask the driver where to get off). From Via Cassia it is a 1km walk to the camp site. A good option is *Village Camping Flaminio (☎ 06 333 26 04, Via Flaminia 821)*, which is about 15 minutes from the city centre by public transport. It costs L13,000/12,400 per person/site. Tents, caravans and bungalows are available for hire. From Stazione Termini catch bus No 910 to Piazza Mancini, then bus No 200 to the camp site. At night, catch bus No 24N from Piazzale Flaminio (just north of Piazza del Popolo).

Hostel

To reach HI *Ostello Foro Italico (☎ 06 323 62 67, Viale delle Olimpiadi 61)* take Metro Linea A to Ottaviano, then bus No 32 to Foro Italico. The hostel has a bar, restaurant and garden and is open year-round. It is closed from 9.30 am to noon. Breakfast and showers are included in the price, which is L24,000 per night. A meal costs L14,000.

The Associazione Italiana Alberghi per la Gioventù (Italian Youth Hostels Association; ☎ 06 487 11 52), Via Cavour 44, has information about all youth hostels in Italy and will assist with bookings to stay at universities during summer. You can also join HI here.

Religious Institutions

A number of religious institutions offer accommodation in Roma, including some near Stazione Termini and Il Vaticano. However, they have strict curfews. If you want to stay in one, you can apply to the nearest Catholic archdiocese in your home town. Otherwise, try the *Domus Aurelia delle Suore Orsoline (Map 2; ☎ 06 393 76 480, fax 06 393 76 480, Via Aurelia 218)*, about 1km west of San Pietro, which has singles/doubles with bathroom for L70,000/ 110,000. From Stazione Termini catch bus No 64 to Largo Argentina, then No 46 to Via Aurelia. The *Padri Trinitari (Map 2; ☎ 06 638 38 88, Piazza Santa Maria alle Fornaci)*, just south of the Basilica di San Pietro, has singles/doubles/triples for L75,000/130,000/ 160,000, including breakfast.

Villa Bassi (Map 2; ☎ 581 53 29, Via Giacinto Carini 24) is at the top of the Gianicolo hill, in the Monte Verde area, very close to both Trastevere and Il Vaticano. Take bus No 75 from Stazione Termini. Clean, simple singles/doubles/triples/quads cost L60,000/80,000/110,000/130,000.

Bed & Breakfast

B&B is a relatively new concept in Roma. However, it is taking off in light of the impending influx of pilgrims for Jubilee 2000, for whom there is just not enough budget accommodation. Lists of private B&B operators can be obtained from the APT. They are also listed in the fortnightly magazine *Wanted in Rome*, which has a useful classified section.

One advantage of B&B accommodation is that Italian houses are invariably spotlessly clean. The drawback is that you are staying in someone's home and will probably be expected to operate within the fam-

ily's timetable. Keys are not always provided. A hotel or pensione would be more suitable for those who expect to be coming in late at night or to be making a lot of noise. Most B&Bs are fairly central, but when making the booking (which should be done well in advance of your stay) make sure you understand fully the location of the accommodation, to avoid finding yourself in an outer suburb which has limited public transport.

Bed & Breakfast Italia (☎ 06 687 86 18, fax 06 687 86 19, email md4095@mclink.it, Corso Vittorio Emanuele II 282) is one of several B&B networks. It offers accommodation in three different price categories. Singles/doubles/triples with shared bathrooms cost L50,000/95,000/130,000, rooms with private bathroom cost L70,000/130,000/ 150,000 and luxurious rooms with private bathroom cost L85,000/160,000/190,000.

Pensioni & Hotels

Roma has a wide range of pensioni and hotels in the budget price range. However, many of these have recently been renovated in preparation for the Jubilee and prices have gone up accordingly.

North-East of Stazione Termini (Map 3)
To reach the pensioni in this area, head to the right as you leave the train platforms, onto Via Marsala, which runs alongside the station.

Hotel Rimini (☎ 06 446 19 91, Via Marghera 17) has singles/doubles with bathroom for L130,000/160,000 including breakfast. *Pensione Giamaica (☎ 06 445 19 63, fax 06 445 19 63, email md0991@mclink.it, Via Magenta 13)* has OK singles/doubles for L50,000/78,000 including breakfast. *Fawlty Towers (☎ 06 445 03 74, Via Magenta 39)* offers hostel-style accommodation. A bed in a four person dorm costs L30,000, single rooms cost L60,000 and doubles start at L85,000. Run by the people at Enjoy Rome (see Tourist Offices earlier in this chapter), it offers lots of information about Roma. Added bonuses are the sunny terrace, communal fridge, microwave and satellite TV.

Nearby in Via Palestro are several reasonably priced pensioni. **Pensione Restivo** (**☎** 06 446 21 72, Via Palestro 55) has large singles/doubles for L70,000/110,000. There is a midnight curfew. **Pensione Katty** (**☎** 06 444 12 16, Via Palestro 35) has basic rooms for L60,000/85,000. **Hotel Ventura** (**☎** 06 445 19 51, fax 446 00 34, Via Palestro 88) has singles/doubles for up to L90,000/130,000. Rooms that look out on the busy road can be very noisy. **Pensione Ester** (**☎** 06 495 71 23, Viale del Castro Pretorio 25) has large, comfortable doubles for L70,000 and triples for L90,000.

There are three good pensioni at Via San Martino della Battaglia 11. **Pensione Lachea** (**☎** 06 495 72 56, fax 06 445 46 65) has large, clean doubles/triples for L65,000/95,000. **Hotel Pensione Dolomiti** (**☎** 06 495 72 56, fax 06 445 46 65) is under the same helpful management and the newly restructured three-star singles/doubles/triples cost L100,000/150,000/210,000 including breakfast. Downstairs is **Tre Stelle** (**☎** 06 446 30 95, fax 06 44 68 29) with singles/doubles/triples for L60,000/90,000/140,000.

Albergo Sandra (**☎** 06 445 26 12, fax 06 446 08 46, Via Villafranca 10), in the road that runs between Via Vicenza and Via San Martino della Battaglia, is clean with dark but pleasant rooms. Singles/doubles cost L80,000/140,000, including the cost of a shower. Prices go down according to the length of your stay.

Albergo Mari 2 (**☎** 06 474 03 71, fax 06 447 03 311, Via Calatafimi 38) has singles/doubles for L60,000/120,000, or L80,000/150,000 with bathroom. **Papa Germano** (**☎** 06 48 69 19, Via Calatafimi 14a) is one of the more popular budget places in the area and has singles/doubles for L50,000/70,000 and doubles with bathroom for L100,000. Nearby, **Hotel Floridia** (**☎** 06 481 40 89, fax 06 444 13 77, Via Montebello 45), has singles/doubles with bathroom for L110,000/160,000. **Hotel Ascot** (**☎** 06 474 16 75, Via Montebello 22) has quiet, old-fashioned singles/doubles with bathroom for L80,000/110,000. Don't worry about the porn cinema opposite; the hotel itself is

fine. Ask for room No 24, which still has its original parquet floor.

Hotel Castelfidardo (**☎** 06 446 46 38, fax 06 494 13 78, Via Castelfidardo 31) is one of Roma's better one-star pensioni. It has clean and pleasant singles/doubles for L60,000/85,000, and triples for L95,000. A double/triple with private bathroom costs L110,000/125,000. Across Via XX Settembre, at Via Collina 48 (a 10 minute walk from the train station), is **Hotel Ercoli** (**☎**/fax 06 474 54 54), offering singles/doubles with bathroom for L115,000/160,000, including breakfast in the sunny breakfast room. In the same building is **Pensione Tizi** (**☎** 06 482 01 28, **☎**/fax 06 474 32 66), with singles/doubles for L55,000/80,000. Doubles with bathroom cost L100,000.

South-West of Stazione Termini (Map 3)

This area is decidedly seedier, but prices remain the same. As you leave the train station, follow Via Gioberti to Via G Amendola (which becomes Via Filippo Turati) and Via Principe Amedeo. There's a concentration of budget pensioni here and you shouldn't have any trouble finding a room. The area improves as you head away from the station and towards the Colosseo and Foro Romano.

A good choice in the area is **Hotel Kennedy** (**☎** 06 446 53 73, fax 06 446 54 17, Via F Turati 62), which has satellite TV and air-conditioning and very comfortable singles/doubles with bathroom for L110,000/180,000. At Via Cavour 47, the main street running south-west from the piazza in front of Stazione Termini, is the newly restructured **Pensione Everest** (**☎** 06 488 16 29). It has expensive rooms for L140,000/220,000 (L80,000/130,000 in the low season). **Hotel Sandy** (**☎** 06 488 45 85, fax 06 445 07 34, Via Cavour 136) is probably the closest thing in Roma to a backpackers crash pad. The hotel is on the 5th floor (no lift). Beds are in dorms for between three and five people (eight in summer) and cost L25,000 per person (L20,000 out of season). There are metal lockers but no keys and the hotel lacks adequate bathroom facilities – so be prepared to queue. Reservations are not accepted and payment is in cash only. **Hotel Il Castello** *(Map 5;* ☎ *06 772 04 036, fax 06 704 90 068, Via Vittorio Amedeo II 9)* is close to the Manzoni Metro station, south of Termini. Singles/doubles cost L70,000/120,000 and dorm beds cost L25,000 per person.

Off Via Nazionale is **Hotel Elide** *(☎ 06 488 39 77, fax 06 489 04 318, Via Firenze 50)*, which has well-maintained rooms. A single without bathroom costs L75,000. A double/triple with bathroom costs L150,000/ 180,000. Ask for room No 18, which has an elaborate, gilded ceiling.

Hotel Galatea *(☎ 06 474 30 70, Via Genova 24)* is through the grand entrance of an old palace. It has well-furnished singles/ doubles for L100,000/130,000. A triple costs around L195,000. Doubles/triples with bathroom go for L160,000/208,000.

City Centre (Map 6) Basically, there aren't any really economical hotels in Roma's historical centre. However, in the areas around Piazza di Spagna, Piazza Navona, the Pantheon and Campo de' Fiori, you do have the convenience and pleasure of staying right in the centre of historic Roma. The easiest way to get to Piazza di Spagna is on the Metro Linea A to Spagna. To get to Piazza Navona and the Pantheon area, take bus No 64 from Piazza dei Cinquecento, in front of Stazione Termini, to Largo di Torre Argentina.

One of the most centrally located and relatively cheap hotels is the **Pensione Primavera** *(☎ 06 688 03 109, fax 06 686 92 65, Piazza San Pantaleo 3)*, on Corso Vittorio Emanuele II, just south of Piazza Navona. A magnificent entrance leads to a pleasant, recently renovated establishment where a double costs L170,000 and triples are a better deal at L60,000 per person, including breakfast. **Albergo Abruzzi** *(☎ 06 679 20 21, Piazza della Rotonda 69)* overlooks the Pantheon. You couldn't find a better location, but the rooms can be very noisy until late at night when the piazza is finally deserted. Basic singles/doubles cost L98,000/ 140,000, including use of the communal

shower. Bookings are essential throughout the year.

Pensione Mimosa *(☎ 06 688 01 753, Via Santa Chiara 61)*, off Piazza della Minerva, has singles/doubles/triples for L85,000/ 120,000/180,000 (plus L15,000 for a private bathroom). Prices include breakfast.

Albergo della Lunetta *(☎ 06 686 10 80, fax 06 689 20 28, Piazza del Paradiso 68)*, north-east of Campo de' Fiori, has doubles for L110,000, or L150,000 with a shower. Bookings are essential. **Hotel Pomezia** *(☎ 06 686 13 71, Via dei Chiavari 12)*, which runs off Via dei Giubbonari from Campo de' Fiori, is reasonably priced, given its location, with basic doubles for L130,000, including breakfast. Use of the communal shower is free.

Near Il Vaticano & Trastevere Although there aren't many bargains in this area, it is comparatively quiet and still close to the main sights. Bookings are an absolute necessity because rooms are often filled with people attending conferences at Il Vaticano. The simplest way to reach the area is on the Metro Linea A to Ottaviano. Turn left into Via Ottaviano, and Via Germanico is a short walk away. Otherwise, take bus No 64 from Stazione Termini to the Basilica di San Pietro and walk away from the basilica, north along Via di Porta Angelica, which becomes Via Ottaviano after the Piazza del Risorgimento. This is a five minute walk.

The best bargain in the area is **Pensione Ottaviano** *(Map 2;* ☎ *06 397 37 253, email gi.costantini@agora.stm.it, Via Ottaviano 6)*, near Piazza del Risorgimento. It has dormitory beds for L30,000 per person (L20,000 out of season) and doubles for L70,000. The owner speaks English. **Hotel Giuggioli** *(Map 2;* ☎ *06 324 21 13, Via Germanico 198)* is very small, but a delight. A double costs L110,000, or L130,000 with bathroom. Rooms are well furnished. There are two other pensioni in the same building. **Hotel Lady** *(☎ 06 324 21 12)*, on the 4th floor, has large, clean singles/doubles for L100,000/ 120,000 (L130,000/150,000 with bathroom). **Pensione Nautilus** *(☎ 06 324 21 18)*, on the

2nd floor, has doubles/triples for L110,000/140,000. Rooms with bathroom are an extra L30,000.

Pensione San Michele (Map 2; ☎ 06 324 33 33, Via Attilio Regolo 19), off Via Cola di Rienzo, has average singles/doubles for L60,000/90,000. The same management run *Pensione Valparaiso (Map 1; ☎ 06 321 31 84, Via Giulio Cesare 47)*, near the Lepanto Metro station. It has clean, simple singles/doubles for the same prices as the San Michele. In Trastevere is the *Carmel (Map 4; ☎ 06 580 99 21, Via Mameli 11)*, where singles/doubles with bathroom cost L90,000/130,000, breakfast included.

PLACES TO STAY – MID-RANGE

All rooms in this section have a private bathroom unless otherwise stated.

Near Stazione Termini (Map 5)

To the south-west of the train station is the *Hotel Igea (☎/fax 06 446 69 11, email igea@venere.it, Via Principe Amedeo 97)*, with singles/doubles/triples for L140,000/200,000/210,000, not including breakfast. *Hotel Acropoli (☎ 06 488 56 85)*, in the same street at No 67, has singles/doubles for L70,000/150,000. *Hotel Dina (☎ 06 474 06 94, fax 06 489 03 614, Via Principe Amedeo 62)* is clean with a friendly management. Singles/doubles cost L90,000/160,000. At No 47 is the *Hotel Sweet Home (☎ 06 488 09 54)*, with singles/doubles for L100,000/140,000, not including breakfast. In the same building is *Albergo Onella (☎ 06 488 52 57, fax 06 488 19 38)*. Its singles/doubles/triples cost L120,000/160,000/220,000, including breakfast.

Hotel Palladium Palace (☎ 06 446 69 18, fax 06 446 69 37, Via Gioberti 36) has been refurbished and the rooms are large, but the feel is impersonal. Singles/doubles/triples cost L200,000/280,000/350,000. The *Hotel d'Este (☎ 06 446 56 07, fax 06 446 56 01, email d.este@italyhotel.com, Via Carlo Alberto 4b)* is a stone's throw from Santa Maria Maggiore and is one of the better medium-range hotels in the area. It has a pleasant roof garden and beautifully furnished, comfortable singles/doubles for up to L260,000/380,000.

North-west of the train station, on Via Firenze, off Via Nazionale, there are a few good-value hotels. *Hotel Seiler (☎ 06 488 02 04, fax 06 488 06 88)*, at No 48, has clean but basic rooms; all have a TV and the price includes breakfast. Singles/doubles cost L160,000/220,000. Triples/quads are also available. *Hotel Oceania (☎ 06 482 46 96, fax 06 488 55 86)*, at No 38, is an ideal family hotel – although it is on the expensive side. Simply furnished singles/doubles are L190,000/245,000, and triples/quads are L310,000/370,000. A room for five costs L410,000. During winter the hotel offers a 20% discount, and a 10% discount can be negotiated at other times.

North-east of the train station is *Hotel Harmony (☎ 06 48 67 38, fax 06 474 39 04, Via Palestro 13)*, which has singles/doubles/triples with breakfast for L100,000/150,000/210,000. *Hotel Positano (☎ 06 49 03 60, fax 06 446 91 01, Via Palestro 49)* has clean, pleasant doubles/triples for up to L160,000/220,000.

City Centre

Albergo del Sole (Map 6; ☎ 06 687 94 46, fax 06 689 37 87, email alb.sole@flashnet.it, Via del Biscione 76), off Campo de' Fiori, has large rooms and a roof terrace. Its singles/doubles are L130,000/200,000, or L105,000/150,000 without bathroom. *Hotel Campo de' Fiori (Map 6; ☎ 06 688 06 865, fax 06 687 60 03, Via del Biscione 6)* has interestingly furnished rooms on its six floors (note that there's no lift), as well as a roof garden with a great view. Singles/doubles/triples with bathroom cost L180,000/220,000/270,000, including breakfast, and doubles/triples without bathroom are L150,000/195,000.

Near Piazza di Spagna is *Hotel Pensione Suisse (Map 3; ☎ 06 678 36 49, fax 06 678 12 58, Via Gregoriana 56)*. It has good-quality singles/doubles priced at L140,000/200,000 and triples for L265,000. Closer to Piazza del Popolo is *Hotel Margutta (Map 2; ☎ 06 322 36 74, fax 06 320 03 95, Via Laurina 34)*, off Via del Corso. The rooms are spotless and clean doubles cost L175,000, including breakfast (prices are negotiable). *Hotel Forte* (Map 3; ☎ 06 320 76 25, fax 06 320 27 07, Via Margutta 61), parallel to Via del Babuino, is comfortable and quiet. Its singles/doubles cost L130,000/200,000, but out of season prices fall by up to L60,000 per person.

The *Hotel Pensione Merano* (Map 3; ☎ 06 482 17 96, fax 06 482 18 10, Via Vittorio Veneto 155) is a lovely old place with singles/doubles/triples for L125,000/175,000/230,000, including breakfast. *Hotel Julia* (Map 3; ☎ 06 488 16 37, fax 06 481 70 44, email hotel.julia@rpilo.it, Via Rasella 29), off Via delle Quattro Fontane, near Piazza Barberini, is a no-frills place but quiet and clean. Singles/doubles cost L170,000/270,000. The price includes breakfast and all rooms have television.

Near Il Vaticano & Trastevere

Virtually next to the wall of Il Vaticano, off Via dei Corridori, is *Hotel Bramante* (Map 2; ☎ 06 688 06 426, fax 06 687 98 81, email bramante@excalhq.it, Vicolo delle Palline 24). It has rooms of reasonable quality costing L132,000/176,000 for a single/double with shower. Without bathroom, they cost L97,000/132,000. *Hotel Prati* (Map 2; ☎ 06 687 53 57, fax 06 688 06 938, email prati @italyhotel.com, Via Crescenzio 89) has singles/doubles/triples priced at L120,000/180,000/240,000. Singles/doubles without bathroom cost L90,000/120,000. The hotel is on four floors and there is no lift. *Hotel Adriatic* (Map 2; ☎ 06 688 08 080, fax 06 689 35 52, email adriatic@ats.it, Via Vitelleschi 25), on the continuation of Via Porcari, off Piazza del Risorgimento, has modern rooms and is good value with singles/doubles/triples/quads for L140,000/180,000/240,000/300,000, excluding breakfast.

At Via Cola di Rienzo 243 there are two good-quality hotels, both excellent value for their location and prices. *Hotel Joli* (Map 2; ☎/fax 06 324 18 54) is on the 6th floor. It has large rooms and is ideal for families. Singles/doubles/triples/quads cost L80,000/120,000/160,000/200,000. *Hotel Florida*

(Map 2; ☎ 06 324 18 72, fax 06 324 18 57) is on the 2nd floor and has singles/doubles/triples for L120,000/160,000/200,000. Discounts are available out of the high season.

Hotel Ticino (Map 2; ☎ 06 324 32 51, Via dei Gracchi 161) has comfortable rooms, some of which are big enough for families. There are showers but no toilets in some rooms. A single/double room costs L125,000/180,000, including breakfast.

Hotel Amalia (Map 2; ☎ 06 397 23 354, fax 06 397 23 365, Via Germanico 66), near the corner of Via Ottaviano, has a beautiful courtyard entrance and clean, sunny rooms. Singles/doubles with bathroom are priced at L150,000/220,000; triples go for L300,000.

In Trastevere there is the *Hotel Cisterna* (Map 4; ☎ 06 581 72 12, Via della Cisterna 7-9), off Via San Francesco a Ripa. It has average, comfortable rooms. Singles/doubles/triples cost L120,000/160,000/215,000.

PLACES TO STAY – TOP END

There is no shortage of expensive hotels in Roma, but many, particularly those near Stazione Termini, are geared towards large tour groups and, while certainly offering all conveniences, tend to be a bit anonymous. The following three and four-star hotels have been selected on the basis of their individual charm, as well as value for money and location. All rooms have bathroom, telephone and TV. Breakfast is usually included in the price, but it is wise to check.

Aventino (Map 4)

If you prefer quieter surroundings and don't mind being a bit out of the centre of town, try the *Aventino* and *Sant'Anselmo Hotels* (☎ 06 574 51 74, fax 06 578 36 04, Piazza di Sant'Anselmo 2). These are four villas run by one company. The Aventino provides two star accommodation; singles/doubles/triples/quads cost L150,000/230,000/250,000/260,000. The other villas are in the three star category, with singles/doubles/triples/quads for L190,000/290,000/340,000/360,000. All prices include breakfast. There are pleasant gardens and courtyards where you can have your breakfast or a drink.

Near Stazione Termini (Map 3)

Hotel Venezia (☎ 06 445 71 01, fax 06 495 76 87, Via Varese 18), on the corner of Via Marghera, is beautifully furnished in antique style. Singles/doubles/triples cost L181,000/ 246,000/332,000. Prices drop in the low season. At *Hotel Montecarlo (☎ 06 446 00 00, fax 06 446 00 06, email info@hotelmonte carlo.it, Via Palestro 17a)* single/double/ triple rooms cost L170,000/250,000/347,000. It also offers generous discounts on rooms in the low season. *Hotel Piemonte (☎ 06 445 22 40, fax 06 445 16 49, Via Vicenza 34)* has very pleasant singles/doubles for up to L200,000/280,000. The bathrooms are particularly nice and discounts are offered in the low season and during August. On the other side of the train station is *Hotel Giada (☎ 06 488 58 63, fax 06 482 03 44, Via Principe Amedeo 9)*. It is a pleasant but impersonal establishment with singles/doubles for L190,000/230,000.

At the end of Via Cavour, in the area close to the Foro Romano, are two very good hotels. Both are on Via Tor de' Conti, which runs behind Via dei Fori Imperiali, and their location is hard to beat. *Hotel Nerva (☎ 06 678 18 35, fax 06 699 22 204)*, at No 3, has singles/doubles for up to L250,000/ 360,000. *Hotel Forum (☎ 06 679 24 46, fax 06 678 64 79, email forum@venere.it)*, at No 25, is a four star hotel with a delightful roof garden and panoramic views of the Foro Romano. Singles/doubles cost up to L360,000/520,000.

City Centre

Near Piazza di Spagna are several of Roma's better hotels. The *Gregoriana (Map 3; ☎ 06 679 79 88, fax 06 678 42 58, Via Gregoriana 18)* has long been an institution for the fashionable set. Its rooms are not numbered, but instead adorned with letters by the 1930s French fashion illustrator Erté. Its singles/ doubles cost up to L220,000/360,000. Magnificently located at the top of the Spanish Steps is *Hotel Scalinata di Spagna (Map 3; ☎ 06 679 30 06, fax 06 699 40 598, Piazza Trinità dei Monti 17)*, which has a roof terrace overlooking the city. It is usually booked up for months in advance, so it's worth contacting them early. It has singles/doubles for up to L380,000/450,000. Opposite is the high-class *Hassler Villa Medici (Map 3; ☎ 06 69 93 40, fax 06 678 99 91, email hassler roma@mclink.it, Piazza Trinità' dei Monti 6)*, one of Roma's top hotels. Doubles cost up to L1,030,000 per night. Around the corner is the small *Hotel Sistina (Map 3; ☎ 06 474 41 76, fax 06 481 88 67, Via Sistina 136)*, with singles/doubles for L260,000/370,000.

Another of Roma's top hotels is *Minerva (Map 6; ☎ 06 699 41 888, fax 06 679 41 65, email minerva@pronet.it, Piazza della Minerva 69)*. It's run by the Crowne Plaza chain and, for around L750,000 a double, you get absolute luxury and comfort. It has a rooftop terrace with a splendid view of the Pantheon. *Hotel Senato (Map 6; ☎ 06 678 43 43, fax 06 699 40 297, Piazza della Rotonda 73)* overlooks the Pantheon. Its comfortable rooms are reasonably quiet, considering the hotel's position, and cost around L250,000/ 345,000. *Albergo Teatro di Pompeo (Map 6; ☎ 06 687 28 12, fax 06 688 05 531, Largo del Pallaro 8)*, near Campo de' Fiori, has plenty of olde-worlde charm – in fact guests have breakfast in the remains of Pompeo's Theatre (55 BC). Its very comfortable doubles start from L310,000.

Near Il Vaticano (Map 2)

Hotel Columbus (☎ 06 686 54 35, fax 06 686 48 74, Via della Conciliazione 33) is in a magnificent 15th century palace in front of Basilica di San Pietro. It is a Renaissance curiosity with its splendid halls and frescoes by Pinturicchio. It has singles/doubles for L300,000/400,000. Also near Il Vaticano is the elegant *Hotel Sant'Anna (☎ 06 688 01 602, fax 06 683 08 717, email santanna@ travel.it, Borgo Pio 133)*. It has doubles for L300,000.

RENTAL ACCOMMODATION

Apartments near the centre of Roma are expensive and you can expect to pay a minimum of L1,500,000 a month for a studio apartment or small one-bedroom place. A room in a shared apartment will cost at least

L600,000 a month, plus bills. Shared apartments are advertised in *Wanted in Rome* and *Porta Portese*, available from newspaper stands. There are also agencies, known as *agenzie immobiliari*, specialising in short-term rentals in Roma, which charge a fee for their services. They are listed in *Wanted in Rome*.

PLACES TO EAT

Roma offers a pretty good range of places to eat. There are some excellent establishments offering typical Roman fare to suit a range of budgets, as well as some good, but usually fairly expensive, restaurants specialising in international cuisines, such as Indian, Chinese, Vietnamese and Japanese. The best areas to look for good *trattorie* are Trastevere and between Piazza Navona and the Tevere. During summer, these areas are lively and atmospheric and most establishments have outside tables. Meal times are generally from 12.30 to 3 pm and 8 to 11 pm, although in summer many restaurants stay open later. If you want to be sure of getting a table (especially one outside), either make a booking or arrive before 8.30 pm.

Antipasto dishes in Roma are particularly good and many restaurants allow you to make your own mixed selection. Typical pasta dishes include: *bucatini all'Amatriciana*, with a usually very salty sauce of tomato and *pancetta* (cured bacon), topped with *pecorino Romano* (matured sheep's cheese); *penne all'arrabbiata*, which has a spicy sauce of tomatoes and chilli; and *spaghetti carbonara*, with pancetta, eggs and cheese. *Saltimbocca alla Romana* (slices of veal and ham) and *abbacchio* (roast lamb seasoned with rosemary) are classic meat dishes, which are followed by a wide variety of vegetables. During winter, try the *carciofi alla Romana* (artichokes stuffed with mint or parsley and garlic) or *carciofi alla giudia*, which are deep-fried. Offal is also very popular in Roma and a local speciality is the *pajata* (pasta with a sauce of chopped veal intestines).

Always remember to check the menu posted outside the establishment for prices and cover and service charges. Expect to pay under L30,000 per person at a simple trattoria, up to L50,000 at an average restaurant and around L100,000 or more at Roma's top eating places. These prices are for a full meal including entrée, main course, dessert and wine. Eating only pasta and salad and drinking the house wine at a trattoria can keep the bill down. If you order meat or, particularly, fish you will push up the bill substantially.

There are hundreds of bars around the city which are good options for cheap, quick meals. A sandwich taken at the bar *(al banco)* will cost between L2500 and L6000. At takeaway *pizzerie*, a slice of freshly cooked pizza, sold by weight, can cost as little as L2000. There are numerous bakeries in the Campo de' Fiori area which are good for a cheap snack. Try a piece of *pizza bianca*, a flat bread resembling *focaccia*, which costs from around L1500 a slice. See Sandwiches & Snacks later in this section for more details.

For groceries and supplies of cheese, *prosciutto*, salami and wine, shop at *alimentari* (grocery stores). For fresh fruit and vegetables, there are numerous outdoor markets, notably the lively daily market in Campo de' Fiori, although it is expensive. Cheaper food markets are held on Piazza Vittorio Emanuele, near Stazione Termini; on Piazza Testaccio, on the other side of the Aventino from the Circo Massimo; and on Via Andrea Doria, near Largo Trionfale, north of Il Vaticano. The huge wholesale food markets on Via Ostiense, some distance from the city centre, are open from 10 am to around 1 pm Monday to Saturday.

Restaurants, Trattorie & Pizzerie

Generally, the restaurants near Stazione Termini are to be avoided if you want to pay reasonable prices for good-quality food. The side streets around Piazza Navona and Campo de' Fiori harbour many good-quality, low-priced trattorie and pizzerie, and the areas of San Lorenzo (to the east of Stazione Termini, near the university) and Testaccio (across the Tevere, near the Piramide di

Cestio mausoleum) are popular eating districts with the locals. Trastevere might be among the most expensive places to live in Roma, but it offers an excellent selection of rustic-style eating places hidden in tiny piazze, and pizzerie where it doesn't cost the earth to sit at a table on the street.

City Centre – Budget A popular eating place with tourists and locals is *Otello alla Concordia (Map 3; ☎ 06 679 11 78, Via della Croce 81)*, between Via Babuino and Via del Corso. You can eat a good Roman-style meal for around L30,000. Nearby in Via Margutta, which runs parallel to Via Babuino, is *Osteria Margutta (Map 3; ☎ 06 323 10 25, Via Margutta 82)*. It has good-quality food for around the same prices as Otello alla Concordia. *Pizzeria il Leoncino (Map 3; ☎ 06 687 63 06, Via del Leoncino 28)*, across Via del Corso from Via Condotti, has good pizzas at low prices. You can eat and drink for around L20,000. *Pizzeria Montecarlo (Map 6; ☎ 06 686 18 77, Vicolo Savelli 12)* is a very traditional pizzeria, with paper sheets for tablecloths. A fine pizza with wine or beer will cost around L18,000. The *Pizzeria da Baffetto (Map 6; ☎ 06 686 16 17, Via del Governo Vecchio 11)* is a Roman institution. Its large pizzas would feed an army and deserve their reputation as among the best in Roma. Expect to join a queue if you arrive after 9 pm and don't be surprised if you end up sharing a table. Pizzas cost around L8000 to L12,000, 1L of wine costs L8000 and the cover charge is only L1500. Farther along the street, at No 18, is a tiny, nameless *osteria* (no telephone), run by Antonio Bassetti, where you can eat an excellent meal for between L20,000 and L30,000. The consistently good food and low prices make it one of the best-value places to eat in Roma. There is no written menu, but don't be nervous: even when very busy, the owner/waiter will try to explain (in Italian) the dishes. It is closed on Sunday.

Trattoria Pizzeria da Francesco (Map 6; ☎ 06 686 40 09, Piazza del Fico 29) has good pasta from L8000, and a variety of antipasti and vegetables. Pizzas range in price from around L9000 to L14,000, and a full meal will cost around L30,000. To reach it take Via del Corallo from Via del Governo Vecchio. *Pizzeria Corallo (Map 6; ☎ 06 683 07 703, Via del Corallo 10)*, off Via del Governo Vecchio, has good pizzas and is open late. A meal will cost around L30,000.

In Piazza della Cancelleria, between Piazza Navona and Campo de' Fiori, is *Grappolo d'Oro (Map 6; ☎ 06 686 41 18)*. It serves excellent traditional Roman food for around L30,000 for a full meal. It's closed on Sunday. Opposite is *Ditirambo (Map 6; ☎ 06 687 16 26)*, where you'll eat very well for around L40,000.

There are several restaurants in the Campo de' Fiori. *Hosteria Romanesca (Map 6; ☎ 06 686 40 24)* is tiny and there are no outdoor tables in winter, so arrive early. A dish of pasta will cost between L8000 and L12,000, and a full meal under L35,000. *La Carbonara (Map 6; ☎ 06 686 47 83)*, also in the campo, is a popular spot and a full meal will cost up to L60,000.

In Piazza de' Ricci, through Piazza Farnese and north along Via di Monserrato, is an excellent little restaurant, *Pierluigi (Map 2; ☎ 06 686 13 02, Piazza de' Ricci)*, where a full meal will cost around L60,000. *Hostaria Giulio (Map 2; ☎ 06 688 06 466, Via della Barchetta 19)*, between Via Giulia and Via di Monserrato, is another good-value eating place. It has two or three tables outside in summer. *Trattoria Polese (Map 2; ☎ 06 686 17 09, Piazza Sforza Cesarini 40)*, just off Corso Vittorio Emanuele, close to the Lungotevere, specialises in traditional Roman dishes, but also has pizza. A full meal costs around L35,000 and you can sit outside.

Filletti di Baccalà (Map 6; ☎ 06 686 40 18, Largo dei Librari), off Via dei Cappellari, serves only deep-fried cod fillets and wine. You can satisfy moderate hunger and thirst for under L10,000. *Il Grottino (Map 6; Via delle Grotte 27)*, off Via dei Giubbonari, near Campo de' Fiori, serves reasonable pizzas for around L7000 to L12,000; 1L of wine costs L6000 and the cover charge is L1500. A full meal will cost around L25,000.

On the other side of Via Arenula, in the

Jewish quarter, is **Sora Margherita** *(Map 6; ☎ 06 686 40 02, Piazza delle Cinque Scole 30)*, so well known and popular with the locals that there isn't even a sign over the door. It is open only for lunch and serves traditional Roman and Jewish food in simple surroundings. A meal will cost around L25,000. Also in the Jewish quarter is **Al Pompiere** *(Map 6; ☎ 06 686 83 77, Via Santa Maria de' Calderari 38)*. Its food is great – try the carciofi alla giudia – and prices are reasonable. A full meal should cost around L35,000. **Da Gigetto** *(☎ 06 686 11 06, Via del Portico d'Ottavia 21a)* is a local institution. Right next to the ancient Roman Portico d'Ottavia, its location can't be beaten, especially if you get a table on the pavement. A meal will cost under L50,000. It's closed on Monday.

City Centre – Mid-Range The very popular **Mario** *(Map 3; ☎ 06 678 38 18, Via della Vite 55)*, off Piazza di Spagna, offers Tuscan food for around L65,000 a full meal. Another good restaurant in the area is **Al 34** *(Map 3; ☎ 06 679 50 91, Via Mario de' Fiori 34)*, which has a menu combining Roman cooking with regional dishes from throughout Italy. A full meal will cost around L55,000. The widely known **Dal Bolognese** *(Map 2; ☎ 06 361 14 26, Piazza del Popolo 1)* is in a prime position to attract tourists, but maintains high culinary standards and reasonable prices. You must book if you want a table outside in summer. A full meal will cost up to L75,000.

Near the Fontana di Trevi is **Al Moro** *(Map 3; ☎ 06 678 34 95, Vicolo delle Bollette 13)*, where a good-quality, traditional Roman meal will come to less than L70,000. **Tullio** *(Map 3; ☎ 06 475 85 64, Via San Nicola da Tolentino 26)*, off Piazza Barberini, serves Roman and Tuscan dishes. It is of a high standard and a full meal will cost around L70,000. Also near Piazza Barberini is **Colline Emiliane** *(Map 3; ☎ 06 481 75 38, Via degli Avignonesi 22)*, a spartan-looking trattoria which serves superb Emilia-Romagnan food. A full meal will cost around L50,000.

A few streets north of the Pantheon is **Il comelli** *(☎ 06 38 35 11, Via di Bruno Emilia*

Bacaro *(Map 6; ☎ 06 686 41 10, Via degli Spagnoli 27)*, a tiny trattoria whose menu reflects what is available fresh on any given day. A meal will cost around L60,000. **La Campana** *(Map 6; ☎ 06 686 78 20, Vicolo della Campana 18)*, at the top end of Via della Scrofa, is believed to be Roma's oldest restaurant and is certainly a favourite. A full meal will cost around L65,000. **Il Cardinale – GB** *(Map 2; ☎ 06 686 93 36, Via delle Carceri 6)*, off Via Giulia, is another well-known restaurant with superb food. A full meal should come to under L80,000.

Vecchia Roma *(Map 6; ☎ 06 686 46 04, Piazza Campitelli 18)* has a well-deserved reputation for good food. Its outside tables are extremely popular in summer. A full meal will cost from L80,000. **Piperno** *(Map 6; ☎ 06 688 06 629, Via Monte de' Cenci 9)* has a menu combining Roman and Jewish cooking and is considered one of Roma's better mid-range restaurants. A full meal will cost from L80,000.

City Centre – Top End Close to Via Vittorio Veneto, **Andrea** *(Map 3; ☎ 06 482 18 91, Via Sardegna 24-28)* is one of Roma's most popular top restaurants. A full meal will cost in the range of L100,000. **Il Convivio** *(Map 6; ☎ 06 686 94 32, Via dell'Orso 44)*, a little north of Piazza Navona, is an elegant restaurant with a creative menu. A full meal will cost around L100,000.

El Toulà *(Map 2; ☎ 06 687 34 98, Via della Lupa 29)* is one of Roma's most prestigious restaurants, a fact reflected in the prices – more than L130,000 for a full meal.

West of the Tevere – Budget The main concentration of good-value restaurants is in Trastevere and the Testaccio district. Most establishments around San Pietro and Il Vaticano are geared towards tourists and can be very expensive.

Osteria dell'Angelo *(☎ 06 38 92 18, Via G Bettolo 24)* is in the Trionfale area (Map 1) – to get there, walk north along Via Leone IV from Il Vaticano. A hearty Roman meal can be had for around L30,000. **Pizzeria Giacomelli** *(☎ 06 38 35 11, Via di Bruno Emilia*

Faà 25) is off Via della Giuliana, past Largo Trionfale (Map 1). The pizzas are good, big and cheap. *Il Tempio della Pizza (Map 2; ☎ 06 321 69 63, Viale Giulio Cesare 91)* is open late and has good-quality food at reasonable prices.

In Trastevere's maze of tiny streets there are any number of pizzerie and cheap trattorie. The area is beautiful at night and most establishments have outside tables. It is also very popular, so arrive before 9 pm unless you want to queue for a table.

Mario's (Map 6; ☎ 06 580 38 09, Via del Moro 53) is a local favourite for its cheap pasta (around L10,000), but you can find better quality elsewhere. *Da Augusto (Map 6; ☎ 06 580 37 98, Piazza dei Renzi 15)* is another great spot for a cheap meal. Try the home-made *fettucine*. If you arrive early there is also a good selection of vegetables. A meal with wine will cost around L20,000. *Da Otello in Trastevere (Map 4; ☎ 06 589 68 48, Via della Pelliccia 47-53)* has excellent antipasti. A hearty meal should cost around L30,000.

Da Giovanni (Map 2; ☎ 06 686 15 14, Via della Lungara 41) is a good 10 minutes walk from the centre of Trastevere. It's a popular eating place and you will probably have to wait for a table. The food is simple and the prices really good. *Da Gildo (Map 2; ☎ 06 580 07 33, Via della Scala 31)* is a pizzeria/trattoria with a range of pizzas and good-quality food. A full meal will cost around L25,000. Nearby is *Da Lucia (Map 4; ☎ 06 580 36 01, Vicolo del Mattonato 2)*, which offers an excellent range of antipasti and pasta. In summer it has tables outside. A meal will cost around L35,000. *Pizzeria Ivo (Map 4; ☎ 06 581 70 82, Via di San Francesco a Ripa 158)* has outdoor tables, but the pizza could be bigger for the price (from L9000). The *bruschetta* is an excellent start to the meal. The house wine comes in bottles and is not a bargain at L8000. *Pizzeria Popi-Popi (Map 4; ☎ 06 589 51 67, Via delle Fratte di Trastevere 45)*, just off Piazza San Cosimato, is very popular among young people, who flock to its outside tables in summer. The pizzas are average but cheap.

Pizzeria da Vittorio (Map 4; ☎ 06 580 03 53, Via di San Cosimato 14) is tiny and you will have to wait if you arrive after 9 pm. A delicious bruschetta and pizza with wine will cost around L20,000. *Panattoni (Map 4; ☎ 06 580 09 19, Viale di Trastevere 53)* stays open late and is always crowded; it is one of the more popular pizzerie in Trastevere. You can eat there for around L15,000.

You won't find a noisier, more popular pizzeria in Roma than *Pizzeria Remo (Map 4; ☎ 06 574 62 70, Piazza Santa Maria Liberatrice 44)*, in Testaccio. A meal will cost around L16,000. *Augustarello (Map 4; ☎ 06 574 65 85, Via G Branca 98)*, off the piazza, specialises in offal dishes. A full meal should cost around L20,000. *Trattoria da Bucatino (Map 4; ☎ 06 574 68 86, Via Luca della Robbia 84)*, is a popular Testaccio eating place, with pasta from L10,000 to L12,000 and pizzas for around the same prices. It also serves Roman fare. A full meal will cost about L30,000.

West of the Tevere – Mid-Range to Top End
In Testaccio *Checchino dal 1887 (Map 4; ☎ 06 574 63 18, Via di Monte Testaccio 30)* serves superb Roman food, including, of course, lots of offal. A full meal will cost around L75,000.

Paris (Map 4; ☎ 06 581 53 78, Piazza San Calisto 7) has developed a reputation for excellent cuisine. A meal will cost up to L80,000.

San Lorenzo to the Foro Romano – Budget
Places to eat in San Lorenzo, being in Roma's university district, are influenced by the student population. One of the more popular places, *Pizzeria l'Economica (Map 3; Via Tiburtina 44)*, serves local fare and good pizzas at prices students can afford. *Formula 1 (Map 3; ☎ 06 445 38 66, Via degli Equi 13)* is another good-value pizzeria, as is *Le Maschere (Map 3; ☎ 06 445 38 05, Via degli Umbri 8)*; both are popular with students. One of the area's more famous trattorie is *Pommidoro (Map 1; ☎ 06 445 26 92, Piazza dei Sanniti 44)*, where an excellent meal will cost around L40,000.

Tram Tram (Map 1; ☎ 06 49 04 16, Via dei Reti 44) has excellent food at moderate prices.

If you have no option but to eat near Stazione Termini, try to avoid the tourist traps offering overpriced set menus. There are many *tavole calde* (literally 'hot tables') in the area, particularly to the west of the train station. These offer *panini* (filled rolls) and pre-prepared dishes for reasonable prices. There is a self-service in the station complex, *La Piazza*, where you can eat good food at reasonable prices, and there are a few good-value restaurants in the area. *Da Gemma alla Lupa (Map 3; ☎ 06 49 12 30, Via Marghera 39)* is a simple trattoria with prices to match: a full meal will cost around L30,000. *Trattoria da Bruno (Map 3; Via Varese 29)* has good food at reasonable prices. *Hosteria Angelo (Map 3; Via Principe Amedeo 104)* is a traditional trattoria with very reasonable prices. *Galilei (Map 5; ☎ 06 731 56 42, Via Galilei 12)*, between the train station and Basilica di San Giovanni in Laterano, is a good, cheap pizzeria.

Towards the Colosseo is *Hostaria di Nerone (Map 3; ☎ 06 474 52 07, Via delle Terme di Tito 96)*. Popular with tourists, it has good food and a full meal will cost around L30,000. Another decent pizzeria is *Alle Carrette (Map 3; ☎ 06 679 27 70, Vicolo delle Carrette 14)*, off Via Cavour, near the Foro Romano; a pizza and wine will come to around L20,000. Just off Via Cavour, on the tiny Via dell'Angeletto, is *Osteria Gli Angeletti (Map 3; ☎ 06 474 33 74)*, an excellent little restaurant. It has outside tables on the Piazza Madonna dei Monti, the heart of the Rione Monti. You'll pay between L10,000 and L14,000 for pasta and around L16,000 for a main course. It's open daily but closes in December.

San Lorenzo to the Foro Romano – Mid-Range Off Via Merulana, a few streets north of Piazza San Giovanni in Laterano, *La Tana del Grillo (Map 3; ☎ 06 704 53 517, Via Alfieri 4-8)* offers Ferrara cuisine, as well as the usual Roman fare. A full meal will cost from L40,000 to L50,000. *Il Dito e la Luna*

(☎ 06 494 07 26, Via dei Sabelli 47-51), in the San Lorenzo district, serves hearty, good-quality meals for around L50,000.

Foreign Restaurants
These are not exactly abundant, but there are some very good restaurants in Roma which serve international cuisine.

Chinese food is very popular, but the food is often heavily salted and can leave a lot to be desired. *Golden Crown (Map 3; ☎ 06 678 98 31, Via in Arcione 85)*, between Via del Tritone and the Palazzo del Quirinale, is a good choice; expect to pay up to L40,000 for a solid meal. For an excellent Japanese meal, head for *Sogo Asahi (Map 3; ☎ 06 678 60 93, Via di Propaganda 22)*, near Piazza di Spagna. It is expensive, however, at around L70,000 a head. It has a sushi bar, for which you have to book. *Suria Mahal (Map 6; ☎ 06 589 45 54, Piazza Trilussa)*, in Trastevere, is an Indian restaurant where a delicious meal will cost around L45,000. Tex Mex food can be found at *Oliphant (Map 6; ☎ 06 686 14 16)*, on the corner of Via della Scrofa and Via delle Coppelle.

If all you really want is a Big Mac, you'll find *McDonald's* outlets on Piazza della Repubblica (with outside tables), Piazza di Spagna, Piazza della Rotonda (with a view of the Pantheon that many a chic eatery would kill for) and Viale di Trastevere (between Piazza Sonnino and Piazza Mastai). At *Marconi (Map 3; Via di Santa Prassede 1)*, just in front of Santa Maria Maggiore, you can munch on fish and chips, baked beans and other assorted stodgy English dishes.

Vegetarian Restaurants
All trattorie serve a good selection of vegetable dishes, but there are other options for vegetarians in Roma. *Centro Macrobiotico Italiano (Map 3; ☎ 06 679 25 09, Via della Vite 14)* charges L8000 membership fee and dishes start at L10,000. At *Margutta Vegetariano (Map 2; ☎ 06 678 60 33, Via Margutta 19)*, parallel to Via del Babuino, décor and prices are upmarket and a meal will cost no less than L40,000. *Il Canestro (Map 4; ☎ 06 574 62 87, Via Luca della Robbia 47)*,

in Testaccio, is another good option. A full meal will cost around L35,000. It also has a health food shop and is closed on Sunday.

Cafés

Remember that prices skyrocket in cafés as soon as you sit down, particularly in major tourist haunts such as the areas around Piazza di Spagna or the Pantheon, where a *cappuccino* at a table can cost as much as L10,000. The same cappuccino taken at the bar will cost around L1600. The narrow streets and tiny piazzas in the area between Piazza Navona and the Tevere have a number of popular cafés and bars.

Those seeking the best coffee in Roma should go to the *Tazza d'Oro (Map 6; Via degli Orfani)*, just off Piazza della Rotonda, and *Bar Sant'Eustachio (Map 6; Piazza Sant'Eustachio)*, near the Pantheon. Fashionable (and expensive) places to drink coffee or tea are the *Caffè Greco (Map 3; Via dei Condotti 86)*, near Piazza di Spagna, *Babington's Tea Rooms (Map 3; Piazza di Spagna 23)* and *Caffè Rosati (Map 2; Piazza del Popolo)*.

At *Caffè del Marzio (Map 4; Piazza Santa Maria in Trastevere)* you will pay L5000 for a cappuccino if you sit down outside, but it's worth it as this is one of Roma's most beautiful and atmospheric piazzas.

Sandwiches & Snacks

Paladini (Map 6; Via del Governo Vecchio 29) might look like a run-down alimentari but it makes mouthwatering pizza bianca on the premises, filled with whatever you want, for L3000 to L5000. Try the prosciutto and fig – an unusual combination but delicious. On Via di Ripetta (which runs off Piazza del Popolo, parallel to Via del Corso) there are several bars and takeaways with good fare. *Caffè Sogo (Map 2; Via di Ripetta 242)* has Japanese snacks and drinks. Next door is a tiny Japanese grocery.

Paneformaggio (Map 2; Via di Ripetta 7) and *M & M Volpetti (Map 6; Via della Scrofa 31)*, near Piazza Navona, are upmarket sandwich bars and *rosticcerie* (roast-meat shops) where you can buy gourmet lunch snacks for

above-average prices. Closer to Termini is *Il Golosone (Map 3; Via Venezia)*, off Via Nazionale, a sandwich bar and tavola calda where you can sit down without paying extra. Another option is *Dagnino*, *(Map 3; Galleria Esedra)*, off Via Orlando.

Among the more famous sandwich outlets in Roma is *Frontoni (Map 4; Viale di Trastevere)*, on the corner of Via San Francesco a Ripa, opposite Piazza Mastai. It makes its panini with both pizza bianca and bread, and you can choose from an enormous range of fillings. Sandwiches are sold by weight and a generously filled one will cost around L6000. It also has excellent pizza by the slice. It is worth making a special trip to Testaccio, to eat lunch at *Volpetti Più (Map 4; Via A Volta 8)*. It's a tavola calda, so you don't pay extra to sit down. The pizza by the slice is extraordinarily good and there are plenty of pasta, vegetable and meat dishes.

Takeaway pizza by the slice is very popular in Roma and there are numerous outlets all over the city. Usually you can judge the quality of the pizza simply by taking a look. Some good places are *Pizza Rustica (Map 6; Campo de' Fiori)*, *Pizza a Taglio (Map 6; Via Baullari)*, between Campo de' Fiori and Corso Vittorio Emanuele II, and *Pizza a Taglio (Map 3; Via delle Muratte)*, just off Piazza di Trevi.

Ice Cream

Gelateria Giolitti (Map 6; Via degli Uffici del Vicario 40) has long been a Roman institution. It was once the meeting place of the local art crowd and writers. Today it remains famous for its fantastic *gelati*. Around the corner, *Gelateria della Palma (Map 3; Via della Maddalena 20)* has a huge selection of flavours and some say the gelati are better than at Giolitti. A cone with three flavours costs around L2500. Both establishments also have cakes and pastries. *La Fonte della Salute (Map 4; Via Cardinal Marmaggi 2-6)*, in Trastevere, has arguably the best gelati in Roma. An atmospheric spot is *Il Ristoro della Salute (Map 5; Piazza del Colosseo)*. Buy a cone or a *frullato* (fruit drink) and wander across the road to the Colosseo.

Bread & Pastries

Bernasconi (Map 6; Piazza B Cairoli 16) has a tempting selection of cakes and great pastries. *Bella Napoli* (Map 6; Corso Vittorio Emanuele 246a) is a bar/pasticceria specialising in Neapolitan pastries. *Valzani* (Via del Moro 37), in Trastevere, is one of Roma's best pasticcerie, as is *Antonini* (Via Sabotino 21-29), near Piazza Mazzini in Prati (Map 1). *La Dolceroma* (Map 6; Via del Portico d'Ottavia 20), between the Teatro di Marcello and Via Arenula, specialises in Austrian cakes and pastries. In the same street, at No 2, is the kosher bakery *Il Forno del Ghetto*, a very popular outlet for cakes and pastries. You will need to look for the street number as there is no sign. Near Stazione Termini is *Panella l'Arte del Pane* (Map 3; Largo Leopardi 2-10), on Via Merulana, with a big variety of pastries and breads.

Groceries

Hundreds of small outlets in the centre of Roma sell cheese, salami, bread and groceries. There is also a growing number of supermarkets in Roma's suburbs. The following are some of Roma's better known gastronomic establishments.

Billo Bottarga (Map 6; Via di Sant'Ambrogio 20), near Piazza Mattei, specialises in kosher food and is famous for its *bottarga* (roe of tuna or mullet). *Castroni* (Map 2; Via Cola di Rienzo 196), in Prati, near Il Vaticano, has a wide selection of gourmet foods, packaged and fresh, including international foods (desperate Aussies will find Vegemite here). It also has an outlet at Via delle Quattro Fontane 38, off Via Nazionale. *Gino Placidi* (Map 6; Via della Maddalena 48), near the Pantheon, is one of central Roma's best alimentari. *Volpetti* (Map 4; Via Marmorata 47), in Testaccio, has high-quality cheese and meats.

Health Foods

Buying muesli, soy milk and the like can be expensive in Italy. The following outlets have a good range of products, including organic fruit and vegetables at relatively reasonable prices.

L'Albero del Pane (Map 6; Via Santa Maria del Pianto 19), in the Jewish quarter, has a wide range of health foods, both packaged and fresh. It has an outlet for organic fruit and vegetables at Via dei Baullari 112, just off Campo de' Fiori. *Emporium Naturae* (Viale Angelico 2) is a well-stocked health-food supermarket (take Metro Linea A to Ottaviano, Map 2). *Il Canestro* (Map 4; Via Luca della Robbia 47), in Testaccio, near the market, also has a large selection of health food, as well as fresh fruit and vegetables and takeaway food.

ENTERTAINMENT

Roma C'è is Roma's primary entertainment guide. It is published every Thursday and there is a small section in English. It costs L2000 and is available at newsstands. *Trovaroma* is a weekly supplement in the Thursday edition of the newspaper *La Repubblica* and provides comprehensive listings, but in Italian only. The newspaper also publishes daily listings for cinemas, theatres and concerts. *Wanted in Rome* is a fortnightly magazine in English that reviews important festivals and events in Roma's English-speaking community. It has entertainment listings, as well as details of bars and pubs, and is available at various newspaper stands in the city centre and from some international bookshops.

Pubs & Bars

Pubs are the new big thing in Roma. They offer a big selection of beers and many have Guinness on tap. A favourite haunt of young foreigners, they're also popular with the locals. In the centre, try *The Drunken Ship* (Map 6; Campo de' Fiori 20) or *Trinity College* (Map 3; Via del Collegio Romano 6). Near Termini, there's *Marconi* (Map 3; Via Santa Prassede 9), serving real pub food such as fish and chips and baked beans, the *Druid's Den* (Map 3; Via San Martino ai Monti 28) or the *Fiddler's Elbow* (Map 3; Via dell'Olmata 43).

There are also plenty of places to enjoy a glass of wine. *Vineria* (Map 6; Campo de' Fiori), also known as Da Giorgio, has a wide selection of wine and beers and was once the gathering place of the Roman literati. Today it is less glamorous, but is still a good place to drink (although cheap only if you stand at the bar). *L'Angolo Divino (Map 6; Via dei Balestrari)*, off Campo de' Fiori, serves a variety of dishes and a good selection of cheeses to complement its equally good selection of wine. *Enoteca Piccolo (Map 6; Via del Governo Vecchio 75)* is a pleasant wine bar serving snacks. Near Via del Governo Vecchio is the *Bar della Pace (Map 6; Via della Pace)*, a popular but expensive place for the young in-crowd. *Cul de Sac (Map 6; Piazza Pasquino 73)*, just off Piazza Navona, at the start of Via del Governo Vecchio, is a popular wine bar which also serves excellent food.

Bevitoria Navona (Map 6; Piazza Navona 72) charges reasonable prices – around L2500 for a glass of average wine and up to L10,000 for better quality wine – although you'll pay more if you sit outside. *Trimani (Map 3; Via Cernaia 37)*, near Stazione Termini, is Roma's biggest wine bar and also serves good-quality food.

A comfortable place to drink is the *San Michele aveva un Gallo (Map 4; Via San Francesco a Ripa)*, across Viale Trastevere, near the corner of Piazza San Francesco d'Assisi. You can also eat light meals here.

Discos & Clubs

Roman clubs are expensive. Expect to pay up to L40,000 to get in, which may or may not include one drink. Hot spots include *Alien (☎ 06 841 22 12, Via Velletri 13)*, *Piper (☎ 06 841 44 59, Via Tagliamento 9)* and *Gilda (Map 3; ☎ 06 678 48 38, Via Mario de' Fiori 97)*. *Locale (Map 6; ☎ 06 687 90 75, Via del Fico 3)* and *The Groove (Map 6; ☎ 06 687 24 27, Vicolo Savelli 10)* are both near Piazza Navona and are very popular among young foreigners and Italians.

Testaccio is alive with clubs, most of which are on Via di Monte Testaccio. One of the more interesting and popular places is *Radio Londra*, at No 65b, and others include *Akab*, at No 69, *Caruso Caffè*, at No 36, and *Caffè Latino*, at No 96. In the same area is *Villaggio Globale (Map 4; Lungotevere Tes-*

taccio), accessible from Largo GB Marzi at the Ponte Testaccio, an alternative hangout for people who really know the meaning of angst. This is one of several *centri sociali* in Roma, a type of squatters club frequented by ageing hippies, New-Age types and people who are still into punk and grunge. Common throughout Italy, these places are often associated with extreme left-wing political activity, although in Roma they are principally places of entertainment.

Gay & Lesbian Venues

Details of Roma's gay and lesbian bars and clubs are provided in gay publications (see Gay & Lesbian Travellers in the Facts for the Visitor chapter) and through local gay organisations. The American-run *Hangar (Map 3; ☎ 06 488 13 97, Via in Selci 69)* is Roma's oldest gay bar and has a mixed clientele. Another choice for gays is *L'Alibi (Map 4; ☎ 06 574 34 48, Via di Monte Testaccio 44)*, regarded by many as Roma's premier gay venue. On Saturday the *Joli Coeur (Map 1; ☎ 06 862 15 827, Via Sirte 5)*, near Via Nomentana, attracts a predominantly young lesbian crowd.

Rock

Rock concerts are held throughout the year and are advertised on posters plastered around the city. Concerts by major performers are usually held at the *Palazzo dello Sport* or *Stadio Flaminia*, both a fair distance from the city centre. For information and bookings, see local listings publications or contact the ORBIS agency (☎ 06 482 74 03), at Piazza Esquilino 37, near Stazione Termini.

Jazz

For jazz and blues try *Alexanderplatz (Map 2; ☎ 06 397 42 171, Via Ostia 9)*, which in July and August moves to the *Villa Celi montana* on the Celio hill (Map 5).

Otherwise there's *Folkstudio (☎ 06 487 10 630, Via Frangipane 42)*, *Big Mama (Map 4; ☎ 06 581 25 51, Vicolo San Francesco a Ripa 18)* in Trastevere or the *Four XXXX (Map 4; ☎ 06 575 72 96, Via Galvani 29)* in Testaccio.

Classical Music

Concerts are given by the *Accademia di Santa Cecilia (Map 2; ☎ 06 688 01 044)* in the auditorium at Via della Conciliazione 4 during the winter months and in the gardens at Villa Giulia in summer. The *Accademia Filarmonica* holds its season at the Teatro Olimpico (☎ 06 323 48 90), at Piazza Gentile da Fabriano 17. From June to September, there are concerts in the ruins of the Teatro di Marcello near Piazza Venezia every evening at 9 pm. They are organised by *Concerti al Tempietto (☎ 06 481 48 00, Via di Teatro Marcello 44)*.

Performances of sacred and classical music are also held in some of Roma's churches. The programmes are generally excellent and not to be missed. Check in *Roma C'è* for details.

Cinemas

Films are shown daily in English at *Il Nuovo Pasquino (Map 4; ☎ 06 580 36 22, Piazza Sant'Egidio)* in Trastevere, just off Piazza Santa Maria in Trastevere, and at *Quirinetta (Map 3; ☎ 06 679 00 12, Via Minghetti 4)*, off Via del Corso. On Monday night you can see films in their original language at *Alcazar (Map 4; ☎ 06 588 00 99, Via Merry del Val)*, off Viale di Trastevere. The *Nuovo Sacher (Map 4; ☎ 06 581 81 16)*, at Largo Ascianghi, between the Porta Portese area and Trastevere, screens films in their original language on Monday and Tuesday.

A popular form of entertainment in the hot Roman summer is outdoor cinema. *Isola del Cinema* is an international film festival that takes place on the Isola Tiberina from late June until the end of August. For *Notti di Cinema a Piazza Vittorio* a huge screen is erected in the Piazza Vittorio Emanuele II, near Stazione Termini. Outdoor screens are also set up at other locations, including on the Celio. Check the listings magazines or the daily press for details of these events.

Theatre

English-language theatre is performed periodically by the International Theatre at *Teatro Agora (☎ 06 687 41 67, Via della*

Penitenza 33) in Trastevere. Other theatres occasionally perform plays in English. Check the listings papers mentioned earlier in this section for details.

Opera

The opera season at the *Teatro dell'Opera (Map 3; ☎ 06 481 60 255, Piazza Beniamino Gigli)* starts in December and continues until June. In summer, opera is performed outdoors in the Stadio Olimpico.

SPECTATOR SPORTS

The city's two football teams, AS Roma and Lazio, play their home matches at Stadio Olimpico at Foro Italico, north of the city centre. Tickets start at around L30,000, but can cost as much as L120,000. They can be bought from the ticket office at the ground (☎ 06 323 73 33) or from agencies such as Orbis (☎ 06 482 74 03), Piazza Esquilino 36.

SHOPPING

Don't feel bad if you find that Roma's shop windows are competing with its monuments for your attention. Just make sure you allocate plenty of time (as well as funds) for shopping. Roma's main shopping districts include: the Piazza di Spagna area for the main clothing, shoes and leather goods designers, Via Nazionale and surrounds for a good mix of affordable clothing, the Via Veneto area for the top names, Via dei Coronari for antiques and Via del Governo Vecchio for second-hand and alternative clothing. If you can time your visit to coincide with the sales, you'll pick up some marvellous bargains. The winter sales run from early January to around mid-February and the summer sales from July to early September. Shops open from around 9.30 am to 1 pm and 3.30 to 7.30 pm (4 to 8 pm in summer). There is a trend towards longer opening hours from 9.30 am to 7.30 pm, but usually only the larger shops or department stores have these hours.

Clothing, Shoes & Leather Goods

All the following are on Map 3 unless otherwise indicated.

Big designer names for clothing include:

Emporio Armani, Via del Babuino 140; MaxMara, Via Condotti 17, Via Frattina 28 and Via Nazionale 28; Fendi, Via Borgognona 36; Valentino, Via Condotti 13; and Cenci, Via Campo Marzio 1-7.

For shoes and leather goods, try: Gucci, Via Condotti 8; Bruno Magli, Via Veneto 70; Fratelli Rossetti, Via Borgonogna 5; Raphael Salato, Via Veneto 149; and Mandarina Duck, Via di Propaganda 1, just off Piazza di Spagna. More affordable shops include Benetton, Sisley and Stefanel, which are on just about every street corner, and Max & Co (Map 2), Via Condotti 46. For cut price designer wear, head for Discount Systems, Via del Viminale 35.

Antiques, Design & Furniture

Wander along Via dei Coronari and Via dei Banchi Nuovi (both Map 2) if you're interested in antiques. Antique prints are sold at Alinari (Map 3), Via Aliberti 16a, and Nardecchia (Map 6), Piazza Navona 25. Designer furniture can be found on Via del Babuino (Map 2). If you're looking for Italian design homewares, try Leone Limentani (Map 6), Via Portico d'Ottavia 47.

For Children

For children's clothes, shop at La Cicogna (Map 3), Via Frattina 138, or PrèNatal (Map 3), Via Nazionale 45. For toys, head for Città del Sole (Map 6), Via della Scrofa 65.

Markets

Everyone flocks to Porta Portese market on Sunday morning. A mishmash of new and old, the market has all manner of incredible deals, but you have to be prepared to drive a hard bargain. The market extends along the side streets parallel to Viale Trastevere (Map 4). Be extremely aware of pickpockets and bag snatchers.

The excellent market on Via Sannio (Map 5), near Porta San Giovanni, sells new and second-hand clothes. It's open to around 1 pm Monday to Saturday. For prints, antiques and books, head for the market at Piazza Fontanella Borghese (Map 2), held every morning except Sunday.

GETTING THERE & AWAY
Air

Roma's main airport is Leonardo da Vinci (☎ 06 6 59 51), also known as Fiumicino, after the town nearby. The city's other airport is Ciampino (☎ 06 79 49 41), where many national and some international, including charter, flights arrive. See the Getting Around section in this chapter for details on getting to and from the airports, and the Getting There & Away chapter for information on flights to and from Roma.

All the airlines have counters in the departure hall at Fiumicino, but their main offices are in the area around Via Vittorio Veneto and Via Barberini, north of Stazione Termini (Map 3). They include:

Air France
   (☎ 06 48 79 11) Via Sardegna 40
Air New Zealand
   (☎ 06 488 07 61) Via Bissolati 54
Alitalia
   (☎ 06 6 56 42) Via Bissolati 20
British Airways
   (☎ 06 524 91 512) Via Bissolati 54
Cathay Pacific
   (☎ 06 482 09 30) Via Barberini 3
Qantas
   (☎ 06 420 12 312) Via Bissolati 54
Singapore Airlines
   (☎ 06 478 55 360) Via Barberini 11
TWA
   (☎ 06 4 72 11) Via Barberini 67
United Airlines
   (☎ 06 489 04 140) Via Bissolati 54

Bus

The main station for intercity buses is on Piazzale Tiburtina, in front of Stazione Tiburtina (Map 1). Take Metro Linea B from Stazione Termini to Tiburtina. Various bus lines run services to cities throughout Italy.

COTRAL buses, which service the Lazio region, depart from numerous points throughout the city, depending on their destination. The company is linked with Roma's public transport system, which means that the same ticket is valid for city and regional buses, trams, the Metro, and train lines. For more detailed information about which companies go to which destinations, go to Stazione

Tiburtina, or the Eurojet agency (☎ 06 474 28 01) in Piazza della Repubblica (Map 3), where you can buy tickets for some bus lines. Enjoy Rome or the APT office can also help (see Tourist Offices earlier in this chapter).

Some useful bus lines include:

ARPA, SIRA, Di Fonzo, Di Febo & Capuani
Services to Abruzzo, including L'Aquila, Pescasseroli and Pescara. Information from Piazzale Tiburtina.
Bonelli
Services to Emilia-Romagna, including Ravenna and Rimini. Information from Piazzale Tiburtina.
COTRAL
Via Ostiense 131 (☎ 800 431 784 toll-free)
Services throughout Lazio. Buses for Palestrina and Tivoli depart from Ponte Mammolo Metro station on Linea B (also stopping at Rebibbia); buses for Bolsena, Saturnia, Toscana and Viterbo depart from Saxa Rubra, on the Ferrovia Roma Nord train line; buses for the Castelli Romani depart from Anagnina, the last stop on the Metro Linea A; buses for the beaches south of Roma depart from the EUR-Fermi station on the Metro Linea B; for Bracciano, Cerveteri and Tarquinia take a bus from the Lepanto station on Metro Linea A.
Lazzi
(☎ 06 884 08 40) Via Tagliamento 27r
Services to other European cities and the Alpi.
Lirosi
Services to Calabria. Information from Eurojet (☎ 06 474 28 01).
Marozzi
Services to Bari and Brindisi (via towns including Alberobello and Matera), Sorrento, the Costiera Amalfitana and Pompei. Information from Eurojet (☎ 06 474 28 01).
SAIS & Segesta
Services to Sicilia. Information at Piazza della Repubblica or Piazzale Tiburtina (☎ 06 481 96 76).
Sena
Services to Siena. Information from Eurojet (☎ 06 474 28 01).
SULGA
Services to Perugia and Assisi, as well as to Fiumicino airport. Information from Eurojet (☎ 06 474 28 01 in Roma).

Train

Almost all trains arrive at and depart from Stazione Termini. There are regular connec-

tions to all the major cities in Italy and Europe. Examples of one-way costs for Intercity trains (rapido supplement included) from Roma are as follows: Firenze L38,500, Napoli L28,500, Milano L68,000 and Venezia L68,000. For train information (in Italian only) ring ☎ 147 88 80 88 from 7 am to 9 pm or go to the information office at the train station, where English is spoken.

Timetables can be bought at most newspaper stands in and around Stazione Termini and are particularly useful if you are travelling mostly by train. Services at Stazione Termini include luggage storage (L1500 per item per day), telephones and currency exchange booths. Metro and city bus tickets are sold at tobacconists inside the train station.

There are eight other train stations scattered throughout Roma. Some northbound trains depart from or stop at Stazione Ostiense and Stazione Trastevere. Remember to validate your train ticket in the yellow machines on the station platforms. If you don't, you may be forced to pay a fine on the train.

Car & Motorcycle

The main road connecting Roma to the north and south of Italy is the Autostrada del Sole, which extends from Milano to Reggio di Calabria. On the outskirts of the city it connects with the Grande Raccordo Anulare, the ring road encircling Roma. From here, there are several arteries into the city.

If you are approaching from the north, take the Via Salaria, Via Nomentana or Via Flaminia exits. From the south, Via Appia Nuova, Via Cristoforo Colombo and Via del Mare (which connects Roma to the Lido di Ostia) all provide reasonably direct routes into the city. The Grande Raccordo Anulare and all arterial roads in Roma are clogged with traffic on weekday evenings from about 5 to 7.30 pm. On Sunday evening, particularly in summer, all approaches to Roma are subject to traffic jams as Romans return home after weekends away.

The A12 goes out to Civitavecchia and then runs north along the coast to Genova (it also connects the city to Fiumicino airport). Signs to the autostrada from the centre of

GREATER ROMA

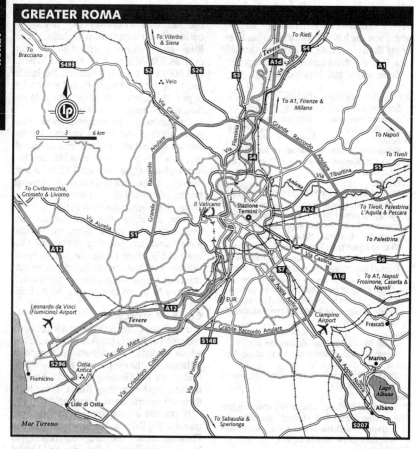

Roma can be vague and confusing, so invest in a good road map. It's best to stick to the arterial roads to reach the Grande Raccordo Anulare and then exit at the appropriate point.

Main roads out of Roma basically follow the same routes as ancient Roman consular roads. The seven most important are:

Via Aurelia (S1)
Starts at Il Vaticano and leaves the city to the north-east, following the Tyrrhenian coast to Pisa, Genova and France

Via Cassia (S2)
Starts at the Ponte Milvio and heads north-west to Viterbo, Siena and Firenze

Via Flaminia (S3)
Starts at the Ponte Milvio; goes north-west to Terni, Foligno and over the Appennini into Le Marche, ending on the Mar Adriatico at Fano

Via Salaria (S4)
Heads north from near Porta Pia in central Roma to Rieti and into Le Marche, ending at Porto d'Ascoli on the Mar Adriatico

Via Tiburtina (S5)
Links Roma with Tivoli and Pescara, on the coast of Abruzzo

Via Casilina (S6)
Heads south-east to Anagni and into Campania, terminating at Capua near Napoli

Via Appia Nuova (S7)
The most famous of the consular roads, it heads south along the coast of Lazio into Campania, and then goes inland across the Appennini into Basilicata, through Potenza and Matera to Taranto in Puglia and on to Brindisi

Hitching

It is illegal to hitchhike on the autostrada, so you have to wait on main roads near autostrada entrances. To head north on the A1, take bus No 319 from Stazione Termini, get off at Piazza Vescovio and then take bus No 135 to Via Salaria. To go south to Napoli on the A1/A2, take the Metro to Anagnina and wait in Via Tuscolana.

There is an International Lift Centre in Firenze (☎ 055 28 06 26) which matches people up with drivers, and Enjoy Rome (see Tourist Offices earlier in this chapter) might also be able to help. Hitching is not recommended, particularly for women, either alone or in groups.

GETTING AROUND
To/From the Airports

To get to the city from Fiumicino airport take the airport-Stazione Termini direct train (L15,000). Follow signs to the train station from the airport arrivals hall. The train arrives at and leaves from track No 22 at Termini and takes about 30 minutes. Tickets can be bought from vending machines at Fiumicino and Termini, from the Alitalia office at track No 22, or at the airport. After the first direct train for Termini, at 7.37 am, the service runs hourly (half-hourly at certain times of the day) from 8.07 am until 10.07 pm. From Termini to the airport, trains start at 6.50 am and run hourly (half-hourly at times) to 9.20 pm.

Another train stops at Trastevere, Ostiense and Tiburtina stations (L8000). From Fiumicino, trains run about every 20 minutes from 6.27 am to 11.27 pm, and from Ostiense from 5.19 am until 10.49 pm. The train does not stop at Termini.

From midnight to 5 am a bus runs from Stazione Tiburtina (accessible by bus No 42N

from Piazza dei Cinquecento, in front of Termini) to the airport.

The airport is connected to the city by an autostrada. Follow the signs for Roma out of the complex and exit from the autostrada at EUR. From there, you'll need to ask directions to reach Via Cristoforo Colombo, which will take you directly into the centre.

If you arrive at Ciampino airport, blue COTRAL buses (running between 5.45 am and 10.30 pm) will take you to the Anagnina Metro station, from where you can get to Stazione Termini. If you arrive late or very early, you have little option other than to take a taxi. Ciampino airport is connected to Roma by the Via Appia Nuova.

Bus

The city bus company is ATAC. Most of the main buses terminate in Piazza dei Cinquecento at Stazione Termini. The information booth in the centre of the piazza gives out a map outlining the bus routes. The Lozzi map of Roma provides a good enough guide to these bus routes. See also Maps in the Orientation section earlier in this chapter.

Another central point for the main bus routes is Largo di Torre Argentina, near Piazza Navona. Buses generally run from about 6 am until midnight, with limited services throughout the night on some routes. Regular travellers to Roma should note that some of the bus routes have been changed in the past few years.

Roma's buses, subway and suburban railways are now part of the same system and tickets are valid for all three modes of transport. This means that individual tickets are now considerably more expensive, but if you manage to get the intended mileage out of them, the savings are high. Single tickets cost L1500 for 75 minutes, daily tickets cost L6000, weekly tickets L24,000 and monthly tickets L50,000. These tickets are valid for city and regional buses, trams, the Metro and train lines.

Tickets must be purchased before you get on the bus or train and then validated in the machine as you enter. The fine for travelling without a validated ticket is L50,000 and the inspectors are growing tired of the same old protestations of ignorance from tourists. You can get tickets on Piazza dei Cinquecento, at tobacconists, at newspaper stands and from vending machines at main bus stops.

Useful routes include:

No 8 (tram)
Largo di Torre Argentina to Trastevere, Stazione Trastevere and Monteverde Nuovo
No 36
Stazione Termini along Via Nomentana (for foreign embassies)
No 44
Piazza Venezia to Trastevere
No 64
Stazione Termini to Basilica di San Pietro
No 116 (small electric bus)
Via Giulia through the city centre to Villa Borghese
No 175
Piazzale Partigiani at Ostiense train station to Stazione Termini
No 218
Piazza San Giovanni in Laterano to the Via Appia Antica and catacombs
No 910
Stazione Termini to the Villa Borghese

Metropolitana

The Metropolitana (Metro) has two lines, Linea A and Linea B. Both pass through Stazione Termini.

Useful Metro stations include:

station	line	attractions
Circo Massimo	Linea B	Circo Massimo, Aventino, Il Celio, Terme di Caracalla
Colosseo	Linea B	Colosseo
Flaminio	Linea A	Villa Borghese
Ottaviano	Linea A	Il Vaticano
Piramide	Linea B	Stazione Ostiense, trains to the airport and the Lido di Ostia
Spagna	Linea A	Piazza di Spagna

See the earlier Bus section for information on tickets. The Metro operates from 5.30 am to 11.30 pm (12.30 am on Saturday) and trains run approximately every five minutes.

Car & Motorcycle

Negotiating Roman traffic by car is difficult enough, but you might be taking your life in your hands if you ride a motorcycle in the city. The rule in Roma is to look straight ahead to watch the vehicles in front, and hope that the vehicles behind are watching you!

Most of the historic centre of Roma is closed to normal traffic, although tourists are permitted to drive to their hotels. Traffic police control the entrances to the centre and should let you through if you have a car full of luggage and mention the name of your hotel. The hotel management should provide a pass which allows you to park in the centre. Traffic police are getting very tough on illegally parked cars. At best you'll get a heavy fine (around L100,000), at worst a wheel clamp or your car towed away. If you park illegally and return to find your car missing, always check first with the traffic police (☎ 06 6 76 91). You'll have to pay about L180,000 to get it back, plus a hefty fine.

A system of parking charges has been introduced around the periphery of Roma's city centre. Spaces are denoted by a blue line in areas including the Lungotevere (the roads beside the Tevere river) and near Termini. You'll need small change to get tickets from vending machines placed every 100m or so along the road, otherwise tickets are available from tobacconists. Parking costs L2000 per hour.

The major parking area closest to the centre is at the Villa Borghese; entry is from Piazzale Brasile at the top of Via Veneto. There's also a supervised car park at Stazione Termini.

Other car parks are at Piazzale dei Partigiani, just outside Stazione Ostiense (the Metro runs from nearby Piramide station to the city centre), and at Stazione Tiburtina, from where you can also catch the Metro into the centre.

Car Rental To rent a car, you need to be at least 21 years old and possess a valid driving licence. It is cheaper to organise a car in advance if you want to rent one for a long period.

See Rental in the Car & Motorcycle section of the Getting Around chapter for a guide to costs. The multinational operators in Roma (Avis, Europcar and Hertz) are slightly cheaper than the local ones.

The major companies are:

Avis
   (☎ 06 793 40 195) Ciampino airport
   (☎ 06 481 43 73) Stazione Termini
Europcar
   (☎ 06 52 08 11) central booking
   (☎ 06 650 10 879) Fiumicino airport
   (☎ 06 488 28 54) Stazione Termini
Maggiore Budget
   (☎ 147 86 70 67) central booking
   (☎ 06 650 10 678) Fiumicino airport
   (☎ 06 488 00 49) Stazione Termini

Motorcycle & Bicycle Rental Motorcycles (as well as scooters or mopeds) and bicycles can be rented from Happy Rent (Map 3; ☎ 06 481 81 85), Via Farini 3. Motorcycle (600cc) rental costs are L160,000 per day and scooters and mopeds (50cc to 125cc) cost up to L140,000 per day. Bicycle rental is from L5000 for one hour to L120,000 for a week. It also rents cars and mini-vans. Baby seats are available for both cars and bicycles.

Another option is Bici e Baci (☎ 06 482 84 43), Via del Viminale 5, near Piazza della Repubblica. Scooter rental starts at L40,000 per day; a bicycle costs L15,000 per day. Bicycles are also usually available for hire on Piazza del Popolo and at the Villa Borghese.

Taxi

Taxis in Roma are on 24 hour radio call. Cooperativa Radio Taxi Romana (☎ 06 35 70) and La Capitale (☎ 06 49 94) are two of many operators. There are major taxi ranks at the airports, Stazione Termini and Largo Argentina, in the historical centre. Surcharges apply to luggage, night service, public holidays and travel to and from Fiumicino airport.

The rate is a minimum charge of L4500 (for the first 3km), then L1200 per kilometre. There are supplements of L5000 from 10 pm to 7 am and L2000 from 7 am to 10 pm on Sunday and public holidays. There is also a L15,000 supplement on travel to and from Fi-

umicino airport because it is outside the city limits. This means the fare will be around L70,000. If you telephone for a taxi, the driver will turn on the meter immediately and you will pay the cost of travel from wherever the driver was when the call was received.

Lazio

Declared a region in 1934, the Lazio area has, since ancient Roman times, been an extension of Roma. Through the ages, the rich built their villas in the Lazio countryside and many towns developed as the fiefdoms of noble Roman families, such as the Orsini, Barberini and Farnese families. Even today, Romans build their weekend and holiday homes in the picturesque areas of the region (the pope, for instance, has his summer residence at Castelgandolfo, south of Roma) and Romans continue to migrate from the chaotic and polluted city to live in the Lazio countryside. This means the region is relatively well-served by public transport and tourists can take advantage of this to visit places of interest.

While the region isn't exactly packed with major tourist destinations, it does offer some worthwhile day trips from the city. A tour of Etruria, the ancient land of the Etruscans, which extended into northern Lazio, is highly recommended. Visits to the tombs and museums at Cerveteri and Tarquinia provide a fascinating insight into Etruscan civilisation. The ruins of Villa Adriana (Hadrian's Villa), near Tivoli, and of the ancient Roman port at Ostia Antica, are both easily accessible from Roma, as is the medieval town of Viterbo, north of the capital. In summer, tired and overheated tourists can head for the lakes north of Roma, including Bracciano, Bolsena and Vico, which are somewhat preferable to the polluted beaches near the city, or head south to the relatively clean and sandy beaches of Sabaudia or Sperlonga.

There are some hill-top towns to the southwest of Roma which are worth visiting, such as Anagni (which has remarkable frescoes in its Romanesque cathedral), Alatri and those of the Castelli Romani in the hills just past

ROMA

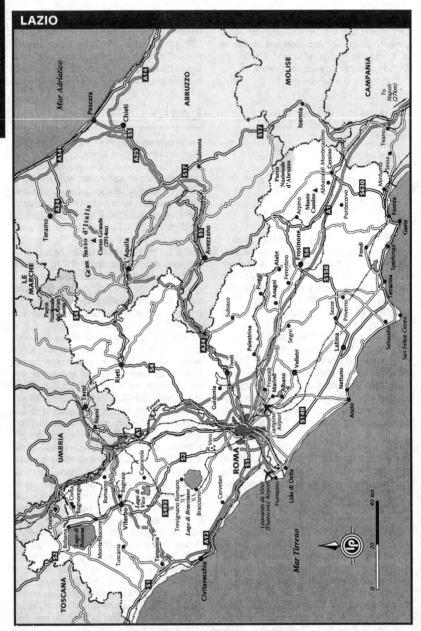

Roma's outskirts. Those interested in Italy's involvement in WWII might want to visit Monte Cassino, the scene of a major battle during the last stages of the war.

If you have your own transport, try to avoid day trips out of Roma on Sunday during summer. On your return in the evening, you are likely to find yourself in traffic jams extending for many kilometres, even on the autostrada.

OSTIA ANTICA

The Romans founded this port city at the mouth of the Tevere river in the 4th century BC and it became a strategically important centre for defence and trade. It was populated by merchants, sailors and slaves and the ruins of the city provide a fascinating contrast to the ruins at Pompei, which was populated by wealthier citizens. After Saracen invasions and the outbreak of malaria it was abandoned, but Pope Gregory IV re-established the city in the 9th century AD.

Information about the town and ruins is available from the APT office in Roma (see Tourist Offices in the Information section at the beginning of this chapter).

Things to See

The ruins are quite spread out and you will need a few hours to see them all. Admission to the city is through the **Porta Romana**, which leads you onto Ostia Antica's main thoroughfare, the **Decumanus Maximus**. The **Porta Marina**, at the other end of the road, once opened onto the seafront. Of particular note in the excavated city are the **Terme di Nettuno** (Neptune's Baths), to your right just after entering the city. Take a look at the black and white mosaic depicting Neptune and Amphitrite. Next is a **Roman theatre** built by Agrippa, which could hold 2700 people. It was restored in 1927 and is now used for staging classical performances and concerts. Behind the theatre is **Piazzale delle Corporazioni**, where Ostia's merchant guilds had their offices, each distinguished by a mosaic depicting their wares.

Returning to the Decumanus Maximus, you reach the **forum**, the **Tempio di Roma e**

Augusto, with its statue of Roma Vincitrice (Victorious Roma), and the **Tempio Rotondo**. Follow the Vico del Pino and Via del Tempio Rotondo to the Cardo Maximus to reach the **Domus Fortuna Annonaria**, the heavily decorated home of one of Ostia's wealthier citizens. Opposite, in the area next to the **Grandi Horrea** (warehouses), are private houses, including the quite well-preserved **Casa di Diana**.

Continue along the Via dei Dipinti to reach Ostia Antica's **museum**, which houses statues, mosaics and wall paintings found at the site. The ruins are open daily except Monday from 9 am to 4 pm between November and February, to 5 pm in March and to 6 pm between April and October. Admission to the excavations and museum costs L8000.

Getting There & Away

To get to Ostia Antica, take the Metro Linea B to Piramide, then the Ostia Lido train from Ostiense. Trains leave approximately every 30 minutes and the trip takes about 20 minutes. It is covered by the standard L1500 ticket. The ruins are also easy to reach by car from Roma. Take the Via del Mare, a fast *superstrada* which runs parallel to the Via Ostiense. There is a car park at the entrance to the site (L4000 flat rate).

TIVOLI

Set on a hill by the Aniene river, Tivoli was a resort town of the Romans and became popular as a summer playground for the rich during the Renaissance. While the majority of tourists are attracted by the terraced gardens and fountains of the Villa d'Este, the ruins of the spectacular Villa Adriana, built by the Roman emperor Hadrian, are far more interesting.

The IAT office (☎ 0774 31 12 49) is on Largo Garibaldi, near the COTRAL bus stop. It is open from 9 am to 3 pm.

Things to See

The **Villa Adriana** was built in the 2nd century AD as the summer residence of Emperor Hadrian and was influenced by the classical architecture of the day. It was successively plundered by the Saracens and Romans for building materials, and many of its original decorations were used to embellish the Villa d'Este. However, enough remains to give an idea of its former splendour. You will need about four hours to see the vast ruins, and you'll be exhausted before you've seen even half the place. Take a break for a picnic, or lunch at the bar in the visitors centre, before resuming your tour.

Highlights include the **Villa dell'Isola** (Island Villa), where Hadrian purportedly spent his more pensive moments, the **Palazzo Imperiale** and its **Piazza d'Oro** (Golden Square), and the floor mosaics of the **Hospitalia**. Even though little remains of Hadrian's **Piccole e Grandi Terme** (Small and Large Baths), it is easy to work out their layout and imagine their former grandeur. Take a look at the model of the villa in the small visitors centre to get an idea of the extent of the complex. The villa is open daily from 9 am to 5 pm between November and January, to 6 pm in February and October, to 6.30 pm in March and September and to 7.30 pm between May and August. Admission costs L8000.

The Renaissance **Villa d'Este** was built in the 16th century for Cardinal Ippolito d'Este, grandson of the Borgia pope, Alexander VI, on the site of a Franciscan monastery. The villa's beautiful gardens are decorated with numerous fountains, which are its main attraction. You will wander through the cardinal's villa on the way to the gardens. Rather than paying too much attention to the fairly drab rooms, take a look out of the windows for a bird's-eye view of the gardens and fountains. The villa is open from 9 am to 7.30 pm Tuesday to Sunday between April and September, and from 9 am to 5.30 pm between October and March. Admission costs L8000.

Getting There & Away

Tivoli is 30km east of Roma and is accessible by COTRAL bus from outside the Ponte Mammolo station on Metro Linea B. The bus leaves every 10 minutes from Monday to Saturday and every 20 minutes on Sunday and public holidays. It stops at the towns of Bagni di Tivoli and Villa Adriana, about 1km

from Tivoli, along the way. Otherwise, catch local bus No 4 to Villa Adriana from Tivoli's Piazza Garibaldi. The fastest route by car is on the Roma-L'Aquila autostrada (A24).

ETRUSCAN SITES

Lazio has a few important Etruscan archaeological sites, most within easy reach of Roma by car or public transport. These include Tarquinia, Cerveteri, Veio and Tuscania (four of the major city-states in the Etruscan League).

The tombs in the area have long supported the illegitimate industry of the *tombaroli* (tomb robbers), who have plundered the sites for centuries and sold their discoveries on the black market. It is said that, since many tombs are still to be excavated, a good number of tombaroli remain active. Prospective buyers of illicit Etruscan artefacts should, however, beware: another notorious activity of the tombaroli is the manufacture of fake treasures.

If you have the time, a few days spent touring at least Tarquinia and Cerveteri, combined with visits to their museums and the Villa Giulia, should constitute one of your most fascinating experiences in Italy. A useful guidebook to the area, *The Etruscans*, is published by the Istituto Geografico de Agostini and has a map. If you really want to lose yourself in a poetic journey, read DH Lawrence's *Etruscan Places* (published by Penguin in *DH Lawrence and Italy*).

Tarquinia

Believed to have been founded in the 12th century BC, and home of the Tarquin kings who ruled Roma before the creation of the republic, Tarquinia was an important economic and political centre of the Etruscan League. The town has a small medieval centre with a good Etruscan museum, but the major attractions here are the painted tombs of the burial grounds.

Orientation & Information By car or bus you will arrive at the Barriera San Giusto, just outside the main entrance to the town (see the later Getting There & Away section). The

APT office (☎ 0766 85 63 84) is on your left as you walk through the medieval ramparts, at Piazza Cavour 1. It is open from 8 am to 2 pm Monday to Saturday. Tarquinia can be seen on a day trip from Roma, but if you want to stay overnight in the medieval town, it is advisable to book.

Things to See The 15th century Palazzo Vitelleschi, on Piazza Cavour, houses the **Museo Nazionale Tarquiniese** (☎ 0766 85 60 36) and a significant collection of Etruscan treasures, including frescoes removed from the tombs. There is a beautiful terracotta frieze of winged horses, taken from the Ara della Regina temple. Numerous sarcophagi found in the tombs are also on display. The museum is open from 9 am to 7 pm Tuesday to Sunday. Admission costs L8000.

The famous painted tombs are at the **necropolis**, a 15 to 20 minute walk away (get directions from the museum). It's open from 9 am to 7 pm Tuesday to Sunday and admission costs L8000. Almost 6000 tombs have been excavated, of which 60 are painted, but only a handful are open to the public. Excavation of the tombs started in the 15th century and continues today. Unfortunately, exposure to air and human interference has led to serious deterioration in many tombs and they are now enclosed and maintained at constant temperatures. The painted tombs can be seen only through glass partitions.

If you have a car, you can get to the remains of the Etruscan acropolis, on the crest of the Civita hill nearby. There is little evidence of the ancient city, apart from a few limestone blocks which once formed part of the city walls, since the Etruscans generally used wood to build their temples and houses. However, a large temple, the **Ara della Regina**, was discovered on the hill and has been excavated this century.

If you have time, wander through the pleasant medieval town of Tarquinia, where there are several churches worth a look.

Places to Stay & Eat There is a camp site, *Tusca Tirrenia* (☎ 0766 86 42 94, Viale delle Nereidi), by the sea at Tarquinia Lido,

5km from the medieval town. It's open from May to October.

There are no budget options in the old town and it can be difficult to find a room if you don't book in advance. *Hotel San Marco* (☎ 0766 84 22 34, Piazza Cavour 10), in the medieval section of town, has singles/doubles for L65,000/100,000. The *Hotel all'Olivo* (☎ 0766 85 73 18, fax 0766 84 07 77, Via Togliatti 15), in the newer part of town, a 10 minute walk downhill from the medieval centre, has singles/doubles for L70,000/ 120,000, including breakfast. Closer to the centre, but more expensive, is *Hotel Tarconte* (☎ 0766 85 61 41, fax 0766 85 65 85, Via Tuscia 19); singles/doubles cost up to L100,000/ 140,000, including breakfast. At Tarquinia Lido, *Hotel Miramare* (☎ 0766 86 40 20, Viale dei Tirreni 36) is a good budget choice. A double room costs L90,000 with bath or L70,000 without.

There are few places to eat in Tarquinia, but for a good, cheap meal go to *Trattoria Arcadia* (Via Mazzini 6). *Cucina Casareccia* is opposite at No 5.

Getting There & Away Buses leave approximately every hour for Tarquinia from Via Lepanto in Roma, near the Metro Linea A Lepanto station, arriving at Tarquinia at the Barriera San Giusto. You can also catch a train from Roma, but Tarquinia's train station is at Tarquinia Lido, approximately 3km from the centre. You will then need to catch one of the regular local buses to the Barriera San Giusto. If you are travelling by car, take the autostrada for Civitavecchia and then the Via Aurelia (S1). Tarquinia is about 90km north-west of Roma.

Buses leave from the Barriera for Tuscania, near Tarquinia, every few hours.

Cerveteri

Ancient Caere was founded by the Etruscans in the 8th century BC and enjoyed a period of great prosperity as a commercial centre from the 7th to 5th centuries BC. The main attractions here are the tombs known as *tumoli*: great mounds of earth with carved stone bases. Treasures taken from the tombs can be seen in the Musei Vaticani, the Museo di Villa Giulia and the Louvre. The Pro Loco tourist office is at Via delle Mura Castellane.

The main necropolis area, **Banditaccia** (☎ 06 994 00 01), is open from 9 am to 4 pm (to 7 pm in summer) daily except Monday. Admission costs L8000. On Saturday and Sunday, a bus leaves the medieval town from the main square at 9, 10 and 11 am; otherwise it is a pleasant 3km walk west from the town.

You can wander freely once inside the area, although it is best to follow the recommended routes to see the best-preserved tombs. One of the more interesting is the **Tomba dei Rilievi**, dating from the 4th century BC. It is decorated with painted reliefs of household items. The tomb has been closed to avoid further damage to its paintings, but can be viewed through a window. Follow the signs to the **Tomba dei Capitali** and the **Tomba dei Vasi Greci**. Signs detailing the history of the main tombs are in Italian, so it is advisable to take a guidebook.

There is also a small **museo archeologico** (☎ 06 994 13 54) with an interesting display of pottery and sarcophagi. It is on Piazza S Maria and is open from 9 am to 7 pm daily except Monday (between November and March you have to ring the bell after 2 pm). Admission is free.

Cerveteri is only 40 minutes north-west of Roma and can be reached by COTRAL bus from Via Lepanto, outside the Lepanto station on Metro Linea A. Alternatively, take the train to Ladispoli. From there, a COTRAL bus will take you the remaining 6km to the town centre. By car, take either Via Aurelia (S1) or the Civitavecchia autostrada (A12).

Veio

This was the largest of the Etruscan League cities. Its proximity to Roma meant there was a traditional rivalry between the two cities and, after a siege lasting 10 years, it finally fell under Roma's dominion in 396 BC and was destroyed. It became a *municipium* under Augustus, but eventually declined in importance and was abandoned.

Little evidence remains of the city. The only things to see are the remains of a swim-

ming pool and the lower section of a temple. However, important finds were made during excavations of the site in the 18th century, including the famous statue of Apollo, now in the Museo di Villa Giulia in Roma.

By car, leave Roma on the Via Cassia, exit at Isola Farnese and follow signs for Veio. Otherwise, take bus No 201 (for Olgiata) from Piazza Mancini, near the Ponte Milvio, to Isola Farnese and ask the bus driver to let you off at the road to Veio (although there is probably not enough to see at Veio to warrant the trouble of taking public transport).

CIVITAVECCHIA

There is little to recommend this busy port and industrial centre to tourists, other than the fact that it is the main point of departure for the daily ferries to Sardegna. Established by Emperor Trajan in 106 AD as the port town of Centumcellae, it was later conquered by the Saracens, but regained importance as a papal stronghold in the 16th century. The medieval town was almost completely destroyed by bombing during WWII. In 1995, the town hit the headlines when a 43cm-high statue of the Madonna, located in the private garden of a local family, started crying tears of blood. Originally brought from Medjugori (in the former Yugoslavia) the statue is now in the Chiesa di Sant'Agostino. Tests revealed the tears were in fact human blood and the statue continues to attract crowds of pilgrims, although Il Vaticano is yet to rule on the authenticity of the miracle.

Orientation & Information

The port is a short walk from the train station. As you leave the station, turn right into Viale Garibaldi and follow it along the seafront. The APT office (☎ 0766 2 53 48) is at Viale Garibaldi 42 and is open from 8.30 am to 1.30 pm and 4 to 7 pm Monday to Friday. It also has an information booth at the port, open from 9 am to 1 pm daily.

Places to Stay & Eat

There should be no need to spend the night in Civitavecchia. It is easily accessible from Roma, and, if you are travelling to Sardegna, it's better to catch a night ferry to save money and time. If you get stuck, try the *Hotel Traghetto* (☎ *0766 2 59 20, Via Braccianese Claudia 2*), near the port. Singles/doubles cost L85,000/109,000, breakfast included.

For food, head for a pizzerie along the waterfront, or try *Trattoria da Vitale* (☎ *0766 2 36 39, Viale Garibaldi 23*). It's not too expensive to eat on the ferry (restaurant meals and snacks are available), but it is wise to take supplies on board if you want to save money. There's a *grocery shop* near the station and a *market* every morning except Sunday on Piazza Regina Margherita in the town centre.

Getting There & Away
COTRAL buses from Roma to Civitavecchia leave from outside the Lepanto station on Metro Linea A about every 40 minutes. Civitavecchia is on the main train line between Roma (1½ hours) and Genova (2½ hours). By car it is easily reached from Roma on the A12. If arriving from Sardegna with your car, simply follow the A12 signs from Civitavecchia port to reach the autostrada for Roma.

Ferries to/from Sardegna Tirrenia operates ferries to Olbia (eight hours), Arbatax (10 hours) and Cagliari (from 14 to 17 hours). Departure times and prices change annually and it is best to check with a travel agency, or with Tirrenia directly, for up-to-date information. At the time of writing, a one-way fare to Olbia was L33,900 for a *poltrona* (airline-type seat), L49,900 for a bed in a 2nd class cabin, L64,000 for a bed in a 1st class cabin and L138,000 to take a small car.

The company operates fast boats (in summer only) from Civitavecchia to Olbia and from Fiumicino to Golfo Aranci in Sardegna. They take only 3½ to 4 hours, but are considerably more expensive than the slower ferries. It costs around L70,000 for 2nd class ticket and L150,000 for a small car. Tickets can be purchased at travel agencies, including CIT, or at the Tirrenia office in Roma (☎ 147 89 90 00), Via Bissolati 41, and at the Stazione Marittima in Civitavecchia.

The Ferrovie dello Stato (FS) also runs two daily ferries to Sardegna, docking at Golfo Aranci (about 20km north of Olbia and accessible by bus or train); the fare is only L18,000 if you are prepared to stand. The downside is that you cannot book in advance and availability cannot be guaranteed. Go to the port at Civitavecchia and try your luck.

VITERBO
Founded by the Etruscans and eventually taken over by Roma, Viterbo developed into an important medieval centre and in the 13th century became the residence of the popes.

Papal elections were held in the town's Gothic Palazzo Papale and stories abound about the antics of impatient townspeople anxious for a decision. In 1271, when the college of cardinals had failed to elect a new pope after three years of deliberation, the Viterbesi locked them in a turreted hall of the palazzo, removed its roof and put the cardinals on a starvation diet. Only then did they manage to elect Gregory X.

Although badly damaged by bombing during WWII, Viterbo remains Lazio's best-preserved medieval town and is a pleasant base for exploring northern Lazio. For travellers with less time, Viterbo is an easy day trip from Roma.

Apart from its historical appeal, Viterbo is famous for its therapeutic hot springs. The best known is the sulphurous Bulicame pool, mentioned by Dante in his *Divine Comedy*.

Orientation & Information
As is the case with most historic centres in Italy, the town of Viterbo is neatly divided between newer and older sections. Hotels are in the newer part of town; you must cross the Piazza del Plebiscito, with its palaces, before reaching medieval Viterbo and the real reason for your visit. There are train stations north and south-east of the town centre; both are just outside the town walls. The intercity bus station is somewhat inconveniently located at Riello, a few kilometres out of town.

The APT office (☎ 0761 30 47 95) is on Piazza San Carluccio, in the medieval quarter, and is open from 9 am to 1 pm and 1.30 to 3.30 pm Monday to Friday and from 9 am to 1 pm on Saturday.

The main post office is on Via F Ascenzi, just off Piazza del Plebiscito. The Telecom office is at Via Cavour 28, off the southern side of the piazza.

Things to See

Piazza del Plebiscito The piazza is enclosed by 15th and 16th century palaces, the most imposing of which is the **Palazzo dei Priori**, with an elegant 17th century fountain in its courtyard. Many rooms are decorated with frescoes, notably the Sala Reggia, which is decorated with a late Renaissance fresco depicting the myths and history of Viterbo.

Cattedrale di San Lorenzo & the Palazzo Papale The 12th century cathedral on Piazza San Lorenzo was rebuilt in the 14th century to a Gothic design, although the interior has just been restored to its original Romanesque simplicity. Also on the piazza is the Palazzo Papale, built in the 13th century with the aim of enticing the popes away from Roma. Its beautiful, graceful loggia is in the early Gothic style. The part facing the valley collapsed in the 14th century, but the bases of some of the columns remain. The hall in which papal conclaves were held is at the top of the steps. If it is not open, ask at the curia (☎ 0761 34 11 24), off the loggia.

Piazza Santa Maria Nuova The Romanesque church on this piazza was restored to its original form after bomb damage in WWII. The cloisters, which are believed to date from an earlier period, are worth a visit.

Medieval Quarter Via San Pellegrino takes you through the medieval quarter into **Piazza San Pellegrino**. The extremely well-preserved buildings which enclose this tiny piazza comprise the finest group of medieval buildings in Italy.

Other Things to See Built in the early 13th century, the **Fontana Grande**, on Piazza Fontana Grande, is the oldest and largest of Viterbo's Gothic fountains.

At the old northern entrance to the town is the **Chiesa di San Francesco**, on the piazza of the same name, a Gothic building which was restored after suffering serious bomb damage during WWII. The church contains the tombs of two popes: Clement IV (died 1268) and Adrian V (died 1276). Both tombs are lavishly decorated, notably that of Adrian, which features Cosmati work, a mosaic technique used in the 12th and 13th centuries.

There's no shortage of museums in town. The **Museo della Macchina di Santa Rosa** (☎ 0761 34 51 57), on Via San Pellegrino, documents the history of the festival that takes place on 3 September each year, when the Viterbesi parade a 30m-high tower around the town. The museum is open from 10 am to 1 pm and 4 to 7 pm Wednesday to Sunday; admission is free. The **Museo Civico** (☎ 0761 34 82 75) has reopened after a 10 year restoration project. It's housed in the convent of the Chiesa di Santa Maria della Verità, just outside the Porta della Verità, on the eastern side of town. Among the works in the museum are the lovely *Pietà* by Sebastiano del Piombo, along with a Roman sarcophagus which is said to be the tomb of Galiana, a beautiful and virtuous woman murdered by a Roman baron after she refused his advances. The museum is open from 9 am to 6 pm daily except Monday from November to March (to 7 pm from April to October) and admission costs L6000.

Places to Stay & Eat

For budget accommodation try *Hotel Roma* (☎ 0761 22 72 74, fax 0761 30 55 07, Via della Cava 26), off Piazza della Rocca. Singles/doubles cost L50,000/75,000 without bathroom and L70,000/105,000 with. Prices include breakfast. For three star accommodation there is *Hotel Tuscia* (☎ 0761 34 44 00, fax 0761 34 59 76, Via Cairoli 41); singles/doubles are L85,000/140,000, with breakfast.

For a reasonably priced meal seek out *All' Archetto* (☎ 0761 32 57 69, Via San Cristoforo), off Via Cavour. A full meal will cost around L25,000. *Il Richiastro* (☎ 0761 22 80 09, Via della Marrocca 18) serves hearty food based on ancient Roman recipes and has outside tables in summer. The speciality soups cost L8000, pasta costs from L10,000 and a meat course is around L14,000.

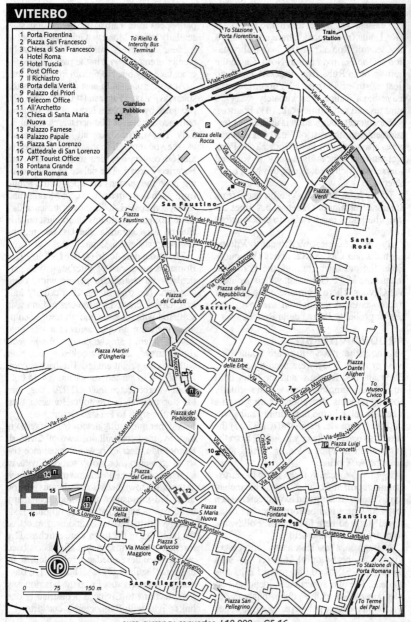

VITERBO

1 Porta Fiorentina
2 Piazza San Francesco
3 Chiesa di San Francesco
4 Hotel Roma
5 Hotel Tuscia
6 Post Office
7 Il Richiastro
8 Porta della Verità
9 Palazzo dei Priori
10 Telecom Office
11 All'Archetto
12 Chiesa di Santa Maria
   Nuova
13 Palazzo Farnese
14 Palazzo Papale
15 Piazza San Lorenzo
16 Cattedrale di San Lorenzo
17 APT Tourist Office
18 Fontana Grande
19 Porta Romana

Getting There & Away

The easiest way to get to Viterbo is by CO-TRAL bus from Roma. There are several a day, leaving Roma from the Saxa Rubra station on the Ferrovia Roma-Nord. Catch the train to Saxa Ruba from Piazzale Flaminio (just north of Piazza del Popolo). Buses leave Saxa Rubra approximately every 30 minutes and the journey takes 1½ hours.

The intercity bus station is at Riello, a few kilometres north-west of Viterbo. However, buses also stop at the Porta Romana and Porta Fiorentina entrances to the city. If you find yourself at Riello, catch city bus No 11 into Viterbo.

Trains from Roma to Viterbo leave from Stazione Termini or Ostiense, but times are irregular and it is advisable to check before you go.

By car, the easiest way to get to Viterbo is on the Via Cassia (S2, about 1½ hours). Enter the old town through the Porta Romana onto Via G Garibaldi, which becomes Via Cavour. There are numerous public car parks scattered throughout the town; the best is probably Piazza della Rocca.

AROUND VITERBO

Viterbo's **thermal springs** are about 3km west of town. They were used by both the Etruscans and Romans, and the latter built large bath complexes, of which virtually nothing remains. Travellers wanting to take a cure or relax in the hot sulphur baths will find the Terme dei Papi (☎ 0761 35 01) the easiest to reach. Take city bus No 2 from the bus station in Piazza Martiri d'Ungheria, near the APT office.

If you have a car, you can reach the **Etruscan necropoli** at Castel d'Asso. The ancient tombs are interesting and have recently been restored. Theatrical performances are occasionally staged here in summer. Follow the signs from the Terme dei Papi.

At Bagnaia, a few kilometres north-east of Viterbo, is the beautiful 16th century **Villa Lante** (☎ 0761 28 80 08), noted for its fine gardens. The two, superficially identical, palaces are closed to the public, but you can wander in the large public park for free or pay

L4000 for a guided tour of the gardens. The park opens from 9 am to one hour before sunset daily except Monday. Guided tours of the gardens leave every half hour. Unfortunately, picnics aren't allowed in the park. From Viterbo, take city bus No 6 from Piazza Caduti.

At Caprarola, south-east of Viterbo, is the splendid **Palazzo Farnese** (☎ 0761 64 60 52). Designed by Vignola, it is one of the most important examples of Mannerist architecture in Italy. You will need to wait for an attendant to take you through rooms richly frescoed in the 16th century by artists such as Taddeo and Federico Zuccari. The palace and surrounding park and gardens are open to the public from 9 am to 4 pm daily except Monday and admission costs L4000. Seven buses a day leave from the Riello bus station just outside Viterbo for Caprarola; the last bus returns from Caprarola at 6.35 pm.

The **Parco dei Mostri** (☎ 0761 92 40 29) at Bomarzo, north-east of Viterbo, will be particularly interesting for people with young children. The park of the 16th century Palazzo Orsini, created for the Orsini family, is scattered with gigantic and grotesque sculptures, including an ogre, a giant and a dragon. Also of interest are the octagonal *tempietto* (little temple) and the crooked house, built without using right angles. The park is open from 8 am to sunset; admission is L15,000. From Viterbo, catch the COTRAL bus from the stop near Viale Trento to Bomarzo, then follow the signs to Palazzo Orsini.

Another interesting detour from Viterbo is the tiny, medieval hilltop town of **Civita di Bagnoregio**, near its newer Renaissance sister, Bagnoregio (north of Viterbo). Civita, in a picturesque area of tufa ravines, is known as the dying town because continuous erosion of its hill has caused the collapse of many buildings. Abandoned by its original residents, who moved to Bagnoregio, most of the buildings in the town were purchased by foreigners and artisans and Civita has been restored and developed as a minor tourist attraction. Regular COTRAL buses serve Bagnoregio from Viterbo. From the bus stop, ask for directions to Civita; a pedestrian bridge links Civita with Bagnoregio's outskirts.

THE LAKES

There are three large lakes north of Roma, all of which are extremely popular recreational spots in summer. The lake shores never seem to get as crowded as Lazio's beaches and their hilly, leafy environment makes them more attractive swimming destinations.

Bracciano

Close to Roma, this lake is easily accessible by public transport. Visit the **Castello Orsini-Odelscalchi** (☎ 06 998 04 348) in the medieval town of Bracciano, or head straight for the lake for a swim. On the northern edge of the lake is the picturesque town of Trevignano Romano, with its pretty waterfront and modest beach.

Eat at the excellent little trattoria *Da Regina*, near the castle in Bracciano, or by the lakeside at *La Tavernetta* (☎ 06 999 90 26, Via Garibaldi 62) in Trevignano Romano.

COTRAL buses, which depart roughly every 30 minutes from outside the Lepanto Metro station in Roma, serve Bracciano directly, arriving in Piazza Roma in the middle of town, or get to Bracciano via Trevignano Romano. By car, take Via Braccianense (S493) for Bracciano or Via Cassia (S2) to Trevignano Romano.

Lago di Vico

This lake, close to Viterbo, is a nature reserve with various recreational facilities, including canoeing. At the lakeside, about 3km from the town of Caprarola, there is a camp site *Natura* (☎ 0761 61 23 47). It's only open in the summer and bookings are recommended.

From Roma, Lago di Vico isn't easy to get to by public transport. Luckily, the COTRAL bus to Caprarola passes nearby. Catch it from Saxa Rubra on the Ferrovia Roma-Nord and ask the driver when to get off. By car, take Via Cassia (S2) to Viterbo and follow signs.

Bolsena

Too far to warrant a day trip from Roma, Bolsena is, however, close to Viterbo. The town was the scene of a miracle in 1263 – a doubting priest was convinced of transubstantiation when blood dripped from the host he was holding during a mass. To commemorate the event Pope Urban IV founded the festival of Corpus Domini. The Pro Loco tourist office (☎ 0761 79 95 80) is at Piazza Matteotti 9.

There are many hotels and camp sites by the lake, including *Villaggio Camping Lido* (☎ 0761 79 92 58), and *Hotel Eden* (☎ 0761 79 90 15, Via Cassia), with singles/doubles for L60,000/90,000.

Bolsena has an interesting medieval section, with a 12th century **castle** which now houses a museum. Of particular interest are the 11th century **Chiesa di Santa Cristina** and the **catacombs** beneath it. Just before the entrance to the catacombs is the **altare del miracolo**, where the miracle of Bolsena occurred. The catacombs are noteworthy because they contain tombs which are still sealed.

If you're touring the area by car, it is worth heading on to **Montefiascone**, which is noted for its white wine, Est, Est, Est. Visit the **duomo** and the nearby Romanesque church of **Sant'Andrea**. On the Orvieto road, in Umbria, is the Romanesque church of **San Flaviano**.

In summer, COTRAL runs a direct bus service to Bolsena from Saxa Rubra in Roma; otherwise you must change at Viterbo. There are regular COTRAL buses to Bolsena from Viterbo, leaving from the Riello bus station.

SOUTH OF ROMA
The Castelli Romani

Just past the periphery of the city are the Colli Albani (Alban Hills) and the 13 towns of the Castelli Romani. A summer resort area for wealthy Romans since the days of the Empire, its towns were mainly founded by popes and patrician families. Castel Gandolfo and Frascati are perhaps the best known; the former is the summer residence of the pope and the latter is famous for its crisp white wine. The other towns are Monte Porzio Catone, Montecompatri, Rocca Priora, Colonna, Rocca di Papa, Grottaferrata, Marino, Albano Laziale, Ariccia, Genzano and Nemi.

For information visit the APT tourist office in Frascati (☎ 06 942 03 31), Piazzale Marconi 1. It is open from 8 am to 2 pm Monday to Saturday and also from 3.30 to 6.30 pm Tuesday to Friday.

The area has numerous villas, including the 16th century **Villa Aldobrandini** in Frascati, designed by Giacomo della Porta and built by Carlo Maderno, which has a beautiful garden. The ancient site of **Tusculum**, near Frascati, is preceded by a stretch of Roman road. There is little to see here, save an excellent view. At Grottaferrata there's a 15th century **abbazia** (abbey) and museum.

Nemi is worth a visit to see the pretty **Lago di Nemi**, in a volcanic crater. In ancient times there was an important sanctuary beside the lake, where the goddess Diana was worshipped. Today, very little remains of this massive temple complex, but it is possible to see the niche walls of what was once an arcade portico. New excavations at the site have just started. The incongruous-looking building at the edge of the lake, near the ruins of the temple, has an interesting story attached to it. It was built by Mussolini to house two ancient Roman boats (one 73m long, the other 71m), which were recovered from the bottom of the lake when it was partly drained between 1927 and 1932. The official story is that retreating German troops burned the ships on 1 June 1944. Locals tell a different story, but you'll have to go there to find out!

There is a delightful trattoria in the town of Nemi – *Trattoria la Sirena del Lago* (☎ *06 936 80 20*), right on the edge of a cliff and overlooking the lake. Signs will direct you there from the centre of town. A simple, but excellent, meal will cost L30,000.

It is really best to tour this area by car: you could see most of the more interesting sights on an easy day trip from Roma. However, most of the towns of the Castelli Romani, including Nemi, are accessible by COTRAL bus from the Anagnina station on Metro Linea A. Trains also leave from the Lazio platform at Stazione Termini for Frascati, Castelgandolfo and Albano Laziale, from where you could catch a bus to Nemi.

Palestrina

A town has existed here since the 7th century BC, making it one of the oldest in the region. Known in ancient times as Praeneste, it is worth visiting for the massive **Santuario della Fortuna Primigenia**. Built by the Romans on a series of terraces which cascade down the hill, the sanctuary was topped by a temple on the summit. The **Palazzo Colonna Barberini** now stands at this point and houses the **Museo Archeologico Nazionale Prenestino**, which contains an important collection of Roman artefacts. Of particular interest is the spectacular **Barberini mosaic**, dating from the second century BC. It depicts the Nile in flood and it is fascinating to study the numerous individual scenes. The view from the sanctuary is excellent and this on its own makes a visit to this town worthwhile.

Palestrina is accessible from Roma by COTRAL bus from the Anagnina station on Metro Linea A. Buses leave about every 30 minutes and the journey takes an hour.

Anagni & Alatri

These medieval towns are in an area known as the Ciociaria, 40 minutes south of Roma. **Anagni**, birthplace of several medieval popes, is of special interest for its lovely Lombard-Romanesque cathedral, built in the 11th century. Its pavement was laid in the Middle Ages by Cosmati marble workers. The crypt has an extraordinary series of vibrant frescoes, painted by Benedictine monks in the 13th century. Depicting a wide range of subjects, the frescoes are considered a major example of medieval painting at the crucial stage of its transition from the Byzantine tradition to the developments culminating in the achievements of Giotto. The frescoes have been restored and certainly warrant a day trip from Roma. The crypt's pavement was also laid by the Cosmati. Visits to the crypt can only be made with a guide, but you shouldn't need to wait longer than 10 minutes.

Alatri has a couple of interesting churches, including the 13th century Chiesa di Santa Maria Maggiore in its main piazza. Its ancient **acropolis** is ringed by huge 6th century BC walls, built by the town's original inhabitants, the Ernici.

Anagni is easily accessible from Roma's Stazione Termini on the Frosinone train line. To get to Alatri, catch the train to Anagni and then the COTRAL bus to Alatri.

Along the Coast

Beaches close to Roma include Fregene, the Lido di Ostia and the long stretch of dune-lined beach between Ostia and Anzio. However, they really are not terribly inviting and the water tends to be heavily polluted. You'll need to go further south to Sabaudia and Sperlonga to find cleaner, more attractive spots for a swim. Sabaudia has the added attraction of sand dunes and the **Parco Nazionale del Circeo**, a wetlands nature reserve along the coast. It is accessible by COTRAL bus from outside the EUR-Fermi station on Roma's Metro Linea B.

Sperlonga This small, increasingly touristy, medieval hilltop town has a pretty beach. The main attraction in the area is the **Grotta di Tiberio**, a cave with a circular pool used by the Roman emperor Tiberius. The remains of his villa are in front of the cave. Statues found in the cave are housed in the nearby museum and include a large group in the style of the *Lacoön* (in the Musei Vaticani).

If you want to stay, try the *Albergo Major* (☎ *0771 54 92 44, Via Romita I 4*). It charges L80,000/100,000, including breakfast, for a single/double in low season, and is open year-round. In high season, half board costs L110,000 per person.

To get there from Roma, take the CO-TRAL bus from the EUR-Fermi station on Metro Linea B, or catch the local train to Napoli (not the Intercity) and get off at Fondi. There are buses approximately every hour to Sperlonga from the station. Otherwise, it's about L25,000 by taxi.

Isole Pontine

International tourists are only just beginning to discover this group of small islands between Roma and Napoli. Only two of the islands – Ponza and Ventotene – are inhabited, and both are popular summer holiday spots for Italians. Ponza is the larger of the two and has a number of hotels and plenty of good restaurants. There are OK beaches at Ponza town and Le Forna, the other main settlement on the island. Ponza is ecologically in pretty poor shape. Almost every inch of the hilly island was terraced and used for farming and now suffers badly from erosion. Bird-hunting is virtually an obsession for the locals; bad news for migrating birds passing over on their journeys between Europe and Africa. Ventotene has a very small permanent population and limited accommodation facilities. Basically, neither of the islands has the fascination or wild beauty of the Isole Eolie or Isole Egadi (off Sicilia), but they're pleasant and accessible from Roma.

There's a tourist office (☎ 0771 8 00 31) in Ponza's main town. Hotels on the island include *Hotel Mari* (☎ *0771 8 01 01, fax 0771 8 02 39, Corso Pisacane 19*), in Ponza town, with singles/doubles for up to L100,000/190,000 in high season, breakfast included. However, numerous locals rent out rooms for much less and you'll find them touting at the port. An excellent place to eat is *Ristorante da Ciro* (☎ *0771 80 83 88, Via Calacaparra*), 1km or so from Le Forna. A meal of fresh seafood will cost around L40,000.

There's a regular local bus service on Ponza. Otherwise, you can hire small motorcycles at the port, either at one of the numerous outlets or from one of the touts who will meet you at the ferry. A hydrofoil runs between Ponza and Ventotene and the islands are accessible by car ferry or hydrofoil from Anzio, Terracina or Formia. Timetable information is available from most travel agencies and in summer it is also published in the *Cronaca di Roma* section of the national daily newspapers *Il Messaggero* and *Il Tempo*.

Liguria, Piemonte & Valle d'Aosta

The north-western corner of Italy has long been a political, economic and intellectual engine room for the country. It was here that the movement for Italian unity took wing; Piemonte was the cradle of Italy's industrial success and the birthplace of its labour movements, while for much of this century the Piemontese capital, Torino, has been a hotbed of intellectual activity. A little farther south, Genova was once a major city port, open to the rest of the world for centuries. Today it is regaining importance.

Torino and Genova resonate with past glories, but they are only one side of the coin. From the ski pistes and walking trails of the Valle d'Aosta and northern Piemonte to the Ligurian coast and the magic of the Cinque Terre (Five Lands), this corner of the country is a microcosm of the best Italy has to offer in natural beauty.

Liguria

The Ligurian coast was inhabited by Neanderthals about one million years ago and many remains have been unearthed in the area. The locals say these early inhabitants were lured by the beaches, which still exert a hold over the hundreds of thousands of tourists who flock to this narrow coastal region each year. There is more to Liguria, however, than its beaches. Stretching from the French border in the west to La Spezia in the east, the coast is dotted with resorts and medieval towns; the mountainous hinterland hides hilltop villages, the occasional piste and plenty of scope for walkers and climbers. Genova, regional capital and one-time sea power, is an important port and a much-overlooked attraction in its own right.

Liguria has been ruled by the Greeks, Saracens, Romans, Venetians, Lombards and

Highlights

- Explore the streets of medieval Genova

- Walk along part or all of the Grande Traversata delle Alpi

- Dodge volleys of oranges at Carnevale in Ivrea

- Contemplate the mystery of the shroud of Turin

- Stroll between the picturesque coastal villages of the Cinque Terre rounding off with dinner in Vernazza

- Tuck into a plate of trenette al pesto and a seafood main in a Genoese trattoria

- Ski the slopes at Courmayeur, or just take the Monte Bianco cable car

- Get away from it all in the Valle d'Aosta

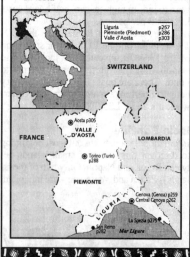

Liguria	p257
Piemonte (Piedmont)	p286
Valle d'Aosta	p303

SWITZERLAND

Aosta p305

VALLE D'AOSTA

FRANCE

LOMBARDIA

Torino (Turin) p288

PIEMONTE

Genova (Genoa) p259
Central Genova p262

LIGURIA

La Spezia p279

San Remo p282

Mar Ligure

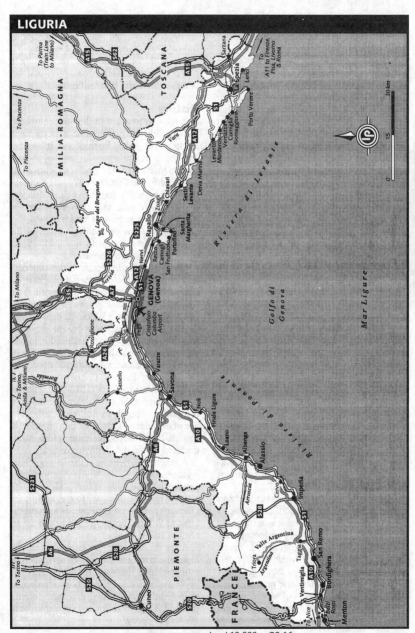

LIGURIA

French, and strong early trade influences from as far afield as Sicilia, Northern Africa and Spain are evident.

Cuisine is marked by the products of the Mediterranean climate – fresh herbs, extra virgin olive oil and seafood. Among the region's culinary creations are *pesto, focaccia* and *farinata,* a chickpea flour bread. A visit to the Cinque Terre is not complete without trying its delicious but rare dessert wine, Sciacchetrà. The Riviera di Ponente is also well known for its wine.

A railway line follows the coast from the French border to La Spezia and beyond, connecting all points along the way. By road you have the choice of good (and expensive) autostrade (the A10 west of Genova, the A12 east) or the Via Aurelia (S1), an often congested but more picturesque state highway.

GENOVA (GENOA)
postcode 16100 • pop 706,000
Travellers who write off Genova as simply a dirty port town and bypass it for the coastal resorts do the city and themselves a disservice. Once a mighty maritime republic and the birthplace of Cristoforo Colombo (Christopher Columbus), the city known as *La Superba* (literally the 'proud', 'haughty') has admittedly lost some of its gloss over the centuries, but none of its fascination. Genova might have had a still greater story behind it had the town founders seen fit to lend an ear to Colombo's exploration ideas; instead, Spain became a Renaissance superpower on the back of wealth discovered in the Americas. This didn't stop Genova from celebrating the 500th anniversary of the discovery of America with an Expo in 1992.

The labyrinth of narrow alleys at the heart of the old city, near the port, is a scrappy zone of some ill-repute, but it is undeniably interesting – full of visiting sailors, prostitutes, delinquents and longtime residents. (Spare a thought for the foreign prostitutes, mostly from Africa – they have generally been brought here under false pretences and stand condemned to years of virtual slavery to 'pay back' the people who smuggled them in.) Turn a corner and you stumble across

medieval churches or well-to-do Renaissance residences converted into museums. During the day, the seamier side of Genovese life mixes with the fashionable set. At night, however, central Genova empties and becomes a decidedly uninviting area.

History
Genova was founded in the 4th century BC and possibly derives its name from the Latin *ianua* (door). A key Roman port, it later became a mercantile power, although often subject to domination by others. Genova was occupied by the French in 774, the Saracens in the 10th century and even by the Milanese in 1353. A famous victory over Venezia in 1298 led to a period of rapid growth, but quarrels between the noble families of the city – the Grimaldis, the Dorias and the Spinolas – caused much internal disruption.

Genova reached its peak in the 16th century under the rule of imperial admiral Andrea Doria and managed to benefit from Spain's American fortunes by financing Spanish exploration. Coinciding happily with the Renaissance, Genova's golden age lasted into the 17th century and produced innumerable magnificent palaces and great works of art. The feverish activity attracted masters of the calibre of Rubens, Caravaggio and Van Dyck. Galeazzo Alessi (1512-72), who designed many of the city's splendid buildings, is regarded as highly as Andrea Palladio. The age of exploration left the writing on the wall, though, and as the Mediterraneo's importance declined, so too did Genova's fortunes.

A leading participant in the Risorgimento – the process of Italian unification and independence in the 19th century – Genova was also the first northern city to rise against the Germans and the Italian Fascists towards the close of WWII, liberating itself before the arrival of Allied troops.

After the war, the city expanded rapidly along the coast and swallowed up numerous villages along the way. However, after the boom years of the 1960s it began to decline as big industries folded and port activity dropped. The waterfront and city centre were allowed to decay.

GENOVA (GENOA)

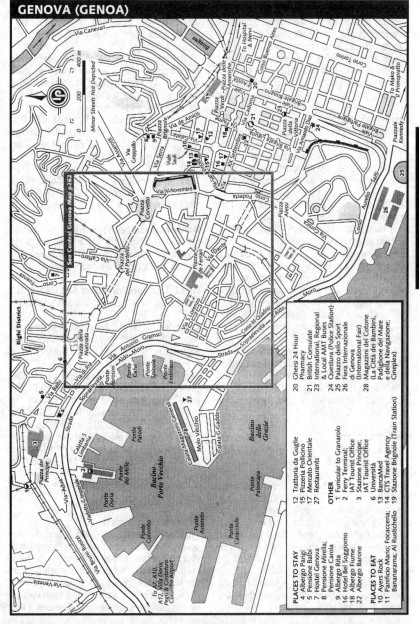

LIGURIA

PLACES TO STAY
4 Albergo Parigi
5 Pensione Balbi
8 Hostel Genova
Pensione Mirella;
Pensione Carola
9 Albergo Rita
16 Hotel Bel Soggiorno
18 Albergo Fiume
22 Albergo Barone

PLACES TO EAT
10 Ayers Rock
11 Panificio Mario; Focacceria;
Bananarama; Al Rustichello

12 Trattoria da Guglie
15 Pizzeria Pollicino
17 Mercato Orientale
27 Restaurants

OTHER
1 Funicular to Granarolo
2 Ferry Terminal;
IAT Tourist Office
3 Stazione Principe;
IAT Tourist Office
6 Università
13 BancaMed
14 CTS Travel Agency
19 Stazione Brignole (Train Station)

20 Ghersi 24 Hour
Pharmacy
21 British Consulate
23 International, Regional
& Local AMT Buses
24 Questura (Police Station)
25 Palazzo dello Sport
26 Fiera Internazionale
di Genova
(International Fair)
28 Magazzini del Cotone
(La Città dei Bambini,
Padiglione del Mare
e della Navigazione;
Cineplex)

The city may now have turned a corner. Vast amounts of money were poured into improvements for the Expo in 1992 and the largely privatised and restructured port operations are registering big increases in container business – a hopeful sign that Genova may yet recover some of its former glory as a trading port.

Orientation

Genova stretches along the Ligurian coast for some 30km and is served by 15 train stations. The city can seem overwhelming on arrival, but the centre is quite compact, tucked in between the two main train stations, Principe and Brignole. The main boulevard, Via XX Settembre, starts a short walk south-west of Stazione Brignole and spills into the city's focal point, Piazza de Ferrari. This area offers the best cheap accommodation.

West towards the port and stretching around the waterfront towards Stazione Principe are the oldest Genovese quarters, within a maze of narrow lanes or *caruggi*. Most of the city's monuments are here, but Genova is no museum – a classic and somewhat weather-beaten port, the streets hum with activity, not all of it salubrious. The Stazione Principe area, close to the port, is dodgy ground for newcomers – local buses run between it and Stazione Brignole.

It is easiest to walk around the old city as most traffic is banned from the centre. Car parks are well signposted.

Information

Tourist Offices The main IAT office (☎ 010 24 87 11) is on Palazzina Santa Maria on the waterfront near Il Bigo and is open from 9 am to 6.30 pm daily. There are branch offices at the airport, ferry terminal and Stazione Principe, open from 8 am to 8 pm Monday to Saturday, and a smaller office in Nervi, which has irregular opening hours. The tourist office Web site is at www.apt.genova.it but it's in Italian only.

Money Most banks will give cash advances and change travellers cheques, and there are plenty of ATMs all around town.

Post & Communications The main post office on Via Dante, just off Piazza de Ferrari, is open from 8.15 am to 7.40 pm Monday to Saturday.

The most central Telecom office, inside the main post office, is open from 6 am until 8.30 pm. There is another at Stazione Brignole, open from 8 am to 9.30 pm daily – it's the only one with telephone directories.

To get on line head for BancaMed (☎ 010 54 00 35) at Via San Vincenzo 101 (next to the CTS travel agency). It's open from 9 am to 7 pm Monday to Friday.

Travel Agencies CTS (☎ 010 56 43 66) is at Via San Vincenzo 119. CIT (☎ 010 29 19 53) has an office at Via XXV Aprile 16.

Bookshops Bozzi, Via Cairoli 2, has a good selection of English and French-language books. Feltrinelli's store at Via Bensa 32r also stocks a reasonable range.

Gay & Lesbian Travellers Arci Gay (☎ 010 545 02 24) is at Salita Salvator Viale 15r.

Laundry La Maddalena coin laundrette at Vico della Maddalena 2 is open from 8 am to 8 pm daily. A 7kg load costs L6000.

Medical Services & Emergency The Ospedale San Martino (hospital; ☎ 010 55 51) is at Largo Rosanna Benci 10, east of the town centre. The Guardia Medica Regione Liguria (☎ 010 35 40 22) operates an after-hours, home-visit medical service from 8 pm to 8 am. The Ghersi pharmacy (☎ 010 54 16 61), Corso Buenos Aires 18, is open 24 hours.

The questura (police station; ☎ 010 5 36 61) is on Via Armando Diaz.

Piazza de Ferrari

Flanked by the **Teatro Carlo Felice**, the imposing **Borsa** (former stock exchange) and **Palazzo Ducale**, Piazza de Ferrari is the focal point of Genova and an obvious starting place for exploration of the city. The palace, once the seat of the city's rulers, has been opened up for cultural exhibitions and houses a few good restaurants (see Restaurants in the Genova Places to Eat section).

Cattedrale di San Lorenzo

A stone's throw west of the Palazzo Ducale (Ducal Palace), the main entrance of which faces Piazza Matteotti, is the city's cathedral. Its distinctively Genovese black and white striped Gothic marble façade, fronted by twisting columns and almost gaudy decoration, is something of a shock every time you turn a corner to see it. Well, it would be if you could see any of it through the scaffolding that was there at the time of writing.

Construction and embellishments were carried out over several centuries. The cathedral was begun in the 12th century, but the bell tower and cupola weren't erected until the 16th century. Inside, **Cappella del Battista** once housed relics of St John the Baptist.

Look out for the museum in the sacristy, which houses the *Sacro Catino*, a cup allegedly given to Solomon by the Queen of Sheba and used by Jesus at the Last Supper (how did a humble prophet/deity manage to get a hold of that cup for his evening nosh-up?). Other relics include the polished quartz platter upon which Salome is said to have received John the Baptist's head. The museum is open from 9 am to noon and 3 to 6 pm daily except Sunday. Admission costs L8000.

Porta Soprana & Casa di Colombo

Head south-east from the Cattedrale di San Lorenzo through Piazza Matteotti and you'll find the impressive remains of Genova's city walls. Porta Soprana (Soprana Gate) was first built in 1155, although what you see is the restored version. In Genova's heyday the city was considered virtually impregnable on the landward side because of its walls.

Casa di Colombo, in the gate's shadow on Piazza Dante, is a much rebuilt house, said to be Colombus' birthplace, or at least the spot where his father lived. There are conflicting opinions about the authenticity of the claims.

Via Garibaldi & Palazzi

Skirting the northern edge of what were once the city limits, Via Garibaldi clearly marks a break between the Middle Ages and the Renaissance, and between poor and rich. Lined with magnificent, if somewhat blackened and unkempt, *palazzi*, it is the place to admire the pick of Genova's museums.

The **Palazzo Rosso** (the Red Palace – it was getting a much needed coat of paint at the time of writing) boasts works from the Venetian and Genovese schools and several paintings by Van Dyck. The **Palazzo Bianco** (the White Palace) features works by Flemish, Spanish and Dutch masters, displaying Genova's international cultural links, but there is plenty of home-grown material too by the likes of Caravaggio and Antonio Pisanello. Look also for Dürer's *Portrait of a Young Boy*. Both galleries are open from 9 am until 1 pm Tuesday, Thursday and Friday; from 9 am to 7 pm Wednesday and Saturday and from 10 am to 6 pm on Sunday. Admission to each costs L6000.

Many of the buildings on Alessi's grand boulevard house banks or other public facilities. Wander in if the gates are open. No 9, the **Palazzo Doria Tursi**, Genova's town hall since 1848, was built in 1564. Inside are the relics of two famous Genovese – fragments of Colombo's skeleton (!) and one of Niccolò Paganini's violins, played occasionally at concerts. The **Palazzo del Podestà**, Via Garibaldi 7, has magnificent frescoes in the courtyard.

Museums

Not far from Via Garibaldi, as you head south into the old town, is the **Galleria Nazionale di Palazzo Spinola**, Piazza Superiore di Pellicceria 1, a 16th century mansion housing Italian and Flemish Renaissance works. It is open from 9 am to 7 pm Tuesday to Saturday, 9 am to 1 pm Monday. The **Galleria di Palazzo Reale**, Via Balbi 10, also features Renaissance works. It's open from 9 am to 7 pm Wednesday to Saturday; to 1.30 pm the rest of the week. Admission to each costs L8000.

The **Museo d'Arte Orientale**, set in gardens next to Piazzale Mazzini, has one of the largest collections of Oriental art in Europe. It's open from 9 am to 1 pm daily but is

LIGURIA

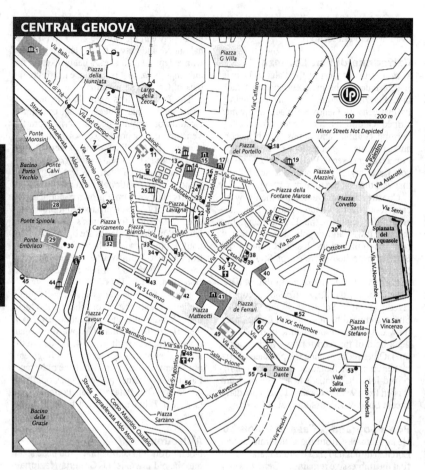

CENTRAL GENOVA

Minor Streets Not Depicted

0   100   200 m

closed Monday and Wednesday. Admission costs L6000. The city also boasts a museum of pre-Columbian art, the **Museo Americanistico F Lunardi**, in the Villa Gruber on Corso Solferino. For information on the museums in the Expo area see Porto Antico later in the chapter; for information on museums in the surrounding area, see Around Genova.

Churches

The **Santissima Annunziata del Vestato**, Piazza della Nunziata, is a rich example of 17th century Genovese architecture and is still being restored. It was virtually destroyed in WWII bombing raids. Look up at the trompe l'oeil in the dome. The **Chiesa di San Siro**, Via San Siro, also badly damaged during WWII, dates back to the 4th century but was rebuilt in the 16th century.

The **Chiesa di San Donato**, Strada S Agostino, was built in the 11th century in pure Romanesque style but was enlarged in the 12th and 13th centuries. The church of the Doria family, **Chiesa di San Matteo**, on Piazza San

LIGURIA

Matteo, was founded in 1125. Andrea Doria's sword is preserved under the altar and his tomb is in the crypt. The **Chiesa del Gesù**, also known as Chiesa di Sant'Ambrogio, is nearby on Via Soprano.

Old City

Medieval Genova is a maze of twisting lanes and dank blind alleys, the core of which is bound by Porta dei Vacca, by the waterfront Vias Cairoli, Garibaldi, XXV Aprile, and by the Porta Soprana around the inland periphery. Beyond this it straggles along the coast in both directions, especially at the northern end up the seedy Via di Prè.

The best way to explore the area is to simply wander about. Most of the prostitution and lowlife is concentrated in the zone west of **Via San Luca**, itself a hip thoroughfare full of cafés and bars with Piazza Bianchi at its southern end. East of the piazza is Via degli Orefici, where you'll find market stalls (especially good for second-hand books), more cafés and a couple of great restaurants and *pasticcerie* (cake shops). As for the narrow Via di Prè, it exerts its own lowlife 'charm'.

Though the area is so busy in daylight just about everything shuts at night. Exceptions are some fine eateries and the 24 hour prostitution and drug trade.

Porto Antico (Old Port)

The 1992 Expo left the Genovese waterfront with some lasting attractions and the area known as the Porto Antico continues to develop. In fact, anyone who has been to Barcelona will find it hard not to draw comparisons between the two cities. Genova built 'Europe's biggest aquarium', so then Barcelona had to build 'Europe's biggest aquarium' (the claim remains disputed). Barcelona converted old dockside warehouses into museums, Genova followed suit. Both have cinema complexes. On the whole, Genova's effort comes a distant second to the Spanish city, but things are way better than they were at the beginning of the 1990s. Note that the cafés around here tend to be rather cheeky – try L3500 for a *cappuccino*!

Stars of the **Acquario** include sharks, dolphins and penguins. Located on Ponte Spinola, the acquario is open from 9.30 am to

The Ocean Blue

From an early age, Cristoforo Colombo (or Christopher Columbus to English-speakers) showed signs of having a bad case of what we might call the 'travel bug'. Born in 1451 and steeped in Marco Polo's writings and Pliny's *Natural History*, he conceived an ambitious project to reach the Orient by sailing west instead of east.

Adventurous as Genova's rulers might have been, this was too much for them, so Colombo went off to look for other patrons. He first tried his luck in Portugal in 1484 but didn't do too well there either. Only after some time knocking on the appropriate door in Spain did he receive a more sympathetic hearing. He got backing from the Catholic Monarchs, Fernando and Isabel, to attempt the journey.

Cristóbal Colón, as the Spaniards know him, set off with 100 men and the three small caravels *Niña, Pinta* and *Santa Maria* on 3 August 1492. Two months later he landed in the Bahamas. Over the following eight years he discovered Cuba, Haiti, Jamaica and some of the Antilles, still convinced he was in Asia.

Sent back to Spain on charges of committing atrocities (although subsequent Spanish colonisers evidently developed a thicker skin in this regard), he was later pardoned. He made one last voyage between 1502 and 1504, tracking the central American coast and reaching Colombia. When he died, forgotten and embittered, two years later in Valladolid, Spain, he still had no idea he had discovered a new world.

Today, of course, he's everyone's hero, from Genova to the USA and from Spain to Latin America. Common lore has him as the son of various cities and, although most accept Genova as his birthplace, there are those in Barcelona, Spain, who insist he is one of theirs. As recently as 1998 a Barcelonese historian said he had sufficient evidence to back the claim. That said, the inauguration of the monument to Colombo in Barcelona in 1888 was attended by Genovese dignitaries.

NICKY CAVEN

Cristoforo Colombo discovered the New World in his caravel *Niña*.

6.30 pm Tuesday to Friday and until 8.30 pm at weekends and holidays. In summer it also opens on Monday. Admission costs L19,000.

A hundred metres south is **Il Bigo**, a derrick built for the sole purpose of hoisting a cylindrical container 200m into the air and allowing its occupants a bird's-eye view of the city. Admission costs L5000 and it operates from 11 am to 1 pm and 2.30 to 4 pm Tuesday to Saturday (until 5 pm Sunday and holidays). Behind it is an ice-skating rink, open from October to April.

The frescoed **Palazzo San Giorgio**, just back from the waterfront, has seen several changes of career over the centuries. Now home to the port authority, it was once a bank. Marco Polo was imprisoned here for a stint and spent his time working on *Il Milione*.

A recent addition to the waterfront is the **Museo Nazionale dell'Antardide**. Featuring videos of Antarctic life (you can listen in Italian, English or French), lots of displays and computers with CD-ROMs to browse through, it's an original, if unspectacular, museum about the great white continent. It is open from 9.45 am until 6.45 pm Tuesday to Saturday; from 10.30 am to 7 pm on Sunday and holidays. Admission costs L10,000.

Walk west past a series of restaurants and you come to the **Magazzini del Cotone**, the one-time cotton warehouses. This long hangar-like building has been converted into a waterside entertainment area, although the conversion seems a little half-hearted. To wander around inside is to get the impression they built the shell but have yet to get the decorators in. Be that as it may, it houses some interesting stuff. The Cineplex has nine cinemas and a few humdrum shops as well.

More engaging is the **Padiglione del Mare e della Navigazione**, a museum dedicated to Genova's proud maritime history. If you like large and intricate model ships, this is for you. If you get lucky you may get to see someone working on the restoration of one of the models. Life-sized dioramas attempt to transport you back to Genova's busy port days. It's open from 10.30 am to 6 pm Tuesday to Friday and an hour longer at weekends and holidays. Admission costs L9000.

La Città dei Bambini has games and interactive gismos thought out for children aged three to five, and a separate section for kids aged up to 14. It's open from 10 am to 6 pm daily except Monday and admission costs L8000. Anklebiters need to be accompanied by an adult. In some cases they might not get so many kicks if they don't speak Italian.

City Walls

The high country leaning protectively over the city bears a 13km long scar of city walls, built to shield the port's landward side. You can get up to the wall and inspect some of its forts. The funicular to Righi from Largo della Zecca was the preferred means for getting there from the city, but it has been shut and it is unclear for how long. The F1 bus runs from Piazza Bandiera (just east of the Santissima Annunziata del Vestato).

Organised Tours

During the summertime the Cooperativo Battellieri del Porto di Genova (☎ 010 26 57 12) runs tours of the port. These tours depart

The Genius of Genova

Born in 1782, Niccolò Paganini knew just about all there was to know about the violin by his 13th year. Two years later, after learning composition in Parma, he launched his concert career which, over the following 40 years, was to take him to every corner of Italy and to the great stages of Europe.

Paganini didn't just play a mean violin. He was a virtuoso on the guitar as well. From the violin he extracted chords, harmonies, arpeggios and rhythms hitherto undreamed of. A prolific composer, his genius was passed on for posterity – he left behind six concertos, 24 quartets for violin, viola, guitar and other strings, 12 sonatas for violin and guitar and a long list of further sonatas. Liszt and Chopin applied much of what they learned from Paganini's genius to the piano.

The virtuoso spent the last days of his restless life a little farther along the coast from his native Genova in Nice, France, where he died in 1840. He is now buried in Parma.

NICKY CAVEN

at 3.15 pm from near the aquarium and cost L10,000.

Since 1998 whale-spotting excursions have been organised by the same company, twice a week, from June to August. The excursions are organised in consultation with the Worldwide Fund for Nature and cost up to L65,000 per person.

City bus tours were scheduled to start in summer 1999, leaving Piazza Caricamento at 3.30 pm. Ask at the tourist office for details.

Places to Stay – Budget

Camping The camp sites on the outskirts of the city are all easily accessible by bus from Stazione Brignole. *Villa Doria (☎ 010 696 96 00, Via al Campeggio Villa Doria 15)*, on the way to Pegli, is open year-round and can be reached by bus No 1, 2 or 3 from Piazza Caricamento. Seven other camp sites and caravan parks are scattered along the coast on either side of the city.

Hostels The HI *Hostel Genova (☎/fax 010 242 24 57, Via Costanzi 120)* is in the Righi area, north of Genova's old centre. B&B costs L22,000 and a meal costs L14,000. Catch bus No 40 from Stazione Brignole to the end of the line or No 35 from Stazione Principe, after which you have to connect with No 40. The hostel is closed from 20 December to 1 February.

Hotels Although the old city, Stazione Principe and the port areas have a fair smattering of budget places, you'll get better value and a greater feeling of security near Stazione Brignole and Via XX Settembre. Prices given are for the high season. They generally come down a lot when things get slow.

Near Stazione Brignole are two hotels in a lovely old building at Via Groppallo 4. Turn right as you leave the train station and go up Via de Amicis to Piazza Brignole. Via Groppallo is on the right. *Pensione Mirella (☎ 010 89 37 22)* has singles/doubles at L38,000/67,000. *Pensione Carola (☎ 010 839 13 40)*, on the 3rd floor, is better, with clean, well-kept rooms for up to L50,000/80,000. Up the road at No 8, *Albergo Rita* offers a variety of

good rooms, ranging from L50,000 for a single without private bathroom to L90,000 for a double with.

Down Via Fiume in front of the Stazione Brignole station, *Albergo Fiume (☎ 010 570 54 60)* has decent, clean rooms with private bathroom costing up to L90,000.

Albergo Barone (☎ 010 58 75 78, Via XX Settembre 2/23) is not as squeaky clean but it's OK; rooms cost L60,000/80,000. You'll find four or five more options on this stretch of street as far as Piazza Santo Stefano.

If it's dirt cheap (and, in some instances, dodgy) you want, the Stazione Principe area is for you. At *Pensione Balbi (☎ 010 28 09 12, Via Balbi 21-3)* singles/doubles cost up to L65,000/90,000, or L40,000/70,000 including a communal bathroom. Several hotels in a similar category are dotted along this street; or you could go one better and head for Via di Prè. *Albergo Parigi (☎ 010 25 21 72, Via di Prè 72)* has secure rooms for L40,000/60,000.

Places to Stay – Mid-Range

For a little more money, the best option is *Hotel Bel Soggiorno (☎ 010 58 14 18, Via XX Settembre 19)*. Singles/doubles with a bathroom, TV and mini-bar start at L70,000/98,000 and rise to L125,000/160,000 in the high season.

Albergo Rio (☎ 010 29 05 51, Via Ponte Calvi 5) charges L90,000/120,000 for rooms with bathroom, TV and phone. It's an interesting part of town in which to stay.

Places to Stay – Top End

One of the grand old establishments of Genovese hospitality is *Bristol Palace (☎ 010 59 25 41, fax 010 56 17 56, Via XX Settembre 35)*. Rooms cost from L150,000 to L400,000.

Places to Eat

The bulk of the good eating is to be done in the old city, although there are exceptions. Don't leave town without trying a pasta with *pesto genovese* (a sauce of basil, garlic, parmesan cheese and pine nuts), *torta pasqualina* (made with spinach, ricotta cheese and eggs), *pansoti* (spinach ravioli with a thick, creamy hazelnut sauce), *trenette al pesto* (a spaghetti with pesto and potato) and, of course, *focaccia*. If you're cooking your own meals, stock up at the **Mercato Orientale** on Via XX Settembre.

Restaurants Via San Vincenzo, near Stazione Brignole, is a short, but busy, food street. *Al Rustichello*, at No 59r, is about the poshest joint; main courses cost L15,000 or more. For cheaper snacks go to *Panificio Mario*, at No 61, the down-to-earth *farinata* specialists *Trattoria da Guglie*, No 64; or the *focacceria* at No 61a. You could end with a delicious ice cream from *Bananarama*, at No 65.

Nearby, *Ayers Rock (Viale Sauli 33)* is a bright self-service buffet joint. *Pizzeria Pollicino (Galleria degli Artigiani 116e)* is in a tiny arcade. It has very few tables, 30 types of pizza and great *torta di verdura* (vegetarian pie).

The waterfront area around Piazza Caricamento is lined with cheap eateries and restaurants, including a couple of Chinese places. More formal, and wedged in at the corner of Via Sottoripa and Via Ponte Calvi, is *Trattoria Le Maschere*.

At *Trattoria da Maria (Vico Testa d'Oro 14)*, off Via XXV Aprile, a meal will cost you L13,000, including wine. The place exudes a simple charm.

The *Gran Caffè Roberti,* in the Palazzo Ducale on Piazza de Ferrari, offers expensive coffee but great food, including several Ligurian specialities. You can get away with about L30,000 for a meal. It should not be confused with the pricier joint upstairs.

Hidden away on the nearby Vico degli Indoratori No 5, just south of Via degli Orefici, *La Santa* is more expensive if you eat à la carte but has a reputation for good regional cooking. It offers a set menu for L20,000 (not including drinks).

Seafood is inevitably a speciality in some restaurants. The *Trattoria Vittorio (Vico del Duca 24)* offers a limited but tasty range; a full meal costs around L30,000.

Ristorante Bruno (Vico Casana 9) has a set menu for L30,000, otherwise you'll pay L50,000 for a range of Ligurian specialties.

I Tre Merli (Vico della Maddalena 26) is a charming addition to this part of town, all uncovered brick and vaults; it's great for a candlelit meal that won't cost over L40,000 per person.

The *restaurants* down on the waterfront near the Magazzini del Cotone are OK, if a little overpriced.

If you feel like heading right out of town (you'll need to take a taxi), *Il Primopiatto (Via del Tritone 12 R)*, just inland from the waterfront in the Sturla area east of the Fiera Internazionale (International Fair), is highly recommended.

Cafés & Pasticcerie Away from the waterfront, central Genova all but shuts down in the evening – 'better to go home and sleep' was the advice of one local.

Mangini & C (Via Roma), at Piazza Corvetto, is renowned as Genova's finest pasticceria. *A Ved Romanengo (Via degli Orefici 31)* has been serving scrumptious pastries since 1805. Nearby, Via San Luca and Campetto are good hunting grounds for cafés and snackbars during the day but are dead at night.

Entertainment

Theatre tickets can be booked through Box Office (☎ 010 59 01 95), Via Fieschi 20r. It is open from 11 am to 6 pm (closed 2 to 3 pm) Tuesday to Saturday.

Opera The opera house, *Teatro Carlo Felice (☎ 010 58 93 29, Piazza de Ferrari)*, opened in 1991 on the site of the original opera house (heavily bombed in WWII) and has a year-round programme.

Theatre The IAT usually has details of theatre programmes and booking details for the city's main theatres. The Genova Theatre Company performs throughout the year at the *Politeama Genovese (☎ 010 831 16 21, Via Piaggio)* and the *Teatro Di Genova (☎ 010 570 24 72, Corte Lambruschini)*. The main season runs from January to May.

The stage of *Teatro della Tosse (☎ 010 247 07 93, Piazza Renato Negri 4)* first saw

LIGURIA

action in 1702 when it was built as the Teatro Sant'Agostino. Some time later, Casanova walked the boards here.

Cinemas Three cinema clubs show films in their original language on selected nights. They are: *Cineclub Chaplin (☎ 010 88 00 69, Piazza Cappuccini 11)*; *Fritz Lang (☎ 010 21 97 68, Via Acquarone 64)*; and *Cineclub Lumière (☎ 010 50 59 36, Via Vitale 1)*.

Bars & Pubs If you like cocktails you could try *Caffetteria le Corbusier (Piazza San Donato)*, which is open until 1 am. A hushed and intimate hideaway for stolen moments over coffee or wine is *Café Madeleine (Via della Maddalena 107)*. It also serves food.

Those sick of Italian lager might pop in to the *Britannia Pub (Vico Casana)*; Guinness costs L8000 a pint.

Quite an experience is *Pub Imperiale* on Il Campeto. Enter by the easternmost door on this square and head upstairs. Observe the neglected extravagance of the ceiling. Just the setting in this extraordinary old mansion is worth the effort. Have a Tetleys and munch on some snacks.

La Polena (Vico del Filo 21r) usually stays open until 3 am and often has music to go with your drinks.

Fitzcarraldo (Piazza Cavour 35r) is also open until 3 am and has live music. Sometimes it's more like cabaret, which is an acquired taste – but at least you can drink.

Discos & Clubs This kind of thing is not Genova's forte. A popular disco is *Mako (Corso Italia 28r)*. You can find a few others, especially in the summer, farther south-east along the waterfront in the Lido area. The bulk of discos and clubs are well out of town.

Getting There & Away

Air The Cristoforo Colombo international airport at Sestri Ponente, 6km west of the city, has regular domestic and international connections but, for flights outside Italy, Milano and Pisa have cheaper options. For general flight information telephone ☎ 010 6 01 51, or call your airline direct.

Bus Buses to international cities go from Piazza della Vittoria, as do limited interregional services and buses for other points in Liguria.

Train Genova is linked by train to Torino, Milano, Pisa and Roma and it makes little difference which of the two train stations (Principe or Brignole) you choose, except for trips along the two Rivieras. Going west to San Remo and Ventimiglia, for example, there are more departures from Stazione Principe than from Brignole.

Car & Motorcycle The A12 connects Genova with Livorno in Toscana and with the A11 for Firenze. The A7 goes to Milano, the A26 to Torino and the A10 to Savona and the French border. Hitchhikers will probably have more luck on the S1 heading in either direction along the coast, or the S35 heading north to Alessandria (and on to Torino). Drivers who hate tolls and are in no hurry should also consider these roads.

Boat The city's busy port is an important embarkation point for ferries to Spain, Sicilia, Sardegna, Corsica and Elba. Most of the maritime activity is from June to September only. All prices given are for one-way, low-season, deck-class tickets; unless mentioned otherwise the boats depart from the main terminal building on Ponte dei Mille. Major companies are:

Corsica Marittima
    (☎ 010 58 95 95) c/o GSA/Cemar, Via XX Settembre 2-10. A subsidiary of SNCM this company sails to Corsica (L34,000 to Bastia).
Grandi Navi Veloci (Grimaldi group)
    (☎ 010 58 93 31) Via Fieschi 17. It has luxury ferries to Sardegna (to Porto Torres or Olbia costs L73,000); Sicilia (to Palermo L123,000) and Spain (to Barcelona costs L98,000). The services to Spain and Sicilia are year-round; to Sardegna they run during the summer only. The ferries leave from Ponte Assereto.
Moby Lines
    (☎ 010 25 27 55) Ponte Assereto. It sails to Corsica (L37,500 to Bastia) and Sardegna via Corsica (overland between Bastia and Bonifacio). The services run from March to September.
SNCM Ferryterranee
    (☎ 010 58 95 95) c/o GSA/Cemar, Via XX Set-

tembre 2-10. It offers a service to Tunisia (Tunis L198,000). The service runs weekly from late June to late September.

Tirrenia
(☎ 010 275 80 41) Ponte Colombo. Ferries and high speed boats operate to Sardegna (Cagliari, Porto Torres, Olbia or Arbatax – to Olbia fares are L46,000); connect to Sicilia from Sardegna.

See the Sicilia and Sardegna Getting There & Away sections for more route details.

Ferries serve towns on the Riviera di Levante, including Camogli, Portofino, Santa Margherita, the Cinque Terre, and San Fruttuoso, from June to September. Cooperativa Battellieri del Golfo Paradiso (☎ 010 577 20 91) ferries sail from a quay in the Mandraccio quarter of the Porto Antico. Alimar (☎ 010 25 67 75) runs Marexpress, a summertime catamaran service to Portofino and Monte Carlo. Frequency depends largely on demand.

Getting Around

To/From the Airport An airport bus service, the AMT's Volabus, leaves from Piazza Verdi, outside Stazione Brignole, and stops at Stazione Principe. It costs L4000.

Bus AMT (☎ 010 599 74 14) operates buses throughout the city. Main termini include the two train stations, Piazza della Vittoria and Piazza Caricamento. A ticket valid for 90 minutes costs L1500; an all-day ticket is L5000. The tickets can also be used on mainline trains within the city limits (as far as Voltri and Nervi).

Taxi For taxis, call Radiotaxi on ☎ 010 59 66.

AROUND GENOVA

Hidden behind the industrial wasteland of Genova's west is **Pegli**, a victim of the city's growth. It lies in a sheltered harbour and offers magnificent views of the city and coastline. The Museo Navale is in the Villa Doria at Piazza Bonavino. The Museo Archeologico, in the Villa Pallavicini on Via Pallavicini, presents a comprehensive overview of Ligurian prehistory. The villa itself is set in a magnificent park modelled on the Genovese gardens of the Renaissance.

At the eastern edge of Genova, **Nervi** has also been absorbed by the growing city. Renowned for its outdoor Festival Internazionale del Balleto at the Teatro ai Parchi in July and an outdoor cinema in the rose garden (Cinema nel Roseto) at the same venue in August, Nervi still manages to retain its own identity. It also boasts the **Museo d'Arte Moderna** (which was closed at the time of writing).

Recco, a little farther east, is the scene of an enormous fireworks display in the first week of September. It goes on for three nights running as part of the Festa della Madonna, which culminates in a grand religious procession on Sunday. Take a train there, as traffic is so tight you could spend all evening in search of a parking spot.

RIVIERA DI LEVANTE

The coast east of the portside sprawl of Genova is not as heavily developed as the area west of the city and even rivals Campania's Costiera Amalfitana in beauty. A sprinkling of small resorts and villages, especially the Cinque Terre, retain a real charm despite their evident popularity, and the surrounding countryside is visually dramatic.

Camogli

Wandering through the alleyways and the long, cobbled streets of Camogli, it is hard not to be taken aback by the painstaking trompe l'oeil decoration – house after house sports meticulously painted columns, balustrades and even windows. This is a feature of many Ligurian towns but Camogli seems to take special pride in this genre of civic art. The esplanade, Via Garibaldi, is a colourful place for a stroll and really comes to life on the second Sunday in May, when local fishermen celebrate the Sagra del Pesce (Fish Festival), frying hundreds of fish for all and sundry in 3m-wide pans along the waterfront.

Camogli means 'house of wives', taking its name from the days when the women ran the town while their husbands were at sea. The town was also a strong naval base and once boasted a fleet larger than Genova's.

Information To the right when leaving the train station is the APT office (☎ 0185 77 10 66) at Via XX Settembre 33. It's supposed to be open from 8.40 am to 12.10 pm and 3.40 to 6.10 pm Monday to Saturday, but don't bet on it.

Activities Luigi Simonetti Nautica (☎ 0185 77 19 21), Via Garibaldi 59, hires out canoes, pedal boats, rowing boats and motorboats.

Places to Stay & Eat Prices given are high season single/double. *Albergo la Camogliese* (☎ *0185 77 14 02, Via Garibaldi 55*) has rooms from L90,000/110,000. The *Augusta* (☎ *0185 77 05 92, Via P Schiaffino 100*) charges upwards of L90,000/120,000, while the *Selene* (☎ *0185 77 01 49, Via Cuneo 15*) has rooms for L65,000/115,000.

Like accommodation, eating out is costly, with most waterfront restaurants charging high prices for ordinary food. Try *Il Faulo* (*Via Garibaldi 98*), which specialises in Genovese fare and has a vegetarian menu; pasta starts at around L13,000. Smaller, less expensive trattorie are tucked in the lanes away from the water, so you'll need to explore.

Getting There & Away Camogli is on the Genova-La Spezia train line and services are regular. Tigullio buses head for Rapallo and Santa Margherita every 20 minutes (L1400) and for Portofino Vetta along a pretty drive known as La Ruta. Drivers can reach Camogli from the A12 or the Via Aurelia (S1). In summer ferries connect Camogli with other towns on the Portofino promontory and the Cinque Terre.

Santa Margherita
postcode 16038

In a sheltered bay on the eastern side of the Portofino promontory on the Golfo di Tigullio, Santa Margherita is an attractive resort town and a potential base for exploring the area. From the jumble of one-time fishing families' houses on the waterfront you can admire the million-dollar yachts at their moorings.

Once home to a considerable coral-fishing fleet that roamed as far afield as Africa, Santa Margherita is now better known for its orange blossoms and lace.

From the train station, head downhill to the port, then along Via Gramsci to Piazza Caprera, from where most buses depart.

Information The IAT office (☎ 0185 28 74 85), at Via XXV Aprile 4 just off Piazza Caprera, is open from 8.30 am to 12.30 pm and 3.30 to 6.30 pm daily (from 9.30 am to 12.30 pm on Sunday and holidays).

The post office is at Via Roma 36 and is open from 8.10 am to 5.30 pm Monday to Friday and Saturday morning.

For medical help Ospedale Civile di Rapallo (☎ 0185 68 31) is at Rapallo in Piazza Molfino. For an ambulance call ☎ 0185 66 91 60 (Croce Rossa); for a night doctor (Guardia Medica) call ☎ 010 35 40 22.

Activities Santa Margherita is a sports playground and the list of activities you'll find includes sailing, water-skiing and diving. Ask at the IAT office, the big hotels or on the waterfront for information – and have a fat wallet handy.

Places to Stay & Eat A clean well-lit place handy to the centre is *Albergo Annabella* (☎ *0185 28 65 31, Via Costasecca 10*), just off Piazza Mazzini, where rooms cost up to L65,000/95,000. At about the same prices, *Albergo Azalea* (☎ *0185 28 81 60, Via Roma 60*) is not as appealing but handy for the train station.

At *Trattoria San Siro* (*Corso Matteotti 137*), 15 minutes up from the seashore, a full meal will cost around L35,000. Try the *pansoti* (round ravioli). At *Ristorante da Alfredo* (*Piazza Martiri della Libertà 38*), near the water, pizzas start at L7000; it's one of many similar places on the esplanade. *Simonetti* (*Via Bottaro 51*) serves good *gelati*.

Getting There & Around Santa Margherita is on the Genova-La Spezia railway line. The A12 passes Rapallo before cutting inland towards Santa Margherita. Viale E Rainusso, which runs off Piazza Vittorio Veneto, joins the Via Aurelia (S1), the secondary road to Genova. Buses leave Piazza Martiri della Libertà for Portofino and Rapallo (every 20 minutes, L1400).

In summer, the Servizio Marittimo del Tigullio (☎ 0185 28 46 70) runs ferries to Portofino (L10,000 return). Other ferries go to San Fruttuoso (L19,000 return) from near the bus stop and the Cinque Terre (L35,000 return). Some services begin in spring and continue into October but dry up in winter.

You can hire bicycles and motor scooters at Agrifogli (☎ 0185 28 70 45), Piazza Martiri della Libertà 40, or from a place opposite the IAT office.

Paraggi

Two kilometres north of Portofino, there's little at Paraggi but a few hotels and one of the area's few slivers of white, sandy beach.

Portofino

Dubbed by the Italian press the 'richest promontory in Italy', Portofino is home (or holiday home) to the mega-rich and powerful. Anyone who is anyone has a villa here, and a host of movers and shakers wheel, deal and play in Portofino.

A certain haughty disdain on the part of many long-standing residents lends the town a healthy air of restraint, and the huddle of pastel-coloured houses around the modest portside piazza is a delight. In summer the piazza, fronted by unassuming but expensive cafés and boutiques, is full of the glitterati, attracted to the most chichi spot in all of Liguria.

OK, it *is* all very nice, but you have to question the motives of the individual responsible for the overblown official sign as you enter town: *Portofino – Gioiello del Turismo Europeo* (Portofino – Jewel of European Tourism). Oh please.

Information The IAT office (☎ 0185 26 90 24), Via Roma 35, just back from the port, is open from 9 am to noon and 3 to 6 pm daily. It can advise on water sports and accommodation, which is scarce and expensive.

Things to See & Do Near the **Chiesa di San Giorgio** a flight of stairs leads up to the 16th century **castle** of the same name. Built over an existing fort by the Genovese, under some pressure from their Spanish allies. The castle occasionally saw action, particularly when occupied by Napoleon and taken by the English in 1814. It offers a great view, but for an even better outlook continue to the **lighthouse**; it's an hour's walk there and back.

Boats can be hired from Giorgio Mussini & C (☎ 0185 26 93 27), Calata Marconi 39.

Places to Stay & Eat The 'cheapest' lodgings are at the *Eden (☎ 0185 26 90 91, Vico Dritto 18)*; singles/doubles cost L160,000/ 200,000 (and rates almost double in high season). The cover charge alone at most restaurants would equal some travellers' daily meal allowance, while a cup of coffee at a table will cost L5000 or more at the waterfront cafés. Don't despair. At *Pizzeria El Portico (Via Roma 21)*, pizzas start at L8000 and the *Panificio Canale*, at No 30, serves decent pastries for about L3000 a slice.

Getting There & Away Portofino can be reached by bus from Santa Margherita and in summer ferries crisscross the gulf from most towns along the coast (see Getting There & Around under Santa Margherita for more details). Drivers must park at the entrance to the town (L7500 for the first hour) as cars are banned farther in.

San Fruttuoso

San Fruttuoso is a fascinating village dominated by the **Abbazia di San Fruttuoso di Capodimonte**, a Benedictine abbey with medieval origins. Built as a resting place for bishop St Fructuosus, martyred in Spain in 259, it was rebuilt in the mid-13th century with the assistance of the Doria family, who used it as a family crypt. It fell into decay with the decline of the religious community and in the 19th century was divided into small living quarters by local fishermen. It's open from 10 am to 6 pm Tuesday to Sunday in summer (until 4 pm in winter, closing altogether in November). Admission is L5000.

LIGURIA

Perhaps more fascinating is the bronze statue of Christ, *Il Cristo degli Abissi*, lowered 15m to the sea bed by locals in 1954 as a tribute to divers lost at sea and to bless the waters. You must dive to see it, but locals say it can be viewed from a boat if the waters are calm. A replica, in a fish tank, is on display in the church adjoining the abbey. A religious ceremony is held over the statue each August.

San Fruttuoso is accessible either by foot from Camogli or Portofino (an exhilarating cliffside walk that takes up to 2½ hours each way from either town), or by ferry (summer only from Santa Margherita and Portofino, year-round from Camogli).

Rapallo

Rapallo is a major resort but is often overlooked for the more illustrious Santa Margherita and Portofino. A bigger place, it has an air of bustle independent of tourists that the towns farther down the promontory lack – all the more so on Thursday, which is market day at Piazza Cile.

With its Roman origins, Rapallo boasts a bridge supposedly used by Hannibal during the Carthaginian invasion of Italy in 218 BC.

More recently, Rapallo enjoyed a brief period of international popularity in the treaty-signing business. In 1920, the Italo-Yugoslav Treaty that defined the borders of the two countries was signed here; two years later the Russians and Germans sealed a peace deal that lasted all of 19 years.

Information The IAT office (☎ 0185 23 03 46), Via Diaz 9, opens from 9.30 am to 12.30 pm and 3.30 to 6.30 pm daily (Sunday morning only).

Things to See & Do A *funivia* (cable car) goes to **Montallegro**, a sanctuary built on the spot where, on 2 July 1557, the Virgin Mary was reportedly sighted. For the funivia follow signs from Corso Assereto; a circuitous 10km road also reaches the site. Just off the Lungomare Vittoria Veneto is a 16th century **castle**.

You can join up for PADI dive courses with Marco Maglia (☎ 0185 26 04 98) or just call for advice on dive sites.

Places to Stay & Eat For the camp sites in the hills near Rapallo take the Savagna bus from the train station. *Miraflores* (☎ 0185 26 30 00, Via Savagna 10) is open from April to October and *Rapallo* (☎ 0185 26 20 18, Via San Lazzaro 4) is open only in summer. The best of the budget hotels in Rapallo is *Bandoni* (☎ 0185 5 04 23, Via Marsala 24), right on the waterfront, where singles/doubles start at L42,000/72,000. If money is the biggest obstacle then maybe the no-frills *Giardino* (☎ 0185 5 07 86, Via Venezia 103) is for you. It is nothing special but rooms cost just L27,000/48,000.

At *Vesuvio (Lungomare Vittorio Veneto 29)* pizzas start at L8000. A more intimate atmosphere makes the *Hostaria Vecchia Rapallo (Via Fratelli Cairoli 24)*, a block farther back from the water, a pleasant alternative. Main courses here cost about L25,000. Another good option is *Trattoria Genovese (Corso Roma 19)*, where a meal shouldn't cost more than around L40,000.

Getting There & Away Regular buses connect Rapallo with Santa Margherita (every 20 minutes, L1400) and Camogli. The trip is more pleasant by bus than by train. For more information see the Santa Margherita section earlier in this chapter.

Chiavari to Levanto

The stretch of coast between the Portofino promontory and the Cinque Terre can come as a bit of a letdown, wedged as it is between two such beauty spots. It does have some of the Riviera di Levante's best beaches, but the resorts of Sestri Levante, Deiva and Levanto become predictably crowded in summer.

Cinque Terre

If you miss the five villages which make up the mountainside Cinque Terre – Monterosso, Vernazza, Corniglia, Manarola and Riomaggiore – you will have bypassed some of Italy's most extraordinary countryside. But blink as the train zips between tunnels and miss them you will.

The mountains, covered wherever possible by terraced vineyards (the locals have set up ingenious monorail mechanisms to ferry themselves up and the grapes back down), do precipitously into the Mediterraneo. They leave little room for the tiny fishing villages that clutter the coves, are tucked into ravines or perched on top of sharp ridges. Fishing and viniculture have been the two main sources of income over the centuries, but tourism now plays a pivotal role too. The position of the villages has hopefully saved them from the thoughtless resort development that blights much of the Ligurian coast.

Oddly, the area is more popular with foreign visitors than Italian tourists. This means that from April until October accommodation can be hard to find, even mid-week. Plenty of locals rent out rooms on a more or less official basis – if you miss the telltale signs, *camere* (rooms) and *affittacamere* (rooms for rent), ask around in the bars. If you fail to find something in the prettiest of the villages, Vernazza and Corniglia, use the handy trains to move to the others and try your luck again.

Prices are not low but neither are they extortionate. Food isn't cheap either, and often mediocre. Try to lay your hands on some local vintages, such as the nationally renowned white and dessert wines *Morasca, Chiaretto del Faro*, and the heavenly, sweet *Sciacchetrà*.

You can drive to all five villages but cars are not permitted beyond the entrance to each town (which can mean a hike of up to 1km). The local La Spezia-Genova trains are regular and by far the most convenient way to get to and around the Cinque Terre.

For those with the time there is a scenic path, known as the Via dell'Amore (Lovers' Lane), connecting all the villages. The going can get strenuous at times, but reasonably fit walkers can cover it fairly comfortably in five or so hours. The stretch between Monterosso and Vernazza is the least scenic and the most difficult. Farther along, the dramatic views of the towns and coast should compensate for any sweat and tears. You'll be pleased you brought some swimming gear too, because the water in some of the pretty little coves is crystal clear.

Monterosso Huge statues carved into the rocks overlook one of the few decent sized beaches in the Cinque Terre, a grey, pebbly affair. Monterosso gets its name from the unusual red colouring of the nearby cliff faces, but it's the least attractive of the villages; it's expensive too. At *Albergo Punta Mesco* (☎ *0187 81 74 95, Via Molinelli 35*), just past the railway bridge and a few minutes walk from the beach, singles/doubles will cost L70,000/110,000 in the high season. The beachside hotels start at about L100,000 for a single with breakfast in the high season.

Vernazza Possibly the most fetching of the villages, Vernazza makes the most of the sea, with a promenade and piazza on the water. The road winding away from the centre is choked with tiny vineyards and patches of lemon grove. Head for the **Castello Doria**, which has sweeping views of the town and surrounding coast from its tower. The main drag, Via Roma, has a laundrette (No 49) and email services at Bar Marlin (No 43).

Albergo Barbara (☎ *0187 81 23 98, Piazza G Marconi 30*) has singles/doubles costing L80,000/90,000 in the high season. *Pensione Sorriso* (☎ *0187 81 22 24, Via Gavino 4*) offers rooms with breakfast for L70,000/90,000. At least half a dozen affittacamere operate in Vernazza. Up on the path to Corniglia is *Ristorante La Torre* (☎ *0187 82 10 82*), which charges up to L100,000 for two people. Some of these places will only take week-long bookings between July and August. Ristorante La Torre isn't a bad place to eat either; otherwise you have several choices clustered about the tiny port.

Corniglia Balanced precariously along a ridge high above the sea, Corniglia is quite an uphill hike from the train station. Four-storey houses, narrow lanes and stairways are woven together on the hill and topped by **La Torre**, a medieval lookout from which you can look south-east to Manarola.

On the path to Manarola, behind the train station, is *Villaggio Marino Europa* (☎ *0187 81 22 79*), a row of self-contained bungalows sleeping up to six people. Open from June to the end of September (cheapest in June and September), they can be rented for a minimum of three days. Local wine grower Domenico Spora (☎ 0187 81 22 93) is just one of several people offering rooms – a quick walk around town will throw up several options. Spora's rooms cost as much as L90,000 for a double in high summer. *A Cantina de Mananan (Via Carruggio 117)* is a cosy little osteria where pasta dishes start at L10,000 and seafood dishes at L17,000.

Manarola Lacking some of the atmosphere of Corniglia and Vernazza, Manarola is nonetheless a captivating village. If you're game for a good uphill walk, take the path off Via Rollandi, near Piazza Castello, through vineyards to the top of the mountain. On a clear day you can see all the villages. *Ostello 5 Terre (☎ 0187 92 02 15, Via Riccobaldi 21)* charges L25,000 per person. In summer you may need to book a month ahead.

Riomaggiore The Via dell'Amore straggles along the cliffside from Manarola to Riomaggiore – a mess of houses slithering down a ravine that forms the main street, with tiny fishing boats lining the shore and stacked in the small square. The older part of town is a few minutes walk south of the train station, through a long tunnel.

More than half a dozen affittacamere are available, some along Via Colombo. *Agostino Franceschetti (☎ 0187 92 00 26, Via del Santuario 96)* offers doubles costing L70,000 in high season. Single occupancy costs less in low season. *Luca Giaccio (☎ 0187 92 03 25, Via Colombo 148)* charges from L80,000 to L90,000 for doubles.

Most restaurants are along Via Colombo, which runs from the waterfront through the centre of the village. Try *Veciu Muin (Via Colombo 83)* for a good pizza. A meal at *La Lanterna*, overlooking the cove, costs about L35,000 a head.

La Spezia
postcode 19100
La Spezia sits at the head of the gulf of the same name – also known as the Gulf of Poets,

in deference to Byron, Dante, DH Lawrence, Shelley, George Sand and others drawn here by its beauty. A decision late in the 19th century to establish Italy's largest naval base here propelled La Spezia from minor port to busy provincial capital; the street grid and venerable public buildings are largely a product of that time. It's still a navy town, with the ubiquitous blue sailor's uniform a constant reminder.

Orientation The city of La Spezia is sandwiched between the naval base to the west and the commercial port to the east. The main street and scene of the ritual *passeggiata* (evening stroll) is the narrow Via Prione, running from the train station to the palm-lined Viale Italia on the waterfront.

Information The IAT office (☎ 0187 77 09 00), Viale G Mazzini 47, is open from 9.30 am to 12.30 pm and 2.30 to 5.30 pm Monday to Saturday. There is another office (☎ 0187 71 89 97) at the train station.

The post office, on Piazza di Giuseppe Verdi, is open from 8.15 am to 7.40 pm Monday to Saturday. An unstaffed Telecom office at Via da Passano 40 is open from 7 am to 10 pm daily.

For medical help out of hours call ☎ 0187 50 77 27. The questura (☎ 0187 53 01) is well away from the centre at Viale Italia 497.

Things to See The star attraction is the **Pinacoteca Civica Amedeo Lia**, on the corner of Via Prione and Via del Vecchio Ospedale. This private art collection contains some 2000 works by such masters as Tintoretto, Tiepolo, Titian, Veronese, Bellini and Sansovino. It's open from 10 am to 6 pm Tuesday to Sunday and admission costs L12,000.

Across the canal from Piazza Domenico Chiodo the **Museo Navale** opens from 2 to 6 pm Monday and Friday, from 8.30 am to 1.15 pm on Sunday and from 9 am to noon and 2 to 6 pm during the rest of the week. Admission costs L2000. Founded in 1870 following the transfer of the Genovese maritime museum to La Spezia, it hosts a phalanx of *polene*, the colourful busts or

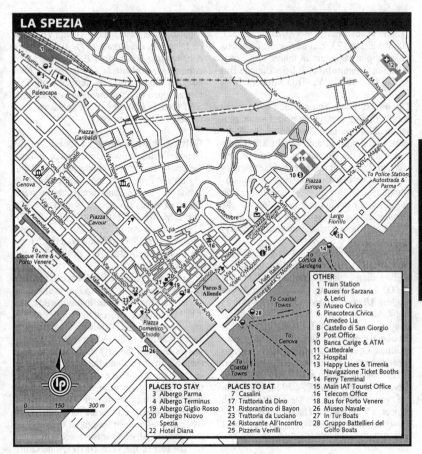

LA SPEZIA

LIGURIA

OTHER
1 Train Station
2 Buses for Sarzana & Lerici
5 Museo Civico
6 Pinacoteca Civica Amedeo Lia
8 Castello di San Giorgio
9 Post Office
10 Banca Carige & ATM
11 Cattedrale
12 Hospital
13 Happy Lines & Tirrenia Navigazione Ticket Booths
14 Ferry Terminal
15 Main IAT Tourist Office
16 Telecom Office
18 Bus for Porto Venere
26 Museo Navale
27 In Tur Boats
28 Gruppo Battellieri del Golfo Boats

PLACES TO STAY
3 Albergo Parma
4 Albergo Terminus
19 Albergo Giglio Rosso
20 Albergo Nuovo Spezia
22 Hotel Diana

PLACES TO EAT
7 Casalini
17 Trattoria da Dino
21 Ristorantino di Bayon
23 Trattoria da Luciano
24 Ristorante All'Incontro
25 Pizzeria Verrilli

statuettes that graced the prows of vessels, and lots of model ships. The adjoining naval base opens to the public on one day each year, 19 March, the festival of the town's patron saint, San Giuseppe.

The most interesting part of the **Museo Civico**, Via Curtatone 9 off Corso Cavour, is the archaeology department, with its hotchpotch of Bronze Age and Iron Age relics and squat, ancient Ligurian *statue-stelae*. It opens from 8.30 am to 1 pm and 2 to 7 pm Tuesday to Sunday. Admission costs L6000.

Activities La Spezia has several walking clubs that offer information on medium to long walks around the coast and into the mountains. Natura Trekking (☎ 0187 50 42 64), Via Bragarina 56/9, can help with maps and information.

The province, which takes in Calice, Luni and Varese Ligure, has more than a dozen horse-riding clubs and many tracks. Ask at the IAT for information on farms that organise horse riding; some offer accommodation, but you don't have to stay overnight.

Scuba diving is popular. The Federazione Italiana Pesca Sportiva (☎ 0187 51 12 22), Via V Veneto 173, can advise on locations and hire places, or get in touch with European Sea Organisation Club Spedizione Blu (☎ 0187 77 04 00), Via Don Minzoni 2.

Places to Stay You shouldn't have any trouble finding reasonably priced accommodation in La Spezia, unless you want a single room – seemingly in short supply. The town's proximity to the Cinque Terre, Porto Venere and Lerici makes it a perfect base, especially as the limited accommodation in the surrounding area often fills up. There is no camp site in La Spezia, but there are plenty in the surrounding towns. You might also ask at the IAT office about *agriturismo* (farm holiday) options.

Albergo Giglio Rosso (☎ 0187 73 13 74, Via Carpenino 31) has perfectly adequate, if slightly dingy, singles/doubles at L35,000/ 55,000 – you'll probably be told there are no singles. *Albergo Nuovo Spezia (☎ 0187 73 51 64, Via Felice Cavallotti 31)* is one block away; rooms cost up to L43,000/55,000 without own bathroom; slightly more with private facilities. Opposite the train station, *Albergo Terminus (☎ 0187 70 34 36, Via Paleocapa 21)* has rooms starting at L37,000/55,000. At *Albergo Parma (☎ 0187 74 30 10, Via Fiume 143)* rooms start at L55,000/90,000, all with shower, TV and phone. *Hotel Diana (☎ 0187 73 40 97, Via Colombo 30)*, near the naval base, usually has doubles only from L80,000.

Places to Eat A *produce market* is held daily on Piazza Cavour, and there's plenty of restaurants, cafés and bars along Via Prione.

For a filling pizza, try *Pizzeria Verrilli (Piazza Domenico Chiodi 32)*, one of a couple of places on the square. It sells generous *pizzette* (good for one person) for about L8000.

Ristorantino di Bayon (Via Felice Cavallotti 23) has a set menu, including wine, that costs L28,000, or you can go à la carte and try the *pennette al salmone norvegese affumicato* (pasta with smoked Norwegian salmon). *Trattoria da Luciano (Via Colombo 27)* offers copious amounts of food for as little as

L20,000. If you want good seafood at a reasonable price, head for the Tuscan *Trattoria da Dino (Via Da Passano 17)*. At *Ristorante All'Incontro (Via Sapri 10)*, tuck into a first course of *spaghetti alla chitarra ai 'batti batti' di Monterosso* (chunky spaghetti in a sauce topped with flavoursome local sea critters) for L14,000. For bread or pastries, try *Casalini (Via Prione 191)*.

Getting There & Away La Spezia is on the Genova-Roma railway line, which follows the coast, and is also connected to Milano, Torino and Pisa. The Cinque Terre and other coastal towns are easily accessible by train, but other towns close to La Spezia can only be reached by ATC buses (☎ 0187 52 25 22). These include Porto Venere (from Via Domenico Chiodo), Sarzana and Lerici (both from the train station). Buy your tickets from the town's tobacconists.

The A12 runs past La Spezia to Genova and Livorno and the A15 to Parma also connects with the main north-south route, the A1. Hitchhikers can catch the Lerici bus and get off at Via Valdilocchi in the port area for access to the A12 and A15. The S1 passes through the city and connects with the S62 for Parma and the north.

Cyclists might like to know that most trains passing through the Apenninni to Parma have bicycle storage.

Ferries depart La Spezia for Genova and other coastal towns throughout the summer and occasionally on pleasant weekends during the rest of the year. Navigazione Golfo dei Poeti (☎ 0187 96 76 76; which has its office in Lerici), Gruppo Battellieri del Golfo (☎ 0187 2 10 10) at Banchina Revel and In Tur (☎ 0187 73 29 87) at Viale Mazzini 21, off Passeggiata C Morin, all run services.

Happy Lines (☎ 0187 56 45 30), Largo Fiorillo, runs ferries to Bastia in Corsica daily from April to October. Tirrenia operates fast summer services to Sardegna. Contact any travel agency.

Porto Venere

It is worth catching the bus from La Spezia for the razor-clam soup Porto Venere has contributed to Ligurian fare. The Romans built Portus Veneris on the western shore of the Golfo della Spezia as a base on the route from Gaul to Spain. From the brightly coloured houses along the waterfront, narrow steps and cobbled paths lead up the hillside towards the **Chiesa di San Lorenzo**, erected in the 12th century and subsequently altered. It lies in the shadow of **Castello Doria**, built in the 16th century on the site as part of the Genovese Republic's defence system. The views from its magnificent terraced gardens are superb.

At the end of the waterfront quay is the 13th century **Chiesa di San Pietro**, built in the Genovese Gothic style with black and white bands of marble, and the **Grotta Arpaia**, once a haunt of Byron, with views towards the Cinque Terre. A plaque celebrates the poet's exploits as a swimmer – he once made a dash across the gulf from Porto Venere to Lerici.

Just off the promontory lie three tiny islands, Palmaria, Tino and Tinetto. Navigazione Golfo dei Poeti (see the La Spezia Getting There & Away section for contact details) runs trips around the islands during the summer for L15,000, and you can hire local boats from the waterfront (haggling advised) to take you to Palmaria and the grottoes along its western shore.

Fishing is supposedly the mainstay of Porto Venere. You can buy all the tackle and gear you want at Lucky Nautica Sport (☎ 0187 79 21 98), Calata Doria 38, which also hires out kayaks for L10,000 per hour.

Places to Stay & Eat Only 12km south of La Spezia, Porto Venere is a straightforward day trip – a good thing as neither accommodation nor food is cheap. If you do want to stay, *Albergo Il Genio* (☎ 0187 79 06 11), in a former castle at the start of the waterfront, has singles/doubles starting at L100,000/ 120,000.

Ristorante Miramare and *Taverna di Venere* are among the half-dozen or so restaurants along Calata Doria, by the sea. The former has a good set menu of seafood for L35,000 including wine; the latter offers a less impressive set menu costing L29,000. Alternatively, try *Bar al Naviglio* (*Via Olive*

73), away from the quay and a relatively inexpensive place for lunch.

Lerici

At the southern end of the Riviera di Levante, 10km and a short bus ride from La Spezia, Lerici is an exclusive summer refuge for wealthy Italians. It is a town of villas with manicured gardens set into the surrounding hills and equally well-kept swimming pools built into the cliffs along the beach. Make your way up to the 12th century **Castello Lerici** for outstanding views of the town and the occasional art exhibition.

If you plan to stay in the area, jump off the bus at the pleasant village of **San Terenzo** (also dominated by a Genovese castle), half an hour's walk from Lerici. In 1822, Percy Bysshe Shelley set sail from here for Livorno (Leghorn), a fateful voyage that cost him his life on the return trip when his boat sank off the coast near Viareggio.

A pleasant 4km walk or bus ride from Lerici along the Fiascherino road takes you past some magnificent little bays towards Tellaro. The area was a haunt of DH Lawrence in the year before WWI broke out. When you reach a huge illuminated sign reading 'Eco del Mare', make for the nearby *spiaggia libera*, the euphemism for a public beach – most others in the area are private.

Tellaro is a quiet fishing hamlet with pink and orange houses cluttered about narrow lanes and tiny squares. Weave your way to the Chiesa di San Giorgio, sit on the rocks and watch the world go by.

Places to Stay & Eat There are three camp sites based in the hills around Lerici. *Gianna* (☎ 0187 96 64 11, Via Fiascherino), just outside the village, is open from Easter to the end of September. *Maralunga* (☎ 0187 96 65 89, Via Carpanini 61), on the Lerici to Tellaro road, and *Senato Park* (☎ 0187 98 83 96, Via Senato 1) both open on 1 June and close at the end of September. The camp sites are accessible by bus from Piazza Garibaldi in Lerici.

Hotels here include *Albergo delle Ondine* (☎ 0187 96 51 31, Via Fiascherino 1), in a good spot at the top of Tellaro. Singles/

LIGURIA

doubles cost L40,000/75,000, or L90,000 for doubles with private bathroom. Outside Tellaro is the affittacamere **Armando Sarbia** (☎ *0187 96 50 49, Via Fiascherino 57*), where doubles cost L60,000. In San Terenzo, the **Pensione Nettuno** (☎ *0187 97 10 93, Via Mantegazza 1*) has singles/doubles with private bathroom from as little as L25,000/ 48,000 (the price doubles in high season).

There are a few pleasant trattorie in San Terenzo. Try **La Palmira** (*Via Angelo Trogu*), where you can dine well for about L30,000. At **Fuoco e Fiamme** (*Piazza Meneghetti 2*) pizzas start at L9000.

Val di Magra

South-east of La Spezia, the Val di Magra forms the easternmost tongue of Ligurian territory before you reach Toscana. **Sarzana**, a short bus ride from La Spezia, was once an important outpost of the Genovese republic. In the cathedral you can see the world's oldest crucifix, painted on wood. In the chapel is a phial said to have contained the blood of Christ. Nearby, the fortress of Sarzanello (also known as Castruccio Castracani) offers magnificent views. Take a pretty detour to the hillside hamlet of **Castelnuovo Magra**, which boasts a medieval castle.

Die-hard fans of all things Roman may be interested in **Luni**, about 6km south-east of Sarzana (1km off the S1 towards the coast; it's not well signposted). Established as a Roman colony in 177 BC on the site of an Etruscan village, it thrived until the 13th century. Excavations have revealed the amphitheatre, forum, temple and other remnants of a classic Roman town, but the ruins are not in top condition. The site and a small museum are open from 9 am to 7 pm Tuesday to Sunday. Admission costs L4000.

RIVIERA DI PONENTE

Stretching west from Genova to France, this part of the Ligurian coast is more heavily developed than the eastern side. It attracts package tour groups from northern Europe as well as Italian summer holiday-makers en masse. However, some of the resorts are not bad at all; several of Genova's historical maritime

rivals retain the architectural trappings of a more glorious past, and the mountains, hiding a warren of hilltop villages, promise cool air and pretty walking and driving circuits.

Savona

When you approach Savona from west or east, it is the sprawl of the port's facilities that first strikes you. However, with a population of only 70,000, Savona doesn't match the chaos of its longtime rival, Genova. The two cities were steady opponents from the time of the Punic Wars and the Genovese destroyed the town in 1528, proving their dominance. Now a provincial capital and bishopric, Savona suffered heavy bombing raids during WWII. The small medieval centre, dominated by the baroque **Cattedrale di Nostra Signora Assunta**, still survives.

Orientation The train station is in a relatively new part of town, south-east of the Letimbro river. Via Collodi, to the right of the train station as you walk out, and Via Don Minzoni, to the left, both lead across the river towards the leafy Piazza del Popolo (which serves as a drug-addicts' hang-out). From here, Via Paleocapa, Savona's elegant main boulevard, runs to the waterfront.

Information The IAT office (☎ 019 840 23 21), Piazza del Popolo, is open from 9 am to 12.30 pm and 3 to 6 pm Monday to Saturday.

Places to Stay & Eat Savona has two youth hostels. The first is in the **Fortezza Priamar** (☎/fax *019 81 26 53, Corso Mazzini*), on the waterfront, and charges L20,000 for B&B; it's open year-round. Take bus No 2 from the train station. The other, **Villa de' Franceschini** (☎/fax *019 26 32 22, Via alla Strà 29, Conca Verde*), charges L15,000 for B&B; phone on arrival in Savona for a free pick-up in its private bus. It is open from 15 March to 30 September.

Otherwise, things are grim for the small spender. **Albergo Ghione** (☎ *019 82 18 20, Piazza del Popolo 51/r*) has a few singles/ doubles going for as 'cheaply' as L60,000/ 90,000. **Albergo Riviera Suisse** (☎ *019 85*

08 53, *Via Paleocapa 24)* charges L98,000/ 145,000 in high season, but prices drop considerably when things are slow.

A smattering of restaurants, trattorie and cafés can be found along Via Paleocapa and in the city centre. *Ristorante da Nicola (Via XX Settembre 43)* offers local specialities, with pasta starting at L8000; it's also the town's oldest pizzeria.

Getting There & Away Trains run to Genova and along the coast to San Remo, but SAR and ACTS buses are the best option for reaching other points farther inland. They go from Piazza del Popolo and the train station.

Corsica Ferries runs boats to Bastia and Île Rousse in Corsica from Porto Vado, just outside Savona. In the summer months there are up to four daily departures both ways. The one-way trip can cost up to L53,000 per person. You can get a shuttle bus to the port from the train station.

Apenninni Savonesi

About a 40 minute bus ride north of Savona, **Sassello** is a tranquil mountain resort close to the regional boundary with Piemonte. A pleasant circuit from Savona to Genova, if you have your own transport, takes you along winding mountain roads to Sassello and past several towns, including Rossiglione, near the border with Piemonte. Sassello's modest monuments include the **Bastia Soprano**, a Doria family castle. **Acqui Terme**, 32km farther north in Piemonte, is an ancient spa built around the ruins of a Roman water system. Enjoy a bath in the natural hot spring.

Noli

An independent republic for 600 years, the seaside town of Noli has little of the Riviera di Ponente's made-to-measure resort atmosphere. Dominated by the ruined walls of the medieval republic, which run up a hill behind the old town and peak in a fort designed to watch for invaders from North Africa, the town sells itself as the original home of a Ligurian culinary singularity, *trofie* (tiny pasta shreds made from potato flour and eaten with pesto sauce). The claim is disputed

by Recco, a town east of Genova. Fishing remains one of Noli's mainstays and the waterfront is often converted into an impromptu seafood market.

The APT office (☎ 019 74 89 31) is on the waterfront at Corso Italia 8.

Again, cheap accommodation is in short supply here, although outside summer you can often bargain prices down. At budget level try **Albergo Rino** (☎ *019 74 80 59 or 0161 47 71 00, Via Cavalieri di Malta 3)*, where rooms cost L60,000/90,000.

For home cooking try *Locanda da Massimo (Piazza Milite Ignoto 2)*. Great gelati are to be had at *Pappus (Piazza Manin 12)*.

Buses run from Finale Ligure and Savona. For even better beaches, stop in **Varigotti**, just past Noli on the way south to Finale Ligure.

Finale Ligure

With a good beach and affordable accommodation, Finale Ligure is worth using as a base for exploring the Riviera di Ponente. If climbing rocks is your idea of fun, pack your ropes and head for the hinterland. Many areas offer good free climbing, and well-organised clubs make maps of the best climbs.

Finale Ligure is divided into three areas. Finalborgo, the original centre, is away from the coast on the Pora river. A clutter of twisting alleys behind medieval walls, it's the most interesting part of the Finale triad. Also atmospheric is the waterfront Finale Marina area, where most accommodation and restaurants are found. Finale Pia, towards Genova, runs along the Sciusa river and is rather suburban. The train station is at Piazza Vittorio Veneto, at Finale Marina's western end. Walk straight down Via Saccone to reach the sea.

Information The APT office (☎ 019 68 10 19) is opposite the beach at Via San Pietro 14.

Activities Rock climbing in the area immediately inland is popular. Rockstore in Via Nicotera, Finalborgo, hires out climbing gear and gives free advice. Another good place to seek information and meet other climbers is the nearby Caffè Centrale.

LIGURIA

Places to Stay & Eat Two camp sites open year-round: *La Foresta* (☎ *019 69 81 03*) and *San Martino* (☎ *019 69 82 50*), both in the same area about 7km north-east of town. Take an ACTS bus from the centre. There's a *youth hostel* (☎ *019 69 05 15, Via Caviglia 46*) as well. Beds with breakfast are L19,000.

The APT can sometimes advise on private rooms or mini-apartments in private houses.

The town boasts 130 hotels. *Marita* (☎ *019 79 34 15, Via Saccone 17*) is close to the train station. Singles/doubles with shared bathroom start at L40,000/60,000. A double with private bathroom costs L80,000.

Pizzeria Le Petit (*Via San Pietro 3*) serves specials galore and pizzas starting at L8000. *Trattoria la Tavernetta* (*Via Colombo 37*) does great *trofie al pesto*.

Getting There & Around SAR buses running along the coast leave from opposite the train station.

Regular local buses link Finale Marina and Finalborgo. Bicycle hire at Oddone (☎ *019 69 42 15*), Via Colombo 22, costs L4000 per hour or L16,000 per day Mountain bikes are also available.

Albenga

Albenga's medieval centre sets it apart from many of the resorts farther west. Settled as far back as the 5th century BC, Albenga grew from its Roman roots to become an independent maritime republic in the Middle Ages, despite being destroyed several times by barbarian invaders. In the 13th century it threw in its lot with Genova.

The Pro Loco tourist office (☎ 0182 55 90 58), on Via Ricci, is open from 9 am to 12.30 pm and 3 to 6.30 pm Monday to Saturday.

Things to See Albenga's **Museo Diocesano**, featuring a painting by Caravaggio, is near the 5th century **baptistry** and Romanesque **cathedral**. The baptistry is somewhat unusual, if only because the 10-sided exterior breaks with the octagonal shape that characterises its counterparts throughout northern Italy.

The **Museo Navale Romano**, Piazza San Michele, has a collection of 1st century amphoras, or wine urns, recovered in 1950 from the wreck of a Roman cargo vessel found 4km offshore. It is one of the world's oldest discovered shipwrecks.

Places to Stay & Eat There are some 20 camp sites in the area around Albenga. The *Delfino* (☎ *0182 5 19 98*), on Via Aurelia (S1), is reasonably close to the train station.

Albergo Italia (☎ *0182 5 04 05, Viale Martiri della Libertà 8*) is in a handy location. Singles/doubles cost L45,000/75,000 including breakfast.

Trattoria la Bifora (*Via delle Medaglie d'Oro 20*) is in the historic heart of town and offers a cheap set menu costing L20,000. *Enoteca Conterosso* (*Via Tortaro 32*), apart from starters and main courses, offers a range of cheeses and *sfiziosità* (all sorts of snacks and mixed platters).

Getting There & Away Albenga is served by trains and SAR buses (main stop on Piazza del Popolo) along the coast.

Alassio

In addition to 3km of white beaches, Alassio boasts its own variety of *baci*, delicious chocolate concoctions that fall somewhere between truffles and biscuits. Though Alassio's chocolates aren't as well known as Perugia's, they're good value – head for *Caffè Talmone Via Mazzini 107*. This is one of the more pleasant beach resorts on this mountainous stretch of the Ligurian coast and there is no shortage of hotels should you decide to stay.

The IAT office (☎ 0182 64 03 46) is at Via Gibb 26. The SAR Autolinee bus information office (☎ 0182 64 05 96) at Piazza della Libertà can organise excursions around the Isola Gallinara nature reserve (you can't step onto the island), as well as day trips inland to Monte Carlo and other destinations.

Cervo

Past Capo Cervo on the way south-west to Imperia, this small fishing village, dominated by a ring of walls and towers around the medieval centre, makes a pretty stop.

Imperia

Dominated by lines of hothouses on the surrounding hillside, Imperia is the main city of the westernmost province of Liguria, commonly known as the Riviera dei Fiori because of the area's flower-growing industry, said to be among the most extensive in Europe. Imperia was founded in 1923 by Mussolini when he bridged the Impero river and unified the towns of Porto Maurizio (to the west) and Oneglia (to the east), although they retain the air of separate towns.

From Porto Maurizio train station, head up the hill to Viale Matteotti or through an underpass to the waterfront, which eventually leads to Corso Garibaldi.

Information The APT office (☎ 0183 29 49 47) is at Viale G Matteotti 54a. There is a post and Telecom office at Via San Maurizio 13 and 15.

Things to See Porto Maurizio, the older of the two towns, is dominated by the **Cattedrale di San Maurizio**, a large neoclassical cathedral in Piazza del Duomo at the highest point on the hill. Across the square is the small **Museo Navale Internazionale del Ponente Liguria**, which is hardly ever open.

Places to Stay & Eat The camp sites, *Eucalyptus* (☎ 0183 6 15 34) and *La Pineta* (☎ 0183 6 14 98) are just off the coast road (S1) and can be reached by bus No 2 or 3 from either train station. There are several others in the area.

Pensione Ambra (☎ 0183 6 37 15, Via Ramblado 9) charges L40,000/65,000 for singles/doubles. You might have to pay for half or even full board. You'll find a few other small places nearby.

Pizzamania (Via XX Settembre 39) serves pizza by the slice and is good for lunch. There are several restaurants and cafés along the esplanade, Via Scarincio. The poshest is the *Lanterna Blù* at No 32, with set menus starting at L45,000.

Getting There & Away Buses for the coast stop virtually in front of the APT office. Tickets are sold in the café next door. Buses connect both train stations and bus No 3 runs through Porto Maurizio. Trains stop at Oneglia and Porto Maurizio stations, but the latter is the handiest.

San Remo
postcode 18038

San Remo gained prominence as a resort for Europe's social elite, especially British and Russian, in the mid-to-late 19th century, when the likes of Empress Maria Alexandrovna (mother of Nicholas II, the last tsar) held court here. Today, although a few hotels thrive as luxury resorts, many from that period are long past their prime and are cut off from the beach by the railway line.

Orientation The old centre, La Pigna, is just north of Corso Matteotti, San Remo's main strip, where the wealthy take their evening stroll. Farther east, past Piazza Colombo and Corso Giuseppe Garibaldi, is the seedier area. Corso Matteotti meets San Remo's other famous strip, Corso Imperatrice, at Piazzale Battisti near the train station.

Information The APT office (☎ 0184 57 15 71) is at Largo Nuvoloni 1, just near the corner of Corso Imperatrice. It's open from 8 am to 7 pm Monday to Saturday and from 9 am to 1 pm S unday. There are plenty of banks, especially along Via Roma.

The main post office at Via Roma 156 is open from 8.15 am to 7.40 pm Monday to Saturday. There are public telephones at the train station and the APT office has the latest telephone books for most of the country.

For medical assistance, head north for the Ospedale Generale (☎ 53 61) at Via Giovanni Borea 56. The questura (☎ 0184 5 90 81) is at Via del Castillo 5.

Things to See & Do The **Russian Orthodox Church** on Piazza Nuvoloni was built for the Russian community, which followed Tsarina Maria Alexandrovna to San Remo. The church, with its onion-shaped domes, was

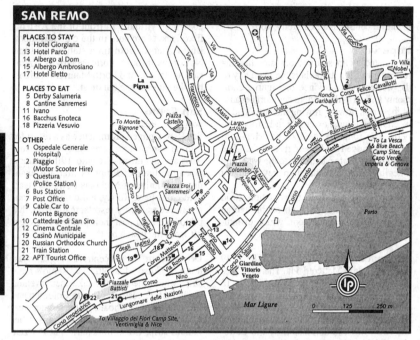

SAN REMO

PLACES TO STAY
4 Hotel Giorgiana
13 Hotel Parco
14 Albergo al Dom
15 Albergo Ambrosiano
17 Hotel Eletto

PLACES TO EAT
5 Derby Salumeria
8 Cantine Sanremesi
11 Ivano
16 Bacchus Enoteca
18 Pizzeria Vesuvio

OTHER
1 Ospedale Generale
   (Hospital)
2 Piaggio
   (Motor Scooter Hire)
3 Questura
   (Police Station)
6 Bus Station
7 Post Office
9 Cable Car to
   Monte Bignone
10 Cattedrale di San Siro
12 Cinema Centrale
19 Casinò Municipale
20 Russian Orthodox Church
21 Train Station
22 APT Tourist Office

designed in 1906 by Josef Choussef who, 20 years later, planned Lenin's mausoleum in Moscow. It's open from 7 to 11.15 am and 3 to 6 pm daily (Sunday hours are longer).

Italy's principal **flower market** is held on Corso Garibaldi from 6 to 8 am daily, June to October. Go to watch the frenetic bidding.

Monte Bignone is a short drive from the centre, or a cable-car ride (if it's working) from Corso degli Inglesi, and offers views over San Remo and as far west as Cannes.

The **Villa Nobel**, former home of Alfred Nobel, the Swedish inventor of dynamite after whom the Nobel prize is named, is at Corso Felice Cavallotti 112. Restoration work was finished at the time of writing, but no-one knew yet when it would reopen.

Activities The APT office has a list of contacts for many sporting activities including diving, windsurfing, sailing and fishing.

Special Events In February, budding and established talents congregate for the Festival della Canzone Italiana (Festival of Italian Songs). It is *the* pop music event and, though most of the tunes are depressingly middle-of-the-road, more than a few local success stories have emerged from the festival.

Places to Stay San Remo is stuffed with hotels and with luck you may strike a reasonable deal. The APT office has a full list, but don't take too much notice of the prices out of high season. Summer is difficult, and some places shut for holidays in September.

Three camp sites are worth considering: *Blue Beach* (☎ 0184 51 32 00, Via al Mare 183), 5km east of San Remo near the small town of Bussana; *La Vesca* (☎ 0184 51 37 75, Corso Mazzini 80), a bit closer; and *Villaggio dei Fiori* (☎ 0184 66 06 35, Via Tiro a Volo 3), all served by bus from the train station.

Albergo al Dom (☎ *0184 50 14 60, Corso Mombello 13)* is a homely place where singles/doubles cost around L40,000/65,000 in the low season; the doubles have shower and toilet. Not far off, the *Albergo Ambrosiano* (☎ *0184 57 71 89, Via Roma 36)* has reasonable doubles costing from L60,000 to L90,000. *Hotel Parco* (☎ *0184 50 96 40, Via Roma 93)* has decent, if unspectacular, rooms available for L45,000/60,000.

Closer to Piazza Colombo, the *Hotel Giorgiana* (☎ *0184 50 69 30, Via San Francesco 37)* has rooms for about L35,000/65,000.

For something a little more upmarket, *Hotel Eletto* (☎ *0184 53 15 48, fax 0184 50 15 06, Corso Matteotti 44)* has a whole range of rooms. Doubles can cost anything from L80,000 to L140,000 depending on the room and season.

Places to Eat Try the local cuisine at *Cantine Sanremesi (Via Palazzo 7)*. It is an old tavern and about the only place with this kind of time-worn character in San Remo. There are many cheaper trattorie around Piazza Colombo and Piazza Eroi Sanremesi.

Another place with a cosy atmosphere is *Ivano Via Corradi 39*, just down from the Cattedrale di San Siro. A pricier option is the *Pizzeria Vesuvio (Via Corradi 5)*. For modestly priced food and a few glasses of wine, you could try the *Bacchus Enoteca (Via Roma 65)*. Self-caterers should head for the *Derby Salumeria (Piazza Colombo)*.

Entertainment With more than 20 clubs, San Remo jumps at night. First and foremost is the grand *Casinò Municipale (Corso degli Inglesi 18)*, with its 'American Games', cabaret shows, roof garden and nightclub – bring your chequebook! The APT office has a list of nightclubs and might be able to advise you on the most happening locations. Locals tend to head for a series of clubs around La Pigna. More sedate are the cafés and bars lining Corso Matteotti.

Getting There & Away San Remo is on the Genova-Ventimiglia railway line and there are regular trains from either city. Riviera

Trasporti buses (☎ 0184 59 27 06) leave from the train station and the main bus station near Piazza Colombo for the French border, Imperia and inland destinations. Other companies operate from the same bus station to destinations such as Torino and Milano. By car, you can reach San Remo quickly on the A10 or more scenically (and less expensively) by following the S1 along the coast.

Getting Around The Piaggio agent Bianchi Emilio (☎ 0184 54 13 17), Corso Felice Cavalotti 39, hires out scooters and motorcycles. In summer, head down to Giardino Vittorio Veneto, by the old port, to hire bicycles.

Valle Argentina

The so-called Silver Valley stretches away from **Taggia**, a charming little place a few kilometres inland from the San Remo-Imperia road, into thickly wooded mountains that seem light years from the coastal resorts. Buses from San Remo go as far as **Triora**, 33km from San Remo and 776m above sea level. This haunting medieval village, the scene of celebrated witch trials and executions in the 16th century, dominates the surrounding valleys, and the trip is well worth the effort. Those with their own transport can explore plenty of other villages. Each of them seems more impossibly perched on a hill crest than the one before.

Bordighera

A few kilometres west of San Remo is built-up Bordighera. Apart from being a one-time favourite haunt of rich British seaside lovers – the collection of charming and costly hotels attests to this – Bordighera's fame rests on a centuries-old monopoly of the Holy Week palm business. Il Vaticano selects its branches exclusively from the palms along the promenade, Lungomare Argentina.

Ventimiglia

If you are coming in from the splendidly rich end of the French Riviera, you may find arrival in Ventimiglia a bit of a letdown. The town is jaded, the grey, pebbly beach is nothing special and the limpid blue water of

Nice seems far away. Typically in this frontier area, French seems almost to have equal status with Italian.

The train station is at the head of Via della Stazione, which continues to the waterfront as Corso della Repubblica. Corso Genova, which runs past the Roman ruins, is the main eastern exit from the city, while its continuation to the west, Via Cavour, runs through the centre and heads to France.

Information The APT office (☎ 0184 35 11 83), Via Cavour 61, is open from 8 am to 7 pm Monday to Saturday. There are several banks (some with ATMs) and also an exchange booth at the train station.

Things to See Ventimiglia's **Roman ruins,** which include an amphitheatre, date from the 2nd and 3rd centuries, when the town was known as Albintimulium. The ruins straddle Corso Genova, a few kilometres east of the train station, but they're only for die-hards; railway lines and traffic kill any atmosphere.

Squatting on a hill on the western bank of the Roia river is the medieval town. A 12th century **cathedral** on Via del Capo rises above the surrounding lanes and neglected houses. There are some breathtaking views of the coast from Corso Giuseppe Verdi.

Places to Stay The town's camp site, *Roma* (☎ *0184 23 90 07, Via Peglia 9),* is near the centre. *Albergo Cavour (☎ 0184 35 13 66, Via Cavour 3)* has singles/doubles costing L50,000/80,000 (add L10,000 for a private bathroom). *Albergo XX Settembre (☎ 0184 35 12 22, Via Roma 16)* can come in quite cheap if you're lucky – at L30,000/60,000. It has a popular restaurant downstairs. Near the waterfront is *Hotel Villa Franca (☎ 0184 35 18 71, Corso della Repubblica 12),* which offers reasonable rooms for L40,000/58,000; those with private bathroom cost more.

Hotel Posta (☎ 0184 35 12 18, Via Sottoconvento 15) is a step up in quality and costs L70,000/110,000.

Places to Eat A series of pizza restaurants lines the beach on Passeggiata G Oberdan.

A nicely placed one is *Il Terrazzino*, which offers pretty views across to the old town and an unspectacular but dirt-cheap set menu for L16,900. There are several down-to-earth places around Via Roma and Piazza della Libertà, and along Via Cavour. For a cosier atmosphere, try *Pergola* (*Via Roma 6a*) where the set menu costs L22,000.

Getting There & Around By bus, Riviera Trasporti (☎ 0184 35 12 51), next to the APT office, connects the city with towns along the coast and into France; frequency drops outside the high season. Trains connect the city with Genova, Nice, Cannes and Marseilles. The A10 (toll) and Via Aurelia (S1) link the town with Genova and the French border, while the S20 heads north into France.

Eurocicli (☎ 0184 35 18 79), Via Cavour 70b, hires out bicycles and tandems.

Balzi Rossi

Right by the Ponte San Lodovico, which crosses into France, 8km west of Ventimiglia, is the Balzi Rossi (Red Rocks) Stone Age site. To enter (with a guide only) the grottoes where Cro-Magnon people once lived, you must buy a ticket for the small **Museo Preistorico**, which features the Triple Burial (a grave of three Cro-Magnon people), pots of weapons and animal remains from the period. It is open from 9 am to 7 pm daily and admission costs L4000. The Riviera Trasporti bus to France that leaves Via Cavour in Ventimiglia three times a day (except Sunday) drops you right at the site.

Villa Hanbury

Overlooking the coast by the village of Mortola are the Giardini Botanici Hanbury. Established in the 19th century by Sir Thomas Hanbury, an English noble, the tumbledown gardens surround his Moorish-style mausoleum, open from 9 am to 6 pm in summer, though hours reduce in the off season. Admission costs L8500. Take the No 1A bus from Via Cavour in Ventimiglia; the bus goes on to the Ponte San Luigi frontier post, from where you could walk down to the Balzi Rossi.

Piemonte (Piedmont)

The region's position against the French and Swiss Alps has helped forge an identity for Piemonte that is quite separate from that of the rest of Italy. Its neat and tidy northernmost reaches could easily be Swiss, while Torino's grand squares, arcades and sophisticated café life owe more to French influence than to anything 'typically' Italian.

The House of Savoy, which ruled Piemonte in the early 11th century, created one of Europe's grand cities in Torino. Vittorio Emanuele II and the Piemontese statesman Count Camillo Cavour were instrumental in achieving Italian unification and succeeded in making Torino the capital of Italy, albeit briefly, for three years from 1861.

Much of Italy's industrial boom this century has its roots in the region, particularly in and around Torino where Fiat started making cars. Today, Piemonte is second only to Lombardia in industrial production and is one of the country's wealthiest regions.

Piemonte's cuisine is heavily influenced by French cooking and uses marinated meats and vegetables. *Bagna caoda* (meat dipped in oil, anchovies and garlic) is popular during winter, and the white truffles of Piemonte are considered the best in Italy. The region accounts for two-thirds of Italy's rice production, so it comes as no surprise that *risotto* is popular in Piemonte. The crisp climate is no hindrance to wine-making and you can find some good reds, notably those from the vineyards of Barolo and Barbera, and sparkling wines from Asti.

Central Torino is an ideal base for exploring the region. The area's main attraction is the Grande Traversata delle Alpi (GTA), a walk of more than 200km through the Alps from the Ligurian border to Lago Maggiore in the north-east of the region.

Note that the APT and IAT offices in Piemonte are gradually being transformed into semi-privatised offices called Agenzia Turismo Locale (ATL).

Walking

Allow yourself a couple of weeks to complete the Grande Traversata delle Alpi, or a couple of days for smaller sections. The walk starts near Viozene, in the south of Piemonte, and follows a network of Alpine rifugi north through the province of Cuneo, the Valle di Susa and the Parco Nazionale del Gran Paradiso. It continues across the north of the region before ending on the banks of Lago Maggiore at Cannobio.

The best months for walking are late June into September, although by the end of summer (officially 21 September) the weather can be unpredictable.

A fold-out map entitled *Percorsi e Posti Tappa GTA* (Routes & Places to Stop), which lists names and locations of rifugi and emergency information, is available from the regional tourist office or the Clup Alpino Italiano office, both in Torino. The information is in Italian only, but addresses and details are easily deciphered. All rifugi are open from July to September and some remain open throughout the winter for cross-country skiers – many are located in or near villages.

The paths described are clearly marked and generally within the grasp of moderately fit people. In various places they link with optional walks inside French territory.

In addition, readers of Italian can buy a wide range of detailed guides to specific areas, published by Club Alpino Italiano.

Emergency There is a 24 hour mountain rescue service. If you're in difficulty and you can get to a phone, call ☎ 118. In dire situations where a helicopter is sent in, signal for help by raising both arms above your head (one up and one down by your side means you don't need help).

Horse Riding

The Alpitrek map *A Cavallo Tra Val & Valsangone* provides information on horse-riding tracks through the Piemontese Alpi. It is available from the Valle di Susa tourist office in Oulx. A second horse-riding map, *In Piemonte a Cavallo*, detailing routes

PIEMONTE

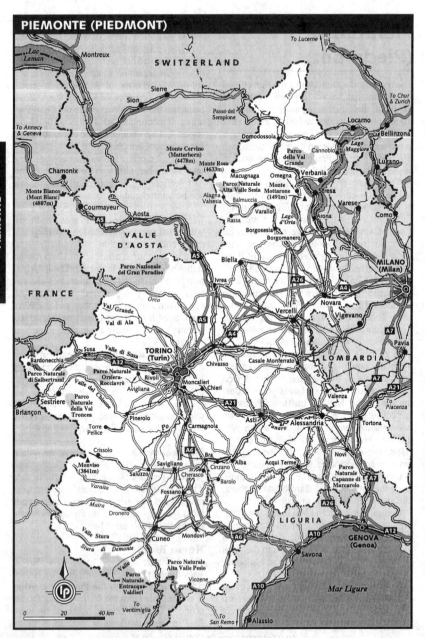

PIEMONTE

starting at Albisola on the Ligurian coast, is also be available at some tourist offices.

Quite a number of places organise horse-riding treks or less exacting rides through some of the region's valleys and national parks. A popular approach is to book places in an agriturismo or rifugio where horse riding is an option. The main tourist office in Torino should be able to give you some tips.

Adventure Sports

Activities as diverse as white-water rafting, bungee jumping and mountain-bike treks are organised by various groups throughout Piemonte, mostly in the summer months. Again, the main tourist office in Torino (and those in the many towns around the region) should be able to provide a list of organisations.

Skiing

Skiing is possible in the north and west of Piemonte – consult skiing entries in this chapter for more details. The tourist offices in these areas have copious amounts of information on pistes, rifugi and ski hire.

TORINO (TURIN)

postcode 10100 • pop 950,000

A gracious city of wide boulevards, elegant arcades and grand public buildings, Torino rests in regal calm beside a pretty stretch of the Po river. Touting itself as Europe's capital of baroque (although a good deal of it tends more to the neoclassical), the city definitely has the air of a capital *manqué* rather than some provincial outpost. Despite all the rain it gets it does look as if it could do with a good scrubbing up.

Although much of the industrial and suburban sprawl, especially west and south of the city centre, is predictably awful, the city is blessed with a green belt in the hills east of the river, with views to the snow-covered Alpi west and north.

Torino, the Savoy capital from 1574, was for a brief period after unification the seat of Italy's parliament. It was also the birthplace of Italian industry. Giants like Fiat (Fabbrica Italiana di Automobili Torino) lured hundreds of thousands of impoverished southern Ital-

ians to Torino and housed them in vast company-built and owned suburbs like Mirafiori to the south. Fiat's owner, the Agnelli family, is one of Italy's most powerful establishment forces, but Torino itself is a left-wing bastion. Industrial unrest on Fiat's factory floors spawned the Italian Communist Party under the leadership of Antonio Gramsci and, in the 1970s, the left-wing terrorist group called the Brigate Rosse (Red Brigades).

History

It is unclear whether the ancient city of Taurisia began as a Celtic or Ligurian settlement. Like the rest of northern Italy, it eventually came under the sway of the Roman Empire, which was succeeded by the Goths, Lombards and Franks.

When Torino became capital of the House of Savoy it pretty much shared the dynasty's fortunes thereafter. The Savoys annexed Sardegna in 1720, but Napoleon virtually put an end to their power and occupied Torino in 1798. Torino suffered Austrian and Russian occupation before Vittorio Emanuele I restored the House of Savoy and re-entered Torino in 1814. Nevertheless, Austria remained the true power throughout northern Italy until unification, when Torino became the capital, an honour it passed on to Firenze three years later.

Torino adapted quickly to its loss of political significance, becoming first a centre for industrial production during the WWI years and later a hive of trade-union activity. Today, it is Italy's second-largest industrial city after Milano.

Orientation

The north-facing Stazione Porta Nuova is the point of arrival for most travellers. Trams and buses departing from the front of the station connect with most parts of the historic centre, which is quite spread out. From the station, walk straight ahead over the main east-west route, Corso Vittorio Emanuele II, through the grand Piazza Carlo Felice and north along Via Roma until you come to the broad café-lined Piazza San Carlo. Piazza Castello and

TORINO (TURIN)

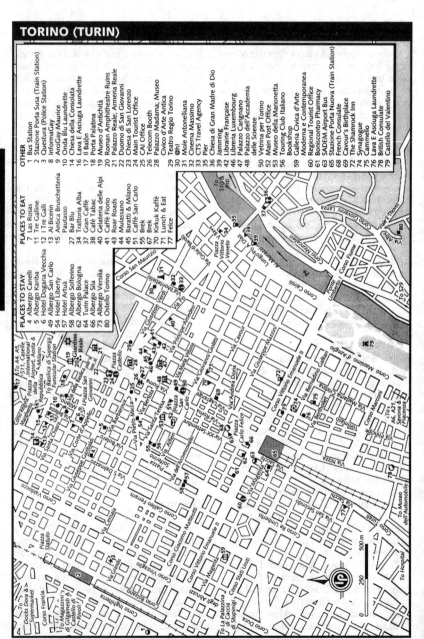

PLACES TO STAY
4 Albergo Canelli
5 Albergo Kariba
6 Hotel Dogana Vecchia
49 Albergo San Carlo
54 Hotel Liberty
57 Hotel Artuà
58 Albergo Solferino
62 Albergo Bologna
64 Turin Palace
66 Albergo Sila
73 Albergo Versilia
80 Ostello Torino

PLACES TO EAT
7 Las Rosas
11 Tre Galline
12 I Tre Galli
13 Al Bicerin
15 Antica Bruschetteria Pautasso
27 Bar Blu
34 Trattoria Alba
37 Gran Caffè
38 Café Tabac
40 Gelateria delle Alpi
41 Caffè Fiorio
43 Roar Roads
44 Mulassano
45 Baratti & Milano
51 Caffè San Carlo
55 Brek
67 Brek
70 Kirkuk Kaffè
71 Lunch & Eat
77 Felce

OTHER
1 Bus Station
2 Stazione Porta Susa (Train Station)
3 Questura (Police Station)
8 InformaGay
9 ArciGay Maurice
10 Onda Blu Laundrette
14 Chiesa della Consolata
16 Lava E Asciuga Laundrette
17 Il Balón
18 Porta Palatina
19 Museo d'Antichità
20 Roman Amphitheatre Ruins
21 Palazzo Reale; Armeria Reale
22 Duomo di San Giovanni
23 Chiesa di San Lorenzo
24 Main Tourist Office
25 CAI Office
26 Telecom Booth
28 Palazzo Madama; Museo Civico d'Arte Antica
29 Teatro Regio Torino
30 @hl
31 Mole Antonelliana
32 Cinema Massimo
33 CTS Travel Agency
35 Pier
36 Chiesa di Gran Madre di Dio
39 Jamming
42 Librairie Française
46 Libreria Luxembourg
47 Palazzo Carignano
48 Palazzo dell'Accademia delle Scienze
50 Vetrina per Torino
52 Main Post Office
53 Museo della Marionetta
56 Touring Club Italiano
59 Galleria Civica d'Arte Moderna e Contemporanea
60 Regional Tourist Office
61 Boniscontro Pharmacy
65 Stazione Porta Nuova (Train Station)
68 French Consulate
69 Cavour's Birthplace
72 The Shamrock Inn
74 Synagogue
75 Cammello
76 Lava E Asciuga Laundrette
78 British Consulate
79 Castello del Valentino

Preparing for the day's catch, Camogli, Liguria.

Fun in the sun, Riomaggiore

Napoleons on parade at the Battaglia delle Arance (Battle of the Oranges), Ivrea, Piemonte

Riding high ...

... and dodging the 'citrus bullets' at the Battaglia delle Arance.

With its wide spaces and colonnaded walkways Piazza Chanoux is the focal point for Aostan life.

Spot the glitterati at Portofino's chichi portside piazza, Liguria.

Whatever you do, don't miss cliffside Riomaggiore or any of the other Cinque Terre villages, Liguria.

the Duomo di San Giovanni (which contains the Shroud of Turin) are farther north along Via Roma. The Mole Antonelliana dominates the horizon to the east, near Via Po (the student area), Piazza Vittorio Veneto and the mighty Po river.

Information

Tourist Offices Torino's main tourist office (☎ 011 53 51 81) at Piazza Castello 161 is open from 8.30 am to 7.30 pm daily, as is a smaller booth at Stazione Porta Nuova (☎ 011 53 13 27). Another at the airport (☎ 011 567 81 24) is open until 11.30 pm. Ideally by the time you read this you'll also be able to get information on the rest of the region at these offices. If not, try the regional tourist office at Via Magenta 12, open from 9.30 am to noon Monday to Friday. Tourist information in Italian is on their Web site at www.turismotorino.org.

For information on all the cultural events in town (theatre, cinema, exhibitions and so on) drop in at Vetrina per Torino (☎ 011 442 47 40), Piazza San Carlo 159.

Money There is a bank with an ATM and an exchange booth at Stazione Porta Nuova. Other banks are along Via Roma and on Piazza San Carlo.

Post & Communications The main post office is at Via Alfieri 10 and is open from 8.15 am to 7 pm Monday to Saturday. There's a branch at Stazione Porta Nuova.

There are unstaffed Telecom booths, both open from 8 am to 10 pm daily, at Via Roma 18 and Stazione Porta Nuova.

You can go on line for L12,000 per hour at @h! (☎ 011 815 40 58), Via Montebello 13.

Bookshops Libreria Luxembourg, Via C Battisti 7, sells a range of English-language books and newspapers. For the French equivalent, try the Librairie Française, Via Bogino 4. For travel stuff, visit the Touring Club Italiano bookshop on Piazza Solferino 3 bis.

Laundry Onda Blu has a laundrette at Piazza della Repubblica 1d, while Lava E Asciuga

has branches at Piazza della Repubblica 5g and Via Sant'Anselmo 9. Onda Blu opens from 8 am to 10 pm daily and the latter two are open until 11 pm. It costs L6000 to wash 7kg of dirty underwear.

Medical Services & Emergency The Ospedale Mauriziano Umberto I (☎ 011 5 08 01) is at Largo Turati 62. The Boniscontro pharmacy (☎ 011 53 82 71), Corso Vittorio Emanuele II 66, is open at night.

The questura (☎ 011 5 58 81) is at Corso Vinzaglio 10.

Other Information The CTS travel agency (☎ 011 812 45 34) is at Via Montebello 2.

For gay and lesbian information, contact ArciGay Maurice (☎ 011 521 11 16), Via della Basilica 5, or InformaGay (☎ 011 521 18 36), Via Santa Chiara 1.

The Club Alpino Italiano (CAI; ☎ 011 53 92 60) is at Via Barbaroux 1.

Piazza Castello

At the heart of Torino's historic centre and surrounded by museums, theatres, cafés and student quarters, this grand square is a logical place to start your exploration of the city. Bordered by porticoed promenades, the piazza is dominated by **Palazzo Madama**, a part-medieval, part-baroque 'castle'. It was built in the 13th century on the site of the old Roman gate. Madama Reale Maria Cristina, the widow of Vittorio Amedeo I, used it as her residence in the 17th century and so it was named after her. The rich baroque façade was added in the following century. Today the palazzo houses the **Museo Civico d'Arte Antica**, at present closed for restoration.

The entire square around the Palazzo Madama and up to the Palazzo Reale was, at the time of writing, being churned up by city workers – let's hope it looks nice when they have finished.

In the north-western corner of the square is the baroque **Chiesa di San Lorenzo**, designed by Guarino Guarini. The richly complex interior compensates for the spare façade.

Farther north, you pass through gates flanked by statues of the Roman deities

PIEMONTE

Castor and Pollux to reach the **Palazzo Reale**. An austere, apricot-coloured building erected for Carlo Emanuele II around 1646, its lavishly decorated rooms house an assortment of furnishings, porcelain and other bits and pieces, including a collection of Chinese vases. The **Giardino Reale** (Royal Garden), east of the palace, was designed in 1697 by André le Nôtre, who also created the gardens at Versailles. The entrance to the **Armeria Reale**, the Savoy Royal Armoury, is under the porticoes just right of the palace gates. It contains what some claim to be the best collection of arms (weapons that is) in Europe. The palace is open from 9 am to 7 pm daily except Monday. The armoury opens from 9 am to 2 pm, except on Tuesday and Thursday, when it opens from 2.30 to 7.30 pm. Admission to both costs L8000, but you are obliged to join a guided tour in the palace. Admission to the gardens is free.

Under Piazza Castello's porticoes you'll find the **Teatro Regio Torino** (see the later Entertainment section for details) and a couple of Torino's more refined cafés.

Duomo di San Giovanni

Torino's cathedral, west of the Palazzo Reale off Via XX Settembre, houses the **Shroud of Turin**, in which Christ's body was supposedly wrapped after his crucifixion. The shroud is usually kept in the **Cappella della Santa Sindone** (Chapel of the Holy Shroud). It was put on public display for a few months in 1998 – the first time in 20 years – but is now safely stored away from prying eyes until 26 August 2000. Then it will be hauled out until 22 October as part of the Millennium celebrations. At other times you can see a decent copy on permanent display in front of the altar. The dome of the duomo remains wreathed in scaffolding after the April 1997 fire that came close to taking the shroud with it – thank goodness for firemen with the faith!

Just to the north of the duomo you can see the remains of a 1st century **Roman amphitheatre** and, a little farther to the north-west, the **Porta Palatina**, the red brick remains of a Roman-era gate.

Across the road at Via XX Settembre 88c is the **Museo d'Antichità**, a trip down 7000 years of memory lane to the earliest Pianura Padana (Po plain) settlements. It's continually expanding and curators say that by the year 2000 there will be 20,000 objects on display. How much you like it depends in part on how much you go for all those itty bitty artefacts. It's open from 9 am to 7 pm Tuesday to Sunday; admission costs L8000.

Mystery Within a Shroud

For centuries experts and fanatics have argued over the authenticity of the Shroud of Turin. It supposedly bears the image of a man buried after crucifixion – thus for centuries many have believed the body of Christ was wrapped in this cloth after he was taken down from the cross.

The earliest recorded reference to the shroud was in the 14th century and the debate has raged ever since. In 1898 the image was made crystal clear in a photographic negative, but its origins remain as clear as mud.

Numerous tests have been carried out on the shroud, but the carbon dating that was done in 1988 was thought to have put a definitive lid on the subject – scientists dated the shroud to around the 13th century.

Not everyone likes the verdict. 'Shroudies' are legion and they are not about to give up. It has now been claimed that a 16th century fire that damaged the shroud could also have had an effect on subsequent carbon dating. For some, the 1988 tests have become inadmissible evidence.

Other examinations revealed DNA contamination of the shroud, leading one scientist to publish a book entitled *The DNA of God?* Some scribblers could not resist the temptation and began speculating on the possibility of cloning Christ!

Anti-shroudies abound too. One lot claim that the image is neither the blood of Christ nor a cheap medieval fake but, rather, the first ever attempt at photography (using a camera obscura) ... by Leonardo da Vinci!

Museums

Perfect for a typical rainy day in Torino are the museums just south of Piazza Castello.

The baroque **Palazzo Carignano**, Via Accademia delle Scienze 5, was the birthplace of Carlo Alberto and Vittorio Emanuele II and the seat of Italy's first parliament, from 1861 to 1864. You can see the parliament as part of the **Museo Nazionale del Risorgimento Italiano**, which has an extensive display of arms, paintings and documents tracing the turbulent century from the revolts of 1848 to WWII. Open from 9.30 am to 6.30 pm Tuesday to Saturday and from 9 am to 12.30 pm Sunday, it's one of the best of this genre in northern Italy (and there are many) but is of limited interest to those who don't read Italian. Admission is L8000. On the topic of the Risorgimento, one of its prime architects, Camillo Benso di Cavour, was born and died at Via Lagrange 25.

On the same street as Palazzo Carignano and housing the **Museo Egizio** is the **Palazzo dell'Accademia delle Scienze**. The museum was established in the late 18th century and is considered one of the best museums of ancient Egyptian art, second only to those in London and Cairo. It is open from 9 am to 7 pm Tuesday to Saturday; from 9 am to 2 pm on Sunday and holidays. Admission costs L12,000. In the same building is the **Galleria Sabauda**, housing the Savoy collection of art, including works by Italian, French and Flemish masters. It's open from 9 am to 2 pm Tuesday to Saturday (from 10 am to 7 pm Thursday) and admission costs L8000.

Farther afield is the **Galleria Civica d'Arte Moderna e Contemporanea**, Via Magenta 31, dedicated to 19th and 20th century artists including Renoir, Courbet, Klee and Chagall. It is open from 9 am to 7 pm Tuesday to Sunday. Admission costs L10,000.

For modern art of a more metallic sheen, head for the **Museo dell'Automobile**, Corso Unità d'Italia 40 (south along Via Nizza). Among its 400 masterpieces is one of the first Fiats and the Isotta Franchini driven by Gloria Swanson in the film *Sunset Boulevard*. It's open from 10 am to 6.30 pm Tuesday to

---

Museum Information

Most of Torino's monuments and museums are closed on Monday and opening hours can vary according to the season. Check at the tourist office for details.

Those intending to do some serious sightseeing should invest in a *Carta Musei*. For L20,000 you get unlimited access to practically every monument and museum in town – at that price you'd be lucky to see inside more than two if you pay as you go. The ticket is valid for two days.

Long-term visitors might want to consider the *Abbonamento Musei*. It costs L60,000 and is valid for a calendar year for admission to 22 of the museums and monuments in and around Torino, including temporary exhibitions.

Sunday. Admission costs L10,000. Take bus No 34 from beside Stazione Porta Nuova.

Back in central Torino, the **Museo della Marionetta**, Via Santa Teresa 5, contains puppets and costumes tracing the history of marionette theatre from the 17th century. It opens from 9 am to 1 pm Tuesday to Friday and from 2 to 6 pm at weekends. With a little luck, you'll see the danglers in action.

Piazzas

The great squares and elegant boulevards lend Torino its air of reserved majesty. Via Roma, Torino's main shopping thoroughfare since 1615, stretches south from Piazza Castello to the grandiose **Stazione Porta Nuova**, built by Mazzucchetti in 1865.

Walking south from Piazza Castello you'll emerge onto **Piazza San Carlo**. Known as Torino's drawing room, and home to several renowned cafés, the piazza is surrounded by characteristic porticoes (central Torino has some 18km of them) and capped at its southern end by two baroque churches, Chiesa di San Carlo and Chiesa di Santa Cristina. Farther down Via Roma you reach **Piazza Carlo Felice**, at once piazza and garden. This piazza, like Via Nizza, which continues south off the piazza past the train station, has seen better days. Now the main axis of Torino's seedier side of life, Via Nizza and the surrounding area is worth exploring but is dodgy territory at night.

If you do happen to be wandering around here, head east a few blocks to admire the Oriental strangeness of the 19th century **synagogue** on Piazzetta Primo Levi.

Another extremely elegant promenade is **Piazza Solferino**, over to the west.

Via Po & Around

The hip young scene, revolving around Torino's university, can be freely enjoyed in the cafés and trattorie along and around Via Po, which connects Piazza Castello with the river, via Piazza Vittorio Veneto.

The single most remarkable sight in the area is the **Mole Antonelliana**, a couple of blocks north of Via Po on Via Montebello. Intended as a synagogue when it was started in 1863, this extraordinary structure comes as something of a shock when you first see it from the surrounding narrow streets. Capped by an aluminium spire, it is a display of engineering as an art form (in a similar vein perhaps to the Eiffel Tower) and quite a spectral sight when lit up at night. At the time of research it was still closed (work was being completed on a new history of cinema museum) but it is due to reopen by 2000.

Walking south along the Po river you come to the **Castello del Valentino**, a mock French-style chateau built in the 17th century. It is closed to the public. The carefully designed French-style park around it opened in 1856 and is one of the most celebrated in Italy – particularly by rollerbladers, cyclists and smooching young romancers. A little farther south a minor Disney-style medieval castle and *borgo* (village) were built for the Esposizione Generale Italiana (Italian General Exhibition) in 1884. The castle and borgo were reopened after restoration in 1996. You can wander around the borgo at will, but admission to the castle (from 9 am to 7 pm Tuesday to Sunday) costs L5000.

East from Piazza Vittorio Veneto, across the Po, is the **Chiesa di Gran Madre di Dio**

church, built between 1818 and 1831 to commemorate the return of Vittorio Emanuele I from exile. Set into the hills, its dome is an unmistakable landmark, but the church is usually closed to the public.

Basilica di Superga

In 1706, Vittorio Amedeo I promised to build a basilica to honour the Virgin Mary if Torino was saved from besieging French and Spanish armies. The city was indeed saved and architect Filippo Juvarra built the church on a hill across the Po river to the north-east of central Torino. It became the final resting place of the Savoys, whose lavish tombs make for interesting viewing.

The spot is now better known as a football shrine. The tomb of the Torino football team, all killed when their plane crashed into the basilica in thick fog in 1949, is at the rear. To get there, take the No 15 tram from Piazza Vittorio Veneto to the end of the line and then the connecting funicular.

If you have a vehicle, the drive up through the thickly wooded Pino Torinese helps give the lie to the belief that Torino is little more than a polluted, industrial town.

La Palazzina di Caccia di Stupinigi

A visit to the Savoys' sprawling hunting lodge, tucked away in manicured grounds beyond the Fiat plants and Mirafiori suburb, is a must. It is slowly being restored with Fiat money and many parts of the building are in original condition. It is open from 9.30 am to noon and 2 to 5.30 pm Tuesday to Sunday. Admission costs L10,000.

Take bus No 4 from along Via San Secondo (near Stazione Porta Nuova) or along its southbound route from Piazza della Repubblica to Piazza Caio Mario. There you have to change to bus No 41 (you need a *suburban* ticket for this one – L1400), which takes you right to the palazzina.

Castello di Rivoli

The preferred residence of the Savoy family lies just outside central Torino in Rivoli. The 17th century building now houses a contemporary art gallery and hosts various temporary exhibits. It is open from 10 am to 5 pm Tuesday to Friday, and to 7 pm at weekends; admission costs L10,000. Take bus No 36 heading south along Corso Francia from near Stazione Porta Susa to the end of the line, from where it is a short walk.

Shopping

Every morning until about noon, Piazza della Repubblica, north of the city centre, is filled with the cries and smells of the main food and clothes market. On Saturday the area north of the same square becomes an antique collector's heaven – it's known as Il Balôn. On the second Sunday of every month it goes one better and becomes Il Gran Balôn, with antique dealers from far and wide. You can buy anything from fine furniture to used old-style petrol pumps.

Organised Tours

Ask about the ATM bus company's Touristibus trips. At the time of writing they offered two daily excursions both departing from the Via Po side of Piazza Castello, one of two hours around town starting at 10 am and another of three hours including one of the royal residences (such as Stupinigi) at 2.30 pm. The ticket in either case costs L12,000 and is also valid for the whole day on all public transport. For details call ☎ 011 576 45 90.

Places to Stay – Budget

Finding a room in Torino can be difficult, and finding a cheap one can be even harder. Call the tourist office in advance for a suggestion. The information booth at Stazione Porta Nuova will make bookings for you.

Camping & Hostels The *Campeggio Villa Rey* (☎ 011 819 01 17, Strada Superiore Val San Martino 27) is away from the centre. Check with the tourist office for directions and opening times.

The youth hostel, *Ostello Torino* (☎ 011 660 29 39, fax 011 660 44 45, Via Alby 1), is in the hills east of the Po river and can be reached by bus No 52 from Stazione Porta Nuova. Ask the driver where to get off. B&B costs L19,000 and a meal is L14,000.

Hotels Near Stazione Porta Nuova, *Albergo Versilia* (☎ 011 65 76 78, Via Sant'Anselmo 4) is basic but not bad value; singles/doubles cost L45,000/65,000.

Albergo Canelli (☎ 011 53 71 66, Via San Dalmazzo 7), off Via Giuseppe Garibaldi, has bare but serviceable rooms starting as low as L25,000/35,000 (L40,000/55,000 in high season). In the same pleasant area, *Albergo Kariba* (☎ 011 54 22 81, Via San Francesco d'Assisi 4) charges L40,000/60,000/90,000 for singles/doubles/triples in slightly more comfortable digs.

Albergo Bologna (☎ 011 562 01 91, Corso Vittorio Emanuele II 60), just across from Stazione Porta Nuova, is in a similar class but is often full. Singles without private bath cost L55,000, but the rooms with bath are overpriced at L100,000/130,000.

At *Albergo San Carlo* (☎ 011 562 78 46, Piazza San Carlo 197) singles/doubles/triples start at L60,000/80,000/110,000 (prices rise in high season) – the location is hard to beat.

Handy for Stazione Port Nuova is *Albergo Sila* (☎ 011 54 40 86, Piazza Carlo Felice 80) where decent rooms start at L65,000/80,000 and rise to L75,000/107,000 in high season.

Places to Stay – Mid-Range & Top End

If you have a little extra to spend, *Hotel Dogana Vecchia* (☎ 011 436 67 52, fax 011 436 71 94, Via Corte d'Appello 4) has well-kept rooms for up to L160,000/200,000 including breakfast. Mozart and Verdi were among its more distinguished guests. If you get lucky, it may have a few cheaper rooms without private bath.

A very pleasant address just off the grand and leafy Corso Umberto I is Via Brofferio. Here you'll find two good mid-range places, *Hotel Artuá* (☎ 011 517 53 01, fax 011 517 51 41, Via Brofferio 1) and *Albergo Solferino* (☎ 011 561 34 44, fax 011 562 22 41, Via Brofferio 3). The latter charges L90,000/130,000; Artuá costs about L10,000 more.

Hotel Liberty (☎ 011 562 88 01, fax 011 562 81 63, Via Pietro Micca 15) is a good central choice. Singles/doubles are L150,000/190,000.

PIEMONTE

Opened in 1872, the **Turin Palace** (☎ 011 562 55 11, fax 011 561 21 87, Via Sacchi 8) is the city's last word in late 19th century luxury. Singles/doubles here start at L290,000/340,000.

Places to Eat

Torino's cuisine is heavily influenced by the French, and the massive migration of southern Italians to the city brought traditions of cooking unmatched anywhere else in the north. Try *risotto alla piemontese* (with butter and cheese) or *zuppa canavesana* (turnip soup) and finish with a Savoy favourite, *panna cotta* (a kind of crème caramel). The wines are largely from the Asti region or the Barolo vineyards.

The area around Via Po is great for cheaper restaurants full of students. Via Giuseppe Garibaldi also hosts a number of cheerful spots for a bite to eat.

Restaurants One of the cheapest self-service restaurants is **Lunch & Eat** (Via Giovanni Giolitti 16). Here you can munch on a two course lunch for just L9500.

The Italian version of fast food is **Brek** (Piazza Carlo Felice 22), a quick stumble from the train station. There's another on Piazza Solferino. A little farther off is **Felce** (Via Sacchi 50), a local favourite for cheap food and snacks. Fancy a weekend brunch on the Po? Head for **Café Tabac** at Ai Murazzi.

Trattoria Alba (Via Bava 2), off Piazza Vittorio Veneto, is a busy, modestly priced place offering solid servings of tasty food – a good meal with wine costs about L25,000.

It would be interesting to know what drugs they were doing when they came up with the name **Roar Roads** (Via Carlo Alberto 3) for a restaurant bar. But they do pretty acceptable meals (pasta up to L10,000). It's a good spot for slurping beers too (see the later Entertainment section).

Las Rosas (Via Bellezia 15f) is a funky little Tex-Mex bar serving decent food and beer.

For a real change, the **Kirkuk Kafè** (☎ 011 53 06 57, Via Carlo Alberto 24d) serves up Kurdish, Turkish, Iraqi and Iranian food – call to book as it's popular, cheap and tiny.

An old favourite in Torino is **Tre Galline** (Three Hens; Via Bellezia 37d), serving traditional Piemontese food at prices perhaps a smidgen out of the budget range. Try the *sottofiletto di fassone con fonduta di Castelmagno e aceto balsamico* (pheasant fillet with cheese fondu and balsamic vinegar; L24,000).

Nearby, **I Tre Galli** (Via Sant'Agostino 25) is a popular haunt, spacious and full of light. You can drink at the bar or tuck into a meal. There are a few good places to eat here – another is **Antica Bruschetteria Pautasso** (Piazza Emanuele Filiberto 4). Expect to pay around L30,000 (excluding wine) for a traditional meal.

Cafés & Bars Perhaps partly due to Torino's legacy of French and Austrian involvement, and maybe also as a result of the indifferent weather, the city has a flourishing and chic café life. Piazzas Castello and San Carlo are loaded with establishments patronised by the well-to-do (where a coffee can easily cost you L4000 or more) and there's great choice along Via Po. Torino's many literary luminaries and political potentates have certainly not wanted for places to chat the day away.

Caffè Fiorio (Via Po 8) was a favourite haunt of Camillo Cavour; it's been operating since 1780. **Mulassano** (Piazza Castello), established in 1900, is a true *belle époque* relic and is popular with the theatre mob from the nearby Teatro Regio Torino. A couple of steps away is the slightly older and more elegant **Baratti & Milano**. Here, by the way, they offer a fine lunch menu with main course, wine, dessert and coffee for around L25,000 – dine in style for peanuts!

Caffè San Carlo (Piazza San Carlo) once played host to a riotous gaggle of pre-unification patriots and other dangerous persons. Today it is more bankers' territory. **Gran Caffè** (Piazza Gran Madre di Dio), just across the Po river , makes for a tranquil change of atmosphere.

Finally, a little off the beaten track, is **Al Bicerin** (Piazza della Consolata 5). People have come here for refreshment since 1763. You must come and try *bicerin*, a drink made up of coffee, thick hot chocolate, milk and whipped cream. It also sells chocolate and other goodies.

Gelaterie There are plenty of gelaterie to choose from. The *Gelateria delle Alpi (Via Po 18)* and *Gelateria Fiorio,* part of Caffè Fiorio, are among the best. *Bar Blu*, on the corner of Piazza Castello and Via Roma, is also good.

Entertainment

On Friday, the newspaper *La Stampa* has an entertainment insert, *Torino Sette*, which lists what's on in town. The city organises Giorni d'Estate, a series of summer concerts and films in various parks and theatres from June until August, and plenty of free music events in September – the tourist office has all the programmes from May. Free noon concerts are usually staged from February to April.

Theatre The cheapest tickets for the opera season at *Teatro Regio Torino (☎ 011 881 52 41, Piazza Castello 215)* go on sale for a minimum of L20,000, an hour before the performances begin, but you'll generally need to queue well before. When they sell out, it is often possible to see the performance for free live on TV in the Teatro Piccolo Regio next door.

There are theatres throughout the city. Check *Torino Sette* and at the tourist office for programmes.

Cinemas Near the Mole Antonelliana, *Cinema Massimo (Via Montebello 8)* offers an eclectic mix of films, mainly in English or with subtitles.

Bars, Discos & Clubs The nightlife in Torino is among the country's best. Many discos and clubs require membership, but you can often join temporarily. The scene changes quickly (pick up the free booklet *News Spettacolo* at the tourist office to get an idea of what's happening; it lists a couple of hundred places), from Irish pubs to Latin American dance clubs, from straight to gay, from innocent to the downright naughty.

A good central spot for trying a very un-Italian selection of beers is *Roar Roads* (see the earlier Places to Eat section). Here they will serve up an odd wooden contraption with eight half pints of all sorts of beers for L30,000. One of the best of the Irish pubs in town is *The Shamrock Inn (Corso Vittorio Emanuele 34)*.

Ai Murazzi, the arcaded riverside area stretching along the Po between Ponte Vittorio Emanuele I and Ponte Umberto I, was once the centre of Torinese nightlife, but it's a shadow of its former self nowadays. Several spots are still open and can be fun: try *Pier* at No 7-9-11 and *Jamming* at No 17.

The scene has tended to spread out in dribs and drabs across the city in the past few years. *Docks Dora (Via Valprato 68)* is north-west of the city centre – it's a good bar with music. You'll find several other places around here. *Supermarket (Via Madonna di Campagna 1)* is also north-west of the town centre; concerts are staged every week. The *Magazzini di Gilgamesh (Piazza Moncenisio)* is another big music venue west of Stazione Porta Susa. There are also several places strung out along the length of the seemingly never-ending Corso Francia.

Via Principe Tommaso has a few happening places. *Cammello*, at No 11, is a beacon, pumping out music and alcohol from 5 pm to 5 am.

Getting There & Away

Air Torino is served by Caselle international airport (☎ 011 567 63 61 for flight information), north-west of the city, with connections to European and national destinations. You can also get to Torino from Milano's Malpensa airport.

Bus Most international, national and regional buses terminate at the main bus station (☎ 011 433 25 25) at Corso Inghilterra 1. You can also get to Milano's Malpensa airport from here.

Train The main train station is Stazione Porta Nuova, Piazza Carlo Felice. Regular trains connect Torino with Milano, Aosta,

PIEMONTE

Venezia, Genova and Roma. Most stop at Stazione Porta Susa as well.

Car & Motorcycle Torino is a major autostrada junction. The A4 connects with Milano, the A5 with Aosta, the A6 with Savona and the Ligurian Coast and the A21 with Piacenza. If you're heading for Genova, take the A21 and then the A7 rather than the expensive and sometimes dangerous A6. For hitchhikers, the S10 heads for Asti, the S24 for Susa and the S11 east for Milano.

Getting Around

To/From the Airport The SADEM bus company (☎ 011 311 16 16) serves the airport every 30 minutes from Stazione Porta Nuova, stopping also at Porta Susa station. The trip costs L3000. Buses for Milano's Malpensa airport leave from the main bus station.

Bus & Tram The city boasts a dense network of buses and trams run by Trasporti Torinesi (☎ 800-01 9152 toll-free), which has an information booth at Stazione Porta Nuova. Day tickets (L4200) are available.

The company also runs Navigazione sul Po (☎ 011 576 45 90), which operates boat rides on the river between June and September.

Car & Motorcycle Major rental agencies include Avis (☎ 011 50 11 07), Corso Turati 37, and Europcar (☎ 011 650 36 03), Stazione Porta Nuova.

Taxi Call ☎ 011 57 37 or 011 57 30 for a cab.

VALLE DI SUSA

West of Torino and easily accessible by car, bus and train, the Valle di Susa takes in the old town of Susa and several ski resorts, including the glamorous but overdeveloped Sestriere. There are some beautiful spots and a few pleasant mountain villages, but they can be thronged during the ski season and at weekends. The roads often become clogged with miles of traffic jams on Friday and Sunday as Torino's weekend escapees pile in and out of the city. Walking oppor-

tunities here are good, but they're even better in the north and near the Parco Nazionale del Gran Paradiso.

Sacra di San Michele

Perched atop Monte Pirchiriano at the mouth of the Valle di Susa, high above the road from Torino, this brooding Gothic-Romanesque abbey dates back to the 11th century. The closest town is Avigliana, a short train ride from Torino, which is connected to the abbey by bus (there are about three a day). A better route is to continue by train to Sant'Ambrogio, at the foot of the hill, and tackle the 90 minute walk up. Check opening times with the main tourist office in Torino before setting out.

Susa

Susa, on the busiest route between Torino and France, Susa started life as a Celtic town (a Druid well remains as testimony) before falling under the sway of the Roman Empire. The modest Roman ruins make it a pleasant stop on the way to the western ski resorts.

In addition to remains of a Roman **aqueduct**, an **amphitheatre** still in use and the **Arco d'Augusto**, the early 11th century **Duomo di San Giusto** is a rare medieval survivor in Piemonte.

Albergo Stazione (☎ 0122 62 22 26, Corso Stati Uniti 2) is as close as Susa comes to cheap accommodation, with singles/doubles for L45,000/65,000.

Sapar buses connect Susa with Torino, Oulx and other valley destinations.

Exilles

Worth a brief look is the forbidding **fort** overlooking the quiet village of Exilles, 14km west of Susa. Its obscure medieval origins, its military role only ended in 1943. It's generally open from 2 to 7 pm, but you should check with a tourist office in the area before making a special trip. Sapar buses stop here.

Oulx

Nothing much in itself, Oulx is, however, a good place to get information on skiing, walking and other activities throughout the Valle di Susa. The tourist office (☎ 0122 83 15 96), Piazza Garambois 5, is the main one for the valley and can help with lodgings, Settimana Bianca (White Week Skiing) packages and walking details. Regular trains run from Torino and Sapar buses connect with destinations along the Susa and Chisone valleys.

Cesana Torinese

Eleven kilometres west of the resort of Sestriere, Cesana makes a much cosier base than its better known neighbour and offers several cheap accommodation possibilities. The IAT office (☎ 0122 8 92 02) is at Piazza V Amedeo 3. Three or four daily buses make the run up to Susa and back.

Sestriere

Conceived by Mussolini and built by the Agnelli clan (of Fiat fame), Sestriere is a cultural desert that has grown to become one of Europe's most fashionable ski resorts. The mountains here are pleasant indeed, and there are several villages on either side of Sestriere that could make more appealing bases, unless of course you feel a need to be seen here in your après-ski garb.

The IAT office (☎ 0122 75 54 44) is at Via Pinerolo 14 and has information on skiing and accommodation. Summer activities include walking, free climbing and mountainbike riding. Out of season, only a couple of three-star hotels remain open.

Buses connect the resort with Oulx, Susa and Torino.

SOUTHERN PIEMONTE

The roads south of Torino to Liguria mark the divide between the low hills and dull plains of most of eastern Piemonte from the slopes that rise in the west to the southern French Alps. It is an area little frequented by foreign tourists, and where numerous valleys slice paths west towards France (although only a few offer access across the border). Not as high as the mountains of the north, the area still provides good walking opportunities and skiing in winter.

Cuneo

Cuneo is a mildly interesting provincial capital and transport junction between Torino and Liguria. The old town lies in the northern wedge of the city, presenting a pleasant if faded picture, although there is not too much to delay the sightseer. Cuneo is useful as a base for exploring the southern valleys of Piemonte, especially for those without their own transport. If you have wheels, a better alternative is Saluzzo, 33km to the north.

The bus station is handily located at the northern tip of the old town, which peters out at the vast central square, Piazza di Duccio Galimberti. The train station lies to the south-west on Piazzale Libertà.

Information The tourist office (☎ 0171 6 66 15), Corso Nizza 17, has extensive information about the province.

Places to Stay & Eat At *Albergo Ciriegia (☎ 0171 69 27 03, Corso Nizza 11)*, decent singles/doubles start at L40,000/70,000. *Albergo Cavallo Nero (☎ 0171 69 20 17, Via Seminario 8)* charges L65,000/80,000, or L20,000 more with private bathroom.

This hotel also has a *restaurant*; or you could try a pizza at the cosy *Ristorante Capri* on the other side of Piazza Seminario. Piazza di Duccio Galimberti and Corso Nizza are the best places to look for cafés.

Getting There & Away Cuneo's big plus is transport. There are regular trains to Saluzzo, Torino, San Remo, Ventimiglia and Nice in France. There is a second train station for the Cuneo-Gesso line, serving small towns in that valley to the south-west. Various bus companies run services to Saluzzo, Torino, Imperia, Savona and along the Valle Stura. By car, take the A6 from Torino towards Savona and exit at Fossano, or follow the S20.

Around Cuneo

Among the valleys that radiate westwards from Cuneo, the **Valle Stura** (the longest) leads to the Colle della Maddalena, crossing into France. The surrounding mountains offer skiing when snowfalls are good, and

euro currency converter L10,000 = €5.16

Cin Cin

One of Italy's best known drinks, Cinzano, has its own museum just 10km west of Alba. In fact, it even has its own town, for the *frazione* (small area) of the hilltop Santa Vittoria d'Alba (3km north off the Alba-Bra highway), which lies right on the highway itself, is called ... Cinzano.

Nestled among the company's main distillery and warehouses you'll find the Museo del Bicchiere; here you can inspect posters, photos and all sorts of artefacts chronicling the history of a company that started as a small distilling operation in the hills of Torino more than two centuries ago.

The Cinzano family got into the vermouth-making business on an industrial scale in the mid-19th century, but it only really took off when the company's representatives started travelling the globe early in the 20th century. Publicity has been the key to worldwide success and long before you reach Cinzano town you can't fail to notice the name on billboards all over the surrounding countryside.

there are several rifugi for walkers. The same can be said of the bare rock mountain slopes that feature along the **Valle Gesso**.

Another attractive option is the **Valle Maira**, which starts to the north-west of Cuneo. **Dronero**, a pretty medieval village with houses topped by precarious-looking grey slate roofs, marks the start of the climb upward and westward.

Saluzzo

About 60km south of Torino, Saluzzo warrants a day trip and is a good base for closer exploration of the valleys and castles of southern Piemonte. Once a feisty medieval stronghold, the town maintained its independence until the Savoys won it in a 1601 treaty with France. One of Saluzzo's better known sons was General Carlo dalla Chiesa, whose implacable pursuit of the Mafia led to his assassination in 1982.

Information The tourist office (☎ 0175 4 67 10), Via Griselda 6, has a range of information about the surrounding valleys.

Things to See & Do Cobbled lanes twist upwards to **La Castiglia**, the sombre castle (used as a prison for a time this century) of the Marchesi, Saluzzo's medieval rulers. La Salita al Castello is lined with medieval houses. Commanding views over the old town's burnt-red tiled rooftops is the **Torre Civica**, a restored 15th century tower that was part of the old *municipio* (town administration). For L2500 you can climb to the top. Pass the contemporary church and convent of San Giovanni on the same square and you reach the **Museo Civico di Casa Cavassa** (admission L5000), a fine example of a 16th century noble's residence. The museum and Torre Civica are open Wednesday to Sunday and a combined admission ticket is L6000.

Places to Stay & Eat There is no really cheap accommodation in Saluzzo. At the *Albergo Persico* (☎ 0175 4 12 13, Vicolo Mercati 10), singles/doubles are L65,000/90,000. The *Perpoin* (☎ 0175 4 23 83, Via Spielberg 19) is good but still pricier at L90,000/150,000 in high season.

The latter has its own restaurant, and there are plenty of little *pizzerie* scattered over the lower part of town. Heading up into the old town, *Osteria dei Mondagli*, on the tiny piazza of the same name (at the base of Via Muletti), is a good bet. In summer you can eat outside and a full meal is likely to cost around L50,000 a head.

Getting There & Away There are regular bus and train connections from Torino and Cuneo. Buses also run up the Pianura Padana.

Around Saluzzo

A few minutes' drive south of Saluzzo is one of the more easily reached castles in the area, **Castello di Manta**. Inquire at the Saluzzo tourist office for up-to-date information.

The Po river doglegs north a few kilometres west of Saluzzo and the valley leading westward to its source, below **Monviso**

(3841m), is an enticing excursion. Should you want to walk around the mountain there are rifugi and a few hotels in the nearby town of **Crissolo**. Take your passport in case you want to cross into France.

Alba

Solid red-brick towers rise above the heart of Alba, a wine town that has kept enough of its medieval past to make it a worthwhile stop.

Alba was first settled in Neolithic times, but its modern claims to fame include cooking with truffles, and a *palio* (contest) on donkeys, inaugurated in 1932 as a snub to nearby Asti, its eternal rival in all things, including wine production. Towards the end of WWII, the town's citizens proclaimed Alba an independent republic for 23 days after partisans liberated it from the Germans.

Orientation & Information The tumble-down Piazza del Risorgimento, dominated by the 15th century Cattedrale di San Lorenzo, leads onto Via Vittorio Emanuele II, Alba's main street and a busy pedestrian zone. It, in turn, is capped by the ample Piazza Savona, where chic cafés line porticoed footpaths.

The tourist office (☎ 0173 3 58 33), Piazza Medford, can be of assistance with sugges-

tions on wineries to seek out in the region. Staff might be able to offer advice on which of the many privately owned castles and medieval manors in the surrounding Langhe and Roero regions can be visited.

Places to Stay & Eat The cheapest place is *Leon d'Oro* (☎ 0173 44 19 01, Piazza Marconi 2). Singles/doubles cost L70,000/90,000 in high season. Many *cafés* and *trattorie* line Piazza Savona and Via Vittorio Emanuele II.

Getting There & Away Alba is accessible by bus from Torino, Cuneo and Asti (30km to the north-east).

Cherasco

The quiet medieval town of Cherasco, 23km west of Alba at the confluence of the rivers Stura di Demonte and Tanaro, boasts a commanding position in the wine-growing hill region of Le Langhe. The local castle was built in 1348 by Luchino Visconti. In September the place comes to life for the traditional celebratory *falò* (bonfire) at harvest time.

The snail is a central part of Langhe cuisine. Some people come here just to savour this delicacy. A good place to do so is the tiny and welcoming *Osteria della Rosa*

Mushroom Magic

When autumn comes to Piemonte, it's time to *andare a funghi* – go mushroom-picking. Mushrooms, especially the popular *porcini* (boletus) and the much harder to come by *tartufo* (truffle), also known as *Tuber magnatum*, are considered something of a delicacy.

So prized are mushrooms that the town of Alba celebrates the Fiera del Tartufo (Truffle Fair) for a couple of weeks each mid-October. This is a delightful occasion for the palate, when Alba's best wines and rival vintages from Asti and the Langhe are brought out to accompany mouthwatering mushroom and truffle recipes dating back to the 17th century. The markets overflow with great slabs of porcini. Some as big as 2kg have been found by avid pickers – that's a lot of mushroom. (The Langhe, by the way, are also famous for hazelnuts, which end up in Gianduiotti chocolates and, more recently, in the chocolate spread Nutella.)

Porcini and other specimens sprout in the dark oak and chestnut-forest floors on sunny days immediately following a good burst of rain. Truffles, on the other hand, incubate for several months, and those who know where to look often take specially trained truffle-sniffing dogs. If you head off mushroom-picking yourself, let someone in the know examine them before you gobble them up – many species are poisonous.

Rossa (☎ *0172 48 81 33*). A meal will cost you from about L40,000 and you may well need to book ahead. Cherasco is on the Alba-Bra (a few kilometres north) bus line.

EASTERN PIEMONTE
Asti
Settled long before it was made a Roman colony in 89 BC, Asti has had a rockier history than its subdued aspect might suggest. An independent city state in the 13th and 14th centuries, it was subsequently passed around between Spain, Austria, Napoleon's France and finally the Savoys, prior to unification.

The largely flat lands around Asti produce grapes that make some of Italy's top sparkling wines.

Information The tourist office (☎ 0141 53 03 57), in the centre of town at Piazza Alfieri 34, has information about the town. It can also assist with itineraries for the wine areas.

Things to See The **cathedral**, on Piazza Cattedrale, is a large, 14th century Gothic construction. The city's other noteworthy church is the **Chiesa di San Secondo**, named after Asti's patron saint. During the late 13th century the region became one of Italy's wealthiest and some 100 towers of the period stand as reminders of its glorious past.

Special Events On the third Sunday of every September, 21 jockeys spur their horses around a chaotic course in Asti; the prize is a banner known as the Palio. The medieval horse race, revived in 1967 and dating back to the 13th century, comes at the end of a week-long wine festival.

Places to Stay & Eat September is a difficult time to find a place to stay. The nearest camp site is *Campeggio Umberto Cagni* (☎ *0141 27 12 38, Via Valmanera 78*), off Corso Volta. At *Albergo Antico Paradiso* (☎ *0141 21 43 85, Corso Torino 329*), singles/doubles with shower cost up to L55,000/80,000. The *Cavour* (☎/fax *0141 53 02 22, Piazza Marconi 18*) has rooms for L55,000/80,000 (or L68,000/100,000 with bathroom).

Asti is something of a culinary centre, with restaurants to suit most budgets; try on and around Piazza Alfieri or pick up a list from the tourist office.

Getting There & Away Trains run to Torino and Genova and the region's bus station is just near the train station. By car, you can take the A21 Torino-Piacenza autostrada. It is also an easy drive from Genova on good roads, starting with the S35.

NORTHERN PIEMONTE
Head north-east from Torino towards Milano and you'll pass through wide plains that largely typify eastern Piemonte – some of it is so flat and wet it's good for growing rice, as is evident on the approach to Vercelli. Turn left here and aim north; the landscape quickly changes as the lower slopes preceding the Swiss Alps come into view. Skiing (even in summer!), walking and white-water rafting are among the treats on offer among the valleys that spread west and north. To the east you can strike out for Lago d'Orta and Lago Maggiore, the first two in a string of lakes across northern Italy (see the Lombardia & the Lakes chapter for further information).

Varallo & the Valsesia
Varallo marks the beginning of the Valsesia, one of the less crowded Piemontese valleys. The tourist office (☎ 0163 5 12 80), Corso Roma 38, has plenty of pamphlets on every conceivable aspect of the area. It's open daily (mornings only on Sunday and Monday).

Varallo is a sensible starting point if only because it's a railhead and bus line junction. A narrow winding road also links the valley directly with the pretty **Lago d'Orta**. See the Lombardia & the Lakes chapter for details.

The *Albergo Monte Rosa* (☎ *0163 5 11 00, Via Regaldi 4)* in Varallo is a delightful place and all the rooms face tree-covered hills. Immaculate singles/doubles are available for L70,000/100,000.

The Valsesia to Monte Rosa From Varallo, at 450m, you can follow the valley up towards Monte Rosa and the Swiss frontier,

Battle of the Oranges

The mildly charming plains town of Ivrea, 35km north-east of Torino, explodes out of its year-round torpor to celebrate the Battaglia delle Arance (Battle of the Oranges) in February – the highpoint of its Carnevale celebrations.

The story goes that back in medieval times, a miller chose another miller's pretty young daughter for his wife. So far so good. But the nasty tyrant, like many other feudal rulers, reserved for himself the right to the first round with any local woman who was about to be married. A feisty individual, the miller's daughter was so upset by this that she sparked a revolt by the impoverished townspeople. On foot and armed only with stones, they launched themselves against the tyrant's troops, pelting them as they rode around the town in horse-drawn carts. This desperate uprising went down in the town's folk history and centuries later provided an excuse for rival gangs from different parts of town to stage an annual riot around Carnevale.

When Napoleon occupied this part of Italy at the beginning of the 19th century, his administrators decided to order everyone to wear red revolutionary bonnets. Just what immediate effect this had on the Carnevale celebrations is hard to say, but the red bonnet became mandatory millinery for anyone on foot at the time of Carnevale. Napoleon's men also put a stop to the fatal nature of the brawling, ordering that from then on the re-enactment of the famous uprising was to be carried out with oranges.

And so today, for three consecutive days in early February, teams of 'revolutionaries' wait at four different piazze for roaming carts laden with helmeted 'soldiers' – and they pound each other with tonnes of oranges specially imported from Sicilia for the occasion. In the midst of the mayhem, a colourful costume procession featuring the miller's daughter (la mugnaia), medieval characters and Napoleonic troops slips and slides its way along a slimy carpet of squashed orange (well-mixed with horse manure). Beware – anyone on the ground caught not wearing some kind of red headgear is considered fair game for a massive orange assault by the 'rebel' squads.

Ivrea is an easy day trip from Torino, accessible by regular trains and occasional buses. The centre of town, where all the fun takes place, is a few minutes walk from the train station.

PIEMONTE

where some peaks exceed 4000m. **Alagna** is the last town along the valley; you can get detailed local skiing information there from Monterosa Ski. Some 20 rifugi dot the area, the Capanna Osservatorio Regina Margherita at Punta Gnifetti (4559m) being the highest. A cable car at Alagna climbs to Punta Indren (3260m). From here it's possible (in summer at least) to walk to many of the various peaks.

Get expert local advice on what can be safely undertaken before setting out, as some of the trails require expert alpine skills and gear. Some of the toughest skiing in Europe is possible here – you could find yourself abseiling down into *couloirs* (canyons) to make it down from the Monte Rosa peak. Off-piste challenges abound.

Some 25 Alpine guides are on the books at Alagna – inquire at the IAT tourist office (☎ 0163 92 29 88), Piazza Grober.

Domodossola

The last main stop before Switzerland, Domodossola may once have been an attractive pre-Alpine town but suburban sprawl and hotels have ruined the effect. Those intending to explore the surrounding valleys should make haste to do so and leave this place behind them.

Information The tourist office (☎ 0324 48 13 08), Corso P Ferraris 49, has detailed information on walking and skiing. It's open from 9 am to noon and 2 to 5 pm Monday to Friday. Most of the resorts are well organised and offer Settimana Bianca packages.

Places to Stay & Eat The town's cheapest hotel, *Albergo Domus* (☎ *0324 24 23 25, Via Cuccioni 12),* is very central; singles/doubles start at L40,000/60,000. *Albergo La Pendola* (☎ *0324 24 37 04),* farther from the centre and train station, has singles from L50,000 and doubles with bathroom for L80,000. Both alberghi have restaurants. Otherwise, *Trattoria Romana (Via Binda 16)* is not unreasonable and specialises in French and Roman cuisine.

Getting There & Away Trains regularly run to Milano and Novara for Torino. You can also board international trains to Switzerland (including the charming run to Locarno) – a trip well worth doing. You can see France, Germany and even the Czech Republic from here (see also Stresa in The Lakes section of the Lombardia & the Lakes chapter).

The bus station is in front of the train station. Milano is 125km to the south-east and Torino is 168km to the south-west of Domodossola.

Valle d'Aosta

Covering a mere 3262 sq km and with a population of only 116,000, the Valle d'Aosta is the smallest of the Italian regions, but one of the wealthiest.

Human settlement in the Valle d'Aosta dates back to 3000 BC and Neolithic and early Bronze Age remains have been discovered. Early Roman sites dot the valley and Aosta is known as the Rome of the Alps. The area's fate was often tied to that of neighbouring French regions. For a century the Valle d'Aosta was part of the kingdom of Bourgogne, and was later made a part of republican France, and then of Napoleon's imperial France. Under Mussolini's regime, massive immigration from other parts of Italy was encouraged in an attempt to bury the region's separate identity.

The Valdestans, as the inhabitants are called, speak a Franco-Provençal patois, and French is afforded equal rights with Italian. Italian was in fact introduced into the region only after it was incorporated into the newly united Italian state in 1861. To the east of the region, the Walser villagers cling to their German dialect, Tich. The valley has always been an important passageway through the Alps and is lined with castles. The opening of the Traforo Monte Bianco (Mont Blanc Tunnel) in 1965, which connects Courmayeur in the west of the Valle d'Aosta with the French resort of Chamonix, turned what had been a quiet valley into a major road-freight thoroughfare and one of Europe's premier skiing areas. Unfortunately, over-development and pollution soon followed, although you can certainly still 'get away from it all' in the valleys running off Valle d'Aosta. The Valle d'Aosta enjoys self-governing status, stemming from its bi-national origins, which means 90% of local taxes are spent in the province.

The cuisine of the Valle d'Aosta makes liberal use of the local cheese, *Fontina*, a curious cross between Gouda and Brie. Traditional dishes include *valpellineuntze*, a thick soup of cabbage, bread, beef broth and Fontina, and *carbonada con polenta*, also a thick soup traditionally made with the meat of the chamois although beef is now generally used. *Mocetta* (dried beef) is popular. The valley also boasts numerous small, government-subsidised cooperative vineyards, most producing reds and *rosatos* (rosé). These wines are generally dry and fruity.

The region shares, with France, Europe's highest mountain, Monte Bianco (Mont Blanc, 4807m) and, with Switzerland, the Matterhorn (Monte Cervino, 4478m). It also takes in Monte Rosa (4633m) and the Gran Paradiso (4061m), which it shares with Piemonte. Its resort towns – Courmayeur, Breuil-Cervinia, La Thuile, Gressoney-St-Jean and Cogne – and valleys offer a feast of year-round activities. Some towns, such as Breuil-Cervinia, are anonymous, custom-built resort towns but others, such as Cogne, retain their mountain village character.

VALLE D'AOSTA

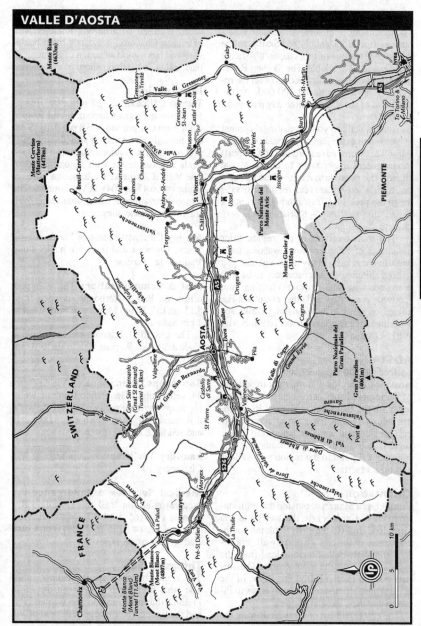

Activities

The mountains offer some formidable skiing options (for more details see Skiing in the Activities sections of this chapter). A range of ski passes is available. The Skipass Rosso gives unlimited seasonal access to all the region's runs and costs L1,190,000. At the other end of the scale, a three day pass costs L146,000.

You can walk to your hamstrings' content in areas such as the Parco Nazionale del Gran Paradiso. More adventurous (and expert) mountaineers might want to tackle Monte Bianco. It is possible to reach 3462m by cable car, from where walkers can set off across the ice to the peak (4807m), although this is for expert climbers only – tourists should stay close to the rifugio.

The tourist offices in the region offer mountains of information on walking trails and rifugi and huts. Many trails will take you to high altitudes, so it is necessary to be well prepared with the correct clothing and footwear, good maps and other essentials. For advice on what to take on long walks see Walking in the Dolomiti in the Trentino-Alto Adige chapter.

AOSTA

postcode 11100 • pop 39,000

Aosta is the capital and the only major city of the region. It lies at the centre of the valley, with the Dora Baltea river at its southern boundary and the Buthier river on its eastern side, and is the transport hub for the region. It has limited attractions but is a jumping-off point to the region's 11 valleys and their resorts.

Orientation

From Piazza Manzetti, outside the train station, Via G Carducci (to the west) and Via Giorgio Carrel (to the east) flank the southern stretch of the city's Roman wall. Via Olletti and Viale della Stazione lead from the train station into the town centre. The former goes to Piazza Narbonne, home of the central post office, and the latter leads to Piazza Chanoux, the main square.

The city is laid out on a grid following the

Roman pattern and most of the historic centre is closed to traffic. Via de Tillier, west of Piazza Chanoux, is Aosta's main boulevard and has a good selection of restaurants, bars, cafés and fashion shops.

Information

Tourist Offices The APT office (☎ 0165 23 66 27) is at Piazza Chanoux 8 and is open from 9 am to 1 pm and 3 to 8 pm daily; 9 am to 1 pm only on Sunday. It provides information on skiing conditions and cheap package deals and can assist with accommodation. The Valle d'Aosta APT also has an office in Roma (☎ 06 474 41 04), at Via Sistina 9. The regional government has an interesting Web site at www.aostavalley.com.

Money Currency exchange booths are on Piazza Chanoux and there are banks along Viale della Stazione.

Post & Communications The main post office, on Piazza Narbonne, is open from 8.15 am to 7.30 pm Monday to Friday and to 1 pm Saturday.

The unstaffed Telecom phone centre at Viale della Pace 9 opens from 8 am to 10 pm daily.

Bookshops Libreria Minerva, Via de Tillier 34, sells Istituto Geografico Centrale walking maps covering pretty much all the Valle d'Aosta region. They are on a 1:25,000 scale and sell for L12,000 apiece.

Laundry You'll find a laundrette at Via Chambery 100.

Medical Services & Emergency For medical attention, call the Ospedale Regionale (☎ 0165 4 14 00), Viale Ginevra. The questura (☎ 0165 26 21 69) is on Corso Battaglione Aosta 169.

Things to See

The main attractions are the Roman ruins. The **Arco d'Augusto** is between the **Porta Pretoria** (the main gate to the Roman city) and the Buthier river bridge at the end of Via

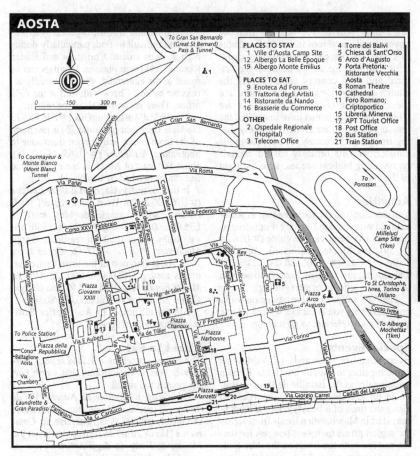

AOSTA

To Gran San Bernardo
(Great St Bernard)
Pass & Tunnel

PLACES TO STAY
1 Ville d'Aosta Camp Site
12 Albergo La Belle Époque
19 Albergo Monte Emilius

PLACES TO EAT
9 Enoteca Ad Forum
13 Trattoria degli Artisti
14 Ristorante da Nando
16 Brasserie du Commerce

OTHER
2 Ospedale Regionale (Hospital)
3 Telecom Office
4 Torre dei Balivi
5 Chiesa di Sant'Orso
6 Arco d'Augusto
7 Porta Pretoria; Ristorante Vecchia Aosta
8 Roman Theatre
10 Cathedral
11 Foro Romano; Criptoportico
15 Libreria Minerva
17 APT Tourist Office
18 Post Office
20 Bus Station
21 Train Station

0   150   300 m

To Courmayeur &
Monte Bianco
(Mont Blanc)
Tunnel

Via Parigi

Via dell'Edelweiss

Viale Gran San Bernardo

Via Roma

To Porossan

Via Ginevra

Corso XXVI Febbraio

Corso Padre Lorenzo

Via della Pace

Viale Federico Chabod

Via Martinet

Viale della Pace

Via Guido Rey

Via di Baillage

Antica Zecca

Sant'Orso

Via Mgr-de-Sales

Via Xavier de Maistre

Via Anselmo

To Millelaci
Camp Site
(1km)

To St Christophe,
Ivrea, Torino &
Milano

Piazza
Giovanni
XXIII

Via Croce di Città

Piazza
Arco
d'Augusto

Corso Ivrea

To Albergo
Mochettaz
(1km)

To Police Station

Piazza
Chanoux

V P Pretoriane

To Laundrette &
Gran Paradiso

Piazza della
Repubblica

Via E Aubert

Via de Tillier

Piazza
Narbonne

Via Ribitel

Via dei Tornaboni

Corso
Battaglione
Aosta

Via
Chambéry

Via Challand

Via Bonifacio Festaz

Via Vramalian

Via Ollietti

Viale della Stazione

Piazza
Manzetti

Via G. Carducci

Via Giorgio Carrel

Caduti del Lavoro

Via Torino

Viale Garibaldi

Bunker

VALLE D'AOSTA

Anselmo. The arch bears a crucifix, added in medieval times. Walk 300m west from the bridge to the Porta Pretoria gate, then north along Via di Baillage to the **Roman theatre**. Part of its 22m-high façade remains intact. Performances are often held in the well-preserved lower section. All that remains of the **Foro Romano**, another couple of blocks to the west beneath the Piazza Giovanni XXIII, is a colonnaded walkway, the **Criptoportico**. The **Torre dei Balivi**, the corner of the Roman wall, was used until recently as a prison.

The **Cattedrale**, also on Piazza Giovanni XXIII, has a neoclassical façade that belies the impressive Gothic interior. The carved wooden choir stalls are particularly beautiful. Two mosaics on the floor, dating from the 12th to 14th centuries, are also worth studying. The cathedral has a museum with religious treasures collected from throughout the region.

Chiesa di Sant'Orso on Via Sant'Orso dates from the 10th century but was altered on several occasions, notably in the 15th century when Giorgi di Challant of the ruling family ordered the original frescoes covered and a new roof installed. Remnants of these frescoes can be viewed by clambering up into the cavity between the original and 15th century ceilings. Ask the church attendant for a tour. The interior and the magnificently carved choirstalls are Gothic, but excavations have unearthed the remains of an earlier church, possibly dating from the 8th century. The Romanesque cloister, with its ornately carved capitals representing biblical scenes, is to the right of the church.

Activities
You can climb on the rocks known as Adrénaline, Polyester and Lipstick. For information, call Cooperativa Interguide (☎ 0165 4 09 39), Via Monte Emilius 13. Aeroclub Valle d'Aosta (☎ 0165 26 24 42) in St Christophe, just outside Aosta, can set you up for hang-gliding or paragliding.

The APT office can give advice on walking trails or put you in contact with an Alpine guide if you prefer not to go it alone.

Special Events
Every October thousands of Valdestans come together to watch cow fights. Known traditionally as the Bataille de Reines (Battle of the Queens), the event is organised along the lines of a beauty contest. Knockouts start in March, when locals from across the region prime their best bovines for battle, and end with the finals on the third Sunday in October, when the queen of the cows is crowned. This might seem a bit strange, but it is a tradition from the days when cows returning from mountain fields would tussle with each other. The losing cow is not injured and the match ends when one pulls away. The queen sells for millions of lire.

The Foire de Sant'Orso, the annual wood fair held on 30 and 31 January in honour of the town's patron saint, brings together craftspeople from all over the valley who display their carvings and then present an item to the saint at the Chiesa di Sant'Orso. It is held near the Porta Pretoria.

Places to Stay
Accommodation in Aosta is generally expensive and difficult to find, particularly during high seasons around Christmas and Easter. Cheaper and more pleasant lodgings can be found in the hinterland, which is usually accessible by bus. Check with staff at the APT office. There are no hostels in the region.

The *Ville d'Aosta* camp site (☎ 0165 36 13 60, Viale Gran San Bernardo 76) is just north of the town centre and is open from June to September. *Milleluci* (☎ 0165 23 52 78), about 1km east of Aosta, is open year-round and can be reached by bus No 11.

In the centre, try *Albergo La Belle Époque* (☎ 0165 26 22 76, Via d'Avise 18), off Via E Aubert, where singles/doubles start at L35,000/60,000 (rising by L25,000 with private bathroom in the high season). *Albergo Mochettaz* (☎ 0165 4 37 06, Corso Ivrea 107), about 1km east of the town centre, has rooms costing L42,000/63,000. At *Albergo Monte Emilius* (☎ 0165 3 56 92, Via Giorgio Carrel 11) rooms start at L50,000/80,000.

Almost all hotels in Aosta offer Settimana Bianca packages.

Places to Eat
The penny-conscious will find several *self-service restaurants* around that won't hurt the pocket too much.

Otherwise, *Ristorante da Nando (Via de Tillier 41)* specialises in *polenta* dishes and is reasonably priced, as is *Brasserie du Commerce (Via de Tillier 10)*. Tucked away at Via Maillet 3, *Trattoria degli Artisti* is recommended – L40,000 should see your way through a satisfying meal.

Head out to the back garden of *Enoteca Ad Forum (Via Mgr de Sales)*, opposite the cathedral, for a sunshine lunch. The food is nothing spectacular but the setting is pleasant.

Ristorante Vecchia Aosta, right inside the arches of Porta Pretoria, is a choice spot to enjoy local cuisine. You can try the set menu for L40,000 or eat à la carte.

Shopping
Tradition has it that Sant'Orso gave carved wooden shoes known as *sabi* to the city's

poor. Valdestans continue to carve shoes, tiny houses and ceremonial pots, all still widely used. Shops throughout the city, particularly along Via Porte Pretoriane, sell these goods.

Getting There & Away
Air Aosta has a small airport that services commuter flights. The airports at Torino and Geneva are both about an hour away by car.

Bus Buses to Milano, Roma, Firenze, Torino and Geneva leave from the bus station (☎ 0165 26 20 27), virtually opposite the train station. Other services cover most of the region; buses to Courmayeur are particularly frequent.

Train The town is served by trains from most parts of Italy, via Torino and Milano. Most travellers to and from Milano must change trains at Chivasso. A limited train service connects Aosta with Pré-St Didier, about 5km short of Courmayeur.

Car & Motorcycle Aosta is on the A5, which connects Torino with the Monte Bianco (Mont Blanc) tunnel; the last stretch of the highway is still being built. Another exit road north of the city leads to the Gran San Bernardo (Great St Bernard) tunnel.

Getting Around
The town is small and all sites are easily reached on foot. *Navetta* (shuttle) buses run through town from the train station. Taxis can be booked on ☎ 0165 3 18 31.

AROUND AOSTA
If you need a break from the slopes, the Aosta valley is peppered with castles, many of them Romanesque and Gothic, just waiting to be explored. Each castle is within view of the next, and messages used to be transferred along the valley by flag signals. East from Aosta is the magnificently restored **Castello di Fénis** (admission L6000), formerly owned by the Challant family and featuring rich frescoes as well as period graffiti. It was never really used as a defensive post but served as a plush residence.

Past St Vincent, the sober **Castello di Verrès** (L6000) is more the real thing, doing sentinel duty atop its rocky perch. About 1km south-west of the Dora Baltea river, below the town of Verrès. The restored 15th century **Castello d'Issogne** (L10,000) was a castle, though you'd hardly know it – it looks for all the world like a stately home.

Farther down the valley still, towards Pont St Martin, the fortress of **Bard** (closed) was a no-nonsense military outpost given short shrift by Napoleon on his first campaign into Italy. Once you are at Pont St Martin, you could strike north for Gressoney-St-Jean. Just near the town is the fairytale **Castel Savoia** (L6000), begun in 1900 for the Italian royals.

Heading west towards Monte Bianco from Aosta, you quickly come upon the **Castello di Sarre** (L10,000). Built in 1710 on the remains of a 13th century fort, King Vittorio Emanuele II bought it in 1869 to use as a hunting residence. The Savoia sold it in 1972 and it now serves as a museum of the royal presence in the region. **Castello di San Pierre** (L4000), which houses a natural history museum, is the last main item of interest on the castle route.

Visitors are sent through the castles at 30 minute intervals. A ceiling of 20 to 50 visitors in any 30 minute period is imposed. The Aosta APT has full timetable information.

Probably the only reason to visit **St Vincent**, Valle d'Aosta's second-biggest city, is for its casino. It is also a stopping-off point for the Valle d'Ayas and Valtournenche, which leads to Monte Cervino.

PILA
This is the closest resort to Aosta (about 18km to the north) and prices are quite reasonable. There is a village at Pila, but most services, such as the tourist office, police and medical services, are handled from Aosta.

Skiing
Pila is among the largest ski areas in the valley, with more than 80km of runs, including about 10km for cross-country skiing. It is served by 13 lifts, one of which connects the

VALLE D'AOSTA

village with Aosta. It offers challenging and difficult black runs and has a competition slalom course, but it also caters for beginners, with many easy runs. The highest slope, in the shadow of Gran Paradiso, reaches 2700m.

Walking

This is not one of the best areas for walking if you like high Alpine country, but the lower slopes leading down into the Dora Baltea valley provide picturesque and easy walks. Of the two rifugi in the Charvensod area a few kilometres south of Aosta, one is open year-round. Some lifts operate in summer for walkers or day-trippers.

Places to Stay

Aosta is a cheaper bet than Pila. The *Soleil et Neige* camp site (☎ 0165 5 99 48), open year-round, is about 7km from the resort on the way to Aosta. At *Hotel La Nouva* (☎ 0165 52 10 05), singles/doubles cost L55,000/90,000 in the high season. *Albergo Chacaril* (☎ 0165 52 12 15) has rooms for L61,000/114,000 (considerably less in off season). The best Settimana Bianca deals are found in Aosta.

Getting There & Away

Two roads lead to Pila, one of them from Aosta and the other from Gressan, a town about 6km west of Aosta. A cable car connects Aosta with the village. SVAP bus Nos 4 and 5 go from Aosta to Charvensod and Gressan respectively, but there is no bus service to Pila.

COURMAYEUR & MONTE BIANCO

With much of the original village intact and set against the backdrop of Monte Bianco, Courmayeur is one of the more picturesque of the skiing resorts in Valle d'Aosta. It is also one of the most expensive. Out of season, wealthy Milanese and Torinese women leave their fur coats in a local furrier's vault – minks and ermines are too valuable to be worn in the streets of their home cities. The resort has more than 140km of downhill and cross-country skiing runs and a feast of summer activities including skiing, horse

riding, hang-gliding, canoeing and 280km of mountain walking trails. A cable-car service leaves from La Palud, near Courmayeur, for Punta Helbronner (3462m) on Monte Bianco – an extraordinary 20 minute ride. It is also possible to organise guided walks up the mountain. See Walking & Climbing later for details.

Information

Tourist Offices The APT office (☎ 0165 84 20 60), Piazzale Monte Bianco 13, opens from 9 am to 7 pm daily in summer. During the winter it is open from 9 am to 12.30 pm and 3 to 6.30 pm Monday to Friday; from 9.30 am to 12.30 pm and 3.30 to 6 pm at weekends.

The Associazione Operatori Turistici del Monte Bianco (☎ 0165 84 23 70), at Piazzale Monte Bianco 3, can assist with finding accommodation.

Medical Services For medical attention and ambulance, call ☎ 0165 84 46 84 or go to the Pronto Soccorso at the Ospedale Regionale d'Aosta (☎ 0165 30 42 56).

Skiing

Monte Bianco offers skiing year-round. The Ski Club Courmayeur Monte Bianco (☎ 0165 84 24 77) is at the Centro Sportivo in Plan des Lizzes. You can reach the skiing school on the same number or at Strada Regionale 51. The best bet if you are just skiing is to book a Settimana Bianca package through an agency such as CIT. Most ski runs, chair lifts and ski lifts are reachable by the Courmayeur, Dolonne and Val Veny cable cars. For details, check with the APT or Cableways Monte Bianco in La Palud (☎ 0165 8 99 25).

Walking & Climbing

The APT has a basic map of walking trails in the Valdigne and on Monte Bianco. You would, however, be better off with the IGC 1:25,000 map No 107. If you walk the higher trails on Monte Bianco or you want to walk on the glaciers, go properly equipped and consider hiring a guide. Many people who take the Punta Helbronner cable car are completely unprepared for what awaits them at almost 3500m. Even if it's sweltering in the valley it could be -10°C at Punta Helbronner. Moral of the story: take heavy winter clothes. Head up early in the morning because by early afternoon heavy weather usually descends onto the summit area.

You can continue from Punta Helbronner down to Chamonix in France (bring your passport and check if you need a visa to enter France). The return fare from La Palud to Punta Helbronner is L40,000 (or L44,000 if you return by bus). You can do a day-long round trip either way between Courmayeur and Chamonix for L100,000; the return leg is by bus. Mont Blanc Tour Operator, Piazzale Monte Bianco 3 in Courmayeur, sells tickets.

Società Guide di Courmayeur (mountain guide association; ☎ 0165 84 20 64), Piazza Henry 2, organises activities including rock-climbing courses and a seven day guided walk up Monte Bianco.

Many rifugi and huts are located along walking trails in the mountains around Courmayeur. They are marked on all walking maps. Those offering hotel-style service and accommodation are usually only open in summer. Unattended huts, or *bivacchi*, are open year-round. The APT publishes a guide to the different huts.

Mountain Biking

To hire a bike, try Noleggio Ulisse (☎ 0165 84 22 55), in front of the Courmayeur chair lift, or Club des Sports (☎ 0165 8 95 70) in Planpincieux, which is about 5km north of Courmayeur.

Other Activities

The Scuola di Canoa e Rafting Courmayeur (☎ 0165 80 00 88) can advise on canoeing. If you want to go ballooning, contact the Club Aérostatique Mont Blanc (☎ 0165 4 02 05).

Places to Stay & Eat

Peak season accommodation in Courmayeur is very expensive if you aren't on a package deal, but the towns along the valleys (of La Palud, Dolonne, Entrèves, La Saxe, Plan

Ponquet, Val Ferret, Pré-St Didier and Morgex) offer reasonably priced rooms. Contact the APT office or the local hotel association, the Associazione Operatori Turistici del Monte Bianco, for assistance.

Campers can head for *Val Veny-Cuignon* (☎ 0165 86 90 73) in the locality of the same name (open July to mid-September), which is within easy reach of Courmayeur. In La Palud, *Albergo La Quercia* (☎ 0165 8 99 31) has doubles costing from L57,000 to L70,000. There are good food shops along Via Roma, in the old part of Cormayeur. Most restaurants are also along Via Roma.

Getting There & Away

Three trains a day from Aosta terminate at Pré-St Didier, with bus connections to the main bus station at Piazzale Monte Bianco in Courmayeur, outside the APT office. Courmayeur is served by long-haul buses from Milano, Torino and Geneva. Local buses connect the resort with Aosta and surrounding towns and villages. By car, take the S26 from Aosta.

The journey from Chamonix through the 11.5km Monte Bianco tunnel may not be possible for some time as a result of the fire that killed 40 people in March 1999. The blaze, which started on a truck, engulfed traffic ploughing into the tunnel and reached temperatures of 1300°C. Firefighters tackling the flames from both the French and Italian sides took days to reach the heart of the fire. The intense heat of the fire severely damaged the tunnel and, even when the damage is repaired, new fire precautions will have to be in place before either the French or Italians feel ready to open it again. The tragedy prompted both sides to inspect all their cross-border tunnels.

VALTOURNENCHE

Stretching from the Valle d'Aosta to Monte Cervino, the Valtournenche takes in several smaller and reasonably priced skiing areas – Antey-St-André, Chamois, La Magdeleine and Torgnon – and culminates in the resorts of Valtournenche and Breuil-Cervinia. The latter is the second-largest resort in Valle d'Aosta and is modern, purpose-built, expensive and fairly ugly, although it offers some of the best skiing in Europe.

Information

The Matterhorn Central Valley APT office (☎ 0166 54 82 66) is in Antey-St-André and the Breuil-Cervinia APT office (☎ 0166 94 91 36) is at Via Carrel 29. In the town of Valtournenche, the APT office (☎ 0166 9 20 29) is at Via Roma 45.

For mountain and Alpine guides, contact the Società Guide del Cervino (☎ 0166 94 81 69), Via Carrel.

Skiing

There are several resorts in the valley, all well equipped with downhill and cross-country runs. From Breuil-Cervinia, 25 cable cars and lifts take skiers into breathtaking terrain. Summer skiing is also possible as several cableways and lifts continue to operate, taking skiers on to the Plateau Rosa. This resort introduced Valle d'Aosta to night skiing, in the Campetto area.

For details, contact the Breuil-Cervinia APT or Sciovia (ski lift) Crétaz (☎ 0166 94 86 76). In Breuil-Cervinia, you can arrange skiing lessons with the Cielo Alto ski school (☎ 0166 94 84 51).

Walking

Basic walking maps are available at the APT offices, but if you want to tackle the Matterhorn you need to be properly dressed and equipped. Get a 1:25,000 walking map, such as the IGC map No 108 (see under Bookshops in the Aosta section for more information).

Places to Stay

Campers in Valtournenche should make for *Glair-Lago di Maen* (☎ 0166 9 20 77). In Breuil-Cervinia, *Albergo Leonardo Carrel* (☎ 0166 94 90 77) has singles/doubles costing up to L65,000/84,000, while *Hotel Sporting* (☎ 0166 94 91 12) can charge anything from L80,000/90,000 to L140,000/180,000. If you're heading there to ski, it is best to arrange a Settimana Bianca package.

Getting There & Away

Buses run from Aosta to the resorts and most ski areas in the valley. SAVDA (☎ 0165 36 12 44) operates services from Courmayeur, Aosta and Châtillon to Breuil-Cervinia and on to other resort villages.

PARCO NAZIONALE DEL GRAN PARADISO

The Gran Paradiso was Italy's first National Park, established in 1922 after Vittorio Emanuele II gave his hunting reserve to the state. This park incorporates the valleys around the Gran Paradiso (4061m), three of which are in the Valle d'Aosta: the Valsavarenche, Val di Rhêmes and the beautiful Valle di Cogne (check out IGC map No 102). On the Piemonte side of the mountain the park includes the valleys of Soana and Orco. By 1945 the ibex had been almost hunted to extinction and there were only 419 left in the park. Today, as the result of a conservation policy, there are almost 4000 living here.

Excellent cross-country skiing trails line the Valle di Cogne, but the park is really devoted to summer activities. There are numerous well-marked trails and rifugi. The main point of departure for the Gran Paradiso peak is Pont in the Valsavarenche.

Information

Tourist Offices The Gran Paradiso Mountain Community Tourist Office (☎ 0165 9 50 55) is at Località Champagne 18 Villeneuve. Cogne's APT (☎ 0165 7 40 40) is at Piazza Chanoux 36. Both have plenty of information about summer and winter activities. If you want a mountain guide, try the APT or the Società Guide di Cogne (☎ 0165 7 43 61), Via Cavagnet 10. Les Amis du Paradis (the Friends of Paradise association, ☎ 0165 7 48 35) in Cogne has reams of information about the area.

Medical Services & Emergency First aid is available in St-Pierre (☎ 0165 90 38 11) and Cogne (☎ 0165 74 91 07). For police in Cogne call ☎ 0165 75 38 32 and in St-Pierre call ☎ 0165 92 78 32.

Activities

If you are interested in a guided, four day walk in the park, contact the Società Guide del Gran Paradiso-Valsavarenche (☎ 0165 9 51 03) or the tourist office. The APT office in Cogne publishes a brief walking guide.

Valle di Cogne is the most picturesque, unspoiled valley with a good range of accommodation in the village of Cogne.

Places to Stay

If you're camping, *Al Sole* (☎ 0165 7 42 37) in the Lillaz area of the Valle di Cogne, is open year-round. In Valsavarenche, *Camping Pont Breuil* (☎ 0165 9 54 58), at Pont, opens from June to September.

There's also a youth hostel in the park, the *Centro di Soggiorno* (☎ 0124 90 11 07), in the *frazione* (small area) of Noasca called Gere Sopra. B&B in this well-looked-after hostel costs L25,000 and there are 36 beds. It's open year-round.

In Cogne, *Hotel du Soleil* (☎ 0165 7 40 33, Viale Cavagnet 24) singles/doubles cost anything up to L58,000/110,000. *Hotel au Vieux Grenier* (☎ 0165 7 40 02, Via Limnea Borealis 32) charges a minimum of around L60,000/110,000.

Getting There & Away

Several bus companies operate reliable services between valley towns and Cogne, running on to Aosta and beyond. Cogne can also be reached by cable car from Pila.

AROUND MONTE ROSA

The Valle di Gressoney, the first of the Valle d'Aosta's eastern valleys, and the parallel Valle d'Ayas are dominated by the massive Monte Rosa. Both valleys are picturesque and popular in summer and winter.

In the Valle di Gressoney, stay in the pretty lake-side mountain village of Gressoney-St-Jean, which retains its traditional atmosphere. Gressoney-La-Trinité is higher up the valley and so is closer to the main walking trails and ski runs, but these days it has been largely taken over by anonymous tourist facilities.

In the Valle d'Ayas the main resort is Champoluc, at the head of the valley, but

Brusson is a good option too, particularly if you want to do easy half or one-day walks. Serious walkers may want to invest in the IGC map No 101.

Information

Tourist Offices There are APT offices in Champoluc (☎ 0125 30 71 13), Brusson (☎ 0125 30 02 40), La Trinité (☎ 0125 36 61 43) and St Jean (☎ 0125 35 51 85). For information about mountain guides, contact the APT offices or the Società Guide di Champoluc-Ayas (☎ 0125 30 89 60).

Medical Services & Emergency For an ambulance anywhere in the valley call ☎ 0125 80 70 67. For police in Brusson call ☎ 0125 30 01 32, in St Jean call ☎ 0125 35 59 80, and in Verrès call ☎ 0125 92 93 24.

Places to Stay

For campers, *La Pineta* (☎ 0125 35 53 70), at Gressoney-St-Jean in the Valle di Gressoney, is open year-round. Hotels in the Valle d'Ayas include *Albergo Cré-Forné* (☎ 0125 30 71 97) in Crest, where singles/doubles cost up to L40,000/60,000, and *Hotel Beau Site* (☎ 0125 30 01 44, Via Trois Villages 2) in Brusson; it charges up to L40,000 per person.

In Gressoney-St-Jean the *Hotel Grünes Wasser* (☎ 0125 35 54 03, Strada Regionale 41, No 14) has rooms costing L50,000 per person, rising to L75,000 in high season. *Hotel Lyskamm* (☎ 0125 35 54 36, Strada Statale 505, No 1) has more upmarket rooms for L70,000/130,000. At Gressoney-La-Trinité, try the *Gasthaus Lysjoch* (☎ 0125 36 61 50, Loc. Föhre 4), where rooms start at L70,000/120,000.

Getting There & Away

Trains running through Aosta stop in St Vincent and Verrès, from where you can catch a bus to either valley. SAVDA operates bus No 33 along the Valle di Gressoney and bus No 35 from Verrès to Champoluc. Bus No 40 connects Aosta with Champoluc, via Col de Joux. Leave the A5, S26 or Aosta-Torino/Milano train at Pont-St-Martin and swing north for the Valle di Gressoney.

euro currency converter L10,000 = €5.16

Lombardia (Lombardy) & the Lakes

From the Alpi to the lush plains of the Po river, Lombardia's often fractious political history is reflected in its geographical diversity. Beyond the financial metropolis of Milano, the region is peppered with affluent towns that preserve a distinct character inherited from the days of the city-states. Mantova, Cremona, Bergamo, Brescia and Pavia have wealth and style, but the northern clime and a degree of orderly self-satisfaction make them staid in comparison with cities farther south. The hard-working people of Milano have built Italy's economic and fashion capital – a businesslike place that more closely resembles the great cities of northern Europe.

Italy's richest and most developed region offers its populace numerous escape routes. The most popular is the stretch of enchanting lakes from Lago d'Orta to Lago di Garda.

Lombardia formed part of Gallia Cisalpina (Cisalpine Gaul) before it fell to Saracen tribes and later to the Germanic Lombards (Langobards). Interference by the Franks under Barbarossa in the 12th century ended when the cities united under the Lega Lombarda (Lombard League). After the Lega collapsed, Lombardia was divided between powerful families – the Viscontis, Sforzas, Gonzagas and Scaligers – and was later invaded by the Venetians, the Austrian Habsburgs and Napoleon.

Lombard cuisine relies heavily on rice and *polenta* and features butter, cream and cheese from the Alpine pastures. Gorgonzola originated just outside Milano. Pasta is fresh and usually stuffed with squash, meat, cheese or spinach. As a dessert it can contain raisins or candied fruit. Meats are predominantly pork and veal – *cotoletta alla milanese* (fillet of veal fried in breadcrumbs) is famous.

Lombardia's sparkling wines are among Italy's best – the Franciacorta red is mellow, while the white is fruity and dry.

Highlights

- Head to La Scala in Milano for a night at the opera
- Contemplate the Gothic complexity of Milano's duomo, then climb up to the roof for views to the mountains
- Take in some jazz and drinks in Milano's Navigli district
- Visit the magnificent Certosa di Pavia monastery, south of Milano
- Wander around Bergamo's *città alta* and listen for the strange *bergamasco* dialect
- Listen to the sounds of violins at the Triennale Internazionale degli Strumenti ad Arco in Cremona
- Chug along in a boat across Lago di Como with a lunch stop in Bellagio, the 'pearl' of the lake

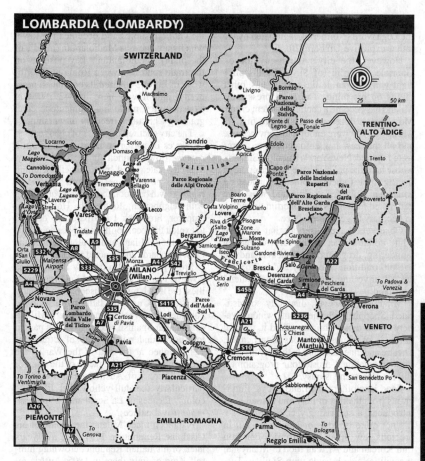

LOMBARDIA (LOMBARDY)

Public transport is excellent and nearly all towns can be reached easily by road or rail.

Milano (Milan)

postcode 20100 • pop 1.6 million

Obsessed with work and money, the Milanese run their busy metropolis with comparative efficiency and aplomb. Indeed, Milano is synonymous with style – the country's economic engine room, it is also the world's design capital and rivals Paris as a leading fashion centre.

Many Milanese have a healthy disregard for Roma and, although Milano is smaller than the ancient imperial capital, it is home to Italy's stock market, most of the country's major corporations and the nation's largest concentration of industry.

Milano's business and political leaders have long railed against corrupt and inefficient government in Roma and the subsidies directed to the south. This sense of protest spawned a separatist party in the late 1980s, the Lega Nord (Northern League), led by the rather explosive Umberto Bossi.

However, the city's tough-guy mayor, Gabriele Albertini (of Silvio Berlusconi's right-wing Forza Italia party), has other things on his mind. The local press feels Milano has become a centre of violent crime. More than a dozen murders in the first six weeks of 1999 were enough to convince one and all that new law enforcement measures were required. New York's Rudolph Giuliani, whose hardline policies have slashed crime in the Big Apple (where recorded homicides are counted in multiples of a hundred) must have had mixed feelings when Albertini turned up in February to get some advice.

Observers have asserted that massive white collar crime, in the form of money laundering, drugs and arms rackets and the age old tradition of bribery and kickbacks, are all alive and well in Italy's financial heartland.

Milano is, however, distinctly sophisticated. Shopping, whether of the window variety or, for those who can afford it, the real thing, is of almost religious significance. Theatre and cinema flourish, the city is top of most international music tour programmes, and the club scene is busy.

Food is another of Milano's joys. Immigrants from the rest of Italy and abroad have introduced a surprisingly eclectic cuisine. It's not quite London or New York but in precious few other Italian cities can you find Korean and African food or Malaysian specialities side by side with Sicilian, Tuscan and Lombard dishes.

The Milanese talk endlessly of getting out of Milano and moving to the country, but deep down you sense they are proud of their city – and few appear to leave. They do depart en masse in August to escape the stifling heat, and you would do well to stay away then too.

History

Milano is said to have been founded by Celtic tribes who settled along the Po river in the 7th century BC. In 222 BC, Roman legions marched into the territory, defeated the Gallic Insubres and occupied the town, which they knew as Mediolanum (middle of the plain). Mediolanum's key position on the trade routes between Roma and northwestern Europe ensured its continued prosperity, and it was here in 313 AD that Constantine I made his momentous edict granting Christians freedom of worship.

The city endured centuries of chaos caused by waves of barbarian invasions, to form a *comune* (town council) in the 11th century. The city-state, ruled by a council including members of all classes, entered a period of rapid growth but soon found itself squabbling with neighbouring towns. The Holy Roman emperor, Frederick I (Barbarossa), decided to exploit the local conflicts and besieged Milano in 1162. Milano and its allies formed the Lega Lombarda and exacted revenge in 1176.

From the mid-13th century the city was governed by a succession of important families: the Torrianis, the Viscontis and finally the Sforzas. Under the latter two it enjoyed considerable wealth and power. Milano came under Spanish rule in 1535 and passed to Austria under the Treaty of Utrecht of 1713, signed at the end of the War of the Spanish Succession. Legacies of the reign of Maria Theresa of Austria are still evident, particularly the dull-yellow (her favourite colour) façades of La Scala and the *palazzo reale* (royal palace).

Napoleon made Milano the capital of his Cisalpine Republic in 1797 and, five years later, of his Italian Republic, crowning himself King of Italy there in 1805. Austria returned in 1814, but this time the occupation was short-lived. Troops under Victor Emmanuel II and Napoleon III crushed the Austrian forces at the Battle of Magenta in 1859 and Milano was incorporated into the nascent Kingdom of Italy.

Heavily bombed in WWII, the city was subsequently rebuilt and quickly grew to acquire its modern industrial prominence.

Orientation

Milano is a sprawling metropolis, but most of its attractions are concentrated in the centre

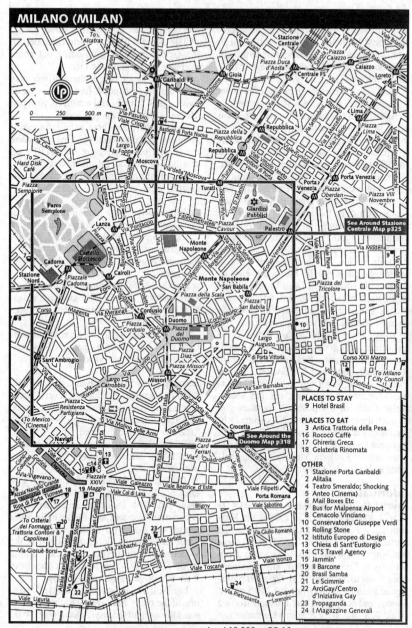

MILANO (MILAN)

LOMBARDIA & THE LAKES

PLACES TO STAY
9 Hotel Brasil

PLACES TO EAT
3 Antica Trattoria della Pesa
16 Rococó Caffè
17 Ghireria Greca
18 Gelateria Rinomata

OTHER
1 Stazione Porta Garibaldi
2 Alitalia
4 Teatro Smeraldo; Shocking
5 Anteo (Cinema)
6 Mail Boxes Etc
7 Bus for Malpensa Airport
8 Cenacolo Vinciano
10 Conservatorio Giuseppe Verdi
11 Rolling Stone
12 Istituto Europeo di Design
13 Chiesa di Sant'Eustorgio
14 CTS Travel Agency
15 Jammin'
19 Il Barcone
20 Brasil Samba
21 Le Scimmie
22 ArciGay/Centro
      d'Iniziativa Gay
23 Propaganda
24 I Magazzine Generali

between the *duomo* (cathedral) and the Castello Sforzesco. The duomo is an unmistakable focal point for your explorations. The city is serviced by an efficient underground railway, the Metropolitana Milanese (MM); where relevant, we have given MM stations in brackets after entries for places of interest. It is easy to get lost, so a map is essential.

Apart from the centre of town, the main areas of interest for tourists are the Brera, immediately north of the duomo, which encompasses many galleries and fashionable shopping streets, and Navigli to the south.

Exiting from Stazione Centrale, built in 1931 and a classic of the Fascist era, you emerge onto Piazza Duca d'Aosta (much cleaned up over the years but still not an ideal place to hang out at night). A good orientation point is the Pirelli building, a slender skyscraper to your right as you leave the train station. Some of the better hotels are clustered here. To the south-east of Stazione Centrale, Via Dom Vitruvio leads to the main area for budget hotels. It meets Piazza Lima at the intersection of Corso Buenos Aires and becomes Via Plinio.

To get from Piazza Duca d'Aosta to the city centre, walk south-west along Via Pisani, through the enormous park-lined Piazza della Repubblica, and along Via Filippo Turati to Piazza Cavour. From here, take Via Alessandro Manzoni, which runs off the south-western side of the piazza. This takes you through the exclusive Monte Napoleone fashion district and on to Piazza della Scala, with its opera house. From there an arcade in the glass-domed Galleria Vittorio Emanuele II leads to Piazza del Duomo.

Information

Tourist Offices The main ATP office (☎ 02 725 24 300, fax 02 725 24 250) at Via Marconi 1, on Piazza del Duomo, provides the useful *Milan is Milano* and *Milano Mese* brochures. It's open from 8.30 am to 5 pm Monday to Friday (usually later in summer), from 9 am to 1 pm and 2 to 6 pm on Saturday and from 9 am to 1 pm and 2 to 5 pm on Sunday and holidays. There is a branch office (☎ 02 725 24 360) at Stazione Centrale.

The Comune di Milano (Milano City Council) operates an information office (☎ 02 869 07 34) in Galleria Vittorio Emanuele II. It's especially good for finding out about events in and around the city.

If you're lucky, one of these offices may have copies of a good free visitors guide (with lots of listings and a mini-map) called *Milano – Dove, Come, Quando*.

Finally, there are three local information numbers in Italian. You can find out where the nearest pharmacies are on ☎ 1100, get cinema and museum information on ☎ 1101, and hotel information and the locations of the nearest ATMs on ☎ 1102.

Publications Those planning to hang out in Milano for a long time may want to pick up the monthly publication *The Informer*, available at the American Bookstore. It is particularly good for advice on dealing with bureaucracy.

Another useful free monthly publication is *Hello Milano*. This English-language magazine is packed with listings, maps and practical information.

If you're planning to live here, *Milanopass* (L19,000) has 300-plus pages of listings. You'll find it in most bookshops.

Money You will find a Banca di San Paolo ATM in Stazione Centrale and several banks on the southern side of Piazza Duca d'Aosta. The Exact currency exchange booth at the Stazione Centrale is open from 7 am to 10.30 pm daily; watch out for the commission. It also offers a Western Union money transfer service.

The Banca Commerciale Italiana has a 24 hour booth, with a currency exchange machine and ATMs inside, on the corner of Via Alessandro Manzoni and Piazza della Scala – you need a cash (or credit) card to get in. There are bureaux de change, open at the weekend, at both airports. American Express (☎ 02 720 03 694), Via Brera 3, is open from 9 am to 5.30 pm Monday to Friday.

For Western Union money transfers, go to one of the many Mail Boxes Etc stores scattered throughout the city. A handy one (☎ 02

670 71 039) is at Piazza Caiazzo 3, not far east of Stazione Centrale. There's another store (☎ 02 290 02 245) at Via Moscova 13.

The Extra Change office at Via Dom Scarlatti 19 can organise MoneyGram transfers.

Post & Communications The main post office is on Piazza Cordusio, although the office (and parcel post) at Via Cordusio 4 is open longer hours: from 8.15 am to 7.30 pm Monday to Friday, to 4.20 pm on Saturday.

The main Telecom office is in Galleria Vittorio Emanuele II; it's open from 8 am to 9.30 pm daily. Another office at Stazione Centrale is open from 8 am to 9.30 pm and has telephone directories for Italy, France, Germany, the UK and other European countries. Neither office is staffed.

Cut-price phone offices are spreading around Stazione Centrale, especially on Via Dom Scarlatti. Phone Centre at No 19 and World Link Phone, across the road, are typical. They also sell a growing range of cheaprate international calling cards. Always check the rates on these services carefully.

The Hard Disk Café (☎ 02 331 01 038), Corso Sempione 44, is an Internet café where you can send email and surf the internet for L10,000 an hour until 9 pm. Its Web site is at www.hdc.it.

Travel Agencies For student and budget travel, CTS has offices at Via San Antonio 2 (☎ 02 58 47 51), Corso di Porta Ticinese 100 (☎ 02 837 26 74) and Via di V Peroni 21 (☎ 02 706 32 059). CIT (☎ 02 86 37 01) is in the Galleria Vittorio Emanuele II.

Bookshops The American Bookstore (☎ 02 87 89 20), Via Camperio 16, has a good selection of English books. Alternatively try the English Bookshop (☎ 02 469 44 68), Via Ariosto. For French books visit the Ile de France Libreria Francese (☎ 02 760 01 767), Via San Pietro all'Orto 10. You could also try Feltrinelli, Via Alessandro Manzoni 12. They sell books published in a variety of languages.

For an extensive range of guidebooks and the best map selection (including complete sets of the Kompass and Tabacco 1:25,000

walking series), try the Touring Club Italiano bookshop (☎ 02 8 52 61) at Corso Italia 10.

Cultural Centres Milano's cultural centres include: the German Goethe Institut (☎ 02 760 05 871), Via San Paolo 10; the Centre Culturel Français (☎ 02 485 91 911), Corso Magenta 63; and for Spain, the Instituto Cervantes (☎ 02 720 23 450), Via Dante 12.

Gay & Lesbian Travellers For information on gay activities, call ArciGay/Centro d'Iniziativa Gay (☎ 02 581 00 399), Via Torricelli 19. The staff can advise on other associations in Milano and throughout Italy.

Laundry There are a few *lavanderie* (laundrettes) in the Stazione Centrale area. The handiest is the Lavanderia Self Service, Via Tadino 4, where washing 7kg of clothes costs L5000. Another, but farther away, is Onda Blu at Via Paisiello 4, off Viale Abruzzi, a short way south of Piazzale Loreto.

Medical Services & Emergency The Ospedale Maggiore Policlinico (hospital; ☎ 02 5 50 31) is at Via Francesco Sforza 35, near the city centre. There's an all-night pharmacy at Stazione Centrale (☎ 02 669 07 35). For a doctor out of hours, call ☎ 02 3 45 67.

The questura (police station; ☎ 02 6 22 61) is at Via Fatebenefratelli 11. Some staff speak English.

Dangers & Annoyances Milano's main shopping areas are popular haunts for pickpockets and thieves.

Lost Property For *oggetti smarriti* (lost property), contact the Milano City Council (☎ 02 546 52 99) at Via Friuli 39. Otherwise try Linate airport (☎ 02 701 24 451), Malpensa airport (☎ 02 748 54 215) or the Ufficio Oggetti Rinvenuti (☎ 02 637 12 667) at Stazione Centrale.

Duomo
Milano's navel, Piazza del Duomo (MM1 or MM3 Duomo), has the atmosphere of London's Piccadilly Circus but the latter's statue

LOMBARDIA & THE LAKES

of Eros doesn't quite compare with Milano's most visible monument, the duomo. Commissioned in 1386 by Gian Galeazzo Visconti, it is the world's fourth largest church.

The first glimpse of this late Gothic wonder is certainly memorable, with its marble façade shaped into pinnacles, statues and pillars, the whole held together by a web of flying buttresses. Some 135 spires and 3200 statues have somehow been crammed onto the roof and into the façade.

The central spire is capped by a gilded copper statue of the Madonna, 108m above the ground. The forest of spires, statuary and pinnacles generally distracts observers from an interesting omission – Milano's duomo has no bell tower.

The huge brass doors at the front bear the marks of bombs that fell near the duomo during WWII. The inside of the duomo features 15th century stained-glass windows on the right and later copies on the left – you will notice a definite contrast between the two.

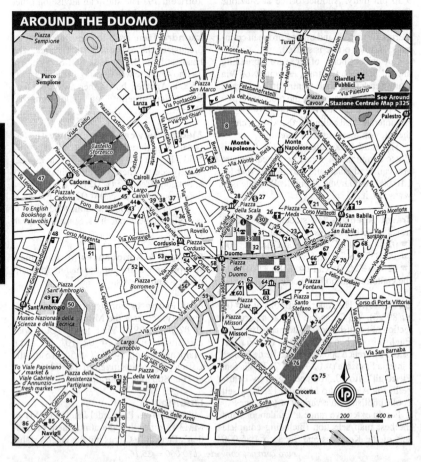

AROUND THE DUOMO

A nail, stored high above the altar, is said to have come from Christ's cross and is displayed once a year in September. Originally lowered using a device made by Leonardo da Vinci called the *nigola*, the nail is now retrieved by more modern means. The nigola is stored near the roof on the right-hand side as you enter the duomo by the main entrance off Piazza del Duomo. Next to the main entrance is a stairwell leading down to an early Christian baptistry that predates the Gothic church. Admission to the duomo is free but admission to the baptistry costs L3000.

The 158 step climb to the roof of the duomo (L6000) is worth the effort – for some locals the roof serves as a sunbathing terrace. You can take the lift for L8000. The entrance is outside the church on the northern flank.

Around the Duomo

At the **Museo del Duomo**, Piazza del Duomo 14, you can study in more detail the church's six centuries of history, plus a rich collection of sculptures, some made for the duomo from the 14th to 19th century. It is open from 9.30 am to 12.30 pm and 3 to 6 pm daily except Monday. Admission costs L10,000.

The **Civico Museo d'Arte Contemporanea** (MM1 Duomo or MM3 Missori), in the restored Palazzo Reale, south of the duomo, is dedicated to works by Italian futurists and lesser-known modern Italian artists. It's open from 9.30 am to 5.30 pm Tuesday to Sunday.

Virtually destroyed in bombing raids during WWII and rebuilt afterwards, the cruciform **Galleria Vittorio Emanuele II** leads north off Piazza del Duomo. The galleria,

AROUND THE DUOMO

PLACES TO STAY		
2	Albergo Commercio	
13	Hotel Manzoni	
38	Hotel London	
43	Hotel Cairoli	
52	Albergo Vecchia Milano	
59	Hotel Speronari	
85	Albergo Cantore	

PLACES TO EAT		
5	Orient Express	
6	Bar Jamaica	
9	Brek	
10	Caffè del Sole	
12	La Bice	
14	Il Salumaio	
15	Don Lisander	
18	Cova	
21	Sunflower Bar; Milan Point	
24	Ristorante di Gennaro	
25	Luini	
31	Savini	
32	Autogrill	
36	Lemantèa Taberna San Tomaso	
37	Vecchia Napoli	
41	Ciao	
42	Antica Osteria Milanese	
45	Viel	
55	Ristorante Peck	
57	Peck	
58	Amico	
60	Pizzeria Dogana	
61	Ciao	

66	Panino Giusto	
70	Ciao	
71	Bar dell'Università	
73	Ristorante Le Cento Pizze	
74	Antica Osteria del Laghetto	
83	Osteria dell'Operetta	
84	Cucchi	
86	Milanodoc	

OTHER		
1	Le Trottoir	
3	Biblos	
4	Club 2	
7	American Express	
8	Palazzo di Brera; Pinacoteca di Brera	
11	British Council; Versace	
16	Museo Poldi-Pezzoli	
17	Feltrinelli Bookshop	
19	Chiesa di San Babila	
20	Ile de France Liberia Francese	
22	Goethe Institut	
23	British Consulate	
26	Chiesa di San Fedele	
27	Banca Commerciale Italiana 24 Hour Booth	
28	Teatro alla Scala (La Scala)	
29	Comune di Milano Information Office	
30	Palazzo Marino	
33	Galleria Vittorio Emanuele II	
34	Telecom Office	
35	Museo Teatrale alla Scala	

39	Instituto Cervantes	
40	Chiariva	
44	American Bookstore	
46	Main Bus Station	
47	Stazione Nord	
48	Bar Magenta	
49	Basilica di Sant'Ambrogio	
50	Università Cattolica	
51	Civico Museo Archeologico; Chiesa di san Maurizio	
53	Post Office	
54	Main Post Office	
56	Pinacoteca Ambrosiana	
62	Main APT Tourist Office; Centro di Guide Turistiche	
63	Palazzo Reale; Civico Museo d'Arte Contemporanea	
64	Museo del Duomo	
65	Duomo	
67	Cinemas	
68	Australian Consulate	
69	Milano Ticket	
72	CTS Travel Agency	
75	Ospedale Maggiore Policlinico (Hospital)	
76	Università Statale	
77	Torre Velasca	
78	Touring Club Italiano Bookshop	
79	British Airways	
80	Chiesa di San Lorenzo Maggiore; Piazza Vetra	
81	Black Friars	
82	Colonial Café	

LOMBARDIA & THE LAKES

designed by Giuseppe Mengoni, was one of the first buildings in Europe to employ mainly iron and glass as structural elements. The four mosaics around the central octagon represent Europe, Africa, Asia and North America. The galleria became known as 'il salotto di Milano' (Milano's drawing room) thanks to its elegant cafés, such as Savini.

South-west of Piazza del Duomo, the **Pinacoteca Ambrosiana**, Piazza Pio XI 2 (MM1 Cordusio), is one of the city's finest galleries and contains Italy's first real still life, Caravaggio's *Canestra di Frutta* (Fruit Basket), as well as works by Tiepolo, Titian and Raphael. Also on show is Leonardo da Vinci's *Musico* (Musician). The library contains many protected Leonardo manuscripts.

On this site in 1609, Cardinal Federico Borromeo founded a fine public library, one of the first in Europe. Nine years later it was followed by the gallery, whose collection was donated by the cardinal. That collection continued to grow in the following centuries and it now spreads out over 24 rooms. The gallery opens from 10 am to 5 pm daily except Monday. Admission costs L12,000.

Behind the gallery lies the **Chiesa di San Sepolcro**, begun in 1030 and featuring a Romanesque crypt. It was dedicated to the Holy Sepulchre during the Second Crusade.

South of the duomo, and best viewed from the church's roof, is one of Milano's more memorable skyscrapers, the **Torre Velasca**, a 20 storey building topped by a six storey protruding block. A classic late 1950s design by Studio BBPR, this building deserves a look.

La Scala & Around

Walk north through the Galleria Vittorio Emanuele II from Piazza del Duomo to Piazza della Scala, dominated by a monument dedicated to Leonardo, and the **Teatro alla Scala** (MM1 or MM3 Duomo). La Scala, as it is commonly known, opened on 3 August 1778 and was the venue for innumerable operatic first nights throughout the 19th and early 20th centuries. Heavily damaged in WWII, it was reopened in 1946 under the baton of Arturo Toscanini, who returned from New York after a 15 year absence.

A Saint of the World

When the future Sant'Ambrogio (Saint Ambrose) was appointed Bishop of Milano in 374, to great public acclaim, his credentials were hardly in order – he hadn't even been baptised. Small matter; this former governor of Liguria had impressed everyone with his skills in umpiring between Catholics and Arians (a Christian sect that denied Christ's oneness with God), so he received all the sacraments and the mitre in an unusually accelerated procedure.

At that time, Milano was the effective capital of the western half of the crumbling Roman Empire and Ambrogio became a leading figure in imperial politics. He and the emperor of the western half of the Roman empire, Gratian, embarked on a crusade to eradicate paganism and the Arian heresy.

His influence grew such that he was later able to challenge the authority of Theodosius – the eastern emperor and guarantor of the western empire after Gratian's assassination – with impunity. In one incident, the emperor had ordered Christians responsible for burning down a synagogue to rebuild it. Ambrogio demanded the order be revoked and, threatening to thump the pulpit and stir popular feeling on the issue, convinced the emperor to see things his way.

Ambrogio, the public functionary who had never been a priest, turned out to be a powerful and charismatic bishop. He was the incarnation of the triumph of spiritual over secular power. He presaged the Church's future political role in European affairs and inspired the composition of the *Te Deum*. He died in 397

The adjoining **Museo Teatrale alla Scala** boasts such curiosities as Verdi's death mask (complete with the maestro's facial hairs). You can wander into the opera house from the museum, which is open from 9 am to noon and 2 to 5 pm daily (closed on Sunday from November to April). Admission costs L6000.

The **Palazzo Marino**, between Piazza della

Milano's blend of old and new

Milano's duomo – a forest of spires and statuary

Flying the flag(s), Piazza del Duomo, Milano

Maria Teresa's legacy, Teatro La Scala, Milano

The neobaroque expanse of Stazione Centrale

The beautiful tranquility of Lago Maggiore

Castello Scaligero, Sirmione

Fish baiting, Lago di Como

Boat for hire – Sirmione provides the perfect base to explore Lago Maggiore.

Scala and Piazza San Fedele, was begun in 1558 by Galeazzo Alessi and is a masterpiece of 16th century residential architecture. Admission is free except during exhibitions.

There are more than 60 grand *palazzi* (mansions) scattered about the city centre – a far cry from the several hundred that were still standing at the end of the 19th century, but impressive enough.

North-east along Via Alessandro Manzoni is the **Museo Poldi-Pezzoli** (MM3 Monte Napoleone), containing a rich collection bequeathed to the city in 1881 by the nobleman Giacomo Poldi-Pezzoli. It's a pleasure wandering the two floors of this old mansion, which are filled with collections of jewellery, porcelain, sundials, tapestries, ancient armaments, period furniture and paintings. Of the latter (most on the 1st floor), you'll find contributions from Tiepolo, Botticelli, Giovanni and Jacopo Bellini, Piero della Francesca, Mantegna, Crivelli, Lorenzo Lotto, Il Pinturicchio, Filippo Lippi and others. It is open from 9.30 am to 12.30 pm and 2.30 to 6 pm daily except Monday (and a little longer on Saturday). Admission costs L10,000.

Castello Sforzesco

At the northern end of Via Dante looms the Castello Sforzesco (MM1 Cadorna or Cairoli, or MM2 Cadorna). Originally a Visconti fortress, it was entirely remodelled by Francesco Sforza in the 15th century; Leonardo aided in designing the defences. Its modern museums house excellent sculpture collections, including Michelangelo's *Pietà Rondanini*. Other collections include an applied arts display and a decent picture gallery, featuring works by Bellini, Tiepolo, Mantegna, Correggio, Titian and a Van Dyck. There's also a museum devoted to ancient Egyptian artefacts. These museums open from 9.30 am to 5.30 pm Tuesday to Sunday. Admission is free. Behind the castle, the **Parco Sempione** is a 47 hectare park featuring a sadly neglected arena inaugurated by Napoleon.

Palazzo di Brera

The sprawling 17th century Palazzo di Brera, on Via Brera, east of the Castello Sforzesco, houses the **Pinacoteca di Brera** (MM2 Lanza). Its extensive treasury of paintings has continued to grow since the gallery was inaugurated at the beginning of the 19th century, but it's a somewhat fusty old place and a little disappointing.

Andrea Mantegna's masterpiece *The Dead Christ* is one of the better known works on display. Also represented are Raphael, Bellini (look for his *Madonna and Child*), Tiepolo, Rembrandt, Goya, Caravaggio, Van Dyck, El Greco and many more. Temporary exhibitions are held regularly. It is open from 9 am to 6 pm Tuesday to Saturday, to 12.30 pm Sunday. Admission costs L8000.

Cenacolo Vinciano

Leonardo da Vinci's masterful mural depicting the Last Supper is in the Cenacolo Vinciano (Vinciano Refectory), next to the **Chiesa di Santa Maria delle Grazie** (MM1 Conciliazione or MM1 or MM2 Cadorna), west of Stazione Nord. Painted between 1495 and 1498 in the refectory of the Convento di Santa Maria delle Grazie, Leonardo's work is believed to capture the moment when Jesus uttered, 'One of you will betray me'. The word *cenacolo* means refectory, the place where Christ and the 12 Apostles celebrated the Last Supper, and also is used to refer to any mural depicting this scene.

Painstaking restoration of the *Last Supper* began in 1977 and was finally completed in May 1999. Centuries of damage from floods, bombing and decay had left the mural in a lamentable state. The method employed by restorers in the 19th century caused the most damage – their alcohol and cotton wool removed a layer from the painting. Even so, Leonardo must take some of the blame, as his experimental mix of oil and tempera was not very durable. Vasari, the 16th century biographer of Italian artists, observed that it was already fading in his time.

Getting to see the *Last Supper* is something of a medieval test of faith. Groups of 25 are sluiced through every 15 minutes, but the real hitch is that you have to book ahead by phone. From within Italy call ☎ 199 199 100. From abroad call ☎ 39 02 894 21 146

LOMBARDIA & THE LAKES

or 39 041 520 03 45. Dialling is the easy part. Operators for both international and national lines appear to speak only Italian. Let's say it's your lucky day and you reach an operator who speaks your language. This is what you'll be up against. Firstly, admission costs L12,000. Then the booking fee is L2000. OK fine. Add the cost of an international phone call (which can go on for a while). Then you can only send your payment by postal order (which also costs). You'd better remember to keep the receipt, because you are bound to arrive in Italy before the postal order. The receipt will be proof you actually sent it. If you are absolutely sure you want to put yourself through all this, summer opening hours, at time of writing, are: from 9 am to 9 pm Tuesday to Friday, until midnight Saturday and until 8 pm Sunday.

We have had reports that it's possible to get in without booking if business is very slack and you are prepared to queue for some time. You could try your luck, but don't bet on it.

South of Castello Sforzesco

The **Civico Museo Archeologico**, Corso Magenta 15 (MM2 Cadorna), features substantial Roman, Greek, Etruscan, Gandhara (ancient north-west Indian) and medieval sections and is housed in the Monastero Maggiore, which is attached to the Chiesa di San Maurizio. It also contains frescoes by Bernardino Luini and is open from 9.30 am to 5.30 pm daily except Monday. Admission is free.

A short stroll south, the Romanesque **Basilica di Sant'Ambrogio** – dedicated to Milano's patron saint, Sant'Ambrogio (Saint Ambrose; see the earlier boxed text 'A Saint of the World') – dominates the piazza of the same name. Founded in the 4th century by Ambrogio, Bishop of Milano, the church has been repaired, rebuilt and restored several times since and is a bit of a hotchpotch of styles. The shorter of the two bell towers dates to the 9th century, as does the remarkable ciborium under the dome inside. It is believed that at least parts of the columns inside date back to the time of Sant'Ambrogio, the saint himself is buried in the crypt. The at-

tached **museum** houses relics dating from the earliest days of the basilica's existence, and is open from 10 am to noon and 3 to 5 pm daily except Tuesday (afternoons only on Saturday and public holidays). Admission to the museum costs L3000.

The Museo Nazionale della Scienza e della Tecnica, Via San Vittore 21 (MM2 Sant'Ambrogio), is one of the world's largest technology museums and features a room dedicated to Leonardo's scientific work. It is open from 9.30 am to 5 pm daily, except non-holiday Mondays (to 6.30 pm on Saturday and public holidays). Admission costs L10,000.

Around Piazza Cavour

The **Civica Galleria d'Arte Moderna**, Via Palestro 16 (MM1 Palestro), in the 18th century Villa Reale which Napoleon temporarily called home, has a wide collection of 19th century works, including many from the Milanese neoclassical period. It opens from 9.30 am to 5.30 pm Tuesday to Sunday; admission is free. In the grounds you can see more recent work in the **Padiglione d'Arte Contemporanea**. To the south, the nearby **Chiesa di San Babila** (MM1 San Babila) is said to have been built on the site of a paleo-Christian church dating from 46 AD.

Around Navigli

The **Chiesa di San Lorenzo Maggiore**, Piazza Vetra (MM3 Missori), an early Christian church built between 355 and 372 on the site of a Roman building, features several 3rd century columns. The **Chiesa di Sant'Eustorgio**, Piazza Sant'Eustorgio, was built in the 9th century and altered in the 11th century; it features a 15th century Cappella Portinari (Chapel of St Peter Martyr). The church's baptistry was designed by Donato Bramante.

Courses

The Linguadue School of Italian (☎ 02 295 19 972), Corso Buenos Aires 43, offers individual or group courses in Italian. It is one of several language schools in Milano.

The Istituto Europeo di Design (☎ 02 579 69 51, fax 02 550 12 613), Via Sciesa 4, runs intensive one-month summer courses in photography, interior design, fashion design and graphic advertising. It also has full-time three-year courses.

If you can't beat 'em, join 'em. Fashion has arrived at the universities. The Università Bocconi (☎ 02 583 62 018), Via Sarfatti 25, 20136 Milano, offers a fashion and design component in its MBA course. The Università Cattolica (☎ 02 7 23 41), Largo GemelliS 1, 20123 Milano, offers a six month postgraduate course interestingly entitled Globalisation, Communication and Metropolitan Professions, part of which is given over to fashion.

Work

If you are so taken with Milano that you'd like to live there, one possible source of work is teaching English. There are many schools but competition is stiff and pay unspectacular. The British Council (☎ 02 77 22 21), Via Alessandro Manzoni 38, is not in the habit of employing people who simply walk in, but it might be able to point you in other directions.

Others wishing to teach their language should contact the relevant cultural centre, listed under Information earlier in this chapter.

Organised Tours

Guided tours around the city and to towns outside Milano can be organised through the Centro di Guide Turistiche (☎ 02 86 32 10), Via Marconi 1. Or call in at a tourist office.

The Autostradale bus company (☎ 02 339 10 794) runs a three hour bus tour of the city from the APT office. Departures are at 9.30 am daily except Monday, and tickets cost a rather extravagant L50,000. Better value, perhaps, is the Ciao Milano tourist tram, a vintage piece from the 1920s that runs four times a day past the main points of interest. It costs L30,000 and you can get on and off as you please. You can buy tickets for both at the APT office.

Special Events

If you needed any convincing of the special place that Sant'Ambrogio occupies in the city's iconography, a quick look around will reveal the omnipresence of the adjective *ambrosiano*, from banks and shops to advertising. See the earlier boxed text 'A Saint of the World'.

The Festa di Sant'Ambrogio, 7 December, is Milano's biggest feast day. Until late 1993, religious celebrations and a traditional street fair were held around the Basilica di Sant'Ambrogio, but they now take place at the Fiera di Milano (MM1 Amendola Fiera), the trade, conference and exhibition centre, north-west of the city centre. La Scala also marks the occasion by opening its opera season on this day.

The first 10 days of June are devoted to the Festa del Naviglio, a smorgasbord of parades, music and other performances. Milano plays year-round host to fairs of all kinds – autumn seems to be the most active time for the fashion fairs.

Places to Stay

Milano's hotels are among the most expensive and heavily booked in Italy. The already obscenely high prices (a 1999 survey found the city the fourth most expensive place to get a room in Europe, after London, Paris and Roma) seem to shoot up constantly at well above the inflation rate. When there is a trade fair on (nearly all the time) many hotels hike the prices up even further. Finding a room during a festival can also be a difficult task.

The area surrounding Stazione Centrale is full of cheapish one and two-star joints, but quality varies and singles/doubles for less than L60,000/90,000 are hard to find.

The main APT office will make recommendations but not bookings – the Stazione Centrale office is more helpful in this respect and will call around if things are tight. You can also try the Centro Prenotazioni Hotels Italia (☎ 800 01 57 72, you can phone from abroad on ☎ 02 295 31 605). They are unlikely to book you into anything with fewer than two stars. Chiariva (☎ 02 8 50 41), Via Dante 8, will book hotels of three star rating and above.

The APT office has lists of private rooms, student accommodation, religious institutions and boarding houses. Most are rented by the

LOMBARDIA & THE LAKES

month. It also offers a deal called Weekend Milano – discounted weekend packages in some of the better hotels.

Places to Stay – Budget

Camping The *Campeggio Città di Milano* (☎ *02 482 00 134, Via G Airaghi 61)* is a fair distance from the centre. Go to De Angeli station (MM1), west of the city centre, and take bus No 72; telephone bookings are advised. By car, leave the Tangenziale Ovest at San Siro-Via Novara. Otherwise, the nearest *camp site* (☎ *039 38 77 71)* is in Monza and is open from April to September.

Hostels & Religious Institutions The HI youth hostel, *Ostello Piero Rotta* (☎ *02 392 67 095, fax 02 330 00 191, Viale Salmoiraghi 1)*, charges L24,000 for B&B. Take the MM in the direction of Molino Dorino (MM1) and get off at QT8 (the name of the station and surrounding area) or take bus No 90 or 91.

Protezione della Giovane (☎ *02 290 00 164, Corso Garibaldi 123)*, east of Parco Sempione, accommodates women aged between 16 and 25. Beds start at L37,000.

Hotels – Stazione Centrale & Corso Buenos Aires Most of the cheaper hotels near the station will not take bookings. Many budget places in this area, although handy, double quietly (and sometimes not so quietly!) as brothels. You could easily sleep in one of these places and be blissfully ignorant – or you could be less fortunate.

One of the better places is *Hotel Due Giardini* (☎ *02 295 21 093, Via Lodovico Settala 46)*. The rooms are simple but fast pricing themselves out of this category (singles/doubles start at L80,000/130,000). However those at the back are separated from the outside world by a cheerful garden – you'd never know you were in a big city.

Hotel Valley (☎ *02 669 27 77, Via Soperga 19)* is not in a great location but the rooms are reasonable and it's friendly enough. Singles/doubles with bathroom, TV and phone cost L80,000/120,000. Singles with shared facilities cost L70,000.

East of Corso Buenos Aires is *Hotel Del*

Sole (☎ *02 295 12 971, Via Gaspare Spontini 6)* where singles/doubles cost L60,000/90,000 and triples are L130,000.

A 10 minute walk south-east of the train station, *Hotel Nettuno* (☎ *02 294 04 481, Via Tadino 27)* has singles/doubles for L50,000/75,000 or L65,000/100,000 with bathroom.

Down near Piazza della Repubblica, the recently renovated *Hotel Casa Mia* (☎ *02 657 52 49, Viale Vittorio Veneto 30)* has something of a family atmosphere. Singles/doubles cost L80,000/130,000.

Verona (☎ *02 669 83 091, Via Carlo Tenca 12)* is also close to Piazza della Repubblica. Singles/doubles cost L80,000/120,000 – this includes TV and breakfast, and you can bargain the price down on longer stays in single rooms.

Hotel Kennedy (☎ *02 294 00 934, Viale Tunisia 6)* has acceptable rooms for L60,000/80,000 (or L120,000 with bathroom), but all rooms are on the 6th floor.

Closer to the city centre, in an interesting location near lots of restaurants and well away from the seedy atmosphere of the train station, is *Hotel Tris* (☎ *02 294 00 674, Via Sirtori 26)*, where basic singles/doubles/triples start at L70,000/100,000/130,000.

There is a crowd of budget and mid-range places along Via Napo Torriani. *Hotel Brasil* (☎*/fax 02 749 24 82, Via Modena 20)* is not a bad place. The rooms are of a reasonable size and clean. Singles/doubles cost L90,000/115,000 with private bathrooms or L70,000/90,000 without.

Hotels – City Centre & Navigli The *Albergo Commercio* (☎ *02 864 63 880, Via Mercato 1)* offers singles/doubles with shower for L60,000/90,000, but it's often full. From Piazza Cordusio, walk north up Via Broletto, which later becomes Via Mercato. The entrance to the hotel is around the corner in Via delle Erbe.

Within spitting distance of Piazza del Duomo is *Hotel Speronari* (☎ *02 864 61 125, Via Speronari 4)*, where comfortable singles/doubles with bathroom start at L90,000/150,000. Not so comfortable rooms without a private bathroom are L70,000/100,000.

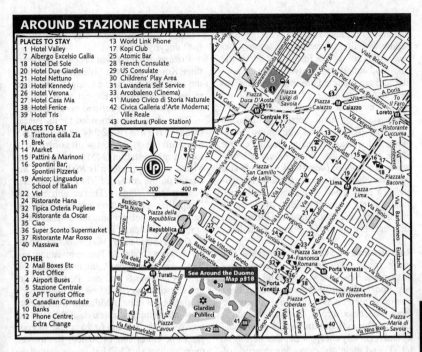

AROUND STAZIONE CENTRALE

PLACES TO STAY
1 Hotel Valley
7 Albergo Excelsio Gallia
18 Hotel Del Sole
20 Hotel Due Giardini
21 Hotel Nettuno
23 Hotel Kennedy
26 Hotel Verona
27 Hotel Casa Mia
38 Hotel Fenice
39 Hotel Tris

PLACES TO EAT
8 Trattoria dalla Zia
11 Brek
14 Market
16 Pattini & Marinoni
16 Spontini Bar;
   Spontini Pizzeria
19 Amico; Linguaude
   School of Italian
22 Viel
24 Ristorante Hana
32 Tipica Osteria Pugliese
34 Ristorante da Oscar
35 Ciao
36 Super Sconto Supermarket
37 Ristorante Mar Rosso
40 Massawa

OTHER
2 Mail Boxes Etc
3 Post Office
4 Airport Buses
5 Stazione Centrale
6 APT Tourist Office
9 Canadian Consulate
10 Banks
12 Phone Centre;
   Extra Change
13 World Link Phone
17 Kopi Club
25 Atomic Bar
28 French Consulate
29 US Consulate
30 Childrens' Play Area
31 Lavanderia Self Service
33 Arcobaleno (Cinema)
41 Museo Civico di Storia Naturale
42 Civica Galleria d'Arte Moderna;
   Ville Reale
43 Questura (Police Station)

LOMBARDIA & THE LAKES

Albergo Cantore (☎ 02 835 75 65, *Corso Porta Genova 25*) is close to Milano's Bohemian zone. Fairly simple singles/doubles cost L40,000/65,000. This place is one of the cheaper deals in town and the location is not bad (although it's hardly handy for transport).

Places to Stay – Mid-Range & Top End
Stazione Centrale & Corso Buenos Aires
The *Hotel Fenice* (☎ 02 295 25 541, fax 02 295 23 942, *Corso Buenos Aires 2*), in the upper three star category, has singles/doubles starting at L160,000/220,000 (more during trade fairs and festivals). The city's most elegant hotel, a stroll back into early 20th century splendour, is *Albergo Excelsior Gallia* (☎ 02 6 78 51, *Piazza Duca d'Aosta 9*). Rooms here start at L446,000/578,000 and then head for the stars.

City Centre The *Albergo Vecchia Milano* (☎ 02 87 50 42, *Via Borromei 4*), near Piazza Borromeo, is a good but slightly expensive two star place where singles/doubles with bathroom cost L90,000/150,000 (when no trade fair or festival is on) including breakfast. *Hotel London* (☎ 02 720 20 166, fax 02 805 70 37, *Via Rovello 3*), off Via Dante, looks swanky but charges reasonable rates. Singles/doubles are L100,000/150,000, or L130,000/200,000 with bathroom.

In a nice area near Castello Sforzesco is *Hotel Cairoli* (☎ 02 80 13 71, *Via Porlezza 4*), just off Via Camperio. Rooms here cost L160,000/245,000 with breakfast; there is a 20% discount if no trade fair or festival is on.

If you want to mix it with the big spenders, *Hotel Manzoni* (☎ 02 760 05 700, fax 02 78 42 12, *Via Santo Spirito 20*) is close to the Versace shop. A room here costs L195,000/250,000, fair or no fair.

Places to Eat

Italians say Lombard cuisine is designed for people who don't have time to waste – because they're always in a hurry for work. Fast-food outlets and sandwich bars are popular and are cluttered around Stazione Centrale and the duomo.

The city has a strong provincial cuisine. *Polenta* (a cornmeal porridge similar to American grits) is served with almost everything, and *risotto* dominates the first course of the city's menus. Try *cotoletta alla milanese* or *ossobuco* (veal shank). Polenta also figures on the sweets menu, but *torta di tagliatelle*, a cake made with egg pasta and almonds, might be more inviting.

Bar snacks are an institution in Milano and most bars lay out their fare from 5 pm daily.

Restaurants – Stazione Centrale
For snacks try *Spontini Bar* (*Corso Buenos Aires 60*), accessible from Via Spontini, or head next door to *Spontini Pizzeria*. *Ciao* (*Corso Buenos Aires 7*) is part of a chain (there are others on Corso Europa, Via Dante 5 and Piazza del Duomo), but the food is good quality and relatively cheap, with pasta starting at L4500 and main dishes costing upwards of L6000. *Brek*, *Amico* and *Autogrill* are similar chains and make quick, cheap but superior alternatives to hamburger-style fast food. Some messy takeover activity is going on among them, so names may change. Several have been marked on the maps in this book.

Ristorante da Oscar (*Via Palazzi 4*) is the place to head for seafood – L15,000 will buy you a gargantuan helping of pasta mixed with watery delights – it's unlikely you'll need a second course. For southern Italian feasting wrap your mouth around the goodies in the *Tipica Osteria Pugliese* (*Via Tadino 5*). The self-serve *antipasti* (starters) are enough to make you drop the main courses.

You can have a taste of Africa at *Ristorante Mar Rosso* (*Via Panfilo Castaldi 42*), which specialises in Eritrean food. A walk through the back streets around here will reveal quite a few other little restaurants. There isn't generally a menu at *Massawa* (*Via Sirtori 6*), you just dig into whatever they put in front of you – various meats and sauces, which you eat with your hands, and *engera* (soft doughy bread).

Ristorante Hana (*Via Lecco 15*) is one of three Korean places in Milano, but probably the best. You can have a straightforward set menu for L20,000. Expect to pay about L50,000 for a more refined evening meal.

Particularly recommended for its Tuscan dishes is *Il Faro* (☎ *02 284 68 38, Piazzale San Materno 8*), a short walk north-east of Loreto metro station (MM1 or MM2). One Metro stop farther east is *Ristorante Cuccuma*, on the corner of Via Pacini and Via Fossati (MM2 Piola). This eccentrically lit Neapolitan place offers excellent seafood and pizzas, often accompanied by someone singing sentimental Italian hits.

Trattoria dalla Zia (*Via Generale Gustavo Fara 5*) is a good little Tuscan restaurant just south-west of Stazione Centrale. Heading farther west towards Stazione Porta Garibaldi and Corso Como you'll find the area haunted at night by a certain Milanese high society crew, all seemingly in search of the most expensive drink. You can find a couple of good places here. For about L50,000, you too can munch where Ho Chi Minh once sampled the best of Lombard food, at *Antica Trattoria della Pesa* (☎ *02 655 57 41, Via Pasubio 10*).

Restaurants – City Centre
The first Milanese pizza was cooked at *Ristorante di Gennaro* (*Via S Radegonda 14*), east of the Galleria Vittorio Emanuele II. Next door at No 16 is one of Milano's oldest fast-food outlets, *Luini*. It sells *panzerotti* (pizza dough stuffed with tomatoes, garlic and mozzarella) for L3000.

Pizzeria Dogana, on the corner of Via Capellari and Via Dogana, near the duomo, serves pasta and pizza for around L10,000.

A good place to head for after the movies is *Panino Giusto* (*Piazza Beccaria*), also known as the *House of Sandwich*. *Bar dell'Università* (*Via Larga 8*), just south of the duomo, serves great-value pizza *al trancio* (by the slice). Not far from here you'll find a few other interesting places. *Ristorante Le Cento Pizze* (*Piazza Santo Stefano 12*) serves up, as the name suggests, an enormous range of pizzas at slightly above-average prices. *Antica Osteria del Laghetto* (☎ 02 760 02 992, *Via Festa del Perdono 1*) has good food in cosy surroundings for about L40,000.

Lemantèa Taberna San Tomaso (*Via San Tomaso 5*), near Via Rovello, has been reborn as a chic restaurant where main courses cost around L25,000; alternatively, you could try the special set menu, *Sette Secoli di Cucina (Seven Centuries of Cooking)* for L70,000. Close by is the more down to earth *Vecchia Napoli* (*Via San Tomaso*), on the corner of Via Rovello, where pizzas start at L9000.

Highly recommended is the charming *Antica Osteria Milanese* (*Via Camperio 12*), where main courses start at L18,000.

One of the city's posher restaurants is *Don Lisander* (☎ 02 760 20 130, *Via Alessandro Manzoni 12A*), which serves Milanese risotto and a host of Tuscan dishes. It's relatively expensive, with main dishes from L32,000.

A good spot for Japanese and Sichuan cuisine is *Ristorante Wu* (☎ 02 46 89 99, *Via Ranzoni 6*), a short walk south-west from Amendola Fiera Metro Station (MM1) or you can take tram No 24.

A favourite with the fashion crowd is *La Bice* (☎ 02 79 55 28, *Via Borgospesso 12*). Expect to part company with L90,000 per person.

If your mouth is watering and money is no object, you could head for *Ristorante Peck* (*Via Cesare Cantù 11*), where main courses start at L32,000.

Restaurants – Navigli There are any number of eateries in and around the Navigli area and the accompanying cafés and bars make it surely the most pleasing part of Milano in which to pass an evening. One outstanding spot, where a full meal with wine will come to as much as L50,000, is *Osteria dell'Operetta* (☎ 02 837 51 20, *Corso di Porta Ticinese 70*).

For good, cheap Greek snacks and meals, you can't beat *Ghireria Greca* (*Ripa di Porta Ticinese 13*).

Farther down on the other side of the canal you'll find a string of enticing restaurants.

Among them, *Osteria dei Formaggi* (*Alzaia Naviglio Grande 54*) is a good choice – meals are made with a whole range of Italian cheeses. Farther down at No 62, *Trattoria Conconi* has an appealing cosy ambience with a wooden interior. The food in both restaurants is of high quality and likely to set you back around L70,000 a head for a full meal with wine.

Cafés & Bars In the Stazione Centrale area is *Pattini & Marinoni* (*Corso Buenos Aires 53*), which sells bread and pizza by the slice for about L3000. The street is lined with small cafés and places to grab a quick *panino* (filled roll).

Cova (*Via Monte Napoleone 8*), in the Monte Napoleone shopping district, is an elegant, but expensive, tearoom where you can mix in with wealthy Milanese. Not as old but just as chichi is *Caffè del Sole* (*Via della Spiga 44*). Close by is another haunt of the fashion-conscious, the slightly less expensive *Sunflower Bar* (*Via San Pietro all'Orto 8*).

Orient Express (*Via Fiori Chiari 8*) is a rather chic spot for a post antique-browsing drink or, on Sunday, brunch (if you can get in). Less rough on the wallet but fairly hip is *Bar Jamaica* (*Via Brera 32*).

South of the duomo, in and around Navigli, is a happening part of town and there are plenty of cafés and bars to check out. *Caffè Cucchi*, at the northern end of Corso Porta Genova, is a fine place for piazza-watching. Head farther south-west and you'll come across *Rococó Caffè*, a cool bistro on the corner of Via Casale and the Alzaia Naviglio Grande.

Gelaterie A popular spot in the trendy Navigli area is *Gelateria Rinomata* (*Viale Gorizia*), on the southern side of Ripa di Porta Ticinese, by the Darsena. Nearby, *Milanodoc* (*Piazza Antonio Cantore*) is also good – try its soya-based *gelati*.

A classic place is *Viel*, near the Castello Sforzesco, a favourite late-night haunt for young Milanese. The gelati are good and the *frullati di frutta* (fruit shakes), better. There's another branch at Corso Buenos Aires 15.

Self-Catering Via Speronari is one of the better areas to shop for bread, salami, cheese and wine. There is also a fresh *produce market* on weekends at Via Benedetto Marcello. The *Super Sconto supermarket* on Via Panfilo Castaldi, just off Corso Buenos Aires, is not a bad place for picking up supplies.

For gourmet eating, head for *Peck*. Its three storey food store is at Via Spadari 9 (just west of Piazza del Duomo). Established in 1883, it is one of Europe's elite gourmet outlets – if anything, more tempting than London's Harrods or Fortnum & Mason – and famous since 1920 for its home-made *ravioli*. Wandering around in here (strongly advised) will open your eyes to undreamed of culinary delights, ranging from cheeses (up to 3500 variations of *Parmigiano* alone) to freshly prepared meals ready to take home. Take a look at the fine wines (three quarters of them Italian), which can cost anything from US$10 to US$1000!

Another Milano institution is *Il Salumaio (Via Monte Napoleone 12)*, a fine delicatessen in the fashion district.

Entertainment

Milano has some of Italy's best clubs, a handful of cinemas screening English-language films and a fabulous year-round cultural calendar, topped by La Scala's opera season. The main season for theatre and concerts opens in October.

Jazz festivals are held at various times of the year – check at the APT office to get the latest details. Look out in particular for the Milano Jazz Festival in November.

The APT office has entertainment listings, as do most daily newspapers. Pick up *Milano Mese*, a monthly entertainment guide available from the APT office.

For some clue as to what's happening in the club scene, *Corriere della Sera* has a reasonable supplement, *ViviMilano*, on Wednesday, while *La Repubblica* counters on Thursday with *Tutto Milano*. Neither is as good as it used to be. Both papers are fine for cinema listings.

Live in Italia is a free monthly publication you can sometimes dig up in the tourist of-

fice. It lists upcoming gigs, although these are mostly international acts. *Hello Milano* (see Tourist Offices under Information earlier in this chapter) is also good if you can get it.

You can obtain tickets for theatre performances, concerts, football matches and other events from Milano Ticket (☎ 02 76 00 91 31, fax 02 76 00 85 47), Via Durini 42 (Scalone 7, 1st floor). You can buy tickets in person or pay for them in advance with a credit card over the phone or through their Web site at www.milanoticket.it. You can also buy tickets for many events in several stores, such as Ricordi in the Galleria Vittorio Emanuele II.

Bars & Pubs There are two areas in particular to search for a drink, some music and the madding crowd. Otherwise, good bars are sprinkled at distant intervals across the city.

Brera The Brera (predictably located around Via Brera) comes alive at night as crowds swirl through the narrow lanes and into watering holes where a beer will cost anything from L8000 to L20,000, depending on the bar and whether or not it has music (usually of the smoke-filled piano bar variety). Among the more popular of these places are *Biblos (Via Madonnina 17)* and *Club 2 (Via Formentini 2)*. As you might have guessed, this is the expensive part of town.

A quirky little spot on the edge of this district is *Le Trottoir*, on the corner of Via Pontaccio and Corso Garibaldi. It also serves food upstairs.

Navigli & Porta Ticinese Head south for Navigli, via Corso di Porta Ticinese, for an alternative to the Brera bars.

One pleasant bar you could start with (if Guinness is good for you) is *Black Friars (Corso di Porta Ticinese 16)*. *Colonial Café (Via De Amicis 12)* is a newer affair, a large, airy place that gets packed at weekends.

The focal point for the truly busy nightlife is Via Cardinale Ascanio Sforza, which runs along the Naviglio Pavese canal. Starting south and moving up, you'll find *Le Scimmie* at No 49, a well-established jazz bar. Where the often filthy dribble of water ends is an even bigger floating bar, *Il Barcone*. Several other places line the same stretch of canal.

Farther to the west, *Capolinea (Via Lodovico il Moro 119)* is Milano's temple to jazz.

For some Brasilian sounds, try out *Brasil Samba (Via Emilio Gola 4)*.

Elsewhere Another traditional meeting place for Milanese night owls is *Bar Magenta (Via Giosue Carducci 13)*, a short walk south of Castello Sforzesco. A good place is *Kopi Club (Via Spontini 6)*, not far from Stazione Centrale. Also within walking distance of the station is *Atomic Bar (Via Casati 24)*, a cool cave with a vaguely grungy New York feel and mean drinks for L10,000.

Discos & Clubs A popular spot in the northern part of Navigli is *Jammin' (Piazzale XXIV Maggio 8)*, although they overdo the Latin theme. *Shocking (Bastioni di Porta Nuova 12)* is practically always open, attracting different crowds with thematic changes in music each evening. Admission costs up to L30,000. *Alcatraz (Via Valtellina 25)* is a fresh addition to the scene. A huge space often used for concerts, it converts into Milano's biggest club on Friday and Saturday nights. Admission costs around L25,000. Another thumping popular new spot is *I Magazzini Generali (Via Pietrasanta 14)*.

Rock Live bands can sometimes be seen at discos like *Propaganda (Via Castelbarco 11)* and *Rolling Stone (Corso XXII Marzo 32)*. Another venue to watch is *Teatro Smeraldo (☎ 02 290 06 767, Piazza XXV Aprile 10)*.

Bigger concerts tend to be held at *Palavobis (☎ 02 334 00 551, Viale Sant'Elia 33)*, near the San Siro stadium (MM1 Lampugnano), or *Filaforum di Assago (☎ 02 48 85 71)*, farther out of town; some recent big names to play here include Lenny Kravitz, Elton John and Massive Attack. To get there, take the MM2 line to Romolo and pick up a shuttle bus put on for concerts.

Opera La Scala's main opera season opens on 7 December, but you can see theatre, ballet and concerts year-round, apart from

the last week or two of July and all of August. The box office (☎ 02 720 03 744), in the portico in Via Filodrammatici on the left-hand side of the building, is open daily from noon to 7 pm and until 15 minutes after curtains up on performance nights.

Book well in advance, as most performances sell out months before. Your only hope may be the 200 standing-room tickets that go on sale at the entrance to the Museo Teatrale alla Scala 45 minutes before the scheduled starting time. These can cost as little as L10,000.

The best seats in the house on premiere night can cost as much as L1,500,000! CIT offices abroad will book tickets, or you can do so on line at www.lascala.milano.it. Note that prebooked tickets carry a 20% surcharge.

Classical Music The *Chiesa di San Maurizio* in the Monastero Maggiore hosts concerts, usually involving small classical ensembles, throughout the year. For information call ☎ 02 760 05 500. Tickets for performances are available at the APT office.

The *Conservatorio Giuseppe Verdi (☎ 02 762 11 101, Via Conservatorio 12)* is the venue for many classical music concerts.

Check out *Milano Mese* for details of other performances around town.

Cinemas English-language films are shown once a week at these cinemas: *Anteo (☎ 02 659 77 32, Via Milazzo 9; MM2 Moscova)*; *Arcobaleno (☎ 02 294 06 054, Viale Tunisia 11; MM1 Porta Venezia)*; and *Mexico (☎ 02 489 51 802, Via Savona 57; MM2 Porta Genova)*. A couple of other cinemas occasionally show *lingua originale* (original language) films.

Theatre At least another 50 theatres are active in Milano; for theatre details check the newspapers and ask at the APT office.

Spectator Sports

Football Milano's two teams, AC Milan and FC Internazionale Milano (known simply as Inter), play on alternate Sundays during the football season at the San Siro stadium, also

LOMBARDIA & THE LAKES

known as Meazza (after Giuseppe Meazza, one of the greats of Italian football). Tram No 24 and bus Nos 95, 49 and 72 run there, or you can take the metro and get off at Lotto metro station (MM1), from where a free shuttle bus runs to the stadium. Tickets are available at the stadium or, for AC Milan matches, from Milan Point (☎ 02 79 64 81), Via San Pietro all'Orto 8, or branches of the Cariplo bank. Buy tickets for Inter matches at Banca Popolare di Milano branches, or call ☎ 02 7 70 01. Tickets cost from L25,000 to L65,000 but can go much higher for big matches.

Motor Racing The Italian Grand Prix is held at the Monza autodrome (☎ 039 248 22 53) each September. The track is several kilometres out of town and can be reached along Viale Monza from Piazzale Loreto.

Shopping

Any item of clothing you ever wanted to buy, but could never afford, can be found in Milano. The streets for clothing, footwear and accessories are behind the duomo around Corso Vittorio Emanuele II, and between Piazza della Scala and Piazza San Babila.

For upmarket and exclusive fashions, head for Via della Spiga, the boutique mecca, Via Monte Napoleone or Via Borgospesso, which runs between the two – all in an area known as the Quadrilatero d'Oro (Golden Quad), or Monte Napo to the in-crowd. Versace is at Via Alessandro Manzoni 38; Krizia is at Via della Spiga No 23. Around the corner in Via San Andrea you'll find Trussardi, Gianfranco Ferré, Prada, Fendi and Kenzo. Valentino, Gucci, Ungaro, Ferretti, Cartier and Louis Vuitton are clustered along Via Monte Napoleone. It sometimes seems as if all Japan's tourists to Italy congregate in this area.

The areas around Via Torino, Corso XXII Marzo and Corso Buenos Aires are less expensive. Markets are held around the canals, notably on Viale Papiniano on Tuesday and Saturday mornings. There is a flea market in

Design

Milano is the world's design capital, although you have to search it out as shops and galleries are spread throughout the city and most products are made for export. The city began to make a name for itself in the design of modern furniture before WWII, but only when the city took off as a postwar industrial powerhouse did Milano's design business come into its own.

The magazine *Interni* occasionally publishes a foldout guide called *Interni Annual*, which lists the names and addresses of most design shops and galleries, as well as upcoming design fairs and exhibitions (of which there are many). The magazine, along with many others that have grown on the back of the industry (such as *Abitare*, *Domus* and *Casa Bella*), is on sale at newspaper stands.

Serious shoppers or design buffs and students wanting to find out where the best showrooms are could look at *A Key to Milan*, a city guidebook published by Hoepli (available in most bookshops for L27,000). It has a good introductory section on design, with a selected list of top showrooms.

Once a year Milano hosts Milano Capitale del Design, a week of expositions, cocktail events and a general celebration of the latest wares on show. *Interni* promotes the week; you can pick up guides to all the events and hordes of design houses across the city at the tourist office. Info also appears on line at www.mondadori .com/interni.

NICKY CAVEN

Viale Gabriele d'Annunzio on Saturday and a decent antique market in Brera at Via Fiori Chiari every third Saturday of the month. Milano's version of Portobello Rd, a huge market where you can buy just about anything, is held on the last Sunday of each month on the Alzaia Naviglio Grande and Ripa di Porta Ticinese (tram No 19).

Getting There & Away

Air The bulk of European and other international flights use one of the two terminals at Malpensa airport, about 50km north-west of the city. Terminal 2, or Nord, is the old one. Malpensa 2000 was inaugurated in late 1998 to cope with increasing air traffic from Europe and the USA.

Most (but not all) domestic and some European flights use Linate airport, about 7km east of the city centre. For flight information for both airports call ☎ 02 748 52 200. You will probably be directed to call one of eight dedicated, computerised information numbers, four for each airport.

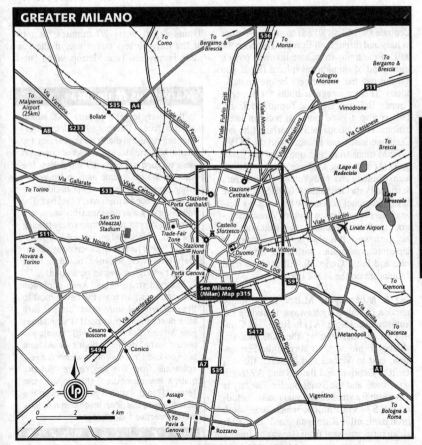

GREATER MILANO

See Milano (Milan) Map p315

0   2   4 km

Major airlines include Alitalia (☎ 02 2 68 51, 02 2 68 52, 02 2 68 53), Corso Como 15, and British Airways (☎ 02 80 98 92), Corso Italia 8.

Bus Bus stations are scattered across the city, so unless you know exactly what you want and where you're going, you're better off on the train. Bear this in mind when considering how to get to Milano as well. Eurolines, Autostradale and several other national and regional companies leave from Piazza Castello, in front of Castello Sforzesco (MM2 Cairoli), to many national and international points.

Train You can catch a train from Stazione Centrale (☎ 147 88 80 88) to all major cities in Italy and throughout Europe. Travel on the bulk of the trains from here involves paying some kind of supplement (plus a fine if you did not pay the supplement before embarkation). There are regular trains for Venezia, Firenze, Bologna, Genova, Torino and Roma. This is also a good point to pick up international connections to Switzerland (the fast Cisalpino train) and France (with the TGV).

FNM trains from Stazione Nord (☎ 02 480 66 771) on Piazzale Cadorna connect Milano with Como, Erba and Varese. Trains from Stazione Porta Garibaldi (☎ 02 655 20 78) are mostly regional services which run to destinations such as Lecco, Como, Varese, Bergamo, Cremona, Mantova, the Valtellina and the north-west. It is always worth comparing departure possibilities with those from Centrale and Porta Garibaldi. All of these train stations are on the MM2 line.

Car & Motorcycle Milano is the major junction of Italy's motorways, including the Autostrada del Sole (A1) to Reggio di Calabria in southern Italy; the A4, aka the Milano-Torino, west to Torino; the Serenissima, east to Verona and Venezia; the A7, south to Genova; and the A8 and A9, north to the lakes and the Swiss border. The city is also a hub for smaller national roads, including the S7 (Via Emilia), which runs south through Emilia-Romagna, and the S11, which runs east-west from Brescia to Torino.

All of these roads meet the Milano ring road, known as the Tangenziale Est and the Tangenziale Ovest. From here, follow signs into the city centre. It should be noted that the A4 in particular is an extremely busy road on which numerous accidents can hold up traffic for hours. From October to April all roads in the area become extremely hazardous because of rain, snow and, especially, fog.

Getting Around

Malpensa Airport The Malpensa Express train (40 minutes, L15,000/20,000 one way/return) between Stazione Nord and Malpensa 2000 began operations in June 1999. Trains depart every 30 minutes for most of the day. Tickets cover use of the Passante Ferroviario (see Metropolitana later).

Marvellous Malpensa

In their hurry to get Malpensa 2000 airport open on time in October 1998, air traffic authorities in Milano didn't do themselves any media favours. The first weeks of operation were plagued by confusion and delays. The icing on the cake came early in November when, one evening, someone decided the runways needed a fresh coat of asphalt. The following day was unseasonably warm and incoming aircraft found themselves landing in a kind of black sludge. Some 40 outward-bound flights had to be cancelled while aircraft tyres were cleaned down – there weren't enough spares to go around!

The odd strike helped keep confusion high and transport from the new airport to the old Terminal Nord (itself blessed with little direct public transport) is scandalous (see Milano Getting Around). Locals expected that all domestic flights would from now on use Linate airport, which is easily accessible from the city centre. But no, quite a few domestic flights depart from Terminal Nord – such a pain that even the slow trains to the deep south begin to look more attractive than flying!

Some early morning and evening services are provided by bus instead (L13,000 one way).

Alternatively, you can take the Air Pullman Malpensa Shuttle bus (☎ 02 400 99 280), from Piazza Luigi di Savoia, outside Stazione Centrale, every 20 to 30 minutes. The big problem is that the old terminal (Malpensa Nord, or Terminal 2) is poorly served. Buses run there infrequently and the only option is to pick up a shuttle bus or taxi from Terminal 1 after catching the train. A taxi from either airport to the centre of town will cost around L100,000.

To/From Linate Airport From Piazza Luigi di Savoia, STAM buses (☎ 02 66 98 45 09) run to Linate airport about every half hour from 5.40 am to 9 pm (20 minutes, L5000). You can also get local bus No 73 from Piazza San Babila (Corso Europa) for L1500.

Metropolitana, Tram & Bus Milano's public transport system, run by the ATM (☎ 800 016857), is efficient. The MM consists of four underground lines (red MM1, green MM2, yellow MM3 and blue *Passante Ferroviario*). Another major line is being considered. Travelling on the underground is the most convenient way to get around, but you may find ATM buses and trams useful too.

A Metropolitana ticket costs L1500, valid for one underground ride or up to 75 minutes travel on buses and trams. You can buy a book of 10 tickets for L14,000 or unlimited one/two-day tickets for bus, tram and MM for L5000/9000. Tickets are available at MM stations as well as at authorised tobacconists and newspaper stands.

Free public transport maps are sometimes available from ATM offices at the Duomo MM station and Stazione Centrale.

Car & Motorcycle Entering central Milano by car is a hassle. The system of one-way streets is aimed to discourage you from entering. Once in, you must pay to park (L2500 per hour) and the limit is two hours. From 7 pm to midnight there is a set parking fee of L5000. You need to buy a blue SostaMilano card from tobacconists and

scratch off the date and hour and put it on the dashboard. Illegally parked cars attract fines and are sometimes towed away.

The city is dotted with expensive car parks (look for signs with a white P on a blue background). You are better off leaving the car farther out near a convenient MM or tram stop.

When parking in the streets (where it is allowed), note that at least once a fortnight the street will be cleaned – you need to shift your car from midnight to allow this operation, otherwise you risk a fine of L117,000 and possibly being towed away.

Hertz, Avis, Maggiore and Europcar all have offices at Stazione Centrale and both airports.

Taxi Don't bother trying to hail taxis as they generally won't stop. Head for taxi ranks (there are 112 throughout the city, marked with a yellow line on the road) which have telephones. A new computerised number for calling up taxis is ☎ 147 81 47 81.

South of Milano

PAVIA
postcode 27100 • pop 85,000
Virtually a satellite of Milano, Pavia is nonetheless a thriving industrial and agricultural centre on the banks of the Ticino river, perhaps best known for its prestigious university. Originally the Roman Ticinum, Pavia later rivalled Milano as the capital of the Lombard kings until the 11th century. Like many cities of the north, Pavia became a pawn of power politics as the Renaissance dawned. Spain occupied it in the early 16th century and only relinquished control under the Treaty of Utrecht in 1713, when the Austrians promptly replaced the Spanish. Austrian rule, interrupted by a few years of Napoleonic French control from 1796, lasted until 1859.

Less than 30 minutes from Milano by train, Pavia warrants a visit – the nearby Certosa di Pavia, a Carthusian monastery founded by the Visconti family, makes such a visit a must.

LOMBARDIA & THE LAKES

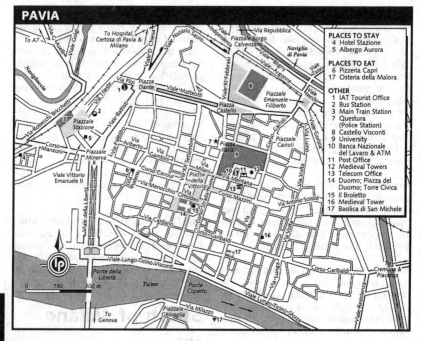

PAVIA

To A7

To Hospital,
Certosa di Pavia &
Milano

Via G Aselli
Viale Golgi
Via G Chiesa
Viale Nazario Sauro
Via Indipendenza
Via Repubblica
Piazzale Borgo
Calvenzano

Navigliaccio
Navigliaccio
Via Filzi
Piazza Dante
Viale D Chiesa
Viale Matteotti
Naviglio
di Pavia
Viale Argonne
Viale Argonne
Viale Ligny
Viale Argonne
Viale Tasso
Viale Necchi

Via Tieste
Via Battisti
Via Bricchetti
Via Robecchi
Piazzale
Stazione
Via Palestro
Luna
Via Ariberto
Via Gambini
Via XI Febbraio
Via Cairoli
Via Luino
Via Gorizia

Piazzale
Emanuele
Filiberto
Piazza
Castello
Piazzale
Cairoli
Corso Cavour

Corso Manzoni
Piazzale
Minerva
Corso Cavour
Via VIII Settembre
Via Milani
Piazza della Vittoria
Via Menocchio
Via Omodeo
Via Cardano
Via Mentana
Corso Mazzini
Via Volta
Via Antonio Scopoli

Viale Vittorio
Emanuele II
Viale della Libertà
Corso Strada Nuova
Corso Garibaldi
Via Volta
Via Moruzzone
Via Lunga

Ponte della
Libertà
Ticino
Viale Lungo-Ticino-Visconti
Ponte
Coperto
Viale Lungo-Ticino-Sforza
Corso Garibaldi
Cremona &
Piacenza
Viale Resistenza

0   150   300 m

To
Genova
Piazzale
Chinaglia
Via Milazzo

| PLACES TO STAY |
| 4 Hotel Stazione |
| 5 Albergo Aurora |

| PLACES TO EAT |
| 6 Pizzeria Capri |
| 17 Osteria della Malora |

| OTHER |
| 1 IAT Tourist Office |
| 2 Bus Station |
| 3 Main Train Station |
| 7 Questura |
| (Police Station) |
| 8 Castello Visconti |
| 9 University |
| 10 Banca Nazionale |
| del Lavaro & ATM |
| 11 Post Office |
| 12 Medieval Towers |
| 13 Telecom Office |
| 14 Duomo; Piazza del |
| Duomo; Torre Civica |
| 15 Il Broletto |
| 16 Medieval Tower |
| 17 Basilica di San Michele |

Orientation

From Piazzale Minerva, across from the main train station at the western edge of the city centre, go north-east along Viale Battisti for about 400m to the IAT office. Corso Cavour, which runs east off Piazzale Minerva, leads directly to Piazza della Vittoria – the duomo is on your right.

Information

The IAT office (☎ 0382 2 21 56), Via Filzi 22, produces a decent map and information brochure. It is open from 8.30 am to 12.30 pm and 2 to 6 pm Monday to Saturday.

The Banca Nazionale del Lavoro on Via Mentana, near the university, has an ATM.

The post office, Piazza della Posta 2, is open from 8 am to 7 pm Monday to Saturday.

The Telecom office at Via Galliano, near the post office, opens from 8 am to 8 pm Monday to Saturday.

For medical assistance, go to the Ospedale San Matteo (☎ 0382 50 11) at Piazza Golgi 2. The questura (☎ 0382 51 21) is at Piazza Italia 5.

Castello Visconti

This forbidding castle, which watches over the northern end of the medieval city (only two of its original four massive towers remain), was in fact only ever used as a residence. It was built in 1360 for Galeazzo II Visconti and now houses the Museo Civico, Museo del Risorgimento and a small gallery of modern art. The castle and museums are open from 9 am to 1.30 pm Tuesday to Saturday and from 9.30 am to 1 pm Sunday. Admission costs L5000.

University

On Corso Strada Nuova is the University of Pavia, which started life as a school in the 9th century and was elevated to university status in 1361. Christopher Columbus was among its notable graduates and the self-taught physicist Alessandro Volta, who discovered the electric volt, lectured here. You can forget the tale claiming Columbus' ashes are held in a safe in the director's office – he is actually buried in Seville, Spain.

Churches

The **duomo**, which boasts the third largest dome in Italy, was started in 1488 but only completed in the 19th century. Both Leonardo and Donato Bramante contributed to the church's design. Today parts of the duomo look the worse for wear – in 1989 its bell tower fell over, killing four people.

The Basilica di San Michele, built in the Romanesque style in 1090 on the site of a 7th century church, was long a preferred location for European coronations. Barbarossa was crowned Holy Roman emperor here in 1155. Although deteriorated, the façade is a masterwork of Romanesque. The statues and restrained floral sculpting on the arches over the main entrance, partly obscured by scaffolding, are as pleasing to the eye today as they must have been a millennium ago.

Medieval Towers

Pavia once boasted some 100 medieval watchtowers. Most have been demolished, but a few remain; a group of three stands on Piazza di Leonardo da Vinci, just behind the post office.

Certosa di Pavia

Nine kilometres north of Pavia, on the road to Milano, is the splendid Certosa di Pavia, a Carthusian monastery and one of the most notable buildings produced during the Italian Renaissance. Founded by Gian Galeazzo Visconti of Milano in 1396 'as a private chapel for the Visconti family and a home for 12 monks, the Charterhouse soon became one of the most lavish buildings in northern Italy.

The interior is Gothic, although some Renaissance decoration is evident. Note the trompe l'oeil high on the nave, which gives the impression that people were watching

the monks. In the former sacristy is a giant sculpture, dating from 1409 and made from hippopotamus teeth, including 66 small bas-reliefs and 94 statuettes.

The small cloisters to the right offer good photo angles of the church, particularly from behind the baroque fountain. Behind the 122 arches of the larger cloisters are 24 cells, each a self-contained living area for one monk. Several are open to the public.

The Charterhouse is open from 9.30 to 11.30 am and 2.30 to 4.30 pm Tuesday to Sunday (or as late as 6 pm from May to September). Admission is free, although you are encouraged to leave a donation.

To get there by car from Milano, take the S35 to Pavia and turn off at Torre del Mangano. The Charterhouse is well signposted. SGEA buses go from Piazza Castello in Milano and from the bus station on Via Trieste, near the train station, in Pavia (L2300). The Charterhouse, a 10 minute walk from the bus stop, is also on the Milano to Pavia train line.

Places to Stay

The choice of accommodation in Pavia is decidedly limited, making a day trip from Milano the most straightforward option.

Hotel Stazione (☎ 0382 3 54 77, *Via Bernardino de Rossi 8*) is OK if you like the sound of passing trains. Adequate singles/doubles cost from L60,000/80,000. The two star *Albergo Aurora* (☎ 0382 2 36 64, *Viale Vittorio Emanuele II 25*) charges L60,000 for a single without private bath and L75,000/105,000 for singles/doubles with private bath. That's as cheap as it gets in Pavia.

You could also stay out of town by the Charterhouse at *Hotel Certosa* (☎ 0382 93 49 45, fax 0382 93 30 04, *Via Togliatti 8*), which has comfortable singles/doubles starting from L130,000/190,000.

Places to Eat

The province produces about one-third of Italy's rice, so risotto is popular – try the favoured local version with small frogs.

Pizzeria Capri (*Corso Cavour 32*) is a reasonable place for a pizza and offers a limited range of simple pasta and meat courses. The

LOMBARDIA & THE LAKES

best place to search for hearty local cuisine is just across the Ponte Coperto. There are at least three places along the river on Via Milazzo and several more a short walk farther south. *Osteria della Malora (☎ 0382 3 43 02, Via Milazzo 79)* offers outdoor dining in the summer and a meal should not set you back more than L50,000 a head.

Getting There & Away
Pavia's bus station is on Via Trieste, opposite the train station. SGEA buses run hourly to Milano arriving at Viale Bligny, south of the centre and also to Certosa di Pavia.

Direct trains also operate to/from Genova, Piacenza and Cremona.

By car, take the A7 autostrada from Milano and exit at the Bereguardo or Gropello C turn-off. The S35 from Milano is a better bet for hitchhikers.

Getting Around
The town is small, but SGEA bus Nos 3 and 6 run from the train station through the main square, Piazza della Vittoria. Most cars are banned from the centre and there are car parks near the station.

East of Milano

BERGAMO
postcode 24100 • pop 118,000
Virtually two cities, Bergamo's walled hilltop *città alta* (upper town) is surrounded by the *città bassa* (lower town), a sprawling modern addition to this magnificent former outpost of the Venetian empire. Although Milano's skyscrapers to the south-west are visible on a clear day, historically, Bergamo was more closely associated with Venezia, which controlled the city for 350 years until Napoleon arrived at the gates. Although long dominated by outsiders, Bergamo has retained a strong sense of local identity, perhaps demonstrated most colourfully by the local dialect, which is all but incomprehensible to visitors. Despite its wealth of medieval, Renaissance and baroque architecture, the city is not a big tourist destination.

Orientation
Viale Papa Giovanni XXIII, which becomes Viale Roma and then Viale Vittorio Emanuele II as it continues uphill towards the old town, forms the city's axis. It is capped at the southern end by the train and bus stations.

Viale Vittorio Emanuele II swings east around the old town walls to enter the città alta at Porta di Sant'Agostino. You can also take a funicular up for the last leg.

Piazza Vecchia is the focal point of the città alta; the main street is Via B Colleoni.

Information
Tourist Offices In the città bassa, the APT office (☎ 035 21 02 04) is at Viale Vittorio Emanuele II 20, while in the città alta it is at Vicolo Aquila Nera 2 (☎ 035 23 27 30). The one in the città alta is handier and opens from 9 am to 12.30 pm and 2.30 to 5.30 pm daily.

Money You'll find several banks in the città bassa and a couple on Via B Colleoni, near the APT office in the città alta.

Post & Communications The main post office in the città bassa is at Via Masone 2A, beyond Piazza della Libertà. It is open from 8.15 am to 8 pm Monday to Friday and from 8.30 am to 12.30 pm Saturday. A branch office on Via San Lorenzo, in the città alta, is open from 8 am to 1.30 pm (5.30 pm in summer) Monday to Saturday.

The Telecom office (unstaffed) in the città alta is just next to the Agnello d'Oro hotel on Piazzetta San Pancrazio. It opens from 8 am to 8 pm daily.

Medical Services & Emergency The Ospedali Riuniti (☎ 035 26 91 11) is at the western edge of town, along Via dello Statuto. The questura is on Via Alessandro Noli.

Things to See & Do
If you have limited time, head straight to the città alta. Bus No 1 from the train station goes to the funicular.

Piazza Vecchia The heart of medieval Bergamo is hard to miss. Whichever way you

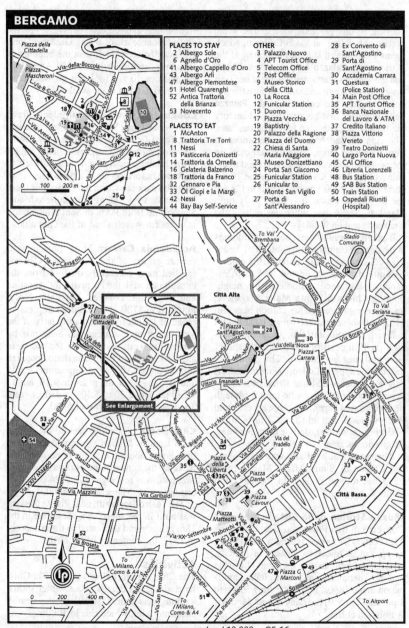

BERGAMO

PLACES TO STAY
2 Albergo Sole
6 Agnello d'Oro
41 Albergo Cappello d'Oro
43 Albergo Arli
47 Albergo Piemontese
51 Hotel Quarenghi
52 Antica Trattoria della Brianza
53 Novecento

PLACES TO EAT
1 McAnton
8 Trattoria Tre Torri
11 Nessi
13 Pasticceria Donizetti
14 Trattoria da Ornella
16 Gelateria Balzerino
18 Trattoria da Franco
32 Gennaro e Pia
33 Öl Giopì e la Margì
42 Nessi
44 Bay Bay Self-Service

OTHER
3 Palazzo Nuovo
4 APT Tourist Office
5 Telecom Office
7 Post Office
9 Museo Storico della Città
10 La Rocca
12 Funicular Station
15 Duomo
17 Piazza Vecchia
19 Baptistry
20 Palazzo della Ragione
21 Piazza del Duomo
22 Chiesa di Santa Maria Maggiore
23 Museo Donizettiano
24 Porta San Giacomo
25 Funicular Station
26 Funicular to Monte San Vigilio
27 Porta di Sant'Alessandro
28 Ex Convento di Sant'Agostino
29 Porta di Sant'Agostino
30 Accademia Carrara
31 Questura (Police Station)
34 Main Post Office
35 APT Tourist Office
36 Banca Nazionale del Lavoro & ATM
37 Credito Italiano
38 Piazza Vittorio Veneto
39 Teatro Donizetti
40 Largo Porta Nuova
45 CAI Office
46 Libreria Lorenzelli
48 Bus Station
49 SAB Bus Station
50 Train Station
54 Ospedali Riuniti (Hospital)

LOMBARDIA & THE LAKES

enter the walled hilltop town, you'll soon find yourself in this gracious square. The white porticoed building on Via B Colleoni, which forms the northern side of the piazza, is the 17th century **Palazzo Nuovo**, now a library and the square's least interesting feature. Turn instead to the south and you will face the imposing arches and columns of the **Palazzo della Ragione**, first built in the 12th century but largely reconstructed four centuries later. The lion of San Marco is a reminder of Venezia's long reign. Note the sun clock in the pavement beneath the arches. Next to the palazzo, the **Torre Civica** still tolls the 10 pm curfew. For L2000 you can climb to the top for wonderful views. It is open daily from March to September, otherwise only at the weekends and on holidays.

Tucked in behind these secular buildings is the core of Bergamo's spiritual life, the Piazza del Duomo. Oddly enough, the modest baroque **duomo**, dedicated to Sant'Alessandro, plays second fiddle to the neighbouring **Chiesa di Santa Maria Maggiore**, an imposing Romanesque church begun in 1137 and whose weather-worn exterior hides a lavish baroque interior. Gaettano Donizetti, a 19th century composer and son of Bergamo, lies buried here. The gaudy Renaissance **Cappella Colleoni** (funeral chapel) is an extravagant addition to the church and is named after the man who built it (though he is not buried here). The chapel opens from 9 am to 12.30 pm and from 2 to 6.30 pm (4.30 pm in winter), daily except Monday. Admission is free.

The octagonal **baptistry** was built inside the Chiesa di Santa Maria Maggiore in 1340 but moved outside in the late 19th century.

Museo Storico della Città In the former Convento di San Francesco (founded in the 13th century), this new museum is still being completed. It traces the history of the city, with special emphasis on the period from the end of Venetian rule in 1797 to Italian unification in the 1860s. It opens from 9.30 am to 1 pm and 2 to 5.30 pm daily except Monday. Admission is free.

Museo Donizettiano A small collection of furnishings and objects belonging to the city's favourite musical son, Gaettano Donizetti, can be seen for free in the building of Bergamo's music institute at Via Arena 9. It opens from 10 am to 1 pm on weekdays; from 2.30 to 5 pm at the weekend.

Lookouts A stroll downhill along Via B Colleoni and then Via Gombito will take you past **Torre Gombito**, a 12th century tower. Carry on along the medieval 'main street' towards the funicular and then turn left to **La Rocca**, a fortress set in a park. The views from the park are worth the effort. For more spectacular views, take the funicular to Monte San Vigilio from Porta di Sant'Alessandro, at the north-western end of the città alta.

Accademia Carrara Make time to visit the art gallery of the Accademia Carrara, reached most pleasantly on foot from the città alta through the Porta di Sant'Agostino and down the cobbled Via della Noca. Founded in 1780, it contains an impressive range of Italian masters, particularly of the Venetian school. An early *St Sebastian* by Raphael is worth looking out for and there are works by Botticelli, Canaletto, Lorenzo Lotto, Andrea Mantegna, Giovanni Tiepolo and Titian. It is open from 9.30 am to 12.30 pm and 2.30 to 5.30 pm daily, except Tuesday. Admission costs L5000.

Città Bassa If heading back to the station for a train to Milano you could do worse than hover about the series of squares that make up the centre of the città bassa. Piazza Matteotti was redesigned in 1924 by a Fascist favourite, Marcello Piacentini.

The **Teatro Donizetti**, near Piazza Cavour, was built in the shape of a horseshoe in the 18th century and dedicated to the composer in 1897, the centenary of his birth.

Activities
The Club Alpino Italiano (CAI), Via Ghislanzoni 15, has details about winter sports, walking and gentle strolls in the nearby Bergamo Alpi, which rise to 1000m.

The APT office also produces several maps of walking trails in the Bergamo province, many of them numbered and quoted with approximate walking times.

Libreria Lorenzelli, Via Guglielmo d'Alzano 3, has a range of walking and cycling guidebooks, in Italian, devoted to the area.

Places to Stay

Bergamo is an easy day trip from Milano, but if you want to stay you must arrive early or telephone ahead – what hotels there are can fill distressingly quickly.

A few cheaper hotels, often full of migrant workers from the south, are scattered about the città bassa, but if you can afford a little extra, some excellent options can be found up the hill. The APT office has a list of camp sites and *rifugi* (mountain refuges) in the nearby Bergamo Alpi and *agriturismo* (tourist accommodation) farms and houses throughout the province.

The *Nuovo Ostello di Bergamo* (☎ 035 36 17 24, Via Galileo Ferraris 1) is several kilometres from the città bassa. Take bus No 14 from the train station. A dorm bed costs L25,000, or you can opt for L30,000 a head in a double or L35,000 a single.

Città Bassa One budget hotel is *Novecento* (☎ 035 25 52 10, Via dello Statuto 23), near the corner of Via Damiano Chiesa, with singles/doubles from L35,000/50,000. It's a bit of a hike from the train station.

Antica Trattoria della Brianza (☎ 035 25 33 38, Via Broseta 61a) is about 20 minutes walk west of the train station, opposite the Coop supermarket. It has modest, clean rooms for L33,000/66,000. Closer to the station and a little more expensive at L35,000/70,000 is *Hotel Quarenghi* (☎ 035 32 03 31, Via Quarenghi 33).

Albergo Piemontese (☎ 035 24 26 29, Piazza G Marconi 11) is one of several three-star places in the area. It charges L90,000/130,000. If you're really out of luck, or have lire to burn, *Albergo Arli* (☎ 035 22 20 14, Largo Porta Nuova 12) has doubles from L148,000. Farther up the scale again, doubles in the *Albergo Cappello d'Oro* (☎ 035 23 25 03, Viale Papa Giovanni XXIII 12) start at L205,000.

Città Alta The *Agnello d'Oro* (☎ 035 24 98 83, Via Gombito 22) could almost pass for an antique shop. Just a short walk from the funicular station, it has attractive rooms from L80,000/135,000. *Albergo Sole* (☎ 035 21 82 38, Via Colleoni 1), just off Piazza Vecchia, has rooms from L90,000/120,000 and is also good. It has a restaurant with a lovely garden out the back – delightful alfresco dining in the summer.

Places to Eat

Like the Venetians, the Bergamaschi are fond of polenta and eat it as a side dish or dessert (*polenta eösei*). They contributed *casonsei*, a ravioli stuffed with meat, to the Italian table and the area is noted for its fine red wines, including Valcalepio.

Città Bassa For a good, cheap bite, *Bay Bay Self-Service* (*Via Tiraboschi 73*) is hard to beat. It's open for lunch only from Monday to Friday. A hundred metres closer to Viale Papa Giovanni XXIII on the same street is *Nessi*, one of a chain of bakeries and pastry shops dotted around the city. Its takeaway pizza is popular – all the school kids swarm in.

Gennaro e Pia (*Via Borgo Palazzo 41*) has pizzas from L6000. *Öl Giopì e la Margì* (*Via Borgo Palazzo 25G*) is expensive (L50,000 for a full meal) but the waiters wear traditional costume, if that's important to you.

Città Alta Cheap food is in short supply here, but you can get pizza and panini at *McAnton* (*Via B Colleoni 22*). *Nessi* has a branch at Via Gombito 34, with a selection of local sweets, including polenta eösei, as well as pizza.

Trattoria da Franco (*Via B Colleoni 8*) has pizzas from around L8000. *Trattoria da Ornella* (*Via Gombito 15*) offers traditional foods, with a full meal costing around L45,000. A cosier spot offering Bergamasco specialities is *Trattoria Tre Torri* (*Piazza Mercato del Fieno*), at the southern end of Via San Lorenzo. You'll need to book ahead.

LOMBARDIA & THE LAKES

Gelateria Balzerino (Piazza Vecchia) is the perfect spot for an ice cream or *granita*. There are a couple of watering holes and cafés along the main street. Try *Pasticceria Donizetti (Via Gombito 17)* for coffee under the porticoes.

Getting There & Away

Air The local airport, Orio al Serio, is a few kilometres south-east of the train station. A handful of international flights land here.

Bus The bus station, on the train line side of Piazzale G Marconi, is served by SAB, which operates services to the lakes and mountains from its own terminal, and a half dozen other lines that go to Milano, Brescia, Cremona, Como and Piacenza, to name a few.

Train The train station is also on Piazzale G Marconi. There are frequent trains for the 50 minute run to Milano and less frequent trains to Brescia and Cremona.

Car & Motorcycle To reach Bergamo by car, take the A4 autostrada from Milano or Venezia, the S11 from Milano or the S42 from Treviglio to the south. On entering Bergamo note that the 'centro' signs refer to the città bassa. If you want to head straight for the old city, follow the 'città alta' signs. Hitchhikers could try the S11.

Getting Around

ATB buses serve the city and you can get free route maps from the office on Largo Porta Nuova. Bus No 1 connects the train station with the funicular to the città alta. Bus No 3 runs from Porta di Sant'Alessandro in the città alta to Via Pietro Paleocapa, in the città bassa. You can buy tickets valid for an hour's travel on buses and funiculars for L1600 or an all-day ticket for L4500. There are machines at the train and funicular stations.

AROUND BERGAMO

There are several small ski resorts in the Bergamo Alpi, notably around the **Val Brembana**, reached from Bergamo along Via Nazario Sauro and **Val Seriana**, reached by

way of Via Borgo Santa Caterina from the città bassa. Each valley boasts seven or eight Alpine rifugi for summer and winter activities, many walking tracks and reasonably priced accommodation (details available from the Bergamo APT office).

VALTELLINA

Covering the band of Alpi across Lombardia's north, the Valtellina is one of Italy's least attractive Alpine regions, although it does have some acceptable skiing and is well set up for walking.

The APT Valtellina has offices in Bormio (☎ 0342 90 33 00), Via Roma 131/b; in Sondrio (☎ 0342 51 25 00), Via C Battisti 12; in Aprica (☎ 0342 74 61 13), Corso Roma 178; in Madesimo (☎ 0343 5 30 15), Via Carducci 27 and in Livigno (☎ 0342 99 63 79), Via de la Gesa 65. See Lonely Planet's *Walking in Italy* guide or pick up a copy of *Trekking in Valtellina* – both guides detail walks and provide rifugio and camping information for the area.

Trains leave Milano for Sondrio, a regional transport hub, and buses connect with the resorts and towns.

BRESCIA

postcode 25100 • pop 197,000

Brescia is a somewhat scruffy provincial capital, arms production centre and transport hub. Although rough around the edges, its student life gives the place a bit of buzz, which is noticeably lacking in other Lombard towns. There are also a few sights worth stopping for.

When the Romans took control of the Gallic town in 225 BC, Brescia (the name derives from a word meaning hill) already had hundreds of years of now obscure history behind it. Charlemagne and his successors were in the driver's seat in the 9th century, followed for 1000 years by a parade of outside rulers. As revolutionary fervour swept Europe in 1848-49, Brescia was dubbed 'The Lioness' for its 10 day anti-Austrian uprising – an unsuccessful prelude to its participation in the movement towards Italian unification a decade later.

Orientation

From the train and bus stations on the south-western edge, the city centre is a 10 minute walk along Viale della Stazione and Corso dei Martiri della Libertà towards Piazza della Vittoria.

Information

Tourist Offices The APT office (☎ 030 4 34 18) at Corso Zanardelli 34 is open from 9 am to 12.30 pm and 3 to 6 pm Monday to Friday and from 9 am to 12.30 pm Saturday. Another tourist office (☎ 030 240 03 55) is at Piazza della Loggia 6. It opens from 9.30 am to 12.30 pm and 2 to 5 pm Monday to Saturday.

Money The Banca San Paolo di Brescia, on Corso Zanardelli, and the Banca Credito Agrario Bresciano, on Piazza Paolo VI, both have reliable ATMs.

Post & Communications The main post office on Piazza della Vittoria is open from 8.15 am to 7 pm Monday to Friday and from 8.15 am to 1 pm Saturday. The Telecom office is at Via Moretto 46 and is open from 8 am to 8 pm Monday to Saturday.

Laundry Give your clothes a tumble at Onda Blu laundry, Via Solferino 8f.

Medical Services & Emergency The Ospedale Civile (☎ 030 3 99 51) is on Piazzale Ospedale at the northern edge of the city. You can get an ambulance on ☎ 030 200 25 22. For late night pharmacies, check the *Giornale di Brescia*. The questura (☎ 030 3 74 41) is on Via Botticelli.

Colle Cidneo & Castello

Brescia's historic centre is dominated by the Colle Cidneo, topped by a rambling *castello* (castle) that has been the core of the city defences for centuries. **Torre Mirabella**, the main round tower, was built by the Viscontis in the 13th century. The rest is a mix of additions and alterations, completed by the city's long series of outside overlords. The castello holds two museums; the **Museo delle Armi Antiche** and the **Civico Museo del Risorgi-**

mento. The former contains one of Italy's most extensive collections of weapons. The latter deals with Italian unification history. Both are open from 10 am to 5 pm daily, except Monday, in summer and 9.30 am to 1 pm and 2.30 to 5 pm the rest of the year. Admission to each costs L5000. You can wander the grounds and much of the castello walls (a smoochers' hang-out) from 8 am to 8 pm.

Cathedrals & Piazzas

The most compelling of Brescia's religious monuments is the **Duomo Vecchio**, or Rotonda, an 11th century Romanesque basilica built over a 6th century circular structure on Piazza Paolo VI. The form of the church is uncommon and there are hints in the mosaics of an even earlier Roman presence here. Next door, the Renaissance **Duomo Nuovo** dwarfs its elderly neighbour but is of less interest (especially while the scaffolding stays up). Also on the square is **Il Broletto**, a medieval town hall with an 11th century tower.

North-west of Piazza Paolo VI is Piazza della Loggia, dominated by the squat 16th century **loggia** (lodge) in which Palladio had a hand. The **Torre dell'Orologio**, with its exquisite astrological timepiece, is modelled on the one in Venezia's Piazza San Marco.

Finally, the Fascist era **Piazza della Vittoria** is well worth a look. Laid out in 1932 by Piacentini, the square and its buildings (like the post office) are a perfect example of the period's monumentalism.

Roman Ruins & Museums

Evidence of the Roman presence in Brescia is still visible. Along Via dei Musei, at the foot of the castle, are the now partly restored and impressive remains of the **Capitolium**, a Roman temple built in 73 AD that now houses the modest **Museo Civico Età Romana**. It was closed at the time of writing, although you can see the ruins from the street. About 50m farther east along the same street is a modest **Roman theatre**.

In some respects more intriguing is the jumbled **Monastero di Santa Giulia and Basilica di San Salvatore**. Roman mosaics have been unearthed here as well. The star piece of

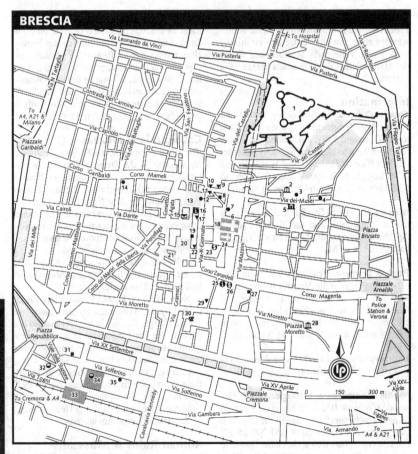

the collection is the 8th century Croce di Desiderio, a Lombard cross encrusted with hundreds of jewels. It was also closed at the time of writing.

Across the street from the Capitolium at Via dei Musei 28 is the **Palazzo Martinengo**; temporary art exhibitions are often held here.

On Piazza Moretto, the **Pinacoteca Civica Tosio-Martinengo** features works by artists of the Brescian school as well as by Raphael. Hours and admission are the same as for the other museums.

Special Events

The International Piano Festival, held from early April until June, is staged in conjunction with nearby Bergamo, while the Estate Aperta festival of music and other activities occupy the summer months. The city's opera season is between October and November.

Places to Stay

There should be no problems finding accommodation in Brescia, particularly in the summer.

BRESCIA

PLACES TO STAY		OTHER		18	Piazza Paolo VI
8	Hotel Duomo	1	Colle Cidneo & Castle	20	Piazza della Vittoria
19	Hotel Vittoria	2	Capitolium;	21	Piazza del Mercato
27	Albergo Regina e		Museo Civico Età Romana	23	Banca Credito Agrario
	Due Leoni	3	Roman Theatre		Bresciano & ATM
31	Albergo Solferino	4	Monastero di Santa Giulia;	24	Duomo Vecchio
			Basilica di San Salvatore	25	Tourist Office
PLACES TO EAT		5	Palazzo Martinengo	26	Banca San Paolo di Brescia (ATM)
9	Al Frate	6	Duomo Nuovo	28	Pinacoteca Civica
10	Caffetteria la Torre	7	Il Broletto		Tosio-Martinengo
11	Vasco da Gama	12	Torre dell'Orologio	30	Telecom Office
17	Hosteria La Vineria	13	Piazza della Loggia	32	Bus Station
22	Spizzico	14	Torre della Pallata	33	Train Station
29	Don Rodriguez	15	Post Office	34	Main Bus Station
		16	Tourist Office	35	Onda Blu Laundry

Albergo Solferino (☎ 030 4 63 00, Via Solferino 1) is near the tram and bus stations and has basic singles/doubles from about L30,000/50,000, although they sometimes charge more.

The budget choice is the **Hotel Duomo** (☎ 030 377 28 78, Via Cesare Beccaria 17), just off Piazza Paolo VI. Some singles are pokey though and prices start at L45,000. Doubles cost from L65,000, but can rise to L100,000. The hotel has a bar and TV room.

Albergo Regina e Due Leoni (☎ 030 375 78 81, Corso Zanardelli), near the APT office, charges L50,000/80,000.

Top of the range, with prices to match, is the somewhat dowdy **Hotel Vittoria** (☎ 030 28 00 61, Via X Giornate 20).

Places to Eat & Drink

Risotto and beef dishes are common in Brescia and the region offers many good wines, including those from Botticino, Lugana and Riviera del Garda.

For fresh produce, locals head for **Piazza del Mercato**. There's a choice of cheap snack places at the bus station, or try **Spizzico**, on the corner of Via IV Novembre and Via X Giornate, for huge fast-food-style pizza slices at about L4500. **Don Rodriguez** (Via Cavallotti 6) serves up reasonably priced pizzas.

Further north, **Hosteria La Viniera** (Via X Giornate 4) offers moderately priced meals and doubles as an *enoteca* (wine boutique).

The happening area of town is along Corso Mameli and Via dei Musei, where there are plenty of restaurants, cafés and bars.

If you're prepared to part with L40,000-plus, **Al Frate** (Via dei Musei 25) serves well-presented regional dishes – it's often full.

Caffetteria la Torre (Via de Musei) is a busy student haunt, while the newer **Vasco da Gama** (Via Beccaria 4) tries to look like an older bar and attracts a crowd revelling in the dim lighting. Both serve food.

Getting There & Away

The main bus station is right across the road from the train station; SIA buses go from another station nearby. Most buses serve Brescia province, Lago di Garda and Lago d'Iseo. Only a few buses go to Milano and Bergamo.

From Milano, frequent trains take 50 minutes. From Brescia there are quite a few trains to Cremona, Venezia, Verona and Bergamo.

By car, the A4 and S11 go west to Milano and east to Lago di Garda and Verona, while the A21 and S45 head south to Cremona.

CREMONA

postcode 26100 • pop 81,000

Home of the Stradivari violin, Cremona today jealously maintains its centuries-old status as premier exponent of the delicate art of making the perfect string instrument. All of the great violin-making dynasties started here – Amati, Guarneri and Stradivari – and

LOMBARDIA & THE LAKES

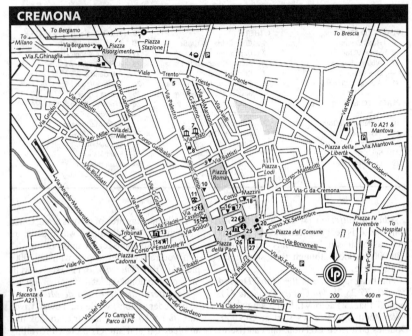

CREMONA

there are plenty of opportunities to get better acquainted with the art of violin making. Not that Cremona is Italy's only centre for violin-makers – rivals in nearby cities will assure you that the only thing better about the Cremonese product is the publicity. For centuries an independent city-state, Cremona boasts a compact but impressive city centre, meriting a stopover, if not necessarily an overnight stay. Cremona is an easy day trip from Milano, Mantova, Brescia and Piacenza.

Orientation
The town is small and easy to navigate. From the train station, walk south along Via Palestro and Corso Campi to the central area around Piazza Cavour, Piazza della Pace and Piazza del Comune. Bus No 1 goes to Piazza Cavour from the train station, but you'll probably travel just as fast on foot. The bus station is off Via Dante, east of the train station.

Information
The APT office (☎ 0372 2 32 33) is at Piazza del Comune 5, opposite the duomo. It's open from 9.30 am to 12.30 pm and 3 to 6 pm Monday to Saturday and from 10 am to 1 pm on Sunday and holidays.

The Banca Popolare di Cremona, on Piazza del Comune, has a money-changing machine, and the Banca Nazionale del Lavoro's ATM on Corso Campi is reliable.

The post office, at Via Verdi 1, opens from 8 am to 7 pm Monday to Friday and to 1 pm Saturday. The unstaffed Telecom office, Via Cadolini 3, opens from 8 am to 8 pm Monday to Saturday. The public hospital (☎ 0372 40 51 11) is on Largo Priori. The questura (☎ 0372 48 81) is at Via Tribunali 6.

Piazza del Comune
Even if violins do not ring your bell, the rust-red heart of Cremona, **Piazza del Comune,**

CREMONA

PLACES TO STAY					
3	Albergo Bologna	16	Ristorante Fou-Lú	13	Palazzo di Giustizia
8	Albergo Touring	18	Ristorante Centrale	14	Questura (Police Station)
17	Hotel Astoria			15	Post Office
19	Albergo Brescia	**OTHER**		20	Duomo
		1	Train Station	21	Torrazzo
PLACES TO EAT		4	Bus Station	22	Banca Popolare di Cremona
2	La Bersagliera	6	Museo Stradivariano	23	Piazza Cavour
5	Pizza al Taglio	7	Museo Civico	24	Palazzo Comunale
9	Pizzeria da Tonino	11	Telecom Office	25	APT Tourist Office
10	Ristorante Marechiaro	12	Banca Nazionale del Lavoro	26	Loggia dei Militi
			& ATM	27	Baptistry

makes at least a brief stop in this quiet town worthwhile.

Medieval Cremona, like most Lombard towns, was an independent comune until the 14th century, when the Viscontis of Milano added it to their growing collection. To keep clear the difference between the secular and the spiritual, the buildings connected with the latter were erected on the eastern side of the square; those concerned with earthly affairs were constructed across the way.

The **duomo** started out as a Romanesque basilica but by the time it was finished in 1190 it had been heavily overtaken by Gothic modishness – best demonstrated by its Latin cross-shaped ground plan. The façade, however, is largely faithful to the original concepts. Inside there is plenty of artwork to admire. Perhaps most interesting are the partial frescoes uncovered in the early 1990s – some, including one of a winged harpy, date to the duomo's first days. Look for work by the Renaissance masters Boccaccino and Bembo. The duomo is open from 7.30 am to noon and 3.30 to 7 pm daily.

The adjoining **Torrazzo**, or bell tower, is connected to the cathedral by a Renaissance loggia, the **Bertazzola**. At 111m, the Torrazzo is said to be the tallest tower of its kind in Italy. It is open from 10.30 am to noon (sometimes 12.30 pm) and 3 to 6 pm (to 7 pm on holidays). Admission costs L6000. To the south is the 12th century **baptistry** which, like many Italian medieval baptistries, has an octagonal base. Alluding to renewal and hence baptism and resurrection, the figure eight appears in much religious decoration – its use in this kind of architecture is no coincidence.

Across the square are the **Palazzo Comunale** and, to its south, the smaller porticoed **Loggia dei Militi**. Both date to the 13th century. The former was and remains the town hall; the latter housed the town's militia.

Museums & Violins
Before you do anything, ask about the *biglietto cumulativo* that allows admission to all

NICKY CAVEN

The Stradivari violin, made by one Cremona's great violin-making dynasties

LOMBARDIA & THE LAKES

of the town's museums. It costs L15,000 and is valid for three months.

While you're at the Palazzo Comunale, take a look at the violin collection, featuring two Amatis, two Guarneris and a 1715 Stradivari. A local maestro occasionally plays the instruments to keep them in working order. To find out if and when he might do so, call the town hall switchboard (☎ 0372 2 21 38) for an appointment. The collection can be viewed from 8.30 am to 6 pm Tuesday to Saturday and from 10 am to 6 pm Sunday and holidays. Admission costs L6000.

As the name suggests, the **Museo Stradivariano**, Via Palestro 17, features items from the Stradivari workshop. Admission times and tickets are the same as for the Palazzo Comunale. Around the corner, the **Museo Civico**, housed in the 16th century Palazzo Affaitati (same hours; admission L10,000), has a mixed bag of paintings and other odds and sods.

If you want to see violins being made, get hold of the APT's list of Cremona's 90-odd workshops. They are commercial operations but you may be able to arrange a visit – discuss it with APT staff.

Special Events
Violin-lovers flock to Cremona for the Triennale Internazionale degli Strumenti ad Arco (International String Instrument Expo). It's held every third October and the next one will be in 2000. The autumn and winter tend to be rich in music programmes and concerts – check with the APT office.

Places to Stay
The **Camping Parco al Po** (☎ 0372 2 71 37, *Via Lungo Po Europa*) is outside the city centre. Head south-west from Piazza Cavour.

Albergo Bologna (☎ 0372 2 42 58, *Piazza Risorgimento 7*), near the train and bus stations, has small singles for L35,000. Closer to the centre, **Albergo Touring** (☎ 0372 3 69 76, *Via Palestro 3*) has singles/doubles for L40,000/90,000. If you're driving in, **Albergo Brescia** (☎ 0372 43 46 15, *Via Brescia 7*) is handy. Decent singles/doubles cost L50,000/60,000. In a small

lane near Piazza Cavour, the **Hotel Astoria** (☎ 0372 46 16 16, *Via Bordigallo 19*) has comfortable singles/doubles with three-star mod cons for L75,000/110,000.

Places to Eat
Cremona's gifts to Italian cuisine include *bollito* (boiled meats) – several varieties exist and *cotechino* with polenta is the speciality. *Mostarda*, often served with bollito, consists of fruit in sweet mustardy goo. Sounds unpalatable, but it's really not bad at all.

For a quick slice of pizza (sold by weight), head for **Pizza al Taglio** (*Viale Trento e Trieste 63*), near the train station. The **Ristorante Marechiaro** (*Corso Campi 49*) serves standard Italian fare, including pizzas for about L9000. **La Bersagliera** (*Piazza Risorgimento 17*) is similar. **Pizzeria da Tonino** (*Via Antico Rodano 9*) is tucked away in a side alley off Corso Campi.

With a little more cash you could try **Ristorante Centrale** (*Via Pertusio 4*), off Corso Mazzini. It's a popular spot, oozing history and charm, where you can try cotechino, admire human-size jars of mostarda and drool over huge drums of fresh local cheese. You can eat well for about L35,000. If you need a change, go to **Ristorante Fou-Lú**, the Chinese establishment on Via Bordigallo, just north of Piazza Cavour.

Getting There & Away
Various bus companies run services to Milano, Brescia and Bergamo and occasionally long-distance buses heading for Genova, Trieste and Venezia call in here.

By train the city can be reached from Milano via Treviglio, from Mantova, Pavia and Brescia, or from the south by changing at Piacenza.

The most direct road from Milano is the S415 (Paullo exit); the A21 takes you to Brescia, where it joins with the A4.

MANTOVA (MANTUA)
postcode 46100 • pop 52,000
On the shores of lakes Superiore, Mezzo and Inferiore (a glorified widening of the Mincio river) is Mantova, a serene and beautiful city.

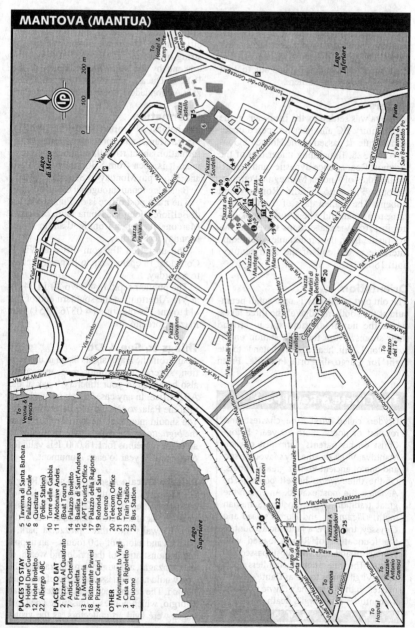

MANTOVA (MANTUA)

LOMBARDIA & THE LAKES

PLACES TO STAY
9 Hotel Due Guerrieri
12 Hotel Broletto
22 Albergo ABC

PLACES TO EAT
2 Pizzeria Al Quadrato
7 Antica Osteria
   Fragoletta
13 La Masseria
18 Ristorante Pavesi
24 Pizzeria Capri

OTHER
1 Monument to Virgil
3 Casa di Rigoletto
4 Duomo
5 Tavena di Santa Barbara
6 Palazzo Ducale
8 Questura
   (Police Station)
10 Torre delle Gabbia
11 Motonave Andes
   (Boat Tours)
14 Palazzo Broletto
15 Basilica di Sant'Andrea
16 APT Tourist Office
17 Palazzo della Ragione
19 Rotonda di San
   Lorenzo
20 Telecom Office
21 Post Office
23 Train Station
25 Bus Station

However, industrial sprawl from its booming petrochemical industry has scarred the surrounding countryside and left the lakes heavily polluted. The city can be visited as a day trip from as far afield as Milano but, to do it justice, spend the night there.

History

Mantova was settled by the Etruscans in the 10th century BC and later prospered under Roman rule. It passed to the House of Gonzaga in 1328, flourishing under one of the foremost Renaissance dynasties and attracting the likes of Andrea Mantegna, Petrarch, Antonio Pisanello, Giulio Romano and Rubens. The golden days of 'La Gloriosa' came to a mean end when Austria took control in 1708. Vienna's troops stayed in control (aside from the predictable Napoleonic interlude at the end of the 18th century) until 1866.

Orientation

The old part of the city is on a small peninsula at the southern edge of the three lakes, while the newer districts spread around their shores. From the train station on Piazza Don Leoni, head a short distance to the right for Largo di Porta Pradella. From there, take a sharp turn left up Corso Vittorio Emanuele II for a 10 minute walk to the city centre. The heart of the centre is a string of five piazzas, capped at the northern end by the sprawling complex of the Palazzo Ducale. The bus station is on Piazzale A Mondadori, south of the train station.

Information

The helpful APT office (☎ 0376 32 82 53), Piazza Mantegna 6, produces a range of information about trips throughout the province. It is open from 8.30 am to 12.30 pm and 3 to 6 pm Monday to Saturday.

Banks are found throughout the city centre.

The main post office is on Piazza Martiri di Belfiore, along Via Roma south of Piazza Marconi. It is open from 8.30 am to 7 pm, Monday to Saturday.

The unstaffed Telecom office at Via F Corridoni 13 opens 8 am to 10 pm, Monday to Saturday.

The public hospital (☎ 0376 20 14 34) is at Via Albertoni, at the southern end of the old town. The questura (☎ 0376 20 51) is at Piazza Sordello 46.

Things to See & Do

Apart from the major sights listed in this section, several other minor museums could also be added to your itinerary – ask at the APT office. In any case, if you only want to visit the Palazzo Ducale and Palazzo del Te, you should inquire at the tourist office about the *biglietto unico*, which gives admission to all of the museums for L18,000. It is valid for one visit in a year to each monument.

Palazzo Ducale Also known as the Reggia dei Gonzaga, after the longtime rulers of Mantova, the Palazzo Ducale occupies a great chunk of the north-eastern corner of the city. Its walls hide three piazze, a park, a basilica and a total of 450 rooms – an imposing demonstration of the pride and wealth of the Gonzagas, although from Piazza Sordello you would never guess the extent of what lies behind. The centrepiece is the **Castello di San Giorgio**, which houses a museum. The Gonzagas were avid art collectors, as the visitor

---

The Chaste & Royal Poet

Dryden called Virgil 'the chastest and royalest of poets'. Born 70 years before Christ on his parents' farm just outside Mantova, Virgil was the city's favourite son and one of ancient Roma's greatest poets. Of the three works he left behind, *The Aeneid* is the most exalted. An epic in the great tradition of the ancient Sumerian myth, *Gilgamesh*, and Homer's *Iliad* and *Odyssey*, the tale is a fantastic account of the foundation of Roma, loaded with symbolism and told with unsurpassed virtuosity. The inspiration of countless poets since, Virgil comes to life as Dante's 'sweet master' in the Florentine's *Divine Comedy*, 14 centuries after Virgil's death.

soon realises. The highpoint is Andrea Mantegna's *Camera degli Sposi*, a series of fine frescoes in one of the castle's towers. This part of the complex is open from 9 am to 2 pm daily except Monday and also from 2.30 to 6 pm Tuesday to Saturday (7 pm in summer). Admission costs L12,000. You are free to wander the rest of the area at will. Occasionally, other exhibitions are held in the cellars of the outer walls, so it is worth taking a stroll outside the city gates and along the palace's lakeside fortifications.

Churches The baroque cupola of the **Basilica di Sant'Andrea**, on Piazza Mantegna, looms over the city in much the same way that St Paul's dominates east London (although the scaffolding around the cupola detracts something from its majesty at the moment).

Designed by Leon Battisti Alberti in 1472, Mantova's principal place of worship houses a much disputed relic: containers said to hold earth soaked by the blood of Christ's spear wound. The very Roman soldier responsible for the wound is said to have scooped up the earth and buried it in Mantova after leaving Israel. The containers are paraded around the town in a grand procession on Good Friday. There is no dispute though about the tomb of the painter Andrea Mantegna, also to be found inside the basilica.

South of the basilica, across the 15th century colonnaded Piazza delle Erbe, is the 11th century Romanesque **Rotonda di San Lorenzo**, sunk below the level of the piazza and believed to be on the site of a Roman temple dedicated to Venus. In the **Palazzo della Ragione**, which runs the length of the square from the Rotonda and was once the seat of secular power in the city, you can occasionally see exhibitions of varying interest – sometimes for free.

The **duomo**, on Piazza Sordello, pales somewhat before the magnificence of the basilica. Its origins lie in the 10th century, but there is little to see of them. The façade was erected in the mid-18th century, while the decoration inside was completed by Giulio Romano after a fire in 1545.

Piazzas Past the 13th century Palazzo della Ragione on Piazza delle Erbe is the **Palazzo Broletto**, which dominates the neighbouring Piazza del Broletto. In a niche on the façade is a figure said to represent Virgil.

Enter Piazza Sordello from the south and on your left you have the grand house of the Gonzagas' predecessors, the Bonacolsi clan. Hapless prisoners used to be dangled in a cage from the tower – aptly known as the **Torre della Gabbia** (Cage Tower). Behind the duomo lies the **Casa di Rigoletto**, which Verdi used as a model set for most of his operas.

Palazzo del Te Mantova's other Gonzaga palazzo, at the southern edge of the centre along Via Roma and Via Acerbi, is a grand villa built by Giulio Romano. It has many splendid rooms, including the **Sala dei Giganti**, one of the most fantastic and frightening creations of the Renaissance. It also houses a modern art collection and an Egyptian museum. It is open from 9 am to 6 pm Tuesday to Sunday and from 1 to 6 pm Monday. Admission costs L12,000.

Boat Tours Boat tours of the lakes and downriver to the confluence with the Po are available. Inquire at Motonave Andes (☎ 0376 32 28 75), Piazza Sordello 8. Cruises of one to 1½ hours cost from L10,000 to L14,000 per person. Motonave Andes' Web site is at www.amerigo.it/ANDES.

Places to Stay
The HI youth hostel was closed at the time of writing. There is also a *camp site* within the grounds, with rates from L5000 per person.

Albergo ABC (☎ *0376 32 33 47, Piazza Don Leoni 25*) has a variety of rooms, ranging from pokey singles for L40,000 to reasonable doubles with bathroom for up to L120,000. The hotel is one of a trio lined up opposite the train station.

If you have a little more money to burn, head for the centre and stay in *Hotel Due Guerrieri* (☎ *0376 32 15 33, Piazza Sordello 52*). The most expensive rooms have views over the square and cost from L75,000/

LOMBARDIA & THE LAKES

105,000. The best doubles can cost as much as L155,000. **Hotel Broletto** (☎ *0376 22 36 78, Via dell'Accademia 1*) also offers good singles/doubles starting at L95,000/140,000.

Places to Eat & Drink

Over a million pigs are reared in the province of Mantova each year and many local dishes incorporate them. Try the *salumi* (salt pork), *pancetta*, *prosciutto crudo* or *salamella* (small sausages), or risotto with the locally grown *vialone nano* rice. Wines from the hills around Lago di Garda are excellent. Try the red Rubino dei Morenici Mantovani.

Pizzeria Capri *(Via Bettinelli 8)*, opposite the train station, has good pizzas and other local dishes, with pasta from L7000. **Pizzeria Al Quadrato** *(Piazza Virgiliana 49)*, overlooking the park, is a pleasant place.

Ristorante Pavesi *(Piazza delle Erbe 13)* is one of the city's better restaurants and inexpensive; a full meal costs around L35,000. If you're around here and just feel like eating pizza, **La Masseria** *(Piazza Broletto 7)* is worth considering.

Check out the **Antica Osteria Fragoletta** *(Piazza Arche 5)*, just off Lungo Lago dei Gonzaga, a simple place that dishes up generous servings of local food – a full meal will come to about L35,000, including wine. The restaurant has changed names a few times – but they claim that food has been served on this site since the 18th century.

The most atmospheric place for a stiff drink is the **Taverna di Santa Barbara**, on Piazza di Santa Barbara inside the Palazzo Ducale.

Getting There & Away

APAM (☎ *0376 32 72 37*) operates bus services, mainly to provincial centres, from the bus station.

The easiest way to get from major cities to Mantova is by train.

By road, Mantova is close to the A22 autostrada – take either the Mantova Nord or Sud exit and follow the 'centro' signs. The S236 runs direct to Brescia and the S10 to Cremona.

Getting Around

The easiest way to get around the city is to walk – the centre is only 10 minutes from the train station. APAM bus Nos 2M and 4 will also get you from the station to the centre.

AROUND MANTOVA
Sabbioneta

About 35km south-west of Mantova, Sabbioneta was created in the second half of the 16th century by Vespasiano Gonzaga Colonna in a failed attempt to build Utopia. You can only enter as part of a guided tour, which is organised by the local tourist office (☎ *0375 5 20 39*), Piazza d'Armi 1, Palazzo Giardino. The tours cost up to L10,000, depending on how many of Sabbioneta's five 16th century monuments you care to visit. Admission is extra to the 19th century synagogue (L4000) and Museo (L6000), which includes the Sala del Tesoro (with a Golden Fleece found in the tomb of Vespasiano Gonzaga) and an art gallery. Several buses run to Sabbioneta from Mantova.

San Benedetto Po

The Benedictine abbey in this small Pianura Padana (Po plain) town, 21km south-east of Mantova, was founded in 1007. Little remains of the original buildings, although the Chiesa di Santa Maria still sports a 12th century mosaic. The star attraction is the Correggio fresco discovered in the refectory in 1984. There are buses to the town from Mantova.

The Lakes

Where the Lombard plains rise into the Alpi, northern Italy is pocked by a series of lakes, among the most beautiful of Italy's natural attractions. Unfortunately, the secret has been out for at least a century – the prices and summer crowds can detract from the pleasure. The lakes are not only the playground of the Milanese rich; tourists from all over northern Europe converge on their favourites. Laghi di Garda, di Como and Maggiore are especially busy, although even the minor lakes are hardly immune to tourism.

Most are within easy reach of Milano and provincial centres such as Bergamo and Brescia. There are plenty of camp sites, hostels and hotels to suit all pockets, as well as many rifugi in the mountains.

LAGO MAGGIORE

The most captivating of the lakes, Maggiore (also known as Lago Verbano) is indeed stunning in parts, although its shores are flatter and less spectacular than those of some of its pre-Alpine counterparts. Fed principally by the Ticino and Tresa rivers, Lago Maggiore is about 65km long. The area becomes stiflingly overcrowded in high season, a good time to stay well away.

Stresa

Extremely popular with British and German tourists, this resort town on the lake's western shore is like one great English tearoom – prim and not unattractive, but staid and insipid. Although commonly touted as a base for visiting the Isole Borromee (see following section) and the lake in general, the islands can in fact be reached from other points around the lake.

Information The IAT office (☎ 0323 3 01 50) is at Via Pietro Canonica 8 and is open daily in summer (mornings only at the weekend; closed Sunday in winter). Other tourist offices are at Arona, Baveno and Verbania. You can pick up the *Trekking per Tutti* booklet here, which outlines, in several languages, 18 walks around the lake.

Things to See & Do Apart from visiting the Isole Borromee, you can take a cable car west to the summit of Monte Mottarone, the highest peak in the vicinity (1491m). Modest skiing possibilities are an added attraction to the views and the nearby **Parco del Mottarone** offers some pleasant walking opportunities. The cable car runs from about 9 am to 5 pm daily, or you can drive up through the park (L6000 per car for use of a private road). The **Villa Pallavicino**, a huge garden with a zoo where the animals roam relatively freely, offers superb views of the lake and the surrounding mountains. Admission costs L11,000.

Places to Stay & Eat The nearest camp site is the **Sette Camini Residence** (☎ 0323 2 01 83, Via Pianezza 7), a few kilometres south-west from Stresa at Gignese. There are some 40 camp sites up and down the western shore of the lake – check with the IAT office in Stresa.

Hotels are plentiful but must be booked well in advance for summer or long weekends. **Orsola Meublé** (☎ 0323 3 10 87, Via Duchessa di Genova 45) has singles/doubles costing up to L60,000/100,000 in high season. **Chez Osvaldo** (☎ 0323 3 19 48, Via A Bolongaro 57) has cheap and cheerful rooms for L50,000/70,000, which is as cheap as it's likely to get here. **Hotel Luina** (☎ 0323 3 02 85, Via Garibaldi 21) is in a slightly busier part of town, a block back from the waterfront. It has good rooms for the same rates as at Orsola Meublé. For big spenders there are 20 hotels in the three to five star range. Alternatively, pick up an agriturismo guide in the Stresa IAT office.

Chez Osvaldo (Via Anna Bolongaro 57) comes through on the eating front too. Pasta costs around L9000 and mains up to L16,000 – try the *scaloppine panna e mele*, veal cooked in an apple and cream sauce. **Ristorante del Pescatore** (Vicolo del Poncivo 3) will whip up a paella of sorts for two for around L50,000.

Getting There & Away Stresa lies on the Domodossola-Milano train line. Buses leave from the waterfront for destinations around the lake and elsewhere, including Milano, Novara and Lago d'Orta.

By car, the A8 autostrada connects Milano with Varese, south-east of Lago Maggiore. Exit at Legnano for the S33 road, which passes the lake's western shore and continues to the Simplon pass. The A8/A26 from Milano has an exit for Lago Maggiore, via Arona.

Ferries and hydrofoils around the lake are

operated by Navigazione Lago Maggiore (☎ 0322 23 32 00), connecting Stresa with Arona, Angera, Baveno, Cannobio, Pallanza, the islands and Locarno (Switzerland). A variety of day tickets (starting at L10,000 and rising, depending on destinations) are available for unlimited trips, but most unhurried visitors find normal single-trip tickets better value. Services are reduced in autumn and winter.

A good trip to take is a circular excursion from Stresa to Domodossola, from where you get a charming little train to Locarno (Switzerland – take your passports) and by ferry back to Stresa. It costs L44,000.

Isole Borromee

The Borromean Islands can be reached from various points around the lake, but Stresa and Baveno are the best departure points. The four islands, Bella, Pescatori (or Superiore), Madre and San Giovanni, form the lake's most beautiful corner.

Isola Bella has long played host to famous holiday-makers – Wagner, Stendhal, Byron and Goethe among them. The **Palazzo Borromeo** is the main draw. Built in the 17th century for the Borromeo family, the sumptuous palace contains works by Giovanni Tiepolo and Anthony Van Dyck as well as Flemish tapestries and sculptures by Canova. The gardens are magnificent and contain plants from around the world – although you must pay L14,000 to see it all. **Isola Madre** provides fertile ground for Italy's tallest palm trees. There is an 18th century palace and even more lavish gardens than Isola Bella. Admission costs L14,000. Both islands' sights open daily from April to late October.

Isola dei Pescatori retains some of its original fishing-village atmosphere. For accommodation the revamped *Albergo Verbano* (☎ 0323 3 04 08) is open year-round, except for January and February, and charges from L200,000 for a double.

Western Shore to Switzerland

Stresa is not the only town on Lago Maggiore and it is worth considering the alternatives. The choice depends a little on your taste, but you should remember that you will never really escape the feeling of being in a somewhat artificial environment.

Verbania, the biggest town on the lake, offers plenty of accommodation in most classes (including a youth hostel), but it's the least inviting place. **Cannero Riviera**, farther north, is a small lakeside village and a good spot for a tranquil break. Just off the coast lie some tiny islets that, before being taken over by the Borromeo family in the 15th century, served as a den for thieves who operated in the area during the 12th century. More interesting is **Cannobio**, 5km short of the Swiss border. The town's spotless cobblestone streets and the waves of Swiss day-trippers could leave you wondering if you've already crossed the frontier!

Camp sites dot the coast and Cannero and Cannobio have about 20 hotels between them – check the IAT office in Stresa or the branches in Arona, Baveno or Verbania for a list. A car ferry links Intra (Verbania) to Laveno on the eastern shore, and all the western shore towns are connected by ferry and bus.

LAGO D'ORTA

Only 15km long and about 2.5km wide, Lago d'Orta is one of the smaller of the Italian lakes. It is actually in the Piemonte region and is separated from its more celebrated eastern neighbour, Lago Maggiore, by Monte Mottarone. Its still waters are surrounded by lush woodlands and, unlike the big lakes, the area is not yet swarming with visitors. It can still become congested though at the weekend and during the summer.

Orta San Giulio

This is undoubtedly the prettiest of the lake's towns and suffers less than places like Stresa from the blandness born of over-tourism. It is difficult to beat sipping a coffee over the morning paper in one of the cafés on the lakeside square. It is the obvious choice as a base, not only for Lago d'Orta but arguably for Maggiore as well (if you have a vehicle at any rate), which you can reach via Monte Mottarone.

Information The APT del Lago d'Orta (☎ 0322 91˙19 37) is on the left just after the intersection that leads onto the little promontory. Staff can advise on walking and accommodation in the area. It opens from 9 am to 1 pm and 2.30 to 8 pm daily from April to October, with reduced opening hours in winter.

Things to See & Do Regular launches make the short trip (L4000 a head return) to the **Isola San Giulio**, named after a Greek evangelist who earned his saintly status by ridding the island of an assortment of snakes and monsters late in the 4th century. A 12th century basilica dominates the island.

Sacro Monte, behind Orta San Giulio, is dotted with a series of small chapels erected to San Francesco d'Assisi over a 200 year period from 1591 – it makes for a pleasant stroll above the town.

The small village of **Armeno**, at the foot of Monte Mottarone, is worth visiting, not least for its umbrella museum.

Places to Stay & Eat The hitch in Orta San Giulio can be finding a place to stay, especially in the high season and at the weekend. Four camp sites stretch along the coast north of Orta San Giulio and another couple inland – ask at the APT office. The nearest is *Camping Orta* (☎ 0322 9 02 67, Via Domodossola 28) and it's open year-round.

Cheap is not a buzzword here. *Hotel Olina* (☎ 0322 90 56 56, Via Olina 40) offers cosy rooms from L75,000/95,000 in low season. The *Creperie (Piazza Motta 33)* might have a couple of rooms – it was shut when we called by.

A charming but minuscule dining choice is *Al Boeuc (Via Bersani 28)*. The stone wall setting houses a wine bar that also does food – a cold meat platter for two costs L22,000.

In Armeno, the *Madonna di Luciago* (☎ 0322 99 90 06) has singles/doubles from L50,000/80,000.

Getting There & Away Orta San Giulio is just off the Novara-Domodossola train line and can also be reached by bus from Stresa.

From the south, take the S32 from Novara, in Piemonte, or the S229, also from Novara, which is not as interesting but much quicker.

LAGO DI COMO

Marie Henri Beyle first set foot on the shores of Lago di Como as a 17-year-old conscript under Napoleon. Years later, as Stendhal, he wrote in *La Chartreuse de Parme* that the blue-green waters of the lake and the grandeur of the Alpi made it the most beautiful place in the world. Pliny the Elder and Pliny the Younger were born here, but are not known to have gushed about the area to the same degree as Stendhal. In any case, many people would no doubt consider Como's other famous son as having achieved quite a deal more for the world: Alessandro Volta, born in 1745, came up with, well, the battery.

The whole town centre of Como becomes one great antiques market on the last Saturday of every month – a nice excuse for a day trip by train from Milano.

Known also as Lago Lario, this immense body of water is enchantingly beautiful, as are its tiny waterside villages, some accessible only by boat. Today, the waters are murky and swimming, although permitted in parts, is inadvisable.

Como
postcode 22100 • pop 90,000

Como gets a lot of bad press but has the advantage over many other lakeside towns of being a real city with its own life. The people you mingle with in the streets might be Italians – even locals – and not the usual crowd of tourists crated in from northern Europe. The town offers a few attractions in its own right and is a good base from which to make excursions around the lake.

Orientation From the main train station at Piazzale San Gottardo, walk east to Piazza Cacciatori delle Alpi and continue along Via G Garibaldi to Piazza Volta. The main square, Piazza Cavour, overlooking the lake, is about 50m farther east along Via Fontana. Tourist boats depart from in front of the piazza and

LOMBARDIA & THE LAKES

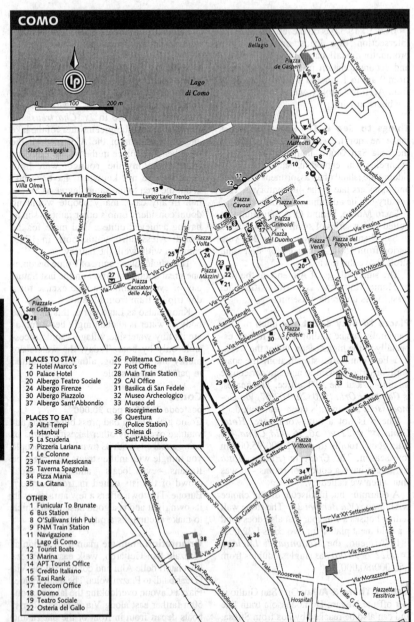

COMO

PLACES TO STAY
2 Hotel Marco's
10 Palace Hotel
20 Albergo Teatro Sociale
24 Albergo Firenze
30 Albergo Piazzolo
37 Albergo Sant'Abbondio

PLACES TO EAT
3 Altri Tempi
4 Istanbul
5 La Scuderia
21 Pizzeria Lariana
21 Le Colonne
23 Taverna Messicana
25 Taverna Spagnola
34 Pizza Mania
35 La Gitana

OTHER
1 Funicular To Brunate
6 Bus Station
8 O'Sullivans Irish Pub
9 FNM Train Station
11 Navigazione
Lago di Como
Tourist Boats
13 Marina
14 APT Tourist Office
15 Credito Italiano
16 Taxi Rank
17 Telecom Office
18 Duomo
19 Teatro Sociale
22 Osteria del Gallo

26 Politeama Cinema & Bar
27 Post Office
28 Main Train Station
29 CAI Office
31 Basilica di San Fedele
32 Museo Archeologico
33 Museo del
Risorgimento
36 Questura
(Police Station)
38 Chiesa di
Sant'Abbondio

regular ferries leave from along the shore. East of Piazza Cavour along Lungo Lario Trieste is the bus station and Stazione Ferrovia Nord Milano (FNM), a smaller train station running shuttles to Milano. The funicular for the mountain settlement of Brunate is farther along at Piazza de Gasperi.

Information The APT office (☎ 031 26 97 12) is at Piazza Cavour 17 and is open from 9 am to 1 pm and 2.30 to 6 pm Monday to Saturday. There is a smaller office in the main train station.

The Credito Italiano just off Piazza Cavour is good for exchanging money and ATMs abound in the centre.

The post office is at Via T Gallio 6 and is open from 8.15 am to 5.30 pm Monday to Friday and from 8.15 am to 1 pm Saturday.

The Telecom office is on a small square off Via Albertolli, south of Piazza Cavour. It is open from 8 am to 8 pm Monday to Saturday.

The Ospedale Sant'Anna (☎ 031 58 51 11) is at Via Napoleona 60. The questura (☎ 031 31 71) is at Viale Roosevelt 7.

Duomo From Piazza Cavour, walk along the arcaded Via Plinio to Piazza del Duomo and the marble-faced cathedral, built and repeatedly altered from the 14th to the 18th centuries. The duomo combines elements of baroque, Gothic, Romanesque and Renaissance design and is crowned with a high octagonal dome. Next to it is the polychromatic **municipio** (town hall), altered in 1435 to make way for the cathedral.

Churches & Museums The **Basilica di San Fedele**, named after the saint who brought Christianity to the Como region, first went up in the 6th century. It has since undergone various changes, including those in the bell tower and façade which took place in the 20th century, although the original lines of the basilica have been largely respected. It's on Via Vittorio Emanuele II, as are the Palazzo Giovio and Palazzo Olginati – the former housing the **Museo Archeologico**, with important prehistoric and Roman remains and the latter the

Museo del Risorgimento (aka Museo Garibaldi), with mementos from Garibaldi's period – he actually stayed in this building for a time. Both are open from 9.30 am to 12.30 pm and 2 to 5 pm daily except Monday, and from 10 am to 1 pm on Sunday. Admission to each costs L4000.

Brunate East of Piazza Cavour, along the waterfront to Piazza de Gasperi, is the funicular railway station for Brunate. Tickets cost L4100 one way or L7200 return. Check the timetable for the last car before you leave. Brunate, at 720m, overlooks Como and the lake and offers a pleasant walk and excellent views from the small town of San Maurizio. You can follow a walking trail up from Como if you want – reckon on spending at least two hours getting up there.

Walking Around Como The APT office has produced a walking map of the area with a 50km walk from Cernobbio, near Como, to Sorico, near the lake's northern edge. It can be broken into four stages. The map shows the location of rifugi and some camp sites. Maps for other walks are available, but are mostly in Italian. Try also the CAI (☎ 031 26 41 77), Via Alessandro Volta 56. See Lonely Planet's *Walking in Italy* guide for planned walks around Como.

Places to Stay With a couple of exceptions, accommodation in the town is reasonably expensive, but the hostel in Como, and the two along the lake, help make a visit affordable for the budget-conscious.

The APT office also has a list of apartments and villas available for rent, but these are not generally cheap.

The *International* camp site (☎ 031 52 14 35, Via Cecilio) is away from both the town centre and the lake, and it's preferable to camp along the lake. The *Villa Olmo* hostel (☎ 031 57 38 00, Via Bellinzona 6), fronting the lake, is 1km from the main train station and 20m from the closest bus stop. Take bus No 1, 6, 11 or 14. B&B costs L16,000 and a meal costs L14,000. The hostel opens from March to November.

euro currency converter   L10,000 = €5.16

LOMBARDIA & THE LAKES

Albergo Teatro Sociale (☎ 031 26 40 42, Via Maestri Comacini 8), on the southern side of the duomo, has dull but clean single/doubles from L35,000/60,000, or doubles with bath for L80,000. *Albergo Piazzolo (☎ 031 27 21 86)* is right in the town centre at Piazzolo Terragni 6 (a tiny square along Via Indipendenza), with just four rooms with bath or shower. It charges L65,000/95,000 for single/double occupancy.

Heading south-east from the train station is *Albergo Sant'Abbondio (☎ 031 26 40 09, Via S Abbondio 7)*, which has basic singles/doubles with shower for L55,000/80,000. In the low season the rooms are generally occupied long-term by students and workers.

A pleasant enough little spot in the midrange is *Hotel Marco's (☎ 031 30 36 28, Via Coloniola 43)*, where well kept if smallish rooms with shower, loo, TV and phone cost L100,000/140,000. A little more will get you into *Albergo Firenze (☎ 031 30 03 33, Piazza Volta 16)*, which occupies a prime spot on this square. Rooms cost L105,000/160,000.

Palace Hotel (☎ 031 30 33 03, Lungo Lario Trieste 16) has singles/doubles for as high as L195,000/295,000, if you want lakeside style.

Places to Eat Como's fare, dominated by the whims of nearby Milano and its daytrippers, is good but rarely cheap. You will, however, find many sandwich bars and self-service restaurants. A plentiful *food market* opens in the morning from Monday to Saturday at Via Mentana 15.

Pizza Mania (Via Milano 20), outside the city wall, sells pizza slices by weight and is quite good value. *Pizzeria Lariana (Via Fiammenghino 4)* is similar. If you're looking for something from a different part of the Mediterraneo, you could pick up a doner kebab at *Istanbul (Lungo Lario Trieste 26)*.

Taverna Spagnola (Via Grassi 8) serves competent Italian dishes and will make a local attempt at paella (L48,000 for two). Equally popular are two places on Piazza Mazzini, Le Colonne and Taverna Messicana, the latter in a lovely old building.

La Gitana (Via Milano 117) is run by an Egyptian who cooks reasonable, if unspectacular, Italian food and, on request, dishes from his homeland.

La Scuderia (Piazza Matteotti 4) is a popular trattoria behind the bus station, but is a little pricey – mains cost around L20,000. Not far away, a classy new addition is *Altri Tempi (Via Coloniola 44)*. Three courses and starter can be expensive, but they do *piatti unici* (single dishes), mostly with a risotto base, for L23,000.

Entertainment Como doesn't exactly hop, but you can get a soothing stout at *O'Sullivan's Irish Pub*, wedged in between the FNM railway and the train station. The *Osteria del Gallo (Via Vitani 20)* is a more genteel and cosy little den for a glass of wine – or simply buy a bottle to take away.

Getting There & Away SPT buses (☎ 031 30 47 44) leave from Piazza Matteotti for destinations along the lake and cities throughout the region. Trains from Milano's Stazione Centrale arrive at Como's main train station and go on to many cities throughout Western Europe. Trains from Milano's Stazione Nord are more frequent and arrive at Como's Stazione FNM – timed to link with the ferries.

By car, Como is on the A9 autostrada, which connects with the A8 to Milano's ring road. The S35 from Como also connects to the ring road.

Ferries and hydrofoils criss-cross the lake. Navigazione Lago di Como (☎ 031 57 92 11), Piazza Cavour, operates boats year-round. A day ticket allowing unlimited trips costs L28,500. A day cruise around the lake with lunch on the boat costs L48,000 (L52,000 at the weekend).

Around Como
Looking like an inverted 'Y', Lago di Como is 51km long and lies at the foot of the Rhetian Alpi. Its myriad towns can easily be explored by boat or bus from Como and are worth at least a two day visit. Highlights include the **Villa d'Este** at Cernobbio, a monu-

mental 16th century villa that is now a hotel; the **Isola Comacina**, the lake's sole island, where Lombard kings took refuge from invaders; and the **Villa Carlotta** near Tremezzo, with its magnificent gardens. The towns farther north are lesser tourist attractions.

There are two youth hostels on Lago di Como, numerous camp sites and many reasonably priced hotels. The *Ostello La Primula* (☎ *0344 3 23 56, Via IV Novembre 86*), at Menaggio, about halfway up the lake on the western side, is close to the bus stop on the route from Como. It's a great hostel and charges L16,000 a night (closed from mid-November to mid-March). Farther north is the *Ostello Domaso* (☎ *0344 9 60 94, Via Case Sparse 12*) at Domaso. It costs L15,000 a night and is on the same bus route. Both are open from March to October. Check with the APT office in Como for lists of the 50 or so camp sites, hotels and agriturismo facilities along the lake shore.

Bellagio Considered the 'pearl' of the lake, Bellagio is indeed a pretty little town sitting more or less on the point where the western and eastern arms of the lake split and head south. The 30km drive from Como is itself rewarding, though the trip down the eastern side towards Lecco is less so. The only drawback to being in Bellagio is the inevitable feeling that you're sharing the pleasure with just a few too many other outsiders – would the real residents of Bellagio please stand up?

Albergo Roma (☎ *0344 95 04 24*) is well situated in the town and has singles/doubles starting at L42,000/66,000 in low season. It's about as cheap as Bellagio gets and opens from March to October only.

The lake's only car ferries connect the eastern and western shores in this area, stopping at Bellagio.

LAGO DI GARDA
The largest and most popular of the Italian lakes, Garda (370 sq km) lies between the Alpi and the Pianura Padana and enjoys a temperate climate. At its northern reaches, Garda is hemmed in by craggy mountains

and resembles a fjord. As it broadens towards the south, the lake takes on the appearance of an inland sea.

There are many large villages around the lake, but most are heavily developed and unpleasant. The picturesque but Disneyland-like resort of Sirmione is worth visiting, as is Gardone Riviera on the lake's western edge. At the northern end, Riva del Garda is a good base for walking in the nearby Alpi.

Getting There & Away
Buses leave Verona, Brescia, Mantova and Milano for the main towns around the lake.

Desenzano del Garda is on the main Milano-Venezia train line.

By car, the A4 autostrada and the S11, which connect Milano with Venezia, pass the southern edge of the lake and the A22 runs parallel with the lake's eastern shore, connecting Verona with Trento. Riva del Garda can be reached by exiting the A22 at Rovereto Sud.

Getting Around
Navigazione sul Lago di Garda (☎ 800 55 18 01), Piazza Matteotti 2, in Desenzano del Garda, operates ferries between most towns on the lake. It has offices or booths in all of the towns it serves and operates year-round. Ask at tourist offices for timetables. Fares range from L2200 to L21,200, depending on the length of the trip and whether you get the *battello* (ferry) or *aliscafo* (hydrofoil).

Sirmione
Catullus, the Roman poet, celebrated Sirmione – a narrow peninsula jutting out from the southern shore of the lake – in his writings and his name is still invoked in connection with the place. It is a popular bathing spot and is often jammed tight with tourists. In spite of this, Sirmione retains a comparatively relaxed atmosphere. The area of interest (watch for the castle) is an islet attached by a bridge to the rest of the peninsula.

Information The main tourist office (☎ 030 91 61 14), Viale Marconi 2, has information on hotels and activities such as walking, skiing, windsurfing and horse riding. There is a Telecom office on Piazza Carducci.

Things to See & Do The Roman villa and baths known as the **Grotte di Catullo** probably had nothing to do with the Roman poet, although Catullus and his family did have a villa in the area. The extensive ruins occupy a prime position on the northern, quieter end of the Sirmione island. The site is open from 9 am to 6.45 pm (4 pm in winter) Tuesday to Sunday. Admission costs L8000.

The **Castello Scaligero**, also known as the Rocca Scaligera, was built by Verona's ruling family, the Scaligeri, as a stronghold on the lake in 1250. There's not a lot inside, but the views from the tower are good. It's open from 9 am to 7 pm daily in summer and from 9 am to 1 pm Tuesday to Sunday in winter. Admission costs L8000.

You can go for a watery spin around the island. Plenty of boats leave from near the castle – at about L25,000 per person. All sorts of vessels will also make any manner of trip around the lake – at a price.

Activities It is possible to swim at the small beaches on the town's eastern side and an array of water activities can be arranged in the town. Windsurfers could try calling Centro Surf Sirmione on ☎ 0338 624 36 50 or Centro Surf Martini (☎ 030 91 62 08). Several places hire out pedalos and kayaks.

Places to Stay & Eat It is hard to believe there are 93 hotels crammed in here. Book ahead or stay away in summer and at long weekends. Four camp sites lie near the town and the APT office can advise on others around the lake. The *Campeggio Sirmione* (☎ 030 91 90 45), on the foreshore at Via Sirmioncino 9, is one of the largest.

Hotels include *Albergo Progresso* (☎ 030 91 61 08, Corso Vittorio Emanuele 18), which is as cheap as you'll find in the heart of old Sirmione. You'll pay L45,000/60,000 for singles/doubles. *Albergo degli Oleandri* (☎ 030 990 57 80, Via Dante 31), near the castle, is in a shady, pleasant location and

has rooms for L65,000/88,000 including breakfast. *Albergo Sirmione* (☎ 030 91 63 31, fax 030 91 65 58, Piazza Castello 19) has rooms for up to L165,000/280,000. Bear in mind that these and most other hotels shut from the end of October to March.

Osteria al Pescatore (Via Piana 18) is one of the better, reasonably priced restaurants and there are loads of takeaway food outlets to be found, especially around Piazza Carducci. This is also where the bulk of the cafés and gelati joints are.

Around Sirmione
Sirmione is about 5km east of Desenzano del Garda, the lake's largest town and a main transport hub (but not really worth a visit). Farther north from Desenzano del Garda is Salò, which gave its name to Mussolini's puppet republic in 1943, after the dictator was rescued from the south by the Nazis. The CAI has an office in Salò, at Via San Bernardino 26, with information on walks and Alpine rifugi in the surrounding mountains.

Heading east, kids will be excited to hear of **Gardaland** (☎ 045 644 97 77), Italy's equivalent of Disneyland. It opens from 9.30 am to 6.30 pm daily from March to October. In summer the hours are extended to midnight. Adults and children over 10 years pay L35,000 to get sick on the various rides. Only toddlers get in for free. The nearest train station is at Peschiera del Garda. The remaining 2km are covered by a free bus service.

Gardone Riviera
On the western edge of the lake at the head of a small inlet is the popular resort of Gardone Riviera. It retains a hint of its past as the lake's most elegant holiday spot but has succumbed to development and the problems of being a group tourist destination.

The APT office (☎ 0365 2 03 47) is at Corso Repubblica 37.

Things to See & Do A visit to the town is a must to see **Il Vittoriale**, the exotic villa of Italy's controversial 20th century poet and screeching nationalist, Gabriele d'Annunzio. He moved in here in 1922 because, he claimed, he wanted to escape the world, which made him ill. Protagonist of clamorous but ineffectual wartime stunts in WWI – he flew a lone raid to drop leaflets over Vienna – he died in 1938 and is buried near the villa among his wartime companions.

One of d'Annunzio's most triumphant and more bizarre feats was to capture, with a band of his soldiers, a battleship from the fledgling Yugoslavia shortly after WWI, when Italy's territorial claims had been partly frustrated in postwar peace talks. The ship's bow protrudes from the villa's gardens and adds to the kitsch flavour of the residence. Il Vittoriale is at the northeastern edge of town and is open from 8 am to 8.30 pm daily April to September and from 9 am to 12.30 pm and 2 to 5.30 pm in winter. Admission costs L16,000 to both the grounds and house or L8000 to visit the gardens and house or L8000 to visit the gardens and museum only. The town also features **botanical gardens**, on the road to d'Annunzio's villa.

Some pleasant and easy walks can be undertaken from here, heading inland to the rifugi at **Monte Spino** or **Monte Pizzicolo**. Ask at the APT office for more details.

Places to Stay & Eat The well located *Albergo Nord* (☎ 0365 2 07 07, *Via Zanardelli 18*) has singles/doubles from L45,000/60,000. *Villa Fiordaliso* (☎ 0365 2 01 58, *Via Zanardelli 132*) was a favourite of Mussolini's mistress, Clara Petacci. It is also one of the lake's most beautiful hotels and best restaurants. Rooms cost from L300,000 and the food is expensive. For more modest food, try *Pizzeria Sans Souci*, near the APT office, which has pizzas from L8000.

Gargnano & Villa
Gargnano is really just another lake resort town. Mussolini was based here for the short life of his Repubblica Sociale Italiana (or Repubblica di Salò). He was guarded by German SS units and the republic was in fact fictitious, as northern Italy was occupied territory after Italy signed an armistice with the Allies in September 1943. The re-

public lasted until 25 April 1945, when the last German troops were finally cleared from Italy. Mussolini and Petacci were lynched three days later near Lago di Como.

Riva del Garda
The most popular of the resort towns around Lago di Garda is Riva del Garda, at its northern edge. It has a pleasant old centre of cobbled lanes and squares and occupies a nice position on the lake. Links with the Germanic world are evident, not only in the bus and car loads of Germans and Austrians, but also in the town's history. Riva was part of Habsburg Austria until it was incorporated into Italy after WWI and was annexed briefly by Nazi Germany in the closing years of WWII. Central European luminaries such as Nietzsche, Kafka and Thomas Mann were wont to put their feet up in Riva.

Information The APT office (☎ 0464 55 44 44) is in the Giardini di Porta Orientale 8, opposite the 'castle'. Staff here can advise on accommodation and sporting activities.

Things to See Three kilometres north of town is the **Cascata Varone**, a 100m waterfall fed by the Lago di Tenno. Admission to the waterfall area costs L7000. Opening hours vary – check with the APT office.

Activities Riva is one of Italy's most popular spots for windsurfing and has four schools that hire out equipment. Bouwmeester Windsurfing Centre (☎ 0464 55 17 30), c/o Hotel Pier, and Nautic Club Riva (☎ 0464 55 24 53), Viale Rovereto 44, also run sailing classes.

The APT office has a list of people who can help with information on free-climbing in the area. For mountain bike hire, try Centro Cicli Pederzolli (☎ 0464 55 18 30), Viale Canella 14, or Girelli (☎ 0464 55 66 02), Viale Damiano Chiesa 15/17. You're looking at between L20,000 and L25,000 a day.

Speedy Gonzales (☎ 0464 55 20 89) runs boat excursions on the lake for L15,000 per person per hour. Boats leave from near the

LOMBARDIA & THE LAKES

APT office. Moby Dick runs excursions for the same price, from the same spot.

The town is a great starting point for walks around Monte Rocchetta, which dominates the northern end of Lago di Garda.

Places to Stay & Eat Several camp sites dot the waterfront, including *Campeggio Bavaria (☎ 0464 55 25 24, Viale Rovereto 100)*. The HI youth hostel, the *Benacus (☎ 0464 55 49 11, Piazza Cavour 10)*, in the centre of town, charges L22,000 for B&B and is open 1 March to 31 October.

Hotels are plentiful, but during the summer it is advisable to book. *La Montanara (☎ 0464 55 48 57, Via Montanara 18)*, in a narrow lane in the centre, is one of the cheapest places. Singles/doubles cost L28,000/54,000 and doubles with bathroom L58,000. The hotel also offers half and full board and has a pleasant trattoria. The nearby *Albergo Vittoria (☎ 0464 55 43 98, Via Dante 39)* has rooms with bath costing L45,000/80,000, although a few cheaper ones are available if you push. *Hotel Portici (☎ 0464 55 54 00, Piazza III Novembre 19)* offers rooms for L80,000/125,000 in the high season (you may be obliged to take full board in the high season). *Hotel Sole (☎ 0464 55 26 86, fax 0464 55 28 11)*, at No 35 overlooking the lake, was Nietzsche's favourite and has rooms ranging from L180,000 to L250,000.

The town has many takeaway places and good delicatessens for picnic supplies. *Leon d'Oro (Via Fiume 26)*, has various Trentino dishes (including *strangolapreti* – 'strangle the priest' – for L10,000). For an exceptional wood oven pizza, head straight for *Bella Napoli (Via dei Fabbri 34)*. There are plenty of lakeside cafés and pastry shops.

Getting There & Away The bus station is on Viale Trento, in the newer part of town, a 10 minute walk from the lake. Regular APT buses connect Riva with Verona, leaving Verona from the Porta Nuova bus station. Atesina buses connect Riva with Trento. Other buses serve various stops around the lake.

LAGO D'ISEO & VALLE CAMONICA

The least known of the large Italian lakes, Lago d'Iseo is possibly the least attractive. Although shut in by mountains, it is scarred in the north-east (around Lovere and Castro) by industry and a string of tunnels.

At the southern end of the Valle Camonica, the lake is fed by the Oglio river and marks the boundary between the provinces of Bergamo and Brescia – getting information about one side from tourist offices on the other is not easy! Farther south stretches the Franciacorta, a patch of rolling countryside that produces good wine. The mountainous hinterland offers decent walking possibilities. Check with the APT office in the lake towns, or at Bergamo or Brescia.

Getting There & Around

Buses connect the lake with Brescia and Bergamo. There are also trains from Brescia to Iseo and several other towns on the lake. Navigazione sul Lago d'Iseo (☎ 035 97 14 83), based in Costa Volpino, operates ferries between (south to north) Sarnico, Iseo, Monte Isola, Lovere and Pisogne. Fares range from L2200 to L9600 per trip and the timetable is substantially reduced in winter. Buses also connect towns around the lake.

Iseo

A pleasant, if somewhat dull, spot fronting the southern end of the lake, Iseo boasts the first monument erected to Garibaldi. The APT del Lago d'Iseo (☎ 030 98 02 09) is at Lungolago Marconi 2.

The area is well supplied with accommodation, particularly camp sites. Iseo has 16 sites, including the *Belvedere (☎ 030 98 90 48, Via Risorgimento 64)*. About the cheapest hotel in the centre of town is *Albergo Milano (☎ 030 98 04 49, Lungolago Marconi 4)* with singles/doubles at L70,000/90,000.

Monte Isola

The best thing to do here is get a boat to Europe's biggest lake island, Monte Isola. Few vehicles are allowed on the streets, so the fishing village is quite peaceful. It has four hotels and a camp site, *Campeggio Monte Isola* (☎ *030 982 52 21, Via Croce 144*).

Eastern Shore

If Iseo seems a little empty and you want to stay on the mainland, there are a few smaller towns farther north. **Sulzano** is small and quiet and on the ferry run to Monte Isola. Farther up the road is **Marone**, from where a side road winds up into the mountains to **Zone**. Walking is the attraction and there are a few rifugi about – inquire at the APT office.

Western Shore

The northern end of the lake you can forget, although some of the driving through the blasted rock face at the water's edge is enjoyable. **Riva di Solto** is a fairly unspoiled village on the western shore but **Sarnico**, towards the southern end of the lake, is better, with hotels and restaurants.

Valle Camonica

The Valle Camonica weaves its way from the north of Lago d'Iseo to the vast **Parco** **dell'Adamello** and, farther north, to the **Parco Nazionale dello Stelvio**. The area borders on Trentino-Alto Adige and takes in the better parts of the Alpi Lombardi. The two national parks offer many walks of varying difficulty and are dotted with Alpine rifugi. See the Trentino-Alto Adige chapter for more details.

About halfway between Darfo and Edolo, lovers of rock-carving will have a field day. The **Parco Nazionale delle Incisioni Rupestri**, at Capo di Ponte, is a 30 hectare open-air museum containing a representative array of engravings going as far back as the Bronze Age. The valley is littered with such carvings. The park is open from 9 am to 5 pm daily except Monday (7 pm in summer); admission costs L8000.

The area from Edolo north offers some reasonable **skiing** in winter, particularly near Ponte di Legno, at the northern end of the valley, and the nearby Passo del Tonale. Brescia's APT is a good place to obtain walking, camping and rifugi information. In the valley there are tourist offices at Darfo Boario Terme (☎ 0364 53 16 09), Edolo (☎ 0364 7 10 65) and Ponte di Legno (☎ 0364 9 11 22).

LOMBARDIA & THE LAKES

Trentino-Alto Adige

This autonomous Alpine region, incorporating much of the spectacular limestone Dolomiti mountain range, is best thought of as two distinct areas. Its provinces, Trentino and Alto Adige, are culturally, linguistically and historically separate.

Alto Adige, or Südtirol (South Tirolo), in the north of the region was part of the Tirolo province of Austria until ceded to Italy in 1918. The people, mostly of Germanic descent, predictably favour the German language (68%) over Italian (28%), although Ladin (4%), an ancient Latin-based language, is also spoken in some zones, mainly the Val Badia (Gadertal) and the Val Gardena (Grödnertal); see the boxed text 'The Ladin Tradition' in the Val Badia section for more information.

Trentino, to the south of Alto Adige, was a reluctant part of the Austrian and Austro-Hungarian empires for about a century until it was returned to Italy after WWI. The population here has a strong Italian identity, although German is widely spoken (more to accommodate the realities of modern tourism than a sign of nostalgia for the days of Austrian rule!).

The marriage of Trentino to Alto Adige, Italian to Tyrolean, has at times created friction, and extreme right-wing political parties have always done well here. Alleanza Nazionale, the descendant of the neo-Fascist MSI (Movimento Sociale Italiano) party, has strong support in the area, but in Alto Adige the Südtiroler Volkspartei (SVP) is the most popular party by far. One of its primary aims is the preservation and development of German and Ladin ethnic groups, but more extreme elements want to secede from Italy. Bombings of railways, power stations and military installations that shook the region in the 1950s, 1960s and 1980s were attributed to radical secessionists.

It was only in 1992 that a long haggled-over deal covering the area's statutes and privileges was formally agreed to by Italy

Highlights

- Enjoy the spectacular views while walking in the Parco Naturale Fanes-Sennes-Braies
- Ski in the Brenta group, the Val di Fassa or just about anywhere in the Dolomiti
- Visit Cortina d'Ampezzo – it is not by chance that it is a favourite with the jet set
- Go mountain biking in the Alpi di Siusi

and Austria, with the blessing of the UN. By the mid-1990s, however, the SVP was pushing to have Alto Adige made a separate region, in complete contravention of the 1992 agreement. This caused much alarm among the people of Trentino, who fear being swallowed up by other regions (such as the Veneto) and losing the benefits gained by the Trentino-Alto Adige joint status as an autonomous region.

Politics aside, tourism throughout the Trentino-Alto Adige is highly organised and travellers will have little difficulty finding good accommodation and extensive information on their choice of activity, including walking and skiing.

Accommodation ranges from hotels and *pensioni* (boarding houses which tend to insist on half or full board), through *garni* (basically B&Bs) to *rifugi* (mountain huts), which can be anything from expensive hotel-restaurants at the top of chair lift routes to simple *bivacchi* (spartan mountain huts). Prices vary greatly according to the season and most Alpine rifugi are only open from late June to late September. If you plan on walking in the mountains during August, book beds at the rifugi before you set out.

Information

The two provincial tourist offices are the APT del Trentino in Trento and the APT for Südtirol in Bolzano. Both are extremely helpful and have lots of information about the region, including updated lists of the rifugi in the area. The APT del Trentino has other offices in Roma (☎ 06 360 95 842), c/o Touring Club Italiano, Via del Babuino 20, and in Milano (☎ 02 864 61 251), Piazza Diaz 5. There is also a 24 hour toll-free information service you can call from anywhere in Italy on ☎ 800 84 50 34.

Email inquiries to the Internet can be sent to apt@provincia.tn.it, or see APT Trentino's Web site at www.provincia.tn.it/apt/.

Getting There & Around

If you want to fly direct to the area, the two nearest airports are Verona and Innsbruck (Austria). The latter is closer to the best of the mountains. If no financially acceptable flights to these two airports are available, you could check out flights to Munich (Germany), as long as you don't mind then doing the train trip south to Bolzano (or taking an express bus to Merano).

Public transport in Trentino-Alto Adige is excellent. The two main companies are SAD (Servizi Autobus Dolomiti) in Alto Adige and Atesina in Trentino. The main towns and many ski resorts can be reached directly from major Italian cities – including Roma, Firenze, Bologna, Milano and Genova. Long-haul bus companies operating such routes include Lazzi, SITA and STAT. Information about these services is available from tourist offices and bus stations throughout Trentino-Alto Adige, or from the following offices: Lazzi Express (☎ 06 884 08 40), Via Tagliamento 27B, Roma; SITA (☎ 055 21 47 21), Autostazione, Via Santa Caterina da Siena 17, Firenze.

For information about the Lazzi/SITA joint service, call ALPI Bus (☎ 055 21 51 55, 055 29 49 55) or go to Piazza Adua 1, Firenze;

An Alpine Coral Reef

The Dolomiti account for a vast portion of the eastern Alpi and are divided between Trentino-Alto Adige and the Veneto. These regions are now all part of Italy; however, during WWI they were divided by the border (and, hence, the front line of combat) between Italy and Austria-Hungary. These spectacular, spiky peaks take their name from the French geologist De Dolomieu, who was the first to identify their composition of sedimentary limestone formed from calcium carbonate and magnesium. The Dolomiti are actually ancient coral reefs, a fact that makes them seem all the more extraordinary. During the Triassic period the entire area was covered with tropical forest and a shallow, warm sea. After millions of years the sea receded at the same time as the Alps were being formed, raising what had once been the seabed to heights of between 2000 and 3000m. During the Ice Age the coral reefs and rocks were eroded by glaciers which, together with normal atmospheric erosion, shaped the fantastic formations seen today in the Dolomiti. It is not unusual to find marine fossils among the pinnacles, towers and dramatic sheer drops of these mountains. Coral reefs are always fascinating, but particularly so when reincarnated as Alpine peaks.

TRENTINO-ALTO ADIGE

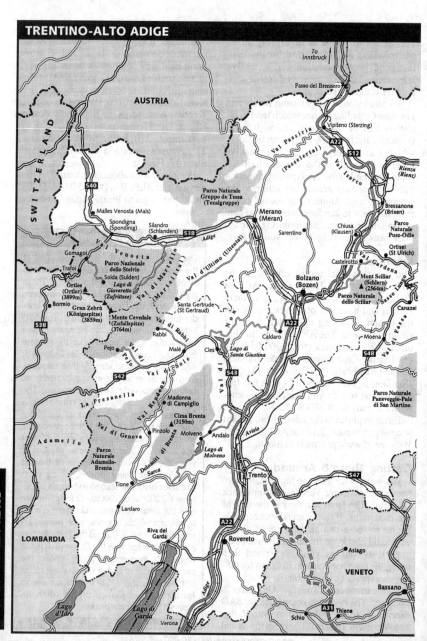

and STAT (☎ 010 58 71 81), Piazza della Vittoria 30/R, Genova.

WALKING IN THE DOLOMITI

The Dolomiti, stretching across Trentino-Alto Adige into the Veneto, provide the most spectacular and varied opportunities for walkers in the Italian Alps – from half-day strolls to walks including more demanding routes that require mountaineering skills.

Trails are generally well marked with numbers on red-and-white painted bands (on trees and rocks along the trails) or inside different coloured triangles for the Alte Vie (High Routes). Numerous rifugi offer overnight lodging and refreshments. Tourist offices usually have maps with roughly marked trails, but walkers planning anything more than the most basic itinerary should use detailed maps. Tourist office staff can advise on the degree of difficulty of each trail.

Preparations

If you plan a serious walk, invest in a good map. The best are the Tabacco 1:25,000 maps, which provide extensive details of trails, altitudes and gradients, as well as marking all rifugi and bivacchi. They are widely available throughout the Dolomiti. An alternative is the Kompass series.

The walking season runs from the end of June to the end of September and, depending on weather conditions, sometimes into October, though rifugi close around 20 September.

Always check weather predictions before setting out and ensure you are prepared for high-altitude conditions. In the Alpi the weather can suddenly change from hot and sunny to cold and wet, even in mid-August. Changes usually occur in the afternoon, so it is best to set out early. Even on the shortest, most popular trails at the height of summer, make sure you have good walking shoes, a warm jacket and plenty of water.

The following is a list of items to carry on high-altitude walks of more than one day:

- comfortable, waterproof walking boots (already worn in)
- light, comfortable backpack

TRENTINO-ALTO ADIGE

- anorak (or pile/wind jacket)
- change of T-shirt, underwear and socks (wool and cotton)
- shorts and long pants
- gloves, wool or pile hat, or headband, and scarf
- water bottle containing at least 1L per person
- hooded raincoat or poncho
- torch (flashlight) and batteries, a pocket knife, a lightweight thermal blanket (for emergencies), suncream, tissues, sunglasses and, if necessary, a sheet or sleeping bag
- slippers or thongs to wear at rifugi (optional)
- some lightweight, energy-producing food

Walking Areas

The best areas for walking in the Dolomiti include:

- the Dolomiti di Brenta (Brenta group) accessible from either Molveno to the east or Madonna di Campiglio to the west
- the Val di Genova and the Adamello group also accessible from Madonna di Campiglio (the Brenta and Adamello groups form the Parco Naturale Adamello-Brenta)
- the Sella group accessible from the Val Gardena to the west, the Val Badia to the north, Livinallongo to the east and the Val di Fassa to the south
- the Alpe di Siusi, the Sciliar and the Catinaccio group accessible from Siusi and Castelrotto
- the Pale di San Martino accessible from San Martino di Castrozza and Fiera di Primiero
- the area around Cortina which straddles Alto Adige and the Veneto and features the magnificent Parco Naturale di Fanes-Sennes-Braies and, to the south, Monte Pelmo, Monte Civetta and the Val di Zoldo area
- the Sesto Dolomiti north of Cortina towards Austria, accessible from San Candido or Sesto in Val Pusteria

There are four Alte Vie in the Dolomiti – walks that can take up to two weeks to complete. The routes link existing trails and, in some places, incorporate new trails created to make difficult sections easier to traverse.

Each route links a chain of rifugi and you can opt to only walk certain sections:

- Alta Via No 1 crosses the Dolomiti from north to south, from the Lago di Braies to Belluno
- Alta Via No 2 extends from Bressanone to Feltre and is known as the Alta Via delle Leggende (High Route of Legends), because it passes through Odle, the mythical kingdom of ancient Ladino fairy tales

- Alta Via No 3 links Villabassa and Longarone
- Alta Via No 4 goes from San Candido to Pieve di Cadore

The Alte Vie are marked by numbers inside triangles – blue for No 1, red for No 2 and orange/brown for No 3; No 4 is marked by normal numbers on red-and-white bands. Booklets mapping out the routes in detail are available at the APT di Belluno, in the Veneto, or the APT in Trento.

People wanting to undertake guided walks, or to tackle the more difficult trails that combine mountaineering skills with walking (with or without a guide), can seek information at Guide Alpine (mountain guide) offices in most towns in the region. See the information in relevant towns in this chapter.

For more information on walking in the Dolomiti, see Lonely Planet's *Walking in Italy* guide.

Three Day Walk in Parco Naturale Fanes-Sennes-Braies

The following is a basic guide for a three day walk, accessible from Cortina d'Ampezzo or Corvara in Badia and incorporating a section of Alta Via No 1 that starts at the Passo di Falzarego and ends at the Passo Cimabanche. The best map is Tabacco No 03 (1:25,000) for Cortina d'Ampezzo e Dolomiti Ampezzane. Estimated times are intended as a guide for walkers who maintain a steady pace. Those who meander could double the time taken to complete each stage and this should be taken into account when aiming for specific rifugi. This trail is suitable for people with little walking experience.

Day One This first stage will take you from the Passo Falzarego to the Rifugio Fanes (four to five hours). The Passo Falzarego (2105m) is accessible by car or bus (three a day; 40 minutes) from Cortina and Corvara. A cable car will then take you up to the Rifugio Lagazuoi (2752m). Enjoy the spectacular view south-west across to the Marmolada glacier, because this is the highest altitude you will reach during the walk.

From the rifugio, head downhill into the wide valley, following the trail marked with a No 1 inside a blue triangle. On reaching the small Lago di Lagazuoi you will find, to the right, the beautiful but tiring ascent to the Forcella del Lago (2486m), from where you start the long descent into the Piano Grande, with a magnificent view of the Conturines mountains to your left. Once in the Piano Grande, a pretty valley of alpine pastures, take the trail to the right. At the end of the Piano Grande, past Passo Tadega (2143m), follow the triangle signs along the dirt road to eventually reach the Lago di

Limo (2159m) at the foot of the Col Bechei (2794m). Follow the trail to the left and you will descend to the picturesque Rifugio Fanes (2060m) or, slightly farther along the trail, the less expensive Rifugio la Varella (2042m). You can eat a meal and spend the night at either one. If you still have the energy, explore the beautiful Fanes high plain, taking trail No 12 to Lago Paron through enchanting scenery of limestone-white and a thousand shades of green, dotted with the colours of alpine flowers.

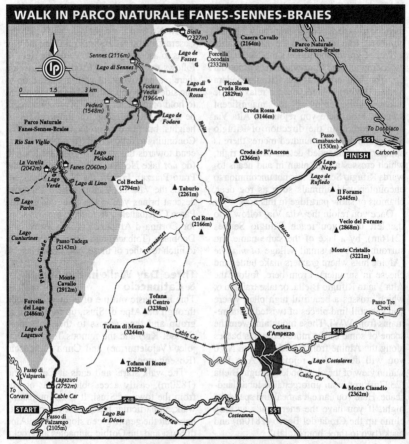

WALK IN PARCO NATURALE FANES-SENNES-BRAIES

TRENTINO-ALTO ADIGE

Day Two This stage will take you from Rifugio Fanes to Rifugio Biella (five to six hours). Following the blue triangular Alta Via signs, head down into the small valley of the San Vigilio river until you reach Lago Piciodèl on your right. Shortly after the lake, again on your right, is a trail that can be taken in preference to the Alta Via route, which, at this point, becomes a long descent to Rifugio Pederù (1548m), from where you climb to 2000m following a road heavily used by 4WD vehicles ferrying tourist groups to the rifugio. For those who want to end their walk now, a road descends from the rifugio into the Val Badia. The detour, on the other hand, is an atmospheric but tiring route, recommended to experienced walkers only. The unnumbered trail leads off to the right just after a river of gravel and follows the lake before ascending into the semi-wilderness, Banc dal Se. You will arrive at the Rifugio Fodara Vedla (1966m), where you can relax on the terrace while enjoying the magnificent scenery. From here you rejoin the Alta Via route, heading in the direction of Rifugio Sennes. After a few hundred metres there is another recommended detour to your right, which crosses a high plain in and heads towards Rifugio Sennes. It is not uncommon to encounter wild animals such as roe deer, chamois or snow partridge in this area.

Once you rejoin the Alta Via, follow it to the left until you reach Rifugio Sennes (2116m), by a lake of the same name and surrounded by a small village of *malghe* (Alpine huts where graziers make butter and cheese in summer). From here, follow the Alta Via to Rifugio Biella, or take trail No 6, which crosses a beautiful high plain where you can still find pieces of twisted metal remains from WWI. These mountains were the scene of some of the more ferocious battles along the Alpine front line. From trail No 6 you will descend to rejoin the Alta Via, within view of the old wooden Rifugio Biella (2327m), set in an unforgettable lunar landscape. Here you can eat a meal and spend the night. If you have the energy, it's an easy climb up the Croda del Becco (2810m) and back (two to three hours total).

Day Three This stage goes from Rifugio Biella to the Passo Cimabanche (five to six hours). Ascend trail No 28, which follows the crest above the rifugio. Here you leave the Alta Via, which descends to the Lago di Braies, a short distance to the north. The route instead heads south-east towards the majestic Croda Rossa (3146m), a beautiful mountain inhabited by golden eagles. Trail No 28 follows the crest until it reaches the Forcella Cocodain, a mountain pass at 2332m. From here you descend to the left, in a northerly direction on the slope of the Prato Piazza. After a short distance you pick up trail No 3 and continue the descent until you reach an intersection with trail No 4. Continuing to follow No 3 to the right, you will reach the Casera Cavallo at 2164m. From here the trail starts to ascend, always towards the right. It follows the face of the Croda Rossa, where there's a narrow point with a sheer drop to one side. Here you will find a fixed iron cord to hold onto for security. This section might be a bit intimidating for those afraid of heights, but presents no technical difficulty. Continuing to follow trail No 3, you will descend towards the valley to meet trail No 18 (do *not* take No 3A, which descends to the Prato Piazza). Follow the No 18 south, towards the Valle dei Canopi, where a slippery descent brings you to the S51 road and the Passo Cimabanche. Here there are bus stops for Cortina d'Ampezzo (15km away) and Dobbiaco (Tolbach) and a bar. It is possible to hitch to either of these towns from here.

Three Day Walk in the Sciliar & Catinaccio

This is a basic outline of a three day walk through the Alpe di Siusi, up to the Sciliar group and then across to the Antermoia (Kessel-Kgl) and the famous Torri del Vajolet (Vajoletturme) and Cima Catinaccio (Rosengarten).

The walk starts and ends at Compaccio (1820m), easily accessible by car or bus from the town of Siusi. It is an interesting walk, in particular because of the contrasts between the gentle green slopes of the Alpe di Siusi and the Gothic pinnacles and rocky

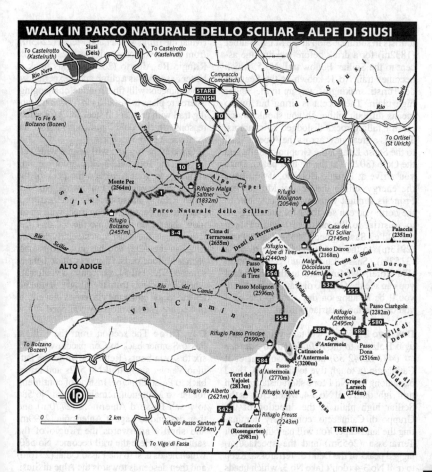

WALK IN PARCO NATURALE DELLO SCILIAR – ALPE DI SIUSI

towers of the Catinaccio group, which give the impression of a fairy-tale castle.

As is the case whenever you walk using the walks detailed in this book, make sure you are correctly dressed and equipped. The directions here should be used as a guide only and you should use Tabacco 1:25,000 map No 05. The second day of the walk is demanding and may present some difficulties for walkers with no experience. However, if you are fit, healthy and cautious you should have no trouble. Book in advance to

sleep at the rifugi, in particular at the small Rifugio Passo Santner (Santnerparshüte).

Day One This first stage will take you from Compaccio to the **Rifugio Bolzano** (☎ 0471 61 20 24) at 2457m (three to four hours). From the big car park at Compaccio, take the trail marked No 10 and follow it until you reach the turning to the left for the Rifugio Malga Saltner (Saltnerhütte; trail No 5). You will be walking through the western part of the Alpe di Siusi, a vast and beautiful area of undulating green pastures, packed full of tourists in summer. Stop at the Malga Saltner (1832m) for a drink before tackling the ascent to the Sciliar. Follow trail No 5, which becomes trail No 1, known as the Sentiero dei Turisti, snaking its way up to the Sciliar high plain. The ascent is tiring but by no means difficult, although you should watch out for falling rocks dislodged by chamois. There is a great view across the Alpe di Siusi to the Sasso Lungo, the Gruppo di Sella and the Odle (3025m at the highest peak). Once you arrive at Rifugio Bolzano, if you have the energy, climb the nearby Monte Pez. From its summit you have a 360° view: to the north you can see the Alpi stretching into Austria; to the north-east you can see the Odle, Sassongher (2665m) and Puez (2913m); to the east is the Gruppo di Sella (3152m), Sasso Lungo and Sasso Piatto (Plattkofel; 2964m); and to the south-east you can see the Gruppo di Catinaccio, where you'll be heading on day two; to the west you can see the Austrian border.

Day Two This track will take you from Rifugio Bolzano to the **Rifugio Passo Santner** (☎ *0471 62 42 30*) under the summit of Il Catinaccio (a tough five to six hours). Head back along trail No 1 for a short distance, then turn right onto trail No 3-4, which crosses the Sciliar high plain in the direction of the Gruppo di Catinaccio, completely dominating the landscape. You will pass the Cima di Terrarossa (2655m) and the spectacular, jagged peaks of the Denti di Terrarossa. Keep to trail No 3-4 (don't take No 3, which heads to the right) to reach the Rifugio Alpe di Tires (2440m), then go south on trail No 3a-554, ascend to the Passo Alpe di Tires and continue on to the Passo Molignon (2596m).

From here you start the difficult and very steep descent on a *ghiaione* (river of gravel) into the lunar landscape of a valley. Before reaching the valley floor the trail forks. Keep to the left and stay on trail No 554, which will take you up to the Rifugio Passo Principe (2599m), under the Catinaccio d'Antermoia (3200m). You can take a break at this tiny refuge. From here, descend into the valley

along the comfortable trail No 584. You'll arrive at the rifugi Vajolet and Preuss (2243m), from where you take trail No 542s up to the Rifugio Re Alberto (2621m). This track is better described as a climb and inexperienced mountaineers will find it quite challenging. There are plans to install a *via ferrata* (climbing trail with permanent steel cord) for safety reasons, which would significantly reduce the excitement of the ascent.

Once at the top you will be in a wide valley with the Torri del Vajolet, famous among climbers, to your right and the peak of the Catinaccio to your left. Follow trail No 542s up to Rifugio Passo Santner, perched on a precipice under the Rosengarten, with an almost sheer drop down into the Val di Tires. It is one of the most spectacularly located rifugi in the Alpi, and has just two rooms, each with four beds. Climbers flock here in summer. The trail 542s becomes a via ferrata where it descends from the rifugio. If you intend to tackle either the via ferrata or a climb, make sure you are properly equipped.

Day Three The section from the Rifugio Passo Santner back to Compaccio will take six to seven hours. Return down to the Rifugio Vajolet along trail No 542s and return back to Passo Principe. Instead of continuing for Passo Molignon, remain on trail No 584 to reach Passo d'Antermoia (2770m) and then descend to Lago d'Antermoia (2490m) and shortly afterwards the rifugio of the same name. Here the trail becomes No 580, which heads east to the Passo Dona (2516m) and then descends towards the Alpe di Siusi. After a relatively short distance the No 580 veers to the right (east), but you will instead continue straight ahead and, at the next fork, take trail No 555, which will take you in a westerly direction along the northern slopes of the Molignon group. At the base of the Molignon, the trail joins a dirt road (trail No 532) near the group of herders' shelters known as Malga Dòcoldaura (2046m). Follow No 532 to the Casa del TCI Sciliar, then go straight ahead along trail No 7, which will take you all the way down to Compaccio. (At Rifugio Molignon, the trail becomes a small road and some distance farther on it becomes trail No 7-12.)

SKIING IN THE DOLOMITI

The Dolomiti boast innumerable excellent ski resorts, including the fashionable Cortina d'Ampezzo (for drop-dead gorgeous people and their weighty wallets), Madonna di Campiglio, San Martino di Castrozza and Canazei, as well as the extremely popular resorts of the Val Gardena.

Accommodation and ski facilities are abundant and you have plenty of scope to choose between downhill and cross-country skiing, as well as *sci alpinismo*, which combines skiing and mountaineering skills on longer excursions through some of the region's most spectacular territory. Snow boarding and other white-stuff activities are also catered for.

Tourist offices abound throughout the region, but the best for general information, including on ski pass prices and Settimana Bianca (White Week skiing and accommodation packages) deals are the APT del Trentino in Trento and the APT for Alto Adige/Südtirol Dolomiti in Bolzano. See Tourist Offices under Information in the Trento and Bolzano sections later in this chapter.

The high season is generally from Christmas to early January and then from early February to April, when prices go up considerably – Settimana Bianca packages are big money-savers (see Activities in the Facts for the Visitor chapter for more details).

If you want to go it alone but plan to do a lot of skiing, invest in a ski pass. Most resort areas offer their own passes for unlimited use of lifts at several resorts for a nominated period (average price in the 1998/99 high season for a six day pass in the most popular resorts was around L250,000). However, the best value is the Superski Dolomiti pass which allows access to 464 lifts and more than 1180km of ski runs. In the 1998/99 high season a Superski pass for seven days cost L309,000 (or L269,000 from 7 to 30 January and again from 14 March). Contact Dolomiti Superski (☎ 0471 79 53 98), Via Cir 8, 39048 Selva Gardena (Alto Adige), or visit

the Web site at www.dolomitisuperski.com for information. Brochures are available at tourist offices throughout the region.

For the latest information on snow in the area, call ☎ 0461 23 89 39. In case of emergency in the mountains, call ☎ 118 for Soccorso Alpino.

The average cost of ski and boot hire ranges from L18,000 to L25,000 per day for downhill skis and up to L18,000 for cross-country skis and boots. In an expensive resort like Cortina, however, prices jump to as high as L40,000 per day to hire downhill skis and boots.

Ski schools operate at all resorts. A six day course can cost up to L190,000, while private lessons will cost at least L50,000 per hour.

OTHER ACTIVITIES

Come summer, you can opt for alternative pastimes such as mountain biking, hang-gliding and rock-climbing. Tourist offices can help you find trails, bike rental outlets and hang-gliding schools.

Gruppi Guide Alpine (Mountain Guide Groups) can be found in most towns and villages – many are listed in this chapter. If no group is listed for a particular area, the local tourist office will assist.

These groups organise guided walks (ranging from family nature walks to challenging walks of up to seven days at high altitudes) and rock-climbing courses, or you can even send the kids away for a few days of adventure. Many groups also offer guided mountain-bike and horse-riding tours.

Families are well catered for throughout the region, but particularly in Alto Adige. Many tourist offices organise special activities for kids in the summer and winter high seasons and some guide groups offer special courses and walks for youngsters. Most of the resort towns in Alto Adige have sports centres and playgrounds and many hotels are equipped for children providing cots, high chairs, special menus, playrooms and so on.

Some information and suggested family walks are given in this chapter, but contact tourist offices for more details.

TRENTINO-ALTO ADIGE

Trentino

TRENTO (TRENT)

postcode 38100 • pop 103,000

This calm, well-organised provincial capital is a good place to start any exploration of the province. Its tourist offices have extensive information on the town and Trentino, and it is convenient for public transport throughout the province.

Known by the ancient Romans as Tridentum, Trento later passed from the Goths to the Lombards and was eventually annexed by the Holy Roman Empire, when it became known as Trento or Trient. From 1027 until the early 19th century it was an episcopal principality, during a period marked by political and territorial conflict with the rulers of Tirolo. The Council of Trent (1545-63) considered the restructuring of the Catholic Church here and launched the Counter-Reformation.

Orientation

The train station and adjacent bus station are close to Trento's compact historic centre, as well as to most of the accommodation. Turn right as you leave the train or bus station and follow Via Andrea Pozzo, which becomes Via Cavour, to the central Piazza del Duomo.

Information

Tourist Offices Cross the park in front of the train station and turn right to reach the APT office (☎ 0461 98 38 80) at Via Alfieri 4. It's open from 9 am to 6 pm Monday to Saturday and to 1 pm on Sunday. The office has lots of information (in English) about the town, including maps.

The provincial tourist office, the APT del Trentino (☎ 0461 83 90 00, email apt@provincia.tn.it), Via Romagnosi 11, has extensive information on Trentino and can advise on skiing, walking and climbing, as well as other activities. See the introduction to this chapter for details of its Roma and Milano offices and Web site.

Post & Communications The main post office is on Via Calepina, at Piazza Vittoria.

Travel Agencies CTS (☎ 0461 98 15 33) is at Via Cavour 21.

Medical Services & Emergency The Ospedale Santa Chiara (hospital; ☎ 0461 90 31 11) is on Largo Medaglie d'Oro, southeast of the centre, off Corso III Novembre. In a medical emergency, call the Guardia Medica (☎ 0461 91 58 09).

The questura (police station; ☎ 0461 89 95 11), is on Piazza della Mostra, which is off Via San Marco near the Castello del Buonconsiglio.

Things to See & Do

The Piazza del Duomo, flanked by the Romanesque **duomo** and the 13th century **Palazzo Pretorio** and its tower, is the natural place to start a tour of Trento. The Council of Trent was held in the duomo (as well as in the Chiesa di Santa Maria Maggiore). In the duomo's transept are fragments of medieval frescoes, and two colonnaded staircases flank the nave. The foundations of an early Christian church were discovered beneath the duomo in the late 1970s.

The area is open from 10 am to noon and from 2.30 to 6 pm Monday to Saturday. Admission costs L2000, or you can pay L5000 for a combined ticket that includes admission to the **Museo Diocesano** in the Palazzo Pretorio. The museum houses paintings depicting the Council of Trent, as well as a collection of Flemish tapestries. Opening hours are the same as for the duomo.

On the other side of the piazza are two Renaissance houses, known as the **Case Cazuffi-Rella**, their façades decorated with frescoes. In the centre of the piazza is the 18th century **Fontana di Nettuno**.

From the piazza, head north along Via Belenzani or Via Oss Mazzurana and turn right into Via Manci to reach the **Castello del Buonconsiglio**. The castle, home of the bishop-princes who once ruled Trento, incorporates the 13th century Castello Vecchio and the Renaissance Magno Palazzo. Inside the castle is the **Museo Provinciale d'Arte**. The castle and museum are open from 9 am to noon and 2 to 5 pm Tuesday

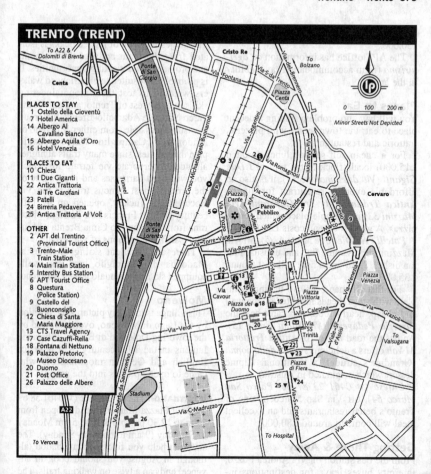

TRENTO (TRENT)

PLACES TO STAY
1 Ostello della Gioventù
7 Hotel America
14 Albergo Al Cavallino Bianco
15 Albergo Aquila d'Oro
16 Hotel Venezia

PLACES TO EAT
10 Chiesa
11 I Due Giganti
22 Antica Trattoria ai Tre Garofani
23 Patelli
24 Birreria Pedavena
25 Antica Trattoria Al Volt

OTHER
2 APT del Trentino (Provincial Tourist Office)
3 Trento-Malè Train Station
4 Main Train Station
5 Intercity Bus Station
6 APT Tourist Office
8 Questura (Police Station)
9 Castello del Buonconsiglio
12 Chiesa di Santa Maria Maggiore
13 CTS Travel Agency
17 Case Cazuffi-Rella
18 Fontana di Nettuno
19 Palazzo Pretorio; Museo Diocesano
20 Duomo
21 Post Office
26 Palazzo delle Albere

to Sunday (from 10 am to 6 pm during the summer). Admission costs L9000.

Ask at the APT about visits to the castles in the valleys around Trento.

Places to Stay

The youth hostel, *Ostello della Gioventù* (☎ 0461 23 45 67, Via Manzoni 17), is near the Castello del Buonconsiglio and charges L21,000 for a dorm bed, L25,000 for a bed in a double room and L30,000 for a single. Prices include breakfast.

Hotel Venezia (☎ 0461 23 41 14, Piazza Duomo 45) is a 1950s-style hotel. Its single/double rooms with bathroom cost L60,000/86,000.

The *Albergo Al Cavallino Bianco* (☎ 0461 23 15 42, Via Cavour 29) has simple rooms costing L65,000/92,000 with private bathroom or L45,000/70,000 without. *Albergo Aquila d'Oro* (☎ 0461 98 62 82, Via Belenzani 76) has good rooms with bathroom for L100,000/140,000 including breakfast. At *Hotel America* (☎ 0461 98 30 10, Via Torre

Verde 50), comfortable rooms cost L110,000/ 150,000.

The APT office has information on *agriturismo* (farm accommodation) availability in the area.

Places to Eat

You will have no problem finding a decent place to eat: the town teems with pizzerie, trattorie and restaurants.

For a cheap self-service lunch (around L15,000) locals flock to the typical *I Due Giganti (Via del Simonino 14)*; it is also an affordable evening restaurant for dinner. *Antica Trattoria ai Tre Garofani (Via Mazzini 33)* is a simple place which serves pizzas. A good set menu costs L30,000.

Patelli (Via Dietro le Mura A1/5), off Via Mazzini, serves some fine and unusual Italian dishes. A full meal here will cost around L35,000.

For that German beer-hall feeling, complete with stags' heads mounted on the wall and cheap, hearty food, you can't beat the *Birreria Pedavena (Via Santa Croce 15)*. Across the road at No 16, *Antica Trattoria Al Volt* offers a delicious *strudel della nonna* (Grandma's strudel, a traditional Alpine dessert which originated in Austria).

Chiesa (☎ 0461 23 87 66, Parco San Marco 64), off Via San Marco, is one of Trento's better restaurants and an excellent meal will come to around L80,000.

Getting There & Away

From the bus station on Via Andrea Pozzo, intercity buses leave for destinations including Madonna di Campiglio, San Martino di Castrozza, Molveno, Canazei and Riva di Garda. Timetables are posted at the bus station. You can also pick up a full guide to Trentino's public transport from the APT del Trentino office.

Regular trains connect Trento with Verona, Venezia, Bologna and Bolzano. The Trento-Male train line (station next to the main station) connects the city with Cles in the Val di Non via scenic routes.

Trento is well linked with Verona to the south and Bolzano to the north on the A22.

DOLOMITI DI BRENTA

This majestic group of jagged peaks is isolated from the main body of the Dolomiti and provides good walking opportunities. It is probably best suited to experienced walkers wanting to test their mountaineering skills. North-west of Trento, and part of the Parco Naturale Adamello-Brenta, the group is easily accessible from either Molveno or Madonna di Campiglio. Walkers should plan their routes, since many trails at higher altitudes incorporate vie ferrate for which you will need harnesses and ropes. One of the group's most famous trails is the Via Bocchetta di Tuckett, opened up by 19th century climber Francis Fox Tuckett, which runs from Molveno to Cima Brenta and includes difficult sections of vie ferrate.

There are excellent skiing facilities at Madonna di Campiglio, and the well-equipped ski resort Andalo is near Molveno.

Molveno

This village is in a very picturesque position by the Lago di Molveno, overshadowed by the towering Dolomiti di Brenta. It became famous in the 19th century as a base for English and German mountaineers who came to open up trails into the group.

Information The APT office (☎ 0461 58 69 24) is at Piazza Marconi 5 and is open from 9 am to 12.30 pm and 3.30 to 5 pm Monday to Saturday (9 am to noon on Sunday). The staff can help you find accommodation (although in August you should book in advance) and can advise on walking trails. The Gruppo Guide Alpine office (☎ 0461 58 60 86) is also in Piazza Marconi.

There is an *ambulatorio medico* (tourist medical service) provided by the *comune* (town council; ☎ 0461 59 60 45) from 9 to 11 am in the Palazzo Comunale (entrance at the rear). If a medical emergency occurs at night, phone the Guardia Medica of Andalo on ☎ 0461 58 56 37.

Activities From the top of the village, a *cabinovia* (two seater cable car) will take you up to the Rifugio Pradel (1400m), from where there's a hike following trail No 340 to the Rifugio Croz dell'Altissimo (1430m), a pleasant and easy one hour walk. Take trail No 340 to the Rifugio Selvata (1630m), then trail No 319 to the rifugi Tosa and Tommaso Pedrotti (2491m; about four hours walk).

From here most of the trails are difficult and you will need to be prepared for vie ferrate or for traversing glaciers. It is best to seek detailed information locally and take a carefully planned route using a good map.

For a less demanding walk, there is a path around the lake which starts at the Camping Spiaggia Lago di Molveno site. Making the entire circle of the lake will take about three and a half hours, but half the route is on the road, so it might be best to double back when the trail ends.

The Gruppo Guide Alpine organises guided walks, some incorporating vie ferrate, as well as rock-climbing courses and, in winter, ski-mountaineering. Of interest to families might be the five-day mountaineering courses for kids aged from eight to 15 years. The course is offered weekly from June to October.

Places to Stay & Eat The APT office will provide a list of the mountain rifugi and their telephone numbers to help you plan your walk. If staying in Molveno, try *Camping Spiaggia Lago di Molveno* (☎ 0461 58 69 78) at the lakeside, which charges up to L9500 per person and L15,000 for a site.

Prices do not vary greatly among the hotels in town and many require that you take full board. Average prices for full board range from L70,000 per person in May and June to around L100,000 per person in the high season (July and August). Try *Zurigo* (☎ 0461 58 69 47, Via Rio Massò 2) or *Hotel Ariston* (☎ 0461 58 69 07) right in the centre of town on Piazza San Carlo. *Grand Hotel Molveno* (☎ 0461 58 69 34) is in a lovely position out of town by the lake, on the road to Trento. Full board costs around L150,000 in the high season.

Getting There & Away Molveno is accessible on FTM (☎ 0561 23 83 50) or Atesina

(☎ 0461 98 36 27) buses from Trento. Atesina buses also connect Molveno with Milano in July and August, leaving from Piazza Castello in Milano on Saturday and/or Sunday (depending on the season).

Madonna di Campiglio & Pinzolo

One of the top ski resorts in the Alpi, Madonna di Campiglio (often simply called Madonna) and the less expensive Pinzolo sprawl along the Val Rendena, on the northwestern side of the Dolomiti di Brenta. Ski lifts are plentiful, as are opportunities for cross-country and alpine skiing.

Information The APT office in Madonna (☎ 0465 44 20 00) is in the centre of the village, off Piazza Brenta Alta. It has lots of information about skiing and walking in the area and can advise on accommodation. It will also mail out hotel lists and other information on request. Otherwise, check out the local Web site at www.aptcampiglio.tn.it. The office of the Gruppo Guide Alpine (☎ 0465 44 26 34) is across the street (open only after 4 pm) and brochures on its summer excursions are available at the APT office.

A tourist medical service (☎ 0465 44 07 55) operates in the winter and summer high seasons. The Guardia Medica is available year-round on ☎ 0465 44 04 30.

Helpful staff at the APT office in Pinzolo (☎ 0465 50 10 07) can give advice on cheap accommodation in this quiet family resort.

Activities A network of chair lifts and cable cars will take you from Madonna to the numerous ski runs or, in summer, to the walking trails. A few kilometres north of the village at Campo Carlo Magno is a cable car that takes you up, in two stages, to the Passo Grostè (2446m), from where walkers can set off into the Dolomiti di Brenta. The return trip on the cable car will cost L24,000. The Via delle Bocchette (trail No 305) leaves from the Rifugio Grostè (2438m) at the cable car station. This is the via ferrata for which the Brenta group is famous; only experienced mountaineers with the correct equipment should attempt it (the equipment can be

TRENTINO-ALTO ADIGE

hired locally). Otherwise, take trail No 316 to Rifugio del Tuckett and Q Sella (2271m). From there, take trail No 328 and then No 318 (sentiero Bogani) to the Rifugio Brentei (2182m; four to five hours from Grostè). All trails heading higher into the group from here cross little glaciers and special equipment is needed.

The interesting 16th century **Chiesa di San Vigilio** at Pinzolo merits a visit for its external painting entitled *La Danza Macabra* (*The Dance of Death*) that measures 20m in length. To the north of Pinzolo there is the entrance to the Val di Genova, often described as one of the most beautiful valleys in the Alpi. A series of spectacular waterfalls along the way enhances its reputation as great walking country, and it's just as tempting for a picnic. Four rifugi strung out along the valley floor make staying overnight an option. The Rifugio Adamello Collini (1641m) is at the end of the road, from where you can take trail No 212-220 to the Rifugio Citta' di Trento (2449m), or trail No 241 to the end of the valley (about 2000m) beneath a huge, receding glacier. From here the trail climbs steeply to the Rifugio Caduti dell'Adamello (3020m) at the edge of the glacier.

If you descend into the Val Rendena for a few kilometres south-west of Madonna you come to the Valli Giudicarie area near Lardaro, where there is a helpful tourist office (☎ 0465 90 12 17). The area is not served by public transport and you will need your own car to explore the spectacular side valleys. The 25km-long Val di Daone road, south-west of Lardaro, brings you to a reservoir. Walk along the edge of the reservoir for about two hours and you arrive at the peaceful Rifugio Val di Fumo (☎ 0465 67 45 25) at the foot of the imposing Carè Alto in the Adamello group. This old-style rifugio recalls the mountain-lover's paradise of the 1950s before the Dolomiti were discovered by the tourists.

Places to Stay & Eat Virtually none of Madonna's accommodation will suit the pockets of budget travellers. Most places require that you pay for half or full board

and in the high season may be reluctant to accept bookings for less than seven days. Prices are given per person per day in the high season unless otherwise stated.

Garni Bucaneve (☎ 0465 44 12 71) is south of Madonna, near Piazza Palù, and offers B&B for L50,000 per person, although prices can rise in early July. The *Bellavista* (☎ 0465 44 10 34), a pleasant establishment uphill from the APT office, near the Funivia Pradalago, charges from L114,000 for full board and L104,000 for half board. *La Baita* (☎ 0465 44 10 66, Piazza Brenta Alta 17) is a comfortable hotel with a good-value restaurant. Prices in July are L100,000 for half board or L700,000 per week for full board.

In the Val di Genova, *Rifugio Fontanabona* (☎ 0465 50 11 75) at 1099m and *Rifugio Stella Alpina* (☎ 0465 50 12 16) at 1450m are both in lovely settings. Full board costs around L80,000 per person in a double room. Both rifugi have excellent restaurants and are open from 20 June to 20 September.

In Madonna, try *Ristorante/Pizzeria Le Roi* on Via Cima Tosa, near Piazza Brenta Alta, where a full meal will cost around L40,000. Around the corner is *Paninoteca Dolomiti*, where hot sandwiches, starting at L4500, should be sufficient for lunch. In the summer and winter high seasons you could try one of the malghe, such as *Malga Ritorto* (☎ 0465 44 24 70), accessible by car in summer and by 'snow cat' service in winter.

Getting There & Away Madonna di Campiglio is accessible from Trento's bus station by regular Atesina bus. Autostradale and SIA operate weekend services from Milano, while Lazzi and SITA between them run services from cities including Firenze and Bologna.

VAL DI NON

The Val di Non is a picturesque valley of apple orchards and castles accessible from Trento by Trento-Male train or bus. The main town is Cles, dominated by the Castel Cles. The local Pro Loco tourist office (☎ 0463 42 13 76) is on Corso Dante, just off the main road through town, and there is an APT office in the nearby village of Fondo (☎ 0463 83 01 33). If you want to stay here on your way north, try **Antica Trattoria** (☎ 0463 42 16 31, Via Roma 13) in Cles, where singles/doubles with bathroom cost L70,000/115,000. A meal in the restaurant costs about L35,000.

SAN MARTINO DI CASTROZZA

Huddled at the foot of the imposing Pale di San Martino – mountains so stark and grey-white that they virtually glow in the dark – San Martino is another of Trentino's top ski resorts. The mountains are part of the Parco Naturale Paneveggio-Pale di San Martino, noted for its alpine vegetation and wildlife, including the roe deer, chamois, marmot, wildfowl and birds of prey such as the golden eagle. It is a magnificent area for skiing or walking, and both San Martino di Castrozza and the nearby Fiera di Primiero are well equipped for tourists.

Information

The APT office (☎ 0439 76 88 67, email info@sanmartino.com), Via Passo Rolle 165, has plenty of information and can advise on walking trails, hotels or apartments. The office is open in the summer and winter high season from 9 am to noon and 3 to 7 pm Monday to Saturday and from 9.30 am to 12.30 pm on Sunday. The Guide Alpine (☎ 0439 76 87 95) staff a desk in the same building from 5.30 to 7.30 pm. There is also a Web site at www.sanmartino.com.

The nearest hospital is at Feltre, although a tourist medical service is available during summer and winter at San Martino (☎ 0439 76 87 39) and Primiero. Full details are available at the APT office.

Activities

The area has excellent ski runs and is part of the extensive Superski Dolomiti region; during winter a special ski bus connects the valley with the various runs. The Pale di San Martino has well-marked walking trails and a reasonable map is available at the APT office. A chair lift and cable car will take you to the Rifugio Rosetta (2600m), from where you can choose between several

relatively easy walks or walks requiring mountaineering skills.

The more ambitious can check out activities with the Guide Alpine. It organises mountaineering ascents (Pala di San Martino, Cima della Madonna and Sass Maor) a 120km-long, high-altitude skiing excursion, as well as walks along vie ferrate and rock climbing courses.

Places to Stay & Eat

Prices vary according to the season and many places require that you pay for half or full board. They may also be reluctant to accept bookings of less than seven days. The APT office will advise on apartments to rent and has a full list of rifugi in the area.

Suisse (☎ 0439 6 80 87, Via Dolomiti 1) has singles/doubles with shower costing L50,000/100,000. **Biancaneve** (☎ 0439 6 81 35) is nearby at No 14 and charges about L50,000 per person for B&B. The newly renovated **Hotel Plank** (☎ 0439 76 89 76, Via Laghetto 35) charges L150,000 per person for full board. Good Settimana Bianca deals are available.

For meals, try **Da Anita** (☎ 0439 76 88 93), a cosy place in the centre of San Martino at Via Dolomiti. Slightly out of town, along Via Fontanelle, is **Caffè Col**. Local food is served at the various malghe around San Martino, which have developed into proper restaurants. Try the traditional-style **Malga Venegiota** (☎ 0462 57 60 44) at 1824m, accessible from Passo Rolle by a trail from Malga Juribello (three hours return) or by a shorter trail that incorporates the Baita Segantini chair lift (2170m).

Getting There & Away

Atesina buses run to San Martino from Trento and Canazei (via Predazzo). Long-haul services connect San Martino with cities such as Padova (SITA) and Venezia (Brusutti), among others.

CANAZEI

This popular ski resort in the Val di Fassa is surrounded by the striking peaks of the Gruppo di Sella to the north, the Catinaccio

(Rosengarten; 2981m) to the west and the Marmolada to the south-east. Canazei, a modern town, and a series of others along the valley to Vigo di Fassa, are geared to summer and winter tourism, although some locals still make a traditional living from dairy farming.

Skiing possibilities include a range of downhill and cross-country runs, as well as some challenging Alpine tours and the Sella Ronda network (see Gruppo di Sella later in this chapter). The Marmolada glacier provides summer skiing. Walkers can approach the Catinaccio group from Vigo di Fassa, 11km south of Canazei. The best approach to the Gruppo di Sella is from the Passo Pordoi, where a cable car will take you up to almost 3000m.

Information

The Canazei APT office (☎ 0462 60 11 13, email apt.fassa@softcom.it), Via Roma 34, has information on skiing, walking and accommodation. There is also a Web site at www.DolomitiSuperski.com/valfassa. For L330,000 your child can stay at the Snow Kindergarden for six days; the price includes a three hour daily skiing lesson.

Places to Stay & Eat

There are hundreds of hotels, garnis and rooms for rent in the Val di Fassa, and plenty enough in Canazei itself. It is advisable to book ahead in August and during the peak ski season. The APT office can provide details of rooms and apartments for rent.

Camping Marmolada (☎ 0462 60 16 60) is on Via Pareda in the town centre and is open in summer and winter.

Finding cheap places to stay is not always easy, and many places prefer you to stay for seven days. There is a cluster of cheaper possibilities on Via Dolomiti in Canazei. *Garni Christian* (☎ 0462 60 13 88), at No 150, charges L55,000 per night for half board. *Hotel Giardino delle Rose* (☎ 0462 60 22 21), at No 174, charges the same, as does *Garni Centrale* (☎ 0462 60 23 40) at No 176. *Garni Ciamorc* (☎ 0462 60 24 26, Via Pareda 41) is another decent option in the same price bracket. The lux-

urious and romantic *Hotel Astoria* (☎ 0462 60 13 02, Via Roma 88) charges L110,000 for half board in the low season.

There are numerous *bars* and *paninoteche* (cafés) in Canazei and a *supermarket* (Via Dolomiti 120). *Osteria La Montanara* (Via Dolomiti 147) serves good meals for around L35,000. Opposite, at No 168, is *Pizzeria/Ristorante Italia*, where pizzas start at L8000.

Getting There & Away

Canazei can be reached by Atesina bus from Trento and by SAD bus from Bolzano and the Val Gardena. Buses do not cross the high mountain passes (such as Passodi Sella) in winter.

GRUPPO DI SELLA

The Sella group, in the western Dolomiti, straddles the border between Trentino and Alto Adige, close to Cortina d'Ampezzo in the Veneto and the spectacular Parco Naturale di Fanes-Sennes-Braies. To the west is the spiky Sasso Lungo (Langkofel; 3181m), which extends to the Alpe di Siusi in Alto Adige. To the east is the Val Badia and its main town, Corvara, while to the south lies the Val di Fassa.

Skiers can complete the tour of the Sella in a single day on a network of runs called the Sella Ronda that covers a total distance of 26km. This long and challenging route is suitable for skiers with some experience and a good level of fitness. The local tourist offices can supply a leaflet that describes the clockwise and anticlockwise routes, including possible variations. The routes are covered by the famous Dolomiti Superski skipass. For walkers there is a summer version of the same leaflet, the *Sella Ronda estiva*. This contains details of the circular route that takes roughly eight hours to complete, at an all-inclusive cost of L30,000.

The walking trails of the Sella and Sasso Lungo can be reached from Canazei or the Val Gardena resorts by bus to Passo Sella or Passo Pordoi. At Passo Sella (2240m), from where you enjoy a magnificent view across the Alpi, a cable car runs to the Rifugio T

Demetz (2996m) on the Sasso Lungo. From here you can pick up trail No 525, which traverses the mountain's jagged peaks to the Alpe di Siusi. From Passo Pordoi (2242m), take the cable car up to Sasso Pordoi (2952m). Here you can get onto the Alta Via No 2, which crosses the group, heads down to the Passo Gardena and then continues into the breathtaking Parco Naturale Puez-Odle.

Alternatively you can take trail No 638 to the Rifugio Piz Fass on Piz Boè (3152m). Continuing along No 638 you will reach a combined chair lift and cable car service down to Corvara in the Val Badia. The cable car and chair lift are open from 8.30 am to 5.30 pm, with a break for lunch (from about 12.15 to 2 pm), and are closed all day Monday. Use a good map (such as the Tabacco 1:25,000 scale) and plan carefully. The Sella also offers challenging walks, some incorporating vie ferrate, for people with mountaineering experience. For further information on the Sella, the Val Gardena and the Val Badia see the following section on Alto Adige.

Alto Adige

This orderly Alpine fairyland owes more to its largely Austrian heritage than to its recent Italian history. Alto Adige (Südtirol) is a year-round attraction for skiers, climbers, walkers or just plain ordinary folk looking to appreciate its natural splendour.

BOLZANO (BOZEN)
postcode 39100 • pop 100,000
The provincial capital, Bolzano is unmistakably Austrian. Forget your *cappuccino* and *brioche* and tuck into some *deutscher Kaffee* (German coffee) with *Sachertorte* (chocolate apricot cake). You'll hear Italian and German spoken (both languages are compulsory subjects in school) but, aside from concessions to the former in street, hotel and restaurant signs, there are precious few reminders of Italian rule here. The town's small historic centre, with its engaging Tyrolean architecture and arcaded streets, harbours numerous outdoor cafés and restaurants, making it a very pleasant place to spend a few days.

Settled in the Middle Ages, Bolzano was an important market town that became a pawn in the power battles between the bishops of Trento and the counts of Tirolo. During the first decades of the 19th century it passed, with the rest of the Tirolo, from Bavaria, to Austria, to Napoleon's kingdom of Italy and, finally, again to Austria. Along with the Südtirol, Bolzano passed to Italy after WWI and was declared the capital of the province in 1927.

Orientation
The old-town centre is Piazza Walther (Waltherplatz), a few minutes walk along Viale Stazione from the train station on Via Garibaldi. The intercity bus station is on Via Perathoner, between the train station and the piazza.

Information
Tourist Offices The Bolzano AAST office (☎ 0471 30 70 00) is at Piazza Walther 8 and is open from 9 am to 6.30 pm Monday to Friday and from 9 am to 12.30 pm on Saturday. It provides a special Visitor's Pass to tourists spending at least three nights in town. The pass covers admission to some sights and museums, a cable car ride and a guided tour of the town.

The provincial tourist office for Alto Adige (☎ 0471 99 38 08) is at Piazza Parrocchia (Pfarrplatz) 11 and is open from 9 am to noon and 2 to 5 pm Monday to Friday. Here you can pick up information about accommodation, activities and transport, as well as walking possibilities. The office's Alpine information desk can help further with planning walks and climbs.

Money Money can be changed at all banks in Bolzano, from 7 am to 8 pm at weekends. There's also a currency exchange booth at the train station.

Post & Communications The post office, on Via della Posta, is open from 8.05 am to 6.30 pm Monday to Friday and from 8.05 am

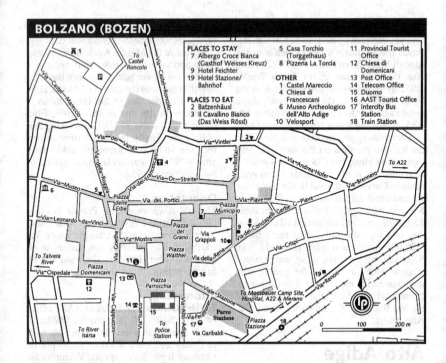

BOLZANO (BOZEN)

PLACES TO STAY
7 Albergo Croce Bianca
   (Gasthof Weisses Kreuz)
9 Hotel Feichter
19 Hotel Stazione/
   Bahnhof

PLACES TO EAT
2 Batzenhäusl
3 Il Cavallino Bianco
   (Das Weiss Rössl)

5 Casa Torchio
   (Torggelhaus)
8 Pizzeria La Torcia

OTHER
1 Castel Mareccio
4 Chiesa di
   Francescani
6 Museo Archeologico
   dell'Alto Adige
10 Velosport

11 Provincial Tourist
   Office
12 Chiesa di
   Domenicani
13 Post Office
14 Telecom Office
15 Duomo
16 AAST Tourist Office
17 Intercity Bus
   Station
18 Train Station

to 1 pm on Saturday. The Telecom office at Piazza Parrocchia 15 is open from 7.30 am to 11 pm daily.

Medical Services & Emergency Ospedale Regionale San Maurizio (☎ 0471 90 81 11) is on Via Lorenz Böhler, some distance from the town centre off the road to Merano, and accessible on city bus No 8 or 10a from the train station.

The questura (☎ 0471 94 76 11) is at Via Marconi 33.

Things to See & Do

While away a few hours at one of the many outdoor cafés on Piazza Walther or along the side streets that lead to Piazza delle Erbe. Otherwise, hire a bike from Velosport, Via Grappoli (Weintraubengasse) 56, near Piazza Walther, for a ride around town.

Start a sightseeing tour with the Gothic

duomo on Piazza Parrocchia, and the nearby **Chiesa di Domenicani** with its cloisters and chapel featuring 14th century frescoes of the Giotto school. Take a walk along the arcaded **Via dei Portici** (Laubengasse), through the charming Piazza delle Erbe (the German name Obstplatz explains what this square is – the daily fresh produce market), to reach the 14th century **Chiesa di Francescani** on Via dei Francescani. It features beautiful cloisters and a magnificent Gothic altarpiece carved by Hans Klocker in 1500 in the Cappella della Beata Vergine (Virgin's Chapel). There are several castles (not open to the public): the 13th century **Castel Mareccio** (Schloss Maretsch) is north along Via della Roggia from Piazza delle Erbe. **Castel Roncolo** (Schloss Runkelstein), out of town on the road to Sarentino (Sarnthein), is the best of a trio in the area. A bike will come in handy for visiting both.

The newly opened **Museo Archeologico dell'Alto Adige** (☎ 0471 98 20 98), at Via Museo 43, houses an important collection of regional treasures, including the mummified body of hunter-traveller 'Ötzi', discovered by chance in the Similaun glacier in September 1991 and dating back 5300 years. His equipment is also on display, accompanied by an exhaustive commentary. The museum is open from 10 am to 6 pm Tuesday to Sunday (from 9 am to 5 pm in winter, to 8 pm on Thursday). Admission costs L10,000.

Places to Stay

There is a wide choice of accommodation in Bolzano, including hotels and pensioni, rooms for rent and agriturismo – the APT office has full listings. There is a camp site, *Moosbauer* (☎ 0471 91 84 92, Via San Maurizio 83), out of town towards Merano.

Albergo Croce Bianca/Gasthof Weisses Kreuz (☎ 0471 97 75 52, Piazza del Grano 3), off Via dei Portici, charges up to L48,000 per person for B&B. The *Hotel Stazione/ Bahnhof* (☎ 0471 97 32 91, Via Renon 23) is in a less pleasant position to the east of the train station, but offers reasonable B&B with bathroom for L50,000. *Hotel Feichter* (☎ 0471 97 87 68, Via Grappoli 15) charges a little more. Out of town at Colle (Kohlern), accessible by road or the Funivia del Colle, is *Klaushof* (☎ 0471 32 99 99), which offers B&B for a more affordable L40,000.

Places to Eat

You can pick up basic supplies (for example fruit and vegetables, bread and cheese) from the open-air *market* held every morning from Monday to Saturday on Piazza delle Erbe. In the same area are numerous *bakeries*, *pastry shops* and *cafés*, as well as a small *supermarket*. While you can eat pizza and pasta if you wish, Bolzano's best restaurants specialise in the Tyrolean-style Austrian cuisine, *Il Cavallino Bianco/Das Weiss Rössl* (Via Bottai 6) is extremely popular and reasonably priced at around L30,000 for a full meal. *Pizzeria La Torcia* (Via dei Conciapelli 25) is cheap and also serves pasta. *Casa Torchio/ Torrgelhaus* (Via Museo 2), just off Piazza

delle Erbe, is a wonderful place with antique glass windows and excellent local specialities at reasonable prices. *Batzenhäusl* (Via Andrea Hofer 30) is a traditional restaurant where a full meal costs up to L50,000.

Getting There & Away

Bus Bolzano is a major transport hub for Alto Adige. SAD buses leave from the bus terminal on Via Perathoner, near Piazza Walther, for destinations throughout the province, including Val Gardena, the Alpe di Siusi, Brunico, Val Pusteria and Merano (where you can change for destinations including the valleys leading up into the Parco Nazionale dello Stelvio).

SAD buses also head for resorts outside the province, such as Canazei and Cortina d'Ampezzo in Trentino and Veneto respectively, (for the latter you have to change at Dobbiaco). Timetables are available from the bus station or the AST office. You can call toll free for bus information on ☎ 800 84 60 47.

Train Regular trains connect Bolzano with Merano, Trento, Verona, Milano, Innsbruck (Austria) and Munich (Germany). You can also catch a train from Bolzano to Brunico and San Candido in the Val Pusteria.

Car & Motorcycle The town is easily accessible from the north and south on the A22.

MERANO (MERAN)

Merano is a rather sedate little place, its typically Tyrolean centre clean and well-tended. The Terme di Merano, a complex of therapeutic baths and treatments, is the main attraction and most tourists tend to be in the older age group. Merano is close to the Parco Naturale Gruppo di Tessa (Texalgruppe), the Parco Nazionale dello Stelvio and the spectacular Ortles (Ortler) mountain range, so you might use the town as a stopover on your way to higher altitudes.

The train and intercity bus stations are on Piazza Stazione (Bahnhofsplatz), a 10 minute walk from the centre of town. As you leave the train station, turn right into Via Europa

TRENTINO-ALTO ADIGE

(Europaallee) and at Piazza Mazzini (Mazziniplatz) take Corso della Libertà (Freiheitsstrasse) to reach the town centre.

Information

The Azienda di Cura, Soggiorno e Turismo (ACST; ☎ 0473 23 52 23, email info@meraninfo.it), Corso della Libertà 35, provides information about the city. It also has a Web site at www.meraninfo.it.

The main post office and Telecom office are at Via Roma (Romastrasse) 2, on the other side of the river from the historic town centre.

Ospedale Provinciale Tappeiner (☎ 0473 26 33 33) is at Via Rossini 5, off Via Goethe.

Things to See & Do

The historic centre of town surrounds the arcaded Via dei Portici (Laubengasse) and the Piazza del Duomo – take any of the streets off Corso della Libertà near the ACST office (leading away from the river). The **Terme di Merano** (therapeutic baths, *Kurbad* in German; ☎ 0473 23 77 24), at Via Piave 9, offers a full range of medical treatments, including hydromassages, and physiotherapy. For L15,000 you can enjoy a healthy radon bath in a small thermal swimming pool. The complex is open Monday to Saturday year-round.

If you're interested in women's clothing past and present, drop in to the **Museo della Donna (Frauenmuseum)** at Via dei Portici 68. The **Museo Civico** (☎ 0473 23 60 15), at Via delle Corse 42, is open from 10 am to 5 pm Tuesday to Saturday and from 10 am to 1 pm on Sunday and public holidays (also from 4 to 7 pm in July and August). Admission costs L2700 for adults and L2000 for children. The **Castello Principesco** (☎ 0473 23 01 02), on Via Galilei, was home to the Princes of Tirolo after 1470; it's one of the better-maintained castles in Alto-Adige. Opening times and prices are the same as for the Museo Civico.

Beer-lovers might be interested in a visit to the **Forst Brewery**, (☎ 0473 26 01 11) at Forst, just outside Merano.

Places to Stay

Accommodation is abundant in Merano – ask at the ACST office for full hotel and apartment lists, including those equipped for children (with services such as babysitting, baby cots and playrooms). Most establishments in the centre are expensive, although *Pension Tyrol (☎ 0473 44 97 19, Via XXX Aprile/30 Aprilstrasse 8)*, off Corso della Libertà, has reasonable rooms starting at about L90,000 for a double (singles are hard to get). The price includes breakfast.

Villa Pax (☎ 0473 23 62 90, Via Leichter 3) is a religious institution which charges L36,000 per person including breakfast. To reach it from Corso della Libertà, cross the river at Piazza D Rena and follow Via Cavour to Via Dante, turn right and then left into Via Leichter. *Conte di Merano/Graf von Meran (☎ 0473 23 21 81, Via delle Corse 78)* is just near the Via dei Portici. Its lovely rooms can cost up to L90,000 per person, including breakfast.

Places to Eat

Ristorante Forsterbräu (Corso della Libertà 90) surrounds a courtyard and serves typical Tyrolean food at reasonable prices. A full meal costs around L30,000. Two restaurants on Via dei Portici serve excellent Tyrolean fare at similar prices: *Rainer* at No 266 and *Hairsrainer* at No 100, notable for its cavernous feel. *Picnic Grill (Via delle Corse 26)* is even more economical, offering pizzas and pre-prepared food.

Getting There & Away

Merano is easily accessible by bus or train from Bolzano (about 40 minutes). SAD buses also connect the town with Monte San Caterina (Katharinaberg) and other villages that give access to the Tessa group, as well as to Silandro (Schlanders) and the valleys leading up into the Ortles range and the Parco Nazionale dello Stelvio. See the section on the Parco Nazionale dello Stelvio for bus information. A direct bus departs Merano for Munich (Germany) every Saturday from late March to early November for DM45 (DM80 return).

PARCO NAZIONALE DELLO STELVIO

If you can tear yourself away from the Dolomiti, this major national park offers more fantastic walking possibilities: at low altitudes in the pretty valleys, Val d'Ultimo (Ultental), Val Martello (Martelltal) and Val di Solda (Suldental), and at high altitudes on spectacular peaks such as the Gran Zebru (Königspitze; 3859m), Cevedale (Zufallspitze; 3769m) and the breathtaking Ortles (3905m), all part of the Ortles range. There is a network of well-marked trails, including routes over some of the range's glaciers. The park incorporates one of Europe's largest glaciers, the Ghiacciaio dei Forni.

The glaciers permit year-round skiing and there are well-serviced runs at Solda and the Passo Stelvio (2757m); the latter is the second-highest pass in the Alpi and is approached from **Trafoi** on one of Europe's most famous roads, a series of tight switchbacks covering 15km with, at times, nerve-wrackingly steep gradients. The road is famous among cyclists, who flock to the park every summer to tackle the ascent.

If you want to stay in Trafoi, there is a *camp site (☎ 0473 61 15 33, 0473 61 16 81 in winter)* and several hotels and garni including *Hochleiten (☎ 0473 61 17 91)*, which charges L40,000 for B&B.

SAD bus No 102 runs to Stelvio village, from Merano change at Spondigna (Spondinig). Buses to the pass run in summer only.

The park straddles Alto Adige and Trentino and can be approached from Merano (from where you have easy access to the Val d'Ultimo, Val Martello, Val di Solda and the Passo Stelvio), or from the Val di Sole in Trentino, which gives easy access to the Valle di Peio and the Val di Rabbi.

Val di Solda

The village of Solda (Sulden), at the head of the Val di Solda, is a small ski resort and a base for walkers and climbers in summer. Challenging trails lead you to high altitudes; these include trail No 28, which crosses the Madriccio pass (3123m) into the Val Martello. The tourist office at Solda (☎ 0473 61 30 15) has information on accommodation and activities.

At Solda try *Pension Nives (☎ 0473 61 32 20)*, which offers B&B for around L40,000 per person, or half board for L65,000. At the top end, *Parc Hotel (☎ 0473 61 31 33)* offers lovely rooms and good food; half board costs around L100,000. The village virtually closes down from October to Christmas.

SAD buses connect Solda with Merano on weekdays during the summer only; you need to change at Spondigna.

Val Martello

This picturesque valley is a good choice for relatively low-altitude walks, with spectacular views of some of the park's high peaks. The real beauty of the valley is that the environment is unspoiled by ski lifts and downhill ski runs. It is a popular base for tackling the glaciers (guided walks can be organised). In winter there is excellent cross-country skiing, and climbers can crawl up the valley's frozen waterfalls from January to March. In spring the valley attracts ski mountaineers, since there is no danger of avalanches.

People with children might like to take trail No 20 up into the Val di Peder. It is an easy walk, with some lovely picnic spots along the way and the chance to see animals, including chamois and deer.

Schoenblick (☎ 0473 74 47 76) is high in the valley (2100m) and offers half board only, costing L62,000 per person. For further accommodation, inquire at the Pro Loco office.

The road into the valley is open year-round, and SAD bus 107 runs to Martello village from Silandro. In summer the bus proceeds to Rifugio Genziana (Enzianhütte).

Valle di Peio

From Peio (also spelt Pejo) Terme (1393m), actually inside Trentino province, chair lifts operate to the Rifugio Doss dei Cembri (2400m), from where you can pick up trail No 105 to the Rifugio Mantova al Vioz (3535m) at the edge of the Forni glacier. If you want to climb Monte Vioz (3645m) or continue onto the glacier, you can hire the necessary equipment in Pejo.

TRENTINO-ALTO ADIGE

The tourist office at Male (☎ 0463 90 12 80), Piazza Regina Elena 19, has extensive information on these valleys, including accommodation, transport and sporting activities, and will advise on walking trails and ski facilities.

Ferrovia Trento-Male buses connect Peio Terme with Madonna di Campiglio and with Male in the Val di Sole. Male is on the Trento-Male train line.

VAL GARDENA

An enchanting alpine valley, Val Gardena (Grödnertal) is hemmed in by the towering peaks of the Parco Naturale Puez-Odle (Naturpark Puez-Geisler), the imposing Gruppo di Sella and Sasso Lungo and the gentle slopes and pastures of the Alpe di Siusi, the largest high plain in the Alpi. It is one of the most popular skiing areas in the

NICKY CAVEN

Val Gardena is one of the best places in Italy to buy wooden carvings and statues.

Alpi because of its relatively reasonable prices and excellent facilities. Be warned though that the valley and its ski runs are packed in the ski season. In the warmer months, walkers have easy access to trails at high and low altitudes.

The valley's main towns, Ortisei (St Ulrich), Santa Cristina (St Christina) and Selva (Wolkenstein), all offer lots of accommodation. Along with the Alpe di Siusi (see that section later in this chapter), the Val Gardena provides excellent facilities for families. The well-organised tourist offices run activities for children in summer and winter, and you'll find sports centres and well-equipped playgrounds.

Along with Val Badia (Gadertal), the Val Gardena is an enclave that has managed to preserve the ancient Ladin language and culture, and a rich tradition in colourful legends (for more details see the boxed text 'The Ladin Tradition' in the Val Badia section later in this chapter). The ancient tradition of woodcarving is also maintained here and the valley's artisans are famed for their statues, figurines, altars and toys. Beware of mass-produced imitations.

Information

There are tourist offices in each of the towns: Ortisei (☎ 0471 79 63 28), Santa Cristina (☎ 0471 79 30 46) and Selva (☎ 0471 79 51 22). All have extensive information on accommodation, ski facilities and walking trails. A guidebook in English is available for each town, along with information on guided walks and rock-climbing schools; alternatively address your queries to info@val-gardena.com. The Web site at www.val-gardena.com also has comprehensive information and pictures of garni and hotels.

Skiing & Walking

In addition to its own fine downhill ski runs, the valley also forms part of the Sella Ronda, a network of runs connecting the Val Gardena, Val Badia, Livinallongo and Val di Fassa. Areas like the Vallunga, near Selva, offer good cross-country skiing. Alpine skiers should consult the tourist offices for detailed

Val Badia, Alto Adige – a mixture of Italian, German and ancient Ladin cultures

STEFANO CAVEDONI

Italy is not just gentle rolling hills – the rugged Via delle Bocchetta, Dolomiti di Brenta.

information. There are stunning trails around Forcella Pordoi and Val Lasties in the Gruppo di Sella, and on the Sasso Lungo.

This is walkers' paradise, with endless possibilities, from the challenging Alte Vie of the Gruppo di Sella and the magnificent Parco Naturale Puez-Odle, to picturesque family strolls in spots like the Vallunga. Just behind Selva, the valley is home to some over-friendly horses who like to harrass picnicking tourists. The walk to the end of the valley takes three to four hours. It is possible to continue from the end of the valley, along trail No 14, to pick up the Alta Via No 2. From here you can continue up into Gruppo di Odle, or double back into Gruppo di Puez and on to the Gruppo di Sella.

Full-Day Walk in the Puez-Odle This is a full-day walk (about eight hours) at high altitude through the Alpe di Cisles, an extraordinarily beautiful landscape dominated by the Odle and Puez mountains. As with all walks, make sure you carry a good map: the Tabacco 1:25,000 No 05 is recommended. Also ensure that you carry the correct items of clothing and plenty of water (for more details see Walking in the Dolomiti earlier in this chapter) and notify your hotel of your planned route.

From Ortisei (about 1250m) in the Val Gardena, take the cable car to Seceda (L16,000, or L27,000 return; which is open from 8.45 am to 4.45 pm) at 2456m. This is the highest point you will reach during the walk and there is a memorable view – one of the most spectacular in the Alpi. Behind you is the Odle group, a series of spiky pinnacles. Take trail No 2a, which follows the slope and passes through what most people would consider a typical alpine environment – lush, green sloping pastures dotted with wooden malghe, used by herders as summer shelters.

This type of environment is, in fact, unusual at such high altitude. Following trail No 2a through the scenic Alpe di Cisles, you will come to an area known as Prera Longia. Huge boulders with surreal forms dot the landscape – who knows how long ago they fell from the mountains. It is

highly likely that you'll see marmot, roe deer and certainly lots of birds here. Follow the trail until you arrive in a valley: at this point you need to descend into the valley (continuing along trail No 2a, making sure you don't follow the signs for Rifugio Firenze) then go up the other side, following the sign for Forces de Sieles. It's a 200m descent and then a very tiring 400m uphill climb. At this point the trail becomes No 2 (there are several trails which branch off to the right – don't follow them), which will bring you to the Forces de Sieles (2505m).

Continue on trail No 2; following it to the left, you'll reach a short section of vie ferrate. Don't panic – you don't need any equipment; just hold onto the cord if you need help to cross this steep section. After a short distance, the trail joins the Alta Via No 2 (marked with the number 2 inside a triangle). Following the trail to the right, you'll pass a crest and then descend to a small, high plain, almost like a rocky balcony above the Vallunga – you are directly beneath the Puez group at this point, the highest peak of which is the Cima Puez (2913m).

Continue along the trail, heading towards Rifugio Puez (Puezhütte), but before you get there you'll find on your right trail No 4, which descends into a broad valley and eventually reaches the Vallunga and trail No 4-14. This is virtually a small road; follow it to the right and meander down the pretty Vallunga, with its alpine vegetation. If you walk quietly, you should come across quite a few animals. The contrast between the majesty of the high mountains and the gentle environment of the valley creates a memorable effect and provides a fitting end to the walk. Once you arrive at the end of the valley, it will take another 15 minutes or so to reach the town of Selva, from where you can catch a bus back to Ortisei.

Places to Stay

The valley has hundreds of hotels and pensioni, but it is still advisable to book in advance, particularly during August and at Christmas and Easter. Many places only offer half or full board, but there are also

TRENTINO-ALTO ADIGE

plenty of B&Bs and *affittacamere* (rooms for rent), as well as apartments. The tourist offices have full lists, including photos and prices, so write or phone to request a booklet in advance. If you arrive in Ortisei without a booking and the tourist office is closed, an electronic table outside the office has the latest info on hotel vacancies.

Ortisei There are plenty of budget places, such as *Gran Cësa* (☎ 0471 79 74 22, Via Zitadella-Strasse 67), where B&B costs up to L47,000.

The *Panoramik* (☎ 0471 79 64 95, Via Vidalong-Strasse 9) offers B&B for around L60,000 in peak season, while *Alpenhotel Rainell* (☎ 0471 79 61 45, Via Vidalong-Strasse 19) offers half board for L100,000 in June and L155,000 in August.

Santa Cristina The *Garni Tyrol* (☎ 0471 79 20 58, Via Plesdinaz-Strasse 113) charges around L43,000 per person for B&B year-round. *Haus Walter* (☎ 0471 79 33 37, Via Val-Strasse 6) has recently been restored and charges L55,000 for B&B. *Pensione Bellavista* (☎ 0471 79 20 39, Via Plesdinaz-Strasse 65) is 1km north of the town and offers B&B/half board for up to L55,000/L75,000, in a panoramic setting. In the town centre is *Hotel Post* (☎ 0471 79 20 78, Via Dursan-Strasse 17), which offers half board for up to L160,000.

Selva About the cheapest place is the affittacamera *Plochof* (☎ 0471 79 55 88, Via Daunëi-Strasse 71), on the edge of town, which charges L32,000 per person. *Garni Zirmei* (☎ 0471 79 52 12, Via Col da Lech-Strasse 60) is more central and charges around L60,000 for B&B. For a long stay try *Residence Katiuscia* (☎ 0471 79 55 08, Via Larciunëi-Strasse 38), near the Vallunga. It's a fair walk from town but in a lovely position. A week's accommodation for two people costs L770,000 in August.

Getting There & Away

The Val Gardena is accessible from Bolzano by SAD bus, as well as from Canazei (summer only). Regular buses connect the towns along the valley and you can reach the Alpe di Siusi by either bus or cable car. Full timetables are available at the tourist offices.

Long-distance bus services (Lazzi, SITA and STAT) to major cities throughout Italy are available in July and August and between Christmas and Easter. Information can be obtained at Alpintourdolomit Viaggi (☎ 0471 79 61 35) in Ortisei.

ALPE DI SIUSI & PARCO NATURALE DELLO SCILIAR

There's something magical about the view across the Alpe di Siusi (Seiser Alm) to the Sciliar (Schlern): the green undulating pastures end dramatically at the foot of these towering peaks. It is a particularly spectacular scene in an area that certainly doesn't lack scenery. The Alpe di Siusi (1700m to 2200m), the largest plateau in Europe, forms part of what is known as the Altipiano dello Sciliar, which also incorporates the villages of Castelrotto (Kastelruth) and Siusi (Seis), lower down at about 1000m.

There is something for walkers of all ages and expertise in this area. The gentle slopes of the Alpe di Siusi are perfect for families with young kids, and you won't need much more than average stamina to make it to the Rifugio Bolzano (Schlernhaus; 2457m), just under Monte Pez (2564m), the Sciliar's summit. If you're after more challenging walks, the jagged peaks of the Catinaccio group and the Sasso Lungo are nearby. These mountains are famous among climbers worldwide.

Information

The area is popular in both summer and winter and its tourist offices are highly organised. All local offices will send out information such as hotel lists and prices. There are four offices of the Associazione Turistica Siusi – Sciliar: Castelrotto (☎ 0471 70 63 33), Piazza Kraus 1; Siusi (☎ 0471 70 70 24), Via Sciliar 8; Compaccio (Compatsch; ☎ 0471 72 79 04) in the Alpe di Siusi; and Fie' allo Scilliar (☎ 0471 72 50 47). Pick up the brochure listing local services from the tourist offices.

For medical assistance call ☎ 0471 70 65 55. The Guardia Medica Turistica (☎ 0471 70 54 44) is based at Telfen, between Castelrotto and Siusi.

Activities

There's no shortage of organised activities or details on how to organise your own. In winter the area offers excellent skiing: downhill, ski-mountaineering and cross-country. It forms part of the Superski Dolomiti network. As in the Val Gardena, the area gets pretty crowded during peak periods. Ask at the tourist offices about walking trails open during the snow season.

In summer the trails in the Alpe di Siusi are crowded with walkers but as soon as you get to higher altitudes they start to thin out. Using a good map and following the tourist office recommendations, you could spend days taking leisurely walks in the Alpe di Siusi, stopping for picnics or planning your walks to ensure that you reach a malga for a lunch break. The tourist offices organise low-priced guided walks of varying length and difficulty. There are also plenty of good trails for mountain bikers. There are plenty of challenging walks, including several vie ferrate. The Catinaccio group can also be approached from the Val di Fassa. See Walking in the Dolomiti at the start of this chapter for details of a three day walk in the Sciliar and Catinaccio.

Courses & Organised Tours The Scuola Alpina Dolomiten (☎ 0471 70 53 43, email dolomit@cenida.it), Via Vogelweider (Vogelweidergasse) 6, Castelrotto, has a summer programme which includes a seven day guided walk across the Dolomiti from the Alpe di Siusi area to the Tre Cime di Lavaredo. Also offered is a week of free-climbing (for experts), a rock-climbing course for beginners and a mountain-bike 'safari' from Bolzano to Sesto. In winter, a beginners' ski-mountaineering course is on offer, as well as a 'Skisafari' for experts, both on and off runs, through the Alpe di Siusi, Val Gardena, Val Badia to Cortina, the Marmolada and the Val di Fassa finish-

ing at the Alpe di Siusi. Its Web site is at www.dolomiten-alpin.com.

Places to Stay

There are plenty of hotels and pensioni in this area, but bookings are recommended during the summer and winter high seasons. If you're travelling with kids, ask staff at the tourist office for information on hotels equipped for, or offering special deals for, children. There's a choice between places in the villages, or up on the Alpe di Siusi. If you choose to stay in the Alpe di Siusi, there is a regular bus service; in summer normal traffic is banned from the plateau. For details see Getting There & Around below.

Try *Albergo Zallinger* (☎ 0471 72 79 47, *Saltria 74)*, at the foot of the Sassopiatto, where half board costs up to L80,000 per person. In Castelrotto, *Garni Villa Rosa* (☎ 0471 70 63 27, *St Annaweg 3)* has B&B in double rooms costing from L38,000 to L55,000 per person, depending on the season. It's about 10 minutes walk to the centre. The traditional *Gasthof zum Wolf* (☎ 0471 70 63 32, *Oswald von Wolkensteinstrasse 5)* is right in the middle of Castelrotto; comfortable B&B costs L62,000 to L97,000 per person in a double room, depending on the season – they may insist on half board (an extra L15,000 per person). In most hotels you'll pay L8000 extra for single occupancy.

Getting There & Around

The Altipiano dello Sciliar is accessible by SAD bus from Bolzano, the Val Gardena and Bressanone. By car, exit the Brennero autostrada (A22) at Bolzano Nord or Chiusa.

From May to October the roads of the Alpe di Siusi are closed to normal traffic. Tourists with a booking at a hotel in the zone can obtain a special permit from the tourist office at Compaccio allowing them to drive between 4 pm and 10 am. It is best to organise your pass before arriving in the area; ask your hotel owner for assistance. A regular bus service operates from Castelrotto and Siusi to Compaccio and from there on to the Alpe di Siusi. Tourists staying in some hotels in the area are given a special Favorit card that

TRENTINO-ALTO ADIGE

entitles them to free bus travel on the Buxi line. For information about the pass and the participating hotels ask at the tourist offices.

VAL BADIA

Along with the Val Gardena, Val Badia is one of the last strongholds of the ancient Ladin culture and language. Most local kids (as well as adults) are aware of the Ladin legends, richly peopled by giants, kings, witches, fairies and dragons. Many are set on the nearby Fanes high plain, which forms part of the magnificent Parco Naturale Fanes-Sennes-Braies. This is one of the most evocative places in the Dolomiti and can be reached easily from the Alta Val Badia, either on foot or by cable car from Passo Falzarego. The towns in the valley include Colfosco (Colfosch), La Villa (La Ila), San Cassiano (San Ciascian) and Corvara.

Corvara

This ski resort is an excellent base for walkers wanting to tackle the peaks enclosing the Alta Badia. Corvara was the central town of the Ladin tribes and today is a pleasant little place, with a well-organised tourist office and plenty of accommodation.

The Associazione Turistica tourist office (☎ 0471 83 61 76, email altabadia@dolomiti superski.com) is on the town's main street. In summer it is open from 8 am to noon and 3 to 7 pm Monday to Saturday and 11 am to 1 pm on Sunday. It has extensive information on ski facilities, walking trails, accommodation and transport. It also has a Web site at www.altabadia-dolomites.com.

For medical assistance, go to the Croce Bianca, set back from Corvara's main street near the tourist office. In an emergency, the nearest public hospital is in Brunico (☎ 0474 58 11 11).

Activities Corvara is on the Sella Ronda ski trail and is part of the Superski Dolomiti network (for more details seeing Skiing in the Dolomiti earlier in this chapter). From the town, you can reach the Passo Falzarego by SAD bus and then take the cable car up into the Parco Naturale Fanes-Sennes-Braies. For more details see the section on Walking in the Dolomiti earlier in this chap-

---

The Ladin Tradition

The Ladin language and culture can be traced back to around 15 BC when the people of the Central Alpi were forcibly united into the Roman province of Rhaetia. The Romans, of course, introduced Latin to the province but the original inhabitants of the area, with their diverse linguistic and cultural backgrounds, modified the language to such an extent that by around 450 AD it had evolved into an independent Romance language, known as raeto-romanic. At one point the entire Tyrol was Ladin but today the language and culture are confined mainly to the Val Gardena and the Val Badia, where in the 1981 census about 90% of the locals declared that they belonged to the Ladin language group. Along with German and Italian, Ladin is taught in schools and the survival of the Ladin cultural and linguistic identity is protected by law.

The Ladin culture is rich in vibrant poetry and legends, set amid the jagged peaks of the Dolomiti and richly peopled by fairies, gnomes, elves, giants, princesses and heroes. Passed on by word-of-mouth for centuries and often heavily influenced by Germanic myths, many of these legends were in danger of being lost. In the first decade of the 20th century, journalist Carlo Felice Wolff, who had lived most of his life in Bolzano, undertook a major project: he spent 10 years gathering and researching the local legends, listening as the old folk, farmers and shepherds recounted the legends and fairy tales. The originality of the legends he eventually published is that, instead of simply writing down what he was told, Wolff reconstructed the tales from the many different versions and recollections he gathered.

ter. Alternatively, you can pick up trail No 12 from near La Villa, or trail No 11, which joins Alta Via No 1, at the Capanna Alpina, a few kilometres off the main road between Passo Valparola and San Cassiano. Either trail will take you up to the Alpe di Fanes and the two rifugi, Lavarella and Fanes.

A combination of cable car and chair lift will take you from Corvara up into the Gruppo di Sella at Vallon (2550m) where you'll get a spectacular view across to the Marmolada glacier. From Vallon you can traverse the Sella or follow the trail that winds around the valley at the top of the chair lift (about one hour). A good area for family walks is around Prelongià (Prelungé) (2138m). Catch the cable car from La Villa and then take trail No 4 and trail No 23 to reach Prelongià. Trail No 23 will take you down to Corvara. Horse riding, mountain biking and hang-gliding are also popular activities in the valley.

Places to Stay & Eat The tourist office can help you find accommodation. Try *Garni Laura* (☎ *0471 83 63 40, Via Col Alt 44)*, back from the main road near the tourist office. B&B costs up to L40,000 per person. At *Ciasa Blancia* (☎ *0471 83 62 96, Via Sassongher 52)* half board costs up to L110,000. *La Tambra* (☎ *0471 83 62 81, Via Sassongher 2)* is a pleasant, child friendly hotel. Full board costs up to L165,000 per person per day. Full meals at the attached *Ristorante/ Pizzeria La Tambra* cost about L40,000.

At the upper end of the scale, try the luxurious *Romantik Hotel La Perla* (☎ *0471 83 61 32, email perla@altabadia.it, Via Col Alt 105)*, whose rooms more than live up to its name. The hotel offers excellent gourmet food and high-quality wine in a traditional, 18th century Ladin-style dining room. It also has two saunas and a swimming pool with water games. The low-season price (end of June) for half board is L168,000.

Getting There & Away SAD buses link Corvara with Bolzano, Merano, Brunico, the Val Gardena, the Passo Sella and Passo Pordoi, Canazei and the Passo Falzarego (note

that buses re-route to avoid crossing the high passes in winter).

CORTINA D'AMPEZZO

Across the Fanes-Conturines range from the Val Badia is the so-called jewel of the Dolomiti, Cortina d'Ampezzo. Italy's most famous, fashionable and expensive ski resort, Cortina is actually situated in the Veneto, but has been included here because of its central location in the Dolomiti. It is one of the best equipped, and certainly the most picturesque, resorts in the Dolomiti. If you are on a tight budget, the prices for accommodation and food will be prohibitive, even in the low season. However, nearby camp sites and Alpine rifugi (the latter open only in summer) provide more reasonably priced alternatives.

Situated in the Ampezzo bowl, Cortina is surrounded by some of the most stunning mountains in the Dolomiti, including (in a clockwise direction) Cristallo, the Gruppo di Sorapiss-Marmarole, Antelao, Becco di Mezzodi-Croda da Lago, the Nuvolau-Averau-Cinque Torri and Tofane. To the south are the Pelmo and the Civetta. Facilities for both downhill and cross-country skiing are first class and the small town's population swells dramatically during the ski season as the rich and famous pour in. The town is also busy during the summer months, because the area offers great possibilities for walking and climbing, with well-marked trails and numerous rifugi.

Information

The main APT office (☎ 0436 32 31, email apt1@sunrise.it), at Piazzetta San Francesco 8 in the town centre, has information on accommodation, skiing facilities and walking trails. It can also provide a full listing of apartments and rooms for rent. The Web site is at www.sunrise.it/dolomiti. There is also a small information office at Piazza Roma 1.

Cortina's Gruppo Guide Alpine (☎ 0436 86 85 05), based at the Casa delle Regole at Corso Italia 69/a, is open from 8 am to noon and 4 to 8 pm. Apart from the usual rock-climbing courses and guided walks for adults, the guides also offer a range of courses and walks for children.

Activities

Apart from the three day walk through Fanes-Sennes-Braies detailed in the Walking in the Dolomiti section earlier in this chapter, the Dolomiti around Cortina offer a network of spectacular trails. A series of three cable cars (L45,000 return) will take you from Cortina up to the Tofana di Mezzo (3243m) in summer only; all of the trails from here are difficult and incorporate vie ferrate, for which you will need to be properly equipped. You can link up with the Alta Via No 1 either at the Passo Falzarego or at the evocative Passo Giau, with the spiky Croda da Lago to the east and the Cinque Torri to the north-west. To get to the Passo Giau you can catch a bus from Cortina to Pocol and then take a taxi.

Another possibility is to take the local bus from Cortina east to Passo Tre Croci (1805m) and take trail No 215 (which is a section of Alta Via No 3) up to the Rifugio A Vandelli (1928m) in the heart of the Sorapis group. From here the Alta Via No 3 continues up to 2316m and then to the left as trail No 242, which leads to the Antelao and Marmarole groups. This section incorporates a section of vie ferrate, as does trail No 215, which heads off to the right.

Not far from Cortina, and accessible by Dolomiti Bus in summer, are the Tre Cime di Lavaredo, one of the most famous climbing locations in the world and also a panoramic place to walk. The fact that you can arrive by bus literally at the foot of the Tre Cime means the area is crawling with tourists in the high season.

Family Walk from Rifugio Malga Ra Stua to Forcella Lerosa

This is a good walk for families because the climb is not too steep, it's fairly short – around four hours up and back, including a picnic stop – and you'll see lots of animals and birds along the way. The area is easily accessible from either the Val Pusteria or Cortina, by car or public transport – from Cortina or Dobbiaco take the S51.

Eight kilometres north of Cortina, take the small road to the left at the first switchback – if you are approaching from Dobbiaco it is the first switchback after Passo Cimabanche. During summer, from mid-June to mid-September, the road up to Ra Stua is closed to normal traffic. You can walk the 3 to 4km from the car park at the switchback (1420m) to Ra Stua (1670m), or use the reasonably priced minibus service which operates from 8 am to 6 pm daily in summer to Ra Stua from another large parking area situated to the west of the main road 900m south of Pensione Fiames, 4km north of the centre of Cortina.

Use the Tabacco 1:25,000 map of Cortina d'Ampezzo e Dolomiti Ampezzane.

If you decide to walk from the car park, take the track that heads uphill from the eastern side of the switchback and follows the slope of the Croda de R'Ancona. The track doesn't have a number but is marked on the map.

Malga Ra Stua is at the beginning of the Val Salata, a lovely alpine environment and perfect for a family walk. Before heading off for a walk in the valley, make sure you let the people running the rifugio know where you are going and check on the departure time of the last minibus.

More serious walkers can walk to the end of the Val Salata, ascend to the Lago di Sennes (2116m) and pick up the walk through the Parco Naturale Fanes-Sennes-Braies which is detailed earlier in this chapter. However, those wishing to do the family walk from Ra Stua, head up along the Val Salata for about 150m and take the dirt road to your right; cross two bridges and you'll come to a signpost. Here, leave the dirt road that continues as a shortcut to Forcella Lerosa and turn right to take track No 8 for Forcella Lerosa – Val de Gotres. This former military road, built by the Austrian army during WWI, is a little bit longer but much easier and more scenic. There is a series of switchbacks winding uphill past ancient fir trees and at certain points there are panoramic views across the Fanes high plain. You will reach a lovely small valley where, if you approach quietly, you might see the resident marmots, chamois and squirrels. Follow the trail around the valley, always keeping to the main track and avoiding the several diversions to the right. The trail will bring you to a little wooden house with a water fountain in a wide valley with a dirt road. From here, Passo Forcella Lerosa (2020m) is a few minutes walk to the right. In front of you now is the majestic Croda Rossa (3146m), one of the most beautiful peaks in the Dolomiti.

One option is to turn right on the dirt road, still numbered as trail No 8, to reach the pass. After a picturesque descent of about 4km you will reach the S51, closer to Dobbiaco and just before Passo Cimabanche.

Alternatively you can turn left at the wooden house and follow the dirt road back down to Ra Stua. This route is the aforementioned shortcut near Ra Stua but is less attractive than the ascent, so there is always the option to return the way you came.

Back at the Malga Ra Stua, try the fantastic hot chocolate topped with fresh cream.

Places to Stay
International Camping Olympia (☎ 0436 50 57) is 3.5km north of Cortina at Fiames and is open year-round. In the high season it charges L30,000 per day for one person and a tent and it also has 25 beds in bungalows for around L35,000 per person, although these are usually fully booked. *Camping Cortina* (☎ 0436 86 75 75, Via Campo 2), 2.5km south of Cortina, is also open year-round and has similar prices.

There are no budget hotels in Cortina; however, one of the best deals is to be found at *Casa Tua* (☎ 0436 22 78, 0335 656 75 57, email casatua@cortinanet.it, Loc. Zuel 100), 3km south of Cortina in a very quiet area with gardens. B&B in clean rooms with bathroom costs from L45,000 to L80,000 per person, depending on the season. To get there take bus No 2, departing every 30 minutes in the high season and hourly during the rest of the year, from Piazzale Roma. Check out the Web site at www.cortinanet.it/casatua/index .html.

Pensione Fiames (☎ 0436 23 66, Via Fiames 13), 4km north of Cortina, is about as cheap and basic as it gets, with doubles costing up to L140,000 for a double in the high season. *Meuble' Montana* (☎ 0436 86 04 98, Corso Italia 94) charges up to L190,000 with breakfast. *Meuble' Cavallino* (☎ 0436 26 14, Corso Italia 142) is in the heart of the town; doubles cost L230,000 including breakfast.

Places to Eat
There are numerous good eating places in and around Cortina, although many are very expensive. The *Standa* supermarket on Via Franchetti is a good place to shop if you have access to a kitchen. For a good pizza, head for *Il Ponte* (☎ 0436 86 76 24, Via Franchetti 8). *Ristorante Pizzeria Croda Café* (☎ 0436 86 65 89, Corso Italia 163) has reasonably priced meals; big salads cost L17,000. Another good pizzeria is *El Bronzin* (☎ 0436 86 70 51, Via Roma 47). Here you'll pay around L30,000. The restaurant *Ra Stua* (☎ 0436 86 83 41, Via Grohmann 2) offers good meals for around L40,000, but guests at Casa Tua can expect a discount. *El Zoco* (☎ 0436 86 00 41, Via Cademai 18) specialises in grills – don't expect much change from L50,000.

Getting There & Away
Cortina's bus station is on Via Marconi. SAD buses connect Cortina with Dobbiaco, where you can change for Brunico and Bolzano. Dolomiti buses run to Belluno, Pocol and Passo Falzarego. There are also bus services to Venezia and Padua (ATVO), Bologna and Milano (Zani). Local services connect the town with International Camping Olympia at Fiames and Pocol.

As mentioned in the walk to Ra Stua, a minibus service connects Fiames with the rifugio Malga Ra Stua from 8 am to 6 pm daily from mid-July to mid-September. A special service for mountain bikers and their bikes also runs from Fiames to various locations. Call ☎ 0436 86 70 88 for information.

VALZOLDANA
Valzoldana lies a mere 50km south of Cortina, south of the imposing Civetta (3220m) and Pelmo (3168m) groups, yet it

TRENTINO-ALTO ADIGE

has none of the tourist trappings displayed by its more illustrious neighbour. Until the last century the Zoldani made their living by exploiting the local resources – metal deposits and water – to make nails for the Venetian Republic; until 1890, that is, when a flood destroyed their makeshift smithies. Many people left the region and emigrated to Munich and Vienna, setting up as travelling ice cream and sorbet salesmen; today many of their descendants run famous ice cream parlours the world over. Since the 1970s the profits from these commercial activities have fostered the growth of the tourism industry.

Information

For details of summer and winter activities and accommodation go to the APT Valzoldana office in Forno di Zoldo (☎ 0437 78 73 49) or in Zoldo Alto (☎ 0437 78 91 45). There is also a Web site at www.dolomiti.it.

Activities

Modern ski runs hug the Civetta group at Zoldo Alto. Eighty kilometres of runs link the valley to the Dolomiti Superski network, allowing skiers to reach the Sella and Marmolada groups. In the lower valley around Forno di Zoldo the landscape is unchanged, the prices and crowds have been kept under control and the food is authentic and excellent.

Walkers might like to take advantage of the extensive network of paths in the area. In six days you can do a round trip through unspoiled woodland beneath the peaks of less 'famous' mountains such as Sfornioi, Bosconero and Pramper.

Places to Stay

There are numerous hotels and camp sites in the valley, including *Hotel Corinna* (☎ *0437 7 85 64, fax 0437 78 75 93, Via ai Pez, email corinna@dolomiti.it*) at Forno di Zoldo (850m). Singles/doubles here cost L80,000/120,000 including breakfast, and half board is L120,000. In Zoldo Alto try the *Hotel al Sole* (☎ *0437 78 92 17*), where half board costs about L110,000. *Rifugio Casera di Bosconero* (1457m), in the conifer forest at the foot of the mountain of the same name, has dorm

beds for L18,000; half board costs L60,000. It is accessible from Forno on the path marked 490A (three to four hours), or from the Lago di Pontesei on paths 490 or 485 (two to three hours).

Getting There & Away

The valley is served by the S251 that descends from the Forcella Staulanza pass (1789m) in the north to Longarone in the south-east. Coming from the south, leave the S51 at Longarone, following signs to Cortina, and then turn left onto the S251.

VAL PUSTERIA & DOLOMITI DI SESTO

On the northern edge of the Dolomiti, the Val Pusteria (Pustertal) is bordered by the magnificent Parco Naturale Fanes-Sennes-Braies and, farther north, by the Parco Naturale delle Dolomiti di Sesto, which includes some of the area's most famous peaks – among them the Tre Cime di Lavaredo (Drei Zinnen). The valley is easily reached from the Val Badia and Cortina d'Ampezzo along the spectacular Valle di Landro (Höhlensteintal). Its main centre is Brunico (Bruneck), a pleasant market town with excellent transport connections that makes a good base for excursions into Fanes-Sennes-Braies. More picturesque options are San Candido (Innichen) and Sesto (Sexten) at the base of the Dolomiti di Sesto.

Information

The tourist office in Brunico (☎ 0474 55 57 22) is at the bus station on Via Europa. In San Candido, the tourist office (☎ 0474 91 31 49) is on Piazza del Magistrato, and in Sesto the tourist office (☎ 0474 71 03 10) is on the main street, Via Dolomiti. All have plenty of information about ski facilities and walking possibilities and will send out brochures about accommodation.

There is an excellent public hospital at Brunico (☎ 0474 58 11 11).

Activities

Easy to get to from the Val Pusteria is the beautiful Lago di Braies, a perfect spot for a picnic, followed by a leisurely walk around the lake. More serious walkers might like to tackle part of the Alta Via No 1, which starts here. The Fanes-Sennes-Braies park is more easily approached from the Val Badia or from Passo Falzarego.

At the other end of the valley, towards Austria, are the Dolomiti di Sesto, where there are some spectacular trails. Good areas for family walks are the Valle Campo di Dentro (Innerfeldtal), near San Candido, and the Val Fiscalina (Fischleintal), near Sesto. Both valleys are very popular spots for cross-country skiing in winter.

From the Val Fiscalina it is a long but easy walk along trail No 102 to Rifugio Locatelli (Drei Zinnen-Hütte; 2405m), from where you will be able to get a great view of the Tre Cime di Lavaredo. You can continue to the Tre Cime along trail No 101 and then down to Rifugio Auronzo (2320m). From there you can catch a Dolomiti Bus down to the Valle di Landro or to Cortino d'Ampezzo. This is one of the highest rifugi in the Dolomiti that is accessible by road.

All of the trails around the Tre Cime are easy enough for first-time walkers and for families. In fact, in July and August the trails here are more like motorways; they are literally packed with tourists, since it is possible to get there by car or bus.

If you do want to walk here, don't be fooled by the crowded trails into thinking that you don't need to come fully prepared. Remember you are walking at high altitude and the weather conditions can change dramatically at any time, so always carry a warm jacket and water and wear proper walking shoes.

An option for serious walkers is to take trail No 103 from the Rifugio Fondo Valle (1548m) at the end of the Val Fiscalina up to Rifugio Comici (Zsigmondy-Hütte; 2224m), then trail No 101 to Rifugio Pian di Cengia (Büllele-Joch-Hütte, 2528m) and to Rifugio Locatelli. From here, trail No 102 descends into the Val Fiscalina.

Places to Stay
In Brunico, *Krone-Corona* (☎ *0474 8 52 67, Via Ragen di Sopra [Oberragen] 8),* in the old town centre, charges L52,000 per person for B&B in the high season. In San Candido, *Residence Obermüller-Fauster Melchior* (☎ *0474 91 34 12, Via Castello [Burgweg] 8)* is in a picturesque position at the back of the town. It has rooms and apartments at reasonable prices of up to L35,000 per person per day. *Villa Waldheim* (☎ *0474 91 31 87, Via Pascolo [Am Erschbann] 1)* offers half board for up to L96,000.

Getting There & Away
By SAD bus you can reach Brunico and San Candido from Bolzano and Merano, the Val Badia and San Vigilio di Marebbe, the Val Gardena (on the Innsbruck bus) and Cortina. Catch a bus from Brunico or San Candido to Dobbiaco, from where you can catch a bus to the Lago di Braies. To get to the Rifugio Auronzo at the Tre Cime di Lavaredo, catch the Cortina bus from San Candido or Dobbiaco then, from Cortina, catch the bus for Misurina and the Tre Cime.

The Val Pusteria is reached by train from Bolzano via Fortezza (where a change is necessary). By road, the valley is easily accessible from the Val Badia, from Cortina via the S51 in the Valle di Landro and from the A22.

TRENTINO-ALTO ADIGE

Most travellers to the Veneto region are so dazzled by Venezia that they neglect the rest, which is a shame. You should try to set aside extra days at least to behold Giotto's extraordinary frescoes in Padova and to take in an opera at Verona's Roman Arena.

Vicenza, which was the home town of the architect Palladio, is also well worth a stopover, perhaps on your way to the northern reaches of il Veneto for a visit to Cortina d'Ampezzo, one of the world's most famous ski resorts, and for some walking in the eastern Dolomiti.

The region's cuisine is founded on rice and corn. Polenta is fried, served with hearty game stews and included in other main course dishes. *Risotto* is cooked with almost everything the countryside and lagoon have to offer, from baby peas to shellfish and game. A local favourite is risotto flavoured with the ink of *seppia* (cuttlefish).

One of il Veneto's best known contributions to the Italian table is *tiramisù*, a rich dessert of mascarpone cheese, Marsala, sponge and chocolate.

The wine list provides some of Italy's most popular drops, including Soave, a fine white that is well known in the USA, the UK and Australia. The light, sparkling Prosecco and Bardolino red wines are also known widely. The Bellini, a cocktail of Prosecco and fresh peach juice, has come a long way since Giuseppe Cipriani first mixed one at Harry's Bar in Venezia in the 1950s.

Getting around is easy. The A4, which runs between Torino and Venezia, bisects the region and there is an efficient bus and train network, meaning few parts are out of reach.

For information about the Veneto region call ☎ 800 01 41 96 toll-free from anywhere in Italy, or check out the Web site at www.veneto.org.

Highlights

- Lose yourself in the back lanes and canals of Venezia
- Visit the lagoon islands of colourful Burano and peaceful Torcello
- Tuck in to a good seafood meal in one of Venezia's osterie
- Marvel at the mosaics of the Basilica di San Marco
- Take a tour of Palladio's villas, from the Brenta to Vicenza
- Catch an opera at Verona's Arena

Il Veneto p395

Venezia (Venice)
Dorsoduro, San Marco & Castello pp406-7
Central Venezia p410
Cannaregio, Santa Croce & San Polo pp414-15

FRIULI-VENEZIA GIULIA

LOMBARDIA

Verona p437   Vicenza p434
Padova (Padua) p429   Venezia (Venice) p399

EMILIA-ROMAGNA

Mar Adriatico

Venezia (Venice)

postcode 30100 • pop 68,200 (292,500 including mainland)

Perhaps no other city in the world has inspired the superlatives heaped upon Venezia by writers and travellers through the centuries.

Forget that Venezia is no longer a great maritime republic and that its buildings are in

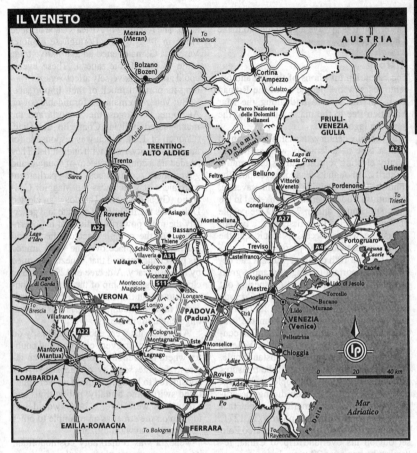

IL VENETO

serious decay and constantly threatened by rising tides. Today, Byron might be reluctant to take his daily swim along the Canal Grande: it is too dirty. But the thoughts of Henry James are as true today as they were a century ago: 'Dear old Venice has lost her complexion, her figure, her reputation, her self-respect; and yet, with it all, has so puzzlingly not lost a shred of her distinction'. La Serenissima (the most Serene Republic), remains a singular phenomenon.

The secret to seeing and discovering the

real romance and beauty of Venezia is to *walk*. Parts of Cannaregio, Dorsoduro and Castello are empty of tourists, even in the high season. You can become lost for hours in the narrow, winding streets between the Ponte dell'Accademia and Stazione Santa Lucia (train station), where the signs that point towards San Marco and the Ponte di Rialto rarely seem to make sense – but what a way to pass the time!

The city's busiest months are between May and September, Christmas and New

Year, during Carnevale (in February), and at Easter, but it is always a good idea to make a hotel booking.

History

The barbarian invasions of the 5th and 6th centuries saw the people from the Roman towns of the Veneto and along the Mar Adriatico flee to the marshy islands of the Venetian lagoon.

In the 6th century the islands began to form a type of federation, with each community electing representatives to a central authority, although its leaders were under the control of the Byzantine rulers in Ravenna. Byzantium's hold over Italy weakened in the early 8th century and in 726 AD the people of Venezia elected their first doge, a type of magistrate, whose successors would lead the city for more than 1000 years.

By the late 10th century, Venezia had become an important trading city and a great power in the Mediterraneo, prospering out of the chaos caused by the First Crusade launched in 1095. During the 12th century the city continued to profit from the crusades and at the beginning of the 13th century, under Doge Enrico Dandolo, Venezia led the Fourth Crusade to Constantinople. Venezia not only kept most of the treasures plundered from Constantinople, it also kept most of the territories won during the crusade, consolidating a maritime might that made it the envy of other powers. In 1271, Venetian merchant and explorer Marco Polo set out on his overland trip to China, returning by sea over 20 years later.

During much of the 13th and 14th centuries, the Venetians struggled with Genova for maritime supremacy, a tussle that culminated in Genova's defeat in 1380 during an epic siege at Chioggia. Their maritime power consolidated, the Venetians turned their attentions to dominating the mainland, capturing most of the Veneto and portions of what are now Lombardia and Emilia-Romagna. However, the increasing power of the Turks forced the Venetians to deploy forces to protect their interests elsewhere. The fall of Constantinople in 1453 and Morea in 1499 gave the Turks control of access to the Mar Adriatico. The rounding of Africa's Cape of Good Hope in 1498 by the Portuguese explorer Vasco da Gama opened an alternative trade route to the Mediterranean. These events could not fail to adversely affect Venezia, robbing its ports of much of their importance.

But Venezia remained a formidable power. At home, the doges, the Signoria and the much-feared judicial Consiglio dei Dieci (Council of Ten), which was responsible for internal security, ruled with an iron fist. They headed up a complex system of councils and government committees, the parliament equivalent of which was the Maggior Consiglio (Great Council). The doge, an elected Duke, was the figurehead of state and generally the most powerful individual in government, but the complex set of checks and balances put in place over the years limited his power and ensured that Venezia was ruled by its aristocracy. A decree of 1297 virtually closed off membership of the Maggior Consiglio to all but the most established of patriarchal families, making Venezia a tightly knit oligarchy until its demise.

All Venetians were encouraged to spy on other Venetians in every city, port and country where the Venetian Republic had an interest, for the security of the state. Acts considered to be against the state were punished swiftly and brutally: public trials and executions were rare; a body would just turn up on the street as an example to other potentially wayward citizens.

Venezia was remarkably cosmopolitan, its commerce attracting people of all nationalities. Although Venezia limited the commercial and social activities of its Jewish community, which it concentrated in one of Europe's earliest ghettos, it did nothing to stifle the Jewish religion. Similarly, the Armenians were permitted religious freedom for centuries and given protection during the Inquisition.

The city's wealth was made all the more conspicuous by the luxury goods traded and produced there. Venezia had a European monopoly on the making of what is now known as Murano glass; its merchants had also

Acque Alte

Venezia can be flooded by high tides during winter. Known as *acque alte*, these mainly occur between November and April, flooding low-lying areas of the city such as Piazza San Marco. The serious floods are announced several hours before they reach their high point by the sounding of 16 sirens throughout the city and islands.

In some areas you can see the water rising up over the canal border, although most of the water actually bubbles up through drains. The best thing to do is buy a pair of *stivali di gomma* (gumboots) and continue sightseeing. *Passerelle* (raised walkways) are set up in Piazza San Marco and other major tourist areas of the city (you can pick up a brochure with a map of the passerelle at the tourist office), but the floods usually last only a few hours. If the flood level exceeds 1.2m, then you can be in trouble, as even the walkways are no use at that level.

Venezia's flooding problems are compounded by the fact that the city is actually sinking: it sank by 23cm during the 20th century. Another major concern is that the waters of the canals are incredibly polluted. Until 20 years ago, the Mar Adriatico natural tidal currents flushed the lagoons and kept the canals relatively clean. But the dredging of a 14m-deep canal in the 1960s, to allow tankers access to the giant refinery at Marghera, changed the currents. Work is now underway to clean the sludge from the city canals.

As though all this was not enough, the salt water – even when unpolluted – is corroding the city's foundations. Alarm bells are ringing and the city fathers have warned that if efforts are not made to counteract the corrosion, canalside buildings could start to collapse.

The so-called Moses plan to install three massive floodgates at the main entrances to the lagoon was first approved by the Italian government in the 1980s, but never seems to get past the starting line. After finally getting approval from various commissions in 1998, the plan was stopped again in December when leftwing and Green politicians in Venezia said the US$2.5 billion plan required further study, as its environmental impact on the lagoon was still unknown. The Ministry of the Environment in Roma put its rubber stamp to the doubts (again!) and said no.

Exasperated by this, Paolo Costa, a Venetian and former public works minister, declared: 'We do not need more doctors at the bedside'. He claimed that the city would be submerged by the end of the 21st century. The Green Party countered that the funds for the project (which would require up to US$10 million worth of maintenance annually) would be better spent cleaning up chemical and oil pollution in the lagoon and dredging silted-up canals.

The pro-Moses camp says that, however imperfect, the project would buy precious time for Venezia. And so Chioggia's town council approved the project in February 1999, leading the Venetians to again rethink – this time setting the final decision date to the year 2000. In the meantime the plan is to be tinkered with and resubmitted for an environmental impact study.

reintroduced the art of making mosaics, and Venetian artisans made fine silks and lace.

But even as her people wallowed in their well-being, Venezia was on the wane. Both the Turks and the Vatican States made gains at the republic's expense during the 16th and 17th centuries, and in 1669 Venezia lost Crete to the Turks after a 25 year battle: its last stronghold in the Mediterraneo was gone. Finally, in 1797 the Maggior Consiglio abolished the constitution and opened the city's gates to Napoleon, who in turn handed Venezia to the Austrians. Napoleon returned in 1805, incorporating the city into his Kingdom of Italy, but it reverted to Austria after his fall. The movement for Italian unification

Saving Venezia

Floods, neglect, pollution and many other factors have contributed to the degeneration of Venezia's monuments and artworks. Since 1969 however, a group of private international organisations, under the aegis of UNESCO, has worked to repair the damage.

The Joint UNESCO-Private Committees Programme for the Safeguarding of Venezia has raised millions of dollars for restoration work in the city: from 1969 to 1992 nearly 100 monuments and more than 900 works of art were restored.

Major restoration projects completed include the Chiesa della Madonna dell'Orto, the façade of the Chiesa di San Zulian, the Chiesa di Santa Maria Formosa, the Chiesa di San Francesco della Vigna and the polyptych by Giovanni Bellini in the Chiesa di SS Giovanni e Paolo.

The funding is provided by 24 private committees representing 12 countries. Apart from restoration works, the programme also funds specialist courses for trainee restorers in Venezia.

spread quickly through the Veneto and, after several rebellions, Venezia was united with the Kingdom of Italy in 1866. The city was bombed during WWI but suffered only minor damage during WWII, when most attacks were aimed at the neighbouring industrial zones of Mestre and Marghera.

The city's prestige as a tourist destination grew during the 19th century, as it was surpassed as a trade port by Trieste. Today, Venezia's modest permanent population (less than half that of the 1950s) is swollen by up to 25 million visitors every year, the majority of them day-trippers.

Orientation

Venezia is built on 117 small islands and has some 150 canals and 409 bridges. Only three bridges cross the Canal Grande (Grand Canal): the Accademia, the Rialto and the Scalzi. The city is divided into six quarters (sestieri): Castello, San Marco, Dorsoduro, Cannaregio, San Polo and Santa Croce. A street is called a calle (sometimes shortened to ca'), ruga or salizzada; little side streets can be called calletta or ramo; a street beside a canal is called a fondamenta; a canal is a rio; and a street which follows the course of a filled-in rio is a rio terrà. A quay is a riva and where a street passes under a building (something like an extended archway) it is called a sotoportego. The only square in Venezia called a piazza is San Marco – all the others are called a campo. On maps you will find the following abbreviations: Cpo for Campo, Sal for Salizzada, cl or C for Calle and Fond for Fondamenta.

You can drive your car to Venezia and park it, but there is nowhere to drive once you arrive. Ferries also transport cars to the Lido, where they can be driven (although buses are more than adequate there). In Venezia itself all public transport is by vaporetto (small passenger boat/ferry) along the canals. To cross the Canal Grande between the bridges, use a traghetto (ferry), a cheap way to get a short gondola ride. Signs will direct you to the traghetto points.

The alternative is to go a piedi (on foot). To walk from Stazione Santa Lucia to Piazza San Marco along the main thoroughfare, the Lista di Spagna (its name changes several times along the way), will take a good half-hour – follow the signs to San Marco.

From San Marco, the routes to other main areas, such as the Rialto, Accademia and the train station, are well signposted but can be confusing, particularly in the Dorsoduro and San Polo areas. The free map provided by the tourist office provides only a vague guide to the complicated network of streets. There are several good maps on sale in bookshops and at newspaper stands, but the best is probably Touring Club Italiano's Venezia (L10,000), which is clear at a scale of 1:5000 and includes maps of the other islands of interest.

Street Numbering System If all that isn't confusing enough, Venezia also has its own style of street numbering. Instead of a

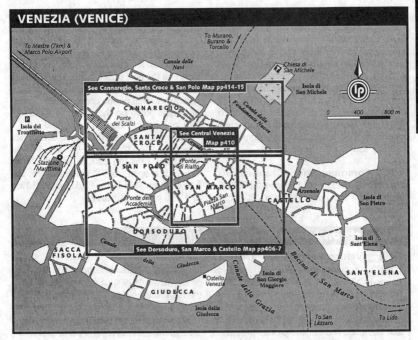

VENEZIA (VENICE)

To Mestre (7km) &
Marco Polo Airport

To Murano,
Burano &
Torcello

Canale delle Navi

Chiesa di
San Michele

Isola di
San Michele

0   400   800 m

See Cannaregio, Santa Croce & San Polo Map pp414-15

CANNAREGIO

Ponte
dei Scalzi

Canale della Fondamenta Nuove

Isola del
Tronchetto

SANTA
CROCE

See Central Venezia
Map p410

Stazione
Marittima

SAN POLO

Ponte
di Rialto

Ponte dell'
Accademia

SAN MARCO

Piazza San
Marco

Arsenale

Isola di
San Pietro

CASTELLO

DORSODURO

Canale

della

See Dorsoduro, San Marco & Castello Map pp406-7

Isola di
Sant'Elena

SACCA
FISOLA

Giudecca

Ostello
Venezia

Isola di
San Giorgio
Maggiore

Bacino di San Marco

SANT'ELENA

GIUDECCA

Canale della Grazia

Isola della
Giudecca

To San
Lazzaro

To Lido

system based on individual streets, there is a long series of numbers for each sestiere. For instance, a hotel might give its address as San Marco 4687, which doesn't help you much. Ask the hotel owner for the actual name of the street. As much as possible, we give actual street names plus the sestiere numbers throughout the chapter.

Information

Tourist Offices There is one central information line in Venezia: ☎ 041 529 87 11. The main APT office is at Piazza San Marco 71/f. The young staff will help with information on hotels, transport and things to see and do in the city. The office opens from 9.40 am to 5.20 pm daily. Hours tend to change regularly, so if in doubt call ahead.

The smaller office at Stazione Santa Lucia opens from 8 am to 7 pm daily in the summer, but again no guarantees – you have to ask yourself why a city with such an influx of tourists puts such a tiny info office at their disposal! There are offices on the Lido, at Viale Santa Maria Elisabetta, and at the airport. In summer five booths are set up in strategic spots around the city.

The useful booklet *Un Ospite di Venezia* (A Guest in Venice), published by a group of Venezia hotel owners, is sometimes available at the tourist offices. If not, you can find it in most of the larger hotels.

Money Most of the main banks are in the area around the Ponte di Rialto and San Marco. There is an Exact Change booth in Stazione Santa Lucia offering good rates; it opens from 8.20 am to 7.40 pm daily. There's another Exact Change booth on Campo San Bartolomeo near the Ponte di Rialto.

The American Express office (Amex; ☎ 041 520 08 44) is at Salizzada San Moisè (exit from the western end of Piazza San Marco on to Calle Seconda dell'Ascensione). The postal address is San Marco 1471. For Amex cardholders there's also an express cash machine. The office is open from 9 am to 5.30 pm Monday to Friday and to 12.30 pm on Saturday. Thomas Cook has two offices: one at Piazza San Marco (☎ 041 522 47 51) and the other at Riva del Ferro 5126 (☎ 041 528 73 58), near Ponte di Rialto. They open from 9.10 am to 7.45 pm Monday to Saturday and to 5 pm Sunday.

Post & Communications The main post office is at Salizzada del Fontego dei Tedeschi, just near the Ponte di Rialto. It opens from 8.15 am to 7 pm Monday to Saturday. Stamps are available at window Nos 11 and 12 in the central courtyard. There is a branch post office at the western end of San Marco.

There is an unstaffed Telecom phone centre in the post office building and a bank of phones nearby on Calle del Galeazza. Other unstaffed phone centres can be found on Strada Nova on the corner of Corte dei Pali, and just off Campo San Luca.

For email and Net hits, try Omniservice Internet Café (☎ 041 71 04 70), Fondamenta dei Tolentini 220, in Sestiere Santa Croce. It is open from 8.30 am to 1 pm and 3 to 6.30 pm Monday to Friday and 9.30 am to 12.30 pm on Saturday.

Discounts on Admission

Rolling Venice Concession Pass

If you are aged between 14 and 29, take your passport and a colour photograph to the Assessorato alla Gioventù (☎ 041 274 76 37), Corte Contarina 1529 (just west of Piazza San Marco), and pick up the Rolling Venice card. It offers significant discounts on food, accommodation, entertainment, public transport, museums and galleries, and costs L5000. The office opens from 9.30 am to 1 pm Monday to Friday and again from 3 to 5 pm on Tuesday and Thursday. You can also pick up the pass at: Associazione Italiana Alberghi per la Gioventù (☎ 041 520 44 14), Calle del Castelforte 3101, San Polo; and Agenzia Arte e Storia (☎ 041 524 02 32), Corte Canal 659, Santa Croce. From July to September it is also available at the tourist offices listed earlier in this section.

Combined & Special Tickets

The *comune* (town council) offers a *biglietto cumulativo* (combined ticket) for L18,000 that covers admission to the Palazzo Ducale (Doge's Palace), Museo Correr, Libreria Sansoviniana, the Museo Vetrario on Murano, Museo del Merletto di Burano (lace museum) and the rather minor Palazzo Mocenigo, which houses a museum dedicated to textiles. The ticket is valid for several months and can be purchased from any of these museums. This ticket does not cover the guided tour of the Palazzo Ducale.

For L18,000 you can get a special ticket to the Gallerie dell'Accademia, the Galleria Franchetti in the Ca' d'Oro and the Museo d'Arte Orientale in Ca' Pesaro. Or L8000 will get you a discounted ticket to the latter two only.

Finally, for the 14 churches where you normally pay L3000 entry (among them the Frari), you can buy a three day pass valid for six of the 14 and pay L15,000 – a saving of L3000 – not a big deal but better than a poke in the eye. You can pick up this at the participating churches.

Museum Opening Hours

Check with the APT office for the latest variations on opening days and hours, as exceptions tend to be greater than any perceptible rule.

Travel Agencies For budget student travel, contact CTS (☎ 041 520 56 60), Ca' Foscari 3252, Dorsoduro.

Bookshops A good selection of English-language guides and books on Venezia is available at Studium, Calle de la Canonica 337a, off the northern end of Piazza San Marco. Late-night readers in need of a paperback (several languages catered for) should make for Libreria Demetra, Campo San Geremia 282 (Cannaregio).

Gay & Lesbian Travellers Arcigay Nove (☎ 041 72 11 97) is at San Giacomo dell'Orio 1507, in Santa Croce.

Laundry Self-service laundries are a comparative novelty in Italy and in Venezia you have the grand choice of one. Bea Vita Lavanderia is in Santa Croce, at Calle de le Chioverete 665b. You pay L6000 to wash 8kg and L1000 per minute to dry. It opens from 8 am to 10 pm.

Medical Services & Emergency The Ospedale Civile (hospital; ☎ 041 529 45 17) is at Campo SS Giovanni e Paolo. Current information on late-night pharmacies is listed in *Un Ospite di Venezia* and daily newspapers such as *Il Gazzettino* or *La Nuova Venezia*.

The questura (police station; ☎ 041 528 46 66) is at Fondamenta di San Lorenzo 5053, Castello. There's a special carabinieri number (☎ 041 520 47 77) for foreigners in trouble.

Lost Property For property lost on trains call ☎ 041 78 52 38; for property left on vaporetti call ☎ 041 272 21 79, or for buses ☎ 041 272 28 38. Otherwise call the *vigili urbani* (local police) on ☎ 041 522 45 76.

Canal Grande

Described by French writer Philippe de Commines in the 15th century as 'the finest street in the world, with the finest houses', the Canal Grande is a little dilapidated these days but still rivals the world's great boulevards. It weaves for 3.5km through the city like a huge, upside-down 'S', with a depth of about 6m and a width ranging from 40m to 100m. Taking a vaporetto is the only way to see the incredible parade of buildings, including more than 100 *palazzi* (mansions), which date from the 12th to the 18th centuries. Board vaporetto No 1 at Piazzale Roma and try to grab a seat on the deck at the back.

Not far past Stazione Santa Lucia and Canale di Cannaregio (the city's second-largest canal) and just after the Riva di Biasio stop (to the right) is one of the most celebrated Veneto-Byzantine buildings, the **Fondaco dei Turchi**. Once a Turkish warehouse and now the Museo Civico di Storia Naturale (Natural History Museum), it was badly restored in the 19th century. It is recognisable by the three-storey towers on either side of its colonnade.

Continue past Rio di San Marcuola to **Palazzo Vendramin Calergi** on the left. Richard Wagner died here in 1883 and it is now a fine Renaissance winter home for the casino. Farther on and to the right, just after the San Stae stop, is the **Ca' Pesaro**, Baldassare Longhena's baroque masterpiece built between 1679 and 1710. Longhena died worrying about the cost and the building was only completed after his death. It houses the Galleria d'Arte Moderna and Museo d'Arte Orientale.

Shortly after, to the left, is the **Ca' d'Oro** (Golden House), acclaimed as the most beautiful Gothic building in Venezia (see the Cannaregio section later in this chapter). To the right, as the boat turns for the Ponte di Rialto, is the **pescheria** (fish market) on Campo della Pescaria, built in 1907. On the other side of the canal is the **Palazzo Michiel dalle Colonne**, with its distinctive colonnade.

On the right, just after the fish market, are the **Fabbriche Nuove di Rialto**, built in 1555 by Jacopo Sansovino as public offices for trade and commerce. Next door is the city's produce market and then the **Fabbriche Vecchie di Rialto**, built in 1522 as a courthouse. Just before the Ponte di Rialto, on the left bank, the **Fondaco dei Tedeschi** was once the most important trading house on the canal and now serves as the main post office. It was rebuilt after a fire in 1505 and frescoes by Titian and Giorgione once adorned its façade.

The stone **Ponte di Rialto** was built in the late 16th century by Antonio da Ponte, who won the commission in a public competition over architects including Palladio. The Renaissance **Palazzo Grimani**, on the left after the bridge and just before the Rio di San Luca, was designed by Sanmicheli. Farther along the same bank, the **Palazzo Corner-Spinelli** was designed in the same period by Mauro Cordussi. On the right, as the canal swings sharply to the left, is the late-Gothic **Ca' Foscari**, commissioned by Doge Francesco Foscari. One of the finest mansions in the city, it is followed on the left by the 18th century **Palazzo Grassi**. Now owned by Fiat, it is used as a cultural and exhibition centre. Opposite, the massive **Ca' Rezzonico**, designed by Baldassare Longhena, houses the city's collection of 18th century art.

You are now approaching the last of the canal's three bridges, the wooden **Ponte dell'Accademia**, built in 1930 to replace a metal 19th century structure. Past it and on the right is the unfinished **Palazzo Venier dei Leoni**, where American heiress Peggy Guggenheim lived until her death in 1979. It is home to her collection of modern art. Two buildings along is the delightful **Palazzo Dario**, built in 1487 and recognisable by the multi-coloured marble façade and its many chimneys.

On the left bank, at the Santa Maria del Giglio stop, is **Palazzo Corner**, an imposing, ivy-covered residence also known as the Ca' Grande and designed in the mid-16th century by Jacopo Sansovino. On the right, before the canal broadens into the expanse facing San Marco, is the magnificent **Basilica di Santa Maria della Salute** by Baldassare Longhena.

San Marco

Piazza San Marco Napoleon thought of Piazza San Marco as the finest drawing room in Europe. Enclosed by the basilica and the arcaded Procuratie Vecchie and Nuove, the square plays host to competing flocks of pigeons and tourists. Stand and wait for the bronze *Mori* (Moors) to strike the bell of the 15th century Torre dell'Orologio, which rises (at the time of writing hidden by scaffolding) above the entrance to the Mercerie, the main thoroughfare from San Marco to the Rialto. Or sit and savour a coffee at Florian or Quadri, 18th century cafés across from each other on the piazza – expect to pay at least L10,000 for a cappuccino and even more if there is music.

Basilica di San Marco The basilica embodies a magnificent blend of architectural and decorative styles, dominated by the Byzantine and ranging through Romanesque to Renaissance.

Venetian merchants stole the body of San Marco from Alexandria, Egypt, in 828 and brought it to Venezia for Doge Giustiniano Participazio, who bequeathed a huge sum of money to build a basilica fitting for such an estimable theft. The honourable merchants were doing nothing more than fulfilling a pious portent – for legend had it that an angel once appeared to San Marco and told him he would be laid to rest in Venezia.

The original church was destroyed by fire in 932 and rebuilt, but in 1063 Doge Domenico Contarini decided it was poor in comparison to the splendid Romanesque churches being raised in mainland cities and had it demolished.

The new basilica, built on the plan of a Greek cross, with five bulbous domes, was modelled on Constantinople's (later destroyed) Church of the Twelve Apostles and consecrated in 1094. It was actually built as the doges' private chapel and remained so until it became Venezia's cathedral in 1807.

For more than 500 years, the doges enlarged and embellished the church, adorning it with an incredible array of treasures plundered from the East, in particular Constantinople, during the crusades.

The arches above the doorways in the façade boast fine mosaics. The one on the left end, depicting the arrival of San Marco's body in Venezia, was completed in 1270. The three arches of the main doorway are decorated with Romanesque carvings, dating from around 1240.

Venezia in a Nutshell

Uneven alleys turn porticoed corners and end in tiny bridges arched over muddied canals. Others lead nowhere. Still others take you along wider waterways and, often enough, you'll emerge to behold yet another wonder of Venezia before you – one of its more than 200 churches or some grand palatial residence. Cheerful *osterie* (restaurants) are tucked away in the most unlikely spots, colourful markets abound and the bustling main streets throng with crowds of locals and visitors window-shopping, parading or simply racing from point A to B.

Venezia is unique for many reasons but where else in the world can you immerse yourself in such activity without having your ears assaulted by the roar of cars? Instead, here you are carried along by the tramp of feet, the music of human discourse echoing through the narrow streets and canals, the lap of the water and the hum of the vaporetti. You could spend months here and never tire of learning your way through the labyrinth. Give yourself as much time as you can.

The main tourist areas are Piazza San Marco, the Rialto and the streets of souvenir shops that connect the two, as well as the main thoroughfare linking Stazione Santa Lucia and San Marco.

But it is easy enough to escape the crowds. Head for the tranquil streets and squares of Dorsoduro and San Polo – while the hordes are cramming into the Basilica di San Marco, you will be virtually alone admiring Tintoretto's paintings in the Scuola Grande di San Rocco or Titian's masterpieces in the adjacent Frari. If you go to the sestiere of Castello, farther away from San Marco, you'll discover relatively little-visited monuments such as the massive Gothic Chiesa dei SS Giovanni e Paolo. Cannaregio, if you keep away from the main thoroughfare, is also really worth exploring.

Before you do anything else, catch the vaporetto No 1 along the Canal Grande, Venezia's main 'street' – see the Canal Grande section for a description of the outstanding grand buildings, or *palazzi*, along the waterway.

On the *loggia* (balcony) above the main door are found copies of four gilded bronze horses: the originals, on display inside, were stolen and brought to Venezia when Constantinople was sacked in 1204, during the Fourth Crusade. Napoleon removed them to Paris in 1797, but they were returned following the collapse of the French Empire.

Through the doors is the **narthex**, or vestibule, its domes and arches decorated with mosaics, mainly dating from the 13th century. The oldest mosaics in the basilica, dating from around 1063, are in the niches of the bay in front of the main door from the narthex into the church proper. They feature the Madonna with the Apostles.

The **interior** of the basilica is dazzling: if you can take your eyes off the glitter of the mosaics, take time to admire the 12th century marble pavement, a geometrical whimsy which has subsided in places, making the floor uneven.

The lower level of the walls is lined with precious eastern marbles, and above this decoration the extraordinary feast of gilded **mosaics** begins. Work started on the mosaics in the 11th century and continued until well into the 13th century. Mosaics were added in the 14th and 15th centuries in the baptistry and side chapels and, as late as the 18th century, mosaics were being added or restored.

To the right of the high altar is the entrance to the sanctuary. San Marco's body is contained in a sarcophagus beneath the altar. Behind the altar is one of the basilica's greatest treasures, the exquisite **Pala d'Oro**, a gold, enamel and jewel-encrusted altarpiece made in Constantinople for Doge Pietro Orseolo I in 976. It was enriched and reworked in Constantinople in 1105, enlarged by Venetian

Making his Mark

The story goes that an angel appeared to the evangelist Marco (St Mark) when his boat put in at Rialto while he was on his way to Roma from Aquileia. The winged fellow informed the future saint that his body would rest in Venezia. We don't know what Marco thought of all this, but he died some years later in Alexandria, Egypt. In 828, two Venetian merchants persuaded the guardians of his Alexandrian tomb to let them have the corpse, which they then smuggled down to their ship in port.

You've got to ask yourself why they would bother with such strange merchandise. In those days, any city worthy of the name had a patron saint. Venezia already had San Teodore, but he was hardly a rousing star in the Christian pantheon. An evangelist, now that would be something quite different. Did the doge order this little mission? We will never know. Whatever the truth behind this story, it seems that *someone's* putrid corpse was transported to Venezia, and everyone rather liked the idea of San Marco in their midst. San Teodore was demoted and the Doge ordered construction of a chapel to house the newcomer. That church would later become the magnificent Basilica di San Marco.

NICKY CAVEN

One of Venezia's emblems – the Lion of San Marco

Legend also has it that, during the rebuilding of the basilica in 1063, the body of San Marco was hidden and then 'lost' when its hiding place was forgotten. In 1094, when the church was consecrated, the corpse (which must have been a picture of frailty by this time) broke through the column in which it had been enclosed. 'It's a miracle,' the Venetians cried. Or was it just a sign of incredibly dodgy plasterwork? San Marco had been lost and now was found. A grateful populace buried the remains in the church crypt. They now lie beneath the basilica's high altar.

goldsmiths in 1209 and reset again in the 14th century. Among the almost 2000 precious stones which adorn it are emeralds, rubies, amethysts, sapphires and pearls.

The **Tesoro** (Treasury), accessible from the right transept, contains most of the booty from the 1204 raid on Constantinople, including a thorn said to be from the crown worn by Christ. Admission to the Pala d'Oro costs L3000 and to the Tesoro L4000.

Through a door at the far right end of the narthex is a stairway leading up to the **Galleria**, which contains the original gilded bronze horses and the **Loggia dei Cavalli** (L3000). The galleria affords wonderful views of the church's interior, while the loggia offers equally splendid vistas of the square.

Although the church is open for longer hours, tourists are restricted to visiting the paying attractions from 9.30 am to 4.30 pm Monday to Saturday and from 2 to 4.30 pm on Sunday and holidays. The mosaics are best seen when illuminated. This means from 11.30 am to 12.30 pm Monday to Friday and 'all day' at the weekend. 'All day' refers to the masses held – as long as a mass is on so are the lights.

The basilica's 99m-tall **bell tower** is in Piazza San Marco. It was built in the 10th century but suddenly collapsed on 14 July

1902 and was later rebuilt brick by brick. You can pay L8000 to get to the top. It opens from 9 am to 7 pm daily (9.30 am to 5.30 pm in winter).

Procuratie The former residence and offices of the Procurators of San Marco, who were responsible for the upkeep of the basilica, the **Procuratie Vecchie** were designed by Mauro Codussi and occupy the entire northern side of the Piazza San Marco.

On the southern side of the piazza are the **Procuratie Nuove**, planned by Jacopo Sansovino and completed by Vincenzo Scamozzi and Baldassare Longhena. Napoleon converted this building into his royal palace and demolished the church of San Geminiano at the western end of the piazza to build the wing commonly known as the Ala Napoleonica, which housed his ballroom.

The Ala Napoleonica is now home to the **Museo Correr**, dedicated to the art and history of Venezia. Through this museum you also access first the **Museo Archeologico**, which houses an impressive, if somewhat repetitive, selection of ancient sculptures, and then the **Libreria Sansoviniana**. Described by Palladio as the most sumptuous palace ever built, the Libreria was designed by Jacopo Sansovino in the 16th century. It takes up the entire western side of the Piazzetta di San Marco. For admission details see the earlier 'Discounts on Admission' boxed text. It is open daily from 9 am to 7 pm.

Piazzetta di San Marco Stretching from Piazza San Marco to the waterfront, the piazzetta features two columns bearing statues of the Lion of San Marco and San Teodoro, the city's two emblems. Originally a marketplace, the area was also a preferred location for public executions and political meetings.

Palazzo Ducale The Palazzo Ducale was not only the doges' official residence, as the name suggests, but also the seat of the republic's government, housed bureaucrats and contained the prisons. Established in the 9th century, the building began to assume its present form 500 years later with

the decision to build the massive **Sala del Maggior Consiglio** for the council members, who ranged in number from 1200 to 1700. It was inaugurated in 1419.

The palace's two magnificent Gothic façades in white Istrian stone and pink Verona marble face the water and Piazzetta di San Marco. Much of the building was damaged by fire in 1577, but it was successfully restored by Antonio da Ponte (who designed the Ponte di Rialto).

The main entrance, the 15th century **Porta della Carta** (Paper Door), to which government decrees were fixed, was carved by Giovanni and Bartolomeo Bon. Leading from the courtyard, the **Scala dei Giganti** (Giants' Staircase) by Antonio Rizzo takes its name from the huge statues of Mars and Neptune, by Jacopo Sansovino, which flank the landing.

Past Sansovino's **Scala d'Oro** (Golden Staircase) are rooms dedicated to the various doges, including the **Sala delle Quattro Porte** on the 3rd floor, where ambassadors would be kindly requested to await their ducal audience. The room's ceiling was designed by Palladio and the frescoes are by Tintoretto. Off this room is the **Anticollegio**, which features four Tintorettos and the *Rape of Europa* by Veronese. Through here, the ceiling of the splendid **Sala del Collegio** features a series of artworks by Veronese. Next is the **Sala del Senato**, graced by yet more Tintorettos.

The indicated route (you have no choice in the matter) then takes you to the immense **Sala del Maggiore Consiglio** on the 2nd floor. It is dominated at one end by Tintoretto's *Paradise*, one of the world's largest oil paintings, measuring 22m by 7m. Among the many other paintings in the hall is a masterpiece, the *Apotheosis of Venice* by Veronese, in one of the central ceiling panels. Note the black space in the frieze on the wall depicting the first 76 doges of Venezia. Doge Marin Falier would have appeared there had he not been beheaded for treason in 1355.

Next, you find yourself crossing the small, enclosed **Ponte dei Sospiri** (Bridge of Sighs) to reach the prisons. The bridge is named because of the sighs prisoners tended to make

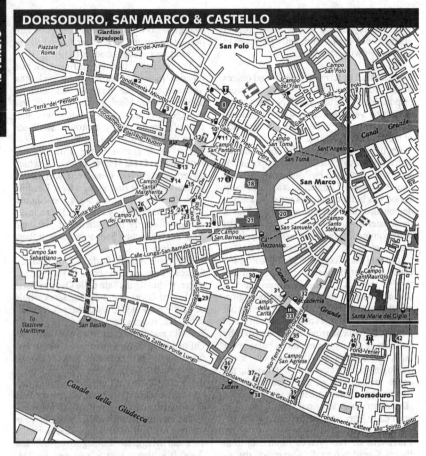

DORSODURO, SAN MARCO & CASTELLO

on their way into the dungeons. The poor unfortunates to make this dismal crossing must have been well behaved indeed not to give more vigorous vent to their displeasure than a mere sigh.

The palace opens from 8.30 am to dusk (up to 7 pm in summer and as early as 4 pm in winter) daily. Infrared radio receivers (which pick up an audio-loop commentary in each room) can be hired near the ticket desk for L7000. See the earlier 'Discounts on Admission' boxed text for admission de-

tails. Note that the sale of tickets stops at 5.30 pm in summer.

Guided tours, known as *itinerari segreti* (secret itineraries), of lesser known areas of the palace, including the original prisons, can be joined. The English-language tour starts at 10.30 am and tickets cost L24,000. You need to book ahead.

San Marco to the Rialto The Mercerie, a series of streets lined with shops, connects Piazza San Marco and the Rialto in a rather

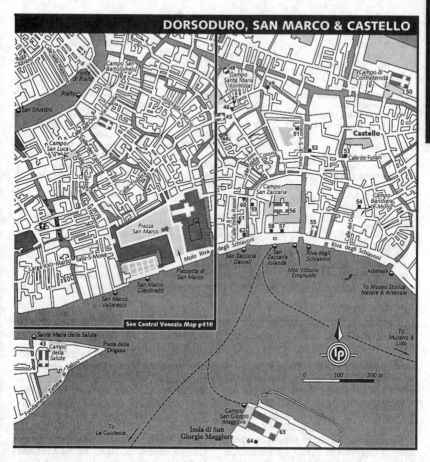

DORSODURO, SAN MARCO & CASTELLO

See Central Venezia Map p410

tortuous manner. The **Chiesa di San Salvatore**, built on a plan of three Greek crosses laid end to end, features Titian's *Annunciation* and Bellini's *Supper in Emmaus*. North of the church and close to the Ponte di Rialto is the bustling **Campo San Bartolomeo**.

San Marco to the Accademia The area immediately west of Piazza San Marco is a rabbit warren of streets and alleys lined with exclusive shops, where, if you search hard enough, you might pick up some interesting

gifts and souvenirs, such as watercolours of the city, marbled paper and carnival masks.

On the way to the Ponte dell'Accademia there are a couple of churches of interest. The Renaissance Chiesa di **San Fantin**, in the campo of the same name, has a domed sanctuary and apse by Jacopo Sansovino. Also in Campo San Fantin stands what's left of the **Teatro la Fenice**, the opera house that opened in 1792 and was largely gutted by fire in January 1996. Several of Verdi's operas had their opening nights here.

euro currency converter L10,000 = €5.16

DORSODURO, SAN MARCO & CASTELLO

PLACES TO STAY
2 Locanda Salieri;
  Brodo di Giuggiole
3 Hotel dalla Mora
4 Albergo Casa Peron
15 Albergo Antico Capon
19 Locanda Fiorita
29 Antica Locanda Montin
30 Albergo Accademia Villa
  Maravege
34 Hotel Galleria
35 Albergo agli Alboretti
39 Pensione Seguso
49 Foresteria Valdese
54 La Residenza
57 Londra Palace
58 Albergo Paganelli
59 Hotel Doni
62 Danieli

PLACES TO EAT
10 Arca
11 Da Silvio
13 Mega 1 Supermarket
14 Il Caffè
23 L'Incontro
24 Gelateria il Doge

25 Green Pub
27 Da Codroma
36 Gelati Nico
46 Pizzeria da Egidio
47 Osteria al Mascaron
60 Trattoria alla Rivetta
61 Al Vecio Penasa

OTHER
1 Intercity Bus Station
5 Associazione Italiana Alberghi
  per la Gioventù
6 Chiesa di Santa Maria
  Gloriosa dei Frari
7 Atelier Pietro Longhi
8 Scuola Grande di San Rocco
9 Caffè Blue Music
12 Chiesa di San Pantalon
16 Istituto Zambler
17 CTS Travel Agency
18 Ca' Foscari
20 Palazzo Grassi
21 Ca' Rezzonico
22 Ca' Macana
26 Scuola Grande dei Carmini
28 Chiesa di San Sebastiano
31 British Consulate

32 Ponte dell'Accademia
  (Accademia Bridge)
33 Gallerie dell'Accademia
37 Chiesa dei Gesuati
38 Alilaguna Ferry to Airport;
  Ferry No 16 to Fusina
40 Il Pavone
41 Palazzo Venier dei Leoni;
  Peggy Guggenheim Collection
42 Palazzo Dario
43 Basilica di Santa Maria
  della Salute
44 Palazzo Querini-Stampalia
45 Chiesa di Santa Maria Formosa
48 French Consulate
50 Chiesa di San Francesco
  della Vigna
51 Questura (Police Station)
52 Società Dante Alighieri
53 Scuola di San Giorgio
  degli Schiavoni
55 Chiesa di Santa Maria
  della Pietà
56 Chiesa di San Zaccaria
63 Chiesa di San Giorgio
  Maggiore
64 Fondazione Cini

Before you go elsewhere, make sure you duck up just north of the Chiesa di San Fantin to admire the wonderful external spiral staircase at the **Palazzo Contarini del Bovolo**.

Return to Calle Larga XXII Marzo and turn right for the **Chiesa di Santa Maria del Giglio**, also known as Santa Maria Zobenigo. Its baroque façade features maps of European cities as they were in 1678. Go on to Campo Francesco Morosini (or Campo Santo Stefano) and the Gothic **Chiesa di Santo Stefano**. Of note are three paintings by Tintoretto in the sacristy: the *Last Supper*, the *Washing of the Feet* and the *Agony in the Garden*.

Dorsoduro

Gallerie dell'Accademia This is a must for anyone with even a passing interest in art. The former church and convent of Santa Maria della Carità, with additions by Palladio, hosts a collection that follows the progression of Venetian art from the 14th to the 18th centuries.

Room 1 contains works by the early 14th century painter Paolo Veneziano, including the *Coronation of the Virgin*. The main feature of Room 2, which covers the late 15th and early 16th centuries, is Carpaccio's altarpiece *The 10,000 Martyrs of Mt Ararat*. It also contains works by Giovanni Bellini. Rooms 4 and 5 feature Andrea Mantegna's *St George*, several paintings of the Madonna and Child by Giovanni Bellini and Giorgione's fabulous *La Tempesta*. Rooms 6 to 10 contain works of the High Renaissance, including Tintoretto and Titian, but one of the highlights is Paolo Veronese's *Feast in the House of Levi* in Room 10. Originally called *The Last Supper*, the painting's name was changed because the leaders of the Inquisition objected to its depiction of characters such as drunkards and dwarfs. The room also contains one of Titian's last works, a *Pietà*. In Room 13 are a number of works by the 18th century painter Giambattista Tiepolo. Giovanni Bellini and Carpaccio appear again in subsequent rooms and the collection ends in Room 24 with Titian's beautiful *Presentation of the Virgin*.

The gallery's opening times are complex. At last check they were Monday from 9 am to 2 pm, Tuesday to Saturday from 9 am to 10 pm and Sunday from 9 am to 8 pm. These are high season times (ie from Easter to end September) and subject to change at any time. Admission costs L15,000.

Peggy Guggenheim Collection Peggy Guggenheim called the unfinished Palazzo Venier dei Leoni home for 30 years until she died in 1979. She left behind a collection of works by her favourite modern artists, representing most of the major movements of the 20th century. Picasso, Mondrian, Kandinsky, Ernst, Chagall, Klee, Miró, Dalì, Pollock, Brancusi, Magritte and Bacon are all represented. The collection is open from 11 am to 6 pm (closed Tuesday), and admission costs L12,000. Take a wander around the sculpture garden (which includes works by Moore, Giacometti and Ernst), where Miss Guggenheim and many of her pet dogs are buried.

Basilica di Santa Maria della Salute Dominating the entrance to the Canal Grande, this beautiful church was built in the 17th century in honour of the Virgin Mary, who was believed to have delivered the city from an outbreak of plague that had killed more than a third of the population. Inside Baldassare Longhena's octagonal church, Titian and Tintoretto left their mark in the Great Sacristy. Every year, on 21 November, a procession takes place from Piazza San Marco to the church to give thanks for the city's good health.

The Zattere The Fondamenta delle Zattere runs along the Canale della Giudecca from Punta della Salute to Stazione Marittima. It is a popular *passeggiata* location. The main sight is the 18th century Santa Maria del Rosario, or **Chiesa dei Gesuati**, designed by Giorgio Massari. Tiepolo's ceiling frescoes tell the story of San Domenico. At the end of the Zattere, over Rio di San Basilio, the **Chiesa di San Sebastiano** was the local church of Paolo Veronese, who provided most of the paintings and lies buried in the church.

Ca' Rezzonico This 17th and 18th century mansion, which faces the Canal Grande, houses the **Museo del Settecento Veneziano**. Designed by Baldassare Longhena and completed by Massari, it was home to several notables over the years, including the poet Robert Browning, who died there. The museum houses a collection of 18th century art and furniture and is also worth visiting for the views over the Canal Grande and the fine ceiling frescoes by Tiepolo – notably the *Allegory of Merit* in the Throne Room. Unfortunately it was closed at the time of writing.

Scuola Grande dei Carmini Tiepolo also had a hand in this 16th century building, near the church of the same name, just west of Campo Santa Margherita. In the Salone, nine ceiling paintings depict the virtues surrounding the *Virgin in Glory*. It opens from 9 am to 6 pm Monday to Saturday and from 9 am to 1 pm on Sunday. Admission costs L7000.

San Polo
Chiesa di Santa Maria Gloriosa dei Frari
This massive Gothic church, rich in art treasures, is one of the highlights of a visit to Venezia. It was built for the Franciscans in the 14th and 15th centuries and decorated by an illustrious array of artists. Titian, who is buried inside, painted the dramatic *Assumption* over the high altar. Another of his masterpieces, the *Madonna di Ca' Pesaro*, hangs above the Pesaro altar (last on the left before the choir). The church opens from 9 am to 6 pm Monday to Saturday and from 1 to 6 pm and on Sunday. Admission costs L3000.

Scuola Grande di San Rocco Built for the Confraternity of St Roch in the 16th century and decorated with more than 50 paintings by Tintoretto, this is one of Venezia's great surprises.

Tintoretto won a competition to decorate the school and spent 23 years on the extraordinary series of paintings. The ground floor

IL VENETO

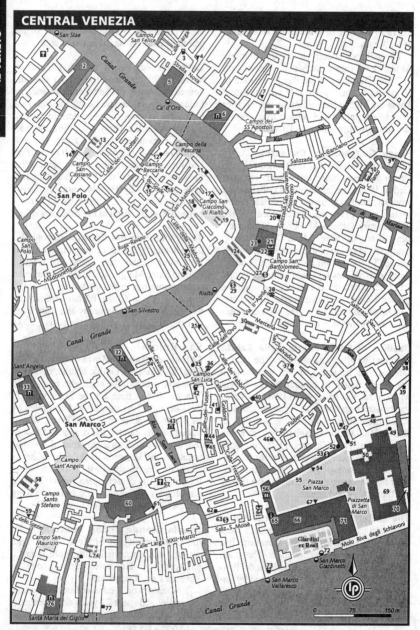

CENTRAL VENEZIA

CENTRAL VENEZIA

PLACES TO STAY					
26	Locanda Sturion	2	Ca' Pesaro	43	Palazzo Contarini del Bovolo
38	Locanda Silva	3	The Fiddler's Elbow	48	Veneziartigiana
39	Locanda Rimedio	5	Ca' d'Oro	49	Studium (Bookshop)
40	Al Gambero	6	Palazzo Michiel dalle Colonne	50	Basilica di San Marco
41	Serenissima	8	Chiesa dei SS Apostoli	51	Torre dell'Orologio
44	Locanda Casa Petrarca	10	Chiesa di Santa Maria	52	Intras Travel Agency
46	Hotel Noemi		dei Miracoli	53	Thomas Cook
47	Hotel ai do Mori	11	Fabbriche Nuove di Rialto	55	Procuratie Vecchie
77	Gritti Palace	12	Pescheria (Fish Market)	56	Museo Correr
		13	Chiesa di San Cassiano	57	Chiesa di San Fantin
PLACES TO EAT		17	Fabbriche Vecchie di Rialto	58	Chiesa di Santo Stefano
4	Osteria dalla Vedova	18	Food Market	60	Teatro la Fenice
7	Pizzeria Casa Mia	19	Chiesa di San Giacomo di Rialto	62	Assessorato alla Gioventù
9	Osteria da Alberto	20	Giacomo Rizzo	63	American Express
14	Al Nono Risorto	21	Main Post Office;	64	Post Office
15	Cantina do Spade		Telecom Office	65	APT Tourist Office
16	Cantina do Mori	22	Phones	66	Procuratie Nuove
25	Trattoria alla Madonna	23	Fondaco dei Tedeschi	68	Bell Tower
31	Antica Carbonera	24	Ponte di Rialto (Rialto Bridge)	69	Palazzo Ducale
34	Enoteca Il Volto	27	Exact Change	70	Ponte dei Sospiri
45	Ristorante da Ivo	28	Phones		(Bridge of Sighs)
54	Caffè Quadri	29	Thomas Cook	71	Libreria Nazionale Marciana;
59	Pasticceria Marchini	30	Chiesa di San Salvatore		Museo Archeologico
61	Vino Vino	32	Palazzo Grimani	72	Alilaguna Ferry to Airport
67	Caffè Florian	33	Palazzo Corner-Spinelli	73	Harry's Bar
		34	Teatro Goldoni	74	Chiesa di Santa Maria
OTHER		36	Telecom Office		del Giglio
1	Chiesa di San Stae	37	Agenzia Kele & Teo	75	Legatoria Piazzesi
		42	Black Jack Bar	76	Palazzo Corner (Ca' Grande)

entrance hall was the last to be painted. It features a series on the life of the Virgin Mary, starting on the left wall with the *Annunciation* and ending with the *Assumption* opposite.

Up the grand staircase, designed by Scarpagnino, is the main hall. Tintoretto painted Old Testament episodes in the ceiling panels and a remarkable series of New Testament scenes around the walls. Pick up one of the hand-held mirrors so you can study the ceiling paintings without getting a sore neck. The small **Sala dell'Albergo**, off the main hall, contains the cycle's most striking paintings, including the *Glorification of St Roch* in the centre of the ceiling. The *Crucifixion*, occupying one wall of the room, is a masterpiece.

The school is open from 9 am to 5.30 pm from Easter to the end of October (from 10 am to 4 pm during the winter). Admission costs L8000.

Towards Ponte di Rialto Heading for Ponte di Rialto from the Frari, you soon arrive in the vast **Campo San Polo**, the city's largest square after Piazza San Marco. Locals bring their children here to play so, if you are travelling with small kids they might appreciate some social contact while you take a cappuccino break.

The area around **Ponte di Rialto**, bursting with the life of the daily produce market, was one of the earliest settled locations in Venezia. Rialto, or *rivo alto*, means high bank and the spot was considered one of the safest in the lagoon. There has been a market here for almost 1000 years – the **Fabbriche Vecchie** along the Ruga degli Orefici and the **Fabbriche Nuove**, running along the Canal Grande, were built by Scarpagnino after a fire destroyed the old markets in 1514.

Although there has been a bridge at the Rialto since the foundation of the city, the present stone bridge by Antonio da Ponte was completed in 1592.

Virtually in the middle of the market, off the Ruga degli Orefici, is the **Chiesa di San Giacomo di Rialto**. According to local legend it was founded on 25 March 421, the same day as the city.

Towards Stazione Santa Lucia Tintoretto fans will want to visit the **Chiesa di San Cassiano** in the campo of the same name, north-west of the Rialto. The sanctuary is decorated with three of Tintoretto's paintings, the *Crucifixion*, the *Resurrection* and the *Descent into Limbo*.

The Renaissance **Ca' Pesaro**, farther north with its façade facing the Canal Grande, houses the **Museo d'Arte Moderna** on the ground floor. Started in 1897, the collection includes works purchased from the Venezia Biennale art festival, held every even-numbered year, and is one of the largest collections of modern art in Italy. The gallery was closed at the time of writing. The **Museo d'Arte Orientale**, in the same building on the top floor, features a collection of Asian and Eastern oddments. It is open from 9 am to 2 pm (closed Monday); admission is L4000.

Continuing north-west past the Chiesa di San Stae you'll find the **Fondaco dei Turchi**, a 12th century building used at one time as a warehouse by Turkish merchants and now housing the **Museo Civico di Storia Naturale**. If it ever reopens, take the kids there to see the impressive 12m-long crocodile.

As you head south, the 13th century **Chiesa di San Giacomo dell'Orio**, near the square of the same name, is worth a visit. Of particular interest is the Old Sacristy, whose walls and ceilings are decorated with a cycle of paintings depicting the *Mystery of the Eucharist* by Palma Giovane.

Cannaregio

The long pedestrian thoroughfare connecting Stazione Santa Lucia and Piazza San Marco crawls with tourists – few venture off it into the peaceful back lanes.

The Carmelite **Chiesa dei Scalzi** (Church of the Barefooted) is next to Stazione Santa

Lucia. There are damaged frescoes by Tiepolo in the vaults of two of the side chapels. Along the Rio Terrà Lista di Spagna, the otherwise uninspiring 18th century **Chiesa di San Geremia** holds the body of Santa Lucia, who was martyred in Siracusa in 304 AD. Her body was stolen by Venetian merchants from Constantinople in 1204 and moved to San Geremia after the Palladian church of Santa Lucia was demolished in the 19th century to make way for Stazione Santa Lucia.

Ghetto Nuovo Most easily accessible from the Fondamenta Pescaria, next to the Canale di Cannaregio, through the Sotoportego del Ghetto, this was the world's original ghetto. The area was once a foundry and it is tempting to think that the Venetian word for foundry *(getto)* gave rise to what would become an unpleasant addition to Europe's cultural vocabulary.

The city's Jews were ordered to move to the small island, which became known as Ghetto Nuovo, in 1516. They were locked in at night by Christian soldiers and forced to follow a set of rules limiting their social and economic activities, but they retained full freedom of religious expression.

Extreme overcrowding combined with building height restrictions means that some apartment blocks have as many as seven storeys, but with very low ceilings. In 1797, after the fall of the republic, Jews were allowed to leave the ghetto to live wherever they chose.

The **Museo Ebraico** (Jewish Museum) on Campo Ghetto Nuovo opens from 10 am to 4.30 pm daily (except Saturday and Jewish holidays). Admission costs L5000. Guided tours (in Italian and/or English; other languages if booked ahead) of the ghetto and three of its synagogues leave from the museum every hour between 10.30 am and 3.30 pm daily, except Saturday, and cost L12,000. Of the 500 or so Jews still living in Venezia, only about 30 remain in the ghetto.

Cross the iron bridge from the Campo Ghetto Nuovo to reach the Fondamenta degli Ormesini and turn right. This is a truly peaceful part of Venezia, almost completely empty of tourists. There are some interesting bars and a couple of good restaurants along the fondamenta.

Chiesa della Madonna dell'Orto This 14th century church was Tintoretto's parish church and contains many of his works. Among them are *Last Judgment* and *Making of the Golden Calf* in the choir and *Vision of the Cross to St Peter* and *Beheading of St Paul*, which flank an *Annunciation* by Palma Giovane in the apse. On the wall at the end of the right aisle is Tintoretto's *Presentation of the Virgin in the Temple*. The artist is buried in the church.

Gesuiti This Jesuit church (its proper name is Santa Maria Assunta) dates from the early 18th century. Its baroque interior features walls with inlaid marble in imitation of curtains. Titian's *Martydom of St Lawrence* is on the first altar on the left, balanced by Tintoretto's *Assumption* in the north transept.

Chiesa di Santa Maria dei Miracoli This particularly beautiful Renaissance church, designed by Pietro Lombardo, boasts magnificent sculptures. Pietro and his son Tullio Lombardo executed the carvings on the choir.

Chiesa dei SS Apostoli This church, at the eastern end of the Strada Nova, is worth visiting for the 15th century Cappella Corner by Mauro Codussi, which features a painting of Santa Lucia by Tiepolo (removed for restoration in 1994).

Ca' d'Oro This magnificent Gothic structure, built in the 15th century, was named Ca' d'Oro (Golden House) for the gilding that originally decorated the sculptural details of the façade. Visible from the Canal Grande, the façade stands out from the remainder of the edifice, rather drab by comparison. It houses the **Galleria Franchetti**, an impressive collection of bronzes, tapestries and paintings, and opens from 9 am to 7 pm daily. Admission costs L6000.

Castello

Chiesa di Santa Maria Formosa This church is in the middle of one of Venezia's most appealing squares, Campo Santa Maria Formosa, a few minutes north-east of Piazza San Marco. Rebuilt in 1492 by Mauro Cordussi on the site of a 7th century church, it contains an altarpiece by Palma Giovane depicting Santa Barbara.

Palazzo Querini-Stampalia This 16th century palace was donated to the city in 1868 by Count Gerolamo Querini. On its 2nd floor, the **Museo della Fondazione Querini-Stampalia** has a collection of paintings and Venetian furniture. It opens from 10 am to 1 pm and 3 to 6 pm Tuesday to Sunday (extended until 10 pm on Friday and Saturday in summer). Admission costs L10,000.

Chiesa dei SS Giovanni e Paolo This huge Gothic church, founded by the Dominicans, rivals the Franciscans' Frari in size and grandeur. Work started on the church in 1333, but it was not consecrated until 1430. Its vast interior is divided simply into a nave and two aisles, separated by graceful, soaring arches. The beautiful stained-glass window in the south transept (the largest in Venezia) was made in Murano to designs by Bartolomeo Vivarini and Girolamo Mocetto in the 15th century.

Around the walls, many of the tombs of 25 doges were sculpted by prominent Gothic and Renaissance artists. Look out for Giovanni Bellini's polyptych of San Vincente Ferrer over the second altar of the right aisle. Still in its original frame, it also features an *Assumption* and *Pietà*. There are several paintings by Paolo Veronese in the Cappella del Rosario at the end of the north transept, including ceiling panels and an *Adoration of the Shepherds* on the western walls.

Chiesa di San Zaccaria The mix of Gothic and Renaissance architectural styles makes this 15th century church interesting. Most of the Gothic façade is by Antonio Gambello, while the upper part, in Renaissance style, is by Codussi. On the second altar of the north

CANNAREGIO, SANTA CROCE & SAN POLO

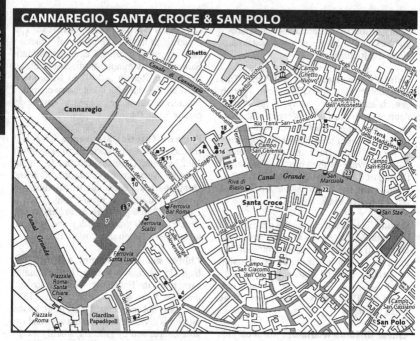

CANNAREGIO, SANTA CROCE & SAN POLO

PLACES TO STAY
10 Hotel Abbazzia
11 Hotel Santa Lucia
12 Hotel Villa Rosa
14 Hotel Rossi
17 Alloggi Calderan;
    Casa Gerotto
18 Hotel al Gobbo
21 Archies

PLACES TO EAT
19 Gam Gam
25 Paradiso Perduto
27 Sahara

28 Standa Supermarket
30 Hostaria Al Ponte

OTHER
1 Intercity Bus Station
2 Omniservice Internet Café
3 Bea Vita Lavanderia
4 Agenzia Arte e Storia
5 Chiesa di San Giacomo
   dell'Orio
6 Ponte dei Scalzi (Scalzi Bridge)
7 Stazione Santa Lucia
8 Chiesa dei Scalzi
9 Tourist Office

13 Park & Playground
15 Chiesa di San Geremia
16 Libreria Demetra
20 Museo Ebraico
22 Fondaco dei Turchi; Museo
    Civico di Storia Naturale
23 Palazzo Vendramin Calergi
24 Wine Bar
26 Chiesa della Madonna
    dell'Orto
29 Gesuiti
31 Ospedale Civile (Hospital)
32 Chiesa dei SS Giovanni
    e Paolo

aisle is Giovanni Bellini's *Madonna with Saints and an Angel Musician.*

Riva degli Schiavoni This walkway extends along the waterfront from the Palazzo Ducale to the Arsenale ferry point at the far south-eastern end of Castello. The exclusive hotels that line it have long been favourites for Venezia's more affluent visitors. About halfway along is Chiesa di Santa Maria della

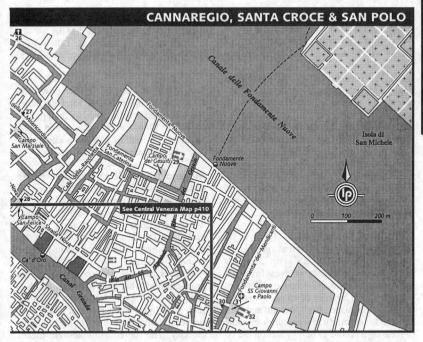

CANNAREGIO, SANTA CROCE & SAN POLO

See Central Venezia Map p410

Pietà, known as **La Pietà**, where concerts are held regularly. Vivaldi was concert master here in the early 18th century. Look for the ceiling fresco by Tiepolo.

Scuola di San Giorgio degli Schiavoni
The school was established by Venezia's Slavic community in the 15th century and this building was erected in the 16th century. The walls of the ground floor hall are decorated with a series of superb paintings by Vittore Carpaccio, depicting events in the lives of the three patron saints of Dalmatia: SS Giorgio, Trifone and Girolamo.

Chiesa di San Francesco della Vigna
Designed and built by Jacopo Sansovino, this 16th century Franciscan church is named for the vineyard that once thrived on the site. Its façade was designed by Palladio and inside, just to the left of the main door, is a triptych

of saints by Antonio Vivarini. The chapel to the left of the choir is decorated with sculpted reliefs by Pietro Lombardo and his school.

Arsenale The city's huge dockyards were founded in 1104 and at their peak were home to 300 shipping companies and employed up to 16,000 people, capable of turning out a new galley every 100 days. Covering 32 hectares and completely enclosed by fortifications, the Arsenale was a symbol of the maritime supremacy of Venezia. Napoleon destroyed it in 1797, but it was later rebuilt and remained in use until WWI as a shipyard for the Italian navy.

The Renaissance gateway surmounted by the Lion of San Marco commemorates the Christian victory over the Turkish fleet in the Battle of Lepanto in 1571, but you may not pass beyond it as the bulk of the Arsenale remains military property.

The **Museo Storico Navale**, towards the Canale di San Marco on the far side of Rio dell'Arsenale, covers the republic's maritime history with a huge exhibition of paraphernalia, model boats, costumes and weapons, and is worth visiting. Among the exhibits is Peggy Guggenheim's gondola, one of the oldest remaining in the city. The museum is open from 8.45 am to 1.30 pm Monday to Saturday (except Thursday, when it opens from 2.30 to 5 pm) and admission is L3000.

At the eastern edge of Venezia, the residential back lanes of Castello are worth walking through to see how the locals live. Beyond, the islands of **San Pietro** and **Sant'Elena** are pools of peace far removed from the busy heart of Venezia.

Islands of the Lagoon

Giudecca Originally known as *spina longa* (long spine) because of its shape, Giudecca's present name probably derives from the word Zudega (*giudicato* – the judged), which was applied to families of rebellious nobles at one time banished from Venezia and later allowed to return. Rich Venetians later came of their own accord to build villas on the island. Its main attraction is the **Chiesa dei Redentore**, built by Palladio in 1577 after the city was saved from a savage outbreak of plague. On the third Saturday in July the doge would pay a visit to the church, crossing the canal from the Zattere on a pontoon (the name Zattere means 'rafts'). The festival of the Redentore remains one of the most important on Venezia's calendar of events.

San Giorgio Maggiore On the island of the same name, Palladio's **Chiesa di San Giorgio Maggiore** has one of the most prominent positions in Venezia and, although it inspired mixed reactions among the architect's contemporaries, it has had a significant influence on contemporary architecture. Built between 1565 and 1580, the church has an austere interior, an interesting contrast to its bold façade. Its art treasures include works by Tintoretto: a *Last Supper* and the *Shower of Manna* on the walls of the high altar, and a *Deposition* in the Cappella dei Morti. Take

the lift to the top of the 60m-high bell tower for an extraordinary view (L3000).

Opening hours are from 9.30 am to 1 pm (to 10.30 am only on Sunday and holidays) and 2.30 to 5 pm daily.

San Michele The city's cemetery was established on Isola di San Michele under Napoleon and is maintained by the Franciscans. The **Chiesa di San Michele in Isola**, begun by Codussi in 1469, was among the city's first Renaissance buildings.

Murano The people of Venezia have been making crystal and glass (the difference between the two lies in the amount of lead employed) since as early as the 10th century, when the secrets of the art were brought back from the East by merchants. The industry was moved to the island of Murano in the 13th century.

Venezia had a virtual monopoly on the production of what is now known as Murano glass and the methods of the craft were such a well-guarded secret that it was considered treason for a glass-worker to leave the city. The incredibly elaborate pieces produced by the artisans can range from the beautiful to the grotesque – but, as the Italians would say, *i gusti son gusti* (each to his own). Watching the glass-workers in action is certainly interesting.

The **Museo Vetrario** contains some exquisite pieces and is open from 10 am to 5 pm every day except Wednesday. Admission costs L8000.

The nearby **Chiesa dei SS Maria e Donato** is a fascinating example of Venetian-Byzantine architecture. Founded in the 7th century and rebuilt 500 years later, the church was first dedicated to the Virgin Mary. It was rededicated to San Donato after his bones were brought there from Cephalonia, along with those of a dragon he supposedly had killed (four of the 'dragon' bones are hung behind the altar). The church's magnificent mosaic pavement was laid in the 12th century, and the impressive mosaic of the Virgin Mary in the apse dates from the same period.

The island can be reached on vaporetto

Impressive Villa Pisani, Strà

Dreamy canals, Venezia

Cross the Grand Canale – by foot over Ponte di Rialto or gondola.

The revealing baroque facade of Palazzo Maffei, Verona

Picture perfect, Isola di Burano

View towards Palladio's prominent Chiesa di San Giorgio Maggiore with its 60m-high bell tower

The four 'masketeers', Carnevale, Venezia

Rich velvet opulence ...

... and cool white elegance, Carnevale, Venezia

No 12, 13 or 42 from Fondamente Nuove (No 42 also leaves from San Zaccaria and Piazzale Roma). No 62 also goes there from Piazzale Roma.

Burano Famous for its lace industry, Burano is a pretty fishing village, its streets and canals lined with bright, pastel-coloured houses. The **Museo del Merletto di Burano** is a museum of lace making and is open from 9 am to 5 pm daily except Tuesday (the ticket window shuts from 3.30 pm). Admission is L8000. If you plan to buy lace on the island, choose with care and discretion, as these days much of it is imported from China. Take vaporetto No 12 from Fondamente Nuove.

Torcello This delightful little island, with its overgrown main square and sparse, scruffy-looking buildings and monuments, was at its peak from the mid-7th century to the 13th century, when it was the seat of the Bishop of Altinum and home to some 20,000 people. Rivalry with Venezia and a succession of malaria epidemics systematically reduced the island's splendour and its population. Today, fewer than 80 people call the island home.

The island's Veneto-Byzantine cathedral, **Santa Maria Assunta**, shouldn't be missed. Founded in the 7th century, it was Venezia's first cathedral. It was rebuilt early in the 11th century and contains magnificent Byzantine mosaics.

On the cathedral's western wall is a vast mosaic depicting the Last Judgment, but its great treasure is the mosaic of the Madonna in the semi-dome of the apse. Starkly set on a pure gold background, the figure is one of the most stunning works of Byzantine art you will see in Italy. The cathedral opens from 10 am to 5.30 pm. Admission is L5000, and includes an information audiotape. You can also climb the bell tower (L3000).

The adjacent tiny **Chiesa di Santa Fosca** was founded in the 11th century to house the body of Santa Fosca. Across the square, in the Palazzo del Consiglio, is the **Museo di Torcello**, which tells the history of the island. It opens from 10 am to 12.30 pm and 2 to 4 pm Tuesday to Sunday. Admission

costs L3000. Take vaporetto No 12 from Fondamente Nuove.

The Lido The main draw here is the beach, but the water can be polluted and the public areas of the waterfront are often unkempt. Alternatively, you can pay a small fortune (between L20,000 and L80,000) to hire a chair and umbrella in the more easily accessible and cleaner areas of the beach.

The Lido forms a land barrier between the lagoon and the Mar Adriatico. For centuries the doges trekked out here to fulfil Venezia's Marriage to the Sea ceremony by dropping a ring into the shallows, celebrating Venezia's close relationship with the sea.

It became a fashionable seaside resort around the late 19th century and its more glorious days are depicted in Thomas Mann's novel *Der Tod in Venedig (Death in Venice)*. The rows of modern apartments and hotels ensure the beaches are crowded, particularly with holidaying Italians and Germans, but the Lido is far from fashionable these days.

The snappy **Palazzo del Cinema** hosts Venezia's international film festival each September (see Special Events later) and the **casino** packs them in during the summer months. Apart from that, there is little to attract you here, unless you are passing through on your way to Chioggia. The Lido can be reached by vaporetto No 1, 6, 14, 52 or 82 and the vehicle ferry from Tronchetto.

Chioggia The second most important city in the lagoon after Venezia, Chioggia lies at the southern end of the lagoon. Invaded and destroyed by the Venetian Republic's maritime rival, Genova, in the late 14th century, the medieval core of modern Chioggia is a crumbly but not uninteresting counterpoint to its more illustrious patron to the north. In no way cute like Murano or Burano, Chioggia is a firmly practical town, its big fishing fleet everywhere in evidence. If your time is limited in Venezia, you can live without Chioggia – the trip can take about two hours each way. City bus No 1, 2, 6 or 7 connects Chioggia with the Sottomarina, saving you the 15 minute walk.

From the Lido, bus No 11 leaves from Gran Viale Santa Maria Elisabetta, outside the tourist office on the Lido; it boards the car ferry at Alberoni and then connects with a steamer at Pellestrina that will take you to Chioggia. Or you can take a bus from Piazzale Roma. The APT (☎ 041 554 04 66) is on the waterfront at the Sottomarina.

Courses

The Società Dante Alighieri (☎ 041 528 91 27), Palazzo Zorzi, Castello 3405, offers both short intensive and longer Italian-language courses from September to June. Monthly courses start at around L350,000.

The Istituto Zambler (☎ 041 522 43 31, fax 041 528 56 28), off Campo Santa Margherita at Dorsoduro 3116a, offers language and one to two-week cooking courses. It also has a course in Venetian history and art involving 12 guided tours of the city. Check out its Web site at www.virtualvenice.net/zambler.

The Fondazione Cini (☎ 041 528 99 00), Isola di San Giorgio Maggiore, runs seminars on subjects relating to the city, in particular music and art.

Gondola Rides

A gondola ride is the quintessence of romantic Venezia, although at L120,000 for 50 minutes (L150,000 after 8 pm) the *official* price is a rather hefty return from the clouds to reality. The rates are for a maximum of six people – less romantic but more affordable. Prices are set for gondola rides but you can negotiate fees for additional services, such as a singer to serenade you during the ride.

Gondolas are available near main canals all over the city, or can be booked in the following areas: San Marco (☎ 041 520 06 85), Rialto (☎ 041 522 49 04), Piazzale Roma (☎ 041 522 11 51) and Stazione Santa Lucia (☎ 041 71 85 43).

Venezia for Children

The kids will certainly enjoy a trip down the Canal Grande on vaporetto No 1. If you can't afford a gondola, at least treat them to a short trip across the canal on a traghetto. They will probably also enjoy a trip to the islands, particularly to see the glass-making demonstrations on Murano. Older kids might enjoy watching the big ships pass along the Canale della Giudecca, so take them to Gelati Nico on the Fondamenta Zattere, where you can relax for half an hour or so.

Children of all ages will enjoy watching the Mori strike the hour at the Torre dell'Orologio on Piazza San Marco. In summer you could spend a few hours on the beach at the Lido, stopping for gelati on the way home.

There are *giardini pubblici* (public gardens) at the eastern end of Castello, at the Giardini vaporetto stop. There is also a small playground tucked in behind the Lista di Spagna just before Campo San Geremia.

Organised Tours

You can join free tours for a biblical explanation of the mosaics in the Basilica di San Marco. Offered by the Patriarcato (the church hierarchy in Venezia), they take place in Italian at 11 am Monday, Tuesday and Thursday to Saturday and at 3 pm on Wednesday. The tours are conducted in English on Monday, Thursday and Friday at 11 am and in French at the same time on Thursday.

Consult *Un Ospite di Venezia* for details of visits to other churches and sights in the city. The APT has an updated list of authorised guides, who will take you on a walking tour of the city. The going rate is L172,000 for a three hour tour for up to 30 people. With tourism projected to just keep on growing, the Veneto regional government is trying to train new guides in various languages just as quickly as it can.

Travel agencies in central Venezia can put you on to one of several city tours, ranging from guided walks for L30,000 to gondola rides with serenade for L50,000 a person.

Special Events

The major event of the year is Carnevale, when Venetians don spectacular masks and costumes for a 10 day street party in the run up to Ash Wednesday.

The APT publishes a list of annual events, including the many religious festivals staged by almost every church in the city. One is held in July at the Chiesa del Redentore (see the earlier Giudecca Island section), and another at the Basilica di Santa Maria della Salute each November (see the earlier Dorsoduro section).

The city next hosts the Historical Regatta of the Four Ancient Maritime Republics in June 2002. The former maritime republics of Genova, Pisa, Venezia and Amalfi take turns to host this colourful event. The annual Regatta del Redentore, held each July on the Canal Grande, is another celebration of the city's former maritime supremacy.

The Venezia Biennale, a major exhibition of international visual arts, started in 1895 and has been held every even-numbered year since the early 20th century. However, the 1992 festival was postponed until 1993 so there would be a festival on the Biennale's 100th anniversary in 1995. It is held from June to October in permanent pavilions in the Giardini Pubblici, as well as in other locations throughout the city. Major art exhibitions are held at the Palazzo Grassi and you will find smaller exhibitions in various venues around the city throughout the year.

The Venezia International Film Festival, Italy's version of Cannes, is organised by the Biennale and held annually in September at the Palazzo del Cinema on the Lido.

Places to Stay

Venezia is an expensive place to stay, it's as simple as that. Even in the depths of low season you won't find more than about a half dozen places offering singles/doubles without bathroom for less than L65,000/95,000. Expect to pay from L150,000 upwards for a decent budget double with bathroom. Most places include breakfast (usually unsatisfactory) whether you like it or not.

Budget travellers have the option of the youth hostel on Isola della Giudecca and a handful of other dormitory style arrangements, some of them religious institutions. They mostly open in summer only.

Most of the top hotels are around San Marco and along the Canal Grande, but it is possible to find bargains tucked away in tiny streets and on side canals in the heart of the city. There are lots of hotels near Stazione Santa Lucia, but it is a good 30 minute walk to San Marco. The Dorsoduro area is quiet and relatively tourist-free.

It's advisable to book well in advance year-round in Venezia, particularly in May, September, during Carnevale and at weekends.

The Associazione Veneziana Albergatori has offices at Stazione Santa Lucia, in Piazzale Roma and at the Tronchetto car park. Staff here will book you a room, but you must leave a small deposit.

By the time you have this guide in your hands, inflation will have sent prices up, but in Venezia more than elsewhere hotel rates also vary wildly for a range of other reasons. Some hotels have the same prices year-round, while others drop them when things are slow (as though that happens a lot). Low season for the average Venetian hotelier means November, early December and January. That's it.

Some of the more expensive hotels operate further price differentials: weekend rates can be higher than during the week. Rooms with views (especially of the Canal Grande) are generally dearer than those without. Finally, proprietors' whim can produce all sorts of results.

The prices that follow should, therefore, be regarded as an orientation at best. Where possible, plan ahead and shop around. Remember that, unless you leave a deposit, many smaller hotels won't feel obliged to hold a room for you all day unless you call to confirm.

Consider using Padova (see Padova in the Around Il Veneto section later in this chapter) as a base, or at least for a day or two while you get oriented in Venezia (it's only 37km, or 30 minutes on most trains, away), to give yourself time to find and book a place that suits.

Places to Stay – Budget

Camping There are numerous camp sites, many with bungalows at Littorale del Cavallino, the coast along the Mar Adriatico, north-east of the city. Camp sites closer to the city are not a very attractive option. The tourist office in San Marco has a full list, but you could try *Marina di Venezia (☎ 041 530 09 55, Via Montello 6)* at Punta Sabbioni, which is open from late April to the end of September.

Hostels The HI *Ostello Venezia (☎ 041 523 82 11, fax 041 523 56 89, Fondamenta delle Zitelle 86)* is on Giudecca. It's open to members only, although you can buy a card there. B&B is L25,000 and full meals are available for L14,000. Take vaporetto No 82, 41 or 42 from Stazione Santa Lucia or Piazzale Roma to Zitelle. It is open from 7 am to midnight (with a break between 9.30 am and 1.30 pm).

The nearby *Istituto Canossiano (☎ 041 522 21 57, Fondamenta del Ponte Piccolo 428)* has beds for women only from L18,000 a night. Take vaporetto No 41, 42 or 82 to Sant'Eufemia on Giudecca.

Foresteria Valdese (☎ 041 528 67 97, Castello 5120) is in an old mansion near Campo Santa Maria Formosa. Head east from the square on Calle Lunga, cross the small bridge and the Foresteria is in front of you. It has a couple of dorms with beds for L27,000 per night, with breakfast included (less if you stay for a few nights). A single costs L35,000, with breakfast included. Book well ahead.

Hotels & Pensioni – Cannaregio There is plenty to choose from here, with many hotels a stone's throw from Stazione Santa Lucia. Quality is not always at a premium, so hunt around.

Just off the Lista di Spagna, *Hotel Santa Lucia (☎ 041 71 51 80, Calle della Misericordia 358)* is in a newish building. A lone traveller can pay L80,000 for a room without bathroom. Doubles with/without bathroom cost L160,000/130,000.

At No 389, *Hotel Villa Rosa (☎ 041 71 65 69)* has 33 comfortable rooms each with bathroom, TV and phone. Out the back is a quiet little garden terrace where you can take your complimentary breakfast. You will pay as much as L150,000/170,000.

Hotel Rossi (☎ 041 71 51 64, Calle delle Procuratie 262) is also near Stazione Santa

Lucia, in a tiny lane off Lista di Spagna. It has pleasant rooms starting at L75,000/120,000.

At *Hotel al Gobbo (☎ 041 71 50 01, Campo San Geremia 312)* singles/doubles without bathroom cost L80,000/115,000 or L105,000/145,000 with. The rooms are nicely decorated and comfortable.

The pick of the crop on this square are *Alloggi Calderan* and *Casa Gerotto (☎ 041 71 53 61, Campo San Geremia 283)*. Together they offer a range of rooms. Small bright singles cost L50,000. Some dorms (separate male and female only arrangements) cost on average L30,000 a head. Doubles without bathroom cost L100,000, or L140,000 with.

At *Archies (Rio Terrà del Cristo 1814b)* they don't like to give out their number, which is OK because they won't take phone bookings anyway. Very basic singles/doubles/triples cost L50,000/66,000/75,000.

Hotels & Pensioni – San Marco Although it's the most heavily touristed part of Venezia, Sestiere San Marco offers some surprisingly good quality budget pensioni.

Just off Piazza San Marco is *Hotel ai do Mori (☎ 041 520 48 17, Calle Larga 658)*. It has attractive rooms, some with views of the basilica and one even has a terrace. Prices for doubles start at L135,000/180,000 without/with bathroom.

Al Gambero (☎ 041 522 43 84, Calle dei Fabbri 4687) is in a great location north of Piazza San Marco. Good singles/doubles without bathroom cost L85,000/140,000 or L165,000/210,000 with.

Hotel Noemi (☎ 041 523 81 44, Calle dei Fabbri 909) has good-sized rooms with phone and satellite TV for L100,000/140,000. None has attached bathroom.

One of the friendliest places to stay in this area is *Locanda Casa Petrarca (☎ 041 520 04 30, San Marco 4386)*, with rooms costing L80,000/120,000 without bathroom. Doubles with loo and shower cost L150,000. To get there, find Campo San Luca, follow Calle dei Fuseri, take the second left and then turn right into Calle Schiavone.

Locanda Fiorita (☎ 041 523 47 54, San Marco 3457a) is set on a wonderful little *campiello* near Campo Santo Stefano. The rooms in this old Venetian pile are simple enough but well maintained, and cost up to L100,000 for a single without bathroom or L170,000 for a double with.

Hotels & Pensioni – Castello This area to the east of San Marco, although close to the piazza, is less heavily touristed. From Stazione Santa Lucia catch vaporetto No 1 and get off at San Zaccaria Danieli.

A stone's throw east of San Marco is a delightful establishment, the *Hotel Doni* (☎ *041 522 42 67, Fondamenta del Vin, Castello 4656*), off Salizzada San Provolo. It has clean, quiet rooms without bathroom for L80,000/120,000. A double with bathroom is L160,000.

Locanda Silva (☎ *041 522 76 43, Fondamenta del Rimedio 4423*), south of Campo Santa Maria Formosa towards San Marco, has pleasant, simple singles/doubles without bathroom for L55,000/85,000, and doubles with bath for L125,000.

Hotels & Pensioni – Dorsoduro, San Polo & Santa Croce The *Locanda Salieri* (☎ *041 71 00 35, Fondamenta Minotto 160*) has singles/doubles from L65,000/110,000. To the east, *Albergo Casa Peron* (☎ *041 528 60 38, Salizzada San Pantalon 84*) has rooms for L75,000/110,000 with own shower. It is a small but characterful place.

Hotel dalla Mora (☎ *041 71 07 03, Santa Croce 42a*) is on a small canal just off Salizzada San Pantalon, near the Casa Peron. It has clean, airy rooms, some (like No 5) with lovely canal views, and there is a terrace. Singles/doubles cost L85,000/140,000 with bathroom.

Ezra Pound favoured the *Antica Locanda Montin* (☎ *041 522 71 51, Fondamenta di Borgo 1147*). Rooms are L110,000/130,000 (or doubles with bathroom for L150,000).

Albergo Antico Capon (☎ *041 528 52 92, Campo Santa Margherita 3004b*) is right on this lovely square and has a variety of rooms for anything up to L150,000.

Hotel Galleria (☎ *041 520 41 72, Accademia 878a*) is the only one star hotel on

the Canal Grande, near the Ponte dell'Accademia. Rooms without bathroom can cost up to L135,000/145,000 and those with cost L165,000/195,000. Book ahead.

Hotels & Pensioni – Lido The *Pensione La Pergola* (☎ *041 526 07 84, Via Cipro 15*), just north off Gran Viale Santa Maria Elisabetta, has a range of rooms. Singles/doubles with bathroom cost L70,000/140,000 in high season, and as little as half that in the low season.

Hotels & Pensioni – Mestre Only 15 minutes away on the regular bus Nos 7 and 2 (the latter passes Mestre train station) or by train, Mestre is a drab, but sometimes necessary, alternative to staying in Venezia. *Giovannina* (☎ *041 92 63 96, Via Dante 113*) charges a maximum of L80,000/100,000. A single without bathroom costs L55,000.

Places to Stay – Mid-Range
Cannaregio The *Hotel Abbazzia* (☎ *041 71 73 33, Calle Priuli detta dei Cavalletti 68*) is in a restored abbey, a one minute walk from Stazione Santa Lucia. Many of the lovely rooms face on to a central garden. Singles/doubles cost up to L295,000/330,000, with bathroom and breakfast. Prices drop considerably out of season.

San Marco The *Serenissima* (☎ *041 520 00 11, Calle C Goldoni 4486*) is tucked away in the area between San Marco and Ponte di Rialto. Singles/doubles cost L190,000/250,000.

Castello The *Locanda Remedia* (☎ *041 520 62 32, Calle Remedia 4412*) is a pearl on a tiny courtyard. Try for the front room with the 16th century ceiling fresco. You'll pay up to L150,000/280,000.

A good deal if you get one of the three waterfront rooms is *Albergo Paganelli* (☎ *041 522 43 24, Riva degli Schiavoni 4182*). Singles/doubles/triples cost L170,000/270,000/320,000 with bathroom and breakfast. For views over the lagoon you must shell out L270,000/360,000 for a double/triple.

La Residenza (☎ *041 528 53 15, Campo*

Bandiera e Moro, Castello 3608) is in a 15th century mansion and has delightful rooms for L160,000/240,000.

Dorsoduro In Dorsoduro, *Albergo Accademia Villa Maravege (☎ 041 521 01 88, Fondamenta Bollani, Dorsoduro 1058)* is set in lovely gardens, with views of the Canal Grande. This popular hotel has singles/doubles for up to L185,000/345,000.

Locanda Sturion (☎ 041 523 62 43, Calle Sturion 679) is two minutes from Ponte di Rialto. It has been a hotel on and off since the 13th century and has superb rooms for L200,000/310,000.

Pensione Seguso (☎ 041 528 68 58, Fondamenta Zattere ai Gesuati 779) is in a lovely quiet position facing the Canale della Giudecca. Singles/doubles here cost up to L195,000/250,000 with bathroom and breakfast.

Albergo agli Alboretti (☎ 041 523 00 58, Rio Terrà Antonio Foscarini 884) is a charming hotel that almost feels like an inviting mountain chalet when you step in. In its category it is one of Venezia's star choices. The management is friendly and the rooms tastefully arranged. They cost up to L160,000/250,000. The restaurant is also of a high standard.

Places to Stay – Top End
San Marco The luxury *Gritti Palace (☎ 041 79 46 11, fax 041 520 09 42, Campo Santa Maria del Giglio 2467)* is one of Venezia's most famous hotels – its façade fronts onto the Canal Grande. If you can afford to pay up to L1,600,000 a double, you'll be mixing with royalty.

Castello Some of the city's finest hotels are on Riva degli Schiavoni. The four star *Londra Palace (☎ 041 520 05 33, fax 041 522 50 32, Riva degli Schiavoni 4171)* has doubles for anything up to L1,000,000 and most rooms have views over the water. Renovated in 1998, the rooms feature 19th century furniture, jacuzzis and marble bathrooms. The luxury-class *Danieli (☎ 041 522 64 80, fax 041 520 02 08)* nearby has rooms for up to L700,000/1,350,000, and most of them look out over the canal.

Giudecca The *Cipriani (☎ 041 520 77 44, fax 041 520 39 30)* is set in lavish grounds on Giudecca, with unbeatable views across to San Marco. In high season you'll hand over up to L1,750,000 for a double room. Prices drop by almost half in the low season. Take the hotel's private boat from San Marco.

Places to Eat
If you've enjoyed the fine cooking of Toscana and Emilia-Romagna and the basic 'down home' style of a Roman meal, you might find the fare in Venezia a bit disappointing. The staples of Veneto cuisine are rice and beans. Try *risi e bisi* (risotto with peas) or *risotto nero*, coloured and flavoured with the ink of *seppia* (cuttlefish). Seafood is popular (but also expensive, read the fine print as most fish is sold by weight). Try *zuppa di pesce* (fish soup) or seppia with polenta. Be sure not to miss a risotto or pasta dish with *radicchio trevisano* (red chicory). *Tiramisù*, the rich mascarpone dessert, is a favourite here.

Search out the little trattorie tucked away in the side streets and squares, since most of the obvious restaurants around San Marco and near Stazione Santa Lucia are tourist traps. Many bars serve filling snacks with lunch-time and pre-dinner drinks. Most also have a wide range of Venetian panini, with every imaginable filling. *Tramezzi* (sandwich triangles) and huge bread rolls cost from L1500 to L5000 if you eat them standing up. A cheaper alternative can be the many *bacari*, also known as *osterie*. (There is more information about osterie later in this section.)

Restaurants Better areas to look for places to eat include the back streets of Cannaregio and San Polo, as well as around Campo Santa Margherita in Dorsoduro.

Cannaregio On Fondamenta della Misericordia locals crowd into several trattorie and bars. Young people will enjoy *Paradiso*

Perduto, at No 2539, a bar with live music and tables outside in summer. For Syrian food and belly-dancing, try *Sahara* at No 2520. *Pizzeria Casa Mia (Calle dell'Oca 4430)* has pizzas and pasta for about L10,000 and main courses for about L18,000.

Gam Gam (Ghetto Nuovo 2884) is great for your tastebuds if you like Israeli-style felafels and other Middle Eastern delicacies. It is kosher.

On the 'frontier' with Sestiere di Castello, the aptly named *Hostaria Al Ponte (Calle Larga G Gallina 6378)* is a highly recommended and rather teeny spot to snack on *cichetti* (small samples of finger-food such as stuffed olives and deep-fried vegetables in batter) and indulge in good wines.

San Marco On Calle Bembo, the continuation of Calle dei Fabbri, *Antica Carbonera* is a small trattoria catering for locals. Pasta starts at around L12,000.

Beside a small canal, *Ristorante da Ivo (Calle dei Fuseri 1809)* specialises in seafood and is recognised as one of Venezia's best restaurants. Consequently it's not cheap: a full seafood meal will cost from around L80,000 to L100,000.

Vino Vino (San Marco 2007) is a popular osteria at Ponte Veste near Teatro la Fenice. The menu changes daily and the pre-prepared food is good quality. Pasta or risotto costs L8000, a main dish L15,000, and there is a good selection of vegetables. Wine is sold by the glass for L2000.

Castello The *Trattoria alla Rivetta (Ponte San Provolo 4625)*, right next to the canal and just before Campo San Provolo, serves Venetian dishes. Pasta costs around L10,000 and a main dish around L17,000.

Pizzeria da Egidio (Campo Santa Maria Formosa 5245) has pizzas from L9000 and you can sit in the piazza.

Santa Croce & San Polo This is a great area for small, cheap places to eat. *Brodo di Giuggiole (Fondamenta Minotto 159)* is small and family-run and offers a quality set-price menu at L45,000. *Trattoria alla Madonna*

(Calle della Madonna), a few streets west of the Rialto off Fondamenta del Vin, is an excellent trattoria specialising in seafood. Prices are reasonable, but a full meal will cost L60,000 or more.

Arca (Calle San Pantalon 3760) serves pasta and pizza for around L8000 to L10,000. It has live music on Tuesday evening. Across the street at No 3748 is *Da Silvio*, a good-value pizzeria and trattoria with outside tables in a garden setting. A full meal here will cost around L35,000.

Al Nono Risorto (Sotoportego de Siora Bettina). Stop in here if only to luxuriate in the canalside garden. *Pesce ai ferri* (grilled fish) is tasty at L25,000. You can precede it with various pasta dishes at around L13,000.

Dorsoduro Typical regional fare is served at *L'Incontro (Rio Terrà Canal 3062)*, between Campo San Barnaba and Campo Santa Margherita. The menu alters daily and a full meal will cost around L40,000.

Islands of the Lagoon On Giudecca and run by the Cipriani hotel, *Harry's Dolci (Fondamenta San Biagio)* has fantastic desserts. Meals in the restaurant cost at least L80,000. There is also a snack bar. *Ristorante All'Isola d'Oro (Riviera Santa Maria Elisabetta 2)*, near the vaporetto landing on Lido, has average-priced meals. *Osteria dalla Mora (Fondamenta Manin 75)* looks out over one of Murano's canals and is worth considering for lunch or dinner. A meal is around L35,000.

Burano may be pretty, but its restaurant prices aren't. One of the better choices is *Ristorante Galuppi (Via B Galuppi 470)* – look for the dolls in the windows. A meal will cost about L40,000 per person. *Locanda Cipriani (Piazza Santa Fosca 29)*, on Torcello, is famous and expensive – expect to shell out L100,000. For something simpler, try *Al Trono di Attila (Fondamenta Borgognoni 7a)*, between the ferry stop and the cathedral, where a full meal costs around L40,000.

Chioggia & Mestre The *Ristorante Vecio Foghero (Calle Scopici 91)*, in Chioggia, serves good pizzas and seafood dishes. *Da*

Bepi Venesian (Via Sernaglia 27), in Mestre, a couple of blocks from Stazione Santa Lucia, offers traditional dishes and a meal will cost around L40,000.

Osterie Venezia's osterie are a cross between bars and trattorie, where you can sample cichetti, generally washed down with a small glass of wine *(ombra)*. Locals often choose to bar-hop from osteria to osteria, a great way to experience a more down-to-earth side of Venezia.

Some osterie serve full meals. *Osteria al Mascaron (Calle Lunga)*, east of Campo Santa Maria Formosa, is a bar/osteria and trattoria. The cichetti are good, but a meal is overpriced. *Osteria dalla Vedova (Calle del Pistor)*, off Strada Nova in Cannaregio, is also called Trattoria Ca d'Or and is one of the oldest osterie in Venezia. The food is excellent and modestly priced – L35,000 will cover you.

In the San Marco area, near Campo San Luca, *Enoteca Il Volto (Calle Cavalli 4052)* has an excellent wine selection and good snacks. On the San Polo side of Ponte di Rialto, *Cantina do Mori (Sotoportego dei do Mori)* offers good evening meals for about L35,000. A few steps away at Calle do Spade 860, *Cantina do Spade* is Venezia's oldest eating house – L40,000 should see you through dinner. Another hidden Venetian jewel along similar lines is *Osteria da Alberto (Calle Gallina 5401)* in Cannaregio. A tranquil option, well away from the madding crowd, is *Da Codroma (Fondamenta Brianti, Dorsoduro 2540)*. It's an old-time bacaro with good cichetti.

Snacks Between Riva degli Schiavoni and Campo SS Filippo e Giacomo is *Al Vecio Penasa (Calle delle Rasse 4587)*, which offers an excellent selection of sandwiches and snacks at reasonable prices.

You'll find several alternatives for snacks and drinks on Campo Santa Margherita, including the *Green Pub* which serves Guinness. *Il Caffè*, on the same square at No 2963, is a lively student bar.

Along the main thoroughfare between Stazione Santa Lucia and San Marco, numerous bars serve sandwiches and snacks.

Cafés If you can cope with the idea of paying from L10,000 (some lucky people have reported being charged as much as L20,000!) for a cappuccino, spend an hour or so sitting at an outdoor table at Florian or Quadri and enjoy the atmosphere of Piazza San Marco. *Caffè Florian* is the most famous of the two cafés – its plush interior has seen the likes of Lord Byron and Henry James taking breakfast (separately) before they crossed the piazza to *Caffè Quadri* for lunch. Both cafés have bars, where you can pay normal prices for a coffee or drink (taken on your feet) and still enjoy the elegant surroundings.

Gelaterie & Pasticcerie The best ice cream in Venezia is at *Gelati Nico (Fondamenta Zattere ai Gesuati 922)*. The locals take their evening stroll along the Zattere while eating their gelati. *Gelateria il Doge (Campo Santa Margherita)* also has excellent gelati. One of Venezia's better cake shops is *Pasticceria Marchini (Calle dello Spezier 2769)*, just off Campo Santo Stefano.

Self-Catering The best *markets* take place on the San Polo side of Ponte di Rialto. *Grocery shops*, where you can buy salami, cheese and bread, are concentrated around Campo Beccarie, which happens to lie next to the city's main fish market. There is a *Standa supermarket* on Strada Nova and a *Mega 1 supermarket* off Campo Santa Margherita.

Entertainment

The Venezia Carnevale (see Special Events earlier) is one of Italy's best known festivals, but exhibitions, theatre and musical events continue throughout the year in Venezia. Information is available in *Un Ospite di Venezia* and the tourist office also has brochures listing events and performances year-round.

Bars & Pubs The *Black Jack Bar (Campo San Luca)* serves a decent Bellini, among other cocktails, for L3500.

The nameless *wine bar* by the bridge at

Rio Terrà della Maddalena in Cannaregio is great for a drink or three – it tends to be a local hangout. *Paradiso Perduto* (see Cannaregio under Places to Eat) is a hip joint with live music. *Caffè Blue Music*, Dorsoduro 3778, is a cool student bar with live music on Friday. It is as good a place as any to try the favourite Veneto drink, a *spritz*. This is one part sparkling white wine, one part soda water and one part bitter (Campari or one of several other variants), topped with a slice of lemon and, if you wish, an olive.

Irish-style pubs are as popular here as anywhere in Europe. *The Fiddler's Elbow* (*Corte dei Pali 3847*), off Strada Nova in Cannaregio, is representative of the genre.

Harry's Bar (*Calle Vallaresso 1323*), off Salizzada San Moisè, is on the western edge of Piazza San Marco. The Cipriani family, which started the bar, claims to have invented many Venetian specialities, including the Bellini cocktail. A meal at the restaurant upstairs will cost you at least L100,000, but it is one of the few restaurants in the city to have been awarded a Michelin star.

Discos & Clubs As far as clubs go, the city's spread is pretty dismal. A drive to Mestre or a boat to the Lido is the best bet, but the latter shuts down in winter. In summer, Jesolo and its beach (to the north of the lagoon) is where a lot of the action takes place.

Cinemas The city doesn't have an English-language cinema. *Summer Arena*, a cinema-under-the-stars on Campo San Polo during July and August, features British and American films, but they are generally dubbed. The time to see cinema in the original language is during the September film festival (see Special Events earlier).

Opera & Classical Music Until it was destroyed by fire in January 1996, *Teatro la Fenice* (☎ *041 521 01 61*) was Venezia's premier opera and classical music stage. Performances are still organised but held in alternative venues. One is the Chiesa di Santa Maria della Pietà on the Riva degli Schiavoni; tickets can be purchased from

Agenzia Kele & Teo (☎ 041 520 87 22), Ponte dei Baratteri, San Marco, or from the church, two days before the event. A contemporary music festival is held annually in October at the *Teatro Goldoni* (☎ *041 520 52 41, Calle C Goldoni, San Marco 4650b*).

Casinos The *Casinò Municipale di Venezia* has two locations. In winter it is at the Palazzo Vendramin Calergi, on the Canal Grande, and in summer it moves to the Palazzo del Casinò on the Lido. Vaporetto No 61 or 62 from San Zaccaria Danieli take you to/from the summer version.

Shopping

When people shop in Venezia they tend to think of Murano glass and there is no shortage of workshops and showrooms full of the stuff, particularly between San Marco and Castello and on the island of Murano. Much of it is designed for tourist groups, so if you want to buy, shop around. Quality and prices vary dramatically and you don't need to go to Murano to find quality stuff. Always haggle, as the marked price is usually much higher than what the seller expects to get. If you do decide to buy Venetian glass, you can have the shop ship it home for you. Remember, it can take a long time for your package to arrive and you are likely to have to pay duty.

Carnevale masks make beautiful souvenirs. Again, quality and price are uneven. Ca' Macana, Calle delle Botteghe, Dorsoduro 5176, is worth a look. You can even see how masks are made. For a more flamboyant display, costume hire and sale and the chance to buy a helmet and sword, try Atelier Pietro Longhi, Rio Terrà, San Polo 2604b.

Venezia is also noted for its *carta marmorizzata* (marbled paper). The oldest store is the Legatoria Piazzesi, Campiello della Feltrina, San Marco 2551c. It employs time-honoured methods to turn out high-quality (and high-priced) items. Il Pavone, Fondamenta Venier dei Leoni 721, Dorsoduro, is another good store.

Many shops (and artists in the city's many squares) sell simple watercolours of typical Venetian scenes. Veneziartigiana,

Calle Larga San Marco 412, is a collective selling works by Venetian artists.

If you want to buy unusual pasta, such as Curaçao blue fettucine, and other culinary delicacies try Giacomo Rizzo, Salizzada S Giovanni Crisostomo 5778.

The main shopping area for clothing, shoes, accessories and jewellery is in the narrow streets between San Marco and the Rialto, particularly the Mercerie and around Campo San Luca. The more upmarket shopping area is west of Piazza San Marco.

You can expect most shops hoping to sell to tourists to open all weekend during the high season (Easter to September).

Getting There & Away

Air Marco Polo airport (☎ 041 260 92 60 for flight details) is just east of Mestre and is served by flights from most major Italian and European cities, and from New York.

Alitalia (☎ 041 258 12 22) is at Via Sansovino 7 in Mestre; the Padova office of British Airways (☎ 049 66 04 44) is the closest to Venezia; Qantas, Canadian Airways and TWA are handled by Clipper Viaggi (☎ 041 98 77 44), Via Lazzari 1, in Mestre.

Bus ACTV buses (☎ 041 528 78 86) leave from Piazzale Roma for surrounding areas, including Mestre and Chioggia. There are also bus connections to Padova and Treviso. Tickets and information are available at the ticket office on the piazza.

Train Stazione Santa Lucia (☎ 147 88 80 88) is directly linked by train to Padova, Verona, Trieste, Milano and Bologna, and is easily accessible from Firenze and Roma. You can also leave from Venezia for major points in Germany, Austria, Slovenia and Croatia.

Orient Express The Venice Simplon Orient Express runs between Venezia and London via Verona, Zurich and Paris twice weekly from March to November. Departures from London are on Thursday and Sunday; from Venezia it leaves on Wednesday and Saturday. The trip in old-world luxury takes about 30 hours and costs from US$1910

one way. You can choose from a couple of alternative routes too. Any travel agency in Venezia can assist, or call the headquarters in London (☎ 020-7928 6000) or check its Web site at www.orient-expresstrains.com.

Car & Motorcycle The A4 passes through Mestre. It's the fastest way to reach Venezia. Take the Venezia exit and follow the signs for the city. The A4 connects Trieste with Torino, passing through Milano. From the south, take the A13 from Bologna, which connects with the A4 at Padova. A more interesting route is to take the S11 from Padova to Venezia.

Once you cross the bridge from Mestre, the Ponte della Libertà, cars must be left at one of the huge car parks on Piazzale Roma or on the island of Tronchetto. Parking is not cheap and you will pay L25,000 or more for every 24 hours. A cheaper alternative is to leave the car at Fusina near Mestre and catch vaporetto No 16 to the Zattere and then the No 52 or No 51 to either San Marco or Stazione Santa Lucia. Ask for information at the tourist office just before the bridge to Venezia.

Avis (☎ 041 522 58 25) is on Piazzale Roma, as are Eurodollar (☎ 041 528 95 51), Hertz (☎ 041 528 3524) and Autonoleggio Venezia (☎ 041 520 00 00). They all have counters at Marco Polo airport too.

Boat Minoan Lines (☎ 041 271 23 45), Porto Venezia, Zona Santa Marta, runs ferries to Greece (Corfu, Igoumenitsa and Patras) from Venezia three times a week in winter and daily in summer. Passengers pay up to L124,000 one way for an airline-style seat, depending on the season.

Strintzis Lines (☎ 041 277 05 59), Stazione Marittima 103, operates up to four ferries a week during summer to the same destinations in Greece. A simple spot on the deck costs from L60,000 a person in lowest season up to L98,000. Airline-style seats cost about the same as with Minoan Lines.

Getting Around

To/From the Airport The airport is accessible by regular *motoscafo* (motorboat) from both San Marco and the Lido (L17,000), operated by the Cooperativa San Marco (☎ 041 522 23 03). The Alilaguna hydrofoil costs L17,000 from Venezia or the Lido to the airport or L8500 from Murano to the airport. Murano to the Lido also costs L8500, as does Murano to Piazzale Roma in Venezia. You can pick up the Alilaguna boat at the Zattere or near Piazza San Marco, in front of the Giardini ex-Reali.

There are also buses operated by the Società ATVO (☎ 041 520 55 30), which cost L5000, or you can take the regular ACTV city bus No 5, both leave from Piazzale Roma. A water taxi from San Marco will cost at least L87,000, and to obtain this official price you may have to haggle.

Vaporetto Vaporetti are the city's mode of public transport. A car ferry transports vehicles from Tronchetto, near Piazzale Roma, to the Lido. From Piazzale Roma, vaporetto No 1 zigzags up the Canal Grande to San Marco and then the Lido. It is a great introduction to Venezia. There are faster and more expensive alternatives if you are in a hurry.

Single vaporetto tickets cost L6000 (plus L6000 for luggage!), even if you only ride to the next station. A 24 hour ticket is good value at L18,000 for unlimited travel. Better still are the three day (L35,000) and weekly (L60,000) tickets. Rolling Venezia passholders can get the three day ticket for L25,000. Those understandably tempted to ride without paying should note that ticket inspectors do *occasionally* make an appearance.

Tickets can be purchased at the ticket booths at most landing stations and should be validated in the machines at each landing station before you get on the boat. Otherwise you can buy them on the boat.

Routes and route numbers can change, so the following list should be taken as a guide:

No 1
  Piazzale Roma, Ferrovia, Canal Grande, Lido
No 12
  Fondamente Nuove, Murano, Burano, Torcello, Punta Sabbioni
No 14
  San Zaccaria, Lido, Litorale del Cavallino (Punta Sabbioni & Treporti)

No 17
  Car ferry from Tronchetto to Lido
No 41
  Circular line – Piazzale Roma, Sacca Fisola, Giudecca, San Zaccaria, San Pietro, Fondamente Nuove, Ferrovia
No 42
  Circular line – in reverse direction to No 41
No 51
  Circular line – San Zaccaria to Lido, Ferrovia, Piazzale Roma, Zattere, San Zaccaria
No 52
  Circular line – in reverse direction to No 51
No 61
  Limited stops circular line – Murano, Ferrovia, Piazzale Roma, San Zaccaria, Lido
No 62
  Limited stops circular line – Ferrovia, Piazzale Roma, San Zaccaria, Lido (extends to casino in summer)
No 71
  Limited stops line (summer only) – San Zaccaria, Murano, Ferrovia, Piazzale Roma, Tronchetto
No 72
  Limited stops line (summer only) – in reverse direction to No 71
No 82
  San Zaccaria, San Marco, Canal Grande, Ferrovia, Piazzale Roma, Zattere, Giudecca, San Giorgio and (in summer only) Lido
N
  All-stops night circuit taking in Piazzale Roma, Tronchetto, Giudecca, San Giorgio, Canal Grande, Lido

Traghetto The poor man's gondola, traghetti are used by locals to cross the Canal Grande where there is no nearby bridge. They operate between: Campo del Traghetto (near Santa Maria del Giglio) and Calle de Lanza; Campo San Samuele, north of the Ponte dell'Accademia, and Calle Traghetto; between Calle Mocenigo, farther north, and Calle Traghetto; between Fondamenta del Vin and Riva del Carbon, near the Ponte di Rialto; and between Campo Santa Sofia and Campo della Pescaria, near the produce market. The ride costs L700 (although some locals round it up to L1000).

Water Taxis Water taxis are prohibitively expensive, with a set L27,000 charge for a maximum of seven minutes, an extra L8000 if you order one by telephone, and various surcharges which make a gondola ride seem cheap.

Porters Getting from the vaporetto stop to your hotel can be difficult if you are heavily laden with luggage. There are several stands around the city where porters (*portabagagli*) can be engaged to escort you to your hotel. They charge L20,000 for one item and roughly L10,000 for each extra one. Prices virtually double to transport your baggage to any of the other islands, including Giudecca. They can be found at points including the Ponte dell'Accademia (☎ 041 522 48 91), Stazione Santa Lucia (☎ 041 71 52 72), Piazzale Roma (☎ 041 520 30 70), Ponte di Rialto (☎ 041 520 53 08) and San Marco (☎ 041 523 23 85).

Around Il Veneto

THE BRENTA RIVIERA

Dotted along the Brenta river, which passes through Padova and spills into the Venetian lagoon, are more than 100 villas built by wealthy Venetian families as summer homes; most are closed to the public. The most outstanding are the **Villa Foscari** (1571), built by Palladio at Malcontenta, and the **Villa Pisani**, also known as the Villa Nazionale, at Strà, which was built for Doge Alvise Pisani. It was used by Napoleon and was the site of the first meeting between Hitler and Mussolini. ACTV buses running between Padova and Venezia stop at or near the villas. Those that open do so with widely varying timetables from May to the end of September. See the later Around Vicenza section for information on other Venetian villas.

The luxurious *Burchiello* barge plied the Brenta river between Venezia and Padova in the 17th and 18th centuries. Today, a reproduction barge ferries tourists for about L120,000, including lunch and short tours. The trip is one way (either way) between Venezia and Strà, with connecting shuttle buses between Strà and Padova. Call ☎ 049 66 09 44 or try travel agencies in Venezia,

for example Intras, Piazza San Marco 145. At least two other ferries cover this stretch of the Brenta – ask at the Padova APT.

PADOVA (PADUA)
postcode 35100 • pop 225,000
Although famous as the city of San Antonio and for its university, one of the oldest in Europe, Padova is often seen as merely a convenient and cheap place to stay while visiting Venezia. However, the city offers a rich collection of art treasures, including Giotto's incredible frescoed chapel, and its many piazzas and arcaded streets are a pleasure to explore.

Padova's wealth grew during the 13th century when it was controlled by the counts of Carrara, who encouraged cultural and artistic prosperity and established the Studium, the forerunner of the university.

Orientation
From the train station, it's a 10 minute walk across the square and up Corso del Popolo (later Corso Garibaldi) to the centre. Bus No 10 will also get you there. Piazza della Frutta and the adjoining Piazza delle Erbe form the lively heart of the old city, bustling with market activity – take some time to drool over all the fine foods. The Basilica del Santo (also known as Basilica di Sant'Antonio) and the vast Prato della Valle are a good 20 minute walk south from the train station.

Information
Tourist Offices The APT office at the train station (☎ 049 875 20 77) opens from 9 am to 7.30 pm Monday to Saturday (9.15 am to 5.45 pm from November to March) and 8.30 am to 12.30 pm on Sunday (9 am to noon from November to March).

Post & Communications The post office, Corso Garibaldi 33, is open from 8.15 am to 7 pm Monday to Saturday (8.30 am to 6.30 pm on Sunday).

Telecom operates an unstaffed phone office at Riviera dei Ponti Romani 38, open from 7 am to 10 pm Monday to Saturday.

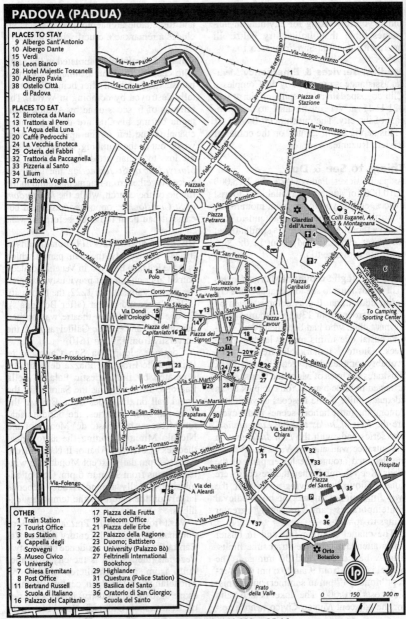

PADOVA (PADUA)

PLACES TO STAY
9   Albergo Sant'Antonio
10 Albergo Dante
15 Verdi
18 Leon Bianco
28 Hotel Majestic Toscanelli
30 Albergo Pavia
38 Ostello Città
    di Padova

PLACES TO EAT
12 Birroteca da Mario
13 Trattoria al Pero
14 L'Aqua della Luna
20 Caffè Pedrocchi
24 La Vecchia Enoteca
25 Osteria dei Fabbri
32 Trattoria da Paccagnella
33 Pizzeria al Santo
34 Lilium
37 Trattoria Voglia Di

OTHER
1   Train Station
2   Tourist Office
3   Bus Station
4   Cappella degli
    Scrovegni
5   Museo Civico
6   University
7   Chiesa Eremitani
8   Post Office
11 Bertrand Russell
    Scuola di Italiano
16 Palazzo del Capitano
17 Piazza della Frutta
19 Telecom Office
21 Piazza delle Erbe
22 Palazzo della Ragione
23 Duomo; Battistero
26 University (Palazzo Bò)
27 Feltrinelli International
    Bookshop
29 Highlander
31 Questura (Police Station)
35 Basilica del Santo
36 Oratorio di San Giorgio;
    Scuola del Santo

0   150   300 m

euro currency converter L10,000 = €5.16

Bookshops Padova is full of bookshops, and if you're looking for anything in languages other than Italian, try Feltrinelli International at Via San Francesco 14.

Medical Services & Emergency Medical assistance is provided by the Complesso Clinico Ospedaliero (hospital clinic; ☎ 049 821 11 11) at Via Giustiniani 1, to the southeast of the city. The questura (☎ 049 83 31 11) is at Via Santa Chiara, on the corner of Riviera Ruzante.

Things to See & Do
A special ticket, Padova Arte, for L15,000 (L10,000 for students), available at tourist offices, admits you to the main monuments – worth considering if you intend to 'do' Padova thoroughly. (There's a similar ticket for lesser sights spread about in the surrounding province too.)

Cappella degli Scrovegni Many art lovers visit Padova just to see this chapel in the Giardini dell'Arena. It was commissioned by Enrico Scrovegni in 1303 as a burial place for his father, who had been denied a Christian burial due to his money lending practices. Giotto's remarkable fresco cycle, probably completed between 1304 and 1306, illustrates the lives of Mary and Christ and is arranged in three bands. You can pick up an adequate guide to the frescoes as you enter. Among the most famous scenes in the cycle are the *Kiss of Judas* and the *Lamentation*. The series ends with the *Last Judgment* on the entrance wall and the Vices and Virtues are depicted around the lower parts of the walls. Keep in mind when the frescoes were done – Giotto was moving away from the two-dimensional figures of his medieval contemporaries and presaging greater things to come.

The chapel is often full and in busier times attendants enforce strict time limits, usually between 20 and 30 minutes. The chapel is open from 9 am to 6 pm daily except Monday (7 pm in summer) and admission costs L10,000. The ticket is also valid for the adjacent **Museo Civico**, whose col-

lection of 14th to 18th century Veneto art and forgettable archaeological artefacts includes a remarkable crucifix by Giotto.

Chiesa Eremitani Completed in the early 14th century, this Augustinian church was painstakingly rebuilt after being almost totally destroyed by bombing in WWII. The remains of frescoes done by Andrea Mantegna during his 20s are displayed in a chapel to the left of the apse. Most were wiped out in the bombing, the greatest single loss to Italian art during the war. The *Martyrdom of St James*, on the left, was pieced together from fragments found in the rubble of the church, while the *Martyrdom of St Christopher*, opposite, was saved because it had been removed before the war.

Historic Centre Via VIII Febbraio leads to the city's **university**, the main part of which is in the Palazzo Bò ('ox' in Venetian dialect, named after an inn that previously occupied the site). Established in 1222, the university is Italy's second oldest (after Bologna's). Europe's first anatomy theatre was opened here in 1594 and Galileo Galilei taught at the university from 1592 to 1610.

Continue along Via San Canziano to Piazza delle Erbe and Piazza della Frutta, separated by the majestic **Palazzo della Ragione**, also known as the Salone, for the grand hall on the upper floor. Built in the 13th and 14th centuries, the building features frescoes by Giusto de' Menabuoi and Niccolò Mireto depicting the astrological theories of Pietro d'Abano. It is open from 9 am to 7 pm daily except Monday; in winter it opens from 9 am to 6 pm. Cost of admission (usually around L7000) depends largely on the nature of the temporary exhibits.

West from here is the Piazza dei Signori, dominated by the 14th century **Palazzo del Capitanio**, the former residence of the city's Venetian ruler. South is the city's **duomo**, built from a much-altered design by Michelangelo. The 13th century Romanesque **battistero** (baptistry) features a series of frescoes of Old and New Testament scenes by Giusto de' Menabuoi, influenced by Giotto.

The duomo is open from 7.30 am to noon and 3.45 to 7.30 pm daily except Monday (slightly longer hours on Sunday and public holidays), while the battistero opens from 9.30 am to 1 pm and 3 to 6 pm (to 7 pm in summer) on the same days. Admission to the battistero costs L3000.

Piazza del Santo In the piazza, in front of the basilica, is the *Gattamelata*, created by Donatello in 1453. This magnificent equestrian statue of the 15th century Venetian *condottiere* (leader) Erasmos da Narni (whose nickname, Gattamelata, translates as 'Honeyed Cat') is considered the first great bronze of the Italian Renaissance.

The city's most celebrated monument is the **Basilica del Santo** (or di Sant'Antonio), which houses the corpse of the town's patron saint and is an important place of pilgrimage. Construction of what is known to the people of Padova as Il Santo began in 1232. The saint's tomb, bedecked by requests for the saint's intercession to cure illness or thanks for his having done so, is in the Cappella del Santo in the left transept. There was a time when the area around the tomb was awash with crutches and other prosthetic devices of the grateful cured – it appears these have been reduced to a symbolic few. Look out for the saint's relics in the apse too. The sculptures and reliefs of the high altar are by Donatello. The basilica opens from 6.30 am to 7 pm daily (to 7.45 pm in summer).

On the southern side of the piazza lies the **Oratorio di San Giorgio**, the burial chapel of the Lupi di Soranga family of Parma, with 14th century frescoes. Next door is the **Scoletta** (or **Scuola**) **del Santo**, containing works believed to be by Titian. The former is closed for restoration but the latter opens from 9 am to 12.30 pm and 2.30 to 7 pm (to 5 pm in winter). Admission costs L3000.

Just south of Piazza del Santo, the **Orto Botanico** is purportedly the oldest botanical garden in Europe. It opens from 9 am to 1 pm and 2 to 6 pm daily (Monday to Saturday mornings only in winter) and admission costs L5000.

Courses

The Bertrand Russell Scuola di Italiano (☎ 049 65 40 51), Via E Filiberto 6, runs one-month language courses for foreigners costing about US$570. Accommodation is extra.

Organised Tours

For tours of Padova, you can get in touch with Xanadu Viaggi (☎ 049 66 42 55) or inquire at the APT office.

Places to Stay

Padova has no shortage of budget hotels, but they fill quickly in summer. The closest camp site, *Camping Sporting Center* (☎ 049 79 34 00, Via Roma 123) at Montegrotto Terme, about 15km south-west of Padova, can be reached by city bus M. *Ostello Città di Padova* (☎ 049 875 22 19, Via dei A Aleardi 30) offers B&B for L20,000. Take bus No 3, 8 or 12 from the train station to Prato della Valle and then ask for directions.

The Koko Nor Association (☎ 049 864 33 94, Via Selva 5) can help you find B&B-style accommodation in family homes starting at around L40,000/70,000.

At *Verdi* (☎ 049 875 57 44, Via Dondi dell'Orologio 7), basic but clean singles/doubles cost L40,000/64,000. Similar sorts of rooms at *Albergo Pavia* (☎ 049 66 15 58, Via Papafava 11) cost L44,000/59,000.

Albergo Sant'Antonio (☎ 049 875 13 93, Via San Fermo 118), at the northern end of Via Dante, has excellent singles/doubles, most with TV and phone, for L58,000/82,000 or L94,000/116,000 with bathroom. Just nearby is the much simpler and cheaper *Albergo Dante* (☎ 049 876 04 08, Via San Polo 5) with rooms for L40,000/57,000.

The three star *Leon Bianco* (☎ 049 875 08 14, fax 049 875 61 84, Piazzetta Pedrocchi 12), near Piazza della Frutta, has rooms from L130,000/169,000 in high season (which is most of the time!). A leafy alternative is *Hotel Majestic Toscanelli* (☎ 049 66 32 44, Via dell'Arco 2), which will set you back up to L195,000/295,000.

Places to Eat

Daily *markets* are held on the piazze around the Palazzo della Ragione, with fresh produce sold in the Piazza delle Erbe and Piazza della Frutta, and bread, cheese and salami sold in the shops that lie beneath the porticoes.

Trattoria al Pero (Via Santa Lucia 72) serves regional dishes and a full meal will come to around L30,000. Across the road at No 91, *L'Aqua della Luna* is a funky sort of place where you can get great pizzas and/or cocktails.

For vegetarian food, try *Birroteca da Mario (Via Breda 3)*. *Osteria dei Fabbri (Via dei Fabbri 13)* is full of atmosphere, although more expensive. Try the *ravioloni di magro*: exquisite, light ravioli done in a butter and sage sauce. *La Vecchia Enoteca (Via San Martino e Solferino 32)* is a swank joint where mouth-watering mains cost around L25,000.

In the area around Prato della Valle, the best choice is *Trattoria Voglia Di (Via Umberto I)*, just before the Prato. You can have a full meal or snack at the bar. *Pizzeria al Santo (Via del Santo 149)* has good pizzas from L7000. Nearby, *Trattoria da Paccagnella (Via del Santo 113)* is a comfortably elegant setting for fine Veneto cuisine – try the *coniglio in casseruola con verdure e origano* (duck casserole with vegetables and oregano). *Lilium*, at No 181, offers wonderful gelati and fine pastries.

Behind the blunt neoclassical façade of the newly refurbished *Caffè Pedrocchi*, just off Via VIII Febbraio, is the former meeting place for 19th century liberals and one of Stendhal's favourite haunts. Today it's more posy than cosy, but maybe that's how it always was.

Entertainment

From July to September each year the city hosts the Notturni d'Arte festival, featuring concerts and outdoor events; many are free. The APT office has details. Some opera and theatrical performances are held at the *Teatro Comunale Verdi (☎ 049 876 03 39, Via Livello 32)*.

Beer-lovers wanting a variation on the Irish theme could strike out for *Highlander (Via San Martino e Solferino 71)* – you guessed it, a 'Scottish' pub. For some tips on discos and the like, start with the APT office's *Dove Andiamo Stasera* brochure.

Getting There & Away

SITA buses (☎ 049 820 68 34) depart from Piazzale Boschetti, 500m south of the train station, and head for Terme Montegrotto, Colli Euganei, Trieste, Venezia (L5100), Este, Mantova, Piacenza and Genova. By train the city is connected to Milano, Venezia (L4100 in 2nd class, L8100 on the fast Intercity trains) and Bologna.

The A4 (Milano-Venezia) passes to the north, while the A13, which connects the city with Bologna, starts at the southern edge of town. The two autostrade are connected by a ring road.

AROUND PADOVA

South-west of Padova, along the A13 or the S16, are the **Colli Euganei** (Euganean Hills), dotted with vineyards and good walking trails: ask at the Padova APT office for information about the trails and accommodation. The Consorzio Vini DOC dei Colli Euganei (☎ 049 521 18 96), Via Vescovi 41 in Luvigliano, can provide details of the vineyards.

If you are driving (which you pretty much have to, as public transport is abysmal in the area), follow the signposted Strada dei Vini dei Colli Euganei (Euganean Hills Wine Road), which will take you on a tour of many vineyards. You can pick up a map and itinerary from the APT in Padova. Most of the vineyards are open to the public and some of them even offer accommodation.

The tourist office (☎ 0429 8 13 20) in the medieval town of **Montagnana** is on Piazza Trieste. The HI youth hostel, *Rocca degli Alberi (☎/fax 0429 807 02 66, Castello degli Alberi)*, is in a former castle and opens from April to mid-October. B&B costs L16,000 and it is close to the town's train station.

VICENZA

postcode 36100 • pop 109,000

Vicenza is the centre of Italian textile manufacturing and a leader in the development and production of computer components, making it one of the country's wealthiest cities. Most tourists come to Vicenza to see the work of Andrea di Pietro della Gondola, better known as Palladio, whose designs have influenced architects worldwide. Vicenza flourished as the Roman Vicentia and in 1404 became part of the Venetian Republic, sharing the city's fortunes, as the many Venetian Gothic mansions demonstrate.

Orientation

From the train station, in the gardens of the Campo Marzo, walk straight ahead along Via Roma into Piazzale de Gasperi. From here, the main street, Corso Andrea Palladio, leads to the duomo and the centre of town.

Information

Tourist Offices The APT office (☎ 0444 32 08 54) is at Piazza Matteotti 12 and opens from 9 am to 1 pm and 2.30 to 6 pm Monday to Saturday; from 9 am to 1 pm on Sunday.

Post & Communications The main post office is at Contrà Garibaldi, near the duomo. A small unstaffed Telecom office is at Contrà Vescovado 2.

Medical Services & Emergency For urgent medical assistance, go to the Ospedale Civile (☎ 0444 99 31 11), Viale Ferninando Rodolfi 37, north of the city centre from Piazza Matteotti. The questura (☎ 0444 54 33 33) is at Viale Giuseppe Mazzini 24.

Things to See & Do

On Piazza Castello are several grand edifices, including the **Palazzo Porto-Breganze** on the southern side, designed by Palladio and built by Scamozzi, one of the city's leading 16th century architects. The main street, Corso Andrea Palladio, runs north-east from the square and is lined with fine buildings. Piazza dei Signori, nearby, is dominated by the immense **Basilica Palladiana**, built by Palladio

from 1549 over an earlier Gothic building – the slender 12th century bell tower is all that remains of the original structure. The basilica is open from 9.30 am to noon and 2.15 to 5 pm Tuesday to Saturday, and from 9 am to 12.30 pm on Sunday. Palladio's **Loggia del Capitaniato**, on the north-western side of the piazza on the corner of Via del Monte, was left unfinished at his death and shows his flair for colour.

South-west from the basilica is the **duomo**, a dull church destroyed during WWII and later rebuilt (some of its artworks were saved). Contrà Porti, which runs north off Corso Andrea Palladio, is one of the city's most majestic streets. The **Palazzo Thiene** at No 12, by Lorenzo da Bologna, was originally intended to occupy the entire block. Palladio's **Palazzo Porto-Barbaran** at No 11 features a double row of columns. He also built the **Palazzo Isoppo da Porto** at No 21, which remains unfinished. His **Palazzo Valmarana**, at Corso Antonio Fogazzaro 18, is considered one of his more eccentric creations. Across the Bacchiglione river is the **Parco Querini**, the city's largest park.

North along Corso Andrea Palladio and left into Contrada di Santa Corona is the **Chiesa di Santa Corona**, begun in 1261 by the Dominicans to house a relic from Christ's crown of thorns. Inside are the *Baptism of Christ* by Giovanni Bellini and *Adoration of the Magi* by Veronese.

Corso Andrea Palladio ends at the **Teatro Olimpico**, started by Palladio in 1580 and completed by Scamozzi after Palladio's death. Considered one of the purest creations of Renaissance architecture, the theatre design was based on Palladio's studies of Roman structures. Scamozzi's remarkable street scene, stretching back from the main façade of the stage, is modelled on the ancient Greek city of Thebes. He created an impressive illusion of depth and perspective by slanting the streets upward towards the rear of the set. The theatre was inaugurated in 1585 with a performance of *Oedipus Rex*, but soon fell into disuse – the ceiling caved in and it remained abandoned for centuries until 1934, when it was restored and reopened.

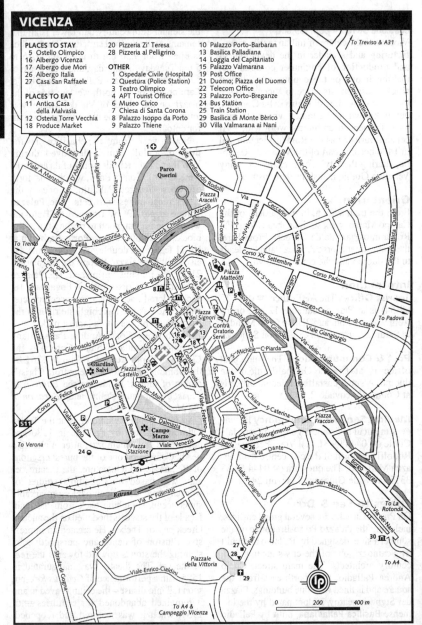

VICENZA

PLACES TO STAY
5 Ostello Olimpico
16 Albergo Vicenza
17 Albergo due Mori
26 Albergo Italia
27 Casa San Raffaele

PLACES TO EAT
11 Antica Casa
      della Malvasia
12 Osteria Torre Vecchia
18 Produce Market

20 Pizzeria Zi' Teresa
28 Pizzeria al Pelligrino

OTHER
1 Ospedale Civile (Hospital)
2 Questura (Police Station)
3 Teatro Olimpico
4 APT Tourist Office
6 Museo Civico
7 Chiesa di Santa Corona
8 Palazzo Isoppo da Porto
9 Palazzo Thiene

10 Palazzo Porto-Barbaran
13 Basilica Palladiana
14 Loggia del Capitaniato
15 Palazzo Valmarana
19 Post Office
21 Duomo; Piazza del Duomo
22 Telecom Office
23 Palazzo Porto-Breganze
24 Bus Station
25 Train Station
29 Basilica di Monte Bèrico
30 Villa Valmarana ai Nani

Since then, the theatre has become a prized performance space for opera and other theatre – it is one of the few working theatres where the performers and audience are eyeball to eyeball. It is open from 9 am to 12.30 pm and 2.15 to 5 pm Monday to Saturday in summer, and from 9.30 am to 12.30 pm on Sunday and holidays; in winter closing times are 15 minutes earlier. Admission costs L5000. The nearby **Museo Civico** in the Palazzo Chiericati, open the same hours, contains works by local artists as well as by the two Tiepolos and Veronese. Admission costs L5000. If you want to see the theatre and museum, get a *biglietto cumulativo* (combined ticket) for L9000.

South of the city, the **Basilica di Monte Bèrico** on Piazzale della Vittoria, set on top of a hill, presents magnificent views over the city. The basilica was built in the 18th century to replace a 15th century Gothic structure, itself raised on the supposed site of two appearances by the Virgin Mary in 1426. An impressive 18th century colonnade runs most of the way along Viale X Giugno to the church on the top of the hill – very handy when it's pouring with rain in autumn. Or catch city bus No 9.

A 20 minute walk part of the way back down Viale X Giugno and then east along Via San Bastiano will take you to the **Villa Valmarana ai Nani**, featuring brilliant frescoes by Giambattista and Giandomenico Tiepolo. The 'ai Nani' (dwarfs) refers to the statues perched on top of the gates surrounding the property. The villa is open every afternoon except Monday from mid-March to early November – check at the APT office or call ☎ 0444 54 39 76. Admission costs L10,000.

Signs mark the path to Palladio's Villa Capra, better known as **La Rotonda**. It is one of Palladio's most admired – and copied – creations, having served as a model for similar buildings across Europe and the USA. The gardens (admission L5000) are open from 10 am to noon and 3 to 6 pm on Tuesday, Wednesday and Thursday from March to November and the villa (admission L10,000) opens on Wednesday

for the same hours. Otherwise, groups of 25 or more (L20,000 a person) can book a visit to the villa and gardens on ☎ 0444 32 17 93. Bus No 8 stops nearby.

Places to Stay

Many hotels close during the summer, particularly in August, so book ahead. At other times you should have no problems getting a room.

The closest camp site, the *Campeggio Vicenza* (☎ *0444 58 23 11, Strada Pelosa 239*) is near the Vicenza Est exit from the A4. The recently opened HI youth hostel, the *Ostello Olimpico* (☎ *0444 54 02 22, Viale Giuriolo 7-9*) is in a fine building right by the Teatro Olimpico. It costs L25,000 per person.

Albergo Italia (☎ *0444 32 10 43, Viale Risorgimento 3*), near the train station, has singles/doubles with bathroom costing upwards of L60,000/80,000 (but this can increase enormously in high season). *Albergo Vicenza* (☎ *0444 32 15 12, Stradella dei Nodari 5-7*), near Piazza dei Signori, has rooms with bathroom for up to L80,000/110,000. The nearby *Albergo due Mori* (☎ *0444 32 18 86, Contrà do Rode 26*), has rooms for up to L65,000/124,000 in the high season. One of the best choices is *Casa San Raffaele* (☎ *0444 54 57 67, Viale X Giugno 10*), in a former convent behind the colonnade leading to Monte Bèrico, with singles/doubles with bathroom for L65,000/95,000.

Places to Eat

A large produce *market* is held each Tuesday and Thursday on Piazza delle Erbe. *Pizzeria Zi' Teresa* (*Contrà San Antonio 1*) has good pizzas from L8000, as does *Pizzeria al Pellegrino* (*Piazzale della Vittoria*).

They say the *Antica Casa della Malvasia* (*Contrà delle Morette 5*) has been around since 1200. In those days, it was the local sales point for Malvasia wine, imported from Greece by Venetian merchants. Nowadays it offers main courses for up to L13,000, accompanied by an array of 80 types of wine and 150 types of grappa!

IL VENETO

Another good destination is the *Osteria Torre Vecchia (Contrà Oratorio Servi 23)*. This elegant old house with high wood ceilings offers fine eating at a high-ish price. The *menù afrodisiaco* costs L40,000.

Entertainment

Concerts are held in summer at the Villa Valmarana ai Nani; check at the APT office for details. For information about performances in the Teatro Olimpico, contact the APT or call ☎ 0444 22 21 11.

Getting There & Around

FTV buses (☎ 0444 22 31 15) leave from the bus station, just near the train station, for Padova, Thiene, Asiago, Bassano, Verona and towns throughout the nearby Monti Berici mountains. Trains connect the city with Venezia, Milano, Padova, Verona, Treviso and smaller towns in the north. By car, the city is on the A4 connecting Milano with Venezia. The S11 connects Vicenza with Verona and Padova. There is a large car park near Piazza Castello and the train station.

The city is best seen on foot, but bus Nos 1, 2, 3 and 7 connect the train station with the city centre.

AROUND VICENZA

As Venezia's maritime power waned in the 16th century, the city's wealthy inhabitants turned their attention inland, acquiring land to build sumptuous villas (see also the Brenta Riviera section earlier in this chapter). Forbidden to build castles by the Venetian senate, which feared a landscape dotted with well-defended forts, the city's patricians set about building thousands of villas, of which about 3000 remain. Most are inaccessible to the public and many are run-down.

The APT office in Vicenza can provide reams of information about the villas, including a booklet entitled *Vicenza – the Villas*. The De Agostini map, *Ville Venete*, sells for about L8000 from newspaper stands and is one of the few complete maps. Drivers should have little trouble planning an itinerary. If you don't have a car, take the FTV bus north from Vicenza to Thiene, passing through Caldogno and Villaverla, and then continue on to Lugo.

The Villa Godi-Valmarana, now known as the **Malinverni**, at Lonedo di Lugo, was Palladio's first villa. A good driving itinerary is to take the S11 through Montecchio Maggiore and continue south for Lonigo, Pojana Maggiore and then head north for Longare and back to Vicenza. A round trip of 100km, the route takes in about a dozen villas.

A few kilometres south of Pojana Maggiore you'll find an HI youth hostel at Montagnana (see the earlier Around Padova section for details).

Check with the APT in Vicenza for details of the Concerti in Villa Estate, a series of classical concerts held in villas around Vicenza each summer. Also ask about accommodation, which is available in some villas.

VERONA

postcode 37100 • pop 250,000

Wander the quiet streets of Verona on a winter's night, and you might almost be forgiven for believing the tragic love story of Romeo and Juliet to be true. Get past the Shakespearean hyperbole, however, and you'll find plenty to keep you occupied in what is without doubt one of Italy's most beautiful cities. Known as *piccola Roma* (little Roma) for its importance in the days of the empire, Verona's truly golden era came during the 13th and 14th centuries under the della Scala family (also known as the Scaligeri). The period was noted for the savage family feuding about which Shakespeare wrote his play.

Orientation

If you count all the sprawl around it, Verona is quite spread out, but the old town is small and easy to find your way around. There is a lot to see and it is a popular base for exploring surrounding towns. Buses leave for the centre from outside the train station; otherwise walk to the right, past the bus station, cross the river and walk along Corso Porta Nuova to Piazza Brà, 15 minutes away. From the piazza, walk along Via G Mazzini and turn left at Via Cappello to reach Piazza delle Erbe.

VERONA

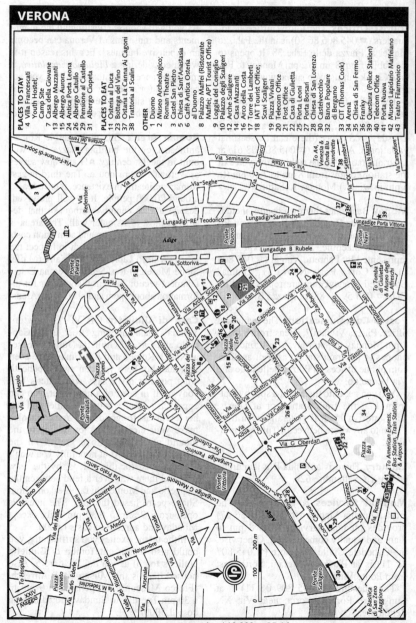

PLACES TO STAY
4 Villa Francescati
   Youth Hostel;
   Camp Site
7 Casa della Giovane
13 Albergo Mazzanti
15 Albergo Aurora
24 Antica Porta Leona
26 Albergo Catullo
29 Pensione al Castello
31 Albergo Ciopeta

PLACES TO EAT
11 Osteria al Duca
23 Bottega del Vino
33 Ostaria La Canna Ai Cagoni
38 Trattoria al Scalin

OTHER
1 Duomo
2 Museo Archeologico;
   Roman Theatre
3 Castel San Pietro
5 Chiesa di Sant'Anastasia
6 Caffè Antica Osteria
   al Duomo
8 Palazzo Maffei (Ristorante
   Maffei; APT Tourist Office)
9 Loggia del Consiglio
10 Palazzo degli Scaligeri
12 Arche Scaligere
14 Casa Mazzanti
16 Arco della Costa
17 Torre dei Lamberti
18 IAT Tourist Office;
   Scavi Scaligeri
19 Piazza Viviani
20 Telecom Office
21 Post Office
22 Casa di Giulietta
25 Porta Leoni
27 Porta Borsari
28 Chiesa di San Lorenzo
30 Castelvecchio
32 Banca Popolare
   di Bergamo
33 CIT (Thomas Cook)
34 Arena
35 Chiesa di San Fermo
36 Franky
37 Questura (Police Station)
40 Telecom Office
41 Porta Nuova
42 Museo Lapidario Maffeiano
43 Teatro Filarmonico

euro currency converter L10,000 = €5.16

Information

Tourist Offices The tourist office headquarters (☎ 045 806 86 80) is in the Palazzo Maffei at Piazza delle Erbe 38. It opens to the public from 8 am to 2 pm Monday to Friday. Check out its Web site at www.verona-apt.net.

The IAT office (☎ 045 806 86 80), in the same building as the Scavi Scaligeri on Piazza dei Signori, is open from 9 am to 7 pm Tuesday to Sunday (there can be seasonal variations). An office (☎ 045 800 08 61) at the train station (to the right before you exit the station) opens from 8 am to 7.30 pm (to 6 pm in winter) Monday to Saturday.

Money Banks dot the town centre, including the Banca Popolare di Bergamo on Piazza Brà, one of several with an automatic exchange machine. American Express is represented by Fabretto Viaggi (☎ 045 806 01 55), Corso Porta Nuova 11. Thomas Cook and MoneyGram are represented by CIT (☎ 045 59 17 88) at Piazza Brà 2.

Post & Communications The main post office, Piazza Viviani 7, opens from 8 am to 7 pm Monday to Saturday. You'll find telephones at the train station as well as Telecom phone offices on Piazza delle Erbe and Via Leoncino.

You can get onto the Net at a spot by platform 1 at the train station or at Diesis, Via Sottoriva 15. It is generally open from 11 am to anywhere between 10 pm and midnight.

Laundry There is an Onda Blu laundrette at Via XX Settembre 62a.

Medical Services & Emergency The city's Guardia Medica (☎ 045 807 56 27) provides medical services from 8 pm to 8 am and usually comes to you. Otherwise, the Ospedale Civile Maggiore (☎ 045 807 11 11) is at Piazza A Stefani, north-west from Ponte Vittoria.

The questura (☎ 045 809 06 11) is at Lungadige Porta Vittoria, near Via XX Settembre.

Things to See & Do

As you will soon see, visiting all the monuments and museums of Verona can become an expensive business. For this reason it is worth considering a *biglietto cumulativo*, a multi-entrance ticket that will give you access to all (or at least a decent selection) of sights for a single reduced price. Ask at a tourist office before bleeding in each place.

Roman Arena This pink marble Roman anfiteatro, on the bustling Piazza Brà, was built in the 1st century AD and now serves as Verona's opera house. The third-largest Roman anfiteatro in existence, it once seated around 20,000 people. It is well preserved, despite a 12th century earthquake that destroyed most of its outer wall. The arena is open from 9 am to 7 pm and admission costs L6000, or L7000 if you wish to inspect the nearby **Museo Lapidario Maffeiano** (Maffei Stone Museum) too. See the Verona Entertainment section later in this chapter for information about opera and plays at the Arena.

Casa di Giulietta Off Via G Mazzini, Verona's main shopping street, is Via Cappello and Casa di Giulietta (Juliet's house) at No 23. Romeo and Juliet may have been fictional, but here you can swoon beneath what popular myth says was Juliet's balcony or, if in need of a new lover, you can approach a bronze statue of Juliet and rub her left breast for good luck. You could also make your eternal mark by adding to the mound of scribbled love grafitti on the walls of the house (but hopefully you won't feel the need for this!). It is, by the way, doubtful there was ever a feud between the Cappello and Montecchi families, on whom Shakespeare based the play. The house is open from 9 am to 6.30 pm daily except Monday and admission costs L6000.

If the theme excites you sufficiently, you could also search out **Tomba di Giulietta** (Juliet's tomb) at Via del Pontiere 5. Also housed here is the **Museo degli Affreschi** (Fresco Museum). It opens from 9 am to 6.30 pm Tuesday to Sunday and admission costs L5000.

Piazza delle Erbe Originally the site of a Roman forum, this piazza remains the lively centre of the city today, but the permanent market stalls in its centre detract from its beauty. The square is lined with some of Verona's most sumptuous buildings, including the baroque **Palazzo Maffei**, at the northern end, with the adjoining 14th century **Torre del Gardello**. On the eastern side is **Casa Mazzanti**, a former residence of the della Scala family, identifiable by its fresco-decorated façade.

Separating Piazza delle Erbe from **Piazza dei Signori** is the **Arco della Costa**, beneath which is suspended a whale's rib. Legend says it will fall on the first 'just' person to walk beneath it. In several centuries, it has never fallen, not even on the various popes who have paraded beneath it. Ascend the nearby 12th century **Torre dei Lamberti** by lift (L4000) or on foot (L3000) for a great view of the city. It's open from 9 am to 6 pm daily.

In Piazza dei Signori, the 15th century **Loggia del Consiglio**, the former city council building, is regarded as Verona's finest Renaissance structure. It is attached to the **Palazzo degli Scaligeri**, once the main residence of the della Scala family.

Through the archway at the far end of the piazza are the **Arche Scaligere**, the elaborate tombs of the della Scala family, which unfortunately may only be viewed from outside.

In the courtyard just behind the Arche you can now see some excavation work being done on this part of Verona. You enter the **Scavi Scaligeri** through the same building as the IAT office. The excavations are not so exciting as to warrant a big detour, so to make them more attractive, the building is used to host international photographic exhibitions. It is open from 10 am to 6 pm (closed Sunday). Admission prices depend on the exhibition.

Churches North from the Arche Scaligere stands the Gothic **Chiesa di Sant'Anastasia**, started in 1290, but not completed until the late 15th century. Inside are numerous artworks, including a lovely fresco in the sacristy, by Pisanello, of *St George Setting out to Free the Princess*. The 12th century **duomo** combines Romanesque (lower section) and Gothic (upper section) styles and has some very interesting features. Look for the sculpture of Jonah and the Whale on the south porch and the statues of two of Charlemagne's paladins, Roland and Oliver, on the west porch. In the first chapel of the left aisle is an *Assumption* by Titian, in an altar frame by Jacopo Sansovino.

At the river end of Via Leoni is **Chiesa di San Fermo**, which is actually two churches: the Gothic church was built in the 13th century over the original 11th century Romanesque structure. The **Chiesa di San Lorenzo** is near the Castelvecchio and the Basilica di San Zeno Maggiore farther to the west (for more on the last of these, see later in this section).

A combined entrance ticket to all these churches costs L8000. Otherwise entrance to each church costs L3000. Opening times vary with the season. Generally the churches are open from 10 am to 1 pm and 1.30 to 4 pm Tuesday to Saturday.

Castelvecchio South-west from Piazza delle Erbe, on the banks of the Adige, is the 14th century fortress of Cangrande II (of the della Scala family). The fortress was damaged by bombing during WWII and restored in the 1960s. It now houses a museum with a diverse collection of paintings, frescoes, jewellery and medieval artefacts. Among the paintings are works by Pisanello, Giovanni Bellini, Tiepolo, Carpaccio and Veronese. Also of note is a 14th century equestrian statue of Cangrande I. The museum opens from 9 am to 6.30 pm daily except Monday and admission costs L6000. The **Ponte Scaligero**, spanning the Adige river, was rebuilt after being destroyed by WWII bombing.

Basilica di San Zeno Maggiore A masterpiece of Romanesque architecture, this basilica in honour of the city's patron saint was built mainly in the 12th century, although its apse was rebuilt in the 14th century and its bell tower, a relic of an earlier structure on the site, was started in 1045. The basilica's magnificent rose window depicts the Wheel of Fortune. Before going inside, take a look at the sculptures on either side of the main doors. The doors themselves are decorated with bronze reliefs of biblical subjects. The highlight inside is Mantegna's triptych of the *Madonna and Saints*, above the high altar. The basilica is north-west of Castelvecchio.

Across the River Across Ponte Pietra is a **Roman theatre**, built in the 1st century AD and still used today for concerts and plays. Take the lift at the back of the theatre to the convent above, which houses an interesting collection of Greek and Roman pieces in the **Museo Archeologico**. On a hill high behind the theatre and museum is the **Castel San Pietro**, built by the Austrians on the site of an earlier castle. Both the museum and theatre open from 9 am to 3 pm (closed Monday). Combined admission costs L5000.

City Gates Near the Casa di Giulietta, on Via Leoni, is the **Porta Leoni**, one of the gates to Roman Verona. The other is **Porta Borsari** at the bottom end of Corso Porta Borsari.

Places to Stay
If you are having problems finding a hotel room, you could try calling the Cooperativa Albergatori Veronesi (☎ 045 800 98 44). They start with two-star hotels and the service is free.

The beautifully restored HI youth hostel, *Villa Francescati* (☎ 045 59 03 60, Salita Fontana del Ferro 15), should be your first choice. B&B is L21,000 a night. Next door is a *camp site*. To reserve a space, speak to the hostel management. Catch bus No 73 from the train station.

Casa della Giovane (☎ 045 59 68 80, Via Pigna 7), off Via Garibaldi, is for women only and costs up to L22,000 for a bed in a triple or quad. A bed in a double or triple with bathroom costs L25,000. Catch bus No 73 and ask the driver where to get off.

About the cheapest place in a central location is *Albergo Catullo* (☎ 045 800 27 86, Via Valerio Catullo 1). Basic singles/

doubles without bathroom start at about L45,000/65,000, but can rise as high as L60,000/90,000. It also has more expensive doubles with bathroom.

Pensione al Castello (☎ 045 800 44·03, Corso Cavour 43) has rooms with bathroom for as much as L90,000/120,000. *Albergo Ciopeta* (☎ 045 800 68 43, Vicolo Teatro Filarmonico 2), near Piazza Brà, is a great little place, but you'll need to book well in advance. Its singles/doubles cost L80,000/120,000.

One of the best located hotels in the city is *Albergo Aurora* (☎ 045 59 47 17, Piazzetta XIV Novembre 2). It has singles without bathroom at L70,000, but you'll be lucky to get this price. Rooms with bathroom start at L110,000/130,000 and can rise another 40%, depending on the season.

Albergo Mazzanti (☎ 045 800 68 13, Via Mazzanti 6), just off Piazza dei Signori, is potentially a better deal. If you can get low-season prices, the rooms are small but clean and not too pricey at L47,000/67,000, or L77,000/97,000 with bathroom. Add up to 50% more in the high season. *Antica Porta Leona* (☎ 045 59 54 99, Corticella Leoni 3) is an excellent hotel, not far from the Casa di Giulietta. Its lovely rooms cost up to L180,000/250,000 in high season.

Places to Eat
Known for its fresh produce, its crisp Soave (a dry white wine) and its boiled meat, Verona offers fine eating at reasonable prices.

Osteria al Duca (Via Arche Scaligere 2), in the so-called Casa di Romeo (actually the former home of the Montecchi, one of the families on which Shakespeare's play is based), has a solid set menu for L20,000, but its reputation is greater than its cooking. More expensive but locally recommended is *Bottega del Vino* (Vicolo Scudo di Francia 3a). The frescoes alone are worth seeing. *Ristorante Maffei* (Piazza delle Erbe 38), in the Palazzo Maffei, has pasta from L16,000 and main dishes from L25,000. It also serves some vegetarian dishes.

Head east across the river for a couple of other treats. *Osteria La Canna Ai Cagoni*

(Via Scrimiari 5) offers *spadellato* (pan-sautéed pasta with various meats, cheese and *rucola*). *Trattoria al Scalin (Via San Vitale 6)* has changed hands and now offers enticing Sicilian cooking.

Entertainment
Throughout the year the city hosts musical and cultural events, culminating in the season of opera and drama from July to September at the *Arena*. Tickets cost from L28,000 to L290,000; bookings on ☎ 045 800 51 51. For more information try the Web site at www.arena.it.

There is a programme of ballet and opera in winter at the 18th century *Teatro Filarmonico (☎ 045 800 28 80, Via dei Mutilati 4)*, just south of Piazza Brà, and Shakespeare is performed at the Roman theatre in summer. Information and tickets for these events are available at the Ente Lirico Arena di Verona (☎ 045 800 51 51), Via Dietro Anfiteatro 6/8.

Caffè Antica Osteria al Duomo (Via Duomo 7) is a cosy tavern with mandolins, balalaikas and other string instruments hanging on the wall. On Wednesday and Friday you can join in for a singalong. Otherwise, just pop in for a drop of *fragolino* (sweet strawberry wine).

For a brighter, more youthful ambience, you could try *Franky (Via San Paolo 5b)*. It has a grunge feel and occasionally you can hear performances of anything from poetry to live music.

Getting There & Away
Verona-Villafranca airport (☎ 045 809 56 66) is just outside the town and accessible by bus. Flights from all over Italy and some European cities arrive here.

The main intercity bus station is in front of the train station, in an area known as Porta Nuova. Buses leave for Mantova, Ferrara, Brescia and provincial destinations. The airport bus also leaves from here.

Verona has rail links with Milano, Venezia, Padova, Mantova, Modena, Firenze, Roma, Austria and Germany and is at the intersection of the Serenissima A4 (Milano-Venezia) and Brennero A22 autostrade.

Getting Around
Bus Nos 11, 12, 13 and 72 (bus No 91 or 98 on Sunday and holidays) connect the train station with Piazza Brà, and bus No 70 with Piazza delle Erbe (tickets cost L1600). Otherwise it's a 15 to 20 minute walk along Corso Porta Nuova. Cars are banned from the city centre in the morning and early afternoon, but you will be given entry if you are staying at a hotel. Free car parks are at Via Città di Nimes (near the train station), Porta Vescovo to the east and Porta Palio to the west, from where there are buses into the city centre. For a taxi, call ☎ 045 53 26 66.

TREVISO
postcode 31100 • pop 85,000
A small, pleasant city with historical importance as a Roman centre, Treviso is worth a stopover if you are heading north for the Dolomiti. There is, however, no decent cheap accommodation in the city. If you can pay higher rates, Treviso can make a good base from which to see the smaller towns leading up into the Alpi. A prosperous town of 85,000, Treviso claims Luciano Benetton as its favourite son. The company's factories can be found around the city.

Information
The APT office (☎ 0422 54 76 32) is at Piazzetta Monte di Pietà 8, adjacent to Piazza dei Signori. It opens from 9 am to 1 pm Monday to Saturday and from 3 to 6 pm Wednesday to Saturday.

Things to See & Do
The APT promotes Treviso as the *città d'acqua* (city of water) and compares it with Venezia. While the Sile river, which weaves through the centre, is quite beautiful in parts, the city is not a patch on La Serenissima. Boat cruises on the *Silis* and *Altino* (☎ 0422 78 86 63, 0422 78 86 71) operate on the Sile between Treviso and the Venetian lagoon, but only during the summer.

The city's other claim to fame is as the *città dipinta* (frescoed city). Get a copy of *Treviso Città Dipinta* (Italian only) from the APT and follow the fresco itinerary, taking in

the **Cattedrale di San Pietro**, with frescoes by
Pordenone, the **Chiesa di San Nicolò**, with
frescoes by Tomaso da Modena, and the deconsecrated **Chiesa di Santa Caterina**, where
there is a fresco cycle by Tomaso.

Places to Stay & Eat
There's not much in the line of cheap accommodation in Treviso. You'll be looking at
around L85,000/120,000 for a single/double
room at the handful of places in central Treviso – the best choice is *Albergo alle Beccherie (☎ 0422 54 08 71, Piazza Ancilotto 8)*,
near Piazza dei Signori. It's also known as the
Campeol and has a good restaurant. *Ristorante al Dante (Piazza Garibaldi 6)* has
good budget options with pasta from L8000.

Getting There & Away
The bus station is at Lungosile Mattei, near
the train station. Lamarca Trevigiani buses
link Treviso with other towns in the
province, and ACTV buses go to Venezia.
Trains (☎ 0422 54 13 52) arrive at Piazzale
Duca d'Aosta and go to/from Venezia, Belluno, Padova and major cities to the south
and west. By car, take the S53 for Venezia
and Padova.

BELLUNO
postcode 32100 • pop 36,000
Belluno is a beautiful little town at the foot
of the Dolomiti and makes a good base for
exploring the mountains. It is worth a day
trip from Venezia, either by train or bus, and
is also easily accessible from Treviso.

The tourist office, the Azienda di Promozione Turistica delle Prealpi e Dolomiti
Bellunesi (☎ 0437 94 00 83), Via Rodolfo
Psaro 21, produces a feast of information on
walking, skiing and other sporting endeavours and should be visited if you are planning to head into the Dolomiti. The
Comunità Montana Bellunese (☎ 0437 94
02 83), Via San Lucano 7, can assist with
details on Alpine *rifugi*.

*Camping Park Nevegal (☎ 0437 90 81
43, Via Nevegal 263)*, open year-round, is
about 10km from the town at Nevegal and
reached by Autolinee Dolomiti bus from
Belluno. The nearest youth hostel is *Ostello
Imperina (☎ 0437 6 24 51)*, 35km north-
west at Rivamonte Agordino. B&B costs
L25,000 and you can get there on the
Agordo bus from Belluno. *Casa per Ferie
Giovanni XXIII (☎ 0437 94 44 60, Piazza
Piloni 11)*, near the centre of Belluno, has
singles for L39,000 and only a few doubles
for L69,000 (they will knock off about
L5000 if you stay a few nights in a row). *Albergo Taverna (☎ 0437 2 51 92, Via Cipro
7)*, has singles/doubles without bathroom
for L30,000/55,000. Most of the town's
restaurants are around the central Piazza dei
Martiri.

Autolinee Dolomiti buses (☎ 0437 94 12
37), Piazzale della Stazione, depart from
the train station on the western edge of town
for Agordo, Cortina d'Ampezzo, Feltre and
smaller towns in the hills and south of town.
Trains are less regular to northern towns but
there are services to Treviso and Venezia.

Friuli-Venezia Giulia

While the Adriatic coast is made up of little more than a series of lagoons and flat wetlands, the Friulian plains and Giulian plateaus lead up to the pine-covered Alpi in the north, bordered by the Veneto to the west, Austria to the north and Slovenia to the east.

Roman rule was followed by that of the Visigoths, Attila's Huns, the Lombards and Charlemagne's Franks. The Patriarchate of Aquileia, formed in the second half of the 10th century, unified the local church and remained autonomous for several centuries.

Parts of Friuli went to Venezia in 1420 but the easternmost area, including Gorizia, was only briefly touched by its influence. By 1797 the whole region was under the control of Habsburg Austria. Most of Friuli joined Italy in 1866 but it was not until after WWI that Gorizia, Trieste (in a roughly defined area known as the Giulia), Istria and Dalmatia were included – and at what cost. The Latin-Germanic-Slav triangle found its bloodiest expression in the trenches of WWI: Italy's 700,000 dead came from as far afield as Sardegna and Sicilia, but a great many of them fell in what would subsequently become Friuli-Venezia Giulia.

After WWII Italy kept Trieste but was obliged to cede Dalmatia and the Istrian peninsula to Tito's Yugoslavia in 1947. The Iron Curtain passed right through the frontier town of Gorizia. Today, road signs in the area around the town are in Italian and Slovene and you can still stumble across the occasional Slovene monument to Yugoslav partisans along the back lanes of the province. The Slovene community is strong but feels, not without reason, that Roma pays little heed to its needs – for years there has been talk of bilingual education for Italian Slovenes, with little or no result.

Relations between Italy and Slovenia are cordial at best. Each side is critical of the other's treatment of their respective Slovene and Italian minorities. Italy is also miffed that its eastern neighbour tends to turn north to-

Highlights

- Tuck into a buffet lunch in Trieste and follow with a lingering afternoon coffee at Caffè San Marco
- Visit the fine Romanesque basilica at Aquileia
- Behold the Lombard artwork in the pretty town of Cividale del Friuli
- Get away for some skiing and walking in the northern Alpi Carniche

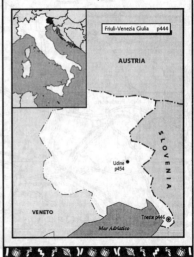

wards Austria and Germany in order to expand trade rather than looking towards Roma.

West from the frontier, the road signs are in Italian and Friulian. Udine bears the marks of Venetian intervention, with Trieste largely a neoclassical creation of Habsburg Austria.

The region is relatively unexplored and its cities and towns are worth a few days of your time. You can mix urban culture with nature by heading for the Adriatic beaches, northern ski slopes or forest walking tracks.

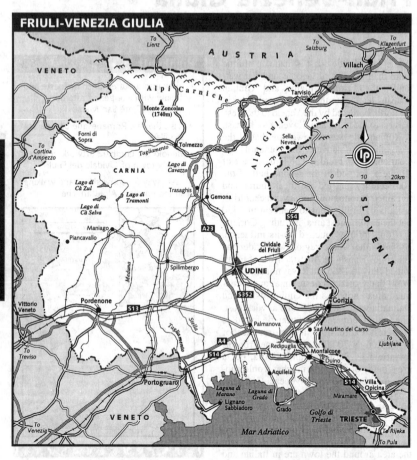

TRIESTE
postcode 34100 • pop 238,000

Sitting snugly between Mar Adriatico and Slovenia, Trieste is an odd city. The faded grandeur of its largely homogenous architecture is owed entirely to its days as the great southern port of the Austro-Hungarian Empire during the 18th and 19th centuries. The city is a kind of microcosm of one of Western Europe's major preoccupations – migrant pressure from east and south. What could be more incongruous, or more eloquent, than the sight of Croatian shoppers (bus and carloads flock to Trieste daily) bargaining fiercely with illegal African immigrants hawking their wares in the streets?

Strangely attractive, although hardly strong on specific tourist sights, Trieste is not a bad place to end an Italian tour and embark on a foray into Slovenia and Croatia. The city, including many restaurants and hotels, closes down almost completely in August.

History

Known in antiquity as Tergeste, the fortified settlement was occupied by a succession of Venetian tribes, Gauls and Celts. The city became prominent under the Roman Empire in the 2nd century BC, but when Aquileia was founded to the west, Trieste fell into an obscurity that was to last until the 18th century.

The Austrian empress Maria Theresa then saw its potential as a port. As the city developed, much of its medieval heart was levelled to make way for a new layer of neoclassical buildings. When Trieste became part of Italy in 1918, the government found the city no match for ports to the south, and once again it fell into decline.

Known as Trst to the Slavs, the city has often been a bone of contention. The poet and ultra-nationalist Gabriele d'Annunzio launched some of his madcap escapades into Yugoslavia from this city after WWI, and in 1945 the Allies occupied Trieste pending settlement of Italy's border disputes with Belgrade. They remained here until 1954. Today, traffic through the port is growing, although its main purpose is as an unloading point for the massive oil tankers supplying a pipeline to Austria.

Orientation

The train and bus stations are at the northern edge of Trieste's historic centre, on Piazza della Libertà. Head south along any main street and you'll be in the grid of the 18th century Borgo Teresiano, home to several budget hotels, as well as plenty of bars and restaurants. South of the Borgo Teresiano (about a 20 minute walk from the train station) is the hilltop Castello di San Giusto. The town's main museums are a little farther to the south-west, while the principal shopping boulevards stretch east off Via Giosue Carducci.

Information

Tourist Offices The APT office (☎ 040 42 01 82) at Stazione Centrale is open from 9 am to 7 pm Monday to Friday and to 2 pm on Saturday. Check out its Web site at www.fvgpromo.it (Italian only).

Money Branches of the Banca Nazionale del Lavoro have ATMs that accept Visa. There are currency exchange booths (open from 9 am to 7 pm daily) at the train and bus stations and at the ferry terminal, Stazione Marittima.

Post & Communications The main post office is on Piazza Vittorio Veneto. It is open from 8 am to 7 pm Monday to Saturday. Unstaffed Telecom offices at Stazione Centrale and Piazza Nicolò Tommaseo 4b are open from 7 am to 10 pm daily.

Travel Agencies Staff at CTS (☎ 040 36 18 79), Piazza Dalmazia 3b, can advise on travel in the Balkans.

Medical Services & Emergency The Ospedale Maggiore (hospital; ☎ 040 399 11 11) is on Piazza dell'Ospedale, south-east of Via Giosue Carducci. The questura (police station; ☎ 040 37 901) is at Via Tor Bandena 6.

Colle di San Giusto

With commanding views across the city and sea, this hill is topped by a rambling 15th century **castello**, largely built over earlier fortifications by the city's Venetian rulers from 1470 onwards. Apart from wandering around the walls, you can visit the **museum**, which houses a small collection of arms and period paraphernalia. The castle is open from 9 am to sunset and admission costs L2000. The museum is open from 9 am to 1 pm Tuesday to Sunday and admission costs L3000.

The **Basilica di San Giusto**, completed in 1400, is the synthesis of two earlier Christian basilicas and blends northern Adriatic and Byzantine styles. The interior contains 14th century frescoes depicting San Justus, the town's patron saint. Down the road a little, the **Civico Museo di Storia ed Arte** has religious artefacts and Egyptian oddments, and opens from 9 am to 1 pm daily except Monday (to 7 pm on Wednesday). Admission costs L3000. The **Orto Lapidario** (Stone Garden), behind the museum, has a collection of bits of classical statues and pottery.

FRIULI-VENEZIA GIULIA

FRIULI-VENEZIA GIULIA

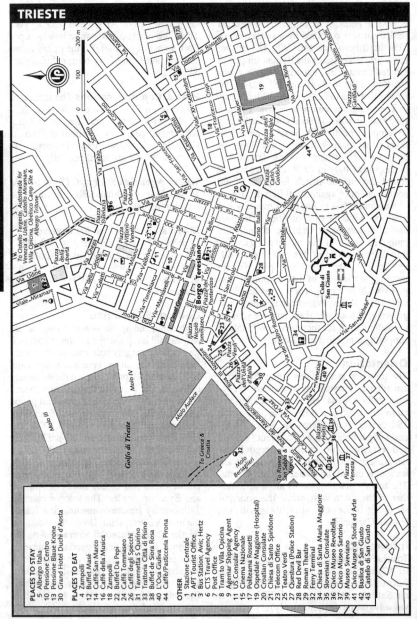

TRIESTE

PLACES TO STAY
5 Albergo Italia
10 Pensione Centro
13 Pensione Blaue Krone
30 Grand Hotel Duchi d'Aosta

PLACES TO EAT
4 Zampolli
12 Buffet Masé
14 Caffè San Marco
16 Caffè della Musica
18 Zampolli
22 Buffet Da Pepi
24 Caffè Tommaseo
26 Caffè degli Specchi
31 Tavernetta S Quirino
33 Trattoria Città di Pisino
38 Buffet de Siora Rosa
40 L'Oca Giuliva
44 Caffè/Pasticceria Pirona

OTHER
1 Stazione Centrale
2 APT Tourist Office
3 Bus Station; Avis; Hertz
6 CTS Travel Agency
7 Post Office
8 Tram to Villa Opicina
9 Agemar Shipping Agent
11 US Consular Agency
15 Cinema Nazionale
17 Politeama Rossetti
19 Ospedale Maggiore (Hospital)
20 Croatian Consulate
21 Chiesa di Santo Spiridone
23 Telecom Office
25 Teatro Verdi
27 Questura (Police Station)
28 Red Devil Bar
29 Roman Theatre
32 Ferry Terminal
34 Chiesa di Santa Maria Maggiore
35 Slovenian Consulate
36 Civico Museo Revoltella
37 Civico Museo Sartorio
39 Museo Sveviano
41 Civico Museo di Storia ed Arte
42 Basilica di San Giusto
43 Castello di San Giusto

To get there bus No 24 leaves from Stazione Centrale. Otherwise, you could walk up from the waterfront area, taking Via F Venezian, Via San Michele and Via San Giusto. Car access is by Via Capitolina.

Around Borgo Teresiano

Going back down Via Capitolina you will come to Corso Italia, the main business thoroughfare. The area of straight boulevards to the north, known as the Borgo Teresiano, was designed by Austrian urban planners in the 18th century for Empress Maria Theresa. The rather pathetic-looking **Canal Grande** that runs through this area marks the northern end of the harbour. The Serbian Orthodox **Chiesa di Santo Spiridone**, on the street of the same name, was completed in 1868 and sports some glittering mosaics.

At its southern end, Corso Italia spills into the grand **Piazza dell'Unità d'Italia**, which is bordered by the most elegant buildings, the results of Austrian town-planning efforts.

Farther in from the waterfront, and also accessible off Corso Italia, is Via del Teatro Romano. Built under Emperor Trajan and only rediscovered in 1938, the **Roman theatre** is today largely overgrown and in poor condition. The nearby baroque **Chiesa di Santa Maria Maggiore** is one of Trieste's finest churches.

Risiera di San Sabba

This was once a rice-husking plant at the southern end of Trieste on Via Valmaura. In 1943 the Germans (with local Fascist help) built a crematorium here and turned it into Italy's only extermination camp. It is believed 20,000 people perished here, including 5000 of Trieste's 6000 Jews. Yugoslav partisans closed it when they liberated the city in 1945 and 20 years later it became a national monument and museum. It is open from 9 am to 1 pm Tuesday to Sunday. You can get there by bus No 10.

Museums

The city's chief museum, the **Civico Museo Revoltella**, Via A Diaz 27, is a worthwhile art gallery. It is open from 9 am to 7 pm daily except Tuesday (it opens until midnight from July to September). Admission costs L5000.

Nearby, the **Civico Museo Sartorio**, Largo Papa Giovanni XXIII, contains an assortment of 19th century furnishings and decorative art. It is open from 9 am to 1 pm daily except Monday and Sunday and admission costs L4000.

Fans of Trieste's rather lugubrious literary figure, Italo Svevo, might like to visit the **Museo Sveviano** at Piazza Hortis 4. It opens from 10 am to noon daily.

Activities

The APT runs a walking tour of the town each Sunday morning. There is a minimum of five people and the guides speak several languages; the tour must be booked on ☎/fax 040 36 62 80. A tour with a slightly different route takes place on Saturday afternoon from February to December. Each walk costs L10,000 per person.

Places to Stay

Finding a room is generally easy, although in August many hotels close. The cheaper places can fill with Croatians in town on shopping sprees. Ask at the APT about 'T For You', a weekend discount deal involving some of the city's better hotels.

The closest camp site to the city centre is *Obelisco* (☎ 040 21 16 55, Strada Nuova per Opicina 47) in Villa Opicina. Take tram No 2 or bus No 4 from Piazza Oberdan. The HI *Ostello Tergeste* (☎/fax 040 22 41 02, Viale Miramare 331) is 5km from the train and bus stations towards Venezia and can be reached by bus No 36. B&B costs L20,000 and it is open year-round.

Pensione Centro (☎ 040 63 44 08, Via Roma 13), has singles/doubles from L40,000/70,000. *Pensione Blaue Krone* (☎ 040 63 18 82, Via XXX Ottobre 12) offers simple rooms starting at L40,000/60,000.

Albergo Italia (☎ 040 36 99 00, Via della Geppa 15) has rooms from L115,000/155,000. If you'd prefer to be by the seaside,

Albergo Tritone (☎ 040 42 28 11, Viale Miramare 133) is a worthwhile choice on the road to the Castello Miramare (bus No 36). Rooms with bath, TV and phone are priced at L100,000/155,000.

To do it in style, try *Grand Hotel Duchi d'Aosta (☎ 040 760 00 11, fax 040 36 60 92, Piazza dell'Unità d'Italia 2).*

Places to Eat

Friulian cuisine has been influenced by many cultures but poverty has contributed the most. One typical dish, *brovada*, could see you eating turnips fermented with the dregs of pressed grapes. Otherwise *gnocchi* (potato, pumpkin or bread dumplings) are popular, as are *polenta* and *bolliti* (boiled meats), eaten in restaurants called *buffets*. They, and the many sausages you can munch on, traditionally come with *cren*, a rather strong horseradish. Wines from the eastern hills of Friuli, stretching from near the city on the Slovene border up into the Alpi, are considered the region's best. Finish dinner with a *resentin*, coffee in a cup rinsed with grappa.

Restaurants If you're in the castello area, head for *L'Oca Giuliva (Via F Venezian 27)*, where L25,000 should ensure a good sample of this place's inventive cuisine – ever tried strudel with goose breast?

Closer to Piazza dell'Unità d'Italia, *Tavernetta S Quirino (Via A Diaz 3b)* has something of the atmosphere of a small English pub and specialises in meat fillets and veal. A meal will cost around L35,000. The surrounding area is traditional fishers' territory, as some of the street names suggest. Try *Trattoria Città di Pisino (Via Alberto Boccardi 7c)* for fish.

One of Trieste's best restaurants is *Antica Trattoria Suban (☎ 040 5 43 68, Via Comic 2)*, in business since 1865. Take bus No 6 from the Stazione Centrale and expect to pay around L40,000 a head.

Buffets About the most authentic buffet in town is *Buffet Da Pepi (Via Cassa di Risparmio 3b)*. Another with a deliberately Germanic ambience is *Buffet Masé (Via*

Valdirivo 32), where you can wash down a plate of German sausage with a huge mug of Munich lager – perfect on a freezing winter night. A wonderful place for a quick lunch (open daily except Saturday) is *Buffet da Siora Rosa (Piazza Hortis 3)*. Try the giant gnocchi or the *involtini* – light pastry filled with ham and several melted cheeses.

Cafés & Bars Triestini take coffee seriously. The elegant *Caffè San Marco (Via Cesare Battisti 18)*, rebuilt after WWI, is by far the most atmospheric – a favourite with students, chess players, newspaper readers and anyone in the mood for Austrian-style *kaffeeklatsch* (gossiping with friends over coffee).

Others of the same ilk that have lost a little charm through refurbishing include *Caffè Tommaseo (Riva III Novembre)* and *Caffè degli Specchi (Piazza dell'Unità d'Italia 7)*. Another pleasant stop is *Caffè della Musica (Via Domenico Rossetti)*, while James Joyce used to seek inspiration in *Caffè/Pasticceria Pirona (Largo Barriera Vecchia 12)*.

For *gelati*, you can't go past *Zampolli (Viale XX Settembre 25)*, which turns out ice-cream creations shaped like pasta and meat dishes. They look bad but taste great. There's another outlet at Via Ghega 10.

Entertainment

Teatro Verdi (☎ 040 672 21 11, Piazza Verdi 1) is the main venue for the city's opera, while *Politeama Rossetti (☎ 040 56 72 01, Viale XX Settembre 45)* is the principal stage for drama. To taste the Slovene side of Trieste's cultural life, see what's on at *Teatro Sloveno* or Kulturni Dom in Slovenian *(Via Petronio 4)*.

For some live rock music, check out *Red Devil* bar *(Via Donota 4)*.

Getting There & Away

Air Some international flights and domestic flights to Roma, Genova and southern Italy land at Ronchi dei Legionari international airport *(☎ 0481 77 32 25)* on Via Aquileia.

Bus All national and international buses operate from the bus station on Piazza della

Libertà. Autolinee Triestine (☎ 040 42 50 20) and Saita (☎ 040 42 50 01) operate services to Udine, Gorizia, Duino, Cividale del Friuli, Venezia, Genova and destinations in Slovenia and Croatia.

Train The Stazione Centrale (☎ 147 8 80 88) on Piazza della Libertà serves trains to Gorizia, Udine, Pordenone, Venezia and main cities to the west and in the south. There are regular trains to Zagreb (Croatia) and less regular trains to Budapest (Hungary) and Slovenia.

Car & Motorcycle Trieste is at the end of the A4 (to Venezia and Milano) and connects with the A23 to Austria. The S14 follows the coast and connects the city with Venezia; it continues into Slovenia, as does the S15. Avis (☎ 040 42 15 21) and Hertz (☎ 040 42 21 22) have offices at the bus station.

Boat Agemar Shipping Agent (☎ 040 36 32 22), Via Rossini 2, is a good place to inquire about ferries to Greece, Croatia and Albania. Anek Lines (☎ 040 322 05 61) runs a summer service to Patras, Igoumenitsa and Corfu, leaving up to four times a week in the high season. From May to the end of September, Adriatica runs motorboats to Lignano and Grado, and on to various points along the Istrian coast in Slovenia and Croatia. Albania was out of the question at the time of writing.

Getting Around

A bus runs from the bus station on Piazza della Libertà to the airport at regular intervals.

ACT operates buses throughout the city. Bus No 30 connects Stazione Centrale with Via Roma and the waterfront, while Bus No 24 goes to the Castello di San Giusto. There are services to Miramare (No 36) and Villa Opicina (tram No 2 or bus No 4).

Taxi Radio Trieste (☎ 040 30 77 30) operates round the clock.

AROUND TRIESTE

About 7km north-west of Trieste is the **Castello Miramare**, a grand, white castle set in fine gardens overlooking the coastline.

Archduke Maximilian of Austria had it built in the mid-19th century, but he never occupied it. After a brief stint as emperor of Mexico for Napoleon III, he was executed by the Mexicans in 1867. His widow Carlotta, who remained at the castle, went mad and it was subsequently rumoured that anyone spending a night at Miramare would come to a bad end. In summer you can see a *suoni e lumi* (sound and light) show recreating all of these events. Take bus No 36 from Trieste or the train. It's open from 9 am to 6 pm daily (4 pm in winter) and admission costs L8000.

Villa Opicina, 5km north of Trieste, boasts the **Grotta Gigante**, the world's largest accessible cave. The interior is spotlit with coloured globes and the 90m-high cavern is worth the effort. Take the Villa Opicina tram No 2 from Piazza Oberdan to Villa Opicina and then the No 45 bus. Opening hours are from 9 am to noon and 2 to 7 pm in summer with reduced hours in winter. Admission costs L13,000.

If you reached Opicina in your own transport, consider heading 5km over the Slovenian border to **Lipica**, the home of Austria's legendary white Spanish thoroughbreds, or Lipizzaners, since 1580. The stud farm opens to visitors from May to September. You can see performances by the four-legged stars on Tuesday and Friday afternoons in July and August.

Several monuments to soldiers who died in WWI were built in Il Carso (Carso Heights) during the 1930s. The **Redipuglia memorial** contains the remains of 100,000 dead and is as sobering a reminder of the idiocy of war as any of the WWI monuments littered across Europe. There is a museum and, a couple of kilometres north, an Austro-Hungarian war cemetery. The area is sprinkled with other monuments, including one on **Monte di San Michele**, the scene of particularly bloody encounters (you can wander through the battlefield today), and the **Sacrario di Olsavia**, north of Gorizia. Redipuglia can be reached by bus or train from Trieste. Your own transport is the best bet for the other sites, which are of less interest.

FRIULI-VENEZIA GIULIA

GORIZIA
postcode 34170 • pop 39,200

That strangely un-Italian feeling you may have picked up elsewhere in Friuli-Venezia Giulia is no more evident than in Gorizia – right on the frontier of the Latin and Slav worlds, with a long history of Germanic/Austrian tutelage. Most locals speak Italian and Slovenian and many road signs are in both languages. Austrian-style café culture (lots of rustling newspapers) rules and not a few of the GO number plates are from Nova Gorica, that post-WWII creation over the border. Only a short train or bus ride from Trieste or Udine, Gorizia is an interesting and quirky place and a stop worth making. The Colleo area surrounding the town produces some of Italy's finest white wines.

History

Settled before the arrival of the Romans, the hilltop castle and surrounding town were always on the periphery of someone else's empire – Roman, Holy Roman and, from the early 16th century, that of the Austrian Habsburgs (to whom it became known as the Nice of the Empire). Apart from a brief spell under Venezia, Gorizia first came under Italian control after WWI. In the wake of the following world war, Italy and Yugoslavia finally agreed to draw a line through the city in 1947, leaving most of the old city in Italian hands, and spurring Tito's followers to erect the soulless Nova Gorica on the other side.

Orientation & Information

The bus station is on Via IX Agosto, off Corso Italia, while the train station is about a kilometre south-west of the centre on Piazzale Martiri Libertà d'Italia, at the end of Corso Italia.

The helpful APT (☎ 0481 38 62 24/25) is at Via Roma 9, on the 1st floor of the government building. The main post office is on the corner of Corso Verdi and Via Oberdan.

Borgo Castello

Gorizia's main sight is its castle, the original nucleus of the town. It has undergone sev-

The Rout of Caporetto

The wanton spilling of young blood in the fight for centimetres of ground during WWI was not restricted to the killing fields of France and Russia. From May 1915, Italy decided to join the massacre, in the hope of ending the campaign for independence begun the century before by booting Austria off 'Italian' soil. The price of this folly, to a nation barely 50 years old, was 700,000 dead and more than a million wounded.

The main Italian front stretched from the Alpi to the Mar Adriatico through Friuli and the Giulia, and Italy made substantial gains in its first offensive – approaching Gorizia (which did not fall until the following year) and advancing as far as Caporetto in the north (in modern Slovenia).

From then on, typical trench warfare set in, with neither side making much progress. Some of the toughest fighting took place on the Carso Heights between Trieste and Gorizia, and the Isonzo river soon became to the Italians what the Somme was to the Allies in France.

In October 1917, disaster struck when the Austro-Hungarians (with the decisive aid of crack German units) crushed the Italians at Caporetto, pretty much throwing them back to their 1915 starting lines, where they hung on grimly until the collapse of the Central Powers the following year. Italians don't meet their Waterloo, they 'have a Caporetto'.

eral transformations and was restored in the 1920s after suffering serious damage in WWI. It makes a pleasant enough excursion and occasional exhibitions are held there. It is open from 9.30 am to 1 pm and from 3 to 7.30 pm Tuesday to Sunday. Admission costs L6000.

There is a small **war museum** about 50m away downhill, but you will need Italian to benefit from the explanations. It opens from 10 am to 7 pm Tuesday to Sunday (6 pm in winter). Admission costs L6000.

Churches

The most outstanding of Gorizia's churches is **Sant'Ignazio** on Piazza della Vittoria. You can't miss the onion-shaped domes – another sign that you're in *Mitteleuropa*. The little 14th century **Chiesa di Santo Spirito**, by the castle, is also worth a quick look. Perhaps more interesting is the 18th century **synagogue**, Via Ascoli 19 – ask at the tourist office about visiting times.

Nova Gorica

It's a hoot to hop across into Slovenia for a brief look at the post-Tito republic. There's nothing much to see, but the difference between the two places has its own fascination, and you may want to visit the **Kostanjevica monastery**, the burial place of the last of the French branch of the Bourbon royal family. You can walk or drive across at two points – formalities are minimal, but have your passport handy (visitors who would usually need visas for Slovenia will need them here).

Places to Stay & Eat

Locanda da Sandro (☎ 0481 53 32 23, *Via Santa Chiara 18)* has good singles/doubles with bathroom for L58,000/85,000. There are a couple of fine *trattorie* scattered about the centre of the old town below the castle.

Getting There & Away

Trains and buses connect with Trieste and Udine. Buses also run to Nova Gorica, from where you can get buses all over Slovenia.

AQUILEIA

postcode 33051 • pop 3400

Once the fourth city of the Roman Empire, Aquileia was founded in 181 BC. Dubbed the Seconda Roma (Second Rome) within 100 years, the city was a major trading link between the imperial capital and the East. By the beginning of the Christian era, Aquileia was the richest market town in Italy and subordinate only to Roma, Milano and Capua. A patriarchate was founded here as early as the 4th century AD and, in spite of repeated assaults by Huns, Lombards and others, Aquileia's religious importance ensured it a privileged position until as late as the 14th century. The 4th century mosaics in the town's Romanesque basilica are quite extraordinary.

What is now a small town lies at the eastern end of the Venetian plains, and the local dialect is a good measure of the influence that the expanding Venetian republic had on Aquileia.

Information

The APT office (☎ 0431 91 94 91), Piazza Capitolo 4, opens daily from 1 April to 1 November.

Things to See & Do

Head straight for the **basilica**, largely rebuilt after the 1348 earthquake. The long-hidden floor of the basilica's 4th century predecessor is a precious and rare pictorial document of Christianity's early days, made up of mosaics depicting episodes in Christ's life, Roman notables and animal scenes. The basilica is open from 8.30 am to 7 pm daily in summer; from 9 am to 12.30 pm and 2.30 to 5 pm in winter. Don't miss out on the two crypts. The Cripta degli Affreschi (near the altar; L1500) boasts some marvellously preserved 12th century frescoes, while the Cripta degli Scavi (closed at time of writing; L1500) reveals the floor mosaics of the 4th century church. The bell tower, erected in 1030, was still closed for restoration at the time of writing.

Scattered remnants of the **Roman town** include ruins of the one-time *porto fluviale* (river port), forum, houses and markets. You can also visit a couple of archaeological museums.

Visit the **Bottega della Grappa** (☎ 0431 9 10 91), Via Julia Augusta 87a, where you can sample local products (for free), and view the making of grappa. You can also visit the Ca' Tullio winery (☎ 0431 91 97 00), Via Beligna 41.

Places to Stay

Camping Aquileia (☎ 0431 9 10 42, *Via Gemina 10)* is the most affordable camp site, open from mid-May to mid-September. The *Albergo Aquila Nera* (☎ 0431 9 10 45,

Piazza Garibaldi 5) has singles/doubles starting from L40,000/60,000 in the low season.

Getting There & Away

Aquileia is a short trip from Trieste and Udine, and regular buses from both cities call in on the way to Grado. The S352 road heads north towards Udine and south to Grado.

PALMANOVA

If you flew over it you'd see what makes this town so special. Venezia built it 10km north of Aquileia as a fortress in the form of a nine-pointed star in 1593. Later Napoleon and the Austrians made use of it and to this day the Italian army maintains a garrison here. Unfortunately the town itself has lost much of its charm – even the hexagonal Piazza Grande has been shorn of its trees by some town-planning bright spark. A few locals are lobbying to have decades of growth peeled back from the defensive walls, the town's real attraction. One day they might just manage it. Meanwhile you can visit a military museum, including some outer defences erected by Napoleon. It's an easy bus ride from Udine.

GRADO

About 14km south of Aquileia, Grado is a not unpleasant Adriatic beach resort, spread along a narrow island backed by lagoons. The small medieval centre, criss-crossed by narrow *calli* (lanes), is a bright spot dominated by a Romanesque **basilica** and surrounded by cheery, tumbledown houses.

The APT office (☎ 0431 89 91) is at Viale Dante Alighieri 72. Grado is a day trip by bus from Udine or Trieste, but if you want to stay in summer, book ahead. There are several camp sites and about 90 hotels, many of which close in winter. *Albergo Zuberti (☎ 0431 8 01 96, Piazza Carpaccio 25)* is one of the cheapest year-round hotels. Rooms start at L45,000/75,000 in the low season.

LIGNANO

The Lignano area is pure resort, dispensing with the trappings of old town centres. Lying on the tip of a peninsula facing Laguna di Marano to the north and Mar Adriatico to the south, **Lignano Sabbiadoro** is the main town. The water here and in the neighbouring resorts is about all there is of any interest. Staff at the APT office (☎ 0431 7 18 21), Via Latisana 42 at Lignano Sabbiadoro, can assist with hotels and camp sites.

UDINE

postcode 33100 • pop 99,000

The region's second-largest city, Udine's topsy-turvy history has left it heir to an oddly mixed Italian, Slavic and Germanic culture. The city lies at the heart of Friuli, and as some inhabitants still speak the local dialect, the town authorities have put up street names in dialect next to the official Italian signs.

The Romans founded Udine as a way-station. By the early 15th century, when it first came under Venetian control, Udine had grown into a substantial city to rival nearby Cividale del Friuli and Aquileia. It is the Venetian influence that most strikes the eye in the town's bright medieval centre. Napoleon's lieutenants briefly took control at the beginning of the 19th century, followed by the Austrians until 1866, when the city joined the Italian kingdom. Udine survived WWII intact, but an earthquake in 1976 caused heavy damage and cost hundreds of lives. The great Renaissance painter Giambattista Tiepolo lived here for many years, leaving a number of works behind, notably in the duomo.

Orientation

The train station is on Viale Europa Unita at the southern edge of the old city centre. The bus station is opposite the train station, slightly to the east. Walk along Via Roma, through Piazza Repubblica and along Via Carducci for the duomo. An alternative route from Piazza Repubblica is to veer north-west along Via Dante and continue to Piazza della Libertà. The massive Piazza I Maggio is to the north-east.

Information

Tourist Offices The APT office (☎ 0432 29 59 72), Piazza I Maggio 7, is open from 9 am to 1 pm and 3 to 5 pm Monday to Friday. It has loads of information on the city and the rest of the region.

Money The central Banca Commerciale Italiana is on Piazza del Duomo, and there are plenty of other banks scattered through the city centre.

Post & Communications The main post office is at Via Vittorio Veneto 42 and is open from 8.15 am to 7.30 pm Monday to Saturday.

The Telecom office is at Via Savorgnana 15. It is open from 7 am to 10 pm daily.

Medical Services & Emergency For medical attention, go to the Ospedale Civile (☎ 0432 55 21), north of the city centre in Piazza Santa Maria della Misericordia. The questura (☎ 0432 59 41) is at Via D Prefettura 16.

Piazza della Libertà
A gem of the Renaissance, Piazza della Libertà lies at the heart of the old town, and

NICKY CAVEN

Every hour two Moorish figures strike the bell atop the Loggia di San Giovanni.

most sights of historical interest are clustered on or near it.

The 15th century Palazzo del Comune (town hall), also known as the **Loggia del Lionello** after its architect, is a clear reminder of Venetian influence, as is the **Loggia di San Giovanni** opposite, which features a clock with Moorish figures that strike the hours – similar to the Mori of Venezia's Torre dell'Orologio.

Castello
The **Arco Bollani** next to the Loggia di San Giovanni was designed by Palladio in 1556 and leads up to the castello, which was used by the Venetian governors. It now houses the **Galleria d'Arte Antica**, whose extensive collection includes works by Caravaggio, Carpaccio and Tiepolo. The complex includes the **Museo Archeologico** and is open from 9.30 am to 12.30 pm and 3 to 6 pm Tuesday to Sunday (closed Sunday afternoon); admission costs L4000. Also on the hill is the 12th century **Chiesa di Santa Maria del Castello**, which originally stood within the walls of the medieval castle.

Around the Duomo
If you head south down Via Vittorio Veneto from Piazza della Libertà you'll reach the Piazza del Duomo and also the 13th century Romanesque-Gothic **duomo**, with several frescoes by Tiepolo. The **Museo del Duomo**, in the *campanile*, contains frescoes by Viale da Bologna but remains closed. South across the street from the duomo is the **Oratorio della Purità**, with a beautiful ceiling painting of the *Assumption* by Tiepolo (under restoration at the time of writing). You can visit the duomo from 7 am to noon and 4 to 8 pm daily. Ask in the duomo if you can get access to the Oratorio.

North-east of Piazza del Duomo is the **Palazzo Arcivescovile** (Archbishop's Palace) on Piazza Patriarcato, where Tiepolo completed a remarkable series of frescoes depicting Old Testament scenes. The palace is open from 10 am to noon and 3.30 to 6.30 pm Wednesday to Sunday. Admission is L7000.

South of Piazza del Duomo on Via B

FRIULI-VENEZIA GIULIA

UDINE

PLACES TO STAY	10	Caffè Delser	4	Castello; Museo Archeologico;	16	Pinocchio
2 Albergo Clocchiatti	15	Pasticceria Carli		Galleria d'Arte Antica	17	Taverna dell'Angelo
25 Albergo Al Vecchio Tram		di L Fogoletto	5	I Piombi	18	Palazzo Arcivescovile
29 Hotel Principe	21	Enoteca Aquila Nera	6	Loggia di San Giovanni	19	Questura (Police Station)
31 Pensione Al Fari	26	Spaghetteria da Ciccio	7	Loggia del Lionello	20	Main Post Office
32 Albergo da Brando	27	All'Allegria	11	Cinema Puccini	22	The Black Stuff (Irish Pub)
			12	Banca Commerciale	23	Chiesa di San Francesco
PLACES TO EAT	OTHER			Italiana	24	Telecom Office
8 Caffè Contarena	1	Galleria d'Arte Moderna	13	Duomo	28	Bus Station
9 Trattoria al Lepre	3	APT Tourist Office	14	Oratorio della Purità	30	Train Station

Odorico is the 13th century **Chiesa di San Francesco**. Although once one of Udine's most striking churches, it is now used as a gallery. A tiny ice-skating rink is erected in the square in front of the church in winter.

Galleria d'Arte Moderna

The Galleria d'Arte Moderna, Piazzale P Diacono 22, features a wide selection of well known 20th century art and also displays works by modern Friulian artists. It opens from 9.30 am to 12.30 pm and 3 to 6 pm; it is free on Sunday morning but closed Sunday afternoon and all day Monday. Admission costs L4000.

Places to Stay

Udine has no youth hostel or camp site, and rooms in many cheap hotels are taken by workers. A map outside the train station pinpoints all hotels. *Albergo da Brando* (☎ 0432 50 28 37, Piazzale Cella 16), west of the station, is the cheapest, charging L25,000 per person. *Albergo Al Vecchio Tram* (☎ 0432 50 25 16, Via Brenari 32), near Piazza Garibaldi, has decent, if slightly malodorous, singles/doubles from L35,000/58,000.

Pensione Al Fari (☎ 0432 52 07 32, Via Melegnano 41), south of the train station, is more comfortable but in something of a residential backwater. Singles/doubles/triples range up to L42,000/66,000/69,000. *Albergo Clocchiatti* (☎ 0432 50 50 47, Via Cividale 29) is east of the city centre and charges from L50,000/80,000 to an exorbitant L80,000/140,000.

If they are charging the latter, you may as well stay at *Hotel Principe* (☎ 0432 50 60 00, Viale Europa Unita 51), which has rooms for up to L100,000/160,000.

Places to Eat

Don't wait too late to eat out, as the city is generally pretty quiet by 10 pm, especially during the week – no Latin excitement in the streets here.

Via Grazzano is not a bad place to look. *Spaghetteria da Ciccio* at No 18 does cheap, filling meals in a cosy atmosphere. *All'Allegria*, at No 11, stays open compara-

tively late and serves quality local cuisine – any place that can make peas taste good is worthy of admiration. Count on spending about L40,000 a head.

Otherwise, *Enoteca Aquila Nera*, on the corner of Via Vittoria Veneto and Via Piave, has first courses for L5000 and seconds for L6500 until midnight – you can wash the food down with a broad selection of wine. A good option is *Trattoria al Lepre (Via Poscolle 29b)*. Try the home-made *tagliatelle ai funghi* (pasta with mushrooms).

The tea-and-cake crowd hangs out at *Caffè Contarena (Via Cavour 1a)*. For an Austrian-style atmosphere and a good read of the newspaper day or night, head for *Caffè Delser (Via Cavour 18a)*. The Germanic influence is clearly visible in the city's sweets; for great cakes and a coffee, try *Pasticceria Carli di L Fogoletto (Via Vittorio Veneto 36)*, in a building dating from 1392.

Entertainment

An army of Udine's youth, and a fair sprinkling of those more advanced in years, meets nightly until 3 am for a pint or six at *The Black Stuff* Irish pub *(Via Gorghi 3)*. Alternatively, head downstairs at *I Piombi (Via Manin 12)* for a wide range of Euro beers and snacks (*focaccia* and pizza). Hipper still is *Pinocchio (Via Lovaria 3a)*, a sprawling bar with low lights and thumping music. A couple of doors down is the characterful *Taverna dell'Angelo (Via Lovaria 3c)*.

Getting There & Away

All buses leave from the bus station (☎ 0432 50 69 41). Ferrari (☎ 0432 50 40 12) operates services to smaller towns in the north of the region and to Trieste and Lignano. Saita (☎ 0432 50 30 04) also serves Trieste and Grado. SAF (☎ 0432 60 81 11) runs to most main centres in the region, and more distant destinations include Belluno, Padova, Venezia, Bolzano and even Taranto.

The train station is on the main Trieste-Venezia train line and services are regular. Connections can be made to Milano and beyond, as well as to Vienna and Salzburg in Austria.

The A23 passes the city to the west and connects the A4 with Austria. The S56 leads to Trieste and the S13 to Austria.

Getting Around

The train and bus stations are a few minutes from the city centre, but most ATM buses pass by. Take bus No 1 for Piazza del Duomo. Radiotaxi (☎ 0432 50 58 58) serves the city all hours.

CIVIDALE DEL FRIULI

postcode 33043 • pop 11,000

A trip to Cividale del Friuli is a must if you make it to Udine. It is one of the most picturesque towns in the region, its small medieval centre managing to survive several devastating earthquakes. Julius Caesar founded the town in 50 BC and in the 6th century AD it became the seat of the first Lombard duchy. About 200 years later, its growing reputation drew the patriarch of Aquileia to Cividale.

The APT office (☎ 0432 73 13 98) at Corso Paolino d'Aquileia 10 (near the Ponte del Diavolo) has information about Cividale, the Natisone valley and walking in several parks and the mountains to the north and east.

Cividale is at its most picturesque where the **Ponte del Diavolo** (Devil's Bridge) crosses the emerald green Natisone River. Take a walk through the cobbled lanes to the **Tempietto Longobardo**, on Borgo Brossano. This 'little temple', also known as the Oratorio di Santa Maria in Valle, was rebuilt after a 13th century earthquake and is an exquisite example of Lombard artwork. It's open from 10 am (an hour earlier in summer) to 1 pm and 3.30 to 5.30 pm (an hour longer in summer) daily. Admission costs L4000. The **duomo**, to the west, is not the most engaging cathedral, but you can continue exploring the Lombard theme in the tiny **museum** – the centrepiece is the Altar of Ratchis, a magnificent example of 8th century Lombard sculpture. Daily opening hours are from 9.30 am to noon and 3 to 6 pm (7 pm in summer, afternoons only on Sunday and holidays).

The town has only three hotels. *Albergo Pomo d'Oro* (☎ 0432 73 14 89, Piazza San

Giovanni 20) is the cheapest, with singles/doubles with private bathroom for L70,000/100,000. A few singles without bath come in at L50,000.

Trains and buses connect the town with Udine and Trieste, or you can drive the 17km from Udine on the S54.

CARNIA

North of Udine, the Friulian lowlands gradually give way to Alpine country on the way to Austria. Known generically as the Carnia, after the people who settled here in around the 4th century BC, the region's prime attractions are walking and skiing – and an agreeable, if only relative, absence of tourists.

The eastern half is characterised by forbidding and rocky bluffs along the valley to **Tarvisio**. This Alpine resort, 7km short of the Austrian border (heading for Villach) and 11km from Slovenia, is not a bad base for skiing and walking. The town itself is a curiosity. The Saturday market attracts hordes of Austrians; the bargains (everything from alcohol to clothes) must be pretty good, because Vienna's visitors are joined by lots of bargain-hunters from as far afield as Budapest, Zagreb and Ljubljana. A few kilometres east are a couple of fairly peaceful lakes, from where you can take forest rambles.

For the more attractive, verdant western half of the Carnia, head off the main north-south road for Tolmezzo, a small town surrounded by industry. Don't bother stopping but make for the west (Forni di Sopra) or north (Monte Zoncolan, for instance). It's a pretty and comparatively undisturbed area.

Information

The AAST office has branches in the towns of Tarvisio (☎ 0428 21 35), Via Roma 10; Forni di Sopra (☎ 0433 88 67 67), Via Cadore 1; and Piancavallo (☎ 0434 65 51 91). The Azienda Regionale delle Foreste (☎ 0432 29 47 11) at Via Manzini 41 in Udine can assist with maps and other details.

Activities

Skiing There are 18 skiing centres across northern Friuli-Venezia Giulia, the most important being (in a rough curve west to east) Piancavallo, Forni di Sopra, Ravascletto-Zoncolan, Sella Nevea and Tarvisio. Daily, weekly and season ski passes are available. A season ski pass *(Cartaneve)* is valid for the whole region and costs L560,000. The main centres have ski schools. There are some pretty decent downhill pistes, all starting at about 1700m or higher. Families tend to be attracted by these resorts and some effort is made to cater for children.

Walking The Udine APT office produces *Rifugi Alpini*, a useful guide to *rifugi* (accommodation in the Alpi) in the region. It's in Italian, but you should be able to make out the salient details. Leaflets suggesting various walking routes are also available. There is plenty of scope: the Tarvisio AAST has a brochure outlining some 70 walks, taking from one to seven hours in the area around the town. You can buy detailed walking maps in local newsagencies.

Cycling Some years back, the Ferrovie dello Stato and some of the northern mountain communities put together a useful guide to eight cycling itineraries in the Carnia. The rides are not too demanding and routes connect with train stations for those who want to ease up on the way. Older kids can cope with at least one of the more laid-back rides. The booklet is as rare as hen's teeth now, but in the hope they might bring it out again one day, ask at the Udine APT office or hunt around the main train stations for *La Pedemontana col Treno*. Although written in Italian, you can follow the routes in conjunction with a decent map.

Places to Stay
Camp sites are sparse. You can try *Val del Lago* (☎ 0432 97 91 64) at Trasaghis or *Tornerai* (☎ 0433 8 80 35) at Località in the Forni di Sopra area.

Most towns have at least a few hotels, and a surprising number are in the one star bracket. At the height of the season you are advised to book ahead – the Udine APT has a full list of the region's accommodation.

Getting There & Away
Tarvisio is connected by up to 10 trains a day to Udine (1¾ hours) and is the most easily accessible town in the region. If you don't have your own transport, you will have to rely on the Olivo bus line that operates infrequent services throughout the Carnia. Drivers heading north from Udine can take the A23 or the S13 – possibly one of the most boring roads in Italy, at least until you pass the chain of supermarkets between Udine and Gemona. The A23 is faster but is a tollway.

Emilia-Romagna & San Marino

Despite its convenient location between the big tourist draws of Toscana to the south and Lombardia and Veneto in the north, Emilia-Romagna is largely overlooked by the visiting masses. The regional capital, Bologna, was one of the most important medieval cities; its university is Europe's oldest, and turned out the likes of Thomas Becket, Erasmus, Copernicus, Dante and Petrarch. Bologna has also long been regarded as Italy's culinary capital, drawing on produce from the fertile Pianura Padana (Po plain) and adding *tortellini* and *lasagne* to the Italian table. It is a sophisticated city, well worth a visit of several days, and makes a good base for short trips to Ferrara, Modena and Parma, all once important Renaissance towns.

The Adriatic towns of Ravenna, which boasts one of the world's best collections of Byzantine mosaics, and Rimini, with its beaches and nightlife, add to the region's diversity, as does the marshland of the Foci del Po (Po delta), which Emilia-Romagna shares with Veneto.

A highlight for those interested in walking is the Grande Escursione Appenninica (GEA), a 25 day walk that cuts a path through the Appennini, taking in *rifugi* (mountain accommodation) and many of the dozens of medieval castles dotting the range.

Emilia, which stretches west of Bologna, and Romagna to the east were joined on Italian unification. Both former papal states, they each retain their own characteristics: the Emilians are an industrious people, and the Romagnoli are known for their entrepreneurial spirit, which finds a special expression in tourism.

Settled by the Etruscans, the area began to prosper after 187 AD, when the Romans built the Via Emilia. Apart from a period of Byzantine rule along the Mar Adriatico coast and the medieval experience of the independent *comuni* (commune), the real boom came with the Renaissance, when some of the country's most notable families

Highlights

- Wander through the historical centre of Bologna
- Study the spectacular mosaics of Ravenna
- Admire the fine Romanesque duomo in Modena
- Feast on lasagne, tortellini, Parma prosciutto, *parmigiano-reggiano* and other specialities of the region

ruled the various towns – the Farnese in Parma and Piacenza, the Este in Ferrara and Modena and the Bentivoglio in Bologna – and built opulent palaces and courts.

Transport along the Via Emilia (S9) is excellent and bus connections enable exploration into the mountains and north along the Po river. The region's prosperity means prices are relatively high, but youth hostels enable even budget travellers to see the entire region without too much trouble. However,

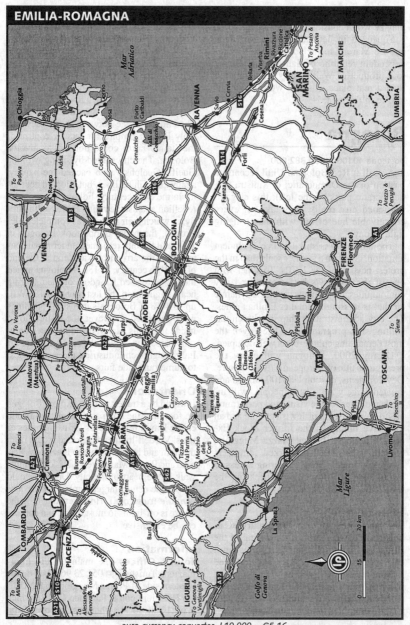

EMILIA-ROMAGNA

accommodation can be difficult to find, so it may be worth considering booking ahead.

Squeezed in between Emilia-Romagna and Le Marche to the south is the tiny independent republic of San Marino. Closer to a product of Walt Disney's imagination than a real place, it's still worth a visit if you're in the area.

Bologna

postcode 40100 • pop 382,000

They call it Red Bologna. Until recently a bastion of the Democratici di Sinistra (the democratic party of the left), this elegant, porticoed city really does take on every conceivable hue of red with the changing light of day.

The university is still a source of student agitation, albeit on a smaller scale than in the protest heyday of the 1970s. Together with one of the country's better organised gay communities, the students provide a dynamic air that is missing in smaller Emilian cities. The city administrators chip in with an unstinting arts programme to keep even the most demanding culture-buffs well occupied. During 2000, Bologna will enjoy the prestigious title of European City of Culture. Developments, costing US$100 million and created largely for young people, will include facilities for the visual and performing arts, a new museum of Jewish culture and an extensive library in the former Stock Exchange building, behind Piazza Maggiore, containing over 900 networked computers and a multimedia arcade offering access to a multitude of information. Check out the Web site www.Bologna2000.it for details.

History

Bologna started life in the 6th century BC as Felsina, for two centuries the capital of the Etruscan Pianura Padana territories until tribes from Gaul took over and renamed it Bononia. They lasted another couple of hundred years before surrendering to the Romans' northward march. As the Western Empire crumbled, Bologna became increasingly exposed to attack from the north, and was sacked and occupied by a succession of Visigoths, Huns, Goths and Lombards.

The city reached its pinnacle as an independent *comune* and leading European university in the 12th century. Wealth brought a building boom and every well-to-do family left its mark by erecting a tower. There were 180 of them in all, of which 15 still stand. The endless tussle between the papacy and Holy Roman Empire for secular control of the Italian north could not fail to involve Bologna. The city started by siding with the Guelfi (Guelphs), who backed the papacy, against the Ghibellines, but adopted neutrality in the 14th century. Following a popular rebellion against the ruling Bentivoglio family, in which their palace was completely destroyed, the papal troops took Bologna in 1506 and the city remained under papal control until the arrival of Napoleon at the end of the 18th century. In 1860, Bologna joined the newly formed Kingdom of Italy. During heavy fighting in the last months of WWII, up to 40% of Bologna's industrial buildings were destroyed. However, the historic town inside the walls survived and has been carefully preserved. Today, the city is a centre for Italy's high-tech industries and it plays host to numerous trade fairs.

Orientation

It would be a travesty not to explore Bologna on foot, and the compactness of the historic centre leaves few excuses for using buses or taxis. Via dell'Indipendenza leads south from the train and bus stations into Piazza del Nettuno and Piazza Maggiore – a brisk 10 minute walk to the heart of the city. Drivers should follow the *centro* target symbol off the *tangenziale* (ring road). However, much of the centre is off-limits to most traffic and parking can be expensive.

Information

Tourist Offices The main Ufficio Informazione Turistica (☎ 051 23 96 60) is on the western side of Piazza Maggiore in the Ufficio Relazioni con il Pubblico (URP), which is run by the local authorities. It is open from

9 am to 7 pm Monday to Saturday, to 2 pm on Sunday and to 1 pm on public holidays. Other offices are at the train station (☎ 051 24 65 41) and at the airport (☎ 051 647 20 36). The latter is closed on Sunday. Staff will assist with finding rooms but will not make bookings. They have stacks of information, free maps and brochures, including *A Guest in Bologna*, compiled by local shopkeepers and hoteliers. There is a ticket for admission to all the museums for L12,000 per day and L16,000 for three days; children up to the age of 14 are admitted free or at a discount.

Money You can change currency (commission-free) at an exchange booth at the train station, open from 7.10 am to 1.30 pm and from 2.10 to 8.30 pm daily. The bank at the main bus station has an ATM that accepts Visa cards. Otherwise, there are branches of the major banks with ATM service on Via Rizzoli, the continuation of Via Ugo Bassi, and on Via Indipendenza.

Post & Communications The main post office is on Piazza Minghetti, south-east of Piazza Maggiore. It is open from 8.15 am to about 5.30 pm Monday to Friday and to 12.20 pm on Saturday.

There are Telecom offices with attendants at Piazza VIII Agosto 24 and in Via Oberdan off Via Rizzoli. They are open from 8.30 am to 7.30 pm daily. The unstaffed office at the train station is open 24 hours.

Gay & Lesbian Travellers ArciGay (☎ 051 644 62 52), Piazza di Porta Saragozza 2, provides information and arranges events.

Medical Services & Emergency There are two hospitals: Ospedale Maggiore (☎ 051 647 81 11) on Via Emilia Ponente and Ospedale Sant'Orsola (☎ 051 636 31 11), at Via Massarenti 9. There is a 24 hour pharmacy on Piazza Maggiore and the pharmacy at the train station is open to 11 pm on weeknights and to 10 pm on Sunday and public holidays. For the Guardia Medica service, call ☎ 147 83 18 31 (west Bologna) or ☎ 147 83 28 32 (east Bologna).

The questura (police station; ☎ 051 640 11 11) is at Piazza Galileo 7.

Dangers & Annoyances The city is only just starting to have problems with street crime such as bag theft and pickpocketing. The area around the university, particularly Piazza Verdi, is a haunt for drug addicts and can be unpleasant at night.

Other Information The Sestante travel agency (☎ 051 26 61 24) is at Piazza del Nettuno 2 and CTS (☎ 051 23 75 01) has an office at Largo Respighi 2, off Piazza Verdi.

Feltrinelli has an Italian bookshop on Via dei Giudei, near the two leaning towers, and an international one at Via Zamboni 7b.

There is a coin laundrette at Via G Petroni 38, open from 9 am to 9 pm daily. There are Onda Blu laundrettes at Via San Donato 4 and Via Saragozza 34ab.

Piazzas Maggiore & Nettuno

At the centre of Bologna's old city, Piazza Maggiore and the adjoining Piazza del Nettuno to the north are lined by some of Bologna's most graceful medieval and Renaissance monuments. The bustling pedestrianised squares are a focal point of city life, with Bolognesi flocking to the cafés and often gathered around the mime artists and buskers who perform on the uneven stone pavement.

Fontana del Nettuno In the area between the two piazzas stands a mighty bronze Neptune, sculpted in 1566 by a Frenchman known to posterity as Giambologna. The four angels represent the winds and the four sirens the continents known at that time.

Palazzo Comunale Lining the western flank of the two piazze is the town hall, sporting an immense staircase attributed to Bramante and built wide enough for horse-drawn carriages to chauffeur their occupants up to the 1st floor. Above the main entrance you'll see a bronze statue of Pope Gregory XIII, a native of Bologna and responsible for the

EMILIA-ROMAGNA

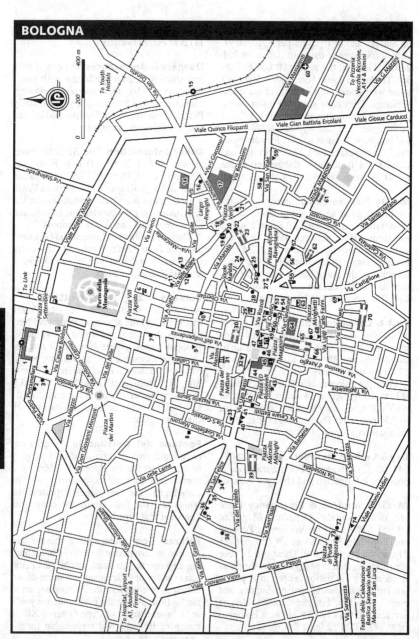

BOLOGNA

PLACES TO STAY	59	Osteria du Madon	28	Feltrinelli Bookshop
8 Albergo Marconi	66	Ristorante Torre de' Galluzzi	29	Telecom Office
21 Albergo Rossini	68	Zanarini	30	Cattedrale di San Pietro
42 Albergo Panorama	69	Osteria dei Poeti	31	Museo Civico Medioevale e
51 Albergo Garisenda	71	Osteria Senzanome		del Rinascimento
52 Albergo Apollo	74	Trattoria da Amedeo	37	Cinema Adriano
58 Albergo San Vitale			38	Cinema Lumière
	OTHER		39	Chiesa di San Francesco
PLACES TO EAT	1	Main Train Station; Tourist Office	43	Questura (Police Station)
9 Diana	2	Avis	44	Palazzo Comunale
10 Marsalino	3	Europcar	45	Main Tourist Office
11 Gelateria Delle Moline	4	Hertz	46	Fontana del Nettuno
13 Le Stanze	5	Main Bus Station; ATM	47	Palazzo del Re Enzo;
20 Caffè al Teatro	6	Telecom Office		Sestante Travel Agency
24 La Mamma	7	Arena del Sole	49	Palazzo del Podestà
32 McDonald's	12	Downtown	55	Vanguard
33 Mercato Ugo Bassi	14	Pinacoteca Nazionale	56	British Council
34 Gelateria Ugo	15	Train Station	60	Ospedale Sant'Orsola (Hospital)
35 Pizzeria Bella Napoli	16	Farmacia dalla Maddalena	61	Basilica di Santa Maria dei Servi
36 Trattoria da Danio	17	University; Palazzo Poggi	62	Basilica di Santo Stefano
40 Bass'8	18	Teatro Comunale	63	Post Office
41 Pizzeria Altero	19	CTS Travel Agency	64	Museo Civico Archeologico
48 Gelateria la Torinese	22	Oratorio di Santa Cecilia	65	Basilica di San Petronio
50 Osteria del Sole	23	Chiesa di San Giacomo Maggiore	67	Archiginnasio
53 Tamburini	25	Feltrinelli International Bookshop	70	Basilica di San Domenico
54 Trattorie da Gianni; Rosa Rose	26	Kinki Disco	72	Cinema Tiffany
57 Caffè Commercianti	27	Le Due Torri	73	ArciGay

Gregorian calendar. You can visit two art collections, the **Collezioni Comunali** (with good views over Piazza Maggiore) and the new **Museo Morandi**, both open from 10 am to 6 pm daily except Monday. Admission costs L8000 for one museum or L10,000 for both.

Note the huge panel outside the palazzo covered with photos of Italian partisans killed in the resistance to German occupation. Such displays are common in the cities and towns of Emilia-Romagna, which was a centre of fierce partisan activity.

Palazzo del Re Enzo Across from the Palazzo Comunale, this palace is named after King Enzo of Sicily, who was confined here for 20 years from 1249.

Palazzo del Podestà Beneath this fine example of Renaissance architecture and behind the cafés facing Piazza Maggiore, there is a whispering gallery at the point at which the two perpendicular passages inter-

sect. Stand diagonally opposite another person and whisper: the acoustics are amazing.

Basilica di San Petronio
Named after the city's patron saint, Bologna's largest house of worship was started in 1392 to plans by Antonio di Vincenzo (who was in fact subordinated to Andrea da Faenza) but never finished.

Originally intended to be larger than the first San Pietro in Roma (the structure destroyed to make way for Roma's present basilica), San Petronio was effectively truncated by the papacy, which decreed it could not be larger than San Pietro's and decided that much of the land should be used for a university. If you walk along Via dell'Archiginnasio on the eastern side of the basilica you can see semi-constructed apses poking out oddly from the building and the incomplete façade. Despite the papal intervention, the basilica is the fifth largest in the world and a fantastic example of Gothic architecture.

The central doorway, by Jacopo della Quercia, dates from 1425 and features carvings from the Old and New Testaments and a beautiful *Madonna and Child*. The chapels inside contain frescoes by Giovanni da Modena and Jacopo di Paolo. A giant sundial, designed by Cassini in 1656, decorates the floor of the northern aisle.

Museo Civico Archeologico

Just east of the basilica along Via dell'Archiginnasio (entrance on Via de' Musei), this museum has impressive collections of Egyptian and Roman artefacts and one of Italy's best Etruscan displays, featuring two burial chambers unearthed near the city. It is open from 9 am to 2 pm Tuesday to Friday and from 9 am to 1 pm and 3.30 to 7 pm on Saturday and Sunday. Admission costs L8000.

Archiginnasio

Site of the city's first university and now its library, the Archiginnasio contains an anatomy theatre carved entirely from wood in 1647. It was destroyed during WWII and completely rebuilt. The theatre and the Sala della Stabat Mater, named after the hymn by Rossini first played here in 1842, can be visited for free from 9 am to 1 pm Monday to Saturday. Just find the attendant.

Museo Civico Medioevale e del Rinascimento

Housed in the Palazzo Ghislardi-Fava at Via Manzoni 4, this museum has a collection of bronze statues and medieval coffin slabs, as well as some armour and a few frescoes by Jacopo della Quercia. It's open from 9 am to 2 pm on weekdays, except Tuesday, and from 9 am to 1 pm and 3.30 to 7 pm at the weekend. Admission costs L8000.

Le Due Torri

The two slender and highly precarious leaning towers that rise above Piazza di Porta Ravegnana are unmistakable landmarks. The taller of the towers is the **Torre degli Asinelli** at 97.6m. Built by the family of the same name in 1109, it has 498 steps which can be climbed from 9 am to 6 pm in summer and

to 5 pm in winter, in spite of the 1.3m lean. It affords marvellous views of the city. Admission costs L3000. The Garisenda family was even less cautious with foundations when erecting its tower, originally designed to compete with its neighbour and later sized down to 48m because of its 3.2m lean. It is closed to the public.

University Quarter

North-east of the towers along Via Zamboni is the **Chiesa di San Giacomo Maggiore**, on Piazza Rossini, open from 7 am to noon and from 3.30 to 6 pm daily. Built in the 13th century and remodelled in 1722, the church contains the Cappella Bentivoglio with frescoes by Lorenzo Costa. Near the church stands the extraordinary **Oratorio di Santa Cecilia**, dubbed the Sistine Chapel of Bologna for its impressive *ciclo* of 10 frescoes describing the life of Santa Cecilia. The decorations, painted by Lorenzo Costa, Amico Aspertini and Francesco Raibolini (known as il Francia) at the end of the 15th century, have recently been restored. Visits can be arranged at the main tourist office. A little farther up the road is the **Teatro Comunale**, where Wagner's works were heard for the first time in Italy.

The university area is worth visiting for the cafés and bars alone. The university has several museums open to the public, mostly in the **Palazzo Poggi**, on the corner of Via Zamboni and Via San Giacomo, details of which can be obtained from the tourist office.

Pinacoteca Nazionale North of the university, at Via delle Belle Arti 56, this art museum concentrates on works by Bolognese artists from the 14th century on. The extensive exhibits include several works by Giotto and also Raphael's *Ecstasy of St Cecilia*. El Greco and Titian are also represented, but by comparatively little-known works. The gallery is open from 9 am to 2 pm Tuesday to Saturday and to 1 pm on Sunday and public holidays. Admission costs L8000.

Basilica di Santo Stefano

From the two towers, head south-east along Via Santo Stefano, long a residential area for Bologna's wealthy and lined with the elegant façades of their palazzi.

Where the street widens into a pretty triangular piazza, you find yourself before the Basilica di Santo Stefano, actually a group of four churches (originally there were seven). On the right are the 11th century, Romanesque **Chiesa del Crocefisso** (Crucifix) and the octagonal **Chiesa del Santo Sepolcro** (Holy Sepulchre), whose shape suggests it started life as a baptistry. Crocefisso houses the bones of San Petronio, Bologna's patron saint. The basin in the small courtyard has long been popularly believed to be the one in which Pontius Pilate washed his hands after he condemned Christ to death. In fact it is an 8th century Lombard artefact.

The city's oldest church is **San Vitale e Agricola**, which incorporates many Roman ruins. The bulk of the building dates from the 5th century, and the tombs of the two saints, 100 years older still, once served as altars in the side aisles (today only one tomb remains). From the **Chiesa della Santa Trinità** you can pass to the modest medieval colonnaded cloister, off which a small **museum** contains a limited collection of paintings and frescoes. The complex is open from 9 am to noon and from 3.30 to 6.30 pm.

Basilica di San Domenico

The basilica, south of the city centre, was erected in the early 16th century to house the remains of San Domenico, the founder of the Dominican order, who had only just opened a convent on the site when he died in 1221.

The **Cappella di San Domenico** contains the saint's elaborate sarcophagus, the reliefs of which illustrate scenes from his life. Designed by Nicolò Pisano in the late 13th century, the chapel was worked on by a host of artists over the following couple of centuries. The angel on the right of the altar was carved by Michelangelo when he was aged 19 and bears a resemblance to *David*, which he sculpted years later. The chapel is also decorated with several paintings of the saint, whose skull lies in a reliquary behind

the sarcophagus. Ask an attendant to let you see the small **museum** and the inlaid wood of the choir stalls behind the main altar of the church.

When Mozart spent a month in the city's music academy, he occasionally played the church's organ. The basilica is closed between 1 and 2 pm.

Chiesa di San Francesco

At the western end of Via Ugo Bassi, at Piazza Marcello Malpighi, the Chiesa di San Francesco is fronted by the elaborate tombs of the *glossatori* (law teachers). The church, one of the first in Italy to be built in the French Gothic style, was completed in the 13th century and contains the tomb of Pope Alexander V. The church is closed between noon and 3 pm.

Basilica Santuario della Madonna di San Luca

The hilltop Basilica Santuario della Madonna di San Luca is visible from most parts of the city. Built in the mid-18th century, it houses a painting of the Virgin Mary supposedly by San Luca (hence the place's name) and transported from the Middle East to Bologna in the 12th century.

The sanctuary lies about 4km south-west of the city centre and is connected to the city walls by a long portico with 666 arches, beginning at Porta Saragozza. Each April a statue of the Virgin is carried along the portico. Take bus No 20 from the city centre to Villa Spada, from where you can get a COSEPURI minibus to the sanctuary (buy the L5000 return ticket on the minibus). On a sunny day it is worth getting off at Meloncello and walking the remaining 2km under the arches.

Work

There is no shortage of foreign-language teachers in Bologna. If you want to try your luck, you could start with Inlingua (☎ 051 23 80 22), Via Testoni 2, or the British Council (☎ 051 22 51 42, email info.bologna@brit coun.it), Corte Isolani 8. The British Council has a Web site at www.britcoun.org/italy.

EMILIA-ROMAGNA

Special Events

Each summer, the city sponsors Bologna Est, a three month festival of events involving museums and galleries, the university and local and national performers. Torri da Estate is another summer programme that takes place at the foot of the modern towers of Kenzo Tange in the Zona Fiera (Fair District), and includes discos. Most events are free and a schedule is available at the tourist office.

Places to Stay

Budget hotels in Bologna are in short supply and it is almost impossible to find a single room. The city's busy trade fair calendar means that hotels are often heavily booked, so always reserve in advance; check with the tourist office to find out when the fairs are on. The city is jammed with expensive hotels catering to business people, but when there are no fairs on some of them offer discounts of up to 50% on doubles.

There are several camp sites within driving distance of the city. Check with the tourist office. You could also ask for student accommodation, but only during university breaks.

Hostels The best options are the two HI youth hostels. *Ostello San Sisto (Via Viadagola 14)* charges L20,000 with breakfast (the hostel has been closed for restoration but was due to reopen by the end of 1999; for information call Ostello Due Torri-San Sisto 2). *Ostello DueTorri-San Sisto 2* (☎ *051 50 18 10*), in the same street at No 5 (same management), charges L21,000. Take bus Nos 93 or 20b from Via Irnerio, off Via dell'Indipendenza near the station, and ask the driver where to alight. From there, follow the signs for the hostel.

There is one other hostel option for groups and families: *Centro Europa Uno (☎/fax 051 625 83 52, Via Emilia 297)* in San Lazzaro di Savena, about 9km south-east of Bologna. Singles/doubles cost L24,000/60,000. It's always open and bookings are essential. Bus No 94 runs to the hostel from central Bologna.

Hotels The pick of the city's cheaper hotels is *Albergo Garisenda (☎ 051 22 43 69,*

Galleria del Leone 1), off the busy Via Rizzoli, with rooms looking out over the leaning towers. Singles/doubles/triples start at L65,000/90,000/120,000. *Albergo Apollo* (☎ *051 22 39 55, Via Drapperie 5)*, in a more attractive and quieter street also off Via Rizzoli, has singles/doubles from L60,000/98,000 and triples with bathroom for L177,000. *Albergo San Vitale (☎ 051 22 59 66, Via San Vitale 94)* is in a lively student area and has clean singles/doubles with bathroom starting at L80,000/110,000.

On the opposite side of town, rooms at *Albergo Marconi (☎ 051 26 28 32, Via Marconi 22)*, on a busy road, start at L52,000/82,000. *Albergo Panorama (☎ 051 22 18 02, Via Livraghi 1)*, off the central Via Ugo Bassi, has roomy, clean singles/doubles with a view for L70,000/95,000 and doubles with bathroom for L120,000.

Albergo Rossini (☎ 051 23 77 16, Via dei Bibiena 11), in the university area, is a good deal with single/doubles from L95,000/150,000 with bathroom and L65,000/100,000 without.

Places to Eat

Some know Bologna as La Grassa (the fat), and the Bolognesi are indeed serious about food and fussy about their pasta. The best pasta is *tirata a mano*, hand-stretched and rolled with a wooden pin, not a machine. It is cooked in many ways and eaten with a multitude of sauces. Everyone knows *spaghetti bolognese*, but the Bolognesi call the meat sauce *ragù*. *Mortadella*, known sometimes as Bologna sausage or baloney, hails from the area. The hills nearby produce the Lambrusco red and a full, dry Sauvignon.

Fortunately, it is cheap to eat in Bologna, particularly in the university district northeast of Via Rizzoli. The city has many good bars and *osterie* (snack bars), where you can get cheap drinks and snacks. Some serve full meals and rarely levy a cover charge.

Restaurants There are several self-service places about town. *La Mamma (Via Zamboni 16)* is the cheapest with its student and soldiers menu for L10,000. A better choice is **Bass'8** *(Via Ugo Bassi 8)*, where a full meal starts from L12,500. For a classy version of the genre, head to **Tamburini** *(Via Caprarie 1)*. Apart from selling some of Bologna's finest food products, it has a self-service restaurant where you can taste some of the goodies without having to cook them yourself. **Osteria Senzanome** *(Via Senzanome 42)* is one of the best known osterie and serves a full meal for around L30,000. **Osteria du Madon** *(Via San Vitale 73d)* is an atmospheric restaurant with pasta dishes starting at L12,000 and a full meal at L40,000. **Osteria dei Poeti** *(Via dei Poeti 1a)* can be more expensive but the food's excellent. It's been in operation since 1600.

Local opinion is divided on the subject of Bologna's top pizza, but you won't go far wrong on price or quality at **Pizzeria Bella Napoli** *(Via San Felice 40)*. A good place for pizza *al taglio* (by the slice) is **Pizzeria Altero** *(Via Ugo Bassi 10)*. **McDonald's** is on the corner of Via dell'Indipendenza and Via Ugo Bassi, if you feel that particular urge.

If you are after quality fish and Neapolitan dishes in Bologna, catch bus No 25 on Via Rizzoli and ask to get off at the corner of Via Pizzardi and Via Mengoli outside the city walls. At **Pizzeria Vecchia Riccione** *(☎ 051 39 18 64, Via Mengoli 30)* a fresh fish meal starts from L30,000 and the pizzas and pastas are delicious.

Trattoria da Danio *(Via San Felice 50)* is targeted by locals for its rustic feel. **Trattoria da Amedeo** *(Via Saragozza 88)* is popular with Bolognesi on a budget and has a lunch menu for L20,000. **Trattoria da Gianni** *(Via Clavature 18)* is recommended for its home-made pasta and charges L50,000 for a full meal, while the adjoining **Rosa Rose** is cheaper.

Ristorante Torre de' Galluzzi *(Corte Galluzzi 5a)*, behind the Basilica di San Petronio, is delightfully located in a medieval tower and has a set menu featuring local meat or fish specialities for around L80,000. **Diana** *(Via dell'Indipendenza 24)*, three blocks north of Piazza del Nettuno, is famous for its tortellini and a full meal will cost at least L70,000.

Cafés The **Osteria del Sole** *(Via Ranocchi 1d)* first opened for business in about 1400 and is the only place left in Bologna which maintains the centuries-old tradition of the osteria as watering hole only. It's also one of Bologna's few early openers, open from 8 am to 2 pm and from 7.30 to 9 pm, although this is not set in stone. If you want to eat, arm yourself with goodies from the surrounding food shops.

Zanarini *(Via Luigi Carlo Farini 2)*, behind the Basilica di San Petronio, is one of the city's finest tearooms and specialises in unusual cakes. Some of its past glory is lost, but the grand décor makes a visit worthwhile, if a little expensive.

Caffè Commercianti *(Strada Maggiore 23)* has become something of a haunt for the city's intelligentsia, apparently inspired by a combination of Umberto Eco and the best Martini in town.

More modest and with plenty of student life is **Caffè al Teatro**, on the corner of Largo Respighi and Via Zamboni. **Marsalino** *(Via Marsala 13d)*, just off Via Indipendenza, provides pasta dishes at lunch and cakes and tea or wines in the evening.

At **Le Stanze** *(Via Borgo San Pietro 1)*, at the corner with Via delle Moline, the young staff offer music and atmosphere in an establishment whose vaulted ceiling, fresco decorations and furniture provide a perfect setting for a chat over an aperitif.

One of the streets mostly frequented by students and young people is Via del Pratello, just off Via Ugo Bassi. It has plenty of cheap bars, *birrerie*, osterie, and trattorie, and in summer the atmosphere recalls that of the movement of the late 1970s, when from a house in this road one of the first free radios, Radio Alice, broadcast the student rebellion of the period.

Gelaterie The **Gelateria Ugo** *(Via San Felice 20)* is one of the city's best for ice-cream. Also well established are **Gelateria la Torinese** *(Via Archiginnasio)*, behind the Palazzo del Podestà, and **Gelateria delle Moline** *(Via delle Moline 13b)*, off Via Indipendenza, specialising in *focaccia* and *gelato* sandwiches.

EMILIA-ROMAGNA

Self-Catering You can shop at the vast *Mercato Ugo Bassi (Via Ugo Bassi 27)*, or just east of Piazza Maggiore the attractive daily produce *market*, centred on speciality food shops in the area around Via Drapperie, Via Orefici and Via Clavature.

Entertainment

The tourist office sometimes has brochures containing plenty of information on theatre, cinema and nightlife. For the latest information on what's on in clubland, buy *Zero-in-Condotta* for L4000.

Bars, Discos & Clubs Bologna has one of the healthiest night scenes in Italy, bolstered by an active student population and gay community.

Downtown (Via delle Moline 16b) is the place to go for loud music for the price of a drink. If techno, hip-hop and the very latest music are your thing, head for *Link (☎ 051 37 09 71, Via Fioravanti 14)*, behind the train station. This former *centro sociale occupato* is now housed in a municipal building and is very popular with young people. At *Vanguard (Vicolo Sampieri 3b)* you can eat, drink and dance until the wee hours. Music ranges from hip-hop to acid jazz, there's no cover charge and it's one of the better inner-city spots. *Kinki (Via Zamboni 1a)* is a long-time favourite disco and welcomes lesbians and gays. It's open on Thursday, Friday and Saturday nights and cover charges are around L30,000.

Cinemas English-language films are shown at *Tiffany (☎ 051 58 52 53, Piazza di Porta Saragozza 5)* and *Lumière (☎ 051 52 35 39, Via Pietralata 55a)*, which shows arthouse movies in all languages. *Adriano (☎ 051 55 51 27, Via San Felice 52)* is a similar place. The public film library promotes the revival of old movies and organises the annual *festival del cinema ritrovato* (festival of rediscovered films). This is an interesting seven day event taking place between June and July in cinemas and open air venues in Piazza Maggiore and the Palazzo Comunale.

Theatre, Opera & Classical Music The *Teatro Comunale (☎ 051 52 99 99, Piazza Verdi)* is the main venue for opera and concerts and has a year-round programme. Other theatres include *Teatro Duse (☎ 051 23 18 36, Via Cartoleria 42)*, *Arena del Sole (☎ 051 27 07 90, Via Indipendenza 44)*, *Teatro delle Celebrazioni (☎ 051 615 33 74, Via Saragozza 236)* and *Teatro Dehon (☎ 051 34 47 72, Via Libia 59)*.

Shopping

If you're intending to do any shopping in Bologna, don't come on Thursday, as all shops shut for the afternoon. At the weekend there's a flea market at the Parco della Montagnola. The main shopping streets are Via Ugo Bassi, Via Rizzoli, Via Marconi, Via dell'Indipendenza, Via Massimo d'Azeglio and Via San Felice.

Getting There & Away

Air Bologna's Guglielmo Marconi airport (☎ 051 647 96 15), north-west of the city at Borgo Panigale, is serviced by mainly European airlines and there are flights to Roma, Venezia, southern Italy, Pisa, London, Paris and Frankfurt.

Bus Services to regional centres such as Ravenna, Ferrara and Modena leave from the depot (☎ 051 29 02 90) opposite Piazza XX Settembre, round the corner from the train station. There are buses to Ancona and Milano and international buses to London, Paris, Amsterdam, Brussels, Prague and Warsaw.

Train Bologna is a major transport junction for northern Italy and trains from Roma and Milano stop here. Many are Eurostar trains.

Car & Motorcycle The city is linked to Milano, Firenze and Roma by the A1 Autostrada del Sole. The A13 heads directly for Ferrara, Padova and Venezia, and the A14 for Rimini and Ravenna. The city is also on the Via Emilia (S9), which connects Milano with the Adriatic coast. The S64 goes to Ferrara.

For car hire, all major companies are represented in the city. Most have offices at the airport. Try Avis (☎ 051 25 50 24) at Via Pietramellara 35, Europcar (☎ 051 24 71 01) at Via G Amendola 12f and Hertz (☎ 051 25 48 52) at Via G Amendola 16a.

Getting Around
ATC Aerobus connects the city with the airport (L7000). It leaves from in front of the train station every 20 minutes from 6.50 am to midnight.

Bologna has an efficient bus system, run by ATC, which has information booths at the train station and on Via Marconi at the junction with Via Ugo Bassi and Via Lame. Bus Nos 30 and 21 are among the many connecting the train station with the city centre.

To book a cab call ☎ 051 37 27 27.

PORRETTA
The tiny thermal spring town of Porretta Terme lies about 50km south of Bologna in the Appennini. Traditionally a sleepy resort for people wanting to take advantage of the therapeutic mineral waters, the town has in recent years become a focal point for soul music lovers from across Europe. Each year, during the third weekend in July, the town hosts the **Sweet Soul Music Festival**, a tribute to Otis Redding and a celebration of the Memphis sound. If you happen to be in the region at the time, it really is worth making the trip to Porretta for the festival, held over three nights in the town's Rufus Thomas Park. For information about the festival and about the town itself, contact the APT di Porretta (☎ 0534 2 20 21), Piazza Protche 4. Places to stay include the one star *Trattoria Toscana (☎ 0534 2 22 08, Piazza della Libertà)* or the four star *Hotel Santoli (☎ 0534 2 32 06, Via Roma)*. Trains leave hourly for Porretta from Bologna. The town is also accessible by train from Firenze.

West of Bologna

MODENA
postcode 41100 • pop 176,600
Some 40km north-west of Bologna, Modena was one of a series of Roman garrison towns established along the Via Emilia in the 2nd century BC, in this case on the site of an already existing Etruscan settlement.

Modena remained an obscure little place until it became a free city in the 12th century and passed to the Este family late in the following century. Prosperity finally came when it was chosen as the capital of a much-reduced Este duchy in 1598, after the family had lost Ferrara to the Papal States. Apart from a brief Napoleonic interlude, the Este remained in control until Italian unification.

Modena is home to Italy's favourite tenor, Luciano Pavarotti, and car manufacturers Ferrari, Maserati, Bugatti, Lamborghini and De Tomaso, who all do their bit to make this town one of the most affluent in the country.

Orientation
To get to the centre from the train station in Piazza Dante, head down Viale Crispi and turn right into Corso Vittorio Emanuele II, which leads to the Palazzo Ducale. Walk around the palazzo to Piazza degli Estensi and then straight ahead along Via L C Farini for Via Emilia, the main drag. The duomo and Piazza Grande are south of Via Emilia, and the bulk of offices, banks, hotels and restaurants are within easy walking distance of the centre.

Information
Tourist Offices The IAT office (☎ 059 20 66 60 – infuriating recorded information only), Piazza Grande 17, opens from 8.30 am to 1 pm and from 3 to 7 pm Monday to Saturday (closed on Wednesday afternoon) and from 9 am to noon on Sunday.

Post & Communications The post office is at Via Emilia 86 and opens from 8.15 am to 7.15 pm. The Telecom office is at Via L C Farini 26 and there's a smaller office at Via dell'Università 23.

Medical Services & Emergency You can call an ambulance or locum doctor on ☎ 059 22 22 08. The main hospital (☎ 059 43 72 71/2) is at Piazzale Sant'Agostino, opposite the Palazzo dei Musei. For late

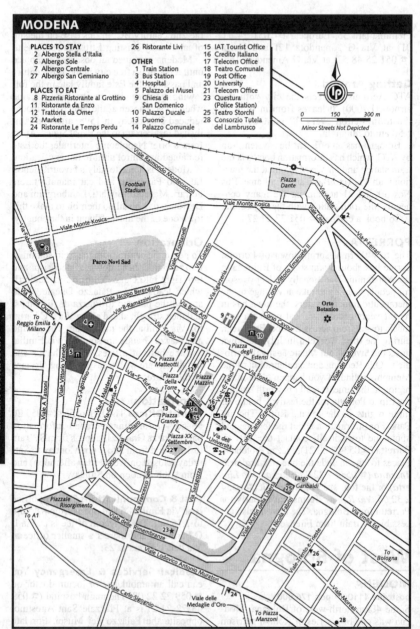

MODENA

PLACES TO STAY
2 Albergo Stella d'Italia
6 Albergo Sole
7 Albergo Centrale
27 Albergo San Geminiano

PLACES TO EAT
8 Pizzeria Ristorante al Grottino
11 Ristorante da Enzo
12 Trattoria da Omer
22 Market
24 Ristorante Le Temps Perdu

26 Ristorante Livi

OTHER
1 Train Station
3 Bus Station
4 Hospital
5 Palazzo dei Musei
9 Chiesa di
   San Domenico
10 Palazzo Ducale
13 Duomo
14 Palazzo Comunale

15 IAT Tourist Office
16 Credito Italiano
17 Telecom Office
18 Teatro Comunale
19 Post Office
20 University
21 Telecom Office
23 Questura
   (Police Station)
25 Teatro Storchi
28 Consorzio Tutela
   del Lambrusco

0   150   300 m

Minor Streets Not Depicted

night pharmacies, check the *Gazzetta di Modena* newspaper.

The questura (☎ 059 41 04 11) is at Viale delle Rimembranza 12.

Duomo

Dedicated to Modena's patron saint, San Geminiano, the duomo was started in 1099 and is one of the finest Romanesque cathedrals in Italy. The façade is adorned with precious bas-reliefs depicting scenes from Genesis by the 12th century sculptor Wiligelmo. The carvings were a common way to inform the illiterate masses about the Old Testament. Although a rare practice in those times, Wiligelmo signed his work (to the left of the main door), as did the building's architect, Lanfranco (in the main apse). Among the many fine carvings are some typical medieval motifs depicting the months and agricultural scenes. The duomo is open from 6.30 am to noon and from 3.30 to 7 pm daily except Monday (it is not possible to visit during religious services). Much of Wiligelmo's work has been removed to the **Museo Lapidario del Duomo**, adjoining the duomo at Via Lanfranco 6.

The duomo's Romanesque **Torre Ghirandina** was started in 1169 and rises to 87m, culminating in a Gothic spire that has quite a lean. It's open from 10 am to 1 pm and from 3 to 7 pm on Sunday and holidays during the summer only. Admission costs L2000.

Palazzo dei Musei

Palazzo dei Musei, in Piazzale Sant'Agostino, houses several galleries, including the city's art collection and the Biblioteca Estense. The **Museo Lapidario Estense** (admission free) contains Roman and medieval stonework, including sarcophagi; it was partly closed for renovation at the time of writing. The **Galleria Estense** (admission L8000) features most of the Este family collection and comprises works by Cosme' Tura, Bernini, Guercino, Guido Reni, Velázquez, Correggio and El Greco. The **Biblioteca Estense** has one of Italy's most valuable collections of books, letters and manuscripts and includes the *Bible of Borso d'Este*, its 1200 pages illustrated by Ferrarese artists and considered the most decorated Bible in existence. It can be seen, but you must leave your passport at the desk. The **Museo Civico del Risorgimento** is a standard display chronicling Italian unification; it was closed for restoration at the time of writing. The **Museo Civico Archeologico Etnologico** (admission L5500) presents a range of Bronze Age exhibits, as well as items from Africa, Asia, Peru and New Guinea. Access is combined with the **Museo Civico d'Arte**, a modest collection of paintings. The opening times are all over the place, although you are safe from 9 am to noon on most days except Monday.

Palazzo Ducale

Started in 1634 for the Este family, this grand baroque edifice is now home to Modena's military academy, whose cadets wear fuchsia-coloured uniforms (looking like they've stepped off a Quality Street chocolate tin) and are considered Italy's crack soldiers. The doors of the palazzo are thrown open to the public on Army Celebration Day (4 November) and every Sunday from 10 to 11 am. You need to book a week ahead on ☎ 059 20 66 60.

Activities

If you're tiring of soaking up culture, the Appennini south of Modena offer lots of scope for outdoor activities, including walking, horse riding, canoeing and skiing. The IAT office has stacks of brochures, with details about walking trails and places to stay, including rifugi and camp sites.

Ask at the IAT office about booking tours of the Maserati and De Tomaso factories.

Special Events

The Settimana Estense in late June and early July is a week of banquets, jousts and other early Renaissance fun, with lots of locals flitting about in period costume.

Places to Stay

Modena is close enough to Bologna to make it a day trip, although the city does have reasonably cheap accommodation.

EMILIA-ROMAGNA

International Camping Modena (☎ *059 33 22 52, Via Cave di Ramo 111)* is a couple of kilometres west of the city in Bruciata. Take bus No 19. It's open from April to the end of September.

Albergo Sole (☎ *059 21 42 45, Via Malatesta 45),* west of Piazza Grande, has singles/ doubles without bathroom for L40,000/ 70,000. *Albergo San Geminiano* (☎ *059 21 03 03, Viale Moreali 41),* a 10 minute walk east of the city centre, has rooms from L65,000/105,000 (and doubles without own bath for L85,000); it also has free parking. *Albergo Stella d'Italia* (☎ *059 22 25 84, Via Paolo Ferrari 3)* has overpriced rooms from L70,000/120,000. If you're going to spend this kind of money – and the choices are limited – you may as well try the *Albergo Centrale* (☎ *059 21 88 08),* Via Rismondo 55. It is close to the heart of town and has perfectly good rooms for L85,000/130,000.

Places to Eat

Like Bologna and Parma, Modena produces excellent *prosciutto crudo* (cured ham). The city's gastronomic speciality is *zampone* (stuffed pig's trotter). It also produces the bulk of Italy's balsamic vinegar, a rich aromatic vinegar using local wine that is sprinkled liberally over salads and meat dishes. Free guided visits to the *acetaie* (where they produce the vinegar) can be arranged through the IAT office. Tortellini is another speciality, as is Lambrusco, one of the more famous Italian sparkling reds, which should be drunk chilled and with everything. The city's Consorzio Tutela del Lambrusco, Via Schedoni 41, can tell you about vineyards and advise on tastings and opening times. The fresh produce *market* is just south of Piazza XX Settembre.

Pizzeria Ristorante al Grottino (*Via Taglio 26),* north of Piazza Matteotti, has pizzas from L6000 to L18,000. *Trattoria da Omer* (*Via Torre 33)* serves supposedly Renaissance dishes that were prepared at the Este court, but a meal could cost L40,000 or more. *Ristorante da Enzo* (*Via Coltellini 17)* is one of the better restaurants, with main courses from L16,000 to L24,000. They

make their own pasta on the premises. For seafood, head for *Ristorante Le Temps Perdu* (*Viale Lodovico Antonio Muratori 163).* *Ristorante Livi* (*Viale Trento e Trieste 71)* is a decent pizzeria.

Entertainment

The city's better bars are along Via Emilia, near the duomo, but check prices, as a beer could cost L10,000.

Sipario in Piazza, held during July and August, features outdoor concerts and ballet in Piazza Grande, with tickets starting at around L10,000. Posters advertise forthcoming events.

The opera season is in winter, with most performances at the *Teatro Comunale* (☎ *059 20 00 10, Corso Canal Grande 85).* Check out the *Teatro Storchi* (☎ *059 22 32 44, Largo Garibaldi 15),* for drama. You can also buy tickets at an office in the same building as the IAT office.

Shopping

On the fourth weekend of every month, excluding July and December, a big antiques fair is held in Parco Novi Sad, 500m northwest of the city centre.

Getting There & Around

The bus station is on Via Fabriani. ATCM and other companies connect Modena with most towns in the region and cities including Cremona and Milano.

The main train station is in Piazza Dante. There are services to Bologna, Mantova, Verona, Roma, Parma and Milano.

The city is at the junction of the A1 Autostrada del Sole, which connects Roma with Milano, and the A22, which heads north for Mantova, Verona and the Brenner pass.

ATCM's bus No 7 connects the train station with the bus station and the city centre. For a taxi, call ☎ 059 37 42 42. Bicycles can be hired next to the train station.

AROUND MODENA
Galleria Ferrari

Enzo Ferrari, who died in 1988, reckoned the Modenese possess a rare combination of

Check out the Ferraris on display at the Galleria Ferrari.

boldness and hard-headedness needed to build racing cars. His factory is in **Maranello**, 17km south of Modena (regular buses run from Modena), but visits are not allowed. The Galleria Ferrari (☎ 0536 94 32 04), the firm's museum, is at Via Dino Ferrari 43. It boasts one of the largest collections of Ferraris on show in the world and is open from 9.30 am to 12.30 pm and 3 to 6 pm daily except Monday. Admission costs L15,000.

Vignola
A lovely medieval village 22km south of Modena, Vignola offers visitors good food and a 14th century castle, with frescoed rooms. In the spring, the countryside around the town is a mass of cherry blossoms.

Carpi
Once the centre of the Pio family territories, Carpi is an impressive Renaissance town, built using the characteristic local red bricks. It's 20km north of Modena and easily reached by train. Its elegant Pio palace incorporates a medieval castle and dominates one of the biggest squares in Italy, which is closed on one side by a system of ancient porticoes. Visit the 16th century duomo and the Romanesque Chiesa di Santa Maria del Castello.

REGGIO EMILIA
postcode 42100 • pop 130,000
Also known as Reggio nell'Emilia, this town started life in the 2nd century BC as a Roman colony along the Via Emilia, which divides it. Nothing remains from those days and much of the present city was built by the Este family during the 400 years it was in control from 1406 on.

Although most of us know the cheese from this area as Parmesan (as in Parma), it is in fact called *parmigiano-reggiano*, reflecting the fact that it's produced across both provinces.

Few tourists bother to stop here, but Reggio has a pleasant centre and makes a functional base for exploring the Appennini to the south – it certainly merits a stop if you're passing through.

Information
Tourist Offices The IAT office (☎ 0522 45 11 52), at Piazza Camillo Prampolini 5c, is 1km west of the train station, along Via Emilia San Pietro, and is open from 8.30 am to 1 pm and 2.30 to 6 pm Monday to Saturday and from 9 am to noon on Sunday.

Post & Communications The post office is at Via Sessi 3 and there's an unstaffed Telecom phone office at Galleria San Rocco 8f.

Medical Services & Emergency The Ospedale Santa Maria Nuova (☎ 0522 29 61 11) is at Viale Risorgimento 80.
 The questura (☎ 0522 45 87 11) is at Via Dante Alighieri 6.

Churches
The city's sights are concentrated around Piazza del Monte (formerly Piazza Cesare Battisti), Piazza Camillo Prampolini and Piazza San Prospero. The latter two are separated by the **duomo**, built in the 13th century in the Romanesque style and completely remodelled 300 years later. The 15th century **Chiesa di San Prospero**, on the piazza of the same name, is fronted by red marble lions. Its striking octagonal bell tower was built in 1537. The baroque **Basilica della Ghiara**, on Corso Garibaldi, houses recently restored frescoes by 17th century Emilian artists including Ludovico Carracci, Gian Francesco Barbieri (called the Guercino), Lionello Spada and Alessandro Tiarini. At the time of writing it was draped in restorers' scaffolding.

Palazzo del Municipio
On the southern side of Piazza Camillo

EMILIA-ROMAGNA

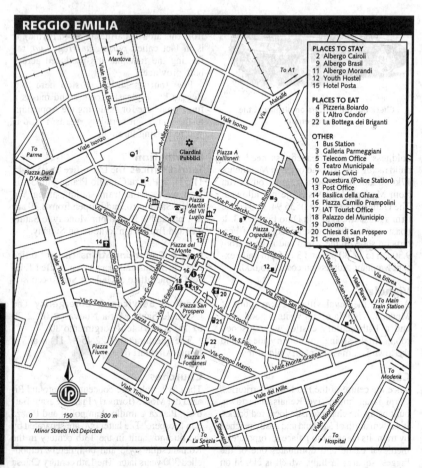

REGGIO EMILIA

PLACES TO STAY
2 Albergo Cairoli
9 Albergo Brasil
11 Albergo Morandi
12 Youth Hostel
15 Hotel Posta

PLACES TO EAT
4 Pizzeria Boiardo
8 L'Altro Condor
22 La Bottega dei Briganti

OTHER
1 Bus Station
3 Galleria Parmeggiani
5 Telecom Office
6 Teatro Municipale
7 Musei Civici
10 Questura (Police Station)
13 Post Office
14 Basilica della Ghiara
16 Piazza Camillo Prampolini
17 IAT Tourist Office
18 Palazzo del Municipio
19 Duomo
20 Chiesa di San Prospero
21 Green Bays Pub

Prampolini, the 14th century town hall contains the **Sala del Tricolore**, the room where the Italian flag was devised during a conference that established Napoleon's short-lived Cispadane Republic in 1797.

Teatro Municipale
On the northern side of Piazza Martiri del VII Luglio, this imposing building could be a royal palace. Built in 1857 as an opera house, it is now mainly used for performances of modern ballet.

Museums
North from Piazza del Monte, facing Piazza Martiri del VII Luglio at Via Secchi 2, the four **Musei Civici** house a collection of 18th century works of art and archaeological discoveries. The museums are open from 9 am to noon Tuesday to Friday and also from 3 to 6 pm at the weekend. Admission is free. The **Galleria Parmeggiani**, at Corso Cairoli 2, has some worthwhile Italian, Spanish and Flemish canvases, including an El Greco. It's open the same hours as the Musei Civici.

Places to Stay & Eat

The Reggio Emilia *youth hostel* (☎ 0522 45 47 95, Via dell'Abbadessa 8), about 500m from the train station in the city centre, has beds for L16,000. For a hotel, try *Albergo Morandi* (☎ 0522 45 43 97, Via Emilia San Pietro 64), which has rooms with bathroom for L68,000/98,000. *Albergo Cairoli* (☎ 0522 45 35 96, Piazza XXV Aprile 2), near the bus station, has rooms for L55,000/80,000 (L70,000/95,000 with bathroom, phone and TV). *Albergo Brasil* (☎ 0522 45 53 76, Via Roma 37) has rooms for much the same price and will discount for longer stays. For sheer luxury in the centre, you can pay L200,000/240,000 at *Hotel Posta* (☎ 0522 43 29 44, fax 0522 45 26 02, Piazza del Monte 2).

There is a produce *market* each Tuesday and Friday on Piazza San Prospero. Shop at the local *alimentari* for delicious typical local snacks such as *erbazzone* (herb pie with cheese or bacon) or *gnocco fritto* (fried salted dough – good ones are as light as air!). For pizza or straightforward meals try *Pizzeria Boiardo* (Gallery San Rocco 3f) and *L'Altro Condor* (Via Secchi 17). *La Bottega dei Briganti* (Via San Carlo 14b) has a wonderful conspiratorial atmosphere and a small leafy courtyard. Pasta and main courses both cost around L12,000 and they are worth every lira.

For a drink you could then retire to the *Green Bays Pub*, up the road at number 10.

Getting There & Around

ACT buses (☎ 0522 92 76 11) serve the city and region from the bus station in Viale A Allegri. The train station is at the eastern end of town on Piazza Marconi and plenty of trains serve all stops on the Milano-Bologna line.

The city is on the Via Emilia (S9) and the A1 passes to the north. The S63 is a tortuous but scenic route that takes you south-west across the Parma Appennini to La Spezia on the Ligurian coast.

You are unlikely to need the ACT's city buses. If you are in a blind hurry, you can call a taxi on ☎ 0522 45 25 45.

AROUND REGGIO EMILIA

South-west of the city along the S63, the **Parco del Gigante** national park is spread along the province's share of the Appennini. There are numerous walking trails, well served by rifugi. Climb or walk around the huge limestone rock called the **Pietra di Bismantova**. The tourist office at **Castelnovo ne' Monti** (☎ 0522 81 04 30), Piazza Martiri della Libertà 12b, can provide details of activities, hotels and camping.

The area's main attractions are three medieval castles, once owned by Matilda, the Countess of Canossa, famed for reconciling the excommunicated Emperor Henry IV with Pope Gregory VII in 1077. The castle of **Canossa**, built in 940 and rebuilt in the 13th century, is open to the public. It houses a small museum, open daily except Monday. From Canossa you can see across to the castle of **Rossena**, which can be visited two days a week (check at Castelnovo's tourist office for details). The other castle, Bianello, is privately owned.

A good base for exploring the Pianura Padana area north of Reggio Emilia is **Guastalla**, as it has a *youth hostel* (☎/fax 051 22 49 13, Via Lido Po 11). B&B costs L16,000. Trains and buses run from Reggio Emilia.

PARMA
postcode 43100 • pop 88,000

Of the Emilian cities west of Bologna, little Parma is the pick of the crop. Straddling the banks of a Po tributary – the Torrente Parma – this well-off, orderly city should not be missed. The bicycle rules in the squares and cobbled lanes of the old town centre and the surrounding countryside is home not only to Parmesan cheese and Parma ham (Italy's best prosciutto), but also to a variety of castles and walking tracks. The city itself is a little expensive, but the budget-conscious can stay at the hostel or camp site.

Verdi and Toscanini composed many of their greatest works here and Stendhal immortalised the city in *La Chartreuse de Parme*.

EMILIA-ROMAGNA

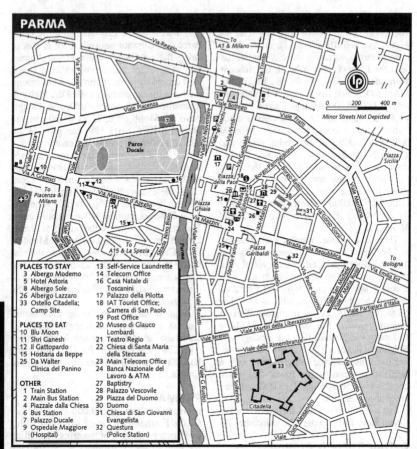

PARMA

To
A1 & Milano

Via Reggio

Via Trento

0   200   400 m

Minor Streets Not Depicted

Via Piacenza

Viale Bottego

Viale Fratti

Piazza
Sicilia

Parco
Ducale

Piazza
della Pace

Piazza
Ghiaia

Piazza
del Duomo

Via Massimo d'Azeglio

To
Piacenza &
Milano

To
A15 & La Spezia

Piazza
Garibaldi

Strada della Repubblica

To
Bologna

Via Emilia Est

Citadella

Viale Partigiani d'Italia

Viale Martiri della Liberazione

Viale delle Rimembranze

PLACES TO STAY
3 Albergo Modemo
5 Hotel Astoria
8 Albergo Sole
26 Albergo Lazzaro
33 Ostello Citadella;
    Camp Site

PLACES TO EAT
10 Blu Moon
11 Shri Ganesh
12 Il Gattopardo
15 Hostaria da Beppe
25 Da Walter
   Clinica del Panino

OTHER
1 Train Station
2 Main Bus Station
4 Piazzale dalla Chiesa
6 Bus Station
7 Palazzo Ducale
9 Ospedale Maggiore
   (Hospital)

13 Self-Service Laundrette
14 Telecom Office
16 Casa Natale di
    Toscanini
17 Palazzo della Pilotta
18 IAT Tourist Office;
    Camera di San Paolo
19 Post Office
20 Museo di Glauco
    Lombardi
21 Teatro Regio
22 Chiesa di Santa Maria
    della Steccata
23 Main Telecom Office
24 Banca Nazionale del
    Lavoro & ATM
27 Baptistry
28 Palazzo Vescovile
29 Piazza del Duomo
30 Duomo
31 Chiesa di San Giovanni
    Evangelista
32 Questura
    (Police Station)

History

Originally Etruscan, Parma achieved importance as a Roman colony on what would become the Via Emilia. As the Romans' authority dwindled, Parma passed to the Goths and later the Lombards and Franks. In the 11th century, as the conflict between the Holy Roman Empire and the papacy gathered steam, Parma threw in its lot with the former, even furnishing two anti-popes. In the following centuries internal squabbling was largely responsible for the city's turbu-

lent fate, as it fell to the Visconti family, the Sforzas, the French and finally the papacy.

The Farnese family ruled Parma in the pope's name from 1545 to 1731, when the Bourbons took control, making Parma one of the pawns in European power games. Don Philip of Bourbon, son of Spain's Philip V, and his wife Louise Elisabeth, daughter of France's Louis XV, ushered in a period of peace and frenetic cultural activity. From the time of Napoleon's incursions into northern Italy at the beginning of the 19th century,

Parma entered a period of instability that ended only with Italian unification. Some 60 years later, the barricades went up as Parma became the only Emilian city to oppose the infamous march on Roma by Mussolini's blackshirts in 1922.

Orientation

From the train station on Piazzale della Chiesa, head south along Via Verdi for the huge Palazzo della Pilotta. Cross Via Garibaldi for the duomo area or walk south for Piazza Garibaldi, the main square.

Information

Tourist Offices The IAT office (☎ 0521 21 88 89), Via Melloni 1a, is open from 9 am to 7 pm Monday to Saturday and to 1 pm Sunday. InformaGiovani (☎ 0521 21 87 48), in the same building, has information for young people and disabled travellers.

Post & Communications The main post office is on Via Melloni, off Via Garibaldi, and is open from 8.15 am to 7 pm Monday to Friday and to 12.30 pm Saturday. The Telecom office is on Piazza Garibaldi; the telephones are down a flight of stairs in front of the office and are available from 7.30 am to midnight daily. There's another office at Via Massimo d'Azeglio 660.

Medical Services & Emergency For a locum doctor at night, call the Guardia Medica on ☎ 0521 29 25 55. The Ospedale Maggiore (☎ 0521 99 11 11) is at Via Gramsci 14, west of the centre.

The questura (☎ 0521 21 94) is at Borgo della Posta.

Laundry There is a self-service laundrette on Via Massimo d'Azeglio 108.

Piazza del Duomo

The **duomo** is a classic example of the area's Romanesque design. It was begun in 1059 but largely rebuilt 60 years later after Parma was hit by an earthquake. Antonio Correggio's *Assunzione della Vergine* (Assumption of the Virgin) graces the inside of the cupola and took the painter six years to complete (from 1524). Take time to look at the restored wood inlay work in the Sagrestia dei Consorziali (sacristy) and, in the southern transept, Benedetto Antelami's delicate sculpture, the *Deposizione* (Descent from the Cross), completed in 1178. The duomo is open from 7.30 am to 12.30 pm and 3 to 7 pm daily.

Antelami was also responsible for the striking pink marble **baptistry** on the southern side of the square. Typically octagonal, it was completed in 1260 and represents the peak of Antelami's work. It is open from 9 am to 12.30 pm and 3 to 7 pm daily. Admission costs L3000.

Palazzo della Pilotta

The hulk of this immense palazzo, shattered by WWII air raids, looms over Piazza della Pace. Built for the Farnese family between 1583 and 1622, and supposedly named after the Spanish ball game of pelota which was played within its walls, it now houses several museums and galleries. The **Galleria Nazionale** is by far the most important. Its collection includes works by Antonio Correggio, Francesco Parmigianino, Fra Angelico and Van Dyck, as well as a sculpture of Empress Marie-Louise, second wife of Napoleon, by Antonio Canova. The gallery is open from 9 am to 2 pm daily and tickets cost L12,000, which includes admission to the **Teatro Farnese**. The theatre, a copy of Andrea Palladio's Teatro Olimpico in Vicenza, is housed in the palace's fencing school. It was completely rebuilt after WWII bombing.

Upstairs, the **Museo Archeologico Nazionale** is devoted partly to Roman artefacts discovered around Parma but also hosts a display of Etruscan artefacts excavated in the Pianura Padana. It is open from 9 am to 7 pm daily except Monday and admission costs L4000.

The **Biblioteca Palatina**, first opened to the public in 1769, contains more than 700,000 volumes and 5000 manuscripts. The **Museo Bodoniano**, which can be visited only by appointment, is devoted to the life of Giambattista Bodoni, who designed the typeface that bears his name.

Piazza Garibaldi

More or less on the site of the ancient Roman forum, Piazza Garibaldi is the centre of Parma. The 17th century Palazzo del Governatore at the northern end hides the **Chiesa di Santa Maria della Steccata**, which contains some of Francesco Parmigianino's most extraordinary work, including the frescoes on the arches above the altar. Many members of the ruling Farnese and Bourbons lie buried in this church, known to locals simply as La Steccata.

Chiesa di San Giovanni Evangelista

Just east of the duomo, this church and convent were built in the early 16th century on the site of a 10th century church. The ornate baroque façade was added a century later, and the magnificent decoration on the cupola is by Correggio. Parmigianino's contribution includes the adornment of the chapels. The church is open from 8.30 am to noon and from 3.30 to 6 pm (slightly longer hours on Sunday and holidays). The cloisters are open from 10 am to 1 pm and from 3.30 to 6 pm.

Visit the convent's ancient pharmacy, the **Spezieria di San Giovanni**, accessible through a small door on the northern side of the church. It opens from 9 am to 2 pm daily and admission costs L4000.

For more Correggio, head for the **Camera di San Paolo**, in the convent of the same name off Via Melloni. It's open from 9 am to 2 pm daily and admission costs L4000.

Museo di Glauco Lombardi

Waterloo meant different things to different people. While Napoleon headed into miserable exile, his second wife, Marie-Louise of Austria, got off pretty lightly. After her heady few years as Empress of the French, she was left with the dukedom of Parma, Piacenza and Guastalla. She ruled until 1847, with a moderation and good sense uncommon for the time.

Several of her belongings, including a portrait of her great husband, ended up in the hands of town notable and collector Glauco Lombardi. An eclectic assortment of Lombardi's artworks and other objects illustrative of life in Parma over the past few centuries now fill the Museo di Glauco Lombardi, at Via Garibaldi 15. It was closed at the time of writing.

West Bank

Spread along the west bank of the Parma (l'Oltretorrente) are the rambling gardens of the **Parco Ducale**, first laid out in 1560 around the Farnese family's **Palazzo Ducale**. The palazzo is now home to the local carabinieri, but groups can visit for free from 8 am to noon Monday to Saturday by calling ahead (☎ 0521 23 00 23) – check at the IAT office. The lovely public gardens are open from dawn to dusk, except in summer, when you can stroll until midnight.

At the south-eastern corner of the park, at Via R Tanzi, is the **Casa Natale di Toscanini**, the birthplace of one of Italy's greatest modern conductors, Arturo Toscanini (1867-1957). His career began almost by accident during a tour in Brazil, when he was asked to take the podium in Rio de Janeiro after the Brazilian conductor had stormed off. In 1908 he joined the New York Metropolitan and from then on split his time between Italy and the US, where he died. The house contains a small free museum dedicated to Toscanini's life and music. It opens from 10 am to 1 pm and from 3 to 6 pm Tuesday to Saturday and from 10 am to 1 pm Sunday. Admission costs L3000.

If in a musical frame of mind, you could visit the tomb of Niccolò Paganini, 2km farther south in the Cimitero della Villetta.

Places to Stay

Cheap accommodation can be difficult to find for most of the year, so bookings are advisable. Within the walls of the giant former fortress, the city's youth hostel, *Ostello Cittadella* (☎ 0521 96 14 34, Parco Cittadella 5), charges L16,000 a night. It's open from the beginning of April to the end of October. Take bus No 9 or 12 from the train station or city centre and ask the driver for directions. There is a *camp site* inside the fortress, run by the same management.

Albergo Sole (☎ 0521 99 51 07, Via Gramsci 15) has basic singles/doubles without bathroom from L50,000/85,000. Take bus No 9 from the train station. *Albergo Lazzaro* (☎ 0521 20 89 44, Via XX Marzo 14) has singles without bath for L55,000 and singles/doubles with bath from L65,000/90,000. The two star *Albergo Moderno* (☎ 0521 77 26 47, Via A Cecchi 4) is handy for the train station and has rooms for L74,000/105,000 with bathroom, but the area is a little unpleasant. *Hotel Astoria* (☎ 0521 27 27 17, Via Trento 9) has all the mod cons and is near the train station. Rooms cost L130,000/188,000 including taxes and breakfast.

Places to Eat

There's a daily produce *market* on Piazza Ghiaia, between the river and Piazza Garibaldi. A decent snack place is *Da Walter – Clinica del Panino* (Borgo Palmia 2d). The *Albergo Lazzaro* has a restaurant that does a L17,000 vegetarian dish and crêpes.

The west bank is a good place to hunt out restaurants. *Il Gattopardo* (Via Massimo d'Azeglio 63a) is one of the city's more popular pizzerie, with big pizzas from L9000 to L14,000. *Shri Ganesh*, at No 81, offers Indian main courses for L15,000. *Blu Moon* (Via Gramsci), a couple of doors down from Albergo Sole, has everything from seafood to pizzas. Main courses start at about L10,000. For a classier meal in a small spot tucked away from the main streets, search out *Hostaria da Beppe* (Strada Imbriani 49b). Delicious main courses cost around L20,000 and they also offer a self-service cold buffet for L8000.

Piazza Garibaldi is as good a spot as any to sip your Campari and read the paper.

Entertainment

Parma's opera, concert and theatre season runs from about October to April. *Teatro Regio* (☎ 0521 21 86 78, Via Garibaldi 16a) offers a particularly rich programme of music and opera, while *Teatro Due* (☎ 0521 23 02 42, Via Salnitrara 10) presents the city's top drama. In summer the city sponsors outdoor music programmes. Inquire at the IAT office for details.

Getting There & Away

TEP (☎ 0521 28 31 78) operates buses throughout the region, including into the Appennini and to Soragna and Busseto (see the following Verdi Country section). Services leave from just in front of the train station on Piazzale della Chiesa. Other services run to Mantova and Sabbioneta.

Frequent trains connect Parma to Milano, Bologna, Brescia, La Spezia and Roma.

Parma is just south of the A1 to Milano and east of the A15, which connects the A1 to La Spezia. It is on the Via Emilia (S9), while the S62 provides an alternative route parallel to the A15.

You can park your car on Piazza della Pace and there's plenty of meter parking near the station and along the main roads around the historic centre. Traffic is restricted in the centre itself.

AROUND PARMA
Verdi Country

Head north-west of Parma along the Via Emilia (S9) and branch north for Fontevivo and Fontanellato, where you will find one of the more interesting of Parma province's 25 castles. Sitting in a murky moat, the **Rocca di Sanvitale** was built in the 16th century by the family of the same name, more as a pleasure dome than a military bastion, as the Sanvitale clan was inclined to more idle pursuits. Parmigianino had a part in the decoration. It is open from 9.30 to 11.30 am and from 3 to 5 pm (longer in summer). Admission to the castle costs L7000, but to see the Parmigianino rooms you pay an extra L5000 for the compulsory guided tour.

Nine kilometres farther on is Soragna, site of the **Rocca Meli Lupi**. It looks more like a stately home than a fortress, but there are Parmigianino works and a display of period furniture. Opening times are 10 am to noon and 3 to 6 pm daily except Monday. Admission (by hourly guided tour only) costs L7000.

EMILIA-ROMAGNA

The Small World of Don Camillo

If postwar Italy was dominated by the squaring off between the church-backed Christian Democrat Party and the communists, no-one captured the essence of that conflict better than humorist Giovanni Guareschi. Emilia-Romagna, the stronghold of Italian communism, became the scene of Guareschi's village scraps between Don Camillo, the local curate with a direct line to God, and Peppone, the town mayor with a striking resemblance to Stalin. Their antics in what became known as Guareschi's Piccolo Mondo, published weekly in satirical magazines and later collected in several volumes (such as *Don Camillo* and *Don Camillo e il Suo Gregge*) were a clever balance between comedy and political satire. They were so successful that several of the stories ended up on film.

A free exhibition dedicated to Guareschi's Piccolo Mondo in the Sala delle Damigiane at Roncole Verdi is scheduled to remain open until the year 2000.

Roncole Verdi, site of the humble home where Giuseppe Verdi came into the world, is 10km on. The Casa Natale di Giuseppe Verdi is open from 9.30 am to 12.30 pm and from 3 to 7 pm daily except Monday. Admission costs L3000.

Next stop is **Busseto**, where the Teatro Verdi opens from 9.30 am to 12.30 pm and from 3 to 7 pm daily except Monday. Admission is L5000. You can also visit a small museum dedicated to Verdi in the run-down Villa Pallavicino and, a few kilometres out of Busseto, his villa at **Sant'Agata**. For more information on the Verdi sights call Busseto's local tourist office on ☎ 0524 9 24 87.

TEP buses from Parma run along this route up to six times a day on weekdays.

South into the Appennini

You could take several routes south of Parma to cross the Appennini into north-western Toscana, stopping at a castle on the way or walking through the hills and around several glacial lakes.

One route roughly follows the Parma river towards Langhirano (a town of 6th century Lombard origin, now the main production centre of the best quality ham). About 5km short of the town rises the majestic **Castello di Torrechiare**, one of many built or rebuilt by Pier Maria Rossi in the 15th century. He romped with his lover Bianca Pellegrino in the Camera d'Oro (Golden Room), where he

could look at a map of all his castles on the ceiling. The castle is open from 9 am to 1.45 pm daily except Monday and admission costs L4000 (plus L2000 for a guide).

From Langhirano, follow the road down the western bank of the Parma, crossing the river at Capoponte and proceeding to **Tizzano Val Parma**, a charming Appennini town that offers pleasant walking in summer and skiing in winter (5km farther on at Schia). Farther south still, the heights around **Monchio delle Corti** offer views to La Spezia on a good day. It's a possible base for exploring some of the 20 glacial lakes that dot the southern corner of the province, bordering Toscana.

The mountains are in fact riddled with walking and cycling tracks and rifugi. If you'd prefer to be carried, there are several organisations in the province that arrange horse-riding excursions. The IAT office in Parma can point you to some of them. An interesting challenge is to follow the **Romea**, an ancient route for pilgrims heading south to Roma, from Collecchio to Fornovo, Bardone, Terenzo, Cassio and Berceto. All these villages have interesting Romanesque remains. The IAT office in Parma has an excellent walking brochure for this route and can advise on appropriate maps.

Of the other 20 or so castles in the province, **Castello Bardi**, about 60km south-west of Parma (not on the above route), is also worth a mention. Soaring

EMILIA-ROMAGNA

Basilica Santuario della Madonna di San Luca, linked to Bologna's city walls by a 666-arched portico

Toscana – not the only wine-producing region, but one of the best

Fortification, Colle di Val d'Elsa

Don't hold your breath waiting for your post in Italy.

The gently rolling landscape of Chianti country, Toscana

above the surrounding town, it dates from 898, although most of the present structure was built in the 15th century.

Getting There & Away

TEP runs buses from Parma to most destinations throughout the province. On weekdays there are four buses a day to Bardi for instance, and at least as many to Monchio delle Corti via Langhirano. At the weekend the La Spezia-Parma train service guarantees space for transporting bicycles.

PIACENZA

postcode 29100 • pop 105,000

In the north-western corner of Emilia, just short of the Lombardia frontier, Piacenza is another prosperous town generally overlooked by tourists. Its few noteworthy monuments certainly make a stop worthwhile, but don't warrant an enormous effort to go out of your way.

Orientation & Information

The train station is on the eastern edge of

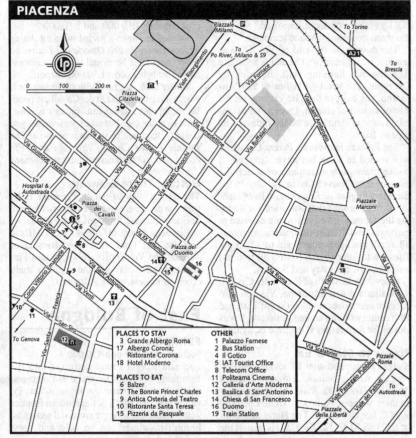

PIACENZA

PLACES TO STAY	OTHER
3 Grande Albergo Roma	1 Palazzo Farnese
17 Albergo Corona;	2 Bus Station
Ristorante Corona	4 Il Gotico
18 Hotel Moderno	5 IAT Tourist Office
	8 Telecom Office
PLACES TO EAT	11 Politeama Cinema
6 Balzer	12 Galleria d'Arte Moderna
7 The Bonnie Prince Charles	13 Basilica di Sant'Antonino
9 Antica Osteria del Teatro	14 Chiesa di San Francesco
10 Ristorante Santa Teresa	16 Duomo
15 Pizzeria da Pasquale	19 Train Station

EMILIA-ROMAGNA

town. From here it's a 20 minute walk to the central square, Piazza dei Cavalli, or you can catch bus No 1, 6 or 8.

The IAT office (☎ 0523 32 93 24), at Piazzetta Mercanti 7, was shut at the time of writing, but may have reopened by the time you read this. A temporary office had been set up in the Palazzo Farnese, but it too looked convincingly shut.

Things to See

Piazza dei Cavalli is dominated by the impressive brick and marble 13th century town hall, also known as Il Gotico. In front of the building, the two equestrian statues of the Farnese dukes Alessandro and his son Ranuccio, by Francesco Mochi, date from 1625 and are masterpieces of baroque sculpture.

The duomo, at the end of Via XX Settembre, was started in 1122 and is a sombre Romanesque building with frescoes by Guercino. The nearby Basilica di Sant'Antonino was built in the 11th century on the site of an earlier church. Its peculiar octagonal tower is claimed to be the oldest of its type in Italy.

The Palazzo Farnese on Piazza Cittadella was started in 1558 but never finished. It houses three little museums, of which the main one, the Museo Civico, is home to the Etruscan Fegato di Piacenza, a liver fashioned from bronze that was used for divining the future. The other two are devoted to carriages and Italian unification memorabilia. All are open from 9 am to 12.30 pm Tuesday to Sunday and from 3.30 to 6 pm on Thursday, Saturday and Sunday.

A few blocks south of Piazza dei Cavalli, the Galleria d'Arte Moderna, Via San Siro 13, contains a decent collection of 18th and 19th century Italian art and sculpture. It was closed for restoration at the time of writing.

Places to Stay & Eat

Budget accommodation is not one of Piacenza's strong points. Albergo Corona (☎ 0523 32 09 48, Via Roma 141) has singles/doubles without bathroom from L40,000/60,000, but call ahead. The Hotel Moderno (☎ 0523 38 50 41, Via Tibini 31) is nearest the

train station (there's no sign) and has rooms with bathroom for L55,000/70,000 (or doubles for L80,000 with own bath), but it's nothing special. If for some reason you want to spend big in Piacenza, you could try the overpriced Grande Albergo Roma (☎ 0523 32 32 01, Via Cittadella 14), where singles/doubles are an astonishing L220,000/280,000. To entice, they throw in breakfast.

You can grab a pizza at Ristorante Corona, beneath the Albergo Corona, for about L10,000. Pizzeria da Pasquale on Piazza del Duomo does a similar deal.

For modestly priced local cuisine, you could try Ristorante Santa Teresa (Corso Vittorio Emanuele II 169f). Main courses cost between L10,000 and L15,000.

One of the town's award-winning dining experiences is Antica Osteria del Teatro, on the corner of Via Verdi and Via Santa Franca. Main meals here cost L30,000 or more.

Balzer café, on Corso Vittorio Emanuele II where it runs into Piazza dei Cavalli, is popular, though the monumental interior is somewhat over the top. For an expensive ale, you could pretend you're somewhere else at The Bonnie Prince Charles (Vicolo Perestrello 10), a pub and restaurant round the corner.

Getting There & Away

The easiest way to get to Piacenza is by train, with direct services from Milano, Torino, Cremona, Bologna and Ancona.

Piacenza is just off the A1 from Milano and the A21 (and S10) from Brescia or Torino. The Via Emilia (S9) runs past Piacenza, passing through the region's main cities on its way to the Adriatico.

East of Bologna

FERRARA
postcode 44100 • pop 150,000

Lucrezia Borgia found marriage into the Este family brought several disadvantages, not least among them the move to this Po valley city, just south of the modern frontier with Veneto. Close to the river and wetlands, Ferrara in winter can be cold and grey,

EMILIA-ROMAGNA

shrouded in cloying banks of fog. As she was used to a warmer climate, Lucrezia's feelings were perhaps understandable, but Ferrara (especially on a sunny day) retains much of the austere splendour of its Renaissance heyday, when it was strong enough to keep Roma and Venezia at arm's length.

History

The Este dynasty ruled Ferrara from 1260 to 1598 and their political and military prowess was matched by an uninterrupted stream of cultural activity. Petrarch, Titian, Antonio Pisanello and the poets Torquato Tasso and Ludovico Ariosto are just some of the luminaries who spent time here under the patronage of the Este dukes.

When the House of Este fell in 1598, Pope Clement VIII claimed the city and presided over its decline. Ferrara recovered some importance during the Napoleonic period, when it was made chief city of the lower Po river. The local government has carefully restored much of the centre since the end of WWII.

Orientation

The most direct route to the centre from the train station in Piazza Stazione, on the western edge of town, is along Via Cassoli and Via Garibaldi. Alternatively, head north along Via Felisatti and turn right into Viale Cavour, the main street. Turn right again at the Castello Estense (impossible to miss) for Piazzetta del Castello. Corso Martiri della Libertà, on the eastern side of the castle, runs into Piazza Cattedrale and Piazza Trento Trieste, the centre of town.

Information

Tourist Offices The main IAT office (☎ 0532 20 93 70, email infotur.comfe@nettuno.it), in the main courtyard of the Castello Estense, is open from 9 am to 1 pm and from 2 to 6 pm Monday to Saturday (morning only on Sunday). The IAT office has a Web site at www.comune.fe.it.

The IAT publishes a useful free mini-guide, *Ferrara*, in various languages. It has information about the sights, as well as practical details. There is a L5000 cumula-

tive ticket available, which is valid to some of the town's museums.

Post & Communications The post office is at Viale Cavour 27, near the castello. The Telecom office is at Largo Castello 30 and is open from 9 am to 12.30 pm and from 3 to 7 pm.

Medical Services & Emergency For the Guardia Medica call ☎ 0532 20 31 31. The Ospedale Sant'Anna (☎ 0532 23 61 11) is at Corso della Giovecca 203.

The questura (☎ 0532 29 43 11) is at Corso Ercole I d'Este 26.

Castello Estense

The imposing castle in the centre of town was started in 1385 for Nicolò II d'Este, primarily to defend the family from riotous subjects, who at one point rebelled over tax increases. By the middle of the following century, the Este family had begun to expand the fortress. Under Ercole I it became the dynasty's permanent residence.

Although sections are now used as government offices, many of the rooms, including the royal suites, are open for viewing. Highlights are the Sala dei Giganti (Giants' Room) and Salone dei Giochi (Games Salon), with frescoes by Camillo and Sebastiano Filippi; the Cappella di Renée de France; and the dungeon. Here, in 1425, Duke Nicolò III d'Este had his young second wife, Parisina Malatesta, and his son, Ugo, beheaded after discovering they were lovers, providing the inspiration for Robert Browning's *My Last Duchess*. The castello is open from 9.30 am to 5.30 pm daily except Monday. Admission costs L8000.

Palazzo Municipale

Linked to the castello, the town hall once also contained Este family apartments. The grand staircase by Pietro Benvenuti degli Ordani is worth seeing. You may be able to see some of the rooms if you ask the attendant.

Cattedrale

Consecrated early in the 12th century, the cathedral features a mixture of Renaissance

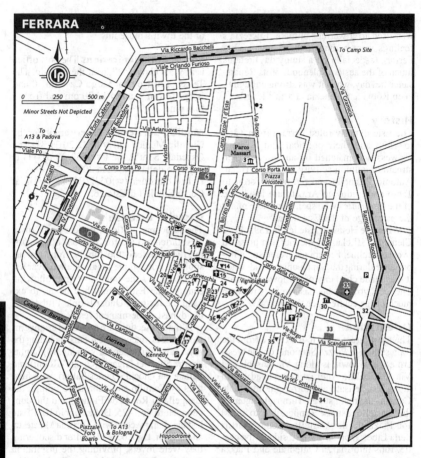

FERRARA

To Camp Site

To A13 & Padova

0   250   500 m

Minor Streets Not Depicted

To A13 & Padova

Via Riccardo Bacchelli

Viale Orlando Furioso

Via Arianuova

Parco Massari

Corso Porta Po

Corso Rossetti

Corso Porta Mare

Piazza Ariostea

Via Mascheraio

Viale Cavour

Via Cassoli

Corso Piave

Via Garibaldi

Corso della Giovecca

Via Vignatagliata

Corso Porta Reno

Cortevecchia

Via Vittoria

Via Savonarola

Canale di Burana

Darsena

Via Darsena

Via Ripagrande

Via Ramparti di San Paolo

Via Kennedy

Via Mulinetto

Via Argine Ducale

Via Borgo di Sotto

Via Scandiana

Via Mayr

Via Baluardi

Viale Volano

Via Fabbri

Via XX Settembre

Via Ungarelli

Piazzale Foro Boario

To A13 & Bologna

Hippodrome

EMILIA-ROMAGNA

and Gothic styles. Note the array of columns along its southern façade.

The **Museo della Cattedrale** has a superb collection of Renaissance pieces, including 15th century illustrated missals and works by Jacopo della Quercia and other Renaissance masters. It is open from 10 am to noon and from 3 to 5 pm Tuesday to Saturday and from 4 to 6 pm Sunday and public holidays. Admission is by donation. The bell tower was started in 1412 by the Florentine architect Leon Battista Alberti.

Museums & Galleries

North of Castello Estense, on Corso Ercole I d'Este, is the Palazzo dei Diamanti (Palace of the Diamonds), named after the shape of its rusticated façade and built for Sigismondo d'Este late in the 15th century by Biagio Rossetti. Regarded as the family's finest palazzo, the building now houses the **Pinacoteca Nazionale**, in which are hung works by artists of the Ferrarese and Bolognese schools, and a series of prints by Andrea Mantegna. The gallery is open from 9 am to 2 pm Tuesday to

FERRARA

PLACES TO STAY		OTHER		13	IAT Tourist Office
18	Albergo Annunziata	1	Porta degli Angeli	15	Cattedrale; Piazza Cattedrale
20	Albergo Centro Storico	2	Certosa (Cemetery)	16	Palazzo Municipale
22	Albergo Nazionale	3	Museo d'Arte Moderna e	19	Market
36	Casa degli Artisti		Contemporanea Filippo de Pisis	23	Parking (Foreign Cars)
		4	Questura (Police Station)	24	Piazza Trento Trieste
PLACES TO EAT		5	Museo del Risorgimento e	25	Credito Romagnolo & ATM
14	Al Brindisi		della Resistenza	28	Casa Romei
17	Dal Mio Fornaio	6	Pinacoteca Nazionale	29	Monastero del Corpus Domini
21	Trattoria Da Settimo	7	Train Station	30	Palazzina di Marfisa d'Este
26	Pizzeria il Ciclone	8	Stadium	31	Ospedale Sant'Anna (Hospital)
27	Guido	9	Bus Station	32	Piazzale Medaglie d'Oro
35	Il Cucco	10	Post Office	33	Palazzo Schifanoia
38	Antica Trattoria del Volano	11	Telecom Office	34	Palazzo di Lodovico il Moro
		12	Castello Estense	37	Tourist Office

Saturday and from 9 am to 1 pm Sunday. Admission costs L8000.

Next door at No 19 is the **Museo del Risorgimento e della Resistenza**, a fairly standard display of decrees, letters and other memorabilia tracing Italian political history from the mid-19th century to WWII. The museum is open from 9 am to 2 pm and 3 to 7 pm Monday to Saturday and from 9 am to noon and 3.30 pm to 6.30 pm Sunday and public holidays. Admission costs L4000.

The **Museo d'Arte Moderna e Contemporanea Filippo de Pisis** is in the Palazzo Massari at Corso Porta Mare 9, east of the Pinacoteca. It is open from 9 am to 1 pm and from 3 to 6 pm daily. Admission costs L4000.

The **Palazzina di Marfisa d'Este**, Corso della Giovecca 170, was built in 1559 and is worth a look for its decoration and furnishings. It is open from 9.30 am to 1 pm and from 3 to 6 pm daily. Admission costs L4000.

Lucrezia Borgia spent many of her Ferrara days in what is now the **Casa Romei**, on the corner of Via Praisolo and Via Savonarola, a typical Renaissance-style house. It is open from 8.30 am to 2 pm Monday to Thursday and to 7 pm Friday to Sunday. Admission costs L4000. Lucrezia is buried in the nearby **Monastero del Corpus Domini** (closed Saturday and Sunday), along with several Este family members.

Via Borgo di Sotto leads to the 14th century **Palazzo Schifanoia**, a sumptuous Este

residence on Via Scandiana. The Salone dei Mesi (Room of the Months), featuring frescoes by Francesco del Cossa, ranks as the finest example of Ferrarese Renaissance mural painting. The palazzo is open from 9 am to 7 pm daily. Admission costs L4000.

South of the palazzo, on the corner of Via Porta d'Amore and Via XX Settembre, is the **Palazzo di Ludovico il Moro**, housing the Museo Archeologico Nazionale. The palazzo was built by local architect Biagio Rossetti for the Duke of Milano and the collection of Etruscan artefacts is worth a look. It is open from 9 am to 2 pm Tuesday to Saturday and to 1 pm Sunday and public holidays. Admission costs L8000.

City Walls

Although not terribly impressive, most of the 9km of ancient city walls are partly intact and a tour makes a pleasant walk. Start with the Porta degli Angeli in the north of the city – the surrounding area is leafy and tranquil.

Special Events

On the last Sunday of May each year, the eight *contrade* (districts) of Ferrara compete in the Palio, a horse race that momentarily turns Piazza Ariostea into medieval bedlam. Claimed to be the oldest such race in Italy, the first official competition was held in 1279.

The Ferrara Buskers' Festival, held late each August, attracts buskers from around

EMILIA-ROMAGNA

the globe, primarily because the city pays travel and accommodation expenses for 20 of the lucky performers. Entry forms are available from the festival organisers (☎ 0532 24 93 37, fax 0532 24 97 51) or write c/o Assessorato Cultura e Turismo, Via dei Romei 3, 44100 Ferrara.

Places to Stay

Accommodation is usually easy to find, although many hotels close during August. The city's only camp site is *Estense* (☎ 0532 75 23 96, Via Gramicia), north of the centre and outside the city walls. Take bus No 1 or 5 from the train station to Piazzale San Giovanni and walk.

The best hotel deal is *Casa degli Artisti* (☎ 0532 76 10 38, Via Vittoria 66), a few minutes walk south of the cathedral; singles/doubles cost from L30,000/56,000. It's wise to book. *Albergo Centro Storico* (☎ 0532 20 97 48, Via Vegri 15), in a pretty medieval street, charges L40,000/60,000. Don't be surprised if you end up sharing your bed with a cat. The modest *Albergo Nazionale* (☎ 0532 20 96 04, Corso Porta Reno 32) has rooms from L75,000/110,000 with bathroom. For well-located luxury, head to *Albergo Annunziata* (☎ 0532 20 11 11, Piazza della Repubblica 5). Doubles start at L250,000.

Places to Eat

Ferrara's cuisine is typical of the region, incorporating meats and cheeses. One of the local specialities is *cappelacci di zucca*, a pasta pouch filled with pumpkin that looks vaguely like a small, floppy hat.

For quick, mouthwatering snacks try the bakery *Dal mio Fornaio* (Piazza Castello 2), in the square behind the castello.

Pizzeria il Ciclone (Via Vignatagliata 11) is a bright place to eat pizza. *Al Brindisi* (Via Adelardi 11), next to the cathedral, dates from 1435 and serves a salami in red-wine dish. Next door at No 9a the self-service *Pappagallo* offers a full meal for between L15,000 and L20,000 (lunch time only). The *Trattoria da Settimo* (Via Cortevecchia 49), close to the southern side of the castle, is good value and popular with locals. The tourist menu

with wine costs from L20,000. More expensive, and perhaps a little better as well, is the *Antica Trattoria del Volano* (Viale Volano 20). Try the cappelacci di zucca. Equally good is *Il Cucco* (Via Voltacasotto), where you'll be looking at L40,000 for a meal. At *Guido* (Via Vignatagliata 61), in the ghetto, a main course starts at L20,000.

Getting There & Around

The bus station is at Via Rampari di San Paolo. ACFT buses (0532 59 94 29) operate services within the city and to surrounding towns such as Comacchio as well as to the Adriatic beaches (some of these leave from the train station).

Frequent services run to Bologna, Venezia, Ravenna and other towns in the region.

Most traffic is banned from the city centre, but there is a small free parking area for foreigners' cars on Largo Castello. There is parking at the southern end of the centre on Via Bologna and the eastern edge near Piazzale Medaglie d'Oro. ACFT runs bus Nos 1, 2 and 9 from the train station to the city centre. You can hire a bike in the square in front of the station or from Corso Giovecca 21, on the opposite (east) side of town.

FOCI DEL PO

Considering the incredibly polluted state of the Po river, the Foci del Po (Po delta), which straddles Emilia-Romagna and Veneto, should be an unpleasant place. However, the stretch of coast where the river spills into the Mar Adriatico is strangely alluring, particularly because the wetlands surrounding its two large lagoons – the Valli di Comacchio in the south and the Valle Bertuzzi in the north – have been designated as nature reserves. The area provides some of Europe's best birdwatching and after years of neglect by tourist authorities it is now drawing quite a crowd. Despite this, swimming is banned and many beaches have perennial problems with sludge-like algae caused by the dumping of phosphates upstream. Another problem is that the area is plagued by mosquitoes in summer, so be sure to have insect repellent, if not mosquito nets, on hand.

Information

Most towns in the area have tourist offices, as at Comacchio (☎ 0533 31 01 47), Via Buonafede 12, although many are open in summer only, for example the Abbazia di Pomposa (☎ 0533 71 91 10) near Codigoro. The offices produce a wealth of information, including cycling itineraries, walking and horse-riding details, and tips on boat excursions, which are the best way to see the delta.

Things to See & Do

The **Abbazia di Pomposa**, 50km east of Ferrara, near Codigoro, is one of the oldest Benedictine abbeys in Italy, with a church dating from the 7th century. It is believed that the monk Guido d'Arezzo invented the musical scale here, and from about 1000 years ago the abbey was one of Italy's supreme cultural centres. Its decline began in the 14th century and in 1652 the abbey was closed. The church is adorned with frescoes from the 14th century Rimini school and works by Vitale di Bologna, and it contains a small free museum. The complex is open from 8.30 am to 7 pm daily in summer and to 4 pm in winter. The abbey stages a music festival, Musica Pomposa (☎ 0533 72 95 84 for information), each July. Sporadic buses connect Codigoro with Ravenna and Comacchio, but plan carefully or you could end up stranded.

Comacchio is a small fishing village that has one attraction – the Trepponti (Triple Bridge, built in 1635. Don't stop unless you must – the city's claim to be a mini-Venezia is a trifle exaggerated.

The delta's information office (☎ 0544 44 68 66) at **Ca' Vecchia**, a wildlife guardians' centre at Via Fossatone in the Stazione Pineta San Vitale park north of Ravenna, opens from 9 am to noon and from 4 to 7 pm in summer and from 10 am to 4 pm in winter. It produces a map detailing the types of birds likely to be found in that part of the delta's Riserva Naturale and in the sanctuaries at Punte Alberete and Valle Mandriole. You can pick up the same map at the IAT office in Ravenna.

For boat trips, try the *Delfinus* (☎ 0533 32 51 02), which leaves from Porto Garibaldi, east of Comacchio, or the *Principessa* (☎ 0533 99 98 15), which leaves from Gorino, on the Po di Goro estuary.

Places to Stay

If you want to stay in the area, *Albergo Luciana (☎ 0533 71 21 40, Via Roma 66)* in Codigoro, which charges L35,000/57,000 for a single/double.

Getting There & Away

Moving around the area using public transport is difficult. From Ferrara to the Abbazia di Pomposa, for instance, there is virtually nothing. You can get as far as Codigoro, but from there you're on your own. Taxis from Codigoro to Pomposa are hard to come by and cost from L10,000 to L15,000.

RAVENNA

postcode 48100 • pop 90,630

Celebrated for the early Christian and Byzantine mosaics that adorn its churches and monuments, Ravenna was in fact the capital of the Byzantine Empire's western regions during the reign of Emperor Justinian and Empress Theodora.

The city had been the capital of the Western Roman Empire from 402, when the ineffectual Emperor Honorius moved his court from Roma because Ravenna's surrounding malarial swamps made it easier to defend from northern invaders. They, however, simply walked around him and marched into Roma in 410. Honorius was unable, or unwilling, to react, preferring to vegetate in Ravenna until his death in 423. The city finally succumbed 50 years later. The Byzantines arrived in 540 and ruled until the Lombards conquered the city in 752. Venetians controlled Ravenna from 1441 to 1509, when it was incorporated into the Papal States.

Under the Romans, Goths and Byzantines, Ravenna gradually rose to become one of the most splendid cities in the Mediterraneo, and its mosaics are matched only by those of Istanbul. In his *Divine Comedy*, Dante described them as a symphony of colour. The city is close to Adriatic beaches, but they are hardly attractive, especially when effluent from the Po is a threat.

EMILIA-ROMAGNA

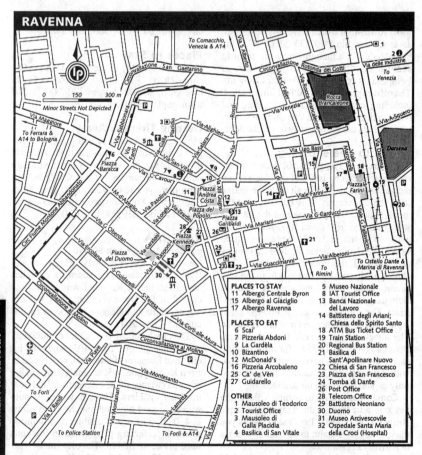

RAVENNA

0   150   300 m

Minor Streets Not Depicted

PLACES TO STAY
11 Albergo Centrale Byron
15 Albergo al Giaciglio
17 Albergo Ravenna

PLACES TO EAT
6 Scai'
7 Pizzeria Abdoni
9 La Gardèla
10 Bizantino
12 McDonald's
16 Pizzeria Arcobaleno
25 Ca' de Vèn
27 Guidarello

OTHER
1 Mausoleo di Teodorico
2 Tourist Office
3 Mausoleo di
Galla Placidia
4 Basilica di San Vitale

5 Museo Nazionale
8 IAT Tourist Office
13 Banca Nazionale
del Lavoro
14 Battistero degli Ariani;
Chiesa dello Spirito Santo
18 ATM Bus Ticket Office
19 Train Station
20 Regional Bus Station
21 Basilica di
Sant'Apollinare Nuovo
22 Chiesa di San Francesco
23 Piazza di San Francesco
24 Tomba di Dante
26 Post Office
28 Telecom Office
29 Battistero Neoniano
30 Duomo
31 Museo Arcivescovile
32 Ospedale Santa Maria
della Croci (Hospital)

EMILIA-ROMAGNA

Orientation

From the train station, on the eastern edge
of town in Piazzale Farini, it's a short walk
along Viale Farini and its continuation, Via
Diaz, into the central Piazza del Popolo.
Nearly everything of interest is within easy
walking distance of here. A few of the
cheaper hotels are near the train station.

Information

Tourist Offices The IAT office (☎ 0544 3
54 04) is at Via Salara 12, off Via Cavour.

It's open from 8.30 am to 7 pm Monday
to Saturday in summer (until 6 pm in winter) and until 4 pm on Sunday and public
holidays. A second office (☎ 0544 45 15
39) is open from April to September at
the Mausoleo di Teodorico, Via delle Industrie 14.

Post & Communications The main post
office is on Piazza Garibaldi and opens
from 8.15 am to 7.10 pm Monday to Friday
and from 8.15 am to 12.50 pm Saturday.

The Telecom office, at Via G Rasponi 22, is open from 8 am to 11 pm daily.

Medical Services & Emergency The Ospedale Santa Maria delle Croci (☎ 0544 40 91 11) is at Via Missiroli 10. The questura (☎ 0544 54 41 11) is some distance from the centre at Via Berlinguer 10-20.

Things to See

A *biglietto cumulativo* (cumulative ticket) allows you into the six main monuments for L10,000. If you intend to view the Museo Internazionale delle Ceramiche in Faenza as well, buy the ticket for L12,000 (not available if there is a visiting exhibition). Opening times given are summer times, which tend to be longer than those during the rest of the year.

Basilica di San Vitale Set back a little from the street of the same name and a few minutes walk north-west of the IAT office, the Basilica di San Vitale was consecrated in 547 by Archbishop Maximian. Its sombre exterior hides a dazzling internal feast of colour, dominated by the mosaics around the chancel, which was constructed between 521 and 548. The **mosaics** on the side and end walls represent scenes from the Old Testament. To the left, Abraham and the three angels and the sacrifice of Isaac are depicted, and on the right, the death of Abel and the offering of Melchizedek. Inside the chancel, the finest mosaics of the series depict the Byzantine Emperor Justinian with San Massimiano and Empress Theodora. The basilica is open from 9 am to 7 pm. Admission costs L6000 (if you don't have the L10,000 ticket).

Mausoleo di Galla Placidia In the same grounds as the basilica lies the mausoleum erected by Galla Placidia, the half-sister of Emperor Honorius, who initiated construction of many of Ravenna's grandest buildings. The light inside, filtered through the alabaster windows, is dim but good enough to illuminate the city's oldest mosaics (same opening hours and admission prices as the basilica).

Museo Nazionale Also near the basilica, this is Ravenna's main museum. Monks began the collection of prehistoric, Roman, Christian and Byzantine artefacts in the 18th century and various items from later periods have been added. The ticket office is open from 8.30 am to 6.30 pm daily and to 10 pm Sunday and public holidays during the summer. Admission costs L8000 and is not covered by the cumulative ticket.

Duomo The town's duomo, on Via G Rasponi, was built in 1733 after its 5th century predecessor was destroyed by earthquake. The duomo itself is unremarkable, but the small adjoining **Museo Arcivescovile** (Episcopal Museum) contains an exquisite 6th century ivory throne of San Maximiano and some beautiful mosaics. More mosaics, of Christ's baptism and the apostles, can be seen in the neighbouring **Battistero Neoniano**. Thought to have started life as a Roman bathhouse, it was converted into a baptistry in the 5th century. The buildings are open from 9.30 am to 6.30 pm. Admission to both the museum and baptistry is L5000 (if you don't have the cumulative ticket).

Tomba di Dante As Dante indicated in the *Divine Comedy* (much of it written in Ravenna), politics is a dodgy business. Following his exile from Firenze in 1302, Dante finally went to live in Ravenna, where he died in 1321. Firenze still supplies the oil for the lamp in Dante's tomb, as a perpetual act of penance for having exiled him. The tomb is next to the Chiesa di San Francesco and there is a small **museum** (admission L3000). A mound placed over his sarcophagus during WWII, to protect it from air raids, is proudly marked and the area around the tomb has been declared a *zona di silenzio*. It is open from 9 am to noon daily except Monday and also from 3.30 to 6 pm in summer.

Still on the subject of literary greats, Lord Byron lived in a house on Piazza di San Francesco in 1819.

Other Churches Those appreciative of mosaics will want to visit the **Basilica di**

Sant'Apollinare Nuovo, off Via di Roma, originally built by the Goths in the 6th century. The high walls in the nave are covered with mosaics; those on the right depict a procession of 26 martyrs and those opposite a procession of virgins. It is open from 9.30 am to 6.30 pm and admission costs L5000 (if you don't have the cumulative ticket).

The Gothic **Battistero degli Ariani** is behind the Chiesa dello Spirito Santo, on Via Diaz.

Five kilometres south-east of the city centre is the **Basilica di Sant'Apollinare in Classe** (take bus No 4 or the train to Classe). The basilica was built in the 6th century on the burial site of Ravenna's patron saint, who converted the city to Christianity in the 2nd century; it features a brilliant mosaic over the altar. Admission costs L4000.

Mosaic Courses

The Centro Internazionale di Studi per l'Insegnamento del Mosaico runs a series of two-week mosaic courses during June, July and August, starting at L600,000. Contact CISIM (☎ 0544 45 03 44, email mosaico@racine.ravenna.it), Via M. Monti 32, 48100 Ravenna, for information or see its Web site at www.mosaico.ravenna.it.

Places to Stay

The city is an easy day trip from Bologna, but staying overnight is no problem (except in summer) as it has a hostel and a few cheap hotels. The closest camp sites are at Marina di Ravenna on the beach (take ATM bus No 70 or follow the S67). *Camping Piomboni* (☎ 0544 53 02 30, Viale della Pace 421) and *Campeggio Rivaverde* (☎ 0544 53 04 91, Viale delle Nazioni 301) have reasonably priced sites.

Ostello Dante (☎ 0544 42 11 64, Via Aurelio Nicolodi 12), the HI youth hostel, is 1km from the train station towards the beach and is served by bus No 1. B&B is L24,000 and a meal L14,000. It has family rooms.

Albergo al Giaciglio (☎ 0544 3 94 03, Via Rocca Brancaleone 42) is one of the cheaper alternatives, with rooms starting at L35,000/52,000. *Albergo Ravenna* (☎ 0544

21 22 04, Viale Maroncelli 12) has rooms with bathroom from L60,000/80,000 and is handy for the train station. It also has parking. Those with looser purse strings could do worse than the central *Albergo Centrale Byron* (☎ 0544 21 22 25, Via IV Novembre 14); it has singles/doubles from L95,000/126,000.

Places to Eat

The city's fresh-produce *Mercato Coperto* (market) on Piazza Andrea Costa, north of Piazza del Popolo, is the best bet for budget food. The self-service *Bizantino*, on the same piazza, is also very cheap. *Pizzeria Arcobaleno* (☎ 0544 21 25 36, Viale Farini 34) has good pizza by the slice. *Pizzeria Abdoni (Via Cavour 31)* has pizza by the slice from L1300, and the *McDonald's* in Piazza del Popolo has a great view.

The *Ca' de Vèn* enoteca *(Via Corrado Ricci 24)* has a good selection of local wines and serves traditional food at reasonable prices in a very nearly medieval atmosphere. At *La Gardèla (Via Ponte Marino 1)* and *Scai' (Via Maggiore 2)* you can eat a meal for about L30,000, while *Guidarello (Via Gessi 9, Via Mentana 33)* specialises in local dishes and charges from L9000 for main courses and L23,000 for a tourist menu.

Entertainment

The Ravennati let it all hang out for the annual *blues festival* in July, which attracts big US names. There is also a busy summer concert calendar, including jazz and opera. Inquire at the IAT office.

Shopping

To see local artisans constructing mosaics in the traditional way, visit Cooperativa Mosaicisti, next to the Museo Nazionale at Via Benedetto Fiandrini 1, which specialises in copies of the city's finer works. Most are for sale.

Getting There & Around

ATM buses (☎ 0544 3 52 88) depart from Piazzale Farini in front of the train station for towns along the coast. Full information is available at the Punto Bus/ATM ticket office on the piazza.

Frequent trains connect the city with Bologna, Ferrara (where you can change for Venezia), Faenza, Rimini and the south coast.

Ravenna is on a branch of the A14 Bologna-Rimini autostrada and the S16 (Via Adriatica) heads south from Ravenna to Rimini and on down the coast. The main car parks are at the train station and behind the Basilica di San Vitale, but there are several others in town.

Ravenna is easy to cover on foot. To see the city by bicycle, hire one at Coop San Vitale, on Piazzale Farini to the left of the station, for L2000 an hour or L15,000 a day.

AROUND RAVENNA
Bicycle Tour
The Ravenna IAT office produces a slim brochure detailing a three day tour beginning and ending in Cervia, on the coast south of the city, which takes you through pine forests and past lagoons in the coastal area up towards the Valli di Comacchio.

Faenza
This Romagnola town has been producing high-grade ceramics for hundreds of years and gave us the word faïence. A 30 minute train ride from Ravenna, the **Museo Inter-** **nazionale delle Ceramiche** (☎ 0546 2 12 40) is worth a visit. It's open from 9 am to 7 pm daily in summer. Admission costs L10,000 or L15,000 if there is a visiting exhibition.

You can get a L12,000 ticket in Ravenna that covers six monuments within that town as well as the Museo Internazionale delle Ceramiche. There's a tourist office (☎ 0546 2 52 31) at Piazza del Popolo 1.

Mirabilandia
This huge amusement park, about 10km south of Ravenna, could be one for the kids. Free buses connect with local trains at the Savio station. Admission costs L34,000 for adults and L27,000 for children. For information, call ☎ 800 85 10 82 toll-free.

RIMINI
postcode 47900 • pop 200,000
Originally Umbrian, then Etruscan and Roman, Rimini sits at the centre of the Riviera del Sole and is now inhabited by beach lovers. The city continued to change hands through the Middle Ages, knowing Byzantine, Lombard and papal rule before ending up in the hands of the Malatesta family in the 13th century. At the beginning of the 16th century Cesare Borgia added the city to his list of short-lived conquests, until it was ruled by Venezia and, finally, again by

EMILIA-ROMAGNA

Remembering Il Duce

It might seem a little odd that Italy's great dictator, Benito Mussolini, should have been born and raised in the traditionally left-wing territory of the Romagna. Predappio, a village overloaded with monumental buildings erected by its most infamous son, is also the Fascist leader's final resting place; his remains were buried here in 1957. About 15km south of Forli (a dull town 45km north-west of Rimini along the Via Emilia), Predappio is the scene of pro-Fascist celebrations each year, when the faithful few mark 31 October, the anniversary of the day Mussolini became prime minister in 1922. Many of the young skinheads and older faithful probably forget that their beloved icon, prior to donning the black shirt, started his political life as a card-carrying socialist and journalist who rarely missed a chance to wave the red rag.

NICKY CAVEN

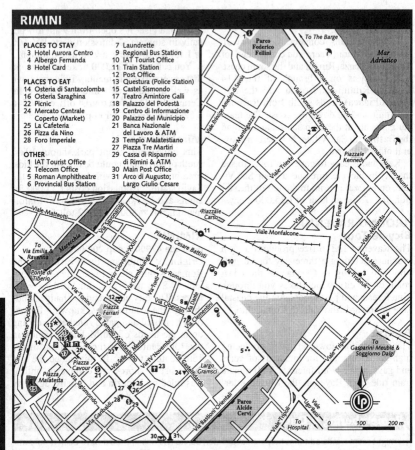

RIMINI

PLACES TO STAY
3 Hotel Aurora Centro
4 Albergo Fernanda
8 Hotel Card

PLACES TO EAT
14 Osteria di Santacolomba
16 Osteria Saraghina
22 Picnic
24 Mercato Centrale
   Coperto (Market)
25 La Cafeteria
26 Pizza da Nino
28 Foro Imperiale

OTHER
1 IAT Tourist Office
2 Telecom Office
5 Roman Amphitheatre
6 Provincial Bus Station

7 Laundrette
9 Regional Bus Station
10 IAT Tourist Office
11 Train Station
12 Post Office
13 Questura (Police Station)
15 Castel Sismondo
17 Teatro Amintore Galli
18 Palazzo del Podestà
19 Centro di Informazione
20 Palazzo del Municipio
21 Banca Nazionale
   del Lavoro & ATM
23 Tempio Malatestiano
27 Piazza Tre Martiri
29 Cassa di Risparmio
   di Rimini & ATM
30 Main Post Office
31 Arco di Augusto;
   Largo Giulio Cesare

EMILIA-ROMAGNA

the Papal States. Rimini joined the Kingdom of Italy in 1860.

The charming old city centre was badly damaged by 400 bombing raids in WWII, but enough remains to warrant a quick look. The town's main attractions are the beach and its frenetic nightlife; young people flock there every weekend from as far as away as Roma. In summer, Rimini fills with Italian and, increasingly, foreign holiday-makers in search of a scrap of beach and nocturnal fun and games – they have more than 100 discos and clubs to choose from. In spite of all this, it remains a ritual family holiday destination for many Italians.

Orientation

The main train station is on Piazzale Cesare Battisti, on the northern edge of the old city centre. From there, Via Dante becomes Via IV Novembre and leads to Piazza Tre Martiri in the city centre. Corso d'Augusto heads north-west from here to the city's other main square, Piazza Cavour. To get to the beach, walk to the north-western edge of Piazzale Cesare Battisti and turn right into Viale Principe Amedeo di Savoia, which broadens into the Parco di Federico Fellini at the waterfront.

Information

Tourist Offices The IAT office (☎ 0541 5 13 31, email iat2@iper.net) at Piazzale Cesare Battisti 1, near the train station, is open from 8 am to 7 pm Monday to Saturday (10 am to 4 pm in winter) and to 2 pm Sunday and public holidays. There's another office (☎ 0541 5 69 02) at Piazzale Federico Fellini 3, open from 8 am to 8 pm in summer and from 9 am to noon and from 3 to 6 pm in winter. The Comune di Rimini (☎ 0541 7 04 12) operates the Centro di Informazione at Corso d'Augusto 156, which opens from 8 am to 1 pm and from 2.30 to 7 pm Monday to Friday and to 1 pm Saturday. They all provide an array of brochures, including the *Agenda Book*, a useful guide to the city. The tourist office has a Web site at www.riminiturismo.it (in Italian only).

Money There are plenty of banks where you can exchange currency. The Banca Nazionale del Lavoro and Cassa di Risparmio di Rimini, both on Corso d'Augusto, have ATMs that accept Visa and several other cards.

Post & Communications The main post office is on Largo Giulio Cesare and is open from 8.10 am to 5.30 pm Monday to Friday and to 1 pm Saturday. There's a branch at Via Gambalunga.

The Telecom office is at Viale Trieste 1 and is open from 8 am to 9.30 pm.

Medical Services & Emergency The Guardia Medica (☎ 0541 70 57 57) operates at night and at weekends. In summer there is a tourist medical service north of the city at Piazzale Pascoli 2. It opens from 8 am to 8 pm. The Ospedale Infermi (☎ 0541 70 51 11) is at Viale Luigi Settembrini 2, southeast of the city centre along Viale Roma and Viale Ugo Bassi.

The questura (☎ 0541 35 31 11) is at Corso d'Augusto 192.

Castel Sismondo

Brooding over the south-western corner of the old town, the castle takes its name from Sigismondo, one of the Malatesta family, which ruled for a couple of centuries until Cesare Borgia took over in 1500. Sigismondo was the worst of a pretty bad lot, condemned to hell by Pope Pius II, who burned an effigy of him in Roma because of his shameful crimes, which included rape, murder, incest, adultery and severe oppression of his people – the usual stuff.

Otherwise known as the Rocca Malatestiana, the building houses the **Museo delle Culture Extraeuropee Dinz Rialto**, a collection of African, Asian and pre-Columbian art. It is open from 8.30 am to 12.30 pm Tuesday to Friday and from 5 to 7 pm Saturday and Sunday. Admission costs L4000.

Roman Remains

Evidence of the Roman presence in the city is found in the **Arco di Augusto** (Arch of Augustus) which was built in 27 BC, at the eastern end of Corso d'Augusto, the evocative **Ponte di Tiberio** (Tiberius' Bridge), at the western end of the same thoroughfare, built in the 1st century AD as testimony to the city's importance to the empire, and the **Roman amphitheatre**, built in the 2nd century AD, at the corner of Viale Roma and Via Bastioni Orientali. Archaeologists have recently dug up Piazza Ferrari to get at a Roman villa once owned by a wealthy surgeon. Their explorations have revealed pavement mosaics and the most complete set of ancient surgical instruments ever discovered on a Roman site. There are plans to open the site to visitors from June to September and on appointment in winter. Ask at the tourist office for information. The Roman forum lay where Piazza Tre Martiri is today.

Tempio Malatestiano

On Via IV Novembre, the temple of the Malatesta clan is the grandest monument in

EMILIA-ROMAGNA

Rimini. Dedicated to San Francesco, the 13th century church was transformed into a personal chapel for the evil Sigismondo Malatesta and his beloved Isotta degli Atti, and is one of the more significant creations of the Renaissance. Most of the work on the unfinished façade was done by Leon Battista Alberti, one of the period's great architects. A crucifix inside is believed to be the work of Giotto, and the church contains a fresco by Piero della Francesca.

Piazza Cavour

This central piazza is lined with the city's finest palazzi, including the **Palazzo del Municipio**, built in 1562 and rebuilt after being razed during WWII. The Gothic **Palazzo del Podestà** was built in the 14th century and is currently undergoing restoration. The **Teatro Amintore Galli** only went up in 1857, in the feverish years leading to unification.

Beaches

Most of the beaches along the coast are either rented to private companies, which in turn rent space to bathers, or are connected to the many nearby hotels. The average daily charge for a deck chair and umbrella is L16,000. Being the kind of resort it is, many people hire changing facilities and chairs for a week or more. Two deck chairs and an umbrella in the front row with cabin facilities would cost L190,000 a week! These private areas are worth it if you have children. They all have bars and small playgrounds and often organise special activities. Otherwise, head for the public areas of the beach without the umbrellas – there is one near the pier.

The Po river pumps its heavily polluted waters into the Adriatico north of Rimini and this occasionally results in green algae washing onto the shores. Beaches have been closed over summer in the past, so check before you swim.

Sailboards can be hired from Bagno Nettuno on the beach near Piazzale Kennedy, while bicycles can be hired at Piazzale Kennedy.

Theme Parks

Rimini is not just for sun-lovers and socialites; there are numerous theme parks for kids and their suffering parents. You could try **Italia in Miniatura** (☎ 0541 73 20 04) in Viserba, a fairly ambitious collection of reproductions of, well, bits of Italy, such as the 6600 sq metres given over to 1:5 scale models of some 120 buildings facing Venezia's Canal Grande and Piazza San Marco. During the high summer season admission costs L24,000 for adults and L18,000 for kids, but prices are lower out of season. Take bus No 8 from Rimini's train station.

Fiabilandia (☎ 0541 37 20 64), in Rivazzura di Rimini, is a fantasy park full of weird and wonderful characters. It costs L23,000 and L18,000 for kids. It's not really suitable for very young children. Take bus No 9 from Rimini's train station.

There are also several **dolphinariums** in the area, including one right on the beach at Rimini (☎ 0541 5 02 98). Admission costs L15,000 for adults and L10,000 for kids over three years old. There is another at Riccione (☎ 0541 60 17 12), which charges L15,000 for adults and L13,000 for kids. Take bus No 11 from Rimini. Waterparks in the area include **Aquafàn** (☎ 0541 60 30 50) at Riccione. Admission costs L35,000 for adults and L20,000 for kids over five years old. There are special bus services at 9 am and 10.15 am from Marina Centro at Rimini but you have to book tickets at a travel agency.

Places to Stay

Unless you have booked in advance, accommodation can be difficult to find and very expensive in summer, as proprietors often make full board compulsory. In winter, many of the 1500 hotels close and the city is dead. Your only hope in summer is the touts, sanctioned by the IAT, who frequent intersections on the outskirts of the city and offer rooms at so-called bargain rates, which can be excessive. For booking ahead, ask the IAT office to send you a hotel list. Otherwise, try Adria Hotel Reservation

(☎ 0541 39 05 30) or Associazione Albergatori (☎ 0541 5 33 99).

The camp site **Maximum** (*☎ 0541 73 23 22*), on Viale Principe Di Piemonte at Miramare, south-east of the city, is accessible by bus No 10 or 11 and is near the water. **Camping Italia International** (*☎ 0541 73 28 82, Via Toscanelli 112*) is north-west of the centre at Viserba and can be reached on bus No 4.

The great majority of hotels close outside the main season. Those listed below are open year-round. During August prices increase significantly. **Hotel Card** (*☎ 0541 2 64 12, Via Dante 50*), on a busy road near the train station, has doubles starting at L64,000. **Gasparini Meuble** (*☎ 0541 38 12 77, Via Boiardo 3*) charges upwards of L76,000 for a double with breakfast. The adjacent **Soggiorno Dalgi** (*☎ 0541 38 57 32, Via Boiardo 5*) has similar prices. They are both out of town to the south-east. **Albergo Fernanda** (*☎ 0541 39 11 00, Via Griffa 2*), on the eastern side of town across Viale Tripoli, has rooms starting at L35,000/70,000, and the restaurant offers fish meals for about L35,000. **Hotel Aurora Centro** (*☎ 0541 39 10 02, Via Tobruk 6*), north of Viale Tripoli, offers singles/doubles with bathroom starting at L45,000/80,000.

Places to Eat
The city is not noted for its culinary contribution to the Italian table and many restaurants offer cheap tourist menus. The **Mercato Centrale Coperto** (produce market) is at Via Castelfidardo. **Picnic** (*Via Tempio Malatestiano 32*) is one of the better budget deals. You can pick up cheap takeaway pizza at **Pizza da Nino** (*Via IV Novembre 9*). **La Cafeteria**, at No 11 on the same street, has good snacks.

Osteria di Santacolomba (*☎ 0541 78 00 48, Via di Duccio 2/4*), off Piazza Malatesta, is in the former bell tower of an 8th century church and serves traditional cuisine, with dishes starting at about L15,000.

The simple **Osteria Saraghina** (*☎ 0541 78 37 94, Via Poletti 32*), just off the central Piazza Malatesta, serves good quality fish dishes from L30,000 to L50,000; alternatively tell the friendly staff how much you want to spend and leave the rest to them.

A good place for people-watching and even a moderately priced meal is **Foro Imperiale** (*Piazza Tre Martiri*).

Entertainment
The most trendy place for locals and tourists is **The Barge** (*Lungomare Tintori 13*), close to Piazzale Fellini; a Romagnola version of the Irish pub. The tasteful decoration and good music, drinks and food are a magnet for fashionable twentysomethings.

The area's discos and clubs are north and south of the centre of Rimini. The most famous is **Cocorico**, at Riccione, a virtual mecca for Italian teenagers. Another is the **Paradiso Club**, at Rimini. Ask at the IAT office for your type of club and also about the special buses which service the discos.

Getting There & Away
The city's Aeroporto Civile (☎ 0541 71 57 11), Via Flaminia, is served by flights from Roma and Milano.

There are regular buses to towns along the coast, including Riccione (No 11) and Cattolica (Nos 11 and 125). Regular services to San Marino run from Rimini's train station (L16,000 return). There's also a direct bus to Roma.

Trains run frequently down the coast to Ancona, Bari, Lecce and Taranto, and up the line through Bologna and on to Milano and Torino.

You have a choice of the A14 (south into Le Marche or north-west towards Bologna and Milano) or the toll-free but often clogged S16.

Getting Around
TRAM buses operate throughout the city and to the airport. Heading north, Bus Nos 10 and 11 pass the station and go through Piazza Tre Martiri, before heading for Piazzale di Federico Fellini. Heading south, Bus No 11 runs between the train station and Riccione.

EMILIA-ROMAGNA

From the end of July to mid-September, TRAM operates special late-night bus services connecting the out of town clubs with the city centre, train station and camp sites. The buses run from about 10.30 pm to 4.30 am, after which you'll have to stay in the clubs or walk.

Taxis (☎ 0541 5 00 20) charge a minimum of L7000, then L1850 per kilometre. You can hire bicycles at Piazzale Kennedy, on the waterfront.

San Marino

postcode 47890 • pop 26,000
What did King Arthur say of Camelot in Monty Python's *The Holy Grail*? 'It is a silly place.' Lying 657m above sea level and only 10km from the Mar Adriatico as the crow flies, the 61 sq km Repubblica di

San Marino seems a little silly as well – one can only speculate as to what Mexico's consul does here! Everybody mocks this place, but it's perhaps a little unfair. True, you are unlikely to see a greater density of kitsch souvenir stands in many other tourist centres, but San Marino is not alone in selling kitsch and although there isn't an awful lot to see, the old town is pleasant and the views all around are quite spectacular.

If you're in Rimini, think of it as just another of the beach resort's theme parks. You can take pictures of the republic's soldiers, buy local coinage (a San Marino version of lira) and send mail with San Marino stamps. Be warned that at the weekend, especially in summer, central San Marino can be choked with visitors.

History

There are innumerable legends describing the founding of this hilly city-state, including one about a stonecutter who was given the land on top of Monte Titano by a rich Roman woman whose son he had cured. At any rate, the inhabitants of the mountain republic are the inheritors of 1700 years of revolution-free liberty; 'Welcome to the Country of Freedom', the signs proclaim. Everybody has left San Marino alone. Well almost. Cesare Borgia waltzed in early in the 16th century, but his own demise was just around the corner and his rule was short-lived. In 1739 one Cardinal Giulio Alberoni took over the republic, but the pope backed San Marino's independence and that was that. During WWII, the republic remained neutral and played host to 100,000 refugees until the Allies marched into the town, in 1944. San Marino joined the European Council in 1988 and the United Nations in 1992.

Orientation

If you arrive by car, you'll have to leave it at one of the numerous car parks and walk or take the series of stairs and elevators to the town. The car parks are expensive and the minimum fee is L7500, even if you stay for only an hour.

SAN MARINO

1 Funivia Station
2 Tourist Office; Telephones
3 Albergo Bellavista
4 Basilica del Santo
5 Palazzo Publico
6 Albergo Diamond
7 Tourist Office; Telephones
8 Bus Station
9 Tourist Office; Telephones
10 La Rocca o Guaita
11 Post Office
12 Cesta o Fratta

Information

In the capital, also called San Marino, the Ufficio di Stato per il Turismo (☎ 0549 88 29 98), in the Palazzo del Turismo, Contrada Omagnano 20, is open from 8.15 am to 2.15 pm daily (to 6 pm on Monday and Thursday afternoons). Two other offices, one at Contrada del Collegio 40 and the other just inside Porta di San Francesco, are open daily. The latter two will stamp your passport for a fee.

The main post office is at Viale Antonio Onofri 87 and is open from 8.15 am to 4.30 pm Monday to Friday. You can buy the republic's special stamps here. There are telephones at the information offices.

Things to See & Do

The best thing to do is wander along the well-kept city walls and drop in at the two fortresses, **La Rocca o Guaita** and **Cesta o Fratta**. Otherwise there are a couple of small **museums** containing ancient weapons, instruments of torture and wax dummies. Below the city, on the road to Rimini in Borgo Maggiore, the small **Museo di Auto d'Epoca** (☎ 0549 90 62 92) is OK if you like looking at cars old and new. Admission costs L5000.

Places to Stay & Eat

There are *camp sites* signposted off the main road (S72) through the republic from Rimini. San Marino city has quite a few hotels should you decide to stay. The cheapest is *Albergo Bellavista* (☎ *0549 99 12 12, Contrada del Pianello 42/44)*, with rooms starting at L60,000/80,000. Only a short walk away is *Albergo Diamond (☎ 0549 99 10 03, Contrada del Collegio 50)*, with singles/doubles starting at L65,000/80,000.

The city centre is dotted with places offering set meals starting at L28,000. The best thing about some of the cafés and snack bars is the views.

Shopping

Nothing is probably the best advice. Liquor stores claim to sell cut-price alcohol, but you would want to be sure about what your poison is worth in Italy before buying here in the belief that you're getting duty-free bargains.

Getting There & Away

Up to nine buses run daily to Rimini. Bonelli (☎ 0541 37 24 32) has a daily service to Urbino. Buses arrive at the parking station in Piazzale Calcigni, better known as Piazzale delle Autocorriere. There are no trains. If you are driving, the S72 leads into the city centre from Rimini. If all the car parks in the city fill up, you are obliged to park near the *funivia* (cable car; ☎ 0549 88 35 90) and catch the latter to the centre (L5000 return). A trip along the winding roads leading south to Urbino in Le Marche is recommended.

Toscana (Tuscany)

The people of Toscana can rightly claim to have just about the best of everything – architecture, the country's greatest collection of art, beautiful countryside bathed in soft pink hues and some of Italy's finest fresh produce and best known wines. It was from Toscana, about 600 years ago, that the effects of the Renaissance began to ripple out across Europe.

The works of Donatello, Michelangelo, Leonardo da Vinci and other 15th and 16th century Tuscan masters remain models for artists worldwide. Tuscan architects – notably Brunelleschi, responsible for the magnificent dome of Firenze's duomo, and Leon Battista Alberti, who designed much of the façade of the Basilica di Santa Maria Novella – have had an enduring influence on the course of architecture.

Dante, Petrarch and Boccaccio planted the seeds for the birth of a unified Italian language with their vigorous literature. Even today the Senesi (Sienese) and the Fiorentini (Florentines) maintain a keen rivalry over who speaks the 'purest' Italian (Italians beyond Toscana would probably dispute that either can take that accolade, since modern Italian is more than simply a derivative of Tuscan).

Most people are drawn to Toscana by the artistic splendour of Firenze and Siena or to view the Torre Pendente (Leaning Tower) in Pisa. But Toscana also features some of Italy's most impressive hill towns, including San Gimignano, Volterra, Cortona and Montepulciano.

The Etruscan sites in the south – around Saturnia and Sovana – will take you away from the mainstream tourist itinerary. Southern Toscana also boasts some of Italy's best beaches – on Monte Argentario and on Isola d'Elba.

Walkers and nature lovers can enjoy the Alpi Apuane, the Garfagnana, the Mugello (north-east of Firenze) and the Parco Naturale della Maremma, near Grosseto.

Highlights

- Admire the duomo and battistero in the heart of Firenze
- Bathe in the ocean of Renaissance art in the Galleria degli Uffizi
- Relax on a beach on the Isola d'Elba
- Meander along the narrow lanes of the glorious medieval city of Siena
- Explore the spectacularly located town of Pitigliano in the south of Toscana
- Tickle your palate with fine Tuscan wines, from Chianti to Montalcino

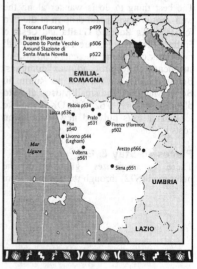

Tuscan cuisine is dominated by bread and the extra virgin olive oil produced in the region's hills. Bread features in every course, including dessert, where it can be topped with egg yolk and orange rind and sprinkled with a heavy layer of powdered sugar.

Crostini (minced chicken liver canapés)

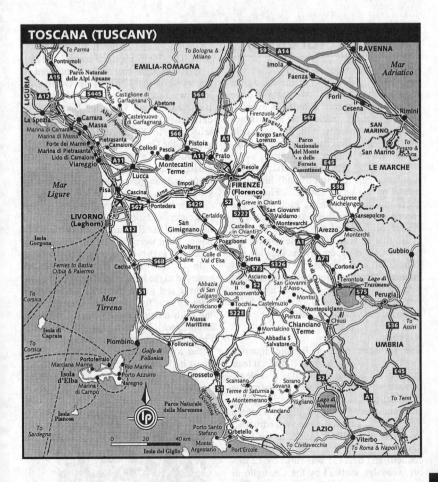

TOSCANA (TUSCANY)

and *fettunta* (a slab of toasted bread rubbed with garlic and dipped in oil) are popular *antipasti* (starters) and hearty soups, such as *ribollita*, thickened with bread, are common first courses.

Meat and poultry are grilled, roasted or fried and may come simply with a slice of lemon (which the Tuscans refer to as sauce). Traditional desserts are simple, such as biscuits flavoured with nuts or spices and served with a glass of the dessert wine *vin santo*.

The region's wines are among the country's best known and include Chianti, the *vino nobile* of Montepulciano, and Brunello di Montalcino. Traditionally, most Tuscan wines are red, but in recent years the vineyards around San Gimignano have produced Vernaccia, a crisp white.

Travelling in Toscana is easy. The A1 and the main train line ensure good north-south connections and most areas are easily accessible by public transport. A car does, however, give you greater flexibility.

Firenze (Florence)

postcode 50100 • pop 461,000

In a valley on the banks of the Arno river and set among low hills covered with olive groves and vineyards, Firenze is immediately captivating. Cradle of the Renaissance and home of Machiavelli, Michelangelo and the Medici, the city seems unfairly burdened with art, culture and history.

Despite the relentless traffic, stifling summer heat, pollution and industrial sprawl on the city's outskirts, Firenze attracts millions of tourists each year. The French writer Stendhal was so dazzled by the magnificence of the Basilica di Santa Croce that he was barely able to walk for faintness. He is apparently not the only one to have felt overwhelmed by the beauty of Firenze – they say Florentine doctors treat a dozen cases of 'Stendhalismo' a year.

You will need at least four or five days to do Firenze any justice at all.

History

The Etruscan city of Fiesole founded Firenze as a colony in about 200 BC. It later became the Roman Florentia, a strategic garrison whose purpose was to control the Via Flaminia linking Roma to northern Italy and Gaul. Along with the rest of northern Italy, the city suffered during the barbarian invasions of the Dark Ages. In the early 12th century it became a free *comune* (town council) and by 1138 was ruled by 12 *priori* (consuls), assisted by the Consiglio di Cento (Council of One Hundred). The council members were drawn mainly from the prosperous merchant class. Agitation among differing factions in the city led to the appointment of a foreign head of state, known as the *podestà*, in 1207.

The first conflicts between the pro-papal Guelfi (Guelphs) and the pro-imperial Ghibellini (Ghibellines) started in the mid-13th century, with power passing from one faction to another for almost a century. The Guelfi eventually formed a government, known as the Primo Popolo, but in 1260

were ousted after Firenze was defeated by Ghibelline Siena at the Battle of Montaperti. The Guelfi regained control in 1289.

If you thought that was complicated, it got worse in the 1290s as the Guelfi split into two factions: the Neri (Blacks) and Bianchi (Whites). When the Bianchi were defeated, Dante was among those driven into exile in 1302. As the nobility lost ground, the Guelf merchant class took control but trouble was never far away. The great plague of 1348 halved the city's population and the government was rocked by growing agitation from the lower classes.

In the late 14th century Firenze was ruled by a caucus of Guelfi under the leadership of the Albizzi family. Among the families opposing them were the Medici, whose influence grew as they became the papal bankers.

In the 15th century Cosimo de' Medici emerged as the head of the opposition to the Albizzi and eventually became Firenze's ruler. His eye for talent and his tact in dealing with artists saw the likes of Alberti, Brunelleschi, Lorenzo Ghiberti, Donatello, Fra Angelico and Fra Filippo Lippi flourish under his patronage. Many of the city's finest buildings are testimony to his tastes.

TRUDI CANAVAN

The *Medusa di Portonaccio* – an example of Etruscan art from the 7th century BC

Savonarola

The Renaissance was a time of extraordinary contrasts. Artists, writers and philosophers of great talent flourished against a backdrop of violence, war, plague and extreme poverty.

In Firenze, the court of Lorenzo de' Medici was among the most splendid and enlightened in Europe. Yet, in the streets and increasingly in Lorenzo's court itself, people had begun to listen intently to the fanatical preachings of a Dominican monk named Girolamo Savonarola.

Born in Ferrara in 1452, Savonarola moved to Firenze in the last years of Lorenzo il Magnifico's rule. An inspired orator, he preached against luxury, greed, corruption of the clergy and against the Renaissance itself. To him the church and the world were corrupt and he accused the ruling class of thinking only 'of new taxes, to suck the blood of the people'.

When the Medici were expelled from Firenze after the French invasion of Italy in 1494 and a republic was proclaimed, Savonarola was appointed its legislator and under his severe, moralistic lead the city underwent a type of religious reform.

His followers included some of the city's greatest humanist philosophers and artists but his enemies were numerous and powerful. Beside the exiled Medici stood the corrupt Pope Alexander VI, against whom the monk preached and who consequently excommunicated Savonarola in 1497. In the ensuing year, the Florentine public began to turn cold on the evangelistic preacher; he came under attack from the Franciscan monks and began to lose the support of political allies.

After refusing to undergo the challenge of an ordeal by fire, Savonarola was arrested and on 22 May 1498 was hanged and burned at the stake for heresy in Piazza della Signoria. His ashes were thrown into the Arno.

Cosimo was eventually followed by his grandson, Lorenzo il Magnifico, whose rule (1469-92) ushered in the most glorious period of Florentine civilisation and of the Italian Renaissance. His court fostered a great flowering of art, music and poetry, turning Firenze into the cultural capital of Italy. Lorenzo favoured philosophers, but he kept up family tradition by sponsoring artists such as Botticelli and Domenico Ghirlandaio; he also encouraged Leonardo and the young Michelangelo, who was working under Giovanni di Bertoldo, Donatello's pupil.

Not long before Lorenzo's death in 1492, the Medici bank failed and two years later the Medici were driven out of Firenze. The city fell under the control of Girolamo Savonarola, a Dominican monk, who led a puritanical republic until he fell from public favour and was fried as a heretic in 1498.

After Firenze's defeat by the Spanish in 1512, the Medici returned to the city but were once again expelled, this time by Emperor Charles V in 1527. Two years later they had made peace and Charles not only allowed the Medici to return to Firenze, but married his daughter to Lorenzo's great-grandson Alessandro de' Medici, whom he made Duke of Firenze in 1530. The Medici then ruled for another 200 years, during which time they gained control of all Toscana.

In 1737 the Grand Duchy of Toscana passed to the House of Lorraine, which retained control (apart from a brief interruption under Napoleon from 1799 to 1814) until it was incorporated into the Kingdom of Italy in 1860. Firenze became the national capital a year later, but Roma assumed the mantle permanently in 1875.

Firenze was badly damaged during WWII by the retreating Germans, who blew all its bridges except the Ponte Vecchio. Devastating floods ravaged the city in 1966, causing inestimable damage to its buildings and artworks. However, the salvage operation led to the widespread use of modern

TOSCANA

FIRENZE (FLORENCE)

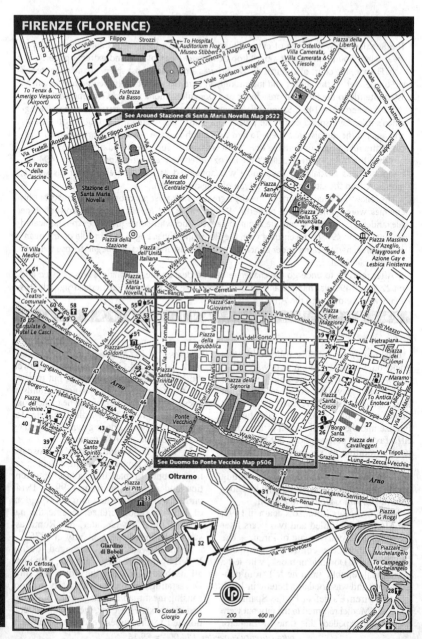

See Around Stazione di Santa Maria Novella Map p522

See Duomo to Ponte Vecchio Map p506

TOSCANA

0   200   400 m

FIRENZE (FLORENCE)

PLACES TO STAY
8 Hotel Due Fontane
37 Istituto Gould
42 Ostello Santa Monaca
53 Pensione Sole;
    Pensione Toscana
54 Pensione Ferretti
56 Ottaviani; Albergo Visconti

PLACES TO EAT
11 Caffelatte
13 Rex Caffé
16 Caffetteria Piansa
18 Antico Noè
19 Il Nilo
20 Osteria Natalino
24 Enoteca Pinchiorri
34 Trattoria Casalinga
35 Cabiria
36 Borgo Antico
38 Trattoria I Raddi
39 Cavolo Nero
44 Angelino
45 Il Caninone di Gallo Nero

51 Da il Latini
57 Sostanza

OTHER
1 Tourist Medical Service
2 Questura (Police Station)
3 Museo di San Marco
4 University
5 Chiesa della SS Annunziata
6 Galleria dell'Accademia
7 Wash & Dry Laundrette
9 Spedale degli Innocenti
10 Museo Archeologico
12 Paperback Exchange Bookshop
14 Teatro della Pergola
15 Cordon Bleu
17 Pongo
21 Teatro Verdi
22 Istituto di Lingua
    e Cultura Italiana per
    Stranieri Michelangelo
23 Casa Buonarroti
25 Comune di Firenze Tourist Office
26 Istituto per l'Arte e il Restauro

27 Basilica di Santa Croce
28 Chiesa di San Salvatore
    al Monte
29 Chiesa di San Miniato al Monte
30 Ponte alle Grazie
31 Dante Alighieri School
    for Foreigners
32 Forte di Belvedere
33 Palazzo Pitti
40 Basilica di Santa Maria
    del Carmine
41 La Dolce Vita
43 Chiesa di Santo Spirito
46 Ponte Santa Trinita
47 Ponte alla Carraia
48 British Consulate
49 Chiesa di Santa Trinita
50 Palazzo Rucellai
52 Wash & Dry Laundrette
55 Fiddler's Elbow
58 Chiesa di Ognissanti
59 French Consulate
60 Europcar
61 Avis

restoration techniques that have saved artworks throughout the country.

Orientation

Whether you arrive by train, bus or car, the central train station, Santa Maria Novella, is a good reference point. Budget hotels and pensioni are concentrated around Via Nazionale, to the east of the station and Piazza Santa Maria Novella, to the south. The main route to the city centre is Via de' Panzani and then Via de' Cerretani, about a 10 minute walk. You'll know you've arrived when you first glimpse the duomo.

Most of the major sights are in easy walking distance – you can stroll from one end of the city centre to the other in about 30 minutes. From Piazza San Giovanni next to the duomo, Via Roma leads to Piazza della Repubblica and continues as Via Calimala and Via Por Santa Maria to the Ponte Vecchio.

Take Via de' Calzaiuoli from Piazza del Duomo for Piazza della Signoria, the historic seat of government – don't be fooled by the copy of Michelangelo's *David* outside the Palazzo Vecchio; the real one is in the Galleria dell'Accademia. The Galleria degli Uffizi is on the piazza's southern edge, near the Arno. Cross the Ponte Vecchio, or the Ponte alle Grazie farther east, to reach Piazzale Michelangelo in the south-east for a view over the city, one of the best vistas in Italy.

You'll find reasonably priced public parking around the imposing Fortezza da Basso, just north of Stazione di Santa Maria Novella and a brisk 10 minute walk to the historic centre along Via XXVII Aprile and Via Cavour. The HI youth hostel is on the city's north-eastern fringe, accessible by bus No 17B from the stazione.

Firenze has two street numbering systems: red or brown numbers indicate commercial premises and black or blue numbers denote a private residence. When written, black or blue addresses are denoted by the number only, while red or brown addresses usually carry an 'r' for *rosso* (red) after the number. It can be confusing, as the black and blue numbers tend to denote whole buildings, while the others may refer to one small part of the same building. When looking for a specific address, keep your eyes on

TOSCANA

both sets of numbers – backtracking is sometimes inevitable.

Information

Tourist Offices The main APT office (☎ 055 29 08 32, fax 055 276 03 83) is just north of the duomo at Via Cavour 1r. It is open from 8.15 am to 7.15 pm Monday to Saturday and from 8.45 am to 1.45 pm on Sunday, from April to October. During the rest of the year it is open until 1.45 pm and closed on Sunday. The branch at Amerigo Vespucci airport (☎ 055 31 58 74) opens from 8.30 am to 10.30 pm daily. APT staff speak English, French, Spanish and German and have extensive, useful information about the city and its services, such as language and art courses, car and bike rental. The APT also offers a special service known as Firenze SOS Turista (☎ 055 276 03 82) from April to October. Tourists needing guidance on matters such as disputes over hotel fees can phone Monday to Saturday from 10 am to 1 pm and 3 to 6 pm. Check out the APT's Web site at www.firenze.turismo.toscana.it.

The Comune di Firenze (city council) operates a tourist office (☎ 055 21 22 45) on Largo Alinari, just outside the south-eastern exit from Stazione di Santa Maria Novella. It generally opens from 8.15 am to 7.15 pm Monday to Saturday in summer. The hours drop to 9 am to 1.45 pm in winter. The Comune di Firenze has another office (☎ 055 234 04 44) at Borgo Santa Croce 29r, open at the same times.

Inside the stazione you can pick up basic information at the Consorzio ITA office (☎ 055 28 28 93). The office's main role is to book hotels. It is open from 8.30 am to 9 pm daily. See Places to Stay later in this section for details on hotel booking services.

One of the handiest commercial maps of the city is the ring bound *Firenze*, published by the Touring Club Italiano. It costs L15,000. There are plenty of cheaper ones around too.

Money A number of banks are concentrated around Piazza della Repubblica. Thomas Cook has a bureau de change (☎ 055 28 97

81) at Lungarno Acciaioli 6r, near the Ponte Vecchio. It opens from 9 am to 7 pm Monday to Saturday and from 9 am to 1 pm Sunday. American Express (Amex) is at Via Dante Alighieri 22r (☎ 055 5 09 81). It opens from 9 am to 5.30 pm Monday to Friday and from 9.30 am to 12.30 pm Saturday.

Post & Communications The main post office is on Via Pellicceria, off Piazza della Repubblica and is open from 8.15 am to 7 pm daily. Fax and telegram services are available, but only faxes sent from other post offices can be received. The APT has a list of private fax services in Firenze.

Amex customers can have their mail forwarded to the Amex office (see under Money).

You will find Telecom phones in the main post office, as well as several booths near the ATAF ticket and information office outside Stazione di Santa Maria Novella. The unstaffed office at Via Cavour 21r is open from 7 am to 11 pm daily and has phone books.

Places to get on line are mushrooming in Firenze. Internet Train has three branches, at Via dell'Oriuolo 25r (☎ 055 263 8968), Via Guelfa 24a (☎ 055 21 47 94) and at Borgo San Jacopo 30r (☎ 055 265 79 35). It costs L12,000 to hook up for an hour (students L10,000).

Travel Agencies Sestante has offices at Via Cavour 56r (☎ 055 29 43 06) and CIT at Piazza della Stazione 51r (☎ 055 28 41 45). At either you can book train and air fares, organise guided tours etc.

CTS (☎ 055 28 95 70) is at Via de' Ginori 25r.

Bookshops The Paperback Exchange, Via Fiesolana 31r, has a vast selection of new and second-hand books in English. Feltrinelli International, Via Cavour 12r, near the APT, has a good selection of books in English, French, German, Spanish, Portuguese and Russian. Internazionale Seeber, Via de' Tornabuoni 70r, also has books in those languages, as well as a fine selection of art books.

TOSCANA

Gay & Lesbian Travellers Azione Gay e Lesbica Finisterrae (☎ 055 67 12 98) is at Via Manara 6, to the east of the city. It is open from Wednesday to Sunday and has a health consultation phone line (☎ 055 48 82 88). It is also possible to arrange to have HIV tests here. The club's Web site is at www.agora .stm.it/gaylesbica.fi.

Laundry The Wash & Dry laundrette chain (☎ 800 23 11 72) has seven branches across the city. You pay L6000 for 8kg of washing and L6000 for drying. They open from 8 am to 10 pm (last wash at 9 pm). Addresses include: Via Nazionale 49, Via della Scala 52/54r and Via dei Servi 105r.

Medical Services The Ospedale Careggi (☎ 055 427 71 11) is the main public hospital and is at Viale Morgagni 85, north of the city centre. There is also the Ospedale Santa Maria Nuova (☎ 055 2 75 81), Piazza Santa Maria Nuova 1, just east of the duomo.

The Tourist Medical Service (☎ 055 47 54 11), Via Lorenzo il Magnifico 59, is open 24 hours and doctors speak English, French and German. The APT office has lists of doctors and dentists who speak various languages.

All-night pharmacies include the Farmacia Comunale (☎ 055 21 67 61), inside the Stazione di Santa Maria Novella, and Farmacia Molteni (☎ 055 28 94 90), in the city centre at Via de' Calzaiuoli 7r.

There is an ambulance station (☎ 055 21 22 22) on Piazza del Duomo.

Emergency The questura (police station; ☎ 055 4 97 71) is at Via Zara 2. You can report thefts at the foreigners office here. There's another station (☎ 055 29 34 62) at Piazza del Duomo 5.

Dangers & Annoyances The most annoying aspect of Firenze is the crowds, closely followed by the summer heat. Pickpockets are active in crowds and on buses. Be aware of the numerous bands of dishevelled women and children carrying newspapers or cardboard. A few will distract you while the others rifle your bag and pockets.

Things to See & Do

Firenze is the proverbial chocolate cake. We won't even try to compete with the battalions of literary greats and other important personages who have spilled rivers of ink in the search for an original superlative.

The city is jammed with sights, mostly confined to a small area. Too little space is available in the confines of this book to do them all justice, although we try to steer you through the 'essentials'.

Museums and monuments tend to close on Monday, though given the hordes of tourists that pour in year-round, quite a few places form an exception to this rule – so much so that the APT has compiled a list of them.

Some sights are state-run or private; others are run by the Comune. Many run by the Comune are secondary on any itinerary, but if you intend to visit the lot, ask about the special *carnet*. It costs L10,000, for which you get an explanatory booklet and discounts of up to 50% on a selection of these sights.

It is always worth checking for discounted or free admission. In some cases EU citizens can get in free, particularly if aged under 18 or over 60.

A Recipe for Stendhalismo

Any list of 'must sees' in Firenze is going to incite cries of protest. How can you recommend that a tour cover the Galleria degli Uffizi, the duomo and the battistero, without including the Museo del Bargello, the Museo di San Marco and the churches of Santa Maria Novella, Santa Croce and SS Annunziata? And what about Masaccio's fresco cycle in Basilica di Santa Maria del Carmine? Or Michelangelo's *David* in the Galleria dell'Accademia and his Medici tombs in the family chapel attached to the Basilica di San Lorenzo? Plan carefully or you could end up with a severe case of Stendhalismo (see the introduction to Firenze). And make sure you carry plenty of L100, L200 and L500 coins for the machines to illuminate the frescoes in the churches.

TOSCANA

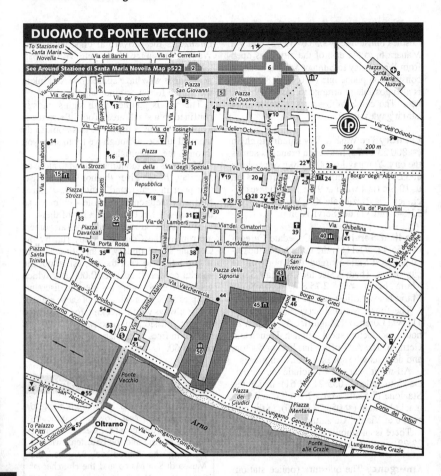

DUOMO TO PONTE VECCHIO

Walking Tours

Here follow a couple of suggested tours of churches, important both architecturally and for the art treasures they contain. The two walks each comprise four churches and the lot could be completed in a day – in morning and afternoon sessions. This works out well, as most churches close for three to four hours in the middle of the day – a handy time to chill out over lunch. The APT office, at Via Cavour 1r, has an updated list of opening hours.

Tour One Start at the **Basilica di Santa Maria Novella**, in the piazza of the same name, just south of the stazione. Begun in the late 13th century as the Florentine base for the Dominican order, the basilica was largely completed by around 1360, but work on its façade and interior continued well into the 15th century. The lower section of the green and white marble façade is transitional from Romanesque to Gothic, while the upper section and the main doorway were designed by Alberti and completed in around 1470. The

DUOMO TO PONTE VECCHIO

PLACES TO STAY		
11	Maxim	
17	Pendini	
20	Albergo Firenze	
21	Pensione Maria Luisa de Medici	
23	Albergo Bavaria	
25	Brunori	
34	Hotel Porta Rossa	
35	Pensione TeTi & Prestige	
46	Bernini Palace	
51	Aily Home	
54	Hotel Alessandra	
57	Pensione la Scaletta	

PLACES TO EAT		
10	Hostaria il Caminetto	
12	Gilli	
13	Ristorante Self-Service Leonardo	
18	Caffè Giubbe Rosse	
19	Festival del Gelato	
22	Trattoria Le Mossacce	
27	Trattoria del Pennello	

29	Ristorante Paoli	
30	Gelateria Perchè No?	
41	Osteria del Gallo e Volpe	
42	Gelateria Vivoli	
48	Fiaschetteria	
49	Angie's Pub	
56	Osteria del Cinghiale Bianco	

OTHER		
1	Questura (Police Station)	
2	Battistero	
3	JJ Cathedral	
4	Ambulance Station	
5	Campanile	
6	Duomo	
7	Museo dell'Opera del Duomo	
8	Ospedale Santa Maria Nuova (Hospital)	
9	Internet Train	
14	Internazionale Seeber Bookshop	
15	Palazzo Strozzi	
16	TWA	

24	Palazzo Pazzi	
26	Casa di Dante	
28	American Express	
31	Chiesa di Orsanmichele	
32	Main Post Office & Telecom Office	
33	Odean Cinehall	
36	Palazzo Davanzati	
37	Mercato Nuovo	
38	Farmacia Molteni	
39	Badia	
40	Palazzo del Bargello; Museo del Bargello	
43	Palazzo Gondi	
44	Loggia della Signoria	
45	Palazzo Vecchio	
47	Kikuya Pub	
50	Galleria degli Uffizi (Uffizi Gallery)	
52	Thomas Cook	
53	Alitalia	
55	Internet Train	

highlight of the Gothic interior is Masaccio's superb fresco of the *Trinity* (1428), one of the first artworks to use the then newly discovered techniques of perspective and proportion. It is halfway along the northern aisle.

The first chapel to the right of the choir, the **Cappella di Filippo Strozzi**, features lively frescoes by Filippino Lippi depicting the lives of San Giovanni Evangelista and San Filippo. Another important work is Domenico Ghirlandaio's series of frescoes behind the main altar, painted with the help of artists who may have included the young Michelangelo. Relating the lives of the Virgin Mary, San Giovanni Battista and others, the frescoes are notable for their depiction of Florentine life in the Renaissance. Brunelleschi's crucifix hangs above the altar in the **Cappella Gondi**, the first chapel on the left of the choir.

The cloisters (entrance on the left of the façade) feature some of the city's best frescoes. The **Chiostro Verde** (Green Cloister) is so named because green is the predominant colour of the fresco cycle by Paolo Uccello. The impressive **Cappellone degli Spagnuoli** (Spanish Chapel) contains frescoes by Andrea di Bonaiuto. However, the basilica was unfortunately closed at the time of writing.

From Piazza Santa Maria Novella head east along Via dei Banchi and take the first street on the left, Via del Giglio. Cross Via de' Panzani and continue straight ahead until you reach Piazza Madonna degli Aldobrandini and the Basilica di San Lorenzo. The streets in this area are lined with market stalls specialising in leather goods and knitwear.

The Medici commissioned Brunelleschi to rebuild the **Basilica di San Lorenzo** in 1425, on the site of a 4th century basilica. It is considered one of the most harmonious examples of Renaissance architecture (Michelangelo prepared a design for the façade that was never executed). It was the Medici parish church and many family members are buried here. The two bronze pulpits are by Donatello, who died before they were completed. He is buried in the chapel featuring Fra Filippo Lippi's *Annunciation*. The entrance to the basilica is on the busy Piazza San Lorenzo, off Borgo San Lorenzo. The basilica is open from 7 am to noon and 3.30 to 6.30 pm daily. Admission is free. The adjoining **Sagrestia Vecchia** (Old Sacristy) was also designed by Brunelleschi and its interior was largely decorated by Donatello.

Visit the **Biblioteca Laurenziana**, which

euro currency converter   L10,000 = €5.16

TOSCANA

can be reached through the cloister. It was commissioned by Cosimo de' Medici to house the Medici library and contains 10,000 volumes. Michelangelo designed the magnificent staircase. The library is open from 9 am to 1 pm daily. Admission is free.

The **Cappelle Medicee** are entered via Piazza Madonna degli Aldobrandini. The **Cappella dei Principi** (Princes' Chapel), sumptuously decorated with precious marble and semiprecious stones, was the principal burial place of the Medici rulers. The graceful and simple **Sagrestia Nuova** (New Sacristy) was Michelangelo's first architectural work. It contains his beautiful sculptures *Night and Day*, *Dawn and Dusk* and the *Madonna with Child*, which adorn the Medici tombs. The chapels are open from 8.30 am to 1.50 pm Tuesday to Sunday (as well as alternating Mondays). Admission costs L10,000.

Next stop is the **Chiesa della SS Annunziata,** on the piazza of the same name. From Piazza San Lorenzo, walk east along Via dei Gori to reach Via Cavour, turn left and walk until you reach Piazza San Marco (about 450m), then turn right into Via Cesare Battisti to reach the Piazza della SS Annunziata. The church was established in 1250 by the founders of the Servite order and rebuilt by Michelozzo and others in the mid-15th century. It is dedicated to the Virgin Mary and in the ornate tabernacle, to your left as you enter the church from the atrium, is a so-called miraculous painting of the Virgin.

The painting, which is no longer on public view, is attributed to a 14th century friar and legend says it was completed by an angel. Also of note are frescoes by Andrea del Castagno in the first two chapels on the left of the church, a fresco by Perugino in the fifth chapel and the frescoes in Michelozzo's atrium, particularly the *Birth of the Virgin* by Andrea del Sarto and the *Visitation* by Jacopo Pontormo. The church is open from 7.30 am to 12.30 pm and 4 to 6.30 pm daily.

Head back to Piazza San Marco for the **Museo di San Marco** in the now deconsecrated Dominican convent and Chiesa di San Marco. The piazza is the centre of the university area. The church was founded in 1299, rebuilt by Michelozzo in 1437 and again remodelled by Giambologna some years later. It features several paintings, but they pale in comparison to the treasures contained in the adjoining convent.

Famous Florentines who called the convent home include the painters Fra Angelico and Fra Bartolomeo, as well as Sant'Antoninus and Girolamo Savonarola. Fra Angelico, who painted the radiant frescoes on the convent walls and Savonarola were of the same religious order – the latter arriving in Firenze almost 30 years after the painter's death in 1455. The convent is a museum of Fra Angelico's works, many of which were moved there in the 1860s. Among them are the *Tabernacolo dei Linaioli*, the *Last Judgment* (painted with his students) and *Descent from the Cross* in the Ospizio dei Pellegrini (Pilgrim's Hospice) and his masterpiece, the *Crucifixion*, in the chapterhouse. Still more of his work can be seen upstairs in the monks' dormitory cells. The museum is open from 8.30 am to 1.50 pm Tuesday to Saturday (as well as alternating Mondays and Sundays). Admission costs L8000.

Tour Two We start at the **duomo**. When you first come upon it from the crowded streets around the square, you will likely stop momentarily in your tracks, somewhat taken aback by the ordered vivacity of its pink, white and green marble façade (slowly but surely getting a long overdue clean, as the modest bits of scaffolding demonstrate). You had probably already spotted Brunelleschi's sloping, brown tiled dome – a dominant feature of Firenze's skyline. For the record, the great temple's full name is Cattedrale di Santa Maria del Fiore. It was begun in 1296 by the Sienese architect Arnolfo di Cambio and took almost 150 years to complete.

Brunelleschi won a public competition to design the enormous **dome**, the first of its kind since antiquity. Although now severely cracked and under restoration, it remains a remarkable achievement of design. When Michelangelo went to work on the Basilica di San Pietro, he reportedly said: 'I go to build a greater dome, but not a fairer one.'

Lorenzo de' Medici & the Pazzi Conspiracy

Plots to ruin the Medici family were nothing new to Firenze but in 1478 Lorenzo de' Medici lost his brother, Giuliano and almost his own life in an incident known as the Pazzi conspiracy.

The Pazzi were a wealthy Florentine family who had been denied the benefits of public office by the Medici. Francesco de' Pazzi, a jealous and bitter priest, plotted to kill the Medici brothers and take power in Firenze. The audacious plan, which had the blessing of Pope Sixtus IV, went into effect in the duomo during Mass.

When all heads were bowed as the host was raised, Francesco and an accomplice struck, stabbing Giuliano to death. Lorenzo escaped into the sacristy and survived the attack, but the city was in uproar. A mob spent days hunting down the conspirators and anyone else believed to be associated with the incident. Hundreds died, including most of the Pazzi family. Surviving members were imprisoned or exiled, the Pazzi name was proscribed and female members of the family were forbidden to marry and have children (Lorenzo later revoked this order). The name, by the way, is also the Italian plural for 'mad, nuts'. Given their fate, medieval Florentine jokes on the family's foolhardiness must have been abundant!

Inside, the cathedral is decorated with frescoes by Vasari and Federico Zuccari and stained-glass windows by Donatello andrea del Castagno, Paolo Uccello and Lorenzo Ghiberti. You can climb up into the dome to get a closer look (enter to the left as you face the altar). The view from the summit over Firenze is unparalleled. The dome is open from 8.30 am to 6.20 pm daily except Sunday and the climb costs L10,000.

The duomo's vast interior, 155m long and 90m wide and its sparse decoration comes as a surprise after the visually tumultuous façade. The sacristies on each side of the altar feature enamelled terracotta lunettes by Luca della Robbia over their doorways. Lorenzo de' Medici hid in the north sacristy after his brother, Giuliano, was stabbed and killed by the Pazzi conspirators.

The two frescoes in the north aisle commemorate the condottieri Sir John Hawkwood and Niccolò da Tolentino, who fought for Firenze. Paolo Uccello painted the former and Andrea del Castagno the latter. Also in the north aisle is a painting of Dante with a depiction of the Divine Comedy, by Domenico di Michelino.

A stairway near the main entrance of the duomo leads to the crypt, where excavations have unearthed parts of the 5th century Basil-

ica di Santa Reparata, which originally stood on the site and Brunelleschi's tomb.

The duomo's multi-coloured marble façade was built in the 19th century in Gothic style to replace Arnolfo di Cambio's uncompleted original, which was pulled down in the 16th century. The duomo may not be entered during Mass.

Giotto designed and began building the graceful and unusual **campanile** (bell tower) next to the duomo in 1334, but died before it was completed. Andrea Pisano and Francesco Talenti continued the work. The first tier of bas-reliefs around the base, carved by Pisano but possibly designed by Giotto, depicts the Creation of Man and the Arts and Industries. Those on the second tier depict the planets, cardinal virtues, the arts and the seven sacraments. The sculptures of the Prophets and Sybils in the niches of the upper storeys are actually copies of works by Donatello and others – the originals are in the duomo's museum. The bell tower is 82m high and you can climb its stairs between 9 am and 6.50 pm daily (to 4.20 pm in winter). Admission costs L10,000.

The Romanesque **battistero** (baptistry) is believed to have been built between the 5th and 12th centuries on the site of a Roman temple. It is one of the oldest buildings in

TOSCANA

Firenze and is dedicated to San Giovanni Battista. Dante was baptised here.

Stripes of white and green marble bedeck the octagonal structure, which is famous for its gilded bronze doors, particularly the celebrated eastern doors facing the duomo, the *Gates of Paradise* by Lorenzo Ghiberti. The bas-reliefs on its 10 panels depict scenes from the Old Testament.

The south door, executed by Pisano and completed in 1336, is the oldest. The bas-reliefs on its 28 compartments deal predominantly with the life of San Giovanni Battista. The north door is by Ghiberti, who won a public competition in 1401 to design it. The design was based on Pisano's earlier door and its main theme is also San Giovanni Battista. The *Gates of Paradise*, however, remain his consummate masterpiece. Most of the doors are copies – the original panels are being gradually removed for restoration and placed in the Museo dell'Opera del Duomo as work is completed. The baptistry is open from noon to 6.30 pm daily. Admission is L5000.

The **Museo dell'Opera del Duomo**, behind the duomo at Piazza del Duomo 9, features most of the art treasures from the duomo, battistero and campanile and is definitely worth a visit.

Displays include the equipment used by Brunelleschi to build the dome, as well as his death mask. Perhaps its best piece is Michelangelo's *Pietà*, which he intended for his own tomb. Vasari recorded in his *Lives of the Artists* that, unsatisfied with the quality of the marble or his own work, Michelangelo broke up the unfinished sculpture, destroying the arm and left leg of the figure of Christ. A student of Michelangelo later restored the arm and completed the figure of Mary Magdalene. The collection of sculpture is considered to be the city's second best after that in the Museo del Bargello. Note in particular Donatello's carving of the prophet Habakkuk (taken from the bell tower) and his wooden impression of Mary Magdalene. The museum is usually open from 9 am to 6.50 pm daily except Sunday (it closes at 6.20 pm in win-

Machiavelli's Manoeuvres

Born in 1469 into a poor branch of what had been one of Firenze's leading families, Niccolò Machiavelli got off to a bad start. His father was a small-time lawyer whose practice had been all but strangled by the city authorities because he was a debtor.

Young Niccolò missed out on the best schools and could consider himself lucky that his father was at least rich in books. The prospects were not sparkling.

Somehow he managed to swing a post in the city's second chancery at the age of 29 and so embarked on a colourful career as a Florentine public servant. His tasks covered a range of internal dealings in Firenze and some aspects of foreign affairs and defence. Our man must have shown early promise, as by 1500 he was in France on his first diplomatic mission. A couple of years later he married Marietta Corsini, with whom he would have five children in the following 12 years.

Impressed by the marshal success of Cesare Borgia and the centralised state of France, Machiavelli came to the conclusion that Firenze needed a standing army. The city, like many others across the length and breadth of the Italian peninsula, had a habit of employing mercenaries to fight their wars. The problem with that system was that mercenaries had few reasons to fight and die for anyone. They took their pay and as often as not did their level best to avoid mortal combat. Machiavelli managed to convince his rulers of the advantages to be had and so, in 1506, he formed a conscript militia. In 1509 he got to try it out on the rebellious city of Pisa, whose fall was in large measure attributed to the troops led by the wily statesman. He was back two years later to dismantle a French-backed schismatic council there. Firenze was not Roma's

ter). Admission costs L8000. It was closed for most of 1999.

From Piazza del Duomo, walk south along Via del Proconsolo and turn left into Borgo degli Albizi and the area known as Santa Croce. When you reach Piazza S Pier Maggiore turn right and walk along Via M Palmieri. Continue straight ahead and turn left into Borgo de' Greci, reaching the Franciscan **Basilica di Santa Croce** on the piazza of the same name. In Savonarola's day, the piazza was used for the execution of heretics, but today it is lined with souvenir shops. Attributed to Arnolfo di Cambio, Santa Croce was started in 1294 on the site of a Franciscan chapel and the façade and bell tower were added in the 19th century. The three-nave interior of the basilica is grand but austere. The floor is paved with the tombstones of famous Florentines of the past 500 years and monuments to the particularly notable were added along the walls from the mid-16th century.

Along the south wall (to your right as you enter the church) is Michelangelo's tomb,

designed by Vasari and a cenotaph dedicated to Dante, who is buried in Ravenna. Further along you will find a monument to the 18th century dramatist and poet Vittorio Alfieri by Antonio Canova, along with a monument to Machiavelli and a bas-relief, *Annunciation*, by Donatello.

The **Cappella Castellani**, in the right transept, is completely covered with frescoes by Agnolo Gaddi. In the Cappella Baroncelli, at the end of the transept, frescoes by his father, Taddeo Gaddi, depict the life of the Virgin. Agnolo Gaddi also painted the frescoes above and behind the altar. Adjoining the sacristy is a corridor by Michelozzo which leads to a Medici chapel, featuring a large altarpiece by Andrea della Robbia. The Bardi and Peruzzi chapels, to the right of the chancel, are completely covered in frescoes by Giotto. In the central chapel of the north transept (also a Bardi chapel) hangs a wooden crucifix by Donatello.

Brunelleschi designed the serene **cloisters** just before his death in 1446. Brunelleschi's

Machiavelli's Manoeuvres

flavour of the month and troops from the Holy See and its allies marched on the city. Machiavelli was now defending not only his hearth but his future – to no avail.

The return of the Medici family to power was a blow for Machiavelli, who was promptly removed from all posts. Suspected of plotting against the Medici, he was even thrown into the dungeon in 1513 and tortured. He maintained his innocence and was freed, but was reduced to penury as he retired to his little property outside Firenze.

It was in these years that he produced his greatest writing. *Il Principe* (The Prince) is his classic treatise on the nature of power and its administration. In it he developed his theories not only on politics and power but on history and human behaviour. What was a thoroughly demoralising time for Machiavelli he turned to good account for generations to come after him. The work and other writings reflect the confusing and corrupt times in which he lived and a desire for strong and just rule in Firenze and beyond.

He ached to get back into active public life too, but in this he was never to be truly satisfied. He was commissioned to write an official history of Firenze, the *Istorie Fiorentine* and towards the end of his life he was appointed to a defence commission to improve the city walls and join a Papal army in its ultimately futile fight against imperial forces. By the time the imperial forces had sacked Roma in 1527, Firenze had again rid itself of the Medici. Machiavelli hoped that he would be restored to a position of dignity, but by now he was suspected almost as much by the Medicis' opponents as he had been years before by the Medici. He died frustrated and, as in his youth, on the brink of poverty, in 1527.

TOSCANA

Cappella dei Pazzi, at the end of the first cloister, is a masterpiece of Renaissance architecture. The **Museo dell'Opera di Santa Croce**, off the first cloister, features a crucifix by Cimabue, which was badly damaged during the disastrous 1966 flood, when more than 4m of water inundated the Santa Croce area. The crucifix was almost completely destroyed and lost much of its paint. It has been partially restored.

The basilica is open from 8 am to 6.30 pm Monday to Saturday in summer (closed from 12.30 to 3 pm in winter) and from 3 to 6 pm on Sunday. The museum is open from 10 am to 12.30 pm and 2.30 to 6.30 pm daily except Wednesday (3 to 5 pm in winter). Admission costs L5000.

We now head for two churches in the **Oltrarno** (over the Arno). Follow Via dei Benci south from Piazza Santa Croce to the Arno. Either cross here at the Ponte alle Grazie or follow the river to your right to reach the Ponte Vecchio. Take Borgo San Jacopo, on your right after you cross Ponte Vecchio and continue along it as it becomes Via di Santo Spirito. Cross Via de' Serragli and take the first left to reach Piazza del Carmine and the **Basilica di Santa Maria del Carmine**. This 13th century basilica was nearly destroyed by a fire in the late 18th century. Fortunately the fire spared the magnificent frescoes by Masaccio in the **Cappella Brancacci**. Considered the painter's finest work, the frescoes had an enormous influence on Florentine art in the 15th century. Masaccio painted them in his early 20s but interrupted the task to go to Roma, where he died aged only 28. The cycle was completed some 60 years later by Filippino Lippi. Earlier frescoes in the cycle were painted by Masolino da Panicale. The frescoes were recently restored and their vibrant colours, combined with Masaccio's vigorous style, create a strong visual impact. Masaccio's work includes the *Expulsion of Adam and Eve from Paradise* and *The Tribute Money* on the upper left wall. The chapel is open from 10 am to 5 pm daily except Tuesday (1 to 5 pm on Sunday and holidays). Admission costs L6000.

Head back towards the Ponte Vecchio, but take Via Santa Monica, which runs off the piazza. Cross Via de' Serragli and continue along Via Sant'Agostino until you come to Piazza Santo Spirito and the **Chiesa di Santo Spirito**. One of Brunelleschi's last commissions, the church is beautifully planned, with a colonnade of 35 columns and a series of semicircular chapels. The chapels' works of art include a *Madonna and Saints* by Filippino Lippi in the right transept. Santo Spirito is open from 8 am to noon and 4 to 6 pm daily except Wednesday afternoon. The piazza outside has developed somewhat of a bohemian feel.

Around Piazza della Signoria

The hub of the city's political life through the centuries and surrounded by some of its most celebrated buildings, the piazza has the appearance of an outdoor sculpture gallery. Ammannati's huge Fountain of Neptune sits beside the Palazzo Vecchio and flanking the entrance to the palace are copies of Michelangelo's *David* (the original is in the Galleria dell'Accademia) and Donatello's *Marzocco*, the heraldic Florentine lion (the original is in the Museo del Bargello). An equestrian statue of Cosimo de' Medici by Giambologna stands towards the centre of the piazza. A bronze plaque marks the spot where Savonarola was hanged and burned at the stake in 1498.

The **Loggia della Signoria** was built in the late 14th century as a platform for public ceremonies and eventually became a showcase for sculptures. To the left of the steps is Benvenuto Cellini's magnificent statue of Perseus holding the head of Medusa. To the right is Giambologna's Mannerist *Rape of the Sabine Women*, his final work.

The **Palazzo Vecchio**, built by Arnolfo di Cambio between 1298 and 1314, is the traditional seat of Florentine government. Its **Torre d'Arnolfo** is 94m high and, with its striking crenellations, is as much a symbol of the city as the duomo. Built for the *signoria*, the highest level of Florentine republican government, it became the palazzo of Cosimo I de' Medici in the mid-16th century, before he moved to the Palazzo Pitti. The

Finish your dash around Firenze's museums and churches with a peaceful walk along the Arno.

Head away from the crowds at the Torre Pendente (Leaning Tower) and relax in Pisa's Orto Botanico.

BETHUNE CARMICHAEL

Ammannati's Fountain of Neptune, Firenze

BETHUNE CARMICHAEL

Take a break in the Giardino di Boboli, Firenze.

JON DAVISON

Belt up at Firenze's famous leather market.

DAMIEN SIMONIS

The marbled duomo and campanile, Firenze

Medici commissioned Vasari to reorganise the interior and create a series of sumptuous rooms. Upstairs from Michelozzo's beautiful courtyard, just inside the entrance, are some lavishly decorated apartments. The **Salone dei Cinquecento** was the meeting room of the Consiglio della Repubblica (Great Council) during Savonarola's time. It was later used for banquets and festivities and features frescoes by Vasari and Michelangelo's *Genius of Victory*, originally destined for Roma and Pope Julius II's tomb.

Vasari designed the Studiolo (Francesco I's study) and several Florentine Mannerist artists decorated it. Farther on is the Cappella di Signoria, decorated by Domenico Ghirlandaio in 1514. The palace is open from 9 am to 7 pm daily (to 2 pm Thursday only). Admission costs L10,000.

Galleria degli Uffizi (Uffizi Gallery)

Designed and built by Vasari in the second half of the 16th century at the request of Cosimo I de' Medici, the Galleria degli Uffizi is in the **Palazzo degli Uffizi**, which originally housed the city's administrators, judiciary and guilds. It was, in effect, an office block (*uffizi* means offices). Vasari also designed the private corridor that links the **Palazzo Vecchio** and the **Palazzo Pitti**. Known as the **Corridoio Vasariano**, it is, at the time of writing, lined with paintings and can be seen only on a guided tour (see the following Corridoio Vasariano section).

Cosimo's successor, Francesco I, commissioned the architect Buontalenti to modify the upper floor of the Palazzo degli Uffizi to house the Medici's growing art collection. The gallery now houses the family's private collection, bequeathed to the city in 1737 by the last of the Medici, Anna Maria Ludovica, on condition that it never leave the city.

Although over the years sections of the collection have been moved to the Museo del Bargello and the city's Museo Archeologico, the Galleria degli Uffizi still houses the world's greatest collection of Italian and Florentine art. Paintings from Firenze's churches have also been moved to the gallery. Sadly, several of its artworks were destroyed and others badly damaged when a car bomb planted by the Mafia exploded outside the gallery's western wing in May 1993.

Partly in response to the bombing, but even more to the gallery's immense popularity (a staggering 1.5 million visitors marched through in 1998), restoration and reorganisation will lead to what promoters have dubbed the 'Grandi Uffizi'. It is hoped that by 2001 all the damaged rooms and others previously closed off will be open to the public.

As a result of all this, the displays remain in a state of flux. However, the principal lines remain the same – the gallery is arranged to illustrate the evolving story of Italian and, in particular, Florentine art. Those rooms marked with * (asterisk) were closed at the time of writing.

The extraordinary wealth of the collection and the sheer number of famous works make one visit insufficient. If you are in Firenze for three or four days and can afford the additional cost, try to spend at least two blocks of three or so hours in the gallery, spread over a few days. Guidebooks to the gallery are on sale all over the city.

Before heading upstairs, visit the restored remains of the 11th century **Chiesa di San Piero Scheraggio**, which was largely destroyed during the construction of the gallery and its apse incorporated into the structure of the palazzo.

Upstairs inside the gallery, the first rooms feature works by Tuscan masters of the 13th and early 14th centuries. Room 2 is dominated by three paintings of the *Maestà* by Cimabue, Giotto and Duccio di Buoninsegna. All three were once altarpieces in Florentine churches. Also in the room is Giotto's polyptych *Madonna col Bambino Gesù, Santi e Angeli* (Virgin and Child with Angels and Saints). Room 3 traces the Sienese school of the 14th century. Of particular note is Simone Martini's shimmering *Annunciazione* (Annunciation), considered a masterpiece of the school and Ambrogio Lorenzetti's triptych *Madonna col Bambino e Santi* (Madonna and Child with Saints). Rooms 5 and 6 house examples of the international Gothic style,

TOSCANA

among them *Adorazione dei Magi* (Adoration of the Magi) by Gentile da Fabiano. Room 7 features works by painters of the early 15th century Florentine school, which pioneered the Renaissance. There is one panel (the other two are in Paris' Louvre and London's National Gallery) from Paolo Uccello's *La Battaglia di San Romano* (Battle of San Romano), as well as Piero della Francesca's portraits *Battista Sforza* and *Federico da Montefeltro* and *Madonna col Bambino* painted jointly by Masaccio and Masolino. In the next room is Fra Filippo Lippi's delightful *Madonna col Bambino e due Angeli* (Madonna and Child with Two Angels).

The Botticelli rooms (Nos 10 to 14) are considered the gallery's most spectacular. Highlights are the *La Nascita di Venere* (Birth of Venus) and *Allegria della Primavera* (Joy of Spring). Room 15 features Leonardo's *Annunciazione*, painted when he was a student of Verrocchio. Room 18, known as the Tribuna, houses the celebrated *Medici Venus*, a 1st century BC copy of a 4th century BC sculpture by the Greek sculptor, Praxiteles. The room also contains portraits of various Medici. The great Umbrian painter, Perugino, who studied under Piero della Francesca and later became Raphael's master, is represented in Room 19*, as well as Luca Signorelli. Room 20* features works from the German Renaissance, including Dürer's *Adorazione dei Magi*. Room 21 has works by Giovanni Bellini and his pupil, Giorgione. Peek through the railings to see the 15th to 19th century works in the Miniatures Room and then cross into the western wing, which houses works of Italian masters dating from the 16th century.

Room 25 features Michelangelo's dazzling *Sacra Famiglia* (Holy Family) and in the next room are works by Raphael, including his *Leo X* and *Madonna del Cardellino*. Room 28 boasts seven Titians, including *Venere d'Urbino* (Venus of Urbino). Rooms 29 and 30 contain works by comparatively minor northern Italian painters, but Room 31 is dominated above all by Venezia's Paolo Veronese, including his *Sacra Famiglia e Santa Barbara* (Holy Family with St Barbara). In Room 32 it is Tintoretto's turn. He is accompanied by a few Jacopo Bassano canvasses. Rooms 33 and 34 were open but still being organised at the time of writing. Room 35 is closed pending reorganisation. For some reason the numbering starts at Room 41* after this. This room is given over mostly to non-Italian masters such as Rubens and Van Dyck. The beautifully designed Room 42, with its exquisite coffered ceiling and splendid dome, is filled with Roman statues. Caravaggio dominates Room 43*, while Rembrandt and Jan Breughel the Elder feature in Room 44*. In Room 45* there are 18th century works by Canaletto, Guardi and Crespi, along with a smattering of foreigners such as the Spaniard Goya.

The gallery is open from 8.30 am to 10 pm Tuesday to Saturday (6.30 pm in winter) and to 8 pm on Sunday (1.50 pm in winter). Admission costs L12,000 and the ticket office is open until 55 minutes before closing time. To avoid the crowds arrive when the gallery first opens, during lunchtime or late afternoon.

Corridoio Vasariano

When Cosimo I de' Medici's wife bought the Palazzo Pitti and the family moved into their new digs, the family wanted to maintain their link – literally – with what from now on would be known as the Palazzo Vecchio. Cosimo commissioned Vasari to build an enclosed walkway between the two palaces, allowing the Medicis to wander between the two without having to deal with the public.

The corridor, now lined with largely minor artworks, has changed considerably over the years. Its present aspect dates from 1923, but it is possible that many of the paintings hung here will be moved to the Grandi Uffizi (see the previous section) in the coming years. To appreciate it all you will want to have a genuine interest in Florentine history and/or a hunger for relatively obscure art. Visits are by guided tour (generally in Italian), which lasts a long 2½ hours. The tour starts in the Palazzo Vecchio, stops at certain points in the Uffizi (but without the scope for looking at the art) and then follows the twists and turns of the corridor to the Palazzo Pitti. Along the way you can peer out for unusual views of Firenze and various paintings are explained, although there is little in the way of 1st class art.

Visits are currently permitted Tuesday to Thursday and Saturday, from March to May and again from September to October. Tours (maximum 35 people) start at 9 and 10.30 am and 1 and 2.30 pm. You need to book ahead on ☎ 055 265 43 21 from 8.30 am to 1 pm Monday to Saturday, or go on line (see the 'Queue Jumping' boxed text). Tickets cost L38,500.

Around Ponte Santa Trinita

From the Galleria degli Uffizi head west along the Arno to the Ponte Santa Trinita, rebuilt after being destroyed by Nazi bombing. Michelangelo is believed to have drawn the original plan but Ammannati built the bridge. Head north along **Via de' Tornabuoni**, one of the city's most fashionable streets, lined with Renaissance mansions and high-class shops including Ferragamo, Gucci and Armani.

In the piazza of the same name, the 13th century **Chiesa di Santa Trinita** features several significant works, including frescoes depicting the life of San Francesco d'Assisi by Domenico Ghirlandaio in the Cappella Sassetti (in the right transept). The altarpiece of the Annunciation in the fourth chapel of the south aisle is by Lorenzo Monaco, who was Fra Angelico's master. Monaco also painted the frescoes on the walls of the chapel.

The **Palazzo Davanzati**, Via Porta Rossa 13, is a well preserved 14th century mansion. It was closed at the time of writing. Just past the palace is the **Mercato Nuovo**, a loggia built in the mid-16th century to house the city's gold and silver trade, that today is home to souvenir stalls and the leather crowd.

Return to Via de' Tornabuoni and head north for the **Palazzo Strozzi**, one of the most impressive Renaissance palazzi in Firenze. The palazzo is today used for art exhibitions. The beautiful **Palazzo Rucellai**, designed by Alberti, is on Via della Vigna Nuova, which branches off to the south-

west. The palace houses a photographic museum dedicated to the vast collection compiled by the Alinari brothers. It was closed at the time of writing.

Continue along Via della Vigna Nuova to reach Piazza Goldoni and then take Borgo Ognissanti to reach the 13th century **Chiesa di Ognissanti**. The church was much altered in the 17th century and has a baroque façade, but inside are 15th century works by Domenico Ghirlandaio and Botticelli. Of interest is Ghirlandaio's fresco above the second altar on the right of the Madonna della Misericordia, protector of the Vespucci family. Amerigo Vespucci, who gave his name to the American continent, is supposed to be the young boy whose head appears between the Madonna and the old man. Ghirlandaio's masterpiece, the *Last Supper*, covers most of a wall in the former monastery's refectory. The church is open from 8 am to noon and 4 to 6 pm daily.

Queue Jumping

If time is precious and money is not a prime concern, you can skip some of the museum queues in Firenze by booking ahead.

For a L2000 fee per ticket, you can book tickets to the Galleria degli Uffizi on ☎ 055 29 48 83. You pick the tickets up at a separate entrance and – hey presto! – you're in like Flynn.

If you prefer the electronic age, Weekend a Firenze is an on-line service where you book tickets for the Galleria degli Uffizi, Galleria dell'Accademia, Galleria Palatina, Museo del Bargello and the Cappelle Medicee. For this you pay L8270 on top of the ticket price. You must book at least five days in advance. You will get an email confirmation that you will have to print out and present at the cashiers desk on the day you go. Check it out at www.weekendafirenze.com.

When you go to the Uffizi with prepaid tickets or confirmation, head for the designated entrance for those with booked tickets.

TOSCANA

South of the Duomo

Take Via de' Calzaiuoli from Piazza del Duomo to reach the **Chiesa di Orsanmichele**. Originally a grain market, the church was formed when the arcades of the market building were walled in the 14th century. Statues of the city guilds' patron saints adorn the exterior. They were commissioned over 200 years and represent the work of many Renaissance artists. Some of the statues are now in the Museo del Bargello but many splendid pieces remain, including *John the Baptist* by Lorenzo Ghiberti and a copy of Donatello's *St George*. The main feature of the interior is the splendid Gothic tabernacle, decorated with coloured marble, by Andrea Orcagna. The church is open from 9 am to noon and 4 to 6 pm (closed first and last Monday of the month).

Just west along Via degli Speziali is the **Piazza della Repubblica**. Originally the site of a Roman forum, it is now home to Firenze's most fashionable and expensive cafés.

Return to Piazza del Duomo and take Via del Proconsolo in the direction of the Arno. Near the intersection of Borgo degli Albizi is the **Palazzo Pazzi**, which is attributed to Brunelleschi and now houses offices. You can wander into the courtyard. From here, head west along Via del Corso to Via Santa Margherita and **Casa di Dante** at No 1, which has a small museum tracing Dante's life. It is open from 10 am to 4 pm daily except Tuesday (to 2 pm on Sunday and holidays). Admission costs L5000.

Palazzo del Bargello Also known as the Palazzo del Podestà, the palace was originally the residence of the chief magistrate when built in 1254 and then a police station. During its days as a police complex, many people were tortured near the well in the centre of the medieval courtyard. It now houses the **Museo del Bargello** and the most comprehensive collection of Tuscan Renaissance sculpture in Italy. The museum is not to be missed.

Several works by Michelangelo grace the ground floor, notably his drunken *Bacchus* (executed when the artist was aged 22), a marble bust of *Brutus*, a tondo of the *Madonna and Child* with the infant San Giovanni and a *David* (or Apollo). Also on the ground floor are many works by Benvenuto Cellini. Don't miss Donatello's stunning bronze *David* on the 1st floor, the first free-standing sculpture since antiquity to depict a fully nude man. Among the many other works by Donatello are *St George*, removed from the façade of the Chiesa di Orsanmichele and replaced with a copy, and the *Marzocco*, which once stood in the Piazza della Signoria and was also replaced with a copy.

The museum is open from 8.30 am to 1.50 pm Tuesday to Saturday and on alternating Sundays and Mondays. Admission costs L8000.

The 10th century **Badia**, opposite the Palazzo Bargello on Via del Proconsolo, was the church of a Benedictine monastery. It is worth a visit to see Filippino Lippi's *Appearance of the Virgin to St Bernard*, to the left of the entrance. Wander into the Renaissance cloister.

Around Piazza della SS Annunziata

For some it is Firenze's most beautiful square. In the university district, the piazza is usually filled with students rather than tourists. Giambologna's equestrian statue of Grand Duke Ferdinando I de' Medici commands the scene. **Spedale degli Innocenti**, on the south-eastern side of the piazza, was founded in 1421 as Europe's first orphanage (hence the 'innocents'). Brunelleschi designed the portico, which Andrea della Robbia decorated with terracotta medallions of a baby in swaddling clothes. To the left of the entrance is the small revolving door where unwanted children were left. A good number of people in Firenze with surnames such as degli Innocenti, Innocenti and Nocentini, can trace their family tree only as far back as the orphanage. A small gallery inside features works by Florentine artists, including Luca della Robbia and Domenico Ghirlandaio. It opens from 8.30 am to 2 pm daily except Wednesday. Admission costs L5000.

About 200m south-east of the piazza, along Via della Colonna, is the **Museo Archeologico**. Most of the Medici hoard of antiquities is on show, including the museum's highlight, a collection of Etruscan artefacts. It is open from 9 am to 2 pm Tuesday to Saturday and to 1 pm Sunday. Admission costs L8000.

Galleria dell'Accademia No tour of Firenze is complete without a visit to this gallery. It houses paintings by Florentine artists spanning the 13th to 16th centuries, but its main draw is Michelangelo's *David*, carved from a single block of marble when the artist was aged only 29. Originally in the Piazza della Signoria, the colossal statue now stands in an alcove at the end of the main hall on the ground floor.

The gallery is open from 8.30 am to 10 pm Tuesday to Saturday (to 8 pm on Sunday) in summer. Closing time is 6.50 pm Tuesday to Saturday and 1.50 pm on Sunday in winter. Admission costs L12,000.

Palazzo Medici-Riccardi Heading back towards the duomo, you will find this extraordinary palace on Via Cavour, just off Piazza San Lorenzo. It is typical of the Florentine Renaissance style and was started by Michelozzo for Cosimo de' Medici in 1444. It served as the Medici residence from 1459 to 1540 and was a prototype for other buildings in the city, such as the Palazzo Pitti. The Riccardi family remodelled it in the 17th century.

The chapel upstairs has beautiful frescoes by Benozzo Gozzoli, with regal scenes featuring members of the Medici clan. The Riccardis built the sumptuously decorated Sala di Luca Giordano. The palace is open from 9 am to 1 pm and 3 to 6 pm Monday to Friday (closed Wednesday) and to 1 pm on Sunday and holidays. Admission to the chapel costs L6000.

Casa Buonarroti
Michelangelo owned this house at Via Ghibellina 70 but never lived in it. Upon his death, the house went to his nephew and eventually became a museum in the mid-

1850s. The collection of memorabilia mostly comprises copies of Michelangelo's works and portraits of the master. On the 2nd floor is Michelangelo's earliest known work, *The Madonna of the Steps*. The museum is open from 9.30 am to 1.30 pm daily except Tuesday. Admission costs L10,000.

The Oltrarno
Ponte Vecchio The 14th century structure has been draped in the glittering wares of jewellery merchants since the time Ferdinando I de' Medici ordered them here to replace the rather malodorous presence of the town butchers – who tended to jettison unwanted leftovers into the river. The views of and from the only bridge to survive Nazi explosives in 1944 are every bit as beguiling as you might expect.

Palazzo Pitti When the Pitti, a wealthy merchant family, asked Brunelleschi to design the family home, they did not have modesty in mind. Great rivals of the Medici, there is not a little irony in the fact that their grandiloquence would one day be sacrificed to the bank account. Begun in 1458, the palace was acquired in 1549 by Eleanora di Toledo, wife of Cosimo I de' Medici. She had it expanded by adding two wings and the Medici, followed later by the grand dukes of Lorraine, made it their home. In the late 19th century it became a residence of the Savoy royal family, who graciously presented it to the state in 1919.

The palace now houses four museums. The **Galleria Palatina** (Palatine Gallery) houses paintings from the 16th to 18th centuries, which are hung in lavishly decorated rooms. The works were collected by the Medici and artists including Raphael, Filippo Lippi, Tintoretto, Paolo Veronese and Rubens are represented. It is a large collection and if visits to the Uffizi, Accademia and Bargello haven't yet worn you out, try to spend at least half a day in the Galleria Palatina. The apartments of the Medici and later of the Savoy, show the splendour in which the rulers lived. The other three galleries are worth a look if you have plenty of

TOSCANA

time. The **Galleria d'Arte Moderna** (Modern Art Gallery) covers Tuscan works from the 18th until the mid-20th century and the **Museo degli Argenti** (Silver Museum), entered from the garden courtyard, has a collection of glassware, silver and semiprecious stones from the Medici collections. The **Galleria del Costume** (Costume Gallery) has costumes from the 18th and 19th centuries.

The Galleria Palatina is open from 8.30 am to 9 pm Tuesday to Friday (6.50 pm in winter), to midnight on Saturday (6.50 pm in winter) and to 8 pm on Sunday (1.50 pm in winter). Admission costs L12,000. The Museo degli Argenti and the Galleria d'Arte Moderna open from 8.30 am to 1.50 pm Tuesday to Sunday and on alternating Mondays and Sundays. The other gallery was closed at the time of writing. A L20,000 combined ticket (valid for one day) will admit you to everything that is open and the Giardino di Boboli. A L12,000 ticket gets you into the Galleria Palatina and Appartamenti Reali (Royal Apartments). Or you can pay L4000 to get into each of the other museums.

Take a break in the palace's Renaissance **Giardino di Boboli**, laid out in the mid-16th century and based on a design by the architect known as Il Tribolo. Buontalenti's noted artificial grotto, with a *Venus* by Giambologna, is interesting. The star-shaped **Forte di Belvedere**, built in 1590 at the southern end of the gardens, is worth a look. The garden is open from 9 am to 7.30 pm daily at the height of summer and to 4.30 pm in winter. Admission costs L4000.

Piazzale Michelangelo Via di Belvedere eventually leads to the piazzale from the Palazzo Pitti, but the road has been closed for some time. Rather than catch a bus, you can head back up Via de' Guicciardini to the Arno and then make the long, uphill walk along Costa San Giorgio: at the top you reach the Forte di Belvedere, from where you can follow the part of Via di Belvedere that is open towards Piazzale Michelangelo. The view from Piazzale Michelangelo makes it worth the effort and should not be missed.

Chiesa di San Miniato al Monte Behind Piazzale Michelangelo, this austere church with its green and white marble façade is one of the best examples of the Tuscan Romanesque style. The church was started in the early 11th century and the façade features a mosaic depicting Christ between the Virgin and San Miniato added 200 years later. Inside, above the altar, is a crucifix by Luca della Robbia and a tabernacle by Michelozzo. The Cappella del Cardinale del Portogallo features a tomb by Antonio Rossellino and a ceiling decorated in terracotta by Luca della Robbia. It is possible to wander through the cemetery outside.

Certosa del Galluzzo

This 14th century monastery is just south of Firenze and well worth a visit. Its great cloister is decorated with tondi by Andrea della Robbia and there are frescoes by Pontormo in the Gothic hall of the Palazzo degli Studi. It can only be visited with a guide; it opens from 9 am to noon and 3 to 6 pm (5 pm in winter) daily except Monday. Take bus No 37 from Stazione di Santa Maria Novella.

Cycling

I Bike Italy (☎ 055 234 23 71) offers reasonably priced full and half-day guided mountain-bike rides in the countryside around Firenze, including in the hills around Fiesole to the north-east of the city. Apart from the dosh, you need some energy and a hardy backside.

If you are interested in cycling, ask for a copy of *Viaggio in Toscana – Discovering Toscana by Bike* at the APT. For where to rent a bike, see Rental under Getting Around later in this section.

Firenze for Children

The tourist offices have information about child day-care services, courses and special activities for kids (organised for local youngsters, not tourists, so seek advice on those most suitable for your children). These options might come in handy if you are planning a few days of hectic sightseeing and your children are museumed-out.

There is a small playground in Piazza Massimo d'Azeglio, about five to 10 minutes walk east of the duomo. Beside the Arno river, about 15 minutes walk to the west of Stazione di Santa Maria Novella, is a massive public park called Parco delle Cascine.

Older children might find the Museo Stibbert entertaining. It features a large collection of antique costumes and armaments from Europe, the Middle East and Asia. It is at Via Federico Stibbert 26, north of the train station and is open from 10 am to 1 pm and 3 to 5 pm daily except Thursday (in winter 10 am to 4 pm on weekdays and 10 am to 6 pm at weekends). Admission costs L8000.

Courses

Firenze has more than 30 schools offering courses in Italian language and culture. Numerous other schools offer courses in art, including painting, drawing, sculpture and art history, plus there are also plenty of schools for cooking courses.

While Firenze is one of the most attractive cities in which to study Italian language or art, it is one of the more expensive. Perugia, Siena and Urbino are cheaper and pleasing alternatives.

The cost of language courses in Firenze ranges from about L450,000 to L900,000, depending on the school and the length of the course (one month is usually the minimum).

Language courses available in Firenze include:

Centro Lorenzo de' Medici
(☎ 055 28 73 60) Via Faenza 43, 50122. This school specialises in art courses for foreigners, but also offers several language programmes – usually taken by students intending to pursue art studies.
Dante Alighieri School for Foreigners
(☎ 055 234 29 86) Via de' Bardi 12, 50125
Istituto di Lingua e Cultura Italiana per Stranieri Michelangelo
(☎ 055 24 09 75) Via Ghibellina 88, 50122. Here you will pay L890,000 for four weeks tuition, but the school will also organise private one-on-one courses, starting at L6,230,000 for two weeks (which includes lunch with the teacher – so you'd better like your teacher!).

Art courses range from one-month summer workshops (costing from L500,000 to more than L1,000,000) to longer-term professional diploma courses. These can be expensive at up to L6,500,000 a semester. Schools will organise accommodation for students, upon request, either in private apartments or with Italian families.

Two art schools you might like to consider are:

Centro Lorenzo de' Medici
(☎ 055 28 73 60) Via Faenza 43, 50122. The school offers a wide variety of courses, from short, intensive dabbles to four-year programmes. The latter costs L36,800,000 (payable in yearly chunks).
Istituto per l'Arte e il Restauro
(☎ 055 234 58 98) Palazzo Spinelli, Borgo Santa Croce 10, 50122

If you're interested in a cooking course, taught in English or French, try:

Centro Lorenzo de' Medici
(☎ 055 28 73 60) Via Faenza 43, 50122. The success this school has had with art and language studies has led it to venture into food, with monthly courses for dilettantes and one-year diploma programmes for those in, or heading into, the business. A one month wine-tasting course with just a lesson a week (no language component) can cost L180,000. A full semester programme goes up to L5,000,000.
Cordon Bleu
(☎ 055 234 54 68) Via di Mezzo 55r, 50123

Brochures detailing courses and prices are available at Italian cultural institutes throughout the world. The Firenze APT also has lists of schools and courses and will mail them on request.

Organised Tours

Walking Tours of Florence (☎ 055 234 62 25) organises city walks led by historians. It does an introductory walk three days a week for L35,000, starting at 10 am at Caffè Giubbe Rosse on Piazza della Repubblica. You can organise all sorts of specific walks to suit your own needs and tastes – at a price. Its Web site is at www.artviva.com.

TOSCANA

Special Events

Major festivals include: the Scoppio del Carro (Explosion of the Cart), when a cart full of fireworks is exploded in front of the duomo on Easter Saturday; the Festa del Patrono (the Feast of San Giovanni Battista) on 24 June; and the lively Calcio Storico (Football in Costume), featuring football matches played in 16th century costume, held in June on Piazza Santa Croce and ending with a fireworks display over Piazzale Michelangelo.

Every two years Firenze hosts the Internazionale Antiquariato, an antiques fair attracting exhibitors from across Europe, held at the Palazzo Strozzi, Via de' Tornabuoni. Call ☎ 055 28 26 35 for information. The next fair will be in September/October 2001.

Places to Stay

The city has hundreds of hotels in all categories and a good range of alternatives, including hostels and private rooms. There are more than 150 budget hotels in Firenze, so even in the peak season when the city is packed with tourists, it is generally possible – if not always easy – to find a room.

You are, however, advised to book ahead in summer and for the Easter and Christmas-New Year holiday periods.

Hotels and pensioni are concentrated in three main areas: near Stazione di Santa Maria Novella, near Piazza Santa Maria Novella and in the old city between the duomo and the Arno.

If you arrive at Stazione di Santa Maria Novella without a hotel booking, head for the Consorzio ITA office (see Information earlier in this chapter). Using a computer network, the office can check the availability of rooms and make a booking. The fee charged ranges from L4500 to L15,000 (for one to five-star places). The office is open from 8.30 am to 9 pm daily.

You can also contact the APT for a list of *affittacamere* (private rooms). Most fill with students during the school year (from October to June) but can be a good option if you are staying for a week or longer.

When you arrive at a hotel, always ask for the full price of a room before putting your bags down. Florentine hotels and pensioni are notorious for bill-padding, particularly in summer. Some may require up to L10,000 extra for compulsory breakfast and others will charge L3000 or more for a shower. Contact the APT's SOS Turista if you have any problems.

Prices listed here are for the high season and, unless otherwise indicated, are for rooms without bathroom. A bathroom will cost from L10,000 to L30,000 extra and sometimes all this means is a shower cubicle. Many places, especially at the budget end, offer triples and quads as well as the standard single/double arrangement. If you are travelling in a group of three or four, these bigger rooms are generally the best value.

High season for those hotels that lift their prices (which is most of them) starts on 15 April and fizzles out by mid-October. Some hotels have an intermediate stage starting on 1 March.

Places to Stay – Budget

Camping The closest camp site to the city centre is *Campeggio Michelangelo* (☎ 055 681 19 77, Viale Michelangelo 80), just off Piazzale Michelangelo, south of the Arno. It opens from April until the end of October. Take bus No 13 from Stazione di Santa Maria Novella. *Villa Camerata* (☎ 055 61 03 00, Viale Augusto Righi 2-4) has a camp site next to HI Ostello Villa Camerata (see Hostels following). There is a camp site at Fiesole, *Campeggio Panoramico* (☎ 055 59 90 69, Via Peramonda 1), which also has bungalows. Take bus No 7 to Fiesole from Stazione di Santa Maria Novella.

Hostels The HI *Ostello Villa Camerata* (☎ 055 60 14 51, fax 055 61 03 00, Viale Augusto Righi 2-4) is one of the most beautiful hostels in Europe. B&B is L24,000, dinner L14,000 and there's a bar. Only members are accepted and it's open from 7 am to midnight, with a break from 9 am to 2 pm. Take bus No 17B, which leaves from the right of Stazione di Santa Maria Novella as you leave the platforms. The journey takes 30 minutes.

The private **Ostello Archi Rossi** (☎ 055 29 08 04, Via Faenza 94r) is another good option for a bed in a dorm room (L24,000) and it is close to the stazione. A bed in a smaller room costs L30,000. **Ostello Santa Monaca** (☎ 055 26 83 38, Via Santa Monaca 6) is another private hostel. It is a 15 to 20 minute walk south of the Stazione, on the other side of the Arno. A bed costs L23,000 and sheets and meals are available.

Ostello Spirito Santo (☎ 055 239 82 02, Via Nazionale 8) is a religious institution near Stazione di Santa Maria Novella. The nuns accept only women and families, and charge L40,000 a person or L60,000 a double. They seem cagey about accepting bookings over the phone – but try in any case. The hostel is open from July to October.

Istituto Gould (☎ 055 21 25 76, Via de' Serragli 49) has clean doubles for L39,000. A bed in a quad costs L33,000, while one in a quintuple costs L28,000.

Hotels – Around Stazione di Santa Maria Novella Many of the hotels in this area are well run, clean and safe, but there are also a fair number of seedy establishments. The area includes the streets around Piazza della Stazione and east to Via Cavour.

Pensione Bellavista (☎ 055 28 45 28, Largo Alinari 15), at the start of Via Nazionale, is small but a knockout bargain if you can manage to book one of the two double rooms with balconies and a view of the duomo and Palazzo Vecchio – they cost L130,000. The pensione has no singles.

Albergo Azzi (☎ 055 21 38 06, Via Faenza 56) has helpful management. Simple, comfortable singles/doubles are L70,000/100,000 or L140,000 for a double with bathroom. The same management runs **Albergo Anna** (☎ 055 239 83 22) upstairs, where prices are similar. Several other budget pensioni in the same building are all habitable.

Soggiorno Nazionale (☎ 055 238 22 03, Via Nazionale 22) has rooms for L70,000/110,000 or L80,000/125,000 if you want rooms with private bathroom.

At No 24 is **Pensione Ausonia & Rimini** (☎ 055 49 65 47), run by an obliging young

couple. Rooms cost L70,000/105,000 or L95,000/125,000 with private bath. The price includes breakfast. The same couple runs the more expensive **Pensione Kursaal** (☎ 055 49 63 24) downstairs.

The **Hotel Globus** (☎ 055 21 10 62, Via Sant'Antonino 24) is a handy little place with reasonable if unspectacular rooms costing up to L80,000/130,000. Everything is kept spotlessly clean.

Albergo Mary (☎ 055 49 63 10, Piazza della Indipendenza 5) has rooms for L90,000/110,000 (add L30,000 for rooms with private bath).

Hotels – Around Piazza Santa Maria Novella This area is just south of the Stazione di Santa Maria Novella and includes Piazza Santa Maria Novella, the streets running south to the Arno and southeast to Via de' Tornabuoni.

Via della Scala, which runs north-west off the piazza, is lined with pensioni. **La Romagnola** (☎ 055 21 15 97) at No 40 has large, clean rooms and a helpful management. Singles/doubles cost L48,000/84,000. Add L8000 for a room with private bath. The same family runs **La Gigliola** (☎ 055 28 79 81) upstairs, with rooms for about the same price. **La Scala** (☎ 055 21 26 29) at No 21 is small and has rooms for L70,000/120,000 with bath.

Pensione Margareth (☎ 055 21 01 38),at No 25, has pleasantly furnished rooms for L65,000/80,000 without private bath and some doubles with bath for L120,000. **Pensione Montreal** (☎ 055 238 23 31) at No 43 has rooms from L60,000/95,000 with bath.

Hidden away on a quiet tiny intersection is the modest **Pensione Ferretti** (☎ 055 238 13 28, Via delle Donne 17). Simple but quiet rooms start at L66,000/105,000 or L85,000/125,000 with bath.

Pensione Sole (☎ 055 239 60 94, Via del Sole 8) is on the 3rd floor. Rooms without bath cost L55,000/75,000 and some doubles with bath cost L95,000. Ask for a quiet room. **Pensione Toscana** (☎ 055 21 31 56), in the same building, has eccentrically decorated rooms for L90,000/120,000 with bathroom.

AROUND STAZIONE DI SANTA MARIA NOVELLA

See Duomo to Ponte Vecchio Map p506

Ottaviani (☎ 055 239 62 23, Piazza degli Ottaviani 1), just off Piazza Santa Maria Novella, has rooms for L70,000/85,000 or doubles with own bath for L105,000, breakfast included. In the same building is *Albergo Visconti* (☎ 055 21 38 77), with a pleasant terrace garden where you can have breakfast. Rooms cost L65,000/96,000. Add about L25,000 to the price for a private bathroom.

Hotels – Duomo to Ponte Vecchio This area is a 15 minute walk south from Stazione di Santa Maria Novella in the heart of old Firenze. One of the best deals is the small *Aily Home* (☎ 055 239 65 05, Piazza Santo Stefano 81), just near the Ponte Vecchio. Rooms cost L35,000/60,000. It has five large rooms, three overlooking the bridge and accepts bookings. The singles are tiny but this has to be about the cheapest hotel option in Firenze.

Pensione Maria Luisa de Medici (☎ 055 28 00 48, Via del Corso 1) is in a 17th century mansion. It has large rooms and caters for families. Doubles/triples without own private bath are L101,000/140,000, or L139,000/179,000 with. Prices include breakfast.

Albergo Firenze (☎ 055 21 42 03, Piazza dei Donati 4), just south of the duomo, has singles/doubles for L90,000/130,000 and breakfast is included. *Brunori* (☎ 055 28 96 48, Via del Proconsolo 5) charges up to L102,000 for doubles with a shower. Singles without start at L48,000. *Albergo Bavaria* (☎ 055 234 03 13, Borgo degli Albizi 26) has rooms for up to L90,000/120,000. A double with bathroom costs L150,000. *Pensione TeTi & Prestige* (☎ 055 239 84 35, Via Porta Rossa 5) has rooms for L90,000/L130,000 with shower and a few doubles with private bathroom for L150,000. The manager is willing to lop off about L20,000 in slack periods.

TOSCANA

AROUND STAZIONE DI SANTA MARIA NOVELLA

PLACES TO STAY		25	Ristorante Lobs	17	ATAF Ticket & Information
2	Albergo Mary	27	Caffè degli Innocenti		Office; ATAF Bus Stop for
3	Pensione Ausonia & Rimini;	28	Il Triangolo delle Bermude		No 7, 13, 62 & 70
	Pensione Kursaal	30	Bondi	18	Telecom Booths
6	Soggiorno Nazionale	33	Mario	19	Comune di Firenze
9	Ostello Archi Rossi	34	Ristorante Zà Zà		Tourist Office
10	Albergo Azzi; Albergo Anna	48	Trattoria il Giardino	20	CIT Travel Agency
22	Pensione Bellavista;	50	Ristorante Dino	21	CAP & COPIT
	Pensione Le Cascine	51	Trattoria il Contadino		Bus Station
23	Ostello Spirito Santo	52	Trattoria da Giorgio	24	Centro Lorenzo
26	Machiavelli Palace	53	La Grotta di Leo		de' Medici
29	Atlantic Palace			32	Market
31	Nuova Italia	**OTHER**		35	CTS Travel Agency
41	Giada	1	Firenze & Abroad	36	Telecom Phone Office
42	Hotel Globus	5	Internet Train	37	Sestante Travel Agency
43	Pensione Accademia	7	Wash & Dry Laundrette	38	APT Tourist Office
47	La Romagnola; La Gigliola	8	Alinari	39	Feltrinelli International
54	Pensione Montreal	11	Lazzi Bus Station		Bookshop
55	Pensione Margareth		& Ticket Office	40	Palazzo Medici-Riccardi
56	La Scala	12	Box Office	44	ATAF Local Bus Stop
57	Giotto	13	ATAF Local Bus Stop	45	Chiesa di Santa Maria Novella
58	Hotel Bellettini	14	Consorzio ITA	46	SITA Bus Station
		15	Deposito	49	Hertz
PLACES TO EAT			(Left Luggage)	59	Cappelle Medicee
4	Trattoria Il Messere	16	Farmacia Comunale	60	Basilica di San Lorenzo

Maxim (☎ 055 21 74 74, Via dei Medici 4) has singles/doubles from L105,000/140,000 and triples from L180,000 and offers substantial discounts in the low season.

Places to Stay – Mid-Range

Around Stazione di Santa Maria Novella The *Pensione Le Cascine* (☎ 055 21 10 66, Largo Alinari 15), near Stazione di Santa Maria Novella, is a two star hotel with nicely furnished rooms, some with balconies. Singles/doubles with bathroom cost L140,000/300,000, including breakfast.

Nuova Italia (☎ 055 26 84 30, Via Faenza 26) is a good choice. Its rooms with bathroom cost up to L125,000/185,000. *Pensione Accademia* (☎ 055 29 34 51, Via Faenza 7) has pleasant rooms and incorporates an 18th century mansion with magnificent stained-glass doors and carved wooden ceilings. The only single costs L130,000 (without own bathroom), while doubles with bathroom cost L200,000, breakfast and television included.

Hotel Bellettini (☎ 055 21 35 61, Via dei

Conti 7) is a delightful small hotel which has well furnished rooms with bathroom for L140,000/190,000.

Giotto (☎ 055 28 98 64, Via del Giglio 13) has doubles with bathroom for L160,000. *Giada* (☎ 055 21 53 17) is in the middle of the open-air leather market at Via Canto de' Nelli 2. The rooms with bathroom are OK and you have the rare luxury of breakfast in your room. Rooms cost L120,000/180,000. *Hotel Le Casci* (☎ 055 21 16 86, Via Cavour 13) has good rooms for L140,000/190,000 with bathroom, breakfast and TV.

Duomo to Ponte Vecchio The *Hotel Alessandra* (☎ 055 28 34 38, Borgo SS Apostoli 17) has lots of character. Singles/doubles cost L100,000/150,000 or L150,000/200,000 with bathroom. *Pendini* (☎ 055 21 11 70, Via Strozzi 2) is another excellent choice. It is furnished with antiques and reproductions, and rooms with bathroom cost L170,000/250,000. *Hotel Porta Rossa* (☎ 055 28 75 51, Via Porta Rossa 19) has large rooms for L170,000/285,000.

TOSCANA

Oltrarno A good choice if you want to stay south of the river is *Pensione la Scaletta* (☎ 055 28 30 28, Via de' Guicciardini 13). It has a terrace with great views. Singles/doubles with bathroom cost L140,000/200,000 including breakfast. Some cheaper rooms looking onto the street cost a little less.

Places to Stay – Top End
Around Stazione di Santa Maria Novella The *Atlantic Palace* (☎ 055 29 42 34, Via Nazionale 12) has rooms for up to L194,000/283,000 with breakfast included – prices here have actually come down!

Machiavelli Palace (☎ 055 21 66 22, Via Nazionale 10) is in a 17th century mansion. Many of its beautiful rooms have terraces. Rooms are worth the price at L240,000/390,000.

East of Stazione di Santa Maria Novella The *Hotel Due Fontane* (☎ 055 21 01 85, Piazza della SS Annunziata 14) is in a fine old building right on this square. The well presented rooms cost L200,000/290,000 a single/double.

Duomo to Ponte Vecchio The *Bernini Palace* (☎ 055 28 86 21, Piazza San Firenze 29) is an excellent hotel in a historic building. Its luxurious rooms are L340,000/500,000 a single/double.

Rental Accommodation
If you want an apartment in Firenze, save your pennies and start looking well before you arrive, as apartments are difficult to come by and can be very expensive. A one room apartment with kitchenette in the city centre will cost from L600,000 to L1,000,000 a month (minimum six months), more for short-term rental. Firenze & Abroad (☎ 055 48 70 04), Via San Zanobi 58, deals with rental accommodation.

Places to Eat
Simplicity and quality describe the cuisine of Toscana. In a country where the various regional styles and traditions have provided a rich and diverse cuisine, Toscana is known for its fine cooking. The rich green olive oil of Toscana, fresh fruit and vegetables, tender meat and, of course, the classic wine, Chianti, are the basics of a good meal in Firenze.

You could start a meal with *fettunta* (known elsewhere in Italy as *bruschetta*), a thick slice of toasted bread rubbed with garlic and soaked with olive oil. Try the *ribollita*, a very filling soup traditionally eaten by the poor of Firenze. It is basically a minestrone with lots of white beans which is reboiled with chunks of old bread and then garnished with olive oil. Another traditional dish is the deliciously simple *fagiolini alla Fiorentina* (green beans and olive oil). Firenze is noted for its excellent beefsteak, known as *bistecca alla Fiorentina* – thick, juicy and big enough for two people.

Many tourists fall into the trap of eating at the self-service restaurants that line the streets of the main shopping district between the duomo and the Arno. Be adventurous and seek out the little eating places in the Oltrarno and near Piazza del Mercato Centrale in the San Lorenzo area, where you'll eat more authentic Italian food. The *market*, open from 7 am to 2 pm Monday to Saturday (also 4 to 8 pm Saturday), has fresh produce, cheeses and meat at reasonable prices. Remember to calculate cover (average about L2000 a head) and service charges (15%) when budgeting.

Restaurants, Trattorie & Pizzerie Eating at a good trattoria can be surprisingly economical – a virtue of the competition for customers' attention.

Around Stazione di Santa Maria Novella & Basilica di San Lorenzo *Mario (Via Rosina 2r)*, a small bar and trattoria near Piazza del Mercato Centrale, is open only for lunch and serves pasta for around L6000 to L8000 and mains from L7000 to L9000. It is very busy. A few doors down is *Ristorante Zà Zà (Piazza del Mercato Centrale 20)*, so popular that it's growing. Try the *ravioli al pesto* – an unusual combination that works well. Prices are similar to those at Mario's. *Trattoria Il Messere (Via Guelfa 52)* is a pleasant little place with first courses costing up to L15,000 and mains ranging from L14,000 to L25,000.

Ristorante Lobs (*Via Faenza 75*) is an excellent fish restaurant. For L60,000 you can enjoy a seafood menu including oysters and Norwegian salmon and Soave wine from the country's north-east. Otherwise mains then cost around L32,000. Round off with *sorbetto al vodka*. Another plus about this joint is that they stop cooking at about 12.30 am – a rare thing in a town where few restaurants serve after 11 pm at the latest.

Around Piazza Santa Maria Novella & Borgo Ognissanti The *La Grotta di Leo* (*Via della Scala 41*) is a pleasant trattoria with a L20,000 set menu or pizzas and pasta from L8000. *Trattoria il Giardino* at No 67 in the same street has a L22,000 set menu and serves good, hearty Tuscan dishes and cheap wine. Nearby is *Trattoria il Contadino* (*Via Palazzuolo 55*) with a L15,000 set menu, including wine. *Trattoria da Giorgio*, at No 54, also has a L15,000 set menu and the food is very good. *Ristorante Dino* (*Via Maso Finiguerra 6-8*) is a good little trattoria, with pasta for up to L12,000 and main courses from L14,000 to L28,000.

Da il Latini (*Via dei Palchetti 4*), just off Via del Moro, is an attractive trattoria serving pasta from L6000 and main courses from L14,000. *Sostanza* (*Via del Porcellana 25r*) offers traditional Tuscan cooking and is one of the best spots in town for bistecca alla Fiorentina. Mains start at L18,000.

City Centre & Towards Santa Croce When it comes to eating while you pinch pennies, it's hard to go past *Ristorante Self-Service Leonardo* (*Via de' Pecori 35r*), where mains cost L7500 for lunch or dinner. *Hostaria il Caminetto* (*Via dello Studio 34*), south of the duomo, has a small, vine-covered terrace. Pasta costs around L7000 and mains from L9000 to L10,000. *Trattoria Le Mossacce* (*Via del Proconsolo 55r*) serves pasta for around L9000 and a full meal with wine will cost up to L40,000.

Trattoria del Pennello (*Via Dante Alighieri 4*) is popular but not as cheap as it once was. Pasta starts at L10,000. *Ristorante Paoli* (*Via dei Tavolini 12*) has magnificent vaulted ceilings and walls covered with frescoes and food to match. It offers a L36,000 set menu and pasta from L12,000.

Among the great little treasures of Firenze is *Angie's Pub* (*Via dei Neri 35r*), east of the Palazzo Vecchio, which offers a vast array of *panini* and *focaccia*, as well as hamburgers, Italian-style with mozzarella and spinach and real bagels. A menu lists the panini, but you can design your own from the extensive selection of fillings; try one with artichoke, mozzarella and mushroom cream. Prices start at around L4000.

At *Fiaschetteria* (*Via dei Neri 17r*) you are even less likely to find a tourist. Try the excellent ribollita for L11,000. A pleasant, reasonably priced little trattoria is *Osteria Natalino* (*Piazza San Pier Maggiore*).

A charming and teeny little place for a long cappuccino over the paper or a tasty lunch – try the *crema di zucca* (pumpkin soup) – is *Caffelatte* (*Via degli Alfani 39r*). It's open until 1 am.

For a cheap and tasty set lunch menu for just L14,500, head for the vaulted *Caffetteria Piansa* (*Borgo Pinti 18r*).

Osteria del Gallo e Volpe, on the corner of Via Ghibellina and Via de' Giraldi, has pizzas from L7000 and pasta from L7500.

One of the city's finest restaurants, *Enoteca Pinchiorri* (*Via Ghibellina 87*) is noted for its Italian-style nouvelle cuisine. A meal will cost L180,000 a head.

Oltrarno The *Osteria del Cinghiale Bianco* (*Borgo San Jacopo 43*), to the right as you cross Ponte Vecchio, specialises in Florentine food. As the name suggests, wild boar is on the menu – the *pappardelle al cinghiale* (a plump kind of pasta in wild boar sauce) are music to your tastebuds on a cold evening.

Angelino (*Via di Santo Spirito 36*) is an excellent trattoria where you can eat a meal, including bistecca, for around L35,000. The pizzeria *Borgo Antico* (*Piazza Santo Spirito*) is a great location in summer, when you can sit at an outside table and enjoy the

TOSCANA

atmosphere in the piazza. *Cabiria* is a popular café that also has outdoor seating.

Trattoria Casalinga (Via dei Michelozzi 9r) is a bustling, popular spot. The food is great and a filling meal of pasta, meat or vegetables plus wine will cost under L25,000. Don't expect to linger over a meal, as there is usually a queue of people waiting for your table.

Trattoria I Raddi (Via Ardiglione 47), just near Via de' Serragli, serves traditional Florentine meals and has pasta from L8000 and main courses from L14,000. Around the bend and further up the same street at No 22, the well hidden *Cavolo Nero* will set you back up to L60,000 a head – try the *carpaccio di Angus con rucola e grana.*

Il Cantinone di Gallo Nero (Via di Santo Spirito 6r) specialises in crostini, starting at L3500. Pasta is from L4500.

Snacks The streets between the duomo and the Arno harbour many *pizzerie* where you can buy takeaway pizza by the slice for around L2000 to L3000, depending on the weight. Another option for a light lunch is *Antico Noè*, a legendary sandwich bar through the Arco di San Piero, just off Piazza San Pier Maggiore. It is take-away only. Just opposite, in the same short tunnel, is *Il Nilo* where you can tuck into fat *felafel* or *shawarma* sandwiches for L4000 to L6000.

Caffè degli Innocenti (Via Nazionale 57), near the leather market around Piazza del Mercato Centrale, has a great selection of prepared panini and cakes for around L3000 to L4000. *Bondi (Via dell'Ariento 85)* specialises in focaccia and offers a variety of toppings. They start at L2500.

Antica Enoteca (Via Ghibellina 142) is one of the city's oldest bars and features hundreds of wines. The owners will gladly open any bottle and engage in a chat while you drink and snack if you have the time. Wines start at L1500 a glass.

Gilli (Piazza della Repubblica) is one of the city's finest cafés and is reasonably cheap if you stand at the bar: a coffee at the bar is L1500 but at a table outside it is L5000.

Gelaterie People queue outside *Gelateria Vivoli (Via dell'Isola delle Stinche)*, near Via Torta, to delight in the gelati widely considered to be the city's best. *Il Triangolo delle Bermude (Via Nazionale 61)*, near the leather market, and *Gelateria Perchè No? (Via de' Tavolini 19r)*, off Via de' Calzaiuoli, are both excellent. *Festival del Gelato (Via del Corso 75)*, just off Via de' Calzaiuoli, offers 90 flavours, including a good selection of semi-frozen ice-cream desserts.

Entertainment

Several publications list the theatrical and musical events and festivals in and around town. The free bimonthly *Florence Today*, the monthly *Firenze Information* and *Firenze Avvenimenti*, a monthly brochure distributed by the Comune, are all available (haphazardly) at the tourist offices. The APT publishes an annual booklet listing the year's events, as well as monthly information sheets. *Firenze Spettacolo*, the city's definitive entertainment publication, is available weekly for L3000 at newsstands. Posters at the tourist offices, the university and in Piazza della Repubblica advertise concerts and other events.

A handy centralised ticket outlet is Box Office (☎ 055 21 08 04) at Via Luigi Alamanni 39. It opens from 3.30 to 7.30 pm Monday and from 10 am to 7 pm Tuesday to Saturday.

Pubs & Bars If you can get hold of the APT's *Firenze per i Giovani* (Florence for Young People) brochure, you'll have a list a mile long of bars and clubs.

Cabiria (Piazza Santo Spirito 4) is a music bar and café popular with young locals, particularly in summer, when you can sit outside.

Another popular bar, with live music and a DJ, is *Pongo (Via Giuseppe Verdi 59r)*. Farther towards the Arno at No 43r, *Kikuya Pub* has a generous happy hour from 7 to 10 pm. You can also hear live music here occasionally.

Foreigners hang out at the *Fiddler's Elbow (Piazza Santa Maria Novella)* and *JJ Cathedral (Piazza San Giovanni)*.

Rex Caffè (Via Fiesolana 25r), in the Sant'Antonio area, is popular with the arts community.

Live Music Some of the bigger venues are well outside the town centre. *Tenax (☎ 055 30 81 60, Via Pratese 46)* is one of the city's more popular clubs and is well out to the north-west of the centre. Bus No 29 and 30 from Stazione di Santa Maria Novella take you close, but you'll need a taxi to get home.

Another venue for bands is *Auditorium Flog (☎ 055 49 04 37, Via M Mercati 24b)* in the Rifredi area, also north of the centre but a little closer than Tenax. Bus Nos 8 and 14 go from the stazione. Depending on who is playing at these venues, admission costs from nothing to L20,000. Then the drinks will cost you on top of that – at least L10,000 for a beer.

Discos & Clubs There aren't too many bars in Firenze that stay open past 2 am. One that does is *Maramao Club (☎ 055 24 43 41, Via de' Macci 79r)*. A fairly small, narrow affair with a minuscule dance area on what could be described as the poop deck at the back, it can get packed beyond comfort at weekends. Admission with one drink costs L20,000. Thereafter drinks cost L10,000.

As for clubs where the emphasis is more on dancing, *La Dolce Vita (Piazza del Carmine 6r)*, south of the Arno, is frequented by foreigners and Italians alike.

Theatre & Classical Music Concerts, opera and dance are performed at various times of the year at the *Teatro Comunale (Corso Italia 16)*, on the northern bank of the Arno. In May and June the theatre hosts Maggio Musicale Fiorentina, an international concert festival. Contact the theatre's box office (☎ 055 21 11 58).

There are also seasons of drama, opera, concerts and dance at the *Teatro Verdi (☎ 055 21 23 20, Via Ghibellina 101)*, from January to April and October to December. There are concert series, organised by the Amici della Musica (☎ 055 60 84 20), from January to April and October to December,

at the *Teatro della Pergola (☎ 055 247 96 51, Via della Pergola 18)*. Several other venues have theatre seasons, including the Teatro della Pergola during the winter.

Cinemas You have a few choices of venue for seeing movies in the original language *(lingua originale)*. *Odeon Cinehall (☎ 055 21 40 68, Piazza Strozzi)* screens such movies every Monday evening.

Shopping

It is said that Milano has the best clothes and Roma the best shoes, but Firenze without doubt has the greatest variety of goods. The main shopping area is between the duomo and the Arno, with boutiques concentrated along Via Roma, Via de' Calzaiuoli and Via Por Santa Maria, leading to the goldsmiths lining the Ponte Vecchio. Window-shop along Via de' Tornabuoni, where the top designers, including Gucci, Saint-Laurent and Pucci, sell their wares.

The open-air market (Monday to Saturday), near Piazza del Mercato Centrale, offers leather goods, clothing and jewellery at low prices, but quality varies greatly. You could pick up the bargain of a lifetime, but check the item carefully before paying. It is possible to barter, but not if you want to use a credit card. The flea market (Monday to Saturday) at Piazza dei Ciompi, off Borgo Allegri near Piazza Santa Croce, specialises in antiques and bric-a-brac.

Firenze is famous for its beautifully patterned paper, which is stocked in the many stationery and speciality shops throughout the city and at the markets.

Getting There & Away

Air Firenze is served by two airports: Amerigo Vespucci (☎ 055 306 17 00), a few kilometres north-west of the city centre at Via del Termine 11; and Galileo Galilei (☎ 055 50 07 07, ☎ 055 21 60 73 at Firenze Air Terminal in Stazione di Santa Maria Novella), near Pisa and about an hour by train or car from Firenze. Amerigo Vespucci caters for domestic and European flights. Galileo Galilei is one of northern

TOSCANA

Italy's main international and domestic air-ports and has regular connections to London, Paris, Munich and major Italian cities.

Several European and some US airlines are represented in the city. Alitalia (☎ 055 2 78 88, ☎ 147 86 56 43) is at Lungarno Acciaioli 10-12r and TWA (☎ 055 239 68 56) is at Via dei Vecchietti 4. British Airways can be contacted on ☎ 147 81 22 66.

Bus The SITA bus station (☎ 055 21 47 21), Via Santa Caterina da Siena 15, is just to the west of Piazza della Stazione. There is a direct, rapid service to Siena and buses leave here for Poggibonsi, where there are connecting buses for San Gimignano and Colle di Val d'Elsa (where you change for Volterra). Direct buses serve Arezzo, Castellina in Chianti, Faenza, Grosseto and other smaller cities throughout Toscana. It also handles some international runs, such as to Zagreb in Croatia.

Several bus companies, including CAP (☎ 055 24 46 37) and COPIT (☎ 055 21 54 51), operate from Largo Alinari, at the southern end of Via Nazionale, with services to nearby towns including Prato and Pistoia.

Lazzi (☎ 166 84 50 10), Piazza Adua 1, next to the stazione, runs services to Roma, Pistoia and Lucca.

Lazzi forms part of the Eurolines network of international bus services. You can, for instance, catch a bus to Paris, Prague or Barcelona from Firenze. A detailed brochure of all Eurolines services is available from the Lazzi ticket office.

In collaboration with SITA, Lazzi operates a service called Alpi Bus, which runs extensive routes to the Alpi. The buses depart from numerous cities and towns throughout Lazio, Umbria, Toscana and Emilia-Romagna for most main resorts in the Alpi. See Getting Around earlier in this book for more details.

Train Firenze is on the Roma-Milano line, which means that most of the trains for Roma, Bologna and Milano are Intercities or the Eurostar Italia, for which you have to pay a supplement. There are also regular trains to and from Venezia (three hours) and

Trieste. For Verona you will generally need to change at Bologna. To get to Genova and Torino, a change at Pisa is necessary. The train information office is in the main foyer at Stazione di Santa Maria Novella – it's open from 7 am to 9 pm daily. A porter service (☎ 055 21 23 19) operates from the train station; they charge L4500 per article to escort your luggage to your hotel.

Car & Motorcycle Firenze is connected by the A1 to Bologna and Milano in the north and Roma and Napoli in the south. The Autostrada del Mare (A11) connects Firenze with Prato, Lucca, Pisa and the coast and a superstrada (no tolls) joins the city to Siena. Exits from the autostrade into Firenze are well signposted and there are tourist offices on the A1 both north and south of the city. From the north on the A1, exit at Firenze Nord and then simply follow the bulls-eye 'centro' signs. If approaching from Roma, exit at Firenze Sud.

The more picturesque S67 connects the city with Pisa to the west and Forli and Ravenna to the east.

Getting Around
To/From the Airports
The No 62 bus runs approximately every 20 minutes from the Stazione di Santa Maria Novella to Amerigo Vespucci airport. The service from the airport runs from 6.30 am to 10.45 pm; from the stazione it runs from 6 am to 10.20 pm. The trip takes 15 minutes. Buy a normal city bus ticket (L1500).

Regular trains leave from platform 5 at the stazione for Galileo Galilei airport near Pisa. Check in your luggage 15 minutes before the train departs. Services are roughly hourly from 7.51 am to 5.05 pm from Firenze and from 10.44 am to 5.44 pm from the airport (only until 4.44 pm at weekends). The trip takes an hour and 20 minutes. When there are no trains there are a couple of bus services which meet flights. Two of these are run by SITA (VOLAinBUS) and depart at 11.15 am and 9.20 pm from near the taxi rank. You are dropped at the SITA terminal on Via Santa Caterina di Siena, just by the train station.

The fare is L20,000. The railways runs a third bus at 12.49 am for late arrivals.

Bus Azienda Trasporti Area Fiorentina (ATAF) buses service the city centre, Fiesole and other areas in the city's periphery. For information, call ☎ 055 565 02 22.

You'll find several main bus stops for most routes around the Stazione di Santa Maria Novella. Some of the most useful lines operate from a stop just outside the southeastern exit of the train station below Piazza Adua. Buses leaving from here include:

No 7	Fiesole
No 13	Piazzale Michelangelo
No 62	Amerigo Vespucci airport
No 70	Night bus for the duomo and the Galleria degli Uffizi

Bus tickets can be bought at tobacconists or automatic vending machines at major bus stops before you get on the bus and must be validated in the machine as you enter. You can buy tickets and pick up a useful routes brochure at the ticket office in among the series of ATAF bus stops on Largo Alinari just outside the south-eastern exit of the train station. Tickets are L1500 for 1 hour and L2500 for three hours. A 24 hour ticket costs L6000.

Car & Motorcycle Traffic is restricted in the city centre and parking is prohibited. Non-residents may only drive into the centre to drop off or pick up luggage from hotels or park in hotel or public garages (the latter will cost you a fortune).

There are several major car parks and numerous smaller parking areas around the fringes of the city centre. If you are planning to spend the day in Firenze, your best option is to park at the Fortezza da Basso, which costs L2000 per hour.

If your car is towed, call ☎ 055 30 82 49. You will have to pay L90,000 to recover it plus whatever fine you are charged.

Rental Avis (☎ 055 239 88 26) is at Borgo Ognissanti 128r, Europcar (☎ 055 29 04 38) at Borgo Ognissanti 53r and Hertz (☎ 055 239 82 05) at Via Maso Finiguerra 33r.

Alinari (☎ 055 28 05 00), Via Guelfa 85r, rents scooters, larger mopeds and bicycles. In summer it also sets up shop at several camp sites – check at the APT for details. Mopeds/scooters cost from L28,000 to L50,000 for five hours or from L35,000 to L80,000 per day. Motorbikes cost up to L180,000 a day. You can hire a bike for L12,000 for five hours, L20,000 per day or L40,000 per weekend.

Taxi Taxis are outside Stazione di Santa Maria Novella or call ☎ 055 42 42, 055 47 98 or 055 43 90. The flagfall is L4400 and then L1430 per kilometre within the city limits (L2540 per kilometre beyond). You are also charged L200 every 20 seconds while stationary and L1000 per item of luggage. There is a night-time surcharge (from 10 pm to 6 am) of L5100 and on public holidays you pay an extra L3100 (but not when paying the night surcharge).

AROUND FIRENZE
Fiesole

Perched in hills about 8km north-east of Firenze, between the valleys of the Arno and Mugnone rivers, Fiesole has attracted the likes of Boccaccio, Carducci, Giovanni Dupré, Marcel Proust, Gertrude Stein and Frank Lloyd Wright, all drawn by the lush olive groves and valleys – not to mention the spectacular view of Firenze. Fiesole was founded in the 7th century BC by the Etruscans and remained the most important city in northern Etruria. It is well worth visiting for the views and is a fabulous spot for a picnic and short walk.

Staff at the APT in Firenze, or in Fiesole (☎ 055 59 87 20), Piazza Mino da Fiesole 36, the centre of this small town, can assist with information about the town and can advise on accommodation, walks and other activities. Most other services are near the tourist office.

Things to See & Do Opposite the tourist office in Piazza Mino da Fiesole is the **duomo**, started in the 11th century and altered in the 13th century, although a 19th century renovation has eradicated many earlier

TOSCANA

features. Behind the duomo is the **Museo Bandini**, featuring an impressive collection of early Tuscan Renaissance works, including Taddeo Gaddi's *Annunciation* and Petrarch's beautifully illustrated *Triumphs*.

Opposite the entrance to the museum on Via Portigiana, the **Zona Archeologica** features a 1st century BC Roman theatre that is used from June to August for the Estate Fiesolana, a series of concerts and performances. Also in the complex are a small Etruscan temple and Roman baths, which date from the same period as the theatre. The small archaeological museum is worth a look, as it includes exhibits from the Bronze Age to the Roman period.

Both museums open from 9 am to 7 pm (5 pm in winter) daily except the first Tuesday of each month. The L10,000 ticket gives admission to both.

If you are planning a picnic or just want a refreshing walk, head uphill along the main street from Piazza Mino da Fiesole to Via Corsica. Take Via Pelagaccio, which eventually becomes a dirt track as it weaves around the mountain overlooking Firenze and winds back into Fiesole.

Places to Stay & Eat The APT advises that you camp in designated areas. There is a camp site at Fiesole, *Campeggio Panoramico* (☎ 055 59 90 69, *Via Peramonda 1*), which also has bungalows. Take bus No 70 from Piazza Mino da Fiesole.

The city has several hotels but most are quite expensive. *Bencistà* (☎ 055 5 91 63, *Via Benedetto da Maiano 4*), about 1km from Fiesole just off the road to Firenze, is an old villa and from its terrace there is a magnificent view of Firenze. Half-board is compulsory at L130,000 per person. It might bust the budget, but for one or two days it's well worth it. Ask for a room with a view.

Casa del Popolo di Fiesole (*Via Antonio Gramsci 25*), up the hill from Piazza Mino da Fiesole, is a cheap pizzeria with great views from the terrace to the mountains to the north and east. Piazza Mino da Fiesole is full of expensive bars – *Blu Bar* is one of the more popular.

Getting There & Away Fiesole is easily reached from Firenze. ATAF bus No 7 from the Stazione di Santa Maria Novella in Firenze connects with Piazza Mino da Fiesole. If you are driving, find your way to Piazza della Libertà, north of the duomo and then follow the signs to Fiesole.

The Medici Villas
The Medici built several opulent villas in the countryside around Firenze as their wealth and prosperity grew during the 15th and 16th centuries. Most of the villas are now enclosed by the city's suburbs and industrial sprawl and are easily reached by taking ATAF buses from Stazione di Santa Maria Novella. Ask for details at the APT office in Firenze about bus numbers and opening times.

Villa Medicea La Petraia, about 3.5km north of Firenze, is one of the finest. Commissioned by Cardinal Ferdinand de' Medici in 1576, this former castle was converted by Buontalenti and features a magnificent garden. **Villa Medicea di Castello**, farther north of the city, was the summer home of Lorenzo il Magnifico and it is possible to visit the park only. Other villas include **Villa di Poggio a Caiano**, about 15km from Firenze on the road to Pistoia and **Villa Medicea di Careggi**.

The Mugello
The area north-east of Firenze leading up to Firenzuola, near the border with Emilia-Romagna, is known as the Mugello and features some of the most traditional villages in Toscana. The Sieve river winds up a valley that is one of Toscana's premier wine areas.

Start with the APT office in Firenze or contact the Comunità Montana del Mugello (☎ 055 849 53 46), Via P Togliatti 45, Borgo San Lorenzo. Promo Mugello (☎ 055 849 42 20), Piazza Martin Luther King 5-6, Borgo San Lorenzo, can help with hotel information and bookings.

The Medici originated from the Mugello and held extensive property in the area. Several Medici family castles, villas and palaces dot the area, some of which are open to the public. Others can be visited with a guide. The APT office in Firenze has information, otherwise contact the Associazione Turismo Ambiente (☎ 055 845 87 93), Piazza Dante 29, Borgo San Lorenzo. If you're interested in a wineries tour, there is a so-called *strada del vino* (wine road) mapped out, which will take you through the areas producing Chianti Rufino and Colli Fiorentini. Again, the Firenze APT office has details. Also ask about the various walking trails through the Mugello.

Northern & Western Toscana

PRATO
postcode 59100 • pop 171,100

Virtually enclosed in the urban and industrial sprawl of Firenze, 17km to the southeast, Prato is one of Italy's main textile centres. Founded by the Ligurians, the city fell to the Etruscans and later the Romans and by the 11th century was an important centre for wool production. It is worth visiting on your way to the more picturesque cities of Pistoia, Lucca and Pisa.

Orientation
The old city centre is small and surrounded by the city wall. The main train station, on Piazza della Stazione, is east of the city centre.

Information
The APT office (☎ 0547 2 41 12) is at Via B Cairoli 48-52, two blocks east of the central Piazza del Comune. It is open from 9 am to 1 pm and 4 to 7 pm Monday to Saturday (2.30 to 6 pm in winter). Ask if there is a *biglietto cumulativo* (combined ticket for the main sights). It should cost L5000 but this may change when the Museo Civico reopens.

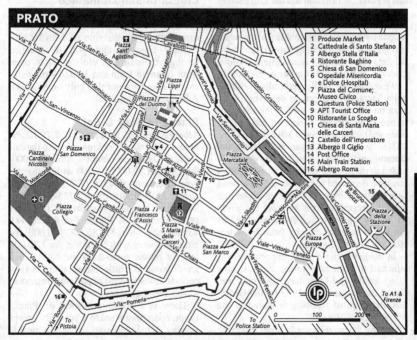

PRATO

1	Produce Market
2	Cattedrale di Santo Stefano
3	Albergo Stella d'Italia
4	Ristorante Baghino
5	Chiesa di San Domenico
6	Ospedale Misericordia e Dolce (Hospital)
7	Piazza del Comune; Museo Civico
8	Questura (Police Station)
9	APT Tourist Office
10	Ristorante Lo Scoglio
11	Chiesa di Santa Maria delle Carceri
12	Castello dell'Imperatore
13	Albergo Il Giglio
14	Post Office
15	Main Train Station
16	Albergo Roma

The main post office is at Via Arcivescovo Martini 8.

For medical emergencies, the Ospedale Misericordia e Dolce (☎ 0547 43 41) is on Piazza dell'Ospedale, south-west of Piazza del Comune. The questura (☎ 0547 55 55) is well out of the centre at Via Cino 10, but operates a small station at Via B Cairoli 29.

Museo Civico

This museum, with its small but impressive collection of largely Tuscan paintings, is housed in the imposing medieval Palazzo Pretorio on Piazza del Comune. Among the artists represented here are Filippo Lippi and Vasari. The museum is open from 10 am to 7 pm daily except Tuesday (morning only on Sunday). Admission costs L10,000. The museum was closed at the time of writing.

Cattedrale di Santo Stefano

Along Via G Mazzoni from Piazza del Comune is Piazza del Duomo and the 12th century Cattedrale di Santo Stefano. The rather simple Pisan-Romanesque façade features a lunette by Andrea della Robbia and the white and green marble banding you will undoubtedly see elsewhere in Toscana (Siena, Pistoia, Lucca). The most extraordinary element, however, is the oddly protruding **Pulpito della Sacra Cintola,** jutting out over the piazza on the right-hand side of the main entrance. The eroded panels of the pulpit, designed by Donatello and Michelozzo in the 1430s, are in the **Museo dell'Opera del Duomo** next door. The pulpit was expressly added so that the *sacra cintola* (sacred girdle) could be displayed to the people five times a year (Easter, 1 May, 15 August, 8 September and 25 December). It is believed the girdle (or belt) was given to San Tomaso by the Virgin and brought to the city from Jerusalem after the Second Crusade.

In medieval times great importance was attached to such holy relics, but just how many girdles did Mary have? Another, declared the real thing in 1953 by the Orthodox Patriarch of Antioch, is stored in the Syrian city of Homs.

Among the magnificent frescoes inside the church, look for those behind the high altar by Filippo Lippi, depicting the martyrdoms of San Giovanni Battista and San Stefano and Agnolo Gaddi's *Legend of the Holy Girdle* in the chapel to the left of the entrance.

Chiesa di Santa Maria delle Carceri

Built by Giuliano da Sangallo towards the end of the 15th century, the interior of this church is considered a Renaissance masterpiece, with a frieze and medallions of the Evangelists by the workshop of Andrea della Robbia.

Also on Piazza Santa Maria Carceri is the **Castello dell'Imperatore**, built in the 13th century by the Holy Roman Emperor Frederick II. The castle is open from 9.30 to 11.30 am and 3.30 to 7 pm daily except Tuesday (3 to 5.30 pm in winter) and is closed on Sunday afternoon.

Chiesa di San Domenico

The main reason for dropping by this church is to have a look at the **Museo di Pittura Murale**, a collection of 14th to 17th century frescoes and graffiti, reached through the church's cloister. It is open from 10 am to 1 pm and 3.30 to 7 pm daily except Tuesday (morning only on Sunday). Admission costs L8000.

Places to Stay & Eat

Albergo Stella d'Italia (☎ 0547 2 79 10, Piazza del Duomo 8), looking across to the cattedrale, has singles/doubles from L60,000/90,000 (or L90,000/115,000 with bath). *Albergo Roma* (☎ 0547 3 17 77, Via G Carradori 1) has rooms from L75,000/90,000. The same people run *Albergo Il Giglio* (☎ 0547 3 70 49, Piazza San Marco 14), where they charge L85,000/110,000 for pleasant rooms with bathroom (or L20,000 less for rooms without private bath). They are disposed to a little horse-trading in slow periods 'in the interest of customer relations' – whatever that means.

There is a *produce market* on Piazza Lippi, open from 8 am to 1 pm daily except Sunday. A most pleasant spot for a meal is

Ristorante Lo Scoglio (Via Verdi 40), where the whole deal will cost you around L40,000 a head. *Ristorante Baghino (Via dell'Accademia 9)* is in much the same vein.

Getting There & Around

CAP and Lazzi buses operate regular services to Firenze and Pistoia from in front of the main train station. Prato is on the Firenze-Bologna and Firenze-Lucca train lines. By car, take the A1 from Firenze and exit at Calenzano or the A11 and exit at Prato.

Several buses, including No 5, connect the main train station with the cattedrale.

PISTOIA

postcode 51100 • pop 90,200

A pleasant city at the foot of the Appennini and 30 minutes north-west of Firenze by train, Pistoia has grown beyond its well preserved medieval ramparts and is today a world centre for the manufacture of trains. In the 16th century the city's metalworkers created the pistol, named after the city.

Orientation & Information

Although spread out, the old city centre is easy to negotiate. From the train station on Piazza Dante Alighieri, head north along Via XX Settembre, through Piazza Treviso and continue heading north to turn right into Via Cavour. Via Roma, branching off the northern side of Via Cavour, takes you to Piazza del Duomo and the APT office (☎ 0573 2 16 22), which is open from 9 am to 1 pm and 3 to 6 pm daily.

The main post office is at Via Roma 5. An unstaffed Telecom phone office is on Corso Antonio Gramsci, near Via della Madonna.

The public hospital (☎ 0573 35 21) is on Viale Giacomo Matteotti, behind the old Ospedale del Ceppo. The questura (☎ 0573 2 67 05) is out of the centre at Via Macallé 23. If you need a doctor fast, call ☎ 0573 36 36.

Piazza del Duomo

Much of Pistoia's visual wealth is concentrated on this central square. The Pisan-Romanesque façade of the **Cattedrale di San Zeno**, also known as the duomo (and like so many buildings across Italy at the time of writing, covered in scaffolding for a pre-2000 clean up), boasts a lunette of the Madonna and Child by Andrea della Robbia, who also made the terracotta tiles that line the barrel vault of the main porch. Inside, in the Cappella di San Jacopo, is the remarkable silver **Altarpiece of San Giacomo**. It was begun in the 13th century, with artisans adding to it over the ensuing two centuries until Brunelleschi contributed the final touch, the two half-figures on the left side.

The venerable building between the duomo and Via Roma is the **Antico Palazzo dei Vescovi**. There are guided tours four times a day through the wealth of artefacts, discovered during restoration work, dating as far back as Etruscan times. Across Via Roma is the **battistero** (baptistry). Elegantly banded in green and white marble, it was started in 1337 to a design by Andrea Pisano.

Dominating the eastern flank of the piazza, the Gothic Palazzo del Comune houses the **Museo Civico**, with works by Tuscan artists from the 13th to 19th centuries. The museum is open from 10 am to 6 pm Tuesday to Saturday and 9 am to 12.30 pm on Sunday and holidays. Admission costs L6000 (free on Saturday afternoon).

The portico of the nearby **Ospedale del Ceppo** will stop even the monument-weary in their tracks – the terracotta frieze by Giovanni della Robbia is unique, depicting *Theological Virtues* and *Seven Works of Mercy*.

Places to Stay & Eat

There are a couple of cheap places to stay. *Hotel Firenze (☎ 0573 2 31 41, Via Curtatone e Montanara)* has singles/doubles for up to L50,000/80,000 or L65,000/100,000 with bathroom. These prices should include breakfast (without the grub you may be able to talk them down a little). You can pick up a pokey room at *Albergo Autisti (☎ 0573 2 17 71, Via le Antonio Pacinotti 89)* for L30,000/50,000 or a slightly better double with bathroom for L70,000.

A *produce market* is open most days on Piazza della Sala, west of the duomo. *Pizzeria Tonino (Corso Antonio Gramsci*

TOSCANA

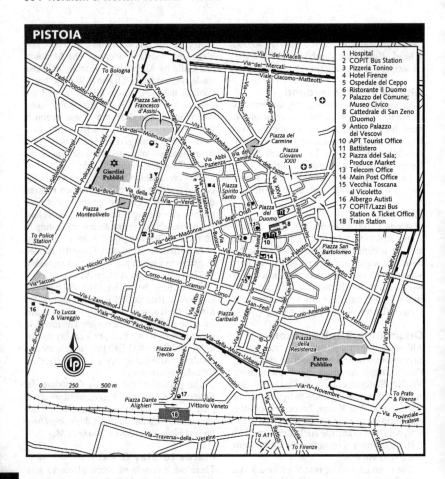

PISTOIA

1 Hospital
2 COPIT Bus Station
3 Pizzeria Tonino
4 Hotel Firenze
5 Ospedale del Ceppo
6 Ristorante Il Duomo
7 Palazzo del Comune;
   Museo Civico
8 Cattedrale di San Zeno
   (Duomo)
9 Antico Palazzo
   dei Vescovi
10 APT Tourist Office
11 Battistero
12 Piazza ddel Sala;
   Produce Market
13 Telecom Office
14 Main Post Office
15 Vecchia Toscana
   al Vicoletto
16 Albergo Autisti
17 COPIT/Lazzi Bus
   Station & Ticket Office
18 Train Station

159) is a pleasant trattoria where a meal will cost around L25,000. *Vecchia Toscana al Vicoletto (Via Panciatichi 4)* is good but slightly more expensive, with pasta from L10,000. *Ristorante Il Duomo (Via Bracciolini 5)* is a cheap self-service buffet place open from noon to 3 pm for lunch only.

Getting There & Around

Buses connect Pistoia with most towns in Toscana. The main ticket office for COPIT and Lazzi buses is on the corner of Viale Vittorio Veneto and Via XX Settembre and most buses leave from just outside (those for Firenze depart from Piazza Treviso). Other COPIT buses leave from Via del Molinuzzo, off Piazza San Francesco d'Assisi.

Trains link Pistoia with Firenze, Bologna, Lucca and Viareggio. By car, the city is on the A11 and the S64 and S66, which head north-east for Bologna and north-west for Parma respectively. Bus Nos 10 and 12 connect the train station with the duomo, although the city is easily explored on foot.

LUCCA

postcode 55100 • pop 87,000

Hidden behind imposing Renaissance walls, Lucca is a pretty base from which to explore the Alpi Apuane and the Garfagnana and is well worth a visit in its own right.

Founded by the Etruscans, Lucca became a Roman colony in 180 BC and a free *comune* during the 12th century, initiating a period of prosperity based on the silk trade. In 1314 it fell under the control of Pisa, but under the leadership of local adventurer Castruccio Castracani degli Anterminelli, the city regained its independence and began to amass territories in western Toscana. Castruccio died in 1325 but Lucca remained an independent republic for almost 500 years.

Napoleon ended all this in 1805. He created the principality of Lucca and, unswerving in his innate sense of democratic values, placed one of the seemingly countless members of his family in need of an Italian fiefdom (this time his sister Elisa) in control. Twelve years later the city became a Bourbon duchy before being incorporated into the Kingdom of Italy.

Lucca remains a strong agricultural centre. The long periods of peace it has enjoyed explain the almost perfect preservation of the city walls – they were rarely put to the test.

Orientation

From the train station on Piazza Ricasoli, just outside the city walls to the south, walk north-west to Piazza Risorgimento and through Porta San Pietro. Head north along Via Vittorio Veneto to the immense Piazza Napoleone and on to Piazza San Michele – the centre of town.

Information

The tourist office (☎ 0583 41 96 89) is on Piazzale Verdi, at the western edge of the walled city in an old city gate, the Vecchia Porta San Donato. It is open from 9 am to 6 pm daily in summer (3 pm in winter, when it also closes on Sunday and holidays).

The Deutsche Bank at Via Fillungo 76 has a user-friendly ATM or you can change currency over the counter.

The main post office is at Via Vallisneri 2, just north of the duomo, and the unstaffed Telecom office is at Via Cenami 19.

The main hospital (☎ 0583 97 01) is on Via dell'Ospedale, beyond the city walls to the north-east. The questura (☎ 0583 45 51) is on Viale Cavour 38, near the train station.

Duomo

Lucca's Romanesque duomo, dedicated to San Martino, dates from the 11th century. The exquisite façade, in the Lucca-Pisan style, was designed to accommodate the pre-existing bell tower. Each of the columns in the upper part of the façade was carved by a local artisan and are all quite different from one another. The reliefs over the left doorway of the portico are believed to be by Nicola Pisano.

The interior was rebuilt in the 14th and 15th centuries with a Gothic flourish. Matteo Civitali designed the pulpit and, in the north aisle, the 15th century tempietto that contains the **Volto Santo**, an image of Christ on a wooden crucifix said to have been carved by Nicodemus, who witnessed the crucifixion. It is a major object of pilgrimage and each year on 13 September it's carried through the streets in a procession at dusk. In the sacristy the tomb of Ilaria del Carretto (wife of the 15th century Lord of Lucca, Paolo Guinigi) is a masterpiece of funerary sculpture executed (if you'll forgive the expression) by Jacopo della Quercia; admission costs L3000. The church contains numerous other artworks, including a magnificent *Last Supper* by Tintoretto, over the third altar of the south aisle.

Chiesa di San Michele in Foro

Equally dazzling is this Romanesque church, built on the site of its 8th-century precursor over a period of nearly 300 years from the 11th century. The wedding-cake façade is topped by a figure of the Archangel Michael slaying a dragon. Look for Andrea della Robbia's *Madonna and Child* in the south aisle.

Opposite the church, off Via di Poggio, is **Casa di Puccini**, where the composer was

TOSCANA

LUCCA

PLACES TO STAY
12 Affittacamere
Centro Storico
19 Piccolo Hotel
Puccini
26 Hotel Diana

PLACES TO EAT
3 Le Salette
6 Trattoria Buralli
8 Di Simo Caffè
21 Piccolo Mondo
22 Ristorante Buca
Sant'Antonio

OTHER
1 Museo Nazionale
Guinigi
2 Chiesa di
San Francesco
4 Chiesa di San
Frediano
5 Chiesa di
Sant'Agostino
7 Chiesa di
San Salvatore
9 Deutsche Bank
& ATM
10 Palazzo Guinigi
11 Torre delle Ore
13 Casa di Puccini
14 Pinacoteca
Nazionale e
Museo di Palazzo
Mansi
15 Tourist Office
16 Hotel Reservation
Office
17 Lazzi Bus Terminal
18 CLAP Bus Terminal
20 Chiesa di San
Michele in Foro
23 Telecom Office
24 Main Post Office
25 Duomo
27 Porta San Pietro;
Piazza Risorgimento
28 Questura
(Police Station)
29 Train Station

TOSCANA

born. It houses a small museum dedicated to his life, which opens from 10 am to 1 pm and 3 to 6 pm daily except Monday. Admission costs L5000.

Via Fillungo

Lucca's busiest street, Via Fillungo, threads its way through the medieval heart of the old city and is lined with fascinating, centuries-old buildings. The **Torre delle Ore** (city clock tower) is about halfway along. In medieval days its possession was hotly contested by rival families.

East of Via Fillungo

You would never know it by simply parading north along Via Fillungo, but just off to the east (accessed from Piazza Scarpellini) is the place where local thespians regularly gathered in Roman days for a spot of outdoor theatre. Centuries later the oval-shaped theatre became **Piazza Anfiteatro** as houses were built on the foundations of the imperial anfiteatro (amphitheatre).

A short walk farther east is **Piazza San Francesco** and the attractive 13th century church of the same name. Along Via della Quarquonia is the Villa Guinigi, which houses the **Museo Nazionale Guinigi** and the city's art collection. It is open from 9 am to 7 pm daily except Monday (to 2 pm on Sunday and holidays). Admission costs L4000.

West of Via Fillungo

Another example of Lucca's adaptation of Pisan Romanesque, the façade of the **Chiesa di San Frediano** features a unique (and much restored) 13th century mosaic. The main feature of the beautiful basilica's interior is the **Fontana Lustrale**, a 12th century baptismal font decorated with sculpted reliefs. Behind it is an *Annunciation* by Andrea della Robbia.

Of some interest are the interior and artworks of the **Pinacoteca Nazionale e Museo di Palazzo Mansi** on Via Galli Tassi. It is open from 9 am to 7 pm daily except Monday (2 pm on Sunday and holidays). Admission is a bit expensive at L8000.

City Walls

If you have the time, do the 4km walk (or jog) along the top of the city walls. These ramparts were raised in the 16th and 17th centuries and are similar to the defensive systems later developed by the French military engineer Vauban.

Courses

The Centro Koinè (☎ 0583 49 30 40), Via A Mordini 60, offers Italian courses for foreigners. A two week summer course costs L650,000, while month-long courses, available year-round, cost nearly L900,000. The school can also arrange accommodation.

Places to Stay

It is always advisable to book ahead, but if you're in a spot try the city's hotel association, the Sindacato Lucchese Albergatori (☎ 0583 49 41 81, Via Fillungo 121). If they fail, there is another hotel reservation office (☎ 0583 31 22 62) at Piazzale Verdi 1.

The city's HI youth hostel, the *Ostello Il Serchio* (☎ 0583 34 18 11, Via del Brennero 673), is outside the walls to the north; take CLAP bus No 1 or 2 from Piazzale Verdi. B&B costs L18,000. It is open from 10 March to 31 October.

A good budget option smack in the heart of town is *Affittacamere Centro Storico* (☎ 0583 49 07 48, Corte Portici 16). It charges L70,000 for doubles and will discount for singles in slack periods. It doesn't accept newcomers after 8 pm. *Hotel Diana* (☎ 0583 49 22 02, Via del Molinetto 11) has singles for L60,000 and doubles with bathroom for up to L105,000. If you can afford the extra, the three star *Piccolo Hotel Puccini* (☎ 0583 5 54 21, Via di Poggio 9) is a better deal, with singles/doubles with bathroom for L90,000/125,000.

Places to Eat

Lucca boasts a good selection of relatively cheap trattorie. For pizza by the slice, go to the small *takeaway* at Via Fillungo 5. *Piccolo Mondo* (Piazza dei Cocomeri 5) is a good spot for a cheap meal – it has a filling if basic set lunch menu for L12,500. Just around the

TOSCANA

corner, **Ristorante Buca Sant'Antonio** *(Via della Cervia 3)* is a rather classier affair where you'll pay about L40,000 a head for a full meal. **Trattoria Buralli** *(Piazza Sant'Agostino 9)* offers a simple but filling tourist menu for L18,000. You'll also find several reasonably priced restaurants and pizza joints, including **Ristorante Le Salette** *(Piazza Santa Maria)*. **Di Simo Caffè** *(Via Fillungo 58)* is a grand bar and gelateria serving local specialities such as buccellato cakes.

Getting There & Away
CLAP buses (☎ 0583 58 78 97) serve the region, including the Garfagnana. Lazzi (☎ 0583 58 48 77) operates buses to Firenze, La Spezia, Carrara, Pisa, Torino and Roma. Both companies operate from Piazzale Verdi.

Lucca is on the Firenze-Viareggio-Pisa train line and there are also services into the Garfagnana. By car, the A11 passes to the south of the city, connecting it with Pisa and Viareggio. The S12, which becomes the S445 at Barga, links the city with the Garfagnana.

Getting Around
Most cars are banned from the city centre, although tourists are allowed to drive into the walled city and park in the residents' spaces (yellow lines) if they have a permit from one of the hotels. There are paid parking areas in piazzas Bernardini, San Martino, Napoleone and Boccherini.

CLAP buses connect the train station, Piazza del Giglio (near Piazza Napoleone) and Piazzale Verdi, but it is just as easy and more pleasurable, to walk.

For a taxi, call ☎ 0583 49 49 89.

THE GARFAGNANA
The heart of the Garfagnana is in the valley formed by the Serchio river and its tributaries. This is an excellent area for walking, horse riding and a host of other outdoor pursuits and the region is well geared for tourism. Staff at the tourist offices in Lucca or Pisa can advise. The most useful organisation in the Garfagnana is Consorzio Garfagnana Turistica (☎ 0583 64 44 73), at the Comunità Montana, Via Vittorio Emanuele

9, in Castelnuovo di Garfagnana. Pro Loco tourist offices in several smaller villages can help with details on hotels and *rifugi* (mountain huts).

Walkers should pick up a copy of *Garfagnana Trekking*, which details a 10 day walk. Another booklet, *Garfagnana a Cavallo*, details guided horse treks that can cost L20,000 an hour or L90,000 a day. Details of these and other aspects of the mountains, including *agriturismo*, are available from the Azienda Agrituristica La Garfagnana (☎ 0583 6 87 05), Località Prade 25, in Castiglione di Garfagnana.

Alpi Apuane
This mountain range is bordered on one side by the stretch of coastline known as the Versilia Riviera and on the other by the vast valley of the Garfagnana. Altitudes are relatively low, in comparison to the Alpi farther north, but the Alpi Apuane are certainly not lacking in great walking possibilities: some trails afford spectacular views to the coastline and the Mar Ligure. The landscape in some areas has been utterly destroyed by marble mining, an industry that has exploited these mountains since Roman times. No environmental laws have been in place to prevent mining companies from literally removing entire peaks in some places. But, in the end, the extent of interference in the natural landscape has created a new environment with a certain aesthetic appeal. You'll find a good network of marked walking trails and several rifugi in the Alpi Apuane. The 1:25,000 *Carta dei Sentieri e Rifugi*, published by Multigraphic of Firenze, is a good map.

You can get information from the Comunità Montana in Castiglione di Garfagnana.

MASSA & CARRARA
These two towns in the northern reaches of Toscana don't really warrant a visit unless you are interested in seeing Italy's famous marble quarries. Massa is the administrative centre of the province and is rather unattractive, although the beachfront extension, Marina di Massa, is popular with holidaying Italians. You might wonder why, if you

happen to stumble onto the overpopulated shores.

Carrara, however, is quite picturesque. At the foothills of the Alpi Apuane, the town appears to be dominated by snowcapped mountains, an illusion created by limestone formations and the vast quarries that virtually cover the hills. The texture and purity of Carrara's white marble is unrivalled and was chosen by Michelangelo for many of his masterpieces. He often travelled to the quarries to personally select blocks of the stone.

The APT has offices at Marina di Massa (☎ 0585 24 00 63), Viale Vespucci 24, and in Carrara (☎ 0585 84 44 03), Via Settembre XX. There is a youth hostel on the coast at Marina di Massa, the *Ostello della Gioventù* (☎ 0585 78 00 34, Via delle Pinete 237), which charges L14,000 for a bed.

Both Massa and Carrara are accessible from the A12 and the S1 Via Aurelia; signs direct you to quarries you can visit and other attractions, such as museums.

PISA
postcode 56100 • pop 98,000
Once, if briefly, a maritime power to rival Genova and Venezia, Pisa now draws its fame from an architectural project gone terribly wrong: its Torre Pendente (Leaning Tower). But the city offers quite a deal more. Indeed, the tower is only one element of the trio of Romanesque beauties astride the green carpet of the Campo dei Miracoli – along with Piazza San Marco in Venezia one of Italy's more memorable squares.

Pisa has a centuries-old tradition as a university town and even today is full of young students. A perhaps unexpectedly beautiful city, it really deserves more than the usual one day stopover planned by the average tourist.

History
Possibly of Greek origin, Pisa became an important naval base under Roma and remained a significant port for many centuries. The city's so-called Golden Days began late in the 9th century when it became an independent maritime republic and a rival of Genova and Venezia. The good

times rolled on into the 12th and 13th centuries, by which time Pisa controlled Corsica, Sardegna and most of the mainland coast as far south as Civitavecchia. The majority of the city's finest buildings date from this period, as well as the distinctive Pisan-Romanesque architectural style.

Pisa's support for the Ghibellini during the tussles between the Holy Roman Emperor and the pope brought the city into conflict with its mostly Guelf Tuscan neighbours, including Siena, Lucca and Firenze. The real blow, however, came when Genova's fleet inflicted a devastating defeat on Pisa at the Battle of Meloria in 1284. The city fell to Firenze in 1406 and the Medici encouraged great artistic, literary and scientific endeavour and re-established Pisa's university. The city's most famous son, Galileo Galilei, later taught at the university.

Orientation
By train you'll arrive at Stazione Pisa Centrale, on Piazza della Stazione at the southern edge of the town. The main intercity bus station is on Piazza Vittorio Emanuele II, a short walk north along Viale Gramsci. The medieval centre is about a 15 minute walk north, across the Arno river and Campo dei Miracoli (aka Piazza del Duomo) is about another 10 minute walk north-west. It is quicker to catch a city bus from outside the stazione (see Getting Around later in this section).

Information
Tourist Offices The main APT office (☎ 050 56 04 64) is in a little cube of a building just outside the city walls. It opens from 8 am to 8 pm Monday to Saturday (9.30 am to noon and 3 to 5.30 pm in the low season). The office at the train station (☎ 050 4 22 91) keeps longer hours in winter (9.30 am to 1 pm and 3 to 6 pm) but has little more than a map and a list of hotels – the most useful items for late night arrivals, however!

Money Avoid the currency exchange booths near the duomo. Change currency at banks along Corso Italia or at Stazione Pisa Centrale.

TOSCANA

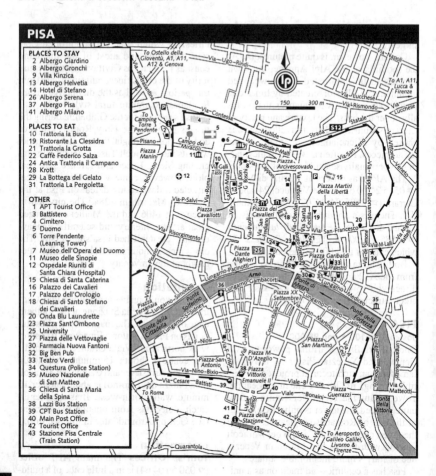

PISA

PLACES TO STAY
2 Albergo Giardino
8 Albergo Gronchi
9 Villa Kinzica
13 Albergo Helvetia
14 Hotel di Stefano
26 Albergo Serena
37 Albergo Pisa
41 Albergo Milano

PLACES TO EAT
10 Trattoria la Buca
19 Ristorante La Clessidra
21 Trattoria la Grotta
22 Caffè Federico Salza
24 Antica Trattoria il Campano
28 Krott
29 La Bottega del Gelato
31 Trattoria La Pergoletta

OTHER
1 APT Tourist Office
3 Battistero
4 Cimitero
5 Duomo
6 Torre Pendente
   (Leaning Tower)
7 Museo dell'Opera del Duomo
11 Museo delle Sinopie
12 Ospedale Riuniti di
   Santa Chiara (Hospital)
15 Chiesa di Santa Caterina
16 Palazzo dei Cavalieri
17 Palazzo dell'Orologio
18 Chiesa di Santo Stefano
   dei Cavalieri
20 Onda Blu Laundrette
23 Piazza Sant'Ombono
25 University
27 Piazza delle Vettovaglie
30 Farmacia Nuova Fantoni
32 Big Ben Pub
33 Teatro Verdi
34 Questura (Police Station)
35 Museo Nazionale
   di San Matteo
36 Chiesa di Santa Maria
   della Spina
38 Lazzi Bus Station
39 CPT Bus Station
40 Main Post Office
42 Tourist Office
43 Stazione Pisa Centrale
   (Train Station)

Post & Communications The main post office is on Piazza Vittorio Emanuele II. You'll find phones scattered throughout the town.

Laundry Clean those smelly socks at Onda Blu self-service laundrette, Via San Francesco 8a.

Medical Services & Emergency The Ospedali Riuniti di Santa Chiara (☎ 050 99 21 11) is a complex at Via Roma 67. The Farmacia Nuova Fantoni, Lungarno Mediceo 51, is open 24 hours. The questura (☎ 050 58 35 11) is on Via Mario Lalli.

Campo dei Miracoli

The Pisans can justly claim that the Campo dei Miracoli is one of the most beautiful squares in the world. Set among its sprawling lawns is surely one of the most extraordinary concentrations of Romanesque splendour – the duomo, the battistero (baptistry) and the Torre Pendente (Leaning Tower). On any day the piazza is teeming with people – students studying or at play, tourists wandering and local workers eating lunch.

A staggered pricing system operates for tickets to enter one or more of the monuments in and around the square. L10,000 admits you to two monuments and L15,000 to four – the two museums, battistero and cimitero (cemetery). The duomo itself is not included and costs an extra L2000.

Opening times are complex. In some cases there are summer, autumn and winter times. What follows below gives the summer and winter 'extremes'.

Duomo The majesty of Pisa's duomo made it a model for Romanesque churches throughout Toscana and even on Sardegna. Begun in 1064, it is covered inside and out with the alternating bands of (now somewhat faded) dark green and cream marble that were to become characteristic of the Pisan-Romanesque style.

The main façade, when not hidden by scaffolding, is a sight to behold, adorned as it is with four tiers of columns. The huge interior is lined with 68 columns in classical style. The bronze doors of the transept, facing the Torre Pendente, are by Bonanno Pisano. The 16th century bronze doors of the main entrance were designed by the school of Giambologna to replace the wooden originals, destroyed in a fire in 1596. The interior was also greatly redecorated after this devastating fire. Important works to survive the blaze include Giovanni Pisano's early 14th century pulpit and an apse mosaic of *Christ in Majesty* completed by Cimabue in 1302. The duomo is open from 10 am to 8 pm on weekdays and 1 to 8 pm daily at weekends. In winter it opens from 10 am to 1 pm and 3 to 5 pm daily.

Torre Pendente Welcome to one of the world's great cockups. The duomo's *campanile* (bell tower) was in trouble from the start. Its architect, Bonanno Pisano, managed to complete only three tiers before the tower started to lean on the southern side. The problem is generally believed to have been

caused by shifting soil and the 'leaning tower' has continued to lean by an average of 1mm a year ever since. Galileo is sometimes claimed to have climbed its 294 steps to experiment with gravity, but today it is no longer possible to follow in his footsteps. The tower has been closed since 1990 while the Italians try to work out how to stop its inexorable lean towards the ground – it now leans 5m off the perpendicular.

Several solutions have been tried without success. In 1998 a plan was approved to wrap cables around the third storey and attach them to A-frames on the northern side. This will hold the tower in place while workers begin to remove small portions of soil on the northern side and create a counter subsidence. The idea is to reduce the lean by 10% and stabilise the tower. No-one knows if it will work. Some believe all the meddling is a mistake. The controversial Italian art historian, Vittorio Sgarbi, once said it would be 'better to see it fall and remember it leaning than see it straightened by mistake'. Was he saying that two wrongs won't set it right?

Battistero The unusual, round baptistery was started in 1153 by Diotisalvi, remodelled and continued by Nicola and Giovanni Pisano more than a century later and finally completed in the 14th century – which explains the mix of architectural styles. At the moment it is shrouded in cleaners' scaffolding. The lower level of arcades is in the Pisan-Romanesque style and the pinnacled upper section and dome are Gothic. Inside, the beautiful pulpit was carved by Nicola Pisano and signed in 1260 and the white marble font was carved by Guido da Como in 1246. The acoustics beneath the dome are quite remarkable too. It is open from 8 am to 9 pm (9 am to 5 pm in winter).

Cimitero Behind the white wall to the north of the duomo, this exquisite cemetery is said to have soil that was shipped from Calvary during the crusades. Many precious frescoes in the cloisters were badly damaged or destroyed during WWII Allied bombing raids. Among those saved were the *Triumph of*

TOSCANA

Death and *Last Judgment*, attributed to an anonymous 14th century painter known as 'The Master of the Triumph of Death'. The cemetery is open from 8 am to 8 pm daily (9 am to 5 pm in winter).

Around Campo dei Miracoli

The **Museo delle Sinopie** houses reddish-brown sketches drawn onto walls as the base for frescoes, discovered in the cemetery after the WWII bombing raids. The *sinopie* have been restored and provide a fascinating insight into the process of creating a fresco, although they are really only worth visiting if you have a particular interest in the subject. The museum is open from 8 am to 8 pm daily (9 am to 1 pm and 3 to 5 pm in winter).

The **Museo dell'Opera del Duomo** on Piazza Arcivescovado, near the Torre Pendente, features many artworks from the tower, duomo and battistero, including a magnificent ivory carving of the *Madonna and Crucifix* by Giovanni Pisano. Another highlight is the bust known as the *Madonna del Colloquio*, by the same artist, taken from the exterior of the battistero. It is open from 9 am to 1 pm and 3 to 7.30 pm daily (5.30 pm in winter).

The City

From Campo dei Miracoli head south along Via Santa Maria and turn left at Piazza Cavallotti for the splendid **Piazza dei Cavalieri**, remodelled by Vasari in the 16th century. The **Palazzo dell'Orologio**, on the northern side of the piazza, occupies the site of a tower where, in 1288, Count Ugolino della Gherardesca, his sons and grandsons, were starved to death on suspicion of having helped the Genovese enemy at the Battle of Meloria. The incident was recorded in Dante's *Inferno*. The **Palazzo dei Cavalieri** on the north-eastern side of the piazza was redesigned by Vasari and features remarkable graffiti decoration. The piazza and palazzo are named for the Knights of Santo Stefano, a religious and military order founded by Cosimo de' Medici. Their church, **Santo Stefano dei Cavalieri**, was also designed by Vasari. The **Chiesa di Santa Caterina**, north of Via San Lorenzo on Piazza

Martiri della Libertà, is a fine example of Pisan-Gothic architecture and contains works by Nino Pisano.

Wander south to the area around **Borgo Stretto**, the city's medieval heart. East along the waterfront boulevard, the Lungarno Mediceo, is the **Museo Nazionale di San Matteo**, a fine gallery. It features works by Giovanni and Nicola Pisano, Masaccio and Donatello. The gallery is open from 9 am to 7 pm Tuesday to Saturday and to 1 pm on Sunday. Admission costs L8000.

Cross the Ponte di Mezzo and head west to reach the **Chiesa di Santa Maria della Spina**, oddly perched on the road along the Arno. It was built in the early 14th century to house a thorn from Christ's crown.

Places to Stay

Pisa has a reasonable number of budget hotels for a small town, but many double as residences for students during the school year, so it can be difficult to find a cheap room.

A camp site, *Camping Torre Pendente*, (☎ 050 56 17 04, *Via delle Cascine 86*) is west of the duomo. The non-HI *Ostello della Gioventù* (☎ 050 89 06 22, *Via Pietrasantina 15*) is a long hike north-west of the duomo. A bed costs L22,000 in a quad. Take bus No 3 from Stazione Pisa Centrale (walking from Campo dei Miracoli is a huge pain).

Albergo Serena (☎ 050 58 08 09, *Via D Cavalca 45*), just off Piazza Dante Alighieri, has singles/doubles for up to L45,000/65,000. *Albergo Helvetia* (☎ 050 55 30 84, *Via Don Gaetano Boschi 31*), south of the duomo, has pleasant rooms without bath for L50,000/65,000 and doubles with bath for L95,000 (prices drop in low season). *Hotel di Stefano* (☎ 050 55 35 59, *Via Sant'Apollonia 35*), near Via Carducci, has good rooms with bath for up to L80,000/115,000 (about L20,000 less without bath).

Albergo Gronchi (☎ 050 56 18 23, *Piazza Arcivescovado 1*) is a steal for its position alone. Rooms cost L30,000/54,000. *Albergo Giardino* (☎ 050 56 21 01, *Piazza Manin 1*), just west of Campo dei Miracoli, was refurbished in early 1999 and charges around L90,000/120,000 for sparkling rooms with bath.

More upmarket is *Villa Kinzica* (☎ 050 56 04 19, fax 050 55 12 04, Piazza Arcivescovado 2), with views of the Torre Pendente and rooms with bathroom and breakfast for L105,000/140,000.

Near Stazione Pisa Centrale, *Albergo Milano* (☎ 050 2 31 62, Via Mascagni 14) has comfortable rooms for L45,000/77,000 (doubles with bath can cost up to L105,000). The two star *Albergo Pisa* (☎ 050 4 45 51, Via Manzoni 22), near Via Francesco Crispi, has a variety of rooms starting at L48,000/64,000.

Places to Eat
Being a university town, Pisa has a good range of eating places. Head for the area north of the river around Borgo Stretto and the university. There is an open-air *food market* on Piazza delle Vettovaglie, off Borgo Stretto.

Antica Trattoria il Campano (Vicolo Santa Margherita), in an old tower near Piazza Sant'Ombono, has loads of atmosphere; a full meal is likely to set you back L40,000. *Trattoria la Grotta* (Via San Francesco 103) is another good choice and similarly priced. It is, as the name suggests, suitably cavernous.

A wonderful sprawling place is *Trattoria La Pergoletta* (Via delle Belle Torri 40), tucked away out of sight just north of the river. Expect to pay about L40,000 a head.

Ristorante La Clessidra (Via Santa Cecilia 34) has excellent food and if the prices look a little steep you can settle for the set meals at L30,000 (meat main course) or L35,000 (seafood). *Trattoria la Buca* (Via Galli Tassi) has pizzas from L8000.

A wonderfully exuberant spot for coffee, gelato, a cocktail or some fine foccacia is *Krott* (Lungarno Pacinotti 2).

One of the city's finest bars is *Caffè Federico Salza* (Borgo Stretto 46), with cakes, gelati and chocolates. Prices inside are one-third of those charged if you eat at the tables outside. For great gelati, head for *La Bottega del Gelato* (Piazza Garibaldi), near the river.

Entertainment
The APT office has a list of discos and events in the city. A couple of UK-style pubs have emerged, which can be quite pleasant if you're in the mood for a soothing pint. One is *Big Ben Pub* (Via Palestro 11).

Opera and ballet are staged at the *Teatro Verdi* (☎ 050 94 11 11, Via Palestro 40) from September to November. Cultural and historic events include the Gioco del Ponte, a festival of traditional costume held on the last Sunday in June. On 17 June, the Arno river comes to life with the Regata Storica di San Ranieri, a rowing competition commemorating the city's patron saint.

Getting There & Away
Air The city's Aeroporto Galileo Galilei (☎ 050 50 07 07), about 2km south of the city centre, is Toscana's main international airport and handles flights to major cities in Europe. Alitalia (☎ 147 86 56 43) and other major airlines are based at the airport.

Bus Lazzi (☎ 050 4 62 88), Piazza Vittorio Emanuele II, operates services to Lucca, Firenze, Prato, Pistoia, Massa and Carrara. CPT (☎ 050 50 55 11), Piazza Sant'Antonio, serves Volterra, Livorno and Lucca.

Train Pisa is connected to Firenze and is also on the Roma-La Spezia train line, with frequent services running in all directions.

Car & Motorcycle Pisa is close to the A12, which connects Parma to Livorno and is being extended south to Roma, although that may yet take some years to complete. The city is also close to the A11 (tollway) and S67 to Firenze, while the north-south S1, the Via Aurelia, connects the city with La Spezia and Roma.

Getting Around
To get to the airport, take a train from the stazione for the four minute journey to Stazione FS Pisa Aeroporto, or the CPT city bus No 3, which passes through the city centre on its way to the airport. For a taxi, call ☎ 050 54 16 00.

TOSCANA

To get from the stazione to the duomo, take CPT bus No 4 or walk the 1.5km.

Large car parks abound in Pisa. The one just north of the duomo is perfect for day-trippers.

Trattoria la Buca (see Places to Eat earlier in this section) hires out bicycles.

LIVORNO (LEGHORN)
postcode 57100 • pop 173,000
Toscana's second-largest city, Livorno is the perfect antidote for those who get too carried away with Toscana's many beauty spots. This place was hammered in WWII and is frankly a bit of a dump. One good reason for coming is to hop on a boat for Sardegna or Corsica and leave again.

Orientation & Information
From the main train station on Piazza Dante, east of the city centre, walk west along Viale Carducci and then Via Grande into the central Piazza Grande. The main APT office (☎ 0586 89 81 11) is at Piazza Cavour 6 (2nd

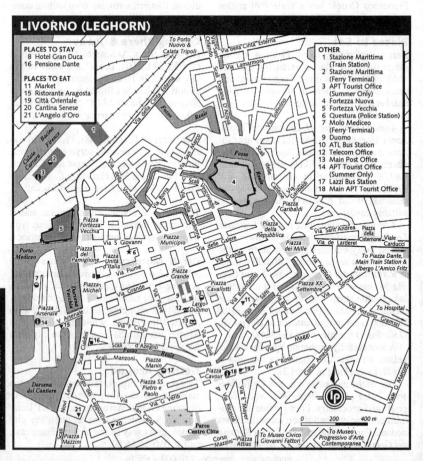

LIVORNO (LEGHORN)

PLACES TO STAY
8 Hotel Gran Duca
16 Pensione Dante

PLACES TO EAT
11 Market
15 Ristorante Aragosta
19 Città Orientale
20 Cantina Senese
21 L'Angelo d'Oro

OTHER
1 Stazione Marittima (Train Station)
2 Stazione Marittima (Ferry Terminal)
3 APT Tourist Office (Summer Only)
4 Fortezza Nuova
5 Fortezza Vecchia
6 Questura (Police Station)
7 Molo Mediceo (Ferry Terminal)
9 Duomo
10 ATL Bus Station
12 Telecom Office
13 Main Post Office
14 APT Tourist Office (Summer Only)
17 Lazzi Bus Station
18 Main APT Tourist Office

floor), to the south. A smaller APT office (☎ 0586 89 53 20) is at Piazza Arsenale, west of Piazza Grande. A third APT office is near the main ferry terminal, in an area known as Calata Carrara, near Stazione Marittima. The main APT office is open from 9 am to 1 pm Monday to Friday (also Tuesday and Thursday from 3 to 5 pm). The smaller offices open mornings and afternoons in summer only.

The main post office is at Via Cairoli 46 and the unstaffed Telecom office at Largo Duomo 14 opens from 8 am to 9.45 pm daily.

The Ospedale Civile (☎ 0586 40 11 29) is at Viale Alfieri 36, near the main train station. The questura (☎ 0586 23 51 11) is in the Palazzo del Governo, Piazza Unità d'Italia.

Things to See
The city does have a few worthy sights. The **Fortezza Nuova**, in the area known as Piccola Venezia (oh please!) because of its small canals, was built for the Medici in the late 16th century. Close to the waterfront is the city's other fort, the **Fortezza Vecchia**, built 60 years earlier on the site of an 11th century building.

Livorno has a couple of extremely modest museums. About the only one perhaps worth your time (if you have some of the latter to kill) is the **Museo Civico Giovanni Fattori**. It's in a pretty park at Via San Jacopo 65 and features works by the 19th century Livorno-based movement led by the artist Giovanni Fattori. The gallery, where temporary exhibitions are also occasionally held, is open from 9 am to 1 pm Tuesday to Sunday. Admission costs L6000. The city's unspectacular **cattedrale** is just off Piazza Grande.

Places to Stay & Eat
Finding accommodation shouldn't be a problem. *Albergo L'Amico Fritz (☎ 0586 40 11 49, Viale Carducci 180)* is near the main train station and offers singles/doubles without bath for L60,000/80,000 and others with bath for L80,000/110,000. Near the waterfront, *Pensione Dante (☎ 0586 89 34 61, Scali d'Azeglio 28)* has modest rooms without private bath for L40,000/58,000. For greater comfort you could try *Hotel*

Gran Duca (☎ 0586 89 10 24, Piazza Micheli), where rooms with all the mod cons will cost L140,000/210,000 including breakfast.

For produce, the *market* is on Via Buontalenti and the area around Piazza XX Settembre is great for bars and cafés. For seafood try *Ristorante Aragosta (Via Arsenale)*, right on the waterfront. Fish mains cost from L12,000 to L20,000. *L'Angelo d'Oro (Piazza Mazzini 15)* is an inexpensive trattoria with pasta from L7000. *Cantina Senese (Borgo dei Cappuccini 95)* is also a popular local eatery and just as inexpensive. There's Chinese at the *Città Orientale (Via Ginori 23)*.

Getting There & Away
Bus ATL buses (☎ 0586 88 42 62) depart from Largo Duomo for Cecina, Piombino and Pisa. Lazzi buses (☎ 0586 89 95 62) depart from Piazza Manin for Firenze, Pisa, Lucca and Viareggio.

Train Livorno is on the Roma-La Spezia line and is also connected to Firenze and Pisa. Trains are less frequent to Stazione Marittima, a second station near the main port. It is usually easier to catch a train to the main train station and then a bus to the ports.

Car & Motorcycle The A12 runs past the city and the S1 connects Livorno with Roma.

Boat Livorno is a major port. Regular departures for Sardegna and Corsica leave from Stazione Marittima (in an area called Calata Carrara, just north of Fortezza Vecchia). In addition, ferries also depart from a smaller terminal known as Porto Mediceo, near Piazza Arsenale, and occasionally from the Porto Nuovo. The first two can be easily reached by bus from the main train station. The third is several kilometres north of the city along Via Sant'Orlando and not well served by public transport. Ask at the APT office for directions.

Ferry companies operating from Livorno can be found in three locations:

TOSCANA

Stazione Marittima
   Corsica Ferries (☎ 0586 88 13 80) Regular services to Corsica (one-way daytime deck-class fares to Bastia range from L29,000 to L47,000 plus L4000 taxes).
   Corsica Marittima (☎ 0586 21 11 01) Services to Corsica (Bastia and Porto Vecchio).
   Sardinia Ferries (☎ 0586 88 13 80) Regular services to Sardegna (one-way deck-class fares to Golfo Aranci, near Olbia, range from L38,000 to L84,000 – the latter fares on summer weekends only).
   Moby Lines (☎ 0586 82 68 23/4/5) Services to Corsica (one-way deck-class fares to Bastia range from L32,000 to L50,000 depending on season) and Sardegna (one-way deck-class fares to Olbia range from L33,000 to L86,000).
Porto Mediceo
   Toremar (☎ 0586 89 61 13) Services to Isola Gorgona, Isola di Capraia.
Porto Nuovo
   Compagnia Sarda Navigazione Marittima (☎ 0586 40 99 25) At Varco Galvani, Calata Tripoli, with ferries to Olbia (Sardegna).
   Grandi Navi Veloci (☎ 0586 40 98 04) At Varco Galvani, Calata Tripoli, Darsena 1, with boats to Palermo in Sicilia (one-way seats range from L103,000 to L161,000).

Getting Around

To get from the main train station to Piazza Arsenale and the Porto Mediceo, take ATL bus No 1. To reach Stazione Marittima take bus No 7. Both these buses and several others pass through Piazza Grande. A ticket costs L1500.

ISOLA D'ELBA
postcode 57307 • pop 29,400

Napoleon should have considered himself lucky to be exiled to such a pretty spot. He arrived in May 1814 and lasted a year. He just had to have another shot at imperial greatness. Well, he met his Waterloo and the rest is history.

Nowadays people willingly allow themselves to be marooned here, to the tune of more than one million tourists a year. They come to swim in its glorious blue waters, lie on the beaches, eat fine food and generally loll about.

Don't come in August (the best thing any sensible being can do in August anywhere in Europe is fly to another hemisphere or stay at home and wait for better days), as it gets unpleasantly crowded.

Elba is growing in popularity among walkers. Its mountainous terrain can provide some tough treks, although there are better places to walk in Toscana.

Just 28km long and 19km across at its widest point, Elba is well equipped for tourists, with plenty of hotels and camp sites. The main towns are Portoferraio on the northern side and Marina di Campo in the south.

Prior to the advent of tourism, its main industry was iron-ore mining. The hordes have only arrived in recent years, so the island is not (as yet) overdeveloped. Which is not to say the people of Elba haven't learned a few tricks of the trade – don't expect to eat well *and* cheaply here. Also, in the height of summer most hotels operate a half board policy – you pay an all-in price per person for room, breakfast and lunch or dinner. This may or may not suit, but is rarely a terribly attractive deal. It is another reason to stay away in high summer (from mid-July to the end of August).

Orientation & Information

Most ferries arrive at Portoferraio, Elba's capital and main transport hub. Ferries from Piombino travel less frequently to Rio Marina, Porto Azzurro and Marina di Campo. The main APT office (☎ 0565 91 46 71), Calata Italia 26, Portoferraio, is open from 8 am to 8 pm daily (to 2 pm on Sunday) from Easter to October. The Associazione Albergatori Isola d'Elba (☎ 0565 91 47 54), Calata Italia 20, will find you a room. Book ahead in summer.

A summer tourist medical service operates at: Portoferraio (☎ 0565 91 42 12) at the public hospital, Località San Rocco; Marina di Campo (☎ 0565 97 60 61), Piazza Dante Alighieri 3; Rio Marina (☎ 0565 96 24 07), Via Principe Amadeo; Marciana Marina (☎ 0565 90 44 36), Viale Regina Margherita; and Capoliveri (☎ 0565 96 89 95), Via Soprana.

Walkers should pick up a copy of *Trekking all'Elba*, which lists walking trails and details each itinerary. For more information about walking, contact Il Genio del Bosco – Centro Trekking Isola d'Elba (☎ 0565 93 03 35) at Portoferraio. The Comunità Montana at Viale Manzoni 4 has contour maps of the island, with paths clearly marked.

Getting There & Away

Unless you have your own boat, the only way to get to Elba is by ferry from Piombino or from Livorno via the island of Capraia. If you arrive in Piombino by train, get the connecting train to the port. Several companies (Moby Lines, Toremar and Elba Ferries) run ferries and have offices at Piombino and Portoferraio. Unless it is the middle of August, you shouldn't have any trouble buying a ticket at the port. Generally you pay L10,000 per person or L50,500 for a small car and driver (other passengers extra). All lines offer a special deal on certain runs (indicated in timetables). The ferry trip takes an hour.

Elba Ferries has a faster catamaran, which carries cars and makes the trip in 25 minutes. Prices on most days are from L12,000 per person and L54,500 for a small car.

Getting Around

Bus The island's bus company, ATL, runs regular services between the main towns. From Portoferraio (the terminus is right by the port), for instance, you can reach all of the main towns, including Marciana Marina, Marina di Campo, Capoliveri and Porto Azzurro, as well as smaller resorts and beaches such as Sant'Andrea, Cavo and Fetovaia. Ask at the tourist office for an updated timetable.

Car, Motorcycle & Bicycle The best way to get around Elba is to hire a mountain bike, scooter or motorcycle. In high season mountain bikes start at L20,000 a day and L100,000 for one week; mopeds (50cc) are from L35,000 to L50,000 a day; motorbikes start at about L100,000 a day. TWN Two Wheels Network (☎ 0565 91 46 66), Viale Elba 32, Portoferraio (branches at Marciana Marina, Marina di Campo, Porto Azzurro

and several other locations) is one of several car rental outlets. Happy Rent (☎ 0565 91 46 65), Viale Elba 5, is another.

Portoferraio

The new part of Portoferraio encompasses the port and is of little interest, so head up to the old town, enclosed by a medieval wall. Here you'll encounter the **Villa dei Mulini**, one of the residences where Napoleon mooched about. It features a splendid terraced garden and his library and is open from 9 am to 7 pm Monday to Saturday and from 9 am to 1 pm on Sunday. Admission costs L8000.

The ticket also allows you admission to the **Villa Napoleonica di San Martino**, Napoleon's summer residence, set in hills about 5km south-west of the town. The villa houses a modest collection of Napoleonic paraphernalia and also hosts an annual exhibition based on a Napoleonic theme. The villa is open the same hours as the Villa dei Mulini.

Places to Stay & Eat The closest camp sites are about 4km west of town in Acquaviva. *Campeggio La Sorgente* (☎ 0565 91 71 39) and *Acquaviva* (☎ 0565 91 55 92) are easily found. *Ape Elbana* (☎ 0565 91 42 45, Salita de' Medici 2), in the old town, has singles/doubles with bathroom from L65,000 per person including breakfast. *Villa Ombrosa* (☎ 0565 91 43 63, Via De Gasperi 3) has singles/doubles with bathroom for around L120,000/150,000. They may insist on taking half board, which is OK as their *Ristorante Villa Ombrosa* serves good Tuscan dishes. A full meal will cost around L40,000.

For about the same money you can eat better still at *Emanuel (Località Enfola)*, out on a headland a few kilometres west of town. For years they have been serving up consistently good Elban dishes – probably the best way to go is the *menù di degustazione* at L45,000, which gives you a rounded experience of the local cuisine.

Marciana Marina

Almost 20km west of Portoferraio, Marciana Marina is slightly less popular with tourists

TOSCANA

and is fronted by some pleasant pebble beaches. It makes a fine base for the island's best walking trails too. The inland villages of **Marciana** and **Poggio**, the latter particularly charming, are easily visited. From Marciana you can take a funicular car to the summit of Monte Capanne, from where you can see across Elba and as far as Corsica to the west.

In Marciana Marina, about the cheapest hotel is *Casa Lupi (☎ 0565 9 91 43, Viale Amedeo)*, about half a kilometre inland on the road to Marciana. Here you shouldn't pay more than L45,000 per person for a room with breakfast. If it all gets too warm for you down on the coast, chill out a little at *Pensione Monte Capanne (☎ 0565 9 90 83)* up in Poggio. You're looking at around L70,000/110,000 depending on the time of year. They may insist on half board.

About halfway between Portoferraio and Marciana Marina, on the road just outside Procchio, is the unassuming *Osteria del Piano (Via Provinciale 24)*. Looks aren't everything. Here they make all their own pasta and serve up some astonishing concoctions, such as black and white spaghetti in a lobster sauce. It's not dirt cheap, but you get what you pay for.

Marina di Campo

Elba's second-largest town, Marina di Campo, is on the Golfo di Campo to the island's south. The beaches are not bad at all (although if you venture further west you will find a few less crowded ones). There are many camp sites around the town and along the coastline. *Albergo Thomas (☎ 0565 97 77 32, Viale degli Etruschi)* is one of the cheapest hotels here and has doubles from L100,000 in low season. In high season they will ask around L95,000 per person for half board. This is a standard story around here.

Porto Azzurro & Capoliveri

Dominated by its fort built in 1603 by Philip III of Spain and now a prison, Porto Azzurro is a pleasant resort town close to some excellent beaches. *Albergo Villa Italia (☎ 0565 9 51 19, Viale Italia)* has doubles for L55,000/85,000.

If you can loosen the purse strings a little around dinner time, try *Ristorante Cutty Sark (Piazza del Mercato 25)*. The *ravioloni alla Cutty Sark* are big ravioli filled with courgettes (zucchini) and shrimp meat and bathed in a shrimp and tomato sauce. You also get to wrestle with seafood critters to extract a sliver of extra flesh.

From Porto Azzurro, take a short trip south to **Capoliveri**, one of the island's little hilltop surprise packets. Wander its narrow streets and enjoy the giddy views before trying out one of the nearby beaches: Barabarca, accessible only by a steep track that winds down a cliff and Zuccale, more easily accessible and perfect for families. The beach of Naregno is a pleasant spot, if your scene is a hotel literally on the beachfront.

Central Toscana

IL CHIANTI

The hills and valleys spreading out between Firenze and Siena are known as Il Chianti. Home to some of the country's best marketed wines, they don't call it Chiantishire for nothing. In some of the small town tourist offices they just assume everyone who wanders in speaks English! Of the wines, Chianti Classico is the most well known. It is a blend of white and red grapes and sold under the Gallo Nero (Black Cockerel) symbol.

The Monti del Chianti, which rise into the Appennini, form Chianti's eastern boundary and comprise some of Toscana's loveliest countryside. Chianti is divided between the provinces of Firenze and Siena, into the areas known as Chianti Fiorentino and Chianti Senese.

Now the Chianti is indeed very pleasant – lots of rolling hills, olive groves and vineyards. Among them stand the many castles of Florentine and Sienese war lords and Romanesque churches known as *pievi*. But perhaps the hype has been just a trifle overdone. In Toscana alone there is plenty of more spectacular country to be seen (around Pitigliano or up in the Alpi Apuane, for instance). Not that we want to put you off, but the Tuscan countryside by no means begins and ends in Il Chianti.

You can get around by bus, but your own wheels make exploration a mighty bit easier. You might like to do it by bicycle or even on foot. You could take a few days to travel along the state road S222, known as the Strada Chiantigiana, which runs between Firenze and Siena.

Budget accommodation is not the area's strong point and you'll need to book well ahead, since it is a popular area for tourists year-round.

Virtually every tourist office in Toscana has good information, but the best is at Radda in Chianti. The tourist office there also has a Web site (see under Radda in Chianti in this section).

Chianti Fiorentino

About 20km south of Firenze on the Chiantigiana is **Greve in Chianti**, the first good base for exploring the area. You can get there easily from Firenze on a SITA bus. The unusual, triangular Piazza Matteotti, is the old centre of the town. An interesting provincial version of a Florentine piazza, it is surrounded by porticoes.

The tourist office (☎ 055 854 52 43) at Via L Cini 1, 500m east of the piazza, opens from 9.30 am to 1 pm daily in summer. Afternoon hours are more erratic (nothing on Sunday and closed at 3 pm on Wednesday, otherwise a safe bet is 2.30 to 5 pm). It can provide maps and information in several languages, including English. If you're looking for a place to stay, try *Giovanni da Verrazzano* (☎ *055 85 31 89, Piazza Matteotti 28)*, with singles/doubles starting at L100,000/130,000. *Del Chianti* (☎ *055 85 37 63)*, at No 86, is less interesting and charges L160,000/180,000.

Montefioralle is an ancient castle-village, only 2km west of Greve. It's worth the walk, particularly to see its church of Santo Stefano, with its precious medieval paintings. From Montefioralle, follow the dirt road for a few hundred metres, then turn off to the right to reach the simple **Pieve di San Cresci**. From here you can descend directly to Greve.

Nearby, in a magnificent setting of olive groves and vineyards, is the evocative **Badia di Passignano**, founded in 1049 by Benedictine monks of the Vallombrosan order. The abbey is a massive towered castle encircled by cypresses.

The abbey church of San Michele has early 17th century frescoes by the artist known as Passignano (so called because he was born here). In the refectory there's a *Last Supper* painted by Domenico and Davide Ghirlandaio in 1476. Take a look at the huge medieval chimney in the kitchen. It is sometimes possible to visit the abbey (☎ 055 807 16 22) at weekends. Food and drinks are available in the tiny village surrounding the abbey.

Travelling south along the Chiantigiana you will pass the medieval village of Panzano; after about 1km, turn off for the Chiesa di San Leolino at **Pieve di Panzano**. Built in the 10th century, it was rebuilt in Romanesque style in the 13th century and a portico was added in the 16th century. Inside, there is a 14th century triptych.

Chianti Senese

Castellina in Chianti is one of the best organised towns for tourists, with lots of hotels and restaurants. Its tourist office (☎ 0577 74 02 01) is at the central Piazza del Comune 1 and open from 10 am to 1 pm and 3.30 to 7.30 pm daily (morning only on Sunday).

You might prefer to head east to **Radda in Chianti**, which has retained much of its charm despite the tourist influx. It is also handy for many of Chianti's most beautiful spots. The tourist office (☎ 0577 73 84 94) at Piazza Ferrucci 1 is very helpful. It has loads of information about places to stay and eat in Chianti, as well as things to see and do, including suggestions for independent walking tours or tours to local wineries, where you can try the local wines before enjoying a traditional lunch. The tourist office has a Web site at www.chiantinet.it and its email address is proradda@chiantinet.it.

For cooking courses in this area, you could consider Posere le Rose (☎ 055 29 45 11), in the village of Poggio San Polo, about

TOSCANA

10km from Radda. One week costs L900,000 (excluding accommodation).

One of the cheapest forms of accommodation in the region is a room in a private house. *Da Giovannino* (☎ *0577 73 80 56, Via Roma 6-8)* is a real family house in the centre of Radda. You'll pay L50,000/80,000 for a single/double. The Radda tourist office can provide details about apartments and the numerous farms and wineries offering accommodation. Prices start at around L100,000 a double.

Getting Around

Buses connect Firenze and Siena, passing through Castellina and Radda, as well as other small towns.

SIENA

postcode 53100 • pop 59,200

Siena is without doubt one of Italy's most enchanting cities. Its medieval centre is bristling with majestic Gothic buildings, such as the Palazzo Pubblico on Il Campo (Piazza del Campo), Siena's main square and a wealth of artwork is contained in its numerous churches and small museums. Like Firenze, Siena offers an incredible concentration of things to see, which simply can't be appreciated in a day trip. A few days at least are needed to get to know the place and its treasures.

Siena also makes a good base from which to explore central Toscana, in particular the medieval towns of San Gimignano and Volterra. Note, however, that it can be difficult to find budget accommodation in Siena unless you book ahead. In August and during the city's famous twice-yearly festival, Il Palio, it is impossible to find any accommodation without a reservation.

History

According to legend Siena was founded by the son of Remus and the symbol of the wolf feeding the twins Romulus and Remus is as ubiquitous in Siena as in Roma. In reality the city was probably of Etruscan origin, although it wasn't until the 1st century BC, when the Romans established a military colony called Sena Julia, that it began to grow into a proper town.

In the 12th century Siena's wealth, size and power grew with its involvement in commerce, banking and trade. Consequently, its rivalry with neighbouring Firenze also grew and led to numerous wars during the first half of the 13th century between Guelf Firenze and Ghibelline Siena. Siena defeated Firenze at the Battle of Montaperti in 1260 but it was a short-lived victory. Only 10 years later the Tuscan Ghibellini were defeated by Charles of Anjou and for almost a century Siena was allied to Firenze, the chief town of the Tuscan Guelf League (supporters of the pope).

During this period Siena reached its peak under the rule of the Council of Nine, a group dominated by the middle class. Many of the fine buildings in the Sienese-Gothic style, which give the city its striking appearance, were constructed under the direction of the Council, including the duomo, the Palazzo Pubblico and Il Campo. The Sienese school of painting had its origins at this time with Guido da Siena and reached its peak in the early 14th century with the works of artists including Duccio di Buoninsegna, Simone Martini and Pietro and Ambrogio Lorenzetti.

A plague outbreak in 1348 killed two-thirds of the city's 100,000 inhabitants and led to a period of decline for Siena.

The plague also put an end to an ambitious plan to dramatically enlarge the duomo. At the end of the 14th century, Siena came under the control of Milano's Visconti family, followed in the century after by the autocratic patrician Pandolfo Petrucci. Under Petrucci the city's fortunes improved, but the Holy Roman Emperor Charles V conquered Siena in 1555 after a two year siege that left thousands dead. Consequently, the city was handed over to Cosimo I de' Medici, who barred the inhabitants from operating banks and thus curtailed Siena's power for good.

Siena was home to Santa Caterina, one of Italy's most famous saints. But saints don't make money. Siena today relies for its prosperity on tourism and the success of its Monte dei Paschi di Siena bank, founded in 1472 and now one of the city's largest employers.

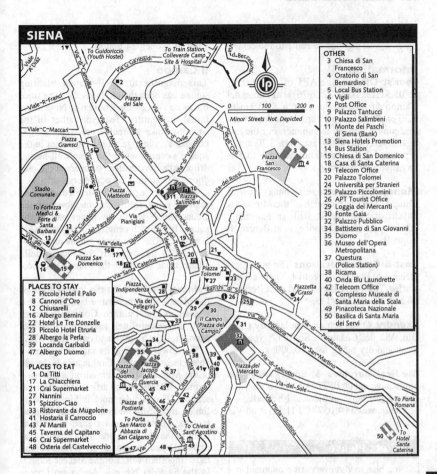

SIENA

OTHER
3 Chiesa di San Francesco
4 Oratorio di San Bernardino
5 Local Bus Station
6 Vigili
7 Post Office
9 Palazzo Tantucci
10 Palazzo Salimbeni
11 Monte dei Paschi di Siena (Bank)
13 Siena Hotels Promotion
14 Bus Station
15 Chiesa di San Domenico
18 Casa di Santa Caterina
19 Telecom Office
20 Palazzo Tolomei
24 Università per Stranieri
25 Palazzo Piccolomini
26 APT Tourist Office
29 Loggia dei Mercanti
30 Fonte Gaia
32 Palazzo Pubblico
34 Battistero di San Giovanni
35 Duomo
36 Museo dell'Opera Metropolitana
37 Questura (Police Station)
38 Ricama
40 Onda Blu Laundrette
42 Telecom Office
44 Complesso Museale di Santa Maria della Scala
49 Pinacoteca Nazionale
50 Basilica di Santa Maria dei Servi

PLACES TO STAY
2 Piccolo Hotel il Palio
8 Cannon d'Oro
12 Chiusarelli
16 Albergo Bernini
22 Hotel Le Tre Donzelle
23 Piccolo Hotel Etruria
28 Albergo la Perla
39 Locanda Garibaldi
47 Albergo Duomo

PLACES TO EAT
1 Da Titti
17 La Chiacchiera
21 Crai Supermarket
27 Nannini
31 Spizzico-Ciao
33 Ristorante da Mugolone
42 Hostaria il Carroccio
43 Al Marsili
45 Taverna del Capitano
46 Crai Supermarket
48 Osteria del Castelvecchio

Orientation

Historic Siena, still largely surrounded by its medieval walls, is small and easily tackled on foot, although the way streets swirl around Il Campo in semi-circles may confuse you. At the city's heart is the gently sloping square, around which curve its main streets: Banchi di Sopra, Via di Città and Banchi di Sotto. By bus you will arrive at Piazza San Domenico, which affords a panoramic view of the city. Walk east along Via della Sapienza and turn right into Banchi di Sopra to reach Il Campo.

From the train station you will need to catch a bus to Piazza Matteotti. Walk southeast out of the piazza on Via Pianigiani to reach Banchi di Sopra, turn right and follow it to Il Campo. Drivers should note that streets within the walls are blocked to normal traffic – even if you are staying at a hotel in the centre of town you will be required to leave your car in a car park after dropping off your bags.

Of the eight city gates through which you can enter Siena, probably the best is Porta

euro currency converter L10,000 = €5.16

San Marco, south-west of the city centre, as it has a well signposted route to the centre.

Information

Tourist Offices The APT office (☎ 0577 28 05 51, fax 0577 27 06 76) is at Piazza del Campo 56 and is open from 8.30 am to 7.30 pm Monday to Saturday and from 9 am to 2 pm on Sunday in summer. For the rest of the year, the hours are from 8.30 am to 1 pm and 3.30 to 6.30 pm Monday to Friday (noon on Saturday).

Money There are several banks near Il Campo. The main branch of the Monte dei Paschi di Siena bank, with an automatic currency exchange service, is at Banchi di Sopra 9.

Post & Communications The main post office is at Piazza Matteotti 1. There are unstaffed Telecom offices at Via dei Termini 40 and Via di Città 113.

Laundry At the self-service laundry Onda Blu, Via del Casato di Sotto 17, you can wash and dry 6.5kg for L10,000.

Medical Services & Emergency The public hospital (☎ 0577 58 51 11) is on Viale Bracci, just north of Siena at Le Scotte.

The questura (☎ 0577 20 11 11) is on Via

Tickets Please

If you plan to visit every last monument in sight, you should consider a seven day *biglietto unico* (cumulative ticket). From 16 March to 31 October it costs L32,000 and gives you access to the Museo Civico, Complesso Museale di Santa Maria della Scala, Museo d'Arte Contemporanea, Museo dell'Opera Metropolitana, Libreria Piccolomini, Battistero di San Giovanni, Chiesa di Sant'Agostino and the Oratorio di San Bernardino. For the rest of the year it costs L7000 less, as the last two of these monuments are shut.

---

del Castoro, between the Duomo and Via di Città. It is open 24 hours.

Il Campo

This magnificent, shell-shaped, slanting square has been the city's civic centre since it was laid out by the Council of Nine in the mid-14th century. Tourists gather in the square to take a break from sightseeing – backpackers lounge on the pavement in the square's centre, while the more well-heeled drink expensive coffees or beers at the outdoor cafés around the periphery.

The square's paving is divided into nine sectors, representing the members of the Council of Nine. In the upper part of the square is the 15th century **Fonte Gaia** (Gay Fountain). The fountain's panels are reproductions – the originals, by Jacopo della Quercia, can be seen in the Palazzo Pubblico.

Palazzo Pubblico At the lowest point of the piazza, this impressive building is also known as the Palazzo Comunale (town hall). Its graceful bell tower, the **Torre del Mangia**, is 102m high and dates from 1297.

The lower level of its façade features a characteristic Sienese-Gothic arcade. Inside is the **Museo Civico**, based on a series of rooms with frescoes by artists of the Sienese school. Of particular note is Simone Martini's famous *Maestà* in the Sala del Mappamondo. Completed and signed in 1315, it features the Madonna beneath a canopy, surrounded by saints and angels. It is one of the most important works of the Sienese school. In the Sala dei Nove is Ambrogio Lorenzetti's fresco series depicting *Allegories of Good and Bad Government*, which are among the most significant to survive from the Middle Ages. There is also a chapel with frescoes by Taddeo di Bartolo.

The opening hours for the Palazzo Pubblico and museum vary throughout the year: in July and August they open from 10 am to 11 pm Monday to Saturday and from 9 am to 1.30 pm on Sunday. At other times of the year they close as early as 4 pm. Admission costs L8000 (students L4000). Climb to the top of the bell tower for a spectacular view (admission L7000). Opening hours for the tower also vary during the year but are roughly 10 am to 6 pm in summer and 10 am to 4 pm in winter.

Duomo

Although it has some Romanesque elements, the duomo is one of Italy's great Gothic churches. Begun in 1196, it was largely completed by 1215, although work continued on features such as the apse and dome well into the 13th century. Work then began on changing, enlarging and embellishing the structure. The magnificent façade of white, green and red polychrome marble was begun by Giovanni Pisano, who completed only the lower section and was finished towards the end of the 14th century. The mosaics in the gables were added in the 19th century. The statues of philosophers and prophets by Giovanni Pisano above the lower section are copies, the originals being preserved in the adjacent Museo dell'Opera Metropolitana.

In 1339 the city's leaders launched a plan to enlarge the duomo and create one of Italy's largest churches. Known as the Nuovo Duomo (New Cathedral), the remains of this unrealised project can be seen on Piazza Jacopo della Quercia, at the eastern side of the duomo. The plan was to build an immense new nave; the present church would have become the transept. The plague of 1348 put a stop to this ambitious plan.

The duomo's interior is rich with artworks and warrants an hour or more of your time. Its most precious feature is the inlaid marble floor, decorated with 56 panels depicting historical and biblical subjects. The earliest panels are the graffiti designs in simple black and white marble, dating from the mid-14th century. The latest panels were completed in the 16th century. Many are roped off, while the most valuable are kept covered and revealed to the public only from 7 to 22 August annually.

The beautiful pulpit was carved in marble and porphyry by Nicola Pisano. Other artworks include a bronze statue of San Giovanni Battista by Donatello, in the northern transept.

Through a door from the northern aisle is another of the duomo's great treasures, the **Libreria Piccolomini**, which Pope Pius III (pope in 1503) built to house the books of his uncle, Enea Silvio Piccolomini, who was Pope Pius II. The walls of the small hall are covered by an impressive series of frescoes by Bernardino Pinturicchio, depicting events in the life of Piccolomini. In the centre of the hall is a group of statues known as the *Three Graces*, a 3rd century AD Roman copy of an earlier Hellenistic work. From mid-March to the end of October, the libreria is open from 9 am to 7.30 pm; at other times of the year it opens from 10 am to 1 pm and 2.30 to 5 pm. Admission costs L2000.

Museo dell'Opera Metropolitana

This museum is next to the duomo, in what would have been the southern aisle of the nave of the Nuovo Duomo. Its great artworks formerly adorned the duomo, including the 12 statues of prophets and philosophers by Giovanni Pisano that decorated the façade. However, the museum's main draw is Duccio di Buoninsegna's striking early 14th century *Maestà*, painted on both sides as a screen for the duomo's high altar. The front and back have now been separated and the panels depicting the Story of the Passion hang opposite the *Maestà*. It is interesting to compare Buoninsegna's work with Martini's slightly later *Maestà* in the Palazzo Pubblico. Other artists represented in the museum are Ambrogio Lorenzetti, Simone Martini and Taddeo di Bartolo. The collection also includes tapestries and manuscripts. The museum is open from 9 am to 7.30 pm daily from 16 March to end of September, to 6 pm in October and to 1.30 pm for the rest of the year. Admission costs L6000.

Battistero di San Giovanni

Behind the duomo and down a flight of stairs is the Battistero di San Giovanni. The baptistry's Gothic façade is unfinished, but its interior is heavily decorated with frescoes. The real attraction is a marble font by Jacopo della Quercia, decorated with bronze panels in relief depicting the life of San Giovanni

Battista by artists including Lorenzo Ghiberti (*Baptism of Christ* and *St John in Prison*) and Donatello (*Herod's Feast*). The baptistry has the same opening hours as the Museo dell'Opera Metropolitana, except that it also opens from 2.30 to 5 pm during the winter months. Admission costs L3000.

Complesso Museale di Santa Maria della Scala

On the south-western side of Piazza del Duomo, this former pilgrims' hospital has frescoes by Domenico di Bartolo in the main ward. The building also houses an impressive collection of Roman and Etruscan remains. The complex is open from 10 am to 6.30 pm in summer, with reduced hours during the rest of the year. Admission costs L8000.

Pinacoteca Nazionale

In the 15th century Palazzo Buonsignori, a short walk south-east of the duomo at Via San Pietro 29, this gallery houses numerous masterpieces by Sienese artists. Look for Duccio di Buoninsegna's *Madonna dei Francescani*, the *Madonna col Bambino* by Simone Martini and a series of Madonnas by Ambrogio Lorenzetti. The gallery is open from 9 am to 7 pm Tuesday to Saturday; from 8 am to 1 pm on Sunday and from 8.30 am to 1.30 pm on Monday. Admission costs L8000.

Chiesa di San Domenico

This imposing Gothic church was started in the early 13th century, but has been much altered over the centuries. It is known for its association with Santa Caterina di Siena, who took her vows in its Cappella delle Volte. In the chapel is a portrait of the saint painted during her lifetime. In the **Cappella di Santa Caterina**, on the southern side of the church, are frescoes by Sodoma depicting events in the saint's life. Santa Caterina di Siena died in Roma and her body is preserved there in the Chiesa di Santa Maria Sopra Minerva. In line with the bizarre practice of collecting relics of dead saints, her head was given back to Siena. It is contained in a tabernacle on the altar of the Cappella di Santa Caterina.

The **Casa di Santa Caterina**, the house where Santa Caterina was born, is on Costa di Sant'Antonio, off Via della Sapienza. The rooms of the house were converted into small chapels in the 15th century and are decorated with frescoes and paintings by Sienese artists, including Sodoma. The house is open from 9 am to 12.30 pm and 2.30 to 6 pm daily. Admission is free.

Other Churches & Palazzi

Also worth investigating when they are open (mid-March to the end of October) are the **Oratorio di San Bernardino**, part of the Chiesa di San Francesco complex (admission L4000 if you don't have the *biglietto unico*) and the **Chiesa di Sant'Agostino** (L3000) on Prato di Sant'Agostino. The former houses a modest museum of religious artworks.

From the Loggia dei Mercanti, northwest of Il Campo, take Banchi di Sotto to the east for the **Palazzo Piccolomini**, the city's finest Renaissance palazzo. It houses the city's archives and a small museum open from 9 am to 1 pm Monday to Saturday. Admission is free. Farther east are the 13th century **Basilica di Santa Maria dei Servi**, with a fresco by Pietro Lorenzetti and the 14th century **Porta Romana**.

Return to the Loggia dei Mercanti and head north along Banchi di Sopra and past Piazza Tolomei, dominated by the 13th century **Palazzo Tolomei**. Farther along there's the Piazza Salimbeni, featuring the **Palazzo Tantucci** to the north, the Gothic **Palazzo Salimbeni** to the east, the head office of the Monte dei Paschi di Siena bank and the Renaissance **Palazzo Spannocchi**. North-east of here, along Via dei Rossi, is the **Chiesa di San Francesco**.

West along Via del Paradiso from Piazza Matteotti is Piazza San Domenico, from where you can see the massive **Forte di Santa Barbara**, built for Cosimo I de' Medici.

Courses

Language Siena's Università per Stranieri (University for Foreigners; ☎ 0577 24 01 11, fax 0577 28 10 30) is at Piazzetta Grassi 2.

The school is open year-round and the only requirement for enrolment is a high-school graduation/pass certificate. The four-week summer courses have no entry requirements. There are several areas of study and courses cost L1,100,000 for 10 weeks. Brochures can be obtained by making a request to the secretary of the university or from the Istituto Italiano di Cultura in your city (see also Useful Organisations in the Facts for the Visitor chapter). The university's Web Site is at www.unistrasi.it.

Non-EU students are usually required to obtain a study visa in their own country; it is important to check with an Italian consulate. See under Visas & Documents in the Facts for the Visitor chapter for more details.

Music The Accademia Musicale Chigiana (☎ 0577 4 61 52, fax 0577 28 81 24), Via di Città 89, offers classical music classes every summer, as well as seminars and concerts performed by visiting musicians, teachers and students as part of the Settimana Musicale Senese. Classes are offered for most classical instruments and range from L280,000 to L1,200,000.

The Associazione Siena Jazz (☎ 0577 27 14 01, fax 0577 28 14 04), Via Vallerozzi 77, offers courses in jazz which start at L380,000. It's one of Europe's foremost institutions of its type.

Organised Tours

The *Treno Natura* is a great way to see the stunning scenery of the Crete Senese, south of Siena. The train line extends in a ring from Siena, through Asciano, across to the Val d'Orcia and the Stazione di Monte Antico, before heading back towards Siena. The line, which opened in the 19th century, was closed in 1994 and trains now run exclusively for tourists.

Trains run on some Sundays during May, June, September and the first half of October. There are usually three per day, stopping at Asciano and Monte Antico and there are connecting trains from Firenze. Tickets cost L20,000. Check at the Siena APT office or at Siena's train station for precise details.

Special Events

The Accademia Musicale Chigiana holds the Settimana Musicale Senese each July, as well as the Estate Musicale Chigiana in July, August and September. Concerts in these series are frequently held at the Abbazia di San Galgano (an imposing former abbey about 20km south-west of the city) and at Sant'Antimo, near Montalcino. Concerts are also held year-round. For information, call ☎ 0577 4 61 52. See also the Abbazia di San Galgano section later in this chapter.

The city hosts Siena Jazz, an international festival each July and August, with concerts at the Fortezza Medici, as well as various sites throughout the city. For details, call ☎ 0577 27 14 01.

Places to Stay

Siena offers a good range of accommodation, but budget hotels generally fill quickly, so it is always advisable to book in advance if you want to pay less than about L130,000 for a double. Forget about finding a room during Il Palio unless you have a booking. For help in finding a room, contact the APT or Siena Hotels Promotion (☎ 0577 28 80 84, fax 0577 28 02 90), Piazza San Domenico. The latter is open from 9 am to 8 pm Monday to Saturday in summer and 9 am to 7 pm in winter.

If you are having trouble finding a hotel room don't despair. The APT office has a list of about 120 affittacamere in town. Agriturismo is well organised around Siena and the APT office has a list of establishments that rent rooms by the week or month.

Colleverde camp site (☎ *0577 28 00 44, Strada di Scacciapensieri 47*) is north of the historical centre (take bus No 3 from Piazza Gramsci) and opens from late March to early November. The cost for one night is L20,000 for adults, L10,000 for children and L25,000 for a site. The non-HI youth hostel *Guidoriccio* (☎ *0577 5 22 12, Via Fiorentina 89, Località Stellino*) is about 2km north-west of the city centre. B&B costs L23,000 and a full meal is L14,000. Take bus No 3 from Piazza Gramsci. If driving, leave the city by Via Vittorio Emanuele II, which is an extension of Via di Camollia.

euro currency converter L10,000 = €5.16

Il Palio

This spectacular event, held twice yearly on 2 July and 16 August, in honour of the Virgin Mary, dates from the Middle Ages and features a series of colourful pageants, a wild horse race around Il Campo and much eating, drinking and celebrating in the streets.

Ten of Siena's 17 *contrade* (town districts) compete for the coveted *palio* (a silk banner). Each of the contrade has its own traditions, symbol and colours plus its own church and palio museum. The centuries-old local rivalries make the festival very much an event for the Sienese, although the horse race and pageantry continue to attract larger crowds of tourists.

On festival days Il Campo becomes a racetrack, with a ring of packed dirt around its perimeter serving as the course. From about 5 pm representatives of each contrada parade in historical costume, each bearing their individual banners.

The race is run at 7.45 pm in July and 7 pm in August. For not much more than one exhilarating minute, the 10 horses and their bareback riders tear three times around Il Campo with a speed and violence that makes your hair stand on end.

Even if a horse loses its rider it is still eligible to win and since many riders fall each year, it is the horses in the end who are the focus of the event. There is only one rule, that riders are not to interfere with the reins of other horses. The Sienese place incredible demands on the national TV network, RAI, for rights to televise the event.

Book well in advance if you want to stay in Siena at this time and join the crowds in the centre of Il Campo at least four hours before the start, or even earlier, if you want a place on the barrier lining the track. If you can't find a good vantage point, don't despair – the race is televised live and then repeated throughout the evening on TV.

If you happen to be in town in the few days immediately preceding the race, you may get to see the jockeys and horses trying out in Il Campo – almost as good as the real thing.

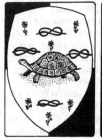

TRUDI CANAVAN

The Tartuca and Drago, two of the traditional banners of the *contrade* (districts) of Siena

In town, try **Hotel Le Tre Donzelle** (☎ 0577 28 03 58, Via delle Donzelle 5), off Banchi di Sotto north of Il Campo. It has clean, simple singles/doubles for L45,000/75,000. A double with bathroom costs L95,000. **Piccolo Hotel Etruria** (☎ 0577 28 80 88, Via delle Donzelle 3) has pleasant rooms for up to L65,000/103,000 with bathroom. **Locanda Garibaldi** (☎ 0577 28 42 04, Via Giovanni Dupré 18), just south of Il Campo, has rooms for L45,000/85,000.

Albergo Bernini (☎ 0577 28 90 47, Via della Sapienza 15) is not a good deal for solo travellers but not bad for people in pairs – a double with/without bathroom is L130,000/110,000. **Albergo la Perla** (☎ 0577 4 71 44, Via delle Terme 25) is a short walk north-west of Il Campo. Small but clean rooms with shower cost L60,000/90,000.

Piccolo Hotel il Palio (☎ 0577 28 11 31, Piazza del Sale 19), a good 15 minute walk from Il Campo, has rooms with bathroom for L130,000/160,000. **Cannon d'Oro** (☎ 0577 4 43 21, Via dei Montanini 28) has rooms with bathroom for L115,000/135,000. The three star *Albergo Duomo* (☎ 0577 28 90 88, *Via Stalloreggi 38)* has lovely rooms, many with views, which cost from L150,000/220,000. Just off Piazza San Domenico is the *Chiusarelli* (☎ 0577 28 05 62, *Viale Curtatone 15)*, which has very pleasant rooms with bathroom for L97,000/135,000. It is in a handy location if you have a car.

A bit of a way out to the south-east is *Hotel Santa Caterina* (☎ 0577 22 11 05, *Via Enea Silvio Piccolomini 7)*. It is small and friendly with good service. You'll pay L175,000/220,000.

Places to Eat

The Sienese claim that most Tuscan cuisine has its origins in Siena and that the locals are still using methods introduced to the area by the Etruscans, namely simple cooking methods and the use of herbs. Among the city's many traditional dishes are soups such as ribollita; *panzanella* (a summer salad of soaked bread, basil, onion and tomatoes); *pappardelle con la lepre* (pasta with hare); and the succulent steaks of the Chianina, cooked over a charcoal grill. Bread is made without salt, as throughout Toscana. *Panforte*, a rich cake of almonds, honey and candied melon or citrus fruit, has its origins in the city. Loosely translated, panforte is heavy bread and it was created as sustenance for the crusaders to the Holy Land.

Restaurants On Il Campo is the cheap self-service *Spizzico-Ciao*. You can eat well here for L20,000 or less. *Hostaria il Carroccio* (*Via Casato di Sotto 32)*, south of Il Campo, has excellent pasta for around L10,000. Try the *pici*, a kind of thick spaghetti, followed by the *friselle di pollo ai zucchini* (bite-sized juicy chicken bits with courgette).

Taverna del Capitano (*Via del Capitano 8)* is good little spot for local food. A full meal will cost about L35,000. More expensive but highly regarded by locals is the nearby *Osteria del Castelvecchio* (*Via Castelvecchio 65)*.

La Chiacchiera (*Costa di Sant'Antonio 4)*, off Via Santa Caterina, is tiny but has a good menu with local specialities. Pasta costs from L8000. A full meal will cost about L35,000.

Al Marsili (*Via del Castoro 3)* is one of the city's better known restaurants and has dishes from L8000 for a first course and from L15,000 for a second. *Ristorante da Mugolone* (*Via dei Pelligrini 8)* is another excellent restaurant, with local specialities. Pasta costs from L10,000 and second courses cost between L15,000 and L25,000.

About a 10 minute walk north of Il Campo, in a less frenetic neighbourhood, are several trattorie and alimentari. *Da Titti* (*Via di Camollia 193)* is a no-frills establishment with big wooden benches where full meals with wine cost around L25,000.

Self-Catering There are *Crai* supermarkets scattered around the town centre, including one at Via di Città 152-156 and another on Via Cecco Angiolieri. *Nannini* (*Banchi di Sopra 22)* is one of the city's finest cafés and pasticcerie.

Shopping

Ricama, a shop at Via di Città 61, promotes the crafts of Siena, in particular embroidery and is worth a visit.

Getting There & Away

Bus Regular buses leave from Piazza San Domenico for Firenze, San Gimignano (change at Poggibonsi) and Volterra (change at Colle di Val d'Elsa), Pienza, Buonconvento, Montalcino and other destinations in the Crete Senese, as well as towns in the Chianti area. Daily buses also connect Siena with Perugia and Roma, leaving from Piazza San Domenico. The Siena APT office has timetables.

Train Siena is not on a major train line, so from Roma it is necessary to change at Chiusi and from Firenze at Empoli, making buses a better alternative. Trains arrive at Piazza F Rosselli, north of the city centre.

Car & Motorcycle From Firenze take the S2 (the *superstrada* which goes direct to Siena). Alternatively, take the S222, also

TOSCANA

known as the Chiantigiana, which meanders its way through the hills of Chianti. From the Firenze-Siena superstrada take the San Marco exit and follow the 'centro' signs.

Getting Around

Tra-in operates city bus services from a base on Piazza Gramsci. From the train station, catch bus No 3 to Piazza Gramsci, about a 10 minute walk from Il Campo. No cars, apart from those of residents, are allowed in the city centre. There are large car parks at the Stadio Comunale and around the Fortezza Medici; both are just north of Piazza San Domenico. Technically, it is necessary to get a special permit to enter the city by car even to just drop off your luggage at your hotel. This can be obtained from the *vigili* on Viale Federico Tozzi, but only if you have a hotel booking. Otherwise, phone your hotel for advice. For a taxi, call ☎ 0577 4 92 22 or, after 9 pm, ☎ 0577 28 93 50.

ABBAZIA DI SAN GALGANO

About 20km south-west of Siena on the S73 is the ruined 13th century San Galgano abbey, one of the country's finest Gothic buildings in its day and now a very atmospheric ruin. A former Cistercian abbey, its monks were among Toscana's most powerful, forming the judiciary and acting as accountants for the comuni of Volterra and Siena. They presided over disputes between the cities, played a significant role in the construction of the duomo in Siena and built themselves an opulent church.

By the 16th century the monks' wealth and importance had declined and the church had deteriorated to the point of ruin. The walls remain standing but the roof collapsed long ago. The abbey is definitely worth a diversion if you are driving, but visiting by public transport is quite difficult. The best option is the bus service between Siena and Massa Marittima, a little farther south-west. The Accademia Musicale Chigiana in Siena sponsors concerts at the abbey during summer. See Special Events in the earlier Siena section.

On a hill overlooking the abbey is the tiny, round Romanesque **Cappella di Monte Siepi**. Inside are badly preserved frescoes by Ambrogio Lorenzetti, which depict the life of San Galgano, a local soldier who had a vision of San Michele on this site. A real-life 'sword in the stone' is under glass in the floor of the chapel, put there, legend has it, by San Galgano.

If you have your own transport, drive via Monticiano towards the S223. Stop off at **Tocchi**, a tiny village with a restored castle nearby, where you can spend the night. You can enjoy an excellent meal of fresh local produce at *Posto di Ristoro a Tocchi* (☎ 0577 75 71 26). A meal will cost around L35,000, B&B from L40,000 a head. You can also get here on the Tra-in bus which travels between Siena and Monticiano. Continue across the valley towards **Murlo**, an interesting medieval fortified village. This was once an important Etruscan settlement and experts claim that DNA tests show that the locals are close relatives of these ancient people.

LE CRETE

Just south-east of Siena, this area of rolling clay hills is a feast of classic Tuscan images – bare ridges topped by a solitary cypress tree flanking a medieval farmhouse, four hills silhouetted one against the other as they fade off into the misty distance. The area of Le Crete changes colour according to the season – from the creamy violet of the ploughed clay to the green of the young wheat, which then turns to gold. If you have the funds to spare, hire a car in Firenze or Siena and spend a few days exploring Le Crete. Another option is the *Treno Natura*, a tourist train which runs from Siena through Asciano and along the Val d'Orcia (see Organised Tours in the Siena section for details).

Apart from the scenery, one of the main attractions in the area is the **Abbazia di Monte Oliveto Maggiore**, a 14th century Olivetan monastery, famous for the frescoes by Signorelli and Sodoma which decorate its Great Cloister. The frescoes illustrate events in the life of the rather severe San Benedetto.

The fresco cycle begins with Sodoma's work on the eastern wall (immediately to the right of the entrance into the church from the cloisters) and continues along the southern wall of the cloisters. The nine frescoes by Signorelli line the western side of the cloisters and Sodoma picks up again on the northern wall. Note the decorations on the pillars between some of Sodoma's frescoes – they are among the earliest examples of 'grotesque' art, copied from decorations found in the then newly excavated Domus Aurea created by Nero in Roma. The monastery is open from 9 am to 12.30 pm and 3 to 6 pm daily. It is possible to stay at the monastery from Easter to the end of September. Call ☎ 0577 70 70 61 for information. They don't take bookings, so it's a case of first in best dressed.

From the monastery, if you have your own transport, head for **San Giovanni d'Asso**, where there's an interesting 11th century church with a Lombard-Tuscan façade and a picturesque *borghetto* with the remains of a castle. Continue on to Montisi and Castelmuzio. Along a side road just outside Castelmuzio is the **Pieve di Santo Stefano in Cennano**, an abandoned 13th century church. Ask for the key at the adjacent farm buildings. Two kilometres past Castelmuzio on the road to Pienza is the 14th century Olivetan monastery of **Sant'Anna in Camprena**. In the refectory there are frescoes by Sodoma that can occasionally be seen. Phone ☎ 0755 74 83 03 for further information or take your chances by turning up (if you have a vehicle). Some restoration work is in progress.

The route from Abbazia di Monte Oliveto Maggiore to Pienza runs almost entirely along a high ridge, with great views of Le Crete.

SAN GIMIGNANO
postcode 53037 • pop 7100
As you crest the hill coming from the east, the 13 towers of this medieval walled town look like some medieval Manhattan. And when you arrive you might feel half of Manhattan's population has moved in – San Gimignano is quite a tourist magnet. Come in the dead of winter, preferably when it's raining, to indulge your imagination a little. In summer most of your attention will probably be focussed on dodging fellow visitors!

There is a reason for all this of course. The towers were symbols of the power and wealth of the city's medieval families and once numbered 72. San Gimignano delle Belle Torri (meaning 'of the Fine Towers') is surrounded by lush and productive land and the setting is altogether enchanting.

Originally an Etruscan village, the town later took its name from the Bishop of Modena, San Gimignano, who is said to have saved the city from the barbarians. It became a comune in 1199, but fought frequently with neighbouring Volterra. The internal battles between the Ardinghelli (Guelfi) and Salvucci (Ghibelline) families over the next two centuries caused deep divisions. Most towers were built during this period – in the 13th century one *podestà* (town chief) forbade the building of towers higher than his (51m).

In 1348 the plague decimated the population and weakened the power of its nobles, leading to the town's submission to Firenze in 1353. Today, not even the plague would dent the summer swarms!

Orientation
The manicured gardens of Piazzale dei Martiri di Montemaggio, at the southern end of the town, are outside the medieval wall and next to the main gate, the Porta San Giovanni. From the gate, Via San Giovanni heads north to Piazza della Cisterna and the connecting Piazza del Duomo, in the city centre. The other major thoroughfare, Via San Matteo, leaves Piazza del Duomo for the main northern gate, Porta San Matteo.

Information
The Associazione Pro Loco (☎ 0577 94 00 08) is at Piazza del Duomo 1, on the left as you approach the duomo. It's open from 9 am to 1 pm and 3 to 7 pm daily (6 pm in winter).

The post office is at Piazza delle Erbe 8, on the northern side of the duomo.

Things to See & Do
Buy the L16,000 ticket, which allows admission to most of San Gimignano's museums, from the ticket offices of any of the city's sights.

TOSCANA

Start in the triangular Piazza della Cisterna, named after the 13th century cistern in its centre. The piazza is lined with houses and towers dating from the 13th and 14th centuries. In the adjoining Piazza del Duomo, the duomo (known as the Collegiata) looks across to the late 13th century **Palazzo del Podestà** and its tower, the **Torre della Rognosa**. The Palazzo del Popolo, left of the duomo, still operates as the town hall.

Collegiata Up a flight of steps from the piazza is the town's Romanesque duomo, its simple façade belying the remarkable frescoes covering the walls of its interior. There are five main cycles. On the left wall as you enter are scenes from the Old Testament by Bartolo di Fredi, dating from around 1367. To the right New Testament scenes by Barna da Siena were completed in 1381. On the inside wall of the façade, as well as an adjoining wall, Taddeo di Bartolo probably scared the daylights out of pious locals with his gruesome depiction of the Last Judgment (1393). In the **Cappella di Santa Fina** are beautiful frescoes by Domenico Ghirlandaio depicting events in the life of the saint. Without the L16,000 general ticket, admission to the chapel costs L6000.

The duomo and chapel are open from 9.30 am to 12.30 pm and 3 to 5.30 pm daily, but tourists cannot enter during mass times.

Palazzo del Popolo From the internal courtyard, climb the stairs to the **Museo Civico**, which features paintings from the Sienese and Florentine schools of the 12th to 15th centuries. Dante addressed the locals in 1299 in the Sala del Consiglio, urging them to support the Guelfi cause. The room contains an early 14th century fresco of the *Maestà* by Lippo Memmi. Climb up the palazzo's **Torre Grossa** for a spectacular view of the town and surrounding countryside.

The palazzo, torre and museum are open from 9.30 am to 7.30 pm daily in summer, with shorter hours during the rest of the year.

Other Things to See The **Rocca**, a short walk to the west of Piazza del Duomo, is the atmospheric ruin of the town's fortress from where you have great views across the valley.

At the northern end of the town is the **Chiesa di Sant'Agostino**. Its main attraction is the fresco cycle by Benozzo Gozzoli in the apse, depicting the life of Sant'Agostino.

Places to Stay

San Gimignano has only a handful of hotels, with eye-popping prices. Coming to the rescue are, apart from the hostel and a camp site, numerous *affittacamere* (rooms for rent) at reasonable prices. The tourist office will provide details, but will not make bookings. The Cooperativa Hotels Promotion (☎ 0577 94 08 09) on Via San Giovanni, just inside the gate of the same name, can place you in a hotel. It will make arrangements months in advance and charges a L3000 fee.

The camp site, *Il Boschetto di Piemma* (☎ 0577 94 03 52), is at Santa Lucia, a few kilometres south of the Porta San Giovanni and is open from Easter to 15 October. Buses leave from Piazzale dei Martiri di Montemaggio. The non-HI *Ostello della Gioventù* (☎ 0577 94 19 91, Via delle Fonti 1) is at the northern edge of town inside the wall. B&B costs L24,000.

Hotel La Cisterna (☎ 0577 94 03 28), on the magnificent Piazza della Cisterna, has singles/doubles from L95,000/170,000. Ask for a room in the medieval section, with a view across the valley.

Places to Eat

A *produce market* is held on Thursday morning on Piazza della Cisterna and Piazza del Duomo. Try the wines at *Il Castello* (Via del Castello 20), a wine bar and restaurant that stays open until midnight; pasta starts at L10,000. *Trattoria La Mangiatoia* (Via Mainardi 5) is one of the town's better restaurants, with pasta from about L9000.

A relative newcomer offering fine food at moderate prices is *Osteria al Carcere* (Via Castello 5). It has an original menu including half a dozen soups, each for L11,000. For a fairly quiet drink and a sampling of one or two of 49 bruschette, try *Locanda Sant'Agostino* on the piazza of the same name.

Ice Festival (Via San Giovanni 113) and *Gelateria di Piazza (Piazza della Cisterna 4)* are great; the latter turns the local wine, Vernaccia, into a delicious ice cream.

Getting There & Around

San Gimignano is accessible from Firenze and Siena by regular buses, but you need to change at Poggibonsi. For Roma and areas such as Perugia and Assisi, you need to get to Siena first. There's also a bus to Volterra. Bus timetables are posted on a pillar to the left as you face the Pro Loco office. Buses arrive in Piazzale dei Martiri di Montemaggio at the Porta San Giovanni. The closest train station is in Poggibonsi.

To reach San Gimignano by car, take the S68 from Colle di Val d'Elsa, which is on the S2 between Firenze and Siena and follow the signs. Signs direct you to large car parks outside the Porta San Giovanni.

VOLTERRA

postcode 56048 • pop 13,400

The Etruscan settlement of Velathri was an important trading centre and remained so under the Romans, who renamed it Volaterrae. A long period of conflict with Firenze started in the 12th century and ended when the Medici took possession of the city in the 15th century.

Perched high on a rocky plateau, the town's well preserved medieval ramparts give Volterra a forbidding air. The city has long had a strong alabaster industry.

Orientation & Information

Driving and parking inside the walled town are more or less prohibited. Park in one of the designated parking areas and enter the nearest city gate – all the main streets lead to the central Piazza dei Priori.

The tourist office (☎ 0588 8 61 50) is at

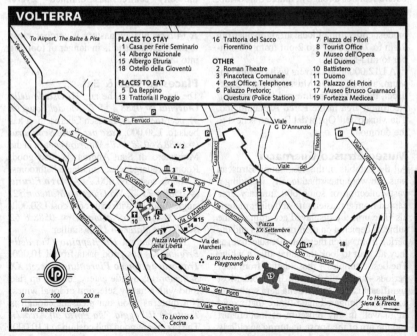

VOLTERRA

To Airport, The Balze & Pisa

PLACES TO STAY
1 Casa per Ferie Seminario
14 Albergo Nazionale
15 Albergo Etruria
18 Ostello della Gioventù

PLACES TO EAT
5 Da Beppino
13 Trattoria Il Poggio

16 Trattoria del Sacco Fiorentino

OTHER
2 Roman Theatre
3 Pinacoteca Comunale
4 Post Office; Telephones
6 Palazzo Pretorio; Questura (Police Station)

7 Piazza dei Priori
8 Tourist Office
9 Museo dell'Opera del Duomo
10 Battistero
11 Duomo
12 Palazzo dei Priori
17 Museo Etrusco Guarnacci
19 Fortezza Medicea

0   100   200 m
Minor Streets Not Depicted

To Livorno & Cecina

To Hospital, Siena & Firenze

TOSCANA

Piazza dei Priori 20. The post office faces it on the northern side of the square. Next door is the questura in the Palazzo Pretorio.

Piazza dei Priori

Piazza dei Priori is surrounded by austere medieval mansions. The 13th century **Palazzo dei Priori** is the oldest seat of local government in Toscana and is believed to have been a model for Firenze's Palazzo Vecchio. The **Palazzo Pretorio**, also dating from the 13th century, is dominated by the Torre del Porcellino (Piglet's Tower), so named because of the wild boar sculpted on its upper section.

Behind the Palazzo dei Priori, along Via Turazza, is the **duomo**, built in the 12th and 13th centuries. Highlights inside include a small fresco by Benozzo Gozzoli, the *Adoration of the Magi*, behind a nativity group in the oratory at the beginning of the left aisle. The 15th century tabernacle on the high altar is by Mino da Fiesole. The 13th century **battistero** features a font by Andrea Sansovino.

The **Pinacoteca Comunale** in the Palazzo Minucci Solaini, Via dei Sarti 1, houses a modest collection of local art. It opens from 9 am to 7 pm daily (to 2 pm from November to mid-March).

A L12,000 ticket covers visits to this museum, as well as the Museo Etrusco Guarnacci, the Roman theatre and the Acropoli/Necropoli area in the Parco Archeologico. The Museo dell'Opera del Duomo is next to the duomo.

Museo Etrusco Guarnacci

All the exhibits in this fascinating Etruscan museum were unearthed locally, including a vast collection of some 600 funerary urns carved from alabaster, tufo and other materials. The urns are displayed according to the subjects depicted on their bas-reliefs and the period from which they date. Be selective, as they all start to look the same after a while. The best examples – those dating from later periods – are on the 2nd and 3rd floors. Most significant is the **Ombra della Sera** sculpture, a strange, elongated nude figure that would fit in well in any museum of modern art and the urn of the **Sposi**, featuring an elderly

couple, their faces depicted in portrait fashion rather than the stylised method usually employed. The museum has the same opening times as the Pinacoteca Comunale.

Fortezza Medicea & Parco Archeologico

Farther along Via Don Minzoni is the entrance to the Fortezza Medicea, built in the 14th century and altered by Lorenzo il Magnifico and now used as a prison.

Near the fort is the pleasant Parco Archeologico, whose archaeological remains have suffered with the passage of time. Little has survived, but it's a good place for a picnic.

Other Things to See

On the city's northern edge is a **Roman theatre**, a well preserved complex that includes a Roman bath.

The **Balze**, a deep ravine created by erosion, about a 20 minute walk north-west of the city centre, has claimed several churches since the Middle Ages after the buildings having fallen into its deep gullies. A 14th century monastery is perched close to the precipice and is in danger of toppling into the ravine.

Places to Stay & Eat

The best deal is at the non-HI *Ostello della Gioventù* (☎ 0588 8 55 77, Via del Poggetto 3), near the Museo Etrusco Guarnacci. It has beds for L30,000. *Casa per Ferie Seminario* (☎ 0588 8 60 28, Viale Vittorio Veneto), in the Monastero di Sant'Andrea, is also good. Rooms are large, clean and have bathrooms. A double costs L64,000. At *Albergo Etruria* (☎ 0588 8 73 77, Via Giacomo Matteotti 32) singles/doubles with bathroom cost L80,000/120,000. *Albergo Nazionale* (☎ 0588 8 62 84, Via dei Marchesi 11) is similar.

The restaurant *Da Beppino* (Via delle Prigioni 13) has good pasta from L10,000. *Trattoria del Sacco Fiorentino* (Piazza XX Settembre) is a little eatery serving up fine food with a happy selection of local wines. Not quite as good but pleasant enough is *Trattoria Il Poggio* (Via Porta all'Arco 7). The pizzas are good and cost up to L10,000.

Getting There & Away

Buses connect the town with Pisa, Siena, Firenze, Cecina and San Gimignano from Piazza Martiri della Libertà. For Siena and Firenze you need to change at Colle di Val d'Elsa. From the small train station in Saline, 9km to the south-west (bus from Volterra), you can get a train to Cecina, from where you can catch trains on the Roma-Pisa line. By car, take the S68 which runs between Cecina and Colle di Val d'Elsa.

CERTALDO

Located in the Val d'Elsa, in a strategic position between Firenze, Siena (40km served by train) and San Gimignano, this small medieval town is definitely worth a visit. Giovanni Boccaccio, one of the fathers of the Italian language, was born here in 1313.

A real find is *Fattoria Bassetto (☎ 0571 66 83 42, 0571 66 49 45, email bassetto@ dedalo.com)*, 2km east of the town on the road for Siena. A 14th century Benedictine convent, it was transformed into a farm by the Guicciardini counts. It is surrounded by a garden complete with swimming pool and offers dorm-style accommodation for L30,000 a night. In the adjacent 19th century manor house, once home of the Guicciardini duchess, there are romantic rooms replete with antique furniture and adjoining bathrooms for L100,000 per person. Advance booking is recommended. You can reach the Fattoria Bassetto on foot from Certaldo train station or contact the owners and arrange to be picked up. See Lonely Planet's *Walking in Italy* for details of a three day walk from Certaldo to San Gimignano and on to Volterra.

Southern Toscana

MAREMMA & ETRUSCAN SITES

The area known as the Maremma extends along the Tuscan coast from just north of Grosseto and south to the border with Lazio, incorporating the Parco Naturale della Maremma (also known as Parco del l'Uccellina) and Monte Argentario. It also extends inland to the extraordinary hill towns of Sovana, Terme di Saturnia and Pitigliano.

Information

Grosseto is the main town in the Maremma area but is of little interest. Its APT office (☎ 0564 45 45 10) is at Via Fucini 43c, a block from the train station. Information about the Parco Naturale della Maremma can be obtained there or at the Centro Visite del Parco Alberese (☎ 0564 40 70 98) on the northern edge of the park. It is open from 9 am to sunset daily (from 7 am mid-June to the end of September). The Associazione Albergatori (☎ 0564 2 63 15), next door to the APT office at Via Fucini 43, can help you find a bed in the province.

The individual towns in the area each have small tourist offices that open daily during summer only.

Parco Naturale della Maremma

Definitely the main attraction in the area, the park incorporates the Monti dell'Uccellina and a magnificent stretch of unspoiled coastline. Admission to the park is limited and cars must be left in designated parking areas. Certain areas can be visited only on particular days and excursions into the park are always limited to set itineraries. Depending on your chosen route, you may see plenty of native animals (including deer, wild boar, foxes and hawks). Certain routes also provide access to the sea. You must buy tickets at the visitors centre in Alberese; they cost L10,000 (which includes bus transport from Alberese to the park entrance) or L7000. There are no shelters, bars and so on within the park, so make sure you carry water and are properly dressed. Cycling is an option (if you bring your own). The park gets crowded in summer, especially at weekends.

Etruscan Sites

If you're heading inland by car, stop off briefly at **Manciano**, a former Sienese fortress and **Montemerano**, a picturesque walled medieval town, where you can buy outstanding Tuscan olive oil at La Piaggia, an agriturismo establishment. Visit the

TOSCANA

town's Chiesa di San Giorgio, which is decorated with 15th century frescoes of the Sienese School. **Saturnia** is more famous for its sulphur spring and baths at **Terme di Saturnia** but its Etruscan remains, including part of the town wall, are worth a diversion. A tomb at Sede di Carlo, just north-east of the town, is one of the area's best preserved. Bring along a bathing costume and take advantage of the curative waters at the picturesque thermal baths.

Sovana This pretty little town has more than its fair share of important Etruscan sites and historical monuments. There's an information office (☎ 0564 61 40 74) in the Palazzetto dell'Archivio on the Piazza del Pretorio.

Pope Gregory VII was born here. Medieval mansions and the remains of a fortress belonging to his family are at the eastern end of the town. The **Chiesa di Santa Maria**, on Piazza del Pretorio, is a starkly simple Romanesque church featuring a magnificent 9th century ciborium in white marble, one of the last remaining pre-Romanesque works left in Toscana. In the church there are also some early Renaissance frescoes.

Walk along the Via del Duomo to reach the imposing Gothic-Romanesque **duomo**, at the far eastern end of the town. The original construction dates back to the 9th century, although it was largely rebuilt in the 12th and 13th centuries. Of particular note are the marble portal and the capitals of the columns that divide the interior into three naves. Several of the capitals feature biblical scenes and are thought to be the work of the Lombard school, dating from the 11th century.

About 1km to the south of the town are a number of Etruscan tombs, the most important being the **Tomba Ildebranda**, the only surviving temple-style tomb and the **Tomba della Sirena**. The area is famous for the spectacular *vie cave*, narrow walkways which were carved like mini-gorges into the rock. The walkways continue for 1km and date from Etruscan times. Other tombs and several necropoli in the area are also worth a visit.

If you'd like to stay in Sovana, try **Hotel Etrusca** (☎ *0564 61 61 83, Piazza Pretorio 16)*, which has singles/doubles for L80,000/ 140,000 with bathroom. *Scilla* (☎ *0564 61 65 31, Via del Duomo 5)*, just off the piazza, has cheaper rooms starting at L45,000/ 70,000 without bathroom or L50,000/ 75,000 with. Both hotels have restaurants.

Sorano High on a rocky spur, this small medieval town has largely retained its original form. Its houses seem to huddle together in an effort not to shove one another off their precarious perch. There's a small tourist office (☎ 0546 63 30 99) on Piazza Busati. The town's main attraction is the newly renovated **Castello Orsini**. It opens from 10 am to 7 pm daily from April to September. During the rest of the year it opens from 10 am to 4 pm Friday to Sunday and on holidays. Admission costs L3000.

You could also climb up **Masso Leopoldino** for a spectacular view of the surrounding countryside. The gate is open at the same times as the castle.

A few kilometres out of Sorano, on the road to Sovana, is the **Necropoli di San Rocco**, an Etruscan burial area.

Pitigliano The visual impact of this town goes one better again than Sorano. It seems to grow out of a high rocky outcrop that rises from a deep gorge. The tourist office (☎ 0564 61 44 33) is at Via Roma 6, just off Piazza della Repubblica.

The town itself is a pleasant stopover – its offerings include the 13th century **Palazzo Orsini** and an imposing 16th century aqueduct. There's a small museum in the palazzo. The town's cathedral dates from the Middle Ages, but its façade is baroque and its interior has been modernised. It is interesting to wander the town's narrow, medieval streets, particularly in the area known as the **Ghetto**, once home to a large Jewish population. You can visit a former synagogue.

For a place to stay, try *Guastini* (☎ *0564 61 60 65, Piazza Petruccioli 4)*, which has singles/doubles with bathroom for L55,000/ 85,000. The place to eat is *Osteria Il Tufo Allegro (Vico della Costituzione 2)*, just off Via Roma. You'll pay about L45,000 for a full meal with wine and dessert. The aromas emanating from the kitchen into the street should be enough to persuade you.

Getting Around

Infrequent Rama buses leave from the train station at Grosseto for Terme di Saturnia, Pitigliano and Sovana. Buses also leave from Orbetello for Pitigliano and Sorano. If you have the funds, hire a car in Grosseto or even in Roma and explore the area for a few days.

MONTE ARGENTARIO

Situated on an isthmus some 120km north-west of Roma, **Orbetello** is a pleasant place, popular with Romans at weekends.

Orbetello's main attraction is its **duomo**, which has retained its 14th century Gothic façade despite being remodelled in the Spanish style in the 16th century. Other reminders of the Spanish garrison that was stationed in the city include the fort and city wall, parts of which are the original Etruscan wall. But the main attraction is the increasingly popular Monte Argentario and its two harbour towns, Port'Ercole and Porto Santo Stefano, both crammed with incredibly expensive boats and yachts.

Around the Peninsula

Monte Argentario is popular with Romans, but not many tourists go there. **Porto Santo Stefano** and **Port'Ercole** are resort towns for the wealthy, but Port'Ercole, in a picturesque position between two forts, retains some of its fishing village character. The main tourist office (☎ 0564 81 42 08) is in Porto Santo Stefano, in the Monte dei Paschi di Siena building, at Corso Umberto 55. It opens from 9 am to 1 pm and 4 to 6 pm Monday to Saturday.

For a pleasant drive, follow the signs to Il Telegrafo, one of the highest mountains in the region and turn off at the **Convento dei Frati Passionisti**, a church and convent

which has sensational views across to the mainland.

There are plenty of good beaches, usually of the pebbly or rocky (rather than sandy) variety. One of the most popular is the long strip of **Feniglia**, between Orbetello and Port'Ercole. Near Port'Ercole the beach is serviced, which means it's clean but cluttered with deck chairs and umbrellas for hire. As you move farther away the beach becomes less crowded but unfortunately it also gets dirtier.

Places to Stay & Eat

Accommodation on the peninsula is generally expensive, although there is a *camp site* (☎ 0564 83 10 90) near Port'Ercole, on the northern fringe at the Feniglia beach.

In Porto Santo Stefano, *Pensione Weekend (☎ 0564 81 25 80, Via Martiri d'Ungheria 3)* is a cosy place which has doubles with bathroom from L100,000. *Albergo Belvedere (☎ 0564 81 26 34, Via del Fortino 51)* is a luxurious complex overlooking the water, where fine singles/doubles cost L120,000/L160,000 in the high season, breakfast included. It has a private beach. Also at Porto Santo Stefano is *Il Veliero (Strada Panoramica 149)*, where an excellent meal will cost around L50,000. At Port'Ercole try *Il Pirata*, a good pizzeria on Lungomare Andrea Doria.

Trattoria Da Siro (Corso Umberto 1 100), just off the waterfront, and *I Due Pini (Località La Soda)*, just outside the port, are both good bets for fine seafood. Remember that at weekends, freshly caught fish is hard to come by – there are simply too many people eating their way through the peninsula then! Cheaper is *Lo Sfizio* on the waterfront road at No 26. You can have bruschetta, pizza or seafood.

Getting There & Away

Rama buses connect most towns on the Monte Argentario with Orbetello (coinciding with the arrival of trains) and Grosseto. By car, follow the signs to Monte Argentario from the S1, which connects Grosseto with Roma.

Eastern Toscana

AREZZO

postcode 52100 • pop 91,700

Heavily bombed during WWII, Arezzo is not the prettiest city in Toscana. That said, the small medieval centre retains some inspiring highlights. The sloping Piazza Grande and the Romanesque jewel that is Pieve di Santa Maria are lesser known perhaps than the frescos by Piero della Francesca in the Chiesa di San Francesco. It is well worth a visit, easily accomplished as a day trip from Firenze.

An important Etruscan town, it was later absorbed into the Roman Empire. A free republic from the 10th century, Arezzo supported the Ghibelline cause in the awful battles between pope and emperor and was eventually subjugated by Firenze in 1384. Sons of whom Arezzo can be justly proud include the poet Petrarch, the writer Pietro Aretino and Giorgio Vasari, the latter most famous for his *Lives of the Artists*.

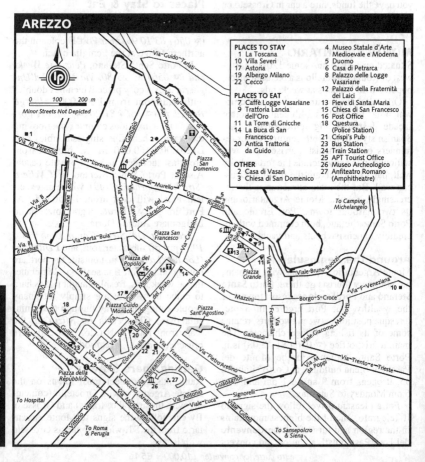

AREZZO

0   100   200 m
Minor Streets Not Depicted

PLACES TO STAY
1 La Toscana
10 Villa Severi
17 Astoria
19 Albergo Milano
22 Cecco

PLACES TO EAT
7 Caffè Logge Vasariane
9 Trattoria Lancia dell'Oro
11 La Torre di Gnicche
14 La Buca di San Francesco
20 Antica Trattoria da Guido

OTHER
2 Casa di Vasari
3 Chiesa di San Domenico
4 Museo Statale d'Arte Medioevale e Moderna
5 Duomo
6 Casa di Petrarca
8 Palazzo delle Logge Vasariane
12 Palazzo della Fraternità dei Laici
13 Pieve di Santa Maria
15 Chiesa di San Francesco
16 Post Office
18 Questura (Police Station)
21 Crispi's Pub
23 Bus Station
24 Train Station
25 APT Tourist Office
26 Museo Archeologico
27 Anfiteatro Romano (Amphitheatre)

To Camping Michelangelo

To Hospital

To Roma & Perugia

To Sansepolcro & Siena

TOSCANA

A widely known antiques fair is held on Piazza Grande and the surrounding streets on the first Sunday of every month, which means accommodation can be difficult to find unless you book well ahead.

Orientation & Information

From the train station on the southern edge of the walled city, walk north-east along Via Guido Monaco to the garden piazza of the same name. The old city is to the north-east and the modern part to the south-east along Via Roma.

The APT office (☎ 0575 37 76 78), near the train station on Piazza della Repubblica, is open from 9 am to 1 pm and 3 to 6.30 pm Monday to Friday and from 9 am to 1 pm Saturday. The post office is at Via Guido Monaco 34.

The Ospedale Civile is outside the city walls on Via A de Gasperi. The questura is on Via Fra Guittone.

Chiesa di San Francesco

The apse of this 14th century church houses one of the greatest works of Italian art, Piero della Francesca's fresco cycle of the *Legend of the True Cross*. This masterpiece, painted between 1452 and 1456, relates the story of Christ's death in 10 episodes. Unfortunately, the frescoes were badly damaged by damp and have been under restoration for some years. You can visit the church from 8.30 am to noon and 2.30 to 6.30 pm. Call ☎ 0575 35 56 68 to book a visit to the restored half of the frescoes (L10,000 per person). Groups of about 15 people are taken in on this basis. Hopes were high that the other half of the frescoes would be restored by some time in the year 2000.

Pieve di Santa Maria

This 12th century church has a magnificent Romanesque arcaded façade reminiscent of the duomo at Pisa (but without the glorious marble facing). Each column is of a different design. Over the central doorway (hidden by scaffolding at the time of writing) are carved reliefs representing the months. The 14th century bell tower, with its 40 win-

dows, is something of an emblem for the city. The stark interior of the church shows a Gothic influence, the only colour coming from the polyptych by Pietro Lorenzetti on the raised sanctuary at the rear of the church.

Piazza Grande & Around

The high end of this lumpy sloping piazza is lined by the porticoes of the **Palazzo delle Logge Vasariane**, completed in 1573. The **Palazzo della Fraternità dei Laici** on the western flank dates from 1375. It was started in the Gothic style and finished after the onset of the Renaissance. Via dei Pileati leads to **Casa di Petrarca**, former home of the poet, which contains a small museum and the Accademia Petrarca.

Duomo

At the top of the hill on Via Ricasoli is the duomo, started in the 13th century and not completed until the 15th century. The Gothic interior houses several artworks of note, including a fresco of Mary Magdalene by Piero della Francesca.

Chiesa di San Domenico & Around

It is worth the walk to the Chiesa di San Domenico to see the crucifix painted by Cimabue, which hangs above the main altar. South-west on Via XX Settembre, the **Casa di Vasari** was built and sumptuously decorated by the architect himself. The house is open from 9 am to 7 pm Monday to Saturday and to 1 pm on Sunday. Down the hill on Via San Lorentino, the **Museo Statale d'Arte Medioevale e Moderna** houses works by local artists, including Luca Signorelli and Vasari, spanning the 13th to 18th centuries. The gallery is open from 9 am to 7 pm daily and admission costs L8000.

Museo Archeologico & Anfiteatro Romano

East of the train station, the museum is in a convent overlooking the remains of the Roman anfiteatro (amphitheatre). It houses an interesting collection of Etruscan and Roman artefacts, including locally produced craftwork and opens from 9 am to 2 pm Monday to Saturday. Admission costs L8000.

Places to Stay

The closest camp site is *Camping Michelangelo* (☎ *0575 79 38 86)* in Caprese Michelangelo, 35km north-east of Arezzo. The non-HI youth hostel, *Villa Severi* (☎ *0575 2 90 47, Via F Redi 13)*, offers B&B for up to L26,000 in a wonderfully restored villa overlooking the countryside.

La Toscana (☎ *0575 2 16 92, Via M Perennio 56)* has simple singles/doubles from L40,000/75,000. *Astoria* (☎ *0575 2 43 61, Via Guido Monaco 54)* has OK rooms for L50,000/80,000. The Soviet-style edifice that is *Cecco* (☎ *0575 2 09 86, Corso Italia 215)*, near the train station, has soulless but clean rooms for L50,000/75,000 or L65,000/95,000 with bathroom and TV. *Albergo Milano* (☎ *0575 2 68 36, Via della Madonna del Prato 83)* is between the train station and the old centre, near Piazza Guido Monaco. It has good rooms for L100,000/150,000.

Places to Eat & Drink

Piazza Sant'Agostino comes alive each Tuesday, Thursday and Saturday with the city's *produce market*. One of the best-value trattorie in town is the unassuming *Antica Trattoria da Guido* (*Via della Madonna del Prato 85)*, next to Albergo Milano. Here you'll eat excellent, home-style food: try the *penne agli asparagi* (pasta in an asparagus sauce). A full meal should come to less than L35,000. *La Buca di San Francesco* (*Via San Francesco 1)*, near the church of the same name, is one of the city's better restaurants; you'll pay up to L50,000 for a full meal.

Not far off Piazza Grande, *La Torre di Gnicche* (*Piaggia San Martino 8)* is a fine old osteria. At *Trattoria Lancia dell'Oro*, in the Logge Vasariane, the food is not quite as good, but it is hard to beat the commanding position over Piazza Grande. Sip a drink at *Caffè Logge Vasariane*, a couple of doors up.

For an evening tipple with young people, try *Crispi's Pub* (*Via Francesco Crispi 10)*. It's not very pub-like but quite fun at weekends.

Getting There & Away

Buses depart from and arrive at Piazza della Repubblica, serving Cortona, Sansepolcro, Monterchi, Siena, San Giovanni Valdarno, Firenze and other local towns. The city is also on the Firenze-Roma train line. Arezzo is a few kilometres east of the A1 and the S73 heads east to Sansepolcro.

SANSEPOLCRO

Along with Arezzo and nearby Monterchi, Sansepolcro is an important stop on an itinerary of Piero della Francesca's work. Both Monterchi and Sansepolcro are easy day trips from Arezzo. Visit **Monterchi** to see the artist's famous fresco *Madonna del Parto* (a pregnant Madonna). It was removed from its original home in the local cemetery for restoration and is currently on display in a former primary school on Via Reglia. Opening hours are 9 am to 1 pm and 2 to 7 pm daily except Monday. Admission is L5000.

Sansepolcro is the birthplace of Piero della Francesca. He left the town when quite young and returned in his 70s to work on his treatises, which included *On Perspective in Painting*.

The small tourist office (☎ 0575 74 05 36) can assist with local information. The itinerary of della Francesca's work takes in other towns in Toscana, Umbria and Le Marche, including Rimini, Urbino, Perugia and Firenze. You can pick up a copy of *Following in Piero della Francesca's Footsteps in Toscana, Marches, Umbria & Romagna* in Arezzo or Sansepolcro.

The **Museo Civico**, in the former town hall, Via Aggiunti 65, is the pride of Sansepolcro and features Piero della Francesca's Renaissance masterpiece, *Resurrection*.

If you need to stay, there are several hotels, including the budget *Orfeo* (☎ *0575 74 20 61, Viale A Diaz 12)*, which charges L45,000/80,000 a single/double. *Albergo Fiorentino* (☎ *0575 74 03 50, Via L Pacioli 60)* has rooms with bathroom for L65,000/95,000 in high season.

SITA buses connect Arezzo with Sansepolcro hourly and the town is on the Terni-Perugia train line.

CORTONA

postcode 52044 • pop 22,500

Set on the side of a hill covered with olive groves, Cortona offers stunning views across the Tuscan countryside and has changed little since the Middle Ages. It was a small settlement when the Etruscans moved in during the 8th century BC. It later became a Roman town. In the late 14th century, it attracted the likes of Fra Angelico, who lived and worked in the town for about 10 years. Luca Signorelli and the artist known as Pietro da Cortona were born here. The city is small, easily seen in a couple of hours and well worth visiting for the sensational view.

Orientation & Information

Piazzale Garibaldi, on the southern edge of the walled city, is where buses arrive. It has a large car park and also offers some of the best views in the city. From the piazzale, walk straight up Via Nazionale to Piazza della Repubblica, the centre of town. The town's streets are disconcertingly steep at times.

The APT office (☎ 0575 63 03 52) is at Via Nazionale 42. It is open from 8 am to 1 pm and 3 to 7 pm Monday to Saturday and from 9 am to 1 pm on Sunday from May to September. The rest of the year it shuts at 6 pm during the week and on Saturday and Sunday afternoons.

Things to See

Start in Piazza della Repubblica with the crenellated **Palazzo Comunale**, which was renovated in the 16th century. To the north is Piazza Signorelli, named after the artist and dominated by the 13th century **Palazzo Pretorio**, also known as the Casanova Palace, whose façade was added in the 17th century. Inside is the **Museo dell'Accademia Etrusca**, which displays substantial local Etruscan finds, including an elaborate 5th century BC oil lamp. The museum is open from 10 am to 7 pm daily except Monday. Admission costs L8000.

Little is left of the Romanesque character of the **duomo**, north-west of Piazza Signorelli. It was completely rebuilt late in the Renaissance and again in the 18th century.

Opposite is the **Museo Diocesano** in the former church of Gesù. Its fine collection includes works by Luca Signorelli and a beautiful *Annunciation* by Fra Angelico.

At the eastern edge of the city centre is the **Chiesa di Santa Margherita**, which features the Gothic tomb of Santa Margherita. Farther up the hill is the 16th century **fortezza**, built for the Medici by Laparelli, who designed the fortress city of Valletta in Malta.

Places to Stay & Eat

The city has several cheap hotels and a hostel, so finding a room shouldn't be a problem. The HI *Ostello San Marco (☎/fax 0575 60 13 92, Via Maffei 57)*, just a short walk east of Piazzale Garibaldi, has B&B for L18,000. It is open from 15 March to 15 October. *Betania (☎ 0575 6 28 29, Via Severini 50)* is a monastery that offers singles/doubles from L35,000/55,000 (it has monthly rates too). *Albergo Italia (☎ 0575 63 02 54, Via Ghibellina 5)*, just off Piazza della Repubblica, is in an old mansion and has rooms with private bathroom, TV and phone for up to L90,000/ 130,000 in high season.

Piazza della Repubblica hosts a *produce market* each Saturday and several *grocery shops* dot the area. At *Trattoria Dardano (Via Dardano 24)* try the *ravioli al burro e salvia* (butter and sage ravioli). A full meal can cost around L30,000. *Il Cacciatore (Via Roma 11)* is one of the city's better restaurants and offers local specialities. Count on paying about L45,000.

Getting There & Away

From Piazzale Garibaldi regular LFI buses connect the city with Arezzo. The city is served by two train stations. Trains from Arezzo stop at the Camucia-Cortona station, in the valley below Cortona and trains for Roma stop at Terontola, about 5km to the south of the Camucia-Cortona station. Shuttle buses connect both stations with Piazzale Garibaldi and a board opposite the APT office entrance details schedules. By car, the city is on the north-south S71 which runs to Arezzo and it is close to the S75 that connects Perugia to the A1.

TOSCANA

Umbria & Le Marche

Dotted with splendid medieval hill towns and offering a chance to flee from the madding crowds to isolated valleys or mountains, the regions of Umbria and Le Marche need to be explored rather than simply visited. Umbria certainly offers some star attractions – the beautifully preserved medieval town of Perugia, San Francesco's home town of Assisi and the extraordinary duomo in Orvieto. The main attraction of Le Marche is Urbino, home of the painter Raphael and Duca Federico de Montefeltro. But in both regions there are a host of smaller, lesser known towns and villages, and plenty of opportunities for nature lovers, walkers and mountain bikers to escape from the standard tourist attractions and get some exercise. This is also prime hang-gliding territory.

Both Umbria and Le Marche were devastated by the 1997 earthquakes which effected around 48 towns, including Norcera Umbra (one of the worst affected areas), Foligno, Bevagna, Montefalco, Assisi, Spello and many small mountain villages. Thirteen people were killed and over 100,000 were left homeless. There has been much criticism that the damage to the cultural patrimony (especially at Assisi) has taken precedence over the devastation that the populace suffered. At the time of writing almost 20,000 people were still living in hastily erected trailer villages. Projects to repair buildings and create new housing are under way, but are progressing slowly. The economic ramifications have also been severe. Tourism, on which both regions depend, virtually ground to a halt after the earthquakes and was only just beginning to return to normal levels in 1999.

Umbria

One of the few landlocked Italian regions, Umbria likes to think of itself as *Il cuore verde dell'Italia* (Italy's green heart). In spring the countryside is splashed with the

Highlights

- Take in some mellow jazz in beautiful Perugia during the Umbria Jazz festival
- Tuck into some typical Umbrian cuisine laced with *tartufi neri* (black truffles)
- Get a sore neck while admiring the magnificent frescoes by Giotto and others in the Basilica di San Francesco in Assisi
- Amble around the streets of Orvieto and check out the magnificent duomo
- Watch a concert, play or dance performance under the stars at Spoleto's Teatro Romano (Roman theatre) during the Festival dei Due Mondi
- Explore the splendid Renaissance town of Urbino
- If the timing is right, attend a concert at the Arena Sferisterio in Macerata

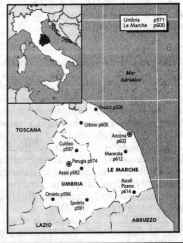

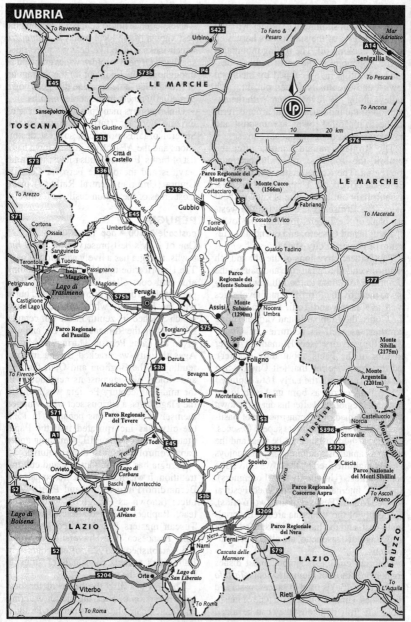

red, pink, yellow, purple and blue of wild flowers, and in summer it explodes with the vibrant yellow of the sunflowers harvested to make cooking oil. The rolling mountains of the Appennini in the north and east descend into hills, many capped by medieval towns, and eventually flatten out into lush valleys along the Tevere river. With the exception of the industrial blight around Terni in the south, most towns are unspoilt and have preserved their medieval centres.

The Romans named Umbria after the Umbrii, the Iron Age tribe who occupied the region. The Roman naturalist Pliny the Elder described the Umbrii as the oldest tribe in Italy but little more is known about them. The Etruscans later settled the western bank of the Tevere, founding the towns of Perugia and Orvieto, and eventually creating 12 powerful city-states.

The Saracen invasions of the 5th and 6th centuries ended Roman rule and caused the Umbrians to retreat to the hill towns, leading to the growth of fortified medieval cities such as Gubbio and Todi. Domination by the Goths, the Lombards and various ruling families, as well as centuries of Guelf-Ghibellini rivalry (see Humanism under History in the Facts about Italy chapter), led to a long decline that left Umbria ripe for papal rule from the early 16th century.

San Francesco was born in Assisi, in the east of the region, and after his death the town was transformed by the construction of Basilica di San Francesco with its superb frescoes. Perugia, a short distance to the west and the region's capital, is a stunning city that enjoys a lively nightlife fired by the city's Università per Stranieri (University for Foreigners). Spoleto's internationally renowned Festival dei Due Mondi (Festival of the Two Worlds), the beauty of the Valnerina area in Umbria's south-east, and the Italian peninsula's largest lake, Lago di Trasimeno, are all powerful attractions.

Umbrian cuisine is simple: most dishes contain only three or four ingredients. *Tartufo* (a type of truffle) is used in sauces, pasta and rice dishes. Umbria's *porcini* (a type of mushroom) are truly delicious; they can be added to pasta or rice, but are best eaten as 'steaks' – an experience not to be missed. Among the best known of the local pastas is *strangozzi*, which looks a little like heavy, square-sided spaghetti. Orvieto's golden wines are popular throughout Italy. Look out for the Sagrantino of Montefalco, a heavy wine that goes down particularly nicely in the cooler months.

Umbria offers many possibilities for agriturismo holidays (farm accommodation). Several organisations can suggest destinations and the APT office in each town has a list of farms. Extensive bus routes, state train services and the private Ferrovia Centrale Umbra (Umbrian Central Railway) make most areas of the region easily accessible.

PERUGIA
postcode 06100 • pop 150,000
One of Italy's best-preserved medieval hill towns, Perugia has a lively and bloody past. The Umbrii tribe inhabited the surrounding area and controlled land stretching from present-day Toscana into Le Marche, but it was the Etruscans who founded the city, which reached its zenith in the 6th century BC. It fell to the Romans in 310 BC and was given the name Perusia. During the Middle Ages the city was racked by the internal feuding of the Baglioni and Oddi families and violent wars against its neighbours. In the mid-13th century Perugia was home to the Flagellants, a curious sect who whipped themselves for religious penance. In 1538 the city was incorporated into the Papal States under Pope Paul III, remaining under papal control for almost three centuries.

Perugia has a strong artistic and cultural tradition. It was home to the fresco painters Bernardino Pinturicchio and Pietro Vannucci (known as Perugino), who was to teach Raphael, and also attracted the great Tuscan masters Fra Angelico and Piero della Francesca. The Università per Stranieri, established in 1925, offers courses in Italian and attracts thousands of students from all over the world.

The town is also the home of the best known version of *baci*, the mouth-watering chocolate-coated hazelnuts made in Perugia.

Orientation

If you arrive in Perugia's main train station, Stazione Fontivegge, you'll find yourself a few kilometres downhill from the historic centre, so the less energetic will prefer to catch a bus. Drivers should follow the Centro signs and park in one of the well-signposted car parks, then take a *scala mobile* (escalator) up to the city centre (for more details see Getting Around later in this section).

Old Perugia's main strip, Corso Vannucci (named after Perugino), runs south to north from Piazza Italia through Piazza della Repubblica and finally ends in the heart of the old city at Piazza IV Novembre, bounded by the duomo and the Palazzo dei Priori. City buses will drop you off either at Piazza della Repubblica or in Piazza Matteotti, just east of Piazza IV Novembre.

Information

Tourist Offices The APT office (☎ 075 572 33 27) is in the Palazzo dei Priori, Piazza IV Novembre 3, opposite the duomo, and is open from 8.30 am to 1.30 pm and 3.30 to 6.30 pm Monday to Saturday and from 9 am to 1 pm Sunday. The monthly publication *Viva Perugia – What, Where, When* (L1000 from the APT office or newspaper stands) lists all events and useful information. InformaGiovani (☎ 075 576 17 24), Via Idalia 1 (off Via Pinturicchio), can assist with tips for young or disabled travellers and provides educational and cultural information.

Money The currency exchange booth at Stazione Fontivegge is open from 7.30 am to 8.30 pm daily. Corso Vannucci is lined with banks, all of which have ATMs; the Cassa di Risparmio di Perugia (Savings Bank of Perugia) at No 39 also has a currency exchange machine.

Post & Communications The main post office is on Piazza Matteotti and is open from 8.10 am to 7.25 pm Monday to Friday and from 8.10 am to 1.45 pm Saturday.

There is a Telecom office in the post office and another on Piazza della Repubblica; both are open from 8 am to 10 pm daily. The Telecom Office is staffed from 9 am to 1 pm and 4 to 7 pm on weekdays.

Medical Services & Emergency The Ospedale Riuniti-Policlinico (hospital; ☎ 075 57 81) is on Viale Bonacci Brunamonti, north-east of the city centre. To find a doctor at night, on Sunday or public holidays, call ☎ 075 3 40 24. The Farmacia San Martino (pharmacy) at Piazza Matteotti 26 is open 24 hours.

The questura (police station; ☎ 075 5 06 21) is on Piazza dei Partigiani, down the scala mobile which starts in the Rocca Paolina at Piazza Italia.

Other Information The CIT travel agency (☎ 075 572 60 61) is at Corso Vannucci 2, while CTS (☎ 075 572 70 50), specialising in budget and student travel, is at Via del Roscetto 21. It will sell ISIC cards to foreigners studying at the university, even to those on short courses.

La Libreria bookshop, Via Oberdan 52, stocks a selection of English-language books.

For information on gay events, try Arci-Gay (☎ 075 572 31 75, 075 573 10 74), Via A Fratti 18.

You can do your laundry at the Onda Blu coin laundrette at Corso dei Bersaglieri 4, on the corner of Via Pinturicchio. It's open from 9 am to 10 pm daily.

Around Piazza IV Novembre

The imposing façades identify Piazza IV Novembre as the old city's main square. Indeed, in the case of the austere **duomo**, size is everything. Started in 1345 and completed in 1430 (although its red and white marble façade was never finished), the Gothic giant offers comparatively little to enthuse over inside. Galeazzo Alessi's magnificent 16th century doorway, facing the Fontana Maggiore in the square, is an exception to the rule. If you happen to be around on 30 July, grab a pew for the annual unveiling of the city's prized relic: the Virgin Mary's wedding ring, locked away in 15 boxes fitted inside each other for added security.

Fra Bevignate designed the **Fontana**

UMBRIA

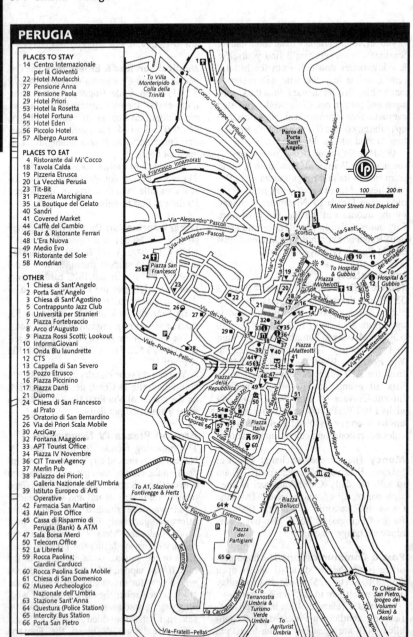

PERUGIA

PLACES TO STAY
14 Centro Internazionale per la Gioventù
22 Hotel Morlacchi
27 Pensione Anna
28 Pensione Paola
29 Hotel Priori
53 Hotel la Rosetta
54 Hotel Fortuna
55 Hotel Eden
56 Piccolo Hotel
57 Albergo Aurora

PLACES TO EAT
4 Ristorante dal Mi'Cocco
18 Tavola Calda
19 Pizzeria Etrusca
20 La Vecchia Perusia
23 Tit-Bit
31 Pizzeria Marchigiana
35 La Boutique del Gelato
40 Sandri
41 Covered Market
44 Caffè del Cambio
46 Bar & Ristorante Ferrari
48 L'Era Nuova
49 Medio Evo
51 Ristorante del Sole
58 Mondrian

OTHER
1 Chiesa di Sant'Angelo
2 Porta Sant'Angelo
3 Chiesa di Sant'Agostino
5 Contrappunto Jazz Club
6 Università per Stranieri
7 Piazza Fortebraccio
8 Arco d'Augusto
9 Piazza Rossi Scotti; Lookout
10 InformaGiovani
11 Onda Blu laundrette
12 CTS
13 Cappella di San Severo
15 Pozzo Etrusco
16 Piazza Piccinino
17 Piazza Danti
21 Duomo
24 Chiesa di San Francesco al Prato
25 Oratorio di San Bernardino
26 Via dei Priori Scala Mobile
30 ArciGay
32 Fontana Maggiore
33 APT Tourist Office
34 Piazza IV Novembre
36 CIT Travel Agency
37 Merlin Pub
38 Palazzo dei Priori; Galleria Nazionale dell'Umbria
39 Istituto Europeo di Arti Operative
42 Farmacia San Martino
43 Main Post Office
45 Cassa di Risparmio di Perugia (Bank) & ATM
47 Sala Borsa Merci
50 Telecom Office
52 La Libreria
59 Rocca Paolina; Giardini Carducci
60 Rocca Paolina Scala Mobile
61 Chiesa di San Domenico
62 Museo Archeologico Nazionale dell'Umbria
63 Stazione Sant'Anna
64 Questura (Police Station)
65 Intercity Bus Station
66 Porta San Pietro

Maggiore in 1278, but it was left to Nicola and Giovanni Pisano to execute the plan. The bas-relief statues represent scenes from the Old Testament and the 12 months of the year. A female figure on the upper basin (facing Corso Vannucci) bears fruit representing fertility, the city's symbol. Hardly surprising then that she is called Perugia. At the time of writing, the fountain had just been unveiled after a three year restoration.

Most eye-catching of all in the square is the 13th century **Palazzo dei Priori**. Long the seat of secular power in Perugia, it still houses the municipal offices. Annexed to these is the **Galleria Nazionale dell'Umbria**, a collection of paintings mostly by Umbrian artists, including Pinturicchio, Perugino and Fra Angelico. It is open from 9 am to 7 pm (often extended to 10 pm in summer) daily and closed on the first Monday of each month. Admission costs L8000, which includes admission to a science museum housed in the same building.

The vaulted **Sala dei Notari**, on the 1st floor of the palazzo, was built in 1296 for the city council and its walls are decorated with colourful frescoes (with particularly charming depictions of animals) by various anonymous artists. To reach it, climb the flight of steps from Piazza IV Novembre. It's open from 9 am to 1 pm and 3 to 7 pm Tuesday to Sunday. Admission is free.

In the Corso Vannucci side of the palazzo is the **Collegio della Mercanzia**, the seat of the city's powerful Renaissance-era merchants. They formed one of several *arti* (guilds) that still exist today (though their power is a shadow of what it was). Reflecting their one-time prestige is the impressive early 15th century, carved-wood panelling inside. Look at the designs closely and it will be hard to escape the impression that they were influenced by Islamic artistry – possibly imported from the Orient via Venezia. A few doors up in the same building is the **Collegio del Cambio**, constructed in 1450 for another guild, the city's moneychangers, and decorated with magnificent frescoes by Perugino. The Collegio della Mercanzia is open from 9 am to 1 pm and 2.30 to 5.30 pm Monday to

Saturday and 9 am to 1 pm Sunday and holidays. The opening hours for the Collegio del Cambio are from 9 am to 12.30 pm and 2.30 to 5 pm Tuesday to Sunday and 9 am to 12.30 pm Sunday. The hours for both *collegi* change at certain times of the year, so check at the APT office first. Admission costs L5000 for the Collegio del Cambio and L2000 for the Collegio della Mercanzia or you can buy a combined ticket for L6000.

West of Corso Vannucci

Head west along Via dei Priori to reach Piazza San Francesco. The 15th century **Oratorio di San Bernardino** has a façade decorated with bas-reliefs by Agostino di Duccio. Next to it is the ruined **Chiesa di San Francesco al Prato**, destroyed over the centuries by various natural disasters. It is used as an atmospheric location for concerts.

Towards the Università per Stranieri

The **Pozzo Etrusco** (Etruscan Well), between Piazza Danti and Piazza Piccinino, dates from the 3rd century BC. From here take Via del Sole to the **Cappella di San Severo**, decorated with Raphael's *Trinity with Saints*, thought to be his first fresco, and frescoes by Perugino. The L3500 ticket admits you to the well and the chapel. Frankly, unless you are desperate to see what *might* be Raphael's first fresco or happen to be an aficionado of large, brown, wet, dank holes in the ground, your L3500 would probably be better spent on a *gelato* (ice cream). The cappella and the well are open from 10.30 am to 1.30 pm and 2.30 to 6.30 pm Monday to Friday (to 5.30 pm Saturday and Sunday and to 4.30 pm daily in winter).

From the cappella, walk back to Piazza Michelotti and turn north into the small Piazza Rossi Scotti, from where you can enjoy a lovely view across the countryside. Take the steps down to Piazza Fortebraccio and the Università per Stranieri, housed in the baroque Palazzo Gallenga. To the south is the **Arco d'Augusto**, one of the ancient city gates. Its lower section is Etruscan, dating from the 3rd century BC; the upper part is Roman and bears the inscription 'Augusta Perusia'. The loggia on top dates from the Renaissance.

Around Corso Giuseppe Garibaldi

North along Corso Giuseppe Garibaldi is the **Chiesa di Sant'Agostino**, with a beautiful 16th century choir by Baccio d'Agnolo. Small signs denote the many artworks carried off to France by Napoleon and his merry men. Farther north along the same thoroughfare, Via del Tempio branches off to the Romanesque **Chiesa di Sant'Angelo**, said to stand on the site of an ancient temple. The columns inside the round church were taken from earlier buildings. Corso Giuseppe Garibaldi continues through the 14th century wall by way of the **Porta Sant'Angelo**. A 10 minute walk takes you to the **Villa Monteripido**, home of the Giuditta Brozzetti fabric company, where you can buy hand-woven linens produced using centuries-old techniques.

South of the Centre

At the southern end of Corso Vannucci are the tiny **Giardini Carducci**, with lovely views of the countryside. The gardens stand atop a once massive 16th century fortress, now known as the **Rocca Paolina**, built by Pope Paul III and standing over a medieval quarter formerly inhabited by some of the city's most powerful families. Destroyed by the Perugini after Italian unification, the ruins remain a symbol of defiance against oppression. A series of scala mobili run through the Rocca and you can wander around inside the ruins, which are often used for exhibitions.

Along Corso Cavour, the early 14th century **Chiesa di San Domenico** is the city's largest church. Perhaps unfortunately, its Romanesque interior, made light by the immense stained-glass windows, was replaced by austere Gothic fittings in the 16th century. Pope Benedict XI, who died after eating poisoned figs in 1325, lies buried here. The convent which adjoins it is the home of the **Museo Archeologico Nazionale dell'Umbria**, which has an excellent collection of Etruscan pieces and a section on prehistory. It is open from 9 am to 7 pm Monday to Saturday (to 1.30 pm Sunday). Admission costs L4000.

Continuing along Corso Cavour you come to the Porta San Pietro. Keep going along Borgo XX Giugno to reach the 10th century **Chiesa di San Pietro**, entered through a frescoed doorway in the first courtyard. The interior is an incredible mix of gilt and marble and contains a *Pietà* by Perugino.

About 5km south-east of the city, at Ponte San Giovanni, is the **Ipogeo dei Volumni**, a 2nd century BC Etruscan burial site discovered in 1840. An underground chamber contains a series of recesses holding the funerary urns of the Volumnio family. Unless you're a big fan of the Etruscans, you'll probably find the tombs at Cerveteri or Tarquinia in Lazio more interesting. It is open from 9.30 am to 12.30 pm and 3 to 5 pm Monday to Saturday (4.30 to 6.30 pm in July and August) and from 9.30 am to 12.30 pm Sunday. Admission costs L4000 and visits are limited to five people at a time, so there can be delays. Take the ASP bus from Piazza Italia to Ponte San Giovanni and walk west from there.

Courses

The list of courses available to locals and foreigners in and around Perugia could constitute a book in itself. You can learn Italian, take up ceramics, study music or spend a month cooking. The APT office has details of all of the courses available.

The Università per Stranieri (☎ 075 5 74 61) is Italy's foremost academic institution for foreigners and offers courses in language, literature, history, art and other subjects. It runs a series of degree courses as well as one, two and three-month intensive courses. The basic language course costs L350,000 per month. For information write to the Università per Stranieri, Palazzo Gallenga, Piazza Fortebraccio 4, Perugia 06122.

The Istituto Europea di Arti Operative (☎ 075 6 50 22), Via dei Priori 14, runs courses in fashion, graphic design, industrial and interior design, drawing and painting.

To study in Perugia you may need to apply for a student visa in your country of residence before arriving in Italy. See Visas & Documents in the Facts for the Visitor chapter for more details.

Special Events
The Umbria Jazz festival attracts international performers for 10 days each July, usually around the middle of the month. Check with the APT office for details. Tickets cost from L15,000 to L50,000 and can be bought in advance from Associazione Umbria Jazz (☎ 075 573 24 32, fax 0175 572 26 56, email umbriajazz@tin.it), Piazza Danti 28, or from Sala Borsa Merci (☎ 075 573 02 71), Via Mazzini 9. See the Web site at www.umbria jazz.com for information (in Italian only).

The Guarda Dove Vai (Watch Where You're Going) festival, held during August, features theatre, music and cinema. Ask at the APT office for a programme.

Places to Stay
Perugia has a good selection of reasonably priced hotels, but if you arrive unannounced during the Umbria Jazz festival or in August, expect problems. The APT office can provide a complete hotel listing. For agriturismo throughout Umbria, try Agriturist Umbria (☎ 075 3 20 28), Via Savonarola 38; Terranostra Umbria (☎ 075 500 95 59), Via Campo di Marte 10; or Turismo Verde Umbria (☎ 075 500 29 53), Via Campo di Marte 14.

About 10 religious institutions and orders offer accommodation in Perugia. Generally rates are cheap and a stay must last at least two days. They have a curfew of 9 pm (10 pm in summer). The APT office can provide a list.

Camping The city has two camp sites, both in Colle della Trinità, 5km north-west of the city and reached by taking bus No 9 from Piazza Italia (ask the driver to drop you off at the Superal supermarket, from where it's a 300m walk to the camp sites). They are *Paradis d'Été* (☎ 075 517 04 88) and *Il Rocolo* (☎ 075 517 85 50). The 'latter is open from 15 June to 15 September only.

Hostels The non-HI youth hostel, *Centro Internazionale per la Gioventù* (☎ 075 572 28 80, Via Bontempi 13) charges L15,000 per night. Sheets (for the entire stay) cost an extra L2000. Its TV room has a fresco-decorated ceiling and the views from the terrace are fantastic. It's closed from mid-December to mid-January.

Pensioni & Hotels Visitors have more than 50 hotels to choose from in Perugia. At *Pensione Anna* (☎/fax 075 573 63 04, Via dei Priori 48), simple singles/doubles cost up to L40,000/60,000 (up to L55,000/80,000 with private bathroom). *Pensione Paola* (☎ 075 572 38 16, Via della Canapina 5) is five minutes from the town centre, down the scala mobile from Via dei Priori; rooms cost L43,000/65,000. Just off Corso Vannucci is *Piccolo Hotel* (☎ 075 572 29 87, Via Luigi Bonazzi 25), which only has doubles (with bathroom) for L75,000, two of which have private balconies. Next door, at No 19, the rather more upmarket *Hotel Fortuna* (☎ 075 572 28 45, fax 075 573 50 40) has rooms for up to L137,000/188,000.

The two star *Albergo Aurora* (☎/fax 075 572 48 19, Viale Indipendenza 21) has doubles with bathroom for L95,000 and a couple of cheaper singles without private bathroom for L55,000 (these overlook a fume-ridden garage). At *Hotel Morlacchi* (☎ 075 572 03 19, Via Tiberi 2), singles/doubles with bathroom are L70,000/100,000 and triples cost L120,000.

Hotel Priori (☎ 075 572 33 78, fax 075 572 32 13, Via Vermiglioli 3), at the corner of Via dei Priori, is in a great location. Pleasant singles/doubles with bathroom cost L90,000/130,000 and triples/quads cost L170,000/200,000. *Hotel Eden* (☎ 075 572 81 02, fax 075 572 03 42, Via Caporali 9) has bright, clean singles/doubles for L60,000/90,000. *Hotel la Rosetta* (☎/fax 075 572 08 41, Piazza Italia 19) is one of Perugia's better hotels. Rooms cost up to L105,000/245,000.

Rental Accommodation If you are planning to study in Perugia, the Università per Stranieri will organise accommodation costing from L400,000 to L800,000 per month, depending on your needs. The weekly *Cerco e Trovo* (L2000 at newspaper stands) lists all available rental accommodation and the APT office can help you to find holiday houses and *affittacamere* (rooms rented on a weekly or monthly basis).

Places to Eat

Restaurants Being a student city, Perugia offers many budget eating options. For great pizza by the slice, there's *Pizzeria Marchigiana (Via dei Priori 3)*, just west of Corso Vannucci. A student pizza haunt is *Pizzeria Etrusca (Via Ulisse Rocchi 31)*. Try the *cuscino*, a closed pizza stuffed with sausage, ham and mozzarella.

Good places for a sit-down pizza are *L'Era Nuova (Via Baldo 6)* and *Tit-Bit (Via dei Priori 105)*. A pizza will cost from L6000 to L10,000 at either restaurant. For a cheap and filling meal, try *Tavola Calda* on Piazza Danti.

Ristorante dal Mi'Cocco (Corso Giuseppe Garibaldi 12) offers a L25,000 set menu featuring local specialities, and is popular with students. *Ristorante Ferrari (Corso Vannucci 43)*, downstairs from the bar of the same name, serves excellent *antipasto* (starters), good pizzas and pasta. A meal will cost around L30,000. For a pizza or salad and ultra modern décor try *Mondrian (Via Luigi Bonazzi 45)*.

Going a little further upmarket, *La Vecchia Perusia (Via Ulisse Rocchi 9)* serves fine local cuisine. It can fill quickly, so be prepared to wait. A full meal will cost close to L40,000. Further upmarket still is the popular *Ristorante del Sole (Via Oberdan 28)*. It's actually down a side alley and, if you aren't dazzled by the views, you'll probably want to just roll around in the antipasto and dessert displays. The food tastes as good as it looks, but expect to pay up to L50,000 for a full meal with wine.

Cafés & Bars The city's finest café, *Sandri (Corso Vannucci 32)* retains a medieval air. Prices are very reasonable. *Caffè del Cambio (Corso Vannucci 29)* is a trendy bar, as is *Medio Evo* on Corso Vannucci at Piazza della Repubblica. The best gelati in town can be had at *La Boutique del Gelato* on the corner of Piazza IV Novembre and Via Calderini.

Self-Catering There is a *covered market* down the stairs from Piazza Matteotti, open from 7 am to 1.30 pm daily except Sunday, where you can buy fresh produce, bread, cheese and meat.

Entertainment

For late-night drinks you could try a Guinness at *Shamrock Pub*, by the entrance to the Pozzo Etrusco or check out *Merlin Pub (Via del Forno 19)* just off Via Fani. *Contrappunto Jazz Club (Via Scortici 4)* is one of the best clubs, and regularly features top-notch Italian and international jazz musicians.

Keep an eye on the notice boards at the Università per Stranieri, as the university often organises free concerts and excursions.

Getting There & Away

Bus Most buses run from Piazza dei Partigiani (take the scala mobile from Piazza Italia). The Perugia-Roma service is operated by SULGA (☎ 075 500 96 41); there are roughly five buses daily (2½ hours) in each direction, and one-way/return tickets, which can be bought on the bus, cost L24,500/38,000. SULGA also operates the Perugia-Firenze service (two hours), which runs daily in each direction, leaving Perugia at 7.30 am and Firenze at 5 pm. Buses also depart from Piazza dei Partigiani for Fiumicino airport, Firenze (Via Stazione), Siena (train station), L'Aquila and cities throughout Umbria, including Assisi, Gubbio and nearby Lago di Trasimeno. Buses also head into Le Marche and as far south as Cosenza in Calabria. The bus to Roma is faster and cheaper than the train and the bus station is closer to the historic centre than Stazione Fontivegge.

Current bus routes, company details and timetables are listed in the monthly booklet *Viva Perugia – What, Where, When*, available from the APT office or at newsstands.

Train The main train station, Stazione Fontivegge (☎ 075 500 74 67), is on Piazza Vittorio Veneto, a few kilometres west of the city centre and easily accessible by frequent buses from Piazza Italia. The city is not on the main Roma-Firenze train line, so you generally need to change at Foligno for Roma (2½ hours, L18,000) or at Terontola for Firenze and the north. There are one or two direct trains each day to Roma and Firenze.

The private Ferrovia Centrale Umbra railway (☎ 075 572 39 47) runs from Stazione Sant'Anna on Piazzale Bellucci and serves Umbertide, Sansepolcro, Terni and Todi.

Car & Motorcycle From Roma, leave the A1 at the Orte exit and follow the signs for Terni. Once there, take the S3b-E45 for Perugia. From the north, exit the A1 at Valdichiana and take the dual-carriageway S75b for Perugia. The S75 to the east connects the city with Assisi.

For car hire, the Hertz office (☎ 075 500 24 39) is at Stazione Fontivegge.

Getting Around
From Stazione Fontivegge catch any bus heading for Piazza Matteotti or Piazza Italia (including Nos 6, 7, 9, 11, 15) to get to the centre. Tickets cost L1500 and must be bought before you board and validated in the machine as you enter.

If you arrive in Perugia by car, following the Centro signs along the winding roads up the hill will bring you to Piazza Italia, where you can leave your car in a metered parking spot (either on the piazza or on the hill immediately preceding it). You are only allowed to stay for one hour, but on Sunday parking is free all day.

The remainder of the city centre is largely closed to normal, non-resident traffic, although tourists may drive to their hotels. Scala mobili to large car parks include the one on Via dei Priori (open from 6.45 am to 12.30 am) that leads to the car parks in Piazza della Cupa and Viale Pompeo Pellini, and the series of scala mobili that descend through the Rocca Paolina to Piazza dei Partigiani. The supervised car park here costs L1500 for the first hour and L2000 per hour thereafter, and is open from 6.15 am to 1 am. If you intend to use the car park a lot, buy an *abbonamento* for tourists (L16,000 for the first two days, then L10,500 per day).

If you park illegally and return to find your

car gone, chances are it has been towed away. Call the Deposito Veicoli Rimossi (☎ 075 577 53 75) to check and be prepared to pay around L200,000 to retrieve your car.

LAGO DI TRASIMENO
The fourth-largest lake in Italy, Lago di Trasimeno is not a bad location for swimming, fishing and other water sports, but hardly comparable with the country's northern lakes. The only blemish is the autostrada along its northern shore.

In 217 BC this area witnessed one of the bloodiest battles in Roman history as Hannibal's Carthaginians routed Roman troops under Consul Flaminius, killing 16,000. The battlefield extended from Cortona and Ossaia (Place of Bones), in Toscana, to the small town of Sanguineto (The Bloody), just north of the lake.

Passignano (or Passignano sul Trasimeno) is the most popular spot for holidaying Italians, so book accommodation in advance for the summer months. More enticing is **Castiglione del Lago**, up on a chalky promontory on the lake's western side, dotted with olive trees and dominated by a 14th century castle.

Information
In Passignano, the APT office (☎ 075 82 76 35), Via Roma 25, can provide details of accommodation and water sports. It's open from 10 am to noon and 3 to 6 pm daily (morning only on Sunday). In Castiglione del Lago, the APT office (☎ 075 965 24 84), Piazza Mazzini 10, is open from 8.30 am to 1.30 pm and 3.30 to 7 pm Monday to Friday, from 9 am to 6 pm Saturday (with a two hour break from 1.30 pm) and from 9 am to 1 pm Sunday. Staff can advise on the many agriturismo options and good walking tracks.

Things to See & Do
Water sports, walking and horse riding are the main reasons to visit the lake. The scenery is agreeable but hardly Umbria's best and the only other attraction is Castiglione del Lago and its **duomo**, which contains several frescoes by Perugino.

The lake's main inhabited island, **Isola Maggiore**, near Passignano, was reputedly a favourite with San Francesco and is noted for its lace and embroidery production. Boats run to the island from the main towns and, though there are no camp sites, you may pitch a tent.

Ask at one of the APT offices for *Tourist Itineraries in the Trasimeno District*, a booklet of walking and horse-riding tracks. Horse-riding centres include the Maneggio Oasi (☎ 0337 65 37 95) in Località Orto, Castiglione del Lago, or Poggio del Belveduto (☎ 075 82 90 76) at Passignano. You'll find other riding centres around the lake.

Places to Stay

Passignano The two camp sites, *Kursaal* (☎ 075 82 80 85, Viale Europa 41) and *Europa* (☎ 075 82 74 05) in San Donato, are open from April to October. At *Pensione del Pescatore* (☎ 075 829 60 63, fax 075 82 92 01, Via San Bernardino 5), singles/doubles cost L50,000/80,000 in high season.

Castiglione del Lago The *Listro* camp site (☎ 075 95 11 93, Via Lungolago) is open from April to September and charges L7000 per person and per tent. About the cheapest hotel you'll find is *Albergo Fazzuoli* (☎ 075 95 11 19, fax 075 95 11 12, Piazza Marconi 11), where singles/doubles cost L60,000/90,000.

Getting There & Around

Passignano is close to the S75b autostrada and is served by regular trains from Perugia and Terontola, making it the most accessible part of the lake. The ASP bus from Perugia to Tuoro, a few kilometres west of Passignano, also stops here and continues to Castiglione.

Castiglione del Lago is on the Firenze-Roma train line, but the Intercity trains don't stop here, so you should instead board a local train (it's slow and stops at every station).

SPNT (☎ 075 82 71 57) operates regular ferry services between the main towns. The company has information offices on the waterfront at each town, where you can pick up a timetable. The return trip to Isola Maggiore from Passignano costs L8500.

DERUTA
postcode 06053 • pop 7400

About 15km south of Perugia, on the S3b-E45 to Terni, Deruta is famed for its richly coloured and intensely patterned pottery. The Etruscans and Romans worked the clay around Deruta but it was not until the majolica glazing technique, with its bright blue and yellow metallic oxides, was imported from Majorca in the 15th century that the ceramics industry took off.

There is not much else to Deruta, but it is probably the place to buy ceramics as prices are lower than in Perugia and other towns. Watch out for low-quality, mass-produced stuff as you browse through the large showrooms in town.

Regular ASP buses connect the town with Perugia and it has a handful of hotels.

TODI
postcode 06059 • pop 17,000

Originally an Etruscan frontier settlement, Todi ended up as a prosperous *comune* in the early Middle Ages – a prosperity reflected in the grandness of its central Piazza del Popolo.

Set atop a craggy hill, Todi seems to have ignored the 20th century, the growing stream of tourists notwithstanding, and getting there by public transport can be quite a slog.

The APT del Tuderte (☎ 075 894 38 67), on Piazza del Popolo, is open in the morning and late afternoon.

Things to See & Do

The 13th century **Palazzo del Capitano** on Piazza del Popolo features an elegant triple window and houses the city's recently restored *pinacoteca* (picture gallery) and museo archeologico. They are open from 9 am to 1 pm and 3 to 6 pm daily. Admission costs L6000. Also facing the square are the 13th century **Palazzo del Popolo** and gloomy **Palazzo dei Priori**.

The **duomo**, at the north-western end of the square, has a magnificent rose window and intricately decorated doorway. The 8th century crypt is worth visiting for the inlaid wooden stalls in the chancel. Spend an hour or two wandering through the medieval labyrinth and popping into some of the other churches. Just outside the city walls is the late Renaissance **Chiesa di Santa Maria della Consolazione**, designed by Bramante in 1508 but not completed until 99 years later.

Special Events

The Todi Festival, held for 10 days each August/September, is a mixture of classical and jazz concerts, theatre, ballet and cinema.

Places to Stay & Eat

If you are planning to stay overnight, expect to spend a lot of money on accommodation. For details of agriturismo opportunities, contact Agritop-Umbria (☎ 075 894 26 27), Via Paolo Rolli 3. The cheapest hotel in Todi is *Tuder* (☎ *075 894 21 84, fax 075 894 39 52, Via Maesta dei Lombardi 13)*, where singles/doubles cost L90,000/150,000 in high season. *Villa Luisa* (☎ *075 894 85 71, fax 075 894 84 72, Via A Cortesi 147)* has rooms costing L100,000/150,000.

Ristorante Umbria (Via Santa Bonaventura 13), behind the APT office, is reasonably expensive but worth it for the view from the terrace over the countryside. If you'd prefer a pizza (and good views if you snaffle the right tables), try *Ristorante Cavour (Corso Cavour 21)*.

Getting There & Away

ASP buses from Perugia terminate in Piazza Iacopone, just south of Piazza del Popolo. Todi is on the Ferrovia Centrale Umbra train line but the train station is inconveniently located 3km east of the town centre in the valley, although city bus B runs there. By road, the city is easily reached on the S3b-E45 which runs between Perugia and Terni.

ASSISI

postcode 06081 • pop 25,000

Despite the millions of tourists and pilgrims it attracts every year, the home town of San Francesco remains a beautiful and tranquil refuge. Since Roman times, its inhabitants have been aware of the visual impact of their city, perched halfway up Monte Subasio (1290m). From the valley its pink and white marble buildings shimmer in the sunlight.

San Francesco was born here in 1182 and his spirit hovers over every aspect of the city's life. He renounced his father's wealth in his late teens to pursue a life of chastity and poverty, founding the order of mendicant friars known as the Frati Minori (Order of Minors; they became known as the Franciscans after San Francesco's death), which attracted a huge following in Europe. One of his disciples, Santa Chiara, born in 1193, was the founder of the Franciscans' female Ordine delle Clarisse (Order of the Poor Clares).

The Basilica di San Francesco is the city's, and possibly Umbria's, main draw. Don't be put off by the prospect of huge crowds, but do check before coming to Assisi that your trip doesn't coincide with a religious celebration, when hotels are likely to be booked out.

Orientation

Piazza del Comune is the centre of Assisi. At the north-western edge of this square, Via San Paolo and Via Portica both eventually lead to the Basilica di San Francesco. Via Portica also leads to the Porta San Pietro and the Piazzale dell'Unità d'Italia, where most intercity buses stop, although ASP buses from smaller towns in the area terminate at Piazza Matteotti. The train station is 4km south-west of the city (use the shuttle bus) in Santa Maria degli Angeli.

Information

Tourist Offices The APT office (☎ 075 81 25 34, fax 075 81 37 27, email aptas@krenet .it), Piazza del Comune 12, is open from 8 am to 2 pm and 3.30 to 6.30 pm Monday to Friday, from 9 am to 1 pm and 3.30 to 6.30 pm Saturday and from 9 am to 1 pm Sunday. It has all the information you'll need on hotels, sights and events. There is a small branch office (☎ 075 81 67 66) just outside Porta Nuova, open from Easter to November.

Money The Cassa di Risparmio di Perugia in Piazza del Comune has an ATM and currency exchange machine.

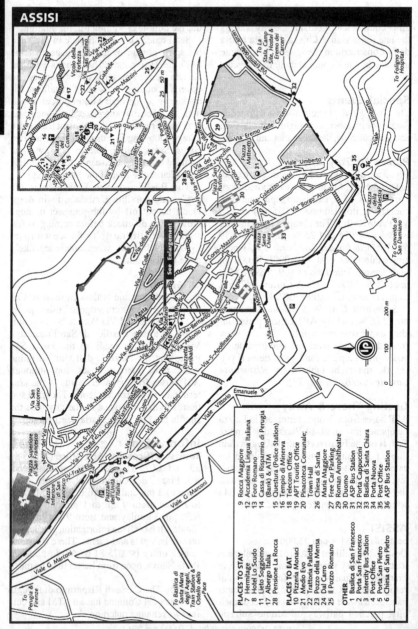

ASSISI

PLACES TO STAY
7 Hermitage
8 Hotel Lo Scudo
11 Lieto Soggiorno
17 Albergo Italia
28 Pensione La Rocca

PLACES TO EAT
10 Pizzeria Monaci
21 Medio Evo
22 Trattoria Pallotta
23 Pozzo della Mensa
24 Dal Carro
25 Il Pozzo Romano

OTHER
1 Basilica di San Francesco
2 Porta San Francesco
3 Intercity Bus Station
4 Post Office
5 Porta San Pietro
6 Chiesa di San Pietro
9 Rocca Maggiore
12 Accademia Lingua Italiana
13 Foro Romano
14 Cassa di Risparmio di Perugia
   (Bank) & ATM
15 Questura (Police Station)
16 Tempio di Minerva
18 Telecom Office
19 APT Tourist Office
20 Pinacoteca Comunale;
   Town Hall
26 Chiesa di Santa
   Maria Maggiore
27 Free Car Parking
29 Roman Amphitheatre
30 Duomo
31 ASP Bus Station
32 Porta Cappuccini
33 Basilica di Santa Chiara
34 Porta Nuova
35 Post Office
36 ASP Bus Station

Post & Communications There are post offices just inside Porta San Pietro and by Porta Nuova. They are open from 8.10 am to 6.25 pm Monday to Friday and to 1 pm at the weekend.

The Telecom office, open from 8 am to 10 pm daily, is next to the APT office on Piazza del Comune.

Medical Services & Emergency The Ospedale di Assisi (☎ 075 813 92 27) is about 1km south-east of Porta Nuova, in Fuori Porta. The questura (☎ 075 81 22 15), or *commissariato della pubblica sicurezza* as it is known here, is on Piazza del Comune.

Basilica di San Francesco
This basilica, comprising two churches, one built on top of the other, suffered extensive damage when two earthquakes struck Umbria and Le Marche in September 1997 (see the introduction to this chapter for more information). Four people died when sections of the vaulted ceiling of the upper church collapsed, and the structure of both churches and the adjoining monastery were damaged.

The lower church was started two years after San Francesco's death in 1228; two years later work began on the upper church on a patch of land known as the Hill of Hell because death sentences were carried out there. The two churches were erected as a compromise after dissent among the Franciscans, some of whom protested against plans for an enormous monument. Appropriately, the name of the hill was changed to Paradise Hill.

The **upper church** (enter from Piazza Superiore di San Francesco) contains a sequence of 28 frescoes depicting the life of San Francesco. These frescoes have been completely restored, apart from the loss of about 30 sq metres from the 5200 sq metre fresco cycle. It has long been claimed that these frescoes were painted by Giotto; however, the latest theories indicate at least three major artists were at work here: Pietro Cavallini, an as-yet unidentified colleague and, it appears, a young Giotto – possibly the author of the final six scenes. Above the

cycle is a series of 32 frescoes depicting scenes from the Old Testament, also attributed to Pietro Cavallini.

The greatest artistic loss caused by the earthquake was the destruction of the frescoes from the ceiling vaults above the entrance doors and above the Papal altar. These included part of Cimabue's frescoes of the four evangelists – San Matteo (St Matthew) was completely lost – and Giotto's fresco of San Girolamo, Doctor of the Church.

The **lower church** did not appear to have been as badly damaged as the upper church and it was reopened relatively soon after the earthquakes. This church's walls are also covered with frescoes. Those by Simone Martini showing the *Life of St Martin*, in the first chapel on the left as you face the altar, are the highlights.

Along the left wall of the left transept are celebrated frescoes by Pietro Lorenzetti depicting scenes of the Crucifixion and the life of San Francesco. Other frescoes above the main altar depict the virtues upon which the Franciscan order was founded – poverty, chastity and obedience. They are attributed to one of Giotto's pupils, dubbed the Maestro delle Vele. In the right transept are works by Cimabue and, below, more scenes by Simone Martini. A small chapel, reached by stairs on the right-hand side of the church, contains various mementos of San Francesco's life, including his shirt and sandals, and fragments of his celebrated *Canticle of the Creatures*. Descend the stairs in the middle of the lower church to reach the crypt containing San Francesco's tomb and those of four of his companions. The crypt was rediscovered in 1818; the coffin had been hidden in the 15th century for fear of desecration.

The basilica's **Tesoreria** (Treasury), accessible from the lower church, contains a rich collection of relics given to the Franciscans over the years.

At the end of 1999, after two years of restoration work, the reopening of the basilica was celebrated with a mass of rededication. New technology was used to make the basilica as earthquake-proof as possible.

Both the basilica (☎ 075 81 90 01) and

Treasury are open from 7 am to 7 pm daily. The basilica is free of charge, however a small charge is payable to enter the Treasury.

Dress rules are applied rigidly in both churches – absolutely no shorts, miniskirts or low-cut dresses.

Other Things to See

From the basilica, take Via San Francesco back to Piazza del Comune, once the site of a **Foro Romano** (Roman Forum), parts of which have been excavated. Access is from Via Portica and admission to the Foro Romano and a small museum costs L4000. It's open from 10 am to 1 pm and 3 to 7 pm daily (2 to 5 pm in winter). The **Tempio di Minerva**, facing the same square, is now a church but retains its impressive pillared façade. Wander into some of the shops on the piazza, which open their basements to reveal Roman ruins. The city's **Pinacoteca Comunale**, in the town hall on the southern side of the piazza, displays Umbrian Renaissance art and frescoes from Giotto's school. Also damaged in the earthquakes, it was still closed at the time of writing.

Off Via Bernardo da Quintavalle is Piazza Vescovado and the Romanesque **Chiesa di Santa Maria Maggiore**, formerly the city's cathedral, with an interesting rose window. South of Piazza del Comune along Corso Mazzini and Via Santa Chiara is the pink and white 13th century Romanesque **Basilica di Santa Chiara**, with a deteriorating but nonetheless striking façade. The body of Santa Chiara is in the crypt. If you believe in talking crosses, cast a glance at the Byzantine crucifix that is said to have told San Francesco to re-establish the moral foundations of the Church. At the time of writing the Basilica di Santa Chiara was closed for an indefinite period for repairs to earthquake damage.

North-east of the Basilica di Santa Chiara, on Piazza San Rufino, the 13th century Romanesque **duomo**, remodelled by Galeazzo Alessi in the 16th century, contains the font at which San Francesco was baptised. The façade is festooned with grotesque figures and fantastic animals typical of this era. The duomo also suffered earthquake damage and was closed at the time of writing.

Dominating the city is the massive 14th century **Rocca Maggiore**, a hill fortress offering fabulous views over the valley and across to Perugia. It is open from 10 am to sunset daily and admission costs L5000, although most of the fortress is closed for a long restoration that will eventually see it converted to an immense art gallery.

A 30 minute walk south from Porta Nuova, the **Convento di San Damiano** was built on the spot where the crucifix spoke to San Francesco and where he wrote his *Canticle of the Creatures*. The convent on this pleasant, bucolic site was founded by Santa Chiara.

About 4km east of the city, reached via the Porta Cappuccini, is the **Eremo dei Carceri**, to which San Francesco retreated after hearing the word of God. The *carceri* (prisons) are the caves that functioned as hermits' retreats for San Francesco and his followers. Apart from a few fences and tourist paths, everything has remained as it was in San Francesco's time, and a few Franciscans actually live here.

In the valley south-west of the city, near the train station, the imposing **Basilica di Santa Maria degli Angeli** was built around the first Franciscan monastery. San Francesco died in its **Cappella del Transito** on 3 October 1226.

Activities

The APT office can provide a map produced by the Club Alpino Italiano (CAI) of walks on nearby Monte Subasio. None is too demanding and the smattering of religious shrines and camp sites could make for an enjoyable excursion of a couple of days.

Courses

If you favour Assisi over Perugia as a place to live and learn Italian, contact the Accademia Lingua Italiana (☎/fax 075 81 52 81), Via Giotto 5. It runs a variety of language and culture courses and can arrange accommodation. Its Web site at www.krenet.it/alia/ gives details.

Special Events

The Festa di San Francesco falls on 3 and 4 October and is the main religious event of the city's calendar. Easter week is celebrated with processions and performances. The Ars Nova Musica festival, held from late August to mid-September, features local and national performers. The colourful Festa di Calendimaggio celebrates the coming of spring in perky medieval fashion, and is normally held over several days at the end of the first week of May.

Places to Stay

Assisi is well-appointed for tourists but in peak periods, such as Easter, August and September, and the Festa di San Francesco, you will need to book accommodation well in advance. Even outside these times many of the hotels will often be full. The APT office has a complete list of private rooms, religious institutions (of which there are 17), flats and agriturismo options in and around Assisi. Otherwise, keep an eye out for *camere* (rooms for rent) signs as you wander the streets. If you fail to find anything in Assisi itself, consider staying in Santa Maria degli Angeli, 4km south-west of Assisi – this way you are near the train station and a half-hourly shuttle bus runs to the city centre.

There is a non-HI *hostel* and *camp site* (both ☎ 075 81 36 36) just east of town at Fontemaggio, reached by walking about 2km uphill along Via Eremo dei Carceri. Beds at the hostel cost L17,000. The HI youth hostel, the *Ostello della Pace* (☎ 075 81 67 67, Via Valecchie 171), is open from 1 March to 10 January. It's spotless and has great pillows. B&B costs L22,000 or L28,000 in family rooms. It is on the shuttle-bus route between Santa Maria degli Angeli and Assisi.

At *Pensione La Rocca* (☎/fax 075 81 22 84, Via Porta Perlici 27), singles/doubles cost L50,000/72,000 with bathroom or L35,000/57,000 without. *Albergo Italia* (☎ 075 81 26 25, fax 075 804 37 49, Vicolo della Fortezza), just off Piazza del Comune, has rooms costing L30,000/50,000 or L45,000/69,000 with bathroom. The two star *Lieto Soggiorno* (☎ 075 81 61 91, Via A Fortini

26), west of Piazza del Comune, has rooms starting at L45,000/75,000 and doubles with bathroom for L95,000. Closer to the Basilica di San Francesco is *Hotel Lo Scudo* (☎/fax 075 81 31 96, Via San Francesco 3). Simple but decent rooms with bath and shower cost up to L60,000/90,000. At the three star *Hermitage* (☎ 075 81 27 6, fax 075 81 66 91, Via degli Aromatari 1), off Via Fontebella, singles/doubles cost L100,000/150,000 and there's car parking.

Places to Eat

For tasty pizza (L8000) try *Pizzeria Monaci*, by the steps on Piazzetta Garibaldi. If pennies are everything, *Il Pozzo Romano* (Via Sant'Agnese 8) serves pizza costing L7000 and under. In the same complex as the camp site at Fontemaggio is *La Stalla*, where you can eat a filling meal under an arbour for about L30,000. *Dal Carro* (Vicolo dei Nepis 2), off Corso Mazzini, is a good bet – the *strongozzi alla norcina* are a marvel and so is the homemade dessert, *tiramisù*. Try also *Trattoria Pallotta* (Via San Rufino 4), where a meal will cost around L30,000. *Pozzo della Mensa* (Via Pozzo della Mensa 11) also specialises in Umbrian dishes; a full meal will come to about L40,000. One of the better restaurants is *Medio Evo* (Via Arco dei Priori 4), where an excellent meal will cost about L50,000.

Getting There & Away

ASP buses connect Assisi with Perugia, Foligno and other local towns, leaving from the bus station on Piazza Matteotti. Most ASP buses also stop on Largo Properzio, just outside the Porta Nuova. Piazzale dell'Unità d'Italia is the terminus for buses for Roma, Firenze and other major cities.

Although Assisi's train station is 4km away at Santa Maria degli Angeli, the train is still the best way to get to many places as the services are more frequent than the buses. It is on the Foligno-Terontola line and is about 35 minutes from Perugia. Change at Terontola for Firenze and at Foligno for Roma.

To reach Assisi from Perugia by road, take the S75, exit at Ospedalicchio and follow the signs.

euro currency converter L10,000 = €5.16

Getting Around

A shuttle bus (L1200) operates every half-hour between Piazza Matteotti and the train station. Normal traffic is subject to restrictions in the city centre and daytime parking is all but banned. If you object to paying for one of the several car parks dotted around the city walls (and connected to the centre by orange shuttle buses), head for Via della Rocca, the road that leads up to Rocca Maggiore. There are no restrictions beyond the P (parking) sign. This leaves you a fairly short, if steep, walk to the duomo and Piazza del Comune.

SPELLO

postcode 06038 • pop 7600

Spello's proximity to Perugia and Assisi makes it well worth a brief trip. Emperor Augustus developed much of the land in the valley, but the Roman ruins are some distance from the town and your time could be better spent wandering Spello's narrow cobbled streets.

There is a small tourist office at Piazza Matteotti 3, or you can pick up information at the APT in Assisi.

The Augustan **Porta Venere** leads to the gloomy **Chiesa di Sant'Andrea** on Piazza Matteotti, where you can admire a fresco by Bernardino Pinturicchio. A few doors down is the 12th century **Chiesa di Santa Maria Maggiore** and the town's real treat, Pinturicchio's beautiful frescoes in the Cappella Baglioni. Also of note is the pavement (dating from 1566) made of tiles from Deruta.

The people of Spello celebrate the feast of Corpus Domini in June (the date changes each year) by skilfully decorating stretches of the main street with fresh flowers in colourful designs. If you want to enjoy it, come on the Saturday evening before the Sunday procession to see the floral fantasies being laid out (from about 8.30 pm) and participate in the festive atmosphere. The Corpus procession begins at 11 am Sunday, but the crowds can make it a stifling event.

Hotels are expensive and there are cheaper options in Assisi and Perugia. *Affittacamere Merulli* (*☎ 0742 65 11 84, fax 0742 65 12 27, Via Belvedere)* has simple singles/doubles

costing L50,000/80,000. Otherwise, you could try *Il Cacciatore* (*☎ 0742 65 11 41, Via Giulia 42)*, where rooms with bathroom cost L80,000/110,000. It also has a restaurant with a large *terrazza*, perfect for a summer lunch. A classy alternative is the exquisite 18th century *Hotel Palazzo Bocci* (*☎ 0742 30 10 21, fax 0742 30 14 64, Via Cavour 17)*, where doubles start at L200,000.

ASP buses running between Perugia and Foligno serve the town and there are also connections to Assisi. Trains are a better option, as Spello is on the line linking Perugia, Assisi and Foligno. A shuttle bus connects the station with central Spello. Spello is on the S75 between Perugia and Foligno.

AROUND SPELLO

Those with time (and, better still, their own wheels) could do worse than undertake a few excursions in the area south-west of Spello. **Bevagna**, about 8km south-west of Foligno (through which you'll pass if you're on public transport), is a charming, medieval hamlet with a couple of Romanesque churches on the central Piazza Silvestri. It comes to life in the last week of June for the Mercato delle Gaite, a bit of a medieval lark where olde-worlde taverns open up and medieval-era handcrafts are brought back to life. The town also boasts a few remnants of its Roman days, including some impressive mosaics at the site of former Roman hot baths.

Seven kilometres to the south-east, **Montefalco** is also known as the Ringhiera dell'Umbria (Balcony of Umbria) for its expansive views. Again, the town is a pleasant medieval backwater graced with several churches. The deconsecrated Chiesa di San Francesco now serves as an overpriced art gallery. Don't leave here without trying the local Sagrantino wine.

GUBBIO

postcode 06024 • pop 32,000

Hitched onto the steep slopes of Monte Ingino and overlooking a picturesque valley, the centuries-old *palazzi* of Gubbio exude a warm ochre glow in the late afternoon sunlight. It doesn't require a great deal of imagination to feel that you have stepped back into the Middle Ages when meandering along the town's quiet, treeless lanes.

Gubbio is famous for its Eugubian Tables, which date from the 3rd century BC and constitute the best existing example of ancient Umbrian script. An important ally of the Roman Empire and a key stop on the Via Flaminia, the town declined during the Saracen invasions. In the 14th century it fell into the hands of the Montefeltro family of Urbino and was later incorporated into the Papal States.

Like many hill towns from Toscana to Le Marche, Gubbio has taken on the feel of a museum, but a day spent here would be well spent.

Orientation

The city is small and easy to explore. The immense traffic circle known as Piazza

Quaranta Martiri, at the base of the hill, is where buses to the city terminate, and it also has a large car park. The square was named in honour of 40 local people who were killed by the Nazis in 1944 in reprisal for partisan activities. From here it is a short, if somewhat steep, walk up Via della Repubblica to the main square, Piazza Grande, also known as the Piazza della Signoria. Corso Garibaldi and Piazza Oderisi are to your right as you head up the hill.

Information

The APT office (☎ 075 922 06 93) on Piazza Oderisi is open from 8.15 am to 1.45 pm and 3.30 to 6.30 pm (3 to 6 pm in winter) Monday to Friday, from 9 am to 1 pm Saturday and from 9.30 am to 12.30 pm Sunday. You can also get information at Easy Gubbio, Via della Repubblica 13, near Piazza Quaranta Martiri.

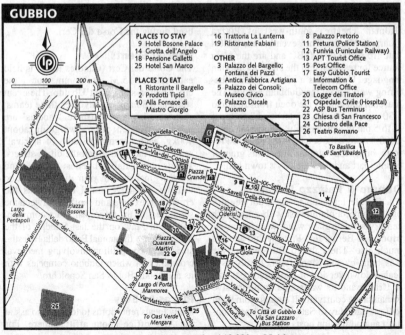

GUBBIO

PLACES TO STAY
9 Hotel Bosone Palace
14 Grotta dell'Angelo
18 Pensione Galletti
25 Hotel San Marco

PLACES TO EAT
1 Ristorante Il Bargello
2 Prodotti Tipici
10 Alla Fornace di Mastro Giorgio

16 Trattoria La Lanterna
19 Ristorante Fabiani

OTHER
3 Palazzo del Bargello; Fontana dei Pazzi
4 Antica Fabbrica Artigiana
5 Palazzo dei Consoli; Museo Civico
6 Palazzo Ducale
7 Duomo

8 Palazzo Pretorio
11 Pretura (Police Station)
12 Funivia (Funicular Railway)
13 APT Tourist Office
15 Post Office
17 Easy Gubbio Tourist Information & Telecom Office
20 Logge dei Tiratori
21 Ospedale Civile (Hospital)
22 ASP Bus Terminus
23 Chiesa di San Francesco
24 Chiostro della Pace
26 Teatro Romano

The main post office, Via Cairoli 11, is open from 8.10 am to 5 pm Monday to Saturday. The Telecom office is at Easy Gubbio.

The Ospedale Civile (☎ 075 9 23 91) is on Piazza Quaranta Martiri. The questura, or *pretura* as it is known here, is at Via XX Settembre 97.

Chiesa di San Francesco

Attributed to Perugia's Fra Bevignate, this church on Piazza Quaranta Martiri features impressive frescoes by a local artist, Ottaviano Nelli. Wander into the **Chiostro della Pace** (Cloister of Peace) in the adjoining convent to view some ancient mosaics.

Piazza Grande

Gubbio's most impressive buildings look out over Piazza Grande, dominated above all by the 14th century **Palazzo dei Consoli**, attributed to Gattapone. The crenellated façade and tower can be seen from all over the town. The building houses the **Museo Civico**, which displays the Eugubian Tables, discovered in 1444 near the Teatro Romano (Roman Theatre) south-west of Piazza Quaranta Martiri. The seven bronze tablets date from 300 to 100 BC and are the main source for research into the ancient Umbrian language. Upstairs is a picture gallery featuring works from the Gubbian school. The museum and gallery are open from 10 am to 1.30 pm (to 1 pm in winter) and 3 to 6 pm (2 to 5 pm in winter) daily. Admission costs L4000. Across the square is the **Palazzo Pretorio**, built along similar lines to its grander counterpart and now the city's town hall.

Duomo & Palazzo Ducale

Via Ducale leads up to the 13th century pink duomo, a plain beast with a fine 12th century stained-glass window, a fresco attributed to Bernardino Pinturicchio and not much else. The Palazzo Ducale opposite was built by the Montefeltro family as a scaled-down version of their grand palazzo in Urbino and its walls hide an impressive Renaissance courtyard. It's open from 9 am to 7 pm Monday to Saturday (to 1 pm Sunday) and admission costs L4000.

Other Things to See

From Piazza Grande, Via dei Consoli leads north-west to the 13th century **Palazzo del Bargello**, the city's medieval police station and prison. In front of it is the **Fontana dei Pazzi** (Fountain of Lunatics), so named because of a belief that if you walk around it three times, you will go mad – on summer weekends the number of tourists carrying out this ritual is indeed cause for concern about their collective sanity. At Via San Giuliano 1-3, just south-east of Palazzo del Bargello, a rather crumbly 15th century mansion houses the **Antica Fabbrica Artigiana**, an exuberant display of fine ceramics – in the Middle Ages one of the city's main sources of income.

South of Piazza Quaranta Martiri, off Viale del Teatro Romano, are the overgrown remains of a 1st century AD **Teatro Romano**. Most of what you see is the result of reconstruction.

From Via San Gerolamo you can ride the curious birdcage *funivia* (funicular) to the **Basilica di Sant'Ubaldo**, an uninspiring church that houses the three huge 'candles' used during the Corsa dei Ceri.

Special Events

The Corsa dei Ceri (Candles Race) is held each year on 15 May to commemorate the city's patron saint, Sant'Ubaldo. The event starts at 5.30 am and involves three teams, each carrying a *cero* (these 'candles' are massive wooden pillars weighing about 400kg, each bearing a statue of a 'rival' saint) and racing through the city's streets. This is one of Italy's liveliest festivals and warrants inclusion in your itinerary, but be wary if you have small children as the crowd gets excited and scuffles between the supporters of the three teams are common.

Also in May, on the last Sunday of the month, there's the annual Palio della Balestra, an archery competition involving medieval crossbows, in which Gubbio competes with its neighbour, Borgo San Sepolchro.

Places to Stay

Many locals rent rooms to tourists, so ask at the APT office about affittacamere. For camping, try the **Città di Gubbio** (☎ 075 927 20 37) in Ortoguidone, a southern suburb of Gubbio, about 3km south of Piazza Quaranta Martiri along the S298 (Via Perugina). It's open from April to September.

All prices given here are for singles/ doubles in the high season, unless otherwise stated.

The cheapest hotel is **Pensione Galletti** (☎ 075 927 77 53, Via Piccardi 1), where rooms start at L36,000/60,000. **Grotta dell'Angelo** (☎ 075 927 17 47, fax 075 927 34 38, Via Gioia 47) has rooms costing upwards of L52,000/75,000 and a charming garden restaurant. **Hotel San Marco** (☎ 075 922 02 34, fax 075 927 37 16, Via Perugina 5) has rooms for up to L100,000/130,000. For a splurge, try **Hotel Bosone Palace** (☎ 075 922 06 88, fax 922 05 52, Via XX Settembre 22), a 14th century palazzo rebuilt in the 18th century. Singles/doubles start at L105,000/140,000 in low season but doubles can rocket as high as L160,000 or more in peak periods.

Out of town on the road connecting Gubbio and Perugia is the agriturismo **Oasi Verde Mengara** (☎ 075 92 01 56), where half board costs up to L75,000, full board L95,000. Its fine restaurant is open to the public and you can eat a memorable and very filling meal for around L30,000. Oasi Verdi Mengara is easily accessible from Gubbio using the regular ASP bus to Perugia, which stops right outside (ask the driver to tell you when to get off). Or at a similar distance south-east of Gubbio at Torre Calzolari is the agriturismo **Azienda Agraria Allevamento San Giovanni** (☎ 075 925 66 46).

Places to Eat

Ristorante Fabiani (Piazza Quaranta Martiri 26) is a good traditional trattoria where a meal will cost around L30,000. You'll pay about the same at **Trattoria La Lanterna** (Via Gioia 23), where local specialities are on hand and many meals feature delicious *tartufi* (truffles). Another good spot frequented by locals is **Ristorante Il Bargello** (Via dei Consoli 37). Try the *pappardelle alla ceraiola*.

One of the better restaurants, **Alla Fornace di Mastro Giorgio** (Via Maestro Giorgio), is also one of the more expensive: most main courses start at L20,000.

The **Prodotti Tipici** shop (Via dei Consoli 41) sells a wide range of locally produced foods and wines.

Getting There & Around

ASP buses run to Perugia (10 daily), Fossato di Vico, Gualdo Tadino and Umbertide, and the company operates daily services to Roma and Firenze. Most buses stop in Piazza Quaranta Martiri, but some terminate at the bus station in Via San Lazzaro. Check the signs or ask at the bus station for which buses stop at which station. You can buy tickets at Easy Gubbio, Via della Repubblica 13.

The closest train station is at Fossato di Vico, about 20km south-east of the city. Trains run from Fossato to Roma, Ancona, Perugia, Terontola, Arezzo and Firenze. ASP buses connect the station with Gubbio, although there are delays between train and bus connections of anything between five minutes and an hour.

By car or motorcycle, take the S298 from Perugia or the S76 from Ancona, and follow the signs. Parking in the large car park in Piazza Quaranta Martiri costs L1000 per hour.

Walking is the best way to get around, but ASP buses connect Piazza Quaranta Martiri with the funivia station and most main sights.

AROUND GUBBIO
Parco Regionale del Monte Cucco

East of Gubbio, this park is a haven for outdoor activities and is dotted with caves, many of which can be explored. It is well set up for walkers, rock climbers and horse riders, and has many hotels and *rifugi* (mountain huts). **Costacciaro**, accessible by bus from Gubbio, is a good base for exploring the area and is the starting point for a walk to the summit of Monte Cucco (1566m).

Maps and brochures are available from the APT office in Gubbio. The Centro Escursionistico Naturalistico Speleologico (☎ 075 917 04 00), Via Galeazzi 5 in Costacciaro, can also help with information about exploring local caves, walking and mountain-bike routes. The CAI produces a walking map,

Carta dei Sentieri Massiccio del Monte Cucco. It is possible to hire mountain bikes at the Coop Arte e Natura (☎ 075 917 07 40), Via Stazione 2, in the village of Fossato di Vico, about 8km south-east of Costacciaro.

There are several horse-riding schools around Gubbio that arrange lessons or treks. One of the schools is Rio Verde (☎ 075 917 01 38), north-east of the city in a hamlet called Fornace; it's open in summer only. Ask for directions when you arrive in these towns.

Alte Valle del Tevere

The northernmost reaches of Umbria, clamped in between Toscana and Le Marche and known as the Alta Valle del Tevere (Upper Tevere Valley), hardly constitute the region's showcase, but there are a few odds and ends to keep you occupied. Among the more interesting spots are **Città di Castello**, which was a powerful centre during the Renaissance, **Umbertide**, with a couple of castles and dominated by a 14th century fortress (closed to the public), and **San Giustino**, whose centre is graced by the Castello Bufalini. The area is connected with Perugia by the private Ferrovia Centrale Umbra railway and the occasional bus. SITA buses also connect the valley with nearby Arezzo in Toscana and then on to Firenze. The best way to see the area is by car or motorcycle.

SPOLETO

postcode 06049 • pop 37,360

Each June and July, this otherwise quiet town takes centre stage for an international parade of drama, music, opera and dance, called the Festival dei Due Mondi.

If you plan to visit Spoleto during the festival, book accommodation and tickets months in advance. When the festival ends, Spoleto goes back to sleep, but it's nonetheless an enchanting town to spend a day exploring.

Orientation

The old part of the city is about 1km south of the main train station – take the orange shuttle bus marked Circolare D for Piazza della Libertà in the centre, where you'll find

the APT office and the Roman-era theatre. Piazza del Mercato, a short walk north-east of Piazza della Libertà, marks the engaging heart of old Spoleto. Between here and Piazza del Duomo you'll find the bulk of the city's monuments and some fine shops.

Information

Tourist Offices The APT office (☎ 0743 22 03 11), Piazza della Libertà 7, has lots of information about the town. It is open from 9 am to 1 pm and 3 to 7 pm daily (10 am to 12.30 pm and 3.30 to 7 pm Sunday and holidays).

Post & Communications The main post office faces Piazza della Libertà, although the entrance is off Viale Giacomo Matteotti. It is open from 8.15 am to 7 pm Monday to Saturday.

The main Telecom office is at Via A Saffi 6, open from 8 am to 10 pm daily.

Medical Services & Emergency The casualty section of the Ospedale di Madonna di Loreto (☎ 0743 21 01) is on Via Madonna di Loreto, west of Porta San Matteo. For an ambulance, call ☎ 0743 4 48 88. The questura (☎ 0743 4 03 24) is on Viale di Trento e Trieste, a block south of the train station.

Roman Spoleto

Pick up a map and walking itinerary from the APT office, and make your first stop the **Teatro Romano** on the western edge of Piazza della Libertà. The 1st century theatre has been rebuilt many times and is currently used for performances during the summer. Have a quick look at the ceramics collection in the **Museo Archeologico** next to the theatre. The theatre and museum are open from 9 am to 1.30 pm and 2.30 to 7 pm Monday to Saturday and from 9 am to 1 pm Sunday. Admission costs L4000.

East of Piazza della Libertà, around Piazza Fontana, are more Roman remains, including the **Arco di Druso e Germanico**, which marks the entrance to the old forum. The excavated **Casa Romana** (Roman house) on Via di Visiale dates from the 1st century. It is open

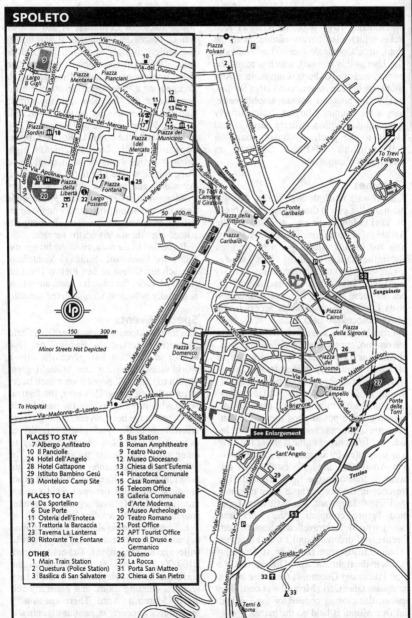

SPOLETO

PLACES TO STAY
- 7 Albergo Anfiteatro
- 10 Il Panciolle
- 24 Hotel dell'Angelo
- 28 Hotel Gattapone
- 29 Istituto Bambino Gesù
- 33 Monteluco Camp Site

PLACES TO EAT
- 4 Da Sportellino
- 6 Due Porte
- 11 Osteria dell'Enoteca
- 17 Trattoria la Barcaccia
- 23 Taverna La Lanterna
- 30 Ristorante Tre Fontane

OTHER
- 1 Main Train Station
- 2 Questura (Police Station)
- 3 Basilica di San Salvatore
- 5 Bus Station
- 8 Roman Amphitheatre
- 9 Teatro Nuovo
- 12 Museo Diocesano
- 13 Chiesa di Sant'Eufemia
- 14 Pinacoteca Comunale
- 15 Casa Romana
- 16 Telecom Office
- 18 Galleria Communale d'Arte Moderna
- 19 Museo Archeologico
- 20 Teatro Romano
- 21 Post Office
- 22 APT Tourist Office
- 25 Arco di Druso e Germanico
- 26 Duomo
- 27 La Rocca
- 31 Porta San Matteo
- 32 Chiesa di San Pietro

from 10 am to 1 pm and 3 to 6 pm daily except Monday. To get in you must buy a L5000 ticket which also covers admission to the Pinacoteca Comunale (see Other Things to See later in this section), which is round the corner, and the **Galleria Comunale d'Arte Moderna**, in Palazzo Spada on Piazza Sordini.

The city boasts a **Roman amphitheatre**, one of the country's largest. Unfortunately it is enclosed within military barracks and closed to the public. Wander along Via dell'Anfiteatro, off Piazza Garibaldi, in search of a glimpse.

Churches

A short walk north through Piazza del Municipio takes you to the 12th century **Chiesa di Sant'Eufemia**, in the grounds of the Archbishop's palazzo. The church is notable for its *matronei* – galleries set high above the main body of the church to segregate the female congregation. Artists from the 15th century Sienese school left behind some striking frescoes. Admission costs L5000, which includes access to the **Museo Diocesano** next door.

From here, it is a quick stroll north-east to the **duomo**, consecrated in 1198 and remodelled in the 17th century. The Romanesque façade is fronted by a Renaissance porch which has been shrouded by restorers' scaffolding for several years. In the 11th century, huge blocks of stone salvaged from Roman buildings were put to good use in the construction of the rather sombre bell tower. Inside, the first chapel to the right of the nave was decorated by Bernardino Pinturicchio, and Annibale Carracci completed an impressive fresco in the right transept. The frescoes in the domed apse were executed by Filippo Lippi and his assistants. Lippi died before completing the work and Lorenzo de Medici travelled to Spoleto from Firenze and ordered Lippi's son, Filippino, to build a mausoleum for the artist. This now stands in the right transept of the duomo. No 8 on Piazza del Duomo, is the house where composer Gian Carlo Menotti was born. The spectacular closing concert of the Festival dei Due Mondi is held on the piazza.

Other Things to See

The **Pinacoteca Comunale** is in the town hall on Piazza del Municipio. Unfortunately the gallery is only accessible by guided tour, although the sumptuous building and some impressive works by Umbrian artists compensate a little. Opening hours are the same as for the Casa Romana (see Roman Spoleto earlier in this section), which is covered by the same L5000 ticket.

Dominating the city is **La Rocca**, a former papal fortress that, until 1982, was a high-security prison housing such notables as Pope John Paul II's attempted assassin, Ali Agca. It is currently closed for restoration.

Along Via del Ponte is the **Ponte delle Torri**, erected in the 14th century on the foundations of a Roman aqueduct. The bridge is named after the towers on the far side.

If you feel like a walk, cross the bridge and follow the lower path, Strada di Monteluco, to reach the **Chiesa di San Pietro**. The 13th century façade, the church's main attraction, is liberally bedecked with sculpted animals.

Special Events

The Italian-American composer Gian Carlo Menotti conceived the Festival dei Due Mondi in 1958. It has given the city a worldwide reputation and brought great wealth to the small population which basks in its reflected glory. However, the festival is not what it once was. For the past decade or so there have been severe funding crises, affecting both the quality and quantity of events. While ticket prices continue to creep up, cutting-edge performances, for which the festival gained its reputation, are now rarely seen. Moreover, in recent years ongoing squabbles between the local authorities and the festival organisers have resulted in threats to relocate the festival.

Events at the festival, held from late June to mid-July, range from opera and theatre to ballet and art exhibitions. Tickets cost from L10,000 to L200,000, depending on the performance and whether you want luxury seats or standing room, and generally sell out by March or April. There are usually several free concerts in various churches.

For information, call ☎ 0743 4 50 28 or 0743 22 03 20, or check out the Web site at www.spoletofestival.net. Bookings can be made from outside Italy by writing to Associazione Festival dei Due Mondi, c/o Teatro Nuovo, 06049 Spoleto, Italy or fax 0743 22 03 21 or email spoletofestival@krenet.it.

Places to Stay

The city is well served by cheap hotels, affittacamere, hostels and camp sites, although if you're coming for the festival you will need to book a room months in advance.

The closest camp site is the *Monteluco* (☎ 0743 22 03 58), just behind the Chiesa di San Pietro, open from April to September. It charges L8000/8000 per person/tent in the high season. *Camping Il Girasole* (☎ 0743 513 35) is about 10km north-west of Spoleto in Petrognano. Buses run to Petrognano from Spoleto's train station.

There are also agriturismo options around Spoleto. The APT office has a booklet with the details.

Istituto Bambino Gesù (☎ 0743 402 32, Via Sant'Angelo 4) is a religious hostel just off Via Monterone; singles/doubles cost L55,000/110,000 in the high season.

At *Albergo Anfiteatro* (☎ 0743 498 53, Via dell'Anfiteatro 14), rooms start at L55,000/75,000. The central *Il Panciolle* (☎ 0743 456 77, Via del Duomo 3) has rooms with bathroom starting at L60,000/90,000. *Hotel dell'Angelo* (☎ 0743 22 23 85, Via Arco di Druso 25) has doubles with bathroom costing from L60,000 to L100,000.

One of the best-located hotels is *Hotel Gattapone* (☎ 0743 22 34 47, fax 0743 22 34 48, Via del Ponte 6); rooms overlooking Ponte delle Torri start at L140,000/170,000 in the low season.

Places to Eat

Spoleto is one of Umbria's main centres for *tartufo nero* (black truffle), used in a variety of dishes. Trying them can be a costly exercise – so check the price before digging in.

A great place in the town centre is *Taverna la Lanterna* (Via della Trattoria 6). It serves a variety of Umbrian pasta dishes and

a full meal shouldn't cost much more than L25,000. *Osteria dell'Enoteca* (Via A Saffi 7) offers a good-value tourist menu incorporating local dishes for around L20,000. You can also buy some typical Umbrian wine and food products there. Nearby, *Trattoria la Barcaccia* (Piazza Fratelli Bandiera 2) offers a L25,000 tourist menu. For pizza, try *Ristorante Tre Fontane* (Via Egio 15), which offers pleasant garden dining.

Outside the old town, *Due Porte* (Piazza della Vittoria 14) is a good, cheap restaurant where pasta dishes start at L7000. At *Da Sportellino* (Viale della Cerquiglia 4), main courses cost from L15,000.

Getting There & Around

Most Società Spoletina Trasporti (SSIT) buses (☎ 0743 21 22 11) depart from Piazza della Vittoria for Monteluco, Foligno, Terni, Roma, Bastardo, Assisi, Perugia and dozens of smaller towns.

Trains from the main station (☎ 0743 485 16), Piazza Polvani, connect with Roma, Ancona, Perugia and Assisi. The city is on the S3, basically the old Roman Via Flaminia, which runs from Terni to Foligno. From Terni, it's a short drive to the A1. There are car parks by all main approaches to Spoleto.

The city is easily explored on foot, although local buses weave through the streets. Orange shuttle bus Circolare D, runs between the train station, Piazza Garibaldi and Piazza della Libertà.

THE VALNERINA

Incorporating most of the lower eastern parts of Umbria, along the Nera river, the Valnerina is a beautiful area. Stretching north-east to the barren summit of Monte Sibilla (2175m) in neighbouring Le Marche, it makes for great walking territory. It also offers a couple of hang-gliding schools in one of the best areas in Europe to learn.

If you want to spend a few quiet days wandering around the valley, try the *Agli Scacchi* (☎ 0743 9 92 21), a pleasant hotel in the pretty medieval village of **Preci**. Singles/doubles cost L55,000/80,000 and half board costs up to L70,000 per person.

The area is criss-crossed by walking trails and you might try to pick up a copy of the aptly titled *20 Sentieri Ragionati in Valnerina* (in Italian; 20 Well-Thought-Out Routes in Valnerina).

If you are driving, the APT Valnerina-Cascia (☎ 0743 711 47), Piazza Garibaldi 1, in Cascia, is a good place to go for information. Tourist bodies in Umbria and Le Marche have erected road signs identifying suggested itineraries.

Getting There & Away

Spoleto is the best point from which to head into the Valnerina. Spoleto's SSIT bus company (☎ 0743 21 22 11) operates several buses a day from Piazza della Vittoria to the terminal at Via della Stazione in Norcia, from where connecting buses run along the Valnerina to Preci and Cascia. Getting to Castelluccio is not so easy, as there are two services from Norcia on Monday and Saturday only.

The S395 from Spoleto and the S209 from Terni join with the S320 and then the S396, which passes through Norcia. The area is also accessible from Ascoli Piceno in Le Marche.

Norcia

This fortified medieval village is the valley's main town and a transport hub of sorts; it also produces what is considered to be the country's best salami. Like the rest of the Valnerina, Norcia has suffered from earthquakes over the centuries; several buildings were damaged in 1997. There is a small tourist office in the central Piazza San Benedetto.

Activities For information on walking and other activities in the surrounding area, head for the Casa del Parco (☎ 0743 81 70 90), Via Solferino 22. It is open from 9.30 am to 12.30 pm and 3 to 6 pm daily.

Hang-gliders should aim for Castelluccio (for more details see Around Norcia).

Places to Stay At *Da Benito* (☎ 0743 81 66 70, Via Marconi 5), singles/doubles start at L50,000/75,000. *Hotel Garden* (☎/fax 0743 81 66 87, Via XX Settembre 2) has rooms for L80,000/120,000 (far less in the low season).

Around Norcia

If you have a car, don't miss the opportunity to visit the vast **Piano Grande**, a high plateau east of Norcia, under Monte Vettore (2476m). It becomes a sea of colour as flowers bloom in early spring.

Perched above the Piano Grande is the tiny, hilltop village of **Castelluccio**, famous for its lentils and *pecorino* and *ricotta* cheeses. If you want to stay overnight, singles/doubles at *Albergo Sibilla* (☎ 0743 87 01 13, Via Piano Grande 2) cost up to L55,000/90,000. About 10km north of Castelluccio at Monte Prata there's a free *camp site* (☎ 0737 98 28), open from 15 June to early October. You may also be able to camp for free on the Piano Grande itself.

The area forms part of the **Parco Nazionale dei Monti Sibillini**, where you can indulge several outdoor whims. Before going off into the Monti Sibillini, at least buy Kompass map No 666 (scale 1:50,000) of walking trails.

If you want to learn hang-gliding, contact Pro Delta (☎ 0743 82 11 56), Via delle Fate 3, in Norcia; it's open in summer only. Another school is Fly Castelluccio, but the office (☎ 0736 25 56 30) is based at Via Iannella 31, Ascoli Piceno, in the neighbouring region of Le Marche. A beginners course of five days will cost about L700,000.

This is also mountain-bike territory. To hire bikes you could try the Associazione Pian Grande (☎ 0743 81 72 79, 0743 81 70 22), Pian Grande di Castelluccio di Norcia, which is open mostly in the afternoons from Easter to October.

TERNI

postcode 05100 • pop 110,484

Terni is a major industrial city, virtually obliterated in WWII bombing raids and subsequently rebuilt. San Valentino was born here and was bishop of Terni until his martyrdom in 269. If you're using public transport you might need to pass through here on the way to the Valnerina, Norcia and the Monti Sibillini.

Terni's APT office (☎ 0744 42 30 47) is south of the main train station and just west of Piazza C Tacito at Viale Cesare Battisti

7, near Largo Don Minzoni. It is closed during the middle of the day and Sunday.

At Easter, Terni's theatres, churches and streets are given over to the Gospel and Soul Festival, a spin-off of the Umbria Jazz festival (see Perugia Special Events earlier in this chapter), which attracts international performers. Ask at the tourist office for details or try the main Umbria Jazz office in Perugia.

If you arrive in Terni by train and need to get to the bus station on Piazza Europa, or vice versa, catch local bus No 1 or 2.

Cascate delle Marmore

About 6km east of Terni, this waterfall was created by the Romans in 290 BC when they diverted the Velino river into the Nera river. These days the waterfall provides hydroelectric power and its flow is confined to certain times of the day. It is worth catching a bus to see it, particularly to witness the arrival of the water after it has been switched on. The falls operate on weekends year-round, usually for an hour or so before noon and again for a couple of hours in the late afternoon and early evening. They also flow for a few hours (usually afternoons around 4 pm) on weekdays from mid-March to the end of August. Ask at the Terni tourist office for the exact times that the water is turned on. The water is illuminated in the course of a sound-and-light show. Whenever the waterfall is switched on, the S79 road connecting Terni with Rieti resembles a car park as drivers stop to gawk at the spectacle. Local bus No 24 runs from the bus station on Piazza Europa to the falls. A number of short walking tracks around the falls allow you to get close up.

ORVIETO
postcode 05018 • pop 21,600

The phalanxes of high-season tourists who crowd into Orvieto are drawn first and foremost by the magnificent duomo, one of Italy's finest Gothic buildings. The town rests on top of a craggy cliff, pretty much in the same spot as its precursor, the Etruscan League city of Velsina. Although medieval Orvieto is the magnet, Etruscan tombs testify to the area's antiquity.

Orientation

Trains pull in at Orvieto Scalo, the modern, downhill extension of the town. From here you can catch bus No 1 up to the old town or the funivia to Piazza Cahen. From the funivia and bus station, walk straight along Corso Cavour, turning left into Via del Duomo to reach the duomo. There's plenty of parking space in Piazza Cahen and in several designated areas outside the old city walls.

Information

The APT office (☎ 0763 34 17 72), Piazza del Duomo 24, is open from 8.15 am to 1.50 pm and 4 to 7 pm Monday to Friday, from 10 am to 1 pm and 4 to 7 pm Saturday and from 10 am to noon and 4 to 6 pm Sunday.

If you plan to spend more than a day in Orvieto, and to see absolutely everything the town has to offer, consider buying the Orvieto Unica card (L20,000) which entitles you to free car parking at Orvieto Scalo train station, unlimited trips on the funivia and city buses, plus admission (entry only once) to the Cappella di San Brizio in the duomo, the Museo Claudio Faina e Civico and the Torre del Moro. The card is valid for one year.

There are several banks, all with Visa and MasterCard-friendly ATMs, on Piazza della Repubblica.

The post office is on Via Cesare Nebbia, off Corso Cavour, and is open from 8.10 am to 6 pm Monday to Saturday. There is an unstaffed Telecom Office at Corso Cavour 119, open from 8 am to 10 pm daily.

The hospital (☎ 0763 30 91) is on Piazza del Duomo. In a medical emergency, call ☎ 0763 34 02 44. The questura (☎ 0763 34 47 93) is on Piazza Cahen.

Duomo

Little can prepare you for the visual feast which is this most remarkable edifice. Started in 1290, the duomo was originally planned in the Romanesque style but, as work proceeded and architects changed, Gothic features were incorporated into the structure. The black and white marble banding of the main body of the church, reminiscent of other great churches you may already have seen in Tuscan cities

ORVIETO

PLACES TO STAY	7	Palazzo del Popolo
6 Albergo Corso	9	Chiesa di San Giovenale
12 Albergo Posta	10	Porta Maggiore
17 Albergo Duomo	11	Chiesa di Sant'Andrea
22 Albergo Virgilio	13	Consorzio Tutela Vino
		Orvieto Classico e Orvieto
PLACES TO EAT	14	Torre del Moro
8 Caffè Montanucci	15	Telecom Office
18 L'Archetto	16	Post Office
23 Cantina Foresi	19	Museo Archeologico
25 Trattoria La Pergola	20	Palazzo dei Papi; Museo
29 La Grotta del Funaro		dell'Opera del Duomo;
		Museo di Emilio Greco
OTHER	21	Duomo
1 Pozzo di San Patrizio	24	Museo Civico Faina
2 Bus Station		e Civico
3 La Rocca	26	APT Tourist Office
4 Funivia Station	27	Hospital
5 Questura (Police Station)	28	Chiesa di San Francesco

To Lago di Trasimeno & A1

Viale-G-Carducci

Piazza XXIX Marzo

Via-A-di-Cambio

Via-Pozzo-di-S-Patrizio

Piazza Cahen

Delle Piagge

To Orvieto Scala Train Station, Orvieto Camp Site & Lago di Corbara

Corso-Cavour

Via-Cavallotti

Via-dell'Olmo

Via-dei-Pecorelli

Via del Popolo

Piazza del Popolo

Piazza Fracassini

Via Malabranca

Via-Malabranca

Via-Magalotti

Piazza della Repubblica

Corso Cavour

Via del Duomo

Piazza Marconi

Via-S-Stefano

Via-Postierla

Via-della-Cava

Via-Ripa-Serancia

Via-Scalza

Via-L-Nebbia

Via-Maitani

Piazza del Duomo

Piazza Clementini

Piazza di Febei

Chiesa di San Francesco

To Viterbo

0   150   300 m

Minor Streets Not Depicted

Piazza Arigelo da-Orvieto

---

like Siena and Pisa, is overshadowed by the
rich rainbow colours of the façade. A harmonious blend of mosaic and sculpture, plain
stone and dazzling colour, it has been likened
to a giant outdoor altar screen.

Pope Urban IV ordered that the duomo be
built, after the so-called Miracle of Bolsena in
1263. A Bohemian priest who was passing
through the town of Bolsena (near Orvieto)
had his doubts about transubstantiation dis-
pelled when blood began to drip from the
Host onto the altar linen while he celebrated
mass. The linen was presented to Pope Urban
IV, in Orvieto at the time, who declared the
event a miracle and set the wheels in motion
for the construction of the duomo. He also declared the new feast day of Corpus Domini.

The building took 30 years to plan and
three centuries to complete. It was probably
started by Perugia's Fra Bevignate and continued by Lorenzo Maitani (responsible for

Firenze's duomo), Andrea Pisano, Nino
Pisano, Andrea Orcagna and Michele
Sammichelli.

The **façade** appears almost unrelated to
the main body of the church, and has greatly
benefited from painstaking restoration, completed in 1995. The three huge doorways are
separated by fluted columns and the gables
are decorated with mosaics that, although
mostly reproductions, seem to come to life
in the light of the setting sun and in the
evening under spotlights. The areas between
the doorways feature 14th century bas-
reliefs of scriptural scenes by Maitani and
his pupils, while the rose window is by Andrea
Orcagna. The great bronze doors, the work
of Emilio Greco, were added in the 1960s.

After the splendour of the exterior, the
interior may at first come as something of a
disappointment. Brace yourself, however: reopened in late 1996 after years of painstaking

restoration, Luca Signorelli's fresco cycle *The Last Judgment*, in the **Cappella di San Brizio** (right of the altar), shimmers with life. Signorelli began work on the series in 1499 and Michelangelo is said to have taken inspiration from it when he began the Cappella Sistina fresco of the same subject 40 years later. Indeed, to some, Michelangelo's masterpiece runs a close second to Signorelli's work. Not to be ignored in the cappella are ceiling frescoes by Fra Angelico. You need a ticket (L3000) to get in; pick it up at the APT office (or in the souvenir shop next to it if the APT office is closed).

The **Cappella del Corporale** houses the blood-stained linen, preserved in a silver reliquary decorated by artists of the Sienese school. The walls feature frescoes depicting the miracle, painted by Ugolino di Prete Ilario.

The duomo and Cappella del Corporale are open from 7.30 am to 12.45 pm and 2.30 to 7.15 pm daily in summer – the hours contract a little in winter. The Cappella di San Brizio is open from 10 am to 12.45 pm and 2.30 to 7.15 pm Monday to Friday and from 2.30 to 5.45 pm Sunday. Be aware, however, that the chapels close when Mass is being said.

Around the Duomo

Next to the duomo, in the **Palazzo dei Papi**, is the **Museo dell'Opera del Duomo**, which houses a clutter of religious relics from the duomo, as well as Etruscan antiquities and works by artists such as Simone Martini and the three Pisanos: Andrea, Nino and Giovanni. The museum has been closed for restoration for an eternity but its reopening was imminent at the time of writing. Check with the APT office for details. Also in the palazzo is the **Museo di Emilio Greco**, displaying a collection of modern pieces donated by the creator of the duomo's bronze doors. It's open from 10.30 am to 1 pm and

The Dove Has Landed

Every year in Orvieto, one 'lucky' dove is picked to star in the town's Pentecostal festivities. The poor thing must wonder how it, the symbol of peace, has managed to end up in what it must find to be an supremely disturbing activity. On Pentecost Sunday (Whit Sunday), the day on which the descent of the Holy Spirit is celebrated, the dove is strapped with red ribbons and tied to a large metal monstrance. This is then set atop the Chiesa di San Francesco, from which a steel cable loops down to a wooden structure erected in front of the duomo. On this is painted a replica of the frescoes depicting the Last Supper in one of the chapels of the duomo.

By noon everything is ready; the crowds have gathered in the Piazza del Duomo, waiting for the big moment of La Palombella (dove), as the spectacle is known. The dove and monstrance are launched down the steel cable in a kind of flightless flight and, when the straitjacketed bird arrives at the duomo, little flames appear on the heads of the apostles and Mother Mary in the Last Supper depiction (Mary wasn't actually at the supper but for the purposes of the feast day this anomaly is overlooked), and a salvo of mortars is let off.

Assuming our little winged friend survives without a heart attack (which it usually doesn't) it is solemnly handed over to the bishop in the Palazzo dei Papi. After much officious speech-making, the bishop then gives the bird to a newlywed couple who are instructed to look after the creature for the remainder of its (hopefully less traumatic) life.

The people of Orvieto have celebrated Pentecost Sunday in this manner since at least 1404. In the old days the whole thing was done inside the duomo. Then in 1846 it was decided to hold the event outdoors, out of respect for the Roman Lateran Council's stipulations forbidding the use of fireworks or flares inside churches. That edict was issued in 1725, so one can only speculate as to why the church authorities of Orvieto delayed its application by a mere 121 years!

3 to 7 pm Tuesday to Sunday (2 to 6 pm in winter). Admission costs L5000 or L8000 for a combined ticket including admission to the Pozzo di San Patrizio (see Other Things to See below). Around the corner, you can see Etruscan antiquities in the **Museo Archeologico**. It's open from 9 am to 7 pm Monday to Saturday, 9 am to 1 pm Sunday and admission costs L4000.

In the unlikely event that your thirst for Etruscan widgets isn't quenched, try the **Museo Claudio Faina e Civico** opposite the duomo. Most of the stuff in here was found in tombs dating back to the 6th century BC near Piazza Cahen. This museo keeps similar hours to the Museo Emilio Greco and admission is rather steep at L8000.

Other Things to See

Head north-west along Via del Duomo to Corso Cavour and you'll see the stout **Torre del Moro**; for L5000 you can climb all 250 steps for sweeping, pigeon-eye views of the city. Back on ground level, continue west to Piazza della Repubblica, where you'll stumble upon the 12th century **Chiesa di Sant'Andrea** and its curious octagonal bell tower. As with many Italian churches it was built over a Roman structure, which itself incorporated an earlier Etruscan building. You can see the ancient foundations in the crypt. The piazza, once Orvieto's Roman forum, is at the heart of what remains of the medieval city.

North of Corso Cavour, the 13th century Romanesque-Gothic **Palazzo del Popolo** presides over the piazza of the same name. At the north-western end of town is the 11th century **Chiesa di San Giovenale**, its interior brightened by 13th and 14th century frescoes.

Standing watch at the town's eastern-most tip is the 14th century **La Rocca**, part of which is now a public garden. Below the fortress, the **Pozzo di San Patrizio** is a well sunk in 1527 on the orders of Pope Clement VII. More than 60m deep, it is lined by two spiral staircases for water-bearing mules. It is open from 10 am to 7 pm daily (6 pm in winter) and admission costs L6000.

Special Events

Umbria Jazz Winter first took place in Orvieto in 1994 and is now well established on the global jazz calendar, attracting top international and Italian artists. It takes place from the end of December to early January. Ask at the APT office for a programme. For more details of Umbria Jazz festivals see under Special Events in the earlier Perugia section.

Places to Stay

You should have no trouble getting a room here during most of the year, but it is always a good idea to book ahead if you're planning to come over New Year, during Umbria Jazz Winter, in summer or at the weekend. Many hotels close in January and February. The closest camp sites are about 10km east of the town, on Lago di Corbara near Baschi. Try the *Orvieto* (☎ *0336 69 10 26*), which charges L8000/7000 per person/tent.

One of the best deals in town is at *Albergo Duomo* (☎ *0763 34 18 87, Via di Maurizio 7*), where singles/doubles cost L43,000/65,000 or L65,000/90,000 with bathroom; some rooms overlook the duomo. *Albergo Posta* (☎ *0763 34 19 09, Via L Signorelli 18*) has rooms costing L50,000/75,000 or L70,000/95,000 with bathroom. At *Albergo Corso* (☎*/fax 0763 34 20 20, Corso Cavour 343*), rooms with bathroom cost L100,000/140,000. The three star *Albergo Virgilio* (☎ *0763 34 18 82, fax 0763 34 37 97, Piazza del Duomo 5*) overlooks the duomo and charges L120,000/165,000 in the high season for rooms with bathroom.

Places to Eat

One of the most pleasant places for a snack is *Cantina Foresi* (*Piazza del Duomo*), a wine cellar with local wines and tables on the piazza, and good sandwiches. *Caffè Montanucci* (*Corso Cavour 21*) is a good place for a sandwich; pasta and other hot dishes start at L7000. Orvieto tends to be a little expensive on the food front, but you can't go wrong at the *Trattoria La Pergola* (*Via dei Magoni 9a*). A fine meal in the back garden will cost about L30,000 – try the *ombrichelli* or the melt-in-your-mouth *gnocchi al modo nostro*.

La Grotta del Funaro (*Via Ripa Seran-cia 41*) is an excellent but rather more pricey restaurant, virtually dug into the city walls. Expect to pay around L40,000 per person.

L'Archetto (*Piazza del Duomo 14*) serves mouth-watering gelati.

Getting There & Away

All buses depart from the station on Piazza Cahen. COTRAL buses connect the city with Viterbo (in Lazio) and Bagnoregio. ATC buses (☎ 0763 34 22 65) run to Baschi, Montecchio, Bolsena, Perugia and Todi. SIRA (☎ 0763 417 30 053) runs a daily service to Roma.

Trains run to Roma (1½ hours) and Firenze; change at Terontola for Perugia. The city is on the A1 and the S71 heads north to Lago di Trasimeno.

Getting Around

A century-old funivia connects Piazza Cahen with the Orvieto Scala train station, with carriages leaving every 15 minutes from 7.15 am to 8.30 pm daily (L1200 or L1500 including the bus from Piazza Cahen to the old town). Bus No 1 also runs up to the old town from the train station (L1200). Once in Orvieto, the easiest way to see the city is on foot, although ATC bus A connects Piazza Cahen with Piazza del Duomo and bus B runs to Piazza della Repubblica.

AROUND ORVIETO

The Etruscans produced wine in the district; the Romans continued the tradition and today the Orvieto Classico wines are among the country's most popular. You can visit 17 vineyards and sample the produce. Unfortunately you need a car, as ATC bus services to most small towns near the vineyards are irregular at best.

Grab a copy of *Andar per Vigne* (in Italian) from the APT office or pop into the Consorzio Tutela Vino Orvieto Classico e Orvieto (☎ 0763 34 37 90), Corso Cavour 36 in Orvieto, for details of its driving tour of the local vineyards.

Le Marche

Characterised by undulating countryside and peppered with quiet and seemingly untouched medieval towns and villages, Le Marche forms a narrow and little travelled band between the Appennini and Mar Adriatico. Now that Toscana has overpriced itself and Umbria is well on the road to doing the same, Le Marche is becoming increasingly popular with Italians and foreigners intent on buying old farmhouses for renovation. Most visitors come for the Renaissance splendour of Urbino or to catch a ferry from Ancona, but the rest of the region deserves at least a few days exploration.

In the south-west, the treeless Monti Sibillini form an impressive and, in parts, forbidding stretch of the Appennini, with plenty to keep even the most die-hard walker busy for days. Unfortunately, much of the coastline has been overdeveloped, with rows of characterless seaside hotels and the beaches swamped with umbrellas in summer, but some of the nooks and crannies outside Ancona and around Senigallia and Pesaro are among the best Mar Adriatico has to offer.

The small hill towns, however, are the region's most enchanting feature. Urbino and Macerata are the best known, but the countryside is littered with little towns and villages, often crowned by an ancient castle or medieval monastery. In the south, Ascoli Piceno boasts a historic centre of elegant squares and several grand monuments in a web of narrow, cobbled lanes.

The Piceni, one of Italy's earliest tribes, were the first inhabitants of the area, which later fell under Roman control. The region prospered in the Middle Ages and boomed during the 15th and 16th centuries, when the powerful Montefeltro family ruled Urbino. Le Marche attracted great Renaissance architects and painters, and Urbino gave the world the genius of Raphael and Donato Bramante.

Local cuisine draws inspiration from two sources. Inland mountain dishes comprise fish, beef, lamb, mushrooms and tartufo; nearer the sea, sole and prawns resembling

LE MARCHE

LE MARCHE

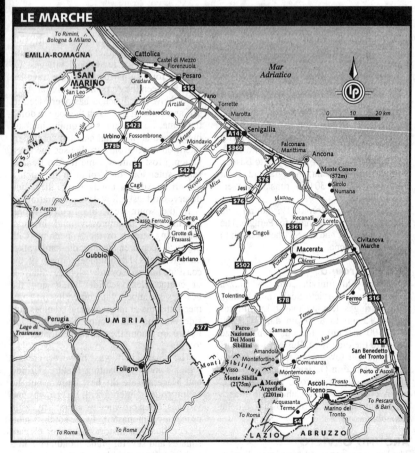

lobsters are popular. *Brodetto* is a tempting fish stew common along the coast, while *vincisgrassi*, a rich lasagne with meat sauce, chicken livers and tartufo nero, is popular inland. The region produces a small amount of wine, with one of the best drops being Vernaccia di Serrapetrona, a sparkling red.

The A14 and S16 (Via Adriatica) hug the coastline, while the inland roads are good and provide easy access to all towns. Inland bus services are frequent and regular trains ply the coast on the Bologna-Lecce line.

ANCONA
postcode 60100 • pop 100,000

Most people visit Ancona in order to head off elsewhere, namely by ferry to Greece, Turkey, Croatia or Albania (although the Albania services mostly remained suspended at the time of writing). A major point of trade with the east since the Middle Ages, Ancona remains the mid-Adriatico's largest port, doing a healthy business in tourists as well as road freight. The old centre was heavily bombed in WWII but it still has a few faded gems to offer the listless voyager waiting for a boat.

Orientation

All trains arrive at the main station on Piazza Nello e Carlo Rosselli and some continue 1.5km north to the ferry terminal, Stazione Marittima (or Molo Santa Maria). From Largo Dogana, near Stazione Marittima, walk uphill south to the central Piazza Roma and east to the city's grand Piazza Cavour. There are several hotels near Piazza Roma and a cluster around the main train station. What remains of the old town stretches in an arc around the waterfront.

Information

Tourist Offices The main APT office (☎ 071 35 89 91, fax 071 358 99 29, email aptancona@tin.it) is inconveniently placed at the eastern end of town at Via Thaon de Revel 4. In summer it is open from 8 am to 8 pm Monday to Saturday; opening hours are shorter during the winter. Branch offices at the train station and Stazione Marittima are open the same hours (the latter only from 1 June to 15 September). There is a useful Web site at www.comune.ancona.it.

Money There are currency exchange booths at the main train station and Stazione Marittima (where there is also an ATM which accepts Visa and MasterCard), but rates are not especially good.

Post & Communications The main post office is on Largo XXIV Maggio and is open from 8.15 am to 7 pm Monday to Saturday. There is a branch office on the corner of Via Ciriaco Pizzecolli and Via della Catena.

The main Telecom office is opposite the main train station and is open from 8 am to 9.45 pm. There is another office, open the same hours, at Piazza Roma 26.

Medical Services & Emergency In a medical emergency, call ☎ 071 20 20 95. The Ospedale Generale Regionale Umberto I (☎ 071 59 61) is at Largo Cappelli 1. The Farmacia Centrale, on the corner of Corso Giuseppe Mazzini and Via Gramsci, has an emergency night service.

The questura (☎ 071 2 28 81) is at Via Giovanni Gervasoni 19, south of the city centre.

Other Information CTS (☎ 071 207 09 63) has an office at Via XXIX Settembre 4/c. There's a laundrette at Corso Carlo Alberto 76.

Piazza del Plebiscito

This elegant piazza was medieval Ancona's main square, which has since been overtaken by grander, if less atmospheric, piazze in the modern town. La Prefettura, the former police station, is in a 15th century palace dominating the piazza and is noted for its beautiful courtyard. At its eastern end stands the baroque **Chiesa di San Domenico**, containing the superb *Crucifixion* by Titian and *Annunciation* by Guercino. Near the chiesa is the 13th century city gate, the **Arco di Garola** (Garola's Arch), also known as Porta San Pietro. Most of the buildings overlooking the piazza went up in the 18th century, largely replacing their medieval precursors.

Museums & Churches

From La Prefettura head north along Via Ciriaco Pizzecolli through the old city's ramparts to Palazzo Bosdari, which houses the **Pinacoteca Comunale** and **Galleria d'Arte Moderna** (☎ 071 222 50 41). The gallery displays works spanning some six centuries include pieces by Guercino, Carlo Crivelli and Lorenzo Lotto. Search out Titian's *Madonna and Saints*. The gallery is open from 9 am to 7 pm Tuesday to Saturday, from 9 am to 1 pm only on Monday and from 3 to 7 pm on Sunday. Admission costs L5000 (people aged under 20 or over 65 free).

A bit farther north along Via Ciriaco Pizzecolli and off to the right is **Chiesa di San Francesco delle Scale**, noteworthy for its 15th century Venetian-Gothic doorway by Orsini. Beyond the chiesa is Vanvitelli's **Chiesa del Gesù** and, nearby, the economics faculty of the city's 13th century university in the **Palazzo degli Anziani**.

At Via Ferretti 1 you'll find the **Museo**

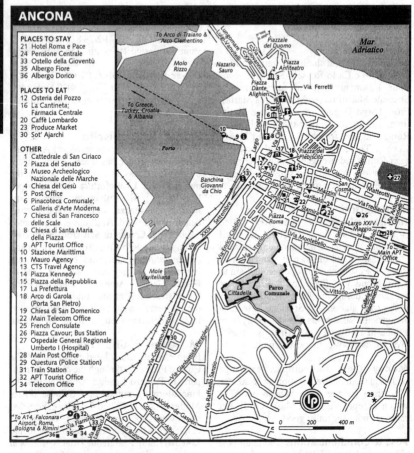

ANCONA

PLACES TO STAY
21 Hotel Roma e Pace
24 Pensione Centrale
33 Ostello della Gioventù
35 Albergo Fiore
36 Albergo Dorico

PLACES TO EAT
12 Osteria del Pozzo
16 La Cantineta;
   Farmacia Centrale
20 Caffè Lombardo
23 Produce Market
30 Sot' Ajarchi

OTHER
1 Cattedrale di San Ciriaco
2 Piazza del Senato
3 Museo Archeologico
   Nazionale delle Marche
4 Chiesa del Gesù
5 Post Office
6 Pinacoteca Comunale;
   Galleria d'Arte Moderna
7 Chiesa di San Francesco
   delle Scale
8 Chiesa di Santa Maria
   della Piazza
9 APT Tourist Office
10 Stazione Marittima
11 Mauro Agency
13 CTS Travel Agency
14 Piazza Kennedy
15 Piazza della Repubblica
17 La Prefettura
18 Arco di Garola
   (Porta San Pietro)
19 Chiesa di San Domenico
22 Main Telecom Office
25 French Consulate
26 Piazza Cavour; Bus Station
27 Ospedale General Regionale
   Umberto I (Hospital)
28 Main Post Office
29 Questura (Police Station)
31 Train Station
32 APT Tourist Office
34 Telecom Office

Archeologico Nazionale delle Marche (☎ 071 20 26 02), in the Palazzo Ferretti, which has been restored twice this century, once after WWII bombing and again after an earthquake in 1972. It includes impressive collections of Greek vases and artefacts from the Iron Age as well as Celtic and Roman remnants.

It is open from 8.30 am to 1.30 pm daily and opening hours are usually extended to 7.30 pm in summer. Admission costs L4000.

Cattedrale di San Ciriaco

Via Giovanni XXIII leads up Monte Guasco to the cattedrale on Piazzale del Duomo – the best spot for sweeping views of the city and across the port. The Romanesque cathedral was built on the site of a Roman temple and has Byzantine and Gothic features. The small **museum** (☎ 071 5 26 88) by the church holds the 4th century sarcophagus of Flavius Gorgonius, a masterpiece of early Christian art. The museum only opens for pre-booked guided tours (free, with donations welcome).

Waterfront

North of Piazza Dante Alighieri along the esplanade Lungomare Luigi Vanvitelli is the **Arco di Traiano** (Trajan's Arch), erected in 115. Vanvitelli's **Arco Clementino** (Clementine Arch), dedicated to Pope Clement XII, is farther on. South of Piazza Dante Alighieri you'll find the small Piazza Santa Maria and the disused, tumbledown **Chiesa di Santa Maria della Piazza**, which retains scraps of 5th and 6th century pavement mosaics.

Places to Stay

A new youth hostel, *Ostello della Gioventù* (π/fax 071 4 22 57, Via Lamaticci 7), has B&B for L23,000. It is closed from 1 to 4 pm. In the centre of town, *Pensione Centrale* (π 071 5 43 88, Via Marsala 10) has singles costing L38,000 and doubles for L90,000/60,000 with/without bathroom. At the *Albergo Dorico* (π 071 4 27 61, Via Flaminia 8) singles/doubles with bath cost L50,000/70,000. *Albergo Fiore* (π 071 4 33 90, Piazza Nello e Carlo Rosselli 24), a few doors down, offers similar accommodation for L40,000/70,000. At the three star *Hotel Roma e Pace* (π 071 20 20 07, fax 207 47 36, Via Leopardi 1), rooms with all mod cons cost L105,000/170,000 including breakfast.

Places to Eat

The *produce market* (Corso Giuseppe Mazzini 130) sells fresh fruit, vegetables and other food. *Osteria del Pozzo* (π 071 207 39 96, Via Bonda 2), just off Piazza del Plebiscito, serves good, reasonably priced food: a meal should cost around L30,000. *La Cantineta* (π 071 20 11 07, Via Gramsci 1/b) is a popular and simple trattoria near the old town centre. Pasta starts at L8000. For seafood (Ancona is a port after all), try *Sot' Ajarchi* (π 071 20 24 41, Via Gugliemo Marconi 93). A full meal will relieve you of about L35,000. *Caffè Lombardo* (Corso Giuseppe Mazzini 59) is a pleasant spot, with tables spilling out onto the street.

Getting There & Away

Air Scheduled flights from London, Roma, Milano and Torino, as well as the odd charter flight (most of them from Russia and the Ukraine), land at Falconara airport (π 071 5 62 57), 10km north-west of Ancona. In summer there are also flights to Olbia on Sardegna.

Bus Most provincial and regional buses depart from Piazza Cavour. COTRAN (π 071 20 27 66) and Reni (π 071 804 65 04) run buses to provincial towns such as Loreto, Recanati and Osimo. Other companies run buses to Macerata, Senigallia, Fano and Pesaro (the last three run by Bucci). Bucci (π 071 79 22 737) also runs a bus to Urbino at 2 pm daily.

Train Ancona is on the Bologna-Lecce line and regular services link it with Milano, Torino, Roma, Bologna, Lecce and most main stops in between. For information, call π 147 88 80 88.

Car & Motorcycle Ancona is on the A14, which links Bologna with Bari. The S16 coastal road runs parallel to the autostrada and is a more pleasant (toll-free) alternative. The S76 connects Ancona with Perugia and Roma.

Boat Ferry operators have booths at Stazione Marittima. Timetables are subject to change, prices fluctuate with the season, and some lines come and go – check at the APT office or at the terminal. Most lines offer discounts on return fares, and the boats are generally roll-on, roll-off car ferries. There is a L5000 port tax added to fares to Albania and Croatia and L10,000 for Greece. Prices listed here are for one-way deck class in the high season:

Adriatica
    (π 071 20 49 15) Adriatica runs two ferries a week to Split in Croatia (L80,000) and Durrës in Albania (services mostly suspended; L155,000).
Anek
    (π 071 207 23 46) This company runs five ferries a week to Igoumenitsa and Patras (L116,000) and charges L200,000 for a car.
Jadrolinija
    (π 071 20 43 05) This operator runs services gularly to Zadar (L69,000) and Split (L76,000).

Minoan Lines
(☎ 071 20 17 08) This company operates about six ferries a week to Patras (L124,000). Most services stop during the winter.

Strintzis Lines
(☎ 071 207 10 68) This operator runs a 32 hour service to Patras via Corfu and Igoumenitsa on Saturday and Sunday, and a 24 hour direct service to Patras on Monday, Tuesday and Wednesday (L98,000 to all destinations).

Superfast
(☎ 071 207 02 40, 071 20 20 33) Superfast operates a daily ferry to Patras, departing at 7 pm and taking 19 hours (L148,000). It charges L208,000 for a small car and offers a 30% discount on a return booking.

Other companies that operate in summer include Dalmacija Express Kvarner and the SEM Maritime Company, both of which have services to Croatia and operate through the Mauro agency, Via della Loggia 6 (☎ 071 5 52 18), which also has a booth at Stazione Marittima (☎ 071 20 40 90).

Getting Around

Conerobus' bus J runs roughly every hour from the main train station to the airport from 6.05 am to 8.30 pm Monday to Saturday. The bus labelled 'Ancona-Aereoporto' does the trip during August and on Sunday and public holidays.

There are about six Conerobus services, including No 1 which connects the main train station with Stazione Marittima and Piazza Cavour (look for the bus stop with the big sign displaying Centro and Porto).

For a taxi, call ☎ 071 4 33 21.

AROUND ANCONA
Loreto

The story goes that angels transferred the house of the Virgin Mary from Palestine to this spot towards the end of the 13th century. Why the angels should have done such a thing is unclear (historians may be able to link this 'miracle' to the pillaging of the Holy Land that occurred during the crusades), but a church was soon built over the site and later expanded to become today's **Santuario della Santa Casa**, an important site for pilgrims. Restoration began in 1468

and additions have been made ever since. The house itself, whatever its origin, is beneath the dome inside the sanctuary and is open all day. Loreto lies about 28km south of Ancona and can be reached easily by bus. Loreto train station (Bologna-Lecce line) is a few kilometres away, but shuttle buses connect it with the town centre.

Beaches

If you are hanging about Ancona for any length of time, head about 20km south along the coast road (take a bus from Piazza Cavour) for **Sirolo** and **Numana**, below Monte Conero. These beaches are among the more appealing on the Mar Adriatico coastline, although they fill up in summer.

URBINO
postcode 61029 • pop 6000

Urbino is the jewel of Le Marche and one of the best-preserved and most beautiful hill towns in Italy. It enjoyed a period of great splendour under the Montefeltro family starting in the 12th century and reached its zenith under Duca Federico da Montefeltro, who hired some of the greatest Renaissance artists and architects to construct and decorate his palace and other parts of the town. The architects Donato Bramante, born in Urbino, and Francesco di Giorgio were among his favourites. Painters in particularly good grace with the duke included Piero della Francesca, who developed his theories on mathematical perspective in Urbino, Paolo Uccello, Justus of Ghent and Giovanni Santi (the father of Raffaello d'Urbino, the great Raphael, who was born in the city).

After Duca Federico lost his right eye and broke his nose in a tournament, he insisted on being portrayed only in profile. The most famous result of this caprice was executed in 1466 by Piero della Francesca and hangs in the Galleria degli Uffizi in Firenze.

The town can be a pain to reach by public transport, but should not be missed. The area to the north, particularly the winding road to San Marino and on into Emilia-Romagna, is a treat and there are plenty of hotels in the small towns along the way.

Orientation

Buses arrive at Piazza Mercatale at the walled city's western edge. From there it's a short walk up Via G Mazzini to Piazza della Repubblica and then back south to Via Vittorio Veneto for Piazza Duca Federico and the sprawling Piazza del Rinascimento. Drivers are most likely to arrive at Piazzale Roma at the city's northern edge, where cars can be parked free of charge. Via Raffaello connects Piazzale Roma with Piazza della Repubblica.

Information

The IAT office (☎ 0722 26 13, fax 0722 24 41, email iat@comune.urbino.ps.it), Piazza Duca Federico 35, is open from 9 am to 1 pm Monday to Saturday. From April to September it's also open from 3 to 6 pm and from 9 am to 1 pm on Sunday morning.

There are several banks around town.

The Banca Nazionale di Lavoro on Via Vittorio Veneto has an ATM.

The main post office is at Via Bramante 18. It's open from 8.30 am to 6.30 pm Monday to Saturday. The Telecom office, at Via Puccinotti 4, is open from 8 am to 10 pm. There's another office, open the same hours, at Piazza di San Francesco 1.

First aid (☎ 0722 30 12 72) is available at the Ospedale Civile (☎ 0722 30 11) on Via Bonconte da Montefeltro, north of the city centre. There is a pharmacy at Piazza della Repubblica 9. The questura (☎ 0722 35 181) is on Piazza Mercatale.

Palazzo Ducale

The grand residence of Urbino's ruling dynasty was completed in 1482 and still dominates the heights of Urbino. Elegant and balanced, it is the most complete and refined early Renaissance palace in Italy. Dalmatian

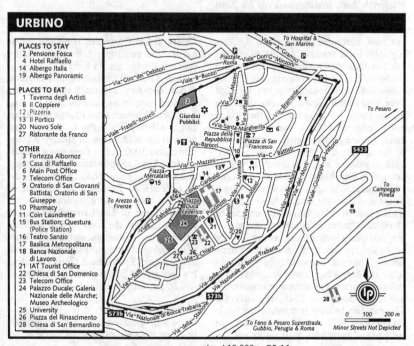

URBINO

PLACES TO STAY
2 Pensione Fosca
4 Hotel Raffaello
14 Albergo Italia
19 Albergo Panoramic

PLACES TO EAT
1 Taverna degli Artisti
8 Il Coppiere
12 Pizzeria
13 Il Portico
20 Nuovo Sole
27 Ristorante da Franco

OTHER
3 Fortezza Albornoz
5 Casa di Raffaello
6 Main Post Office
7 Telecom Office
9 Oratorio di San Giovanni Battista; Oratorio di San Giuseppe
10 Pharmacy
11 Coin Laundrette
15 Bus Station; Questura (Police Station)
16 Teatro Sanzio
17 Basilica Metropolitana
18 Banca Nazionale di Lavoro
21 IAT Tourist Office
22 Chiesa di San Domenico
23 Telecom Office
24 Palazzo Ducale; Galeria Nazionale delle Marche; Museo Archeologico
25 University
26 Palazza del Rinascimento
28 Chiesa di San Bernardino

To Hospital & San Marino

To Pesaro

To Campeggio Pineta

To Arezzo & Firenze

To Fano & Pesaro Superstrada, Gubbio, Perugia & Roma

Minor Streets Not Depicted

0   100   200 m

architect Luciano Laurana drew up the original design, but several masters had a hand in its construction, including the ruling Duca Federico who commissioned it. From Corso Garibaldi you get the best view of the complex with its unusual **Facciata dei Torricini**, a three storey loggia in the form of a triumphal arch, flanked by circular towers. The palace now houses the Galleria Nazionale delle Marche, a formidable art collection, and the less inspiring Museo Archeologico.

A monumental staircase, one of Italy's first, leads to the *piano nobile* (literally 'noble floor') and the Ducal Apartments. The best-preserved room is Duca Federico's **Studiolo**. Intricately worked intarsia (inlaid wood) decorates the entire room, creating illusory perspectives and depicting books which look real, cupboard doors that seem to be hanging open and even a letter that appears to be lying in a desk drawer.

Among the paintings in the **Galleria Nazionale delle Marche**, look out for Piero della Francesca's masterpiece, *Flagellation*, and *The Ideal City*, long held to be by Piero but now attributed to Laurana. Another highlight is the remarkable portrait of Federico and his son Guidobaldo, attributed to the Spanish artist Pedro Berruguete. The art collection, which continues on the 2nd floor, also features several works, including a large number of drawings, by the Urbino artist Federico Barocci. The mildly interesting **Museo Archeologico**, on the far side of the Cortile d'Onore, the palace courtyard, is worth a look – you may as well as admission is included in the L8000 ticket.

The palazzo is open from 9 am to 7 pm Tuesday to Saturday and 9 am to 2 pm on Sunday and Monday, although times can be extended or restricted depending on the season. A booking system introduced in 1997 for peak tourist periods also means that at certain times of the year (particularly between February and May when school groups visit the palazzo) you need to make a reservation for admission, staged at 20-minute intervals. This can only be done in person at the booking office (☎ 0722 32 90 57), which is in the palazzo and open from 8.30 am to 5.40 pm

Tuesday to Saturday and 8.30 am to 12.40 pm on Sunday and Monday. If in doubt, ask at the ticket office or IAT office for details.

Basilica Metropolitana

Rebuilt in the early 19th century in neoclassical style after Francesco di Giorgio Martini's original Renaissance building was destroyed by an earthquake, the interior of Urbino's basilica commands greater interest than its austere façade. Particularly memorable is Federico Barocci's *Last Supper*. The basilica's **Museo Albani** contains further paintings, including Andrea da Bologna's *Madonna del Latte* (Madonna Breastfeeding), along with an engaging assortment of articles collected from Urbino's churches over the centuries. The basilica is next to the Palazzo Ducale and is open from 9.30 am to noon and 2.30 to 6 pm daily (although at the time of writing it was closed for restoration). Admission costs L3000.

Churches & Oratories

Opposite the Palazzo Ducale, the medieval **Chiesa di San Domenico** is notable for its lunette, the panel above the 15th century doorway, by Luca della Robbia.

On Via Barocci the 14th century **Oratorio di San Giovanni Battista** features brightly coloured frescoes by Lorenzo and Giacomo Salimbeni. It's open from 10 am to 12.30 pm and 3 to 5.30 pm Monday to Saturday and from 10 am to 12.30 pm on Sunday. Admission costs L3000. A few steps away, the **Oratorio di San Giuseppe** (same opening hours and admission price) boasts a stucco *Nativity* by Federico Brandani. At the time of writing it was closed for restoration.

The **Chiesa di San Bernardino**, outside the city walls to the south-east along Viale Giuseppe di Vittorio, houses the mausoleum of the Dukes of Urbino, designed by Donato Bramante and Francesco di Giorgio Martini. It's open from 8.30 am to 12.30 pm and 2.30 to 6.30 pm daily. Admission is free.

Casa di Raffaello

If you want to have a look at where Raphael first saw the light of day, the house of his birth (☎ 0722 32 01 05) is north of Piazza della Repubblica at Via Raffaello 57. In spring and summer it is open from 9 am to 1 pm and 3 to 7 pm Monday to Saturday and from 10 am to 1 pm on Sunday. From 1 November to 5 March it's open from 9 am to 2 pm Monday to Saturday and from 10 am to 1 pm on Sunday. Admission costs L5000.

Courses

The university offers an intensive course in language and culture for foreigners during August at a cost of L660,000 and it can arrange accommodation for L300,000 for the month. For information call ☎ 0722 30 52 50 or 0722 22 89 (mornings only) or write to the Segreteria dell'Università, Via Saffi 2, Urbino 61029. You can get details and make a booking from March to 19 July.

Places to Stay

The IAT office holds a full list of private rooms. *Campeggio Pineta* (☎ 0722 47 10), the only camp site, is 2km east of the city in San Donato. At *Pensione Fosca* (☎ 0722 32 96 22, Via Raffaello 61), singles/doubles cost L40,000/60,000. *Albergo Italia* (☎ 0722 27 01, Corso Garibaldi 32) enjoys a good position behind the Palazzo Ducale, but at the time of writing it was under restoration; call to see if it's reopened. *Albergo Panoramic* (☎ 0722 26 00, Strada Nazionale 192), to the east of the city walls, has rooms starting at L60,000/80,000 but it's awkward to reach without your own transport. Heading up the scale in price, *Hotel Raffaello* (☎ 0722 47 84, fax 0722 32 85 40, Via Santa Margherita 40) charges L100,000/150,000 for singles and L150,000/200,000 for doubles in the low/high season.

Places to Eat

Don't miss the *strozzapreti al pesto*, available in most restaurants; these worm-like shreds of pasta were designed to choke priests – sounds horrid but they're delicious. There are numerous *bars* around Piazza della Repubblica and near the Palazzo Ducale that sell good *panini* (filled rolls). Try the *pizzeria* (*Via Vittorio Veneto 19*) for takeaway pizza

by the slice. For cheap Chinese food head to *Nuovo Sole* (☎ 0722 25 21, Via F Budassi 64). For *bruschetta*, salads and light meals try *Il Portico* (☎ 0722 27 22, Via G Mazzini 7), which is both a bookshop and *osteria* (snack bar). *Ristorante da Franco* (☎ 0722 24 92, Via del Poggio 1), just off Piazza Rinascimento and next to the university, has a self-service section where lunch costs less than L20,000.

Taverna degli Artisti (☎ 0722 26 76, Via Bramante 52) serves good pasta and meat dishes; a meal will set you back around L30,000, less if you choose one of their giant pizzas, served on huge wooden slabs and big enough to feed an army. For more elegant dining, head for *Il Coppiere* (☎ 0722 32 23 26, Via Santa Margherita 1). A meal in this cosy 1st floor restaurant will cost around L50,000.

Entertainment

The *Teatro Sanzio* hosts a variety of drama and concerts, particularly from July to September. Pick up a brochure at the IAT office.

La Festa del Duca (The Festival of Dukes) takes place on the third Sunday in August. The town's streets become the setting for a costume procession and the re-enactment of a tournament on horseback in celebration of the splendid era of Duca Federico.

Getting There & Around

Two Pesaro-based companies, Bucci (☎ 0721 3 24 01) and SAPUM (☎ 0721 2 23 33), run up to 13 services daily between Urbino and Pesaro (SAPUM's are more direct). Bucci also runs two buses a day to Roma and services to Ancona and Arezzo. Busturs has services to San Marino and Rimini in summer only (check with the IAT office for details).

Take the bus to Pesaro to pick up trains (see Pesaro Getting There & Away later in this chapter for details).

An autostrada and the S423 connect Urbino with Pesaro, and the S73b connects the town with the S3 for Roma.

Most motor vehicles are banned from the walled city. Small shuttle buses operate in both directions between Piazza Mercatale and Piazza della Repubblica. Taxis (☎ 0722 25 50) operate from Piazza della Repubblica and Piazza Mercatale. There are car parks outside the city gates. Note that there's no parking on Piazzala Roma on Saturday morning as it's market day.

AROUND URBINO
San Leo
Machiavelli, who knew a thing or two about such matters, thought the fortress of San Leo, about 60km north-west of Urbino, 'quite impregnable'. He was probably right – it is difficult to see how the walls perched defiantly on a high outcrop of stone could be assailed.

Part of the Montefeltro duchy, San Leo was first fortified by the Romans, who erected a temple to Jupiter here. The temple was later replaced by the 12th century **duomo**, and nearby you can also admire the pre-Romanesque **pieve**, an 11th century basilica. The Papal States converted the fortress into a prison and the Fascists used it as an aircraft-spotting post during WWII.

Without your own transport, San Leo is a little difficult to reach. Although it is in Le Marche, the most reliable bus route is actually from Rimini, in Emilia-Romagna.

PESARO
postcode 61100 • pop 90,000
Like other resort towns on the Mar Adriatico, Pesaro offers an expanse of beach, the remains of a medieval centre and not much else. In mid-summer you can't move for the crowds, and out of season the waterfront has a sad air about it – maybe it's all the tacky concrete hotel blocks boarded up for the winter. It is, however, a handy transport junction and the best place to get a bus for Urbino, an hour's drive inland.

Orientation
The train station is south-west of the centre, away from the beach. From the station, walk along Viale del Risorgimento, through Piazza Lazzarini and continue to Piazza del Popolo, the town's main square. Via Rossini takes you to Piazzale della Libertà and the waterfront.

Information
Tourist Offices The IAT office (☎ 0721 6 93 41), on Piazzale della Libertà, is open from 9 am to 1 pm and 3.30 to 7.30 pm daily in summer (July to September) and from 9 am to 1 pm Monday to Friday (also from 3.30 to 6.30 pm on Tuesday and Thursday) October to June.

Money There are plenty of banks around town. The Banca Nazionale del Lavoro on Piazza del Popolo has an ATM.

Post & Communications The main post office is on Piazza del Popolo and opens from 8.15 am to 7.40 pm Monday to Saturday.

The Telecom office is on Piazza Matteotti, south-east of Piazza del Popolo, and is open from 7 am to 11 pm daily in summer (the hours are reduced in the low season).

Laundry There's an Onda Blu laundrette at Piazzale I Maggio 12.

Medical Services & Emergency In a medical emergency try *pronto soccorso* on ☎ 0721 3 29 57 The Ospedale San Salvatore (☎ 0721 36 11) is on Piazzale Albani.

The questura (☎ 0721 38 61 11) is at Via Giordano Bruno 5.

Things to See
The 15th century **Palazzo Ducale**, dominating Piazza del Popolo, housed the ruling Della Rovere family. Today it houses bureaucracy and is closed to the public. The splendid windows that grace its façade are by Domenico Rosselli.

Head north-west along Corso XI Settembre for Via Toschi Mosca and the town's **Musei Civici**, which also contains the **Museo delle Ceramiche** and **Pinacoteca**. The production of ceramics has long been a speciality of Pesaro and the museum has a worthy collection, while the pinacoteca's prize is Giovanni Bellini's magnificent altarpiece depicting the *Coronation of the Virgin*. The complex is open from 8.30 am to 1.30 pm Tuesday to Sunday and admission costs L8000. Your ticket is also valid for the

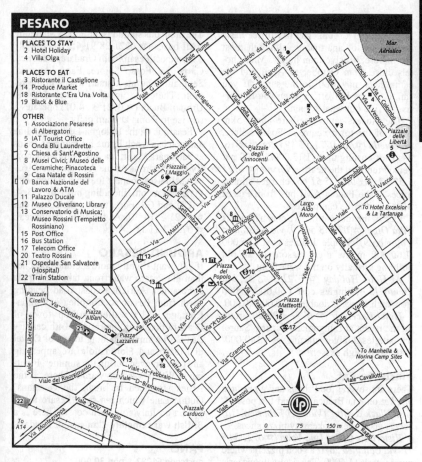

PESARO

PLACES TO STAY
2 Hotel Holiday
4 Villa Olga

PLACES TO EAT
3 Ristorante il Castiglione
14 Produce Market
18 Ristorante C'Era Una Volta
19 Black & Blue

OTHER
1 Associazione Pesarese
  di Albergatori
5 IAT Tourist Office
6 Onda Blu Laundrette
7 Chiesa di Sant'Agostino
8 Musei Civici; Museo delle
  Ceramiche; Pinacoteca
9 Casa Natale di Rossini
10 Banca Nazionale del
   Lavoro & ATM
11 Palazzo Ducale
12 Museo Oliveriano; Library
13 Conservatorio di Musica;
   Museo Rossini (Tempietto
   Rossiniano)
15 Post Office
16 Bus Station
17 Telecom Office
20 Teatro Rossini
21 Ospedale San Salvatore
   (Hospital)
22 Train Station

Casa Natale di Rossini at Via Rossini 34.
The composer Rossini was born in Pesaro
in 1792 and this small museum contains
various personal effects and his spinet. It's
open from 8.30 am to 1.30 pm Tuesday to
Sunday.

The **Chiesa di Sant'Agostino** on Corso
XI Settembre features intricate 15th century
inlaid-wood choir stalls. The modest
Museo Oliveriano on Via Mazza contains
archaeological finds from the area, including a child's tomb from the Iron Age, com-

plete with miniature utensils such as eating
implements. Apply for admission at the adjoining **library**, which has a collection of
ancient coins, manuscripts and medals. The
museum is open from 4.30 to 7.30 pm Monday to Saturday from 1 July to 15 September and from 9 am to noon only on the same
days for the rest of the year.

Places to Stay

The town's hotel association, the Associazione
Pesarese di Albergatori (☎ 0721 6 79 59),

has an office at Viale Marconi 57/1 and will help you find a room. The IAT office has a lengthy list of apartments, although most are more expensive than hotels. Many hotels close from October to April and the camp sites may well do the same. If you can, go to the IAT office when you first arrive to find out what's open.

The closest camp sites are about 5km south of the town centre at Fosso Sejore. *Marinella* (*☎/fax 0721 5 57 95*), on the S16, has sites costing up to L13,000/26,500 per person/tent and the nearby *Norina* (*☎ 0721 5 57 92, fax 0721 5 51 65*) charges similar prices. Take Fano's AMI bus from Piazza Matteotti for the camp sites.

One of the more attractive cheap hotels is *Villa Olga* (*☎ 0721 3 50 29, Via Cristoforo Colombo 9*). Simple doubles cost L55,000 (L60,000 in the high season) in an old building virtually on the waterfront.

At *Hotel Holiday* (*☎ 0721 3 48 51, Via Trento 159*), singles cost L50,000/65,000 (low/high season), doubles L70,000/90,000.

Hotel Excelsior (*☎ 0721 3 27 20*), right on the beach at Lungomare Nazario Sauro, has singles/doubles starting at L140,000/180,000 in high season.

Places to Eat

There are several food shops and a *produce market* on Via Branca, behind the post office. *Black & Blue* (*Viale XI Febbraio 11a*) serves good cheap takeaway pizza slices.

Ristorante C'Era Una Volta (*☎ 0721 3 09 11, Via Cattaneo 26*) is a good pizzeria where pizzas start at L6000. The ristorante/pizzeria *La Tartaruga* (*☎ 0721 3 41 23, Viale Trieste 31*) serves typical local fare as well as the standard pizza menu and a full meal will set you back around L40,000. If you're prepared to part with about L60,000, you could eat at *Ristorante il Castiglione* (*☎ 0721 6 49 34, Via Trento 148*), a posh place with the air of a small castle set in rambling gardens.

Entertainment

In honour of Rossini, the town hosts a series of concerts each August at the *Teatro Rossini* on Piazza Lazzarini.

Getting There & Around

The main bus station is on Piazza Matteotti. AMI buses (*☎ 0721 28 91 45, 0721 37 48 62*) connect Pesaro with Gradara, Cattolica, Carpegna, Fosso Sejore, Fano, Ancona, Senigallia and most small towns in the region. There are up to 10 buses daily to Urbino. Bucci (*☎ 0721 3 24 01*) operates a service to Roma at 6 am daily.

Pesaro is on the Bologna-Lecce train line and you can reach Roma by changing trains at Falconara Marittima, just before Ancona. By car, Pesaro is on the A14 and the S16.

AMI buses connect the train station with Piazza Matteotti, including bus Nos 1, 3, 4, 5, CD and CS. For a taxi in the centre call *☎ 0721 3 14 30*. At the train station call *☎ 0721 3 11 11*.

AROUND PESARO

If you want slightly more secluded beaches than the Pesaro waterfront, take the Strada Panoramica Adriatica coast road heading north from Pesaro to Cattolica in Emilia-Romagna. The walled, hilltop town of **Gradara** boasts an impressive 14th century castle. The smaller fishing towns of **Castel di Mezzo** and **Fiorenzuola** are appealing and quieter, even during the summer. Fighting in WWII was heavy around here, as the Allies struggled to break the Germans' Gothic Line which ran from Pesaro to La Spezia on Italy's western coast. There is a **British war cemetery** 2km east of Gradara.

FANO
postcode 61032 • pop 30,000

Only 12km south-east of Pesaro, Fano is a fairly sedate beach resort that nevertheless fills up in the summer rush. The ancient village took its name from the Fanum, the Temple of Fortune, and its pleasant historic centre retains several reminders of its Roman and medieval past, warranting a brief stop if you're passing through.

Information

The IAT office (*☎ 0721 80 35 34*) is at Viale Cesare Battisti 10. There are other tourist offices (open in summer only) in the smaller nearby towns of Torrette (☎ 0721 88 47 79), at Via Boscomarina 10, and Marotta (☎ 0721 9 65 91), at Viale Colombo 31.

Things to See

A **triumphal arch** built in 2 AD for Augustus still stands despite losing part of its masonry to surrounding buildings over the centuries. Sections of the Roman and medieval **walls** also remain. The 16th century **Corte Malatestiano** contains a museum with works produced by local artists over the centuries.

Places to Stay

Cheap accommodation is in short supply along this stretch of coastline, making Pesaro a more economical base. Five *camp sites* at the southern end of Fano's seashore all charge L7500/10,500 per person and L14,000/18,500 per tent in low/high season. Try the *Fano* camp site (☎ 0721 80 26 52), or pick up the accommodation list from the IAT office.

AROUND FANO

If you're staying for a while, a couple of excursions inland are worth considering. **Mondavio** is a charming Renaissance town about 35km south of Fano. Several buses run from Fano. If driving, take the S16 south to Marotta, from where you head inland to San Michele; Mondavio is a few kilometres to the north.

Some 38km south-west of Fano is **Mombaroccio**, a pleasant 15th century hill town. The main attraction is the view from the old castle walls. Take the S3 west from Fano and turn north at Calcinelli.

SENIGALLIA

postcode 60019 • pop 30,000

Senigallia's aptly named Spiaggia di Velluto (Velvet Beach) is reputedly one of the best lidos on the Mar Adriatico.

The IAT office (☎ 071 792 27 25), at Piazzale Morandi 2, is between the beach and the train station.

Apart from sea and sand, the main draw is the **Rocca Roveresca**, whose four stout, crenellated towers make it hard to miss.

Built for Duca Federico da Montefeltro's son-in-law, its plush Renaissance interior makes a visit well worthwhile if you have a spare hour or two.

Places to Stay

If you're having trouble finding a room, which in summer would come as no surprise, try the Associazione Alberghi e Turismo (☎ 071 6 53 43) at Viale IV Novembre 2.

At *Helios* camp site (☎ 071 6 91 69, Lungomare Italia 3b), pitches start at L8000/25,000 per person/tent in high season. *Liana* (☎ 071 6 52 06, Lungomare Leonardo da Vinci 54) charges similar prices. At *Albergo del Sole* (☎ 071 6 34 67, Lungomare Alighieri 118), on the waterfront, singles/doubles start at L65,000/75,000.

Getting There & Away

All buses stop at the main train station which is in the town centre on Via Rafaele Sanzio. Bucci buses operate along the S16 coastal road to Ancona, Fano and Pesaro. Plenty of trains also service on the same stretch.

GROTTE DI FRASASSI

In September 1971 a team of climbers stumbled across an aperture in the hill country around Genga, about 50km south-west of Ancona, and decided to drop in. What they found were the biggest known caves in Europe containing a spectacle of stalactites and stalagmites, some of them 1.4 million years old.

Three years later they were opened to the public, with a 1.5km-long trail carefully laid through five chambers. **Ancona Abyss**, the first chamber, is almost 200m high, 180m wide and 120m long, and could easily accommodate Milano's duomo.

Tour groups are taken through the caves every couple of hours. Tours last about an hour and cost L16,000. The ticket area and car park are just outside San Vittore Terme, and the entrance to the caves is 600m farther west. For L50,000, you can get rigged up in caving gear to explore the remaining chambers, while for L70,000 you can have a more exciting and challenging experience. This has to be booked well in advance by calling the

Consorzio Grotte di Frasassi (☎ 0732 9 00 80, toll free ☎ 800 01 38 28). Should you need to stay overnight nearby, there are a couple of hotels in San Vittore Terme and Genga.

To reach the caves, take the S76 from Ancona, or the train for Genga (Roma-Ancona line), about 2km from the caves' ticket area; a shuttle bus runs from the train station in summer.

MACERATA
postcode 62100 • pop 42,000
This bustling provincial capital is one of Italy's better kept secrets. Situated atop a rise between the Potenza river valley to the north and the Chienti river in the south, Macerata was established in the 10th century. It is as impressive as many Umbrian and Tuscan hill towns but lacks the tourists, and makes a good base for exploring the surrounding countryside – some of the region's most picturesque.

Orientation
Piazza della Libertà is the focal point of the medieval city, contained within the 14th century walls above the sprawl of the more modern development. Buses arrive at the huge Giardini Diaz,which is a stone's throw from the Porta Romana (the main gate) and the IAT office. A shuttle bus links the train station, which is west of the city centre, to Piazza della Libertà. There is parking virtually right around the walls and you may even find a space on one of the main squares inside the old city.

Information
The main IAT office (☎ 0733 23 04 49, fax 0733 23 44 87) is at Via Garibaldi 87, above the Standa supermarket, and is open from 9 am to 1 pm Monday to Friday and also from 3 to 6 pm on Tuesday and Thursday. A second office (☎ 0733 23 48 07), Piazza della Libertà 12, is open all day during the summer and the same hours as the main IAT office during the rest for the year.

The post office is at Piazza Oberdan 1-3 and is open from 8 am to 7 pm Monday to Saturday. The Telecom office at Galleria del Commercio 33 is open from 8 am to 7 pm daily.

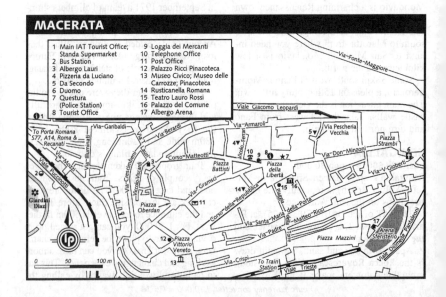

MACERATA

1 Main IAT Tourist Office; Standa Supermarket	9 Loggia dei Mercanti
2 Bus Station	10 Telephone Office
3 Albergo Lauri	11 Post Office
4 Pizzeria da Luciano	12 Palazzo Ricci Pinacoteca
5 Da Secondo	13 Museo Civico; Museo delle Carrozze; Pinacoteca
6 Duomo	14 Rusticanella Romana
7 Questura (Police Station)	15 Teatro Lauro Rossi
8 Tourist Office	16 Palazzo del Comune
	17 Albergo Arena

Things to See

Piazza della Libertà is adorned with one of the city's finest buildings, the 16th century Renaissance **Loggia dei Mercanti**, built by the Farnese pope, Paul III. In the courtyard of the **Palazzo del Comune** are archaeological remains from Helvia Recina, a Roman town 5km north of Macerata, which was destroyed by the Goths.

Corso della Repubblica, the main boulevard where locals take their late-afternoon strolls, spills into Piazza Vittorio Veneto. Here, in the same building, you will find the **Museo Civico**, the **Museo delle Carrozze** and the **Pinacoteca**, with a good collection of early Renaissance works, including a 15th century *Madonna* by Carlo Crivelli. The complex is open from 9 am to 1 pm and 5 to 7.30 pm Tuesday to Saturday, from 5 to 7.30 pm on Monday and from 9 am to 1 pm on Sunday. Admission is free.

The rather ordinary baroque **duomo** is unfinished and worth visiting only if you have some spare time.

Places to Stay & Eat

At *Albergo Lauri* (☎ *0733 23 23 76, Via T Lauri 6)*, singles/doubles start at L55,000/ 100,000. *Albergo Arena* (☎ *0733 23 09 31, Vicolo Sferisterio 16)* has singles starting at L60,000/75,000 and doubles from L90,000/ 120,000 in the low/high season.

Several pizzerie, such as *Rusticanella Romana (Corso della Repubblica 13)* and *Pizzeria da Luciano* (☎ *0733 26 01 29, Vicolo Ferrari 12)*, serve quick takeaway food. One of the better restaurants in town is *Da Secondo* (☎ *0733 26 09 12, Via Pescheria Vecchia 26)*, where a full meal is about L50,000.

Entertainment

The Stagione Lirica (Lyric Festival) is one of Italy's most prestigious musical events, attracting big names to the superb open-air *Arena Sferisterio*, off Piazza Mazzini, between 15 July and 15 August every year. At the same time, the private *Palazzo Ricci Pinacoteca*, in the street of the same name, organises a national exhibition of 20th century Italian art.

Getting There & Away

Several bus companies operate services to Roma, Firenze, Siena, Ancona, Ascoli Piceno, Civitanova Marche and Foligno. The train station (☎ 0733 24 03 54) is at Piazza XXV Aprile 8/10. The S77 connects the city with the A14 to the east and roads for Roma in the west.

AROUND MACERATA

About 20km north-east of Macerata on the road to Ancona, **Recanati** is a pretty little town which straggles along a high ridge. A pleasant enough stop, the town owes a special place in Italian literary history to its most famous son – the early 19th century poet Giacomo Leopardi. A small museum is dedicated to his life in the Palazzo Leopardi.

ASCOLI PICENO
postcode 63100 • pop 55,000

Legend has it that a woodpecker was responsible for the founding of this southern Le Marche town by leading the prehistoric first settlers to the site. The extensive old centre is

---

Giacomo Leopardi

Born in Recanati on 29 June 1798 of well-to-do parents, Giacomo Leopardi became the greatest romantic poet to emerge from Italy. From 1822, when he left home for the first time, until his death in Napoli in 1837, Leopardi travelled extensively through Italy, although he returned to Recanati regularly during his life. The most penetrating of his poetry, often erudite and always demanding, reflects the pain, anxiety and fragile bittersweet moments of joy that seem to have been the substance of the man's life. Leopardi was steeped in a classical education from a precocious age and his verse, however much it belongs to the stormy age of the Romantics, remains firmly planted in the disciplined framework of classicism. The pick of his work is the *Canti*, first published between 1824 and 1835, and now a standard element of Italian literary education.

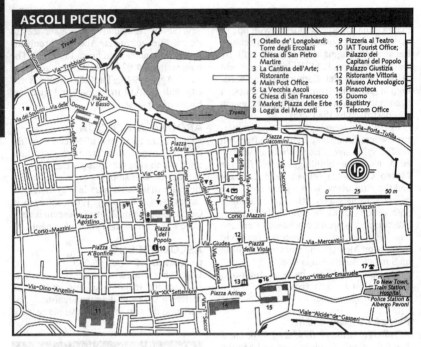

ASCOLI PICENO

1 Ostello de' Longobardi;	9 Pizzeria al Teatro
Torre degli Ercolani	10 IAT Tourist Office;
2 Chiesa di San Pietro	Palazzo dei
Martire	Capitani del Popolo
3 La Cantina dell'Arte;	11 Palazzo Giustizia
Ristorante	12 Ristorante Vittoria
4 Main Post Office	13 Museo Archeologico
5 La Vecchia Ascoli	14 Pinacoteca
6 Chiesa di San Francesco	15 Duomo
7 Market; Piazza delle Erbe	16 Baptistry
8 Loggia dei Mercanti	17 Telecom Office

bounded by the Tronto river to the north and the Castellano river to the south and east, and is dominated by nearby mountains leading into the Appennini. The city is among the region's most interesting after Urbino and deserves more attention than it gets.

Woodpecker stories aside, Ascoli Piceno was probably settled by the Piceni tribe in the 6th century BC. The salt trade eventually brought the city into contact with the Romans, to whom it fell after clamorous defeats in the battlefield in 268 BC. By the 6th century AD, the Goths and then the Lombards had come to supplant the Romans. The city flourished in the Middle Ages, despite being ransacked by troops of Holy Roman Emperor Frederick II after a long siege in 1242.

Orientation

The old town and its modern extension are separated by the Castellano river. The train station is in the new town, east of the river. From the station, head west across Ponte Maggiore, along Corso Vittorio Emanuele and past the duomo. Any of the narrow cobbled lanes to the north of Via XX Settembre will eventually take you to Piazza del Popolo, the heart of the medieval city.

Information

The IAT office (☎ 0736 25 30 45), at Piazza del Popolo 17, is open from 8 am to 1.35 pm and 3 to 7 pm Monday to Friday and from 9 am to 12.30 pm on Saturday.

The main post office is on Via Crispi. It is open from 8.15 am to 7.40 pm Monday to Saturday.

The Telecom office is on Corso Vittorio Emanuele and is open from 9 am to 1 pm Monday to Friday.

The Ospedale Generale Mazzoni (☎ 0736 35 81) is in Monticello, a newly built area

4km to the east of town. The questura (☎ 0736 355 111) is at Viale della Repubblica 8.

Piazza del Popolo

The heart of medieval Ascoli and the town's forum in Roman times, Piazza del Popolo is dominated on the western side by the 13th century **Palazzo dei Capitani del Popolo**. The seat of Ascoli's rulers, it was burned to the ground in 1535 during a bitter local feud and rebuilt 10 years later. The statue of Pope Paul III above the main entrance was erected in recognition of his efforts to bring peace to the town. The building's colourful history did not end there, as it was the headquarters for the local branch of the Fascists from 1938 and became the seat of the partisan Comitato di Liberazione in 1945.

Closing off the piazza to the north, **Chiesa di San Francesco** was started in 1262 and features a 15th century wooden crucifix and 16th century works by Cola dell'Amatrice. Virtually annexed to the church is the **Loggia dei Mercanti**. It looks suspiciously Tuscan, but was in fact built by Lombard masons in the 16th century. Merchants hawk their wares there to this day.

Pinacoteca

The second-largest art gallery in Le Marche is inside the 17th century Palazzo Comunale on Piazza Arringo, south-east of Piazza del Popolo. The Pinacoteca (☎ 0736 29 82 13) boasts 400 works, including paintings by Van Dyck, Titian, Carlo Crivelli and even Turner. Among the prints and drawings is an etching by Rembrandt. The gallery was founded in 1861 with works taken from churches and religious orders that were suppressed in the wake of Italian unification. It is open from 9 am to 1 pm daily. It is also open from 3.30 to 7.30 pm (excluding Sunday) during the summer. Admission costs L6000. Across Piazza Arringo, the **Museo Archeologico** (☎ 0736 25 35 62) has a collection of implements used by the ancient Piceni tribe. It is open from 8.30 am to 1.30 pm Monday to Saturday and admission costs L4000.

Duomo

Standing on the eastern flank of Piazza Arringo, Ascoli's cathedral is a lavish example of baroque excess, embellished in what some connoisseurs consider to be a less than tasteful manner. In compensation for the overkill, you will encounter what is possibly Carlo Crivelli's best work, *Virgin and Saints*, in the **Cappella del Sacramento**. The baptistry next to the duomo, something of a traffic barrier today, has remained unchanged since it was constructed in the 11th century.

Vecchio Quartiere

The town's Old Quarter stretches from Corso Mazzini (the main thoroughfare, or *decumanus*, of the Roman-era settlement) to the Tronto river. Its main street is the picturesque Via delle Torri, which eventually becomes Via Solestà. This is a perfect spot to put away the guidebooks and just wander where your whim takes you. Worth watching for on the curiously named Via delle Donne (Women Street) is the 14th century **Chiesa di San Pietro Martire**, dedicated to the saint who founded the Dominican community at Ascoli. The chunky Gothic structure houses the Reliquario della Santa Spina, containing what is said to be a thorn from Christ's crown of thorns. This church is one of about a dozen in Ascoli dating to at least the 15th century.

The 40m-high **Torre degli Ercolani** on Via dei Soderini, west of the Chiesa di San Pietro, is the tallest of the town's medieval towers. Abutting it is the **Palazzetto Longobardo**, a 12th century Lombard-Romanesque defensive position and now a youth hostel (see Places to Stay for details). Just to the north is the well-preserved **Ponte Romana**, a single-arched Roman bridge.

Special Events

The town's big festival is Quintana, a medieval pageant held on the first Sunday of every August. Hundreds of locals dressed in traditional costume fill the town centre for jousting, parades and other medieval doings. The summer months also come alive with shows and concerts during the city's Stagione Lirica.

Places to Stay

The town's HI *Ostello de' Longobardi* (☎ 0736 25 90 07, *Via dei Soderini 26*) charges L18,000 for B&B. Otherwise, your options for budget accommodation are not extensive.

At the central affittacamere *La Cantina dell'Arte* (☎ 0736 25 11 35, *Rua della Lupa 8*), singles/doubles cost L50,000/70,000. The owner also runs a very cheap restaurant opposite. Five kilometres out of town in Marino del Tronto is *Albergo Pavoni* (☎ 0736 34 25 75, 0736 34 25 87, *Via Navicella 135*), where rooms cost L45,000/70,000. Take bus No 3 from Piazza Arringo.

Places to Eat

Ascoli is responsible for a delicious idea for a starter. *Olive all'ascolana* are olives stuffed with meat and deep-fried.

For a really cheap meal, try the *restaurant* opposite La Cantina dell'Arte (see Places to Stay). A full meal with meat costs around L15,000.

For abundant helpings of good local cuisine, try *La Vecchia Ascoli* (☎ 0736 25 11 44, *Via dei Sabini 10*). A full meal costs around L30,000. At *Pizzeria al Teatro* (☎ 0736 25 35 49, *Via delle Sette Soglie 1*), pizzas start at L6000 and mains cost from about L10,000. A full meal at *Ristorante Vittoria* (☎ 0736 25 95 35, *Via dei Bonaccorsi 7*) will come to L35,000 a head.

There is an outdoor *market* on Piazza delle Erbe, near Piazza del Popolo, every morning except Sunday.

Getting There & Away

Buses leave from Piazzale della Stazione, in front of the train station, which is in the new part of town on the eastern side of the Castellano river. Cotravat (☎ 0736 34 22 43) runs three buses daily to Roma and serves Ancona as well as small towns in the Tronto river area. Cameli (☎ 0736 25 90 91, 06 49 16 43 in Roma) also has buses to Roma. In Roma, Cotravat and Cameli buses leave from Via San Martino della Battaglia, 800m north of Stazione Termini, off Piazza Indipendenza. Mazzuca (☎ 0736 40 22 67) serves Montemonaco, Amandola and other towns near the

Monti Sibillini range. Amadio (☎ 0736 34 27 05, 0736 34 23 40) runs a service to Firenze via Perugia and Siena, and the Abruzzo bus company ARPA (☎ 0736 34 10 49) serves Pescara and Teramo (change there for L'Aquila).

A spur train line connects Ascoli Piceno with Porto d'Ascoli and San Benedetto del Tronto, both of which are on the Bologna-Lecce line.

The S4 connects Ascoli Piceno with Roma and the Mar Adriatico coastline.

MONTI SIBILLINI

Rising bare and forbidding in the lower south-west of Le Marche, and reaching into neighbouring Umbria, the stark Monti Sibillini range is one of the most beautiful stretches of the Appennini. Dotted with caves and lined with walking trails, the mountains are also the scene of more energetic sporting activities such as hang-gliding and horse riding. The range is littered with rifugi and offers reasonable skiing in winter.

Amandola makes a good centre from which to explore the area, but lacks cheap accommodation. It is one of the prettiest villages in Le Marche and is just north of Montefortino. **Montefortino** is a good base for walking as it's reasonably close to the serious walking areas around Montemonaco, at the base of Monte Sibilla.

Montemonaco is an out-of-the-way town and not easily reached by public transport, although you'll be surprised by the number of tourists in summer. Many are there for the Gola dell'Infernaccio (Gorge of Hell), one of the easiest and most spectacular walks in Le Marche.

To reach the range, take the S4 from Ascoli Piceno and follow the signs. Buses connect the area with Ascoli Piceno and various cities throughout Le Marche. See also The Valnerina in the Umbria section earlier in this chapter for details about hang-gliding and how to get to the mountains from Umbria.

Information

If approaching from the north, along the S78 from Ancona, stop at the IAT office (☎ 0733

65 71 44) at Largo Ricciardi 1 in Sarnano. It sometimes has limited walking and climbing information. The CAI publishes a detailed guide to the mountains (in Italian), complete with maps: *Parco Nazionale dei Sibillini – Le Più Belle Escursioni*, by Alberico Alesi and Maurizio Calibani.

Places to Stay

There is a camp site just south of Montefortino at Ceretana. *Montespino* (☎ 0736 85 92 38) has sites costing L7000/12,000 per person/tent and is open from 1 June to 30 September. Montemonaco offers accommodation at good rates. *Albergo Sibilla* (☎ 0736 85 61 44, Via Roma 52) charges L65,000/75,000 per person including breakfast in the low/high season. *Rifugio della Montagna* (☎ 0736 85 63 27), in Foce, just near Montemonaco, charges L40,000 per person without breakfast or L35,000 if you stay two or more nights.

Abruzzo & Molise

Abruzzo, along with neighbouring Molise, is one of the few parts of Italy to be spared the influx of mass tourism. Although neither region is as rich in artistic and cultural heritage as their more illustrious neighbours, there is still plenty to explore, especially in Abruzzo.

Until administratively divided in 1963, Abruzzo and Molise were known as the Abruzzi, a term still commonly used to describe the two. The earthquake-prone region was particularly hard-hit in 1915, when a massive jolt left 30,000 people dead.

Abruzzo

The wild beauty of Abruzzo's mountain terrain is captivating – the bald, craggy peaks of Gran Sasso d'Italia are capped by the Corno Grande (at 2914m the highest mountain in the Appennini) and have perilous drops of up to 1000m. Farther south, wolves and bears still roam protected in the forests of the Parco Nazionale d'Abruzzo.

The region isn't just for nature-lovers. The medieval towns of L'Aquila and Sulmona are well worth visiting, and the countryside is speckled with an array of castles and isolated, hilltop *borghi* (cluttered towns and villages little changed over hundreds of years).

In antiquity, Abruzzo was famed for its witches, wizards and snake-charmers – members of a tribe known as the Marsi, who lived around modern-day Avezzano. Even today, snakes feature in a bizarre annual religious festival in the mountain village of Cocullo, near Sulmona.

Traditionally Abruzzo is a farm and grazing territory and its sheep farmers still play an important role in the local economy. A key agricultural area is the Piana del Fucino (Fucino Plain), east of Avezzano, which was created by draining the vast Lago Fucino in the late 19th century. Prince Torlonia undertook the project on the condition that he would have title to the land and completed it during

Highlights

- Walk up Corno Grande of the Gran Sasso d'Italia, the highest peak in the Appennini

- Get close to some wolves at Civitella Alfedena in the Parco Naturale d'Abruzzo

- Take part in the Processione dei Serpari (Snake-Charmers' Procession) in Cocullo

- Visit the Roman ruins at Saepinum

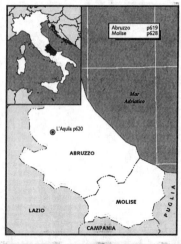

the Fascist period. It was not until the 1950s that the Italian government took over the plain and parcelled it out to local peasants.

Torlonia's efforts were not a first. The ancient Romans had a shot at draining the lake in what proved a remarkable, yet disastrous, feat of engineering. Under the orders of Emperor Claudius, the Romans built a tunnel about 10km long to drain the lake into a neighbouring valley. Unfortunately, when the

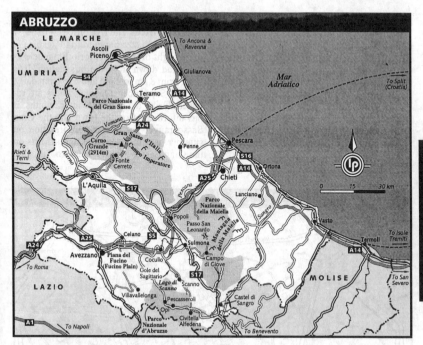

ABRUZZO

outlet tunnel was opened, it proved too small for the massive volume of water in the lake and thousands of spectators, including the emperor himself, almost drowned.

L'AQUILA
postcode 67100 • pop 60,000

The evening sun casts an opaque rose light over the Gran Sasso d'Italia, just to the north of L'Aquila – an encouraging counterpoint to the somewhat gloomy regional capital. In spite of repeated earthquakes, the medieval core of the city remains an interesting place to explore, but L'Aquila's curious beginnings are perhaps more intriguing still. Emperor Frederick II founded the city in 1240, it is said, by drawing together the citizens of 99 villages. Whether true or not, the number 99 became the city's symbol. The citizens of L'Aquila (meaning the Eagle – a reference to the eagle in the imperial coat of arms) estab-

lished 99 churches and 99 piazzas, as well as a fountain with (almost) 99 spouts. Earthquakes, especially one in 1703, have destroyed most of the churches and piazzas, but the medieval fountain survives and, every evening, the town hall bell chimes 99 times.

L'Aquila's people have a rebellious spirit but have frequently backed the wrong horse. King Manfred destroyed the city in 1266 because the people supported the pope, and it came close to a repeat under siege by the Aragonese, in the fight over the Kingdom of Napoli against the House of Anjou. Twice L'Aquila rose against Spanish rule in the 16th and 17th centuries (the first time allied with Francis I of France) and both times the city was crushed. The 1703 earthquake all but finished L'Aquila off. Revolt finally proved fruitful when, in 1860, the city was made regional capital for its efforts towards national unity.

Orientation

L'Aquila's train station is some distance downhill from the old centre, but the regular No 79 bus will take you there. Get off in Corso Federico II, the continuation of the elegant old main boulevard, Corso Vittorio Emanuele. The intercity bus station is on Piazza Battaglione Alpini L'Aquila, and from there it's a short walk down Corso Vittorio Emanuele to the tourist offices and, farther along the Corso, to the Piazza del Duomo and the centre of town.

Information

Tourist Offices The IAT office (☎ 0862 41 08 08) is at Piazza Santa Maria Paganica 5, to the right off Corso Vittorio Emanuele as you head down from the bus station. It is open from 8 am to 2 pm and 3 to 6 pm daily, May to September. Opening hours are reduced during the autumn/winter months. It has information on the town and the Gran Sasso range. For specific information on summer or winter activities and ski lifts on the Gran Sasso, go to the Centro Turistico

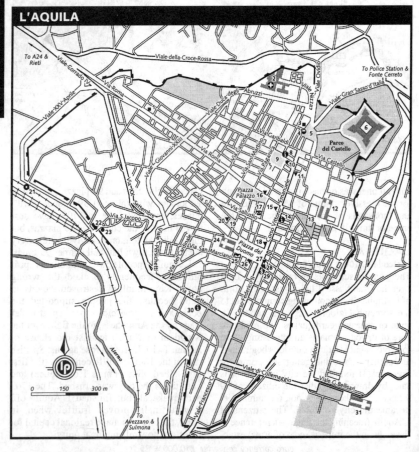

Gran Sasso (☎ 0862 2 21 47) at Corso Vittorio Emanuele 49. It is open from 9 am to 1 pm and 4 to 7 pm Monday to Friday and to 1 pm only Saturday. It also operates as a travel agency with a booking service. The other IAT office (☎ 0862 2 23 06), Via XX Settembre 10, is open from 8 am to 2 pm and 3.30 to 6 pm Monday to Saturday (in summer also from 9 am to noon Sunday).

Post & Communications The main post office is on Piazza del Duomo; it's open from 8.15 am to 7.40 pm Monday to Saturday.

The Telecom office is on Via Patini, off Via Sallustio in front of the bar Sette Nani, and is open from 8 am to 9 pm daily.

Medical Services & Emergency The Ospedale San Salvatore (hospital; ☎ 0862 77 81) is north of the town centre on Viale Nizzi. The questura (police station; ☎ 0862 43 01) is at Via Strinella 2, well out of the centre.

Castello

This massive edifice of steep, blanched battlements sunk deep into a now empty moat is without doubt L'Aquila's most impressive monument. Overlooking the old city's northeastern perimeter out to the Gran Sasso d'Italia, it was first built by the Spaniards after they'd put down a rebellion by the locals. Today, L'Aquila's citizens seem to have singled out the path around the castle as the ideal place for a *passeggiata* (evening stroll)

and endless chat. The castello houses the **Museo Nazionale d'Abruzzo** (☎ 0862 63 31), with the usual collection of local religious artworks. The main draw, however, is the skeleton of a mammoth, found near the town in the early 1950s. The museum is open from 9 am to 7 pm (to 8 pm Sunday) and from 9 pm to midnight, daily except Monday in the summer. It closes at 2 pm (at 1 pm Sunday) during the winter. Admission costs L8000.

Basilicas

Fronted by a magnificent three-tiered, cream-coloured façade, the 15th century **Basilica di San Bernardino** is one of the city's finest churches. You'll find it on the piazza of the same name, east of Corso Vittorio Emanuele. The most outstanding internal features are the exquisite gilded woodwork ceiling (a baroque gem) and the intricate detail of the relief decoration of San Bernardino's mausoleum, the work of local artisan Silvestro dell'Aquila. San Bernardino, originally of Siena, spent his last years in L'Aquila, where he died.

The Romanesque **Basilica di Santa Maria di Collemaggio**, south-east of the centre along Viale di Collemaggio, has an equally imposing façade, its rose windows encased by a quilt pattern of pink and white marble. The basilica was built at the instigation of a hermit, Pietro da Morrone, who was elected pope at the age of 80 in 1294. Pietro took the name Celestine V, but this unworldly and

ABRUZZO

L'AQUILA

PLACES TO STAY		OTHER		14	Centro Turistico
1	Locanda Orazi	2	Ospedale San Salvatore		Gran Sasso Tourist Office
3	Hotel Castello		(Hospital)	17	Telecom Office
28	Hotel Duomo	4	Intercity Bus Station	19	Piazza San Biagio
		5	Piazza Battaglione	21	Train Station
PLACES TO EAT			Alpini L'Aquila	22	Porta Rivera
10	Trattoria del Giaguaro	6	Castello & Museo	23	Fontana della
11	Pizza Marchigiana		Nazionale d'Abruzzo		99 Cannelle
15	Gran Caffè Eden	7	Porta Castello	24	Duomo
16	La Perla Nera	8	IAT Tourist Office	25	Post Office
18	Sorelle Nurzia	9	Piazza Santa Maria	29	BNL Bank & ATM
20	Trattoria San Biagio		Paganica	30	IAT Tourist Office
26	Ristorante Renato	12	Basilica di San Bernadino	31	Basilica di Santa Maria
27	Caffé Fratelli Nurzia	13	Piazza San Bernardino		di Collemaggio

---

euro currency converter L10,000 = €5.16

trusting man was no match for the machinations of courtiers and politicians and he was eventually forced to abdicate. His successor, Pope Boniface VIII, saw Celestine as a threat and threw him into prison, where he died. As founder of the Celestine order, he was canonised seven years later and his tomb lies inside the basilica.

Fontana delle 99 Cannelle

A symbol of the city, the 'Fountain of the 99 Spouts' was erected in the late 13th century. No-one knows where the water originates, but it was the town's lifeblood until well into the 20th century. Count the various stone faces, gargoyles and the like – they don't seem to add up to the magic number!

Places to Stay

The only cheap place in L'Aquila is *Locanda Orazi* (☎ 0862 41 28 89, *Via Roma 175*). It has singles/doubles for L40,000/60,000.

The pleasant *Hotel Duomo* (☎ 0862 41 08 93, *fax 0862 41 30 58, Via Dragonetti 6*), one street along from Via Cimino, has singles/doubles with bathroom, telephone and TV at L95,000/150,000. The less inspiring *Hotel Castello* (☎ 0862 41 91 47, *Piazza Battaglione Alpini L'Aquila*) has rooms with the same facilities for around L100,000/140,000.

Places to Eat

Traditional local dishes include *maccheroni alla chitarra*, thick macaroni cut by feeding them through a contraption the strings of which apparently reminded someone of a guitar. Lamb also makes a regular appearance, either roasted or grilled. Fresh produce is sold in the *market* held most days in Piazza del Duomo.

For snacks, you can try pizza slices for L2000 to L3000 at *La Perla Nera* (*Corso Principe Umberto 5*). Otherwise, for full pizza check out *Pizza Marchigiana* (*Corso Vittorio Emanuele 117*).

At *Trattoria San Biagio* (*Piazza San Biagio*), along Via Sassa from Piazza del Duomo, you can dine well on local specialities for around L25,000. Another good choice for a low-priced meal is *Trattoria del Gi-*

NICKY CAVEN

A great way to pass some time – can you count 99 spouts on the Fontana delle 99 Cannelle?

aguaro (*Piazza Santa Maria Paganica 4*). A more expensive option is *Ristorante Renato* (☎ 0862 2 55 96, *Via dell'Indipendenza 9*). You will pay about L35,000 for a full meal.

Cafés, Bars & Pasticcerie The *Gran Caffè Eden* is one of the more elegant bars along Corso Vittorio Emanuele, but for sweet food you should make straight for *Sorelle Nurzia*, at No 38. It specialises in a chocolate variety of *torrone*, a scrumptious nougat confection. For the competition, try *Caffè Fratelli Nurzia* (*Piazza del Duomo 74*), in business since 1835.

Entertainment

An annual season of concerts is held from October to May by, among others, the Società Aquilana dei Concerti. Staff at the IAT offices can provide information. If you're in town during the summer, ask about the special concert, ballet and drama performances.

Getting There & Away

ARPA buses (☎ 0862 41 28 08, ☎ 06 44 23 39 28 in Roma) for Roma (L16,900; terminates at Stazione Tiburtina) and Pescara (L14,000) leave from the bus station on Piazza Battaglione Alpini L'Aquila. ARPA buses also connect the city with Avezzano and Sulmona. By train, the town is accessible from Roma via Sulmona or Terni, and from Pescara via Sulmona. From the train station, take local ASM bus No 79 to the centre. The A24 links L'Aquila with Roma, and the A25 leads to Pescara. If heading north, the S17 to Rieti is a pretty route from which you can proceed to Terni and into Umbria.

GRAN SASSO D'ITALIA

The rocky peaks of the Gran Sasso d'Italia are close to L'Aquila. Try the city's tourist offices for details on walking trails and *rifugi* (mountain accommodation). A funicular leaves **Fonte Cerreto** every 30 minutes for Campo Imperatore (2117m), giving access to decent walking trails and a small, but popular, ski resort of the same name. Chair and ski lifts operate on the runs at **Campo Imperatore** and there is more skiing at nearby Monte Cristo (1930m), as well as Campo Felice.

There is a cheap camp site, the *Funivia del Gran Sasso (☎ 0862 60 61 63)*, at Fonte Cerreto, open from 1 May to 15 September, at Easter and at Christmas, and a network of rifugi in the area. Hotel accommodation is limited and expensive. For reasonable prices at high altitude try the *Campo Imperatore (☎ 0862 40 00 00, fax 0862 41 32 01)*, at Campo Imperatore, which charges L60,000 for B&B and L85,000 for half board.

From L'Aquila, take bus No 6 (seven daily) from Via Castello to the funicular at Fonte Cerreto.

SULMONA

Sulmona, the birthplace of Ovid, is an understated but charming little town, hemmed in by mountains. The medieval centre invites one to wander, and the town is well placed to serve as a base for touring southern Abruzzo.

Its modern claim to fame is the *confetti* industry – the making of elaborate flower-shaped arrangements of sugar almonds, a must at traditional Italian weddings.

Orientation & Information

The town's main street, Corso Ovidio, runs from the small park at Piazzale Tresca to the vast Piazza Garibaldi, a five minute walk. Sulmona's IAT office (☎/fax 0864 5 32 76), Corso Ovidio 208, opens from 9 am to 1 pm and 3.30 to 6.30 pm Monday to Saturday. It also opens Sunday morning in summer.

Things to See

Sulmona's main attraction is the **Palazzo dell'Annunziata** on Corso Ovidio, which combines Gothic and Renaissance styles. Note the beautifully carved frieze halfway up the façade. The building houses a small **museum** dedicated to the work of Sulmona's Renaissance goldsmiths. Next to the palazzo is a baroque church of the same name, rebuilt after the 1703 earthquake. Also along Corso Ovidio, on Piazza XX Settembre, is a statue of Ovid.

Piazza Garibaldi is the scene of a colourful market every Wednesday and Saturday mornings. When the bustle of the market clears, you can take a closer look at the austere Renaissance **Fontana del Vecchio** and the medieval **aqueduct**, which borders the piazza on two sides. The most interesting feature of the

---

Ovid

The Augustan poet, considered by some as being second only to Virgil, has a mixed and not altogether flattering reputation. Born in Sulmona in 43 BC and sent at an early age to Roma to study rhetoric and make himself a comfortable career in the cesspit of Roman politics, Ovid preferred to write poetry instead. His early erotic verse, such as *Amores* and *Ars Amatoria*, gained him quick popularity in Roman high society. Possibly his most ambitious work was the *Metamorphosis*, a kind of extended cover version of a whole gamut of Greek myths which culminated in descriptions of Caesar's transformation into a star and the apotheosis of Augustus, ruler at the time. This last piece of sycophancy did not stop the emperor from banishing him to the Black Sea in 8 AD for reasons which are not entirely clear. He died in Tomi, in modern Romania, 10 years later.

ABRUZZO

Chiesa di San Martino, also on the piazza, is its Gothic entrance. On the adjacent Piazza del Carmine, the Romanesque portal is all that remains of **Chiesa di San Francesco della Scarpa**, destroyed in the 1703 earthquake.

Places to Stay & Eat

Hotel Traffico (☎ 0864 5 40 80, Via degli Agghiacciati 17), off Corso Ovidio, has singles/doubles without bathroom for L35,000/50,000. The pleasant *Hotel Italia (☎ 0864 5 23 08, Piazza Salvatore Tommasi 3)*, through Piazza XX Settembre from Corso Ovidio, has doubles with/without bathroom for L80,000/65,000.

For a square meal with no frills (about L30,000 a head), try *Ristorante Stella (Via Mazara 18)*. For more ambience (and for more money!) head for *Ristorante Italia (Piazza XX Settembre 23)*.

Getting There & Away

From Piazza Tresca, walk along Via di Circonvallazione Orientale to reach the bus station, off Via Japasseri. ARPA buses link Sulmona to L'Aquila (nine daily), Pescara (five daily), Napoli (two daily), Scanno (10 daily) and other nearby towns. ARPA buses also head for Cocullo, Castel di Sangro and Pescasseroli, which is in the Parco Nazionale d'Abruzzo.

The train station is about 2km downhill from the historic centre, and the half-hourly bus No A runs between the two. Regular trains link the town with Roma and Pescara.

AROUND SULMONA
Cocullo

The tiny mountain village of Cocullo only warrants a visit on one day of the year – the first Thursday in May, when its inhabitants celebrate the feast day of San Domenico in a truly original and weird fashion. A statue of the saint is draped with live snakes and carried in procession through the village, accompanied by villagers also carrying live snakes. Known as the Processione dei Serpari (Snake-Charmers' Procession), the festival has pagan origins and is an unforgettable experience.

The village has no accommodation, but is close to Sulmona and Scanno and linked to both by ARPA buses. Plan to arrive in the village early on the day of the festival, as it has attracted increasingly large crowds in recent years. Festivities usually start at around 10 am, culminating in the procession at noon and then continuing through the afternoon.

Ask at the tourist offices in Sulmona or Scanno for details on buses to Cocullo, since services are increased for the event.

Scanno

This village was assaulted by various photographers after WWII and made into an example of traditionalism in the modern world. As a result, Scanno has become something of a minor tourist mecca for Italians. The handful of elderly women who still skittle about in traditional costume must, you can't help thinking, take some affront at having become individual mobile tourist 'sights'.

Scanno was long a centre of wool production, and for centuries an exclusive supplier to the Franciscan order. Today the cheerfully jumbled medieval village is surrounded by an outcrop of uninspired modern 'suburbia', much of which is given over to hotel space.

Scanno is worth the effort, especially if you have made it this far into Abruzzo. The drive south from Sulmona through the Gole del Sagittario (Sagittarius Gorges) and past the peaceful Lago di Scanno is delightful, and beyond Scanno the road takes you right into Parco Nazionale d'Abruzzo. Two hundred metres from the centre of Scanno there is a chair lift leading up to small ski fields served by a network of lifts.

Information The IAT office (☎ 0864 7 43 17), Piazza Santa Maria della Valle 12, is on the edge of the medieval town centre.

Places to Stay & Eat If you plan to stay overnight, there is a camp site at the Lago di Scanno, *Camping I Lupi (☎ 0864 74 01 00)*, open year-round. The village is crammed with hotels. Try *Pensione Nilde (☎ 0864 7 43 59, Viale del Lago 101)*, which has singles/doubles for L45,000/80,000 or *Pen-*

sione Margherita (☎ 0864 7 43 53, Via Domenico Tanturri 100), offering rooms with bath for L55,000/85,000 and a full board option for L75,000 per person. *Hotel Vittoria (☎ 0864 7 43 98, fax 0864 74 71 79, Via Domenico di Rienzo 46)* is a more up-market option at L80,000/110,000 with bathroom. Most will want to charge for full board, but there is no obligation.

For a meal, the *Ristorante Gli Archetti (☎ 0864 7 46 45, Via Silla 8)* and *Trattoria Lo Sgabello (☎ 0864 74 74 76, Via dei Pescatori 45)*, both in the medieval village, are decent spots.

Getting There & Away ARPA buses connect Scanno with Sulmona. An Autolinee Schiappa bus leaves Stazione Tiburtina in Roma for Scanno three times a day. Departure times are noon, 3 and 5.30 pm.

Skiing
Some modest ski fields lie east of Sulmona. About 18km of tortuous driving brings you to **Campo di Giove**, around which you'll find 15km of downhill runs and also some cross-country trails. It is the first in a series of small ski areas (the next is at Passo San Leonardo, about 10km north of Campo di Giove) leading up into the Montagna della Maiella and the Parco Nazionale della Maiella.

PARCO NAZIONALE D'ABRUZZO
Established in 1923 with a former royal hunting reserve as its nucleus, the Parco Nazionale d'Abruzzo now incorporates about 40,000 hectares of the Appennini (plus an external protected area of 60,000 hectares). It is the last refuge in Italy of the Marsican brown bear and the Apennine wolf, although it is difficult to spot one of these now rare native animals. At the last count there were an estimated 80 bears roaming wild here. The park is also home to golden eagles, a herd of chamois and the odd wildcat. There are plans to reintroduce the lynx, which became extinct in this area in the early 20th century. The park's forests and meadows are perfect for family excursions and long-distance walks, but leaving the marked trails is prohibited.

The most convenient base is the town of **Pescasseroli**, in the centre of the park. The local IAT office (☎ 0863 91 04 61), at Via Piave 2, is open from 9 am to 1 pm and 4.30 to 6.30 pm daily except Sunday. Before setting off to explore, buy a detailed map of the park for L10,000 at the local Ufficio di Zona (☎ 0863 9 19 55), Via Consultore 1. The map shows the walking trails and locations of rifugi. The visitors centre nearby on Viale Santa Lucia is open from 10 am to 1 pm and 3 to 7 pm daily. For L10,000 you can visit its museum and zoo (more a veterinary station for sick and wounded animals), where you can see at least one of most of the park's species up close, including a wolf, a Marsican brown bear and a lynx. The majority of these animals are, once well, released back into the wild.

Another possible base is the mountain village of **Civitella Alfedena** (☎ 0864 89 03 60 for information), on the park's eastern edge. Less touristy than Pescasseroli, it has a visitors centre called Centro Lupo (admission L5000) and a large *area faunistica*, for housing wolves in semi-captivity. In a smaller enclosure lurks a little family of three lynx.

Places to Stay & Eat
Free-camping is forbidden in the park, but there are several camp sites, open from 15 June to 15 September, including *Campeggio dell'Orso (☎ 0863 9 19 55)*, 1km from Pescasseroli on the road to Opi. There are also five rifugi in the park, but to stay you must obtain permission and a key from the Ufficio di Zona in Pescasseroli. To access the rifugi *Fonti Astuni* and *L'Aceretta*, contact the Centro di Visita Cervo (☎ 0863 94 92 61), Via Colle di Marcandrea in Villavallelonga, north-west of the park borders.

In Pescasseroli *Hotel Pinguino (☎ 0863 91 25 80, Via Collachi 2)* has singles/doubles with bathroom and half board for L90,000/ 140,000. *Hotel Cristiana (☎ 0863 91 07 95, Via Collachi 3)*, just outside the town, has doubles for L80,000. For the hungry, try *Pizzeria San Francesco* on Via Isonzo.

If you want to stay overnight in Civitella Alfedena, the best choice is *Albergo La Torre*

ABRUZZO

(☎ 0864 89 01 21, Via Castello 3) in the middle of the old town. It has rooms for L30,000 per person and half board from L55,000 (in low season) to L70,000 (in August).

Getting There & Away
Pescasseroli, Civitella Alfadena and other villages in the park are linked by ARPA bus to Avezzano (and from there to L'Aquila) and to Castel di Sangro (reached from Sulmona by bus or train). In summer an ARPA bus leaves from Piazza della Repubblica in Roma for Pescasseroli (go to the APT office on Via Parigi in Roma for information).

PESCARA
postcode 65100 • pop 123,000
A heavily developed beach resort and commercial centre, Pescara's only attraction is the beach and even that is nothing to write home about. However, travellers to Abruzzo are likely to pass through Pescara since it is also the main transport hub of the region, with trains connecting it to Bologna, Ancona, Roma and Bari, and buses running from it to towns throughout Abruzzo.

Staff at the tourist office can provide information about the jazz festival held in the second half of July at the Teatro D'Annunzio, in the public park by the beach east of the city centre. If you're desperate for something to do, you could visit the Museo Ittico, a fishery museum on the waterfront at Via Raffaele Paolucci.

Orientation
From the FS train and intercity bus stations on Piazzale della Repubblica, the beach is a short walk north-east down Corso Umberto I.

Information
The IAT office (☎ 085 42 90 01) is at Via Nicola Fabrizi 171. It is open from 9 am to noon Monday to Saturday and also from 4 to 7 pm and Sunday morning in the summer. In the peak summer months another information booth normally opens at the train station.

The post office is at Corso Vittorio Emanuele II 106, to the right off Piazzale della Repubblica, and opens from 8.15 am to 7.40 pm Monday to Saturday. Telecom public telephones are located throughout the centre.

The Ospedale Civile (☎ 085 42 51) is at Via Fonte Romana 8, south-west of the train station, off Via del Circuito. The questura (☎ 085 20 571) is on Piazza Italia.

Places to Stay & Eat
A fairly simple place is the **Pensione Roma** *(☎ 085 421 16 57, Via Piave 142)*. Singles/doubles cost a mere L30,000/50,000 – just don't expect any frills. *Hotel Alba* (☎ 085 38 91 45, Via Michelangelo Forti 14), near the train station, has decent rooms with bathroom for L70,000/110,000 (less for a stay of a few days). *Hotel Natale* (☎ 085 422 28 85, Via del Circuito 175) has pleasant singles/doubles for L50,000/80,000 and bargaining is possible.

For a reasonably priced meal, try **Pinguino** *(Corso Manthonè 36)*, across the Pescara river. A meal at **Cantina di Jooz**, in the parallel Via delle Caserme, will cost around L45,000.

Getting There & Away
Bus ARPA buses leave from the train station on Piazzale della Repubblica for L'Aquila, Sulmona and anywhere else you like in Abruzzo, as well as for Roma Stazione Tiburtina (about 2½ hours) at 4 and 6.15 am and 6.15 pm. Di Febo-Capuani buses (☎ 085 421 18 91) leave for the same destination at 9.30 am and 2.30 pm. Di Fonzo also operates a service to Roma at 8.15pm. ARPA/SATAM have a daily service to Napoli Piazza Garibaldi (about five hours) at 2.55 pm. Timetables are posted at the ARPA ticket office (☎ 085 421 50 99) on the piazza.

Train Pescara is on the main train line along the Adriatic coast and is easily accessible for towns such as Bologna, Ancona, Foggia and points farther south, as well as L'Aquila, Sulmona and Roma.

Car & Motorcycle Heading north or south along the coast, you can choose between the A14 and often busy S16. Those heading for Roma, L'Aquila or Sulmona should take the A25 or S5.

Boat The Jadrolinjia high-speed catamaran (passengers only) operates services to the Dalmatian islands and Split in Croatia Monday, Wednesday, Friday and Saturday from 14 June to 18 September (also Tuesday in August). It leaves at 3.30 pm from the small port of Pescara and takes from 5½ to 6½ hours (with intermediate stops) to reach Split. The one-way/return fare is L180,000/260,000 (tourist class). For full timetable information go to Agenzia Sanmar (☎ 085 6 52 47) at the ferry terminal, just south of the Pescara river, or the tour operator Pentatour (☎ 085 421 32 01), Viale Bovio 106, in town.

Molise

Hived off in 1963 from its bigger northern sibling, Abruzzo, Molise is a small, hilly and rather undistinguished region. A kind of cultural bridge from north to south, it has a low ranking on the tourist trail.

Largely rural and repeatedly shaken by devastating earthquakes, its towns are prosaic and of little interest. In fact, the traveller moving north to south will notice, perhaps for the first time, those great clumps of hideous concrete blocks that seem to pass for a kind of standard in modern Mediterranean 'architecture', whether in southern Italy, Spain, Morocco or Egypt.

It's not all bad news. You can wander through the Roman provincial town ruins of Saepinum, south-west of Campobasso, and there are good walking opportunities in the Monti del Matese. Excavations in Isernia have unearthed what is believed to be the oldest village in Europe, and the small beach resort of Termoli is a jumping-off point for the Isole Tremiti, bunched together off the coast of northern Puglia (see the Puglia section of the Puglia, Basilicata & Calabria chapter).

CAMPOBASSO

postcode 86100 • pop 42,500

Molise's regional capital, Campobasso is predominantly modern and basically unappealing, but makes a good base for exploring nearby Saepinum. The national carabinieri

training school is here, as is a high-security prison.

The EPT office (☎ 0874 41 56 62) is at Piazza della Vittoria 14, open from 8.30 am to 1.30 pm Monday to Saturday. From the train station, turn left into Via Cavour, right into Via Gazzani and left again into Corso Vittorio Emanuele to reach it.

You can kill a couple of hours wandering up into the older part of town to take a look at the Romanesque churches of **San Bartolomeo** (13th century) and **San Giorgio** (12th century). The castle you can see from a distance looks impressive until you get close.

If you need a bed for the night, try *Albergo Belvedere (☎ 0874 6 27 24, Via Colle delle Api 32)*, which has singles/doubles with bathroom for up to L38,000/58,000 and triples for L68,000. From the train station, take bus No 1N and ask the driver to let you off there.

Campobasso is connected by bus to Termoli, Isernia and Pescara. By train it can be reached from Roma via Cassino or from Napoli via Benevento.

AROUND CAMPOBASSO

One of the least visited Roman ruins in Italy, **Saepinum** is handy to Campobasso and worth a visit. An unimportant provincial town, it survived into the 9th century before being sacked by Arab invaders. Surrounded by small farms, the ruins are well preserved and include the town walls, a temple, a triumphal arch and the foundations of numerous houses. The area has not been developed for tourism and consequently admission is free.

To reach Saepinum by public transport, you need to take one of the infrequent provincial buses to Altilia, next to the archaeological zone, or Sepino, a 3km walk away.

The **Monti del Matese**, south-west of Campobasso, offer good walking in summer and adequate skiing in winter. Take a bus from Campobasso to Campitello Matese or a train from Campobasso or Isernia to Bojano. From either point there are trails into the mountains. From Bojano, the last bus leaves for Campitello at 2.30 pm.

Campitello Matese is the centre for winter sports and has several hotels, but there's

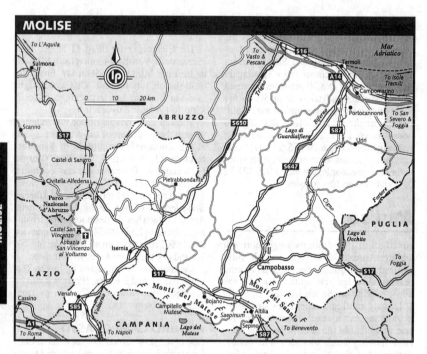

MOLISE

[Map of Molise showing towns including Sulmona, Scanno, Castel di Sangro, Isernia, Campobasso, Termoli, Venafro, with surrounding regions Abruzzo, Lazio, Campania, Puglia, and the Mar Adriatico]

nothing cheap about them. The *Lo Sciatore* (☎ 0874 78 41 37) charges up to L110,000 per person (no singles), including full board. The only slightly cheaper option is *Albergo Kristiana* (☎ 0874 78 41 97), with single rooms ranging from L70,000 to L80,000.

ISERNIA

If you want to see a town held together by scaffolding, then the earthquake-battered old centre of Isernia is the place for you. Otherwise it's modern and dull. In 1979 evidence was discovered here of a village thought to be up to 700,000 years old, possibly the most ancient settlement in Europe, but this is unlikely to make your stay any more exciting. Excavations continue, and stone tools discovered at the site are on display at the town's small **Museo Santa Maria delle Monache**, Corso Marcelli 48 (head to the left along Corso Garibaldi from the train station). It is open

from 9 am to 1 pm and 3 to 7 pm Tuesday to Sunday and admission costs L4000.

Isernia's EPT office (☎ 0865 39 92) is at Via Farinacci 9, a short walk from the train station (turn left into Corso Garibaldi and right into Via Farinacci). It is open from 8 am to 2 pm Monday to Saturday.

For a place to stay, try *Hotel Sayonara* (☎ 0865 5 09 92, *Via G Berta 131*), which has single/double rooms with bathroom for L60,000/90,000. Try bargaining if you plan to stay for several nights.

Isernia is easily reached by bus from Campobasso and Termoli and by train from Sulmona, Pescara and Campobasso.

AROUND ISERNIA

Provincial buses will take you to local hilltop villages. Of interest are the remains of a pre-Roman village, including a Greek-style theatre, just outside **Pietrabbondante**, about

30km north-east of Isernia. It was settled by the Samnites, who controlled the area before Roman domination. Three buses a day connect Isernia and Pietrabbondante.

Near Castel San Vincenzo, about 20km north-west of Isernia, is the **Abbazia di San Vincenzo al Volturno** (take the bus for Castel San Vincenzo from Isernia and then walk 1km to the abbey). Founded in the 8th century, this Benedictine abbey was destroyed by Arabs and rebuilt several times. However, a cycle of 9th century Byzantine frescoes survive in the crypt and these merit a visit. The abbey **museum** normally opens from 9 am to 1 pm and 3 to 7 pm but hours can be irregular; inquire at Isernia's EPT office for advice.

TERMOLI

More low-key compared with some of its northern rivals, Termoli makes a relaxing if unexciting beach stop. The tiny medieval borgo will keep you occupied for a wee while with its 12th century **cathedral** and 13th century Swabian **castle**, built by Frederick II. Termoli is also a year-round jumping off point for the Isole Tremiti. The town is filled with holiday-makers in summer, and accommodation, especially for the budget conscious, is tight. Things don't improve in winter, as much of Termoli shuts down.

The AAST office (☎ 0875 70 67 54) is in Piazza Bega, a short walk along Corso Umberto I from the train station. It is open from 8 am to 12.30 pm and 5 to 6 pm Monday to Friday and in the morning only Saturday.

Places to Stay & Eat

There are camping facilities at *Cala Saracena* (☎ 0875 5 21 93), on the S16 Adriatica to Pescara road (also known as Europa 2) at No 174. It can be reached by local bus from the train station.

Villa Ida (☎ 0875 70 66 66, *Via Mario Milano 27*), a modest hotel 150m from the train station, has singles/doubles with bathroom for L70,000/95,000. It is closed in winter.

Hotel Meridiano (☎ 0875 70 59 46) overlooks the beach on Lungomare Cristo-

foro Colombo and has singles/doubles with bathroom for L110,000/130,000.

For a reasonable fish meal and some rough wine, try *Da Antonio (Corso Umberto I59)*. A full meal will cost about L40,000.

Getting There & Away

Bus The main intercity bus station is on Piazza Bega. SATI buses link Termoli to Campobasso and Pescara, and Isernia can be reached with the Cerella company. Buses also serve Roma and Napoli (the AAST office has full details of bus timetables).

Train Termoli is on the main Bologna-Lecce train line along the Adriatic coast.

Car & Motorcycle Termoli is on the A14 and S16 that follow the coast north to Pescara and beyond and south to Bari. The S87 links Termoli with the Campobasso area overlooking the Cigno river valley.

Boat Termoli is the only place that operates a daily ferry service to the Isole Tremiti year-round (see the Puglia section of the Puglia, Basilicata & Calabria chapter). Inquire at Adriatica Navigazione (☎ 0875 70 53 41), Corso Umberto I, 93; Navigazione Libera del Golfo, c/o Agenzia Di Brino (☎ 0875 70 39 37), Corso Umberto I, 23; or at ticket booths at the ferry terminal. There is at least one departure a day (at 7 am and 2 pm Tuesday and Saturday, at 9.15 am on the other days), and return tickets cost L26,000. Hydrofoils and hydrojet run at least three times a day from June to September for about L46,000 return.

ALBANIAN TOWNS

Several villages to the south of Termoli form an Albanian enclave dating back to the 15th century. These include Campomarino, Portocannone, Ururi and Montecilfone. Although the inhabitants shrugged off their Orthodox religion in the 18th century, locals still use a version of Albanian incomprehensible to outsiders as their first language. The towns can be reached by bus from Termoli.

Campania

CAMPANIA

Presided over by Napoli, the magnificent, chaotic capital of the south, Campania has everything the traveller could want. With the only true metropolis in the Mezzogiorno (literally 'midday', the evocative name for Italy's south), Campania is also blessed with some of the most dramatic coastline in the country, a sprinkling of magical islands and a rich heritage set in ancient ruins.

In the shadow of Vesuvio (Mt Vesuvius) lie the ruins of Pompei and Ercolano (Herculaneum), Roman cities buried by the volcano and so preserved for posterity – both a short excursion south-east of Napoli. There is plenty more for the classicist to explore, including the Campi Flegrei (Phlegraean Fields) to the west, with its reminders of the world celebrated in the writings of Homer and Virgil and, to the south-east, the Greek temples of Paestum, which are among the best preserved in the world.

Many writers have sought to do justice to the natural beauty of the Costiera Amalfitana (Amalfi Coast), farther south of Pompei and also to the islands in the Golfo di Napoli (Bay of Naples), particularly Capri.

Travel inland to Caserta and you will discover the grand Palazzo Reale of the Spanish Bourbons, set in magnificent gardens and modelled on Versailles.

Campania is alive with myth and legend. Stories tell how sirens (sea nymphs) lured sailors to their deaths off Sorrento, how islands in the Golfo di Napoli were the domain of mermaids and that Lago d'Averno (Lake Avernus), in the Campi Flegrei, was believed, in ancient times, to be the entrance to the underworld. Ulysses, Aeneas and other characters of classical storytelling and history have also left their mark (real or imagined) here.

Napoli is the most densely populated area of Campania, although the city itself started life humbly, first as a Greek settlement and later as a pleasure resort for Roma's high society. Little touched by Vesuvio's eruption in 79 AD, which wiped out Pompei and neigh-

Highlights

- Marvel at the famous Toro Farnese and losing yourself among the Graeco-Roman artefacts in Napoli's Museo Archeologico Nazionale

- Wander the lanes and explore the Grotta Azzurra on the Isola di Capri

- Spy on the ancient Roman lifestyle at perfectly preserved Pompei

- Gaze down at the sparkling Costiera Amalfitana from hilltop Ravello's Villa Rufolo

- Wonder at the beauty and size of the (relatively) undiscovered Certosa di San Lorenzo near Padula

Campania	p631
Napoli (Naples)	
Around Spaccanapoli	p638
Mergellina, Vomero & Santa Lucia	p642
Around Piazza Garibaldi	p645

bouring towns, Napoli also survived several Saracen assaults. It was an independent city-state ruled by dukes until southern Italy came under the sway of the Normans in the mid-12th century. The short-lived kingdom of the Normans, with its capital in Palermo (Sicilia),

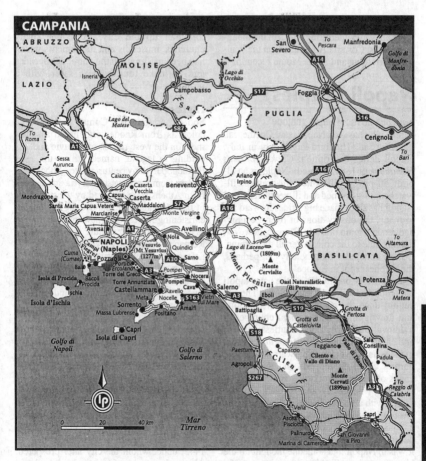

CAMPANIA

changed hands and dimensions regularly but always comprised the bulk of southern Italy, including all Campania. Under Spanish Bourbon rule in the 18th century, Napoli was one of the great capitals of Europe.

Campanian cooking is simple – its greatest contribution to world cuisine is the pizza. In Napoli especially, you can get a quick pizza anywhere and savour its unmistakable, rich, tomato sauce. Campania produces some decent wines, including the popular white Falanghina and various tipples under the Greco

di Tufo name. Limoncello (the bright-yellow lemon liqueur) is a regional speciality. Produced along the Costiera Amalfitana, around Sorrento and on Capri and the other Golfo di Napoli islands, it is best drunk chilled and in small doses – it's definitely an acquired taste.

Napoli is on the main train line from Roma and is a regional transport hub, which makes travel quite easy and cheap. Most places of interest to the traveller in Campania are accessible by train. This is an advantage as tracking down buses can become tiresome.

For the more adventurous and energetic there are some interesting walks in the mountains of the Costeria Amalfitana, on the Penisola Sorrentina and in the Monte Picentini.

Napoli (Naples)

postcode 80100 • pop 1,206,000

A man who has seen Napoli, said Goethe, can never be sad. The third-largest city in Italy, Napoli defies description. *Cook's Tourist's Handbook* of 1884 declared: 'Naples is an ill-built, ill-paved, ill-lighted, ill-drained, ill-watched, ill-governed and ill-ventilated city.' Napoli has since made big strides forward but to many, the observations of over a century ago retain a grain of truth. There is, however, another side to the coin. After all the carping, Cook's concludes that the city 'is, perhaps, the loveliest spot in Europe'.

Beautifully positioned on the bay, Napoli encompasses a little of everything. The old centre, once the heart of ancient Neapolis and now jammed with ancient churches, a medieval university and countless eateries and cafés, pulsates to the life of noisy street markets and their clientele, swarms of people darting about on mopeds and the general chaos of a city at work.

Nothing is orderly and regulation is observed with absolute discretion. Traffic lights are routinely ignored, as are one-way signs and just about every other road rule. When it became mandatory in Italy to wear seatbelts, it was in Napoli that someone thought up the idea of wearing a T-shirt with an imprint of a seatbelt sash. It is not unusual to see a whole family aboard a single Vespa or children buzzing about, dangerously fast, on mopeds.

Napoli is the centre of a booming counterfeit clothes racket and the base for much of Italy's contraband cigarette smuggling. This industry involves the Camorra, Napoli's brand of the Mafia, whose other specialities are bank hold-ups, controlling the local fruit and vegetable markets and the massive *toto nero* (illegal football pools).

Since the election in 1993 of the proactive, left-wing mayor Antonio Bassolino, there have been huge and successful efforts to clean up the city, to reopen many churches, museums and monuments which had been off-limits to the public for decades and to make tourist areas safer with a prominent police presence.

History

Soon after founding Cumae in 1000 BC, colonists from Rhodes established a settlement on the western side of Vesuvio and, according to legend, named it after the siren Parthenope. Many centuries later, Phoenician traders from north-western Syria and Greeks from Athens were attracted by the splendour of the coast and so expanded the settlement, christening it Neapolis (new city). It thrived as a centre of Greek culture and later, under Roman rule, became a favourite for such notables as Pompey, Caesar and Tiberius.

After successive waves of invasion by the Goths and a couple of spells associated with Byzantium, Napoli was an independent dukedom for about 400 years until taken by the Normans in 1139. They, in turn, were replaced by the German Hohenstaufens, whose Swabian dynasty lasted until 1266 and gave the city many new institutions, including the university. After the defeat and death of Manfred (King of Sicily) in the battle of Benevento in 1266, Charles I of Anjou took control of the Kingdom of Sicily and turned Napoli into its de facto capital. The Angevins were in turn succeeded, after a period of disorder, by the Spanish house of Aragon in 1442, under whom the city later prospered. Alfonso I of Aragon, in particular, introduced new laws and a more modern concept of justice and also promoted the arts and sciences.

In 1503 Napoli and the Kingdom of Sicily were absorbed by the Spanish empire, which sent viceroys to rule as virtual dictators. Notwithstanding their heavy-handed rule, Napoli flourished artistically and acquired much of its splendour during this period. Indeed, it continued to flourish when the Spanish Bourbons re-established Napoli as capital of the Kingdom of the Two Sicilies in 1734 (the Kingdom of the Two Sicilies encompassed part of the Italian peninsula and Sicily

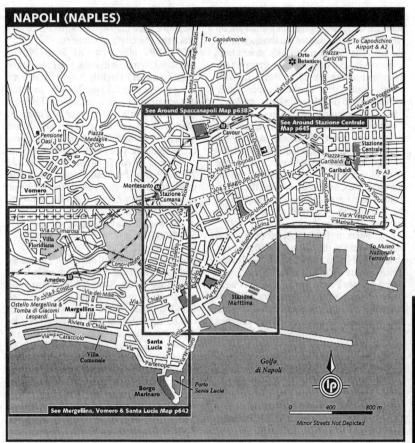

NAPOLI (NAPLES)

from the mid-15th to mid-19th centuries). Aside from a Napoleonic interlude under Joachim Murat from 1806 to 1815, the Bourbons remained in the saddle until unseated by Garibaldi and the Kingdom of Italy in 1860. One of Europe's greatest cities, Napoli was a serious but unsuccessful, contender for capital of the new nation.

The city was heavily damaged during WWII in more than 100 bombing raids and marks can still be seen on many monuments. The Allies subsequently presided over a fairly disastrous period of transition from war to peace – many observers have since attributed the initial boom in the city's organised crime, at least in part, to members of the occupying forces. A severe earthquake in 1980 and the dormant, but not extinct, Vesuvio looming to the east, remind Neapolitans of their city's vulnerability.

Orientation

Napoli stretches along the waterfront and is divided into *quartieri* (districts); most street signs bear the name of the district as well. Stazione Centrale and the bus station are off Piazza Garibaldi, east of Spaccanapoli, the old city. The piazza and its side streets form an enormous and unwelcoming transport terminus and street market. The area is distinctly seedy. Quite a few of the cheaper hotels, some of which double as brothels, are here.

A wide shopping street, Corso Umberto I, skirts the southern edge of Spaccanapoli, the ancient heart of Napoli, on its way south-west from Piazza Garibaldi to Piazza Bovio. From here Via A Depretis runs to the huge Piazza Municipio, dominated by the unmistakable Castel Nuovo. From the waterfront behind the castle you can find boats to the bay islands, Palermo and other long-distance destinations.

The Palazzo Reale, the former royal palace, is next to the castle. From the palace, go north to Napoli's main street, Via Toledo, which becomes Via Roma for a short stretch after it crosses Piazza Carità, to reach Piazza Dante, on the western boundary of Spaccanapoli. The road continues as Via Pessina, then Via Santa Teresa degli Scalzi and then Corso Amedeo di Savoia, before reaching the Parco di Capodimonte north of the centre.

The extensions of two of Napoli's more original streets, Via Benedetto Croce (which becomes Via San Biagio dei Librai) and Via dei Tribunali, eventually meet Via Roma. Much of Napoli's street life, artisans and a host of good, cheap restaurants can be found in this area. Via San Biagio dei Librai is part of an almost straight run from near Stazione Centrale through Spaccanapoli to the foot of the hilltop Vomero district.

To the south and west extend broad boulevards and majestic squares leading to Santa Lucia and chic Mergellina. Above it all, sits Napoli's upper-middle class in the relative calm of Vomero, a natural balcony with grand views across the city and bay to Vesuvio.

Information

Tourist Offices Napoli has several tourist offices which stock *Qui Napoli*, a free monthly listings brochure which includes details of the opening hours for museums and other places to see in Napoli. You can pick up a good map at the tourist office plus guides to the city's monuments.

The EPT office (☎ 081 26 87 79) at Stazione Centrale will book hotel rooms and some staff speak English. It opens from 9 am to 1 pm and 3 to 7.30 pm Monday to Saturday and from 9 am to 1 pm Sunday. The main EPT office (☎ 081 40 53 11) is at Piazza dei Martiri 58 (open from 8.30 am to 2.30 pm Monday to Friday). There are branch offices at the Mergellina train station and the airport.

There is an AAST office (☎ 081 552 33 28) on Piazza del Gesù Nuovo, south-east of Piazza Dante, which opens from 8.30 am to 7.30 pm Monday to Saturday and until 3.30 pm Sunday.

The student travel centre, CTS (☎ 081 552 79 60), is at Via Mezzocannone 25.

Money The city is full of currency exchange booths and the rates offered are usually lower than at the banks. Some banks charge commission to change travellers cheques, so ask first. Visa, MasterCard or Eurocheque cards can be used at most banks with ATMs, including the Banca Nazionale del Lavoro at Via Firenze 39 and Monte dei Paschi di Siena, around the corner on Corso Novara. Banks open from about 8 am to 1 pm and then 3 to 4.30 pm Monday to Friday. American Express is represented by Every Tour (☎ 081 551 85 64) at Piazza Municipio 5-6.

Post & Communications The main post office is at Piazza Matteotti, off Via A Diaz, in a grand, Fascist-era building. It is open from 8.15 am to 7.30 pm Monday to Friday and to 1 pm Saturday.

The main Telecom office is at Via A Depretis 40, open from 9 am to 10 pm daily. Internetbar, Piazza Bellini 74, provides email and Internet access.

Medical Services For an ambulance, call ☎ 081 752 06 96. Each district has a Guardia Medica with a doctor on duty at night and weekends. Tourist offices have a list of phone numbers and they are also listed in *Qui Napoli*. The Ospedale Loreto-Mare (hospital;

☎ 081 20 10 33), Via Amerigo Vespucci, is on the seafront about three minutes by taxi from the Stazione Centrale. The pharmacy at Stazione Centrale is open from 8 am to 8 pm daily, or check the daily *Il Tempo di Napoli* for details of an open pharmacy in your area.

Emergency The questura (police station; ☎ 081 794 11 11) is at Via Medina 75, off Via A Diaz. It has an office for foreigners where you can report thefts etc. To report a stolen car, call ☎ 081 794 14 35.

Dangers & Annoyances Petty crime is a big problem in Napoli, so a few precautions are necessary. Carry your money and documents in a money belt and never carry a bag or purse if you can help it – moped bandits just love them. Be very aware of pickpockets on crowded buses.

Car and motorcycle theft are also problems in Napoli, so think twice before bringing a vehicle to the city.

Women should be careful walking alone in the streets at night, particularly near Stazione Centrale and Piazza Dante. Never venture into the dark side streets at night unless you are in a group. The area west of Via Toledo and as far north as Piazza Carità can be particularly threatening.

Take care when crossing roads. There are few functioning traffic lights and pedestrian crossings and Neapolitans rarely stop anyway. When facing a green light they drive with caution, believing that those facing the red light will not stop. Vehicles and pedestrians simply slip around each other in a kind of unwritten code of road 'courtesy' that can be a little unnerving at first.

Walking Tour

You'll never walk all of Napoli in a day but the following itinerary will take you through the heart of it and help you get your bearings.

Starting from Piazza Garibaldi, head a short way down Corso Umberto I before veering right into Via Egiziaca a Forcella. Cross Via P Colletta and follow the main street as it veers to the left into Via Vicaria Vecchia. Where this runs into the busy cross street, Via Duomo, you have the **Chiesa di San Giorgio Maggiore** on your left and, two blocks north-west up Via Duomo, the **duomo** itself. Virtually opposite is the **Chiesa dei Girolamini**. Walk back south-east to where you emerged on Via Duomo. Turn west off Via Duomo into Via San Biagio dei Librai, one of the liveliest roads in Spaccanapoli. You'll pass the **Ospedale delle Bambole** (Dolls' Hospital) and the churches of **SS Filippo e Giacomo** and **Sant'Angelo a Nilo**.

On Piazza San Domenico Maggiore stands the important church of the same name. Note that the not-to-be-missed **Cappella di San Severo** is just off this square in a lane east of the church. Here you are faced with at least two choices.

You could head south along Via Mezzocannone past the **university** and rejoin Corso Umberto I, turning right and following it into Piazza Bovio. From here, Via A Depretis leads south-west to Piazza Municipio and the round-towered **Castel Nuovo**. Walk west from here and you will come to an elegant series of squares and the surrounding **Palazzo Reale**, the **Teatro San Carlo**, the **Galleria Umberto I** and the **Chiesa di San Francesco di Paola**. From here you could follow the waterside around to Santa Lucia and beyond to Mergellina, or turn north from Piazza Trento e Trieste up **Via Toledo** (named after the Spanish viceroy who had it laid out as part of his urban expansion programme in the mid-16th century), leading back to Spaccanapoli.

Alternatively, from Piazza San Domenico Maggiore continue west along Via B Croce, past the **Palazzo Filomarino** and the **Basilica di Santa Chiara** as far as Piazza del Gesù Nuovo and the **Chiesa del Gesù Nuovo** (as well as the AAST office). Then backtrack to the first intersection and turn left (north) along Via S Sebastiano. At the next intersection on your left a short street leads down to the **Port'Alba**, a city gate built in 1625 and Piazza Dante. Ahead of you is Piazza Bellini and to your right Piazza Luigi Miraglia. The latter becomes Via dei Tribunali and intersects with Via Duomo. This was the **decumanus**, or main street, of the original Greek and later Roman, town. Two-thirds of the

CAMPANIA

way along stood the Greek **agora**, or central market and meeting place, in what is now Piazza San Gaetano.

Piazza Bellini, by the way, is a good place to rest your weary feet in one of several cafés and while you're at it, you could inspect the remains of the ancient Greek city walls under the square. After that you could then proceed farther north along Via Santa Maria di Costantinopoli right up to the grand **Museo Archeologico Nazionale**.

Spaccanapoli

Duomo Built on the site of earlier churches, which were themselves preceded by a temple of Neptune, this grand cathedral was begun by Charles I of Anjou in 1272. Largely destroyed in 1456 by an earthquake, it's undergone numerous alterations. The neo-Gothic façade is the result of late 19th century cosmetic surgery. Above the wide central nave inside is an ornately decorated panel ceiling.

Of central importance to Napoli's religious (some would say superstitious) life is the 17th century baroque **Cappella di San Gennaro** (St Januarius; also known as the Cappella del Tesoro or Chapel of the Treasury), to the right after you enter the duomo. The chapel houses the head of the saint, as well as two phials of his congealed blood, kept behind the opulent high altar. San Gennaro, the city's patron saint, was martyred at Pozzuoli, near Napoli, in 305 AD and tradition holds that two phials of his congealed blood liquefied when his body was transferred back to Napoli. Three times a year, thousands gather in the duomo to pray for a miracle, namely, that the blood will again liquefy and save Napoli from any potential disaster. The saint is said to have saved the city from disaster on numerous occasions, although the miracle failed to occur in 1941 when Vesuvio erupted. See Special Events later in this section.

The next chapel contains an urn with the saint's bones and various other relics. Below the duomo's high altar lies the **Cappella Carafa**, also known as the Crypt of San Gennaro, a Renaissance chapel built to house the saint's relics.

To the left and rear of the duomo, a passageway leads to what is effectively a separate church, the 10th century **Basilica di Santa Restituta**. Also much altered over time, it is now part of the duomo's so-called archaeological zone, to which admission costs L5000. It's open from 9 am to noon and 4.30 to 7 pm Monday to Saturday and from 9 am to noon Sunday.

Around the Duomo Virtually opposite the duomo is the entrance to the **Chiesa dei Girolamini**, or San Filippo Neri, a rich baroque church with two facades. Its 18th century façade, facing Via dei Tribunali, is now closed. A small picture gallery in the adjoining convent features works from the 16th to 18th centuries. It is open from 9.30 am to 12.30 pm and 2 to 5.30 pm daily; admission is free.

Duck around the corner into Via dei Tribunali and you'll soon come across the **Chiesa di San Lorenzo Maggiore**, to the left in Piazza San Gaetano. The interior of the church, begun by Provençal architects under the Franciscans in the 13th century, is French Gothic. Catherine of Austria, who died in 1323, is buried here and her mosaic-covered tomb is among the most eye-catching of the church's adornments. You can pass through to the cloisters of the neighbouring convent, where Petrarch sojourned in 1345. There is also a museum housing relics, dating back as far as Greek Neapolis, which were discovered during excavations. Admission is free.

Across Via dei Tribunali is the **Chiesa di San Paolo Maggiore**, built in the late 16th century on the site of a temple of the Dioscuri. The opulent interior houses the tomb of San Gaetano (St Cajetan).

While you're in the area, the **Chiesa di San Giorgio Maggiore**, where Via San Biagio dei Librai meets Via Duomo, is worth a quick look for its austere interior.

Across the road is the 15th century **Palazzo Cuomo**, built by Tuscan artists. The building was moved several metres in 1881 when the street was being widened. It now contains the Museo Gaetano Filangieri, with an extensive collection of arms, furniture and china, as well as paintings of the Neapolitan school. It is open from 9 am to

2 pm Tuesday to Saturday and to 1 pm Sunday; admission costs L5000.

Via San Biagio dei Librai Take a look at the Ospedale delle Bambole at No 81. This 'dolls' hospital' looks a little macabre, with little heads piled up in the windows, but you'd be hard pressed to find too many places like it anywhere in the world for buying or repairing dolls. In fact, this whole street and its continuation, Via B Croce, the parallel Via dei Tribunali to the north and the labyrinth of side alleys, is thronged with craftspeople of all kinds. You'll find not only goldsmiths and other jewellers, but makers of the famous Neapolitan *presepi* (Christmas nativity scenes) – some of them are extraordinarily elaborate.

Farther along from the dolls' hospital is the **Palazzo Marigliano**, which features a magnificent Renaissance entrance hall and façade. You then pass the **Palazzo di Carafa di Maddaloni** and **Chiesa di SS Filippo e Giacomo** with their contrasting Renaissance and Rococo styles.

The entrance to the **Chiesa di Sant'Angelo a Nilo** is on Vico Donnaromita 15, off Via San Biagio dei Librai. Built in 1385 and remodelled in the 18th century, the church contains the monumental Renaissance tomb of one Cardinal Brancaccio, to which Donatello contributed.

The Gothic **Chiesa di San Domenico Maggiore**, along Via B Croce in the piazza bearing its name, was completed in 1324 by the Dominican order and was favoured by the Aragonese nobility. The church's interior, a cross between Baroque and 19th century neo-Gothic, features some fine examples of Renaissance sculpture. In the sacristy are 45 coffins of the princes of Aragon and other nobles.

The deceptive simplicity of the **Cappella di San Severo**, on Via de Sanctis, a narrow lane east of the church, is a dazzling contrast to the treasure chest of sculpture inside. Giuseppe Sanmartino's *Cristo Velato* (Veiled Christ), for instance, still confounds experts, who cannot agree on how he created the apparently translucent veil. Also baffling is Corradini's *Pudicizia* (Modesty),

which makes no attempt to hide the erotic. Also known as the Cappella di Santa Maria della Pietà dei Sangro, the chapel is the tomb of the princes of Sangro di San Severo and is open from 10 am to 5 pm daily except Tuesday. Admission costs L8000.

Around Piazza del Gesù Nuovo From Piazza San Domenico Maggiore the road continues west, following the course of the old Roman main street under the name of Via Benedetto Croce. Croce, Italy's foremost philosopher and historian in the first half of the 20th century, lived and died in the **Palazzo Filomarino**, a grand Renaissance building on the right just before you reach Via San Sebastiano.

Across Via San Sebastiano you come to the **Basilica di Santa Chiara**, a church and convent partly incorporating a Roman wall that was extended around the convent to protect the nuns. Built between 1310 and 1328 under the Angevin dynasty, it suffered from earthquakes and baroque alterations in the 18th century ('overloaded with excessive ornamentation' according to one British observer in the late 19th century). Incendiary bombs burned out the church and destroyed many works of art in 1943. Since the end of WWII it has been returned more or less to its original spare Gothic appearance and is one of Napoli's principal medieval monuments. The nuns' cloisters behind the church consist of four paths that form a cross, bordered by a long parapet entirely covered in decorative ceramic tiles, depicting 64 landscapes and scenes from the nuns' lives.

A few steps west, Piazza del Gesù Nuovo opens before you, with its *guglia*, a kind of ground-level baroque steeple, dripping with opulent sculptural decoration. You'll see several of these around the city. The 16th century **Chiesa del Gesù Nuovo**, on the northern side of the piazza, is one of the city's greatest examples of Renaissance architecture, particularly the lozenge-shaped rustication of its façade. The interior was redecorated in Neapolitan baroque style by Cosimo Fanzango after a fire in 1639.

The **Chiesa di Sant'Anna dei Lombardi**,

euro currency converter L10,000 = €5.16

AROUND SPACCANAPOLI

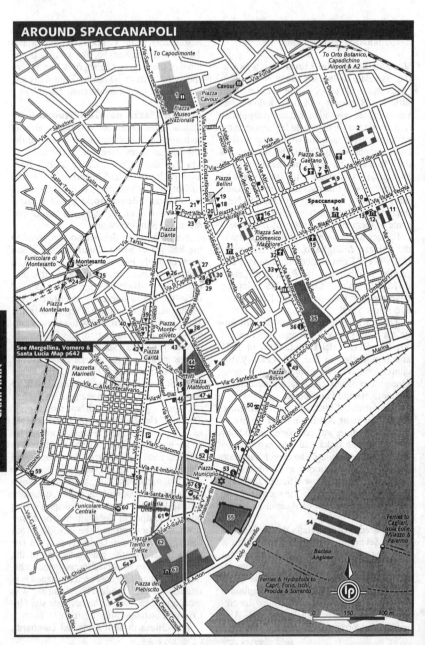

AROUND SPACCANAPOLI

PLACES TO STAY
- 4 Bellini
- 5 Albergo Fiamma
- 10 Duomo
- 38 Candy
- 46 Oriente Grand Hotel
- 49 Hotel Orchidea

PLACES TO EAT
- 7 Trattoria da Carmine
- 8 Pizzeria di Matteo
- 19 Intra Moenia
- 20 Ristorante Bellini
- 21 Caffè dell'Epoca
- 23 Pizzeria Port'Alba
- 25 Friggitoria Fiorenzano
- 26 Ristorante Hong Kong
- 33 Il Pizzicotto
- 37 Minipizza
- 39 La Taverna del Buongustaio
- 40 Pizzeria al 22
- 41 Lo Sfizietto
- 42 Gelateria Azzurra
- 48 La Nova Club
- 58 Pintauro
- 64 Gambrinus

OTHER
- 1 Museo Archeologico Nazionale
- 2 Duomo
- 3 Chiesa dei Girolamini
- 6 Chiesa di San Paolo Maggiore
- 9 Chiesa di San Lorenzo Maggiore
- 11 Chiesa di San Giorgio Maggiore
- 12 Palazzo Cuomo
- 13 Ospedale delle Bambole (Dolls' Hospital)
- 14 Palazzo Marigliano
- 15 Chiesa di SS Filippo e Giacomo
- 16 Cappella di San Severo
- 17 Chiesa di San Domenico Maggiore
- 18 Internetbar
- 22 Port'Alba (City Gate)
- 24 Stazione Cumana; Funicolare di Montesanto
- 27 Chiesa del Gesù Nuovo
- 28 Piazza del Gesù Nuovo
- 29 AAST Tourist Office
- 30 Basilica di Santa Chiara

- 31 Palazzo Filomarino
- 32 Chiesa di Sant'Angelo a Nilo
- 34 Museo della Mineralogia; Museo Zoologico
- 35 University
- 36 CTS Travel Agency
- 43 Chiesa di Sant'Anna dei Lombardi
- 44 Main Post Office
- 45 Tourcar (Travel Agency)
- 47 Questura (Police Station)
- 50 Telecom Office
- 51 Qantas; Gastaldi
- 52 Alitalia
- 53 CIT Travel Agency
- 54 Stazione Marittima; SNAV Ferries
- 55 Castel Nuovo; Museo Civico
- 56 SITA Bus Station
- 57 Every Tour (American Express)
- 59 Otto Jazz Club
- 60 Funicular to Vomero
- 61 Box Office (Ticket Sales)
- 62 Teatro San Carlo
- 63 Palazzo Reale
- 65 Chiesa di San Francesco di Paola

CAMPANIA

south-west of Piazza del Gesù Nuovo, was founded in 1414 by Origlia and features fine Renaissance sculpture, including a superb terracotta *Pietà* (1492) by Guido Mazzoni.

Around Piazza del Carmine South of Stazione Centrale, the **Basilica del Carmine Maggiore**, on the waterfront in Piazza del Carmine, was the scene of the 1647 Neapolitan Revolution led by Masaniello. Inside is the much-worshipped *Madonna Bruna* (Brown Madonna). Each year on 16 July a fireworks display celebrates the festival of the Madonna by simulating the *incendio simolato del campanile* (the burning of the church).

Museo Archeologico Nazionale

Housed in a vast red building that dominates the northern fringe of Spaccanapoli, the archaeological treasures of Napoli's principal museum form one of the most comprehensive collections of Graeco-Roman artefacts

in the world. You could easily lose yourself in here for several hours. Originally a cavalry barracks and later the seat of the city's university, the museum was established by Charles of Bourbon in the late 18th century to house the rich collection of antiquities he had inherited from his mother, Elizabeth Farnese, as well as the treasures which had been discovered at Pompei and Ercolano. It also contains the Borgia collection of Etruscan and Egyptian relics.

Many items from the Farnese collection of classical sculpture are featured on the ground floor, including the impressive *Toro Farnese* (Farnese Bull) in the room of the same name. It is most likely a Roman copy of the Greek original dating from 150 BC. The sculpture is an enormous group of figures depicting the death of Dirce, Queen of Thebes, who in Greek mythology was tied to a bull and torn apart over rocks. The group was carved from a single block of marble and later restored by Michelangelo.

On the mezzanine floor is a gallery of mosaics, mostly from Pompei, including the *Battle of Alexander*, the best known depiction of the great Macedonian emperor. It once paved the floor in the Casa del Fauno at Pompei and is just one of a series of remarkably detailed and lifelike pieces depicting animals, scenes from daily life, musicians and even Plato with his students. In all, the mosaics are an eloquent expression of ancient artistic genius.

The 1st floor is largely devoted to discoveries from Pompei, Ercolano, Stabiae and Cumae. The displays range from numerous murals and frescoes, rescued from the sites, to gladiators' helmets, household items, ceramics and glassware. One room is dedicated to an extraordinary collection of vases of mixed origins, many of them carefully reassembled. The Egyptian collection is in the basement.

The museum is on Piazza Museo Nazionale and is open from 9 am to 2 pm Tuesday to Saturday and to 1 pm Sunday. In summer it often stays open to 7 pm. Admission costs L12,000.

South of Spaccanapoli
Castel Nuovo When Charles I of Anjou took over Napoli and the Swabians' Sicilian kingdom, he found himself in control not only of his new southern Italian acquisitions, but possessions in Toscana, northern Italy and Provence (France). It made sense to base the new dynasty in Napoli rather than Palermo and Charles launched an ambitious construction programme to expand the port and city walls. His plans included converting a Franciscan convent into the castle that still stands in Piazza Municipio. Also dubbed the Maschio Angioino, its crenellated round towers make it one of the most striking buildings in Napoli.

The 'New Castle' was erected in three years from 1279, but what you see today was the result of renovations by the Aragonese two centuries later, as well as a meticulous restoration effort prior to WWII. The heavy grey stone that dominates the castle was imported from Mallorca. The two storey Renaissance triumphal arch at the entrance, the

Torre della Guardia, was completed in 1467 and commemorates the triumphal entry of Alfonso I of Aragon into Napoli in 1443.

Spread across several halls on the ground, 1st and 2nd floors is the **Museo Civico**. Frescoes and sculpture from the 14th and 15th centuries, on the ground floor, are of most interest. The other two floors offer a range of paintings, either by Neapolitan artists or overwhelmingly with Napoli or Campania as subjects, covering the 17th to the early 20th centuries. The castle and museum are open from 9 am to 7 pm Monday to Saturday. Admission to the museum costs L7000.

North-east of the Castel Nuovo on Piazza Bovio is the **Fontana di Nettuno**, dating from 1601. Gianlorenzo Bernini sculpted its sea creatures and Naccherini the figure of Neptune.

Piazza Trento e Trieste This is one of Napoli's more elegant squares, fronted on the north-eastern side by Italy's largest and oldest opera house, the **Teatro San Carlo**, famed for its perfect acoustics. Loclas proudly boast that it was built in 1737 by Charles of Bourbon – 40 years before La Scala. San Carlo was destroyed by fire in 1816 and later restored. It is home to one of the oldest ballet schools in Italy. The French writer Stendhal wrote: 'The first impression one gets is of being suddenly transported to the palace of an oriental emperor. There is nothing in Europe to compare with it.' It is open in the early morning and midafternoon, although an attendant might show you through at other times. Inquire at the box office for exact times.

Across Via San Carlo is one of the four entrances to the imposing glass atrium of the **Galleria Umberto I**, built in 1890 and opened in 1900. The Galleria is the humble cousin of Milano's truly impressive Galleria Vittorio Emanuele II.

Palazzo Reale Facing the grand **Piazza del Plebiscito**, this magnificent palace was built around 1600. It was completely renovated in 1841, but suffered extensive damage during WWII. The statues of the eight most im-

Watch out for the 'wild life' – including some 80 bears – in the Parco Nazionale d'Abruzzo.

The olive tree, considered a symbol of peace

Isolated hilltop village in the Gran Sasso d'Italia

Sulmona – home to the sweet confetti industry

Dramatic cliffs, clear waters, cute houses, expensive shops, seafood restaurants – Positano has it all.

portant kings of Napoli were inserted into niches in the façade in 1888.

After entering the courtyard, a huge double staircase (under a dome) leads to the royal apartments, which house the **Museo del Palazzo Reale**, a rich collection of furnishings, porcelain, tapestries, statues and paintings. The museum is open from 9 am to 1.30 pm Tuesday to Sunday and also from 4 to 7.30 pm at weekends. Admission is L8000.

The palace has also, since 1925, been home to the **Biblioteca Nazionale**, which includes the vast Farnese collection brought to Napoli by Charles of Bourbon, with more than 2000 papyri discovered at Ercolano and fragments of a 5th century Coptic Bible. Admission is free.

The **Chiesa di San Francesco di Paola**, at the eastern end of the piazza, was begun by Ferdinand I in 1817 to celebrate the restoration of his kingdom after the Napoleonic interlude. Flanked by semicircular colonnades, the church is based on Roma's Pantheon and is a popular wedding spot.

Santa Lucia

Castel dell'Ovo The so-called Castle of the Egg is on the small rocky island off Santa Lucia, known as Borgo Marinaro and connected by a bridge from Via Partenope. Folklore states that the name came about after part of the island collapsed, likened by locals to Virgil's story of the breaking of an egg. The castle occupies the site of a Roman villa. Built in the 12th century by the Norman king William I, the castle became a key fortress in the defence of Campania. You can wander through the small lanes on the island (mostly occupied by restaurants) but the castle, restored in the 1970s, is opened only for meetings and exhibitions.

The **Fontana dell'Immacolatella**, at the end of Via Partenope, dates from the 17th century and features statues by Bernini and Naccherini.

Mergellina

West of Santa Lucia, Via Partenope spills into Piazza della Vittoria, marking the beginning of the Riviera di Chiaia, which runs along the northern edge of the **Villa Comunale**, a large park marked off on the seaward side by Via Francesco Caracciolo. The **acquario** (aquarium) in the park was founded in the late 19th century by German naturalist Anton Dohrn. Its 30 tanks contain specimens of sea life exclusively from the Golfo di Napoli area. Ask to see the frescoes on the 1st floor. The aquarium is open from 9 am to 6 pm Monday to Saturday and from 10 am to 6 pm Sunday in summer, from 9 am to 5 pm Monday to Saturday and to 2 pm Sunday in winter. Admission costs L3000.

Close by, at Riviera di Chiaia 200, is the **Museo Pignatelli**, an old patrician residence containing mostly 19th century furnishings, china and other knick-knacks. A pavilion set in the villa's gardens houses a coach museum and contains English and French carriages. Both museums are open from 9 am to 2 pm Tuesday to Sunday. Admission costs L4000.

Farther west, a short stroll from Piazza Sannazzaro and the Mergellina train station, is the **Tomba di Giacomo Leopardi**, the 19th century poet who died in Napoli in 1837 and an Augustan-age Roman monument that has come to be known as the **Tomba di Virgilio**, although it has nothing to do with the ancient bard, who died in Brindisi in 19 BC. The tombs lie behind the Chiesa di Santa Maria di Piedigrotta and can be visited from 9 am to 1 pm daily. Admission is free.

Vomero

Visible from all over the city, the Vomero hill (pronounced 'Vom-e-ro') is quite a world apart, a serene and well-to-do residential quarter that rises above the chaos of the great metropolis below. Several funicular lines connect Vomero with the city.

Castel Sant'Elmo Commanding spectacular views across the city and bay, this austere, star-shaped castle was built over a stronghold first established in 1329. The present structure was built under Spanish vice-regal rule in 1538. Impressive though it is, the castle has seen little real action, serving more often than not as a prison. It is open from 9 am to 2 pm Tuesday to Sunday;

CAMPANIA

admission costs L4000. These details can vary when temporary exhibitions are held.

Certosa di San Martino Barely 100m from the castle lies this Carthusian monastery, established in the 14th century and rebuilt in the 17th century by Fanzango in Neapolitan baroque style. It houses the **Museo Nazionale di San Martino**, which features a section on naval history, an area dedicated to the history of the Kingdom of Napoli as well as an extensive art collection. Of particular interest is the Sezione Presepiale, several rooms devoted to a collection of Neapolitan presepi, elaborate nativity scenes sculpted in the 18th and 19th centuries. Not all of the monastery is open to the public, but you can enjoy the tranquil baroque Chiostro Grande, or main cloisters, whose manicured gardens are ringed by elegant porticoes.

Adjacent is the monastery's church, virtually an art gallery in itself, whose original Gothic character is still evident. It contains exquisite marblework and a good number of

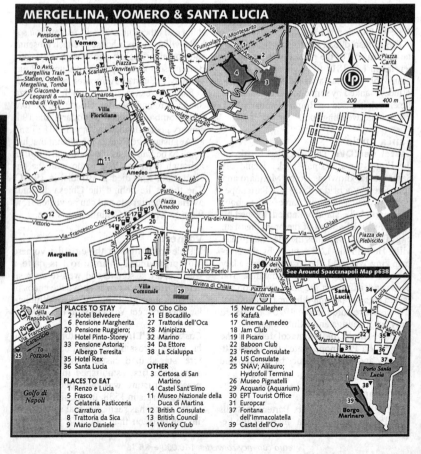

MERGELLINA, VOMERO & SANTA LUCIA

See Around Spaccanapoli Map p638

PLACES TO STAY		10 Cibo Cibo	15 New Callegher
2 Hotel Belvedere		21 El Bocadillo	16 Kafafà
6 Pensione Margherita		27 Trattoria dell'Oca	17 Cinema Amedeo
20 Pensione Ruggiero;		28 Minipizza	18 Jam Club
Hotel Pinto-Storey		32 Marino	19 Il Picaro
33 Pensione Astoria;		34 Da Ettore	22 Baboon Club
Albergo Teresita		38 La Scialuppa	23 French Consulate
35 Hotel Rex			24 US Consulate
36 Santa Lucia		**OTHER**	25 SNAV; Alilauro;
		3 Certosa di San	Hydrofoil Terminal
PLACES TO EAT		Martino	26 Museo Pignatelli
1 Renzo e Lucia		4 Castel Sant'Elmo	29 Acquario (Aquarium)
5 Frasco		11 Museo Nazionale della	30 EPT Tourist Office
7 Gelateria Pasticceria		Duca di Martina	31 Europcar
Carraturo		12 British Consulate	37 Fontana
8 Trattoria da Sica		13 British Council	dell'Immacolatella
9 Mario Daniele		14 Wonky Club	39 Castel dell'Ovo

frescoes and paintings, particularly by 17th century Neapolitan artists. There is a magnificent view from the terraced gardens and from Largo San Martino (the car park) outside. The museum is open from 9 am to 2 pm Tuesday to Sunday and admission is L8000.

Villa Floridiana The verdant grounds of this public park spread down the slopes from Via Domenico Cimarosa in Vomero to Mergellina. The stately home at the bottom end of the gardens was built in 1817 by Ferdinand I for his wife, the Duchess of Floridia. Today it contains the **Museo Nazionale della Ceramica Duca di Martina**, which holds an extensive collection of European, Chinese and Japanese china, ivory, enamels and Italian majolica. The museum is open from 9 am to 2 pm Tuesday to Saturday and to 1 pm Sunday. Admission costs L4000. The park is open from 9 am to one hour before sunset daily except Monday and admission is free.

Capodimonte

Palazzo Reale di Capodimonte Work on a new palace for Charles of Bourbon started in 1738 and took almost a century to complete. On the northern edge of the city, the distinctive pinky-orange and grey palace is set in extensive parklands that were once the noble's hunting grounds. In 1860 the palace passed to the Savoia and in 1947 to the state. It was reopened to the public in 1957 and since 1990 has been extensively restored. The palazzo houses the **Museo e Gallerie di Capodimonte**, which displays the important Farnese collection (see the boxed text 'Voracious Collecting, Farnese Style'). The paintings hang in the royal galleries on the 1st floor and are divided into periods and schools; there are informative panels in each room in both Italian and English. The collection is extensive and boasts works by Bellini, Botticelli, Caravaggio, the Carracci, Correggio, Domenichino, Artemesia Gentileschi, El Greco, Guercino, Angelica Kauffmann, Filippino Lippi, Claude Lorrain, Mantegna, Simone Martini, Masaccio, Perugino, Giulio Romano, Pinturicchio, Signorelli and Sodoma. One of the most famous paintings in the collection is Masaccio's *Crocifissione* (Crucifixion). Another of the highlights is Bellini's

---

Voracious Collecting, Farnese Style

The Farnese collection was founded by Cardinal Alessandro Farnese. On becoming Pope Paul III in 1534, he first gathered art treasures for Il Vaticano and then turned his attention to the decoration of the family seat, Palazzo Farnese, in Roma. Through papal influence, the Farnese family monopolised excavations around the city. In 1540 the *Toro Farnese* (Farnese Bull) was discovered near the Terme di Caracalla and installed in the gardens of Palazzo Farnese. It remained there until its removal in 1787 to the Museo Archeologico Nazionale in Napoli, now the home of other famous Farnese treasures such as *Venere Callipigia* and *Ercole a riposo*.

The future pope's religious vows didn't prevent him from fathering three sons and a daughter. One of the most interesting paintings at the Palazzo Reale di Capodimonte is an unfinished portrait by Titian of Paul III with his two grandsons – Ottavio, who became the Duke of Parma and Piacenza, and Gran Cardinale Alessandro, who later became a serious collector in his own right. Grandson Alessandro continued the collection, commissioning works from Michelangelo, El Greco, Zuccari, Jacopo Bertoia, Salviati and Guglielmo della Porta.

The collection was transferred to Capodimonte from the Farnese family's power base in Parma and Piacenza in 1759, after Charles of Bourbon, the son of Philip V of Spain and Elisabetta Farnese, renounced the Spanish throne for that of Napoli. Many paintings were subsequently sold off by the Bourbon heirs in the early 19th century and the entire collection removed to what is now the Museo Archeologico Nazionale. The paintings were returned to Capodimonte in 1957.

CAMPANIA

Trasfigurazione (Transfiguration), as are the nine works by Titian, including several portraits and an erotic *Danae*.

Also on the 1st floor are the **royal apartments**, which house an extensive collection of armour, ivories, bronzes, porcelain and majolica (including a whole room covered in porcelain decoration), tapestries and other works of art.

The 2nd floor galleries, reopened in 1999, contain work by Neapolitan artists from the 13th to 19th centuries.

The palace is open from 10 am to 7 pm Tuesday to Saturday and from 9 am to 2 pm Sunday. Admission costs L9500. Entrance to the park surrounding the palace is free.

Catacombe di San Gennaro The catacombs are just below the palace – enter from Via di Capodimonte. Dating from the 2nd century, they are quite a different experience from the dark, claustrophobic catacombs characteristic of Roma: a mix of tombs, corridors and broad vestibules held up by columns and arches and decorated with frescoes and mosaics. San Gennaro was buried here. Guided tours begin at 9.30, 10.15, 11 and 11.45 am daily and cost L5000.

Orto Botanico
Head north along Via Duomo to Via Foria and turn right to reach the Orto Botanico (☎ 081 44 97 59) at No 223, near Piazza Carlo III. The botanical gardens were founded in 1807 by Joseph Bonaparte and are part of the Napoli university. Visits are by appointment only.

Napoli for Children
Kids of all ages will enjoy visiting Napoli's various castles. They will also enjoy a visit to the acquario (see the Mergellina section earlier) and older kids should appreciate the archaeological museum (see the Museo Archeologico Nazionale section earlier).

The Museo Nazionale Ferroviario, in a restored railway building on the waterfront at Corso San Giovanni a Teduccio, is another option. It was founded by Ferdinand II of Bourbon in the 19th century to house his collection of railway memorabilia, including engines and carriages. It is open from 9 am to 2 pm Monday to Saturday. Admission is free.

The **Museo della Mineralogia**, on Via Mezzocannone 8 between Via B Croce and Corso Umberto I, features minerals, meteorites and quartz crystals collected from the Vesuvio region. The building also holds the **Museo Zoologico**. Both museums open from 9 am to 1 pm Monday to Friday and from 10 am to 1 pm at weekends. Admission to each museum costs L1000 or L2000 for families.

Work
The Centro di Lingua e Cultura Italiana (☎ 081 551 43 31), Vico Santa Maria dell'Aiuto 17, is one of several language schools in the city. If you want to teach English, start your inquiries at the British Council (☎ 081 66 74 10), Via Crispi 92.

Organised Tours
Excursions to the Golfo di Napoli's islands and inland to Pompei and Vesuvio are organised by CIT (☎ 081 552 54 26), Piazza Municipio 70; Cima Tours (☎ 081 554 06 46), Piazza Garibaldi 114; and Tourcar (☎ 081 552 04 29), Piazza Matteotti 1. A half-day tour to Pompei costs about L50,000.

For something completely different, you could head underground. A warren of cisterns, wells and stone quarries lie below the city's surface splendour and can be visited with the Libera Associazione Escursionisti Sottosuolo (☎ 081 40 02 56), Via Santa Teresella degli Spagnoli 24. At the time of writing they met at Gambrinus (Piazza Trieste e Trento) at 10 am on Saturday and Sunday and at 9 pm Thursday.

Special Events
Napoli's main festivals honour San Gennaro. On the first Sunday in May, on 19 September and on 16 December each year, thousands gather in the duomo to pray that the saint's blood, held in two phials, will liquefy: a miracle said to save the city from potential disasters. Get there early, as police turn back the crowds when the duomo is full. See the Duomo section earlier in this chapter.

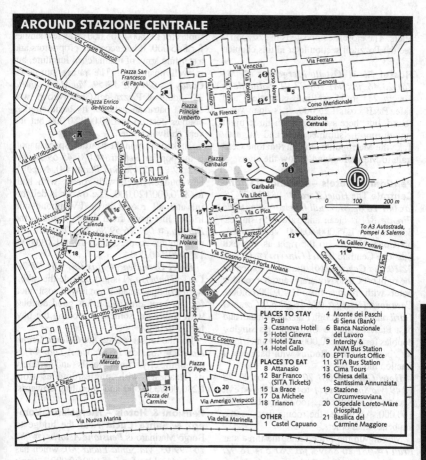

AROUND STAZIONE CENTRALE

PLACES TO STAY
2 Prati
3 Casanova Hotel
5 Hotel Ginevra
7 Hotel Zara
14 Hotel Gallo

PLACES TO EAT
8 Attanasio
12 Bar Franco
   (SITA Tickets)
15 La Brace
17 Da Michele
18 Trianon

OTHER
1 Castel Capuano

4 Monte dei Paschi
   di Siena (Bank)
6 Banca Nazionale
   del Lavoro
9 Intercity &
   ANM Bus Station
10 EPT Tourist Office
11 SITA Bus Station
13 Cima Tours
16 Chiesa della
   Santissima Annunziata
19 Stazione
   Circumvesuviana
20 Ospedale Loreto-Mare
   (Hospital)
21 Basilica del
   Carmine Maggiore

CAMPANIA

Other important festivals are the Madonna del Carmine held on 16 July in Piazza del Carmine, which culminates in a fireworks display and the Madonna di Piedigrotta (5 to 12 September). At Christmas, thousands of elaborate nativity scenes are erected around the city.

Places to Stay

Napoli is surprisingly cheap, in comparison to the north of the country, although most of the budget hotels are clustered near Stazione Centrale in a rather unsavoury area. Staff at the EPT office at Stazione Centrale will recommend and book hotels. You should avoid the hawkers who may harass you around the station – they are on commission and generally pushing less reputable establishments. Many cheaper hotels double as brothels.

Room prices should always be read in Italy as a guide rather than gospel truth, but this is even more the case in Napoli. The following prices are a fair indication. Unfortunately some hotels only have doubles and often are not willing to offer lower prices for solo travellers. The closest camp site is in Pozzuoli – see the Pozzuoli section later in this chapter.

Hostel The HI *Ostello Mergellina* (☎ 081 761 23 46, fax 081 761 23 91, Salita della Grotta 23) in Mergellina, is modern and safe. B&B costs L25,000. It is open year-round, but there's a maximum three night stay during the summer (July and August). Take the Metropolitana from Stazione Centrale to Mergellina and follow the signs.

Pensioni & Hotels – Around Stazione Centrale The *Hotel Zara* (☎ 081 28 71 25, fax 081 26 82 87, email hotelzar@tin.it, Via Firenze 81) is clean and safe with singles/doubles from L35,000/60,000. Via Firenze is off Corso Novara, to the right as you exit Stazione Centrale. *Hotel Ginevra* (☎ 081 28 32 10, Via Genova 116), the second street to the right off Corso Novara, is another reliable hotel with rooms from L40,000/65,000. *Casanova Hotel* (☎ 081 26 82 87, Corso G Garibaldi 333), through Piazza Garibaldi and past Piazza Principe Umberto, has singles/doubles for about L30,000/64,000 and triples for about L90,000. Rooms with bath cost a fraction more.

Hotel Gallo (☎ 081 20 05 12, fax 081 28 18 49, Via Spaventa 11), to the left as you exit Stazione Centrale, has rooms for L110,00/160,000. Ask to see the rooms first – some are better than others.

Moving up the price scale, the three star *Prati* (☎ 081 26 88 98, fax 081 554 18 02, email hotelprati@napleshotels.na.it, Via C Rosaroll 4) has rooms for L140,000/170,000 and is one of the area's best hotels.

Pensioni & Hotels – Around Spaccanapoli Many hotels in this area are near Piazza Dante, which you can reach by bus No R2 from Stazione Centrale or by the Metropolitana (take the train from track No 4 and get off at Piazza Cavour – from there the area is a five minute walk; see the Getting Around section later in this chapter).

Albergo Fiamma (☎ 081 45 91 87, Via Francesco del Giudice 13), off Via dei Tribunali near Piazza Bellini, has basic doubles/triples for L80,000/105,000 and a few singles for L45,000. It has eccentric proprietors and a startling array of mismatched furniture, but is well positioned. The rather run-down *Candy* (☎ 081 552 13 59, Via Monteoliveto 13), south of Piazza del Gesù Nuovo, was once a patrician palazzo. Its basic singles/doubles cost up to L60,000/80,000 but it's very chilly in winter.

Tucked away in the heart of Spaccanapoli is the popular *Bellini* (☎ 081 45 69 96, fax 081 29 22 56, Via San Paolo 44), Napoli's best budget hotel, with rooms with bath for L70,000/120,000. The owner is delightful and all rooms have TV, phone and fridge. Just down from the cathedral is the *Duomo* (☎ 081 26 59 88, Via Duomo 228), with doubles/triples/quads from L100,000/120,000/140,000.

Hotel Orchidea (☎ /fax 081 551 07 21, Corso Umberto 7) is just outside the rabbit warren of Spaccanapoli and is well positioned for the ferry terminal. It has good doubles with bathroom, some overlooking the bay, for L140,000.

For the looser wallet, the *Oriente Grand Hotel* (☎ 081 551 21 33, Via A Diaz 44) is one of the city's finest hotels (and certainly its cleanest), with singles/doubles from L230,000/330,000 and spiralling upwards.

Pensioni & Hotels – Mergellina, Vomero & Santa Lucia Near the bridge to Borgo Marinaro is *Pensione Astoria* (☎ 081 764 99 03, Via Santa Lucia 90), which has singles/doubles for L45,000/70,000 – don't expect much in the line of comfort. In the same building is *Albergo Teresita* (☎ 081 764 01 05) with rooms for L45,000/70,000. It's not unlike walking into a Fellini film.

Just nearby, but further up the price scale, the *Hotel Rex* (☎ 081 764 93 89, fax 081 764 92 27, Via Palepoli 12) has rooms from L140,000/170,000, including breakfast. The *Santa Lucia* (☎ 081 764 06 66, Via Partenope 46), probably Napoli's best hotel, overlooks the bay and Vesuvio in sumptuous style. Doubles cost up to L439,000, depending on the view.

In Vomero, **Pensione Margherita** (☎ 081 556 70 44, Via Domenico Cimarosa 29) is a few doors from the funicular station. Rooms cost L50,000/90,000, including breakfast. Take a L50 coin for the lift. For great views, the **Hotel Belvedere** (☎ 081 578 81 69, Via Tito Angelini 51) stands below the walls of the Castel Sant'Elmo and has sweeping vistas of the city and bay, but it's pretty basic.

Farther out (if everything is full), try **Pensione Oasi** (☎ 081 578 74 56, fax 081 579 82 92, Via Mariano d'Amelio 69) with rooms for L45,000/65,000.

In Mergellina, just off Piazza Amedeo, is **Pensione Ruggiero** (☎ 081 66 03 62, fax 081 66 35 36, Via Martucci 72). Clean and bright rooms with shower start at L115,000/150,000. It's in a good location for restaurants and bars. In the same building is the pricier **Hotel Pinto-Storey** which has rooms for L190,000/240,000.

Places to Eat

Neapolitan street food is among Italy's best. The pizza topped with *mozzarella* cheese and fresh tomato sauce is standard fare, as is the related *calzone*, a puffed up version with the topping becoming a filling instead. *Misto di frittura* – deep-fried potato, aubergine (eggplant) and courgette (zucchini) flowers – tempts from tiny stalls in tiny streets, as does mozzarella in *carozza* – mozzarella deep-fried in bread. Seafood, particularly clams, is a speciality (although it is best to avoid uncooked shellfish as the bay is very polluted).

Qui Napoli has listings (but no descriptions) of restaurants, trattorie and pizzerie.

Restaurants – Spaccanapoli & Stazione Centrale

The *Trattoria da Carmine* (Via dei Tribunali 92) is one of dozens of small family trattorie in this area. It has good value pasta and main dishes and cheap alcohol. It is open for lunch but closes around 8 pm. **Da Michele** (Via Cesare Sersale 1) serves Napoli's (and probably Italy's) best pizza – quite an achievement. There are only two types, *margherita* (mozzarella and tomato) or *marinara* (mozzarella and garlic). The pizzas cost L8000 or L12,000 for an extra large one.

The restaurant is always crowded – make sure you get a numbered ticket and don't be surprised if you have to wait. *Pizzeria di Matteo* (Via dei Tribunali 94) is another excellent option, with pizzas from L4000 – try the pizza lasagne with ricotta and the misto di frittura. It also does takeaway.

Il Pizzicotto (Via Mezzocannone 129) is a bright place with pasta for around L5000 and main dishes from L6000. For a quick pizza, try **Minipizza**, on the corner of Via Santa Chiara and Largo Banchi Nuovi.

The Perfect Pizza

There is great rivalry between the Neapolitans and the Romans for pizza supremacy. Yet the two products really couldn't be more different. Pizzas in Napoli have a soft doughy base, while true Roman pizzas tend to have very thin crusts. The only consensus is that both are delicious.

The Neapolitans regard their version as the authentic one – after all pizza was invented in Napoli in the 18th century – and are proud of it. Pizzerie in Napoli serving the 'real thing' have a sign on the door indicating that you will find *la vera pizza napolitana* (the real Neapolitan pizza). It's not just for show – to be worthy of the seal of approval the pizza maker has to conform to strict requirements. For a Margherita, named after Queen Margherita (1851-1926, wife of King Umberto of Savoy), the cheese must be mozzarella (preferably made from buffalo milk), the olive oil must be extra virgin and the only salt permitted is sea salt. Rolling pins are banned (the dough must be tossed by hand) and the pizza has to be cooked in a wood-fired oven at a temperature of between 420 and 480 °F.

Do some research. For the best pizza in Napoli, head for Da Michele near Stazione Centrale and in Roma, try Pizzeria Remo in Testaccio (see the relevant Places to Eat sections). Sample the produce and decide for yourself. One warning: you might need to eat more than one. Buon appetito!

CAMPANIA

There is another branch in the Mergellina area at Via Bausan 1a.

Trianon (Via Pietro Colletta 46) has a wide selection of pizzas from L5000 and isn't far from Stazione Centrale. It's been going since 1925 and was for years a favourite with Italian celebrities such as film director Vittorio de Sica and comic actor Totò. *La Brace (Via Silvio Spaventa 14),* off Piazza Garibaldi is a recommended no-nonsense eatery where you can fill up for under L25,000.

Ristorante Bellini (Via Santa Maria di Costantinopoli 79-80) is one of Napoli's better restaurants and a full meal will cost from L35,000. Seafood is a house speciality. Virtually around the corner, at Via Port'Alba 18, is *Pizzeria Port'Alba*. Founded in 1830, it's one of the oldest pizzerie in Napoli.

Near the main post office is *La Nova Club (Via Santa Maria La Nova 9)*. It offers excellent food at reasonable prices – you can even tell the waiter your upper limit and he will help you order accordingly. You might need to ring the doorbell. *La Taverna del Buongustaio (Vico Basilico Puoti 8),* tucked in off the western side of Via Toledo, is about as basic a place as you'll find. It has excellent seafood (try the grilled calamari) and is good value. *Pizzeria al 22 (Via Pignasecca 22)*, off Piazza Carità, has takeaway pizzas from L4000.

If you want something other than Italian, *Ristorante Hong Kong (Vico Quercia 5A),* off Via Roma south of Piazza Dante, does good Chinese cuisine for about L15,000 per person.

Restaurants – Santa Lucia The restaurants on Borgo Marinaro are often overpriced but *La Scialuppa* is good value and popular with the locals.

Marino (Via Santa Lucia 118) is a typical Neapolitan restaurant/pizzeria with a huge antipasto (starter) spread and good pizzas. You'll pay around L25,000 for a meal. Farther along the same street at No 56 is *Da Ettore*. It serves delicious *pagnotiello*, a sort of calzone stuffed with mozzarella, ham and mushrooms, for L8500 and good pizzas from L7000 to L10,000.

Restaurants – Mergellina & Vomero
Head for the area around Piazza Amedeo. The surrounding streets down to the waterfront are filled with bars, cafés and restaurants of varying descriptions, as well as some Neapolitan nightlife. A full meal at *Trattoria dell'Oca (Via Santa Teresa 11)* costs around L15,000. For Spanish and Latin American fare, try *El Bocadillo (Via Martucci 50)*.

In Vomero, *Trattoria da Sica (Via Bernini 17)* has basic décor and excellent Neapolitan dishes. The spaghetti *alle vongole e pomodorini* (with clams and cherry tomatoes) and the *pasta genovese* (with pesto) are superb. *Frasco (Via Raffaele Morghen 12)* is one of Vomero's more popular spots, with pizzas and pasta from about L8000. It has a pleasant garden for alfresco dining in summer; pasta costs from L6000. *Mario Daniele (Via A Scarlatti 104)* is a bar with a restaurant upstairs. Lively *Cibo Cibo (Via D Cimarosa 150)* does light meals and drinks at the bar.

In front of the Certosa di San Martino, *Renzo e Lucia (Via Tito Angelini 33a)* offers spectacular views over the city and lofty prices to match. Expect to part with at least L30,000. To reach the restaurant, you could go for a 30 minute uphill walk from Via Roma (not recommended at night) or take bus No V1 from Piazza Vanvitelli.

Snacks One of several food stalls scattered throughout the Spaccanapoli area is *Friggitoria Fiorenzano* on Piazza Montesanto. It sells deep-fried vegetables for L250 a piece – the aubergine slices are especially good. For more substantial snacks and deep-fried food, *Lo Sfizietto*, off Piazza Carità, has goodies for under L1000.

Cafés If sitting around in a bar is your idea of fun, one of the more interesting is *Intra Moenia (Piazza Bellini 69-70)*, an arty/gay/leftist café/bookshop in one of the city's more beautiful piazze. Virtually across the road at Via Santa Maria di Costantinopoli 81, the *Caffè dell'Epoca* has been going since 1886. For something more elegant, head for *Gambrinus*, where Via Chiaia runs into Piazza Trento e Trieste, the oldest café in the city.

Gelaterie & Pasticcerie For good *gelati*, head for *Gelateria Azzurra (Piazza Carità 4)* or *Gelateria Pasticceria Carraturo (Via Bernini)* in Vomero.

Sfogliatelle is the great Neapolitan pastry, a vaguely sweet ricotta-filled number that tastes best straight out of the oven. *Attanasio (Vico Ferroviario 1-4)*, near Stazione Centrale, is deservedly famous throughout Italy for it. *Pintauro (Via Toledo)*, opposite the side entrance to the Galleria Umberto I, serves sfogliatelle fresh from the oven throughout the day.

Entertainment

The monthly *Qui Napoli* and the local newspapers are the only real guides to what's on. You can buy tickets for most sporting and cultural events at The Box Office (☎ 081 551 91 88), Galleria Umberto I 16. Ask here or at the tourist office about what is happening during your stay.

Each May the city authorities organise Maggio dei Monumenti, a month of concerts and cultural activities in various museums and monuments around town. Most of these are free. From May until September there are open-air concerts in various locations. Ask at the tourist offices for details.

Cinema Finding films screened in English is not easy, but you might have luck at *Cinema Amedeo (Via Martucci 69)*, something of an art-house place showing lots of classics.

Theatre & Classical Music The *Teatro San Carlo (☎ 081 797 21 11)* has year-round performances of opera, ballet and concerts. Tickets start at around L20,000 then spiral upwards and always sell quickly. Adjacent to the theatre in the Palazzo Reale (to the left of the main entrance and up the grand staircase) is the *Teatro di Corte*, which is slightly avant-garde but still expensive. Watch out for posters; you can buy tickets at the theatre.

Bars, Discos & Clubs Young, hip Neapolitans stand around their cars and mopeds eating gelati at Piazza Amedeo before going on to jazz joints and trendy (some might say tacky) clubs. Some clubs charge hefty admission or membership fees (up to L80,000), which usually include a drink.

The area around Piazza Amedeo is worth investigating, as there are several watering holes, clubs and live music venues sprinkled in among the trattorie and cafés. Try Via Martucci, where you'll find several choices including the *Jam Club* at No 87, *Il Picaro* at No 81, *Wonky Club* at No 43, *New Callegher* at No 39, *Baboon Club* at No 32 and *Kafafà* at No 49.

The *Otto Jazz Club (Piazzetta Cariati 23)*, west of Piazza Trento e Trieste, features Neapolitan jazz.

In Vomero, *Exclusive (Via Sgambati 59)*, also known as Kiss Kiss, is well-established and expensive, while *La Belle Epoque (Via Andrea d'Isernia 33)*, near the Riviera di Chiaia, has rock, blues, jazz and soul on different nights.

There are several venues for live music. The *Palapartenope (☎ 081 570 68 06, Via Barbagallo)* gets Italian and international acts. Heading out of town, *Havana* (exit No 12 from the Tangenziale to Pozzuoli) hosts live acts and also the plastic stuff, mostly garage and underground material. Similar is *Dynamik Area*, on the Strada Provinciale Grumo/Sant'Arpino in Frattamaggiore.

Spectator Sports

For football, Napoli's home matches are played at the Stadio San Paolo in the western suburb of Mostra d'Oltremare. Call ☎ 081 61 56 23 for details. See also the boxed text 'Goooooooooooaaaaaaaaaalllllll!' in the Facts for the Visitor chapter.

Shopping

They say you can buy anything in Napoli and you can see why after a little time spent wandering around the city centre. From designer stores to improvised stalls with goods straight off the back of a truck, Napoli certainly seems to have it all.

In particular, Napoli is renowned for its gold and Christmas items such as presepi (nativity scenes) and *pastori* (shepherds). The nativity scenes can take on huge proportions,

CAMPANIA

becoming fantastic models of all Bethlehem. Most artisans are in Spaccanapoli, in particular along Via dei Tribunali, Via B Croce and the side streets and lanes. Many goldsmiths and *gioiellerie* (jewellery shops) are clustered around Via San Biagio dei Librai and their wares are well advertised. Be warned, some inflate prices for tourists. If you like old dolls, head for the Ospedale delle Bambole, Via San Biagio dei Librai 81.

The city's more exclusive shops are in Santa Lucia, behind Piazza del Plebiscito, along Via Chiaia to Piazza dei Martiri and down towards the waterfront. Young people shop along Via Roma and Via Toledo.

Street markets where you can buy just about everything are scattered across the city centre, including Piazza Garibaldi and along Via Pignasecca, off Piazza Carità.

Getting There & Away

Air Capodichino airport (☎ 081 789 62 28), on Viale Maddalena, about 5km north-east of the city centre, is southern Italy's main airport and links Napoli with most Italian and several major European cities.

Airlines represented in Napoli include:

Alitalia
  (☎ 081 542 53 33, 147 86 56 42 for international flights) Via Medina 41-42
British Airways
  (☎ 081 780 29 52) Capodichino airport
Qantas (Gastaldi Travel)
  (☎ 081 552 30 01) Via A Depretis 108
TWA
  (☎ 081 764 58 28) Via Cervantes 55

Bus Buses leave for Italian and some European cities from Piazza Garibaldi in front of Stazione Centrale. Look carefully for the buses or ask, because there are no signs.

SITA (☎ 081 552 21 76) has a daily service to Bari, departing from outside the SITA ticket office on Via Pisanelli. It also operates a service to Germany. Maco (☎ 080 310 51 85) has two buses to Bari. Miccolis (☎ 099 735 37 54) has buses to Taranto, Lecce and Brindisi, while CLP (☎ 081 531 17 07) has four buses to Foggia.

Within Campania, SITA runs buses to Pompei, Ercolano (Herculaneum), the Costiera Amalfitana and Salerno. You can buy tickets and catch buses either from the main office on Via Pisanelli (near Piazza Municipio) or from Via G Ferraris, near Stazione Centrale (tickets at Bar Franco, Corso Arnaldo Lucci). Regular buses leave for Caserta, Benevento and Avellino from Piazza Garibaldi.

Curreri (☎ 081 801 54 20) runs a Capodichino airport-Sorrento service twice a day.

Train Napoli is the hub for the south and many trains originating in the north pass through Roma and terminate here. The city is served by regionale, diretto, Intercity and the superfast Eurostar trains. They arrive and depart from Stazione Centrale (☎ 081 554 31 88, 147 88 80 88) or Stazione Garibaldi (on the lower level). There are up to 30 trains a day to Roma.

Car & Motorcycle Napoli is on the major north-south Autostrada del Sole, known as the A1, to Roma and Milano and the A3 to Salerno and Reggio di Calabria. The A30 rings Napoli to the north-east, while the A16 heads north-east to Bari.

When approaching the city, the autostrade meet the Tangenziale di Napoli, a major ring road around the city. The multi-lane ring road, Tangenziale Ovest di Napoli, hugs the city's northern fringe, meeting the A1 for Roma and the A2 to Capodichino airport in the east and continues for Pozzuoli and the Campi Flegrei to the west. The A3 for Salerno and Reggio di Calabria can be reached from Via Galileo Ferraris, off Corso Arnaldo Lucci, south-east of Piazza Garibaldi.

Boat Ferries and hydrofoils leave for Capri, Sorrento, Ischia, Procida and Forio from Molo Beverello in front of the Castel Nuovo.

Ferries to Palermo, Cagliari, Milazzo and the Isole Eolie (Aeolian Islands) leave from the Stazione Marittima, next to the Molo Beverello. Some hydrofoils leave for the Golfo di Napoli islands from Mergellina and Alinauro and SNAV also operate services to most destinations from Mergellina.

Qui Napoli lists current timetables for Golfo di Napoli services. Ferry companies and the routes they service are as follows:

Alilauro
(☎ 081 761 10 04) Via F Caracciolo 11 (Mergellina). It operates hydrofoils to Ischia (one way, L16,000) and Sorrento (one way, L12,000).

Caremar
(☎ 081 551 38 82) Molo Beverello. It serves Capri (one way, ferry, L9800; one way, hydrofoil, L16,500), Ischia (same fares) and Procida (return ferry, L8300; hydrofoil, L13,900).

Linee Lauro
(☎ 081 551 33 52) Linked with Alilauro, it has ferries to Ischia (return, L10,000) and summer boat services direct from Napoli to Tunis. Deck class, one-way high season, L170,000; *poltrona* – an airline-style seat, L180,000; bed in 2nd class cabin, L220,000. It also has direct runs to Sardegna and Corsica in summer.

Navigazione Libera del Golfo
(☎ 081 552 72 09) Molo Beverello. It services Capri (return, L30,000) year-round and Sorrento (summer only).

Siremar
(☎ 091 690 25 55) Part of the Tirrenia group, it operates a service to the Isole Eolie and Milazzo. The service is infrequent in the low-season and up to five days a week in the high season.

SNAV
(☎ 081 761 23 48) Via F Caracciolo 10 (Mergellina). It runs hydrofoils to Capri (one way, L16,000), Procida (L13,000) and Ischia (L16,000). In summer there are daily services to the Isole Eolie.

Tirrenia
(☎ 147 89 90 00) It has a daily service to Palermo at 8 pm (poltrona, one way, L70,600; bed in a 2nd class cabin, L90,500; small car, L140,500) and a Thursday service (also Tuesday in summer) to Cagliari (poltrona, one way, L71,500; 2nd class cabin, L98,500; small car, L140,500) on Thursday. From Palermo and Cagliari there are connections to Trapani and on to Tunisia.

Getting Around

To/From The Airport To get to the airport take bus No 14 or 14R from Stazione Centrale, or CLP's airport bus (☎ 081 531 17 07), every 30 minutes from Piazza Municipio, Via Depretis, Piazza Borsa or Piazza Garibaldi (L3000). The same buses run to the city centre from outside Arrivals.

Tickets Giranapoli tickets can be bought from ANM booths and tobacconists. A ticket costs L1500 and is valid for 90 minutes of unlimited bus or tram trips, or, one trip on either the Metropolitana, funicular, Ferrovia Cumana or Circumflegrea. A daily tourist ticket is good value at L4500. These tickets are not valid to Pompei or Ercolano on the Circumvesuviana train line.

Bus & Tram Most city ANM buses operating in the central area depart from and terminate in front of Stazione Centrale, although the bus stops there are not well signposted. The city produces one rather vague bus map and it is difficult to find decent information. There is an ANM bus information office at Stazione Centrale.

There are four frequent routes (R1, R2, R3 and R4) which connect to other (less frequent) buses running out of the centre. Useful buses include:

R1
From Piazza Medaglie d'Oro to Piazza Carità, Piazza Dante and Piazza Bovio

R2
From Stazione Centrale, along Corso Umberto I, to Piazza Bovio, Piazza Municipio and Piazza Trento e Trieste

R3
From Mergellina along the Riviera di Chiaia to Piazza Municipio, Piazza Bovio, Piazza Dante and Piazza Carità

No 14 & 14R
From Piazza Garibaldi to the airport and the north of the city

No 24
From the Parco Castello and Piazza Trento e Trieste along Via Toledo, Via Roma to Capodimonte

No 110
From Stazione Centrale to the Museo Archeologico Nazionale, past Capodimonte and farther north

No 137R
From Piazza Dante north to Capodimonte, farther north and then back to Piazza Dante

No 401
A night bus operates from midnight to 5 am (hourly departures on the hour), from Stazione Centrale, through the city centre to the Riviera di Chiaia and on to Pozzuoli, returning to Stazione Centrale.

CAMPANIA

Trams No 1 and 1B operate from east of Stazione Centrale, through Piazza Garibaldi, the city centre and along the waterfront to Riviera di Chiaia. Tram No 2B travels from Piazza Garibaldi to the city centre along Corso G Garibaldi.

Train The city has four train systems: the Metropolitana (underground railway), the Ferrovia Cumana, the Circumflegrea and the Circumvesuviana. For a long time the only Metropolitana (underground railway) line has been little more than an ordinary train running from Gianturco, east of Stazione Centrale, with stops at Stazione Centrale, Montesanto, Piazza Cavour, Piazza Amedeo, Mergellina, Fuorigrotta, Leopardi, Campi Flegrei, Pozzuoli and Solfatara. A new underground line has been partly completed with EU funds. It runs north from Piazza Vanvitelli to Piazza Medaglie d'Oro and seven stops beyond, but will only become truly useful to travellers when the extension connecting Piazza Garibaldi, the duomo, piazzas Bovio, Carità and Dante, the Museo Archeologico Nazionale and Piazza Vanvitelli is completed.

The Ferrovia Cumana and the Circumflegrea (☎ 081 551 33 28), based at Stazione Cumana in Piazza Montesanto, 500m southwest of Piazza Dante, operate services to Pozzuoli and Cuma every 20 minutes. Giranapoli tickets (see under Tickets earlier in this section) can be used for one journey only.

The Circumvesuviana (☎ 081 772 24 44), about 400m south-west of Stazione Centrale on Corso G Garibaldi (take the underpass from Stazione Centrale), operates trains to Sorrento via Pompei (L3100), Ercolano (L2200) and other towns along the coast. There are about 40 trains a day running between 5 am and 11 pm (reduced services on major public holidays). Giranapoli tickets are not valid to Pompei or Ercolano.

Funicular Railway The Funicolare Centrale from Via Toledo connects the city centre with Vomero (Piazza Fuga). The Funicolare di Chiaia travels from Via del Parco Margherita to Via Domenico Cimarosa, also in Vomero.

The Funicolare di Montesanto travels from Piazza Montesanto to Via Raffaele Morghen. All three can be used to reach the Certosa di San Martino and the Vomero area. The Funicolare di Mergellina connects the waterfront at Via Mergellina with Via Manzoni. Giranapoli tickets are valid for one trip only on the funicular.

Car & Motorcycle Forget it unless you have a death wish. Park your car at one of the car parks, most of which are staffed and walk around the city centre. Try Supergarage, Via Shelley 11, in the city centre.

Apart from the headaches you will suffer trying to negotiate the city's chaotic traffic, car theft is a major problem in Napoli. Although it is said that Neapolitans observe some caution when driving behind or near cars with foreign numberplates, the risk of being in an accident is quite high if you fail to deal with the local system of not (necessarily) stopping at traffic lights. See also Dangers & Annoyances under Information earlier in this chapter.

Rental Avis has offices at Via Piedigrotta 44 (☎ 081 761 13 65) and Stazione Centrale (☎ 081 554 30 20). Europcar (☎ 081 570 84 26) is at Via Scarfoglio 10. Both have offices at the airport.

It is impossible to hire a moped in Napoli because of theft. You can hire them in Sorrento (see the Sorrento Getting Around section later in this chapter).

Taxi Taxis generally ignore kerb-side arm wavers. You can arrange one through Radiotaxi (☎ 081 556 44 44) or else at taxi stands on most piazze in the city. The minimum fare is L6000 and a short trip can cost up to L20,000 because of traffic delays.

Neapolitan drivers will often tell you that their meter is broken. This means that they don't turn them on and will often estimate (read inflate) the price of the fare. However, you can and should insist that they put the meter on – you might find it miraculously works again. As an indication, from Piazza Garibaldi to Santa Lucia, when there's not too much traffic, it should cost around L15,000. As in Roma, there are extra charges for journeys at night and for baggage.

Around Napoli

CAMPI FLEGREI

The area west of Napoli is known as the Campi Flegrei (Phlegraean – 'Fiery' – Fields), a classical term for the volcanic activity that has made it one of the globe's most geologically unstable areas. The Campi Flegrei includes the towns of Pozzuoli, Baia and Cuma (Cumae) and it was partly through this region that Greek civilisation arrived in Italy. Homer believed the area to be the entrance to Hades and Virgil wrote of it in *The Aeneid*. Now part of suburban Napoli, it bears some reminders of the ancient Greeks and Romans plus it is easily accessible, making it worth a half-day visit.

Getting There & Away

Although there is an ANM bus from Piazza Garibaldi in Napoli to the Campi Flegrei and also CTP and SEPSA buses from near Stazione Centrale, the train is still the more straightforward option. See the Napoli Getting Around section for information about the Metropolitana, Ferrovia Cumana and Circumflegrea rail services.

The Tangenziale di Napoli runs through the area; exit at Pozzuoli. Alternatively, take Via Francesco Caracciolo along the Napoli waterfront to Posillipo, then on to Pozzuoli.

Caremar (☎ 081 526 13 35) runs frequent car and passenger ferries from Pozzuoli to the islands of Ischia and Procida, as well as one hydrofoil per day to Procida. Another ferry company is Traghetti Pozzuoli (☎ 081 526 77 36). Road signs will direct you to the port.

POZZUOLI

Now a grubby-looking suburb south-west of Napoli, Pozzuoli still has some impressive Roman ruins. It is famous for being the birthplace of the actress Sofia Loren. The tourist office (☎ 081 526 50 68), Via Campi Flegrei 3, is about 1km uphill from the train station.

There is a crowded *camp site* (☎ *081 526 74 13*) at Via Solfatara 47.

Things to See

Close to the remains of the Roman port of Puteoli is the **Tempio di Serapide** (Temple of Serapis), which was simply a market of shops and, according to some sources, skilfully designed toilets. It has been badly damaged over the centuries by the seismic activity known as bradyseism (slow earthquake), which raises and lowers the ground level over long periods. The nearby church of Santa Maria delle Grazie, along Via Roma, is sinking at a rate of about 2cm a year because of this.

The **duomo**, at the top of Via del Duomo, was built over a temple of Augustus. Earthquake activity and excavation have revealed six of the temple's columns.

North-east along Via Rosini are the substantial ruins of the **Anfiteatro Flavio** (amphitheatre), which had seating for 40,000 people and could be flooded for mock naval battles. It's open from 9 am to two hours before sunset daily and admission costs L4000.

Farther along, Via Rosini becomes Via Solfatara and continues to the **Solfatara Crater**, about a 2km walk (or jump on any city bus heading uphill). Known to the Romans as the Forum Vulcani and bearing some remnants of ancient spa buildings, the crater occasionally ejects steam jets and bubbling mud. The entire crater is a layer of rock supported by the steam pressure beneath. Pick up a boulder, cast it into the air and listen to the rumblings as it hits the ground. The site is open from 9 am to one hour before sunset daily and admission costs L8000.

To the south of the crater is the **Chiesa di San Gennaro**, where Napoli's patron saint was beheaded in 305 AD.

BAIA & CUMA

Twenty minutes north-west of Pozzuoli, on the Ferrovia Cumana train or by the SEPSA bus, is Baia, once a fashionable Roman bathing resort, the remains of which are now submerged about 100m from the shore. You can take a glass-bottomed boat out to

CAMPANIA

the extensive ruins. There are frequent boat trips at weekends from April to September.

Beyond Baia is Bacoli, with more Roman remains and Cuma (Cumae), the earliest Greek colony in Italy. A visit to the **Antro della Sibilla Cumana** (Cave of the Cumaean Sybil), home of one of the ancient world's greatest oracles, is a must. Inland is **Lago d'Averno** (Lake Avernus), the mythical entrance to the underworld where Aeneas descended to meet his father. Cuma is easily accessible from Baia by a regular bus service. The site is open from 9 am to two hours before sunset daily and admission costs L4000.

CASERTA
postcode 81100 • pop 69,400

Probably founded by the Lombards in the 8th century, on the site of a Roman emplacement atop Monte Tifata, Caserta spread onto the plains below from the 12th century on. The construction of the Bourbons' grand palace assured the town a certain grandeur it would otherwise never have known.

The tourist office (☎ 0823 32 11 37) in the Palazzo Reale produces a guide to the palace.

Palazzo Reale

Also known as the Reggia di Caserta, this splendid palace was built by the Bourbons of Napoli. Work started in 1752 after Charles III of Bourbon decided he would build himself a palace similar to Versailles. Neapolitan Luigi Vanvitelli was commissioned for the job and established his reputation as one of the leading architects of the time after working on the palace.

Covering 51,000 sq metres, with a façade stretching 250m, the building is of massive proportions, with 1200 rooms, 1790 windows and 34 staircases. After entering by Vanvitelli's immense staircase, you follow a path through the royal apartments, most of them richly decorated with tapestries, furniture, mirrors and crystal. After the library is a room containing a vast collection of presepi, played out in several huge cabinets and featuring hundreds of hand-carved characters.

A walk in the elegant landscaped **gardens** is a must. Some 3km long, the best bet

is probably to take the special bus to the far end (L1500 return), marked by a waterfall and the so-called fountain of Diana and then amble your way back. Guides take groups through one garden, the **Giardino Inglese**, which is sprinkled with rare plants, little lakes and fake Roman ruins – all very much the taste of the day.

The apartments are open from 9 am to 2 pm Tuesday to Saturday (also from 3 to 7 pm Thursday to Saturday in summer) and from 9 am to 8 pm on Sunday. Admission is L8000. The gardens are open until 5.30 pm (2.30 pm in winter) daily and admission costs L4000.

Getting There & Away

CPTC buses connect Caserta with Napoli (Piazza Garibaldi) about every 30 minutes from 8 am to 8 pm. Some Benevento services also stop in Caserta. Caserta is on the main train line between Roma and Napoli. Both the bus and train stations are near the Palazzo Reale entrance, which is signposted at the stations.

AROUND CASERTA

About 2km north-west of the Palazzo Reale (buses run from the train station) is the **San Leucio silk factory**, built by Ferdinand IV and still working today and open for visits. About 10km to the north-east (CPTC bus) lies **Caserta Vecchia**, the decayed nucleus of the original town, including the remains of a 9th century castle and a 13th century cathedral.

The modern city of **Santa Maria Capua Vetere** (ancient Capua), about 12km west of Caserta, was populated by the Etruscans, the Samnites and later the Romans. Ruins include a 1st century AD anfiteatro, the largest in Italy after the Colosseo in Roma, which hosted a gladiator school. The famous gladiators' revolt led by Spartacus originated here.

There are also remains of the **Arco d'Adriano** (Hadrian's Arch), under which passed the Via Appia. Most of the artefacts from the area are now in the Museo Provinciale Campano, in the modern town of Capua, 4km away. Regular CPTC buses run from the Caserta train station to Santa Maria Capua Vetere.

BENEVENTO

postcode 82100 • pop 64,700

A provincial capital about 60km north-east of Napoli, Benevento is on the Via Appia (S7). After a period as a Lombard duchy, when it controlled much of southern Italy, the town was transferred to the control of the papacy in the 11th century and remained mostly under papal rule until 1860. The tourist office (☎ 0824 31 99 38) is at Piazza Roma 11.

Things to See

The town was heavily bombed in WWII and the Romanesque **duomo** had to be largely rebuilt. Its elaborate façade was severely damaged. South-west of the cathedral is a Roman theatre, dating from Hadrian's time but it has been repeatedly restored at intervals since. The **Arco di Traiano** (Trajan's Arch), built in 114 AD, commemorated the opening of the Via Traiana. The **obelisk** in Piazza Matteotti is a reminder of the Napoleonic period. The **Chiesa di Santa Sofia**, near the piazza, adjoins what was once a Benedictine abbey. Founded in 762, its main entrance dates from the 12th century. The abbey contains the **Museo del Sannio**, which houses remnants of

a temple dedicated to Isis, dating from 88 AD, along with a gallery devoted to medieval paintings.

Places to Stay

Should you need to stick around overnight, *Albergo Genova* (☎ 0824 42 926, Via Principe di Napoli 103) is close to the train station and charges L25,000/40,000 for singles/doubles.

Getting There & Away

FBN operates trains and buses from Napoli (leaving from Stazione Centrale). For information call ☎ 0824 32 07 56 (trains) or ☎ 0824 32 07 64 (buses). FS trains operate via Caserta. Buses also link Benevento with Roma and Campobasso. Benevento is on the S7 (the Via Appia) and close to the A16.

AVELLINO

postcode 83100 • pop 55,800

About 50km east of Napoli is the largely modern town of Avellino. Napoli and Avellino are connected by buses which run every 20 minutes. The EPT office (☎ 0825 747 32) is at Piazza Libertà 50. A day trip

---

The Battle of Benevento

At the close of 1250, Emperor Frederick II died in Puglia leaving his kingdom in southern Italy to his son Conrad, who was at the time in Germany. For the next eight years Conrad and his son fought the papacy for control of the kingdom until Manfred, a bastard son of Frederick, finally took the reins and eventually asserted his mastery over the entire kingdom.

Roma, however, was not idle and in 1265 reached an agreement with Charles I of Anjou, brother of King Louis IX of France, that gave the Frenchman the kingdom in the name of the Church in exchange for the removal of Manfred and his Swabians.

Manfred assembled an army to meet the threat and on 25 February 1265, he was waiting for the French on the Grandella plain north of Benevento. Charles had hoped to take the city by surprise and gain control of the road to Napoli. His 30,000 troops were exhausted by the long march and so he decided to stay put. Manfred, with only half that number of men, calculated that his only real chance was to attack immediately, abandoning his favourable, defensive position.

At dawn the following day, his Saracen archers and German cavalry stormed Charles' camp, but when the latter's French horsemen entered the fight, things began to go awry. Manfred, seeing his chances of victory fade, charged into the mêlée, but at this vital instant he was abandoned by many of his barons. Manfred and a handful of die-hards pressed on. Every one of them fell. Manfred was 34, and with him passed the short, but illustrious, Swabian line.

CAMPANIA

from Napoli is the best idea, as accommodation options are poor.

The mountainous area south-west of Avellino, particularly around the towns of **Quindici** and **Sarno**, was the scene of horrific mudslides in 1998, in which over 130 people died. The mudslides were caused by the geological instability of the area and excessive rain, but irresponsible deforestation and unauthorised building on the hills also contributed to the disaster.

Things to See & Do
The attraction in the area is the vertiginous summit of **Monte Vergine** and the sanctuary devoted to the Virgin Mary, north of the city (there are daily buses in summer). A young pilgrim, Guglielmo di Vercelli, erected a church here in the 12th century and so began a tradition of pilgrimage that continues to the present day. His remains were finally laid to rest in the crypt of a modern basilica here in 1807.

From the summit (1493m) you can see Napoli on a clear day and the twisting drive up from Avellino is pleasant. If you are in the province in winter, skiing is possible but not great at Lago di Laceno about 30km south-east of Avellino.

Golfo di Napoli (Bay of Naples)

ISOLA DI CAPRI
postcode (Capri) 80073 • postcode (Anacapri) 80071 • pop 7500
Despite the boatloads of tourists who pour onto the Marina Grande each day and restaurants that boast *würstl* (German sausages), real English butter and Maxwell House coffee, Capri remains an enchanting island haven in the Golfo di Napoli. Its breathtaking caves, luxuriant vegetation and the charming narrow lanes of its small towns have attracted visitors for centuries. The best time to visit is in spring (April to early June) or mid-autumn (October) after the summer crowds have ebbed away.

History
Already inhabited in the Palaeolithic age, Isola di Capri was eventually occupied by the Greeks. Roma's Emperor Augustus made it his private playground and his successor Tiberius retired there in 27 AD. Augustus is believed to have founded the world's first palaeontological museum, in the Villa Augustus, to house fossils and Stone Age artefacts unearthed by his workers.

Tiberius, a victim of Tacitus' pen, has gone down in history as something of a porn king on the island, although there is little evidence to back the lurid claims concerning the emperor's orgies. The mud stuck, however, and until modern times his name has been equated by the islanders with evil. When the eccentric Swedish doctor Axel Munthe first began picking about the ruins of Roman palaces and villas on the island in the late 19th century, locals would observe that it was all '*roba di Timberio*' (Tiberius' stuff).

Despite their sleepy, rustic appearances, the people of Capri and Anacapri have continually been at loggerheads and are always ready to trot out their respective patron saints to ward off the *malocchio* (evil eye) of their rivals.

Orientation
About 5km from the mainland, Isola di Capri is a mere 6km long and 2.7km wide. As you approach, there is a lovely view of the town of Capri with the dramatic slopes of Monte Solaro (589m) to the west, hiding the village of Anacapri.

All hydrofoils and ferries arrive at Marina Grande, a small settlement that is virtually part of Capri town. Buses connect the port with the towns of Capri and Anacapri, departing from Via Marina Grande (L1700), just to the right as you leave the pier. A funicular (L1700) also connects the marina with Capri town. Otherwise, follow Via Marina Grande for a 3km uphill walk. Turn left (east) at the junction with Via Roma for the centre of Capri town or right (west) for Via Provinciale di Anacapri, which eventually becomes Via G Orlandi as it reaches the town of Anacapri.

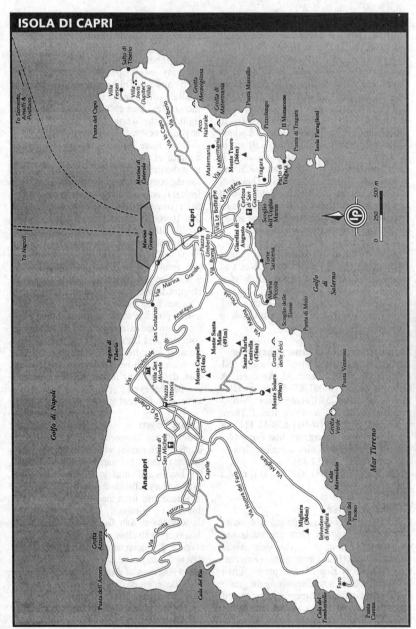

ISOLA DI CAPRI

Information

Tourist Offices There are three AAST tourist offices: at Marina Grande (☎ 081 837 06 34), Banchina del Porto; at Piazza Umberto I (☎ 081 837 06 86), in the centre of Capri; and at Piazza Vittoria (☎ 081 837 15 24), in Anacapri. The offices at Marina Grande and Capri open from 9 am to 1 pm and 3.30 to 6.40 pm Monday to Saturday. In summer they open from 8.30 am to 8.30 pm Monday to Saturday and from 8.30 am to 2.30 pm on Sunday. The Anacapri office is open from 9 am to 3 pm (8.30 am to 8.30 pm in summer) Monday to Saturday. They provide a vague map and walking guide as well as a publication, *Capri È*, listing restaurants and other useful information. On-line information can be found at www.capri.it.

Post & Communications The main post office is on Via Roma, to the left as you enter Capri town. Another post office is at Viale de Tommaso in Anacapri.

There are Telecom offices at Piazza Umberto I in Capri and at Piazza Vittoria 4, in Anacapri.

Medical Services & Emergency In summer there is a tourist medical service (☎ 081 837 50 19) at Via Capri 30, Anacapri. A Guardia Medica (☎ 081 837 50 19) operates at Via Cimino in Capri, at night and at weekends and public holidays year-round. There is a public hospital (☎ 081 838 11 11) and *pronto soccorso* (emergency first aid; ☎ 081 837 81 49). There is also a helicopter ambulance (☎ 081 584 14 81).

The questura (☎ 081 837 72 45) is at Via Roma 70.

Grotta Azzurra

Capri's craggy coast is studded with more than a dozen grottoes, most accessible and spectacular, but none as stunning as the Grotta Azzurra (Blue Grotto). Two Germans, writer Augustus Kopisch and painter Ernst Fries, are credited with discovering the grotto in 1826, but in fact they merely rediscovered and renamed what the locals had long called Grotta Gradola. Remains of Roman work inside, including a carved ledge towards the rear of the cave, were found later.

It is believed the cave sank to its present height, about 15 to 20m below sea level, blocking every opening except the 1.3m-high entrance. This causes the refraction of sunlight off the sides of the cavity, creating the magical blue colour and a reflection of light off the white sandy bottom, giving anything below the surface a silvery glow.

Boats leave from the Marina Grande and a return trip will cost about L25,000 (which includes the cost of a motorboat to the grotto, rowing boat into the grotto and the admission fee). It is only slightly cheaper to catch a bus from Anacapri (L1500 each way and double that if you're coming from Capri), since you'll still have to pay for the rowing boat and admission fee. The visit is worth the money. The 'captains' expect a tip, but you've already paid enough. Tours start at 9 am. The grotto is closed if the sea is too choppy, so check with the tourist office that it's open before making your way there.

It is possible to swim into the grotto before 9 am and after 5 pm, but do so only in company and if the sea is completely calm. Because of tidal flows through the small entrance, it can be quite dangerous but locals, despite their fear of the dragons and witches believed to inhabit the cave, have swum in it for centuries.

Capri Town

From Piazza Umberto I, in the centre of Capri, an afternoon can be whiled away wandering through the narrow lanes with their tiny houses and villas. In the square itself, the 17th century **Chiesa di Santo Stefano** contains remnants from the Roman villas. Head down Via D Birago, or Via V Emanuele, for the **Certosa di San Giacomo**, a Carthusian monastery with cloisters dating from the 14th century. It is open from 9 am to 2 pm Tuesday to Sunday. The nearby **Giardini di Augusto** (Gardens of Augustus) command one of the better views of the Isola **Faraglioni**, the rock stacks along the southern coast.

The **Museo del Centro Caprese I Cerio**, at Piazzetta Cerio 8a, houses a collection of

Neolithic and Palaeolithic fossils discovered on the island. A long restoration was nearing completion at the time of writing.

Villa Jovis

East of the town centre, an hour's walk along Via Tiberio leads to Villa Jovis (Jupiter's Villa), the residence of Emperor Tiberius. The largest and best preserved of the Roman villas on the island, it was in its heyday a vast complex including imperial quarters, entertainment areas, baths, grand halls, gardens and woodland. It is open from 9 am to one hour before sunset and admission is L4000.

The stairway behind the villa leads to **Salto di Tiberio** (Tiberius' Leap), a cliff from where he is believed to have had out-of-favour subjects pitched into the sea. A pleasant walk down Via Matermania passes the **Arco Naturale**, a rock arch formed by the pounding sea. From there you can head farther down a long series of steps and follow the path south and back east into town, passing Punta di Tragara and the Isola Faraglioni on the way.

Anacapri

Villa San Michele Many of the island's visitors are lured here, above all by the words of one of its most troubled inhabitants, Dr Axel Munthe. The house he built on the ruined site of a Roman villa remains immortalised in his book *The Story of San Michele*. The villa houses Roman sculptures from the period of Tiberius' rule and is a short walk north of Piazza Vittoria in Anacapri. Opening hours are from 9 am to 6 pm daily in summer and from 10.30 am to 3.30 pm in winter; admission costs L6000. The pathway behind the villa offers superb views over Capri and the (often closed) stairway of 800 steps was the only link between Anacapri and the rest of the island until the mountain road was built in the 1950s.

Monte Solaro

From Piazza Vittoria in Anacapri, take the chair lift to the top of Monte Solaro where, on a (rare) clear day, you can see for miles. The chair lift is open from 9 am to two hours before sunset and costs L7000 return.

From Anacapri, take a bus to Faro (L1700), a less crowded spot, with one of Italy's tallest lighthouses.

Activities

For scuba diving, try Sercomar (☎ 081 837 87 81) at Marina Grande, or Capri Diving Club (☎ 081 837 34 87) at Faro. Both run certificate courses and hire out scuba equipment. Alberino Gennaro (☎ 081 837 71 18), Via Colombo, also hires out scuba equipment.

Bagni Le Sirene (☎ 081 837 69 70), Marina Piccola, hires out canoes and motorised dinghies and can take you water-skiing. For sailboards and catamarans, contact Banana Sport (☎ 081 837 51 88) at Marina Grande.

The main places to swim are at Bagno di Tiberio, a small inlet west of Marina Grande, where the emperor himself dipped; a rocky area at Marina Piccola; at Faro; off concrete ledges at the Grotta Azzurra (only before 9 am or after 5 pm); and farther west of the grotto below the restaurants. There are no private beaches on the island and the best areas can only be reached by hired boat or by traversing tracks, particularly around Pizzolungo.

Special Events

The main non-religious festival is from 1 to 6 January, when local folk groups perform in Piazza Diaz and Piazza Umberto I.

Places to Stay

Hotel rooms are at a premium in the summer and many close during the winter. There are few really cheap rooms at any time of the year. Beware of the compulsory breakfast in summer and haggle for a better price in the low season.

During the summer months and occasionally in winter, hundreds of young people flock to Capri to party on Friday and Saturday nights, usually around Piazza Umberto I. So if you want peace and quiet at night, avoid this area!

Camping is forbidden and offenders are either prosecuted or 'asked' to relocate to a hotel. You might want to inquire at the tourist office about renting a room in a private home.

euro currency converter L10,000 = €5.16

Marina Grande One place to try is *Italia* (☎ 081 837 06 02, *Via Marina Grande*) which has doubles with bathroom for L175,000. Nearby, *Belvedere e Tre Re* (☎ 081 837 03 45, *Via Marina Grande*) has good views, with singles from L60,000 to L100,000 and doubles from L120,000 to L180,000.

Capri Right in the noisy heart of town is *Stella Maris* (☎ 081 837 04 52, fax 081 837 86 62, *Via Roma 27*), just off Piazza Umberto I. Doubles range from L100,000 to L160,000, with extra beds in rooms for L40,000. The Art Nouveau-style *Esperia* (☎ 081 837 02 62, fax 081 837 09 33, *Via Sopramonte*) is a crumbling villa with spectacular views. Doubles with bathroom start at L180,000.

La Reginella (☎ 081 837 05 00, fax 081 837 68 29, *Via Matermania*) is pleasantly located and has singles/doubles with bathroom starting at L90,000/160,000. Further upmarket, *La Vega* (☎ 081 837 04 81, *Via Occhio Marino*) has doubles with bathroom from L300,000. There is a spectacular view from the hotel pool.

Villa Luisa (☎ 081 837 01 28, *Via D Birago 1*) is a private house with a couple of rooms for rent (with great views) costing L90,000 for a double.

Anacapri One of the better hotel deals can be found at *Loreley* (☎ 081 837 14 40, fax 081 837 13 99, email loreley@mbox.caprinet.it, *Via G Orlandi*), starting at L75,000/130,000 for singles/doubles and triples for L160,000, with bathroom and breakfast included. Some rooms have views across to Napoli. *Caesar Augustus* (☎ 081 837 33 95, fax 081 837 14 44, *Via G Orlandi*) has the best view in town, with a terrace overlooking the bay. The hotel is generally not cheap, with rooms with bathroom starting at L150,000/200,000 but, in the low season, may significantly discount smaller vacant rooms. Anacapri virtually closes during the winter.

Places to Eat
Food is good and reasonably priced (although watch out for inflated cover and service charges) and even the food in the expensive-looking bread and cheese shops isn't exorbitant. *Insalata caprese*, a delicious salad of fresh tomato, basil and mozzarella, has its origins here. Some of the local wines are a bit rough but generally drinkable.

Capri Locals do their fruit and vegetable shopping at the *mercatino* (small market), below the Capri bus stop (take the stairs). *Sfizi di Pane* (*Via le Botteghe 4*) has local breads and cakes and the *cheese shop* opposite, sells caprese cheese, a cross between mozzarella and ricotta.

Ristorante Settanni (*Via Longano 5*) has a bay view and pasta dishes from about L8000. *La Cisterna* (*Via M Serafina 5*) is one of several cosy restaurants in the lanes off Piazza Umberto I and has pizza from L5000. Another restaurant nearby is *Il Tinello* (*Via l'Abate 1-3*). *Da Giorgio* and *Moscardino*, virtually beside each other at Via Roma 34 and 28, have great views and a cover charge to match (L3000, plus 12% service charge). A full meal at either is likely to set you back at least L40,000. One of the island's best traditional restaurants is *La Capannina* (*Via le Botteghe 12*) but a meal could cost up to L70,000 per person.

On the way to Arco Naturale, *Ristorante le Grottelle* (*Via Arco Naturale*) has pasta from L7000 and mains from L9000.

Anacapri Set in a garden, *Il Solitario* (*Via G Orlandi 54*), has pasta dishes from L7000. *La Giara* (*Via G Orlandi 69*) has good pizzas from L7000, as well as a full menu. *Trattoria Il Saraceno* (*Via Trento e Trieste 18*) serves *ravioli caprese* for L8000 and the owners serve their own wine. *Pizzeria Materita* (*Via G Orlandi 140*) has pizzas from L7000. It faces onto Piazza Diaz, as does *Mamma Giovanna* (*Via Boffe 3-5*), with pasta from L6000.

Entertainment
Capri For a drink you could head for *Guarracino* (*Via Castello 7*). Nightlife on Isola di Capri is a bit thin on the ground. In Capri, try *Atmosphere* or *Number Two*, both in

Via Camerelle 61b and 1 respectively or the slightly more modern (if that is possible) *Pentothal* (*Via Vittorio Emanuele 45*).

Anacapri In Anacapri, sit around in *Piazza Diaz* or shoot pool at *Bar Materita* (*Via G Orlandi 140*). For nightlife, the *Zeus* and *New Planet* discos, at Via G Orlandi 103 and 101, might get your blood rushing. The only other real option is *Underground*, at No 259.

Shopping
The island is covered with ceramic tiles displaying street names, numbers and romantic scenes. Massimo Goderecci, Via P Serafino Cimino 8, just off Piazza Umberto I, takes credit for most of these and will bake you a tile for about L100,000.

The island is famous for its perfume and *limoncello*. The former smells like lemons and the latter tastes like vodka. Visit Limoncello Capri at Via Capodimonte 27 in Anacapri and taste the liqueur. The perfumeries are everywhere.

Getting There & Away
See the Napoli and Sorrento Getting There & Away sections for details of ferries and hydrofoils. Call Eli Ambassador (☎ 081 789 62 73) for helicopter flights between the island and Napoli, which can cost several hundred thousand lira.

Getting Around
You can take your car or moped to Capri, but there is no hire service on the island. The best way to get around is by bus, with tickets costing L1700 on the main runs between Marina Grande, Capri, Anacapri, Grotta Azzurra and Faro. Buses run between Capri and Anacapri until past midnight. A funicular links Marina Grande with Capri (L1700).

A taxi ride between any of the villages can cost up to L20,000 and from the Marina to Capri, about L12,000 – the open-topped 1950s Fiats are very inviting. For a taxi in Capri, call ☎ 081 837 05 43 and in Anacapri, call ☎ 081 837 11 75.

ISOLA D'ISCHIA
postcode 80077 • pop 17,800

Isola d'Ischia manages to retain some sense of its past, despite being the largest and most developed of the islands in the Golfo di Napoli and a major tourist destination. Away from the uglier towns, people still work the land as if they'd never seen a tourist, itself an improbable proposition. Although Ischia is especially loved by Germans today, it was the Greeks who first colonised the island in the 8th century BC, calling it Pithecusa. The largely volcanic island is noted for its thermal springs and in summer is frequented as much for the curative powers of its waters and mud as for its beaches.

The main centres are the touristy towns of Ischia and Ischia Porto, Casamicciola Terme, Forio and Lacco Ameno, all fairly unattractive and overcrowded compared to the picturesque towns of Ischia Ponte, Serrara Fontana, Barano d'Ischia and Sant'Angelo. Sant'Angelo is very picturesque, as well as quiet – no cars are allowed in the town. Hotel prices and camping make the island affordable and its size means you might just be able to get away from the August crowds.

Orientation
Ferries dock at Ischia Porto, the main tourist centre. It is about a half-hour walk from the pier to Ischia Ponte, an attractive older centre that culminates in the islet bearing the castle.

Information
Tourist Offices The tourist office (☎ 081 507 42 31, 081 507 42 11) on Via Iasolino (Banchina Porto Salvo) at the main port, is open in summer from 9 am to 1.30 pm and from 3 to 7.30 pm daily. The times are flexible and it often opens in the mornings only and not on Sunday in winter. Get a hotel list, which has the tourist office's best attempt at a map. You can also get limited information on line from www.ischiaonline.it.

Money There are several banks and currency exchange booths dotted around the island. The Monte dei Paschi di Siena, Via Sogliuzzo 50, has an ATM.

CAMPANIA

Medical Services & Emergency For medical assistance go to the hospital (☎ 081 99 40 44) at Lacco Ameno and for the questura call ☎ 081 99 13 36.

Things to See & Do

The ruins of the **Castello d'Ischia**, an Aragonese castle complex on a small islet that includes a 14th century cathedral and several smaller churches, make for an interesting visit while you are in Ischia Ponte. Admission costs L10,000. It is closed in winter.

Monte Epomeo (788m) is the island's highest mountain and can be reached on foot from the towns of Panza and Serrara Fontana (about 1½ hours). It offers superb views of the Golfo di Napoli.

Among the better beaches is the Lido dei Maronti, south of Barano. If you're interested in diving, Gator Sub (☎ 081 98 52 11), near the tourist office in Ischia Porto, has equipment for hire and runs courses.

Places to Stay

Call the tourist office in advance for room availability during summer; few hotels open in winter. From October to May, prices can drop considerably. During the peak period, watch for the compulsory breakfast and extra charge for the showers.

Camping There are three camp sites on the island. Perhaps the best placed is *Mirage* (☎ 081 99 05 51, Lido dei Maronti 37) on the beach south of Barano. A site costs L14,000 plus L15,000 per person per night. The others, open in high season only, are *La Valle dell'Eden* (☎ 081 98 01 58, Casamicciola Terme) and *Eurocamping dei Pini* (☎ 081 98 20 69, Via delle Ginestre 28) in Ischia.

Hotels The simple *Locanda Sul Mare* (☎ 081 98 14 70, fax 081 99 15 08, Via Iasolino 68) is handy for the port and has singles/doubles from L45,000/75,000. *Villa Antonio* (☎ 081 98 26 60, Via San Giuseppe della Croce), a 20 minute walk from the port, has rooms with bathroom and breakfast for L85,000/140,000. Prices drop out of season.

In Sant'Angelo, try *Conchiglia* (☎ 081 99 92 70, Via Chiaia delle Rose). It is perched over the water and prices start at L55,000 per person for B&B in a room with bathroom. In July and August half board is compulsory and costs from L90,000 per person. On the promontory of Sant'Angelo, *Pensione Francesco* (☎ 081 99 93 76, Via Nazario Sauro 42) offers doubles including breakfast for L100,000.

In Barano, *Da Franceschina* (☎ 081 99 01 09, Via Corrado Buono 51) has rooms for L40,000/70,000.

Places to Eat

Cicco e Domingo (Via Luigi Mazzella 80) in Ischia is a pleasant trattoria offering pasta and seafood dishes. A full meal with wine will cost you around L25,000 per person. *Pirozzi (Via Seminario 53)* in Ischia Ponte has pizza from L7000.

For a delicious seafood meal in Sant'Angelo, try *Lo Scoglio (Via Cava Ruffano)*, on the road before the promontory. You'll part with about L25,000 for a full meal.

Getting There & Away

See the Napoli Getting There & Away section for details. You can catch ferries direct to Capri and Procida from Ischia.

Getting Around

The main bus station is at Ischia Porto and the most useful lines are the CS (Circo Sinistra; Left Circle) and CD (Circo Destra; Right Circle), which circle the island in opposite directions, passing through each town and leaving every 30 minutes. All hotels and camp sites can be reached by these bus lines, but ask the driver for the closest stop. Taxis and micro-taxis (Ape three-wheelers) are also available.

The best way to see the island is by car or moped. You can either bring your own onto the island, or hire one. Autonoleggio Balestrieri (☎ 081 98 10 55), at Via Iasolino 35 (near the port), has small Fiats from L50,000 a day and scooters from L35,000 a day. Autonoleggio Ischia (☎ 081 99 24 44), at Via A De Luca 61, offers similar deals. Fratelli del Franco (☎ 081 99 13 34), at Via A De Luca

121, hires out mopeds and mountain bikes. The vehicles cannot be taken off the island.

PROCIDA
postcode 80077 • pop 10,000

The pinks, whites and yellows of Procida's tiny cubic houses, cluttered along the waterfront, make for a colourful introduction to the island. The beauty of the Golfo di Napoli's smallest island is immediately apparent. There are only a few hotels and six camp sites, making it attractive for backpackers, particularly during the peak tourist season in July and August when the other islands are crowded.

Orientation & Information

Marina Grande is the hop-off point for ferries and hydrofoils and forms most of the tourist showcase. There is an information office (☎ 081 810 19 68) right by the boat ticket office on Via Roma.

Things to See & Do

The 16th century Palazzo Reale d'Avalos, more recently used as a prison, dominates the island and is worth exploring. It is possible to explore the island on foot, but the island's narrow roads are usually full of cars – one of Procida's only drawbacks. Walk or catch a bus to Chiaolella for lunch, then explore Vivara, a smaller island reached by a bridge. Vivara is a nature reserve and a good place for birdwatching or simply strolling. The Procida Diving Centre (☎ 081 896 83 85) hires out boats and diving equipment and will organise tours around the island by boat.

Special Events

Visit Procida at Easter to see the colourful procession of the Misteri; which takes place on Good Friday. Locals dress in special costumes, the men wear blue tunics and white hoods covering their heads and faces and many locals carry young children dressed as the Madonna Addolorata. Preparations for the procession begin months in advance, as designs are prepared for the Misteri (basically life-size scenes using plaster and papier mâché figures) which illustrate the events

leading up to the crucifixion of Christ – many are made with considerable artistic licence. On Thursday night there is a re-enactment of the Last Supper at the church of Congreca dei Turchini. Good Friday's activities begin before dawn at the Chiesa di San Michele a Terra Murata and the procession departs from the castello at around 8 am.

Places to Stay & Eat

Camp sites are dotted around the island. *Vivara* (☎ 081 896 92 42, *Via IV Novembre*) and *La Caravella* (☎ 081 896 92 30) are on the eastern side of the island, while *Ciraccio* (☎ 081 896 94 01) and *Graziella* (☎ 081 896 77 47), both on Via Salette, are near the better beaches of Ciraccio on the western side.

For a hotel, try *Riviera* (☎ 081 896 71 97) which has singles/doubles for L50,000/ 100,000 or *Crescenzo* (☎ 081 896 72 55) with rooms including breakfast and bathroom for L75,000/99,000, both at Marina di Chiaolella. The Crescenzo has a very pleasant restaurant overlooking the small harbour.

Savoia (☎ 081 896 76 16), near Centane, has doubles from L70,000. A great place to stay if you're travelling with family or friends is *La Rosa dei Venti* (☎ 081 896 83 85, Via Vincenzo Rinaldi 32). It's a group of self-contained cottages sleeping up to six people, set in a large garden on a clifftop overlooking the sea. The cost can be as little as L35,000 per person if you fill a cottage. Ask at the port, or ask the bus driver for directions.

Good restaurants can be found along the waterfront near the port, including *L'Approdo*, where you'll eat good, fresh seafood at reasonable prices. It also serves pizzas. *Il Cantinone* is another good choice, with meals for around L25,000. For coffee and cake, head for *Bar Il Cavaliere*. There are *grocery shops* in the area around Via Vittorio Emanuele.

Getting There & Around

Procida is linked by boat and hydrofoil to Napoli, Pozzuoli and Ischia. See the Napoli and Campi Flegrei Getting There & Away sections earlier in this chapter for details.

CAMPANIA

SEPSA runs a limited bus service, with four lines covering most of the island, from the port where the ferries and hydrofoils arrive. L1 buses connect the port and Chiaiolella. The small open micro-taxis can be hired for two to three hours for about L20,000 or L30,000, depending on how hard you bargain. You can hire boats from Barcheggiando (☎ 081 810 19 34), although the local fishermen will take you out for between L10,000 and L20,000 per person, depending on the size of your group.

South of Napoli

ERCOLANO (HERCULANEUM)
postcode 80056 • pop 63,500

According to the legend, this Greek settlement was founded by Hercules. Whatever the truth of this, it later passed to the Samnites before becoming a Roman town in 89 BC. Twelve kilometres south-east of Napoli, modern Ercolano is a congested, tangled suburb of the city. Ercolano was a previously peaceful fishing and port town of about 4000 and something of a resort for wealthy Romans and Campanians.

History
The fate of the city paralleled that of nearby Pompei. Destroyed by earthquake in 63 AD, it was completely submerged in the 79 AD eruption of Vesuvio. The difference was that Ercolano was buried by a river of volcanic mud, not the tufa stone and ash that rained on Pompei. The mud helped preserve it for posterity. When the town was rediscovered in 1709, amateur excavations were carried out intermittently until 1874 and much of the material found was carted off to Napoli to decorate the houses of the well-to-do or to end up in museums. Serious archaeological work was begun in 1927 and excavation continues today.

Orientation & Information
Ercolano's main street, Via IV Novembre, leads from the Stazione Circumvesuviana, at the modern town's eastern edge, to Piazza Scavi and the main ticket office for the excavations – an easy walk.

There is a tourist office (☎ 081 788 12 43) at Via IV Novembre 84, but it has little more to offer than a brochure with a map of the ruined city. The *Amedeo Maiuri* guide to Ercolano is sold at some tourist stands for about L10,000 and is considered one of the better guides.

The Ruins
The site is divided into 11 *insulae* (islands) carved up in a classic Roman grid pattern. From the main entrance and ticket office you follow a path above and around the site, until you arrive at the entrance to the ruins proper in the south-western corner. To leave the site, you must go all the way back to the ticket office. After your tickets have been checked you'll probably be gently assailed by would-be guides – if you really want one, make sure you understand what kind of fee or 'gift' is expected at the end. Some of the houses are closed, but an attendant may be able to open them on request. The two main streets, Decumano Massimo and Decumano Inferiore, are crossed by Cardo III, IV and V. On entering, you first encounter **Casa di Aristide** on your left on Cardo III. Immediately next door is **Casa d'Argo**, a well preserved example of a Roman noble family's house, equipped with a porticoed garden, *triclinium* (dining area) and a partly excavated peristyle hall.

The most extraordinary mosaic to have survived intact is in the *nyphaeum* (fountain and bath) in the **Casa di Nettuno ed Anfitrite**, on Cardo IV. Neptune and Amphitrite are depicted in colours so rich they make you realise what the interior of other well-to-do households must have been like. If mosaics are your thing, make your way to the city's public baths, **Terme del Foro**, with separate sections for men and women. The floor mosaics are in pristine condition. While women passed from the *apodyterium* (changing rooms; note the naked figure of Triton adorning the mosaic floor) through the *tepidarium* (warm room) to the *caldarium* (steam bath), men had the added bracing option of the *frigidarium* – a cold bath.

You can still see the benches where bathers sat and the wall shelves for clothing.

Casa del Atrio Mosaico, an impressive mansion on Cardo IV, also has extensive floor mosaics – time and nature have left the floor uneven to say the least.

Behind it and accessible from Cardo V, **Casa dei Cervi** (House of the Deer) is probably the most imposing of the nobles' dwellings. The two storey villa, built around a central courtyard, contains various murals and still-life paintings, as well as the marble

groups of deer assailed by dogs. In one of the rooms stands a statue of a drunken Hercules.

On the corner of the Decumano Inferiore and Cardo V is **Casa del Gran Portale**, named after the elegant brick Corinthian columns that flank its main entrance. Inside are some well preserved wall-paintings.

Off the main street, the Decumanus Massimo, is **Casa del Bicentenario**, so named because it was excavated 200 years after digging at Ercolano first began. A room upstairs contains a crucifix, indicating that

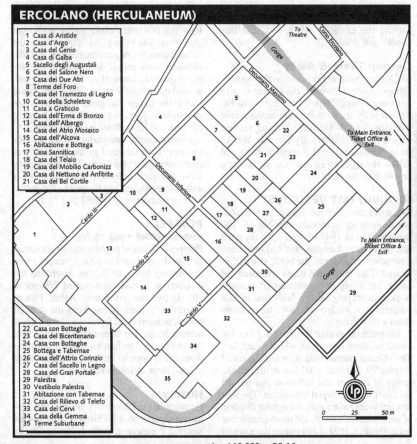

ERCOLANO (HERCULANEUM)

1 Casa di Aristide
2 Casa d'Argo
3 Casa del Genio
4 Casa di Galba
5 Sacello degli Augustali
6 Casa del Salone Nero
7 Casa dei Due Atri
8 Terme del Foro
9 Casa del Tramezzo di Legno
10 Casa della Scheletro
11 Casa a Graticcio
12 Casa dell'Erma di Bronzo
13 Casa dell'Albergo
14 Casa dell'Atrio Mosaico
15 Casa dell'Alcova
16 Abitazione e Bottega
17 Casa Sannitica
18 Casa del Telaio
19 Casa del Mobilio Carbonizz
20 Casa di Nettuno ed Anfitrite
21 Casa del Bel Cortile

22 Casa con Botteghe
23 Casa del Bicentenario
24 Casa con Botteghe
25 Bottega e Tabernae
26 Casa dell'Attrio Corinzio
27 Casa del Sacello in Legno
28 Casa del Telaio
29 Palestra
30 Vestibolo Palestra
31 Abitazione con Tabernae
32 Casa del Rilievo di Telefo
33 Casa dei Cervi
34 Casa della Gemma
35 Terme Suburbane

To Theatre

To Main Entrance, Ticket Office & Exit

To Main Entrance, Ticket Office & Exit

CAMPANIA

0   25   50 m

there might have been Christians in the town before 79 AD. As you exit the ruins, to the left along Corso Ercolano, you will see the remains of a **theatre**, dating from the Augustan period.

The archaeological area is open from 9 am to one hour before sunset daily in summer, but closes as early as 2.45 pm in winter. Admission costs L12,000.

Places to Stay & Eat

Like Pompei, Ercolano is a convenient day trip from Napoli. Otherwise, *Albergo Belvedere* (*☎ 081 739 07 44*) is close to the train station and has decent singles/doubles for L50,000/80,000. There are several bars around the entrance where you can buy snacks and drinks.

Getting There & Away

SITA buses stop at Ercolano on the Napoli-Pompei route. However, the easiest way to get from central Napoli or Sorrento to Ercolano is by train on the Circumvesuviana (see the Napoli Getting Around section earlier in this chapter). By car, take the A3 from Napoli, exit at Ercolano Portico and follow the signs to car parks near the main entrance to the site.

VESUVIO (MT VESUVIUS)

The still active volcano dominates the landscape, looming ominously over Napoli. The last eruption in 1944 blasted open the cone and the plume of smoke, that had long been a constant reminder of the peril, also disappeared. This may have eased the minds of some, but living in the shadow of Vesuvio is akin to staying on the fault line in Los Angeles – scientists consider more eruptions a sure thing.

Its name is probably derived from the Greek *besubios* or *besbios*, which means fire. The volcano erupted with such ferocity on 24 August 79 AD that it all but destroyed the towns of Pompei and Ercolano and pushed the coastline out several kilometres. The subsequent years have witnessed regular displays of the mountain's wrath, the more destructive being those of 1631, 1794 (when the town of

Torre del Greco was destroyed), 1906 and, most recently, 1944, when poverty-stricken Napoli was struggling back onto its feet under Allied occupation.

To reach the summit of Vesuvio you can catch a Trasporto Vesuviano bus from Ercolano train station. There are five a day leaving at 8.30, 9.30 and 11 am and 12.40 and 1.40 pm from Pompei. If you are travelling by car, take the A3 and exit at Ercolano Portico. You can follow the signs through the town, but a road map would also be handy.

The bus will take you to the summit car park, from where you walk a distance of 1.5km (it takes 30 minutes if you're quick). Work on a funicular railway to replace the long out-of-service chair lift is yet to get underway. You must pay L9000 to enter the summit area and be accompanied by a guide, although some people do sneak through unaccompanied. Once there, you can walk around the top of the crater. There are several bars at the summit car park. Those with cars can drive on past the turn-off for the summit car park and head closer up to the crater.

L'osservatorio Vesuviano (Vesuvian Observatory), on the road to the summit, was commissioned by Ferdinand II of Bourbon in 1841. It is a research centre for seismologists and volcanologists and is open to the public by appointment only (*☎ 081 583 21 11*).

POMPEI

postcode 80045 • pop 25,700

Pompei is the most popular tourist attraction in Italy. Ever since Pliny the Younger wrote his moving letters to Tacitus describing the eruption of Vesuvio that buried Pompei in 79 AD (see the boxed text 'Ashes, Fire & Brimstone'), the city has been the stuff of books, scholarly and frivolous and a perfect subject for the big screen. Much of the site, the richest insight into the daily life of the Romans, is open to the public and requires at least three or four hours to visit.

History

Founded in the 7th century BC by the Campanian Oscans on a prehistoric lava flow of Vesuvio, Pompei eventually fell to the Greeks

Ashes, Fire & Brimstone

One of the most descriptive accounts of the eruptions of Vesuvio was by Pliny the Younger, in the form of a letter to the historian Publius Cornelius Tacitus, written in 100 AD. In it Pliny describes how his uncle, Pliny the Elder, a naval commander and natural historian, met his death when he was trying to help people in the area.

He embraced his terrified friend, cheered and encouraged him, and thinking he could calm his fears by showing his own composure, gave orders that he was to be carried to the bathroom. After his bath he lay down and dined; he was quite cheerful, or at any rate pretended he was, which was no less courageous.

Meanwhile on Mount Vesuvius broad sheets of fire and leaping flames blazed at several points, their bright glare emphasised by the darkness of the night. My uncle tried to allay the fears of his companions by repeatedly declaring that these were nothing but bonfires left by the peasants in their terror, or else empty houses on fire in the districts they had abandoned. Then he went to rest and certainly slept, for as he was a stout man his breathing was rather loud and heavy and could be heard by people coming and going outside his door. By this time the courtyard giving access to his room was full of ashes mixed with pumice stones, so that its level had risen, and if he had stayed in the room any longer he would never have got out. He was wakened, came out and joined Pomponianus and the rest of the household who had sat up all night. They debated whether to stay indoors or take their chance in the open, for the buildings were now shaking with violent shocks, and seemed to be swaying to and fro as if they were torn from their foundations. Outside on the other hand, there was the danger of falling pumice stones, even though these were light and porous; however, after comparing the risks they chose the latter. In my uncle's case one reason outweighed the other, but for the others it was a choice of fears. As a protection against falling objects they put pillows on their heads tied down with cloths.

Elsewhere there was daylight by this time, but they were still in darkness, blacker and denser than any ordinary night, which they relieved by lighting torches and various kinds of lamp. My uncle decided to go down to the shore and investigate on the spot the possibility of any escape by seas, but he found the waves still wild and dangerous. A sheet was spread on the ground for him to lie down, and he repeatedly asked for cold water to drink. Then the flames and smell of sulphur which gave warning of the approaching fire drove the others to take flight and roused him to stand up. He stood leaning on two slaves and then suddenly collapsed, I imagine because the dense fumes choked his breathing by blocking his windpipe, which was constitutionally weak and narrow and often inflamed. When daylight returned on the 26th – two days after the last day he had been seen – his body was found intact and uninjured, still fully clothes and looking more like sleep than death.

and later, in the 5th century BC, came under the influence of the Samnites. It became a Roman colony in 80 BC and prospered as a major port and trading town, adorned with grand temples, villas and palaces, until it was devastated by an earthquake in 63 AD. Pompei had been largely rebuilt when Vesuvio, overshadowing the town to the north, erupted in 79 AD and buried it under a layer of lapilli (burning fragments of pumice stone).

Although the town was completely covered by the shower, only about 2000 of its 20,000 inhabitants are believed to have per-ished. Later, Emperor Titus considered rebuilding the city and the Roman Emperor Severus (from 193-211) plundered a little, but Pompei gradually receded from the public eye.

The Pompei area was wholly abandoned during the period of Saracen raids and its remains were further shaken by subsequent earthquakes. In 1594, the architect Domenico Fontana stumbled across the ruins during the construction of a canal. Though the discovery was recorded, substantial excavation was not conducted until 1748, in the time of Charles

CAMPANIA

of Bourbon, who was interested above all in retrieving items of value. Credit for most of the major discoveries belongs to Giuseppe Fiorelli, who worked under the auspices of the Italian government from 1860.

Work continues, but most of the ancient city has been uncovered. Many of the mosaics and murals have been removed and taken to the Museo Archeologico Nazionale in Napoli and other museums around the world.

Pompei has suffered in recent decades from overtourism and underfunding and the deterioration is alarming. Archaeologists warn that many of its treasures are in grave danger of being lost forever. The inclusion of the site on UNESCO's World Heritage List, in the late 1990s, coincided with a new Italian law enabling Pompei to manage its own money and to strike sponsorship deals. It is hoped that private sector contributions will guarantee that Pompei is conserved properly – something that government funds alone cannot hope to do.

Orientation

Arriving by train on the Circumvesuviana, you are deposited at either of the main entrances to the site, Stazione Pompei-Santuario or Pompei-Villa dei Misteri; by car, signs direct you to the *scavi* (excavations) and car parks. There are several camp sites, hotels and none-too-cheap restaurants in the vicinity, although the choice is better in and near the modern town of Pompei itself.

Information

Tourist Offices There are two AAST offices: one in modern Pompei at Via Sacra 1 and the other just outside the excavations at Piazza Porta Marina Inferiore 12, near the Porta Marina entrance. Both share a central

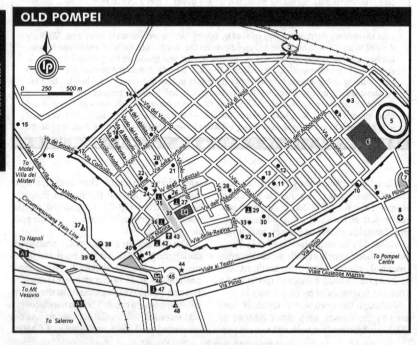

telephone line (☎ 081 850 72 55) and are open from 8 am to 7.30 pm Monday to Saturday. Pick up a map to the excavations.

A good guidebook is essential as it is easy to miss important sites. *How to Visit Pompeii* (L7000) is small but comprehensive. The *Guide d'Agostini – Pompei* (L12,000) is probably the best.

Organised Tours The tourist offices warn against the dozens of unauthorised guides who swoop at tourists, charging exorbitant prices for brief and generally inaccurate tours. Authorised guides wear identification tags and belong to one of three cooperatives: Asso (☎ 081 850 88 55), Cast (☎ 081 856 21 75) and Gata (☎ 081 861 56 61). A group of up to 25 people can take a guide for two hours at a cost of L157,500 (L3750 more for each extra person). Official attendants on the site should open many of the closed sites upon request. But be careful if visiting out-of-the-way ruins, unless you're in a group, even if you are accompanied by an official guide.

The Ruins

The town was surrounded by a wall with towers and eight gates; you can now gain access to the town through several of the gates. The south-western sea gate, the **Porta Marina**, was considerably closer to the water before the eruption. Immediately as you enter you see on the right the remains of an imperial villa with lengthy porticoes. The **antiquarium** above it contains remnants gathered from the city and, in one room, body casts formed by hollows left in the hardened tufa by decayed corpses, depicting their final moments of horror.

Farther along Via Marina you pass the striking **Tempio di Apollo**, built originally by the Samnites in the Doric style and then enter the **foro** (forum), the centre of the city's life. To the right, opposite the Tempio di Apollo, is the **basilica**, the city's law courts and exchange. Dating back to the 2nd century BC, it was one of Pompeii's greatest buildings. Among the fenced-off ruins to the left as you enter, are more gruesome body casts. The various buildings around the foro include **Tempio di Giove** (Temple of Jupiter), one of whose two flanking triumphal arches remains, the **market**, where you can see the remains of a series of shops and **Edificio di Eumachia**, which features an imposing marble doorway.

Taking the street to the right of Edificio di Eumachia, Via dell'Abbondanza, wander along and turn right into Via dei Teatri and enter the **Foro Triangolare**, which is surrounded by the remains of a Doric colonnade.

OLD POMPEI

PLACES TO STAY	11 Casa di Menandro	30 Teatro Piccolo
37 Camping Zeus	12 Casa di Sacerdote Amandus	31 Caserma dei Gladiatori
48 Camping Pompei	13 Casa del Criptoportico	32 Foro Triangolare
	14 Porta di Vesuvio	33 Teatro Grande
PLACES TO EAT	15 Villa dei Misteri	34 Edificio di Eumachia
23 Snack Bar	16 Villa di Diomede	35 Forum
	17 Porta Ercolano	36 Tempio di Apollo
OTHER	18 Casa di Apollo	38 Bus Station
1 Stazione Pompei-Santuario	19 Casa dei Vettii	39 Stazione Pompei-Villa dei Misteri
2 Porta Nola Entrance	20 Casa del Fauno	
3 Villa di Giulia Felice	21 Lupanaro	40 Porta Marina Entrance
4 Casa di Venere	22 Casa del Poeta Tragico	41 Antiquario
5 Amphitheatre	24 Terme del Foro	42 Tempio di Venere
6 Grande Palestra	25 Tempio di Giove	43 Basilica
7 Piazza Anfiteatro & Entrance	26 Market	44 Police Booth
8 First Aid Post	27 Tempio di Vespasiano	45 Piazza Esedra & Main Entrance
9 Necropoli	28 Terme Stabiane	46 Post Office
10 Porta Nocera	29 Tempio di Iside	47 Tourist Office

To your left is the entrance to the **Teatro Grande**, originally built in the 2nd century AD and capable of seating 5000 spectators. Adjoining it is the more recent **Teatro Piccolo**, also known as the Odeon, which is used for music and mime. The **Caserma dei Gladiatori** (Gladiators' Barracks), behind the theatres, is surrounded by a portico of about 70 columns. You may wander around the theatres, but the attendants become testy if they see you climbing the ruins.

From the pre-Roman **Tempio di Iside** (Temple of Isis), rebuilt after the 63 AD earthquake and dedicated to the Egyptian goddess, return to Via dell'Abbondanza, which intersects with Via Stabiana. The **Terme Stabiane** is a large complex with many rooms, some featuring original tiling and murals. Several body casts are located here. Farther along Via dell'Abbondanza are the newer excavations. An attempt has been made in this area to keep frescoes (now behind glass) and artefacts exactly where they were found in some of these buildings. Look for **Casa del Criptoportico**, **Casa di Sacerdote Amandus** (House of the Priest Amandus) and **Casa di Menandro**, which are all well preserved.

Towards the north-eastern end of Via dell'Abbondanza, the **Casa di Venere** (House of Venus) stands out because of its remarkable fresco of the goddess standing in her conch shell. The next block is occupied by the so-called **Villa di Giulia Felice**, a rambling affair that includes a private residence, a public bath, various shops and an inn. Behind it lies the **anfiteatro**, the oldest such Roman amphitheatre known and, at one time, capable of holding an audience of 12,000. The nearby **Grande Palestra** is an athletic field which has an impressive portico and the remains of a swimming pool in its centre.

Return along Via dell'Abbondanza and turn right into Via Stabiana (which becomes Via del Vesuvio) to see some of Pompei's grandest houses. Turn left into Via della Fortuna and the **Casa del Fauno** is on your right. One of the best houses in Pompei which featured a magnificent mosaic, now in Napoli's Museo Archeologico Nazionale. A couple of blocks farther along Via della Fortuna is the **Casa del Poeta Tragico** which still contains some decent mosaics. The nearby **Casa dei Vettii**, on Vicolo di Mercurio, sports some well preserved paintings and statues. Across the road from the Casa del Fauno, along Vicolo Storto, was the **Lupanaro**, a brothel with eye-opening murals. A good place for Pompei's rakes to head for after the Lupanaro was probably the **terme del foro** (forum baths), a short walk away in Via Terme.

From the terme del foro you could continue to the end of Via Terme and turn right into Via Consolare, which takes you out of the town through Porta Ercolano at Pompei's north-western edge. Once past the gate, you pass Villa di Diomede, then turn right and you'll come to **Villa dei Misteri**, one of the most complete structures left standing in Pompei. The Dionysiac Frieze, which spans the walls of the large dining room, is one of the largest paintings from the ancient world, depicting the initiation of a bride-to-be into the cult of Dionysus (the Greek god of wine). These are the most important frescoes left on the site.

The **Museo Vesuviano**, Via San Bartolomeo, south-east of the excavations, contains an interesting array of artefacts.

The ruins are open from 9 am to one hour before sunset. Admission costs L12,000.

Places to Stay

Pompei is best visited on a day trip from Napoli, Sorrento or Salerno as, apart from the excavations, there is little else to see.

Camping Zeus (☎ *081 861 53 20, Viale della Villa dei Misteri*), near Stazione Pompei, has sites from L7000 per person plus L5,000 for tent space. *Camping Pompei* (☎ *081 862 28 82, Via Plinio*) has bungalows from L60,000.

There are some 25 hotels around the ruins and in the nearby modern town. *Motel Villa dei Misteri* (☎ *081 861 35 93*), near the villa itself, has doubles for L80,000. Heading up the scale, the *Hotel Vittoria* (☎ *081 536 90 23*) is a pleasant, old building that has singles/doubles with bathroom for L70,000/110,000, breakfast included.

Places to Eat

Snacks are available at a bar in the ruins' site but for meals, you're best off making the effort to get into town. Via Roma, the continuation of Via Plinio, is a busy street with several options. *Á Dó Giardiniello*, at No 89, is a no-nonsense pizzeria with prices to match. *Ristorante Tiberius (Viale della Villa dei Misteri 1B)*, near the villa, has pasta from L6000.

Getting There & Away

Bus SITA (see the earlier Napoli Getting There & Away section) operates regular bus services between Napoli and Pompei, while ATACS (see the later Salerno Getting There & Away section) runs buses from Salerno. Marozzi (see the Getting There & Away section in the Roma chapter) offers services between Pompei and Roma. Buses arrive and depart from the bus station on Viale della Villa dei Misteri.

Train The quickest route from Napoli is on the Circumvesuviana to Sorrento, which travels via Pompei. Get off at Stazione Pompei-Villa dei Misteri, near the Porta Marina entrance. Alternatively, take the Circumvesuviana to Poggiomarino, alighting at Stazione Pompei-Santuario (see the Napoli Getting Around section).

Car & Motorcycle Take the A3 from Napoli, a trip of about 23km, otherwise you could spend hours weaving through narrow streets and traffic snarls all the way. Use the Pompei exit and follow the signs to Pompei Scavi. Car parks are clearly marked.

SORRENTO

postcode 80067 • pop 17,300

According to ancient Greek legend, the area around Sorrento was known as the Temple of the Sirens. Sailors of antiquity were powerless to resist the beautiful song of these maidens-cum-monsters who, without fail, would lure them and their ships to their doom on the reefs. Homer's Ulysses escaped the sirens' deadly lure by having his oarsmen plug their ears and strapping himself to the mast of his ship as he sailed past the fatal place.

Today's visitors to Sorrento have less to fear and in the high season this unashamed resort town is bursting with holiday-makers, predominantly from Britain and Germany. However, there is still enough southern Italian charm to make a stay here enjoyable and it is handy for Capri (15 minutes away) and the Costiera Amalfitana. The road to Pompei is pretty in parts, but has unfortunately been spoiled by expanding residential and industrial sprawl.

Orientation

Piazza Tasso, bisected by Sorrento's main street, Corso Italia, is the centre of town. The piazza is about a 300m walk north-west of the train station, along Corso Italia. From Marina Piccola, where the ferries and hydrofoils arrive, walk south along Via Luigi de Maio. A walk from the port involves climbing about 200 steps to reach the piazza. Corso Italia becomes the S145 on the way east to Napoli and changes its name to Via del Capo when it heads west.

Information

The AAST office (☎ 081 807 40 33), Via Luigi de Maio 35, is inside the Circolo dei Forestieri (Foreigners' Club), an office and restaurant complex. The AAST is open from 8.45 am to 2.30 pm and 4 to 6.45 pm from Monday to Saturday (slightly shorter hours out of season).

The Deutsche Bank, on Piazza Angelina Lauro, has an ATM that accepts credit cards. American Express is at Acampora Travel (☎ 081 807 23 63), Piazza Angelina Lauro 12.

The post office is at Corso Italia 210. The Telecom office is at Piazza Tasso 37, near Via Correale.

For medical emergencies, contact the Ospedale Civile (☎ 081 533 11 11), which is on Via Fuoro, west of Piazza Tasso.

Things to See & Do

The **duomo** on Corso Italia has a Romanesque façade and its rather odd bell tower rests on an archway supported by four ancient

CAMPANIA

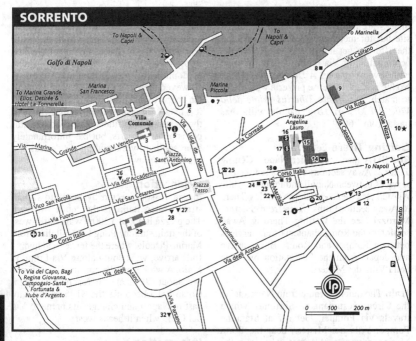

SORRENTO

PLACES TO STAY
6   Excelsior Grand
    Hotel Vittoria
8   Loreley et Londres
11 La Caffetteria (Youth Hostel)
12 Pensione Linda
19 Albergo Nice
24 Hotel City

PLACES TO EAT
4   Foreigners' Club
13 Gastronomia
15 Self Service Angelina Lauro
22 Red Lion

23 Standa Supermarket
26 Giardinello
27 Osteria la Stalla
28 Gatto Nero
32 Caruso

OTHER
1   Ferry Terminal to Napoli
    & Capri
2   Hydrofoil Terminal to Napoli
    & Capri
3   Chiesa di San Francesco
5   AAST Tourist Office
7   Sic Sic (Boat Hire)

9   Palazzo Correale;
    Museo Correale
10 Questura (Police Station)
14 Post Office
16 Deutsche Bank & ATM
17 American Express
    (Acampora Travel)
18 Sorrento Rentacar
20 Bus Station
21 Train Station
25 Telecom Office
29 Cathedral
30 Goldentours International
31 Ospedale Civile (Hospital)

columns. The 18th century **Palazzo Correale**
has some interesting murals and houses the
Museo Correale, which contains a small collection of 17th and 18th century Neapolitan
art, as well as an odd assortment of Greek and

Roman artefacts. The gardens offer views of
the bay and steps lead down to the water.

The **Chiesa di San Francesco**, near the
Villa Comunale park and the AAST office,
boasts a beautiful, if modest, cloister and is

GUY MOBERLY

JOHN HAY

JOHN HAY

Destroyed by the 79 AD eruption of Vesuvius, Pompei is now one of Italy's most popular tourist attractions. Excavations have revealed a city frozen in time.

Trulli – Alberobello's unique stone houses, Puglia

Trani, Puglia – once an important medieval port

Three churches in one, Trani cathedral, Puglia

The mysterious conical-roofed and white-washed *trulli* dot Puglia's flat and highly fertile land.

set in lovely gardens – the views up and down the coast are breathtaking.

If you want a **beach**, head for Marina Grande, a 15 minute walk west from Piazza Tasso, which has small strips of sand and is very popular. The jetties nearby, with ubiquitous umbrellas and deck chairs, will cost up to L25,000 a day. **Bagni Regina Giovanna**, a 20 minute walk west along Via del Capo (or take the bus for Massalubrense), is more picturesque, set among the ruins of the Roman Villa Pollio Felix. To the east is a small beach at Marinella.

From May to October, Sic Sic (☎ 081 807 22 83), at Marina Piccola, hires out a variety of boats (starting at around L35,000 an hour) and organises boat cruises. Goldentours International (☎ 081 878 10 42), Corso Italia 38E, offers tours to the Costiera Amalfitana, Pompei, Capri and other destinations.

Special Events
The Sorrento Film Festival, regarded as the most important in the country for Italian-produced cinema, is held annually, usually in September/October.

The city's patron saint, Sant'Antonio, is remembered on 5 February each year with processions and huge markets. The saint is credited with having saved Sorrento during WWII when Salerno and Napoli were heavily bombed.

Places to Stay
Most accommodation is in the town centre or clustered along the Via del Capo, which is about 3km west of the centre (most of the accommodation here has views over the bay). To reach this area, catch the SITA buses for Sant'Agata or Massalubrense from the train station. Book early for the summer season.

Camping The SITA bus serves two local camp sites. *Campogaio-Santa Fortunata* (☎ 081 807 35 79, Via del Capo 39a) has sites from L9000 and charges from L10,000 per person. Nearby is the *Nube d'Argento* (☎ 081 878 13 44, Via del Capo 21), which is slightly dearer.

Hostel The hostel *La Caffetteria* (☎ 081 807 29 25, Via degli Aranci 160), near the bus and train stations, is run by the comune. It's open year-round and B&B costs L25,000 per person. Some private singles/doubles are also available.

Hotels *Hotel City* (☎ 081 877 22 10, Corso Italia 221) has singles/doubles with bathroom from L75,000/105,000. *Albergo Nice* (☎ 081 878 16 50, Corso Italia 257) has rooms with bathroom for L80,000/120,000. *Pensione Linda* (☎ 081 878 29 16, Via degli Aranci 125) is a very pleasant establishment, with rooms with bathroom for L60,000/100,000. *Loreley et Londres* (☎ 081 807 31 87, Via Califano 12) overlooks the sea and has doubles with bathroom from L140,000.

Near Marina Grande is *Elios* (☎ 081 878 18 12, Via del Capo 33), which has doubles with views from L70,000. Next door, *Desirée* (☎ 081 878 15 63, Via del Capo 31) has singles/doubles/triples/quads from L80,000/140,000/165,000/190,000, all with bathrooms and including breakfast. The hotel has an elevator to a private beach. *Hotel La Tonnarella* (☎ 081 878 11 53), at the same address, has doubles with bathroom from L200,000.

For a touch of Sorrento's former glory, try the venerable old *Excelsior Grand Hotel Vittoria* (☎ 081 807 10 44, Piazza Tasso 34), which takes up a huge block overlooking the ferry terminal. Rooms here start at about L430,000.

Places to Eat
One of the cheapest options is *Self Service Angelina Lauro* (Piazza Angelina Lauro), with pasta from L5000. It serves full English breakfasts and is one of several snack places on the square. *Giardinello* (Via dell'Accademia 7) has pizzas from about L6000. *Osteria la Stalla* (Via Pietà 30) has main courses from L10,000. *Gatto Nero*, a cosy little place a couple of doors down, will do you a full meal with wine for about L25,000. *Caruso* (Via Sant'Antonio 12) is one of the town's best restaurants and one of its most expensive; it's easy to spend L45,000 per person.

CAMPANIA

The *Foreigners' Club (Via Luigi de Maio 35)*, in the same building as the AAST, offers bay views and cheap food. *Red Lion (Via Marziale 25)* offers a set menu for L15,000 or a pizza and a beer for L9000. *Gastronomia (Via degli Aranci)*, opposite Pensione Linda, is a no nonsense pizzeria.

Pick up picnic supplies at the *Standa supermarket*, on the corner of Corso Italia and Via Marziale.

Entertainment

Outdoor concerts are held during the summer months in the cloisters of the *Chiesa di San Francesco*.

Nightclubs include the *Kan Kan (Piazza Sant'Antonino 1)*, which is about the best of a bad bunch and is not overrun by the tourist hordes.

Getting There & Away

SITA buses leave from outside the Circumvesuviana train station and their office is near the bar in the station. They service the Costiera Amalfitana, Napoli and Sant'Agata. It is possible to catch the buses throughout the town, although you must buy tickets from shops bearing the blue SITA sign.

For more bus and train details, see the Napoli Getting There & Away and Getting Around sections earlier in this chapter.

The city can be reached by the S145, which meets a spur from the A3 at Castellammare.

Navigazione Libera del Golfo (☎ 081 807 18 12) and Alilauro (☎ 081 807 30 24) run hydrofoils to Capri from Sorrento, while Caremar (☎ 081 807 30 77) operates ferries. The 15 minute run in the hydrofoils costs L9000 one way and L18,000 return, while the ferry costs L10,000 return. Alilauro has up to six boats a day to Napoli (L14,000 one way) and Navigazione Libera del Golfo has one.

Getting Around

Sorrento Rentacar (☎ 081 878 13 86), Corso Italia 210, hires out scooters from L50,000 for 24 hours or L280,000 for a week. Its cheapest car, a Fiat Uno, will set you back L98,000 a day plus petrol or L460,000 for

five days. This is one of several rental companies and it is worth shopping around. For a taxi, call ☎ 081 878 22 04.

COSTIERA AMALFITANA (AMALFI COAST)

This 50km stretch of coastline which runs from Sorrento to Salerno is one of the most beautiful in Europe. A narrow asphalt ribbon bends and winds along cliffs that drop into crystal-clear blue waters, connecting the beautiful towns of Positano, Amalfi and the hillside village of Ravello. The coast is jampacked with wealthy tourists during the summer, prices are inflated and finding a room is impossible. The moral is that you are much better off coming during spring and autumn. The Costiera Amalfitana all but shuts down over winter, but you can still find places to stay. The area is famous for its ceramics.

Getting There & Away

Bus SITA operates a bus service along the Costeria Amalfitana (S163), from the Sorrento train station to Salerno and vice versa, with buses leaving every 50 minutes. Tickets must be bought in advance from the bar at the Sorrento train station or the SITA bus station in Salerno, or else in bars near the bus stations in the towns along the coast (Via G Marconi in Positano and Piazza Flavio Gioia in Amalfi). Buses also leave from Roma for the Costiera Amalfitana, terminating at Salerno (see the Getting There & Away section in the Roma chapter for details).

Train Take the Circumvesuviana from Napoli to Sorrento or the train to Salerno and then take the SITA bus along the coast.

Car & Motorcycle The coastal road is breathtakingly beautiful, if a little hairy at times, as buses from each direction manoeuvre past each other on narrow sections. In summer, it becomes a 50km traffic jam and can take hours to navigate as the hordes flock to the coast. From Napoli, take the A3 and exit near Castellammare, or follow the signs to Sorrento. The coast road, the S145, passes through Sorrento and becomes the

S163 Amalfitana. A short cut over the hills beyond Meta can save about 30 minutes. To join the coastal road from Salerno follow the signs to Vietri sul Mare or Amalfi.

Boat Navigazione Libera del Golfo (☎ 081 552 72 09), based in Napoli, operates hydrofoils between Amalfi, Positano and Capri. Alilauro (☎ 081 761 10 04) serves the coast from both Salerno and Napoli. Amalfi Navigazione (☎ 089 87 31 90), Via Nazionale 17, Amalfi, operates services between Amalfi and Positano, Capri and Salerno, as does Avenire (☎ 089 87 76 19), also in Amalfi, at the ticket booth by the ferry terminal. Most companies operate in summer only. See the Napoli Getting There & Away section earlier in this chapter for more details.

POSITANO
postcode 84017
Exuding a rather Moorish flavour, Positano is the most picturesque of the coastal towns and some might think the most precious, with its cute houses and expensive shops.

Orientation
Positano is virtually divided in two by the cliff which bears the Torre Trasita (tower). West is the smaller and more pleasant Spiaggia del Fornillo beach area and the less expensive side of town, east is Spiaggia Grande, which gives way to the town centre.

Navigating is easy, if steep. Via G Marconi, part of the S163 Amalfitana, runs north around and above the town, which itself cascades inside this fold in the mountain down to the water. The one-way Viale Pasitea winds down off Via G Marconi from the west to the town centre before climbing back up and above the town, becoming Via Cristoforo Colombo as it travels down to join Via G Marconi. Follow Via G Marconi east to join the S163 to Amalfi, Praiano and Salerno or north-west back to Positano and the S163 to Sorrento and Napoli.

Information
The small APT office (☎ 089 87 50 67), Via del Saraceno 4, near Spiaggia Grande, has a map of the area plus brochures. It is open from 8.15 am to 2 pm Monday to Saturday and also opens in the afternoon in summer.

For changing currency, the Ufficio Çambio is on Piazza dei Mulini, although the Deutsche Bank, Via Cristoforo Colombo 75, may offer better rates and has an ATM.

The post office is on Via G Marconi where it meets Viale Pasitea. It's open from 8.20 am to 2 pm Monday to Saturday.

For medical emergencies at night, on Sunday or during holidays, call the Guardia Medica ☎ 089 81 14 44. Its headquarters is on Via G Marconi, near Via Cristoforo Colombo.

The carabinieri (police; ☎ 089 87 50 11) are on Via G Marconi where it intersects with Viale Pasitea.

Things to See & Do
Positano's main sight is the **Chiesa di Santa Maria Assunta**, just back from the Spiaggia Grande. Inside you'll find a 13th century Byzantine *Black Madonna*. The church is closed in the afternoon and admission is free.

Boating isn't cheap. Head for the 'To Rent' signs on the Spiaggia Grande and expect to pay from L20,000 an hour for a rowing boat or L40,000 an hour for a small motor boat, both cheaper by the half or full day.

Hiring a chair and umbrella on the fenced-off areas of the **beaches** can cost around L25,000 per day, but the crowded public areas are free.

Places to Stay
Positano has several one-star hotels, although in summer they are usually booked well in advance. Out of peak season, haggle with the guest-starved proprietors. Ask at the APT office about rooms in private houses, which are generally expensive, or apartments for rent.

All of the following hotels have rooms with private bathrooms. The pick of the cheaper hotels is *Villa Maria Luisa* (☎ 089 87 50 23, Via Fornillo 40), which has large doubles with terraces and magnificent views for L120,000 (L90,000 low season). Singles are L60,000. It's less appealing in winter. *Pensione Italia* (☎ 089 87 50 24),

CAMPANIA

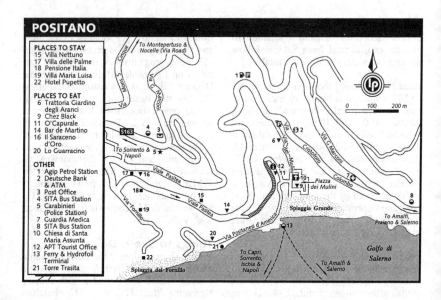

POSITANO

PLACES TO STAY
15 Villa Nettuno
17 Villa delle Palme
18 Pensione Italia
19 Villa Maria Luisa
22 Hotel Pupetto

PLACES TO EAT
6 Trattoria Giardino
  degli Aranci
9 Chez Black
11 O'Capurale
14 Bar de Martino
16 Il Saraceno
  d'Oro
20 Lo Guarracino

OTHER
1 Agip Petrol Station
2 Deutsche Bank
  & ATM
3 Post Office
4 SITA Bus Station
5 Carabinieri
  (Police Station)
7 Guardia Medica
8 SITA Bus Station
10 Chiesa di Santa
  Maria Assunta
12 APT Tourist Office
13 Ferry & Hydrofoil
  Terminal
21 Torre Trasita

off Viale Pasitea, is one of about 20 affitta-camere in Positano. It has doubles only, for L90,000. *Villa delle Palme* (☎ 089 87 51 62), around the corner, charges L120,000 for a double in low season and L130,000 in the peak period, breakfast included.

Villa Nettuno (☎ 089 87 54 01, Viale Pasitea 208) has doubles from L100,000 (L110,000 in high season) and most rooms have balconies or open onto a terrace. *Hotel Pupetto* (☎ 089 87 50 87), overlooking Spiaggia del Fornillo, is pricier, with doubles available at L180,000 in the low season and L210,000 in high season; all the rooms have views.

Places to Eat

Most restaurants are overpriced for the food they serve and you should always check the cover and service charges before you sit down. Many restaurants close over winter, making a brief reappearance for Christmas and New Year. *Il Saraceno d'Oro (Viale Pasitea 254)* has pizzas from L5000 and is close to most of the cheaper hotels. *Lo Guarracino (Via Positanesi d'America)*, on

the waterfront path connecting the two beaches, has pasta from about L7000.

Near the main beach, *O'Capurale (Via Regina Giovanna)* serves local dishes, with pasta from L8000. Overlooking the beach is *Chez Black (Spiaggia Grande)*, a popular spot specialising in seafood. A full meal could cost up to L45,000. *Trattoria Giardino degli Aranci (Via dei Mulini 22)*, although still not cheap, is a little more modest and serves good meals. A great place for a coffee is the *Bar de Martino* which has commanding views of the town and sea.

Getting Around

If you don't mind a climb, there are dozens of small stairways throughout the town, making walking relatively easy. A small orange bus does a complete circuit of the town, passing along Viale Pasitea, Via Cristoforo Colombo and Via G Marconi. Stops are clearly marked and tickets can be bought on board. The bus also stops near the S163 Amalfitana at the town's western edge, where you can also meet the SITA bus to Salerno or back to Sorrento (stopping along the way).

AROUND POSITANO

The hills overlooking Positano offer some great walks if you tire of lazing on the beach. The APT office in Positano has a brochure listing four routes, including the **Sentiero degli Dei** (Trail of the Gods), which heads into the hills from the hamlet of Nocelle and on to the Agerola, towards Amalfi. From the small village of Montepertuso, you can reach Santa Maria al Castello and Monte Sant'Angelo e Tre Pizzi (1444m). The latter is quite a walk.

Visit **Nocelle**, a tiny and still relatively isolated village to the west of Positano, accessible by a short walking track from the end of Via Mons S Clinque from Positano. Have lunch at *Trattoria Santa Croce* (☎ 089 81 12 60), which has a terrace with panoramic views. It is open for lunch and dinner in summer, but at other times of the year it is best to phone and check in advance. Nocelle is accessible by a local bus from Positano, via Montepertuso; buses run roughly every half-hour in summer from 7.50 am to midnight.

The coastal town of **Praiano** is not as scenic as Amalfi, but has more budget accommodation options, including the only camp site on the Costeria Amalfitana, *La Tranquillità* (☎ 089 87 40 84, fax 089 87 47 79, email contraq@contraqpraiano.com), along the coastal road on the Amalfi side of Praiano. It has a pensione and bungalows, as well as a small camp site, a restaurant and a swimming pool. A site for two people and tent costs L50,000 and a double room or bungalow costs from L100,000. The SITA bus stops outside.

AMALFI

postcode 84011

At its peak in the 11th century, Amalfi was a supreme naval power, a bitter enemy of the northern maritime republics, Pisa and Genova and had a population of 70,000. Its navigation tables, the *Tavole Amalfitane*, formed the world's first maritime code and governed all shipping in the Mediterranean for centuries.

Amalfi was founded in the 9th century and soon came under the rule of a doge. Thanks to its connections with the Orient, the city claims to have introduced to Italy such modern wonders as paper, coffee and carpets. The small resort still bears many reminders of its seafaring and trading heyday and is now one of Italy's most popular seaside spots.

Orientation

Most hotels and restaurants are around Piazza Duomo or along Via Genova and its continuation, Via Capuano, which snakes north from the cathedral.

Information

The AST office (☎ 089 87 11 07), at Corso Roma 19 on the waterfront, opens from 8 am to 2 pm Monday to Friday (also from 3 to 8 pm in summer) to 1 pm on Saturday.

There's a Deutsche Bank on Corso Roma with an ATM.

The post office, at Corso Roma 29, is open from 8.15 am to 6.30 pm Monday to Friday and to 12.15 pm on Saturday.

For medical treatment, go to the Municipio Pronto Soccorso (☎ 089 87 27 85) on Piazza Municipio, near the AST office. The questura (☎ 089 87 10 22) is at Via Casamare 19.

Things to See

The **Duomo Sant'Andrea**, an imposing sight at the top of a sweeping flight of stairs, dates from early in the 10th century, but the façade has been rebuilt twice. Although the building is a hybrid, it is the Arab-Norman style of Sicilia that predominates, particularly in the two-tone masonry and the bell tower. The interior is mainly baroque and the altar features statues believed to be by Gianlorenzo Bernini and Naccherini, along with 12th and 13th century mosaics.

The **Chiostro del Paradiso**, next door, was built in the 13th century in Arabic style to house the tombs of noted citizens. It opens from 9 am to 8 pm, with a break of about two hours from 1 pm. Admission costs L1000.

The **Museo Civico**, behind Corso Roma in the town hall building, contains the *Tavole Amalfitane* and other historical documents. It opens from 8 am to 2 pm Monday to Saturday. Admission is free. The restored

CAMPANIA

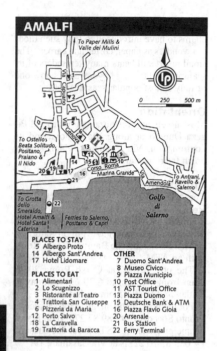

AMALFI

To Paper Mills &
Valle dei Mulini

0   250   500 m

To Ostello's
Beata Solitudo,
Positano,
Praiano &
Il Nido

To Antrani,
Ravello &
Salerno

Amendola

Corso Roma

Marina Grande

To Grotta
dello
Smeraldo,
Hotel Amalfi &
Hotel Santa
Caterina

Golfo
di
Salerno

Ferries to Salerno,
Positano & Capri

PLACES TO STAY
5   Albergo Proto
14 Albergo Sant'Andrea
17 Hotel Lidomare

PLACES TO EAT
1   Alimentari
2   Lo Scugnizzo
3   Ristorante al Teatro
4   Trattoria San Giuseppe
6   Pizzeria da Maria
12 Porto Salvo
18 La Caravella
19 Trattoria da Baracca

OTHER
7   Duomo Sant'Andrea
8   Museo Civico
9   Piazza Municipio
10 Post Office
11 AST Tourist Office
13 Piazza Duomo
15 Deutsche Bank & ATM
16 Piazza Flavio Gioia
20 Arsenale
21 Bus Station
22 Ferry Terminal

CAMPANIA

Arsenale of the former republic, the only ship building depot of its kind in Italy, is to the left of Porta della Marina.

Two **paper mills** still operate in Amalfi. One is at Via Cartoleria 2. The other is also on Via Cartoleria, but is farther away from Piazza Duomo. Called the Cartier d'Amatruda, it still makes paper in the traditional way and can be visited. The town also has a **paper museum** in Valle dei Mulini, set up in a 13th century paper mill (the oldest in Amalfi) and it's open from 9 am to 1 pm daily, except Monday and Friday.

The many ceramics shops, mostly clustered around Piazza Duomo, testify to Amalfi's traditional promotion of this art. Visit the **Bottega d'Arte** on Piazza Duomo and see items being made and glazed.

About 6km along the coast towards Positano is the **Grotta dello Smeraldo**, so-called for the emerald colour of its sandy floor. Just

a shadow of the Grotta Azzurra on Capri, it can be reached by SITA bus from either direction along the Costiera Amalfitana. It opens from 9 am to 4 pm daily and admission costs L5000. On 24 December and 6 January, skin divers make their traditional pilgrimage to the ceramic crib in the grotto.

The Regatta of the Four Ancient Maritime Republics, which rotates between Amalfi, Venezia, Pisa and Genova, is held on the first Sunday in June. Amalfi last hosted it in 1997 and should next host it in 2001.

Activities
In the hills above Amalfi, on the way to Ravello, are dozens of small paths and stairways connecting the coastal towns with mountainside villages. The CAI in Salerno publishes a map with eight long walks in the area, stretching from Salerno to Sorrento. A book titled *Walks from Amalfi – The Guide to a Web of Ancient Italian Pathways* (L10,000) is available from most bookshops in the town.

Boats can be hired in summer at the Marina Grande area, the Spiaggia Santa Croce and the Grotta dello Smeraldo.

Places to Stay
The HI *Ostello Beata Solitudo* (☎ 081 802 50 48, Piazza G Avitabile) in Agerola (off the S163 to Positano) is open year round. A bed is L17,000 and you can use the kitchen. *A'Scalinatella* (☎ 089 87 14 92, Piazza Umberto I) in Atrani, a 15 minute walk north-east of Amalfi, has hostel-style accommodation for L20,000 per person (L25,000 in August) or you can camp for L15,000 per person.

In Amalfi itself, *Albergo Proto* (☎ 089 87 10 03, Salita dei Curiali 4) has doubles/triples with breakfast in high season for L125,000/175,000 or L140,000/200,000 with bathroom. *Hotel Lidomare* (☎ 089 87 13 32, fax 089 87 13 94, Piazza Piccolomini) has spacious and homely singles/doubles for L75,000/131,000 including breakfast. *Albergo Sant'Andrea* (☎ 089 87 11 45), off Piazza Duomo, has rooms from L75,000/ 120,000 in summer.

Il Nido (☎ 089 87 11 48), about 2km west of the centre, has attractive doubles from

L130,000, but no singles. *Santa Caterina* (☎ *089 87 10 12, Strada Amalfitana, S163, 9*) is one of the best hotels on the coast and is the place to stay if you want to splurge. It is set in extensive grounds and commands a magnificent view of the coast. An added attraction is its salt-water swimming pool by the sea. Lovely rooms cost upwards of L490,000.

Places to Eat
Porto Salvo, just off Piazza Duomo, does fantastic pizza and *panozzo* (pizza stuffed with mozzarella and tomatoes) by the slice and has outside tables where you don't pay extra. *Pizzeria da Maria (Via Lorenzo d'Amalfi)* has pizzas from L5000 and a set menu for L25,000. *Trattoria San Giuseppe (Salita Ruggiero II 4)*, off Via Amalfi, has excellent pasta and decent main meals for around L25,000. *Trattoria da Baracca*, overlooking Piazza dei Dogi, is almost as good and prices are similar. For a sit-down pizza, you could do worse than *Ristorante al Teatro (Via Marini 19)*, where you're looking at about L8000. *La Caravella (Via Matteo Camera 12)* is one of Amalfi's finest restaurants, but L50,000 per person is about the minimum you'll pay. On Via Capuano is an *alimentari* for picnic supplies and just down the road is *Lo Scugnizzo*, a pasticceria that makes great cakes.

RAVELLO
Ravello sits like a natural balcony overlooking the Golfo di Salerno from where you can peer down on Amalfi and the nearby towns of Minori and Maiori. The 7km drive from Amalfi along the Valle del Dragone passes through the soaring mountains and deep ravines that characterise the area – watch the hairpin turns. You can continue inland across the mountains and down to Nocera to link up with the A3 to Napoli and Salerno.

Ravello's tourist office (☎ 089 85 79 77), on Piazza Vescovado, is open from 8 am to 8 pm Monday to Saturday in summer (to 7 pm the rest of the year) and has limited information.

Things to See & Do
The **duomo** in Piazza Vescovado dates from the 11th century and features an impressive marble pulpit with six lions carved at its base. There is a free museum in the crypt containing religious artefacts.

Overlooking the piazza is **Villa Rufolo**. Its last resident was the German composer Wagner, who wrote the third act of *Parsifal* there. The villa was built in the 13th century for the wealthy Rufolos and housed several popes, as well as Charles I of Anjou. From the terraces there is a magnificent view over the gulf. The villa's gardens are the setting for the Festivale Musicale di Ravello held each July, when international orchestras and special guests play a selection that always features Wagner. Tickets start at L40,000 and can go as high as L250,000 for some performances. The city hosts a smaller Wagner festival in early July and the patron saint, San Pantaleon, is celebrated with fireworks in late July.

Away from the Piazza Vescovado is the **Villa Cimbrone**, built this century and set in beautiful gardens.

You can visit the city's vineyards: the Casa Vinicola Caruso on Via della Marra, Vini Episopio at the Hotel Palumbo on Via Toro and Vini Sammarco on Via Nazionale. Or you can arrange to visit places where limoncello, the local lemon liqueur, is produced – ask at the tourist office.

Places to Stay & Eat
Accommodation and food are too expensive to make Ravello an overnight option for most travellers. Book well ahead if you're planning to visit Ravello during the Festivale Musicale in July. The small *Toro* (☎ *089 85 72 11, Viale Wagner 3)* has doubles with bathroom from L115,000. The delightful *Parsifal* (☎ *089 85 71 44, Via d'Anna 5)*, in a former convent, has obligatory half board at L145,000 per person (high season) or L112,000 (low season).

Pizzeria la Colonna (Via Roma 20) serves regional cuisine, with pasta from L8000. *Cumpà Cosimo (Via Roma 42-44)* is a little more expensive, but the food is excellent. A meal will cost from L30,000.

CAMPANIA

Ristorante La Marra (Via della Marra 7) will possibly give you the best meal of your trip. There's a tourist menu for L35,000 or you can splash out.

Getting There & Away

To reach the town by car, take the S163 Amalfitana for Salerno and turn off about 2km after Amalfi. SITA operates about 15 buses in each direction daily from the bus station on Piazza Flavio Gioia in Amalfi, departing from 6 am to about 9 pm. Cars are not permitted in Ravello's town centre, but there is adequate parking in supervised car parks.

FROM AMALFI TO SALERNO

If you're coming from the west, life on the Costiera Amalfitana doesn't end at the town of Amalfi. The 20km drive to Salerno, although marginally less exciting than the 16km stretch to Positano and beyond, is dotted with a series of little towns that could make useful alternative bases.

Atrani, a mere kilometre away from Amalfi, round a point, is a pretty extension of the town with a little beach. Farther on are the towns of **Minori** and **Maiori**. Although lacking much of the charm of its better-known partners up the road, both have plenty of hotels and Maiori has a fairly decent-sized beach. Perhaps most attractive on this run is the fishing village of **Cetara**. Shortly before you reach Salerno, you pass through **Vietri sul Mare**, set on a rise commanding views over the town. If all else fails, you could even use this as a local base without really feeling cheated. It is also a good place to buy the local ceramics. The town has plenty of workshops and showrooms and, if you shop around, you'll find some good buys.

SALERNO

postcode 84100 • pop 160,000

After the picturesque little towns of the Costiera Amalfitana, the urban sweep of Salerno and its port along the Golfo di Salerno (Gulf of Salerno) might come as a shock. Salerno is one of southern Italy's many victims of earth tremors and even land-slides, but was also left in tatters by the heavy fighting that followed the landings of the American 5th Army, just to the south of the city, in 1943. With the exception of a charming, tumbledown medieval quarter, the city today is largely unexciting, although there have been successful efforts to smarten it up. It is, however, an important transport junction and an excellent base for exploring the Costiera Amalfitana to the west and Paestum and the Costiera Cilentana to the south-east.

Originally an Etruscan and later a Roman colony, Salerno flourished with the arrival of the Normans in the 11th century. Robert Guiscard made it the capital of his dukedom in 1076 and under his patronage the Scuola Medica Salernitana gained a lot of fame as one of medieval Europe's greatest medical institutes.

Orientation

The train station is on Piazza Vittorio Veneto, at the eastern end of town. Most intercity buses stop here and there are a number of hotels in this area too. Salerno's main shopping strip, the car-free Corso Vittorio Emanuele, leads off to the north-west to the medieval part of town. Running parallel and closer to the sea is Corso Garibaldi, which becomes Via Roma as it heads north-west out of the city for the Costiera Amalfitana. The tree-lined Lungomare Trieste, on the waterfront, changes its name to Lungomare Marconi at the massive Piazza della Concordia on its way out of town south-east towards Paestum.

Information

Tourist Offices The EPT office (☎ 089 23 14 32) is near the train station on Piazza Vittorio Veneto and opens from 8 am to 8 pm (generally closing around 1.30 pm for an hour) Monday to Saturday. The staff are extremely helpful and can provide good maps and a guide, called *Agenda del Turista*, listing accommodation options and transport details, which are also on its TurismoOnline Web site, www.crmpa.it/ept. There is an AAST office (☎ 089 22 47 44) at the other end of town, at Via Roma 258. It is open

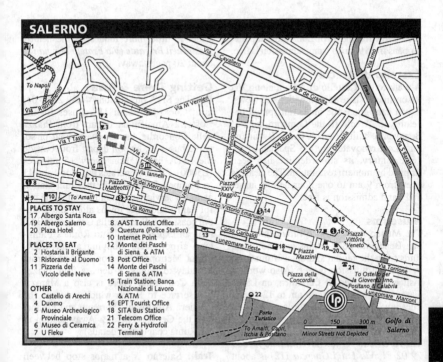

SALERNO

To Napoli

To Amalfi

PLACES TO STAY
17 Albergo Santa Rosa
19 Albergo Salerno
20 Plaza Hotel

PLACES TO EAT
2 Hostaria il Brigante
3 Ristorante al Duomo
11 Pizzeria del
 Vicolo delle Neve

OTHER
1 Castello di Arechi
4 Duomo
5 Museo Archeologico
 Provinciale
6 Museo di Ceramica
7 U Fleku

8 AAST Tourist Office
9 Questura (Police Station)
10 Internet Point
12 Monte dei Paschi
 di Siena & ATM
13 Post Office
14 Monte dei Paschi
 di Siena & ATM
15 Train Station; Banca
 Nazionale di Lavoro
 & ATM
16 EPT Tourist Office
18 SITA Bus Station
21 Telecom Office
22 Ferry & Hydrofoil
 Terminal

Piazza
Matteotti
Piazza dei Mercanti
Piazza
XXIV
Maggio
Corso Vittorio Emanuele
Corso Garibaldi
Lungomare Trieste
Piazza
Mazzini
Piazza della
Concordia
Porto
Turistico
To Amalfi, Capri,
Ischia & Positano

Piazza
Vittoria
Veneto
Via Torrione
To Ostello der
la Gioventù Irno,
Positano & Calabria
Lungomare Marconi

0   150   300 m
Minor Streets Not Depicted

Golfo di
Salerno

CAMPANIA

from 9 am to 1 pm and 4.30 to 7 pm daily except Sunday.

Money There is a Banca Nazionale di Lavoro ATM inside the train station. There are several banks with ATMs on Corso Vittorio Emanuele, including the Monte dei Paschi di Siena, which has another branch at Via Roma 118.

Post & Communications The main post office at Corso Garibaldi 203 is open from 8.15 am to 7.15 pm Monday to Saturday.

The Telecom office is at Corso Garibaldi 31. An Internet café, Internet Point, is at Via Roma 26.

Medical Services & Emergency The Ospedale Ruggi d'Aragona (☎ 089 67 11 11) is at Via San Leonardo. The questura (☎ 089 61 31 11) is at Piazza Amendola.

Duomo
The city's duomo, on Piazza Alfano north of Via dei Mercanti, is dedicated to San Matteo (Saint Matthew), whose remains were brought to the city in 954 and later buried in the crypt. Flanked by a Romanesque bell tower and an atrium featuring 28 Roman columns, the duomo was erected by the Normans under Robert Guiscard in the 11th century and remodelled in the 18th century. It sustained severe damage in the 1980 earthquake. The Cappella delle Crociate (Chapel of the Crusades), so called because crusaders' weapons were blessed here, is named after Pope Gregory VII. He lived in exile in Salerno until his death in 1085 and is buried under the altar. The 12th century mosaic and sculptural decoration on the left side of the central nave is among the most eye-catching. Next door the **Museo Diocesano**, with a modest collection of artworks encompassing items

dating back as far as the Norman period and even a few fragments of Lombard sculpture. It opens from 9 am to 6 pm; admission is free.

Castello di Arechi

A walk to the Castello di Arechi along Via Risorgimento is rewarded with good views, if you can ignore the industrial sprawl beneath you. Arechi II, the Lombard duke of Benevento, built the castle over a Byzantine fort. Last renovated by the Spanish in the 16th century, its slow decline has been stopped by modern restoration. The castle is open from 9 am to one hour before sunset daily and admission is free.

Museums

The **Museo Archeologico Provinciale**, Via San Benedetto 28, contains archaeological finds from the region and opens from 9 am to 1 pm. Admission is free. Also worth a visit is the **Museo di Ceramica**, on Largo Casavecchia, open from 9 am to 12.30 pm Tuesday, Thursday and Saturday.

Places to Stay

The HI *Ostello per la Gioventù Irno* (☎ 089 79 02 51, Via Luigi Guercio 112) is about 500m east of the train station and open year-round. B&B is L17,500 and a meal costs L10,000.

Albergo Santa Rosa (☎ 089 22 53 46, Corso Vittorio Emanuele 14), near the train station, has singles/doubles for L45,000/65,000. Opposite is *Albergo Salerno* (☎ 089 22 42 11, Via G Vicinanza 42), with rooms from L43,000/75,000 or L70,000/87,000 with bathroom. Pricier is the *Plaza Hotel* (☎ 089 22 44 77, Piazza Ferrovia 42), at L80,000/140,000 for comfortable rooms with bathroom, telephone and TV.

Places to Eat & Drink

The 500-year-old *Pizzeria del Vicolo delle Neve* (Vicolo delle Neve 24), off Via dei Mercanti, serves traditional fare and a meal could cost about L20,000. For a soothing ale afterwards, you could try *U Fleku* pub at No 5.

Ristorante al Duomo has a terrace overlooking Piazza al Duomo, but you're looking at about L30,000 for two courses and wine. A little more modest is the nearby *Hostaria il Brigante (Via Fratelli Minguiti 2)* about 20 paces away.

Getting There & Away

Bus The SITA bus station (☎ 089 22 66 04) is at Corso Garibaldi 117. Buses for the Costiera Amalfitana depart from Piazza della Concordia, usually every hour or so, while buses for Napoli depart from outside the SITA bus station every 15 minutes (L5000). ATACS operates bus Nos 4 and 41 to Pompei, from outside the train station and also services to Paestum (catch the bus for Sapri) and other towns along the southern coast from Piazza della Concordia. BAT runs an express service to Roma's Fiumicino airport, also stopping at the EUR-Fermi Metropolitana stop in Roma, from Monday to Friday. It departs from Piazza della Concordia. There is also a Marozzi bus service to Roma which goes via the Costiera Amalfitana, Sorrento and Pompei (see the Getting There & Away section in the Roma chapter for details).

Train Salerno is a major stop between Roma, Napoli and Reggio di Calabria and is served by all types of trains. It also has good services to the Adriatic coast and inland.

Car & Motorcycle Salerno is on the A3 between Napoli and Reggio di Calabria, which is toll-free from Salerno south. From Roma, you can bypass Napoli by taking the A30.

Boat Cooperativa Sant'Andrea (☎ 089 87 31 90) operates ferries from Salerno's Porto Turistico to Capri, Positano and Amalfi from April to October and to Ischia in summer only. Hydrofoils to these destinations, operated by Alilauro, run in summer only. Contact the EPT or AAST offices for the latest details.

Getting Around

Walking is the most sensible option but ATACS buses do run from the train station through the town centre.

PAESTUM

The evocative image of three Greek temples standing in fields of poppies is not easily forgotten and makes the trek to this archaeological site well worth the effort. The temples are among the world's best preserved monuments of the ancient Greek world, remnants of Magna Graecia, as the Greeks called their colonies in southern Italy and Sicilia. The small town is close to some of Italy's better beaches and just south of where US forces landed in 1943.

Paestum, or Poseidonia as the city was first known, was founded in the 6th century BC by Greek settlers from Sybaris, on the Golfo di Taranto farther east. Conquered by the Lucanians from Basilicata in the 4th century BC, it came under Roman control in 273 BC and became an important trading port. The town was gradually abandoned after the fall of the Roman Empire, periodic outbreaks of malaria and savage raids by the Saracens in

TAMSIN WILSON

One of the metopes from the Tempio di Argive Hera, now in the Museo di Paestum

871. The temples were rediscovered in the late 18th century by road builders who subsequently ploughed right through the ruins. The road did little to alter the state of the surrounding area though, which remained full of malarial swamps teeming with snakes and scorpions, until well into the 20th century.

This state of affairs belongs to the past and the site is now easily traversed by foot. All public transport is within walking distance. The tourist office (☎ 0828 81 10 16) on Via Aquilia, opposite the main site, has maps.

The Ruins

The first temple you come across when you enter the site from the northern end, near the tourist office, is the **Tempio di Cerere** (Temple of Ceres), which dates from the 6th century BC. It is the smallest of the three temples and was used as a Christian church for a time. The basic outline of the **foro** (the centre of the ancient city) is evident as you head south. Among the buildings, parts of which remain, are the Italic temple, the Greek theatre, the Bouleuterion, where the senate met and, farther south, the anfiteatro, through which the road was built.

The **Tempio di Nettuno** (Temple of Neptune), dating from about 450 BC, is the most impressive of the remains and the largest and best preserved, with only parts of the inside walls and roof missing. From a distance, its structure gives the impression that the columns are leaning outward. Virtually next door, the so-called **basilica** is the oldest surviving monument in Paestum, dating from the middle of the 6th century BC. With nine columns across and 18 along the sides, it is a majestic building. In the front of the building you can make out remains of the sacrificial altar.

The city was ringed by 4.7km of walls, built and rebuilt by Lucanians and Romans. The most intact section is west of the ruins, but the area to the east makes for a pleasant walk through the local farmland. The ruins are open from 9 am to an hour before sunset and admission costs L8000.

The **Museo di Paestum**, opposite the site, houses a collection of metopes, including

euro currency converter L10,000 = €5.16

CAMPANIA

33 of the original 36 from the **Tempio di Argive Hera** (Temple of Argive Hera), 9km north of Paestum. Wall paintings from tombs on the site are the highlight, but admission is rather steep (L8000) after you have already paid to see the ruins. The museum is open from 9 am to 7 pm.

Places to Stay & Eat
Paestum is a short trip from Salerno, which offers a better range of accommodation. There are more than 20 camp sites in the area, including *Intercamping Apollo* (☎ *0828 81 11 78, Via Principe di Piemonte 2*), close to the ruins and near the beach. There is a HI hostel nearby at Agropoli (see the later Agropoli section). *Albergo Villa Rita* (☎ *0828 81 10 81, Via Principe di Piemonte 39*) is pleasantly located back from the main road but close to the ruins. Smart singles/doubles including breakfast cost L100,000/110,000 in summer and L80,000/100,000 out of season. There are a few cafés and snack bars near the temples, or you could eat at the *Ristorante Museo* or *Ristorante delle Rose* on Via Magna Grecia, which runs between the temples and the museum.

Getting There & Away
ATACS runs buses from Salerno to Paestum (and on to Agropoli), departing hourly from Piazza della Concordia.

Paestum is on the train line from Napoli through Salerno to Reggio di Calabria. Many trains stop at the Stazione di Capaccio, nearer the new town (about 6km from the site) and less frequently at the Stazione di Paestum, a short walk from the temples. Trains are less frequent than the ATACS buses.

Take the A3 from Salerno and exit for the S18 at Battipaglia, or follow the S163 Amalfitana out of Salerno. Paestum is 36km from Salerno.

PARCO NAZIONALE DEL CILENTO E VALLO DI DIANO
The area south-east of Salerno to the regional borders with Basilicata and Calabria is known as the Parco Nazionale del Cilento e Vallo di Diano. The World Wide Fund for

Nature has a wildlife sanctuary, the **Oasi Naturalistica di Persano**, about 20km north-east of Paestum on the Sele river. It is one of the few protected natural environments in southern Italy. Consisting mainly of wetlands, it is home to a wide variety of birds. The sanctuary (☎ 0828 97 46 84) is open from September to April and signs direct you there from the S18.

The **Grotte di Pertosa**, 40km east of Paestum, were discovered in the late 19th century. You can wander through about 1700m of caves full of stalagmites and stalactites. Admission is with a guide only and tours leave hourly from 9 am to 7 pm in summer (to 4 pm in winter). There's a SITA bus at about 9 am from Piazza della Concordia in Salerno; another one will take you back in the afternoon. By car, the caves can be reached via the A3 from Salerno.

About 20km farther down the A3 towards Calabria, the pretty medieval hill town of **Teggiano** makes a pleasant stop. Just outside the small town of Padula, 10km farther south, is the **Certosa di San Lorenzo**, a monastery begun in the 14th century and finished 500 years later. Many of the monks who lived here were from wealthy aristocratic families and no expense was spared in its construction – as the elaborate chapels, huge central courtyard, impressive wood panelled library and the original kitchens all reveal. Lamanna buses run from Salerno to Padula and (less frequently) to Teggiano.

COSTIERA CILENTANA (CILENTO COAST)
South-east of the Golfo di Salerno, the coastal plains begin to give way to more rugged territory, a foretaste of what lies farther on in the stark hills and mountains of Basilicata and the more heavily wooded peaks of Calabria. This southernmost tract of the Campania littoral lends itself little to summer seaside frolics (with some exceptions), although snorkellers will appreciate some of the rocky points. Despite an irregular splattering of camp sites and the like, the beaches are not as popular as those farther north-west or south-east into Basilicata and Calabria. ATACS

buses leave Salerno for Sapri, on the regional boundary between Campania and Basilicata and trains south from Salerno also stop at most towns on the Costiera Cilentana. By car, take the S18 which connects Agropoli with Velia via the inland route, or the S267, which hugs the coast.

Agropoli

This modern coastal town south of Paestum has a small medieval core. Perched on a high promontory overlooking the sea and topped by a crumbling old castle, it is a rewarding stop and could even be a base for travel to the temples at Paestum and also to the clean, sandy beaches to the north-west.

Camping Villaggio Arco delle Rose (☎ 0974 83 82 27, Via Isca Solofrone) is a tacky tourist village but has camp sites. There is an HI youth hostel, *La Lanterna* (☎ 0974 83 80 03, Via Lanterna 8), just out of Agropoli in località San Marco. It opens from March to October and has B&B for L16,000. Family rooms cost L17,000 per person and meals cost L14,000.

Hotel Carola (☎ 0974 82 30 05, Via Pisacane 1), near the harbour, has singles/doubles for L55,000/75,000, but closes from November to March. *Ristorante U Sghizu*, on Piazza Umberto I, the main square of the old town, bakes a pizza for L4500 or more. A full meal will cost around L20,000.

Velia

The ruins of the Greek settlement of Elea, founded in the mid-6th century BC and later a popular spot for wealthy Romans, are worth a visit if you have the time. Its decline matches that of Paestum, but as the town was never an important trading centre, it was considerably smaller than its north-western rival and its ruins are in a far worse state.

The closest town with accommodation is Ascea, with several camp sites and hotels. *Camping Alba* (☎ 0974 97 23 31), near Marina di Ascea, is close to the sea and a few kilometres downhill from the main town. *Albergo Elea* (☎ 0974 97 15 77) has singles/doubles for L50,000/75,000 and is near the water.

The train station for Ascea is at Marina di Ascea. To get to the ruins, wait for a local bus to Castellamare di Velia.

South to Sapri

From Ascea to Sapri, a dowdy seaside town a few kilometres short of Basilicata, the road climbs, dips and curves its way through country that, while not Italy's prettiest, is rarely dull and at times spectacular. The beaches along this part of the coast are good and the water usually crystal clear.

Pisciotta, 12km south-east of Ascea, is an attractive medieval village that clings to the mountainside. A bargain place to stay and eat is *Agriturismo San Carlo* (☎/fax 0974 97 61 77, Via Noce 8), which offers beds and full board for L60,000 per person year-round (L100,000 in August). It also produces a remarkable olive oil from the unique local Pisciotta olive trees.

Another 25km or so farther on are some striking white sandy **beaches** south-east of the resort town of Palinuro (in and around which are camp sites and several hotels). A little farther still, where the road turns steeply inland to pass through San Giovanni a Piro, is Marina di Camerota, a small medieval centre. From there, it's another 25km to Sapri. If you get this far you should really make the effort to continue the short distance into Basilicata (see the Maratea section in the Puglia, Basilicata & Calabria chapter).

Puglia, Basilicata & Calabria

A good number of visitors to Italy, drawn by the beauty of the Costiera Amalfitana and Capri, summon up the gumption to proceed south of Roma to Napoli, but few venture much beyond the boundaries of Campania. Those who do are rewarded.

These southern regions are Italy's poorest, but also the least populated – a decided advantage for travellers wanting to get off the beaten tourist track for a while. Accommodation and food are often more affordable than in other parts of the country and foreign travellers are a definite minority – a welcome change. Above all, it is the dramatic and varied natural beauty – including some of Italy's most spectacular coastline – which will leave its impression, as will the warm welcome of the hospitable southern Italians.

While you won't find the sumptuous artistic treasures of Roma or Firenze, the Mezzogiorno beyond Campania nevertheless retains many reminders of the march past of several civilisations since the Greeks first established the colonies of Magna Graecia along the coast of Calabria, Basilicata and Puglia.

Of the three, Puglia came out best from the eras of Norman, Swabian, Angevin and Spanish rule, all of which left behind a surprisingly diverse heritage in churches, fortresses and other monuments. The same rulers pretty much left Basilicata and Calabria to their own devices. That sense of abandonment created a vacuum that has all too often allowed petty overlords to maintain a violent grip on their local territories. Great strides towards improving living standards have been made since the end of WWII, especially in Puglia, but much remains to be done.

Puglia (Apulia)

Encompassing the 'spur' and 'heel' of Italy's boot, Puglia is bordered by two seas, the Adriatico to the east and the Ionio (known as the Golfo di Taranto), to the south.

Highlights

- Explore Puglia's Romanesque cathedrals, particularly the ones at Trani, Ruvo di Puglia and Barletta
- Drive through the trulli-dotted countryside around Alberobello
- Admire the elegant baroque architecture of Lecce, then head down Penisola Salentina to the tip of Italy's heel
- Waste a few pleasant days in seaside Vieste and explore the rest of the Promontorio del Gargano
- Step back in time in fascinating Matera with its *sassi* (cave dwellings) and churches hewn out of the rocks
- Eat seafood meals in the various coastal settlements of Maratea
- Soak up some early summer rays on the beaches near Tropea and Capo Vaticano
- Walk and ski in Calabria's Sila Massif mountain range

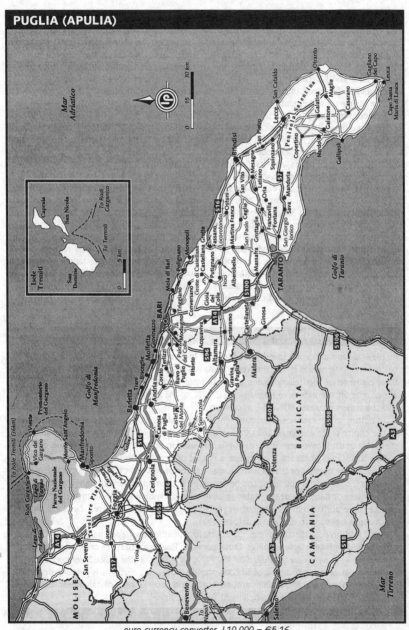

PUGLIA (APULIA)

Puglia's strategic position as the peninsula's gateway to the east made it a major thoroughfare and a target for colonisers and invaders. Today it is a gateway for illegal immigrants from the Balkans, Turkey, the Middle East and North Africa.

The ancient Greeks founded Magna Graecia in a string of settlements on the Ionian coast, including Taranto, which was settled by Spartan exiles. Brindisi marks the end of the Roman Via Appia; the Norman legacy is seen in magnificent Romanesque churches across the region; Foggia and its province were favoured by the great Swabian king, Frederick II, several of whose castles remain; and Lecce, the Firenze of baroque, bears the architectural mark of the Spanish colonisers.

Coloured by its diverse history, the region holds many surprises, including the fascinating sanctuary dedicated to San Michele Arcangelo (St Michael the Archangel) at Monte Sant'Angelo; the *trulli* (conical-roofed, stone houses of Alberobello); and the extraordinary floor mosaic in Otranto's cathedral. Then there are the Isole Tremiti, which remain unspoiled by tourism, the ancient Foresta Umbra on the Promontorio del Gargano and the pleasant beaches of the Penisola Salentina (Salentine Peninsula) at the tip of the heel.

Intensive efforts to crank up industry, improve communications and education and to spur economic growth over the past 30 years have made Puglia the richest of Italy's southern regions, but high unemployment remains a grinding problem. The latter may have had a hand in the growth of Mafia-style organised crime run by the Sacra Corona Unità in the south and La Rosa in the north.

If you want to explore Puglia, you will need your own transport or lots of time, since many sights are in or near small towns and villages that are not always well serviced by public transport. The best option is to base yourself in the main towns and set out on daily expeditions. For instance, many of the more important Romanesque churches are reasonably close to Bari. Puglia lends itself to cyclists as much of the region is flat.

A Taste of Puglia

Puglia is a food and wine lover's paradise – no matter how hard you try, it's difficult to eat badly here. One reason is that the fresh produce is of such high quality. Indeed, many of the basic elements of the Italian kitchen originate from Puglia – a huge proportion of Italy's fish are caught off the extensive Puglian coast, 70% of the country's olive oil is produced here and the region provides 80% of Europe's pasta.

Tomatoes, green cauliflower, chicory, fennel, figs, melons, cherries and grapes are just some of the choice fruits and vegetables that you'll find, often sold at bargain prices on roadside stalls. Almonds, grown near Ruvo di Puglia, are used in many traditional cakes and pastries.

Like their Greek forbears, the Pugliese eat a lot of *agnello* (lamb) and *capretto* (kid). The meat is usually roasted or grilled with aromatic herbs or served in tomato-based sauces.

Fish and seafood are abundant and better priced than in other parts of Italy. Raw fish (such as anchovies or baby squid) marinated in olive oil and lemon juice is not uncommon. *Cozze* (mussels) are prepared in a variety of ways. One recipe from the Bari area, *tiella alla barese*, has mussels baked with rice and potatoes.

You'll find *orecchiette* (sometimes called *strascinati*; little ear-shaped pasta) in most places, often served with vegetable toppings. Other common Pugliese pastas are *cavatelli* and *capunti*.

Many quality wines are produced on the Penisola Salentina (the Salice Salentino is one of the best reds), in the trulli area around Locorotondo (home to a particularly pleasing dry white of the same name) and in the plains around Foggia and Lucera. Some of Italy's best rosé wines hail from Puglia and perfectly complement Pugliese cuisine.

FOGGIA

postcode 71100 • pop 156,470

Set in northern Puglia's patchwork land-scape of the broad Tavoliere Plain, Foggia is an important transport junction and a not unlikeable place, but has little to hold the traveller for long. In the 12th century, the town was one of Frederick II's favourite cities, but later began to decline under the rule of the Spanish house of Aragon. Like much of the region, Foggia has been a fre-quent victim of earthquakes and what was left standing of the old city centre was effi-ciently flattened under Allied bombardment in WWII. The town's location makes it a possible launch pad for excursions to the forest and beaches of the Promontorio del Gargano and to two small towns to the west worth visiting: Troia for its beautiful Puglian-Romanesque cathedral and Lucera for its Swabian-Angevin castle.

Orientation

The train and bus stations are on Piazza Vit-torio Veneto, in the northern rim of town. Viale XXIV Maggio leads directly south into Piazza Cavour and the main shopping area. Several hotels, restaurants, as well as the post and telephone offices, can all be found on and around Viale XXIV Maggio. From Piazza Cavour, Via Lanza leads to Corso Vit-torio Emanuele and the oldest part of town.

Information

Tourist Offices The EPT office (☎ 0881 72 31 41) is about 20 minutes walk from the train station at Via Senatore Emilio Perrone 17. It has limited information, including hotel lists. From the station, walk straight ahead along Viale XXIV Maggio to Piazza Cavour and continue along Corso P Gian-none. Turn left into Via Cirillo (which be-comes Via Bari) and follow it to Piazzale Puglia – Via Perrone is on the right. Other-wise, take bus MD from the station. It is open from 8.30 am to 1.30 pm Monday to Friday and also from 5 to 7 pm on Tuesday.

Post & Communications The post office is on Viale XXIV Maggio and there is a tele-phone office (open from 8 am to 9 pm daily) at Via Piave 29 (off Viale XXIV Maggio).

Things to See

The **cathedral**, off Corso Vittorio Eman-uele, is about the only noteworthy sight. Built in the 12th century, the lower section remains true to the original Romanesque style. The top half, in the noticeably differ-ent baroque style of six centuries later, was grafted on after an earthquake. Most of the cathedral's treasures were lost in the quake, but you can see a Byzantine icon preserved in a chapel inside the church. The icon was supposedly discovered in the 11th century by shepherds, in a pond over which burned three flames. The flames are now the sym-bol of the city.

The **Musei Civici** on Piazza Nigri (take Via Arpi to the right off Corso Vittorio Emanuele) houses archaeological finds from the province, including relics from the Roman and medieval town of Siponto. Three portals in the side of the building, one featuring two suspended eagles, are all that remain of Frederick II's local palazzo.

Places to Stay & Eat

Albergo Centrale (☎ 0881 77 18 62, *Corso Cairoli 5*) has singles/doubles (no bath) for L35,000/68,000.

Near the station, *Hotel Venezia* (☎ 0881 77 09 03, *Via Piave 40*) is basic, with sin-gles starting at L40,000 without bath and top-of-the-range doubles available for L70,000.

Hotel Europa (☎ 0881 72 67 83, *Via Monfalcone 52*) has more upmarket singles/doubles from L100,000/150,000 and *Hotel Cicolella* (☎ 0881 68 88 90, *Viale XXIV Maggio 60*) has rooms from L150,000/260,000. Directly opposite the station is *Pizza e Panini*, which serves exactly that.

There are several *trattorie* in side streets to the right off Viale XXIV Maggio (walk-ing away from the station). *Ristorante Margutta* (*Via Piave 33*) has pizzas from L6500. You'll eat well at *Ristorante L'An-golo Preferito* (*Via Trieste 21*) for about L25,000.

PUGLIA

Getting There & Around

Bus Buses depart Piazzale Vittorio Veneto, in front of the train station, for towns throughout the province of Foggia. SITA has buses to Vieste on the Promontorio del Gargano (up to six daily), Monte Sant'Angelo (eight daily), San Giovanni Rotondo (hourly), Lucera (five daily), Manfredonia and Campobasso (in Molise; twice daily). Ferrovie del Gargano runs buses to Manfredonia, Vieste, Troia and Barletta. Tickets for both companies are available at window 10 or the tobacconist at the train station, or from the bar opposite the station on Viale XXIV Maggio. Four direct services (CLP) also connect Foggia with Napoli (buy tickets on the bus).

Train Foggia is connected by train to other major towns in Puglia, including Bari, Brindisi and Lecce. The town is easily accessible from points along the Mar Adriatico, including Ancona and Pescara.

Car & Motorcycle Take the S16 south for Bari or north for the Adriatic coast to Termoli, Pescara and beyond. The Bologna-Bari A14 also passes Foggia. The S90 south-west will put you on the road to Napoli.

Central Foggia is a confusing tangle of one-way streets. Follow the 'stazione' signs for the train station and get oriented from there, especially if you are planning to stay.

LUCERA

Less than 20km west of Foggia (and a much nicer place to spend the night), Lucera has the distinction of having been re-created as an Arab city by Frederick II.

Surrounded, like Foggia, by the flat plains of the Tavoliere, the site was first settled by the Romans in the 4th century BC and named Luceria Augusta. The fall of empire meant decay for the town, but Frederick II resuscitated it in the 13th century. Arab bandits had become a growing problem in Sicilia and Frederick decided to remove the thorn from his side by relocating all of them to Puglia. Some 20,000 ended up in Lucera, where the emperor allowed them to build mosques and practise Islam freely. He recruited his famous

Saracen bodyguard from the Arabs of Lucera, who accompanied him on his journeys between castles and even to the crusades.

Charles I of Anjou conquered Lucera in 1269 and the new French arrivals replaced many of the town's mosques with Gothic churches. In 1300 Charles II had the Arabs slaughtered.

Things to See

The imposing **castle** was built by Frederick II in 1233. Its external walls were later added by Charles of Anjou, forming a pentagon topped with 24 towers. The remains stand in the north-eastern corner of the enclosure. Excavations have also revealed the remains of Roman buildings. The castle is open until dusk daily. Admission is free, but the guard will expect a small tip.

The **duomo**, in the centre of the old town, was begun by Charles II of Anjou in 1300 and is considered the best example of Angevin architecture in southern Italy. The Gothic **Chiesa di San Francesco** was also erected by Charles II. On the eastern outskirts of town is a poorly maintained 1st century BC **Roman amphitheatre**, open from 7 am to 1 pm and 2 pm until dusk. Admission is free, but tip the guard.

Places to Stay

The pick here is the *Albergo Al Passetto* (☎ 0881 54 22 13) next to the old city gate on Piazza del Popolo. Singles/doubles with bath cost from L35,000/60,000 and there is a restaurant downstairs.

Getting There & Away

Lucera is easily accessible from Foggia (a 30 minute trip) by SITA and FS buses, that terminate in Piazza del Popolo.

TROIA

The village of Troia, 18km south of Lucera, has nothing to do with the Troy of legend. However, its beautiful Puglian-Romanesque **cathedral** merits the (hardly strenuous) effort of getting there. The façade is splendidly decorated with a rose window and in among the gargoyles and other creatures that adorn the exterior of the church are hints of Oriental influence – look particularly for the geometric designs across the top of the eastern façade. The bronze doors are also of particular note.

If you want to stay, try *Albergo Alba d'Oro* (☎ 0881 97 09 40, Viale Kennedy 30) on the way out of town towards Lucera. It has singles/doubles with bathroom for L45,000/70,000.

MANFREDONIA
postcode 71043 • pop 58,300

Founded by the Swabian king Manfred, Frederick II's illegitimate son, this port town has little to attract tourists other than as a transport junction on the way to the Promontorio del Gargano. Intercity buses terminate in Piazza Marconi, a short walk along Corso Manfredi from the AAST office (☎ 0884 58 19 98) at No 26. It is open from 8 am to 2 pm Monday to Friday. You can get limited information on the promontorio.

Things to See
If you have time, head to the other end of Corso Manfredi for a look at the majestic **castle** started by Manfred and completed by Charles of Anjou (open from 9 am to 1 pm and 5 to 7 pm Tuesday to Sunday). The **Museo Archeologico Nazionale del Gargano** inside has a display of ancient artefacts discovered in the area around Manfredonia.

About 2km south of town is **Siponto**, an important port from Roman to medieval times, abandoned in favour of Manfredonia because of earthquakes and malaria. Apart from the **beaches**, the only thing of interest is the distinctly Byzantine-looking 11th century Romanesque **Chiesa di Santa Maria di Siponto**.

Places to Stay & Eat
There are four camp sites south of town. Of the hotels in town, *Albergo Sipontum* (☎ 0884 54 29 16, Viale di Vittorio 229) only has doubles for L80,000. Rooms at *Hotel Azzurro* (☎ 0884 58 14 98, Viale di Vittorio 56) start at L55,000/ 80,000 for a single/ double. For a good meal, try *Al Fuego (Via dei Celestini)*, just off Corso Manfredi.

Getting There & Away
SITA buses connect Manfredonia with Foggia, Vieste and Monte Sant'Angelo, leaving from Piazza Marconi. Tickets and timetable information are available at Bar Impero on Piazza Marconi, near the corner of Corso Manfredi.

PROMONTORIO DEL GARGANO (GARGANO PROMONTORY)
The 'spur' of the Italian boot is made up of limestone mountains, ancient forests and beautiful beaches. For centuries an important destination for religious pilgrims, the Promontorio del Gargano has more recently become a popular tourist playground. Its beach resorts, including Vieste and Peschici, are developing rapidly to accommodate the annual influx of sun-and-fun seekers.

The ancient beeches and oaks of the **Foresta Umbra** in the promontorio's mountainous interior make up one of Italy's last remaining original forests. Walkers will find plenty of well-marked trails and there are several picnic areas. Strictly speaking, overnight camping isn't permitted, but it seems to be tolerated. Public transport to and from the forest can be tricky, but not impossible.

The promontorio also has two important religious sanctuaries: that of San Michele Arcangelo at Monte Sant'Angelo and the burial place of Padre Pio at San Giovanni Rotondo.

Monte Sant'Angelo
For centuries this isolated mountain town overlooking the south coast of the Gargano has been the last stop on a gruelling religious pilgrimage. The object of devotion is the Santuario di San Michele. Here, in 490 AD, San Michele Arcangelo is said to have appeared in a grotto before the Bishop of Siponto. The legend goes that a local man who had lost his prize bull eventually found it at the entrance to a cave. He could not make the animal move, so shot an arrow at it. But the arrow turned and hit the man, who then went to the bishop for advice. San Michele later appeared to the bishop at the grotto, ordering him to consecrate a Christian altar there in place of a pagan shrine.

PUGLIA

During the Middle Ages, the sanctuary marked the end of the pilgrim Route of the Angel, which began in Normandy and passed through Roma. In 999 AD Holy Roman Emperor Otto III made a pilgrimage to the sanctuary to pray that prophecies of the end of world in the year 1000 would not be fulfilled. The sanctuary's fame grew after the much-predicted apocalypse did not eventuate.

Information There is a Pro Loco office on the town's main street, Via Reale Basilica, which can provide limited information about the town. It's open from 9 am to 1 pm and 2.30 to 5 pm Monday to Saturday in summer only.

Things to See & Do Like so many great pilgrimage destinations, the **Santuario di San Michele** has become big tourist business. Those who forget the religious nature of the place are quickly reminded: dress rules are strictly enforced (absolutely no shorts, miniskirts or revealing tops – even bare arms are frowned upon) and don't be surprised if you are asked to put on a special coat to cover offending exposed skin.

A flight of stone steps leads down to the grotto. As you descend, note the graffiti that fills the walls, some of it the work of 17th century pilgrims. San Michele Arcangelo is said to have left a footprint in stone inside the grotto, so it became customary for pilgrims to carve outlines of their feet and hands and leave accompanying messages. Magnificent Byzantine bronze and silver doors open onto the grotto itself.

Inside, a 16th century statue of the archangel covers the spot where he is said to have left his footprint. The main altar stands at the site of the first altar consecrated by the bishop of Siponto to San Michele and behind it is a small fountain of legendary 'healing' waters which you can no longer drink. The grotto also has a beautiful marble bishop's chair, resting on two lions.

Once outside, head down the short flight of steps opposite the sanctuary to the **Tomba di Rotari**, which is not a tomb but a 12th century baptistry. Enter through the church

façade with the lovely rose window, all that remains of the **Chiesa di San Pietro**, destroyed by an earthquake in the 19th century. The portal of the adjacent 11th century **Chiesa di Santa Maria Maggiore** is interesting but the church's interior is disappointing.

Commanding the highest point of the town is a Norman **castle** with Swabian and Aragonese additions which is worth a look. The serpentine alleyways and jumbled houses of this town are perfect for a little aimless ambling. Take the time to head for the **belvedere** for sweeping views of the coast to the south.

Places to Stay & Eat Finding rooms can be decidedly difficult in Monte Sant'Angelo. Ask at the tobacconist's near the sanctuary if there are any cheap beds to be had. The only hotel is the comfortable if charmless three star *Rotary Hotel (☎ 0884 56 21 46, Via Pulsano)*, 1km downhill from town, which has singles/doubles for L80,000/110,000.

There are plenty of takeaways and trattorie, especially on Via Reale Basilica. *La Jalantuúmene (Piazza de Galganis 5)* has excellent food and tables spilling into a picturesque square in summer. Don't leave without tasting the local sweets, *ostie ripiene* (literally, 'stuffed Hosts') – two wafers like Hosts used in the Catholic Communion with a filling of caramelised almonds.

Getting There & Away Monte Sant'Angelo is accessible from Foggia, Manfredonia, Vieste and San Giovanni Rotondo by SITA bus. If you have your own transport, you can take the road to/from Vico del Gargano, which cuts through the Foresta Umbra.

San Giovanni Rotondo

When Padre Pio, an ailing Capuchin priest in need of a cooler climate, arrived in 1916, San Giovanni Rotondo was a tiny, isolated medieval village in the heart of the Gargano. In the following years, Pio gained a reputation as a mystic and miracle-worker and San Giovanni Rotondo underwent something of a miraculous transformation itself, expanding well beyond its original limits.

Up to 200,000 pilgrims crowd into the town every year to pay homage to the priest (who was beatified in May 1999) and spend up in the souvenir shops. Aside from the 14th century **Chiesa di Sant'Onofrio**, a **baptistry** and the 16th century **Chiesa di Santa Maria delle Grazie**, you can visit the **tomb of Padre Pio** in the modern church (Santuario) nearby.

If you want to stay, there are more than 20 hotels, although pilgrims can fill a good number of them early.

SITA buses run five times daily to and from Monte Sant'Angelo and hourly from Manfredonia.

Vieste

The most popular seaside resort on the promontorio and the best equipped with tourist facilities, Vieste is a bright little place. The better beaches are to the south, between Vieste and Pugnochiuso and to the north, between Vieste and Peschici, particularly in the area known as La Salata. There are several camp sites along both stretches of coastline.

Orientation & Information Intercity buses terminate in Piazza Manzoni, a few minutes walk along Via XXIV Maggio from the entrance to the old town and the IAT office (☎ 0884 70 71 30) at Piazza Kennedy 1, in the pink building by the sea. The office is open from 8.30 am to 1 pm and from 3.30 to 8 pm Monday to Saturday in summer. Out of season it is usually open only in the morning.

The post office is on Piazza Vittorio Veneto and there are rows of public telephones there too.

Things to See & Do The old town, with its whitewashed houses and winding medieval streets, offers a couple of sights of interest, although tourists come here for the beaches rather than the history. The **duomo** is Puglian-Romanesque, but underwent alterations in the 18th century.

Head down Via Cimaglia to the **Chianca Amara** (Bitter Stone), on which thousands of citizens were beheaded when the Turks sacked Vieste in the 16th century. Nearby, at the town's highest point, is a **castle**, built

by Frederick II, now occupied by the military and closed to the public.

The **Museo Malacologico**, Via Pola 8, contains a huge collection of seashells from all over the world. Admission is free.

If you want to head for a beach and don't have your own transport, the **Spiaggia del Castello** is just south of the town.

Places to Stay Most of Vieste's many hotels and pensioni are scattered along the beach-front roads to the north and south of town. Camp sites (around 80) abound, particularly along Lungomare E Mattei to the south. A good one is *Campeggio Capo Vieste* (☎ 0884 70 63 26) at La Salata on the road between Vieste and Peschici. It is accessible by Ferrovie del Gargano bus. Another good option is *Villaggio Baia di Campi* (☎ 0884 70 00 00) near Pugnochiuso on the coast road between Vieste and Mattinata.

Pensione al Centro Storico (☎ 0884 70 70 30, Via Mafrolla 32), a former convent in the medieval centre (from Via XXIV Maggio, walk through Piazza Vittorio Emanuele and then follow Via Pola), has singles/doubles for up to L60,000/100,000 (much less in low season). The terrace makes up for the basic rooms. Also in the old town is *Hotel del Seggio* (☎ 0884 70 81 23, fax 0884 70 87 27, Via Vieste 7). It has a private pool and sunbathing terraces and charges up to L140,000 for a double in the high season. *Albergo Punta San Francesco* (☎ 0884 70 14 22, fax 0884 70 14 24, Via San Francesco 2) is in an old olive oil factory and costs from L37,500 per person. It has good deals on large rooms/mini-apartments that sleep four. *Vela Velo* (☎/fax 0884 70 63 03, email velavelo@vieste online.it, Lungomare Europa 19) is north of the old town and has friendly management. Rooms with breakfast cost L40,000/60,000 in the low season, rising to L140,000 for a double (high season), which includes use of the private beach and a mountain bike.

Places to Eat You'll have no trouble eating well in Vieste. For a snack, try *Il Fornaio* at the end of Via Fazzini near the entrance to the old town, which serves pizza by the slice, or

PUGLIA

Chianca Amara (Via Cimaglia 4) for typical local cakes and pastries. A panoramic spot for a cool drink is *Sapori di Mare*, overlooking the sea on Piazzetta Petrone, downhill along Via Cimaglia. *La Ripa (Via Cimaglia 16)* is a pleasant rustic trattoria where a full meal will cost about L25,000. At *Osteria degli Angeli (Via Celestino V)*, near the duomo, a good meal will cost around L30,000. Try the delicious *troccoli dell'angelo* (pasta speciality with prawns). There's fine food at *Osteria degli Archi (Via Ripe 2)* and a full meal costs from L40,000. *Enoteca Vesta (Via Duomo 14)* has an excellent selection of Pugliese wines and good food.

Getting There & Away SITA buses connect Vieste with Foggia and Manfredonia, while the Ferrovie del Gargano bus and train network connects the town with Peschici and Rodi Garganico, as well as other towns on the promontorio. Buses terminate in Piazza Manzoni and timetables are posted outside the town hall nearby. Bus services connecting the towns along the coast are frequent in summer and almost non-existent at other times of the year.

Vieste's port is just north of the old town, about a five minute walk from the IAT office. Boats to the Isole Tremiti (summer only) are run by several companies, including Adriatica and Motonave, which have ticket offices at the port. The cost is L35,000 return on the *monostab* (a sleek high-speed cruise boat). It is also possible to make a boat tour of the coast near Vieste, which includes visits to some of the area's grottoes. Inquire at the port for timetables and tickets. Agenzia SOL (☎ 0884 70 15 58), Via Trepiccioni 5, can also provide tickets as well as information on walking, cycling and horse-riding excursions, plus car, mountain bike and boat hire, as well as transport to the Foresta Umbra.

Peschici

On a rocky outcrop above a sparkling bay, Peschici is a fast-developing resort, but remains relatively unspoiled.

Strongly recalling villages of the Greek islands, with whitewashed houses and a sunny aspect, Peschici has cobbled alleyways with suggestive names – Vico Purgatorio (Purgatory Lane), Via Malconsiglio and Via Buonconsiglio (Bad Advice and Good Advice Streets). Their origins are anyone's guess; Vico Stretto (Narrow Lane) is more straightforward.

Peschici's sandy beaches and hotels fill up in summer, so book well in advance.

Orientation & Information While the medieval part of town clings to the cliff top at the point of the bay, the newer parts of town extend inland and around the bay. Buses arrive at the sports ground uphill from the town's main street, Corso Garibaldi. Turn right into the Corso and walk straight ahead to reach the old town.

The Pro Loco office (☎ 0884 96 44 25) at Corso Garibaldi 57, near the entrance to the old town, can provide information about accommodation, but little else.

Places to Stay & Eat Peschici has several hotels and pensioni, but prices are usually on the expensive side, particularly in summer. Numerous camp sites dot the coast on either side of Peschici. Try *Baia San Nicola* (☎ 0884 96 42 31), close to town, or *Camping Parco degli Ulivi* (☎ 0884 96 34 04), a few kilometres west on the road to Rodi Garganico.

The pick in old Peschici is *Locanda al Castello* (☎ 0884 96 40 38, Via Castello 29), right by the seaward cliffs. It has singles/doubles with bath for L50,000/95,000. In the new town, *Albergo La Pineta* (☎ 0884 96 41 26, Viale Libetta 85) has rooms for L40,000/ 80,000, while next door, *Hotel Timiana* (☎ 0884 96 43 21) offers doubles with full board for L65,000 to L115,000.

To stock up on supplies, shop at the *Supermercato Crai* at the far end of Corso Garibaldi from the medieval section. *Locanda al Castello* has a good, reasonably priced pizzeria and trattoria. Other restaurants in the old part of town include *Ristorante La Taverna (Via Malconsiglio 6)*, off Via Castello, where a full meal will cost up to L40,000 and *Ristorante Vecchia Peschici (Via Roma 31)* where an excellent meal on the terrace overlooking the sea costs around L35,000.

Getting There & Away Peschici is accessible by Ferrovie del Gargano buses from Vieste and Rodi Garganico and the original Ferrovie del Gargano local trains (infrequent) from San Severo (with connections to/from Foggia). From April to September, daily boats leave Peschici's port for the Isole Tremiti. For information and tickets, go to Ondazzurra (☎ 0884 96 42 34) at Corso Umberto I.

Rodi Garganico

Once a simple fishing village, Rodi Garganico and the beach stretching east to the hamlet of San Menaio are rapidly filling up with hotels, camp sites and apartments and the area is the least agreeable of the resorts. Should you really want to go, Ferrovie del Gargano buses link it with Peschici and other towns on the promontorio.

ISOLE TREMITI

postcode 71040 • pop 370

This small archipelago 36km north of the Promontorio del Gargano consists of three main islands: San Domino, San Nicola and Capraia. A convict station until the 1930s, the islands are becoming increasingly popular, but for now remain relatively low-key. Out of season most of the islands' tourist facilities close down and the 370 or so permanent residents resume their isolated, quiet lives.

The islands have an ancient history. Legend says that Diomedes, a Greek hero of the Trojan War, was buried here and that a rare local species of bird, the Diomedee, continues to mourn his death. Early in the 11th century, the Abbazia e Chiesa di Santa Maria (Abbey of Santa Maria) was founded on San Nicola by Benedictine monks, who wielded power in the region until the arrival of the Spanish Bourbons in the 18th century. King Ferdinand IV used the abbey as a jail, a tradition continued by the Fascists, who sent political exiles to the islands in the 1920s and 1930s.

Easily defensible, San Nicola was always the administrative and residential centre of the islands, while the lusher San Domino was used to grow crops. With the risk of pirate attack no longer a preoccupation, you will find most of the islands' accommodation and other facilities on San Domino.

Depending on the boat you catch, you will arrive on either San Domino or San Nicola. Don't panic if you think you have been dropped off on the wrong island, since small boats regularly make the brief crossing (L1800 one way – no exact timetable, you just have to wait). Confirm the departure point of your boat.

Things to See & Do

San Nicola It is interesting to wander around the abbey on San Nicola, noting in particular the **Chiesa di Santa Maria**, which features an 11th century floor mosaic, a painted wooden Byzantine crucifix brought to the island in 747 AD and a black Madonna, which was almost certainly transported here from Constantinople in the Middle Ages.

San Domino San Domino has the only sandy beach on the islands and it becomes extremely crowded in summer. However, numerous small coves where you can swim off the rocks dot the coastline. Some are accessible on foot, while others can be reached only by boat.

If you are feeling energetic, a walking track around the island starts at the far end of San Domino village, past Pensione Nassa. Alternatively, you could hire a bicycle from IBIS Cicli at Piazzetta San Domino. Motorised rubber dinghies are available for hire at the port for about L130,000 per day (go to the Il Piràta bar). Boats leave from San Domino's small port on tours of the island's grottoes; tickets cost around L20,000.

Places to Stay & Eat

You will need to book well in advance for summer. If you intend to arrive out of season, phone to check that hotels are open. In the high season, most hotels require that you pay full-board – a good idea, since the options for eating out are not extensive.

Al Faro (☎ *0882 46 34 24, Via della*

PUGLIA

Cantina Sperimentale), on San Domino, has doubles for around L80,000, while **Locanda La Nassa** (☎ *0882 46 33 45)* has doubles for up to L100,000. *Hotel Gabbiano* (☎ *0882 46 34 10)* has a terrace restaurant overlooking San Nicola from San Domino and very pleasant singles/doubles for around L70,000/140,000.

On San Nicola, you could eat at *Diomedea*, where a simple meal costs around L20,000.

Getting There & Away

Adriatica Navigazione (☎ 0875 70 53 43) runs a year-round daily ferry between the islands and Termoli (in Molise). From October to April the same ferry calls in at Vieste once a week. The return fare is L27,200. From late May to late September, *aliscafi* (hydrofoils) also run between Termoli and the islands, with occasional runs to Ortona (in Abruzzo). The return fare for Termoli to Tremiti is L46,800. Tickets should be purchased at the port.

There are regular services from the towns on the Gargano coast to the islands during the peak summer period, generally by the *monostab*. It links Manfredonia to Vieste, Rodi Garganico and the Isole Tremiti. Services are reduced out of season.

Tickets can be purchased at the ports (preferably 24 hours in advance) or at the following agents:

Manfredonia
    Antonio Galli e Figlio (☎ 0884 58 28 88, 0884 58 25 20) Corso Manfredi 4
Ortona (Abruzzo)
    Agenzia Marittima Fratino e Figli (☎ 085 906 38 55) Via Porto 34
Peschici
    Ondazzurra (☎ 0884 96 42 34) Corso Umberto I
Tremiti
    Adriatica Navigazione (☎ 0882 46 30 08) Via degli Abbati 10
Vasto (Abruzzo)
    Massacesi – Agenzia Viaggi e Marittima (☎ 0873 36 26 80) Piazza Diomede 3
Vieste
    Gargano Viaggi (☎ 0884 70 85 01) Piazza Roma 7

TRANI

postcode 70059 • pop 50,500

A vigorous facelift and a magnificent port-side cathedral have made Trani one of those little jewels that turn up where you least expect to find them. Some 40km north-west along the coast from Bari, this compact and easily manageable town makes a good base for exploring this part of Puglia including Barletta, Molfetta and the Castel del Monte.

Trani was important in the Middle Ages – the modern world's earliest written maritime code, the Ordinamenta Maris, was drawn up here in 1063 – and it flourished during the rule of Frederick II.

Orientation

The train and bus stations are on Piazza XX Settembre. From here, Via Cavour leads past the AAST office to the main central square, the tree-lined Piazza della Repubblica. Continue along Via Cavour to Piazza Plebiscito and the public gardens and, to the left, the port area. Across the small harbour is the cathedral, spectacularly located on a small promontorio.

Information

The AAST office (☎ 0883 58 88 25), at Via Cavour 140, opens from 8.30 am to 12.30 pm and 3.30 to 5.30 pm Monday to Friday (until noon only on Saturday). A booth on Piazza della Repubblica, when staffed, has similar hours.

Cathedral

Started in 1097 on the site of a Byzantine church, the cathedral was not completed until the 13th century. Dedicated to San Nicola Pellegrino (St Nicholas the Pilgrim), it is one of the most beautiful churches in Italy. Its simple but imposing façade is decorated with blind arches. The original bronze doors of the main portal (now on display inside the church for conservation reasons) were cast around 1180 by Barisano da Trani, an accomplished artisan of whom little is known, other than that he also cast the bronze doors of the cathedral at Ravello and the side doors of the cathedral at Monreale.

The grand interior of the cathedral was recently restored to its original Norman austerity. Near the main altar, take a look at the remains of a 12th century floor mosaic, similar in style to the one at Otranto. Below the church is the crypt, a forest of ancient columns, where the bones of San Nicola are kept beneath the altar.

Around the Cathedral

The cathedral crypt opens onto the Byzantine **Chiesa di Santa Maria della Scala**. Of note here is the **Madonna Dolorata**, a life-size statue of the Madonna, dressed in black velvet, a dagger protruding from her heart. Down another flight of stairs is the **Ipogèo San Leucio**, a chamber believed to date from the 6th century.

Near the cathedral is the 13th century **castle**, built by Frederick II. It was altered by the Angevins and until recently was used as a prison.

Around the Port

Several interesting palazzi and churches are sprinkled over the port area. Note the 15th century Gothic **Palazzo Caccetta** and the nearby 12th century **Chiesa di Ognissanti** (All Saints' Church), both on Via Ognissanti close to the cathedral. The Templars built the church as part of a hospital complex used for knights injured in the crusades. Also worth searching out is the **Palazzo della Quercia**, on Piazza Quercia at the other end of the port area.

Places to Stay

By far the most evocative place to spend a night is the newly renovated *Hotel Regia* (☎ 0883 58 45 27, *Piazza Duomo 2*) in the 18th century Palazzo Filisio just across the road from the cathedral. Luxurious singles/doubles with bathroom cost L125,000/175,000. There is also a good restaurant. Better priced, but about 3km out of town (accessible by blue bus for Corato from the station) is *Hotel Capirro* (☎ 0883 58 07 12), a characterless place with secure rooms for L45,000/80,000 (with TV and telephone). Further upmarket, *Hotel Royal* (☎ 0883 58

87 77, *Via De Robertis 24*), about 500m from the port, has rooms from L125,000/198,000.

Places to Eat

To pick up supplies, shop at the *market*, held every Monday to Saturday morning on Piazza della Libertà, to the left along Via Pagano from Piazza della Repubblica.

Pizzeria Al Faro (*Via Statuti Marittimi 50*), at the port, is a good choice – try their seafood pizza. *La Darsena*, at the port in the 18th century Palazzo Palumbo, is more expensive.

Caffè Nautico Club (*Via Statuti Marittimi 18*) is actually a private club but also an excellent little restaurant. If you're lucky, the owner/chef might whip up a delightful seafood meal for around L35,000. Closer to the centre of town, *Ristorante La Nicchia* (*Corso Imbriani 22*) serves up some very decent nosh for around L25,000.

Getting There & Away

AMET buses connect Trani with points along the coast and inland, including Barletta, Canosa di Puglia, Ruvo di Puglia and Andria. Timetables and tickets are available at Agenzia Sprint, opposite the train station in Piazza XX Settembre and at the AAST office.

Three buses from Trani leave in time to connect with the 8.30 am service from Andria to Castel del Monte (see later in this chapter). The return run to Andria leaves the castle at 3 pm. Check with the AAST office for updated times.

Trani is on the main train line between Bari and Foggia and is easily reached from towns along the coast.

The S16 runs through Trani, linking it to Bari and Foggia, or you can hook up with the A14 Bologna-Bari autostrada.

AROUND TRANI
Barletta

About 13km north-west along the coast from Trani, Barletta is more faithful to the stereotype of a grubby neglected port town. It is worth a quick visit for its cathedral, castle and the so-called Colossus, a rather stout Roman-era bronze statue in the town centre.

PUGLIA

Orientation & Information From the train station, walk down Via Giannone across the gardens to Corso Garibaldi then turn right to reach Barletta's centre. From the bus station on Via Manfredi, walk to Piazza Plebiscito and turn into Corso Vittorio Emanuele. The AAST office (☎ 0883 53 15 55) is at Via Ferdinando d'Aragona 95.

Things to See The 12th century Puglian-Romanesque **duomo**, along Corso Garibaldi from the town centre, is among the region's better preserved examples of this architectural style and has recently been restored. It has an impressive canopy over the high altar.

The imposing waterside **castle** – one of Italy's largest – was initially built by the Normans, rebuilt by Frederick II and fortified by Charles of Anjou. It boasts an impressive cannon room which, due to its conical shape, has a stereophonic echo effect. The castle also houses the city's not unimpressive art collection, including over 90 works by Barletta's famous son, De Nittis, who was influenced by the French Impressionists. There is also a display of Sicilian puppets. The castle is open from 9 am to 1 pm daily (except Monday). Admission costs L4000.

Back in the town centre, just off Corso Garibaldi on Corso Vittorio Emanuele, is the **Colossus**, a 5.11m bronze Roman statue believed to be of Emperor Valentinian I. The statue was plundered during the sacking of Constantinople in 1203 and snapped up by Barletta after the ship carrying it sank off the Puglian coast. The statue stands next to the 12th century **Basilica del Santo Sepolcro** (Basilica of the Holy Sepulchre). Originally Romanesque, this church subsequently underwent Gothic and baroque facelifts. The manner in which it appears to have sunk below the level of the square is uncannily reminiscent of the cathedral in Modena (Emilia-Romagna).

Special Events The main event on the town's calendar is the Disfida (Challenge) of Barletta, held annually on the last Sunday in July. One of Italy's best known medieval pageants, it re-enacts a duel between 13 Italian and 13 French knights on 13 February 1503, when the town was besieged by the French. The Italians won and the chivalrous French decamped.

Getting There & Away From the bus station on Via Manfredi, ATAF buses link Barletta with Foggia; there are regular AMET buses to Trani and Molfetta; and SITA buses head for Manfredonia and Bari. Barletta is on both the Bari-Foggia coastal train line and the Bari-Nord train line and is easily accessible from Trani and other points along the coast, as well as inland towns.

Castel del Monte

Castel del Monte, standing like a royal crown on a hilltop, is one of Puglia's most prominent landmarks and visible for miles around. It is in the Murge, a long limestone plateau stretching west and south of Bari. You have to be fairly enthusiastic to make the journey to the castle without your own transport, but it's worth the effort.

The stronghold was built by Frederick II, probably for his own pleasure and to his own design, in the mid-13th century. It appears that the castle's most bellicose use was as a hunting lodge – in Frederick's day the surrounding country was heavily forested and teeming with game. The absence of a moat or other system of defence suggests that it was not a defensive fort.

The castle is built on an octagonal base, each corner equipped with an octagonal tower. Completely restored some years ago, its interconnecting rooms have decorative marble columns and fireplaces and the doorways and window frames are adorned with corallite stone which once covered the entire lower floor. The castle is open from 9 am to 7 pm daily in summer. It opens from 9 am to 1 pm from October to March. Admission costs L4000.

Getting There & Away The easiest way to get to the castle is via Andria. A bus leaves Piazza Municipio in Andria at 8.30 am Monday to Saturday for the castle, returning at

The Castle that Frederick Built

Legend has it that during the construction of Castel del Monte, Frederick II dispatched one of his courtiers to Puglia to check on its progress. However, the courtier was waylaid in Melfi, where he fell in love with a beautiful woman 'whose eyes caused him to forget Castel del Monte and his sovereign'. He remained in Melfi until a messenger from Napoli arrived with orders for him to make his report at once. Rather than admit his negligence to duty, the courtier recounted to Frederick that the castle was 'a total failure as to beauty and utility, and the architect an impostor'. Receiving news of Frederick's anger and displeasure, the architect threw himself to his death from one of the castle's towers rather than face the emperor's wrath. Hearing of these events, Frederick set out for Castel del Monte with the dishonest courtier. Seeing the magnificent building and incensed with rage at the death of the architect, Frederick hauled the courtier up to one of the towers and threw him to his death, as a sacrifice to the memory of an innocent and talented man.

3 pm. The town is also is in easy reach of Trani by bus, or of Bari via the Bari-Nord line. The Andria-Spinazzola bus (several a day) passes close to the castle – ask the driver to let you off. See also the Getting There & Away sections under Trani and Bari.

BARI
postcode 70100 • pop 342,000
Unless you are planning to catch a ferry to Greece, Bari won't be high on your destination list – but it does offer a handful of interesting sights and can make a good base for exploring neighbouring towns such as Ruvo di Puglia, Molfetta, Bitonto, Altamura and even Alberobello and the trulli area. The city's Stop Over in Bari programme makes it still more attractive for under-30s (see the later Information section).

The capital of Puglia and the second most important city in the south after Napoli, it can be a frenetic sort of place – the peak hour traffic is choking. It was an important Byzantine town and flourished under the Normans and later under Frederick II. Bari is a long way from the North Pole, but it is here that San Nicola di Myra, otherwise known as Father Christmas, was finally laid to rest. His remains, contained in a liquid known as the manna (said to have miraculous powers), were stolen from Turkey in 1087 and interred in the Basilica di San

Nicola, built especially for the purpose. It is still an important place of pilgrimage.

Occupied by the Allies during WWII, the port city endured heavy German bombing.

Orientation
Bari is surprisingly easy to negotiate. The FS and Bari-Nord train stations are at the vast Piazza Aldo Moro, in the newer (19th century) section of the city, about a 10 minute walk south of the old town (called Bari Vecchia). Via Crisanzio, a block north of Piazza Aldo Moro and running east to west, has a fair choice of hotels.

This newer part of Bari is on a grid plan. Any of the streets heading north from Piazza Aldo Moro, including Via Sparano, will take you to Corso Vittorio Emanuele II, which separates the old and new cities. Corso Cavour is the main shopping strip.

Information
Tourist Offices The IAT office (☎ 080 540 48 11) is about five minutes walk from the train station, at Via Bozzi 45 and is officially open from 10 am to noon, but it is usually staffed throughout the day and has information such as maps and hotel lists. Limited information can also be obtained from the APT headquarters (☎ 080 540 48 11) at Piazza Aldo Moro 33a (1st floor).

If you are aged under 30 you can take

PUGLIA

BARI

PLACES TO STAY
19 Grand Hotel d'Oriente
26 Albergo Moderno
28 Albergo Romeo; Pensione Giulia
32 Hotel Adria

PLACES TO EAT
3 Al Pescatore
9 Vini e Cucina
16 Il Sorso Preferito
17 Taverna Verde
20 Ristorante Porta d'Oro da Enzo
29 Ristorante OK
30 Yogofrutteria

OTHER
1 Ferry Terminal
2 Basilica di San Nicola
4 Castello Svevo
5 Questura (Police Station)
6 Cathedral
7 Sedile; Colonna della Giustizia
8 Fish Market
10 CIT Travel Agency
11 Deutsche Bank & ATM
12 Banca di Roma & ATM
13 Airport Bus Station
14 SITA & Ferrotranviaria Bus Station; Piazza Eroi del Mare
15 Teatro Petruzzelli
18 IAT Tourist Office
21 Banca Nazionale del Lavoro & ATM
22 Feltrinelli Bookshop
23 Telecom Office
24 OTE Office
25 Post Office
27 CTS Travel Agency
31 APT Tourist Office
33 Main Train Station
34 Bari-Nord Train Station
35 Appulo-Lucane Train Station
36 Marozzi Bus Office
37 SITA & Ferrovie Appulo-Lucane Bus Station

advantage of Stop Over in Bari, an initiative that aims to attract youth tourism to the city. The programme operates from June to September, offering a package that includes low-priced accommodation in small hotels or private homes, or free accommodation in the Pineta San Francesco camp sites, free use of the city's buses, free admission to museums, cut-rate meals, a free bike service and information centres for young travellers.

OTE, Stop Over's main office (☎ 080 521 45 38), is at Via Nicolai Beatillo 47 and there is an information booth on Piazza Aldo Moro and at the ferry terminal. The staff are helpful, speak English and have loads of information about Bari. While only under-30s can take advantage of the package, anyone is welcome to seek information. Get updated details on line from www.inmedia.it/StopOver.

Money There is no shortage of banks, most with ATMs that will accept Visa, MasterCard and Eurocheque cards. Alternatively, there are currency exchange booths at the main train station and the ferry terminal – watch the exchange rates. American Express's representative is Morfimare (☎ 080 521 00 22) at Corso di Tullio 36-40.

Post & Communications The main post office is on Piazza Cesare Battisti, on Via Cairoli. Its counters are open from 8.20 am to 6.30 pm, Monday to Saturday. There is a Telecom office at Via Marchese di Montrone 123, open from 8 am to 9.45 pm daily.

Travel Agencies CTS (☎ 080 521 32 44), which is good for student travel and discounted flights, is at Via Fornari 7. There is a CIT office at Via Abate Gimma 150-152, on the corner of Via De Rossi. OTE (see the earlier Tourist Offices section) can also assist with budget travel arrangements.

Medical Services & Emergency There is a *pronto soccorso* (casualty centre) at Ospedale Consorziale Policlinico (hospital; ☎ 080 547 31 11), Piazza Giulio Cesare, south of the town centre, on the other side of the train

lines. In an emergency, call an ambulance on ☎ 080 504 17 33. For home visits, call the Guardia Medica on ☎ 080 524 23 89.

The questura headquarters (police; ☎ 080 529 11 11) is at Via G Murat, near the castle.

Dangers & Annoyances Bari has a reputation as a drug and crime centre – this means a high rate of petty crime. Don't leave anything in your car, don't display valuable jewellery, wear a money belt and avoid carrying a bag. Don't overdo the paranoia, but be particularly careful when visiting the historic centre (Bari Vecchia) and avoid it altogether at night.

Bari Vecchia
Bari's main churches, the **Basilica di San Nicola** and the **cathedral**, are discussed in the later boxed text 'A Little Romanesque Tour of Puglia'. Both are in the old town – San Nicola in the piazza of the same name and the cathedral is nearby on Piazza Odegitria.

You could start your exploration of Bari Vecchia at Piazza Mercantile, at the northern end of Corso Cavour. In the piazza is the **Sedile**, the medieval headquarters of Bari's Council of Nobles. Set aside in one corner of the piazza is the **Colonna della Giustizia** (Column of Justice), to which it is thought debtors were tied. A fresh produce market is held in the piazza every Monday to Saturday morning. Head along Via della Vecchia Dogana and the Lungomare Imperatore Augusto to reach the Basilica di San Nicola.

Squeezed into the uneven little alleyways of what is a small historic town centre, are some 40 churches and more than 120 little shrines dedicated to the Madonna and various saints. The inhabitants of this part of town appear to live much as their forebears did and Bari Vecchia is certainly worth investigating.

Castello Svevo
Just beyond the perimeter of Bari Vecchia broods the so-called Swabian Castle, which represents four levels of history. A Norman structure was built over the ruins of a Roman fort (now being excavated). Frederick II then incorporated parts of the Norman castle into

PUGLIA

his own design, including two towers that still stand. The bastions with corner towers overhanging the moat were finally added in the 16th century during Spanish rule. Inside you'll find the **Gipsoteca**, a collection of plaster copies of Romanesque monumental decoration from throughout the region. The castle is open from 9 am to 1 pm and 3.30 to 7 pm daily in summer and admission costs L4000. Most of the castle is, however, closed to the public.

Special Events

Bari's big annual event is the Festival of San Nicola, which takes place during the first weekend in May. If you can manage to be in town at the time, it's quite a spectacle. On Saturday evening a procession of people in Norman costume leaves the castle for the Basilica di San Nicola, where they re-enact the delivery of the saint's bones to the Dominican friars. The next day, with a statue of the saint in pride of place, a procession of boats sets off along the coast.

Places to Stay

There are several reasonably priced accommodation options in Bari. The HI youth hostel, *Ostello del Levante* (☎ 080 530 02 82), is just west of Bari by the sea at Palese. B&B is L16,000 per night and a meal costs L14,000. The hostel closes from 20 December to 15 January. The No 1 bus goes there from outside Teatro Petruzzelli on Corso Cavour.

If you choose to stay in a hotel, it is best to pay a bit more for security. The following are all reliable. *Albergo Romeo* (☎ 080 523 72 53, Via Crisanzio 12) has singles/doubles/triples for L60,000/95,000/120,000, all with bathroom. In the same building is *Pensione Giulia* (☎ 080 521 66 30), where rooms cost from L65,000/90,000 with bathroom and breakfast.

Hotel Adria (☎ 080 52 66 99, fax 080 521 32 07, Via L Zuppetta 10), to the right of the station, has comfortable rooms with bathroom for L65,000/100,000. *Albergo Moderno* (☎ 080 521 33 13, Via Crisanzio 60) has rooms for L70,0000/115,000. *Grand Hotel d'Oriente* (☎ 080 524 40 11,

Corso Cavour 32) is a lovely, old-style hotel, with grand prices: L130,000/200,000, breakfast included.

Places to Eat

You will find it difficult to eat a meal more cheaply in Bari than at *Vini e Cucina* on Strada Vallisa, just off Piazza del Ferrarese in the old city (it's best to avoid the area at night; see the earlier Dangers & Annoyances section). It's hard to get much more basic than its cave-like atmosphere and paper tablecloths, though you come close at *Ristorante OK* (Via de Cesare 19), off Piazza Aldo Moro. A two course lunch with wine costs around L15,000.

Taverna Verde (Via Cognetti 18) has excellent pizzas and very reasonably priced pasta and main dishes. A full meal will come to under L35,000. Nearby, *Il Sorso Preferito* (Via Vito Nicola de Nicolò 40) is a roomy old restaurant with loads of character. Again, you're looking at about L35,000.

Ristorante Porta d'Oro da Enzo (Via Principe Amedeo 12), off Corso Cavour, has excellent meals for less than L30,000. *Al Pescatore* (Piazza Federico II di Svevia 8) is next to the castle and specialises in seafood and Puglian dishes. The grilled squid is memorable. A full meal will cost around L50,000.

For great frozen yoghurt head for *Yogofrutteria* (Via Nicola dell'Arca 5).

Getting There & Away

Air Bari's airport (☎ 080 538 23 70) is several kilometres west of the city centre and services domestic flights. You can get there on the Bari-Nord train line. There is also an Alitalia airport bus, which leaves from a terminal at Via Calefati 37 and from the train station. Buses depart 80 minutes before flight times and you must show your plane ticket.

Bus Intercity buses leave from several locations around the town, depending on where you are going and with which company.

SITA buses (☎ 080 556 24 46, 080 574 18 00) leave from Via Capruzzi, on the southern side of the main train station, for destinations including Acquaviva, Canosa, Cassano, Laterza and Spinazzola. SITA buses leave Piazza Eroi del Mare for Andria, Barletta, Molfetta, Trani and Margherita di Savoia. Buy tickets at window No 1 at the train station.

Ferrotramviaria buses (☎ 080 523 22 02) leave from Piazza Eroi del Mare for Andria, Barletta, Ruvo di Puglia, Bitonto and Terlizzi. Ferrovie Appulo-Lucane buses (☎ 080 542 65 52) serve Altamura, Gravina, Matera and Potenza and leave from Via DeVito Francesco. Ferrovie del Sud-Est (FSE) buses (☎ 080 542 65 52) leave from Largo Ciaia, south of Piazza Aldo Moro, for places including Alberobello, Brindisi, Castellana Grotte, Locorotonda, Martina Franca, Polignano, Ostuni and Taranto.

Marozzi buses (☎ 080 521 60 04, 080 521 03 65) for Roma leave from Piazza Aldo Moro. The company's office is at Corso Italia 32.

It is not unheard of for enterprising locals to organise private buses in summer to ferry tourists direct from Bari to Castel del Monte (see the earlier Around Trani section) – check with the tourist office.

Train As with buses, an array of train lines connects Bari with the outside world.

From the main train station (☎ 147 88 80 88) national FS trains go to Milano, Bologna, Pescara, Roma and cities across Puglia, including Foggia, Brindisi, Lecce and Taranto.

There are also private train lines. The Bari-Nord line (☎ 080 521 35 77) connects the city with the airport, Bitonto, Andria and Barletta, and the train station is next to the main station in Piazza Aldo Moro. The Appulo-Lucane line (☎ 080 572 25 11) links Bari with Altamura, Gravina and Matera and Potenza in Basilicata. The station is on Corso Italia, just off Piazza Aldo Moro.

FSE trains (☎ 080 546 21 11) head for Alberobello, Castellana, Locorotondo, Martina Franca and Taranto, leaving from the station in Via Oberdan – cross under the train tracks south of Piazza Luigi di Savoia and head east along Via Giuseppe Capruzzi for about half a kilometre. You can also pick up an FSE train for Martina Franca from the main station on platform 10.

Car & Motorcycle Bari is on the A14 autostrada, which heads north-west to Foggia, south to Taranto and connects with the A16 to Napoli at Canosa di Puglia. Exit at Bari-Nord to reach the centre of town. The easiest way to orient yourself is to follow the 'centro' signs to the centre and then the 'stazione' signs for the main train station and Piazza Aldo Moro.

Boat Ferry traffic to/from Bari is busy year-round, especially to Greece, but also to Albania, Croatia and Egypt. All ferry companies have offices at the ferry terminal, accessible from the train station on bus No 20. Fares to Greece from Bari tend to be only marginally cheaper than from Brindisi and the trip is two hours longer.

Once you have bought your ticket and paid the embarkation tax, you will be given a boarding card, which must be stamped by the police at the ferry terminal.

The main companies and routes they served at the time of writing were:

Adriatica
(☎ 080 553 03 60) c/o Agestea at the ferry terminal or Via Liside 4. It has boats to Durrës (Albania) on Monday, Wednesday, Friday and Saturday (deck class, L110,000; *poltrona* – an airline-type chair, L120,000; bed in a shared cabin, L155,000; car, L180,000).

Superfast
(☎ 080 528 28 28) c/o Portrans at the ferry terminal and Corso de Tullio 6. It has daily ferries to Patras and Igoumenitsa (deck class, L88,000; car, L98,000).

Transeuropa Lines
(☎ 080 521 00 22) c/o Morfimare, Corso De Tullio 36/40 and at the ferry terminal. Three boats a week to Bar in Montenegro (deck class, L75,000; poltrona, L85,000; bed in a shared cabin, L95,000 to L125,000) and two boats to Durrës (deck class, L90,000; poltrona, L100,000; bed in a shared cabin, L130,000 to L150,000).

Ventouris Ferries
(☎ 080 524 43 88) c/o P Lorusso & Co at the ferry terminal or at Via Piccinni 133. It has regular services to Corfu and Igoumenitsa (deck class, L73,000; poltrona, L90,000; bed in a shared cabin L165,000; small car, L100,000).

PUGLIA

A Little Romanesque Tour of Puglia

Of 18 important Romanesque churches in Puglia, only nine have been preserved in the original style. These include the cathedrals at Bari, Altamura, Barletta, Bitonto, Molfetta, Ruvo di Puglia and Trani. Another church that should be added to the list is the Basilica di San Nicola in Bari, used as a model for many of the churches built in the Puglian-Romanesque style and of exceptional architectural value.

With some careful planning, you can visit all these churches on day trips from Bari, although the town of Trani is worth a visit in its own right. If you want to make a full tour of the towns and cities where the churches are located, consider hiring a car for two or three days. This would also enable you to take in a couple of the less important Romanesque churches in the province, and include a trip to the Castel del Monte, the stunning octagonal castle of Frederick II of Swabia, about 40km west of Bari.

The itinerary starts in **Bari** with the Basilica di San Nicola (Saint Nicholas), built in the 11th century on the ruins of a Byzantine palazzo to house the miracle-working bones of San Nicola, stolen by Bari mariners from their resting place in Myra (in what is now Turkey). The basilica has a stark, imposing façade, simply decorated with blind arches and mullioned windows and flanked by two bell towers. Look for the Lion's Doorway on the basilica's northern side, decorated with beautiful sculptures and bas-reliefs depicting chivalric scenes. Inside the three-naved interior is a splendid 12th century tabernacle, as well as a bishop's throne, known as Elia's Pulpit, sculpted in the second half of the 12th century. The remains of San Nicola are housed in the crypt, under the transept.

Bari's 12th century cathedral was built on the remains of a Byzantine cathedral. It retains its elegant Romanesque shape and bell tower, but has been much altered over the centuries.

The cathedrals of Bitonto, Ruvo di Puglia and Molfetta lie west of Bari and can be easily reached by public transport. **Trani** and **Barletta** are farther along the coast; Trani makes the better base – see the Trani and Around Trani sections for more details. If you have the time, take a look at the cathedrals in **Conversano** and **Palo del Colle.**

The cathedral of **Bitonto** is a particularly stunning example of Puglian-Romanesque architecture and one of the most beautiful in the region. Built in the late 12th century on the model of San Nicola in Bari, it is dedicated to San Valentino. Note the carved animals and plants that decorate the capitals on the side walls. The cathedral has been closed for some time and is not expected to reopen in the foreseeable future due to work being carried out under its main pavement. While in Bitonto, spare a moment to inspect the 17th century Chiesa di Purgatorio, near the cathedral. Above the main door people are depicted burning in purgatory, and to the sides are two large figures of Death, dancing in what seems to be delight at these poor souls' fate. You can get to Bitonto from Bari on the private Bari-Nord train line. From the station, walk directly ahead along Via Matteotti (about 1km) until you reach the medieval part

These are high season (roughly July to September) fares; they decrease by about L20,000 for the rest of the year. In high season it may be possible to get a boat to Turkey via Greece. There is a L10,000 embarkation fee to Greece/Yugoslavia and L5000 per person plus L5000 per vehicle to Albania.

Getting Around

Central Bari is quite compact – a 15 minute walk will take you from Piazza Aldo Moro to the old town. Useful city buses are No 20 from the train station to the ferry terminal and No 1 from Teatro Petruzzelli to the youth hostel.

A Little Romanesque Tour of Puglia

of town. You'll see an Angevin tower and there are signs directing you to the cathedral, with tourist maps posted at various points.

The graceful cathedral in **Ruvo di Puglia** has a particularly striking façade and boasts a fine rose window and three portals. The delicately carved central portal features columns supported by griffins, resting on (now very worn) lions, themselves supported by telamons. Ruvo is on the Bari-Nord train line. Otherwise you can take a Ferrotramviaria bus from Bari's Piazza Eroi del Mare (approximately every half-hour daily, except Sunday), which arrives at Cortugno, just off Ruvo's main piazza. The same bus also goes to Bitonto, Andria and Barletta. From the bus stop, walk to the left

TRUDI CANAVAN

The exquisite rose window from the Cattedrale di Ruvo di Puglia

through the piazza and turn right into Corso Giovanni Jatta. Once you reach the park, turn right and then right again when you reach the tower, which is at the rear of the cathedral.

Molfetta is worth a stop not only for its impressively simple cathedral, but also for its largely abandoned, tumbledown medieval centre. Known as the Duomo Vecchio, the cathedral was started in 1150 and completed at the end of the 13th century. It has a stark, undecorated white façade flanked by two bell towers. The interior is a mix of Romanesque, Byzantine and Islamic architecture. The medieval quarter, or Borgo Vecchio, stretches out behind the cathedral and is in a state of great disrepair, although sections are being restored. Molfetta is on the main Bari-Foggia train line, about 20 minutes from Bari. From the station, ask for directions to Via Dante and *il porto* (the port), near which you'll find the cathedral at Via Chiesa Vecchia.

Altamura is about 45 minutes south-west of Bari and easily accessible on the Appulo-Lucane train line (see the Bari Getting There & Away section). Its 13th century cathedral was erected during the reign of Frederick II but was badly damaged by an earthquake in 1316, and later suffered some baroque renovations when the beautiful medieval main portal and elegant rose window were moved from their original position to what had been the apse. The cathedral is in the old town's main street, Via Federico II di Svevia. From the train station, walk straight ahead along Viale Regina Margherita to Piazza Unità d'Italia and enter the old town through Porta Bari. Ferrovie Appulo-Lucane buses also connect Bari and Altamura, arriving in Piazza Santa Teresa. From the piazza, turn right and walk to Piazza Unità d'Italia.

THE TRULLI AREA

Trulli are unusual, circular houses made of whitewashed stone without mortar, with conical roofs. The roofs, which are topped with pinnacles, are tiled with concentric rows of grey slate – these are known locally as *chiancarella*. Many trulli have astrolog-ical or religious symbols painted on the roof.

The trulli area, in the Itria Valley, extends from Conversano and Goia del Colle in the west to Ostuni and Martina Franca in the east, but the greatest concentration of these houses is in and around Alberobello.

PUGLIA

Grotte di Castellana

These spectacular limestone caves are among Puglia's prime attractions. The series of subterranean caves, with their at times breathtaking formations of stalactites and stalagmites, were known as far back as the 17th century and were probably partially investigated in the 18th century. In the 1930s, Italian speleologist Franco Anelli explored about 3km of the caves and today tourists can follow his path with a guide. After descending by elevator to a huge cavern known as La Grave, you are taken on a tour through several caves, culminating in the magnificent **Caverna Bianca**.

The caves (☎ 080 499 82 11 for information) are open from 8.30 am to 7.30 pm daily and tours leave roughly every hour. You can enter only with a guide. There are two tours: a 1km, one hour trip (L15,000) that does not include the Caverna Bianca and the full 3km, two hour trip (L27,000).

You can reach the Grotte on the FSE train line (Bari-Taranto). The station is about 150m from the entrance.

Alberobello

This pretty town virtually exists for tourism these days but, with whole quarters covered with nothing but trulli, it is quite unusual. The town was declared a zone of historical importance in 1924 and many of the trulli are now souvenir and wine shops, boutiques and restaurants.

The Pro Loco office is just off Piazza del Popolo at Corso Vittorio Emanuele 15 in the town centre.

A few kilometres west of the town is the **Chiesa di Santa Maria di Barsento**, accessible only if you have a vehicle (or by hitching). Founded in 591 AD as an abbey, the small complex features one of the oldest churches in Puglia. It is now part of a farm, but the owner is proud to show tourists around the property – which he makes available for wedding receptions. Take the road from Alberobello to Putignano and after 6km turn left into the road for Noci. After 3km you will see Barsento (signposted) to your right.

Places to Stay The *Camping dei Trulli* (☎ 080 932 36 99) is just out of town on Via Castellana Grotte. Charges are L6000 per person and up to L18,000 for a site. In the town centre is *Hotel Lanzillotta* (☎ 080 432 15 11, Piazza Ferdinando IV 31) with singles/doubles for L60,000/90,000. The town's top hotel is *Hotel dei Trulli* (☎ 080 432 35 55, fax 080 432 35 60, Via Cadore 32), which is a complex of trulli. They are self-contained, with bathroom and living area and the cost is L170,000 per person per day for half-board.

Trulli are also available for rent through various agencies, with charges ranging from around L100,000 per day and L600,000 for a week. For further information contact Agenzia Immobiliare Fittatrulli (☎ 080 432 27 17) at Via Duca d'Aosta 14, Alberobello.

Getting There & Away The easiest way to get to Alberobello is on the FSE private train line (Bari-Taranto). From the station, walk straight ahead along Via Mazzini, which becomes Via Garibaldi, to reach Piazza del Popolo.

Locorotondo

The completely circular town of Locorotondo is perched on a hill above the Valle dei Trulli, about 8km from Alberobello. It is an easy detour for those with private transport and is on the FSE train line (Bari-Taranto).

La Taverna del Duca (Via Papatodero 3) in the heart of the centre serves home-style local food. A delicious, hearty meal will set you back around L30,000.

Martina Franca

Founded in the 10th century by refugees fleeing the Arab invasion of Taranto, Martina Franca flourished in the 14th century after it was granted tax exemptions (*franchigie*, hence the name Franca) by Philip of Anjou.

The town is at the edge of the trulli area and you'll see few of the conical constructions here, but it has an interesting historical centre, with a medieval quarter and several specimens of baroque architecture.

Orientation & Information The FSE train station is downhill from the historic centre. City buses go to Piazza XX Settembre and the entrance to the old town, or you can walk to the right along Viale della Stazione, continuing along Via Alessandro Fighera to Corso Italia; continue to the left along Corso Italia to Piazza XX Settembre. The tourist office (☎ 080 70 57 02) is at Piazza Roma 37, where you can get a map of the town and advice on accommodation.

Things to See & Do Next to the tourist office on Piazza Roma is the 17th century **Palazzo Ducale**, a vast edifice now used as the municipal offices. Several frescoed rooms on the 3rd floor are open to the public (free admission).

From the piazza, follow the narrow Corso Vittorio Emanuele into Piazza Plebiscito and the heart of the historic centre. Of note here is the baroque façade of the 18th century **Chiesa di San Martino**.

Special Events The town stages the annual Festival of the Itria Valley in July and August, with concerts and opera. Information and tickets are available through the tourist office.

Places to Stay & Eat The cheapest accommodation options are both out of the town. *La Cremaillere (☎ 080 480 00 52)* is about 6km away at San Paolo on the road to Taranto. It charges from L70,000 for doubles with bathroom. *Da Luigi (☎ 080 430 13 24, fax 080 430 16 66)* is about 3km out on the road to Taranto and charges L40,000/60,000 for single/double rooms with bathroom. Both are accessible by FSE bus from Piazza Crispi.

In town all hotels are expensive, including *Park Hotel San Michele (☎ 080 480 70 53, fax 080 480 88 95, Viale Carella 9)* which charges L115,000/160,000 (with breakfast).

For a meal, *Trattoria La Tavernetta (Corso Vittorio Emanuele 30)* serves great food at decent prices.

Getting There & Away The easiest way to reach the town is on the FSE train line (Bari-Taranto). FSE buses also connect the town with Taranto, Alberobello, Castellana Grotte and Bari, arriving in Piazza Crispi, off Corso Italia.

Ostuni

This stunning town of stark, whitewashed buildings is set on three hills east of Martina Franca and about 40km north-west of Brindisi. The seemingly disordered tangle of narrow cobblestone streets, many little more than arched stairways between the houses, is reminiscent of a North African Arab *medina*. Rising above it all in sombre brown stone is the 15th century Gothic **cathedral**. Its distinctive cupolas, covered in green, yellow and white slate tiles, act like a beacon among the surrounding buildings.

Orientation & Information From Piazza della Libertà, take the narrow Via Cattedrale uphill to the cathedral. From the tiny piazza in front of the cathedral, turn right for a view across to the Adriatico, or turn left to get lost in Ostuni's whitewashed lanes.

Ostuni's AAST office (☎ 0831 97 12 68) is on Piazza della Libertà, downhill from the cathedral in the newer part of town. It is officially open from 9.30 am to 12.30 pm and 6.30 to 9 pm Monday to Friday, but operates shorter hours in winter.

Places to Stay & Eat Ostuni is an easy day trip from Brindisi, but if you want to stay, try *Albergo Tre Torri (☎ 0831 33 11 14, Corso Vittorio Emanuele 298)*. It has rooms for L68,000/92,000 for a single/double. *Hotel Orchidea Nera (☎ 0831 30 13 66, Via Mazzini)*, near the train station, has rooms for L70,000/90,000.

There are some excellent eating places in the old town. *Osteria del Tempo Perso* is tucked away behind the cathedral. To find it, head up Via Cattedrale and, when you reach the wall of the cathedral, turn right through the archway into Largo Giuseppe Spennati and follow the signs to the restaurant.

Getting There & Away Società Trasporti Pubblici (STP) buses run between Ostuni and Brindisi about every two hours, arriving

euro currency converter L10,000 = €5.16

PUGLIA

in Piazza Italia in the newer part of Ostuni. STP buses also connect the town with Martina Franca. However, the easiest way to reach Ostuni is on the main train line from Brindisi or Bari. The No 1 city bus will take you from the station into the centre.

BRINDISI
postcode 72100 • pop 95,400

Travellers associate Brindisi with waiting. The major embarkation point for ferries from Italy to Greece, the city swarms with people in transit. What's more, there really is very little to do here other than wait. Most backpackers gather at the train station, at the port in the ferry terminal, or in Piazza Cairoli in between the two.

Settled in ancient times and taken over by Roma in 3 BC, Brindisi is a natural safe harbour that prospered under the Romans and retained its importance until after the crusades. Invasion, plague and earthquake brought about decline, but today it is a busy merchant and passenger port.

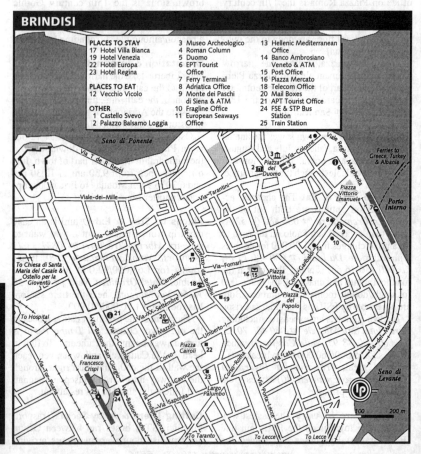

BRINDISI

PLACES TO STAY
17 Hotel Villa Bianca
19 Hotel Venezia
22 Hotel Europa
23 Hotel Regina

PLACES TO EAT
12 Vecchio Vicolo

OTHER
1 Castello Svevo
2 Palazzo Balsamo Loggia
3 Museo Archeologico
4 Roman Column
5 Duomo
6 EPT Tourist Office
7 Ferry Terminal
8 Adriatica Office
9 Monte dei Paschi di Siena & ATM
10 Fragline Office
11 European Seaways Office
13 Hellenic Mediterranean Office
14 Banco Ambrosiano Veneto & ATM
15 Post Office
16 Piazza Mercato
18 Telecom Office
20 Mail Boxes
21 APT Tourist Office
24 FSE & STP Bus Station
25 Train Station

Orientation

The port is about 10 minutes walk from the train station along Corso Umberto I, which becomes Corso Garibaldi. There are numerous takeaway food outlets along the route, as well as a bewildering array of ferry companies and travel agencies.

Information

Tourist Offices There is a tourist office (☎ 0831 52 30 72) at Viale Regina Margherita 12, a short walk from the end of Corso Garibaldi and the ferry terminal (turn left once you reach the waterfront). It is open from 8.30 am to 12.30 pm and 4.30 to 7.30 pm Monday to Saturday. An APT office (☎ 0831 56 21 26) is at Via Cristoforo Colombo 88, close to the train station.

Money There are numerous currency exchange offices between the station and the port. Check the rates and pick the best. Otherwise, good old-fashioned banks also abound. The Banco Ambrosiano Veneto, near the post office, has an ATM, as does Monte dei Paschi di Siena at Corso Garibaldi 112.

Post & Communications The main post office is on Piazza Mercato and opens from 8.15 am to 7.40 pm Monday to Saturday.

The Telecom office, is at Via XX Settembre 6 and opens from 9.15 am to 12.50 pm and 3.30 to 6.30 pm.

Medical Services The Ospedale Generale Antonio di Summa (☎ 0831 51 05 10), is on Piazza Antonio di Summa, west of the train station, between Via Appia and Via Arione. The same number is good for ambulances.

Dangers & Annoyances Brindisi is a thieves' paradise – so valuables should be carried in a money belt and nothing of remote interest should be left unattended in your car. Women are advised not to walk through the town alone at night.

Brindisi is extremely busy in summer, so if you arrive by car, allow extra time for the eternal traffic jam around the port.

Travellers arriving late in the evening are perfect victims for the line 'If you get a taxi, you might just make the last ferry'. Keep your cool and walk right down to the port (if your bags will allow it), as the roundabout ride in the taxi will probably take longer. When you arrive and the ferry has inevitably left, you will of course be offered further rides to hotels.

Things to See & Do

For the Romans, Brindisi was the end of the line or, more specifically, of the Via Appia. For centuries, two great columns marked the end of the imperial highway. One remains, near the waterfront (the other was removed to Lecce and only its pedestal remains). Tradition has it that the Roman poet Virgil died in a house near here after returning from a voyage to Greece.

A little farther in from the waterfront, the modest **duomo** was originally built in the 11th century but substantially remodelled about 700 years later. Nearby is a small **Museo Archeologico**. Across the quiet little square is Palazzo Balsamo, an otherwise undistinguished building that sports a noteworthy **loggia**.

If you are hanging around Brindisi for any length of time, you might cast your eye over the **Castello Svevo**, another of Frederick II's monuments to militarism. Turn left from the train station and walk straight on to get there.

The town's main sight is the **Chiesa di Santa Maria del Casale**, 4km north of the centre. Built by Prince Philip of Taranto around 1300, it is a Romanesque church with Gothic and Byzantine touches. To get there, follow Via Provinciale San Vito round the Seno di Ponente bay. The road becomes first Via E Ciciriello and then Via R de Simone.

Places to Stay

Ostello per la Gioventù (☎ 0831 56 80 24) is about 2km out of town at Via N Brandi 2. B&B costs L18,000 per night. Take bus No 3 or 4 from Via Cristoforo Colombo near the train station.

Hotel Venezia (☎ 0831 52 75 11, Via Pisanelli 4) has singles/doubles for L25,000/

PUGLIA

45,000. Turn left off Corso Umberto I onto Via San Lorenzo da Brindisi. *Hotel Villa Bianca (☎ 0831 52 12 48, Via Armengol 21)*, farther on along Via San Lorenzo da Brindisi, has rooms for L37,000/53,000 and doubles with bathroom for L63,000. *Hotel Europa (☎ 0831 52 85 46, Piazza Cairoli)* has clean, basic rooms for L45,000/60,000 or L65,000/90,000 with bathroom. More up-market is *Hotel Regina (☎ 0831 56 20 01, Via Cavour 5)*, which costs from L90,000/110,000. Take Via Cappellini off Piazza Cairoli and turn left.

Places to Eat

For supplies for the boat trip, shop at the *Sidis supermarket* on Piazza Cairoli. A colourful fresh food *market* is held every morning from Monday to Saturday on Piazza Mercato, just around the corner from the post office.

For a proper feed, head for the side streets off the train station-port route. Try *Vecchio Vivolo (Vico D'Orimini 13)*, which has a good value L14,000 tourist menu.

Entertainment

Musical and cultural events are held in Brindisi year-round, including Estate Insieme in July and August. Get a brochure from the tourist office if you're in town for a while.

Getting There & Away

Bus STP (☎ 0831 52 37 31) and FSE buses connect Brindisi with Ostuni and towns throughout the Penisola Salentina. Most leave from Via Bastioni Carlo V, in front of the train station.

Marozzi has three daily express buses to Roma (Stazione Tiburtina). The trip takes up to nine hours. Appia Travel (☎ 0831 52 16 84), on the waterfront at Viale Regina Margherita 8-9, sells tickets.

Train Brindisi is on the main FS train line, with regular services to Bari, Lecce and Taranto, as well as to Ancona, Bologna, Milano, Napoli and Roma.

Car & Motorcycle Brindisi is easy to reach by road. Watch out for the superstrada exit

for the 'porto' or 'Grecia' (Greece). Allow plenty of time to board your ferry.

Boat Ferries leave Brindisi for Greek destinations including Corfu (nine hours), Igoumenitsa (10½ hours), Patras (approximately 17 hours) and Cefalonia (approximately 16 hours). From Patras there is a bus to Athens. Ferries also service Turkey and Albania. Companies sometimes change hands or names and many only operate in summer. When you get to Brindisi, shop around. Most agents can sell tickets for most lines – ask to see the company brochures. The main companies are given below:

Adriatica
(☎ 0831 52 38 25) Corso Garibaldi 85-87 and at the ferry terminal. It is one of the few companies to run ferries to Greece (Corfu, Igoumenitsa and Patras) year-round (deck class, L100,000; poltrona, L120,000; bed in shared cabin, L170,000; car, L120,000). The price is the same for all three destinations, while it can vary with other companies.

Fragline
(☎ 0831 59 03 34) Corso Garibaldi 88. It operates ferries to Corfu and Igoumenitsa from March to October. Its fares are among the most competitive (deck class, L39,000 to L80,000, depending on the season).

Hellenic Mediterranean Lines
(☎ 0831 52 85 31) Corso Garibaldi 8. It has services to a wide range of destinations in Greece running from March to September. Its prices are similar to those offered by Adriatica.

Illyria Lines
(☎ 0831 59 02 05) c/o Agenzia Ionian, Via de Flagilla 12. It has daily services to Durrës and Vlora.

Italian Ferries
(☎ 0831 59 03 21, 0831 59 03 05) Corso Garibaldi 96-98. It has departures from Brindisi for Corfu and Igoumenitsa from April to September and also to Paxos from July to September (deck class, L32,000 to L58,000; poltrona, L63,800 to L99,000; car, L44,000 to L88,000).

Adriatica and Hellenic are among the most reliable. They are the only lines that can officially accept Eurail passes and Inter-Rail passes, which means you pay only L19,000 to go deck class. For an additional L29,000 you can have an poltrona and for L45,000 a cabin bed. If you want to use your Eurail or Inter-Rail pass, you may need to reserve some weeks in advance, particularly in summer. You can usually get a discount (of up to 35%) on the return leg if you buy it with the outgoing trip.

You must check in at least two hours prior to departure or risk losing your reservation (a strong possibility in the high season). There's a L10,000 port tax.

Several companies offer travellers with camper vans the option of paying deck class and sleeping in their vehicles on the open deck. Fares increase by up to 40% in July and August (prices listed in this section are for the high season – ferry services also increase during this period).

Bring warm clothing and a sleeping bag if you're planning to travel deck class. All boats have the usual over-priced snack bars and restaurants.

Bicycles can usually be carried free of charge. At the time of writing, Adriatica's fares for other types of vehicles to Corfu/Igoumenitsa were L50,000 for motorcycles, L120,000 for cars and L210,000 for minibuses and caravans.

LECCE
postcode 73100 • pop 100,900

Baroque architecture can be grotesque, but never in Lecce. The style here is so refined and particular to the city that the Italians call it *barocco leccese* (Lecce baroque). There is a more prosaic explanation for why the Leccesi went to such ornate lengths. The local stone is particularly malleable, but after it's been quarried it hardens – the perfect building and sculpting material.

A graceful and intellectual university town, close to both the Mar Adriatico and Mar Ionio, Lecce makes an agreeable base from which to explore the Penisola Salentina and the numerous bars and restaurants are a pleasant surprise in such a small city.

History

A settlement of ancient origins, Lecce was overrun in the 3rd century BC by the Romans, who named it Lupiae. While rela-

tively little is known of this period, Lecce boasts the remains of an imposing anfiteatro Romano (Roman amphitheatre) which stands in the main square, Piazza Sant'Oronzo. The city passed to the Byzantines, Normans and Swabians, but it was in the 16th to 18th centuries that it really came into its own, when it was embellished with splendid Renaissance and, most notably, baroque buildings.

Orientation

The train station is about 1km south-west of Lecce's historic centre. To get to the centre, walk straight ahead from the station and turn right into Viale Gallipoli, then left at Piazza Argento into Viale Francesco Lo Re. At the end of this street, turn left again to reach Piazza Sant'Oronzo and the city centre. Regular local buses run from the station to Viale Marconi (get off when you see the castle). From the STP bus station in Via Adua, turn left and walk to the Porta Napoli. Turn right and follow Via G Palmieri, turn left into Corso Vittorio Emanuele and continue until you reach Piazza Sant'Oronzo.

If you have a car, the easiest point to enter the city centre is through the Porta Napoli, a 16th century gate into the old city, just off the ring road. From the gate, follow Via Principe di Savoia and turn right into Corso Umberto I to reach the Piazza Sant'Oronzo.

Information
Tourist Offices The AAST office (☎ 0832 24 80 92) is at Corso Vittorio Emanuele 24. It is open from 8 am to 8 pm (occasionally closing for a couple of hours at lunch time) Monday to Saturday. It also has a useful Web site at www.clio.it/Provincialecce.

Money Branches of the main banks are on Piazza Sant'Oronzo, including the Banca Nazionale del Lavoro at No 39, which has an ATM friendly to Visa, MasterCard and Eurocheque cards.

Post & Communications The main post office is on Piazza Libertini, along Via Salvatore Trinchese from Piazza Sant'Oronzo.

PUGLIA

LECCE

PLACES TO STAY		7	Palazzo del Governo
18	Hotel Risorgimento	8	Basilica della Santa Croce
31	Grand Hotel	12	Telecom Office
32	Hotel Cappello	13	Post Office
		14	Castle
PLACES TO EAT		16	Banca Nazionale del
4	Caffè Paisiello		Lavoro & ATM
6	Osteria Angiolino Picione	17	Antifeatro Romano
9	Pizzeria Dolomiti	20	Chiesa di Sant'Irene
10	Snack Bar da Guido e Figli	22	AAST Tourist Office
11	Ristorante da Guido e Figli	23	Chiesa di Santa Chiara
15	Caffè Alvino	24	Duomo
19	Ristorante Da Dominga	25	Palazzo Vescovile
21	Carlo Quinto	26	Seminario
		27	Chiesa di Santa Teresa
OTHER		28	Chiesa del Rosario
1	Chiesa di SS Nicolò e Cataldo	29	FSE Bus Station
2	Porta Napoli	30	Museo Provinciale
3	STP Bus Station	33	Local Buses to Centre
5	CTS Travel Agency	34	Train Station

There is a Telecom office, with telephones outside, at Via Oberdan 13.

Medical Services Ospedale Vito Fazzi (☎ 0832 66 11 11) is on Via San Cesario, 2km south of the centre on the road to Gallipoli. For an ambulance, call ☎ 0832 66 54 11.

Basilica della Santa Croce

Little can prepare you for the opulence of the most celebrated example of Lecce baroque. Artists including Cesare Penna, Francesco Antonio Zimbalo and Giuseppe Zimbalo worked for 150 years through the 16th and 17th centuries to decorate the building, creating an extraordinarily ornate façade, divided in two by a large balcony supported by 13 caryatids and fantastic figures. The interior is more faithful to the Renaissance style but merits a look if you can recover from the impact of the exterior. The church was under restoration at the time of writing. Giuseppe Zimbalo also left his mark in the former Convento dei Celestini, north of the basilica and now known as the **Palazzo del Governo**.

Piazza del Duomo

Although it falls short of the Basilica della Santa Croce, the baroque feast continues in Piazza del Duomo. The almost unassuming 12th century **duomo** was completely restored in the baroque style by Giuseppe Zimbalo, who was also responsible for the 70m-high **bell tower**. Also in the piazza is the 15th century **Palazzo Vescovile** (Episcopal Palace), which was reconstructed in 1632. Of note is its beautiful 1st floor loggia. Opposite the cathedral is the **Seminario** (seminary), designed by Giuseppe Cino and completed in 1709. Its elegant façade features two levels of windows balanced by a fine portal. Cino also designed the well in the seminary courtyard.

Other Churches

On the way from the duomo to Piazza Sant'Oronzo, on Corso Vittorio Emanuele, you'll see another example of Lecce baroque, the **Chiesa di Sant'Irene**, completed in 1639. Other baroque churches of interest include **Santa Teresa** and **Rosario** (the last work of

Giuseppe Zimbalo) on Via G Libertini and the **Santa Chiara** on Piazza Vittorio Emanuele. The **Chiesa di SS Nicolò e Cataldo** was built by the Normans in 1180 and rebuilt in 1716 by Cino, who retained the Romanesque rose window and portal. The church is along Via San Nicola from the Porta Napoli.

Roman Remains

Excavated below the level of Piazza Sant'Oronzo is the 2nd century AD **Roman amphitheatre**, discovered in the 1930s. Virtually next door stands the **Colonna di Sant'Oronzo**, one of the two columns that marked the end of the Via Appia at Brindisi. After it was moved to Lecce a statue of the city's patron saint was placed on top of it.

The remains of a **Roman theatre**, also uncovered in the 1930s, can be seen near the Chiesa di Santa Chiara. The rows of seats are still remarkably intact. Both the Roman amphitheatre and the Roman theatre were closed for restoration at the time of writing. Ask at the AAST office for an update.

Museo Provinciale

In Viale Gallipoli near the train station, this museum houses a collection of Roman artefacts and religious treasures from later periods. It's open from 8.30 am to 1.30 pm and 2 to 7 pm Monday to Friday. Admission is free.

Places to Stay

Cheap accommodation is nonexistent in Lecce, but you could try camp sites elsewhere in the Penisola Salentina. Near Lecce is *Torre Rinalda* (☎ 0832 38 21 62), near the sea at Torre Rinalda. It costs L10,000/15,000 per person/site. You can get there by STP bus from the station in Via Adua. Another option is Lecce's only *affittacamere* (rooms for rent), *Goffredo Andreina* (☎ 0832 30 46 54, Via Taranto 31), with singles/doubles/triples for L40,000/70,000/95,000.

In town, *Hotel Cappello* (☎ 0832 30 88 81, Via Montegrappa 4) has rooms for L53,000/85,000 with bathroom. *Grand Hotel* (☎ 0832 30 94 05, Viale Oronzo 28) is an old-fashioned place with rooms for L75,000/

PUGLIA

140,000 including bathroom and breakfast. *Hotel Risorgimento (☎ 0832 24 21 25, Via Imperatore Augusto 19)* has very pleasant rooms (with bathroom) for L97,000/160,000.

Places to Eat

Eating in Lecce is a pleasure and needn't be expensive. There is a fresh produce *market* every morning from Monday to Saturday on Piazza Libertini. *Caffè Alvino (Piazza Sant'Oronzo 30)* is a good café for breakfast and *Caffè Paisiello (Piazzetta Bonifacio IX)* is another of the many fine cafés you'll find around town.

Da Guido e Figlio (Via Trinchese 10) is popular for a quick bite from 11.30 am to 3.30 pm Monday to Saturday. The restaurant of the same name around the corner at Via XXV Luglio 14 serves good local food at around L8000 for pasta or a pizza and L10,000 for a meal. For a decent pizza, eat in or takeaway, try *Pizzeria Dolomiti (Viale A Costa 5)*. A cheerful, moderately priced establishment with a garden dining area is the *Ristorante Da Dominga (Corso Vittorio Emanuele 48)*. *Osteria Angiolino Picione (Via Principe di Savoia 24)* serves up typical local food at around L15,000 for a full meal.

Entertainment

Seasons of theatre and music are held throughout the year. Get information from the AAST office.

Getting There & Away

STP buses connect Lecce with towns throughout the Penisola Salentina, including Galatina and Leuca; they leave from the station on Via Adua. FSE buses for towns including Gallipoli, Otranto and Taranto leave from Via Boito, the continuation of Viale Don Minzoni, off Viale Otranto.

Lecce is directly linked by train to Bari, Brindisi, Roma, Napoli and Bologna. FSE trains also depart from the main station for Taranto, Bari, Otranto, Gallipoli and Martina Franca.

Brindisi is 30 minutes away from Lecce by superstrada and the S7 goes to Taranto.

Getting Around

The historic centre of Lecce is easily seen on foot. However, useful buses include Nos 1, 3 and 4, which run from the train station to Viale G Marconi. Ask the bus driver to let you off near Piazza Sant'Oronzo.

AROUND LECCE

The small town of **Galatina**, 18km south of Lecce, was a Greek colony up until the Middle Ages and the Greek language and customs only disappeared at the beginning of the 20th century. It is almost the only place where the ritual of tarantulism – a frenzied dance that was meant to rid the body of the poison from a tarantula spider bite – is still practised. The tarantella folk dance evolved from this. Each year, on the feast day of San Pietro and San Paolo (29 June), the ritual is performed at the (now deconsecrated) church dedicated to the saints.

The town's undiscovered gem is the late 14th century **Basilica di Santa Caterina d'Alessandria**, one of the rare examples of Gothic architecture in Puglia. The earlier Romanesque façade has three intricate portals and a lovely rose window. But hold your breath for the interior, whose five naves and gothic pointed arches are almost entirely covered in frescoes – scenes from the Old and New Testaments and the lives of the Madonna and Santa Caterina d'Alessandria – some of which are thought to be by Giotto's pupils and are similar to frescoes at the Basilica di San Francesco in Assisi. The frescoed 15th century cloister attached to the church is also worth a look.

The STP bus runs to Galatina from Lecce.

OTRANTO
postcode 73028 • pop 5100

Founded in antiquity and long a base of Byzantine power, Otranto is Italy's easternmost settlement. In 1480 the Turks, the Byzantines' successors, landed in Otranto and massacred the inhabitants in an event known as the Sack of Otranto.

Otranto makes a good place to start a coastal tour of the Penisola Salentina. It's obviously easier for those with their own transport, but travellers without wheels will find that local bus companies manage to link all the towns in the peninsula. Otranto is overrun in summer with Italian holiday-makers.

The tourist office (☎ 0836 80 14 36) is at Via Rondachi 8 next to the cathedral.

Things to See

First built by the Normans in the 11th century and subsequently subjected to several face-lifts, the Romanesque **cathedral** has several attractions, including a restored 12th century floor mosaic. Depicting the tree of life and other scenes of myth and legend, it is a masterpiece unrivalled in southern Italy. Rex Arturis (King Arthur as he is more commonly known to Anglo-Saxons) is depicted on horseback near the top of the mosaic. An earlier mosaic from the 4th century, discovered 40cm below the surface, is to go on display.

In the chapel to the right of the altar is one of the south's more bizarre sights. The walls are lined with glass cases filled with hundreds of skulls and other bones, the remains of the victims (said to be 800) of the terrible Sack of Otranto. The cathedral is open from 8 am to noon and 3 pm to sunset. Next door is a small **museum**, open from 10 am to noon and 4 to 8 pm (3 to 6 pm in winter).

The tiny Byzantine **Chiesa di San Pietro** contains some well preserved Byzantine paintings.

The Aragonese **castle**, at the eastern edge of town beside the port, is typical of the squat, thick-walled forts you'll find in coastal towns throughout Puglia. Built in the late 15th century, it is characterised by cylindrical towers that widen towards the base. It has been under restoration for years. Admission is free.

Places to Stay & Eat

There are several camp sites in or near Otranto. *Hydrusa* (☎ 0836 80 12 55) near the port is basic and cheap. Of the dozen or so hotels in the area, *Il Gabbiano* (☎ 0836 80 12 51, Via Porto Craulo 5) is the cheapest at L48,000/87,000 for singles/doubles. *Bellavista* (☎ 0836 80 10 58, Via Vittorio Emanuele 19) has rooms for L89,000 per person for half-board.

There are *fruit and grocery shops* along Corso Garibaldi, on the way from the port to the town centre. A bright place for a meal or just a drink is *La Duchesca* on the cheery square in front of the castle.

Getting There & Away

A Marozzi bus runs daily from Roma to Brindisi, Lecce and Otranto, arriving at the port. Otranto can be reached from Lecce by FSE train or bus.

Ferries leave from here for Corfu and Igoumenitsa in Greece. For information and reservations for both ferries and the Marozzi bus, go to Ellade Viaggi (☎ 0836 80 15 78) at the port.

AROUND OTRANTO

The road south from Otranto takes you along a wild coastline. The land here is rocky and when the wind is up you can see why it is largely treeless. This is no Costa Azzura or Costiera Amalfitana, but it gives you a feeling which is rare in Italy – that of being well off the beaten tourist track. Many of the towns here started life as Greek settlements and the older folk still speak Greek in some parts. There are few monuments to be seen but the occasional solitary tower appears, facing out to sea. When you reach **Santa Maria di Leuca**, you've hit the bottom of the heel of Italy and the dividing line between the Mar Adriatico and Mar Ionio. Here, as in other small Salentine towns, summer sees an influx of Italians in search of seaside relaxation and the Ionian side of the Penisola Salentina in particular is spattered with reasonable beaches. There are few cheap hotels in the area, but you'll stumble across a lot of camp sites around the coast.

GALLIPOLI

postcode 73014 • pop 20,090

Jutting into the Mar Ionio 50km north-west of Santa Maria di Leuca, the picturesque old town of Gallipoli is actually an island connected to the mainland and modern city by a bridge. An important fishing centre, it has a history of strong-willed independence, being the last Salentine settlement to

PUGLIA

succumb to the Normans in the 11th century. The Cooperativa Kale' Polis (☎ 0833 26 40 86), Piazza Imbriani, near the port, will help with information about the town.

The entrance to the medieval island-town is guarded by an Angevin **castle**. On the other side of the bridge, in the modern part of the town, is the so-called **Fontana Ellenistica**. Reconstructed in the 16th century, it is doubtful that any of what you see is truly Hellenistic. Through the maze of narrow lanes in the old town, you will find the 17th century baroque **cathedral**, crammed with paintings by local artists. A little farther west, the **Museo Civico** contains a mixed bag of ancient artefacts, paintings and other odds and ends. A walk around the town perimeter is a pleasant diversion.

Should you want to stay, the pick is *Al Pescatore* (☎ 0833 26 43 31), Riviera Colombo, in the old town. Spacious, modern singles/doubles/triples cost L65,000/110,000/140,000. You can also get dinner there for around L40,000. Otherwise, try *Trattoria La Tonnara (Via Garibaldi 7)* near the cathedral. It's one of several restaurants in the old town and dinner costs around L35,000 per head.

FSE buses and trains link Gallipoli to Lecce. There are train stations at the port and in the modern town at Via XX Settembre.

TARANTO
postcode 74100 • pop 232,300

In an ideally protected location, the port of Taranto has always looked to the sea. Founded around the beginning of the 7th century BC by exiles from Sparta, Taras (as it was then known) became one of the wealthiest and most important colonies of Magna Graecia. At the height of its power, the city was home to some 300,000 people. In the 3rd century BC it was conquered by Roma and its name changed to Tarentum, although Greek customs and laws were maintained.

Taranto is Italy's second naval port after La Spezia and during WWII the bulk of Italy's fleet was bottled up there by the British. One of the city's more interesting claims to fame is that it is alleged to be the point where the first cat landed on European shores.

Orientation
Taranto can be divided in two. The old city is on an island between the port and train station to the west and the new city to the east. You'll find the more expensive hotels, APT office and banks in the modern grid of the new city.

From the train station, take bus No 1, 2 or 8 to the centre of the new town. It is not advisable to walk through the old city with a backpack or carrying luggage.

If you arrive in Taranto by car, particularly from the east, you will find the drive from the state road into the centre of town a long one. Simply follow the familiar 'centro' signs and aim to reach Lungomare Vittorio Emanuele III, a good point of reference.

Information
Tourist Offices Taranto's APT office (☎ 099 453 23 92) is at Corso Umberto I 113, on the corner of Via Acclavio. It's open from 9.30 am to 1 pm and 5 to 7 pm Monday to Friday (4.30 to 6.30 pm in winter) and from 9.30 am to 1 pm Saturday.

Post & Communications The main post office is on Lungomare Vittorio Emanuele III, a short distance from the Canale Navigabile that separates the new and old cities. There is a public Telecom office slightly farther along the Lungomare.

Medical Services Ospedale Annunziata (☎ 099 98 51) is on Via Bruno. Follow the Lungomare Vittorio Emanuele III and turn left at Via de Noto.

Dangers & Annoyances Travellers need to be alert in Taranto, particularly in the old city. Carry all valuables in a money belt and be especially cautious at night in the old city.

Città Vecchia
Taranto's old city is in an extremely dilapidated state, although recent years have seen some efforts to renovate its palazzi and churches. The **Castello Aragonese**, at the island's southern extreme on the Canale Navigabile, was completed in 1492. It is occupied by the Italian navy.

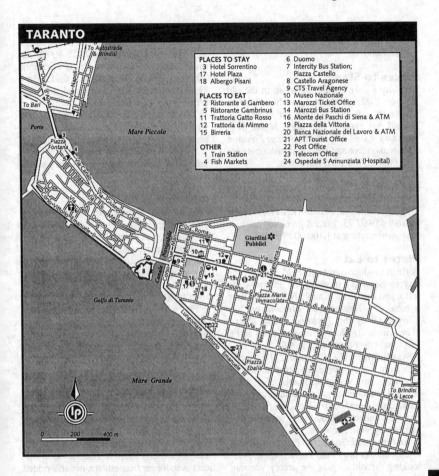

TARANTO

PLACES TO STAY
3 Hotel Sorrentino
17 Hotel Plaza
18 Albergo Pisani

PLACES TO EAT
2 Ristorante al Gambero
5 Ristorante Gambrinus
11 Trattoria Gatto Rosso
12 Trattoria da Mimmo
15 Birreria

OTHER
1 Train Station
4 Fish Markets

6 Duomo
7 Intercity Bus Station;
   Piazza Castello
8 Castello Aragonese
9 CTS Travel Agency
10 Museo Nazionale
13 Marozzi Ticket Office
14 Marozzi Bus Station
16 Monte dei Paschi di Siena & ATM
19 Piazza della Vittoria
20 Banca Nazionale del Lavoro & ATM
21 APT Tourist Office
22 Post Office
23 Telecom Office
24 Ospedale S Annunziata (Hospital)

The 11th century **duomo**, in the centre of the old city on Via del Duomo, is one of the oldest Romanesque churches in Puglia. Remodelled in the 18th century, its three nave interior is divided by 16 ancient marble columns with Romanesque and Byzantine capitals. Its Cappella di San Cataldo is a fine example of baroque architecture and is decorated with frescoes and inlaid marble. The whole cathedral is dedicated to San Cataldo, Taranto's patron saint.

Visit Via Cariati's **fish markets**, where the morning's remarkably varied catch is on display. Taranto has been famous since antiquity for its seafood, in particular its shellfish.

Museo Nazionale

In the new city, the archaeological museum at Corso Umberto I 41 is one of the most important in Italy. It houses a fascinating collection that traces the development of Greek Taras and includes sculpture and pottery, as well as a display of magnificent gold jewellery found in local tombs. The museum

PUGLIA

also houses Roman sculpture and mosaics. It is open from 9 am to 2 pm daily. Admission costs L8000.

Places to Stay

The city's only cheap hotels are in the old city, on Piazza Fontana near the bridge to the train station. Women on their own should not stay in this area. *Hotel Sorrentino* (☎ 099 470 74 56, Piazza Fontana 7) is reasonable and has singles/doubles for L45,000/60,000 with bathroom.

In the new city, *Albergo Pisani* (☎ 099 453 40 87, Via Cavour 43) is safe and clean; singles/doubles/triples cost L40,000/75,000/105,000. A little more upmarket, *Hotel Plaza* (☎ 099 459 07 75, Via d'Aquino 46) has better rooms starting at L100,000/140,000.

Places to Eat

A fresh produce *market* is held every Monday to Saturday morning on Piazza Castello, just across the Canale Navigabile. For a meal, try *Trattoria da Mimmo* on Via Giovinazzi or the *Trattoria Gatto Rosso* (Via Cavour 2). Both offer good food and a full meal costs around L25,000.

At *Birreria* (Via d'Aquino 27) you can pick from self-service, pizza or the full menu; all prices are very reasonable. For fresh seafood at moderate prices, head straight for *Ristorante Gambrinus* (Via Cariati 24). A dish costs about L10,000 and, with the fish markets opposite, how can you go wrong?

Ristorante al Gambero (Piazzale Democrate), across the Ponte Porta Napoli overlooking the old city, is the pricey version. You won't get away with paying under L50,000 for a full meal.

Getting There & Around

FSE buses connect Taranto with Martina Franca, Alberobello, Castellana Grotte and Bari (leaving from Piazza Castello), as well as Ostuni (leaving from Via Magnaghi, in the east of the new city) and smaller towns in the area. SITA buses leave from Piazza Castello for Matera (stopping at Castellaneta) and Metaponto. Chiruzzi buses also leave Piazza Castello for Metaponto. STP and FSE buses

connect Taranto with Lecce. For full details on other intercity bus services, ask at the APT office. Marozzi (☎ 099 459 40 89) has several express services to Roma's Stazione Tiburtina, or you can pick them up for Bari. They leave from Via Cavour and the ticket office is at Corso Umberto I 67.

Trains (both FS and FSE) connect Taranto with Brindisi, Bari, Martina Franca and Alberobello, as well as Napoli and Roma.

AMAT bus Nos 1, 2 and 8 will come in useful for the trip from the station to the new city.

AROUND TARANTO

Fans of that great Latin lover Rudolph Valentino might be interested to know that he was born at **Castellaneta**, about 40km west of Taranto. A plaque on Via Roma marks the birthplace of the silent movie star. A memorabilia **museum** dedicated to Valentino is at Via Municipio 19 and is open from 10 am to 1 pm and 4 to 6 pm.

The whitewashed houses and flagstone lanes of the old town are not entirely without charm and you can get there from Taranto by the SITA bus for Matera (from Piazza Castello). It is also on the FSE train line.

Basilicata

This small and much neglected region spans Italy's 'instep', incorporating the provinces of Potenza and Matera and brief strips of coastline on the Mar Tirreno and Mar Ionio. Basilicata is no longer the desolate, malaria-ridden land of poverty-stricken peasants so powerfully described by Carlo Levi in his novel *Christ Stopped at Eboli*, but it retains a strong sense of isolation and is still one of Italy's poorest regions. The discovery in the mid-1990s of a reservoir of crude oil – the biggest of its kind in mainland Western Europe – in the mountainous area south of Potenza, might change Basilicata's fortunes.

Known to the Romans as Lucania (a name revived by Mussolini during the Fascist period), Basilicata is a mountainous region with large tracts of barren and eroded waste-

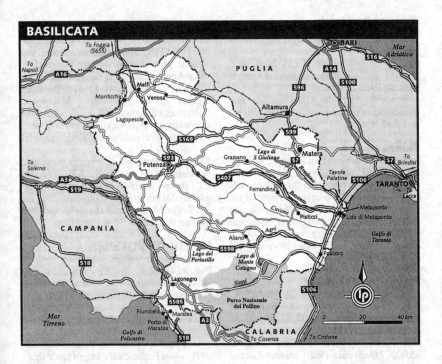

BASILICATA

land, the result of systematic deforestation over the centuries. Government subsidies and industrialisation programmes since the boom of the 1960s, have rid Basilicata of malaria and other diseases and have improved communications, but economic progress has been slow. You don't have to wander far off the main arteries to see peasants working this ungiving land or driving small raggedy herds of sheep across the stony hills in much the same way as their predecessors. A positive aspect of this is the quality of the produce. You'll find excellent bread, really flavoursome fruit and vegetables (used in a huge array of *antipasto* dishes) and arguably the best *ricotta* cheese in the country, still made according to traditional techniques.

Don't come to Basilicata expecting to find a treasure chest of art, architecture and ancient history. The region's dramatic landscape, particularly the Tyrrhenian coast and its close connection with the culture that Levi recorded, along with the fascinating city of Matera, is its main attraction.

POTENZA
postcode 85100 • pop 65,700
Basilicata's regional capital is an unlovely place, but if you're travelling in the region you may pass through it. Badly damaged in repeated earthquakes, especially in 1980, Potenza has lost most of its medieval buildings. Its altitude makes the town cloyingly hot in summer and it can be bitterly cold in winter.

The centre of town straggles east to west across a high ridge. To the south lie the main FS and FCL train stations and local buses make the trip to the centre.

Information
The APT office (☎ 0971 2 18 12) is at Via Alianelli 4, just off the main square, Piazza

Pagano. It can provide a wealth of information including accommodation lists for the entire region.

The post office is on Via IV Novembre. You can find telephones outside the neighbouring INPS building.

Banca Popolare del Materano, Via Vescovado 30, is open from 8.30 am to 1.30 pm and 3.15 to 4 pm.

Things to See

In the old centre of town a couple of modest churches remain, including the **cathedral**, originally erected in the 12th century but rebuilt in the 18th century. North of the town centre is the **Museo Archeologico Provinciale**, housing a collection of ancient artefacts found in the region, but it has been closed for years and no-one knows if it will ever reopen.

Places to Stay & Eat

La Casa dello Studente (☎ 0971 44 27 08, fax 0971 44 52 33, Piazza Don Bosco) has basic singles/doubles for L35,000/60,000. At *Albergo Europa (☎ 0971 3 40 14, Via Giacinto Albini 3)* rooms cost from L25,000/45,000. *Monticchio (Via Caserma Lucana 32)* is a reasonable restaurant, where a meal will cost about L20,000.

Getting There & Away

The transport system in the region is provided by many different companies. Check with the APT office for the best means to reach your destination.

Bus Various companies operate out of several places; the APT office has a comprehensive list of destinations and services.

Grassani (☎ 0835 72 14 43) has two buses daily to Matera, leaving at 2.05 and 5.45 pm. SITA (☎ 0971 2 29 39) has an office at Via Gabet 1 and has daily services to Melfi, Venosa and Maratea. Buses leave from Via Appia 185 and also stop near the Scalo Inferiore FS train station.

Liscio (☎ 0971 5 46 73) has services to destinations including Roma, Napoli, Salerno and Perugia.

Train To pick up a train on the main FS line from Taranto to Napoli, go to Potenza Inferiore (☎ 147 88 80 88 for information). If you want to go to Bari or Matera use the Ferrovie Appulo-Lucane at the Potenza Superiore station (☎ 0971 41 15 61). There are regular services to Taranto, Metaponto, Salerno and Foggia (a different line) and occasionally direct to Napoli. To get to Matera, change at Ferrandina on the Metaponto line.

Car & Motorcycle Potenza is connected to Salerno in the west by the A3, also called E45 (take the E847 branch east at Sicignano). Metaponto lies south-east along the S407. For Matera, take the S407 and then turn north onto the S7 at Ferrandina.

NORTH OF POTENZA

Known as the **Vulture**, the area north of Potenza is characterised by verdant, rolling hills and is dotted with several interesting sites, but it's difficult to explore without your own wheels. It is the home of Basilicata's best wine, Aglianico del Vulture, a robust red that complements the region's hearty cuisine.

Lagopesole, 28km from Potenza (take the S93), boasts Frederick II's largest castle (built over a Norman fortress). The lakes at **Monticchio** provide a popular recreation spot in summer. **Melfi**, 62km north of Potenza, was an important medieval town and a favourite residence of Frederick II's roaming court. It is surrounded by 4km of Norman walls and dominated by a solid castle, largely refashioned by Frederick. The castle has been under restoration for 40 years, but its museum has an excellent archaeological collection of objects found in the area, some dating from the 8th century BC and an astonishing Roman sarcophagus dating from the 2nd century AD. The cathedral, a repeated victim of earthquakes, still has its 12th century bell tower.

Venosa, 25km further east, was once a thriving Roman colony and the birthplace of the Roman poet Quintus Horatius Flaccus, better known as Horace. At the northeastern end of town you can wander around the sparse remains of the original Roman settlement (free admission) that include a baths complex and an anfiteatro. Next to the ruins is the Abbazia della Santissima Trinità, the most impressive structure left by the Normans in Basilicata. The complex consists of the abbey palazzo and two churches, one of them never completed. The Aragonese castle in the centre of town contains a small archaeological museum.

Melfi and Venosa can be reached by bus from Potenza.

MATERA
postcode 75100 • pop 55,000

This ancient city evokes powerful images of a peasant culture that lasted until well after WWII. Its famous *sassi* – the stone houses built in the two ravines that slice through Matera – were home to more than half of the populace (about 20,000 people) until local government built new residential areas in the late 1950s and forcefully relocated the entire population.

Probably the most striking account of how these people lived is given in Carlo Levi's *Christ Stopped at Eboli*. It had taken more than 50 years and vast amounts of development money to eradicate malaria and starvation in Basilicata. Today people are returning to live in the sassi – but now it is a trend rather than a necessity.

Orientation
The centre of the new city is Piazza Vittorio Veneto, a short walk down Via Roma from the train station and intercity bus station off Piazza Matteotti. The ravine housing the sassi zone opens up to the east of Piazza V Veneto.

Information
Tourist Offices The APT office (☎ 0835 33 19 83) is at Via De Viti De Marco 9, off Via Roma. It is open from 9 am to 1.30 pm Monday to Saturday and also 4 to 6.30 pm Monday to Thursday. It has excellent maps, brochures and complete hotel lists. There are also three information offices run by the Comune di Matera (☎ 0835 24 12 60) on Via Madonna delle Virtù (in the sassi), Piazza Matteotti and Via Lucana. These are open from 9.30 am to 12.30 pm and from about 4 to 7 pm daily in summer.

The tourist offices can put you in contact with groups that provide guides to the sassi. One such group, Itinera (☎ 0835 26 32 59,

---

Living in Matera's Sassi

Carlo Levi, a doctor who loved to paint and write, quotes the reactions of his sister to the conditions she observed while passing through Matera on her way to visit him in nearby Aliano, where he was forced to live in the years 1935-36 as punishment for his criticism of the Fascist regime. Describing the stone dwellings of Sasso Caveoso and Sasso Barisano as 'a schoolboy's idea of Dante's Inferno', she went on to say:

The houses were open on account of the heat, and as I went by I could see into the caves, whose only light came in through the front doors. Some of them had no entrance but a trapdoor and ladder. In these dark holes with walls cut out of the earth I saw a few pieces of miserable furniture, beds, and some ragged clothes hanging up to dry. On the floor lay dogs, sheep, goats, and pigs. Most families have just one cave to live in and there they sleep all together; men, women, children, and animals. This is how twenty thousand people live.

She depicted children suffering from trachoma or:

with the wizened faces of old men, their bodies reduced by starvation almost to skeletons, their heads crawling with lice and covered with scabs. Most of them had enormous, dilated stomachs, and faces yellow and worn with malaria.

---

euro currency converter L10,000 = €5.16

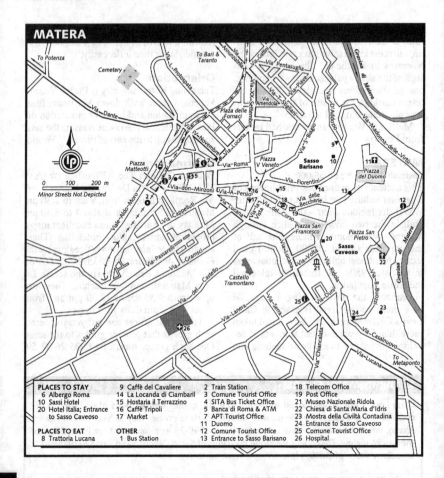

MATERA

Minor Streets Not Depicted

0   100   200 m

To Potenza

Cemetery

To Bari &
Taranto

Plaza delle
Fornaci

Piazza
Matteotti

Piazza
V Veneto

Sasso
Barisano

Piazza
del Duomo

Piazza San
Francesco

Piazza San
Pietro

Sasso
Caveoso

Castello
Tramontano

To
Metaponto

PLACES TO STAY	9 Caffè del Cavaliere	2 Train Station	18 Telecom Office
6 Albergo Roma	14 La Locanda di Ciambaril	3 Comune Tourist Office	19 Post Office
10 Sassi Hotel	15 Hostaria il Terrazzino	4 SITA Bus Ticket Office	21 Museo Nazionale Ridola
20 Hotel Italia; Entrance	16 Caffè Tripoli	5 Banca di Roma & ATM	22 Chiesa di Santa Maria d'Idris
to Sasso Caveoso	17 Market	7 APT Tourist Office	23 Mostra della Civiltà Contadina
		11 Duomo	24 Entrance to Sasso Caveoso
PLACES TO EAT	OTHER	12 Comune Tourist Office	25 Comune Tourist Office
8 Trattoria Lucana	1 Bus Station	13 Entrance to Sasso Barisano	26 Hospital

email arttur@tin.it), organises guided tours in English for groups of one to five people for L40,000 an hour, L70,000 for two hours and L90,000 for three hours. In summer there are also group tours which depart at fixed times (but not always led by English-speaking guides) for L12,000 per person.

An excellent book about the sassi is *Sassi e Secoli* (Stones and Centuries) by R Guira Longa. It is available in English from Libreria dell'Arco, Via Ridola 36, near Sasso Caveoso.

Post & Communications The main post office is on Via del Corso, off Piazza Vittorio Veneto. The Telecom office, just before the post office, is open from 9 am to 12.30 pm and 2.30 to 6 pm Monday to Friday.

Money The Banca di Roma, Via Roma 57, has an ATM that takes Visa and MasterCard.

Medical Services The public hospital (☎ 0835 24 32 12) is on Via Lanera, south of the city centre. If you need a doctor to come to you, contact the Guardia Medica on ☎ 0835 24 35 38.

The Sassi

The two Sassi wards, known as **Barisano** and **Caveoso**, had no electricity, running water or sewerage system until well into the 20th century. The oldest sassi are at the top of the ravine and the dwellings in the lower sections of the ravine, which appear to be the oldest, were in fact established this century. As space ran out in the 1920s, the population started moving into hand-hewn or natural caves.

The sassi zones are accessible from several points around the centre of Matera. There is an entrance just off Piazza Vittorio Veneto or follow Via delle Beccherie to Piazza del Duomo and follow the tourist itinerary signs to enter either Barisano or Caveoso. Sasso Caveoso is also accessible from Via Ridola, by the stairs next to the Hotel Italia.

Caveoso is the most picturesque area to wander around and the most important rock churches are here, including **Santa Maria d'Idris** and **Santa Lucia alla Malva**, both with amazingly well preserved Byzantine frescoes. The tourist offices have detailed sassi maps with suggested itineraries which are well signposted. A formal tour (see the earlier Tourist Offices section) will provide access to some of the more interesting churches.

A couple of sassi have been preserved exactly as they were when their inhabitants left. The best is **Mostra della Civiltà Contadina**, off Via B Buozzi. It is hard to believe that people lived like this only 40 years ago. Many of the sassi are now being renovated and used, with the encouragement of the city authorities, for tourism purposes.

Town Centre

Recent excavations in Piazza Vittorio Veneto have yielded some remarkable discoveries. Beneath the piazza lie the ruins of parts of Byzantine Matera, including a rock church with frescoes, a castle, a large cistern and numerous houses. At the time of writing the excavations were about to be opened to the public. Ask at the tourist office for details.

The 13th century Puglian-Romanesque **cathedral**, on Piazza del Duomo, overlooking Sasso Barisano, is a cacophony of baroque overdecoration but worth a visit to see the side chapel carved out of the rock.

The **Museo Nazionale Ridola** at Via Ridola 24 (☎ 0835 31 12 39) is in the ex-convent of Santa Chiara, dating from the 17th century and houses an interesting collection of prehistoric and classical artefacts. It is open from 9 am to 7 pm daily. Admission costs L4000. Diagonally opposite on Piazzetta Pascoli, is the **Centro Carlo Levi** (☎ 0835 31 42 35) in Palazzo Lanfranchi (free admission) which houses paintings by Levi including an enormous mural depicting peasant life in Matera.

Special Events

Matera celebrates the feast day of Santa Maria della Bruna (the city's patron saint) on 2 July. The festival culminates in a colourful procession from the cathedral and a statue of the Madonna is carried along in an ornately decorated cart. When the procession ends (and the statue has been removed), the crowd descends on the cart in a ceremony known as the *assalto al carro*, tearing it to pieces in order to take away relics.

Places to Stay & Eat

Sassi Hotel (☎ 0835 33 10 09, fax 0835 33 37 33, Via San Giovanni Vecchio 89) is both a hostel, with dormitory beds for L24,000, and a hotel with singles/doubles for L80,000/140,000. The basic *Albergo Roma* (☎ 0835 33 39 12, Via Roma 62) has rooms for L40,000/60,000. The pleasant *Hotel Italia* (☎ 0835 33 35 61, Via Ridola 5) overlooks the sassi and has rooms with bathroom from L130,000/160,000.

A fresh produce *market* is held daily, just south off Piazza Vittorio Veneto. There is a *Divella supermarket* virtually opposite the APT office where you can pick up supplies.

Trattoria Lucana (Via Lucana 48) has a good selection of vegetables. Try the house specialities, such as *orecchiette alla materana* (fresh pasta with a tomato, aubergine and courgette sauce). *Hostaria il Terrazzino* (Vico San Giuseppe 7), behind the Telecom

BASILICATA

office, has a good reputation and the typical local food is excellent. Expect to spend around L35,000 at either.

If you want to eat in a renovated sasso, try *Caffè del Cavaliere (Via D'Addozzio)* off Via Fiorentini, in Sasso Barisano, a bar/café which serves cakes and light meals, or *La Locanda di Ciambaril (Via Fiorentini 66)*, an elegant restaurant where an excellent meal will cost about L35,000. *Caffè Tripoli (Piazza V Veneto 17)* serves the best gelato and coffee in town.

Getting There & Away

Bus The bus station is on Piazzale Aldo Moro, near the train station of Ferrovie Appulo-Lucane. SITA buses (☎ 0835 33 28 62) connect Matera with Taranto (six a day) and Metaponto (up to five daily to the beach in summer; fewer in winter), as well as the many small towns in the province. Grassani (☎ 0835 72 14 43) has two buses a day to Potenza at 6.25 am and 2.30 pm.

Marozzi (☎ 06 225 21 47) runs buses (three a day) between Roma and Matera. Ask for tickets and information at the Kronos Travel Agency (☎ 0835 33 46 53), Piazza Matteotti 8. SITA and Marozzi run a joint special service leaving directly for the northern cities of Siena, Firenze, Prato, Pistoia and Pisa via Scalo Grassano and Potenza. It leaves at 10.35 pm and booking is essential.

All buses leave from Piazza Matteotti.

Train The city is on the private Ferrovie Appulo-Lucane line, which connects with Bari and Altamura. FAL runs regular trains and buses to Bari from its station off Piazza Matteotti (☎ 0835 33 28 61). To get to Potenza, you can take an FAL bus to Ferrandina and connect with an FS train or go to Altamura to link up with FAL's Bari-Potenza run.

Car & Motorcycle If arriving from Bari or Taranto, follow Via Nazionale, which becomes Via Annunziatella, until you reach Via XX Settembre, which connects with Piazza Vittorio Veneto and the city centre. From Metaponto, follow Via Lucana into the city centre.

ALIANO

Not one of Italy's – or even Basilicata's – great tourist stopovers, this tiny hilltop village south of Matera, might attract those who have read *Christ Stopped at Eboli* and have their own transport. When he was exiled to Basilicata during 1935-36 for his opposition to Fascism, Levi lived first in Grassano and then in Aliano. In the novel, he called the town Gagliano and little has changed since he was interned here. The landscape is still as he described it – an 'endless sweep of clay, with the white dots of villages, stretching out as far as the invisible sea' – and you are just as likely to see the locals riding a donkey as driving a car.

Wander to the edge of the old village to see the house where he stayed or you can try getting information at the Pro Loco office (☎ 0835 66 80 74) at Via Stella 65. Two museums have been established in the town, one devoted to Levi (who is buried in Aliano) and another to the peasant tradition of the area.

For the extra keen, Aliano is accessible by a SITA bus that leaves from Matera, but you will have to change in Pisticci Scalo.

METAPONTO

Founded by Greek colonisers between the 8th and 7th centuries BC, the city of Metaponto prospered as a commercial and grain producing centre. One of the city's most famous residents was Pythagoras, who established a school here after being banished from Crotone (in what is now Calabria) towards the end of the 6th century BC.

After Pythagoras died, his house and school were incorporated into a Temple of Hera. The remains of the temple – 15 columns and sections of pavement – are known as the Tavole Palatine (Palatine Tables), since knights, or paladins, are said to have gathered there before heading to the crusades.

Overtaken politically and economically by Roma, Metaponto met its end as a result of the Second Punic War. Hannibal had made it his headquarters after Roma retook Tarentum (Taranto) in 207 BC and he is said to have relocated the town's population to spare it the fate of the people of Tarentum, who were sold into slavery by the Romans for backing the Carthaginians.

Modern Metaponto's only real attraction is a sandy beach, Lido di Metaponto, that attracts loads of summer holiday-makers. It's about 3km east of the train station.

Things to See

You either have to be really keen on ancient ruins or have your own transport to make traipsing around the sparse ruins worth your while. From the train station, walk straight ahead for about 2km. Signposted to your right is the **Parco Archeologico** and to the left is the **Museo Archeologico Nazionale** (☎ 0835 74 53 27); it's a 1km walk to both. The park is actually the site of ancient Metapontum, where you can see what little remains of a **Greek theatre** and the Doric **Tempio di Apollo Licio** (admission is free). The museum houses artefacts from Metapontum and other sites. It is open from 9 am to 7 pm daily; admission costs L4000.

Once back on the main road between Metapontum and the museum, you have a 3km walk to the most memorable reminder of this ancient city-state, the **Tavole Palatine**. Follow the slip road for Taranto onto the S107 highway. The temple ruins are north, just off the highway, behind the old Antiquarium that used to house the museum.

Places to Stay

There are several camp sites but virtually nothing opens in winter. *Camping Magna Grecia* (☎ *0835 74 18 55, Via Lido*) is close to the sea. *Hotel Kennedy* (☎ *0835 74 19 60, Viale Ionio 1*) has singles/doubles at L60,000/80,000. *Sacco* (☎ *0835 74 19 55, Piazzale Lido 7*) charges from L95,000 for a double.

Getting There & Away

Metaponto is accessible from Taranto's Piazza Castello by SITA or Chiruzzi buses and from Matera by SITA bus. Metaponto is on the Taranto-Reggio di Calabria line and trains also connect with Potenza, Salerno and occasionally Napoli. The station is 3km west of the Lido di Metaponto. If you don't want to walk, you could wait for one of the SITA or Chiruzzi buses to pass by on the way to the beach.

AROUND METAPONTO

If you get as far as Metapontum, consider continuing about 17km south down the coast to **Policoro**, originally the Greek settlement of Eraclea. The ruins are not much more complete than those of Metapontum itself, but its museum is worth the visit alone – a fabulous display of artefacts excavated in the area, including two complete tombs with skeletons surrounded by the objects and jewellery with which they were buried. It is open from 9 am to 7 pm daily and admission costs L4000.

SITA buses run down the coast from Metaponto to Policoro but are frequent only in summer.

TYRRHENIAN COAST

Basilicata's Tyrrhenian coast is short (about 20km) but sweet. The S18 threads its way between craggy mountains on the inland side and cliffs that drop away into the sea to the west, making for one of the prettiest drives on the Tyrrhenian coast – but one that curiously peters out virtually as soon as you leave Basilicata in either direction.

About halfway between the Campanian and Calabrian frontiers and a short, steep ride up from the coast, lies the small town of **Maratea**. Watched over by a 22m-tall statue of Christ (at the Santuario di San Biagio), Maratea has been done no harm by tourism. The high part of town, as so often along the south Tyrrhenian coast, forms the historic core, below which has spread an as yet unobtrusive extension.

Maratea is the administrative centre of a series of coastal villages, the prettiest of which are probably **Fiumicello** and **Maratea Porto** which has plenty of bars and restaurants and buzzes until the early hours in summer. Most of the accommodation is down in these coastal settlements and each has at least one small protected beach.

The APT office (☎ 0973 87 69 08) is at Piazza Gesù 32 in Fiumicello. It's open from 8 am to 2 pm and from 3 to 8 pm daily in summer. Hours are reduced in winter. It

BASILICATA

NICKY CAVEN

The 22m-tall statue of Christ at Santuario di San Biaggio watches over the town of Maratea.

has a list of accommodation options including rooms for rent and can also point you in the right direction for boat or moped hire.

One of the cheapest places to stay is the fairly simple *Albergo Fiorella* (☎ 0973 87 69 21) in Fiumicello. *Villa degli Aranci* (☎ 0973 87 63 44) is prettier, but rooms start at about L100,000/120,000 a single/double. Half board is compulsory in summer, at L120,000 per person.

SITA buses link Maratea to Potenza. They also run up the coast to Sapri in Campania and south to Praia a Mare in Calabria. Intercity and nonexpress trains on the Roma-Reggio di Calabria line stop at Maratea train station, below the town. Local trains run infrequently between Praia a Mare, Maratea's various coastal settlements and Sapri. Local buses connect the coastal towns and Maratea train station with the old centre of Maratea and run frequently in summer (get your tickets on the bus or at bars or tobacconists).

Calabria

With some of the country's better beaches and a brooding, mountainous interior, the 'toe' of the Italian boot represents for many travellers little more than a train ride down the Tyrrhenian coast on the way to/from Si-

cilia. Although it may not loom large on the average visitor's list of Italian destinations, Calabria is worth a little exploration. The beaches are among the cleanest in Italy and lovers of ancient history can explore the sparse reminders of the civilisation of Magna Graecia. The downside is the spread of ugly holiday villages along parts of the Ionian and Tyrrhenian coasts and sometimes you have to settle for pebbles rather than sand. Along the roads heading inland you'll encounter some magnificent natural beauty and, every now and then, picturesque and long ignored medieval villages huddled on hill tops.

Sparsely inhabited in Paleolithic times, the area was first settled by Greeks from Sicilia who founded a colony at what is now modern Reggio di Calabria. The process of colonisation spread along the Ionian coast, with Sibari and Crotone the most important settlements. Siding with Hannibal against Roma turned out to be a mistake and with the general's departure for Carthage in 202 BC, the cities of Magna Graecia came under Roma's permanent control. Later, as Roma faded away, the Byzantines took superficial control. Their ineffectual rule and the appearance of Arab raiders (the so-called Saracens) off the coast, favoured a decline in the area which was never really arrested; Calabria continued to be a backwater for a succession of Norman, Swabian, Aragonese, Spanish and Bourbon rulers based in Napoli. Although the brief Napoleonic incursion at the end of the 18th century and the arrival of Garibaldi and Italian unification inspired hope for change, Calabria remained chained to a virtually feudal treadmill.

The province's history of misery has sparked numerous revolts. It also caused, from the 1870s onwards, the rise of highway robbery, which has slowly grown into pervasive organised crime. Calabria's Mafia, known as the 'ndrangheta, incites fear in much of the region's population (although tourists are rarely the target of its aggression). For many, the only answer has been to get out and for at least a century, Calabria has seen its young people emigrate to the north or abroad in search of work.

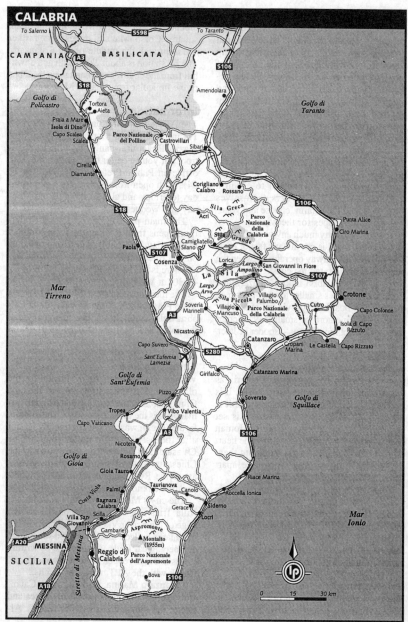

CALABRIA

To Salerno • S598 • To Taranto

CAMPANIA · A3 · BASILICATA · S106

Golfo di Policastro

Amendolara

Golfo di Taranto

Tortora
Aieta
S518
Praia a Mare
Isola di Dino
Capo Scalea
Scalea
Parco Nazionale del Pollino
Castrovillari
Sibari

Cirella
Diamante
Crati
Corigliano Calabro · Rossano
Sila Greca
Punta Alice
Ciro Marina
Acri
S518
S106
Paola
Camigliatello
Silano
Sila Grande · *Neto*
S107
Cosenza
Lorica
Largo Ampollino
San Giovanni in Fiore
S107
La Sila
Largo Arvo
Sila Piccola
Villagio Palumbo
Crotone
Capo Colonne
Mar Tirreno
Soveria Mannelli
Villagio Mancuso
Parco Nazionale della Calabria
Cutro
Isola di Capo Rizzuto
A3
Nicastro
Catanzaro
Capo Suvero
S280
Cropani Marina
Le Castella
Capo Rizzuto
Sant'Eufemia Lamezia
Golfo di Sant'Eufemia
Girifalco
Catanzaro Marina
Pizzo
Soverato
Golfo di Squillace
Tropea
Vibo Valentia
Capo Vaticano
A3
S106
Nicotera
Rosarno
Golfo di Gioia
Gioia Tauro
Riace Marina
Palmi
Taurianova
Canolo
Roccella Ionica
Costa Viola
Bagnara Calabria
Scilla
Gerace
Siderno
Locri
Mar Ionio
Villa San Giovanni
Gambarie
Aspromonte
▲ Montalto (1955m)
A20
MESSINA
SICILIA
Reggio di Calabria
Parco Nazionale dell'Aspromonte
Stretto di Messina
A18
Bova
S106

0   15   30 km

CALABRIA

While mostly tacky, the many tourist villages along the coast can offer excellent package deals and should not be rejected out of hand. There are plenty of camp sites along the coast, but with the exception of some of the more popular coastal towns, budget accommodation is thin on the ground and much of it closes from October to April. Arm yourself with provincial hotel lists from tourist offices before venturing into the backblocks. If you plan to visit in summer, book in advance or at least try to turn up early.

The food is simple, peasant fare and relies heavily on what is produced in the region. It would not be unusual to eat in a restaurant where the owners themselves have produced the salami, cheese and vegetables and the grapes for the wine.

You can get pretty much anywhere by public transport, but it is not always fast or easy. The national FS railway operates between the main cities and around the coast. The private Ferrovie della Calabria links Catanzaro and Cosenza and serves smaller towns in between by train and bus. Blue provincial buses, belonging to a plethora of small private companies, connect most towns – sooner or later.

CATANZARO
postcode 88100 • pop 96,600
Catanzaro replaced Reggio di Calabria as the regional capital in the early 1970s. It is generally overlooked by tourists – and it is not difficult to see why. Catanzaro is set atop a rocky peak 13km in from the Ionian coast on the way north to La Sila. The heart of the old city is pleasant enough, but there is precious little to draw you there apart from the town's transport connections.

Evidence of the city's Byzantine origins is virtually non-existent. Positioned to deter raiders and prevent the spread of malaria, Catanzaro has suffered repeatedly from a different curse – earthquake. As a result of the severe jolts of 1688, 1783 and 1832 there's nothing much of historical interest left.

Orientation
The train station for the private Calabrian railway, Ferrovie della Calabria, is just north of the city centre. Walk south along Via Indipendenza for Piazza Matteotti, the main square. Corso Mazzini takes you farther south through the middle of old Catanzaro. The FS station is about 2km south and downhill from the centre – you can take a local bus or the funicular from Piazza Marconi.

Information
The APT administration office (☎ 0961 85 11) in the Galleria Mancuso, just north of Piazza Prefettura, can help with information, but you're better off going to the APT office on Piazza Prefettura (☎ 0961 74 17 64). Both open from 8.30 am to 1 pm Monday to Friday and also from 3 to 5 pm Monday and Wednesday.

The main post office, on Piazza Prefettura, opens from 8.30 am to 5 pm Monday to Saturday. The public telephone office is on Via Buccarelli.

There is a CTS travel agency (☎ 0961 72 45 30) at Via Indipendenza 26.

The main hospital (☎ 0961 72 67 19) is on Viale Pio X, north of the Ferrovie della Calabria train station. In a police emergency, call the police headquarters (☎ 0961 88 91 11) on Piazza Cavour.

Things to See
Wander south along Corso Mazzini for the older and more interesting parts of the city. Of its churches, the baroque **Basilica dell'Immacolata** is the most impressive. The **duomo**, farther south, was almost completely rebuilt after the last war and is quite ordinary. The **Chiesa di San Domenico** (also known as the Chiesa del Rosario) nearby contains several attractive Renaissance paintings by comparative unknowns.

The city's **Museo Comunale** is inside the Villa Trieste, a large garden on the eastern edge of town near Via Jannoni. The museum has a large collection of coins and some local archaeological finds. At the time of writing it was about to reopen after years of closure. Check with the APT office for details.

Catanzaro Marina, also known as Catanzaro Lido, is the city's access to the sea and one of the Ionian coast's major resorts. Al-

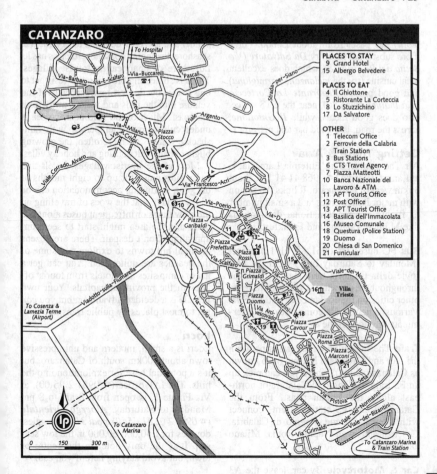

CATANZARO

PLACES TO STAY
9 Grand Hotel
15 Albergo Belvedere

PLACES TO EAT
4 Il Ghiottone
5 Ristorante La Corteccia
8 Lo Stuzzichino
17 Da Salvatore

OTHER
1 Telecom Office
2 Ferrovie della Calabria
   Train Station
3 Bus Stations
6 CTS Travel Agency
7 Piazza Matteotti
10 Banca Nazionale del
   Lavoro & ATM
11 APT Tourist Office
12 Post Office
13 APT Tourist Office
14 Basilica dell'Immacolata
16 Museo Comunale
18 Questura (Police Station)
19 Duomo
20 Chiesa di San Domenico
21 Funicular

though heavily developed, it is less tacky than others and the beaches stretching off in both directions are among the best on the coast.

Places to Stay & Eat

If you are coming from Cosenza, the HI youth hostel *La Pineta* (☎ *0968 66 21 15*) is at Soveria Mannelli on the S19 inland Catanzaro-Cosenza road, 43km north of Catanzaro. It is set in woodlands within striking distance of La Sila and B&B costs L18,000. It's 4km from the nearest train sta-

tion but buses between Cosenza and Catanzaro can drop you nearby.

Catanzaro has few hotels and they are generally expensive. *Albergo Belvedere* (☎ *0961 72 05 91, Via Italia 33*) has singles/doubles from L60,000/100,000. It's basic but you can get a room with a view. *Grand Hotel* (☎ *0961 70 12 56, Piazza Matteoti*) has bland but comfortable rooms for L140,000/190,000 with breakfast.

The best bets for cheap food are the city's bars, where you can grab a cheap sandwich.

CALABRIA

The self-service *Lo Stuzzichino (Piazza Mat-teotti)* has pasta from about L6000. For a more substantial meal try *Da Salvatore (Via Salita del Rosario 28)*, which does excellent local cuisine (try the *melanzane parmigiana*) and good pizzas. *Ristorante La Corteccia (Via Indipendenza 30)*, near the CTS office, also does good meals, while *Il Ghiottone*, across the road, is a good bar and pizzeria.

Getting There & Away

Air The airport, Sant'Eufemia Lamezia, is at Lamezia Terme (☎ 0968 41 41 11), about 35km west of Catanzaro. It links the region with major Italian cities and a small number of flights serve international destinations like Munich, London and Frankfurt.

Bus FC buses (☎ 0961 89 61 11) depart (Monday to Saturday only) from the Fer-rovie della Calabria train station to towns throughout the province, Catanzaro Marina, other cities on the Ionian coast and La Sila. Various other small companies have ter-minals throughout the town.

Train The FC railway runs trains between the city and Catanzaro Marina (also known as Catanzaro Lido), where you can pick up an FS train to Reggio di Calabria or north-east along the Ionian coast. From the Catanzaro city FS station, trains connect with Lamezia Terme, Reggio di Calabria, Cosenza and even Napoli, Roma, Milano and Torino.

Car & Motorcycle By car, leave the A3 autostrada at Lamezia Terme and head east on the S280 for the city. If approaching from along the Ionian coast, follow the 'centro' signs off the S106.

Getting Around

Catanzaro's new funicular railway (tickets L2000) connects the FS train station with Piazza Marconi in the city centre. Other-wise, take a city bus (No 10, 11, 12 or 13). The Circolare Lido bus connects the city centre, the FS train station and Catanzaro Marina.

IONIAN COAST

Wilder and less crowded than the Tyrrhenian seashore, the Ionian coast nevertheless has its fair share of unappealing tourist villages. There is something brooding and resistant to outsiders about this territory, especially if you venture into the hills and valleys away from the coast. Much of the land near the sea is under cultivation, interspersed with ram-shackle villages or, more often, the growing blight of half-built housing and holiday villas.

Most of the tourist villages, hotels and camp sites close for up to eight months of the year, so finding accommodation can be tricky. Add to that the woes of travelling on the slow trains or infrequent buses along the coast and the area might start to seem un-appealing. Don't despair. There are dozens of small hill towns to explore and some of the beaches are quite good. You can get a list of camp sites and hotels from tourist of-fices in the provincial capitals. Your own vehicle is a decided advantage, but you *can* get to most places by public transport.

Locri

Locri is a small, modern and unimpressive town about 100km south of Catanzaro, but it's a potential base for exploration into the hills. The IAT office (☎ 0964 2 96 00), at Via Fiume 1, is open from 8 am to 8 pm Monday to Saturday. *Albergo Orientale (☎ 0964 2 02 61, Via Tripodi 31)* has singles/doubles for L40,000/60,000 in the low sea-son. It is the only hotel in the centre of town, but avoid staying here if you can.

Gerace

About 10km inland from Locri on the S111, Gerace is an immaculately preserved medi-eval hill town that, perhaps sadly, is becom-ing a routine stop on the tourist circuit. It boasts Calabria's largest Romanesque **cath-edral**, high up in the town. It was first laid out in 1045 and later alterations have robbed it of none of its majesty. There is a Pro Loco office (☎ 0964 35 68 88) at Piazza Tribuna 10. *Ristorante a Squella (Viale della Res-istenza 8)* is an excellent traditional restaur-ant and a meal will cost about L25,000.

Farther inland is **Canolo**, a small hamlet seemingly untouched by the 20th century. Buses connect Gerace with Locri.

Isola di Capo Rizzuto

Isola di Capo Rizzuto, 40km north-east of Catanzaro Marina, is one of the best locations along the Ionian coast for camping. *La Fattoria (☎ 0962 79 11 65, Via del Faro)* is one of about 15 sites near the small town and charges L10,000 per person and L10,000 for a site. *Pensione Aragonese (☎ 0962 79 50 13)*, on Via Discesa Marina, is about 10km south-west of town on the waterfront and opposite a rather lonely looking Aragonese castle at Le Castella. It has singles/doubles for L50,000/65,000 and full board for L95,000.

At the northern tip of this zone, whose shore was declared a marine reserve in 1991, is **Capo Colonne**, marking the site of the Greek fortress complex of Hera Lacinia. Only a solitary column belonging to a Doric temple remains to testify to the spot's former splendour.

Crotone

About 10km north of Isola di Capo Rizzuto, Crotone was founded by the Greeks in 710 BC and reached its zenith in the following century, when it virtually controlled all Magna Graecia. In more recent times it has regained influence as one of the region's heavyweight industrial centres and ports.

The APT office (☎ 0962 2 31 85) is at Via Torino 148. It's open from 9 am to 1 pm Monday to Friday and also from 3 to 5 pm Monday and Wednesday.

The town's **Museo Archeologico Statale**, on Via Risorgimento, is one of Calabria's better museums. It's open from 9 am to 1 pm and from 4 to 6 pm Tuesday to Sunday. Nearby (and open similar hours) is a restored 15th century **castle**, typical of the cylindrically towered fortresses erected by the Aragonese in southern Italy's main coastal cities.

Albergo Italia (☎ 0962 2 39 10, Piazza Vittoria 12) has comfortable enough rooms ranging from L40,000 to L70,000 and is open year-round.

North of Crotone

The coastline from Crotone to Basilicata is the region's least developed, partly because the beaches are not terribly good and public transport is generally irregular, although the coast road is decent (and being upgraded).

Cirò Marina About 30km north of Crotone, Cirò Marina is a decent-sized town with plenty of hotel rooms and good beaches despite the huge cement breakwaters nearby. *Albergo Atena (☎ 0962 3 18 21, Via Bergamo)* has singles/doubles from L60,000/80,000. *Punta Alice (☎ 0962 3 11 60)* camp site is at **Punta Alice**, a couple of kilometres north of the town.

Rossano Rossano, 56km north of Cirò, is really two towns – Lido Sant'Angelo, the standard beach resort and coastal extension of the modern plains town of Rossano Scalo, and the original hill town itself, 6km inland.

The transformation over such a short drive is remarkable. The snaking road takes you through verdant countryside, an invitation in itself to head farther inland to a tranquil and picturesque old town, once an important Italian link in the Byzantine empire's chain.

Various reminders of Rossano's ties to the city of Constantinople remain. The **cathedral**, remodelled several times, holds a 9th century Byzantine fresco of the Madonna. For more proof, try the **Museo Diocesano** next door, which houses a precious 6th century codex containing the gospels of San Matteo and San Marco in Greek. The museum is open from 10 am to noon and 5 to 7 pm daily except Sunday, when it is closed in the afternoon (admission costs L2000). Ask around for the custodian if you're having trouble getting in.

Albergo Scigliano (☎ 0983 51 18 46, Viale Margherita 257), near the station, has rooms from L100,000/150,000 with breakfast and there's a camp site, *Camping Torino (☎ 0983 51 00 80)*, at Marina di Rossano.

Rossano is on the Taranto-Reggio di Calabria train line. If you want to head inland, the S177 makes a pretty drive across La Sila

CALABRIA

Ancient Minorities

Possibly Calabria's richest testament to the era of Magna Graecia can be found not in the sparse ruins of abandoned ancient settlements along the coast, but in the hill towns east of Reggio di Calabria – for in the towns of Bova, Condofuri and Roccaforte del Greco (most easily reached from the coastal road), you can still hear the older folk speaking Greek as their native tongue. It is not, say some experts, a dialect of modern Greek, but rather a descendant of the ancient language of Pythagoras. Sceptics claim it is the Greek of the much later Byzantine empire. Even so, it is remarkable to think that this linguistic time capsule has survived for so many hundreds of years.

More numerous and more recently arrived are the Albanians, who began fleeing Muslim persecution in the mid-15th century. You'll find them mostly in small towns scattered about the Piana di Sibari, 50km south of the border with Basilicata on the Ionian coast. Not only have they preserved their language, but in many cases they remain faithful to the Greek Orthodox rite in this bastion of Catholicism.

to Cosenza, although it could be a bit dangerous, especially for women on their own.

Sibari About 25km farther north, among reclaimed farmland, is Sibari. The town is near what was once the seat of the ancient Sybarites, about whose wealth and genius much has been written. This great Greek city state was destroyed by Crotone under Pythagoras in the 6th century BC and excavations since the 1960s have brought only a glimmer of its glory to light (there is a small museum).

COSENZA
postcode 87100 • pop 86,600

Seated at the confluence of two rivers, the Crati and Busento, the medieval core of Cosenza is an unexpected pleasure, with its narrow *vicoletti* (alleys), some no more than

steep stairways, winding past elegant, if much decayed, multistorey apartment houses.

A university town since 1968, Cosenza is without doubt the most attractive of Calabria's three provincial capitals and possibly the only one that seriously merits a stop. What's more, if you're coming from the north, it has the appeal of being a gateway into La Sila and on across to the Ionian coast. As a transportation hub, the city makes a good base for the mountains.

Orientation

The main drag, Corso Mazzini, runs south from Piazza Fera (near the bus station) and intersects Viale Trieste before meeting Piazza dei Bruzi. What little there is in terms of accommodation, food, banks and tourist assistance is all within about a 10 minute walking radius of the intersection. Head farther south and cross the Busento river to reach the medieval part of town.

Information

Tourist Offices There are two APT offices, one on Piazza Rossi (☎ 0984 3 13 88), at the roundabout north of Viale della Repubblica (useful for drivers coming in off the A3), the other (☎ 0984 2 74 85) at Corso Mazzini 92, near Viale Trieste. Among the odds and ends on offer is a guide (with map) to the agriturismo accommodation throughout the province. These places in the country are worth considering as an alternative to the usual hotel grind and often sell farm produce and offer activities such as horse riding. Both offices are open from 7.30 am to 1.30 pm Monday to Friday and also from 2 to 5 pm Monday to Wednesday.

Post & Communications The main post office is on Via Vittorio Veneto on the city centre's western edge. The Telecom office is at the bus station off Piazza Fera.

Medical Services & Emergency The Ospedale Civile (☎ 0984 68 11) is on Via Felice Migliori, behind the post office. In a police emergency contact the questura (☎ 0984 7 26 13) at Via Frugiuele 10.

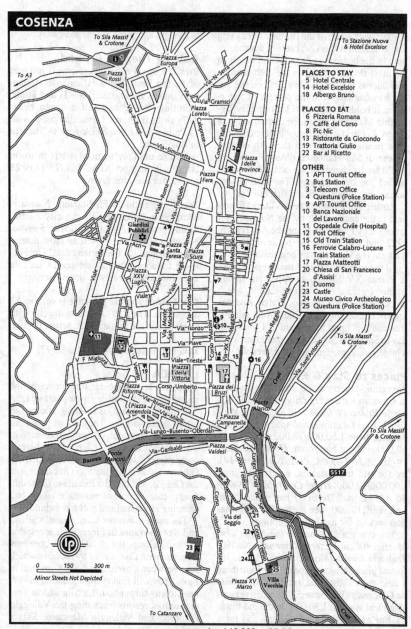

COSENZA

To Sila Massif & Crotone

To A3

Piazza Europa

Piazza Rossi

Via-N-Serra

Via-Gramsci

Via-P-Rossi

Corso-d'Italia

Calopreste

Via-Simonetta

Piazza Loreto

Piazza Fera

Piazza I delle Province

Viale–Roma

Via–Frugliele

Giardini Pubblici

Via–Acri

Piazza Santa Teresa

Piazza Scura

degli Alimena

Via-Medaglie-di-Cro

Via della Republica

Piazza XXV Luglio

Viale

Parisio

Viale

Via–Monte-Santo

Via-Monte–San–Michele

Corso-Mazzini

Via-XXIV-Maggio

Via–Isonzo

Via–Piave

Viale–Trieste

Piazza I della Vittoria

Corso Umberto

Piazza dei Bruzi

To Stazione Nuova & Hotel Excelsior

Piazza Matteotti

V F Migliore

Via V Veneto

Piazza Riforma

Via-Rivocati (Piazza Amendola)

Via-Mileli

Via-Lungo-Busento-Oberdan

Via-Garibaldi

Ponte Mancini

Busento

Piazza Valdesi

Crati

Via–Popilia

Via–Reggio Calabria

Via-Sant'Antonio

To Sila Massif & Crotone

Ponte Alarico

To Sila Massif & Crotone

SS17

Corso Telesio

Lungo Crati de' Seta

Corso Telesio

Via del Seggio

Corso Telesio

Via Vittorio Emanuele

Piazza XV Marzo

Villa Vecchia

Crati

Ponte

PLACES TO STAY
5 Hotel Centrale
14 Hotel Excelsior
18 Albergo Bruno

PLACES TO EAT
6 Pizzeria Romana
7 Caffè del Corso
8 Pic Nic
13 Ristorante da Giocondo
19 Trattoria Giulio
22 Bar al Ricetto

OTHER
1 APT Tourist Office
2 Bus Station
3 Telecom Office
4 Questura (Police Station)
9 APT Tourist Office
10 Banca Nazionale del Lavoro
11 Ospedale Civile (Hospital)
12 Post Office
15 Old Train Station
16 Ferrovie Calabro-Lucane Train Station
17 Piazza Matteotti
20 Chiesa di San Francesco d'Assisi
21 Duomo
23 Castle
24 Museo Civico Archeologico
25 Questura (Police Station)

0   150   300 m

Minor Streets Not Depicted

To Catanzaro

Things to See

A short walk south of the Busento river along Corso Telesio is the 12th century **duomo**, rebuilt in the baroque style (although hardly in the most florid fashion) in the 18th century. The duomo is unexceptional, but on the left is a baroque chapel in the process of restoration. It holds a copy of a 13th century Byzantine Madonna. From the duomo you can follow Via del Seggio through an enchanting little medieval quarter to the 13th century **Chiesa di San Francesco d'Assisi**, in which you'll find a chapel of the original structure behind the right transept. The cloister also bears some remnants of the first building.

Farther south along Corso Vittorio Emanuele is the **castle**, built by the Normans, rearranged by Frederick II and the Angevins in 1222 and left in disarray by several earthquakes. The views are its best feature.

At the southern edge of the old city centre is Piazza XV Marzo, an appealing square fronted by the Accademia Cosentina, which houses the city's **Museo Civico Archeologico**, containing local finds. Admission is free and it is open from 9 am to 1 pm Monday to Saturday. South of the piazza stretches a huge public garden, the **Villa Vecchia**.

Places to Stay & Eat

Accommodation can be a prickly business in Cosenza – there are only four hotels. *Albergo Bruno* (☎ *0984 7 38 89, Corso Mazzini 27*) has functional and spacious singles/doubles from L50,000/70,000 or L35,000/50,000 without bathroom. *Hotel Excelsior* (☎/fax *0984 7 43 83, Piazza Matteotti 14*), by the old train station, has rooms from L60,000/90,000. *Hotel Centrale* (☎ *0984 7 36 81, Via del Tigrai 3*) has rooms from L88,000/118,000. See the earlier Information section for agriturismo options.

You can grab a snack at *Pic Nic* (*Corso Mazzini 108*) or *Pizzeria Romana* at No 190. *Trattoria Giulio* (*Viale Trieste 93*) is an informal place for simple meals. For something a little more substantial, head for *Ristorante da Giocondo* (*Via Piave 53*), where a reasonable meal is about L30,000. In the old town, try *Bar al Ricetto* (*Corso Telesio 29*) for a quick bite. *Caffè del Corso* (*Corso Mazzini*) is a bright spot for a coffee and pastry.

Getting There & Around

Bus The city's main bus station is just east of Piazza Fera. Services leave for Catanzaro, towns throughout La Sila and Paola. Autolinie Preite has half a dozen buses daily along the north Tyrrhenian coast as far as Praia a Mare and SITA goes to Maratea in Basilicata.

You're unlikely to need a bus in town, but it is best to get ATAC bus No 27 or 28 to or from Stazione Nuova.

Train The national FS Stazione Nuova is about 2km north-east of the city centre. Trains go to Reggio di Calabria, Salerno, Napoli and Roma, as well as most destinations around the Calabrian coast. The Ferrovie Calabro Lucane line serves La Sila and other small towns around Cosenza.

Car & Motorcycle Cosenza is off the A3 autostrada. The S107 connects the city with Crotone and the Ionian coast, across La Sila.

Taxi For a taxi, call ☎ 0984 2 88 77.

LA SILA

Though less spectacular than many of the mountain ranges farther up the peninsula, La Sila (the Sila Massif) is still magnificent and offers good walking. The highest peaks are around 2000m; much of them are covered in what amounts to a vast forest, but there is some winter skiing in the central Sila Grande. Other main areas are the Sila Greca, north of the Grande, and the Sila Piccola to the south. Sadly, there are few mountain *rifugi* and camping in the national parks is forbidden.

The main towns are Camigliatello Silano and San Giovanni in Fiore, both accessible by bus along the S107 that connects Cosenza with Crotone, or by the train which runs between Cosenza and San Giovanni in Fiore. You will find accommodation in various towns throughout La Sila and at several tourist resorts, including the Villaggio Palumbo and Villaggio Mancuso. Skiers can use lifts around Camigliatello Silano and near Lorica, on Lago Arvo.

Information
Unfortunately, the tourist offices can help you with little more than vague maps and accommodation lists. Most brochures are in Italian only.

Camigliatello Silano
Ordinary enough in summer, Camigliatello looks quite cute under snow. It is a popular local skiing resort, but won't host any international competitions. A few lifts operate on Monte Curcio about 3km to the south.

The town has about 15 hotels, including *Miramonti* (☎ *0984 579 06 70, Via Forgitelle*), near the tourist office, which has singles/doubles from L52,000/65,000. The three star *Aquila & Edelweiss* (☎ *0984 57 80 44, fax 0984 57 87 53, Viale Stazione 11*) has rooms from L100,000/150,000.

San Giovanni in Fiore
Although this is the biggest town in La Sila, it really has little to recommend it. The provincial accommodation guide lists a lot of hotels here, but most of them are scattered about in the nearby small villages – some as far away as Lorica, 20km to the south-west.

Lorica
A peaceful little spot on Lago Arvo amid thick woods, Lorica is a minor ski resort, with a lift operating nearby. There are several camp sites in the area including *Camping Lorica* (☎ *0984 53 70 18*), on the lake, which charges L10,000 per person. Otherwise try *Albergo La Trota* (☎ *0984 53 71 66*) which has doubles for L80,000. You may have to pay full board (L85,000 per person) in the winter and summer high season.

Villaggio Palumbo
About 15km south of San Giovanni in Fiore, this is a tourist village resort on Lago Ampollino. There is a similar venture about 25km farther south on the road to Catanzaro, **Villaggio Mancuso**. They both offer weekend package deals including food and accommodation and are set up for skiing, horse riding and the like.

REGGIO DI CALABRIA
postcode 89100 • pop 177,600
As you gaze across the strait from the elegant tree-lined Lungomare Matteotti to the twinkling night lights of Messina in Sicilia, you could almost be forgiven for thinking you are in a rather romantic spot. However as you drive through miles of half-built and semi-inhabited concrete slum tenements, you can hardly feel anything but pity for the bulk of this city's people. Rocked repeatedly by earthquakes, the last time devastatingly in 1908, this once proud ancient Greek city has plenty of other woes as well, among them, organised crime. You may notice an awful lot of Carabinieri and Alpine soldiers (Italy's elite troops) in the streets. Wander up to Piazza Castello where heavily armed guards surround the law courts and you begin to gauge the depth of the problem.

Orientation
The main train station is at the southern edge of town on Piazza Garibaldi, where most buses also terminate. Walk north along Corso G Garibaldi, the city's main street, for the APT office and other services. Corso Garibaldi is a kind of de facto pedestrian zone in the evening, as streams of Reggians parade in the ritual *passeggiata* (evening stroll).

Information
Tourist Offices The APT office has branches at the train station (☎ 0965 2 71 20), the airport (☎ 0965 64 32 91) and on the autostrada near the Rosarno Ovest exit. In town the head office is at Via Roma 3 (☎ 0965 2 11 71) and there's a branch at Corso Garibaldi 329 (☎ 0965 89 20 12 or toll free ☎ 800 23 40 69) in the Teatro Comunale building. Most offices purport to open from 8 am to 8 pm, Monday to Saturday, but it's perhaps wiser to use the 2 pm closing time of the head office as a guide.

Post & Communications The main post office is at Via Miraglia 14, near Piazza

CALABRIA

REGGIO DI CALABRIA

Ferries & Hydrofoils
to Sicilia & isole Eolie
(Aeolian Islands)

To Villa San
Giovanni

To Villa San Giovanni
& A3 North

Annunziata

Porto

Via-Santa-Caterina

Via-Italia

Viale-Libertà

Via-Georgia

Via-Vittorio-Veneto

Via-Giuseppe

Via-Giovanni-Amendola

Via-Cardinale-Portanova

Portanova
Exit

Via-XXV-Luglio

Viale-Genoese-Zerbi

Viale-Nava

Via-Roma

Parco
Caserta

Via-Demetrio-Tripepi

Via-Aschenez

Via-Melacrino

Rada
dei
Giunchi

Piazza
de Nava

Mar
Ionio

Corso-Vittorio-Emanuele-III

Corso-Giuseppe-Garibaldi

Via-Giuseppe-Melacrino

Via-Tortona

Via-Demetrio-Tripepi

Via-Reggio-Campi

A3

S106

Stretto di
Messina

Via-Osanna

Piazza
Italia

Lungomare-Corso-Matteotti

Via-Crocefisso

Via-Campanella

Via-Giulia

Spirito
Santo Exit

Via-Francesco-di-Paola

Corso-Giuseppe-Garibaldi

Villa
Comunale

Piazza
del Duomo

Via-Crocefisso

Via-Colt-Agosto

Via-A-Cimino

Via-S-Spirito

Calopinace

To Aeroporto Civile
Minniti (Airport) &
S106 South

To Aeroporto Civile Minniti
(Airport) & S106 South

Reggio
Sud Exit

0   250   500 m

PLACES TO STAY
4   Albergo Noel
14 Grande Albergo
    Miramare
17 Hotel Diana

PLACES TO EAT
8   Antica Gelateria
    Malavenda
11 Ristorante Il Ducale
12 Ristorante Rodrigo
13 Ristorante la Pignatta
15 London Bistro
22 Paninoteca Charlie
23 Pizzeria Rusty

OTHER
1   Ferry Terminal
2   Ferry Terminal
3   Ferry Terminal
5   Main APT Tourist
    Office
6   Sea Point
    (Internet Café)
7   Ospedale Riuniti
    (Hospital)
9   Museo Nazionale
10 Stazione Lido
16 Post Office
18 Banca Nazionale
    del Lavoro & ATM
19 Castle Ruins;
    Piazza Castello
20 Duomo
21 Piazza del Duomo
24 Bus Station;
    Piazza Garibaldi
25 Stazione Centrale

CALABRIA

Italia, and is open from 8.15 am to 6 pm Monday to Saturday. The Telecom office is on Via Marina. There is an Internet café, Sea Point (☎ 0965 2 93 87), at Via Roma 3 (in the same building as the APT office).

Money There is no shortage of banks in Reggio. The Banca Nazionale del Lavoro at Corso Garibaldi 431 is one of several with a user-friendly ATM.

Medical Services & Emergency The Ospedali Riuniti (☎ 0965 39 71 11) is on Via Melacrino. For an ambulance, call ☎ 0965 2 00 10 or 0965 2 44 44. For the Guardia Medica (visiting doctors, at night and on holidays), call ☎ 0965 34 71 05. For the questura, contact their headquarters (☎ 0965 41 11) on Via Santa Caterina.

Things to See & Do
Reggio was completely rebuilt after the 1908 earthquake that devastated southern Calabria and few historic buildings remain. Apart from wandering along Lungomare Matteotti and gazing at Sicilia or participating in one of the most serious passeggiatas you're likely to see, there's little to see or do.

The big exception is housed in a predictably pompous Fascist-era building on Piazza de Nava, at Corso Garibaldi's northern end. The **Museo Nazionale** holds a wealth of finds from Magna Graecia, crowned by the *Bronzi di Riace*, two bronze statues that were hauled up off the Ionian coast near Riace in 1972 and are among the world's best examples of ancient Greek sculpture. There was pressure for the statues to go to Roma, but Calabria won in the end. The sculptor remains unknown, but probably lived in the 5th century BC. There's also work by southern Italian artists in one of the Mezzogiorno's best collections. The museum is open from 9 am to 6.30 pm daily (except the first and third Mondays of the month). Admission is L8000.

The **duomo** in Piazza del Duomo, just off Corso Garibaldi, appears unspectacular until you realise it was rebuilt from rubble. Northeast of the duomo is Piazza Castello and the ruins of a 15th century Aragonese **castle**.

Places to Stay & Eat
Finding a room should be easy, as most visitors to Reggio pass through on their way to Sicilia. *Albergo Noel (☎ 0965 89 09 65, Via G Zerbi 13)* has singles/doubles from L50,000/70,000. *Hotel Diana (☎ 0965 89 15 22, Via Vitrioli 12)* offers perfectly adequate rooms from L50,000/100,000. For a sumptuous stay and a view of Mt Etna, *Grande Albergo Miramare (☎ 0965 81 24 44, fax 0965 81 24 50, Via Fata Morgana 1)* has rooms giving on to Lungomare Matteotti, starting at L180,000/250,000.

There are plenty of places to buy a snack along Corso Garibaldi, including a bar in the Villa Comunale, a large park off the Corso. *Pizzeria Rusty (Via Crocefisso)*, beside the duomo, has pizza by the slice from L2000, while *Paninoteca Charlie (Via Generale Tommasini)*, next to the Red Cross, is good for cheap snacks. *Ristorante la Pignatta (Via Demetrio Tripepi 122)* is a bright place offering local dishes with pasta from around L7000. *Ristorante Il Ducale (Corso Vittorio Emanuele III 13)*, near the museum, offers good meals for L30,000. *Ristorante Rodrigo (Via XXIV Maggio 25)* specialises in Calabrian cuisine, and a full meal will cost in excess of L50,000.

For the town's richest gelati, you can't surpass *Antica Gelateria Malavenda*, on the corner of Via Romeo and Viale Amendola, or *Cesare*, a kiosk on the Lungomare near the museum.

Getting There & Away
Air The city's airport, the Aeroporto Civile Minniti (☎ 0965 64 22 32) at Ravagnese, about 4km to the south, has two flights a day from Roma and one from Milano, as well as the occasional charter flight. Alitalia is represented by Simonetta travel agency (☎ 0965 33 14 44) at Corso Garibaldi 521.

Bus The bus station is on Piazza Garibaldi, in front of the train station. Several different companies operate to towns in Calabria and beyond. ATAM (☎ 0965 62 01 29 or toll free ☎ 800 43 33 10) serves the Aspromonte Massif, with regular bus No 127 to Gambarie.

CALABRIA

Salzone (☎ 0965 75 15 86) has buses to Scilla every hour. Lirosi (☎ 0965 5 75 52) has three daily runs to Roma and three to Catanzaro.

Train Trains stop at Stazione Centrale (☎ 147 88 80 88 for information) and less frequently at Stazione Lido, near the museum. Reggio is the terminus for trains from Milano, Firenze, Roma and Napoli.

Car & Motorcycle The A3 ends at Reggio di Calabria. If you are heading south, the S106 hugs the coast round the 'toe' and up along the Mar Ionio.

Boat Boats from Reggio di Calabria to Messina leave from the port (just north of Stazione Lido). In high season SNAV (☎ 0965 2 96 58) has up to 20 hydrofoils per day (L5500 one way). In low season there are only two (9 am and 1.25 pm). Some boats proceed on to the Isole Eolie. The FS national railways (☎ 147 88 80 88) runs up to 19 big hydrofoils a day from the port to Messina (L2200 one way).

Meridiano (☎ 0965 71 22 08) and NGI (☎ 0335 84 27 84) run car ferries from Reggio to Messina. Meridiano charges L24,000 return for a car; passengers don't pay.

Ferries for cars and foot passengers cross to Messina around the clock from Villa San Giovanni, 20 minutes farther north along the rail line. Caronte (☎ 0965 79 31 31) runs regular ferries throughout the year, which depart every 15 to 20 minutes. Caronte charges L33,000 one way for a standard car, L59,000 return (valid 60 days). Passengers don't pay; motorcycles cost L10,000 each way. The crossing takes about 20 minutes.

Getting Around

Orange local buses run by ATAM (☎ 0965 62 01 29 or toll free ☎ 800 43 33 10) cover most of the city. For the port, take No 13 or 125 from Piazza Garibaldi outside the station. The Porto-Aeroporto bus runs from the port, via Piazza Garibaldi to the airport and vice-versa. Tickets cost L1000 per trip or L1500 for 90 minutes. Buy them at ATAM offices, tobacconists or newsstands.

ASPROMONTE MASSIF

Inland from Reggio di Calabria rises the Aspromonte massif. Its highest peak, **Montalto** (1955m), is dominated by a huge bronze statue of Christ and offers sweeping views across to Sicilia.

The APT office in Reggio may have information and a map of the Montalto area, now a national park, which has some walking trails, albeit not quite as spectacular, or difficult, as those in La Sila.

To reach the Aspromonte's main town of Gambarie, take ATAM city bus No 127 from Reggio di Calabria (four a day). Most of the roads inland from Reggio eventually hit the main S183 road that runs north to the town.

TYRRHENIAN COAST

The region's western seashore is a mixture of the good, the bad and the ugly. Certain stretches are crammed with tacky package resorts that attract holidaying Italians by the thousand each summer. But there are several small towns that are pleasant to stay in, along with the odd cove with a protected sandy beach.

The drive along the Costa Viola, from Rosarno to Scilla and on towards Reggio di Calabria, is one of Italy's great coastal drives, with breathtaking views of Sicilia.

The best sources of information about the coast are the tourist offices in Cosenza and Reggio di Calabria. They'll probably recommend you stay at one of the tourist villages – don't be immediately put off. Many offer excellent value and all have private beaches, generally some of the best on the coast.

Out of season, most hotels, camp sites and tourist villages close. In summer many of the hotels are full, although you should have an easier time with the camp sites.

Most coastal towns are on the main train line between Reggio and Napoli and the S18 road hugs the coast for much of the way. The A3 from Reggio di Calabria to Salerno is farther inland.

Scilla

After the urban confusion of Reggio and Villa San Giovanni, the S18 brings you to a striking stretch of Calabria's coastline. The highlands of the Aspromonte extend right to the coast and the views from the cliffs across to Sicilia can fuel the imagination.

Coming from the north, the drive is even better (especially if you take it slowly on the S18). Wedged in there and arching around a small beach is the picturesque town of Scilla, its northern end dominated by the rock associated with Scylla, the mythical sea monster who drowned sailors as they tried to navigate the Stretto di Messina (and if she didn't get them, Charybdis, across in Sicilia, would).

The HI *hostel*, in the castle, has been closed for renovation for several years. When it reopens (check with the APT office in Reggio di Calabria for details) it will be one of the most atmospheric places to stay on the coast. You could try *Pensione le Sirene* (☎ 0965 75 40 19, *Via Nazionale 55*) with singles/doubles for L46,000/82,000. Just north of the castle, there is a row of houses built into the water which are worth seeing.

Promontorio di Tropea

The Promontorio di Tropea, 50km north of Scilla, is like a bunion on the 'bridge' of Italy's foot. It stretches from Nicotera in the south to Pizzo at the northern end and boasts Calabria's best sandy beaches and crystal-clear aquamarine seas. About 8km south of Pizzo and slightly inland, is the pretty town of **Vibo Valentia**, good for a brief roam and a useful transport hub. The APT office (☎ 0963 4 20 08) on Via Forgiari (behind the Galleria Vecchia) provides several guides to the area and a list of hotels and tourist villages.

Nicotera, at the southern end of the promontorio, is dominated by a medieval castle. At least one camp site functions year-round – *Camping Sayonara* (☎ 0963 8 19 44) at Nicotera Marina, with good ocean views. It charges about L10,000 per person, plus the cost of a site.

About 20km north-west of Nicotera at **Capo Vaticano** are dozens of tourist villages, including *Costa Azzurra* (☎ 0963 66 31 09). Like most of the villages in this area, it closes in winter and generally imposes a full-board arrangement.

Just north of Capo Vaticano, **Tropea** is a picturesque little town perched high above the coast. Probably the prettiest spot on Calabria's Tyrrhenian coast, it has several long sandy beaches within walking distance of the town and plenty of bars, pizzerie and trattorie. There is a Pro Loco office (☎ 0963 6 14 75) in the town centre.

Most of the 10 or so hotels are in the higher price bracket and many close for winter. *Hotel Virgilio* (☎ 0963 6 19 78, fax 0963 6 23 20, *Viale Tondo 27*) has singles/doubles from L62,000/95,000 and is open year-round. The *Stromboli* tourist village (☎ 0963 66 90 93) charges from L65,000 to L115,000 per person for full board on a sliding scale from winter to super-high season (August). The best fish soup on the promontorio can be had at *L'Arca* (*Largo San Giuseppe*), in the centre of town.

A coastal railway runs around the promontorio from Rosarno and Nicotera to Vibo Marina and Pizzo. SAV buses also connect most resorts with Tropea and Pizzo.

Pizzo

In the bars of Pizzo, you will find possibly Italy's best *tartufo*, a type of chocolate ice-cream ball.

Inside the town's **duomo** lies the tomb of Joachim Murat, king of Napoli from 1808 until 1815, when he was defeated by the Austrians and the Bourbons were restored to the Neapolitan throne. Although he was the architect of various enlightened reforms, the locals seemed to prefer the Bourbon devil they had known and showed no great concern when Murat was imprisoned and executed here after one last attempt to regain power in September 1815.

Just north of the town, the **Chiesa di Piedigrotta** was literally carved into the sandstone near the beach by Neapolitan shipwreck survivors in the 17th century. The church was later added to (the statue of Fidel Castro kneeling before a medallion of Pope John XXIII is an obvious recent addition), but the place is crumbling away and there is no move afoot to stop the rot.

Wander through Piazzetta Garibaldi, the

CALABRIA

picturesque old centre of Pizzo overlooking the water, before settling in at **Bar Ercole** for an ice-cream fix. For a typical seafood meal **La Nave**, in a rusting boat on the waterfront, has good main courses from L20,000.

Paola

The 80km coast between Pizzo and Paola is mostly overdeveloped and ugly. Paola is the main train hub for Cosenza, about 25km inland and is a large, comparatively nondescript place. Watched over by a crumbling castle, its main attraction is the **Santuario di San Francesco di Paola**. The saint, who lived and died in Paola in the 15th century, was known as a miracle-worker in his lifetime and the sanctuary he and his followers carved out of the bare rock has for centuries been the object of pilgrimage. You can wander through the spartan chambers but there is precious little to see and a church and monastery has been erected over them. A chapel in the church contains a reliquary of the saint. The sanctuary is open from 6 am to 12.30 pm and 2 to 5.30 pm.

There are several hotels near the station but it might be preferable to stay in towns farther north along the coast.

Diamante to Praia a Mare

Diamante and Cirella mark the southern end of a largely uninterrupted stretch of wide, grey pebbly beach that continues for about 30km to Praia a Mare, just short of Calabria's regional boundary with Basilicata. Although popular with the locals, it is for the most part uninspiring. Backed by rows of camp sites and growing development projects, the coast lacks much of the scenic splendour to the north in Basilicata or indeed south towards Reggio di Calabria.

Il Fortino (☎ 0985 8 60 85, Via Vittorio Veneto), in Cirella, is one of several camp sites along the coast.

If you do find the coast a little flat, head for Scalea and the hills. The old centre of **Scalea**, about 15km south of Praia, is one of the more eye-catching towns along the northern coast. Climb the stairway lanes past the muddle of tumbledown houses or stop in Piazza de Palma for a beer at the Tarì Bar.

Back in the anonymous modern urbanscape below, you could stay at the **Camping la Pantera Rosa** (☎ 0985 2 15 46, Corso Mediterraneo). In August it costs L12,000/10,000 per person/site, but the price drops on either side of this high season. There are also bungalows for up to eight people available for weekly rent.

Praia a Mare

A couple of kilometres short of the border with Basilicata, Praia a Mare is a modern and not terribly appealing town built to serve Italian holiday-makers. At least the surrounding landscape takes a more dramatic tone here, with the S18 coastal highway climbing away behind the town up into Basilicata. The **Isola di Dino**, just off the coast south of the town, is blessed with an easily accessible **grotto** every bit as impressive as Capri's better known Grotta Azzurra and the grey beach is expansive.

If you plan to stay in Praia, your best bet is the tourist village **La Mantinera** (☎ 0985 77 90 23, fax 0985 77 90 09, email mantiner@labnet.it) at the southern end of town in the Fiuzzi area. Full board in high season runs from L105,000 to L160,000. However, you might be better off in Maratea, across the regional frontier in Basilicata (see Maratea in the earlier Tyrrhenian Coast section).

Autolinee Preite operates five or six buses a day in each direction between Cosenza and Praia a Mare. SITA goes north to Maratea.

Aieta & Tortora

The hill villages of **Aieta** and **Tortora**, about 12km and 6km inland from Praia, belong to another world. Infrequent local buses serve both villages, but this is really only a practical excursion for people with their own transport or a lot of time and patience. The towns are precariously perched upon ridges that must have been hard going before asphalt days. Aieta is higher up than Tortora and the journey constitutes much of the reward for going there. When you arrive, walk up to the 16th century Palazzo Spinello at the end of the road and take a look into the ravine behind it.

Sicilia (Sicily)

Think of Sicilia and two things come to mind: beaches and the Mafia. There is no doubt its beaches are beautiful and that organised crime has a powerful impact on Sicilian society. But the island is too diverse to be so easily summed up. It is a place of contrasts, from the crumbling grandeur of the capital, Palermo, to the upmarket glitz of the tourist resort, Taormina. There are Greek ruins at Siracusa, Agrigento, Selinunte and Segesta, and the volcanic Isole Eolie (Aeolian Islands) off Sicilia's northern coast have a wild beauty matched only by the spectacular Mt Etna on the island's eastern coast.

Sicilia is the largest island in the Mar Mediterraneo and its strategic location made it a prize for successive waves of invaders. As well as Greek temples, there are Roman ruins, Norman churches and castles, Arab and Byzantine domes and splendid baroque churches and *palazzi* (mansions).

History

It is believed the earliest settlers were the Sicanians, Elymians and Siculians, who came from various points around the southern Mediterranean; they were followed by the Phoenicians. Greek colonisation began in the 8th century BC with the foundation of Naxos. The cities of Siracusa, Catania, Messina and Agrigento grew and still dominate the island. By 210 BC, Sicilia was under Roman control, with power eventually passing to the Byzantines and then to the Arabs, who had settled in by 903 AD.

Norman conquest of the island began in 1060, when Roger I of Hauteville captured Messina. Mastery of Sicilia subsequently passed to the Swabians and the Holy Roman Emperor Frederick II, known as Stupor Mundi (Wonder of the World). In the 13th century, the French Angevins provided a period of misrule that ended with the revolt known as the Sicilian Vespers in 1282. The island was ceded to the Spanish Aragon family and, in 1503, to the Spanish crown. After

Highlights

- Take in the view of Mt Etna from the Teatro Greco in Taormina

- Visit the Parco Archeologico in Siracusa, the ancient Greek city that once rivalled Athens

- Wander through the remains of Greek temples in the Valle dei Templi near Agrigento

- Marvel at the mosaics of the Cappella Palatino and those of the gorgeous cattedrale of Monreale

- Make the journey to Piazza Armerina to see the fabulous floor mosaics at the Villa Romana del Casale

- Admire the patchwork landscape of Sicilia's interior from the ramparts of the Norman Castello di Venere at Erice

- Climb Stromboli at night (with a guide, of course)

- Visit the Isole Egadi during the *mattanza*, the traditional annual tuna catch

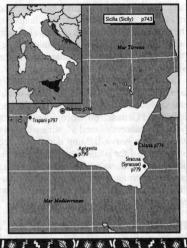

TAMSIN WILSON

Garibaldi won the imagination of Italians striving for independence.

short periods of Savoy and Austrian rule in the 18th century, Sicilia again came under the control of the Spanish Bourbons of Napoli in 1734, who united the island with southern Italy in the Kingdom of the Two Sicilies.

On 11 May 1860, Giuseppe Garibaldi landed at Marsala with his One Thousand and began the conquest that eventually set the seal on the unification of Italy. Life did not greatly improve for the people and between 1871 and 1914 more than one million Sicilians emigrated, mainly to the USA.

In 1943, some 140,000 Allied troops under General Dwight Eisenhower landed on southeastern Sicilia. Initially blocked by dogged Italian and German resistance, Eisenhower's field commanders entered Messina within six weeks, after heavy fighting had devastated many parts of the island. The Allied occupation lasted until early 1944. In 1948 Sicilia became a semi-autonomous region and, unlike other such regions in Italy, it has its own parliament and legislative powers.

The Mafia

The overt presence of the Italian army in Sicilia (you'll see armed soldiers at 'strategic' spots here and there) has done little to dent the Mafia's activities. However, since the arrest of the Sicilian 'godfather' Salvatore ('Toto') Riina in 1993 and his successor, Giovanni 'The Pig' Brusca, in 1996, Mafia *pentiti* (grasses, or turncoats) have continued to blow the whistle on fellow felons, politicians, businessmen and others, right up to former prime minister Giulio Andreotti. At two separate trials in 1997 Andreotti stood accused of supporting the Sicilian Mafia, helping fix court cases and ordering, or consenting to, the murder of an investigative journalist. In 1999 Andreotti was cleared of both charges. Some fear the pentiti are inventing confessions to settle private scores, but there must be something in it, otherwise the Cosa Nostra, as the Sicilian Mafia is known, would not be 'discouraging' pentiti by bumping off their relatives. Tommaso Buscetta, the most famous pentito of them all, has lost at least 33 relatives, his wife and three sons included. There were more than 1000 pentiti in 1997, waiting to give evidence in return for immunity or leniency and protection. However, evidence has surfaced that some pentiti have been continuing their criminal activities while under state protection – which has thrown the witness protection programme into confusion. The Italian author Luigi Barzini once wrote: 'The phenomenon has deep roots in history, in the character of the Sicilians, in local habits. Its origins disappear down the dim vistas of the centuries.'

Sicilians feel offended that the image abroad of their proud island is one portrayed in blood. There is no need to fear that you will be caught in the crossfire of a gang war while on Sicilia. The 'men of honour' have little interest in foreign tourists. (See The Mafia in the Facts about Italy chapter.)

Orientation & Information

Although some industry has developed and tourism is a fast-growing sector, the island's economy is still largely agricultural and the people remain strongly connected to the land. Along the eastern coast especially, there is mile upon mile of citrus groves.

The coastal landscape ranges from rugged

and windswept shores to long stretches of sandy beach, while rolling hills, mountains and dry plateaus dominate the interior. The temperate climate brings mild weather in winter, but summer is relentlessly hot and the beaches swarm with holiday-makers. The best times to visit are spring and autumn, when it is warm enough for the beach but not too hot for sightseeing.

Sicilian food is spicy and sweet – no doubt part of the island's long contact with Arab colonisers. The focus along the coast is on seafood, notably swordfish, and fresh produce. Some say fruit and vegetables taste better on Sicilia. The cakes and pastries can be works of art, but are very sweet. Try the *cassata*, a rich cake filled with ricotta and candied fruits (there is also cassata ice cream); *cannoli*, tubes of pastry filled with cream, ricotta or chocolate; and *dolci di mandorle*, the many varieties of almond cakes and pastries.

Like the Spaniards, Sicilians have a penchant for marzipan, which they make just as well as their Iberian cousins. Then there is *granita*, a drink of crushed ice flavoured with lemon, strawberry or coffee, to name a few flavours – perfect on a hot Sicilian day.

Dangers & Annoyances

Sicilians are generally welcoming and sociable, but women might find the local men a little too friendly. Female tourists should take a hint from local women and avoid walking around at night alone in the bigger cities such as Palermo, Catania and Messina. Exercise caution elsewhere too.

You won't have to worry about confronting the Godfather but petty criminals abound, especially in the bigger centres. Pickpockets and motorcycle-mounted snatch thieves are the worst – the latter love handbags and small day-packs. If you have to

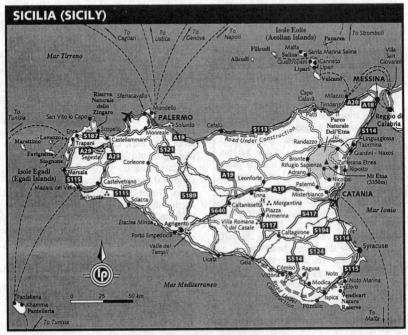

carry one of these items, keep a firm hold on it. Don't wear jewellery and keep all your valuables in a money belt or in your hotel.

Car theft is a problem in Palermo, so using private, guarded car parks is advisable.

Shopping

As in Spain and Portugal, the Arabs brought to Sicilia a rich tradition of ceramic production. Although the modern products are directed at tourists, as souvenirs go, they are evocative of the island. Simple designs with blues and yellows as base colours best reflect the ceramics' artisanal roots; more luridly decorated plates, vases, pots and bowls can be found all over the island. Or you could go for a ceramic *trinacria*, a face surrounded by three legs representing the three-pointed island. Major ceramics centres include Caltagirone and Santo Stefano di Camastra.

Since the 18th century, Sicilia's *carretti* (carts) have been a byword for the island. Used for transport until the arrival of the motorcar, the wooden carts were lovingly sculpted and bedecked with brightly coloured illustrations of mythic events, local characters or even family histories. You'd be lucky to see one in action now, but they are occasionally hauled out as tourist attractions. For the ultimate in memento kitsch, however, you could always buy one of the models on sale in virtually every souvenir shop.

Getting There & Away

Air Flights from all over mainland Italy and major European cities land at Palermo and Catania. Palermo's airport, renamed Falcone-Borsellino after the two anti-Mafia judges assassinated in the city in 1992, is at Punta Raisi, about 32km west of the city, while Catania's airport is 7km south. Buses run from both airports into the respective city centres. See the Palermo and Catania Getting There & Away and Getting Around sections for further details. To obtain information on flights to/from Sicilia, contact Sestante or Alitalia offices.

Bus Direct bus services from Roma to Sicilia are operated by two companies – SAIS Trasporti (☎ 091 617 11 41), Via Balsamo 20, Palermo, and Segesta (☎ 091 616 90 39), Via P Balsamo 26, Palermo. In Roma, the buses leave from Stazione Tiburtina.

The Segesta bus runs direct to Palermo and on to Trapani (two hours from Palermo) leaving Roma at 9.30 pm daily (L65,000 one way). The SAIS bus runs between Roma (leaves 8 pm daily) and Messina (arrives 4.30 am), Catania (arrives 6.15 am) and Agrigento (arrives 9.30 am). In Catania the bus connects with others to Palermo (L75,000 one way), Siracusa, Ragusa and Enna. Going the other way, the bus leaves Agrigento at 5 pm daily and Messina at 9.30 pm daily, arriving in Roma at 6.30 am. One-way tickets from Roma to Catania cost L75,000.

In Roma, inquire at Agenzia Viaggi Eurojet (☎ 06 474 28 01), Piazza della Repubblica 54, or go to Biglietteria Piccarrozzi, Via Guido Mazzoni 12, near the bus station at Piazzale Tiburtina. Booking is obligatory. See Palermo and Roma Getting There & Away sections for more details.

Gelato

It is difficult to get a bad gelato in Italy. Instead, the challenge is to find the best! It is not surprising that many travellers to Italy become obsessed with the country's ice cream. It really is so good and comes in so many flavours that it seems a shame not to eat at least two or three a day. Serious gelato eaters should search out the *gelaterie* that make their ice cream on the premises, particularly the few establishments that actually make their gelato from scratch using fresh ingredients (many places use industrial powdered flavours these days). You only need to try one of the fruit flavours to be able to tell the difference.

Most Italians would agree that the best gelato in the country is found on Sicilia and if you locate a good gelateria, you will realise that you have probably never before eaten a gelato *that* good!

Train Direct trains run from Milano, Firenze, Roma, Napoli and Reggio di Calabria to Messina and on to Palermo, Catania and other provincial capitals – the trains are transported from the mainland by ferry from Villa San Giovanni. Be prepared for long delays on Intercity trains on this route.

Boat Regular car/passenger ferries cross the strait between Villa San Giovanni (Calabria) and Messina. Hydrofoils run by the railways and snappier jobs run by SNAV connect Messina directly with Reggio di Calabria. See the Messina and Reggio di Calabria (Calabria) sections for details.

Sicilia is also accessible by ferry from Genova, Livorno, Napoli and Cagliari, and from Malta and Tunisia. The main company servicing the Mediterranean is Tirrenia and its services to/from Sicilia include Palermo-Cagliari, Palermo-Napoli, Trapani-Cagliari and Trapani-Tunisia.

Grandi Navi Veloci by Grimaldi runs more upmarket and luxury ferries from Livorno (three a week) and Genova (daily) to Palermo.

Ustica Lines runs summer ferries from Trapani to Napoli via Ustica and from Trapani to Pantelleria.

SNAV (☎ 081 761 23 48) runs a summer ferry from Palermo to Napoli (four hours). See the Palermo Getting There & Away section for details.

Ferry prices are determined by the season and jump considerably in summer (Tirrenia's high season varies according to destination, but is generally from July to September). Timetables can change dramatically each year. Tirrenia publishes an annual booklet listing all routes and prices, which is available at Tirrenia offices and agencies.

In summer, all routes are busy and, unless you book in advance, you may literally miss the boat. Tickets can be booked through the company concerned or travel agencies throughout Italy. Offices and telephone numbers for the ferry companies are listed in the Getting There & Away sections for the relevant cities.

The following is a guide to fares, based

on high-season travel at the time of writing. For an airline-type seat, fares were: Genova-Palermo on Grandi Navi Veloci L180,000 (20 hours), Napoli-Palermo on Tirrenia L70,600 (11 hours), Palermo-Cagliari on Tirrenia L66,500 (14 hours) and Trapani-Tunisia on Tirrenia L92,000 (11 hours). For a 2nd class cabin (shared with up to three other people and often segregated by gender), fares were: Genova-Palermo on Grandi Navi Veloci L206,000, Napoli-Palermo on Tirrenia L90,500, Palermo-Cagliari on Tirrenia L90,500 and Trapani-Tunisia on Tirrenia L116,000.

Fares for cars vary according to the size of the vehicle. High-season charges for the Palermo-Cagliari route ranged from L140,500 to L170,500; motorcycles under 200cc cost L40,000 (L60,000 for 200cc and above) and bicycles, surf boards and canoes cost L18,000.

There are also ferry and hydrofoil services, mainly operated by Siremar (☎ 091 690 25 55), from Sicilia to the small groups of islands off the coast (Isole Eolie, Isole Egadi, Isole Pelagie, Pantelleria and Ustica). See the relevant Getting There & Away sections in this chapter for details.

Getting Around

Bus The best mode of public transport on Sicilia is the bus. Numerous companies run services connecting the main towns around the coast including Messina, Catania, Siracusa, Agrigento, Trapani and Palermo. Services also connect these cities with the smaller towns along the coast and in the interior. The companies with the most extensive networks are SAIS and AST. See the Getting There & Away and Getting Around sections for each town.

Train The coastal train service between Messina and Palermo and between Messina and Siracusa is efficient and the run between Palermo and Agrigento is also generally OK. However, train services to elsewhere in the interior can be infrequent and slow, and it is best to do some research before deciding between train and bus. The service from Noto to Ragusa, for instance, is picturesque but very slow.

Car & Motorcycle There is no substitute for the freedom your own vehicle can give you, especially for getting to places not well served by public transport. Roads are generally good and autostrade connect most major cities. It is possible to hitchhike on Sicilia, but don't expect a ride in a hurry. Single women should not hitchhike under any circumstances.

Palermo

postcode 91100 • pop 730,000

At one time an Arab emirate and seat of a Norman kingdom, and in its heyday regarded as the grandest city in Europe, Palermo today is in a remarkable state of decay. It was heavily bombed in WWII and has been much neglected since. It is noted more for the Mafia trials of the 1980s, the assassinations in 1992 of Giovanni Falcone and Paolo Borsellino,

the top anti-Mafia judges, and the upsurge in gangland killings in the mid-1990s.

Beneath the grime enough evidence of its golden days remains for Palermo to be a compelling city to visit, if only as a crossroads between east and west. Cultural cross-fertilisation finds expression in the city's architectural mix, obvious in such monuments as the adjacent churches of La Martorana and San Cataldo.

Palermo's superb position by the sea at the foot of Monte Pellegrino, with the fertile Conca d'Oro valley behind it, has long made it a rich prize for Sicilia's colonisers. Around the 8th century BC the Phoenicians established the town of Ziz here, on the site of a prehistoric village. It remained a relatively minor town under Roman, and later

Byzantine, domination and it was not until 831 AD, when it was conquered by the Arabs, that the city truly flourished and became a jewel of the Islamic world.

When the Normans took control in 1072, things only improved. The seat of the kingdom of Roger I of Hauteville, Palermo was hailed as one of the most magnificent and cultured cities of 12th century Europe. After Roger's death the monarchy foundered, eventually passing to the German Hohenstaufens and the Holy Roman Emperor Frederick II, still remembered as one of Sicilia's most enlightened rulers. After his death, Palermo and all of Sicilia passed to the French Anjou family, themselves later deposed following the Sicilian Vespers revolt in 1282, which started in Palermo. By

PALERMO

PLACES TO STAY
8 Hotel Principe di Belmonte
15 Grand Hotel Le Palme
16 Hotel Petit
20 Hotel Libertà; Hotel Elite; Hotel Boston-Madonia
21 Hotel Tonic
35 Hotel Moderno
46 Grande Albergo Sole
48 Centrale Palace Hotel
57 Albergo da Luigi
58 Hotel Confort
68 Albergo Corona
70 Hotel Sicilia
71 Albergo Piccadilly; Albergo Concordia
72 Albergo Rosalia Conca d'Oro
73 Albergo Orientale
74 Pensione Vittoria

PLACES TO EAT
3 Roney
5 Osteria lo Bianco
7 Hostaria Al-Duar
22 Hostaria la Sella
25 Charleston
27 Dal Pompiere
33 I Grilli
37 Trattoria Shanghai; Vucciria Market
38 Casa del Brodo
39 La Cambusa
41 Trattoria Il Crudo e Il Cotto

44 Antica Focacceria di San Francesco
59 Hostaria da Ciccio
64 Trattoria dai Vespri
65 Trattoria Stella

OTHER
1 CTS Travel Agency
2 CIT Travel Agency
4 Teatro Politeama Garibaldi
6 Pietro Barbaro (SNAV Agents)
9 American Express
10 Stazione Marittima; Molo Vittorio Veneto
11 Tirrenia
12 Siremar
13 Grandi Traghetti & Grimaldi
14 Tunisian Consulate
17 APT Tourist Office
18 Monte dei Paschi di Siena (Bank)
19 Record Viaggi Travel Agency
23 British Consulate
24 Telecom Office
26 Teatro Massimo
28 Feltrinelli Bookshop
29 Opera dei Pupi
30 Museo Archeologico Regionale
31 Post Office
32 Banca Nazionale del Lavoro
34 Chiesa di San Domenico

36 Teatro Biondo
40 Palazzo Chiaramonte-Steri
42 Chiesa di San Francesco d'Assisi
43 Oratorio di San Lorenzo
45 Chiesa di San Matteo
47 Quattro Canti
49 Duomo
50 Porta Nuova
51 Palazzo dei Normanni; Cappella Palatina
52 Chiesa di San Giovanni degli Eremiti
53 AST Bus Station
54 Questura (Police Station)
55 Chiesa di San Giuseppe dei Teatini
56 Fontana Pretoria
60 Chiesa di Santa Caterina
61 Palazzo del Municipio
62 Chiesa di San Cataldo
63 La Martorana
66 Lo Spasimo
67 La Magione (Chiesa della SS Trinità)
69 Chiesa del Gesù
75 Night Pharmacy
76 Telecom Office
77 Urban Bus Station
78 Stazione Centrale
79 Intercity Bus Station
80 APT Tourist Office
81 Ospedale Civico (Hospital)

then eclipsed by Napoli, Palermo sank into a long, slow decline.

Orientation

Palermo is a large but manageable city. The main streets of the historical centre are Via Roma and Via Maqueda, which extend from Stazione Centrale in the south to Piazza Castelnuovo, a vast square in the northern, modern part of town and a 20 minute walk from the train station. Around Stazione Centrale are most of the cheaper *pensioni* and hotels. It's a grimy and chaotic area, but behind the decaying *palazzi* lining the main streets is a fascinating maze of narrow lanes and tiny piazze where you will find markets and *trattorie* and, unfortunately, get an even better idea of just how decrepit Palermo is.

The area around Piazza Castelnuovo seems a world away, with its malls, outdoor cafés and designer shops. Intersecting Via Maqueda and Via Roma are Corso Vittorio Emanuele and Via Cavour, the main thoroughfares to the port and Stazione Marittima (about a 10 minute walk east of Via Roma).

Information

Tourist Offices The main APT office (☎ 091 58 61 22, 091 58 38 47) is at Piazza Castelnuovo 35. The staff speak English and you can pick up a map of the city and a monthly calendar of cultural, theatrical and musical events. Ask for the *Palermo Flash Guide* booklet. The office is open from 8.30 am to 2 pm and from 2.30 to 6 pm Monday to Friday and to 2 pm on Saturday. There is a branch office at Stazione Centrale (☎ 091 616 59 14), open the same times as the main office, and another at the Falcone-Borsellino airport (☎ 091 59 16 98), open from 8 am to 10 pm daily.

Money The currency exchange booth at Stazione Centrale is open from 8 am to 8 pm daily, and there's another at the airport (Banca di Sicilia). Banks are generally open from 8.30 am to 1.15 pm. Several have ATMs, including Banca Nazionale del Lavoro, Via Roma 297, and Monte dei Paschi di Siena, off Via Sant'Oliva. American Express

(Amex) is represented by Ruggieri & Figli (☎ 091 58 71 44), Via Emerico Amari 40.

Post & Communications The main post office is at Via Roma 322. It is open from 8.30 am to 7 pm (to 1.30 pm on Saturday) and has fax and telex services.

There is a Telecom office virtually opposite Stazione Centrale on Piazza G Cesare. It is open from 8 am to 9.30 pm daily. Another Telecom office is on Piazzale Ungheria.

Travel Agencies Sestante CIT (☎ 091 58 63 33), where you can book train, ferry and air tickets, is at Via della Libertà 12. There is a CTS travel agency (☎ 091 611 07 13) at Via N Garzilli 28/G. A bit more convenient is Record Viaggi (☎ 091 611 09 10), Via Mariano Stabile 168 (between Via Ruggero Scttimo and Via Roma).

Bookshops & Newsstands Feltrinelli (☎ 091 58 77 85), Via Maqueda 399, has a foreign-language section that includes English. Several stands around Piazza Giuseppe Verdi sell foreign newspapers.

Medical Services & Emergency The Ospedale Civico (public hospital; ☎ 091 666 22 07) is on Via Carmelo Lazzaro or ring for an ambulance on ☎ 091 30 66 44. There is an all-night pharmacy, Lo Cascio (☎ 091 616 21 17), at Via Roma 1 near Stazione Centrale.

The questura (police station; ☎ 091 21 01 11) is on Piazza della Vittoria.

Dangers & Annoyances Despite a strong police presence in Palermo's historic centre, petty crime continues to be a major problem. Avoid wearing jewellery or carrying a bag, and keep your valuables in a money belt. The risk of being robbed is particularly high in the area from the Vucciria market towards the port. Women should not walk alone in the historic centre at night and all travellers would be best to avoid the area between Via Roma and the port at night. Watch out for pickpockets and bag snatchers around the main intercity bus station on Via Balsamo and in the city's side streets.

Quattro Canti

The busy intersection of Corso Vittorio Emanuele and Via Maqueda marks the Quattro Canti (the 'Four Corners' of Palermo), the centre of the oldest part of town. A 17th century Spanish baroque façade decorated with a fountain and a statue is on each corner. On the south-western corner is the baroque **Chiesa di San Giuseppe dei Teatini**, its interior bursting with marble.

Piazza Pretoria

This piazza hosts the eye-catching **Fontana Pretoria**, created by Florentine sculptors in the 16th century. At the time of its unveiling, the shocked populace named it the Fountain of Shame because of its nude figures. Take time to study the numerous figures that decorate its every corner. Closing off the eastern side of the piazza is the baroque **Chiesa di Santa Caterina**, while the **Palazzo del Municipio**, also known as the Palazzo delle Aquile because of the eagle sculptures that guard each corner of the roof, fronts the southern side of the square.

Chiesa di San Matteo

On the northern side of Corso Vittorio Emanuele, just before it crosses Via Roma, this baroque church has a richly decorated interior. The four statues in the pilasters of the dome represent the Virtues and were carved by Giacomo Serpotta in 1728.

La Martorana

This is one of Palermo's most famous churches and is on Piazza Bellini, a few steps south of Piazza Pretoria. It is also known as Chiesa di Santa Maria dell'Ammiraglio. Although the original 12th century structure has been much altered, it retains its Arab-Norman bell tower and the interior is richly decorated with Byzantine mosaics. Totally in keeping with the decoration, the Greek eastern rite Mass is still celebrated here. Try to time your visit to avoid the many weddings celebrated in the church. It is open from 8.30 am to 1 pm and 3.30 to 5.30 pm Monday to Saturday and from 8 am to 1 pm on Sunday and public holidays. Admission is free.

Chiesa di San Cataldo

Next to La Martorana is this tiny, simple church dating from the period of the Norman domination of Sicilia. Its battlements and red domes are another fusion of Arab and Norman styles. You'll need to get the key from the custodian who sits at a small table to the right as you enter La Martorana. Opening times are the same as for La Martorana and admission is free.

Duomo

Despite its hotchpotch of styles, Palermo's duomo, west of the Quattro Canti along Corso Vittorio Emanuele, is certainly grand.

Built in the late 12th century, the duomo has been modified many times since, most disastrously in the 18th century when the dome was added, spoiling the architectural harmony of the building. In the same period the interior was restored. Although the only part conserved in purely original Norman style is the apse, the church remains an impressive example of Norman architecture. Arab influences in some of the geometric decoration are unmistakable and the graceful Gothic towers distract the eye from that dome. Inside are royal tombs, and among those interred in porphyry sarcophagi are Roger II, Henry VI of Hohenstaufen, Constance de Hauteville and Frederick II of Hohenstaufen. The ashes of Santa Rosalia, patron saint of Palermo, are contained in a silver urn in one of the church's numerous chapels. The duomo is open from 7 am to 7 pm Monday to Saturday and from 8 am to 1.30 pm and 4 to 7 pm on Sunday and public holidays. Admission to the treasury is L1000.

Palazzo dei Normanni

Across Piazza della Vittoria and the gardens is the Palazzo dei Normanni, also known as the Palazzo Reale (Royal Palace). Built by the Arabs in the 9th century, it was extended by the Normans and restructured by the Hohenstaufens. It is now the seat of Sicilia's regional government.

Enter from Piazza dell'Indipendenza to see the **Cappella Palatina**, a magnificent example of Arab-Norman artistic genius, built during the reign of Roger II and decorated with Byzantine mosaics. The chapel was once described as 'the finest religious jewel dreamt of by human thought', its mosaics rivalled only by those of Ravenna and Istanbul. While the mosaics demonstrate the Byzantine influence on Palermitan art, the geometric tile designs are a clear reminder of Arab input. The carved wooden ceiling is a classic example of intricate, Arab-style stalactite design. The chapel is open from 9 am to 12.30 pm and 3 to 5 pm Monday to Friday and in the morning only on Saturday. It is open from noon to 1 pm on Sunday, but overrun by tour groups, so it's better to visit on another day, if possible. Admission is free.

The **Sala di Ruggero** (King Roger's Room), the former king's bedroom, is also worth visiting, only possible with a guide (free of charge), as it is decorated with 12th century mosaics. Go upstairs from the Cappella Palatina. There are guided tours of the palazzo itself, but you'll need to book with Mrs Zichichi a few days in advance by faxing 091 705 47 37. However, preference is given to groups and school trips – lone travellers can have difficulty booking, especially when the regional assembly is in session.

Next to the palazzo is the **Porta Nuova**, built to celebrate the arrival of Charles V in Palermo in 1535.

Chiesa di San Giovanni degli Eremiti

South of the palazzo, this church is a simple and tranquil refuge from the chaos outside. On Via dei Benedettini, St John of the Hermits is another example of the Sicilian Arab-Norman architectural mix. Built under Roger II, it is topped by five red domes and set in a pretty, atmospheric garden with cloisters. The bare interior of the now deconsecrated church features some badly deteriorated frescoes. It opens from 9 am to 1 pm and 3 to 7 pm Monday to Saturday and to 12.30 pm on Sunday and public holidays. Admission costs L4000.

Museo Archeologico & Around

A block north of the main post office on Via Roma is the **Museo Archeologico Regionale**.

To enter, turn left onto Via Bara all'Olivella and onto Piazza Olivella. The museum holds a collection of Greek metopes from Selinunte, the Hellenistic *Bronze Ram of Siracusa* and finds from archaeological sites throughout the island. Although there is not a lot to see apart from the metopes, the museum is definitely worth a visit. It is open from 9 am to 1.50 pm Monday to Saturday (also from 3 to 6.30 pm on Tuesday and Friday) and to 12.30 pm on Sunday and public holidays.

About 200m south on Via Roma is the **Chiesa di San Domenico**. The grand 17th century structure houses the tombs of many important Sicilians and a wealth of paintings.

Towards Piazza Marina

Plunge into the streets heading towards the waterfront from the intersection of Via Vittorio Emanuele and Via Roma and you'll find a few more architectural gems. The **Oratorio di San Lorenzo**, Via dell'Immacolatella, is decorated with stuccoes by Giacomo Serpotta (his greatest work). Caravaggio's last known piece, a Nativity, once hung over the altar. It was stolen in 1969 and has never been recovered. Virtually next door, the 13th century **Chiesa di San Francesco d'Assisi** features a fine rose window and Gothic portal that have survived numerous restorations and restructuring.

Palazzo Chiaramonte-Steri

This imposing 14th century palazzo on Piazza Marina boasts an imposing façade that served as a model for many other buildings on Sicilia. The island's Grand Parliament sat here in the 16th century and, for many years, so did the Holy Office of the Inquisition. The palazzo is open during exhibitions and other such events; otherwise call ☎ 091 33 41 39 to arrange a visit.

Lo Spasimo

South of Piazza Marina, across Via Alloro, this complex of buildings includes the **Chiesa di Santa Maria dello Spasimo**, a typical example of the late-Gothic style, although it was actually built during the Renaissance. Building work on the church extended as far as the walls and the soaring apse, but it has stood for centuries without a roof and its interior is host to a couple of tall *Ailanthus altissima* trees. Restored and opened to the public in 1995, the complex is an atmospheric venue for concerts, performances and exhibitions. It is open from 8 am to midnight daily and admission is free.

Across a vast piazza from Lo Spasimo is the **Chiesa della SS Trinità**, also known as La Magione, a fine Norman church, dating from 1193. It is open from 8 to 11.30 am and 3 to 6.30 pm Monday to Saturday and from 8 am to 1 pm on Sunday.

Catacombe dei Cappuccini

For centuries, Sicilians of a certain social standing who didn't want to be forgotten on their death were embalmed by Capuchin monks. The catacombs in the Capuchin convent on Piazza Cappuccino, west of the city centre, contain the mummified bodies and skeletons of some 8000 Palermitans who died between the 17th and 19th centuries. Although time has been unkind to most (some are just skeletons with suits on), a few are remarkably intact. Rosalia Lombardi, who died at the age of two in 1920, has auburn hair tied in a yellow bow, and looks as though she could be sleeping – even if she is rather pallid. The catacombs are open from 9 am to noon and 3.30 to 5.30 pm daily. You'll be required to make a donation on entry – L2000/3000 is acceptable.

La Zisa

In the same area is this 12th century Arab-Norman castle. The name, which means 'the Splendid', testifies to its magnificence. It was built for William I and completed by William II, and is open from 9 am to 1 pm and 3 to 6.30 pm Monday to Saturday and to 12.30 pm on Sunday and holidays. Admission costs L4000.

La Cuba

Built in 1180, this castle was once part of an enormous park planned by William II, which also incorporated La Zisa. La Cuba has long been engulfed by an army barracks

on Corso Calatafimi, but you can visit it daily from 9 am to 1 pm and 3 to 4.30 pm (closed Sunday afternoon). Admission costs L4000.

Teatro Massimo

Overlooking Piazza Giuseppe Verdi, the proud and haughty 19th century theatre finally reopened in 1997 following a 20 year restoration programme. You can visit the teatro from 8.30 am to 12.30 pm and 4 to 8 pm Monday to Saturday, although if rehearsals are under way entry can be disallowed.

Markets

Palermo's historical ties with the Arab world and its proximity to North Africa are reflected in the noisy street life of the city's ancient centre and nowhere is this more evident than in its markets.

Several markets are spread through the tangle of lanes and alleys of central Palermo. The most famous is the **Vucciria**, winding south from the Chiesa di San Domenico. Here you can purchase anything your taste buds desire (and several items they may recoil at – slippery tripe and all sorts of fishy things) as well as a host of off-the-back-of-a-truck-style bargains. This is another place where it is a bad idea to carry bags or purses: keep your money in a money belt.

Places to Stay

You should have little trouble finding a room in Palermo at whatever price you choose. Staff at the tourist office will make recommendations, but not bookings.

Head for Via Maqueda or Via Roma, between Stazione Centrale and Quattro Canti, for the bulk of the cheap rooms, some of which are in old apartment buildings. Rooms facing onto either street will be noisy. Women on their own should be wary about staying in the area near Stazione Centrale. Prostitutes from time to time bring clients to the cheaper hotels, though as a rule this is not really a problem. The area around Piazza Castelnuovo offers a higher standard of accommodation with fewer budget options (catch bus No 101 or 107 from Stazione Centrale to Piazza Sturzo).

Places to Stay – Budget

Camping The best camp site is *Trinacria* (☎ 091 53 05 90, Via Barcarello 25), by the sea at Sferracavallo. It charges L9000/9500/5000 per person/site/car. Catch bus No 616 from Piazza A de Gasperi (which can be got to by bus No 101 from Stazione Centrale).

Hotels Near Stazione Centrale, try *Albergo Orientale* (☎ 091 616 57 27, Via Maqueda 26), in an old and somewhat decayed building with a once grand courtyard. Basic singles/doubles/triples cost L35,000/60,000/90,000. Just round the corner is *Albergo Rosalia Conca d'Oro* (☎ 091 616 45 43, Via Santa Rosalia 7), with ancient but clean singles/doubles for L40,000/60,000 and triples for L90,000. *Pensione Vittoria* (☎ 091 616 24 37, Via Maqueda 8) is close to the station and has still more spartan singles/doubles for L35,000/55,000 (no bath or shower).

There are a few hotels in one building at Via Roma 72. *Albergo Piccadilly* (☎ 091 617 03 76) has clean rooms (even if there are holes in the bedspreads). Singles cost L35,000 without bath and doubles cost L70,000 with bathroom. *Albergo Concordia* (☎ 091 617 15 14) is also reasonable value with singles/doubles at L30,000/50,000, while doubles with bathroom cost L60,000.

Albergo Corona (☎ 091 616 23 40, Via Roma 118) has clean, pleasant rooms for L35,000/50,000; a double with bathroom is L65,000. *Albergo da Luigi* (☎ 091 58 50 85, Corso Vittorio Emanuele 284), next to the Quattro Canti, has rooms for L30,000/50,000 without bath. Prices with bath start at L40,000/60,000 and depend on the room – ask for one with a view onto Piazza Pretoria and its fountain.

Hotel Sicilia (☎ 091 616 84 60, Via Divisi 99), on the corner of Via Maqueda, has large rooms of a reasonable standard, though they can be noisy. Singles/doubles/triples cost L50,000/75,000/100,000, all with bathroom.

Near Piazza Castelnuovo, *Hotel Petit* (☎ 091 32 36 16, Via Principe di Belmonte 84) has comfortable rooms. There is only one single (without bathroom) for L35,000. Doubles/triples with bathroom cost L65,000/L90,000.

Places to Stay – Mid-Range

Near Corso Vittorio Emanuele, *Hotel Confort* (☎ 091 33 17 41, Via Roma 188) is an agreeable and clean establishment. Rooms cost L38,000/60,000 or L50,000/80,000 with bathroom. Farther north, *Hotel Moderno* (☎ 091 58 86 83, Via Roma 276) has good rooms for L75,000/105,000 and triples with bathroom for L140,000.

Near Piazza Castelnuovo, *Albergo Libertà* (☎ 091 32 19 11, Via Mariano Stabile 136) is a good choice. It has singles/doubles for L50,000/80,000 or L80,000/100,000 with bathroom; triples with bathroom are L140,000. There are several other hotels in the same building. *Hotel Elite* (☎ 091 32 93 18) has singles/doubles for L80,000/110,000 and triples for L140,000, all with bathroom. *Hotel Boston-Madonia* (☎ 091 58 02 34) has doubles with bathroom for L98,000, or for about L70,000 for single occupancy. *Hotel Tonic* (☎ 091 58 17 54, Via Mariano Stabile 126) has decent singles/doubles with bathroom for L90,000/120,000.

Hotel Principe di Belmonte (☎ 091 33 10 65, Via Principe di Belmonte 25) has rooms for L50,000/80,000 or L70,000/94,000 with bathroom.

Places to Stay – Top End

Grande Albergo Sole (☎ 091 58 18 11, fax 091 611 01 82, Corso Vittorio Emanuele 291) has attractive rooms for L150,000/200,000.

The four star **Grand Hotel Le Palme** (☎ 091 58 39 33, fax 091 33 15 45, Via Roma 398), at the Piazza Castelnuovo end of town, is one of the ritziest hotels in Palermo. Its beautiful rooms cost L210,000/300,000, including breakfast.

The four star **Centrale Palace Hotel** (☎ 091 33 66 66, fax 091 33 48 81, Corso Vittorio Emanuele 327) has elegantly furnished rooms and full services; breakfast is included. Singles cost L230,000, doubles L350,000 and triples L435,000.

Places to Eat

With more than 300 officially listed restaurants and eateries to choose from in the city and surrounding area, you should have little trouble finding something to suit your taste and budget.

Palermo's cuisine takes advantage of the fresh produce of the sea and the fertile Conca d'Oro valley. One of its most famous dishes is the tasty *pasta con le sarde*, with sardines, fennel, peppers, capers and pine nuts. Swordfish is served here sliced into huge steaks. A reflection of Sicilia's proximity to North Africa is the presence of couscous on menus, basically a bowl of steamed semolina with a sauce.

Palermitans are late eaters and restaurants rarely open for dinner before 8 pm.

Places to Eat – Budget

Dal Pompiere (Via Bara all'Olivella 107), just up the road from the Opera dei Pupi puppet theatre, has a simple, but filling, set-menu lunch for L13,000. **Hostaria la Sella** (☎ 091 58 53 21, Via Cavour 97) also has a good lunch for L17,000.

If you want to try an age-old Palermitan snack – a *panino* with *milza* (veal innards) and ricotta cheese – head for **Antica Focacceria di San Francesco** (☎ 091 32 02 64, Via A Paternostro 58). It's one of the city's oldest eating houses and worth seeking out; it also serves pizza slices and similar snacks.

Another Palermitan institution is **Casa del Brodo** (☎ 091 32 16 55, Corso Vittorio Emanuele 175). For more than 100 years it has been serving up various broths and boiled meat dishes, all much appreciated by locals. A meal costs around L30,000. **Osteria lo Bianco** (☎ 091 58 58 16, Via Emerico Amari 104) has a menu that changes daily; a full meal will cost around L20,000. **Trattoria Stella** (☎ 091 616 11 36, Via Alloro 104) is in the courtyard of the old Hotel Patria, as it Palermitans used to call it. In summer, the entire courtyard is filled with tables. A full meal will come to around L40,000.

Trattoria dai Vespri (☎ 091 617 16 31, Piazza Santa Croce dei Vespri 8), off Via Roma, past Chiesa di Santa Anna, has excellent food and atmosphere for around L35,000 for a full meal. It has outside tables and meat and seafood are cooked on an outdoor barbecue in summer.

Hostaria da Ciccio (☎ 091 32 91 43, Via Firenze 6), just off Via Roma 178, is one of Palermo's best-loved cheaper eating places – and the food really is great. A meal will cost from around L30,000.

Trattoria Shanghai (☎ 091 58 97 02, Vico Mezzano 34), in the middle of the Vucciria market, is a very basic and less than clean little place with tables on an atmospheric terrace overlooking the busy market. Despite its Chinese name, the trattoria serves typical Sicilian food, which is reasonably priced but not the best you can eat in Palermo.

La Cambusa (☎ 091 58 45 74) and **Trattoria Il Crudo e Il Cotto** (☎ 091 616 92 61), both on Piazza Marina near the port, are popular and serve good meals for around L30,000. The former sometimes has a set, all-inclusive seafood menu for L35,000.

If you feel like a Tunisian night out, with couscous and other typical North African dishes, try **Hostaria Al-Duar** (Via Ammiraglio Gravina 31A), the first street south of Via E Amari. It has a L18,000 set menu.

Places to Eat – Mid-Range & Top End

Most of the posher restaurants are on the outskirts of Palermo or in nearby towns.

I Mandarini (☎ 091 671 21 99, *Via Rosario da Patanna 18*) is at Pallavicino, near Mondello beach. The food is good and a meal will cost at least L45,000. The locals head for Mondello to eat seafood.

Also try *La Barcaccia* (☎ 091 45 15 19, *Via Piano di Gallo 4*). Again, you will be lucky to eat for under L50,000. A popular but pricey fish restaurant at Sferracavallo is *Al Delfino* (☎ 091 53 02 82, *Via Torretta 80*). Don't expect much change from L100,000.

Charleston is one of Palermo's classiest restaurants. Its main establishment is in Palermo at Piazzale Ungheria 30 (☎ 091 32 13 66). In summer it generally closes and its Mondello branch takes over, with outdoor eating on Viale Regina Elena (☎ 091 45 01 71). Expect to pay around L100,000 per head for a memorable meal.

Cafés

On Via Principe di Belmonte (which is closed to traffic between Via Ruggero Settimo and Via Roma) there are numerous cafés with outdoor tables where you can linger over breakfast or lunch. If you want to spend less, buy a panino in one of the many bars along Via Roma. For an expensive afternoon tea, head for *Roney* (*Via della Libertà 13*), Palermo's most fashionable and best-known *pasticceria*. *I Grilli* (☎ 091 58 47 47, *Piazza Cavalieri di Malta 11*) is a popular cocktail bar (and restaurant) north-east of the Vucciria market.

Self-Catering

The *Vucciria market* is held daily except Sunday in the narrow streets between Via Roma, Piazza San Domenico and Corso Vittorio Emanuele. Here you can buy fresh fruit and vegetables, meat, cheese and seafood. Or you can just watch as huge, freshly caught swordfish and tuna are sliced up and sold in minutes. Numerous stalls sell steaming-hot boiled octopus. Although the best known, the Vucciria is far from the only such market around town. For other grocery supplies, try *Standa supermarket* (*Via della Libertà 30*).

Entertainment

Theatre For opera and ballet, the main venue is *Teatro Politeama Garibaldi* (☎ 091 605 32 49, *Piazza Ruggero Settimo*). *Teatro Massimo* (see earlier) has a summer programme. If your Italian is up to it, you can see plays at *Teatro Biondo* (☎ 091 743 43 41, *Via Roma*). The daily paper *Il Giornale di Sicilia* has a listing of what's on.

Opera dei Pupi At *Opera dei Pupi* (☎ 091 32 34 00, *Via Bara all'Olivella 95*), south of Via Cavour, puppet theatre is performed by the Cuticchio family. It is an enchanting experience and something of a Sicilian speciality. It's a good break for young kids, and the elaborate old puppets will endear themselves to adults too. You can generally expect shows to be staged at 5.30 pm at weekends. Tickets cost L10,000 (children L5000). At No 40, in the same street, is one of several artisans who makes and repairs the puppets.

Getting There & Away

Air Falcone-Borsellino airport is at Punta Raisi, 32km west of Palermo. For 24 hour information about domestic flights, call Alitalia on ☎ 147 86 56 41, and for international flights, call ☎ 147 86 56 42. Alitalia has an office (☎ 091 601 93 33) at Via della Libertà 39. It's usually possible at any time of year to hunt down charter flights to major European cities such as London – shop around.

Bus The main Intercity bus station is around Via Paolo Balsamo, to the east of the train station.

See the Getting There & Away section at the beginning of this chapter for details of Segesta and SAIS main services. In addition to those, SAIS Trasporti runs services twice a day to Cefalù. SAIS Autolinee (☎ 091 47 53 20) also services Catania (more than 15 a day), Enna (six a day), Piazza Armerina (four a day), Messina (via Catania, every two hours). Interbus runs to Siracusa (six a day). Between them for Marsala, go to Salemi (☎ 091 617 54 11), Via Rosario Gregorio 44. Cuffaro and Fratelli Camilleri have about 10 buses a day to Agrigento.

AST (☎ 091 680 00 11), away from the main terminal on the corner between Viale delle Scienze and Via Brasa 31, near Piazza dell'Indipendenza and the university, runs four daily buses to Ragusa. It also operates services to Corleone, Cefalù, Palazzo Adriano and Montelepre.

Numerous other companies service points throughout Sicilia and most have offices in the Via Paolo Balsamo area. Their addresses and telephone numbers, as well as destinations, are listed in *Palermo Flash Guide*, available at the APT office.

Train Regular trains leave from Stazione Centrale for Milazzo, Messina, Catania, Siracusa and Agrigento, as well as nearby towns such as Cefalù. There are also Intercity trains heading for Reggio di Calabria, Napoli and Roma. Train timetable information is available in English at the station. There is a Transalpino office inside the station, as well as luggage-storage and bathing facilities.

Car & Motorcycle Palermo is accessible by autostrada from Messina (only partially completed) and from Catania via Enna (this route is quicker). Trapani and Marsala are also easily accessible from Palermo by autostrada, while Agrigento and Palermo are linked by a good state road through the interior of the island.

Rental Europcar has offices at Stazione Centrale (☎ 091 616 50 50) and the airport (☎ 091 59 12 27). All major rental companies are represented in Palermo.

Boat Ferries leave from Molo Vittorio Veneto, off Via Francesco Crispi, for Cagliari (Sardegna), Napoli, Livorno and Genova (see the Getting There & Away section at the beginning of this chapter for further details). The Tirrenia office (☎ 147 89 90 00, 091 602 11 11) is at the port in Palazzina Stella Maris, Calata Marinai d'Italia. Siremar (☎ 091 690 25 55, 091 58 24 03) runs ferries and hydrofoils to Ustica; its office is at Via F Crispi 118. SNAV's main office is in Napoli (☎ 081 761 23 48). It is represented in Palermo by the Pietro Barbaro agency (☎ 091 33 33 33) at Via Principe di Belmonte 55. It runs a summer hydrofoil service to the Isole Eolie. It also operates a ferry service to Napoli, departing at 9 am and arriving at 1 pm daily (going the other way it leaves from Napoli at 5.30 pm) from April to October. Tickets cost L96,000 each way and L120,000 in July, August and September.

Grandi Navi Veloci (☎ 091 58 74 04), part of the Grimaldi Group at the port in Calata Marinai d'Italia, runs ferries from Palermo to Genova (daily) and Livorno (three a week). It also has a Web site at www.grimaldi.it.

The *deposito bagagli* (left luggage) at Stazione Marittima is open from 7 am to 8 pm daily.

Getting Around

To/From the Airport Taxis to the airport cost upwards of L70,000. The cheaper option is to catch one of the regular blue buses run by Prestìa e Comandè (☎ 091 58 04 57), which leave from outside Stazione Centrale, in front of Hotel Elena, roughly every hour from 5 am to around 10.45 pm. Buses run from the airport to Stazione Centrale from 7.30 am to 0.30 am (or until the arrival of the last flight). The timetable is posted at the bus stop outside Stazione Centrale, to your right as you leave the station. Buses also stop on Piazza Ruggero Settimo, in front of Teatro Politeama Garibaldi. The trip takes one hour and costs L6500.

Bus Palermo's city buses (AMAT) are efficient and regular, and most stop in front of Stazione Centrale. Tickets must be purchased before you get on the bus and are available from tobacconists or the booths at the terminal. They cost L1500 and are valid for one hour. A day pass is L5000. Useful routes are:

No 101
  From Stazione Centrale along Via Roma to Teatro Politeama, then past the Giardino Inglese to Piazza A de Gasperi, from where there are connecting buses to Mondello and Sferracavallo
No 105
  From under the trees diagonally left across the piazza from Stazione Centrale to Piazza

SICILIA

dell'Indipendenza, from where there are connecting buses to Monreale and the Convento dei Cappuccini
No 107

From Stazione Centrale along Via Roma to Teatro Politeama Garibaldi, near Piazza Castelnuovo, and on to the Giardino Inglese up Via della Libertà
No 124

From Teatro Politeama to the Castello della Zisa
No 139

From Stazione Centrale to the port
No 327

From Piazza dell'Indipendenza to the Convento dei Cappuccini
No 389

From Piazza dell'Indipendenza to Monreale
No 603

From Piazza A de Gasperi to Mondello (year-round)
No 614

From Piazza A de Gasperi to Mondello
No 628

From Piazza A de Gasperi to Sferracavallo-Isola delle Femmine
No 812

From near Teatro Politeama to Monte Pellegrino (at the time of writing the service had been temporarily suspended due to a landslide)
No 812

From Piazza Giuseppe Verdi to Monte Pellegrino (at the time of writing the service had been temporarily suspended due to a landslide)
No 833

From Piazza Don Sturzo to Mondello, along the coast (summer only)
No GT

From Piazza Giuseppe Verdi to Mondello (summer only)

Metropolitana Palermo's metro system won't be of much use to most people, as its 10 stations radiating out from Stazione Centrale are a good hike from any destinations of tourist interest. There is talk of expanding the system to Falcone-Borsellino airport, which would be useful. A single trip ticket is L1500.

Car & Motorcycle If you have dealt with Roma or Napoli in your own vehicle, Palermo will present no difficulties. Theft of and from vehicles is a problem, however, and you are advised to use one of the attended car parks around town if your hotel has no parking space. You'll be looking at

L15,000 to L20,000 for 24 hours. Some hotels have small car parks, but they are often full; check with your hotel proprietor.

AROUND PALERMO

There are beaches north-west of the city at Mondello and Sferracavallo, but if you're really into spending some time by the sea, you'd be better off heading farther afield, to Scopello, for example. **Mondello** is popular with Palermitans, who crowd the beachfront Viale Regina Elena for the evening stroll. There are numerous seafood restaurants and snack stalls along the avenue. For bus information, see the Palermo Getting Around section.

Between Palermo and Mondello is Monte Pellegrino and the **Santuario di Santa Rosalia**. Palermo's patron saint Santa Rosalia lived as a hermit in a cave on the mountain, now the site of a 17th century shrine. The water, which is channelled from the roof of the cave into a large font, is said to have miraculous powers. Whatever your beliefs, this is a fascinating place to visit, but remember that it is a shrine, not a tourist haunt. The sanctuary (☎ 091 54 03 26) is open from 7 am to 7 pm daily. See the Palermo Getting Around section for bus details. At the time of writing it was not possible to reach the sanctuary by road because of a landslide.

On the northern side of Monte Pellegrino, at Addaura, is the **Grotta dell'Addaura**, where several cave drawings from the Palaeolithic period have managed to survive. The cave is open to visitors from 9 am to noon on Friday and Saturday by prior arrangement through the Palermo *sovrintendenza* ☎ 091 696 12 92.

Monreale

An absolute must is a visit to the **cattedrale** at Monreale, about 8km south-west of Palermo and accessible by frequent city buses. See the Palermo Getting Around section earlier in this chapter.

The magnificent 12th century Norman cathedral was built for William II. It is said he did not want to be inferior to his grandfather, Roger, who was responsible for the duomo in Cefalù and the Cappella Palatino in Palermo. Considered the finest example of Norman architecture on Sicilia, the cathedral in fact incorporates Norman, Arab, Byzantine and classical elements and, despite renovations over the centuries, remains substantially intact. The central doorway has bronze doors by Bonanno Pisano and its northern door is by Barisano di Trani. The interior of the cathedral is almost entirely covered by dazzling gilded mosaics, the work of Byzantine artisans, representing the complete cycle of the Old and New Testaments. Over the altar is a towering mosaic of Jesus Christ.

Outside the cathedral is the entrance to the **cloisters**, which were part of a Benedictine abbey once attached to the church. There are 228 twin columns with polychrome ornamentation. Each of the Romanesque capitals is different, depicting plants, animals and fantastic motifs. The capital of the 19th column on the west aisle depicts William II offering the cathedral to the Madonna.

The cathedral (☎ 091 640 44 13) is open from 8 am to noon and 3.30 to 6 pm daily. The cloisters are open from 9 am to 1.30 pm Monday to Saturday (also 3 to 7 pm Monday, Tuesday and Thursday) and 9 am to 12.30 pm on Sunday. Admission costs L4000.

Solunto

About 17km east of Palermo are the remains of the Hellenistic-Roman town of Solunto (☎ 091 90 45 57). Although the ancient city is only partially excavated, what has been brought to light is well worth the trip. Founded in the 4th century BC on the site of an earlier Phoenician settlement, Solunto was built in a particularly panoramic position on Monte Catalfano, overlooking the sea. Wander along the main street and take detours up the steep, paved side streets to explore the ruined houses, some of which still sport their original mosaic floors. Take particular note of the teatro and the House of Leda (if you can find it), which has an interesting floor mosaic.

The site is open from 9 am to 6 pm Monday to Saturday and 9 am to 12.30 pm on Sunday. To get there, take the train from Palermo to the Santa Flavia-Solunto-Porticello

stop and ask for directions. It's about a half-hour uphill walk. Admission costs L4000.

Ustica

Almost 60km north of Palermo lies the lonely island of Ustica. In 1980, a passenger jet crashed near the island in mysterious circumstances, leaving 81 people dead. Investigators suspect the military was involved, and a dozen Italian airforce officers stand accused of a cover-up.

Ustica is otherwise a tranquil place with barely more than 1000 inhabitants, most living in the mural-bedecked village of the same name. The best months to come are June and September. To visit during August is sheer lunacy. Parts of the rocky coast have been declared a *riserva marina* (marine reserve) and the limpid waters, kept sparkling clean by an Atlantic current through the Straits of Gibraltar, are ideal for diving and underwater photography.

There is an information office (☎ 091 844 94 56) for the riserva marina on Piazza Umberto I, part of an interlocking series of squares in the centre of the village. It is open from 8 am to 1 pm and 4 to 6 pm Monday to Friday and from 8 am to 2 pm Saturday and Sunday (to 9 pm during summer). The staff can advise on activities – they have a list of the island's dive centres. For medical emergencies the Pronto Soccorso can be contacted on ☎ 091 844 92 48. For police, call the carabinieri on ☎ 091 844 90 49.

Activities Among the most rewarding dive sites are the Secca Colombara, to the north of the island, and the Scoglio del Medico, to the west. Note that Zone A of the riserva marina, taking in a good stretch of the western coast north of Punta dello Spalmatore, is protected. Fishing, diving and even swimming are forbidden in the area without permission. The riserva's information office can organise seawatch diving excursions into the zone. The only dive hire outlet, Ailara Rosalia (☎ 091 844 91 62), Banchina Barresi, operates in summer. Otherwise, bring your own gear.

You can also hire a boat and cruise around the island, visiting its many grottoes and tiny beaches. Hotel Ariston (☎ 091 844 90 42), Via della Vittoria 5, is one of several agencies where you can organise boat trips and diving (it also rents motorcycles) or you could try Scubaland (☎ 091 844 92 16), Via Petriera 7, to hire a boat or dinghy.

Places to Stay & Eat There are eight hotels and several *affittacamere* on Ustica. *Pensione Clelia (☎ 091 844 90 39, email clelia@telegest.it, Via Magazzino 7)* is a decent place with rooms for L55,000/105,000. In the high season, prices rocket to L89,000 per head for half board. It has a good little restaurant and the village centre has many others.

Getting There & Around From April to December there is at least one Siremar hydrofoil a day from Palermo. A car ferry runs daily year-round (in winter there is nothing on Sunday). One-way passenger fares are L30,000 (hydrofoil) and L16,500 (ferry) in the high season. The Siremar office (☎ 091 844 90 02) is on Piazza Capitano V di Bartolo, in the centre of Ustica. In summer you can also pick up the Trapani-Favignana-Ustica-Napoli hydrofoil, run by Ustica Lines three days a week. The journey from Napoli to Ustica takes four hours and costs L120,000 one way.

Orange minibuses run around the island from the village, or you can hire a moped at Hotel Ariston in town.

Northern Coast

PARCO DELLE MADONIE

This 40,000 hectare park, between Palermo and Cefalù, incorporates the Madonie mountain range and some of the highest mountains on Sicilia after Etna (the highest peak in the range is Pizzo Carbonara at 1979m). Instituted in 1989 by the Regione Sicilia, the park also takes in several small towns and villages and plenty of farms and vineyards. It is an inhabited area, rather than simply a nature reserve – so you can combine walking with visits to some of the more interesting towns in the park, such as Geraci Siculo and Petralia Soprana and Sottana. There are information offices of the Ente Parco delle Madonie (the body responsible for the park) in Petralia Sottana (☎ 0921 68 40 11) and Isnello (☎ 0921 66 27 95) with details about the park and several one-day walks, as well as information about transport and accommodation.

There are several *rifugi* in the park, including *Rifugio Ostello della Gioventù (☎ 0921 4 99 95)*, Piano della Battaglia, località Mandria Marcate. *Madonie (☎ 0921 64 11 06, Corso Paolo Agliata 81)*, at Petralia Sottana, is another option. If you're looking for something more characteristic, there are excellent agriturismo-style establishments in the area. *Tenuta Gangivecchio (☎ 0921 68 91 91)* is in a former Benedictine convent, dating from the 14th century, just out of the town of Gangi towards the interior of Sicilia. Children under 10 years aren't accepted at Easter and New Year. Half/full board costs L100,000/120,000. *Fulgy Barone d'Aspermont (☎ 0921 67 41 28)*, near San Mauro Castelverde and close to Cefalù, has accommodation in small apartments with kitchens. Half board costs from L80,000 per person.

Transport could be a problem in the Madonie unless you have a car. The towns within the park are serviced by SAIS and AST buses from Palermo, but if you want to reach some of the more secluded parts of the park, you might find that hitching a ride is the only option.

CEFALÙ

Just over an hour by train or bus from Palermo, Cefalù is an attractive beachside village backing onto the rocky frontage to the Madonie mountains. Something of a tourist magnet, it is unspoiled and makes for a relaxing day trip from the capital.

From the train station, turn right into Via Moro to reach Via Matteotti and the old town. If you are heading for the beach, turn left and walk along Via Gramsci, which becomes Via V Martoglio. The AAST office (☎ 0921 42 10 50) is at Corso Ruggero 77 and is open from 8 am to 2 pm and 4 to 7 pm Monday to Friday and to 2 pm on Saturday.

Things to See & Do

Roger II built the **duomo** in the 12th century to fulfil a vow to God after his fleet was saved during a violent storm off Cefalù. The twin pyramid towers of the cathedral stand out over the town centre, but the real beauty is inside. A towering figure of Christ Pancrator in the apse is the focal point of the elaborate Byzantine mosaics. The columns of the twin aisles support Arab-style pointed arches and have beautiful capitals.

Off Piazza del Duomo, at Via Mandralisca 13, is the private **Museo Mandralisca** (☎ 0921 42 15 47). Its collection includes Greek ceramics and Arab pottery, as well as paintings, notably the *Portrait of an Unknown Man* by Antonello da Messina. Opening hours vary according to the time of year, but are roughly 9 am to 12.30 pm and 3.30 to 7.30 pm daily. It opens to midnight during July and August. Admission costs L5000.

From the old town's main street, Via Matteotti, look for the sign pointing uphill to **Tempio di Diana** and make the one hour climb to the castle. Both are ruins that can be visited, but the main attraction is the panoramic view.

Places to Stay & Eat

There are several camp sites in the area, including *Costa Ponente Internazionale* (☎ 0921 42 00 85), about 4km west of the town at Contrada Ogliastrillo. It charges L9500 per person, up to L8000 for a site and L6000 for a car. Catch the bus from the train station heading for La Spisa.

In town, the only really cheap option is *Locanda Cangelosi* (☎ 0921 42 15 91, Via Umberto I 26) with doubles for L70,000. *La Giara* (☎ 0921 42 15 62, Via Veterani 40), uphill from the beach and off Corso Ruggero, has singles/doubles for L52,000/100,000. *Baia del Capitano* (☎ 0921 42 00 05) is in an olive grove near the beach at Mazzaforno, a few kilometres out of town towards Palermo. Its pleasant rooms cost L130,000/210,000.

Trattoria La Botte (☎ 0921 42 43 15, Via Veterani 6), just off Corso Ruggero, serves full meals for around L30,000. Otherwise,

there are plenty of *restaurants* and several *bars* along Via Vittorio Emanuele.

Getting There & Away

SAIS buses leave Palermo for Cefalù twice daily (see the Palermo Getting There & Away section). Trains are more frequent, if a little slow.

TINDARI

At Capo Tindari, farther along the coast towards Milazzo, are the ruins of ancient Tyndaris, founded in 396 BC as a Greek settlement on a rocky promontory. It was later occupied by the Romans and destroyed by Arab invaders. Today, fragments of the city's ramparts, a Greek theatre and Roman buildings, including a house and public baths, remain. A museum houses a collection of Hellenistic statues as well as Greek and Roman pottery. The site is open from 9 am to one hour before sunset. Admission is L4000.

Nearby is the **Santuario della Madonna Nera**. Built in the 20th century to hold a statue of a black Madonna revered since Byzantine times, the sanctuary is a place of pilgrimage. From the Oliveri beach you can reach the Laghetti di Marinello Riserva Naturale, visible from the square in front of the sanctuary.

To get to Tyndaris, catch a train to Patti (on the Palermo-Messina line) and then a bus to the site from outside the station (three a day, with increased services in summer).

MILAZZO

This is not the prettiest sight on Sicilia, but it has its share of baroque churches and palazzi. Most people aiming for the Isole Eolie pass through here. The APT office (☎ 090 922 28 65), Piazza C Duilio 10, is behind Via Crispi. You could head to the northern end of town for a peek at the 16th century Spanish **castle** (☎ 090 922 12 91), open from 10 am to 7 pm daily except Monday in summer, with shorter hours in winter. Guided tours of the inside run at 11 am, noon and 3, 4 and 5 pm.

There are several hotels near the port if you get stuck for the night. *Central* (☎ 090 928 10 43, Via del Sole 8) has basic singles/doubles for L40,000/75,000.

euro currency converter L10,000 = €5.16

SICILIA

Milazzo is easy to reach by bus or train from Palermo and Messina. See Getting There & Away in the Messina section. Intercity buses terminate on Piazza della Repubblica, a five minute walk back along Via Crispi to the port. The train station is a little farther away, on Piazza Marconi, connected to the port by AST buses.

Isole Eolie (Aeolian Islands)

The seven islands of this volcanic archipelago stretching north of Milazzo offer the developed tourist resort of Lipari and the understated jet-set haunt of Panarea, rugged Vulcano, the spectacular scenery of Stromboli and its fiercely active volcano, the fertile vineyards of Salina, and the solitude of outlying Alicudi and Filicudi. Also known as the Lipari Islands, the Isole Eolie have been inhabited since the Neolithic era, when people travelled there for the valuable volcanic glass, obsidian.

The ancient Greeks believed the islands were the home of Aeolus, the god of the wind, and Homer wrote of them in his *Odyssey*. Characterised by their rich colours and volcanic activity, the rugged coastlines are at times lashed by violent seas. As attractive as all this may appear to the modern traveller, the Isole Eolie have traditionally made for a difficult living environment. From the 1930s to the 1950s many inhabitants migrated to Australia (often referred to here as the eighth Isole Eolie), virtually abandoning the outer islands and leaving behind only a small contingent on the others.

Cinema fans might like to see Nanni Moretti's *Caro Diario* (Dear Diary). Part of this quirky film is set in the islands and Moretti captures their essence well. While you are there, look out for the distinctive murals depicting local scenes by Brescian artist Armando Pacchiani which seem to crop up in the most unlikely places.

You will need to book accommodation well in advance in the July/August high sea-

son. The best time to come is in May and early June or late September and October. Ferries and hydrofoils operate year-round, but winter services are much reduced and sometimes cancelled – to the outer islands at any rate – due to heavy seas.

Getting There & Away

Ferries and hydrofoils leave regularly from Milazzo and all the ticket offices are along Via L Rizzo, at the port. Note that there is a L1500 port fee for vehicles. All the following prices were one-way high-season fares at the time of writing.

Both SNAV and Siremar run hydrofoils (L19,500) to Lipari and on to the other islands. SNAV hydrofoils also connect the islands with Messina (L31,000) and Reggio di Calabria (L32,900) year-round, as well as Napoli and Palermo, in summer only.

Siremar runs ferries from Milazzo for about half the price of the hydrofoil (L12,500, cars from L32,500 to L46,500 depending on size), but they are slower and less regular. Siremar also runs ferries to Napoli. NGI Traghetti also runs a limited car ferry service for around the same rates.

Regular hydrofoil and ferry services operate between the islands, but they can be disrupted to the outer islands by heavy seas. Lipari's two ports are separated by the castello – hydrofoils arrive at and depart from Marina Corta, while ferries service Marina Lunga. Siremar and SNAV have ticket offices in the same building at Marina Corta. Siremar also has a ticket office at Marina Lunga. Full timetable information is available at all offices. On the other islands, ticket offices are at or close to the docks.

Examples of one-way fares and sailing times from Lipari are:

Alicudi
    L27,000, 1½ hours (hydrofoil)
    L17,500, 3¼ hours (ferry)
Panarea
    L13,000, 30 minutes (hydrofoil)
    L7500, one hour (ferry)
Stromboli
    L25,500, 50 minutes (hydrofoil)
    L15,000, 2¾ hours (ferry)

LIPARI

postcode 98050 • pop 11,000

The largest and most developed of the islands, Lipari is also the most popular with tourists. The main town, of the same name, is typically Mediterranean, with pastel-coloured houses huddled around its two harbours. A thriving exporter of obsidian in ancient times, it is now a centre for pumice stone (another volcanic product) mining. It's the best equipped base for exploring the archipelago.

Orientation

The town of Lipari's two harbours, Marina Lunga and Marina Corta, are on either side of the cliff-top castle, which is surrounded by 16th century walls, and the town centre extends between them. The main street, Corso Vittorio Emanuele, runs roughly north-south to the west of the castle. From Marina Corta you should walk to the right across the piazza to Via Garibaldi and follow the 'centro' signs for Corso Vittorio Emanuele.

Information

Tourist Offices The AAST office (☎ 090 988 00 95) is at Corso Vittorio Emanuele 202. It is the main tourist office for the archipelago, although offices open on Stromboli, Vulcano and Salina in summer. Staff here will assist with accommodation, which is useful in the busy summer months. Pick up a copy of *Ospitalità in blu*, which contains details of accommodation and services on all the islands. The office is open from 8 am to 2 pm and 4 to 7.30 pm (to 6.30 pm in low season) Monday to Saturday and from 8 am to 2 pm on Sunday and holidays in summer.

Money There are several banks in Lipari, including the Banca del Sud on Corso Vittorio Emanuele. You should have no trouble using Visa, MasterCard or Eurocheque cards for cash advances. Outside banking hours, exchange facilities can be found at the post office and several travel agencies.

Note that banking facilities on the other islands are limited.

Post & Communications The post office (☎ 090 981 13 79) is at Corso Vittorio Emanuele 207, near the AAST office, and opens from 8.30 am to 6.30 pm Monday to Friday and to 1 pm on Saturday. Public telephones can be found throughout the town.

Medical Services For medical emergencies, contact the hospital (☎ 090 9 88 51) or Pronto Soccorso (☎ 090 988 52 67). Both are on Via Sant'Anna.

Things to See & Do

The **castello**, surrounded by massive walls built in the 16th century after Turkish pirates raided Lipari, stands on the site of an ancient acropolis, now part of the **Parco Archeologico**. Buildings dating from before 1700 BC have been unearthed. Also within the castello complex is the **cattedrale**, built by the Normans and sent up in flames during a 1544 pirate raid. Rebuilt a century later, the interior is baroque. Excavations have uncovered part of the original 12th century Norman cloisters.

The **Museo Archeologico Eoliano** (☎ 090 988 01 74) boasts well-organised exhibits that trace the volcanic and human history of the islands and include a collection of Neolithic pottery. It is open from 9 am to 1.30 pm Monday to Saturday and to 1 pm on Sunday. The classical section is open from 3 to 6 pm. Admission to the museum (including the classical section) costs L8000.

It is worth exploring the island, in particular for views of Salina, Alicudi and Filicudi from the rugged, windy cliffs of Lipari's north-western corner. Sunbathers and swimmers head for **Canneto**, a few kilometres north of Lipari town. The beach is accessible by a track just north of Canneto. Farther north are the pumice mines of **Pomiciazzo** and **Porticello**, where there is another beach. The village of Quattropani and the lookout known as Quattrocchi, south of Pianoconte, are good spots to drink in the views.

Scuba diving and sailing are popular. For information on courses, contact the Centro Nautico Eoliano (☎ 090 981 26 91), Salita San Giuseppe 8, or the AAST office.

Viking (☎ 090 981 25 84), Vico Himera 3

SICILIA

(a ticket booth is at Marina Corta), conducts boat tours of all the islands from March to October, including one to Stromboli by night for L45,000 to see the Sciara del Fuoco (Trail of Fire).

Places to Stay

Lipari provides plenty of options for a comfortable stay, from budget level to luxurious. However, prices soar in summer, particularly in August. If all else fails in peak season, AAST staff will billet new arrivals in private homes on the island. Don't reject offers by touts when you arrive, as they often have decent rooms in private houses.

To rent an apartment, contact the AAST office for a list of establishments.

Places to Stay – Budget

The island's camp site, *Baia Unci* (☎ 090 981 19 09), is at Canneto, about 2km out of Lipari town and accessible by bus from the Esso service station at Marina Lunga. Low-season prices are reasonable at L14,000 per person (there is no fee for the tent site) or L12,000 per person in a caravan plus L16,000 for the site, but in high season prices rise to L18,000 per person or L14,000 per person in a caravan plus L20,000 for the site. The HI *youth hostel* (☎ 090 981 15 40, Via Castello 17) is inside the walls of the castello. B&B costs L18,500 per person and L15,000 for a meal – or you can cook your own. It is open from March to October.

Cassarà Vittorio (☎ 090 981 15 23, Vico Sparviero 15), off Via Garibaldi near Marina Corta, costs L50,000 per person or L55,000 with private bathroom. There are also small apartments for L60,000 per person. Use of the kitchen costs L5000 and there are two terraces with views. You'll find the owner (unless he finds you first) at Via Garibaldi 78, on the way from Marina Corte to the city centre.

Diana Brown (☎ 090 981 25 84, fax 090 981 32 13, Vico Himera 3) is also very close to Marina Corta. It has rooms with bathroom and air-conditioning or apartments for L20,000 per person in the low season and up to L60,000 in August. *Enzo il Negro* (☎/fax 090 981 31 63, Via Garibaldi 29) has

spotless, comfortable digs for up to L60,000 per person in the high season. All rooms have bathroom, air conditioning, a fridge and balcony, and there is a large terrace.

Places to Stay – Mid-Range

Pensione Neri (☎ 090 981 14 13, Via G Marconi 43), off Corso Vittorio Emanuele, is in a lovely old, renovated villa. In the low season, a double costs L110,000 and triples/quads L148,000/270,000. In summer, prices jump to L200,000 a double and L270,000/340,000 a triple/quad. All rooms have a bathroom and breakfast is included.

Next door *Hotel Oriente* (☎ 090 981 14 93, Via G Marconi 35) has a bar, garden and very comfortable rooms. Prices vary according to the season, ranging from L55,000 to L130,000 for singles, L100,000 to L220,000 for doubles, L135,000 to L280,000 for triples and L170,000 to L340,000 for quads. All rooms include a bathroom, air-conditioning and breakfast. A new tourist residence, *Costa Residence Vacanze* (☎ 090 988 07 40), at San Leonardo, has one and two-room apartments for L200,000/330,000 per day.

Places to Stay – Top End

Lipari's top hotel is *Villa Meligunis* (☎ 090 981 24 26, Via Marte), on a hill overlooking Marina Corta. Room rates range from L160,000 to L340,000, depending on the season. The price includes breakfast.

Places to Eat

Try pasta prepared with the island's excellent capers and be prepared to spend big to eat the day's sea catch, particularly swordfish. The waters of the archipelago abound in fish, including tuna, mullet, cuttlefish and sole, all of which end up on restaurant tables at the end of the day. The local wine is the sweet, white Malvasia.

People with access to a kitchen can shop for supplies at the *grocery shops* along Corso Vittorio Emanuele.

Although prices go up in the high season, you can still eat cheaply by sticking to the pizzerie along Corso Vittorio Emanuele. *Il Galeone* (☎ 090 981 16 43, Corso Vittorio

Emanuele 222) has good pizzas for around L10,000 or a set lunch for L22,000. *Zum Willi* (☎ 090 981 14 73), on the corner of Corso Vittorio Emanuele and Via Umberto I, is basically a bar that serves pizzas for L6000 to L12,000. For a fuller meal, try *Trattoria d'Oro* (☎ 090 981 25 91, *Corso Umberto I 28-32)*. For a good set menu you'll pay around L20,000, or about L35,000 à la carte.

Da Bartolo (☎ 090 981 17 00, *Via Garibaldi 53)* is certainly one of the island's better trattorie and a good choice for seafood. A full meal is worth around L35,000.

On Via Roma, near Marina Corta, there are a couple of no-nonsense trattorie, including *Nenzyna* (☎ 090 981 16 60, *Via Roma 2)* where you can eat for around L25,000.

Getting There & Around
See the earlier Getting There & Away section for the Isole Eolie.

Urso Guglielmo buses leave from the Esso service station at Marina Lunga for Canneto (10 a day, more frequently in summer), Porticello (seven a day) and Quattropani (eight a day). The company also offers special round trips of the island. Contact the AAST office for timetables.

Boats and scooters are available for hire at Foti Roberto (☎ 090 981 23 52), Via F Crispi 31, to the right as you leave Marina Lunga. A moped costs L40,000 a day and a scooter up to L60,000 a day. A three-seater motorised rubber dinghy costs L100,000 per day and a 14-seater L450,000.

VULCANO
postcode 98050 • pop 800

Just south of Lipari and the first port of call for ferries and hydrofoils from Milazzo, Vulcano is known for its therapeutic mud baths and hot springs. To the ancients, the island of Thermessa, Terasia or Hiera – as Vulcano was variously known – must have inspired a good deal of respect, if not downright fear. Not only did the god of fire, Vulcan, have his workshop here, but Aeolus, the god of the wind, also swirled about.

Of Vulcano's three volcanoes, the oldest lies on the island's southern tip and was already extinct in ancient times. The youngest, Vulcanello, next to the mud baths at the island's north-eastern end, rose from the sea in the 2nd century BC, according to Pliny. The only active volcano, Gran Cratere, has a number of fumaroles; its broad, smoking crater broods over the port. A tranquil place, Gran Cratere hasn't blown for more than four centuries, but you'll notice on arrival the all-pervading stench of sulphurous gases.

Orientation & Information
Boats dock at the Porto di Levante. To the right, as you face the island, is the small Vulcanello peninsula. All facilities are concentrated between the Porto di Levante and the Porto di Ponente, where you will find the Spiaggia Sabbia Nera (Black Sand Beach), the only smooth, sandy beach on the islands.

A tourist office (☎ 090 985 20 28) is open from June to October.

Things to See & Do
Climbing **Gran Cratere** is the main attraction. Follow the signs south along Via Provinciale out of town. A track is then signposted off the road. Take the left fork and head up – about an hour's scramble. The views from the top are reward enough for the sweat.

Even if you don't need a skin cure, a wallow in the hot, sulphurous mud pool of **Laghetto di Fanghi** can be a relaxing way to pass the time, if slightly offensive to the nose (don't wear your best bathing costume, as you'll never get the smell out). It's next to Vulcanello, and when you've had enough you can hop into the water at the adjacent beach where underwater hot springs create a natural Jacuzzi effect.

Paddle boats are usually available for hire on the beach.

Viking offers a boat trip around the island for around L20,000 per person. Information is available on Lipari.

Pino Marturano (☎ 090 985 24 19), Via Comunale Levante, near Porto di Levante in front of the tobacconist, organises boat trips around the island for L20,000 and to Stromboli (approximately eight hours) for L45,000. The proprietor of Gioielli del Mare

(☎ 090 985 21 70) at Porto di Levante organises bus tours (about two hours) around the island for groups of at least 12 people. The price is L20,000 per person. Make a booking and hope a large enough group will form.

Places to Stay & Eat

Pensione Agostino (☎ 090 985 23 42, Via Favaloro 1) is close to the mud baths (and their smell) and has doubles for L50,000/100,000 with bathroom in low/high season. *Pensione la Giara (☎ 090 985 22 29, Via Provinciale 18)* is towards Gran Cratere. A pleasant spot, its rooms cost around L45,000/90,000 per person, although the management prefers to charge by the week.

Sea House Residence (☎ 090 985 22 19), which is close to the mud baths, is a complex of self-contained two, three, four and five-bed apartments in a garden setting. Prices start at L30,000 per person for a double in the low season and rise to L120,000 in August. It opens from April to October. Hotel *Arcipelago (☎ 090 985 20 02)* has a beautiful position on the northern coast of Vulcano. Half board in July is L185,000 per day or L160,000 if you stay more than six days.

For a decent meal, try *Da Maurizio* or *Da Vincenzino*, both on Via Porto di Levante. Another good option is *Il Caimano*.

Getting There & Away

Vulcano is an intermediate stop between Milazzo and Lipari and a good number of vessels go both ways throughout the day.

SALINA

postcode 98050 • pop 850

Just north-west of Lipari, Salina is the most fertile of the islands and consists of two extinct volcanoes, Monte dei Porri and Monte Fossa delle Felci. Its high coastal cliffs are topped with vineyards, where most of the islands' Malvasia wine is produced.

Orientation & Information

Boats dock at Santa Marina Salina, where you will find most accommodation, or at Rinella, a fishing hamlet on the southern coast. The other main villages on the island are Malfa, on the northern coast, and Leni, slightly inland from Rinella.

In summer there are AAST booths at Rinella, Malfa and Santa Marina Salina. For medical assistance, call ☎ 090 984 40 05. For the police, phone ☎ 090 984 30 19.

Things to See & Do

If you are feeling energetic, you could climb the Fossa delle Felci volcano and visit the riserva naturale. From Santa Marina Salina, head for Lingua, a small village 3km south, from where paths lead up the mountain.

The **Santuario della Madonna del Terzito** at Valdichiesa, just south of Malfa, is a place of pilgrimage, particularly around the Feast of the Assumption on 15 August.

Rinella is a popular underwater fishing spot. For information, contact the AAST booths. Boats are available for hire from June to August at Nautica Levante (☎ 090 984 30 83), Via Lungomare, Santa Marina Salina.

Don't miss a trip to the beach at Pollara, the setting for much of Massimo Troisi's last film, *Il Postino*. The climb down is a bit tricky but the beach itself with its backdrop of cliffs is absolutely unbeatable.

Places to Stay & Eat

Camping Tre Pini (☎ 090 980 91 55) is on the beach at Rinella. It costs L12,000 per person, plus L15,000 for a site. *Pensione Mamma Santina (☎ 090 984 30 54, Via Sanità 40)* is in Santa Marina Salina. Head for Via Risorgimento (the narrow main street of town) and walk north for a few hundred metres. The pensione is uphill along a winding lane to your left. Singles/doubles cost L40,000/60,000 per person. From June to September half board for up to 140,000 per person is obligatory.

Hotel L'Ariana (☎ 090 980 90 75, Via Rotabile 11) is in a late 19th century villa overlooking the sea at Rinella. It has terraces and a bar. Half board (with bathroom) costs L85,000/150,000 in the low/high season; full board costs from L115,000 to L180,000.

There are several *restaurants* clustered around the docks at Santa Marina Salina or you could try the one at *Albergo Punta*

Barone, with views out to sea, at the northern exit of town.

Getting There & Around

Hydrofoils and ferries service Santa Marina Salinaand Rinella. You'll find ticket offices at both.

Regular buses run from Santa Marina Salina to Malfa and Lingua and from Malfa to Leni and Rinella. Timetables are posted at the ports. Motorcycles are available for hire from Antonio Bongiorno (☎ 090 984 34 09), Via Risorgimento 240, Santa Marina Salina. A Vespa costs L40,000 a day and a moped L35,000 a day – less if you hire for longer periods.

PANAREA

postcode 98050 • pop 320

Easily the most picturesque of the Isole Eolie, tiny Panarea is 3km long and 2km wide. Boats dock at San Pietro, where you'll find most of the accommodation.

After wandering around San Pietro, head south to Punta Milazzese, about a half-hour walk (there is a small beach along the way), to see the Bronze Age village discovered in 1948. Pottery found at the site is now in the museum at Lipari. Hire a boat at the port to explore the coves and beaches of the island, which are otherwise inaccessible.

Locanda Rodà (☎ 090 98 30 23, *Via San Pietro*), uphill from the port and to the left, is about as close as you'll come to a cheap hotel. Singles/doubles cost L50,000/100,000 and half board is L110,000/145,000 in the low/high season. It has a pizzeria/trattoria that charges average prices. *La Sirena* (☎ 090 98 30 12, *Via Drautt 4*), on the way to the Bronze Age village, has doubles with bathroom for L120,000 and a pleasant trattoria. In July and August half board at L160,000 is obligatory. In the same area is *Trattoria da Pina* (☎ 090 98 30 32) with a terrace overlooking the sea. A meal should cost no more than L40,000.

Hydrofoils and the occasional ferry link the island with Stromboli to the north and Salina (and on to Lipari and Milazzo) to the south.

STROMBOLI

postcode 98050 • pop 500

Stromboli's almost constant eruptions of fiery molten rock make an unforgettable spectacle at night. Lava flow is confined to the Sciara del Fuoco (Trail of Fire) on the volcano's north-western flank, leaving the villages of San Bartolo, San Vincenzo and Scari (which merge into one town) to the east and Ginostra to the south quite safe. Until the massive eruption of 1930, some 5000 people lived on the island, but most took fright and left. Permanent residents now number about 500. The volcano's most recent eruption was in March 1996 and, although minor, left several people injured.

Stromboli, the most captivating of the islands, is inconveniently placed and boat services are prone to disruption. There's a fair choice of accommodation and a stay is more than recommended.

Orientation & Information

Boats arrive at Scari/San Vincenzo, downhill from the town. Accommodation is a short walk up the Scalo Scari to Via Roma, or, if you plan to head straight for the crater, follow the road along the waterfront (see the following section for details).

A tourist office is open in summer. The post office is on Via Roma and the one bank, on Via Nunziante at Ficogrande, is open from June to September only. Otherwise, currency exchange facilities are available at the travel agency, Le Isole e Terme d'Italia, on Via Roma near the port.

Climbing the Volcano

From the port, follow the road along the waterfront, continuing straight past the beach at Ficogrande. Once past the village the path heads uphill, deviating after about 20 minutes to a bar/pizzeria and observatory. Alternatively, follow it through a slightly confusing section of reeds until it starts to ascend to the crater. About halfway up is a good view of the Sciara del Fuoco, although in daylight the glow of the molten lava is imperceptible. The path eventually becomes quite steep and rocky. Note the warning

SICILIA

signs at the summit and do not go too close to the edge of the crater. The round trip from the village should take about four hours.

The climb is a totally different experience at night, when darkness throws the molten lava of the Sciara del Fuoco and volcanic explosions into dramatic relief. It is possible to make the climb during the day without a guide, although the tourist office says it is forbidden. We strongly advise that night climbers go with a guide.

Experienced guides can be contacted through the Alpine Guides office (☎ 090 98 62 63), just off Piazza San Vincenzo. It takes groups of 10 people or more to the crater at 4.30 pm daily (depending on weather conditions and whether a group can be formed), returning at 11.30 pm (about L30,000 per person). Contact the office around noon to make a booking. For the night climb, you will need heavy shoes and clothing for cold, wet weather, a torch (flashlight), food and a good supply of water. Even during the day, you will need wet-weather clothing, as conditions are unpredictable.

See Lonely Planet's *Walking in Italy* for more detailed descriptions of walks on Stromboli, both on the volcano and around the island.

The Società Navigazione Pippo (☎ 090 98 61 35), Via Roma 47, organises nightly boat trips to view the Sciara del Fuoco from the sea. The boat, *Pippo*, leaves at 10 pm from the port and at 10.10 pm from Ficogrande. The tour lasts 2½ hours and costs L25,000 per person. The same company also runs two daytime trips, leaving at 10 am and 3 pm. Viking offers a similar boat trip, starting in Lipari and departing from the Stromboli ferry port for the Sciara del Fuoco at 8 pm. The same boat also heads out to **Strombolicchio**, a towering rock rising out of the sea north of San Vincenzo. The rock is a popular spot for underwater fishing.

Water Sports
La Sirenetta Diving Center (☎ 090 98 60 25), Via Marina 33, at La Sirenetta Park Hotel, offers diving courses.

Alternatively, make your way to the beach

of rocks and black volcanic sand at Ficogra'nde to swim and sunbathe.

Places to Stay & Eat
There's nothing much in the dirt cheap bracket on Stromboli. One of the cheapest options is *Casa del Sole* (☎ 090 98 60 17, *Via Soldato Cincotta*), off the road to the volcano, before you reach Ficogrande. It is popular with young people and has rooms for L25,000/30,000 in the low season, including use of the kitchen. Prices go up by L10,000 in the high season. You'll also find a few affittacamere, charging from L40,000 per person for a room in the high season. *Locanda Stella* (☎ 090 98 60 00, *Via Fabio Filzi 14*) has doubles for L85,000; it charges L140,000 for obligatory full board in July/August. *Barbablù* (☎ 090 98 61 18, *Via Vittorio Emanuele 17*) is a pleasant pensione charging from L120,000 to L260,000 for a double with breakfast, depending on the season.

Hotel Villaggio Stromboli (☎ 090 98 60 18, *Via Regina Elena*) has rooms in the high season for L145,000/250,000. It is on the beach front and has a terrace bar/restaurant. *Park Hotel la Sirenetta* (☎ 090 98 60 25, fax 090 98 61 24) is perfectly sited on the beach at Ficogrande in front of Strombolicchio. It has a swimming pool, a panoramic terrace with a restaurant and one of the best chefs on the island. Half board in July costs L170,000 per person and L210,000 in August.

For a reasonably priced meal, try *La Trottola* on Via Roma. *Punta Lena* on the Lungomare, walking away from the port towards the volcano, is more expensive and has a terrace overlooking the sea. The *pizzeria* at the observatory, about 20 minutes walk up the lower slope of the volcano, is also reasonable.

Getting There & Away
Ticket offices for SNAV and Siremar are at the port. Bear in mind the cost of the trip and distance if you're considering a day visit – which in any case will rob you of the opportunity of a night climb up the volcano. Heavy seas can cause cancellation of ferry and hydrofoil services.

FILICUDI & ALICUDI
postcode 98050 • pop 400

You will need a strong desire to get away from it all to stay on either of these islands west of Lipari. Facilities are limited (severely on Alicudi) and boats can be cancelled due to heavy seas, even in summer.

Filicudi is the larger of the two and its attractions include Grotta del Bue Marino (Grotto of the Monk Seal) and La Canna rock pinnacle, about 1km off the island towards Alicudi. On Capo Graziano, south of the port, are the remains of a prehistoric village dating from 1800 BC. Boats are available for hire if you want to explore the grotto and scuba-diving courses are available in summer.

The island has two hotels. *La Canna* (☎ 090 988 99 56, Via Rosa 43), just uphill from the port, has doubles for L80,000 and half board for L115,000 per person in the high season. *Phenicusa* (☎ 090 988 99 46, 090 988 99 55, Via Porto) has compulsory half board at L90,000 in July.

Alicudi is the farthest from Lipari and the least developed of the Eolie group. There is only one hotel and restaurant, *Ericusa* (☎ 090 988 99 02, Via Regina Elena). Doubles cost L105,000 and half board is L105,000 per person. It is open only during the summer months and bookings are strongly advised.

While on the island, walk up Monte Filo dell'Arpa to see the crater of the extinct Montagnola volcano and the Timpone delle Femmine, huge fissures where women are said to have taken refuge during pirate raids.

Eastern Coast

MESSINA
postcode 98050 • pop 268,000

For most, Messina is the point of arrival on Sicilia and you could hardly imagine a less auspicious introduction. Devastated many times over the centuries, the modern city is pretty much bereft of any hint of its past. Known to the ancient Greeks as Zankle (Sickle) for its beautiful, curved harbour, Messina grew into a splendid city as a Greek colony and later thrived under Roman, Byzantine and Norman rule. Since the 18th century, Messina has been something of a disaster area – hit first by plague, then cholera and finally by earthquakes, including the massive 1908 jolt that all but destroyed the city and killed more than 80,000 people in the region. The city had barely been rebuilt when it was flattened by bombing during WWII.

If you're stuck in Messina, don't despair. The city centre, with its wide avenues, is a pleasant place to wandér around and there remain a couple of vestiges of happier days.

Orientation
The train station is on Piazza della Repubblica, at the southern end of the long waterfront. FS car and truck ferries also arrive here. The main intercity bus station is outside the train station, to the left on the piazza. To get to the city centre from Piazza della Repubblica, walk either straight across the piazza and directly ahead along Via I Settembre to the Piazza del Duomo or turn left into Via G La Farina and take the first right into Via Cannazzaro to reach Piazza Cairoli.

Those coming by hydrofoil from Reggio di Calabria arrive about 1km north of the city on Corso Vittorio Emanuele II, while drivers on the private car ferry from Villa San Giovanni land a few kilometres farther along, just north of the trade fair area (Fiera).

Information
Tourist Offices There is an information office (☎ 090 292 32 92) at Piazza Cairoli 45, which opens from 8 am to 2 pm Monday to Friday. The AAPIT office (☎ 090 67 42 36), to the right as you leave the train station, is a bit farther along at Via Calabria 301. Both have extensive information on Messina, its province and Sicilia in general.

Money There are numerous banks in the city centre – several with ATMs – and a currency exchange booth at the timetable information office at the train station.

Post & Communications The main post office is on Piazza Antonello, on Corso

Cavour near the cathedral. It is open from 8.30 am to 6.30 pm Monday to Saturday.

There is a Telecom office on Corso Cavour, near Via Cannazzaro.

Travel Agencies There's a CTS travel agency (☎ 090 292 67 61) at Via U Bassi 93.

Medical Services The Ospedale Piemonte (☎ 090 22 22 11) is on Viale Europa; at night, call ☎ 090 67 50 48. A booklet, available at the tourist office, lists pharmacies open at night on a rotation basis.

Things to See & Do

The Norman **duomo**, built in the 12th century, was almost completely destroyed by the combined effects of the 1908 earthquake and WWII bombing. Rebuilt virtually from scratch, its fine 15th century doorway is one of the few original elements. The clock tower houses what is believed to be the world's largest astronomical clock, which strikes at noon.

On Piazza del Duomo is the **Fontana di Orione**, an elegant 16th century work by Angelo Montorsoli. Nearby, on Piazza Catalani, off Via Garibaldi, is the 12th century **Chiesa della Santissima Annunziata dei Catalani**, a jewel of Arab-Norman construction. The statue in front of it's a monument to Don John of Austria, who beat the Turks at the Battle of Lepanto in 1571. Farther north, where Via Garibaldi spills into Piazza dell'Unità d'Italia, is Messina's other great fountain, the 16th century **Fontana del Nettuno**.

The **Museo Regionale** (☎ 090 36 12 92) is a long walk along Viale della Libertà at No 465 (or take bus No 8 from the train station) and houses works of art including the *Virgin & Child with Saints* by Antonello da Messina, born here in 1430, and two masterpieces by Caravaggio – *Adorazione dei pastori* and *Resurezione di Lazzaro*. It is open from 9 am to 1.30 pm daily and, obscurely, from 4 to 6.30 pm on every second day in summer and 3 to 5.30 pm in winter. Admission costs L8000.

If you have your own transport, the drive north along the coast from Messina to Capo Peloro and then round to the east is pretty, and there are some reasonable **beaches** between the cape and Acquarone. Where the coast road meets the A20 heading for Milazzo, take the tollway, as the S113 can be incredibly congested from this point.

Places to Stay & Eat

Two hotels are convenient for the train station. *Touring (☎ 090 293 88 51)* charges around L35,000/65,000 for singles/doubles without bathroom and L60,000/100,000 with bathroom. *Mirage (☎ 090 293 88 44, Via N Scotto 3)* charges around L40,000/70,000 for singles/doubles and L98,000 for a double with bathroom. *Hotel Cairoli (☎ 090 67 37 55, Viale San Martino 63)* is of a higher standard and charges L86,000/140,000 for singles/doubles with bathroom and breakfast.

La Trappola (Via dei Verdi 39) has good, reasonably priced, but not rock-bottom, meals. *Trattoria al Padrino (Via Santa Cecilia 54)* is a simple place, where a meal will cost around L30,000.

Getting There & Away

Bus Interbus (☎ 090 66 17 54) runs a regular service (approximately every hour, last bus leaves at 8 pm) to Taormina (L5000 one way), Catania (L10,500 one way) and Catania's airport. The company's office and bus station are at Piazza della Repubblica 6, to the left as you leave the train station. There is a direct connection to Roma (see Getting There & Away at the beginning of this chapter). Giuntabus (☎ 090 67 37 82) runs a service to Milazzo (for ferries and hydrofoils to the Isole Eolie) roughly every hour from Via Terranova 8, on the corner of Viale San Martino.

Train Regular trains connect Messina with Catania, Taormina, Siracusa, Palermo and Milazzo, but buses are generally faster. The train stations for Milazzo and Taormina are inconveniently located some distance from the city centre.

Car & Motorcycle If you arrive in Messina by FS ferry with a vehicle (see following section), it is simple to make your way out of town. For Palermo (or Milazzo and the Isole Eolie), turn right from the docks and follow Viale Garibaldi along the waterfront. After about 1km, turn left into Viale Boccetta and follow the green autostrada (tollway) signs for Palermo. To reach Taormina and Siracusa, turn left from the docks into Via La Farina and follow the autostrada signs for Catania.

If you arrive by private ferry, turn right along Viale della Libertà for Palermo and Milazzo and left for Taormina and Catania – follow the green autostrada signs. You can also take the S114 (busy in summer).

Boat The FS railway runs car ferries to Villa San Giovanni, about 10km north of Reggio di Calabria, from next to the train station. The private Caronte company does the same run from docks a few kilometres up the waterfront, just north of the Fiera (trade fair centre), and services are more frequent. It costs L28,000 one way to take a small car on Caronte (FS prices are similar). The trip takes about 20 minutes, with departures around the clock.

There are also big FS hydrofoils to Reggio di Calabria (L5000 one way). SNAV (☎ 090 36 40 44) runs up to 20 hydrofoils on weekdays to Reggio di Calabria (15 minutes, L5500 one way). SNAV hydrofoils also connect Messina with the Isole Eolie (Lipari L31,000 one way).

SOUTH TO TAORMINA

Those driving the Messina-Taormina route should consider a brief excursion into the foothills of the Monti Peloritani. Head for **Savoca**, 4km of winding road inland from the grey pebble beaches of Santa Teresa di Riva, which takes you through lemon and almond groves to a quiet village with a few medieval churches and a Capuchin monastery, containing **catacombs**. Some eerie-looking skeletons in raggedy 18th century rig are all that remain of local nobles who paid good money for this kind of 'immortality'. The catacombs are open from 9 am to 1 pm and 4 to 7 pm from April to September; 9 am to noon and 3 to 5 pm October to March. Admission is free but visitors are expected to make a donation. AST buses run between Savoca and Santa Teresa di Riva.

TAORMINA
postcode 98039 • pop 11,000

Spectacularly located on a terrace of Monte Tauro, dominating the sea and with views westwards to Mt Etna, Taormina is easily Sicilia's most picturesque town. From its foundation by the Siculians, Taormina remained a favourite destination for the long line of conquerors who followed. Under the Greeks, who moved in after Naxos was destroyed during colonial wars in the 5th century BC, Taormina flourished. It later came under Roman dominion and eventually became the capital of Byzantine Sicilia, a period of grandeur that ended abruptly in 902 when the town was destroyed by Arab invaders. Taormina remained an important centre of art and trade throughout the subsequent Norman, Spanish and French rules.

Long ago discovered by the European jet set, Taormina is an expensive and heavily touristed town. It is well served by hotels, pensioni and eating places, but some travellers might find the glitz and kitsch a little overwhelming. It would be a shame to miss this place though, as its magnificent setting, Teatro Greco and nearby beaches remain as seductive as they were for the likes of Goethe and DH Lawrence.

Orientation

The train station (Taormina-Giardini) is at the bottom of Monte Tauro. You'll need to get an Interbus bus to the bus station (for local and intercity buses – where you'll arrive anyway if you catch the bus from Messina) on Via Pirandello. A short walk uphill from there brings you to the old city entrance and Corso Umberto I, which traverses the town.

Information

Tourist Offices The AAST office (☎ 0942 2 32 43) is in Palazzo Corvaja, just off Corso Umberto I, near Largo Santa Caterina. It is open from 8 am to 2 pm and 4 to 7 pm Monday to Saturday and from 9 am to 1 pm on Sunday.

euro currency converter   L10,000 = €5.16

Money There are several banks in Taormina, mostly along Corso Umberto I. You'll also find currency exchange places along the same street. Check on commissions. Several banks, such as Monte dei Paschi di Siena on Piazza del Duomo, have ATMs. Amex is represented by La Duca Viaggi (☎ 0942 62 52 55), Via Don Bosco 39.

Post & Communications The main post office is on Piazza Sant'Antonio, just outside the Porta Catania, at the far end of Corso Umberto I from the AAST office. There are public telephones in the Avis office (☎ 0942 2 30 41), Via San Pancrazio 7, to your right off Via Pirandello at the entrance to the old town.

Medical Services There is a free nighttime medical service in summer for tourists (☎ 0942 62 54 19) on Piazza San Francesco di Paola. The Ospedale San Vincenzo (☎ 0942 5 37 45) is on Piazza San Vincenzo, just outside the Porta Catania. Call the same number for an ambulance.

Things to See & Do

The **Teatro Greco** at the end of Via Teatro Greco, off Corso Umberto I, was built in the 3rd century BC. Later expanded and remodelled by the Romans, what you see is pretty much a Roman structure, despite its name. In the final years of the empire the amphitheatre was given over solely to gladiator fighting – the sword was mightier at the box office than the pen. The structure has been much tampered with over the centuries – the family of the Spanish Costanza d'Aragona built its home in the 12th century over part of the theatre (to the right as you face the stage). However, it remains a most atmospheric place. Film buffs might note that Woody Allen filmed the Greek chorus scenes here for his film *Mighty Aphrodite*. The view of Mt Etna and the sea through what was once the stage area is breathtaking. There are concerts here in summer. The theatre is open from 9 am to 7 pm in summer (to 4.30 pm in winter). Admission costs L4000.

From the teatro, wander down to the beautiful **villa comunale** (public gardens) on Via Bagnoli Croci. Opening hours are similar to the teatro. Take a picnic and enjoy the panorama.

Back in the town centre is the **Odeon**, a small Roman theatre, badly preserved and partly covered by the adjoining Chiesa di Santa Caterina. It was discovered and excavated in the late 19th century and is believed to have been erected on the site of a Greek temple of Apollo. Taormina's **duomo**, on Piazza del Duomo along Corso Umberto I, was built in the early 15th century.

There are several mansions in Taormina, including **Palazzo Corvaja**. Begun by the Arabs as a defence tower in the 11th century, it was extended several times and includes halls dating from the 14th and 15th centuries. **Palazzo Duca di Santo Stefano**, at the other end of town, is an important example of Sicilian Gothic architecture, with a fanciful mix of Arab and Norman styles. **Badia Vecchia** (Old Abbey), nearby, is a 14th century Gothic building, again with Norman-Arab elements.

Just wandering along the main drag, Corso Umberto I, you can see a smattering of stately old buildings, some dating from the 15th century.

The peak of **Monte Tauro** is adorned by the lonely, windswept ruins of the town's medieval castle, 3km from the town centre along the road to Castelmola (see the later Around Taormina section) or accessible by climbing the linking stairs. The views are great.

You can reach the beaches at **Isola Bella** and **Mazzarò** directly under Taormina by cable car from Via Pirandello. It costs L5000 return and runs from 8.30 am to 1.30 am in summer (to 8.15 pm in winter). Both beaches are largely taken up by private operators (a space with deckchairs and umbrella costs up to L20,000 a day), but there is some space for free bathing. Interbus buses also connect the beaches with the upper town.

Organised Tours

CST (☎ 0942 2 33 01), Corso Umberto I 101, runs excursions to various places. Destinations include Mt Etna (L35,000), Agrigento (L62,000), Siracusa (L55,000) and Lipari

(L75,000). Prices exclude admission to museums and archaeological sites. These are winter prices; expect rises in summer. SAT (☎ 0942 2 46 53, fax 0942 2 11 28), Corso Umberto I 73, also runs tours to Mt Etna.

Special Events

Festivals, theatre and music concerts are organised throughout the summer during Taormina Arte. The Raduno del Costume e del Carretto Siciliano, featuring parades of traditional Sicilian carts and folkloric groups, is usually held in autumn – ask at the AAST office for details.

Places to Stay

Taormina has plenty of accommodation, but in summer you should book in advance as rooms fill rapidly, particularly during August (a good time to stay away). In winter you can sometimes get prices brought down a tad. You can camp near the beach at *Campeggio San Leo* (☎ 0942 2 46 58, Via Nazionale) at Capo Taormina; the cost is L8000 per person.

There are numerous private rooms in Taormina and the tourist office has a full list. *Il Leone* (☎ 0942 2 38 78, Via Bagnoli Croci 127), near the gardens, charges L45,000 per person with breakfast. Some rooms have terraces and great views of the sea.

Pensione Svizzera (☎ 0942 2 37 90, Via Pirandello 26, email svizzera@tau.it), on the way from the bus station to the town centre, has simple, pleasant singles/doubles with bathroom starting at L50,000/70,000 (prices rise to L80,000/120,000 in the high season), including a buffet breakfast. Farther up the same road, *Pensione Inn Piero* (☎ 0942 2 31 39), at No 20, has comfortable singles with bathroom for L72,000/84,000 and doubles for L94,000/120,000.

Pensione Villa Gaia (☎ 0942 2 31 85, Via Fazzello 34) is near the duomo and has rooms for L45,000/95,000 (breakfast included). It is closed in winter.

Villa Nettuno (☎ 0942 2 37 97, Via Pirandello), in front of the Funivia, has singles/doubles for L65,000/110,000 and triples for L140,000 with bathroom.

Villa Fiorita (☎ 0942 2 41 22, Via Piran-

dello 39) is one of Taormina's nicer mid-range hotels. It is well-furnished and comfortable, with a garden, swimming pool, terraces and rooms with sea views. Doubles cost from L185,000 with breakfast.

Hotel Villa Belvedere (☎ 0942 2 37 91, Via Bagnoli Croci 79) has a swimming pool and garden and all rooms and terraces face Mt Etna. Singles/doubles with full services cost up to L163,000/257,000.

If you want to stay near the beach at Mazzarò, try *Villa Caterina* (☎ 0942 2 47 09, Via Nazionale 155), which has pleasant rooms for L60,000 per person.

Places to Eat

Those on a tight budget will be limited in their choice of eating places. There are several gourmet *grocery shops* along Corso Umberto I, where prices are high. Alternatively, try the side streets between Via Teatro Greco and the villa communale, where you can buy picnic supplies at several *grocery* and *pastry shops*. There is a *Standa supermarket* on Via Apollo Arcageta, just up from the post office. Quite a few restaurants close in winter.

For a quick takeaway, you could do worse than *Myosotis (Corso Umberto I 113)*. It has pizzas, *arancini* (deep fried orange rice balls stuffed with meat and peas) and panini for around L5000. For a light meal and pizza try *Shelter Pub (Via Fratelli Bandiera 10)*, off Corso Umberto I. *Time Out (Via San Pancrazio 19)* is a decent little bar and eatery. For pizza at L10,000 to L12,000, *Mamma Rosa (Via Naumachia 10)* is a safe bet.

Trattoria Rosticepi (Via San Pancrazio 10), at the top of Via Pirandello, has good meals for under L25,000 per person. *Ritrovo Trocadero (Via Pirandello 1)* makes pizzas to appeal to tourists – with names like Hawaiian and Mexican – for around L6000 to L14,000. For an excellent meal in lovely surroundings, head for *Ristorante La Piazzetta (Via Paladini 5)*, in a tiny piazza downhill from Corso Umberto I. A full meal will cost L30,000 or more. *Il Baccanale (☎ 0942 62 53 90, Piazzetta Filea)*, off Via Giovanni di Giovanni, is a popular restaurant moderately priced by Taormina standards.

SICILIA

For a quiet drink, head for *Arco Rosso-Da Micio* *(Via Naumachia 7)*, off Corso Umberto I, which serves very good Sicilian wine or walk farther down to the busier *Da Rita (Via Calapitrulli 3)* for excellent salads. Many of the cafés on Corso Umberto I charge extortionately in the high season. At the pretty *Bam Bar (Via di Giovanni 45)*, delicious Sicilian granite cost L4000 and large toasted sandwiches L6000.

Getting There & Around

Bus The bus is the easiest means of reaching Taormina. Interbus (☎ 0942 62 53 01) services leave for Messina (1½ hours, L5500) and Catania (about the same) at least hourly from about 6 am to 7 pm.

Train There are also regular trains, but the awkward location of Taormina's station is a strong disincentive. If you arrive this way, catch an Interbus bus up to the town. They run roughly every 30 to 90 minutes (much less frequently on Sunday).

Car & Motorcycle Taormina is on the A18 tollway and S114 between Messina and Catania. Parking can be a problem in Taormina, particularly in summer. The Lumbi car park is open 24 hours daily and there is a shuttle service to the centre from Porta Messina.

There are several car rental agencies in Taormina, including Avis, Hertz and Maggiore. California (☎ 0942 2 37 69), Via Bagnoli Croci 86, hires out cars and motorcycles at reasonable prices. A small car will cost between L400,000 and L487,000 a week. A Vespa costs L60,000 a day or L370,000 a week.

AROUND TAORMINA

Panorama fanatics should head 5km up the hill to **Castelmola**, literally the high point of the area, with a ruined castle and sweeping views of, well, everything. Several buses run from Taormina.

There is an **archaeological park** south of Taormina at Giardini-Naxos (follow the 'scavi' signs), the site of the first Greek settlement on Sicilia. Founded in 735 BC, it was

destroyed by Dionysius, the tyrant of Siracusa, in 403 BC. There is not a lot to see, but the park is a pleasant green refuge. It is open from 9 am to one hour before sunset Monday to Saturday and to 1 pm on Sunday. Admission costs L4000. Regular buses leave from the Taormina bus station on Via Pirandello for Giardini-Naxos. Giardini's AAST office (☎ 0942 5 10 10) is at Via Tysandros 76E.

Fans of Francis Ford Coppola's *The Godfather* might be interested to know that the wedding scene was shot at **Forza d'Agrò**, near Taormina (three buses a day from Taormina).

A relatively short drive (Interbus buses from Taormina at 9.30 and 11.30 am Monday to Friday only, return to Taormina at 2.20 and 3.20 pm; L8500 return) gets you to the **Gole Alcantara**, a series of modest lava gorges on the river of the same name, a few kilometres short of Francavilla. You could stop in here on your way to Mt Etna. There is lift access to the gorges (L4000) and you can hire wading boots (L13,000), which you'll need if you want to do anything more than peer into the gorges; otherwise, take your swimmers. It is also possible to reach the gorges by the stairs on the main road 200m uphill from the lift entrance. It is forbidden to enter the gorges from around November to May because of the risk of unexpected floods.

CATANIA
postcode 95100 • pop 376,000

Catania's crumbling appearance, chaotic traffic and reputation as a major crime centre may make it seem an intimidating and uninviting place on arrival (the ugly location of the train and bus stations doesn't help), but the city merits the benefit of the doubt. You may end up using it as a base for visiting Mt Etna, so take the time to look around its grand, if poorly maintained, baroque palazzi and chiese. It is well served by hotels and pensioni and the food is good and cheap.

A busy industrial and commercial port town, Catania has an unfortunate history. Situated at the foot of Mt Etna, it was partially destroyed in a massive eruption in 1669 and, as reconstruction began, was shaken to the ground in 1693 by an earthquake that devastated much of south-eastern Sicilia. The 18th century project to rebuild the city in grand baroque style was largely overseen by the architects Giovanni Vaccarini and Stefano Ittar.

Orientation

The main train station and Intercity bus terminal are near the port at Piazza Giovanni XXIII. From here, Corso Martiri della Libertà heads west towards the city centre, about a 15 minute walk. Follow the road to Piazza della Repubblica and continue along Corso Sicilia to Via Etnea, the main thoroughfare running north off Piazza del Duomo. Most sights are concentrated around and west of Piazza del Duomo, while the commercial centre of Catania is farther north around Via Pacini and Via Umberto I.

Information

Tourist Offices The APT office (☎ 095 730 62 22, 095 730 62 23, email apt@apt-catania .com) is at Via Cimarosa 10-12. It is open from 9 am to 7 pm Monday to Saturday. There are branches at the train station (☎ 095 730 62 55) on platform No 1, open roughly the same hours, and at the airport (☎ 095 730 62 66), open from 8 am to 10 pm daily. There is also a Web site at www.apt.catania.com.

Money Banks are concentrated along Corso Sicilia, including Credem Bank and Banca Nazionale del Lavoro, both with reliable ATMs, and several have currency exchange offices, open from 8.30 am to 1.30 pm and 2.30 to 4 pm Monday to Friday. There is a currency exchange booth at the train station and another one on Piazza Università. Amex is represented by La Duca Viaggi (☎ 095 31 61 55), Via Etnea 63-65, with another office at Piazza Europa 1.

Post & Communications The main post office is at Via Etnea 215, between Via Pacini and Via Umberto I. The Telecom office, at Corso Sicilia 67, is open from 9 am to 1 pm and 4 to 7.30 pm Monday to Saturday.

Travel Agencies The CIT travel agency (☎ 095 715 10 04) is at Via S Giuliano 208.

Medical Services In a medical emergency, go to the Ospedale Vittorio Emanuele (☎ 095 743 52 56), Via Plebiscito 268, off Via Vittorio Emanuele II, or try the Ospedale Garibaldi (☎ 095 759 43 71) on Piazza San Maria di Gesù 5/7. The all-night pharmacy, Del Centro (☎ 095 31 36 85), at Via Etnea 107, is open year-round except August. There are also a number of chemists that open at night on a rotational basis.

Piazza del Duomo & Around

Catania's most atmospheric square is easy to identify, as its centrepiece is the **Fontana dell'Elefante**, which was assembled by Vaccarini. The lava statue, carved possibly in the days of Byzantine rule, carries an Egyptian obelisk on its back. The architect worked on the square after the 1693 earthquake. He remodelled the 11th century **duomo** (recently restored), incorporating the original Norman apses and transept, and designed the **Palazzo del Municipio** (town hall) on the northern side of the piazza. It features an elegant baroque façade and, in keeping with a theme, is also known as the Palazzo degli Elefanti. Across Via Vittorio Emanuele II from the duomo is the **Badia di Sant'Agata** (a convent), yet another Vaccarini masterpiece, whose cupola dominates the city centre.

A few blocks north-east you'll stumble onto **Piazza Bellini** – the theatre of the same name is an eye-catching example of the city's architectural richness, a richness unfortunately buried beneath deep layers of grime.

North along Via Etnea from Piazza del Duomo are several buildings of interest. Facing each other on Piazza dell'Università are two designed by Vaccarini, **Palazzo dell'Università** to the west and **Palazzo San Giuliano** to the east.

Roman Ruins & Churches

West along Via Vittorio Emanuele II, at No 226, is the entrance to the ruins of a **Roman theatre** and **Odeon** (small rehearsal theatre). They are open from 9 am to one hour before sunset daily. From Piazza San Francesco, just before the entrance to the ruins, head north along Via Crociferi, which is lined

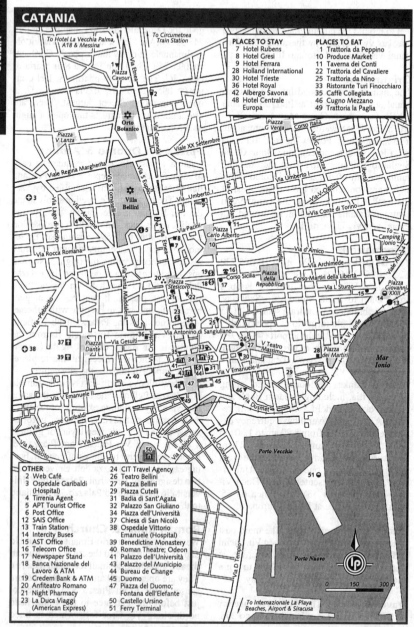

CATANIA

PLACES TO STAY
7 Hotel Rubens
8 Hotel Gresi
9 Hotel Ferrara
28 Holland International
30 Hotel Trieste
36 Hotel Royal
42 Albergo Savona
48 Hotel Centrale
   Europa

PLACES TO EAT
1 Trattoria da Peppino
10 Produce Market
11 Taverna dei Conti
22 Trattoria del Cavaliere
25 Trattoria da Nino
33 Ristorante Turi Finocchiaro
35 Caffè Collegiata
46 Cugno Mezzano
49 Trattoria la Paglia

OTHER
2 Web Café
3 Ospedale Garibaldi (Hospital)
4 Tirrenia Agent
5 APT Tourist Office
6 Post Office
12 SAIS Office
13 Train Station
14 Intercity Buses
15 AST Office
16 Telecom Office
17 Newspaper Stand
18 Banca Nazionale del Lavoro & ATM
19 Credem Bank & ATM
20 Anfiteatro Romano
21 Night Pharmacy
23 La Duca Viaggi (American Express)
24 CIT Travel Agency
26 Teatro Bellini
27 Piazza Bellini
29 Piazza Cutelli
31 Badia di Sant'Agata
32 Palazzo San Giuliano
34 Piazza dell'Università
37 Chiesa di San Nicolò
38 Ospedale Vittorio Emanuele (Hospital)
39 Benedictine Monastery
40 Roman Theatre; Odeon
41 Palazzo dell'Università
43 Palazzo del Municipio
44 Bureau de Change
45 Duomo
47 Piazza del Duomo; Fontana dell'Elefante
50 Castello Ursino
51 Ferry Terminal

with baroque churches. Turn left into Via Gesuiti and follow it to Piazza Dante and the sombre **Chiesa di San Nicolò all'Arena**. The largest church on Sicilia, its façade was never completed. Next to the church is an 18th century Benedictine monastery, the biggest in Europe after that of Mafra in Portugal, but in poor shape. It is now part of the university and slowly being restored. Wander in for a look at the cloisters – the beauty is faded, but it's there.

North of Piazza del Duomo more leftovers from Roman days include a modest **anfiteatro** (amphitheatre) on Piazza Stesicoro. For relief from the madding crowd, continue north along Via Etnea and cut in to the left behind the post office for the lovely gardens of **Villa Bellini**, named in memory of one of Catania's most famous sons, the composer Vincenzo Bellini.

Castello Ursino
Built in the 13th century by Frederick II, one of the great castle-builders of the Middle Ages, this grim-looking fortress, surrounded by a moat, is in an equally grim neighbourhood, where it is best to travel in pairs or groups. It's south-west of Piazza del Duomo, just over the train line. There are a few rooms open in the **Museo Civico** inside. Admission is free.

Special Events
Catania celebrates the feast of its patron saint Agata from 3 to 5 February. During this period one million Catanians and tourists follow as the *Fercolo* (a silver reliquary bust of the saint covered in marvellous jewels) is carried along the main street of the city. There are also spectacular fireworks during the celebrations.

Places to Stay
Camping facilities are available at *Internazionale La Playa* (☎ 095 34 83 40, *Viale Kennedy 47*), with a private sandy beach, on the way out of the city towards Siracusa (take bus No 527 from Piazza Borsellino). *Camping Jonio* (☎ 095 49 11 39, *Via Villini a Mare 2*), about 5km out of the city, is close to a

beautiful rocky beach. Charges are L10,000 per person and L10,000 for a site. To get there, catch bus No 334 from Via Etnea.

Budget hotels are located around the centre and, if you are low on money, Catania is a good place to hole up. There are several places with rock-bottom prices, including *Hotel Trieste* (☎ 095 32 71 05, *Via Leonardi 24*), near Piazza Bellini, which charges about L25,000 a person for a no-frills room.

Holland International (☎ 095 53 36 05, *Via Vittorio Emanuele II 8*) is closer to the train station, just off Piazza dei Martiri, and has singles/doubles for L35,000/60,000 and doubles with bathroom for L75,000.

A little further upmarket, *Hotel Rubens* (☎ 095 31 70 73, *Via Etnea 196*) has rooms at L38,000/50,000 or L50,000/72,000 including bath, while *Hotel Ferrara* (☎ 095 31 60 00, *Via Umberto I 66*) has rooms for L40,000/63,000 or L58,000/78,000 with bathroom. *Hotel Gresi* (☎ 095 32 37 09, *Via Pacini 28*) has singles/doubles for L60,000/80,000 and triples with bathroom for L110,000.

Just off Piazza del Duomo are two hotels with a little more class. *Albergo Savona* (☎ 095 32 69 82, *Via Vittorio Emanuele II 210*) has singles/doubles for L41,000/67,000 or for L78,000/126,000 with bathroom and breakfast. *Hotel Centrale Europa* (☎ 095 31 13 09, *Via Vittorio Emanuele II 167*) comes in at L45,000/70,000 and has doubles with bathroom for L98,000.

Hotel Royal (☎ 095 31 34 48, *Via di San Giuliano 337*) is on the corner with Via dei Crociferi near beautiful baroque churches and has rooms for L80,000/130,000 with bathroom and breakfast. *Hotel La Vecchia Palma* (☎ 095 43 20 25, *Via Etnea 668*) has nice rooms for L80,000/130,000 with bathroom and breakfast. Take bus No 1-4 or 1-5 from Piazza Università.

Places to Eat
Every morning except Sunday, Piazza Carlo Alberto is flooded by the chaos of a *produce market*, known locally as La Fiera. You can pick up supplies of bread, cheese, salami, fresh fruit and all manner of odds and ends. The other major fresh produce

market is *La Pescheria*, off Piazza del Duomo, selling fresh fish. It is open until 2 pm daily (except Sunday) and is well worth a visit.

Don't miss the savoury *arancini*, the superior Sicilian version of the lesser Italian *suppli* (breaded rice balls filled with *ragù* and peas and fried), *cartocciate* (focaccia stuffed with ham, mozzarella, olives and tomato) or baked onions, available for around L2500 apiece from a *tavola calda*, found all over town; or stop at a pasticceria to try the mouthwatering Sicilian sweets.

Eating out can be pleasant and inexpensive in Catania. Students head for the area around Via Teatro Massimo, where there are several sandwich bars and 'pubs'. The area between here and the duomo is littered with small restaurants and trattorie, but some open only for lunch.

Trattoria da Peppino (☎ 095 43 06 20, Via Empedocle 35) serves good antipasti and pasta. A complete meal costs around L30,000. For a seafood meal, go to *Trattoria La Paglia (☎ 095 34 68 38, Via Pardo 23)*, just behind Piazza del Duomo. *Taverna dei Conti (☎ 095 31 00 35, Via G Oberdan 41-43)* serves Sicilian antipasti, fish and seafood. *Trattoria del Cavaliere (☎ 095 31 04 91, Via Paternò 11)*, downtown close to Piazza Stesicoro, serves excellent Sicilian food, including grilled fish and horse meat.

Trattoria Da Nino (☎ 095 31 13 19, Via Biondi 19) has reasonably priced, good meals. Pricier but very pleasant is *Ristorante Turi Finocchiaro (☎ 095 715 35 73, Via Euplio Reina 13)*.

One of the city's better restaurants is *Cugno Mezzano (☎ 095 71 58 710, Via Museo Biscari 8)*, in the old cellar of Palazzo Biscari. Not surprisingly, it is big on wine but is quite expensive.

There are several decent *cafés* along Via Etnea, especially down the Piazza del Duomo end. For a touch of elegance, look in at *Caffè Collegiata*, at No 3 on the street of the same name. For an Internet point and a good beer check out *Web Café (Via Caronda 166)*.

Getting There & Around

Air Catania's airport, Fontanarossa, is 7km south-west of the city centre and services domestic and European flights (the latter all via Roma or Milano). In summer you may be able to dig up the odd direct charter flight to London or Paris. Take the special Alibus from outside the train station.

Bus Intercity buses terminate in the area around Piazza Giovanni XXIII, in front of the train station. SAIS (☎ 095 53 62 01), Via d'Amico 181-187, serves Siracusa, Palermo (two hours 40 minutes via autostrada, L20,000) and Agrigento. It also has a service to Roma (L75,000 one way) leaving at 8 pm. AST (☎ 095 72 30 536), Via Luigi Sturzo 232, also services these destinations and many smaller provincial towns around Catania, including Nicolosi, the cable car on Mt Etna and Noto. Interbus-Etna Trasporti (☎ 095 53 27 16), at the same address as SAIS, runs buses to Piazza Armerina, Taormina, Messina, Enna, Ragusa, Gela and Roma.

Many of the more useful AMT city buses terminate in front of the train station. These include: Alibus, station-airport; Nos 1-4 and 1-6, station-Via Etnea; and Nos 4-7 and 4-6, station-Piazza del Duomo. Buy a daily ticket for L3500. In summer, a special service (D) runs from Piazza G Verga to the sandy beaches. Bus No 334 from Via Etnea takes you to the Riviera dei Ciclopi and the beautiful Norman castello at Acicastello (admission is free).

Train Frequent trains connect Catania with Messina and Siracusa (both 1½ hours) and there are less frequent services to Palermo (3¼ hours), Enna (1¾ hours) and Agrigento (an agonisingly slow four hours). The private Circumetnea train line circles Mt Etna, stopping at the towns and villages on the volcano's slopes. See the later Mt Etna Getting There & Away section.

Car & Motorcycle Catania is easily reached from Messina on the A18 and from Palermo on the A19. From the A18, signs for the centre of Catania will bring you to Via Etnea.

Boat Tirrenia (☎ 095 31 63 94), Via Androne 43, runs car ferries to Livorno (Toscana), four days a week. Gozo Channel, represented by Fratelli Bonanno (☎ 095 31 06 29) at Via Anzalone 7, runs boats to Malta. The ferry terminal is south of the train station along Via VI Aprile.

MT ETNA

Dominating the landscape in eastern Sicilia between Taormina and Catania, Mt Etna (approximately 3350m) is Europe's largest live volcano and one of the world's most active. Eruptions occur frequently, both from the four live craters at the summit (one, the Bocca Nuova, was formed in 1968) and on the slopes of the volcano, which is littered with crevices and old craters.

The volcano's most devastating eruption occurred in 1669 and lasted 122 days. A huge river of lava poured down its southern slope, engulfing a good part of Catania and dramatically altering the landscape. In 1971 an eruption destroyed the observatory at the summit, and another in 1983 finished off the old cable car and tourist centre (you can see where the lava flow stopped on that occasion). Nine people died in an explosion at the southeastern crater in 1979, and two died and 10 were injured in an explosion at the crater in 1987. Its most recent eruption was in 1992, when a stream of lava pouring from a fissure in its south-eastern slope threatened to engulf the town of Zafferana Etnea. The town was saved, but not before one family lost their home and others much of their farmland.

The volcano's unpredictability means people are no longer allowed to climb to the craters. Only a rope marks the point where it becomes unsafe, but it would be foolish to ignore the warning signs and go any farther.

On the northern side of the volcano is a Pro Loco tourist centre (☎ 095 64 30 94), Piazza Annunziata 7 in Linguaglossa. It has information about skiing and excursions to the craters, as well as an exhibition of the flora, fauna and rocks of the Parco Naturale dell'Etna. It is possible to hire a 4WD and guide to tour the volcano. On the southern side, try the APT office in Catania for information. NeT Natura e Turismo (☎ 095 33 35 43, email natetur@tin.it), Via R Quartararo 11, organises tours of the volcano with a volcanologist or expert guide.

To the Craters

South With a daily bus link from Catania via Nicolosi, the southern side of the volcano presents the easier option for an ascent towards the craters. From Rifugio Sapienza (the locality has taken its name from the rifugio that used to be here), the closest the surfaced road comes to the summit, a cable car (SITAS, ☎ 095 91 41 41) climbs to 2600m. It operates from 9 am to 3.30 pm year-round (L34,000 return). In summer, 4WD vehicles then take you through the eerie lava-scape close to the 3000m level. The price for cable car, 4WD and guide was L65,000 return at the time of writing. In winter you are expected to ski back down (snow permitting) – there is no transport beyond the cable car. A day ski pass costs L35,000.

Some tourists make the long climb from Rifugio Sapienza to the top (3½ to four hours on a track winding up under the cable car and then following the same road used by the minibuses).

North Several ski lifts run at Piano Provenzana, snow permitting (a day ski pass costs up to L25,000). From the lifts you're looking at about an hour's walk to come close to the top – a difficult proposition on snow. Inquire about hiring a guide and the feasibility of the walk in winter at the Linguaglossa Pro Loco.

In summer, the lifts don't operate but 4WDs make the same journey. Again, consider a guide for the hour's scramble from where the vehicles stop. At Piano Provenzana, Le Betulle/STAR (☎ 095 64 34 30) charges L60,000 for the three hour return trip to 3100m with a 4WD and guide.

Places to Stay

There's a *camp site* at Nicolosi (☎ *095 91 43 09, Via Goethe*). *Hotel Corsaro* (☎ *095 91 41 22*) at Rifugio Sapienza on the southern side, 200m from the cable car, has singles/doubles for L90,000/130,000.

At Piano Provenzana, a small ski resort on the northern side, *Rifugio Nord-Est (☎ 095 64 79 22)* has beds for L40,000 a night and half board for L65,000.

There are small *hotels* at Piano Provenzana and in some of the towns along the Circumetnea train line, including Linguaglossa and Randazzo. For details, contact the Catania APT office.

Getting There & Away

Having your own transport will make life much easier around Mt Etna, but there are some public transport options. The easier approach is from the south.

South An AST bus (☎ 095 53 17 56) departs the car park in front of the main train station in Catania at 8.15 am for Rifugio Sapienza via Nicolosi. It returns from the rifugio at 4.30 pm. The return ticket costs L7000. The AST office (☎ 095 91 15 05), at Via Etnea 32 in Nicolosi, is open from 8 am to 2 pm Monday to Saturday. You can also drive this route (take Via Etnea north out of town and follow the signs for Nicolosi and Etna).

North SAIS and FCE buses connect Linguaglossa with Fiumefreddo on the coast (from where other SAIS buses run north to Taormina and Messina and south to Catania). Unless the FCE puts on a winter ski-season or summer bus to Piano Provenzana, your only chance from Linguaglossa is your thumb. If driving, follow the signs for Piano Provenzana out of Linguaglossa.

Around the Mountain Another option is to circle Mt Etna on the private Circumetnea train line. It starts in Catania at the train station at Corso delle Province 13, opposite Corso Italia. Go to the ticket office (☎ 095 37 48 42) for information. Catch bus No 628, 448 or 401 from the main train station to Corso delle Province. The line runs around the mountain from Catania to the coastal town of Riposto, passing through numerous towns and villages on its slopes, including Linguaglossa. You can reach Riposto (or neighbouring Giarre) from Taor-

mina by train or bus if you want to make the trip from that end.

Catania-Riposto is about a 3½ hour trip, but you needn't go that far. If you're leaving from Catania, consider finishing the trip at Randazzo (two hours), a small medieval town noted for the fact that it has consistently escaped destruction despite its proximity to the summit. Randazzo is mildly interesting itself, with a couple of churches to punctuate a brief stroll along a few quiet streets, some lined with Aragonese apartments. A good example of lava architecture are the walls of the Norman Cattedrale di Santa Maria, while the Chiesa di Santa Maria della Volta preserves a squat 14th century campanile.

An FS railway branch line connects Randazzo with Taormina/Giardini Naxos, but services are subject to cancellation. The infrequent SAIS buses are more reliable.

South-Eastern Sicilia

SIRACUSA (SYRACUSE)
postcode 96100 • pop 121,000

Once a powerful Greek city rivalling Athens, Siracusa is one of the highlights of a visit to Sicilia. The city was founded in 734 BC by colonists from Corinth, who established their settlement on the island of Ortigia. Ruled by a succession of tyrants from the 5th century BC, Siracusa became a dominant sea power in the Mediterraneo, prompting Athens to attack it in 413 BC. In one of history's great maritime battles, the Athenian fleet was sent to the bottom of the sea.

Siracusa reached its zenith under the rule of Dionysius and attracted luminaries from all around, Plato among them. He apparently so bored Dionysius with his diatribes that the tyrant tried to sell the philosopher as a slave.

The Romans marched into Siracusa in 212 BC, but the city remained important and enlightened under the new administration. Less sensitive handling came from the barbarians in the 5th century AD, later succeeded by the Byzantine empire. Siracusa's fate followed

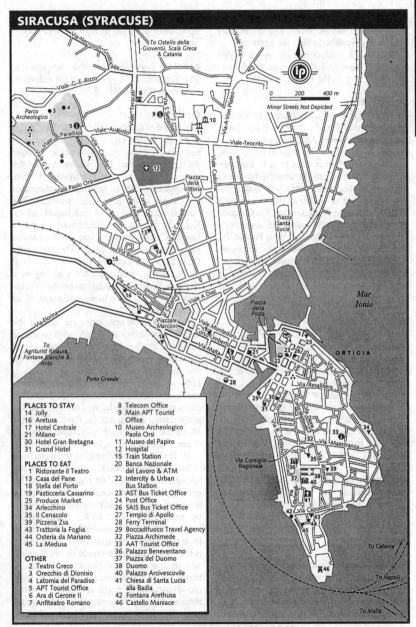

SIRACUSA (SYRACUSE)

To Ostello della Gioventù, Scala Greca & Catania

Parco Archeologico

Piazza della Vittoria

Piazza Santa Lucia

0   200   400 m

Minor Streets Not Depicted

Mar Ionio

Piazza della Posta

ORTIGIA

To Agriturist Rinaura, Fontane Bianche & Noto

Porto Grande

Via Consiglio Regionale

To Catania

To Napoli

To Malta

PLACES TO STAY
14 Jolly
16 Aretusa
17 Hotel Centrale
21 Milano
30 Hotel Gran Bretagna
31 Grand Hotel

PLACES TO EAT
1   Ristorante il Teatro
13 Casa del Pane
18 Stella del Porto
19 Pasticceria Cassarino
25 Produce Market
34 Arlecchino
35 Il Cenacolo
39 Pizzeria Zsa
43 Trattoria la Foglia
44 Osteria da Mariano
45 La Medusa

OTHER
2   Teatro Greco
3   Orecchio di Dionisio
4   Latomia del Paradiso
5   APT Tourist Office
6   Ara di Gerone II
7   Anfiteatro Romano

8   Telecom Office
9   Main APT Tourist
    Office
10 Museo Archeologico
    Paolo Orsi
11 Museo del Papiro
12 Hospital
15 Train Station
20 Banca Nazionale
    del Lavoro & ATM
22 Intercity & Urban
    Bus Station
23 AST Bus Ticket Office
24 Post Office
26 SAIS Bus Ticket Office
27 Tempio di Apollo
28 Ferry Terminal
29 Boccadifuoco Travel Agency
32 Piazza Archimede
33 AAT Tourist Office
36 Palazzo Beneventano
37 Piazza del Duomo
38 Duomo
40 Palazzo Arcivescovile
41 Chiesa di Santa Lucia
    alla Badia
42 Fontana Arethusa
46 Castello Maniace

euro currency converter   L10,000 = €5.16

that of much of the island, witnessing the arrival of the Arabs, Normans, Swabians, French and Spaniards over the centuries.

The Greek mathematician Archimedes was born here and the apostle Paul converted the city to the Christian faith.

Orientation

The main sights of Siracusa are in two areas: on the island of Ortigia and 2km across town in the Neapolis Parco Archeologico (archaeological zone). From the train station, walk east along Via Francesco Crispi to Piazzale Marconi. Heading straight through the piazza to Corso Umberto will bring you to Ortigia, just a five minute walk. Alternatively, turn left from Piazzale Marconi into Via Catania, cross the train line and follow the busy shopping street, Corso Gelone, to Viale Paolo Orsi and the Parco Archeologico. If you arrive by bus, you'll be dropped in or near Piazza della Posta in Ortigia. Most accommodation is in the newer part of town, to the west, while the better eating places are in Ortigia.

Information

Tourist Offices The main APT office (☎ 0931 6 77 10), Via San Sebastiano 45, opens from 8.30 am to 1.30 pm Monday to Saturday. There's also a branch office at the Parco Archeologico.

The AAT office (☎ 0931 46 42 55), on Ortigia at Via Maestranza 33, deals specifically with Siracusa and is probably the most convenient office at which to pick up a map and hotel list. It is open from 8.30 am to 2 pm and 2.30 to 5.30 pm Monday to Friday.

Money Numerous banks line Corso Umberto, including the Banca Nazionale del Lavoro at No 29, which has ATMs. There are others on Corso Gelone. The rates at the train station currency exchange booth are generally poor.

Post & Communications The post office is on Piazza della Posta, to your left as you cross the bridge to Ortigia. It is open from 8.30 am to 6.30 pm Monday to Friday and to 1 pm on Saturday.

The Telecom office, Viale Teracati 46, is open from 8.30 am to 7.30 pm Monday to Saturday.

Medical Services The public hospital is at Via Testaferrata 1. For medical emergencies, ring ☎ 0931 6 85 55.

Ortigia

The island of Ortigia is the spiritual and physical heart of the city. Its buildings are predominantly medieval, with some baroque palazzi and chiese. The 7th century **duomo** was built on top of a Greek temple of Athena, incorporating most of the original columns of the temple in its three-aisled structure. The duomo is a melting pot of architectural styles. Rebuilt after various earthquakes, it has a Gothic-Catalan ceiling, a baroque façade and baroque chapels and altars. The towers on the left side of the church's exterior were built by the Arabs, who used the building as a mosque. Some of the columns on the left side have shifted on their bases, the result of an earthquake in 1542.

Piazza del Duomo, once the site of the Greek acropolis, is lined with baroque palazzi, including **Palazzo Beneventano** and **Palazzo Arcivescovile** (Archbishop's Palace), and is one of the finest baroque squares in Italy. At the southern end is **Chiesa di Santa Lucia alla Badia**, dedicated to St Lucy, the city's patron saint, who was martyred at Siracusa during the reign of the Roman Emperor Diocletian. The church's baroque façade is decorated with a wrought-iron balustrade.

Walk down Via Picherali to the waterfront to find **Fontana Aretusa**, a natural freshwater spring only metres from the sea. Greek legend says the nymph Arethusa, pursued by the river god Alpheus, was turned into a fountain by the goddess Diana so she could escape. Undeterred, Alpheus turned himself into the river that feeds the spring. Next to the spring is the **Foro Vittorio Emanuele II**, where locals take their evening constitutional. At the entrance to Ortigia, on Piazza Pancali, lies **Tempio di Apollo** (Temple of Apollo). Little remains of the 6th century BC Doric structure, apart from the bases of a few columns.

Parco Archeologico

For the classicist, Siracusa is summed up in one image – that of the sparkling white, 5th century BC **Teatro Greco**, hewn out of the rock in what for the Greek settlers was Neapolis (New City). A masterpiece, the ancient theatre could seat 16,000 people.

Near the theatre is **Latomia del Paradiso** (Garden of Paradise), which was a former limestone quarry run by the Greeks along the lines of a concentration camp, where prisoners cut blocks of limestone in subterranean tunnels for building projects. Most of the area remained covered by a 'roof' of earth, which collapsed during the 1693 earthquake. After this, the garden of citrus and magnolia trees was created.

In the garden is **Orecchio di Dionisio** (Ear of Dionysius), an ear-shaped grotto 23m high and 65m deep. It was named by Caravaggio, who, during a visit in the 17th century, was much impressed by its extraordinary acoustics. Caravaggio mused that the tyrant must have taken advantage of them to overhear the whispered conversations of his prisoners. Next to it, the **Grotta dei Cordari** (Cordmakers' Cave) is so named because it was used by cordmakers to practise their craft. The cave has been closed for some years.

Back outside this area and opposite the APT office you'll find the entrance to the 2nd century AD **Anfiteatro Romano**. The amphitheatre was used for gladiator fighting and horse races. Roman punters used to park their chariots in the area between the amphitheatre and Viale Paolo Orsi. The Spaniards, little interested in archaeology, largely destroyed the site in the 16th century, using it as a quarry to build the city walls of Ortygia. West of the amphitheatre is the 3rd century BC **Ara di Gerone II** (Altar of Hieron II). The monolithic sacrificial altar was a kind of giant abattoir where 450 oxen could be killed at one time.

The Parco Archeologico is open from 9 am to one hour before sunset daily (in the depths of winter to 3 pm). Admission costs L4000 and you can stay for up to an hour after the ticket window shuts. To get here, catch a bus (No 1 and several others) from Riva della Posta on Ortigia.

Museo Archeologico Paolo Orsi

This museum is in the grounds of Villa Landolina, about 500m east of the Parco Archeologico, off Viale Teocrito. It contains the best organised and most interesting archaeological collection on Sicilia and certainly merits a visit. It is divided into three sections: Section A deals with proto and prehistoric Sicilia, Section B has an excellent collection from the ancient Greek colonies of Megara Hyblea and Siracusa itself and Section C looks at Syracusan sub-colonies such as Eloro, as well as several Hellenised indigenous towns, and Agrigento and Gela. The museum (☎ 0931 46 40 22) is open from 9 am to 1 pm and 3.30 to 6.30 pm daily except Monday. Admission costs L8000.

Museo del Papiro

This small museum (☎ 0931 6 16 16) at Viale Teocrito 66 has exhibits including papyrus documents and products. The plant grows in abundance around the Ciane river, near Siracusa, and was used to make paper in the 18th century. The museum is open from 9 am to 2 pm Tuesday to Sunday. Admission is free.

Special Events

Since 1914, in every even-numbered year, Siracusa has hosted a festival of Greek classical drama in May and June. Performances are given in the Teatro Greco theatre and prices range from around L20,000 for unreserved seats in the rear to L80,000 for reserved seats close to the stage. Tickets are available from the APT office or at a booth at the theatre entrance. You can call for information on ☎ 0931 6 53 73. At the time of writing the organisation that runs the festival was in financial difficulty and the future of the event was uncertain.

Places to Stay – Budget

Camping There are camping facilities at *Agriturist Rinaura* (☎ 0931 72 12 24), about 4km west of the city; catch bus No 21, 22 or 24 from Corso Umberto. It costs L8000 per person and around L19,000 for a site (including electricity and car space). *Fontane Bianche* (☎ 0931 79 03 33) is about 18km south-west of Siracusa, at the beach of the same name. It is slightly more expensive than Agriturist Rinaura and is open from April to October. Catch bus No 21 or 22.

Hostels The non-HI *Ostello della Gioventù* (☎ 0931 71 11 18, Viale Epipoli 45) is 8km west of Siracusa; catch bus No 11 or 25 from Piazza Marconi. A bed costs L25,000.

Hotels Close to the train station is *Hotel Centrale* (☎ 0931 6 05 28, Corso Umberto 141). It has small, basic singles/doubles for L35,000/50,000. *Milano* (☎ 0931 6 69 81, Corso Umberto 10), near Ortigia, has no-frills rooms for L30,000/55,000 or L50,000/80,000 with bathroom.

The two star *Aretusa* (☎/fax 0931 2 42 11, Via Francesco Crispi 75) is close to the train station and has comfortable singles/doubles for L45,000/70,000. With bathroom, they're L50,000/80,000.

Hotel Gran Bretagna (☎ 0931 6 87 65, Via Savoia 21) is pleasant and has rooms for L53,000/87,000 or L63,000/99,000 with bathroom.

Places to Stay – Mid-Range & Top End

Scala Greca (☎ 0931 75 39 22, fax 0931 75 37 78, Via Avola 7) is north of the Parco Archeologico and has singles/doubles with bathroom for L75,000/98,000. It is, like several other better hotels, quite a distance from the centre. *Jolly* (☎ 0931 46 11 11, fax 0931 46 11 26, Corso Gelone 45) is a very good choice. It is near both the train station and the Parco Archeologico. Fully-serviced, sound-proofed rooms cost up to L215,000/270,000.

The newly restored *Grand Hotel* (☎ 0931 46 46 00, fax 0931 46 46 11, Viale Mazzini 12) on Ortigia has top-class rooms for L240,000/350,000.

Places to Eat

In the streets near the post office, there's a *produce market* until 1 pm daily except Sunday. There are several *grocery shops* and *supermarkets* along Corso Gelone.

For snacks, try the excellent takeaway pizza and focaccia at *Casa del Pane* (Corso Gelone 65).

In the new part of town, *Stella del Porto* (☎ 0931 6 05 82, Via Tripoli 40), off Via Malta, is a simple trattoria with a small menu concentrating on seafood. Try the *pesce spada* (spaghetti with swordfish). A full meal will cost about L25,000. At *Trattoria la Foglia* (☎ 0931 6 62 33, Via Capodieci 21), the eccentric owner/chef and her vegetarian husband serve whatever seafood and vegetables are fresh on the day and bake their own bread. A full meal will cost around L40,000. *Arlecchino* (☎ 0931 6 63 86, Via dei Tolomei 5), near the waterfront, is one of the city's better restaurants. You'll be lucky to pay less than L45,000 a head.

Ristorante Osteria da Mariano (☎ 0931 6 74 44, Vicolo Zuccalà 9), on Ortigia, serves very good traditional Sicilian fare. *Pizzeria Trattoria Zsà* (☎ 0931 2 22 04, Via Roma 73) serves 65 different kinds of pizzas, antipasti and pasta. In both places a full meal costs around L25,000. A good pizzeria is *Il Cenacolo* (☎ 0931 6 50 99, Via del Consiglio Regionale 10). For good fish and Tunisian food go to *La Medusa* (☎ 0931 6 14 03, Via Santa Teresa 23). In the Parco Archeologico, close to the Teatro Greco, *Ristorante il Teatro* (☎ 0931 2 13 21, Via Agnello 8) has a good tourist menu for L22,000. For Sicilian sweets such as cannoli di ricotta and cassata go to *Pasticceria Cassarino* (☎ 0931 6 80 46, Corso Umberto 86).

Getting There & Away

Bus Unless you're coming from Catania or Messina, you'll find buses faster and more convenient than trains. INTERBUS buses (☎ 0931 6 67 10) leave from Riva della Posta or near their office at Via Trieste 28. They connect with Catania and its airport, Palermo (three to four hours, L20,000), Enna and surrounding small towns, including Noto. INTERBUS also has a daily service to Roma, leaving Siracusa at 7.45 am and connecting with the Roma bus at Catania. A single ticket costs L67,000 or L57,000 for people under 26 and over 60.

AST buses (☎ 0931 46 48 20) leave for

SICILIA

Catania, Piazza Armerina, Noto, Modica and Ragusa from their office at Riva della Posta 9/11.

Train More than a dozen trains depart daily for Messina (three hours) via Catania (1½ hours). Some go on to Roma, Torino, Milano and other long-distance destinations. There is only one direct connection to Palermo, leaving at 6.40 am and taking five hours. If you insist on using trains and miss this one, you'll have to go to Catania and wait for a connection. There are several slow trains to Modica and Ragusa.

Car & Motorcycle By car, if arriving from the north, you will enter Siracusa on Via Scala Greca. To reach the centre of the city, turn left at Viale Teracati and follow it around to the south; it eventually becomes Corso Gelone. There is ongoing confusion over the superstrada connection between Catania, Siracusa and towns such as Noto farther along the coast. An autostrada is supposed to connect the towns but starts and ends virtually in the middle of nowhere some kilometres out of Siracusa. You'll need to follow the signs to find it.

Boat Maltese companies run summer ferry and catamaran services to Siracusa. For information try the Boccadifuoco travel agency (☎ 0931 46 38 66), Viale Mazzini 8.

Getting Around
Only a few kilometres separate the Parco Archeologico and Ortigia, about a 20 minute walk. Otherwise, bus Nos 1 and 2 make the trip from Piazza della Posta.

NOTO
postcode 96017 • pop 23,000
Flattened by the 1693 earthquake, picturesque Noto was rebuilt in grand baroque style by its noble families. The warm gold and rose hues of the local stone tone down the heavily embellished palazzi and chiese. However, many of Noto's most important buildings are in a state of extreme disrepair – the result of decades of neglect and plenty of

minor earth tremors. The town was shocked in early 1996 when the dome and roof of its splendid baroque cattedrale collapsed – apparently local authorities knew that the dome was cracked, but nothing was done. Fortunately, it was empty at the time. The absence of the dome has dramatically altered the town's skyline, since the original designers of baroque Noto had taken particular account of the town's visual impact as a whole.

Noto is also good for your tastebuds and particularly known for its cakes and pastries. Be aware that accommodation is a problem.

Orientation & Information
Intercity buses drop you in the Porta Reale, which is at the beginning of Corso Vittorio Emanuele, the town's main street. You can get a map at the APT office (☎ 0931 57 37 79) on Piazza XVI Maggio. It is open from 8 am to 2 pm and 3.30 to 7 pm. The public hospital is on Via dei Mille, on the way out of town towards Noto Antica. In a medical emergency call ☎ 0931 57 12 25.

Things to See & Do
The collapse of the cattedrale dome revealed that previous restoration work done on the city's monuments had been very superficial – a significant problem, since the local white *tufo* stone is very soft and, as a building material, requires constant maintenance. The situation is so bad that several buildings remain standing only because they're held up by wooden supports. Lots of money has been allocated in the past, only to remain unspent, or to evaporate into the ether. However, it seems that the authorities are now serious and numerous projects are under way to restore the cathedral and other important buildings in the city centre. There has also been a move to have Noto added to UNESCO's World Heritage List.

Most of the important monuments line Corso Vittorio Emanuele. Overlooking Piazza XVI Maggio are **Chiesa di San Domenico** and the adjacent **Dominican convent**, both designed by Rosario Gagliardi, a Sicilian architect who made a big contribution to the town's reconstruction. Back towards the

Porta Reale is **Palazzo Villadorata** (also known as Palazzo Nicolaci), on Via Corrado Nicolaci. On the third Sunday in May the street is transformed into a sea of flowers for the **Infiorata**, a festival to welcome the spring. Each of the palazzo's richly sculpted balconies is decorated differently, sporting a veritable menagerie of centaurs, horses, lions, sirens and tragic masks. Once the home of the princes of Villadorata, it is now partly used as municipal offices and some rooms are open to the public.

The **cattedrale** stands at the top of a sweeping staircase overlooking Piazza Municipio. The façade is imposing, but less extravagant than most of Noto's other baroque monuments. Next to the cattedrale is **Palazzo Landolina**, now abandoned, but belonging to the Sant'Alfano, Noto's oldest noble family. Across the piazza is **Palazzo Ducezio**, the town hall, which has been buried in scaffolding for years.

Farther Corso Vittorio Emanuele are the **Chiesa del Santissimo Salvatore** and an adjoining **monastery**. The interior of the church is the most impressive in Noto. The monastery was reserved for the daughters of local nobility. The fountain suspended on a wall next to the monastery was left there after Noto's streets were lowered in 1840 to facilitate the movement of carriages.

Places to Stay

Albergo Stella (☎ 0931 83 56 95), on the corner of Via F Maiore and Via Napoli, near the public gardens, has singles/doubles for L35,000/70,000. *L'Arca* (☎ 0931 89 42 02, Via R Pirri 14), close to Corso Vittorio Emanuele, has rooms for L70,000/95,000. It has a Web site at www.polosud.it/arca. At the end of Corso Vittorio Emanuele, *Al Canisello Rooms* (☎ 0931 83 57 93, Via Pavese 1) is a quiet farmhouse with rooms for L80,000/100,000.

The remaining tourist accommodation is by the sea at Noto Marina, a 15 minute drive or bus trip (buses run only in summer). Hotels include *Albergo Korsal* (☎ 0931 81 21 19), which has rooms for L60,000/95,000, and *President* (☎ 0931 81 25 43), with a

higher standard of rooms for L105,000/170,000.

Places to Eat

The people of Noto are serious about their food, so take time to enjoy a meal and follow it up with a visit to one of the town's excellent bars/pasticcerie. *Caffè Sicilia* (☎ 0931 83 50 13, Corso Vittorio Emanuele 125) and *Corrado Costanzo* (☎ 0931 83 52 43, Via Silvio Spaventa 9), round the corner, are neck and neck when it comes to the best gelato and dolce in Noto. Both make superb *dolci di mandorle* (almond cakes and sweets), real cassata cake and *torrone* (nougat), as well as heavenly gelati and granita – try the one made with *fragolini* (tiny wild strawberries).

Trattoria del Carmine (☎ 0931 83 87 05, Via Ducezio 9) serves excellent home-style meals for about L25,000 a head (try the *coniglio alla stimpirata*), as does *Trattoria del Giglio* (Piazza Municipio 8-10). *Ristorante Neas* (☎ 0931 57 35 38, Via Rocco Pirri 30), close to Corso Vittorio Emanuele, serves typical Sicilian fare.

Shopping

If you are interested in taking home a few pieces of Sicilian ceramics, All'Angolo, on the corner of Piazza dell'Immacolata and Corso Vittorio Emanuele, has an excellent selection of pieces from Caltagirone and Santo Stefano di Camastra.

Getting There & Away

Noto is easily accessible by AST and INTERBUS buses from Catania and Siracusa. Buses run frequently between Noto and Noto Marina from June to August only (in winter there is a school bus service).

AROUND NOTO

The beach at **Noto Marina** is pleasant and, as yet, has not been subject to the overdevelopment characteristic of most Italian resorts. Nearby, and accessible only by car or by making the 45 minute walk, is **Eloro**, the site of a Greek settlement later occupied by the Romans. Uncompleted excavations have revealed a city square and sacred area. On either side of the hill where the sparse ruins lie are long, sandy beaches comparatively free of the usual crowds. Unfortunately, a storm-water drain spills into the sea at the beach to the south of Eloro.

Farther along the coast is the **Riserva Naturale di Vendicari**, a haven for water birds, with special observatories. There is also a superb, long, sandy beach that is popular in summer but never overcrowded. It is possible to reach the park by SAIS bus connecting Noto and Pachino or by INTERBUS (☎ 0931 83 50 23) from Largo Pantheon behind the public gardens.

If you have a car, there are several interesting places to visit within an hour or two of Noto. At **Palazzolo Acreide**, the site of the ancient Akrai, one of the early colonies of Greek Siracusa, there is a Parco Archeologico with the ruins of a Greek theatre, temples and a series of interesting rock carvings called **santoni**, figures connected to ancient goddess worship. Admission costs L4000. About 30km from Palazzolo are the necropoli of **Pantalica**, which are definitely worth a visit. This has been identified as the site of ancient Hybla, one of the oldest settlements in eastern Sicilia, dating back to the Bronze Age. The necropoli are in a deep gorge. It is possible to walk down into the gorge – even to swim in its icy waters. Of interest are the sparse ruins of the *anaktoron*, a monumental royal palace, similar to a Mycenaean *megaron*.

Closer to Noto is **Cava d'Ispica**, just outside the town of Ispica, a Parco Archeologico above a deep gorge. There are traces of prehistoric, Byzantine and medieval settlements. The area was abandoned after the 1693 earthquake.

AST buses leave from Piazza della Posta in Siracusa for Palazzolo Acreide and Ispica. There are also regular trains from Siracusa for Ispica. AST buses leave from Siracusa for Ferla and Sortino, 11km and 6km from Pantalica respectively. There are no buses connecting these towns to Pantalica itself. The Siracusa APT office has timetables and more information.

RAGUSA & RAGUSA IBLA
postcode 97100 • pop 68,000
This prosperous provincial capital is virtually two towns in one: Ragusa Ibla, a curious cocktail of medieval and baroque, and the 18th century 'new' town, simply known as Ragusa.

Orientation & Information
The lower town, Ibla, has most of the sights, but transport and accommodation are in the newer upper town. The train station is on Piazza del Popolo and the Intercity bus station is on the adjacent Piazza Gramsci. From the train station, turn left and head along Viale Tenente Lena, across the bridge (Ponte Nuovo) and straight ahead along Via Roma to reach Corso Italia, the upper town's main street. Turn right on Corso Italia and follow it to the stairs to Ibla or follow the winding road to the lower town.

The tourist office (☎ 0932 62 14 21), at Via Capitano Bocchieri 33 in Palazzo La Rocca, is open from 9 am to 1.30 pm Monday to Saturday. The Ospedale Civile (☎ 0932 62 39 46 for the Guardia Medica) is across Piazza del Popolo from the train station. For an ambulance, call ☎ 0932 62 14 10.

Things to See & Do
The stairs linking the upper and lower towns are next to **Chiesa di Santa Maria delle Scale**. The church, rebuilt after the 1693 earthquake, retains parts of the original 15th century structure, including the campanile and doorway. Take in the panoramic view of Ibla before heading down the stairs.

The **Basilica di San Giorgio**, at the top of a flight of stairs on the Piazza del Duomo, dominates Ibla. Designed by Rosario Gagliardi and built in the late 18th century, it has the boisterous, 'wedding-cake' appearance of high baroque.

Follow Corso XXV Aprile downhill, past **Chiesa di San Giuseppe**, which bears similarities to San Giorgio, until you reach the **Giardino Ibleo**, the town's pleasant public gardens, where you can have a picnic.

In the upper town, visit the early 18th century **duomo** on Piazza San Giovanni off

Corso Italia and **Museo Archeologico Ibleo** (☎ 0932 62 29 63) on Via Natalelli, off Via Roma. The museum is open from 9 am to 1.30 pm and 4 to 7.30 pm Monday to Saturday. Admission costs L4000.

Places to Stay & Eat

All of Ragusa's accommodation is in the upper town and there are no budget hotels. *Hotel San Giovanni (☎ 0932 62 10 13, Via Traspontino 3)* has singles/doubles for L40,000/60,000 or L60,000/96,000 with bathroom. To get there from Piazza del Popolo, head down Viale Leonardo da Vinci, turn left at Via Ingegnere Migliorisi and follow it to the footbridge.

Hotel Rafael (☎ 0932 65 40 80, Corso Italia 40) is a pleasant establishment; rooms with bathroom are L80,000/120,000. Nearby *Hotel Montreal (☎ 0932 62 11 33, Corso Italia 70)* has good singles/doubles with bathroom and breakfast for L90,000/125,000.

There is a *Standa supermarket (Via Roma 187)*, near the bridge. *Trattoria la Bettola (☎ 0932 65 33 77, Largo Camerina 7)*, downhill to the left off Piazza del Duomo, is pleasant and meals are priced at around L30,000. *La Rusticana (☎ 0932 22 79 81, Via XXV Aprile 68)* is another reasonable little place. *U Saracinù (☎ 0932 24 69 76, Via del Convento 9)*, off Piazza del Duomo, has a L25,000 tourist menu; otherwise a full meal will come to around L40,000.

Getting There & Around

Ragusa is accessible by not-so-regular trains from Siracusa, Noto and Agrigento. Buses are better. Etna Trasporti (☎ 0932 62 34 40), a subsidiary of SAIS (information and tickets at Gran Bar Puglisi, Via Dante 94, opposite the train station), runs eight buses per day to Catania.

AST (☎ 0932 68 18 18) serves Palermo (four buses a day) and runs more regularly to Noto and Siracusa (seven a day). An AST timetable is posted at the spot on Piazza Gramsci where AST and SAIS buses stop.

City bus Nos 1 and 3 run from Piazza del Popolo in the upper town to Piazza Pola and the gardens in the lower town of Ragusa Ibla.

MODICA

About 20km east of Ragusa, Modica seems to be a close cousin. It has the same sun-bleached colour and is also divided into two sections: Modica Alta (High Modica) and, you guessed it, Modica Bassa (Low Modica).

The highlight is **Chiesa di San Giorgio** in the upper part of town (local buses run by from the lower end), easily one of the most extraordinary baroque churches in the province. A majestic stairway sweeps up to a daringly tall façade, erected by Rosario Gagliardi in the early 18th century – it looks as if it was meant to be a tower. There are regular AST buses from Ragusa.

Central & South-Western Sicilia

ENNA

postcode 94100 • pop 29,000

High on a commanding ridge in the sun-scorched centre of Sicilia, Enna is somewhat isolated from the main tourist route around the coast. Known since Greek times as the 'umbilicus' of Sicilia, the journey itself is rewarding, from whichever direction you approach. The exercise becomes more tempting still if combined with an excursion to nearby Piazza Armerina for the extraordinary mosaics of the Villa Romana (see Piazza Armerina later in this section).

Enna, 931m above sea level, has been an ideal defensive position and lookout post since prehistoric times. First settled by the Sicani, Enna later became Greek, submitting to the tyranny of Siracusa in 307 BC and thereafter falling into Carthaginian and Roman hands. In Byzantine times it became a fortress and one of the main bulwarks against the Arabs, who nonetheless managed to capture the town in 859. Today it is an important agricultural and mining centre.

Orientation

The principal road into the town is Via Pergusa, which eventually links with Via Roma, the main street of historic Enna. The intercity bus station is on Viale Diaz. To get to the town centre, turn right from the station and follow Viale Diaz to Corso Sicilia, turn right again and follow it to Via Sant'Agata to the left, which heads down to Via Roma.

Information

The AAPIT office (☎ 0935 52 82 28) is at Via Roma 413. The staff are helpful and have maps and information on the city and province. The office is open from 9 am to 1 pm and from 3 to 7 pm Monday to Saturday. The AAST office (☎ 0935 50 08 75), next to Albergo Sicilia in nearby Piazza Cola-janni 6, has information mainly on the city itself and is open from 8 am to 2 pm daily.

The post office is at Via Volta 1, just off Piazza Garibaldi. Public telephones are scattered around the town or you can try Albergo Sicilia.

There are several banks on Piazza VI Dicembre, a short walk downhill from the AAPIT office.

For medical assistance, go to the Ospedale Civile Umberto I on Via Trieste or call ☎ 0935 4 51 11. Out of hours, the Guardia Medica is on ☎ 0935 50 08 96.

Castello di Lombardia

Enna's most visible monument, the medieval castello, crowns the town's highest point at the eastern end. Built by the Swabians and altered by Frederick III of Aragon, it was one of the most important defensive structures in medieval Sicilia. It retains six of its original 20 towers and the views of the surrounding countryside are spectacular – you can make out Mt Etna in the distant north-east. Closer and across the valley rises the town of Calascibetta, erected by the Arabs in the 9th century. It forms the northern sentinel over a valley which now contains the Palermo-Catania A19 and railway. The castello, now part theatre, is open from 9 am to 1 pm and from 3 to 5 pm daily. Admission is free.

Duomo

Back along Via Roma, the 14th century duomo retains, despite remodelling in the 15th and 16th centuries, its Gothic apse and transept. Behind the duomo on Via Roma is the **Museo Alessi**, which houses the contents of the cathedral's treasury. It is open from 9 am to 1.30 pm and from 4 to 6 pm daily; admission costs L2000.

Across Via Roma on Piazza Mazzini, the **Museo Archeologico** (also known as Museo Varisano) has a small collection of ancient artefacts found in the area. It is open from 9 am to 1.30 pm and from 3 to 7.30 pm daily. Admission costs L4000.

Other Things to See & Do

On Piazza Vittorio Emanuele, the most impressive element of the **Chiesa di San Francesco** is its 15th century campanile, adorned with fine Gothic windows. The tower once formed part of the city's defence system. You could head over to the new part of town to the chunky **Torre di Federico** in the villa comunale, also part of the old system. The octagonal tower, standing 24m high, was once linked by a secret passage to the castello. At the time of writing it was closed for restoration.

For a pleasant evening stroll, head for Piazza Francesco Crispi and wander along Viale Marconi to enjoy the view.

Special Events

During Holy Week at Easter, Enna is the setting for colourful, traditional celebrations. On Good Friday, thousands of people wearing hoods and capes of different colours participate in a solemn procession to the duomo.

Places to Stay & Eat

There is no cheap accommodation, so be prepared. Enna itself has only one hotel, *Albergo Sicilia* (☎ 0935 50 08 54, Piazza Colajanni 7). Singles/doubles with breakfast cost L90,000/155,000.

For other options, catch city bus No 5 from Piazza Vittorio Emanuele to Lago di Pergusa (a small, touristy lake with beaches about 10km south). The cheapest is *Miralago* (☎ 0935 54 12 72), with rooms for L50,000/70,000. It is the first place you pass on the right before entering the town proper along Via Nazionale.

There is a *market* every Monday to Saturday morning on Via Mercato Sant'Antonio, where you can find fresh produce. *L'Ariston* (☎ 0935 2 60 38, Via Roma 353) is a good restaurant and *San Gennaro* (☎ 0935 2 40 67, Viale Marconi 6) is quite a pleasant trattoria/pizzeria. It has outdoor tables and a view, and prices are reasonable.

Ristorante Centrale (☎ 0935 50 09 63, Piazza VI Dicembre 9) serves traditional Sicilian food, but is more expensive at around L40,000 for a full meal. The menu changes daily. *Grotta Azzurra* (☎ 0935 2 43 28, Via Colajanni 1) is small but pleasant.

Getting There & Away

SAIS buses (☎ 0935 50 09 02) connect Enna with Catania (and on to Roma), Palermo and Siracusa. It is possible to reach Agrigento via Caltanisetta. Buses terminate on Viale Diaz. Regular SAIS buses also run to Piazza Armerina. Don't take a train – the station is miles away at the foot of the mountain-top town.

PIAZZA ARMERINA

A pleasant town less than an hour by bus or car from Enna, Piazza Armerina boasts an interesting baroque **cathedral**. This self-proclaimed *città dei mosaici* (city of mosaics) is the nearest town to the wonderful treasure that lies in the Villa Romana del Casale, a Roman villa some 5km away.

The AAST office (☎ 0935 68 02 01) is at Via Cavour 15, in the town centre, uphill along Via Umberto I or Via Garibaldi from the Intercity bus stops. It is open from 8 am to 2 pm Monday to Saturday. Get the brochure on the villa here; it explains the layout of the ruins and the mosaics and is often unavailable at the site. SAIS buses connect Enna and Piazza Armerina (about 10 a day). There is also a daily AST bus from Siracusa.

Villa Romana del Casale

Built between the end of the 3rd and mid-4th century, the villa was probably the home or hunting lodge of a Roman dignitary. Buried under mud in a 12th century flood, it remained hidden for 700 years before its magnificent floor mosaics were revealed.

Covering about 3500 sq metres, the villa was designed in line with the lie of the hill on which it stands, creating three main areas. The mosaics cover almost its entire floor and are considered unique for their narrative style of composition, range of subject and variety of colour – much of them clearly influenced by African themes.

The villa is well organised to cope with hordes of tourists and, by following the raised walkways, you will see all the main areas. The most captivating of the mosaics include the erotic depictions in what was probably a private apartment on the northern side of the great peristyle. One of the richest mosaics in terms of colour and action, the *Little Hunt*, is in the largest room. Next door is the villa's most famous piece, illustrating 10 girls clad in what must have been the world's earliest bikinis.

The eastern side of the peristyle opens onto a long corridor, its floor carpeted with the splendid mosaic of the *Great Hunt*, depicting the chase for exotic wild animals. On the other side of the corridor is a series of apartments, whose floor illustrations reproduce scenes from Homer, as well as mythical subjects such as Arion playing the lyre on a dolphin's back, and Eros and Pan wrestling. There is also a lively circus scene.

The villa is open from 9 am to one hour before sunset daily. Arrive early if you want to avoid the large tourist groups that start arriving at around 9.30 am. Admission is L4000.

Three ATAN buses (☎ 0935 68 22 72) leave for the villa from Piazza Senatore Marescalchi in Piazza Armerina at 9, 10 and 11 am and 4, 5 and 6 pm from May to September. Buses leave the villa for Piazza Armerina at 9.30, 10.30 and 11.30 am and 4.30, 5.30 and 6.30 pm. If you have a car, you will be charged L2000 to park outside the entrance.

Places to Stay & Eat

If you want to stay in Piazza Armerina, about the cheapest accommodation is *Villa Romana* (☎ 0935 68 29 11, Via A de Gasperi 18), which has singles/doubles for L80,000/130,000 including breakfast. *Hotel Mosaici*

(☎ 0935 68 54 53), 3km out of town on the way to the villa, has rooms for L60,000/ 80,000. *Azienda Agriturista Savoca* (☎ 0337 88 90 52, fax 0935 68 30 78) is 3km out of Piazza Armerina, on the road to Mirabella. It has pleasant rooms for L80,000 a double, with bathroom and breakfast included. Ask for a room in the older building, in preference to the newer rooms under the swimming pool.

Totò (☎ 0935 68 01 53, Via Mazzini 29) is a typical Sicilian restaurant and serves a good meal for L25,000. Otherwise, try *Del Teatro* (☎ 0935 8 56 62, Piazza del Teatro 1), close to the theatre.

MORGANTINA

About 16km north-east of Piazza Armerina, just beyond the town of Aidone, the remains of what started life as a rich Siculian town have been unearthed. What you see of its agora, theatre and other buildings owes more to subsequent Greek occupation than to the Siculians, however. That the remains are not more spectacular is largely the fault of the Romans, who destroyed the town in 211 BC. Set in pleasant country with wide views to Mt Etna, the Morgantina site is an easy detour if you have your own transport, but a difficult proposition without. It is open from 9 am to one hour before sunset daily and admission costs L4000.

AGRIGENTO

postcode 92100 • pop 52,000

This pleasant medieval town, set high on a hill, overlooks both the Mediterranean and the spectacular Valle dei Templi (Valley of the Temples), a significant ancient Greek site. Founded in 582 BC by settlers from Gela, themselves originally from Rhodes, the town became powerful in the 5th century BC and most of the temples date from then. The Greek poet Pindar described the town as 'the most beautiful of those inhabited by mortals'.

Sacked and destroyed by the Carthaginians in 406 BC, Akragas, as it was known, was conquered and rebuilt by the Romans in the 3rd century BC. The newcomers renamed the town Agrigentum and it continued to prosper under Byzantine and Arab rule. On the road

between Agrigento and Porto Empedocle is Caos, where the playwright Luigi Pirandello (1867-1936) was born.

The Greek temples are the obvious reason to come to Agrigento, but don't overlook the town itself.

Orientation

Intercity buses arrive on Piazza Rosselli and the train station is slightly south on Piazza Marconi. Lying between the two is the green oasis of Piazzale Aldo Moro, at the eastern end of Via Atenea, the main street of the medieval town. Frequent city buses run to Valle dei Templi below the town. See the Getting Around section.

Information

Tourist Offices The AAST office (☎ 0922 2 04 54), Via Cesare Battisti 15, is open from 8.30 am to 1.30 pm and 4.30 to 7 pm Monday to Friday and from 8.30 am to 1 pm on Saturday.

Money Banks are generally open from 8.30 am to 1.30 pm (larger banks also open from 3 to 4 pm) and the Monte dei Paschi di Siena at Piazza Vittorio Emanuele 1 has an ATM. Out of hours there's a currency exchange booth at the post office and another at the train station – watch the rates.

Post & Communications The post office, on Piazza Vittorio Emanuele, is open from 8.30 am to 6.30 pm Monday to Friday and to 12.30 pm on Saturday.

There is a Telecom office at Via A de Gasperi 25, open from 9 am to 7 pm Monday to Friday.

Medical Services The Azienda Ospedaliera San Giovanni di Dio (☎ 0922 49 21 11) is on Via Rupe Atenea 1. For an ambulance, call ☎ 0922 40 13 44.

Valle dei Templi

The five main Doric temples along the 'valley' (actually a ridge) were built around the 5th century BC and are in various states of ruin, due to earthquakes and vandalism.

euro currency converter   L10,000 = €5.16

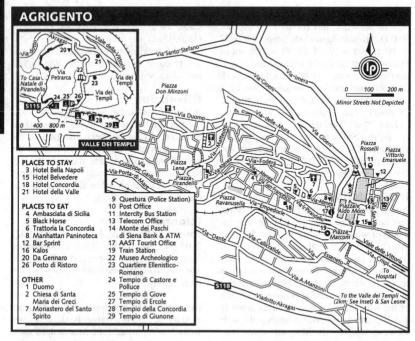

AGRIGENTO

0   100   200 m
Minor Streets Not Depicted

VALLE DEI TEMPLI

PLACES TO STAY
3 Hotel Bella Napoli
15 Hotel Belvedere
18 Hotel Concordia
21 Hotel della Valle

PLACES TO EAT
4 Ambasciata di Sicilia
5 Black Horse
6 Trattoria la Concordia
8 Manhattan Paninoteca
12 Bar Sprint
16 Kalos
20 Da Gennaro
26 Posto di Ristoro

OTHER
1 Duomo
2 Chiesa di Santa
   Maria dei Greci
7 Monastero del Santo
   Spirito

9 Questura (Police Station)
10 Post Office
11 Intercity Bus Station
13 Telecom Office
14 Monte dei Paschi
   di Siena Bank & ATM
17 AAST Tourist Office
19 Train Station
22 Museo Archeologico
23 Quartiere Ellenistico-
   Romano
24 Tempio di Castore e
   Polluce
25 Tempio di Giove
27 Tempio di Ercole
28 Tempio della Concordia
29 Tempio di Giunone

The area is divided into two sections. East of Via dei Templi are the most spectacular temples. The first you will come to is **Tempio di Ercole** (Temple of Hercules), built towards the end of the 6th century BC and believed to be the oldest of the temples. Eight of its 38 columns have been raised and you can wander around the remains of the rest. The **Tempio della Concordia** (Temple of Concord) is the only one to survive relatively intact. Built around 440 BC, it was transformed into a Christian church in the 6th century AD. Its name is taken from a Roman inscription found nearby. The **Tempio di Giunone** (Temple of Juno) stands high on the edge of the ridge, a five minute walk to the east. Part of its colonnade remains and there is an impressive sacrificial altar. This section of the valley is open to 9 pm.

Across Via dei Templi is what remains of the massive **Tempio di Giove** (Temple of Jupiter), actually never completed. Now totally in ruin, it covered an area 112m by 56m, with columns 20m high. Between the columns stood *telamoni* (colossal statues), one of which was reconstructed and is now in the Museo Archeologico. A copy lies on the ground among the ruins, giving an idea of the immense size of the structure. Work began on the temple around 480 BC and it was probably destroyed during the Carthaginian invasion in 406 BC. The nearby **Tempio di Castore e Polluce** (Temple of Castor and Pollux) was partly reconstructed in the 19th century, although probably using pieces from other constructions.

This area is open from 9 am to one hour before sunset daily and admission costs L4000. All the temples are lit up at night (until closing time).

The **Museo Archeologico** (☎ 0922 49 72 21), on Via dei Templi just north of the temples, has a collection of artefacts from the area worth inspecting. It is open from 8 am to 1 pm Monday to Sunday and also from 2 to 5 pm Wednesday to Saturday. Admission costs L8000.

Just opposite the museum, the **Quartiere Ellenistico-Romano**, or Hellenistic-Roman quarter, constituted part of urban Agrigento. Some of its structures date from the 4th century BC, while others were built as late as the 5th century AD.

West of the temples is the country house in Caos where Luigi Pirandello was born. Now a small museum, the **Casa Natale di Pirandello** (☎ 0922 51 11 02) is open from 8.30 am to 7.30 pm daily. Take bus No 1 from the station. The house is just short of Porto Empedocle and overlooks the sea. Admission costs L4000.

Medieval Agrigento

Roaming around the town's narrow, winding streets is relaxing after a day among the temples. The **Chiesa di Santa Maria dei Greci**, uphill from Piazza Lena, at the end of Via Atenea, is an 11th century Norman church built on the site of a 5th century BC Greek temple. Note the remains of the wooden Norman ceiling and some Byzantine frescoes.

A not so relaxing walk farther uphill is to the fragile-looking **duomo** on Via Duomo. Built in the year 1000, it has been restructured many times. The campanile was erected in the 15th century and the panelled ceiling inside dates from the 17th century.

Back towards Piazza Vittorio Emanuele, the **Monastero del Santo Spirito** was founded by Cistercian nuns at the end of the 13th century. Giacomo Serpotta is responsible for the stuccoes in the chapel. There is a small ethnographic museum (☎ 0922 59 03 71) above the old church which is open from 9 am to 1 pm and 4 to 7 pm Monday to Saturday. Admission is free. You can buy cakes and pastries from the nuns. See the later Places to Eat section.

Special Events

Agrigento's big annual shindig is the Sagra del Mandorlo in Fiore (Festival of the Al-

mond Blossom), a folk festival set on the first Sunday in February in the Valle dei Templi.

Places to Stay

You can camp by the sea at San Leone, a few kilometres south of Agrigento, at *Camping Nettuno* (☎ 0922 41 62 68) or at *Camping Internazionale* (☎ 0922 41 61 21), which are open year-round. Take bus No 2 or 2/ from Agrigento or drive down Via dei Templi, continue along Viale Emporium towards the sea and turn left at Lungomare Akragas.

Hotel Bella Napoli (☎ 0922 2 04 35, Piazza Lena 6) is uphill off Via Bac Bac. It has clean, basic singles/doubles for L25,000/ 55,000 or L44,000/75,000 with bathroom. *Hotel Belvedere* (☎ 0922 2 00 51, Via San Vito 20) is in the newer part of town, uphill from Piazza Vittorio Emanuele. It has singles from L50,000 to L68,000 and doubles with bathroom from L70,000 to L98,000, depending on the season. *Hotel Concordia* (☎ 0922 59 62 66, Piazza San Francesco 11), just off Via Atenea. It has rooms for L30,000/60,000 or L45,000/70,000 with bathroom.

Most of Agrigento's better hotels are out of town around the Valle dei Templi or near the sea. *Hotel Akrabello* (☎ 0922 60 62 77) is in the Parco Angeli area, east of the temples. It is modern and comfortable and has rooms for up to L130,000/180,000 with breakfast.

Hotel della Valle (☎ 0922 269 66, Via dei Templi) has lovely rooms with full services, a pool and gardens. Rooms cost up to L150,000/220,000. *Hotel Kaos* (☎ 0922 59 86 22) is by the sea, about 2km from the temples. It is a large resort complex in a restored villa. Rooms cost up to L200,000/280,000.

Places to Eat

The daily *produce market* is held on Piazza San Francesco. A good choice for a light lunch is *Manhattan Paninoteca*, up Salita M Angeli from Via Atenea. For the best pastries, and just for the experience, go to *Santo Spirito* at the end of Via Foderà. The nuns have been making heavenly cakes and pastries to a secret recipe for centuries and their dolce di mandorle (almond cake) is particularly special (and expensive). Press the door bell and say 'Vorrei comprare qualche dolce', and see how you go.

Black Horse (☎ 0922 232 23, Via Celauro 8) serves good, reasonably priced meals. *Ambasciata di Sicilia* (☎ 0922 2 05 26, Via Giambertoni 2) offers typical Sicilian fare and an enjoyable meal will cost under L30,000. Another good restaurant for traditional Sicilian food is *Kalos* (☎ 0922 2 63 89, Via Salita Filino 1), where a full meal costs around L50,000. A reasonable place specialising in fish is *Trattoria Concordia* (☎ 0922 22 26 68, Via Porcello 8).

If you have a car, head for *Trattoria-Pizzeria Kokalo's* (☎ 0922 60 64 27, Viale C Magazzeni 3), east of the temples, where they dish up the area's best pizza.

One of Agrigento's better restaurants is *Le Caprice* (☎ 0922 2 26 46), between the town and temples. A full meal will cost between L40,000 and L50,000. Take any bus heading for the temples and get off at Hotel Colleverde, from where it's a short walk (signposted). *Da Gennaro (Via Petrarca)*, again downhill from the town, also maintains high standards. A full meal, including seafood, will cost around L70,000.

Getting There & Away

Bus For most destinations, bus is the easiest way to get to and from Agrigento. The Intercity station is on Piazza Rosselli, just off Piazza Vittorio Emanuele, and timetables for most services are posted in Bar Sprint on the piazza. Autoservizi Cuffaro (☎ 0922 41 82 31) and Camilleri & Argento (☎ 0922 47 27 98) both run buses to Palermo. SAIS buses serve Roma, Catania, and Caltanissetta. Information about SAIS buses (☎ 0922 59 52 60) can be obtained at Via Ragazzi del '99 12.

Train Trains run to Palermo (two hours), Catania (3½ hours) and Enna. For Palermo, the train is fine, if a little slow. For anywhere else you should consider the bus.

Car & Motorcycle Agrigento is easily accessible by road from all of Sicily's main towns. The S189 links the town with Palermo, while the S115 runs along the coast,

west towards Sciacca and east for Gela and eventually Siracusa. For Enna, take the S640 via Caltanissetta. There is plenty of parking on Piazza Vittorio Emanuele in the centre.

Getting Around

City buses run down to the Valle dei Templi from in front of the train station. Take bus No 1, 1/, 2, 2/ (every 30 minutes) or 3 and get off at either the museum or farther downhill at Piazzale dei Templi. The Green Line (Linea Verde) bus runs every hour from the train station to the duomo, for those who prefer not to make the uphill walk. Tickets cost L1000 and are valid for 1½ hours.

ERACLEA MINOA

A colony within a colony, Eraclea Minoa lies about halfway between Agrigento and Selinunte to the west, atop a wild bluff overlooking a splendid, sandy beach and the magnificent Capo Bianco cliff. Founded by Selinunte in the 6th century BC, the ruins are comparatively scanty and the 4th century theatre's seating has been covered in moulded plastic to protect the crumbling remains. They are open from 9 am to one hour before sunset daily and admission costs L4000.

You can also visit the Riserva Naturale del Fiume Platani. Buses between Sciacca and Agrigento will drop you at the turn-off, from where it's a 4km walk. In summer, buses go from Cattolica Eraclea (which can be reached from Agrigento and Sciacca) to the site.

If you want to stay, try the camp site *Eraclea Minoa Village* (☎ 0922 84 60 23), open from 15 June to 15 September. Charges are L16,000 per person including the site. It is not particularly exciting but the turquoise blue waters in front of the camp site are among the island's most attractive.

ISOLE PELAGIE (PELAGIC ISLANDS)
postcode 92010 • pop 5000

Some 240km south of Agrigento, this tiny archipelago lies farther from mainland Sicilia than Malta, and in many respects has more in common with nearby Tunisia or Libya than Italy. Indeed Libya's Colonel Gaddafi is so convinced of this that he launched a couple of wobbly missiles its way in 1987. Of the three islands, which rise on the African continental shelf, only Lampedusa is of any interest. Linosa has nothing to offer and Lampione is little more than an uninhabited pimple on the sometimes rather tempestuous surface of the Canale di Sicilia, the stretch of Mar Mediterraneo separating Africa from Sicilia.

Lampedusa, a rocky, sparsely covered and, in winter, wind-whipped place, is becoming increasingly popular with Italians looking for an early tan, and the water is enticingly warm. Of the several beaches on the southern side of the 11km-long island, the best known is Isola dei Conigli (Rabbit Island), where Caretta-Caretta turtles lay their eggs between June and August. These timid creatures generally only come in when no-one's about. There are several dive rental outlets; for more information go first to the Pro Loco office (☎ 0922 97 14 77) at Piazza Comm-Brignone 12 (closed at the time of writing). Orange minibuses run hourly from near the Pro Loco to the beach or you could hire a Vespa from one of several outlets around town (look for the *autonoleggio* signs).

Places to Stay

Cheap accommodation can be hard to find. The little pensioni are often full in summer and closed in winter. You could try *Albergo Le Pelagie* (☎ 0922 97 02 11, Via Bonfiglio 11), off Via Roma, a 30 minute walk west along the waterfront from the port (alternatively ring when you get to the port and they will come and pick you up). It has singles/doubles for L90,000/180,000 but, like most places, makes at least half board compulsory in summer.

Getting There & Away

A year-round Siremar ferry leaves Porto Empedocle (7km south-west of Agrigento) at midnight daily except Friday. It takes six hours to reach Linosa and another two to reach Lampedusa; the one-way fare to the latter is L64,000. A car up to 3.5m long costs L89,000. You can buy tickets at the Siremar booth (☎ 0922 63 66 83) at the

port, open from 9 am to 1 pm, 4 to 7 pm, and 9 pm to midnight. Orange buses from Agrigento arrive at Piazza Italia, from where it's a quick walk down Via Quattro Novembre to the port entrance (the last bus from Porto Empedocle leaves for Agrigento at about 9 pm). Boats from Lampedusa (and Linosa) leave daily (10.15 am from Lampedusa). Trips can be cancelled due to bad weather, especially in winter. There are also flights between Lampedusa and Palermo.

SCIACCA
postcode 92019 • pop 40,000
Sciacca started life as a Roman settlement but only really took off with the arrival of the Arabs. The Normans fortified this prosperous farming town, which later came to be ruled alternately by local feuding families. Today a bustling fishing port, the centre of town has a few monuments worthy of a quick look, including the **duomo**, which was erected by the Normans in the 12th century, the peculiar 15th century **Steripinto** building, the neo-Gothic **Palazzo San Giacomo** and the ruins of a **castello** dominating the town. The time to come is February, when the townsfolk let their hair down for Carnevale. The AAST office (☎ 0925 2 27 44) is at Corso Vittorio Emanuele 84. *Paloma Blanca* (☎ 0925 2 51 30, Via Figuli 5), on the eastern side of town, has singles/doubles for L50,000/80,000.

Buses for Palermo leave from Viale della Vittoria (tickets at No 22). Others, run by the Lumia company, serve Trapani, Agrigento and destinations between from Via Agatocle.

SELINUNTE
The ancient Greek city of Selinus, founded in the 7th century BC, was long a prosperous and powerful city, but its standing rivalry with Segesta to the north was to be its undoing. In 409 BC, the latter called in a powerful ally, Carthage, whose troops destroyed Selinunte. The city later recovered under the Siracusans and then Carthaginians, but in 250 BC its citizens delivered the *coup de grâce* to prevent it passing to the Romans. What they left standing, mainly temples, was finished off by an earthquake in the Middle Ages.

Things to See

One of the more captivating ancient sites in Italy, Selinunte once fairly bristled with temples. They are known today simply by the letters A to G, O and M. Five are huddled together in the acropolis at the western end of the site, accessible by road from the ticket office, across the depression known as the Gorgo di Cottone – once Selinunte's harbour. Of particular note is **Temple C** – several of the metopes in Palermo's archaeological museum came from this temple, and there is also a reconstruction of the temple's clay roof at the museum.

Temple E, reconstructed in 1958 amid much criticism, stands out for its recently acquired completeness. Built in the 5th century BC, it is the first of three temples you'll come to at the eastern end of the site. The more outstanding metopes in Palermo's archaeological museum came from this temple. The northernmost **Temple G** was built in the 6th century BC and, although never completed, was one of the largest in the Greek world. Today it is a massive pile of rubble, but evocative nonetheless. The site is open from 9 am to one hour before sunset daily. Admission costs L4000. The ticket office shuts two hours before closing time.

Places to Stay & Eat

Selinunte is close to the village of Marinella di Selinunte, where you can find accommodation. *Il Maggiolino* (☎ 0924 4 60 44) is one of a couple of camp sites; charges are L8000 per person, L5000 per tent and L5000 per car. *Pensione Costa d'Avorio* (☎ 0924 4 62 07, Via Stazione 10) has singles/doubles for L35,000/50,000 or L40,000/80,000 with bathroom. It also has a trattoria. *Hotel Alceste* (☎ 0924 4 61 84, Via Alceste 23) has more upmarket rooms for L90,000/120,000 with bathroom. *Hotel Garzia* (☎ 0924 46 6 60, Via Pigafetta 8), overlooking the sea, has nice rooms for L80,000/130,000 with breakfast.

There are some pleasant little restaurants along the beachfront. Try *Lido Azzurro*, also known as Baffo's, where you can eat good pizzas, pasta and fresh seafood virtually beside the water's edge.

Getting There & Away

AST buses link Marinella to Castelvetrano, which can be reached by Lumia buses from Agrigento, Mazara del Vallo, Marsala and Trapani.

North-Western Sicilia

MARSALA

postcode 91025 • pop 80,000

Best known for its sweet dessert wines, Marsala is a surprisingly pleasant town, with an interesting historic centre. If you have a car, it's a good alternative to Trapani as a base for exploring Sicilia's north-west. Founded as Lilybaeon on Cape Lilibeo by Carthaginians who had fled nearby Mozia (or Motya) after its destruction by Siracusa, the city was eventually conquered by the Arabs, who renamed it Marsa Allah (Port of God). It was at Marsala that Garibaldi landed with his One Thousand in 1860.

Information

Marsala's APT office (☎ 0923 71 40 97) is at Via XI Maggio 100, just off Piazza della Repubblica, in the centre of town. It is open from 8 am to 2 pm and 3 to 8 pm Monday to Saturday. The public hospital (☎ 0923 71 60 31) is on Piazza San Francesco, just west of the city centre. For a medical emergency, call ☎ 0923 95 14 10.

Things to See & Do

Visit the **duomo** on Piazza della Repubblica, built in the 17th and 18th centuries, and its **Museo degli Arazzi** (☎ 0923 71 29 03) at Via Giraffa 57, open from 9 am to 1 pm and 4 to 6 pm daily except Monday. In the museum are eight 16th century tapestries, woven for the Spanish King Philip II and depicting scenes from the war of Titus against the Jews. Admission costs L2000.

The **Museo Lilibeo** (☎ 0923 95 25 35), on Via Boeo in the Baglio Anselmi by the sea (follow Via XI Maggio to Piazza della Vittoria and turn left along Via N Sauro), houses a partly reconstructed Carthaginian warship, which may have seen action in the First Punic War. It was found off the coast north of Marsala in 1971. The museum is open from 9 am to 1.30 pm daily (1 pm on Sunday), as well as from 4 to 7 pm on Wednesday and Saturday. Admission costs L4000. North of the museum, along Viale Vittorio Veneto, is the partly excavated **Insula Romana**, which was a 3rd century AD Roman house.

Pay a visit to Marsala's open-air **market**, open every Monday to Saturday morning in a piazza off Piazza dell'Addolorata, next to the *comune* (municipal offices). In this small, lively marketplace, you'll likely be serenaded by a fruit vendor.

Tipplers should head to **Florio** (☎ 0923 78 11 11) on Lungomare Florio (bus No 16 from Piazza del Popolo) – this is the place to buy the cream of Marsala's wines. Florio opens its doors to visitors to explain the process of making Marsala and to give you a taste of the goods, from 9 am to noon and 2.30 to 5 pm Monday to Thursday and in the morning only on Friday. Pellegrino, Rallo, Mavis and Intorcia are four of the other producers in the same area, and all have an *enoteca* (wine bar), where you can select a bottle or two (usually open from about 9 am to 12.30 pm). Booking is recommended. For free tasting try the enotecas Luminario or La ruota, both at Via Boeo 36.

If you're travelling with small children, they might enjoy the small playground on Piazza della Vittoria, at the end of Via XI Maggio.

Special Events

Marsala's most important annual religious event is the *Processione del Giovedi Santo* (Holy Thursday Procession). A tradition dating back centuries, the procession of actors depicts the events leading up to Christ's crucifixion. Many children participate in the procession, dressed in colourful costume as saints. If you're visiting the area at Easter, be sure to attend both this procession and Trapani's own version on Good Friday.

Places to Stay & Eat

Garden (☎ 0923 98 23 20, Via Gambini 36), near the train station, has basic singles/doubles for L55,000/85,000. *Hotel CAP 3000* (☎ 0923 98 90 55, Via Trapani 161) is outside the historical centre, on the road to Trapani. It has rooms with bathroom, phone and TV for L90,000/150,000. Another option is *Aziendza Agrituristica Samperi* (☎ 0923 74 13 13, Contrada Fornara 13), an agritourism establishment just south of Marsala.

Trattoria Garibaldi (☎ 0923 95 30 06, Piazza dell'Addolorata 5) specialises in fish and a full meal costs about L35,000. You can also eat well for a bit less at *Trattoria Alfayer* (☎ 0923 71 30 30, Via Lungomare Boeo 38).

Getting There & Away

Buses head for Marsala from Trapani (AST or Lumia, eight a day), Agrigento (Lumia, four a day) and Palermo (Salemi). Palermo buses arrive at Piazza del Popolo, off Via Mazzini, in the centre of town. All other buses stop on Piazza Pizzo. The Agrigento buses generally stop at Castelvetrano, from where you can get another to Selinunte.

Trains serve Marsala from Trapani and Palermo, although from the latter you have to change at Alcamo.

How Sweet it Is

The Marsala wine was 'discovered' by Englishman John Woodhouse who, after landing in the city in 1773 and tasting the local product, decided it should be marketed throughout Europe. His first competitor was Benjamin Ingham, who established his own factory in the town and began exporting the wine to the USA and Australia.

One particularly interesting figure in the Marsala-producing business was Ingham's nephew, Joseph Whitaker, who bought the island of San Pantaleo, where the ancient site Mozia (Motya) was based, and built a villa there (it is still in his family today). Whitaker was responsible for renewing interest in the archaeological site of Mozia and for the few excavations carried out.

Between June and September, Sandokan (☎ 0923 71 20 60, 0923 95 34 34) runs a boat service from Molo Dogana to the Isole Egadi.

BETWEEN MARSALA & TRAPANI

The site of ancient **Mozia**, on the island of San Pantaleo in the lagoon known as the Stagnone, is about 11km north along the scenic coast from Marsala. The island is accessible by boat (Arini e Pugliese, L5000 return from 9 am to 1 pm and 3 pm to around 6 or 7 pm, mornings only in winter – there's a L500 charge onto the island). Mozia was the site of one of the most important Phoenician settlements in the Mediterranean, coveted for its strategic position and eventually destroyed by Dionysius the Elder, tyrant of Siracusa in 379 BC.

Today, it is the island's picturesque position in the area known as the *saline* (salt flats) that attracts visitors. The salt flats extend along the coast between Marsala and Trapani and are dotted with windmills and piles of salt covered with terracotta tiles. Very little remains of the city Mozia, but it is interesting to follow the path around the island to visit the various excavations, including the ancient port and dry dock, as well as numerous buildings. Note the submerged road at the port, which connects the island to the mainland. The island hosts the Whitaker Museum (☎ 0923 71 25 98) – its main treasure is *Il Giovinetto di Mozia*, a 5th century BC Phoenician statue of a young boy. Admission costs L5000.

Bus No 11 from Piazza del Popolo in Marsala runs in summer only; bus No 4 drops you close to the boat and runs year-round.

The island and lagoon form part of the Riserva Naturale di Stagnone, a noted humid zone which has a large population of water birds. The *saline* form part of an adjacent riserva naturale known as the **Saline di Trapani e Paceco** (☎ 0923 86 74 42), which includes a small museum at Nubia, a few kilometres south of Trapani. There are plans to develop better facilities for tourists in the area of the saline – such as cycling and walking tracks. Guided nature tours are available from 9 am to 6 pm.

TRAPANI
postcode 91100 • pop 72,000

Although not one of Sicilia's top attractions, Trapani is a comfortable base from which to explore the north-west. From the ancient Greek city of Segesta and the medieval town of Erice to the beaches of the Golfo di Castellammare, the Riserva Naturale dello Zingaro and the Isole Egadi, this small corner is a smorgasbord of Sicilia's main delights.

A Carthaginian and later a Roman city, Trapani thrived as a trading centre under Arab and Norman rule and, after the arrival of the Spanish, enjoyed a period as western Sicilia's most important town. Since then, slow decline has reduced it to a coastal backwater, kept afloat by moderate sea traffic and some fishing. A handful of baroque churches and piazzas warrant some exploration and the town's Easter celebrations are a high point of the year.

Orientation

The main bus station is on Piazza Montalto, with the train station around the corner on Piazza Umberto I. The cheaper hotels are in the heart of the old centre, about 500m west. Make for Piazza Scarlatti down Corso Italia.

Information

Tourist Offices The APT office (☎ 0923 2 90 00, email appt@mail.cinet.it) on Piazza Saturno, off Piazza Scarlatti, opens from 8 am to 8 pm Monday to Saturday and from 9 am to noon on Sunday. It's usually shut for a couple of hours from 2 pm and closes earlier in winter. The Web site is www.cinet.it/apt.

Post & Communications The main post office on Piazza Vittorio Veneto is open from 8.20 am to 7 pm Monday to Saturday. The Telecom office is at Via Agostino Pepoli 47.

Money There are several banks in the town. The Banca di Roma, on Corso Italia, and Monte dei Paschi di Siena, at Via XXX Gennaio 80, have ATMs.

Medical Services & Emergency The Ospedale Sant'Antonio Abate (☎ 0923 80 91

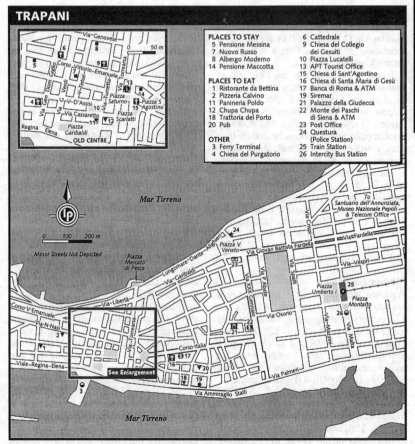

TRAPANI

PLACES TO STAY
5 Pensione Messina
7 Nuovo Russo
8 Albergo Moderno
14 Pensione Maccotta

PLACES TO EAT
1 Ristorante da Bettina
2 Pizzeria Calvino
11 Panineria Poldo
12 Chupa Chupa
18 Trattoria del Porto
20 Pub

OTHER
3 Ferry Terminal
4 Chiesa del Purgatorio

6 Cattedrale
9 Chiesa del Collegio dei Gesuiti
10 Piazza Lucatelli
13 APT Tourist Office
15 Chiesa di Sant'Agostino
16 Chiesa di Santa Maria di Gesù
17 Banca di Roma & ATM
19 Siremar
21 Palazzo della Giudecca
22 Monte dei Paschi di Siena & ATM
23 Post Office
24 Questura (Police Station)
25 Train Station
26 Intercity Bus Station

OLD CENTRE

Mar Tirreno

Minor Streets Not Depicted

To Santuario dell'Annunziata, Museo Nazionale Pepoli & Telecom Office

Mar Tirreno

11) is on Via Cosenza, some distance from the centre of town. Dial the same number for an ambulance. Pronto Soccorso is on ☎ 0923 80 94 50. For the Guardia Medica, Piazza Generale Scio 1, phone ☎ 0923 2 96 29.

The questura (☎ 0923 59 81 11) is on Via Virgilio, off Piazza Vittorio Veneto.

Things to See

The 16th century **Palazzo della Giudecca** on Via Giudecca, with its distinctive façade, stands out among the general decay of the old and run-down Jewish quarter. Cross Corso Italia to reach the **Chiesa di Santa Maria di Gesù** on Via San Pietro, whose exterior has both Gothic and Renaissance features. The 14th century **Chiesa di Sant' Agostino**, on Piazza Saturno, is worth a look for its fine Gothic rose window and portal. Continue along Corso Vittorio Emanuele, noting the 17th century town hall and **Chiesa del Collegio dei Gesuiti**, before reaching the **cattedrale**, with its baroque façade. Off the corso, on Via Generale D Giglio, **Chiesa del**

SICILIA

Purgatorio houses the Misteri, 18th century life-size wooden figures depicting Christ's Passion. On Good Friday they are carried in procession (see Special Events in the Facts for the Visitor chapter).

Trapani's major sight is the 14th century **Santuario dell'Annunziata**, some way from the centre on Via A Pepoli. Remodelled in baroque style in the 17th century, it retains its original Gothic rose window and doorway. The Cappella della Madonna, behind the high altar, contains the venerated *Madonna di Trapani*, carved, it's thought, by Nino Pisano.

The adjacent **Museo Nazionale Pepoli** (☎ 0923 55 32 69), in a former Carmelite monastery, has an archaeological collection, statues and coral carvings. It is open from 9 am to 1.30 pm Tuesday to Saturday and also from 3 to 6.30 pm on Monday and Thursday. It is open from 9 am to 12.30 pm on Sunday. Admission costs L8000.

Places to Stay

Pensione Messina (☎ *0923 2 11 98, Corso Vittorio Emanuele 71*) is on the 3rd floor of a 17th century building and its rooms are very basic; the cost per person is L25,000. *Pensione Maccotta* (☎ *0923 2 84 18, Via degli Argentieri 4*), off Piazza Sant'Agostino, has higher standard singles/doubles for L30,000/50,000 or L40,000/70,000 with bathroom.

Albergo Moderno (☎ *0923 2 12 47, Via Genovese 20*) has simple rooms for L45,000/67,000 with bathroom. *Nuovo Russo* (☎ *0923 2 21 66, Via Tintori 4*) has rooms, some of them classics of the 1950s, from L40,000/70,000 or L65,000/110,000 with bathroom.

Places to Eat

Sicilia's Arab heritage and Trapani's unique position on the sea route to Tunisia has made couscous (or cuscus as they spell it here) something of a speciality, particularly when served with a fish sauce that includes tomatoes, garlic and parsley.

The area around Piazza Lucatelli is a pleasant place for a sandwich and coffee. *Panineria Poldo* serves good sandwiches. For a decent ice cream, try *Chupa Chupa*, also in the piazza. An open-air *market* is held every Monday to Saturday morning on Piazza Mercato di Pesce, on the northern waterfront.

Pizzeria Calvino (*Via N Nasi 77*), towards the port off Corso Vittorio Emanuele, is the town's favourite takeaway pizza and pasta place. You can eat a set lunch at the self-service *Pub* (*Via della Luce 8*) for L15,000. *Trattoria del Porto* (*Via Ammiraglio Staiti 45*), on the southern waterfront, is more up-market with good meals for around L35,000. Similarly priced is *Ristorante Da Bettina* (*Via San Francesco d'Assisi 69*).

Getting There & Away

Air Trapani has a small airport, 16km out of town at Birgi. AST buses leave from Piazza Montalto to coincide with flights. Segesta has a daily bus for the island's main airport at Punta Raisi. It's timetable changes regularly, so check with the APT office.

Bus Express buses connect Trapani with Palermo (Segesta) and Agrigento (Lumia-Egatur, ☎ 0923 2 17 54). All intercity buses use Piazza Montalto, from where AST buses serve Erice (approximately every hour), Castellammare del Golfo (four a day), Castelvetrano (seven a day), Marsala and Mazara del Vallo (four a day) and San Vito lo Capo (six a day). Autoservizi Tarantola runs a bus service to Segesta and Calatafimi.

Train Trains connect Trapani to Palermo, Castelvetrano and Marsala. For Segesta, you can either get off at Segesta Tempio (one train a day), from where you'll have to walk 3km to the temple, or Calatafimi (many) on the way to Palermo. The stations are roughly equidistant from the ancient Greek site.

Boat Siremar runs ferries and hydrofoils to the Isole Egadi. The high-season one-way fare to Favignana, the main island, and also to Levanzo is L9500 on the hydrofoil (journey time is 20 minutes). The journey to Marettimo costs L22,000. Tickets are cheaper on the slower car ferries. Siremar's ticket office (☎ 0923 54 54 55, email siremar@gestel net.it) is at Via Ammiraglio Staiti 61 and there is a Web site at www.siremar.gestelnet.

The same company runs a daily ferry to Pantelleria at midnight. There is no service weekends except in summer. The high-season fare for the six hour trip is L42,000, with booking it goes up to L59,000. The boat returns (usually) at 11 am, reaching Trapani at 5 pm.

Ustica Lines (☎ 0923 2 22 00) runs regular hydrofoils to the Isole Egadi (L10,000), as well as a service from Napoli to Trapani (L150,000 one way), via Ustica (L116,000) and the Isole Egadi (L140,000). It also has a ferry to Pantelleria (L59,000). At the time of writing, the ferry to Kelibia in Tunisia had been temporarily suspended. Get tickets at Egatours, Via Ammiraglio Staiti 13, or directly at the Ustica Lines embarkation point.

Tirrenia runs weekly ferries to Tunisia from Trapani, leaving at 9 am on Monday. Tickets for the eight hour trip cost L92,000 for an airline-type seat and L116,000 for a bed in a 2nd class cabin in the high season. The return boat leaves Tunisia at 8 pm. There is also a weekly Tirrenia service to Cagliari, leaving at 9 pm on Tuesday. Tickets cost L66,500 for an airline-style seat and L92,000 for a bed in a 2nd class cabin. Tickets can be purchased at Salvo Viaggi (☎ 0923 54 54 11), Corso Italia 48, or directly from the Stazione Marittima-Molo Sanità (☎ 0923 54 54 33).

ERICE
postcode 91016 • pop 28,000

This dramatic medieval town, 750m above the sea, is about 40 minutes from Trapani by bus and should not be missed on any account. Settled by the Elymians, an ancient mountain people who also founded Segesta, it was an important religious site associated with the goddess of fertility – first the Carthaginian Astarte, then the Greek Aphrodite and finally the Roman Venus. It has unfortunately become a bit of a tourist trap (watch out for exorbitant charges for food and drinks), but manages to maintain a relatively authentic medieval atmosphere.

The tourist office (☎ 0923 86 93 88) is at Viale Conte Pepoli 56. It is open from 8 am to 2 pm and from 4 to 7 pm weekdays.

Things to See

The triangular-shaped town is best explored by pottering around its narrow streets and peeking through the doorways into courtyards. On the hilltop is the Norman **Castello di Venere** (Castle of Venus). Built in the 12th and 13th centuries over an ancient temple of Venus, the castello is open from 8 am to 7 pm daily; admission is free. Not much more than a ruin, the castello is upstaged by the panoramic vistas north-east to San Vito Lo Capo and Monte Cofano and west to Trapani.

Of the several churches and other monuments in the small, quiet town, the 14th century **Chiesa Matrice**, on Via V Carvini just inside Porta Trapani, is probably the most interesting by virtue of its separate campanile with mullioned windows. The interior of the church was remodelled in neo-Gothic style in the 19th century, but the 15th century side chapels were conserved.

Places to Stay & Eat

If you want to stay overnight, there is an HI youth hostel, *G Amodeo* (☎ 0923 55 29 64), just out of town and open year-round. B&B costs L19,000 and a meal L14,000. Otherwise the options are expensive. *Edelweiss* (☎ 0923 86 91 58, Cortile Vincenzo 5) has singles/doubles for L100,000/130,000.

For a meal, the atmospheric **Ristorante La Pentolaccia** (☎ 0923 86 98 99, Via G Guarnotta 17) is in a 16th century former monastery.

Getting There & Away

There are regular AST buses (hourly in summer) to Trapani (Piazza Montalto).

SEGESTA

The ancient Elymians must have been great aesthetes if their choice of sites for cities is any indication. Along with Erice and Entella, they founded Segesta on and around Monte Barbaro. The Greeks later took over and it is to them that we owe the two outstanding survivors: the teatro high up on the mountain with commanding views out to sea (how did spectators concentrate on the show with such a backdrop?) and the tempio.

The city was in constant conflict with Selinunte in the south and this rivalry led it to seek assistance from a succession of allies, including Carthage, Athens, Siracusa and the Romans, and eventually Selinunte was destroyed. Time has done to Segesta what violence inflicted on Selinunte, and little remains save the theatre and the never completed Doric **tempio**, the latter dating from around 430 BC and remarkably well preserved. The Hellenistic **teatro** is also in a fair state of repair and the only structure inside the old city walls to have survived intact. Nearby are ruins of a castello and church built in the Middle Ages. The site is open from 9 am to an hour before sunset daily. A shuttle bus runs every 30 minutes from the entrance 1.5km uphill to the teatro and costs L2000. Admission to the site costs L4000.

During July and August of every odd-numbered year (alternating with Siracusa), performances of Greek plays are staged in the teatro. For information, contact the APT office in Trapani.

Segesta is accessible by Autoservizi Tarantola bus (☎ 0924 3 10 20) from Piazza Montalto in Trapani (at approximately 8 and 10 am and 2 pm in summer) or from Palermo (Piazza Marina) at 7.50 am and 2 pm. Otherwise catch an infrequent train from Trapani or Palermo to Segesta Tempio; the site is then a 20 minute walk away.

GOLFO DI CASTELLAMMARE
Saved from development and road projects by local protests, the tranquil and wildly beautiful **Riserva Naturale dello Zingaro** (☎ 0924 54 11 97) is the star attraction on the gulf. A stroll up the coast between San Vito lo Capo and the little fishing village of Scopello will take about four hours along a clearly marked track. There are also several trails inland, which are detailed on maps available for a small fee at the information offices at the park's two entrances (near Scopello and near San Vito lo Capo). **Punta della Capreria** is a pebble beach in a tiny cove about 15 minutes walk from the Scopello entrance to the park.

Once home to tuna fishers, **Scopello** now mainly hosts tourists – although its sleepy village atmosphere remains unspoilt. Its port is interesting to visit, with an abandoned *tonnara* (tuna processing plant) and *faraglione* (rock towers rising out of the sea).

Camp sites include **Camping Soleado** (☎ 0923 97 21 66) and **Camping La Fata** (☎ 0923 97 21 33) at San Vito lo Capo, and **Camping Baia di Guidaloca** (☎ 0924 54 12 62) and **Camping Ciauli** (☎ 0924 3 90 49) on the coast road south of Scopello. There are numerous pensioni and hotels at touristy **San Vito lo Capo** and at **Castellammare del Golfo**, a busy coastal town with an interesting medieval core 10km south of Scopello. The APT office at Trapani has a full list. In Scopello itself, *Pensione Tranchina* (☎ 0924 54 10 99, Via Diaz 7) is an excellent choice. It has comfortable rooms with bathroom for L65,000/90,000 and half board from L80,000 per person. The hotel also has a restaurant which serves whatever fish is fresh that day – unless you're a hotel guest you'll need to make a booking to eat there.

AST buses run to San Vito lo Capo and Castellammare del Golfo from Trapani's Piazza Montalto. From Castellammare it is possible to catch a bus to Scopello. There is no road through the Zingaro park.

ISOLE EGADI (EGADI ISLANDS)
For centuries the Egadi islanders have lived from tuna fishing. Nowadays tourism looks set to be the main earner – even the *mattanza*, the almost ritual slaughtering of tuna, is becoming a spectator sport (see the boxed text 'La Mattanza'). Made up of three islands, the archipelago is only a short hop from Trapani. Windswept Monte Santa Caterina dominates the otherwise flat main island of **Favignana**. It is pleasant to explore, with plenty of rocky coves and crystal-clear water. Wander around the tonnara at the port. It was closed at the end of the 1970s due to the general crisis in the local tuna fishing industry. A lack of funding has blocked plans to turn the building into a complex which would include a school and art and craft shops.

There is a Pro Loco office (☎ 0923 92 16 47) at Piazza Matrice 8 in Favignana town

Check out Tempio di Giunone's altar, Agrigento.

Rich farmland near Segesta's Greek ruins, Sicilia

Not to be missed – Monreale cattedrale, Sicilia

When visiting Marsala, Sicilia, take a tipple of the town's renowned sweet dessert wine.

Enjoy the delights of Catania's fish market.

Slippery things for sale, Vucciria market, Palermo

Sicilia owes much of its heritage – architecture, food, way of life – to the Arab invaders of 903 AD.

La Mattanza

A centuries-old tradition, the Isole Egadi's *mattanza* (the ritual slaughter of tuna) still survives. Schools of tuna have used the waters of western Sicilia as a mating ground for centuries and locals can recall the golden days of the islands' fishing industry, when it wasn't uncommon to catch giant breeding tuna of between 200 and 300kg. Fish that size are rare these days and the annual catch is increasingly smaller, due to general overfishing of tuna worldwide. But, even though the Egadi's fishing industry is in severe crisis as a result, the tradition of the mattanza goes on.

Now that the slaughter of tuna can no longer support the islands' economy, it is reinventing itself as a tourist attraction. From around 20 May to 10 June, tourists flock to the Isole Egadi to witness the event. For a fee you can join the fishers in their boats and watch them catching the tuna at close hand – note that you'll need a strong stomach. This is no ordinary fishing expedition: the fishers organise their boats and nets in a complex formation designed to channel the tuna into a series of enclosures that culminate in the *camera della morte* (room of death). Once enough tuna are imprisoned there, the fishers close in and the mattanza begins (the word is derived from the Spanish word for killing). It is a bloody affair – up to eight or more fishers at a time will sink huge hooks into a tuna and drag it aboard. Anyone who has seen Rossellini's classic *Stromboli* will no doubt recall the famous mattanza scene.

or contact Signora Guccione at Albergo Egadi in Favignana. You'll find dive hire outlets and bicycles for rent around town and the small harbour.

Levanzo, 4km north of Favignana, is known for the **Grotta del Genovese**, whose walls bear Palaeolithic etchings of bison and deer and a series of fascinating figures dating from the Neolithic period. The figures of women and men were 'painted' using animal fat and carbon. Interestingly, there is also a representation of a tuna fish – indicating that tuna fishing in the Isole Egadi is indeed an ancient tradition. If you have the time, this is an experience not to be missed. Contact Signor Castiglione, the custodian, on ☎ 0923 92 40 32. Alternatively, ask at the Pro Loco on Favignana. The custodian will take you to the cave by boat – on the way back, ask him to drop you off at the small beach known as *il faraglione*. The trip costs L15,000 per person.

Marettimo, the most distant of the islands, is also the least modern. A few hundred people live mostly in the tiny village on the eastern coast and there are no roads. You can go with fishing boats along the coast or follow mule tracks into the scenic hills.

Places to Stay & Eat

There's plenty of accommodation on Favignana, although during the period of the mattanza and in August you'll have trouble finding a bed without a booking. Many local people rent out rooms. Try *Bouganville* (☎ 0923 92 20 33, Via Cimabue 10), which has singles/doubles for L45,000/80,000. In summer half board is obligatory and costs L90,000 per person. *Villaggio Quattro Rose* (☎ 0923 92 12 23), Località Mulino a Vento, has camping facilities and bungalows. *Albergo Egadi* (☎ 0923 92 12 32, Via Colombo 17), just off Favignana town's main piazza, has comfortable singles/doubles for L50,000/100,000 and also offers half board for L110,000 per person. It has an acclaimed restaurant, where you'll eat one of your best meals in Italy, at very reasonable prices.

Levanzo has only two pensioni. *Paradiso* (☎ 0923 92 40 80), on the seafront, charges L40,000/80,000 for rooms with bathroom. It has a restaurant where you'll eat very well for around L40,000 a head. There are no hotels on Marettimo, but you should be able to dig up a room with the locals. In summer, you'll probably be asked to pay full board wherever you stay.

SICILIA

Getting There & Away

Ferries and hydrofoils run between the islands and to Trapani. See the Trapani section for more details.

PANTELLERIA

Known to the Carthaginians as Cossyra, the island fell to the Romans in 217 BC and five centuries later to the Arabs. The Arab presence lives on in the names of various localities. Pantelleria is a curious place that lies closer to Tunisia than Sicilia. It has sea and sunshine and a mountainous, volcanic interior, with thermal springs and remnants of several ancient settlements, such as Mursia, a few kilometres south of the main town.

There is nothing cheap here, especially in summer, when it is best to book ahead. *Albergo Myriam* (☎ 0923 91 13 74, *Corso Umberto 1*) offers singles for L75,000/95,000 and doubles for L120,000/140,000 in the low/high season. You can also rent *dammusi*, the characteristic domed houses of the island. Siremar boats go to Trapani (see the Trapani Getting There & Away section for more details) and Alilauro's summer season Trapani-Tunisia boat generally calls in at Pantelleria on the way.

Sardegna (Sardinia)

The second largest island in the Mar Mediterraneo, Sardegna has always been considered an isolated land. Even today, its people and culture maintain a separate identity from the mainland, which they call *il continente* (the continent).

The island is dotted with some 7000 *nuraghi*, the conical megalithic stone fortresses that are the only remnants of the island's first inhabitants, the Nuraghic people. These sheep-rearing people lived in separate communities led by warrior-kings and their culture flourished from around 1800 BC.

Sardegna's coast was visited by Greeks and Phoenicians, first as traders then as invaders and the island was colonised by the Romans. They, in turn, were followed by the Pisans, Genoese, Spanish, Austrians and finally, the Royal House of Savoia, the future kings of a united Italy. In 1948 Sardegna became a semiautonomous region.

Despite the succession of invaders and colonisers, it is often said that the Sardinians (known as the Sardi) were never really conquered, they simply retreated into the hills. The Romans were prompted to call the island's central-eastern mountains the Barbagia (from the Latin word for barbarian) because of the uncompromising lifestyle of the warrior-shepherds, who never abandoned their Nuraghic customs. Even today, the Sardi of the interior speak an ancient Latin-based dialect and proudly maintain traditional customs and costume. Until the late 1980s many of the island's shepherds spent long periods in almost complete isolation, living in traditional conical shelters of stone and wood called *pinnettas*. These days the shepherds reach their sheep by 4WD and sometimes walkers are given permission to use the shelters as refuges.

Sardegna's cuisine is as varied as its history. Along the coast most dishes feature seafood and there are many variations of *zuppa di pesce* (fish soup) and pasta. Inland you will find *porcheddu* (roast sucking pig),

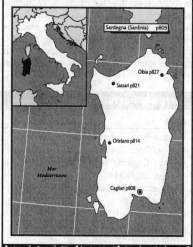

Sardegna (Sardinia) p805
Olbia p827
Sassari p821
Oristano p814
Mar Mediterraneo
Cagliari p808

kid goat with olives and even lamb trotters in garlic sauce. The Sardi eat *pecorino* (sheep's milk cheese) and you will rarely find Parmesan here. The preferred bread throughout the island is the paper-thin *carta musica*, also called *pane carasau*, often sprinkled with oil and salt.

SARDEGNA

Sardegna's 'savage, dark-bushed, sky-exposed land', as it was described by DH Lawrence, has incredibly beautiful gorges and highlands and kilometres of unspoiled coastline with salt lakes and herons. Hunters have always been active in Sardegna, but some wildlife remains, notably the wild pig, the Golden and Bonelli's eagles, the Peregrine falcon, pink flamingoes, the Sardegnan deer and a colony of griffon vultures on the west coast. Miniature horses are raised on the Giara di Gesturi plain in the south-west. Unfortunately, the famous colony of Mediterranean monk seals previously found at the Grotta del Bue Marino, near Cala Gonone, has not been sighted for some years.

The island offers visitors a wide range of attractions, from spectacular beaches and archaeological treasures to the isolated interior, perfect for the more adventurous traveller. If you do venture into the interior, you will find the people extremely gracious and hospitable, although you might find it difficult to make initial contact. Try to avoid coming to the island in August, when the weather is very hot and the beaches are overcrowded. Warm weather generally continues from April to October.

Getting There & Away

Air The airports at Cagliari, Olbia, Alghero and Arbatax-Tortoli link Sardegna with major Italian and European cities.

Boat The island is accessible by ferry from Genova, La Spezia, Civitavecchia, Fiumicino, Napoli, Palermo, Trapani, Bonifacio (Corsica) and Tunisia, as well as Toulon and Marseille in France. The departure points in Sardegna are Olbia, Golfo Aranci, Palau and Porto Torres in the north, Arbatax on the east coast and Cagliari in the south.

The main ferry company is Tirrenia. See the boxed text 'Tirrenia Ferry Services' below for details of routes and prices.

Ferrovie dello Stato (FS) runs a slightly cheaper ferry service between Civitavecchia and Golfo Aranci. Other companies include Moby Lines, which runs ferries from Livorno to Olbia as well as between Sardegna and

Tirrenia Ferry Services

route	fares	duration
Genova-Porto Torres or Olbia	L76,500/96,500/124,500	13 hours
Genova-Porto Torres or Olbia (Fast Ferry)	L131,000/171,000	6 hours
Genova-Cagliari (Summer Only)	L95,500/122,500/156,500	20 hours
Civitavecchia-Olbia	L33,900/49,900/64,800	8 hours
Civitavecchia-Cagliari	L70,500/88,500/118,500	14½ hours
Napoli-Cagliari	L71,500/98,500/132,500	16 hours
Palermo-Cagliari	L66,500/90,500/120,500	13½ hours
Genova-Arbatax	L78,500/100,500/143,500	19 hours
Civitavecchia-Arbatax	L58,500/74,500/104,500	10½ hours
Cagliari-Tunis	L107,000/135,000/205,000	11½ hours
Trapani-Cagliari	L66,500/90,500/132,500	11½ hours
Fast Ferry Civitavecchia or Fiumicino-Olbia or Golfo Aranci (summer only)	L80,000/110,000	4 hours

Fare prices are listed in the following order: *poltrona* (seat) in a 2nd class cabin; bed in a 2nd class cabin; and bed in a 1st class cabin. The cost of taking a small car to Cagliari on a normal ferry can be up to L140,500, or L160,000 on a fast one to Olbia or Golfo Aranci.
Services run year-round unless specified otherwise.

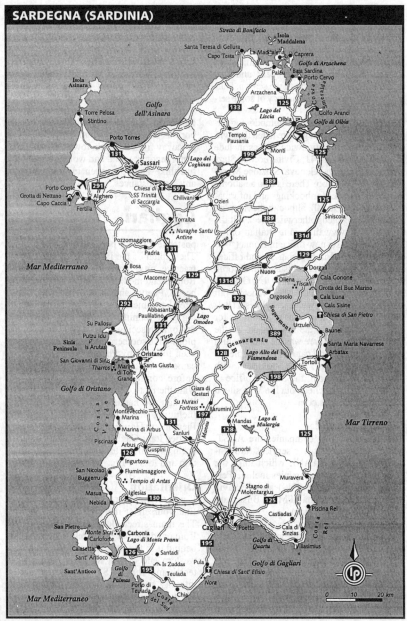

SARDEGNA (SARDINIA)

euro currency converter L10,000 = €5.16

Corsica and Sardegna Ferries, operating from Livorno or Civitavecchia to Golfo Aranci. Brochures detailing Moby Lines, Sardegna Ferries and Tirrenia services are available at most travel agencies. Note that timetables change dramatically every year and that prices fluctuate according to the season. During the low season the frequency of some services is reduced.

Addresses and telephone numbers for Tirrenia's offices in Sardegna are listed throughout this chapter. Nationwide offices include Roma, Via Bissolati 41; Civitavecchia, Stazione Marittima; and Genova, Stazione Marittima Ponte Colombo. There is also a national telephone number for bookings and information (☎ 147 89 90 00), although the lines are frequently engaged; otherwise check out the Web site at www.tirrenia.it (Italian only). Moby Lines has a new office in Roma (☎ 06 42 01 14 55) at Via Bissolati 33 and offices and agents throughout the island. In Livorno it operates through the agency LV Ghianda (☎ 0586 82 68 23), Via Vittorio Veneto 24. It also has a Web site at www.mobylines.it (Italian only). The company has special fares for daytime passages in the low season. At the time of writing, the fare was L279,000 return (Livorno-Olbia) for a car and two people.

For information and bookings with Sardegna Ferries, call the Savona office at ☎ 019 21 55 11 or check out the Web site at www.corsicaferries.com.

Getting Around

Bus The main bus companies are ARST, which operates extensive services throughout the island and PANI, which links the main towns. Other companies include Ferrovie della Sardegna (FdS) and Ferrovie Meridionale Sardegna (FMS). Buses are generally faster than trains.

Train The main Ferrovie dello Stato (FS) train lines link Cagliari with Oristano, Sassari and Olbia and are generally reliable. The private railways which link smaller towns throughout the island can be very slow. However, the Trenino Verde (Green Train) which runs from Cagliari to Arbatax through the Barbagia is a relaxing way to see part of the interior (for more details, see Getting There & Around in the Cagliari section).

Car & Motorcycle The only way to really explore Sardegna is by road. Rental agencies are listed under Cagliari and some other towns around the island.

Hitching You might find hitchhiking laborious because of the light traffic once you get away from the main towns. Hitchhiking is not recommended and women should not hitchhike alone, or even in groups, under any circumstances.

Cagliari

postcode 09100 • pop 250,000
The capital of the island, Cagliari is an attractive city, notable for its interesting Roman and medieval sections, its beautiful beach, Poetto, and its wide marshes populated by numerous species of birds, including pink flamingoes. The city warrants a day of sightseeing and is a good base for exploring the southern coast. Believed to have been founded by Phoenicians, Cagliari became an important Carthaginian port town before coming under Roman control. As with the rest of the island, the city passed through the hands of various conquerors, including the Pisans, Spanish and the Piemontese House of Savoia, before joining unified Italy. Cagliari was savagely bombed during WWII, suffering significant destruction and loss of life.

Orientation

If you arrive by bus, train or boat, you will find yourself at the port area of Cagliari. The main street along the harbour is Via Roma and the old city stretches up the hill behind it to the fortified area. At the northwestern end of Via Roma is Piazza Matteotti and the AAST office, the ARST intercity bus station and the train station. Most of the budget hotels and restaurants are close to the port area.

Information
Tourist Offices The Ente Sardo Industrie Turistiche (ESIT) office (☎ 800 01 31 53, fax 070 66 46 36), covering all of Sardegna, is at Via Goffredo Mameli 97. It is open from 8 am to 8 pm daily from 15 May to 15 September, while in the low season the opening hours are reduced.

The AAST office (☎ 070 66 92 55), at Piazza Matteotti 9, is open from 8 am to 8 pm daily during summer and from 8 am to 2 pm in other months. It has a reasonable amount of information about the town and will advise on accommodation. There is also a provincial tourist information booth at the airport (☎ 070 24 02 00) that opens from 8 am to 8 pm daily between 15 June and 15 September and from 9 am to 1 pm and 4 to 6 pm the rest of the year.

Money There are several major banks on Largo Carlo Felice, which runs uphill from Piazza Matteotti. They usually open from 8.20 am to 1.20 pm and from 3 to 4.30 pm Monday to Friday. There is also a currency exchange office at the train station, open from 8 am to 8 pm daily. The airport has a post office that will change money, open from 8.10 am to 5.30 pm Monday to Friday (to 4 pm on the last day of the month) and to 12.20 pm on Saturday (noon on the last Saturday of the month) and a bank, which is open from 8.20 am to 1.20 pm and 2.30 to 3.30 pm Monday to Friday.

Post & Communications The main post office (☎ 070 6 03 11) is on Piazza del Carmine, up Via la Maddalena from Via Roma. It's open from 8 am to 6.30 pm Monday to Friday and to 1.20 pm on Saturday. You can also change money there. The Telecom phone centre at Via G Angioj, off Piazza Matteotti, is open from 8 am to 10 pm daily.

Travel Agencies There is a CTS office (☎ 070 48 82 60) at Via Cesare Balbo 4.

Medical Services & Emergency Ospedale Civile (hospital; ☎ 070 609 22 67) is on Via Ospedale. To report thefts, go to the questura (police station; ☎ 070 6 02 71) at Via Amat 9.

Things to See & Do
The **Museo Archeologico Nazionale** on Piazza Arsenale, in the Cittadella dei Musei area, has a fascinating collection of Nuraghic bronzes. It is open from 9 am to 7 pm daily except Monday between April and October and from 9 am to 2 pm and 3.30 to 8 pm for the rest of the year. Admission costs L5000. On the 2nd floor is the **Pinacoteca Nazionale**, whose collection includes local and Spanish renaissance paintings. It opens from 8.30 am to 7.30 pm daily and admission costs L4000.

In front of the museum in Piazza Arsenale stands the **Torre di San Pancrazio**. This Pisan tower is open from 9 am to 1 pm and from 3.30 to 7.30 pm daily except Monday (no admission charge).

It is enjoyable to wander through the nearby medieval quarter. The Pisan-Romanesque **duomo** was originally built in the 13th century but later remodelled. Its two precious Romanesque pulpits, carved in 1160, were gifts of the Pisan rulers.

There is a good view of the city and harbour from the **Bastione di San Remy**, in the centre of town in Piazza Costituzione; it once formed part of the old city's fortifications.

Carved into the white limestone of an old quarry, the Anfiteatro Romano is considered the most important Roman monument in Sardegna. It's open from 9 am to 1 pm and 5 to 8 pm daily in summer and from 8.30 am to 5.30 pm in winter. Admission is free. The **Orto Botanico** (botanical gardens), along the way on Viale Fra Ignazio, are a lovely spot for a quiet rest. They are open from 8 am to 1.30 pm and from 3 to 6.30 pm in summer and admission costs a token L1000.

You can spend a day at Poetto beach, east of the centre, where several small bars have outside tables, or wander across to the salt lake of Molentargius, just west of Poetto, to see the pink flamingoes.

Special Events
The Festival of Sant'Efisio is held annually from 1 May. It's a colourful festival, mixing

SARDEGNA

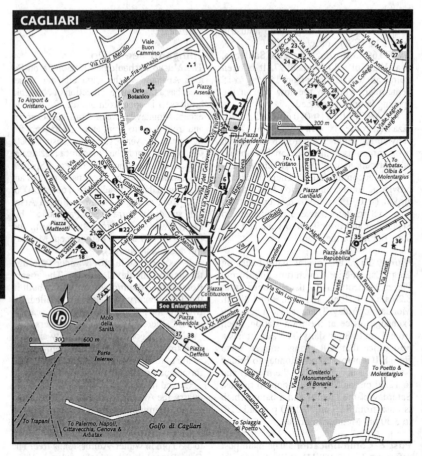

CAGLIARI

the secular and the religious and the highlight is when an effigy of the saint is carried in procession to the small church of Sant'Efisio in the nearby town of Nora (see Around Cagliari later in this chapter).

Places to Stay

There are numerous budget hotels in the old city near the station. Try the pleasant *Locanda Firenze* (☎ 070 65 36 78, *Corso Vittorio Emanuele 50*), which has singles/doubles for L40,000/54,000. *Locanda Mira-*

mare (☎/fax 070 66 40 21, *Via Roma 59*) has rooms for L55,000/70,000. *Albergo Centrale* (☎ 070 65 47 83, *Via Sardegna 4*) charges L40,000/60,000 and the nearby *Albergo La Perla* (☎ 070 66 94 46, *Via Sardegna 18*) has rooms for L48,000/60,000.

Pensione Vittoria (☎ 070 65 79 70, fax 070 66 79 70, *Via Roma 75*) is a very pleasant establishment, with rooms for L55,000/85,000 or L62,000/99,000 with bathroom. *Hotel Quattro Mori* (☎ 070 66 85 35, fax 070 66 60 87, *Via G Angioj 27*) has good rooms for

PLACES TO STAY	OTHER		15	Piazza del Carmine
12 Locanda Firenze	1	Anfiteatro Romano	16	Train Station
22 Hotel Quattro Mori	2	Cittadella dei Musei;	17	Hertz
23 Albergo Centrale		Museo Archeologico	18	ARST Bus Station
24 Hotel Italia		Nazionale; Pinacoteca	19	Stazione Marittima
25 Albergo La Perla		Nazionale		(Ferry Terminal)
30 Pensione Vittoria	3	CTS Travel Agency	20	AAST Tourist Office
32 Locanda Miramare	4	Torre di San Pancrazio	21	Telecom Phone Centre
	5	Former Museo	26	Bastione di San Remy
PLACES TO EAT		Archeologico	27	Piazza dei Martiri
10 Ristorante Il Corso	6	Duomo	31	Ruvioli
13 Trattoria Umberto	7	Piazza Palazzo	35	Ferrovie della Sardegna
28 Trattoria Gennargentu	8	Ospedale Civile (Hospital)		Train Station
29 Trattoria Ci Pensa Cannas	9	Chiesa di San Michele	36	Questura (Police Station)
33 Trattoria da Serafino	11	ESIT Tourist Office	37	Piazza Darsena
34 Corsaro	14	Post Office	38	PANI Bus Station

SARDEGNA

L65,000/90,000 or L70,000/120,000 with bathroom. *Hotel Italia (☎ 070 66 04 10, fax 070 65 02 40, Via Sardegna 31)* has more up-market, comfortable rooms for L105,000/145,000.

Places to Eat

There are several reasonably priced *trattorie* in the area behind Via Roma, particularly around Via Cavour and Via Sardegna. If you want to buy picnic supplies, head for Via Sardegna, where there are several good *alimentari*, as well as a *forno* (bakery).

Trattoria da Serafino (Via Lepanto 6), on the corner of Via Sardegna, has excellent food at reasonable prices. *Trattoria Gennargentu (Via Sardegna 60)* has good pasta and seafood and a full meal will cost around L35,000. *Trattoria Ci Pensa Cannas*, down the street at No 37, is another good choice, with similar prices.

A full meal at *Trattoria Umberto (Via Sassari 86)* will cost around L35,000. *Ristorante Il Corso (Corso Vittorio Emanuele 78)* specialises in seafood and a full meal will cost around L40,000.

Corsaro (Viale Regina Margherita 28) is one of the city's top seafood restaurants. A full meal will cost at least L80,000. In summer it opens a branch at the Marina Piccola at Poetto beach, including a cheaper pizzeria section.

Getting There & Around

Air Cagliari's airport is 8km north-west of the city at Elmas and has a tourist office (☎ 070 24 02 00). ARST buses leave regularly from Piazza Matteotti to coincide with flights. There's an Alitalia office at the airport (☎ 070 24 00 79), otherwise contact the Alitalia central office on ☎ 147 86 56 43 for the cost of a local call. Meridiana is another airline with an office at the airport (☎ 070 24 01 69).

Bus ARST buses leave from the bus station (☎ 070 409 83 24 or ☎ 800 86 50 42 if you are in Sardegna) on Piazza Matteotti for nearby towns, including Pula, the Costa del Sud and Teulada, south-west of Cagliari, as well as Villasimius and the Costa Rei to the east. PANI buses leave from farther along Via Roma on Piazza Darsena for towns such as Sassari, Nuoro, Oristano and Porto Torres. The PANI ticket office (☎ 070 65 23 26) is at Piazza Darsena 4.

If you want to head for the beach at Poetto, take bus PF or PQ from Piazza Matteotti.

Train Regular trains leave for Oristano, Sassari, Porto Torres and Olbia. The private FdS train station is on Piazza della Repubblica.

For information about the Trenino Verde, which runs along a scenic route between Cagliari and Arbatax, contact the ESIT office (see Tourist Offices earlier) or FdS directly

(☎ 070 58 02 46). The most interesting and scenic section of the route is between Mandas and Arbatax.

Boat Ferries arrive at the port just off Via Roma. Bookings for Tirrenia can be made at the Stazione Marittima in the port area (☎ 070 66 60 65). The office opens from 8.30 am to 6 pm Monday to Friday (7 pm for the line to Sicilia) and from 8.30 am to noon and from 3.30 pm until the boat sails on Saturday. Ferries connect Cagliari with Palermo, Trapani, Napoli, Civitavecchia and Genova, as well as Tunisia (via Trapani). See the Getting There & Away section at the beginning of this chapter for further information.

Car & Motorcycle If you want to hire a car or motorcycle, try Hertz (☎ 070 66 81 05), Piazza Matteotti 1, or Ruvioli at Elmas airport (☎ 070 24 03 23) and in the town at Via dei Mille 11 (☎ 070 65 89 55).

AROUND CAGLIARI
Costa Rei
There are good beaches on the largely undeveloped Costa Rei which can be visited on day trips from Cagliari. The area is dotted with camp sites and (generally expensive) hotels.

Villasimius is the most developed town in this area and makes a comfortable base for exploring the attractive coastline. Try *Albergo Stella d'Oro* (☎ 070 79 12 55, Via Vittorio Emanuele 25), which has singles/doubles for L55,000/90,000. Note that half board is obligatory in August (L135,000 per person). Nearby on the beach is *Camping Spiaggia del Riso* (☎ 070 79 10 52), which charges L14,000/24,000 per person/site. Other camp sites in the area include *Garden Cala Sinzias* (☎ 070 99 50 37), on the coast near Castiadas and, farther north, *Piscina Rei* (☎ 070 99 10 89), not far from Muravera.

Slightly farther along the coast west of Villasimius, in the locality of Campus, is *Hotel Cormoran* (☎ 070 79 81 01), a lovely resort hotel with a private sandy beach. Full board costs up to L290,000 in the high season. Bungalows for two people are available for around L2,590,000 per week and bungalows for five people cost up to L2,800,000 per week in the high season. For full details on camping and other accommodation along the coast, contact the tourist office at Cagliari. Regular daily ARST buses connect Cagliari with Villasimius and places along the Costa Rei, including camp sites.

Nora
Founded in the 9th century BC by the Phoenicians, on the coast south-west of Cagliari, Nora was considered important for its strategic position and eventually came under Roman control. The ruins of the city extend into the sea and offer evidence of both civilisations, including temples, houses, a Roman theatre and baths. The ruins are open from 9 am to 8 pm daily in summer and from 9 am to 6 pm out of season. Admission costs L5000. For information call ☎ 070 920 91 38. To get to the ruins, take an ARST bus from Cagliari to Pula, then a local bus (Autolinee Murgia) to Nora (only three a day).

Costa del Sud
The small town of **Chia** marks the start of the beautiful Costa del Sud, which is protected from further development by special ordinances – private homes can be built only in certain zones. There is one large hotel complex which blights the coastline about halfway between Chia and Teulada, the four star *Grand Hotel Baia delle Ginestre* (☎ 070 927 30 05, 0342 90 47 77 in winter). Half board costs from L1,050,000 per week, depending on the season. Apartments are also available for rent.

Those happy to settle for something simpler can try *Camping Comunale Portu Tramatzu* (☎ 070 928 30 27), just past Porto di Teulada. The camp site is by the sea and has a supermarket, bar, pizzeria and restaurant. Costs are L12,500/15,000 per person/site and it is open from April to October. To get to the camp site, take the ARST Cagliari-Teulada bus, get off at Porto di Teulada and then walk the short distance from the port (signs will point you in the right direction).

The town of **Teulada** has your only other option, *Hotel Sebera* (☎ 070 927 08 76), a pleasant establishment 7km from the sea, in the central piazza where buses stop. Full board costs L75,000/90,000 a single/double.

At **Porto di Teulada** there is a very pleasant *bar/trattoria* which specialises in fresh seafood. You can enjoy lunch in the small courtyard for around L50,000.

Regular ARST buses connect Cagliari with Chia and about eight a day continue on to Teulada.

If you have a car, you can make a detour to the **Is Zuddas caves** (☎ 0781 95 57 41), 6km south of Santadi on the road to Teulada. The series of caves has interesting stalagmite and stalactite formations and is open from 9 am to noon and from 2.30 to 6 pm daily between April and September (closing earlier on Sunday and public holidays in winter). Admission costs L10,000 (guided tours only).

Another deviation could include the remains of the Phoenician/Carthaginian city on **Monte Sirai**, just out of Carbonia (☎ 0781 6 40 44). This 7th century BC fort town commanded a view for miles around. The site is still being excavated from 9 am to 1 pm and from 4 to 8 pm daily except Monday (9 am to 5 pm in winter); admission costs L5000 for adults and L3000 for people aged under 16 and over 60.

Southern Sardegna

SANT'ANTIOCO & SAN PIETRO

These islands, off the south-western coast of Sardegna, have sandy beaches and quiet coves, as well as the pleasant towns of Calasetta (Sant'Antioco) and Carloforte (San Pietro), both with whitewashed or pastel-coloured houses lining narrow streets. The town of Sant'Antioco is more developed.

Information

The Pro Loco office (☎ 0781 8 20 31) in the town of Sant'Antioco is at Via Roma 41. It can provide information and advice on accommodation, including apartments for rent.

You can request information by writing (in English) to the Associazione Turistica Pro Loco, 09017 Sant'Antioco. Pro Loco also has an office in Calasetta (☎ 0781 8 85 34). San Pietro has a separate tourist office (☎ 0781 85 40 09) at Carloforte in Corso Tagliafico 1, opposite the port.

Places to Stay

There are camping facilities on Sant'Antioco at *Campeggio Tonnara* (☎ 0781 80 90 58) at Calasapone. It is by the sea, away from the town and accessible on the orange FMS buses that service both islands.

In Sant'Antioco, try *Hotel Moderno* (☎ 0781 8 31 05, Via Nazionale 82), which has singles/doubles for L60,000/90,000 with bathroom. You will need to book well in advance. In Calasetta, the best choice is *Fiby Hotel* (☎ 0781 8 84 44, Via Solferino 83), a very pleasant establishment which has rooms with bathroom for L82,000/93,000 in the high season. It also offers half board/full board for L110,000/L120,000.

In Carloforte on San Pietro, *Hieracon Hotel* (☎ 0781 85 40 28, Corso Cavour 62), facing the port, charges L105,000 per person for half board in the high season and L90,000 a double in other months.

Places to Eat

There is a *Coop* supermarket in the town of Sant'Antioco on the corner of the Lungomare and Via Eleonora d'Arborea. In Carloforte you can pick up supplies at the *Mercato Super Crai (Via Diaz)*.

In Sant'Antioco there are several good trattorie and restaurants, including the pizzeria ristorante *Il Cantuccio (Viale Trento)*, near Piazza Repubblica. In Calasetta, try the pizzeria ristorante *L'Anfora (Via Roma 121)* or the trattoria *Da Pasqualino (Via Roma 99)*. A full meal at either will cost around L30,000, more if you eat fish.

In Carloforte, *Barone Rosso (Via XX Settembre 26)* is the place to go for a sandwich; otherwise, try *Osteria della Tonnara*, on the waterfront, a short walk from the yacht harbour.

SARDEGNA

Getting There & Around

Sant'Antioco is connected to the mainland by a land bridge and is accessible by FMS bus from Cagliari and Iglesias. Regular ferries connect Calasetta and Carloforte.

Orange FMS buses link the small towns on Sant'Antioco and the camp site and isolated groups of houses on San Pietro. In the town of Sant'Antioco you can hire scooters/mountain bikes for L50,000/20,000 a day from Euromoto (☎ 0781 84 09 07), Via Nazionale 57 and make your own tour of the island. At Carloforte, Viracarruggi (☎ 0368 305 55 54), Corso Cavour 28, has mountain bikes/scooters for L15,000/50,000 a day. Both outlets hire motorised rubber dinghies for around L200,000 a day. For boat hire contact Cantiere Sifredi (☎ 0781 85 44 37) or ask in the shop Boutique Mare at the port at Carloforte. Prices range from L100,000 to L300,000 a day, depending on the size of the boat.

IGLESIAS

This mining centre, slightly inland from Sardegna's south-western coast, is left off most tourist itineraries but it's well worth a stopover. Iglesias is in a zone rich in minerals, including lead, zinc and some silver and gold and its mining history extends back to Roman and Carthaginian times. From the 13th century it was occupied by the Pisans, who called it Argentaria (the Place of Silver) after the rich silver deposits discovered there during that period. However, it was the Spanish Aragons who left a greater mark on the town.

The tourist office (☎ 0781 4 17 95), Via Gramsci 9/11, in the centre of town, is open from 9 am to 1 pm and from 4 to 6.30 pm.

Things to See

The **duomo**, on Piazza del Duomo, opposite the municipal offices, dates from the period of Pisan domination and was built in Romanesque-Gothic style. Nearby, on Piazza San Francesco, is the Gothic **Chiesa di San Francesco**. Above the old town, along Via Campidano, there are the remains of Pisan towers and fortified walls.

Places to Stay & Eat

Artu (☎ 0781 2 24 92, Piazza Quintino Sella 15), east of the old part of town, has singles/doubles with bathroom for L95,000/145,000. There are numerous *pastry shops*, *takeaways* and *grocery shops* in the shopping area around Via Martini and Via Azuni, a short walk from Piazza del Duomo. A good meal at *Gazebo Medievale* (☎ 0781 3 08 71, Via Musio 21), off Via Corso Matteotti, will cost you around L50,000.

Getting There & Away

The bus station is on Via Oristano, off Via XX Settembre, south-east of the old town, and tickets can be purchased at Sulcis Agenzia Viaggi, Via Roma 52 (parallel to Via Oristano). Regular FMS buses link Iglesias with Cagliari, Carbonia, Sant'Antioco and Calasetta. Two FMS buses a day head for Arbus, from where you can pick up connections to the Costa Verde. Iglesias is also accessible by train from Cagliari, Carbonia and Oristano and the train station is in Via Garibaldi, a 15 minute walk along Via Matteotti from the town centre.

AROUND IGLESIAS

The Phoenician-Roman **Tempio di Antas** is about 15km north of Iglesias towards Fluminimaggiore. Set in a wide, picturesque valley, the small temple was dedicated to a god of fertility and hunting by the Phoenicians, while the Romans dedicated it to a local Nuraghic divinity. Six columns remain standing. Those without their own transport can take the FMS bus from Iglesias for Fluminimaggiore and get off just after the village of Sant'Angelo. The temple is then a 3km walk along a dirt road. For information contact the local Pro Loco office (☎ 0781 58 10 40).

Western Sardegna

COSTA VERDE

This magnificent stretch of coastline remains almost entirely unspoiled, despite the fact that much of the area has been extensively mined. Former mining towns such as Buggerru, Masua and Nebida are now seeking to make their fortunes as small coastal resorts.

The Costa Verde starts just north of Buggerru at Capo Pecora and continues to Montevecchio Marina. Laws have been passed to protect much of the coastline from development and the area remains a paradise for lovers of secluded beaches. Discreet campers will find that they can free-camp in the area without any hassle. The isolation of much of the coast makes it difficult, but not impossible, for people to reach without their own transport.

Buggerru

This is a good place to make your base. It doesn't have any hotels as yet, but there is space set aside for camping by the waterfront and you can free-camp along the coast to the south of the town. Many residents rent out rooms and apartments and by asking at one of Buggerru's bars or supermarkets you will easily find a bed for the night (although most will be booked out in August). FMS buses run to Buggerru from Iglesias and you can contact the Pro Loco office on ☎ 0781 5 45 22.

San Nicolao

North of Buggerru, this is a long, sandy beach and, unlike many other public beaches in Italy, it's clean. In addition, the rows of deck chairs and umbrellas characteristic of the private beaches in other parts of the country are missing. San Nicolao is accessible by FMS bus from Iglesias.

Piscinas

In the heart of the Costa Verde, at the mouth of the Piscinas river, this magnificent unspoiled beach is backed by a vast protected area of 100m-high sand dunes, which support a rich variety of wildlife. An organised parking area for camper vans has been established behind the dune area, just off the road from Ingurtosu, about 2km from the sea and is due to open in the summer of 2000. Camping is strictly prohibited on the beach and in the sand dunes.

The only building in the area, set right on the beach, is *Le Dune* (☎ 070 97 71 30), an atmospheric three star hotel featuring the mineral deposits of the mines that now lie in ruins along the valley. It offers excellent food and can organise guided tours to the island's most important archaeological sites, as well as to the nearby mining village of Montevecchio. Out of season, full board costs from L130,000 per person and half board is from L115,000. Prices are as high as L200,000 for half board in peak periods.

To reach Piscinas from Guspini (Pro Loco ☎ 070 9 76 01), take the road for Ingurtosu, then take the dirt road to the right where you see the sign for the hotel Le Dune. The distance from the turn-off to the sea is 7km, but if you're on foot the walk is interesting, as you'll pass the ruins of the numerous mines which once operated in the valley. ARST buses run a twice-daily service between Guspini and Ingurtosu, at 6.30 am and 2.05 pm – ask the driver where to get off. ARST buses also run from Cagliari and Oristano to Guspini. The hotel will pick you up from the port or the airport in Cagliari if you can spare the L160,000 fare (a public taxi will probably cost you more).

Marina di Arbus (Pro Loco ☎ 070 975 91 23), also known as Gutturu Flumini, is several kilometres north and is more developed. Accommodation possibilities include *Camping Costa Verde* (☎ 070 97 70 09), which charges L14,000 per person and L20,000 for a site. Getting to Marina di Arbus is not simple by public transport. You will need to catch an ARST bus from Oristano or an FMS bus from Iglesias to Arbus, then from Arbus a bus from Via della Repubblica to Marina di Arbus, operational in summer only, at 7.30 am and 2.20 pm, returning to Arbus in the evening.

ORISTANO

postcode 09170 • pop 32,000

Originally inhabited by the Nuraghic people, the area around what is now Oristano was colonised by the Phoenicians, who established the port town of Tharros, later controlled by the Carthaginians and then the Romans.

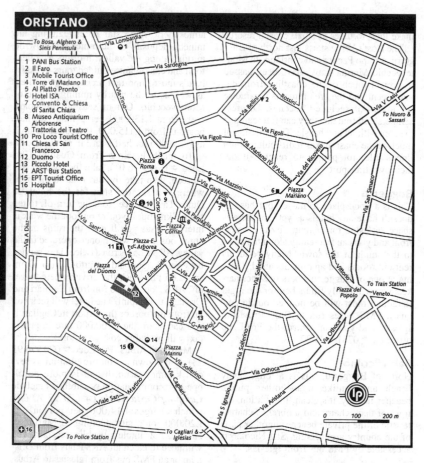

ORISTANO

1 PANI Bus Station
2 Il Faro
3 Mobile Tourist Office
4 Torre di Mariano II
5 Al Piatto Pronto
6 Hotel ISA
7 Convento & Chiesa di Santa Chiara
8 Museo Antiquarium Arborense
9 Trattoria del Teatro
10 Pro Loco Tourist Office
11 Chiesa di San Francesco
12 Duomo
13 Piccolo Hotel
14 ARST Bus Station
15 EPT Tourist Office
16 Hospital

Oristano is believed to have been founded sometime in the 7th century AD by the people of Tharros, who abandoned their ancient town, probably to escape raids by Moorish pirates. Oristano grew to prominence in the 14th century, particularly during the rule of Eleonora d'Arborea, who opposed the Spanish occupation of the island and drew up a body of laws known as the *Carta de Logu*, a progressive legal code which was eventually enforced throughout the island. The code is also considered im-

portant because it acts as a record of the ancient Sardegnan language, in which it was written.

Orientation

A good point from which to orient yourself is Piazza Roma, not far from the PANI bus station, off Via Tirso in Via Lombardia and a five minute walk from the ARST bus station in Via Cagliari, just off Piazza Mannu. The train station is a 20 minute walk away in Piazza Ungheria. To reach Piazza Roma from the station, follow Via Vittorio Veneto to Piazza Mariano and then take Via Mazzini.

Information

Tourist Offices A mobile tourist office opens daily in Piazza Roma during summer and has loads of information on the town and the province and will advise on accommodation and transport. There is a Pro Loco office (☎ 0783 7 06 21) at Via Vittorio Emanuele 8, open from 9 am to 12.30 pm and from 5 to 8.30 pm Monday to Friday in summer and from 9 am to noon on Saturday. The EPT office (☎ 0783 7 31 91) at Via Cagliari 278 is open from 8 am to 2 pm Monday to Friday and also from 4 to 7 pm on Tuesday and Wednesday.

Post & Communications The main post office is on Via Liguria, north-west of Piazza Roma along Via Tirso and opens from 8.15 am to 7.30 pm Monday to Saturday. There are some Telecom public telephones throughout the town.

Medical Services & Emergency For an ambulance, call ☎ 0783 7 82 22 or 0783 7 43 18. There is a public hospital (☎ 0783 31 71) at Via Fondazione Rockefeller, along Viale San Martino from Piazza Mannu.

The questura (☎ 0783 2 14 21) is at Via Beatrice d'Arborea 2, behind the playing fields not far from the hospital.

Things to See

On Piazza Roma is the 13th century **Torre di Mariano II**, which is also known as the Torre di San Cristoforo. From here, walk along Corso Umberto until you get to **Piazza Eleonora d'Arborea**, where you will find a 19th century statue of Oristano's heroine. The neoclassical **Chiesa di San Francesco** is adjacent. Of note inside the church are a 15th century polychrome wooden crucifix, a 14th century marble statue of San Basilio by Nino Pisano and a 16th century polyptych by Pietro Cavaro.

Follow Via Eleonora d'Arborea or Via Duomo to reach the **duomo**, built in the 13th century but completely remodelled in the 18th century. It has a baroque bell tower, topped by a multicoloured dome.

Also of interest is the 14th century **Convento & Chiesa di Santa Chiara**, between Via Parpaglia and Via Garibaldi.

The **Museo Antiquarium Arborense** in Palazzo Parpaglia on Piazza Corrias in the heart of the town contains interesting finds from the ancient Phoenician port of Tharros. It is open from 9 am to 8 pm daily. The L4000 entrance fee includes a guided tour of the museum in English and entrance to some of the town's monuments, including the Torre di Mariano II (also part of the guided tour). Call ☎ 0783 7 44 33 or 0783 79 12 62 for information.

About 3km south of Oristano at Santa Giusta and easily accessible by local ARST buses, is the **Basilica di Santa Giusta**. Built in around 1100, the church is Romanesque, with Pisan and Lombard influences.

Special Events

The most important festival in Oristano is the colourful Sa Sartiglia, held on the last Sunday of carnival (late February or early March) and repeated on Shrove Tuesday. Probably one of the island's most beautiful festive events, the Sartiglia had its origins in a military contest performed by the knights of the Second Crusade. It developed into a festival during the period of Spanish domination and now involves masked, costumed riders who parade through the town before participating in a tournament, where they must pierce the centre of a silver star with their swords while riding at full speed.

Places to Stay & Eat

Oristano is not exactly bursting with hotels and there are no budget options. There is a camp site, the *Camping Torregrande* (☎ 0783 2 22 28) at Marina di Torre Grande, about 7km west of Oristano (regular ARST buses connect the two towns – see Getting There & Around later in this section). It is open from May to October, but may be full during August.

In town, *Piccolo Hotel* (☎ 0783 7 15 00, *Via Martignano 19*) has singles/doubles for

L60,000/100,000. *Hotel ISA (☎ 0783 36 01 01, Piazza Mariano 50)* has rooms with bath for L78,000/125,000.

Agriturismo is very well organised in the province, with half board in a double room costing around L60,000 per person. It is organised by the Consorzio Agriturismo di Sardegna (☎ 0783 7 39 54, fax 0783 7 39 24).

For a quick snack or meal, try *Al Piatto Pronto (Via Mazzini 21)*, near Piazza Roma, which has a wide range of pre-prepared dishes. *Trattoria del Teatro (Via Parpaglia 11)* has full meals for around L40,000, while *Il Faro (Via Bellini 25)* is considered one of Oristano's better and more expensive restaurants, with a meal costing L90,000.

Getting There & Around

The terminal for ARST buses, which service the province, is on Via Cagliari, opposite the EPT office. Regular buses head for Marina di Torre Grande, Putzu Idu and Su Pallosu; during summer they also serve San Giovanni di Sinis and the ruins of Tharros. Four buses a day leave for Bosa.

The PANI bus station is on Via Lombardia, outside the Blu Bar at No 30 (where you can check timetables). There are connections to Cagliari, Sassari and Nuoro.

Oristano is accessible by train from Cagliari, Sassari and Olbia.

The city is easy to negotiate on foot, although urban bus No 2 Circolare Destra (clockwise) or Sinistra (anticlockwise) is handy for getting around. Small buses will also take you into the old town.

AROUND ORISTANO

Just west of Oristano is the **Sinis Peninsula**, with some lovely sandy beaches (which have been awarded a coveted Blue Flag for cleanliness by the EU), the opportunity to see lots of flamingoes and the ruins of the ancient Phoenician port of Tharros. If you have the time, spend a few days relaxing here. There are only a couple of hotels, but rooms are available for rent and several places participate in the local agriturismo programme. Check at the tourist office in Oristano for details.

At the village of **San Giovanni di Sinis** is the 5th century Byzantine church of the same name, where mass is still celebrated. Nearby, in a tiny village of whitewashed houses with pastel-coloured doors, is the tiny church of **San Salvatore**, built over a pagan temple.

Tharros, just outside San Giovanni at the southernmost end of the peninsula, was originally a Phoenician and later a Roman port town. The important ruins, discovered in 1851 by an English archaeologist, yielded significant treasures and are well worth a visit. They are open from 9 am to 8 pm in summer and from 9 am to 5.30 pm in winter. The ticket costs L8000 or L4000 for under 16s. For information call ☎ 0783 37 00 19.

San Giovanni and Tharros can be reached from Oristano by regular ARST buses during summer.

At the northern end of the peninsula are the villages of **Putzu Idu** and **Su Pallosu**, both offering peaceful surroundings and lovely beaches. Between the two villages are marshes which are home to hundreds of pink flamingoes, as well as other water birds. The loveliest beach on the peninsula is nearby at **Is Arutas**.

If you want to stay at Putzu Idu, try *Da Cesare (☎ 0783 5 20 15)*, which has singles/doubles for around L110,000/130,000. Half board, costing L145,000 per person, is obligatory in the high season. A short walk away is the quieter Su Pallosu and *Hotel Su Pallosu (☎ 0783 5 80 21)*, which has rooms for around L75,000/110,000. It offers special deals on half board (from L65,000) at certain times of the year.

Both villages and the beach of Is Arutas are accessible by ARST bus from Oristano.

An event of particular interest, especially for those who want to experience Sardegna's wilder side, is the Sa Ardia in **Sedilo**. This spectacular festival is held on 6 and 7 July in honour of San Costantino and features a fascinating and at times dangerous, ritualised horse race, run just out of town around the country church of **San Costantino**. Thousands of spectators witness the event, with some firing guns (only blanks are used) into the ground and air to excite the horses. Needless to say, there are injuries every year. The race starts at 6 pm on 6 July and is rerun the following morning at about 7 am. Information about the event is available at the provincial tourist office in Oristano. Sedilo is about 50km north-east of Oristano, near Abbasanta and Lago Omodeo.

On the S131 north of Oristano, a few kilometres before Paulilatino, you will find the important Nuraghic **Pozzo Sacro di Santa Cristina** (☎ 0785 5 54 38). This fascinating old well and the Nuraghic village are open from 8.30 am to 9.30 pm daily and the ticket costs L4000. Further along the S131, before you reach Abbasanta, there's the **Nuraghe Losa** (☎ 0785 5 48 23), one of the tallest and best conserved nuraghe in Sardegna. You can visit it free of charge from 8 am to 8 pm.

BOSA
The only town of the Nuoro province on the west coast, Bosa is fast becoming a popular tourist destination, but it is yet to show signs of becoming touristy. The town's historic centre has a pleasant architectural balance which is uncommon in Sardegna. For local information try the town council (☎ 0785 37 31 14, 0785 37 34 10) or go to SWS travel agency (☎ 0785 37 43 91), Corso Vittorio Emanuele 45, which also offers a ticket-booking service.

A medical service for tourists is available in summer only at Bosa Marina at ☎ 0785 37 46 15. The Guardia Medica is at the hospital (☎ 0785 37 31 07).

Things to See & Do
Bosa has a fascinating town centre with lovely little squares and elegant baroque churches. The imposing medieval castle was built in 1112 by the Malaspina, a noble Tuscan family, to control the valley of the Temo river. The Temo, with its 8km of navigable waters, made a local tanning industry possible. Also of interest is the Romanesque church of San Pietro Extramuros, 2km from the old bridge on the south bank of the Temo.

The coastline between Bosa and Alghero is stunning, with rugged cliffs dropping down to unspoiled beaches. The coastline is accessible between **Sa Badrucche** and **Torre Argentina**, a Spanish guard tower. The beaches here are often busy on summer weekends, but the area remains a paradise for walkers in all seasons. However, the only way to really explore the coast is by car or motorcycle. Don't leave anything in your car: thieves patrol the coast looking for easy targets such as unattended cars loaded with luggage.

Also near Bosa is one of the last habitats of the griffon vulture. It is quite an experience if you are lucky enough to spot one of these huge birds whose wingspan can reach 2m.

Places to Stay and Eat
There are hotels in Bosa and at nearby Bosa Marina, an anonymous, modern resort town at the mouth of the Temo river. Nearest to the centre is *Hotel Perry Clan* (☎ 0785 37 30 74, Via Alghero 3), charging L50,000/80,000 for a single/double with bathroom. *Hotel Mannu* (☎ 0785 37 53 06, Via Alghero 28), with clean, modern rooms and a good restaurant, charges around L70,000/120,000 for a room and L50,000 for a seafood meal. All hotels in Bosa can organise guided tours and boat and bicycle rental, as well as a shuttle service to the best beaches on the rocky coastline.

For a good meal try *Tatore (Piazza IV Novembre 13b)*, where you'll spend around L60,000. A more economical option is *Taverna Sant'Ignazio (Via Sant'Ignazio 33)*, in the medieval quarter of Sas Costas.

Getting There & Away
Regular ARST buses link Bosa with Sassari and Oristano, arriving at and departing from Piazza Zanetti. There is a daily bus connection to Alghero, Porto Torres and Olbia, the latter coinciding with the Civitavecchia ferry.

Central Sardegna

AROUND BARUMINI
There are innumerable Nuraghic sites on the island, but some of the most interesting are in the interior and are often very difficult to reach without your own transport. The most

important is the **Su Nuraxi** fortress (☎ 0337 81 30 87), 1km west of Barumini and about 60km north of Cagliari. This vast complex consists of a castle and village and is open from 8.30 am to 7.30 pm (from 9 am to 5 pm in winter); admission costs L7000. On a day trip you will probably spend most of your time travelling if you use public transport.

A better option than spending hours trying to juggle bus timetables is to stay overnight in the nearby town of **Gergei** (10km east of Barumini) at the delightful *Hotel Dedoni* (☎ *0782 80 80 60, Via Marconi 50*), which offers a very high standard of accommodation and traditional food at reasonable prices: L50,000 per person for B&B and L90,000 for full board. The hotel organises day trips and overnight excursions in the area. These can incorporate horse riding, cycling and travel on the Trenino Verde. They will also pick you up from Cagliari or Olbia for L120,000 or L250,000 respectively.

Although Gergei itself is pretty anonymous, it is a perfect base from which to explore the Su Nuraxi site and the nearby plain of **Giara di Gesturi**, inhabited by wild ponies. North of Gergei is the **Giara di Serri**, a high-plain area which, like the Giara di Gesturi, is a great place for walking. Also in this area is the Nuraghic sanctuary of **Santa Vittoria di Serri**, less well known than Su Nuraxi but certainly worth visiting. Of particular interest in this ancient complex is the *recinto delle feste*, a large enclosure lined with small rooms where, it is believed, cult objects and other goods were displayed and sold.

East of Gergei, not far from Orroli, in a lovely, isolated position on the ridge of the Flumendosa gorge, stands the imposing **Nuraghe Arrubiu** (☎ Coop Jaras 0782 84 72 69, 0330 43 55 51). Recently restored, this obscure Nuraghic fortress is a characteristic red thanks to the lichen that has colonised the outside. It is open from 9.30 am to 1 pm and from 3 to 8.30 pm in summer and from 8 am to 5 pm in winter. Admission costs L7000.

A few kilometres south of Barumini, off the road to Cagliari, are the spiky ruins of a 12th century castle, protruding from a hill at **Las Plássas**.

There is an ARST bus from Cagliari to Barumini, but to return you will need to catch an FdS bus to Sanluri and then an ARST bus to Cagliari. FdS buses also serve Gergei. To avoid being stranded, check the latest bus timetables at the Cagliari tourist office. The Trenino Verde which runs between Cagliari and Arbatax passes nearby at Mandas. The section between Mandas and Arbatax is the most scenic part of the railway, so it might be worthwhile catching the train there if you have the time.

Northern Sardegna

ALGHERO
postcode 07041 • pop 40,000
On the island's north-western coast, in the area known as the Coral Riviera, Alghero is one of the most popular tourist resorts in Sardegna. The Catalan Aragonese won the town from Genova in 1354 and even today the locals speak a dialect strongly linked to the Catalan language. Alghero is a good base from which to explore the magnificent coastline that links it to Bosa to the south and the famous Grotta di Nettuno nearby (see the Around Alghero section later in the chapter).

Orientation
Alghero's historic centre is on a small promontory jutting into the sea, with the new town stretching out behind it and along the coast to the north. Intercity buses arrive in Via Catalogna, next to a small park just outside the historic centre. The train station is about 1km north, on Via Don Minzoni and connected to the centre by a regular bus service.

Information
Tourist Offices The AAST office (☎ 079 97 90 54) is at Piazza Porta Terra 9, near the port and just across the gardens from the bus station. They have maps of the town and will help you find a hotel. The old town and most hotels and restaurants are in the area west of the AAST office.

Post & Communications The main post office is at Via XX Settembre 108. Public phones are on Via Vittorio Emanuele, on the other side of the park from the AAST office.

Medical Services During summer there is a tourist medical service (☎ 079 93 05 33) on Piazza Venezia Giulia in Fertilia, just north of Alghero. It is open from 9 am to 12.30 pm and from 4.30 to 7.30 pm, although for emergencies you can telephone 24 hours a day. Otherwise go to the Ospedale Civile (☎ 079 99 62 33) on Via Don Minzoni.

Things to See & Do

Wander through the narrow streets of the old town and around the port. The most interesting church is the **Chiesa di San Francesco**, Via Carlo Alberto. The **cattedrale** has been ruined by constant remodelling, but its bell tower remains a fine example of Gothic-Catalan architecture.

There are three defensive towers in the town. The **Torre del Portal**, on Piazza Porta Terra, was furnished with a drawbridge and moat and was one of the two entrances to the walled town. The **Torre de l'Esperò Reial** was one of the bastions of Alghero's fortified wall. The octagonal **Torre de Sant Jaume**, also known as the Torre dei Cani (Dogs' Tower), was used as a pound for stray dogs.

Special Events

In summer Alghero stages the Estate Musicale Algherese in the cloisters of the Chiesa di San Francesco. A festival, complete with firework display, is held annually on 15 August for the Feast of the Assumption.

Places to Stay

It is virtually impossible to find a room in August unless you book months in advance. At other times of the year you'll have little trouble. Camp sites include **Camping Calik** (☎ 079 93 01 11) in Fertilia, about 6km north of town, where charges in the high season are L20,000/14,000 per person/site. The HI **Ostello dei Giuliani** (☎ 079 93 03 53, Via Zara 1) is also in Fertilia. B&B is L14,000 a night, plus L4000 for hot water; a meal is L14,000.

It is open year-round. To get there take the hourly bus AF from Via Catalogna to Fertilia.

In the old town, **Hotel San Francesco** (☎ 079 98 03 30, Via Ambrogio Machin 2) has singles/doubles for L65,000/110,000 with bathroom. **Pensione Normandie** (☎ 079 97 53 02, Via Enrico Mattei 6) is out of the centre. Follow Via Cagliari (which becomes Viale Giovanni XXIII). It has slightly shabby, but large, rooms for L45,000/80,000.

Miramare (☎ 079 97 93 50, Via G Leopardi 15), south along the Lungomare Dante from the old town, has good rooms with bathroom. **La Margherita** (☎ 079 97 90 06, Via Sassari 70) has rooms with bathroom for up to L90,000/150,000.

Places to Eat

There are numerous supermarkets, including **Mura** in Via Lamarmora. For good sandwiches, head for **Paninoteca al Duomo**, next to the cathedral in Piazza Civica. The best ice cream is at **Paradiso 2**, through the Porta a Mare from Piazza Civica.

At **Ristorante La Piconia** (☎ 079 97 80 01, Via Principe Umberto 29), a full meal will cost around L50,000. **Trattoria Il Vecchio Mulino** (☎ 079 97 72 54, Via Don Deroma 7) is a pleasant establishment, where a full meal will cost about L45,000. **Posada del Mar** (☎ 079 97 95 79, Vicolo Adami 29) serves good pasta for around L12,000 and pizzas for around L9000. **La Lepanto** (☎ 079 97 91 16, Via Carlo Alberto 135) overlooks the sea. A good full meal will cost around L50,000.

La Palafitta (☎ 079 95 21 72, Viale I Maggio) is right on the beach at Spiaggia di Maria Pia, a few kilometres north of Alghero, on the way to Fertilia. Look for the sign and then walk through the small area of pine trees to the restaurant. A full meal will cost around L40,000, a pizza with a beer around L20,000 and you can follow it up with a moonlit walk along the beach.

Getting There & Away

The airport, inland from Fertilia, has domestic flights from major cities throughout Italy. Regular buses leave from Piazza della Mercede to coincide with flights.

SARDEGNA

Intercity buses terminate in Via Catalogna, next to the public park. ARST buses leave for Sassari and Porto Torres and FdS buses serve Sassari as well. There is a special service to Olbia, leaving at 8 pm, to coincide with the 10 pm ferry departure. FdS also runs a service between Alghero and Bosa. Regular buses leave for Capo Caccia and Porto Conte. Timetables are posted in the ticket office (☎ 079 95 01 79) near a bar beside the bus stop area in Via Catalogna.

Alghero is on the local FdS railway line linking it with Sassari and the main FS Cagliari-Oristano-Olbia line. Trains run to Sassari about ten times a day Monday to Saturday (less frequently on Sunday and public holidays).

Getting Around

Urban bus No AF runs hourly between Alghero and Fertilia from 7 am to 9.40 pm. The more regular A0 goes only as far as the Spiaggia di Maria Pia. Some FdS buses run between the port and the train station, a distance of about 1km, also serviced by urban bus Nos AP or AF.

If you want to hire a bicycle or motorcycle to explore the coast, Cicloexpress (☎ 079 98 69 50), Via Garibaldi Porto, has bicycles/mountain bikes/mopeds/scooters at L15,000/20,000/35,000/60,000 per day. Velosport (☎ 079 97 71 82), Via Vittorio Veneto 90, is another option and its prices are slightly lower.

AROUND ALGHERO

There are good beaches north of Alghero, including the **Spiaggia di San Giovanni** and the **Spiaggia di Maria Pia**, easily accessible on the Alghero-Fertilia bus.

The **Grotta di Nettuno** (Neptune's Cave) on Capo Caccia, west of Alghero, is reached by sea with regular boats operated by various companies from Alghero (L17,000) or by SFS bus from Via Catalogna (L6300 return). If you arrive by bus you descend to the cave by a staircase carved into the rock (remember you have to make the arduous 650 step climb on the way back). Guides offer hourly tours from 9 am to 7 pm. Admission is L13,000 for adults and L6000 for children aged under 12.

If you have your own means of transport, explore the Capo Caccia area and visit the **Nuraghe di Palmavera**, about 10km out of Alghero on the road to Porto Conte and the **Necropoli di Anghelu Ruju** (Coop S.i.l.t. ☎ 079 98 07 50) on the road to Porto Torres.

SASSARI

postcode 07100 • pop 120,000

The capital of Sardegna's largest province and the island's second-largest city after Cagliari, Sassari is a pleasant town but is best regarded as a convenient stopover on the way to the northern coast. However, it is worth visiting in May for the Sardegnan Cavalcade, one of Sardegna's most important festivals.

Orientation

Sassari has a compact centre concentrated around its cathedral, but most services are in the busy newer part of town in the area around the vast 18th century Piazza Italia. Most intercity buses stop in the central Corso Margherita di Savoia, opposite Emiciclo Garibaldi, before reaching the main bus station in Via XXV Aprile, south of the train station. To reach Piazza Italia from the bus stop in the city centre, head up Via Brigata Sassari to Piazza Castello and turn right.

The train station is about 10 minutes walk from the centre. From the station, head north to Piazza Sant'Antonio and then follow Corso Vittorio Emanuele to Piazza Castello.

Information

Tourist Offices The AAST office is at Via Roma 62 (☎ 079 23 17 77, fax 079 23 75 85), near the Museo Sanna. It opens from 9 am to 1.30 pm and from 4 to 6 pm Monday to Friday. The EPT office (☎ 079 29 95 44, fax 079 29 94 15), Viale Caprera 36, is open from 8 am to 2 pm Monday to Friday and also from 4 to 7 pm on Tuesday and Wednesday. There is another EPT office at the Fertilia airport (☎/fax 079 93 51 24).

Money You can exchange travellers cheques and can obtain cash advances on Visa and MasterCard at Banca Commerciale Italiana in Piazza Italia.

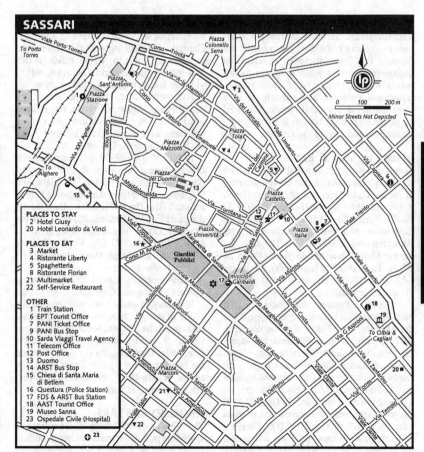

SASSARI

PLACES TO STAY
2 Hotel Giusy
20 Hotel Leonardo da Vinci

PLACES TO EAT
3 Market
4 Ristorante Liberty
5 Spaghetteria
8 Ristorante Florian
21 Multimarket
22 Self-Service Restaurant

OTHER
1 Train Station
6 EPT Tourist Office
7 PANI Ticket Office
9 PANI Bus Stop
10 Sarda Viaggi Travel Agency
11 Telecom Office
12 Post Office
13 Duomo
14 ARST Bus Stop
15 Chiesa di Santa Maria
   di Betlem
16 Questura (Police Station)
17 FDS & ARST Bus Station
18 AAST Tourist Office
19 Museo Sanna
23 Ospedale Civile (Hospital)

Post & Communications The main post
office is at Via Brigata Sassari 13, just off
Piazza Castello. There are Telecom payphones throughout the town.

Medical Services & Emergency The
Ospedale Civile (☎ 079 206 10 00) is on
Via E De Nicola, off Viale Italia. For emer-
gencies (☎ 079 206 16 21) enter by the
Viale Italia entrance (follow the sign Pronto
Soccorso). The questura (☎ 079 28 35 500)
is at Viale Coppino 1.

Things to See
Sassari's **duomo** is in the old town on Piazza del Duomo. Built in Romanesque style
in the 13th century, it was remodelled and
given a baroque façade in the 17th century.
Also worth a look is the **Chiesa di Santa
Maria di Betlem**, on Viale Coppino near the
station. It has a 13th century façade and
lovely 14th century cloisters.

   Museo Sanna, Via Roma 64, is of considerable interest for its Nuraghic collection,
as well as its display of traditional costumes.

Special Events

The Cavalcata Sarda (Sardegnan Cavalcade) is generally held on the penultimate Sunday in May (although the day can change from year to year). It attracts participants from all over the island, who dress in traditional costume and participate in a large and quite colourful parade, followed by equestrian competitions. It's well worth visiting Sassari during the festival.

Places to Stay & Eat

Hotels and pensioni are not abundant in Sassari and if you plan to arrive in high summer, or for the Cavalcade, it is advisable to book a room in advance. *Hotel Giusy (☎ 079 23 33 27, Piazza Sant'Antonio 21)* is close to the station and has singles/doubles with bathroom for L55,000/75,000. The more upmarket *Hotel Leonardo da Vinci (☎ 079 28 07 44, Via Roma 79)* has quality rooms for L120,000/170,000 including breakfast and private bathroom.

An outdoor *fresh-produce market* is held each Monday to Saturday morning on Via del Mercato, near Piazza Colonnello Serra. Alternatively, shop at *Multimarket* supermarket on Via Amendola near the south-eastern corner of Piazza Marconi. You can get good sandwiches at either of the *sandwich shops* on Via Turritana, off Via Brigata Sassari.

There is a *Spaghetteria (Via Usai 10a)* off Largo Felice Cavallotti, where a dish of pasta costs between L5000 and L12,000. There's a *self-service restaurant* on Viale Italia, near the hospital, where you can eat for L20,000. *Ristorante Liberty* is in a restored palazzo on Piazza Sauro, off Corso Vittorio Emanuele. A full meal will cost around L40,000. *Ristorante Florian (Via Bellieni 27)*, off Piazza Italia, has a good reputation. A full meal will cost around L60,000.

Getting There & Around

ARST buses connect with towns such as Bosa, Pozzomaggiore, Porto Torres and Santa Teresa di Gallura and leave from the southern end of Via XXV Aprile, at the corner with Piazza Santa Maria di Betlem. Services also connect with flights to Fertilia

airport. ARST buses also stop on Corso Margherita di Savoia, opposite Emiciclo Garibaldi. Tickets are available from some central bars and at the ARST office (☎ 079 263 92 20) at Emiciclo Garibaldi, where you can also get timetable information.

FdS (☎ 079 24 13 01) buses run to Tempio Pausania, Alghero, Fertilia, Bosa, Olbia and Palau. You can check timetables at the company's ticket office (shared with ARST) at Emiciclo Garibaldi.

PANI (☎ 079 23 69 83) long-distance buses connect Sassari with Porto Torres, Nuoro, Olbia and Oristano, Macomer, Cagliari, leaving from the Via Roma side of Piazza Italia. The PANI ticket office is near the piazza at Via Bellieni 25, next to Ristorante Florian. The Sarda Viaggi travel agency (☎ 079 23 47 84), Via Cagliari 30, off Piazza Castello, provides a booking service and information.

Trains connect Sassari to Porto Torres, Olbia, Oristano and Cagliari.

It is easy to make your way around the centre of town on foot, but the No 8 is a useful bus as it heads from the station to Piazza Italia, travelling along Corso Vittorio Emanuele. If arriving by car, you will find the familiar centro signs to direct you to the centre, where there are numerous supervised daytime car parks.

AROUND SASSARI

The **Chiesa di SS Trinità di Saccargia**, a splendid Pisan-Romanesque church built in 1116, is set in a bare landscape near the town of Codrongianus, about 18km southeast of Sassari along the S131. You should have little trouble reaching Codrongianus by ARST bus from Sassari, but you do have to ask the driver to stop at the church if you don't want to walk the whole 2km from the village.

The **Nuraghe Santu Antine** (Coop La Pintadera ☎ 079 84 71 45) is just off the S131 near Torralba, about 40km south of Sassari. Said to be the most beautiful nuraghe in Sardegna, it is well worth a visit. It can be reached from Sassari on the ARST bus heading for Padria, which stops at Torralba.

PORTO TORRES

This port town and major petrochemical centre has three main attractions other than the ferry: a megalithic altar (4500 BC), 6km out of town on the road to Sassari, the only example of its kind on Sardegna; a well preserved Roman bridge (1st century BC) and Roman thermal baths; and the Pisan-Romanesque **Basilica of San Gavino** dating from the 11th century. To the north-west is the fast-developing beach resort of Stintino, a former fishing village which has managed to retain some of its atmosphere.

The town's main street is Corso Vittorio Emanuele, which is directly in front of you as you face away from the port. The tourist office (☎ 079 51 50 00), Piazza XX Settembre 2, opens from 8.30 am to 12.30 pm and from 3.30 to 5.30 pm Monday to Friday between June and mid-September. In April and the second half of September it's open only in the morning.

Places to Stay & Eat

If you find it necessary to spend the night in Porto Torres, try *Albergo Royal* (☎ 079 50 22 78, Via Sebastiano Satta 8), which has singles/doubles with bathroom for L60,000/110,000 and triples for L130,000 in summer (prices drop by half out of season).

There are numerous places where you can buy sandwiches or snacks, including takeaway pizza by the slice at Via Ponte Romano 54. For a simple meal, try *Poldiavolo (Piazza XX Settembre 7)* in front of the tourist office.

Getting There & Away

Regular ARST buses connect Porto Torres with Sassari and Stintino. The bus station is on Piazzale Colombo at the port and the ticket office is at the Acciaro Bar, Corso Vittorio Emanuele 38. Regular trains connect Porto Torres with Sassari. A new train station has been built about 2km to the west of the port.

Tirrenia runs daily ferries to Genova (three a day in summer). Its office (☎ 079 51 41 07) is in the ferry terminal at the port. Grimandi-Grandi Navi Veloci also runs a daily ferry to Genova in summer (departure 9.30 am, ar-

rival 7 pm). The French line SNCM runs four or five ferries per month to Toulon and Marseille, some via Bastia in Corsica from the end of March to September. The agent for SNCM and Grimaldi in Porto Torres is Agenzia Paglietti/Petertours (☎ 079 51 44 77, fax 079 51 40 63), Corso Vittorio Emanuele 19.

STINTINO

A picturesque fishing village turned tourist resort, Stintino is very crowded in summer. A few kilometres north of the town, facing Isola Asinara, is a magnificent sandy beach, the **Spiaggia di Pelosa**, at Torre Pelosa, although in recent years it has been badly eroded by storms.

If you want to spend a few days in Stintino, try *Albergo Silvestrino* (☎ 079 52 30 07, Via Sassari 14), in the centre of the village. It has singles/doubles with bathroom for L75,000/110,000 and half board for L115,000 (L155,000 in August) per person (closed in January). *Hotel Lina* (☎ 079 52 30 71, Via Lepanto 38), which faces the village's small port, has doubles only from L70,000 to L100,000 depending on the season.

Stintino is accessible from Porto Torres by ARST bus (five a day in summer).

SANTA TERESA DI GALLURA

Together with Palau, about 20km to the east, this seaside resort is an affordable alternative to the jet-set hangouts on the Costa Smeralda. It is a very pleasant spot to pass a few relaxing days, especially if the magnificent coves, rock pools and small beaches of nearby Capo Testa appeal. From the town you can see across the Stretto di Bonifacio to Corsica and you can catch one of the regular ferries which make the crossing to Bonifacio on Corsica's southern tip.

Information

Santa Teresa's AAST office (☎ 0789 75 41 27, fax 0789 75 41 85) is in the town centre at Piazza Vittorio Emanuele 24. It's open from 8.30 am to 1 pm and 3.30 to 8 pm daily in summer and from 8.30 am to 1 pm and 3.30 to 6.30 pm Monday to Friday and from 8.30 am to 1 pm on Saturday from October to

SARDEGNA

May. The helpful staff can provide loads of information and will assist in finding accommodation. You can ring ahead for information on hotels, as well as rooms and apartments for rent, or you can write (in English) to: AAST, Piazza V Emanuele 24, 07028 Santa Teresa di Gallura, Sassari.

You can exchange money daily at the port or at the bank on Piazza V Emanuele.

For medical attention, go to the Guardia Medica (☎ 0789 75 40 79) on Via Carlo Felice, on the corner of Via Eleonora d'Arborea, a short walk from the town centre.

Things to See & Do

The main reason for a visit to this area is to spend time on the beach. There is the small **Spiaggia Rena Bianca** next to the town, but it is recommended that you head for **Capo Testa**, a small cape connected to the mainland by an isthmus, about 5km west of Santa Teresa. There are lovely little beaches on either side of the cape, as well as a large sheltered rock pool. The road ends just below the lighthouse; the path to the right leads to the rock pool and the path to the left leads to a small cove and sandy beach. The cape is actually a military zone, but you'll only have problems if you try to get to the lighthouse.

Motorised rubber boats for up to six people are available for hire at Santa Teresa's port from L150,000 to L250,000 a day. GULP Immobiliare (☎ 0789 75 56 89), Via Nazionale 58, rents apartments, villas as well as cars and motorcycles, which are handy for exploring the area. A moped costs around L38,000 a day and a scooter L60,000.

Places to Stay

Santa Teresa offers extensive accommodation possibilities, including rooms and apartments for rent (contact the AAST office or GULP Immobiliare). It's advisable to book if you plan to arrive during late July or August.

Camping facilities are all out of town. Try **La Liccia** (☎ 0789 75 51 90), about 6km from Santa Teresa towards Palau, 400m from the beach. Charges in August are L17,500/12,500/25,000 per adult/child/site.

In town, **Albergo Da Cecco** (☎ 0789 75 42 20, Via Po 3) has pleasant singles/doubles with bathroom for L90,000/120,000. To get there take Via XX Settembre from the AAST office and turn right at Via Po. **Hotel Bacchus** (☎ 0789 75 45 56, Via Firenze 5) is a quiet place in the new town and is known for its restaurant. It has rooms for L85,000/105,000 and half board for L145,000. **Hotel al Porto** (☎ 0789 75 41 54, Via del Porto 20), on the port, has rooms for L55,000/80,000 and half board for L80,000.

At Capo Testa there's **Bocche di Bonifacio** (☎ 0789 75 42 02), which has rooms for L70,000/105,000 and half board for L110,000 per person.

Places to Eat

There are plenty of good bars and sandwich shops where you can buy sandwiches, including **Poldo's Pub** (Via Garibaldi 4). For good pizza, try **Pizzeria-Ristorante Lungoni** (Via Nazionale) and **Pizzeria La Cambusa** (Via Firenze). **Marinaro**, at the Hotel Marinaro on Via Angioj, has good meals for around L35,000. Restaurant **La Torre** (Via del Mare) charges about L40,000 for a seafood meal. If visiting Capo Testa, try the **trattoria** at the Bocche di Bonifacio hotel.

Getting There & Away

Regular ARST buses connect Santa Teresa with Olbia, Golfo Aranci and Palau, arriving in Via Eleonora d'Arborea, a short walk to the centre. There are also four buses a day to Sassari. Tickets can be purchased at the Bar Baby on Via Lu Pultani, running perpendicular to Via Nazionale, near the bus stop.

Ferry services to Corsica are run by two companies, Moby Lines (☎ 0789 75 14 49) and Saremar (☎ 0789 75 41 56); both have small offices at the port. Together, the two companies run between seven and 14 services a day, depending on the season.

PALAU & AROUND

Close to the Costa Smeralda, Palau is little more than a conglomeration of expensive hotels and private apartment blocks and is much less pleasant than Santa Teresa.

Just off the coast there are two islands

connected by a road bridge: **La Maddalena**, site of a US navy base and **Caprera**, which was given to the hero of Italian unification, Giuseppe Garibaldi, by Vittorio Emanuele II. Garibaldi spent his last years there and it is possible to visit his house. Most of the island is a nature reserve, which means that camping is forbidden.

La Maddalena has an attractive main town, several good beaches and is popular with campers.

Information

Palau's tourist office (☎/fax 0789 70 95 70) is at Via Nazionale 96. It has little in the way of tourist information, but staff can assist with accommodation, including apartments and rooms for rent. La Maddalena's tourist office (☎ 0789 73 63 21, fax 0789 73 66 55) is at Piazza Barone de Geneys.

Places to Stay

Just east of Palau is the seaside *Camping Capo d'Orso* (☎ 0789 70 20 07), on the cape of the same name. In August it charges L12,000/35,500 per person/site. It also has bungalows to rent for two/three/four people for L126,000/138,000/208,000 per day. Out of season, prices are significantly reduced.

There are numerous hotels and rooms for rent in town, but you should book ahead for July and August. *Hotel Serra* (☎ 0789 70 95 19, Via Nazionale 17) has singles/doubles with bathroom for L55,000/75,000. *La Roccia* (☎ 0789 70 95 28, Via dei Mille 15) has rooms for L70,000/110,000. If you're looking for luxury accommodation, try *Hotel Palau* (☎ 0789 70 84 68, Via Baragge), which has doubles for up to L340,000.

On La Maddalena there is *Villaggio Camping La Maddalena* (☎ 0789 72 80 51) at Moneta and *Campeggio Abbatoggia* (☎ 0789 73 91 73), on the other side of the island at Lo Strangolato, close to a lovely beach. Both are reasonably cheap and accessible by local bus from the town of La Maddalena. In town, *Hotel Il Gabbiano* (☎ 0789 72 25 07, Via Giulio Cesare 20) has rooms with bathroom for L110,000/140,000 in August. *Club Méditerranée* (☎ 0789 72 70 78, fax 02 78 37

83) on Caprera charges around L154,000 per day for a bungalow for two people.

Places to Eat

In Palau, you can buy supplies at the *Minimarket da Gemma (Via Nazionale 66)*. There are several decent places to eat, including *L'Uva Fragola (Piazza Vittorio Emanuele)*, just off Via Nazionale near the port, which serves good pizzas as well as salads for around L20,000. *Da Robertino (Via Nazionale 22)* is a good trattoria where a full meal costs around L45,000. At *La Taverna (Via Rossini)*, off Via Nazionale, you can eat an excellent seafood meal for about L80,000.

Getting There & Around

Palau is easily accessible by ARST bus from Sassari, Santa Teresa di Gallura and Olbia and Turmotravel operates a service to the airport at Olbia. FdS operate a year-round bus service to Tempio Pausania and Sassari and in the summer Autoservizi Caramelli buses also run to Porto Torres and connect Palau with places along the Costa Smeralda, including Baia Sardinia and Porto Cervo. Buses stop at Palau's small port. Timetables are posted inside the ferry terminal at the port and at the tourist office.

Traghetti Isole Sarde (TRIS) ferries connect Palau with Genova. Linee Lauro operates to Napoli three days a week from April to January. Contact the Bulciolu agency in Palau (☎ 0789 70 95 05), Via Fonte Vecchia 11, for more details.

Ferries make the short crossing between Palau and La Maddalena every 20 minutes during summer, less frequently in the off season. It is not possible to take your car to La Maddalena; there is a car park just outside Palau, where you can leave the car if you want to catch a ferry to La Maddalena and a bus shuttle service will take you to the port. While it is not obligatory to use the car park, it may be difficult to find a parking spot in town during summer.

Once on the island, catch one of the blue local buses which leave from the port every half-hour and make a round trip of the island. Buses for Caprera leave from the

SARDEGNA

piazza at the end of Via Giovanni Amendola, to the right of the port.

COSTA SMERALDA (EMERALD COAST)

For the average tourist, the Costa Smeralda is out of reach. There are no hotels of less than three stars, which means that prices for a double room start at around L180,000 a day. The coast was purchased in 1962 by a group of international investors led by Prince Karim Aga Khan and was basically developed from scratch. Its resorts include Baia Sardegna, Liscia di Vacca and Porto Cervo, all bearing a stronger resemblance to Disneyland than traditional seaside towns. The coastline is certainly beautiful, but it is not the real Sardegna and unless you have money to burn, or very rich friends with an apartment, it is better to spend the day on one of its beaches and continue your journey.

Those who would like to stay on the Costa Smeralda can obtain information about accommodation from the tourist office at Arzachena (☎ 0789 8 26 24, fax 0789 8 10 90), Via Paolo Dettori 43 (inside the ERSAT building).

The coast is accessible by ARST, FdS and Autoservizi Caramelli buses from Palau and Olbia.

OLBIA

postcode 07026 • pop 43,000

This busy port and industrial centre will very likely be the first glimpse of Sardegna for many tourists. It is a major port for ferries arriving from Civitavecchia, Genova and Livorno and while it is not particularly unpleasant, it is not particularly interesting either and is best passed through quickly.

Orientation

If arriving by ferry, you will find yourself at a well organised port complete with a new ferry terminal and a local bus (No 3) to take you into the centre of town (only about 1km). Trains run from the station to the port to coincide with ferry departures. Intercity buses terminate at the end of Corso Umberto. Head east along Corso Umberto to reach the town centre. The train station is close by on Via Pala, off Piazza Risorgimento.

Information

Tourist Offices The AAST office (☎ 0789 2 14 53, fax 0789 2 22 21) is at Via Catello Piro 1, off Corso Umberto. In summer it opens from 8 am to 7 pm daily; the rest of the year it is open from 8 am to 2 pm and from 3.30 to 6.30 pm Monday to Friday and in the morning only on Saturday. The staff are very keen to help and will advise (in English) on places to stay and eat and can provide information about accommodation and places to visit throughout Sardegna.

Money There are three major banks on Corso Umberto, including the Banca Commerciale Italiana at No 191, which does cash advances on both Visa and MasterCard.

Post & Communications The main post office is on Via Acquedotto, off Piazza Matteotti and there is a row of Telecom payphones on Via de Filippi.

Medical Services & Emergency The Ospedale Civile (☎ 0789 55 22 00) is on Viale Aldo Moro, about a 15 minute walk north of the centre along Via Porto Romano and Via Gabriele d'Annunzio. The police station, called the Commissariato (☎ 0789 22 081), is at Via Piemonte 5-7.

Places to Stay

Albergo Terranova (☎ 0789 2 23 95, Via Giuseppe Garibaldi 6) has singles/doubles for L105,000/145,000. *Hotel Minerva (☎ 0789 2 11 90, Via Mazzini 7)* has doubles for L70,000 and singles/doubles with bathroom for L65,000/90,000.

Hotel Gallura (☎ 0789 2 46 48, Corso Umberto 145) is pleasant, with rooms with bathroom costing L100,000/140,000. *Hotel Centrale (☎ 0789 2 30 17, Corso Umberto 85)* has rooms for L120,000/160,000.

Places to Eat

If you want to stock up on food supplies, head for the *Mercato Civico* on Via Acque-

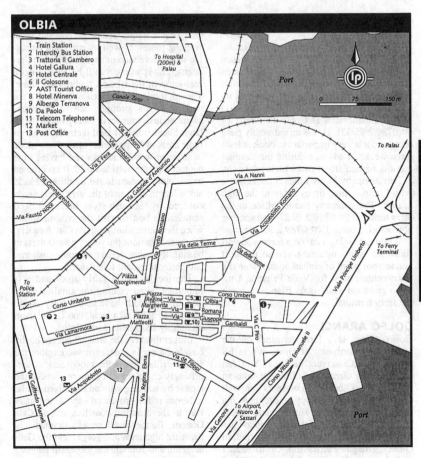

OLBIA

1 Train Station
2 Intercity Bus Station
3 Trattoria Il Gambero
4 Hotel Gallura
5 Hotel Centrale
6 Il Golosone
7 AAST Tourist Office
8 Hotel Minerva
9 Albergo Terranova
10 Da Paolo
11 Telecom Telephones
12 Market
13 Post Office

dotto. At *Il Golosone (Corso Umberto 41)*, you can buy good sandwiches, crêpes and gelati. For more substantial fare try *Da Paolo* (☎ 0789 2 16 75, *Via Cavour 22*), near Hotel Minerva, where a full meal will cost about L40,000. For an excellent meal, try *Trattoria il Gambero* (☎ 0789 2 38 74, *Via Lamarmora 6*), off Piazza Matteotti; a full meal will cost over L50,000. One of Olbia's better restaurants is *Ristorante Gallura (Corso Umberto 145)*, at Hotel Gallura, where a full meal will cost around L90,000.

Getting There & Away

Olbia's airport, a few kilometres south-east of the town, has flights to/from Italy's main cities. To get to the airport take city bus No 8. Contact the local transport company ASPO (☎ 0789 2 73 97) for information.

ARST buses depart from both the port (coinciding with ferry arrivals) and the bus station in the centre for Arzachena and the resorts of the Costa Smeralda, Palau, Santa Teresa di Gallura, Sassari and Nuoro.

There are some train connections to the

major towns, including Sassari, Cagliari and Oristano.

Tirrenia ferries make the eight hour crossing to Civitavecchia daily in the high season and the fast service runs twice a day, departing at 8.30 am (arrival 12.30 pm) and midnight (arrival 6 am). The company has an office at the ferry terminal (☎ 0789 2 46 91) and at Cosmorama at Corso Umberto 17 (☎ 0789 2 85 33). This is an extremely busy route and it is very important to book at least three weeks in advance during the summer months, particularly if you want to take a car.

Ferries run by Moby Lines connect Olbia with Livorno three times a day in the high season. The company has an office at the ferry terminal (☎ 0789 2 79 27) and another at Corso Umberto 1 (☎ 0789 2 35 72).

If you are taking a car on a ferry, you will find clear signs directing you to the port and to your point of embarkation. From the town centre, head for Viale Principe Umberto and then Viale Isola Bianca to reach the ferry terminal.

GOLFO ARANCI

Golfo Aranci is a ferry terminal on the promontory north-east of Olbia, where FS ferries from Civitavecchia dock. You can catch a train directly to Olbia, or take an ARST bus to Olbia, Palau or Santa Teresa di Gallura. It's possible to buy a ticket in Roma (at Stazione Termini or any Sestante office) which covers the cost of the train trip to Civitavecchia, the ferry crossing and the train to Olbia. Sardegna Ferries link Golfo Aranci with Livorno (day and night services) and Civitavecchia (three daytime services including two fast runs) from April to September. For booking and information call the Livorno office on ☎ 0586 88 13 80, Golfo Aranci on ☎ 0789 4 67 80, or Civitavecchia on ☎ 0766 50 07 14. Sometimes there are special prices for two people and a car on daytime trips.

Eastern Sardegna

Nuoro province, about halfway up the east coast of Sardegna, encompasses the area known as the Barbagia. It has unspoiled, isolated beaches, spectacular gorges and great walking routes, as well as important Nuraghic sites. More than in any other part of Sardegna, this is where you'll be able to get a real sense of the island's traditional culture. Though tourism in the area is increasing, the people remain strongly tied to traditions swept aside by tourism in other parts of the island. Shepherds still tend their flocks in remote areas of the province, often living alone in stone or wooden shacks and having little contact with the outside world. It is common to see older women in the traditional black, ankle-length dresses of the area, their heads covered by Spanish-style black, fringed shawls. It's best to visit the area in spring when the patron saint feast days are frequent. On these occasions the young people dress in beautifully embroidered traditional costumes and perform ancient folk dances.

The locals remain fairly aloof and it is important when visiting the smaller, more remote towns to behave respectfully. If you manage to befriend a local, you'll find them incredibly hospitable and helpful.

Larger towns in the area are accessible by bus, but a car is a necessity to explore the smaller villages and the mountains. A surprisingly cheap way to explore parts of the area is by walking with an organised guide.

Nuoro is the provincial capital and gateway to the beautiful coastline around Cala Gonone, Baunei and Urzulei's dramatically beautiful highlands and gorges and the Gennargentu and Supramonte mountain ranges.

NUORO
postcode 08100 • pop 50,000

There is not a lot to see and do in Nuoro, but it is a good starting point for an exploration of the Barbagia. The old centre of town is around Piazza delle Grazie, Corso Garibaldi and Via Italia, near the tourist office. From Piazza delle Grazie, walk along Via IV Novembre and Via Dante. ARST buses terminate in Via Lucania, near the train station. The station is about a 20 minute walk from Piazza delle Grazie along Via La Marmora (turn left as you leave the station).

Information

The EPT office (☎ 0784 3 00 83) is at Piazza Italia 19. It is open daily from 9 am to 1 pm and from 4 to 6.30 pm (from 3 to 7 pm Saturday and Sunday) in summer. The main post office is on Piazza Crispi, between Corso Garibaldi and Piazza Dante and there is a Telecom office at Via Brigata Sassari 6.

Things to See

While in town, take a look at the neoclassical **cattedrale** in Piazza Santa Maria della Neve and the monument and square dedicated to the local poet Sebastiano Satta. The **Museo della Vita e delle Tradizioni Popolari Sardi** (Museum of the Life and Traditions of the Sardegnan People), at Via Antonio Mereu 56, south of the cathedral, is well worth a visit. It opens from 9 am to 1 pm and from 3 to 7 pm in winter and from 9 am to 8 pm in summer and houses a collection of traditional costumes and masks.

Places to Stay

There are no real budget options, but you could try **Mini Hotel** (☎ 0784 3 31 59, Via Brofferio 13), a pleasant little place which has singles/doubles with bathroom for L60,000/78,000. It is off Via Roma, near Piazza Sebastiano Satta. **Hotel Grillo** (☎ 0784 3 86 78, Via Monsignor Melas 14) is in an ugly building, but its rooms are pleasant. Rooms with bathroom are L86,000/112,000 and half board is L102,000.

Places to Eat

To pick up supplies, shop at the **Emanuela market** in Via Isonzo, off Via Trieste just near Piazza Italia, or at the great little **grocery shop** (Corso Garibaldi 168) and the **cheese shop** next door. Otherwise try **Pizzeria-Trattoria Il Rifugio** (☎ 0784 23 23 55, Vico del Pozzo 4), in a narrow street parallel to Via La Marmora in the old centre near Le Grazie.

Getting There & Away

ARST (☎ 0784 29 41 73) buses connect Nuoro with Cagliari (one a day), Olbia (six a day) and Sassari (one a day), as well as towns throughout the province, including Oliena (hourly), Orgosolo (10 a day), Dorgali and Cala Gonone (seven a day) and Baunei (two a day). PANI buses head for Cagliari, Sassari and Oristano. The train reaches Macomer and Bosa on the west coast, where there are connections with the main north-south line.

OLIENA

The value of visiting Oliena, or Orgosolo farther south, is to get a better idea of how locals live in Sardegna's interior. Neither town offers much in the way of tourist facilities or sights, although both, in their own way, provide an alternative travel experience.

Oliena is about 12km south-east of Nuoro and is easily accessible by regular ARST bus. For the more adventurous, it is a place from which to set out on a walking exploration of the Supramonte area to the south or to the isolated Nuraghic site at **Tiscali**, either alone or, even better, with a guide. The Tiscali site is supervised by a guardian and is open from 9 am to 5 pm in winter and to 7 pm from May to September. Admission costs L5000. Remember that there are very few clearly marked trails and that the area is full of goat tracks, so orientation is a serious problem.

On Easter Sunday morning a traditional festival, S'Incontru, dating back to the time of Spanish domination, takes place. In separate processions, the women of the town carry a statue of the Madonna and the men carry a statue of Christ on the cross. They meet in Oliena's main piazza and the place goes crazy, as every man and boy in town greets the *incontru* (meeting of the statues) by shooting a gun into the air.

For information on guided walks, contact Levamus Viaggi (☎ 0784 28 51 90), Corso Vittorio Emanuele 27. They speak English and offer a wide range of possibilities, from a one day 4WD guided tour to a guided walk in the Supramonte. Ask for Murena, a local guide who can take you on a three day walk from there, through the Gola di Gorropu to the beach at Cala Luna. Murena doesn't speak English, but this doesn't generally present a problem.

Barbagia Insolita (☎ 0784 28 81 67), Via Carducci 25 in Oliena, organises guided tours to out-of-the-way areas in the Barbagia by 4WD, as well as on foot. You can choose between demanding or more manageable walks to places including Tiscali, the Gola di Gorropu, Monte Corrasi and the Codula di Luna valley.

Places to Stay & Eat
Accommodation options are limited. Try *Ci Kappa* (☎ *0784 28 87 33, Via Martin Luther King 2*), with singles/doubles for L55,000/77,000 and half board for L70,000. It also has a very good pizzeria-ristorante. A few kilometres east of town, at the beginning of the beautiful Lanaittu valley, is the four star *Su Gologone* (☎ *0784 28 75 12*), near an impressive underground spring that supplies its swimming pool. The hotel is in a lovely setting and is a particularly good option for people wanting to explore the area, as it organises guided tours, walks and even horse-riding expeditions. Rooms cost L130,000/190,000 out of season. In the high season half board costs up to L175,000 per person and full board up to L195,000. Its restaurant serves excellent traditional local dishes and is justifiably renowned throughout the island.

ORGOSOLO
About 18km farther south and reached from Nuoro on an ARST bus, Orgosolo is famous for its tradition of *banditismo* (banditry), but this isn't a subject you will find the locals willing to discuss openly. This tradition was immortalised by the 1963 Italian film *The Bandits of Orgosolo*. One of the town's more notorious *banditi* was released from prison in 1992 and acted as an unofficial negotiator in the much-publicised kidnapping of the son of a Costa Smeralda hotelier (and a relative of the Aga Khan). The child was eventually released in the countryside close to the town.

Orgosolo is also interesting for the series of leftist and nationalistic murals which decorate the façades of many of its buildings. The brainchild of a local art teacher, Francesco del Casino, a native of Siena who has lived in Orgosolo for many years, the murals started appearing in 1973. Generally designed by him, they have been painted by local students as well as other artists. The murals originally reflected fairly extreme political views on a range of international issues, such as the war in Vietnam, apartheid in South Africa and the Palestinian question, but they now deal mainly with domestic social issues.

Places to Stay & Eat
Try *Petit Hotel* (☎ *0784 40 20 09, Via Mannu*), which has singles/doubles with bathroom for L45,000/65,000.

A local group organises lunches in the countryside just outside town, where you can enjoy one of Sardegna's most traditional dishes, porcheddu. The travel agency Avitur (☎ 0789 5 32 30), Corso Umberto 142b in Olbia, organises guided trips by bus from Olbia to Orgosolo, including the lunch, for L84,000 a head. Otherwise you can arrange to attend a lunch by contacting the organisers in Orgosolo directly on ☎ 0784 40 20 71. The cost for lunch only is L30,000 a head.

CALA GONONE & AROUND
This fast-developing seaside resort is an excellent base from which to explore the coves along the coastline, as well as the Nuraghic sites and rugged terrain inland. There is a Pro Loco office (☎ 0784 9 36 96) on Viale del Bue Marino, where you can pick up maps, a list of hotels and information to help you explore the area. There is also a tourist office (☎ 0784 9 62 43), Via La Marmora 108, in the nearby town of **Dorgali**, through which you will probably pass on your way to Cala Gonone.

If you are travelling by car, you will need a detailed road map of the area. One of the best is published by the Istituto Geografico de Agostini. The tourist office has maps which detail the locations of the main sights.

Things to See & Do
Cala Gonone is within easy reach of the Nuraghic sites of **Serra Orrios**, **Tiscali** and **Nuraghe Mannu** or the **Grotta Ispinigoli**. Ask at the tourist office for information. From Cala Gonone's small port, you can catch a boat to the spectacular entrance of

the **Grotta del Bue Marino** (Cave of the Monk Seal), where a guide will take you on a 1km walk to see vast caves with stalagmites, stalactites and lakes. The caves were one of the last habitats of the rare monk seal which has not been sighted for some years. The return boat trip costs L10,000 and admission to the caves costs L10,000.

There are also boats to the beautiful **Cala Luna** (between L14,000 and L25,000 return, depending on the season). This isolated beach is accessible only on foot or by boat (the journey can be combined with a trip to the Grotta for L19,000 return). In August the beach is crowded with sunbathers and camping is forbidden. At other times it is deserted and you can ask for permission to camp near the only building in the area, the restaurant Su Neulagi (☎ 0784 9 33 92). If the weather is unsuitable for swimming, walk along the **Codula di Luna**, a long valley stretching from Cala Luna to the S125 Orientale Sarda near Urzulei (four to six hours). Boats also head along the coast to beaches at **Cala Sisine** (from L22,000 to L25,000 return, depending on the season) and **Cala Mariolu** (from L28,000 to L38,000).

There is a walking track along the coast linking Cala Gonone and Cala Luna (about two hours). The Dorgali tourist office has information about other trails in the area, including how to reach the Nuraghic village of Tiscali (see Oliena earlier in this section).

If you want to explore the spectacular **Gola di Gorropu** (Gorropu Gorge), about 15km south of Dorgali, ask at the Dorgali tourist office or at the Società Gorropu (see Baunei & Urzulei later in this section) about hiring a guide, since you'll need to use ropes and harnesses to descend some sections of the gorge. However, it is possible to walk into the gorge from its northern entrance for about 1km before it becomes impossible to proceed.

To get to the entrance, go south from Dorgali along the road for Urzulei for a couple of kilometres. After the turn-off to the left for Cala Gonone, there is a dirt road to the right, which heads for the Hotel Sant'Elene (see the following Places to Stay & Eat section). Follow this into the valley for about 8km (don't head

uphill for the hotel) and you'll get to a small bridge. Here you'll have to park the car and continue on foot. Walk for about an hour and a half, to reach two small lakes and the entrance to the gorge – one of the most spectacular and romantic landscapes in Sardegna. The huge boulders scattered around the entrance to the gorge are a reminder that nature can be harsh as well as beautiful in Sardegna. Even if you have your own car, allow a full day for the expedition, which will give you time for the walk, a picnic and a swim in the lakes. If you're on foot, but want to explore the gorge, you could stay at the Hotel Sant'Elene and walk to its entrance from there.

Coop Ghivine (☎ 0336 32 69 57, fax 0784 9 67 21) organises guided walks in the Gola di Gorropu or the Codula di Luna. There are several Nuraghic sites in the area and, the Dorgali tourist office can provide maps and advice on how to reach them. See also the Oliena section earlier in this chapter for information about a guided walk that approaches this area from the west.

For boat hire or charter cruises, there are plenty of options at the port. For diving courses, contact Dimensione Mare (☎ 0784 9 67 66), on Via La Marmora, Dorgali.

Places to Stay & Eat

Try *Camping Cala Gonone* (☎ 0784 9 31 65, Via Collodi 1), which charges up to L26,000 per person. Free-camping is strictly forbidden in the area.

Hotels include *Piccolo Hotel* (☎ 0784 9 32 32, Via Cristoforo Colombo), near the port, which has some very pleasant singles/doubles including bathroom for L60,000/99,000. *Hotel La Playa* (☎ 0784 9 31 06, Via Collodi) has rooms for up to L95,000/135,000. At *Pop Hotel* (☎ 0784 9 31 85, Via Marco Polo), close to the port, half board is L110,000 and full board L125,000. It also runs an inexpensive restaurant.

Just out of Dorgali, at the start of the road to Gola di Gorropu, is *Hotel Sant'Elene* (☎ 0784 9 45 72, Località Sant'Elene). Singles/doubles/triples go for L50,000/110,000/150,000. It also has an excellent restaurant with a reasonably priced tourist menu.

euro currency converter L10,000 = €5.16

SARDEGNA

At *Due Chiacchiere* (☎ *0784 9 33 86, Via Acquadolce 13*), a ristorante/pizzeria overlooking the sea near the port in Cala Gonone, a full meal will cost around L30,000. The nearby *Ristorante Il Pescatore* (☎ *0784 9 31 74)* is more expensive. You'll pay around L40,000 or more.

Getting There & Away

Six daily ARST buses run from Nuoro to Cala Gonone via Oliena and Dorgali. There is only one daily run to Tortoli (inland of Arbatax) leaving from Dorgali at 3 pm. The bus stop in Dorgali is on Via La Marmora, in front of the post office.

BAUNEI & URZULEI

These small villages on the S125 between Dorgali and Arbatax provide a good base for exploring the spectacular Gola di Gorropu (Gorropu Gorge, near Urzulei) and the high plain known as the Golgo (near Baunei), where you'll find the ancient **Chiesa di San Pietro**. This beautiful area has an almost magical atmosphere and is where you can see evidence of the ancient Nuraghic civilisation. The rustic church of San Pietro, for centuries a place of pilgrimage, stands isolated in the countryside and is surrounded by a wall lined with pilgrims' shelters. Nearby are the Nuraghic *betili*, conical sacred stones that were carved to indicate feminine forms.

To get to the high plain and church from Baunei, you need to take a very steep road, which winds uphill to the north of the town centre; the road is not served by public transport. A sign indicates San Pietro, but you'll probably need to ask directions. It is about 8km to the church. On the way, 1km before the church uphill on the left, is *Golgo* (☎ *0782 61 06 75, 0337 81 18 28)*, a restaurant designed to blend into its natural surroundings. You can camp here for L10,000 a day if you want to explore the area. A filling, traditional-style Sardegnan meal at the restaurant will cost up to L40,000. The complex opens from Easter to the end of September.

Farther north, about 300m before you reach the church of San Pietro (visible from the road), a road to the left leads to a group

of low buildings. This is the base of *Cooperativa Goloritzé* (☎ *0782 61 05 99, email goloritze@tiscalinet.it)*, a well organised service company, run by young locals, that offers guided treks in the area – on foot, on horseback, or, if you prefer, by donkey. Call them and they will pick you up by car at Baunei for around L15,000 per person (less if you are in a group). Their programme includes a day on horseback exploring the Golgo high plain (L100,000 per person), a two day walk from Golgo to Cala Sisine (L120,000 per person) and a one week walk from the Lanaittu Valley near Oliena to Santa Maria Navarrese (L850,000 per person). Four wheel drives carry in fresh food to camp sites each night and there is a boat shuttle service for walks which end at the sea. If you like the idea of a rustic lunch at a traditional shepherd's hut, they can organise that for L35,000 a head.

From the church, a trail continues on for around 10km to Cala Sisine; otherwise head back to Golgo and take the walking trail down to the sea at Cala Goloritze (one hour). The beauty of the scenery will take your breath away.

For inexpensive and efficient guided tours and walking in the Urzulei area call Società Gorropu (☎ *0347 775 27 06, 0782 64 92 82*, email franc@tiscali.it), a group of young expert guides based at Sa Domu E s'Orcu, a bar-restaurant on the S125 near Urzulei. They can help you make the exciting descent of the Gola di Gorropu (the use of cords is required for part of the descent) or explore the area's fascinating underground caves and rivers.

There are no hotels at either Baunei or Urzulei. If you want to stay in either town, it is possible to rent rooms in private homes – ask the Società Gorropu guides for information. This is an excellent way to get a feel for the real Sardegna. Expect to pay around L25,000 per night (breakfast not included). If you are looking for a good traditional meal at Urzulei, try *Ristorante La Ruota* (☎ *0782 64 90 94, Via San Giorgio 14)*.

On the coast, 10km south of Baunei, is the small and pleasant seaside town of **Santa Maria Navarrese**. This family-style

The stunning yet unpredictable Mt Etna, one of the world's most active live volcanoes

Experience the wilder side of Sardegna at Sedilo's traditional horse race in early July.

What a way to end the walk from Baunei – at Cala Goloritze's magnificent beach.

holiday resort was developed in the 1970s around an ancient church and a medieval tower. The town has a small tourist port and a very long sandy beach dotted with rocky outcrops. Unlike many beaches in Italy, this one is quite undeveloped – although there are a few bars and restaurants.

Albergo Santa Maria (☎ *0782 61 53 15, fax 0782 61 53 96, Via Plammas 30, email albergosantamaria@tiscalinet.it)* is open from the April to the end of October. It offers half board from L80,000 per person in June and late September, up to L135,000 in August. The staff are particularly friendly and helpful. The hotel reserves a section of beach for use by guests and it offers van and boat services to shuttle the guests to the beginning and end of walks or to the more secluded beaches in the area.

Baunei, Santa Maria Navarrese and Urzulei are accessible by ARST bus from Olbia, Nuoro, Dorgali and Cagliari, but it is easier to reach them from Tortoli and Arbatax.

ARBATAX

If you're planning to explore the Barbagia this small port town, not far from Baunei, towards Cagliari, is probably the most convenient place to arrive by ferry. Tirrenia ferries dock here from Civitavecchia twice a week, as do the fast ferries from Fiumicino in summer (19 July to 5 September). If you're heading north to Baunei, Cala Gonone, Dorgali or Nuoro, you will need to catch an ARST bus or walk 4km to Tortoli, where you can catch the direct once-daily ARST bus for Nuoro (via Lanusei). It's best to check at the tourist offices in Dorgali or Nuoro for up-to-date information. Buses leave from Arbatax for Cagliari two or three times a day, but don't necessarily coincide with ferry arrivals. Another, more extravagant, option would be to catch the Trenino Verde to Cagliari (see Getting There & Away in the Cagliari section).

For accommodation, try *Il Gabbiano* (☎ *0782 62 35 12)* in the Porto Frailis area a few kilometres away, which has singles/ doubles with bathroom for L90,000/100,000.

Language

Italian is a Romance language related to French, Spanish, Portuguese and Romanian. The Romance languages belong to the Indo-European group of languages, which include English. Indeed, as English and Italian share common roots in Latin, you will recognise many Italian words.

Modern literary Italian began to develop in the 13th and 14th centuries, predominantly through the works of Dante, Petrarch and Boccaccio, who wrote chiefly in the Florentine dialect. The language drew on its Latin heritage and many dialects to develop into the standard Italian of today. Although many dialects are spoken in everyday conversation, standard Italian is the national language of schools, media and literature and is understood throughout the country.

There are 58 million speakers of Italian in Italy; 500,000 in Switzerland, where Italian is one of the official languages; and 1.5 million speakers in France, Slovenia and Croatia. As a result of migration, Italian is also spoken in the USA, Argentina, Brazil and Australia.

Visitors to Italy with more than the most fundamental grasp of the language need to be aware that many older Italians still expect to be addressed by the third person formal, ie *lei* instead of *tu*. Also, it is not considered polite to use the greeting *ciao* when addressing strangers, unless they use it first; it's better to say *buon giorno* (or *buona sera*, as the case may be) and *arrivederci* (or the more polite form, *arrivederla*). We have used the formal address for most of the phrases in this guide. Use of the informal address is indicated by 'inf' in brackets. Italian also has both masculine and feminine forms (they usually ending in 'o' and 'a' respectively). Where both forms are given in this guide, they are separated by a slash, the masculine form first.

If you'd like a more comprehensive guide to the language, get a copy of Lonely Planet's *Italian phrasebook*.

Pronunciation

Italian pronunciation isn't difficult to master once you learn a few easy rules. Although some of the more clipped vowels, and stress on double letters, require careful practice for English speakers, it is easy enough to make yourself understood.

Vowels

Vowels are generally more clipped than in English:

a	as in 'art', eg *caro* (dear); sometimes short, eg *amico/a* (friend)
e	as in 'tell', eg *mettere* (to put)
i	as in 'inn', eg *inizio* (start)
o	as in 'dot', eg *donna* (woman); as in 'port', eg *dormire* (to sleep)
u	as the 'oo' in 'book', eg *puro* (pure)

Consonants

The pronunciation of many Italian consonants is similar to that of their English counterparts. Pronunciation of some consonants depends on certain rules:

c	as 'k' before 'a', 'o' and 'u'; as the 'ch' in 'choose' before 'e' and 'i'
ch	as the 'k' in 'kit'
g	as the 'g' in 'get' before 'a', 'o', 'u' and 'h'; as the 'j' in 'jet' before 'e' and 'i'
gli	as the 'lli' in 'million'
gn	as the 'ny' in 'canyon'
h	always silent
r	a rolled 'rr' sound
sc	as the 'sh' in 'sheep' before 'e' and 'i'; as 'sk' before 'a', 'o', 'u' and 'h'
z	as the 'ts' in 'lights', except at the beginning of a word, when it's as the 'ds' in 'suds'

Note that when **ci**, **gi** and **sci** are followed by **a**, **o** or **u**, the 'i' is not pronounced unless the accent falls on the 'i'. Thus the name 'Giovanni' is pronounced 'joh-**vahn**-nee'.

Word Stress

A double consonant is pronounced as a longer, more forceful sound than a single consonant.

Stress generally falls on the second-last syllable, as in spa-**ghet**-ti. When a word has an accent, the stress falls on that syllable, as in cit-**tà** (city).

Greetings & Civilities

Hello.	*Buongiorno.*
	Ciao. (inf)
Goodbye.	*Arrivederci.*
	Ciao. (inf)
Yes.	*Sì.*
No.	*No.*
Please.	*Per favore/Per piacere.*
Thank you.	*Grazie.*
That's fine/	*Prego.*
You're welcome.	
Excuse me.	*Mi scusi.*
Sorry (forgive me).	*Mi scusi/Mi perdoni.*

Small Talk

What's your name?	*Come si chiama?*
	Come ti chiami? (inf)
My name is ...	*Mi chiamo ...*
Where are you from?	*Di dov'è?*
	Di dove sei? (inf)
I'm from ...	*Sono di ...*
I (don't) like ...	*(Non) Mi piace ...*
Just a minute.	*Un momento.*

Language Difficulties

Please write it down.	*Può scriverlo, per favore?*
Can you show me (on the map)?	*Può mostrarmelo (sulla carta/pianta)?*
I understand.	*Capisco.*
I don't understand.	*Non capisco.*
Do you speak English?	*Parla inglese?*
	Parli inglese? (inf)
Does anyone here speak English?	*C'è qualcuno che parla inglese?*
How do you say ... in Italian?	*Come si dice ... in italiano?*
What does ... mean?	*Che vuole dire ...?*

Paperwork

name	*nome*
nationality	*nazionalità*
date of birth	*data di nascita*
place of birth	*luogo di nascita*
sex (gender)	*sesso*
passport	*passaporto*
visa	*visto*

Getting Around

What time does ... leave/arrive?	*A che ora parte/ arriva ...?*
the aeroplane	*l'aereo*
the boat	*la barca*
the (city) bus	*l'autobus*
the (intercity) bus	*il pullman*
the train	*il treno*

I'd like a ... ticket.	*Vorrei un biglietto ...*
one-way	*di solo andata*
return	*di andata e ritorno*
1st class	*prima classe*
2nd class	*seconda classe*

I want to go to ...	*Voglio andare a ...*
The train has been cancelled/delayed.	*Il treno è soppresso/ in ritardo.*
the first	*il primo*
the last	*l'ultimo*
platform number	*binario numero*
ticket office	*biglietteria*
timetable	*orario*
train station	*stazione*

I'd like to hire ...	*Vorrei noleggiare ...*
a bicycle	*una bicicletta*
a car	*una macchina*
a motorcycle	*una motocicletta*

Directions

Where is ...?	*Dov'è ...?*
Go straight ahead.	*Si va sempre diritto.*
	Vai sempre diritto. (inf)
Turn left.	*Giri a sinistra.*
Turn right.	*Giri a destra.*
at the next corner	*al prossimo angolo*
at the traffic lights	*al semaforo*
behind	*dietro*
in front of	*davanti*
far	*lontano*
near	*vicino*
opposite	*di fronte a*

Signs

INGRESSO/ ENTRATA	ENTRANCE
USCITA	EXIT
INFORMAZIONE	INFORMATION
APERTO/CHIUSO	OPEN/CLOSED
PROIBITO/ VIETATO	PROHIBITED
POLIZIA/ CARABINIERI	POLICE
QUESTURA	POLICE STATION
CAMERE LIBERE	ROOMS AVAILABLE
COMPLETO	FULL/NO VACANCIES
GABINETTI/BAGNI	TOILETS
UOMINI	MEN
DONNE	WOMEN

Around Town

I'm looking for ...	Cerco ...
a bank	un banco
the church	la chiesa
the city centre	il centro (città)
the ... embassy	l'ambasciata di ...
my hotel	il mio albergo
the market	il mercato
the museum	il museo
the post office	la posta
a public toilet	un gabinetto/ bagno pubblico
the telephone centre	il centro telefonico
the tourist office	l'ufficio di turismo/ d'informazione

I want to change ...	Voglio cambiare ...
money	del denaro
travellers cheques	degli assegni per viaggiatori

beach	la spiaggia
bridge	il ponte
castle	il castello
cathedral	il duomo/la cattedrale
church	la chiesa
island	l'isola
main square	la piazza principale
market	il mercato

mosque	la moschea
old city	il centro storico
palace	il palazzo
ruins	le rovine
sea	il mare
square	la piazza
tower	la torre

Accommodation

I'm looking for ...	Cerco ...
a guesthouse	una pensione
a hotel	un albergo
a youth hostel	un ostello per la gioventù

Where is a cheap hotel?	Dov'è un albergo che costa poco?
What is the address?	Cos'è l'indirizzo?
Could you write the address, please?	Può scrivere l'indirizzo, per favore?
Do you have any rooms available?	Ha camere libere/C'è una camera libera?

I'd like ...	Vorrei ...
a bed	un letto
a single room	una camera singola
a double room	una camera matrimoniale
a room with two beds	una camera doppia
a room with a bathroom	una camera con bagno
to share a dorm	un letto in dormitorio

How much is it ...?	Quanto costa ...?
per night	per la notte
per person	per ciascuno

May I see it?	Posso vederla?
Where is the bathroom?	Dov'è il bagno?
I'm/We're leaving today.	Parto/Partiamo oggi.

Shopping

I'd like to buy ...	Vorrei comprare ...
How much is it?	Quanto costa?

I don't like it.	*Non mi piace.*
May I look at it?	*Posso dare un'occhiata?*
I'm just looking.	*Sto solo guardando.*
It's cheap.	*Non è caro/a.*
It's too expensive.	*È troppo caro/a.*
I'll take it.	*Lo/La compro.*
Do you accept ...?	*Accettate ...?*
credit cards	*carte di credito*
travellers cheques	*assegni per viaggiatori*
more	*più*
less	*meno*
smaller	*più piccolo/a*
bigger	*più grande*

Time, Date & Numbers

What time is it?	*Che (ora è/ore sono)?*
It's (8 o'clock).	*Sono (le otto).*
in the morning	*di mattina*
in the afternoon	*di pomeriggio*
in the evening	*di sera*
When?	*Quando?*
today	*oggi*
tomorrow	*domani*
yesterday	*ieri*
Monday	*lunedì*
Tuesday	*martedì*
Wednesday	*mercoledì*
Thursday	*giovedì*
Friday	*venerdì*
Saturday	*sabato*
Sunday	*domenica*
January	*gennaio*
February	*febbraio*
March	*marzo*
April	*aprile*
May	*maggio*
June	*giugno*
July	*luglio*
August	*agosto*
September	*settembre*
October	*ottobre*
November	*novembre*
December	*dicembre*

0	*zero*
1	*uno*
2	*due*
3	*tre*
4	*quattro*
5	*cinque*
6	*sei*
7	*sette*
8	*otto*
9	*nove*
10	*dieci*
11	*undici*
12	*dodici*
13	*tredici*
14	*quattordici*
15	*quindici*
16	*sedici*
17	*diciassette*
18	*diciotto*
19	*diciannove*
20	*venti*
21	*ventuno*
22	*ventidue*
30	*trenta*
40	*quaranta*
50	*cinquanta*
60	*sessanta*
70	*settanta*
80	*ottanta*
90	*novanta*
100	*cento*
1000	*mille*
2000	*due mila*

one million   *un milione*

Emergencies

Help!	*Aiuto!*
Call ...!	*Chiami ...!*
	Chiama ...! (inf)
a doctor	*un dottore/ un medico*
the police	*la polizia*
There's been an accident	*C'è stato un incidente!*
I'm lost.	*Mi sono perso/a.*
Go away!	*Lasciami in pace!*
	Vai via! (inf)

Health

I'm ill.	*Mi sento male.*
It hurts here.	*Mi fa male qui.*

I'm ...	*Sono ...*
asthmatic	*asmatico/a*
diabetic	*diabetico/a*
epileptic	*epilettico/a*

I'm allergic ...	*Sono allergico/a ...*
to antibiotics	*agli antibiotici*
to penicillin	*alla penicillina*

antiseptic	*antisettico*
aspirin	*aspirina*
condoms	*preservativi*
contraceptive	*anticoncezionale*
diarrhoea	*diarrea*
medicine	*medicina*
sunblock cream	*crema/latte solare (per protezione)*
tampons	*tamponi*

FOOD
Basics

breakfast	*prima colazione*
lunch	*pranzo*
dinner	*cena*
restaurant	*ristorante*
grocery store	*un alimentari*

What is this?	*(Che) cos'è?*
I'd like the set lunch.	*Vorrei il menù turistico.*
Is service included in the bill?	*È compreso il servizio?*
I'm a vegetarian.	*Sono vegetariano/a.*

Menu
This glossary is intended as a brief guide to some of the basics and by no means covers all of the dishes you're likely to encounter in Italy. Names and ingredients of dishes often vary from region to region, and even pizza toppings can change. Most travellers to Italy will already be well acquainted with the various Italian pastas, which include spaghetti, fettucine, penne, rigatoni, gnocchi, lasagne, tortellini and ravioli. The names are the same in Italy and no further definitions are given here.

Useful Words

affumicato	smoked
al dente	firm (as all good pasta should be)
alla brace	cooked over hot coals
alla griglia	grilled
arrosto	roasted
ben cotto	well done (cooked)
bollito	boiled
cameriere/a	waiter/waitress
coltello	knife
conto	bill/cheque
cotto	cooked
crudo	raw
cucchiaino	teaspoon
cucchiaio	spoon
forchetta	fork
fritto	fried
menù	menu
piatto	plate
ristorante	restaurant

Staples

aceto	vinegar
burro	butter
formaggio	cheese
limone	lemon
marmellata	jam
miele	honey
olio	oil
olive	olives
pane	bread
pane integrale	wholemeal bread
panna	cream
pepe	pepper
peperoncino	chilli
polenta	cooked cornmeal
riso	rice
risotto	rice cooked with wine and stock
sale	salt
uovo/uova	egg/eggs
zucchero	sugar

Meat & Fish

acciughe	anchovies
agnello	lamb
aragosta	lobster
bistecca	steak
calamari	squid
coniglio	rabbit

cotoletta	cutlet or thin cut of meat, usually crumbed and fried
cozze	mussels
dentice	dentex (type of fish)
fegato	liver
gamberi	prawns
granchio	crab
manzo	beef
merluzzo	cod
ostriche	oysters
pesce spada	swordfish
pollo	chicken
polpo	octopus
salsiccia	sausage
sarde	sardines
sgombro	mackerel
sogliola	sole
tacchino	turkey
tonno	tuna
trippa	tripe
vitello	veal
vongole	clams

Vegetables

asparagi	asparagus
carciofi	artichokes
carote	carrots
cavolo/verza	cabbage
cicoria	chicory
cipolla	onion
fagiolini	string beans
melanzane	aubergines
patate	potatoes
peperoni	peppers
piselli	peas
spinaci	spinach

Fruit

arance	oranges
banane	bananas
ciliegie	cherries
fragole	strawberries
mele	apples
pere	pears
pesche	peaches
uva	grapes

Soups & Antipasti

brodo – broth
carpaccio – very fine slices of raw meat
insalata caprese – sliced tomatoes with mozzarella and basil
insalata di mare – seafood, generally crustaceans
minestrina in brodo – pasta in broth
minestrone – vegetable soup
olive ascolane – stuffed, deep-fried olives
prosciutto e melone – cured ham with melon
ripieni – stuffed, oven-baked vegetables
stracciatella – egg in broth

Pasta Sauces

alla matriciana – tomato and bacon
al ragù – meat sauce (bolognese)
arrabbiata – tomato and chilli
carbonara – egg, bacon and black pepper
napoletana – tomato and basil
panna – cream, prosciutto and sometimes peas
pesto – basil, garlic and oil, often with pine nuts
vongole – clams, garlic, oil and sometimes with tomato

Pizzas

All pizzas listed have a tomato (and sometimes mozzarella) base.

capricciosa – olives, prosciutto, mushrooms and artichokes
frutti di mare – seafood
funghi – mushrooms
margherita – oregano
napoletana – anchovies
pugliese – tomato, mozzarella and onions
quattro formaggi – with four types of cheese
quattro stagioni – like a capricciosa, but sometimes with egg
verdura – mixed vegetables; usually courgette (zucchini) and aubergine (eggplant), sometimes carrot and spinach

Glossary

AAST – Azienda Autonoma di Soggiorno e Turismo; local tourist office
abbazia – abbey
ACI – Automobile Club Italiano; Italian Automobile Association
acque alte – high water (flooding that occurs in Venezia during winter, when the sea level rises)
affittacamere – rooms for rent (cheaper than a *pensione* and not part of the classification system)
affresco – the painting method in which watercolour paint is applied to wet plaster
agriturismo – tourist accommodation on farms
AIG – Associazione Italiana Alberghi per la Gioventù; Italian Youth Hostel Association
albergo (s), **alberghi** (pl) – hotel (up to five stars)
alimentari – grocery shop
aliscafo (s), **aliscafi** (pl) – hydrofoil
Alleanza Nazionale – National Alliance (neo-Fascist political party)
alloggio – lodging (cheaper than a *pensione* and not part of the classification system)
al trancio – served by the slice
alto – high
ambasciata – embassy
ambulanza – ambulance
anfiteatro – amphitheatre
antipasto (s), **antipasti** (pl) – starter
APT – Azienda di Promozione Turistica; provincial tourist office
ASL – Azienda Sanitaria Locale; Provincial Health Agency
Associazione Cattolica al Servizio/ Protezione della Giovane – Catholic Association for the Protection of the Young
autostrada (s), **autostrade** (pl) – motorway (highway)

bancomat – ATM or automated teller machine
battistero – baptistry
benzina – petrol
benzina senza piombo – unleaded petrol

biglietto – ticket
biglietto chilometrico – kilometric card (train pass)
bivacchi – unattended mountain hut
borgo (s), **borghi** (pl) – cluttered towns and villages, little changed over hundreds of years
BR – Brigate Rosse; Red Brigades (terrorist group)
bruschetta – bread with various toppings

cabinovia – two-seater cable car
calcio – football (soccer)
calle – street (Venezia)
camera – room
campanile – bell tower
cappella – chapel
carabinieri – police with military and civil duties
carnevale – carnival period between Epiphany and Lent
carta d'identità – identity card
carta telefonica – phonecard
cartoleria – shop selling paper goods
casa religiosa per l'ospitalità – religious institution that offers accommodation
castello – castle
cattedrale – cathedral
cena – evening meal
cenacolo – refectory
centro – city centre
chiesa (s), **chiese** (pl) – church
chiostro – cloister; covered walkway, usually enclosed by columns, around a quadrangle
cichetti – snacks
cima – summit
CIT – Compagnia Italiana di Turismo; Italy's national travel agency
codice fiscale – tax number
colazione – breakfast
colonna – column
comune – equivalent to a municipality or county; town or city council; historically, a commune (self-governing town or city
consolato – consulate

contrada – district
coperto – cover charge in restaurants
corso – main street
croda – a mountain with a square peak
CTS – Centro Turistico Studentesco e Giovanile; Centre for Student and Youth Tourists
cuccetta – couchette
cupola – dome

DC – Democrazia Cristiana; Christian Democrats (political party)
Decumanus – main street (Greek)
deposito bagagli – left luggage
diretto – through, slow train
DS – Democratici della Sinistra; Democrats of the Left (political party)
duomo – cathedral

engera – doughy bread
ENIT – Ente Nazionale per il Turismo; Italian Tourist Board
enoteca – wine bar
EPT – Ente Provinciale per Il Turismo; local tourist bureau
ES – Eurostar; very fast train
espresso – express mail; express train; short black coffee
estiva – summer

farmacia – chemist's shop, pharmacy
fermo posta – poste restante
ferramenta – hardware store
ferrovia – train station
festa – feast day; holiday
Feste di Pasqua – Holy Week
fiume – river
fondamenta – street beside a canal
fontana – fountain
foro – forum
Forza Italia – Go Italy (political party)
francobollo – postage stamp
frazione – small area
fresco – see *affresco*
frullati di frutta – fruit shakes
FS – Ferrovie dello Stato; State Railways
funicolare – funicular railway
funivia – cable car

gabinetto – toilets, WC

garni – B&Bs
gasauto or **GPL** – liquid petroleum gas (LPG)
gasolio – diesel
gelaterie – ice-cream parlours
gettoni – telephone tokens
Giubileo – Jubilee of Christ's birth
golfo – gulf
grotta – cave
guardia di finanza – military body responsible for enforcing the law on income tax and monopolies
guardia forestale – forest ranger

IAT – Informazioni e Assistenza ai Turisti; local tourist office
IC – Intercity; fast train
IDP – International Driving Permit
interregionale – long-distance train that stops frequently
IVA – Imposta di Valore Aggiunto; value-added tax of around 19%

lago – lake
largo – (small) square
lavanderia – laundrette
Lega Nord – Northern League, federalist political party
lido – beach
limoncello – bright-yellow lemon liqueur from Campania
lingua originale – original language
locanda – inn, small hotel (cheaper than a *pensione*)
loggia – covered area on the side of a building; porch
lo sci – downhill skiing
lungomare – seafront road, promenade

malghe – Alpine huts
mar or **mare** – sea
mercato – market
merceria – haberdashery shop
Metropolitana – the Roma and Napoli underground systems
Mezzogiorno – literally midday; name for the south of Italy
MM – Metropolitana Milano; Milano underground system
monte – mountain

motoscafo – motorboat
MSI – Movimento Sociale Italiano; Italian Social Movement (neo-Fascist political party)
municipio – town hall
musico – musician

Natale – Christmas
nave (s), **navi** (pl) – large ferry, ship
negozio di alimentari – grocery shop
Neapolis – Latin for Naples meaning 'new city'
necropoli – (ancient) cemetery, burial site
nuraghi – megalithic stone fortresses on Sardegna

oggetti smarriti – lost property
ossobuco – veal shank
ospedale – hospital
ostello per la gioventù – youth hostel
osteria or **bacari** – a snack bar/cheap restaurant

Pagine Gialle – the Yellow Pages (phone directory)
palazzo (s), **palazzi** (pl) – mansion, palace; large building of any type, including an apartment block
palio – contest
panetteria – bakery
panino (s), **panini** (pl) – bread roll with filling
paninoteche – cafés
parco – park
passeggiata - traditional evening stroll
passerelle – raised walkway
pasticceria – cake shop
patrician – a member of the hereditary aristocracy of ancient Rome
PCI – Partito Comunista Italiano; Italian Communist Party (political party)
PDS – Partito Democratico della Sinistra; Democratic Party of the Left (political party)
pensione – small hotel, often offering board
permesso di lavoro – work permit
permesso di soggiorno – permit to stay in Italy for a nominated period
piazza (s), **piazze** (pl) – square
piazzale – (large) open square

pietà – literally pity or compassion; sculpture, drawing or painting of the dead Christ supported by the Madonna
pieve (s), **pievi** (pl) – Romanesque church
pinacoteca – art gallery
pizzeria (s), **pizzerie** (pl) – pizza restaurant
podestà – town chief, head of state
polenta – cornmeal porridge
polizia – police
Polo per le Libertà – Freedom Alliance; right-wing political coalition (political party)
poltrona – airline-type chair on a ferry
ponte – bridge
pontile – jetty
portico – portico; covered walkway, usually attached to the outside of buildings
porto – port
posta – post office
PRC – Partito Rifondazione Comunista; Refounded Communist Party
presepio – nativity scene
pronto soccorso – first aid, casualty ward
PSI – Partito Socialista Italiano; Italian Socialist Party (political party)

quartieri – districts
questura – police station

reale – royal
regionale – slow local train
rifugio (s), **rifugi** (pl) – shelter; accommodation in the Alpi
risotto – (grain) rice
riva – river bank
rocca – fortress
ronda – roundabout
rosso – red
rosticceria – shop selling roast meats

sagra – festival, feast
salumeria – delicatessen
Samnites – a southern Italian people related to the Oscans
santuario – sanctuary
sassi – stone houses built in two ravines in Matera (Basilicata)
scala mobile – escalator, moving staircase
scalinata – staircase
sci alpinismo – ski mountaineering

sci di fondo – cross-country skiing
servizio – service charge in restaurants
sestiere – city section (Venezia)
Settimana Bianca – White Week; skiing package
soccorso stradale – highway rescue
sovrintendenza – supervisor
spiaggia – beach
stazione – station
stazione di servizio – petrol or service station
stazione marittime – ferry terminal
strada – street, road
strada provinciale – main road; sometimes just a country lane
strada statale – main road; often multilane and toll free
superstrada – expressway; highway with divided lanes
supplemento – supplement, payable on a fast train

tabaccheria – tobacconist's shop
tavola calda – literally 'hot table'; pre-prepared meat, pasta and vegetable selection, often self-service
teatro – theatre
tempio – temple
terme – thermal baths
tesoro – treasury

torre – tower
torrente – stream
Torre Pendente – Leaning Tower
toto nero – illegal football pools
traghetto (s), **traghetti** (pl) – small ferry
trattoria (s), **trattorie** (pl) – cheap restaurant
tramezzino – sandwich
treno – train

ufficio postale – post office
ufficio stranieri – (police) foreigners bureau
uffizi – offices
UDR – Unione Democratica per la Repubblica; Democratic Union for the Republic (centre political party)

via – street, road
vico – alley, alleyway
via cave – narrow walkways which are carved like mini-gorges into rock
via ferrate – climbing trail with permanent steel cords
vigili del fuoco – fire brigade
vigili urbani – traffic police, local police
villa – town house or country house; also the park surrounding the house

Zona Rimozione – vehicle removal zone

Acknowledgments

Many thanks to the travellers (apologies if we've misspelt your name) who used the last edition and wrote to us with helpful hints, useful advice and interesting anecdotes:

AF Siraa, Akos Szoboszlay, Alan Adams, Alberto Rossi, Alessandro Pascale, Alison Kubler, Allan & Janet Warman, Alpenroyal Sporthotel, Alyn McNaughton, Amanda Tinker, Ana Steiner, Anas Alghazzi, Andrea Sebastiano, Andy Semmler, Anita Bocquee, Anna Lucke, Anne Marieke Plantinga, Annika Tomberg, Anthea Grimshaw, Anthony Alps, Antonia Bortolotti, Antonio Zingali, Ari Gaitanis, Armin Baum, Aubree Gordon, Audrey Coyle, Azienda Agrituristica Montali

Barb & Gus King, Barbara Forbes, Barrett Feldman, Baylor Lancaster, Becky Pearson, Belinda Clapperton, Belinda Howard, Bernard Novak, Bernice Klinger, Boaz UR, Bob Hanenberg, Bob Klepner, Brad Simmons, Brian Downey, Brian Harland, Brian Lapinski, Brodie Woodland

C Czecher, C Hyslop, Camela Ruby, Camella James, Carlo Cheric, Carol & Brian Little, Carole & Robert Sheesley, Caroline Harkin, Charles Booth, Charlie Clancy, Cheryl Burghardt, Chia Teck Wee, Chris Pecaraio, Christina Miller, Christine Hamel, Christopher R Barnes, Christopher Vuturo, Christy Chan, Ciara O'Mahony, Clancy Broxton, Colin Cha Fong, Concetta Kincaid, Coral Goward, Corrado Bina, Craig Freeman, Craig Z, Cristina Taddei, Crystal Hogg

D Richard Owen, D Trevino, Daniel Walfish, Daniela Cima, Dara Levine, Dave Mountain, David Daniels, David Ingram, David Messineo, David Motamed, David Silva, David Vest, Davide Cavina, Deborah Sheridan, Della Johnston, Detlef Geerlings, Didomizio Joel, Dominic & Sam Guest, Don Bennett, Donna Drago, Dorie Iwata, Douglas Silton, Dr Chris Higson, Dr M Isac, Dubray Books

E Bridgman, Ed Dobosz, Ed Gonzales, Elaine Clance, Elena Martorana, Elsbeth Limberg, Emily Dirks, Emma Beechey, Esther Gutierrez, Eugene See

F Blackwood, Fay Wylie, Fernando Zaidan, Filip Blazek, Flavius I Handrea, Fragiscos Anevlavis, Franca Mirella, Francis E Rodis, Franklin Murillo, Frederico Rigoni, Freek Bos, Fujio Mizuoka

GG Dakin, Gabriel Saffioti, Gariele Valentini, Gerard Regan, Giavi Lara, Gillian Bolan, Giorgia Lanzoni, Giovanni Antonucci, Giovanni Bogani, Giovanni Longo, Gloria Edwards, Gordon Davis, Grace Marcinkoski, Guy Moshe

Hadley M Cave, Hannes Piroth, Hans van der Made, Heiko Mattern, Helen & Don Burns, Helen Milner, Holly Hinton

IM Dawson, Ido & Tair Harpas

J Dudley, J Goddard, J Hamson, J Houley, Jacqueline Pereira, Jan & Ian Scott, Jane Rudge, Janine Brookes, Jasper Lloyd, Jean Dhont, Jennifer Kylstad, Jennifer Wong, Jenny Haddad, Jeremy Ingall, Jeri Cunningham, Jerome Tymms, Jessica Ellis Stouffer, Joanna Drakes, Joanna Walker, Joe Tambe, Joel Burken, Johan Christen Ekman, John Gee, John Ward, Jonathan B Rivera, Jonathan Jaffe, Josephine Hsieh, Josh Gonze, Joyce Kuppinger, Judi Goglia, Judith Brennan, Judith Leshner, Julie Rutberg, Justine Curgenven, Justine Law, Justine Waddington

K Harry, K Rei, Karine Saucier, Kate Milleker, Kathy Kronenberg, Ken Steele, Keri Krupp, Kevin P Pidduck, Kirsten F, Kylie Jeans

L Norgrove, Lars D Myklevoll, Laura Ell, Laura Poggiolini, Laura Pratt, Laurie Stott, Leigh Sarti, Lex Beije, Lindsay Bligh, Lionel Choi, Lisa Bertoluzza, Lisa Glover, Lisa Morey, Lisa Wessler, Liz Eagan, Liz Linden, Luca Cico, Lucinda Croskell, Luisa Chelotti, Lyn & Roge Killen, Lynn Fowler

M & D Pennington, MB Riley, M Behm, M Brown, Makoto Hosoya, Marco Cavalieri, Marg Ewin, Margaret Cowan, Mari Borghesi, Maria Michakzvk, Maria Salas, Marilyn Flax, Marina Prisciandaro, Marion Simon, Mark Briem, Mark Rutherford, Marleen Enschedé, Marta Llimona Broto, Martin Pdehl, Marty Faigin, Mary Baran, Mary Wells, Massimo Bisiacchi, Max Miller, Melinda Sewell, Melissa Anderson, Merryn & David Thomae, Michael Chambers, Michael Jasper, Michael Ledwidge, Michele de Barros, Michelle Kidd, Michelle Rudden, Mike Foale, Mike Valitchka, Mitro Hood, Munindra Khaund

Nancy Lobdell, Natasha Markovic, Niamh Warde,

Nicola McGrade, Nicole Douglas, Nina Holm, Nina Rojas

Olatubosun Oduneye

P Haselgrove, PJ & HW Milkins, Paal Andersen, Paddy Murray, Pam Anders, Pamela Robertson, Paola Alfiero, Paola de Antonellis, Paolo Noseda, Paolo Pietropaolo, Pat Music, Patricia Sampaio d'utra Vaz, Patrick Mornsey, Paul Garner, Paul Gioffi, Paul W Gioffi, Per-Axel Frielingsdorf, Peter Addlem, Peter Cocks, Peter Fraone, Peter Kunkel, Peter M Henriksen, Peter Sluijter, Peter Strazzabosco, Peter Wildrins, Phil & Sally Laing, Philip Harper, Philip Scheir, Piergiorgio Pescali, Pietio Dall'oplis, Pietro Ceribelli, Piran &c Montford

RJ Woollett, R Samways, Rafal Freyer, Rajnish Dhall, Ralph Kuehn, Rebecca Sedgwick, Rebekah Hoare, Regina Pichetti, Rev John Baker, Ricarda & Andreas Daberkow, Richard Folley, Rob Lance, Robert C McLaughlin, Robert Wojtkowski, Robert Youker, Rodolfo Calderari, Rodrigo Riveri, Rolf Palmberg, Romana & Jan Danser, Rona Fergusson, Rose Magers S Rembado, Sandy Wubben, Sanjiv Khamgaonkar, Sarah Douglas, Sarah Murphy, Saskia Cornes, Scott Alkire, Scott Lawrence, Scott Warren, Sean Wight-

man, Sharon Pitardi, Sharon Stock, Sheila McGrath, Silvia Estivill Carraps, Sonia Rebecchi, Sook Fang, Sophie Langella, Sruesh Dhargalkar, Stacey Avard, Stefanou Yiannis, Stephanie Gill, Stephen Iacono, Steve Tarring, Stuart Curtis, Stuart Laurie, Stuart Michael, Sudarat Prachasri, Sue O'Reilly, Sue Walker, Sui-Linn White, Susana Fortini, Susanne Afke van Dijkum

Tamasin Garland, Tara Kneafsey, Tasha Tudor, Teresa Schneider, Terry Portus, Tessa Blaber, Teva R Gayon, Theodora W Simons, Thng Hui Hong, Thomas D Baldwin, Tim Kodek, Tim Morton, Tina Murphy, Tina Perry, Tom Renders, Tom Torchia, Tommy Johansson, Tony Weston, Tricia Cypher

Udo Herrmann

Valerie Reichel Moberg, Vanessa Greatorex, Victor Lawrence, Vince Dimasi, Virginia Saffioti, Vittorio Parisi

Wan-Cheng Wong

Yarden Agari

Zambelli Udine, Zannah Robinson, Zen Parry, Zoe Lee

LONELY PLANET

Phrasebooks

onely Planet phrasebooks are packed with essential words and phrases to help travellers communicate with the locals. With colour tabs for quick reference, an extensive vocabulary and use of script, these handy pocket-sized language guides cover day-to-day travel situations.

- handy pocket-sized books
- easy to understand Pronunciation chapter
- clear & comprehensive Grammar chapter
- romanisation alongside script to allow ease of pronunciation
- script throughout so users can point to phrases for every situation
- full of cultural information and tips for the traveller

'...vital for a real DIY spirit and attitude in language learning'
– *Backpacker*

'the phrasebooks have good cultural backgrounders and offer solid advice for challenging situations in remote locations'
– *San Francisco Examiner*

Arabic (Egyptian) • Arabic (Moroccan) • Australian *(Australian English, Aboriginal and Torres Strait languages)* • Baltic States *(Estonian, Latvian, Lithuanian)* • Bengali • Brazilian • British • Burmese • Cantonese • Central Asia • Central Europe *(Czech, French, German, Hungarian, Italian, Slovak)* • Eastern Europe *(Bulgarian, Czech, Hungarian, Polish, Romanian, Slovak)* • Ethiopian (Amharic) • Fijian • French • German • Greek • Hebrew phrasebook • Hill Tribes • Hindi/Urdu • Indonesian • Italian • Japanese • Korean • Lao • Latin American Spanish • Malay • Mandarin • Mediterranean Europe *(Albanian, Croatian, Greek, Italian, Macedonian, Maltese, Serbian, Slovene)* • Mongolian • Nepali • Pidgin • Pilipino (Tagalog) • Quechua • Russian • Scandinavian Europe *(Danish, Finnish, Icelandic, Norwegian, Swedish)* • South-East Asia *(Burmese, Indonesian, Khmer, Lao, Malay, Tagalog Pilipino, Thai, Vietnamese)* • South Pacific Languages • Spanish (Castilian) *(also includes Catalan, Galician and Basque)* • Sri Lanka • Swahili • Thai • Tibetan • Turkish • Ukrainian • USA *(US English, Vernacular, Native American languages, Hawaiian)* • Vietnamese • Western Europe *(Basque, Catalan, Dutch, French, German, Greek, Irish)*

Lonely Planet Journeys

J OURNEYS is a unique collection of travel writing – published by the company that understands travel better than anyone else. It is a series for anyone who has ever experienced – or dreamed of – the magical moment when they encountered a strange culture or saw a place for the first time. They are tales to read while you're planning a trip, while you're on the road or while you're in an armchair, in front of a fire.

These outstanding titles explore our planet through the eyes of a diverse group of international writers. JOURNEYS books catch the spirit of a place, illuminate a culture, recount a crazy adventure, or introduce a fascinating way of life. They always entertain, and always enrich the experience of travel.

MALI BLUES
Traveling to an African Beat
Lieve Joris (translated by Sam Garrett)
Drought, rebel uprisings, ethnic conflict: these are the predominant images of West Africa. But as Lieve Joris travels in Senegal, Mauritania and Mali, she meets survivors, fascinating individuals charting new ways of living between tradition and modernity. With her remarkable gift for drawing out people's stories, Joris brilliantly captures the rhythms of a world that refuses to give in.

THE GATES OF DAMASCUS
Lieve Joris (translated by Sam Garrett)
This best-selling book is a beautifully drawn portrait of day-to-day life in modern Syria. Through her intimate contact with local people, Lieve Joris draws us into the fascinating world that lies behind the gates of Damascus. Hala's husband is a political prisoner, jailed for his opposition to the Assad regime; through the author's friendship with Hala we see how Syrian politics impacts on the lives of ordinary people.

THE OLIVE GROVE
Travels in Greece
Katherine Kizilos
Katherine Kizilos travels to fabled islands, troubled border zones and her family's village deep in the mountains. She vividly evokes breathtaking landscapes, generous people and passionate politics, capturing the complexities of a country she loves.

'beautifully captures the real tensions of Greece' – *Sunday Times*

KINGDOM OF THE FILM STARS
Journey into Jordan
Annie Caulfield
Kingdom of the Film Stars is a travel book and a love story. With honesty and humour, Annie Caulfield writes of travelling in Jordan and falling in love with a Bedouin with film-star looks.

She offers fascinating insights into the country – from the tent life of traditional women to the hustle of downtown Amman – and unpicks tight-woven Western myths about the Arab world.

LONELY PLANET

Lonely Planet Travel Atlases

Lonely Planet has long been famous for the number and quality of its guidebook maps. Now we've gone one step further and produced a handy companion series: Lonely Planet travel atlases – maps of a country produced in book form.

Unlike other maps, which look good but lead travellers astray, our travel atlases have been researched on the road by Lonely Planet's experienced team of writers. All details are carefully checked to ensure the atlas corresponds with the equivalent Lonely Planet guidebook.

- full-colour throughout
- maps researched and checked by Lonely Planet authors
- place names correspond with Lonely Planet guidebooks
- no confusing spelling differences
- legend and travelling information in English, French, German, Japanese and Spanish
- size: 230 x 160 mm

Available now: Chile & Easter Island • Egypt • India & Bangladesh • Israel & the Palestinian Territories • Jordan, Syria & Lebanon • Kenya • Laos • Portugal • South Africa, Lesotho & Swaziland • Thailand • Turkey • Vietnam • Zimbabwe, Botswana & Namibia

Lonely Planet TV Series & Videos

Lonely Planet travel guides have been brought to life on television screens around the world. Like our guides, the programs are based on the joy of independent travel, and look honestly at some of the most exciting, picturesque and frustrating places in the world. Each show is presented by one of three travellers from Australia, England or the USA and combines an innovative mixture of video, Super-8 film, atmospheric soundscapes and original music.

Videos of each episode – containing additional footage not shown on television – are available from good book and video shops, but the availability of individual videos varies with regional screening schedules.

Video destinations include: Alaska • American Rockies • Argentina • Australia – The South-East • Baja California & the Copper Canyon • Brazil • Central Asia • Chile & Easter Island • Corsica, Sicily & Sardinia – The Mediterranean Islands • East Africa (Tanzania & Zanzibar) • Cuba • Ecuador & the Galapagos Islands • Ethiopia • Greenland & Iceland • Hungary & Romania • Indonesia • Israel & the Sinai Desert • Jamaica • Japan • La Ruta Maya • The Middle East (Syria, Jordan & Lebanon • Morocco • New York • Northern Spain • North India • Outback Australia • Pacific Islands (Fiji, Solomon Islands & Vanuatu) • Pakistan • Peru • The Philippines • South Africa & Lesotho • South India • South West China • South West USA • Trekking in Uganda • Turkey • Vietnam • West Africa • Zimbabwe, Botswana & Namibia

The Lonely Planet TV series is produced by: Pilot Productions
The Old Studio
18 Middle Row
London W10 5AT, UK

LONELY PLANET

Lonely Planet On-line

Whether you've just begun planning your next trip, or you're chasing down specific info on currency regulations or visa requirements, check out Lonely Planet On-line for up-to-the-minute travel information.

As well as mini guides to more than 250 destinations, you'll find maps, photos, travel news, health and visa updates, travel advisories, and discussion of the ecological and political issues you need to be aware of as you travel. You'll also find timely upgrades to popular guidebooks which you can print out and stick in the back of your book.

There's also an on-line travellers' forum where you can share your experience of life on the road, meet travel companions and ask other travellers for their recommendations and advice.

And of course we have a complete and up-to-date list of all Lonely Planet travel products including travel guides, diving and snorkeling guides, phrasebooks, atlases, travel literature and videos, and a simple on-line ordering facility if you can't find the book you want elsewhere.

Lonely Planet Diving & Snorkeling Guides

Beautifully illustrated with full-colour photos throughout, Lonely Planet's Pisces Books explore the world's best diving and snorkelling areas and prepare divers for what to expect when they get there, both topside and underwater.

Dive sites are described in detail with specifics on depths, visibility, level of difficulty, special conditions, underwater photography tips, and common and unusual marine life present. You'll also find practical logistical information and coverage on topside activities and attractions, sections on diving health and safety, plus listings for diving services, live-aboards, dive resorts and tourist offices.

LONELY PLANET

Guides by Region

L onely Planet is known worldwide for publishing practical, reliable and no-nonsense travel information in our guides and on our Web site. The Lonely Planet list covers just about every accessible part of the world. Currently there are 16 series: Travel guides, Shoestring guides, Condensed guides, Phrasebooks, Read This First, Healthy Travel, Walking guides, Cycling guides, Watching Wildlife guides, Pisces Diving & Snorkeling guides, City Maps, Road Atlases, Out to Eat, World Food, Journeys travel literature and Pictorials.

AFRICA Africa on a shoestring • Cairo • Cairo City Map • Cape Town • Cape Town City Map • East Africa • Egypt • Egyptian Arabic phrasebook • Ethiopia, Eritrea & Djibouti • Ethiopian (Amharic) phrasebook • The Gambia & Senegal • Healthy Travel Africa • Kenya • Malawi • Morocco • Moroccan Arabic phrasebook • Mozambique • Read This First: Africa • South Africa, Lesotho & Swaziland • Southern Africa • Southern Africa Road Atlas • Swahili phrasebook • Tanzania, Zanzibar & Pemba • Trekking in East Africa • Tunisia • Watching Wildlife East Africa • Watching Wildlife Southern Africa • West Africa • World Food Morocco • Zimbabwe, Botswana & Namibia
Travel Literature: Mali Blues: Traveling to an African Beat • The Rainbird: A Central African Journey • Songs to an African Sunset: A Zimbabwean Story

AUSTRALIA & THE PACIFIC Auckland • Australia • Australian phrasebook • Australia Road Atlas • Bushwalking in Australia • Cycling Australia • Cycling New Zealand • Fiji • Fijian phrasebook • Healthy Travel Australia, NZ and the Pacific • Islands of Australia's Great Barrier Reef • Melbourne • Melbourne City Map • Micronesia • New Caledonia • New South Wales & the ACT • New Zealand • Northern Territory • Outback Australia • Out to Eat – Melbourne • Out to Eat – Sydney • Papua New Guinea • Pidgin phrasebook • Queensland • Rarotonga & the Cook Islands • Samoa • Solomon Islands • South Australia • South Pacific • South Pacific phrasebook • Sydney • Sydney City Map • Sydney Condensed • Tahiti & French Polynesia • Tasmania • Tonga • Tramping in New Zealand • Vanuatu • Victoria • Walking in Australia • Watching Wildlife Australia • Western Australia
Travel Literature: Islands in the Clouds: Travels in the Highlands of New Guinea • Kiwi Tracks: A New Zealand Journey • Sean & David's Long Drive

CENTRAL AMERICA & THE CARIBBEAN Bahamas, Turks & Caicos • Baja California • Bermuda • Central America on a shoestring • Costa Rica • Costa Rica Spanish phrasebook • Cuba • Dominican Republic & Haiti • Eastern Caribbean • Guatemala • Guatemala, Belize & Yucatán: La Ruta Maya • Havana • Healthy Travel Central & South America • Jamaica • Mexico • Mexico City • Panama • Puerto Rico • Read This First: Central & South America • World Food Mexico • Yucatán
Travel Literature: Green Dreams: Travels in Central America

EUROPE Amsterdam • Amsterdam City Map • Amsterdam Condensed • Andalucía • Austria • Baltic States phrasebook • Barcelona • Barcelona City Map • Belgium & Luxembourg • Berlin • Berlin City Map • Britain • British phrasebook • Brussels, Bruges & Antwerp • Brussels City Map • Budapest • Budapest City Map • Canary Islands • Central Europe • Central Europe phrasebook • Corfu & the Ionians • Corsica • Crete • Crete Condensed • Croatia • Cycling Britain • Cycling France • Cyprus • Czech & Slovak Republics • Denmark • Dublin • Dublin City Map • Eastern Europe • Eastern Europe phrasebook • Edinburgh • Estonia, Latvia & Lithuania • Europe on a shoestring • Finland • Florence • France • Frankfurt Condensed • French phrasebook • Georgia, Armenia & Azerbaijan • Germany • German phrasebook • Greece • Greek Islands • Greek phrasebook • Hungary • Iceland, Greenland & the Faroe Islands • Ireland • Istanbul • Italian phrasebook • Italy • Krakow • Lisbon • The Loire • London • London City Map • London Condensed • Madrid • Malta • Mediterranean Europe • Mediterranean Europe phrasebook • Moscow • Mozambique • Munich • the Netherlands • Norway • Out to Eat – London • Paris • Paris City Map • Paris Condensed • Poland • Portugal • Portuguese phrasebook • Prague • Prague City Map • Provence & the Côte d'Azur • Read This First: Europe • Romania & Moldova • Rome • Rome City Map • Russia, Ukraine & Belarus • Russian phrasebook • Scandinavian & Baltic Europe • Scandinavian Europe phrasebook • Scotland • Sicily • Slovenia • South-West France • Spain • Spanish phrasebook • St Petersburg • St Petersburg City Map • Sweden • Switzerland • Trekking in Spain • Tuscany • Ukrainian phrasebook • Venice • Vienna • Walking in Britain • Walking in France • Walking in Ireland • Walking in Italy • Walking in Spain • Walking in Switzerland • Western Europe • Western Europe phrasebook • World Food France • World Food Ireland • World Food Italy • World Food Spain
Travel Literature: A Small Place in Italy • After Yugoslavia • Love and War in the Apennines • On the Shores of the Mediterranean The Olive Grove: Travels in Greece • Round Ireland in Low Gear

LONELY PLANET

Mail Order

Lonely Planet products are distributed worldwide. They are also available by mail order from Lonely Planet, so if you have difficulty finding a title please write to us. North and South American residents should write to 150 Linden St, Oakland, CA 94607, USA; European and African residents should write to 10a Spring Place, London NW5 3BH, UK; and residents of other countries to Locked Bag 1, Footscray, Victoria 3011, Australia.

INDIAN SUBCONTINENT Bangladesh • Bengali phrasebook • Bhutan • Delhi • Goa • Healthy Travel Asia & India • Hindi & Urdu phrasebook • India • Indian Himalaya • Karakoram Highway • Kerala • Mumbai (Bombay) • Nepal • Nepali phrasebook • Pakistan • Rajasthan • Read This First: Asia & India • South India • Sri Lanka • Sri Lanka phrasebook • Tibet • Tibetan phrasebook • Trekking in the Indian Himalaya • Trekking in the Karakoram & Hindukush • Trekking in the Nepal Himalaya
Travel Literature: The Age of Kali: Indian Travels and Encounters • Hello Goodnight: A Life of Goa • In Rajasthan • A Season in Heaven: True Tales from the Road to Kathmandu • Shopping for Buddhas • A Short Walk in the Hindu Kush • Slowly Down the Ganges

ISLANDS OF THE INDIAN OCEAN Madagascar & Comoros • Maldives • Mauritius, Réunion & Seychelles
Travel Literature: Maverick in Madagascar

MIDDLE EAST & CENTRAL ASIA Bahrain, Kuwait & Qatar • Central Asia • Central Asia phrasebook • Dubai • Farsi (Persian) phrasebook • Hebrew phrasebook • Iran • Israel & the Palestinian Territories • Istanbul • Istanbul City Map • Istanbul to Cairo on a shoestring • Jerusalem • Jerusalem City Map • Jordan • Lebanon • Middle East • Oman & the United Arab Emirates • Syria • Turkey • Turkish phrasebook • World Food Turkey • Yemen
Travel Literature: Black on Black: Iran Revisited • The Gates of Damascus • Kingdom of the Film Stars: Journey into Jordan

NORTH AMERICA Alaska • Boston • Boston City Map • Boston Condensed • British Columbia • California & Nevada • California Condensed • Canada • Chicago • Chicago City Map • Deep South • Florida • Great Lakes • Hawaii • Hiking in Alaska • Hiking in the USA • Honolulu • Las Vegas • Los Angeles • Los Angeles City Map • Louisiana & The Deep South • Miami • Miami City Map • Montreal • New England • New Orleans • New York City • New York City City Map • New York Condensed • New York, New Jersey & Pennsylvania • Oahu • Out to Eat – San Francisco • Pacific Northwest • Puerto Rico • Rocky Mountains • San Francisco • San Francisco City Map • Seattle • Southwest • Texas • Toronto • USA • USA phrasebook • Vancouver • Virginia & the Capital Region • Washington DC • Washington, DC City Map • World Food Deep South, USA • World Food New Orleans
Travel Literature: Caught Inside: A Surfer's Year on the California Coast • Drive Thru America

NORTH-EAST ASIA Beijing • Beijing City Map • Cantonese phrasebook • China • Hiking in Japan • Hong Kong • Hong Kong City Map • Hong Kong Condensed • Hong Kong, Macau & Guangzhou • Japan • Japanese phrasebook • Korea • Korean phrasebook • Kyoto • Mandarin phrasebook • Mongolia • Mongolian phrasebook • Seoul • Shanghai • South-West China • Taiwan • Tokyo • World Food – Hong Kong
Travel Literature: In Xanadu: A Quest • Lost Japan

SOUTH AMERICA Argentina, Uruguay & Paraguay • Bolivia • Brazil • Brazilian phrasebook • Buenos Aires • Chile & Easter Island • Colombia • Ecuador & the Galapagos Islands • Healthy Travel Central & South America • Latin American Spanish phrasebook • Peru • Quechua phrasebook • Read This First: Central & South America • Rio de Janeiro • Rio de Janeiro City Map • Santiago • South America on a shoestring • Santiago • Trekking in the Patagonian Andes • Venezuela
Travel Literature: Full Circle: A South American Journey

SOUTH-EAST ASIA Bali & Lombok • Bangkok • Bangkok City Map • Burmese phrasebook • Cambodia • Hanoi • Healthy Travel Asia & India • Hill Tribes phrasebook • Ho Chi Minh City • Indonesia • Indonesian phrasebook • Indonesia's Eastern Islands • Jakarta • Java • Lao phrasebook • Laos • Malay phrasebook • Malaysia, Singapore & Brunei • Myanmar (Burma) • Philippines • Pilipino (Tagalog) phrasebook • Read This First: Asia & India • Singapore • Singapore City Map • South-East Asia on a shoestring • South-East Asia phrasebook • Thailand • Thailand's Islands & Beaches • Thailand, Vietnam, Laos & Cambodia Road Atlas • Thai phrasebook • Vietnam • Vietnamese phrasebook • World Food Thailand • World Food Vietnam

ALSO AVAILABLE: Antarctica • The Arctic • The Blue Man: Tales of Travel, Love and Coffee • Brief Encounters: Stories of Love, Sex & Travel • Chasing Rickshaws • The Last Grain Race • Lonely Planet Unpacked • Not the Only Planet: Science Fiction Travel Stories • Lonely Planet On the Edge • Sacred India • Travel with Children • Travel Photography: A Guide to Taking Better Pictures

Index

Text

Bold indicates maps.

Bold indicates maps.

Boxed Text

MAP LEGEND

BOUNDARIES

———·—·—·—·— International
——·——·——·—·— Provincial
——·——·——·—·— Regional

HYDROGRAPHY

Coastline, Lake
River, Creek
Canal
Swamp

Building
Urban Area

ROUTES & TRANSPORT

Freeway
(under construction)
Highway
Major Road
Minor Road
Unsealed Road
City Freeway
City Highway
City Road

City Street, Lane
Pedestrian Mall
Tunnel
Train Route & Station
Metro & Station
Cable Car or Chair Lift
Walking Track
Walking Tour
Ferry Route

AREA FEATURES

✿ Park, Gardens
+ × × Cemetery
Market
Beach, Desert

MAP SYMBOLS

✈ Airport
Ancient or City Wall
∴ Archaeological Site
⊖ Bank
ㅅ Beach
⚊ Castle or Fort
⌒ Cave or Grotto
✚ Cathedral, Church
Cliff or Escarpment
○ Embassy or Consulate
⊕ Hospital
※ Lookout
⚐ Monument
▲ Mountain or Hill
Mountain Range

○ **ROMA** National Capital
◉ **MILANO** Provincial Capital
● **La Spezia** City
● **Varazze** Town
● **Arenzano** Village

● Point of Interest

■ Place to Stay
Å Camp Site
Caravan Park
⌂ Hut or Chalet

▼ Place to Eat
⚑ Pub or Bar

🏛 Museum
♁ National Park
P Parking
)(Pass
Petrol Station
★ Police Station
✉ Post Office
🏠 Stately Home
Synagogue
☎ Telephone
Temple
Tomb
ℹ Tourist Information
Transport
Zoo

Note: not all symbols displayed above appear in this book

LONELY PLANET OFFICES

Australia
Locked Bag 1, Footscray, Victoria 3011
☎ 03 8379 8000 fax 03 8379 8111
email: talk2us@lonelyplanet.com.au

USA
150 Linden St, Oakland, CA 94607
☎ 510 893 8555 TOLL FREE: 800 275 8555
fax 510 893 8572
email: info@lonelyplanet.com

UK
10a Spring Place, London NW5 3BH
☎ 020 7428 4800 fax 020 7428 4828
email: go@lonelyplanet.co.uk

France
1 rue du Dahomey, 75011 Paris
☎ 01 55 25 33 00 fax 01 55 25 33 01
email: bip@lonelyplanet.fr
www.lonelyplanet.fr

World Wide Web: www.lonelyplanet.com or AOL keyword: lp
Lonely Planet Images: lpi@lonelyplanet.com.au